Revised Office Readings

Year One

According to
The New Revised Standard Version

The Church Hymnal Corporation
445 Fifth Avenue, New York, N.Y. 10016

5 4 3 2 1

Introduction

Revised Office Readings is published in two volumes, one for each year of the Daily Office Lectionary of the Book of Common Prayer. Scripture readings are taken from The New Revised Standard Version, authorized for public use by the 1991 General Convention of the Episcopal Church. The NRSV, like its parent translation, The Revised Standard Version, enjoys wide use in the congregations of the Episcopal Church.

The readings in this edition have, when necessary, been edited for liturgical use. For example, if the context of a particular passage is not immediately clear, an opening sentence or phrase has been added to aid readers and listeners. Such modifications have been made in accordance with the directions on page 888 of the Prayer Book.

The Prayer Book lectionary sometimes offers an abridgement to a reading by indicating the omissible portion in parentheses in the citation. In this book, those optional passages have been set off in separate indented paragraphs highlighted by a vertical rule in the left margin. On occasion, the lectionary also offers an alternate reading or readings for a particular day. All alternate readings have been included here.

On certain feast days and their eves, and on Good Friday and Holy Saturday, the readings in the lectionary are clearly specified for use in either the morning or the evening. The reader will find them so indicated in this book as well.

For those few times when a lesson has been appointed for use more than once during the year, it appears in this book on the first date of its use. On subsequent occasions, a page reference will guide the reader to the lesson's original appearance.

The psalm citations for each day, with page references to the Prayer Book, appear before the day's readings. Psalmody intended for use in the morning is listed before the ❖ symbol, and evening psalmody is listed after the symbol.

For convenience in leading public worship, complete readings for the major Holy Days appear at the end of both volumes of *Revised Office Readings*. In accordance with the Prayer Book, the Holy Day lections and psalms are clearly divided between Morning Prayer and Evening Prayer.

The publishers hope that the use of *Revised Office Readings* will enhance the worship of the Church by helping its ministers, both lay and ordained, in the effective and worthy proclamation of God's holy Word.

Year One

Week of 1 Advent

Sunday

Psalm 146 [page 803], *Psalm 147* [page 804] ❖
Psalm 111 [page 754], *Psalm 112* [page 755],
Psalm 113 [page 756]

A Reading (Lesson) from the Book of Isaiah [1:1–9]

The vision of Isaiah son of Amoz, which he saw concerning
Judah and Jerusalem in the days of Uzziah, Jotham, Ahaz,
and Hezekiah, kings of Judah. Hear, O heavens, and listen,
O earth; for the LORD has spoken: I reared children and
brought them up, but they have rebelled against me. The ox
knows its owner, and the donkey its master's crib; but Israel
does not know, my people do not understand. Ah, sinful
nation, people laden with iniquity, offspring who do evil,
children who deal corruptly, who have forsaken the LORD,
who have despised the Holy One of Israel, who are utterly
estranged! Why do you seek further beatings? Why do you
continue to rebel? The whole head is sick, and the whole
heart faint. From the sole of the foot even to the head, there

is no soundness in it, but bruises and sores and bleeding wounds; they have not been drained, or bound up, or softened with oil. Your country lies desolate, your cities are burned with fire; in your very presence aliens devour your land; it is desolate, as overthrown by foreigners. And daughter Zion is left like a booth in a vineyard, like a shelter in a cucumber field, like a besieged city. If the LORD of hosts had not left us a few survivors, we would have been like Sodom, and become like Gomorrah.

A Reading (Lesson) from the Second Letter of Peter [3:1–10]

This is now, beloved, the second letter I am writing to you; in them I am trying to arouse your sincere intention by reminding you that you should remember the words spoken in the past by the holy prophets, and the commandment of the Lord and Savior spoken through your apostles. First of all you must understand this, that in the last days scoffers will come, scoffing and indulging their own lusts and saying, "Where is the promise of his coming? For ever since our ancestors died, all things continue as they were from the beginning of creation!" They deliberately ignore this fact, that by the word of God heavens existed long ago and an earth was formed out of water and by means of water, through which the world of that time was deluged with water and perished. But by the same word the present heavens and earth have been reserved for fire, being kept until the day of judgment and destruction of the godless. But do not ignore this one fact, beloved, that with the Lord one day is like a thousand years, and a thousand years are like one day. The Lord is not slow about his promise, as some think of slowness, but is patient with you, not wanting any to perish, but all to come to repentance. But the day of the Lord will come like a thief, and then the heavens will pass away with a loud noise, and the elements will be dissolved with fire, and the earth and everything that is done on it will be disclosed.

A Reading (Lesson) from the Gospel according to Matthew [25:1–13]

Jesus said to the disciples, "Then the kingdom of heaven will be like this. Ten bridesmaids took their lamps and went to meet the bridegroom. Five of them were foolish, and five were wise. When the foolish took their lamps, they took no oil with them; but the wise took flasks of oil with their lamps. As the bridegroom was delayed, all of them became drowsy and slept. But at midnight there was a shout, 'Look! Here is the bridegroom! Come out to meet him.' Then all those bridesmaids got up and trimmed their lamps. The foolish said to the wise, 'Give us some of your oil, for our lamps are going out.' But the wise replied, 'No! there will not be enough for you and for us; you had better go to the dealers and buy some for yourselves.' And while they went to buy it, the bridegroom came, and those who were ready went with him into the wedding banquet; and the door was shut. Later the other bridesmaids came also, saying, 'Lord, lord, open to us.' But he replied, 'Truly I tell you, I do not know you.' Keep awake therefore, for you know neither the day nor the hour."

Monday

Psalm 1 [page 585],   *Psalm 2* [page 586],
Psalm 3 [page 587] ❖ *Psalm 4* [page 587],
Psalm 7 [page 590]

A Reading (Lesson) from the Book of Isaiah [1:10–20]

Hear the word of the LORD, you rulers of Sodom! Listen to
the teaching of our God, you people of Gomorrah! What to
me is the multitude of your sacrifices? says the LORD; I have
had enough of burnt offerings of rams and the fat of fed
beasts; I do not delight in the blood of bulls, or of lambs, or
of goats. When you come to appear before me, who asked
this from your hand? Trample my courts no more; bringing
offerings is futile; incense is an abomination to me. New
moon and sabbath and calling of convocation—I cannot
endure solemn assemblies with iniquity. Your new moons
and your appointed festivals my soul hates; they have
become a burden to me, I am weary of bearing them. When
you stretch out your hands, I will hide my eyes from you;
even though you make many prayers, I will not listen; your
hands are full of blood. Wash yourselves; make yourselves
clean; remove the evil of your doings from before my eyes;
cease to do evil, learn to do good; seek justice, rescue the
oppressed, defend the orphan, plead for the widow. Come
now, let us argue it out, says the LORD: though your sins are
like scarlet, they shall be like snow; though they are red like
crimson, they shall become like wool. If you are willing and
obedient, you shall eat the good of the land; but if you
refuse and rebel, you shall be devoured by the sword; for the
mouth of the LORD has spoken.

*A Reading (Lesson) from the First Letter of Paul
to the Thessalonians* [1:1–10]

Paul, Silvanus, and Timothy, to the church of the
Thessalonians in God the Father and the Lord Jesus
Christ: Grace to you and peace. We always give thanks to
God for all of you and mention you in our prayers,

constantly remembering before our God and Father your work of faith and labor of love and steadfastness of hope in our Lord Jesus Christ. For we know, brothers and sisters beloved by God, that he has chosen you, because our message of the gospel came to you not in word only, but also in power and in the Holy Spirit and with full conviction; just as you know what kind of persons we proved to be among you for your sake. And you became imitators of us and of the Lord, for in spite of persecution you received the word with joy inspired by the Holy Spirit, so that you became an example to all the believers in Macedonia and in Achaia. For the word of the Lord has sounded forth from you not only in Macedonia and Achaia, but in every place your faith in God has become known, so that we have no need to speak about it. For the people of those regions report about us what kind of welcome we had among you, and how you turned to God from idols, to serve a living and true God, and to wait for his Son from heaven, whom he raised from the dead— Jesus, who rescues us from the wrath that is coming.

A Reading (Lesson) from the Gospel According to Luke [20:1–8]

One day, as he was teaching the people in the temple and telling the good news, the chief priests and the scribes came with the elders and said to him, "Tell us, by what authority are you doing these things? Who is it who gave you this authority?" He answered them, "I will also ask you a question, and you tell me: Did the baptism of John come from heaven, or was it of human origin?" They discussed it with one another, saying, "If we say, 'From heaven,' he will say, 'Why did you not believe him?' But if we say, 'Of human origin,' all the people will stone us; for they are convinced that John was a prophet." So they answered that they did not know where it came from. Then Jesus said to them, "Neither will I tell you by what authority I am doing these things."

Tuesday

Psalm 5 [page 588], *Psalm 6* [page 589] ❖
Psalm 10 [page 594], *Psalm 11* [page 596]

A Reading (Lesson) from the Book of Isaiah [1:21–31]

How the faithful city has become a whore! She that was full of justice, righteousness lodged in her—but now murderers! Your silver has become dross, your wine is mixed with water. Your princes are rebels and companions of thieves. Everyone loves a bribe and runs after gifts. They do not defend the orphan, and the widow's cause does not come before them. Therefore says the Sovereign, the LORD of hosts, the Mighty One of Israel: Ah, I will pour out my wrath on my enemies, and avenge myself on my foes! I will turn my hand against you; I will smelt away your dross as with lye and remove all your alloy. And I will restore your judges as at the first, and your counselors as at the beginning. Afterward you shall be called the city of righteousness, the faithful city. Zion shall be redeemed by justice, and those in her who repent, by righteousness. But rebels and sinners shall be destroyed together, and those who forsake the LORD shall be consumed. For you shall be ashamed of the oaks in which you delighted; and you shall blush for the gardens that you have chosen. For you shall be like an oak whose leaf withers, and like a garden without water. The strong shall become like tinder, and their work like a spark; they and their work shall burn together, with no one to quench them.

A Reading (Lesson) from the First Letter of Paul to the Thessalonians [2:1–12]

You yourselves know, brothers and sisters, that our coming to you was not in vain, but though we had already suffered and been shamefully mistreated at Philippi, as you know, we had courage in our God to declare to you the gospel of God in spite of great opposition. For our appeal does not spring from deceit or impure motives or trickery, but just as we have been approved by God to be entrusted with the message of the gospel, even so we speak, not to please mortals, but to please God who tests our hearts. As you know and as God is our witness, we never came with words of flattery or with a pretext for greed; nor did we seek praise from mortals, whether from you or from others, though we might have made demands as apostles of Christ. But we were gentle among you, like a nurse tenderly caring for her own children. So deeply do we care for you that we are determined to share with you not only the gospel of God but also our own selves, because you have become very dear to us. You remember our labor and toil, brothers and sisters; we worked night and day, so that we might not burden any of you while we proclaimed to you the gospel of God. You are witnesses, and God also, how pure, upright, and blameless our conduct was toward you believers. As you know, we dealt with each one of you like a father with his children, urging and encouraging you and pleading that you lead a life worthy of God, who calls you into his own kingdom and glory.

*A Reading (Lesson) from the Gospel according to
Luke* [20:9–18]

Jesus began to tell the people this parable: "A man
planted a vineyard, and leased it to tenants, and went to
another country for a long time. When the season came,
he sent a slave to the tenants in order that they might give
him his share of the produce of the vineyard; but the
tenants beat him and sent him away empty-handed. Next
he sent another slave; that one also they beat and insulted
and sent away empty-handed. And he sent still a third;
this one also they wounded and threw out. Then the
owner of the vineyard said, 'What shall I do? I will send
my beloved son; perhaps they will respect him.' But when
the tenants saw him, they discussed it among themselves
and said, 'This is the heir; let us kill him so that the
inheritance may be ours.' So they threw him out of the
vineyard and killed him. What then will the owner of the
vineyard do to them? He will come and destroy those
tenants and give the vineyard to others." When they heard
this, they said, "Heaven forbid!" But he looked at them
and said, "What then does this text mean: 'The stone that
the builders rejected has become the cornerstone'?
Everyone who falls on that stone will be broken to pieces;
and it will crush anyone on whom it falls."

Wednesday

Psalm 119:1–24 [page 763]   ❖   *Psalm 12* [page 597],
Psalm 13 [page 597],   *Psalm 14* [page 598]

A Reading (Lesson) from the Book of Isaiah [2:1–11]

The word that Isaiah son of Amoz saw concerning Judah
and Jerusalem. In days to come the mountain of the LORD's

house shall be established as the highest of the mountains, and shall be raised above the hills; all the nations shall stream to it. Many peoples shall come and say, "Come, let us go up to the mountain of the LORD, to the house of the God of Jacob; that he may teach us his ways and that we may walk in his paths." For out of Zion shall go forth instruction, and the word of the LORD from Jerusalem. He shall judge between the nations, and shall arbitrate for many peoples; they shall beat their swords into plowshares, and their spears into pruning hooks; nation shall not lift up sword against nation, neither shall they learn war any more. O house of Jacob, come, let us walk in the light of the LORD! For you have forsaken the ways of your people, O house of Jacob. Indeed they are full of diviners from the east and of soothsayers like the Philistines, and they clasp hands with foreigners. Their land is filled with silver and gold, and there is no end to their treasures; their land is filled with horses, and there is no end to their chariots. Their land is filled with idols; they bow down to the work of their hands, to what their own fingers have made. And so people are humbled, and everyone is brought low—do not forgive them! Enter into the rock, and hide in the dust from the terror of the LORD, and from the glory of his majesty. The haughty eyes of people shall be brought low, and the pride of everyone shall be humbled; and the LORD alone will be exalted in that day.

A Reading (Lesson) from the First Letter of Paul to the Thessalonians [2:13–20]

We also constantly give thanks to God for this, that when you received the word of God that you heard from us, you accepted it not as a human word but as what it really is, God's word, which is also at work in you believers. For you, brothers and sisters, became imitators of the churches of God in Christ Jesus that are in Judea, for you suffered the same things from your own compatriots as they did from the Jews, who killed both the Lord Jesus and the prophets, and drove us out; they displease God and oppose everyone by hindering us from speaking to the Gentiles so that they may be saved. Thus they have constantly been filling up the measure of their sins; but God's wrath has overtaken them at last. As for us, brothers and sisters, when, for a short time, we were made orphans by being separated from you—in person, not in heart—we longed with great eagerness to see you face to face. For we wanted to come to you—certainly I, Paul, wanted to again and again—but Satan blocked our way. For what is our hope or joy or crown of boasting before our Lord Jesus at his coming? Is it not you? Yes, you are our glory and joy!

A Reading (Lesson) from the Gospel according to Luke [20:19–26]

When the scribes and chief priests realized that Jesus had told this parable against them, they wanted to lay hands on him at that very hour, but they feared the people. So they watched him and sent spies who pretended to be honest, in order to trap him by what he said, so as to hand him over to the jurisdiction and authority of the governor. So they asked him, "Teacher, we know that you are right in what you say and teach, and you show deference to no one, but teach the way of God in accordance with truth. Is it lawful for us to pay taxes to the emperor, or not?" But he perceived their craftiness and said to them, "Show me a denarius. Whose head and whose title does it bear?" They said, "The emperor's." He said to them, "Then give to the emperor the things that are the emperor's, and to God the things that are God's." And they were not able in the presence of the people to trap him by what he said; and being amazed by his answer, they became silent.

Thursday

Psalm 18:1–20 [page 602] ❖ *Psalm 18:21–50* [page 604]

A Reading (Lesson) from the Book of Isaiah [2:12–22]

The LORD of hosts has a day against all that is proud and lofty, against all that is lifted up and high; against all the cedars of Lebanon, lofty and lifted up; and against all the oaks of Bashan; against all the high mountains, and against all the lofty hills; against every high tower, and against every fortified wall; against all the ships of Tarshish, and against all the beautiful craft. The haughtiness of people shall be humbled, and the pride of everyone shall be brought low; and the LORD alone will be exalted on that day. The idols shall utterly pass away. Enter the caves of the rocks and the holes of the ground, from the terror of the LORD, and from the glory of his majesty, when he rises to terrify the earth. On that day people will throw away to the moles and to the bats their idols of silver and their idols of gold, which they made for themselves to worship, to enter the caverns of the rocks and the clefts in the crags, from the terror of the LORD, and from the glory of his majesty, when he rises to terrify the earth. Turn away from mortals, who have only breath in their nostrils, for of what account are they?

*A Reading (Lesson) from the First Letter of Paul
to the Thessalonians* [3:1–13]

When we could bear it no longer, we decided to be left
alone in Athens; and we sent Timothy, our brother and
co-worker for God in proclaiming the gospel of Christ, to
strengthen and encourage you for the sake of your faith,
so that no one would be shaken by these persecutions.
Indeed, you yourselves know that this is what we are
destined for. In fact, when we were with you, we told you
beforehand that we were to suffer persecution; so it turned
out, as you know. For this reason, when I could bear it no
longer, I sent to find out about your faith; I was afraid
that somehow the tempter had tempted you and that our
labor had been in vain. But Timothy has just now come to
us from you, and has brought us the good news of your
faith and love. He has told us also that you always
remember us kindly and long to see us—just as we long to
see you. For this reason, brothers and sisters, during all
our distress and persecution we have been encouraged
about you through your faith. For we now live, if you
continue to stand firm in the Lord. How can we thank
God enough for you in return for all the joy that we feel
before our God because of you? Night and day we pray
most earnestly that we may see you face to face and
restore whatever is lacking in your faith. Now may our
God and Father himself and our Lord Jesus direct our way
to you. And may the Lord make you increase and abound
in love for one another and for all, just as we abound in
love for you. And may he so strengthen your hearts in
holiness that you may be blameless before our God and
Father at the coming of our Lord Jesus with all his saints.

A Reading (Lesson) from the Gospel according to Luke [20:27–40]

There came to Jesus some Sadducees, those who say there is no resurrection, and asked him a question, "Teacher, Moses wrote for us that if a man's brother dies, leaving a wife but no children, the man shall marry the widow and raise up children for his brother. Now there were seven brothers; the first married, and died childless; then the second and the third married her, and so in the same way all seven died childless. Finally the woman also died. In the resurrection, therefore, whose wife will the woman be? For the seven had married her." Jesus said to them, "Those who belong to this age marry and are given in marriage; but those who are considered worthy of a place in that age and in the resurrection from the dead neither marry nor are given in marriage. Indeed they cannot die anymore, because they are like angels and are children of God, being children of the resurrection. And the fact that the dead are raised Moses himself showed, in the story about the bush, where he speaks of the Lord as the God of Abraham, the God of Isaac, and the God of Jacob. Now he is God not of the dead, but of the living; for to him all of them are alive." Then some of the scribes answered, "Teacher, you have spoken well." For they no longer dared to ask him another question.

Friday

Psalm 16 [page 599], *Psalm 17* [page 600] ❖
Psalm 22 [page 610]

A Reading (Lesson) from the Book of Isaiah [3:8–15]

For Jerusalem has stumbled and Judah has fallen, because
their speech and their deeds are against the LORD, defying
his glorious presence. The look on their faces bears witness
against them; they proclaim their sin like Sodom, they do
not hide it. Woe to them! For they have brought evil on
themselves. Tell the innocent how fortunate they are, for
they shall eat the fruit of their labors. Woe to the guilty!
How unfortunate they are, for what their hands have done
shall be done to them. My people—children are their
oppressors, and women rule over them. O my people, your
leaders mislead you, and confuse the course of your paths.
The LORD rises to argue his case; he stands to judge the
peoples. The LORD enters into judgment with the elders and
princes of his people: It is you who have devoured the
vineyard; the spoil of the poor is in your houses. What do
you mean by crushing my people, by grinding the face of the
poor? says the Lord GOD of hosts.

*A Reading (Lesson) from the First Letter of Paul
to the Thessalonians* [4:1–12]

Finally, brothers and sisters, we ask and urge you in the
Lord Jesus that, as you learned from us how you ought to
live and to please God (as, in fact, you are doing), you
should do so more and more. For you know what
instructions we gave you through the Lord Jesus. For this
is the will of God, your sanctification: that you abstain
from fornication; that each one of you know how to
control your own body in holiness and honor, not with
lustful passion, like the Gentiles who do not know God;
that no one wrong or exploit a brother or sister in this
matter, because the Lord is an avenger in all these things,
just as we have already told you beforehand and solemnly

warned you. For God did not call us to impurity but in holiness. Therefore whoever rejects this rejects not human authority but God, who also gives his Holy Spirit to you. Now concerning love of the brothers and sisters, you do not need to have anyone write to you, for you yourselves have been taught by God to love one another; and indeed you do love all the brothers and sisters throughout Macedonia. But we urge you, beloved, to do so more and more, to aspire to live quietly, to mind your own affairs, and to work with your hands, as we directed you, so that you may behave properly toward outsiders and be dependent on no one.

A Reading (Lesson) from the Gospel according to Luke [20:41—21:4]

Jesus said to the scribes, "How can they say that the Messiah is David's son? For David himself says in the book of Psalms, 'The Lord said to my Lord, "Sit at my right hand, until I make your enemies your footstool."' David thus calls him Lord; so how can he be his son?" In the hearing of all the people he said to the disciples, "Beware of the scribes, who like to walk around in long robes, and love to be greeted with respect in the marketplaces, and to have the best seats in the synagogues and places of honor at banquets. They devour widows' houses and for the sake of appearance say long prayers. They will receive the greater condemnation." He looked up and saw rich people putting their gifts into the treasury; he also saw a poor widow put in two small copper coins. He said, "Truly I tell you, this poor widow has put in more than all of them; for all of them have contributed out of their abundance, but she out of her poverty has put in all she had to live on."

Saturday

Psalm 20 [page 608],   *Psalm 21:1–7(8–14)* [page 608]   ❖
Psalm 110:1–5(6–7) [page 753],   *Psalm 116* [page 759],
Psalm 117 [page 760]

A Reading (Lesson) from the Book of Isaiah [4:2–6]

On that day the branch of the LORD shall be beautiful and
glorious, and the fruit of the land shall be the pride and
glory of the survivors of Israel. Whoever is left in Zion and
remains in Jerusalem will be called holy, everyone who has
been recorded for life in Jerusalem, once the Lord has
washed away the filth of the daughters of Zion and cleansed
the bloodstains of Jerusalem from its midst by a spirit of
judgment and by a spirit of burning. Then the LORD will
create over the whole site of Mount Zion and over its places
of assembly a cloud by day and smoke and the shining of a
flaming fire by night. Indeed over all the glory there will be a
canopy. It will serve as a pavilion, a shade by day from the
heat, and a refuge and a shelter from the storm and rain.

*A Reading (Lesson) from the First Letter of Paul
to the Thessalonians* [4:13–18]

We do not want you to be uninformed, brothers and
sisters, about those who have died, so that you may not
grieve as others do who have no hope. For since we
believe that Jesus died and rose again, even so, through
Jesus, God will bring with him those who have died. For
this we declare to you by the word of the Lord, that we
who are alive, who are left until the coming of the Lord,
will by no means precede those who have died. For the
Lord himself, with a cry of command, with the archangel's
call and with the sound of God's trumpet, will descend

from heaven, and the dead in Christ will rise first. Then we who are alive, who are left, will be caught up in the clouds together with them to meet the Lord in the air; and so we will be with the Lord forever. Therefore encourage one another with these words.

A Reading (Lesson) from the Gospel according to Luke [21:5-19]

When some were speaking about the temple, how it was adorned with beautiful stones and gifts dedicated to God, Jesus said, "As for these things that you see, the days will come when not one stone will be left upon another; all will be thrown down." They asked him, "Teacher, when will this be, and what will be the sign that this is about to take place?" And he said, "Beware that you are not led astray; for many will come in my name and say, 'I am he!' and, 'The time is near!' Do not go after them. When you hear of wars and insurrections, do not be terrified; for these things must take place first, but the end will not follow immediately." Then he said to them, "Nation will rise against nation, and kingdom against kingdom; there will be great earthquakes, and in various places famines and plagues; and there will be dreadful portents and great signs from heaven. But before all this occurs, they will arrest you and persecute you; they will hand you over to synagogues and prisons, and you will be brought before kings and governors because of my name. This will give you an opportunity to testify. So make up your minds not to prepare your defense in advance; for I will give you words and a wisdom that none of your opponents will be able to withstand or contradict. You will be betrayed even by parents and brothers, by relatives and friends; and they will put some of you to death. You will be hated by all because of my name. But not a hair of your head will perish. By your endurance you will gain your souls."

Week of 2 Advent

Sunday

Psalm 148 [page 805],   *Psalm 149* [page 807],
Psalm 150 [page 807],   ❖   *Psalm 114* [page 756],
Psalm 115 [page 757]

A Reading (Lesson) from the Book of Isaiah [5:1–7]

Let me sing for my beloved my love-song concerning his vineyard: My beloved had a vineyard on a very fertile hill. He dug it and cleared it of stones, and planted it with choice vines; he built a watchtower in the midst of it, and hewed out a wine vat in it; he expected it to yield grapes, but it yielded wild grapes. And now, inhabitants of Jerusalem and people of Judah, judge between me and my vineyard. What more was there to do for my vineyard that I have not done in it? When I expected it to yield grapes, why did it yield wild grapes? And now I will tell you what I will do to my vineyard. I will remove its hedge, and it shall be devoured; I will break down its wall, and it shall be trampled down. I will make it a waste; it shall not be pruned or hoed, and it shall be overgrown with briers and thorns; I will also command the clouds that they rain no rain upon it. For the vineyard of the LORD of hosts is the house of Israel, and the people of Judah are his pleasant planting; he expected justice, but saw bloodshed; righteousness, but heard a cry!

*A Reading (Lesson) from the Second Letter of
Peter* [3:11–18]

Since all these things are to be dissolved in this way, what
sort of persons ought you to be in leading lives of holiness
and godliness, waiting for and hastening the coming of the
day of God, because of which the heavens will be set
ablaze and dissolved, and the elements will melt with fire?
But, in accordance with his promise, we wait for new
heavens and a new earth, where righteousness is at home.
Therefore, beloved, while you are waiting for these things,
strive to be found by him at peace, without spot or
blemish; and regard the patience of our Lord as salvation.
So also our beloved brother Paul wrote to you according
to the wisdom given him, speaking of this as he does in all
his letters. There are some things in them hard to
understand, which the ignorant and unstable twist to their
own destruction, as they do the other scriptures. You
therefore, beloved, since you are forewarned, beware that
you are not carried away with the error of the lawless and
lose your own stability. But grow in the grace and
knowledge of our Lord and Savior Jesus Christ. To him
be the glory both now and to the day of eternity. Amen.

*A Reading (Lesson) from the Gospel according to
Luke* [7:28–35]

Jesus spoke to the crowds concerning John: "I tell you,
among those born of women no one is greater than John;
yet the least in the kingdom of God is greater than he."
(And all the people who heard this, including the tax
collectors, acknowledged the justice of God, because they
had been baptized with John's baptism. But by refusing to
be baptized by him, the Pharisees and the lawyers rejected
God's purpose for themselves.) "To what then will I

compare the people of this generation, and what are they like? They are like children sitting in the marketplace and calling to one another, 'We played the flute for you, and you did not dance; we wailed, and you did not weep.' For John the Baptist has come eating no bread and drinking no wine, and you say, 'He has a demon'; the Son of Man has come eating and drinking, and you say, 'Look, a glutton and a drunkard, a friend of tax collectors and sinners!' Nevertheless, wisdom is vindicated by all her children."

Monday

Psalm 25 [page 614] ❖ *Psalm 9* [page 593],
Psalm 15 [page 599]

A Reading (Lesson) from the Book of Isaiah [5:8–12,18–23]

Ah, you who join house to house, who add field to field, until there is room for no one but you, and you are left to live alone in the midst of the land! The LORD of hosts has sworn in my hearing: Surely many houses shall be desolate, large and beautiful houses, without inhabitant. For ten acres of vineyard shall yield but one bath, and a homer of seed shall yield a mere ephah. Ah, you who rise early in the morning in pursuit of strong drink, who linger in the evening to be inflamed by wine, whose feasts consist of lyre and harp, tambourine and flute and wine, but who do not regard the deeds of the LORD, or see the work of his hands! Ah, you who drag iniquity along with cords of falsehood, who drag sin along as with cart ropes, who say, "Let him make haste, let him speed his work that we may see it; let the plan of the Holy One of Israel hasten to fulfillment, that we may know it!" Ah, you who call evil good and good evil, who put darkness for light and light for darkness, who put bitter for sweet and sweet for bitter! Ah, you who are wise in your own eyes, and shrewd in your own sight! Ah, you who are heroes in drinking wine and valiant at mixing drink, who acquit the guilty for a bribe, and deprive the innocent of their rights!

A Reading (Lesson) from the First Letter of Paul to the Thessalonians [5:1–11]

Now concerning the times and the seasons, brothers and sisters, you do not need to have anything written to you. For you yourselves know very well that the day of the Lord will come like a thief in the night. When they say, "There is peace and security," then sudden destruction will come upon them, as labor pains come upon a pregnant woman, and there will be no escape! But you, beloved, are not in darkness, for that day to surprise you like a thief; for you are all children of light and children of the day; we are not of the night or of darkness. So then let us not fall asleep as others do, but let us keep awake and be sober; for those who sleep sleep at night, and those who are drunk get drunk at night. But since we belong to the day, let us be sober, and put on the breastplate of faith and love, and for a helmet the hope of salvation. For God has destined us not for wrath but for obtaining salvation through our Lord Jesus Christ, who died for us, so that whether we are awake or asleep we may live with him. Therefore encourage one another and build up each other, as indeed you are doing.

A Reading (Lesson) from the Gospel according to Luke [21:20–28]

In the hearing of all the people Jesus said to his disciples, "When you see Jerusalem surrounded by armies, then know that its desolation has come near. Then those in Judea must flee to the mountains, and those inside the city must leave it, and those out in the country must not enter it; for these are days of vengeance, as a fulfillment of all that is written. Woe to those who are pregnant and to those who are nursing infants in those days! For there will be great distress on the earth and wrath against this people; they will fall by the edge of the sword and be taken away as captives among all nations; and Jerusalem will be trampled on by the Gentiles, until the times of the Gentiles are fulfilled. There will be signs in the sun, the moon, and the stars, and on the earth distress among nations confused by the roaring of the sea and the waves. People will faint from fear and foreboding of what is coming upon the world, for the powers of the heavens will be shaken. Then they will see 'the Son of Man coming in a cloud' with power and great glory. Now when these things begin to take place, stand up and raise your heads, because your redemption is drawing near."

Tuesday

Psalm 26 [page 616], *Psalm 28* [page 619] ❖
Psalm 36 [page 632], *Psalm 39* [page 638]

A Reading (Lesson) from the Book of Isaiah [5:13–17, 24–25]

My people go into exile without knowledge; their nobles are dying of hunger, and their multitude is parched with thirst. Therefore Sheol has enlarged its appetite and opened its mouth beyond measure; the nobility of Jerusalem and her multitude go down, her throng and all who exult in her. People are bowed down, everyone is brought low, and the eyes of the haughty are humbled. But the LORD of hosts is exalted by justice, and the Holy God shows himself holy by righteousness. Then the lambs shall graze as in their pasture, fatlings and kids shall feed among the ruins. Therefore, as the tongue of fire devours the stubble, and as dry grass sinks down in the flame, so their root will become rotten, and their blossom go up like dust; for they have rejected the instruction of the LORD of hosts, and have despised the word of the Holy One of Israel. Therefore the anger of the LORD was kindled against his people, and he stretched out his hand against them and struck them; the mountains quaked, and their corpses were like refuse in the streets. For all this his anger has not turned away, and his hand is stretched out still.

A Reading (Lesson) from the First Letter of Paul to the Thessalonians [5:12–28]

We appeal to you, brothers and sisters, to respect those who labor among you, and have charge of you in the Lord and admonish you; esteem them very highly in love because of their work. Be at peace among yourselves. And we urge you, beloved, to admonish the idlers, encourage the faint hearted, help the weak, be patient with all of them. See that none of you repays evil for evil, but always seek to do good to one another and to all. Rejoice always, pray without ceasing, give thanks in all circumstances; for this is the will of God in Christ Jesus for you. Do not quench the Spirit. Do not despise the words of prophets, but test everything; hold fast to what is good; abstain from every form of evil. May the God of peace himself sanctify you entirely; and may your spirit and soul and body be kept sound and blameless at the coming of our Lord Jesus Christ. The one who calls you is faithful, and he will do this. Beloved, pray for us. Greet all the brothers and sisters with a holy kiss. I solemnly command you by the Lord that this letter be read to all of them. The grace of our Lord Jesus Christ be with you.

A Reading (Lesson) from the Gospel according to Luke [21:29–38]

In the hearing of all the people, Jesus told the disciples a parable: "Look at the fig tree, and all the trees; as soon as they sprout leaves you can see for yourselves and know that summer is already near. So also, when you see these things taking place, you know that the kingdom of God is near. Truly I tell you, this generation will not pass away until all things have taken place. Heaven and earth will pass away, but my words will not pass away. Be on guard so that your hearts are not weighed down with dissipation and drunkenness and the worries of this life, and that day does not catch you unexpectedly, like a trap. For it will come upon all who live on the face of the whole earth. Be alert at all times, praying that you may have the strength to escape all these things that will take place, and to stand before the Son of Man." Every day he was teaching in the temple, and at night he would go out and spend the night on the Mount of Olives, as it was called. And all the people would get up early in the morning to listen to him in the temple.

Wednesday

Psalm 38 [page 636]   ❖   *Psalm 119:25–48* [page 765]

A Reading (Lesson) from the Book of Isaiah [6:1–13]

In the year that King Uzziah died, I saw the Lord sitting on a throne, high and lofty; and the hem of his robe filled the temple. Seraphs were in attendance above him; each had six wings: with two they covered their faces, and with two they covered their feet, and with two they flew. And one called to another and said: "Holy, holy, holy is the LORD of hosts; the whole earth is full of his glory." The pivots on the thresholds shook at the voices of those who called, and the house filled with smoke. And I said: "Woe is me! I am lost, for I am a man of unclean lips, and I live among a people of unclean lips; yet my eyes have seen the King, the LORD of hosts!" Then one of the seraphs flew to me, holding a live coal that had been taken from the altar with a pair of tongs. The seraph touched my mouth with it and said: "Now that this has touched your lips, your guilt has departed and your sin is blotted out." Then I heard the voice of the Lord saying, "Whom shall I send, and who will go for us?" And I said, "Here am I; send me!" And he said, "Go and say to this people: 'Keep listening, but do not comprehend; keep looking, but do not understand.' Make the mind of this people dull, and stop their ears, and shut their eyes, so that they may not look with their eyes, and listen with their ears, and comprehend with their minds, and turn and be healed." Then I said, "How long, O Lord?" And he said: "Until cities lie waste without inhabitant, and houses without people, and the land is utterly desolate; until the LORD sends everyone far away, and vast is the emptiness in the midst of the land. Even if a tenth part remain in it, it will be burned again, like a terebinth or an oak whose stump remains standing when it is felled." The holy seed is its stump.

A Reading (Lesson) from the Second Letter of Paul to the Thessalonians [1:1–12]

Paul, Silvanus, and Timothy, to the church of the Thessalonians in God our Father and the Lord Jesus Christ: Grace to you and peace from God our Father and the Lord Jesus Christ. We must always give thanks to God for you, brothers and sisters, as is right, because your faith is growing abundantly, and the love of everyone of you for one another is increasing. Therefore we ourselves boast of you among the churches of God for your steadfastness and faith during all your persecutions and the afflictions that you are enduring. This is evidence of the righteous judgment of God, and is intended to make you worthy of the kingdom of God, for which you are also suffering. For it is indeed just of God to repay with affliction those who afflict you, and to give relief to the afflicted as well as to us, when the Lord Jesus is revealed from heaven with his mighty angels in flaming fire, inflicting vengeance on those who do not know God and on those who do not obey the gospel of our Lord Jesus. These will suffer the punishment of eternal destruction, separated from the presence of the Lord and from the glory of his might, when he comes to be glorified by his saints and to be marveled at on that day among all who have believed, because our testimony to you was believed. To this end we always pray for you, asking that our God will make you worthy of his call and will fulfill by his power every good resolve and work of faith, so that the name of our Lord Jesus may be glorified in you, and you in him, according to the grace of our God and the Lord Jesus Christ.

A Reading (Lesson) from the Gospel according to John [7:53—8:11]

Jesus went to the Mount of Olives. Early in the morning he came again to the temple. All the people came to him and he sat down and began to teach them. The scribes and the Pharisees brought a woman who had been caught in adultery; and making her stand before all of them, they said to him, "Teacher, this woman was caught in the very act of committing adultery. Now in the law Moses commanded us to stone such women. Now what do you say?" They said this to test him, so that they might have some charge to bring against him. Jesus bent down and wrote with his finger on the ground. When they kept on questioning him, he straightened up and said to them, "Let anyone among you who is without sin be the first to throw a stone at her." And once again he bent down and wrote on the ground. When they heard it, they went away, one by one, beginning with the elders; and Jesus was left alone with the woman standing before him. Jesus straightened up and said to her, "Woman, where are they? Has no one condemned you?" She said, "No one, sir." And Jesus said, "Neither do I condemn you. Go your way, and from now on do not sin again."

Thursday

Psalm 37:1–18 [page 633] ❖ *Psalm 37:19–42* [page 634]

A Reading (Lesson) from the Book of Isaiah [7:1–9]

In the days of Ahaz son of Jotham son of Uzziah, king of Judah, King Rezin of Aram and King Pekah son of Remaliah of Israel went up to attack Jerusalem, but could not mount an attack against it. When the house of David heard that Aram had allied itself with Ephraim, the heart of Ahaz and the heart of his people shook as the trees of the forest shake before the wind. Then the LORD said to Isaiah, Go out to meet Ahaz, you and your son Shear-jashub, at the end of the conduit of the upper pool on the highway to the Fuller's Field, and say to him, Take heed, be quiet, do not fear, and do not let your heart be faint because of these two smoldering stumps of firebrands, because of the fierce anger of Rezin and Aram and the son of Remaliah. Because Aram—with Ephraim and the son of Remaliah—has plotted evil against you, saying, Let us go up against Judah and cut off Jerusalem and conquer it for ourselves and make the son of Tabeel king in it; therefore thus says the Lord GOD: It shall not stand, and it shall not come to pass. For the head of Aram is Damascus, and the head of Damascus is Rezin. (Within sixty-five years Ephraim will be shattered, no longer a people.) The head of Ephraim is Samaria, and the head of Samaria is the son of Remaliah. If you do not stand firm in faith, you shall not stand at all.

A Reading (Lesson) from the Second Letter of Paul to the Thessalonians [2:1–12]

As to the coming of our Lord Jesus Christ and our being gathered together to him, we beg you, brothers and sisters, not to be quickly shaken in mind or alarmed, either by spirit or by word or by letter, as though from us, to the effect that the day of the Lord is already here. Let no one deceive you in any way; for that day will not come unless the rebellion comes first and the lawless one is revealed, the one destined for destruction. He opposes and exalts himself above every so-called god or object of worship, so that he takes his seat in the temple of God, declaring himself to be God. Do you not remember that I told you these things when I was still with you? And you know what is now restraining him, so that he may be revealed when his time comes. For the mystery of lawlessness is already at work, but only until the one who now restrains it is removed. And then the lawless one will be revealed, whom the Lord Jesus will destroy with the breath of his mouth, annihilating him by the manifestation of his coming. The coming of the lawless one is apparent in the working of Satan, who uses all power, signs, lying wonders, and every kind of wicked deception for those who are perishing, because they refused to love the truth and so be saved. For this reason God sends them a powerful delusion, leading them to believe what is false, so that all who have not believed the truth but took pleasure in unrighteousness will be condemned.

A Reading (Lesson) from the Gospel according to Luke [22:1-13]

Now the festival of Unleavened Bread, which is called the Passover, was near. The chief priests and the scribes were looking for a way to put Jesus to death, for they were afraid of the people. Then Satan entered into Judas called Iscariot, who was one of the twelve; he went away and conferred with the chief priests and officers of the temple police about how he might betray him to them. They were greatly pleased and agreed to give him money. So he consented and began to look for an opportunity to betray him to them when no crowd was present. Then came the day of Unleavened Bread, on which the Passover lamb had to be sacrificed. So Jesus sent Peter and John, saying, "Go and prepare the Passover meal for us that we may eat it." They asked him, "Where do you want us to make preparations for it?" "Listen," he said to them, "when you have entered the city, a man carrying a jar of water will meet you; follow him into the house he enters and say to the owner of the house, 'The teacher asks you, "Where is the guest room, where I may eat the Passover with my disciples?" ' He will show you a large room upstairs, already furnished. Make preparations for us there." So they went and found everything as he had told them; and they prepared the Passover meal.

Friday

Psalm 31 [page 622]   ❖   *Psalm 35* [page 629]

A Reading (Lesson) from the Book of Isaiah [7:10–25]

Again the LORD spoke to Ahaz, saying, Ask a sign of the
LORD your God; let it be deep as Sheol or high as heaven.
But Ahaz said, I will not ask, and I will not put the LORD to
the test. Then Isaiah said: "Hear then, O house of David! Is
it too little for you to weary mortals, that you weary my
God also? Therefore the Lord himself will give you a sign.
Look, the young woman is with child and shall bear a son,
and shall name him Immanuel. He shall eat curds and honey
by the time he knows how to refuse the evil and choose the
good. For before the child knows how to refuse the evil and
choose the good, the land before whose two kings you are in
dread will be deserted. The LORD will bring on you and on
your people and on your ancestral house such days as have
not come since the day that Ephraim departed from
Judah—the king of Assyria." On that day the LORD will
whistle for the fly that is at the sources of the streams of
Egypt, and for the bee that is in the land of Assyria. And
they will all come and settle in the steep ravines, and in the
clefts of the rocks, and on all the thornbushes, and on all the
pastures. On that day the Lord will shave with a razor hired
beyond the River—with the king of Assyria—the head and
the hair of the feet, and it will take off the beard as well. On
that day one will keep alive a young cow and two sheep,
and will eat curds because of the abundance of milk that
they give; for everyone that is left in the land shall eat curds
and honey. On that day every place where there used to be a
thousand vines, worth a thousand shekels of silver, will
become briers and thorns. With bow and arrows one will go
there, for all the land will be briers and thorns; and as for all

the hills that used to be hoed with a hoe, you will not go there for fear of briers and thorns; but they will become a place where cattle are let loose and where sheep tread.

A Reading (Lesson) from the Second Letter of Paul to the Thessalonians [2:13—3:5]

We must always give thanks to God for you, brothers and sisters beloved by the Lord, because God chose you as the first fruits for salvation through sanctification by the Spirit and through belief in the truth. For this purpose he called you through our proclamation of the good news, so that you may obtain the glory of our Lord Jesus Christ. So then, brothers and sisters, stand firm and hold fast to the traditions that you were taught by us, either by word of mouth or by our letter. Now may our Lord Jesus Christ himself and God our Father, who loved us and through grace gave us eternal comfort and good hope, comfort your hearts and strengthen them in every good work and word. Finally, brothers and sisters, pray for us, so that the word of the Lord may spread rapidly and be glorified everywhere, just as it is among you, and that we may be rescued from wicked and evil people; for not all have faith. But the Lord is faithful; he will strengthen you and guard you from the evil one. And we have confidence in the Lord concerning you, that you are doing and will go on doing the things that we command. May the Lord direct your hearts to the love of God and to the steadfastness of Christ.

A Reading (Lesson) from the Gospel according to Luke [22:14–30]

When the hour for the Passover came, Jesus took his place at the table, and the apostles with him. He said to them,

"I have eagerly desired to eat this Passover with you before I suffer; for I tell you, I will not eat it until it is fulfilled in the kingdom of God." Then he took a cup, and after giving thanks he said, "Take this and divide it among yourselves; for I tell you that from now on I will not drink of the fruit of the vine until the kingdom of God comes." Then he took a loaf of bread, and when he had given thanks, he broke it and gave it to them, saying, "This is my body, which is given for you. Do this in remembrance of me." And he did the same with the cup after supper, saying, "This cup that is poured out for you is the new covenant in my blood. But see, the one who betrays me is with me, and his hand is on the table. For the Son of Man is going as it has been determined, but woe to that one by whom he is betrayed!" Then they began to ask one another which one of them it could be who would do this. A dispute also arose among them as to which one of them was to be regarded as the greatest. But he said to them, "The kings of the Gentiles lord it over them; and those in authority over them are called benefactors. But not so with you; rather the greatest among you must become like the youngest, and the leader like one who serves. For who is greater, the one who is at the table or the one who serves? Is it not the one at the table? But I am among you as one who serves. You are those who have stood by me in my trials; and I confer on you, just as my Father has conferred on me, a kingdom, so that you may eat and drink at my table in my kingdom, and you will sit on thrones judging the twelve tribes of Israel."

Saturday

Psalm 30 [page 621],   *Psalm 32* [page 624]   ❖
Psalm 42 [page 643],   *Psalm 43* [page 644]

A Reading (Lesson) from the Book of Isaiah [8:1–15]

Then the LORD said to me, Take a large tablet and write on
it in common characters, "Belonging to Maher-shalal-hash-
baz," and have it attested for me by reliable witnesses, the
priest Uriah and Zechariah son of Jeberechiah. And I went
to the prophetess, and she conceived and bore a son. Then
the LORD said to me, Name him Maher-shalal-hash-baz; for
before the child knows how to call "My father" or "My
mother," the wealth of Damascus and the spoil of Samaria
will be carried away by the king of Assyria. The LORD spoke
to me again: Because this people has refused the waters of
Shiloah that flow gently, and melt in fear before Rezin and
the son of Remaliah; therefore, the Lord is bringing up
against it the mighty flood waters of the River, the king of
Assyria and all his glory; it will rise above all its channels
and overflow all its banks; it will sweep on into Judah as a
flood, and, pouring over, it will reach up to the neck; and its
outspread wings will fill the breadth of your land, O
Immanuel. Band together, you peoples, and be dismayed;
listen, all you far countries; gird yourselves and be
dismayed; gird yourselves and be dismayed! Take counsel
together, but it shall be brought to naught; speak a word,
but it will not stand, for God is with us. For the LORD spoke
thus to me while his hand was strong upon me, and warned
me not to walk in the way of this people, saying: Do not call
conspiracy all that this people calls conspiracy, and do not
fear what it fears, or be in dread. But the LORD of hosts, him
you shall regard as holy; let him be your fear, and let him be
your dread. He will become a sanctuary, a stone one strikes
against; for both houses of Israel he will become a rock one
stumbles over—a trap and a snare for the inhabitants of
Jerusalem. And many among them shall stumble; they shall
fall and be broken; they shall be snared and taken.

*A Reading (Lesson) from the Second Letter of Paul to the
Thessalonians* [3:6–18]

Now we command you, beloved, in the name of our Lord
Jesus Christ, to keep away from believers who are living
in idleness and not according to the tradition that they
received from us. For you yourselves know how you ought
to imitate us; we were not idle when we were with you,
and we did not eat anyone's bread without paying for it;
but with toil and labor we worked night and day, so that
we might not burden any of you. This was not because we
do not have that right, but in order to give you an
example to imitate. For even when we were with you, we
gave you this command: Anyone unwilling to work should
not eat. For we hear that some of you are living in
idleness, mere busybodies, not doing any work. Now such
persons we command and exhort in the Lord Jesus Christ
to do their work quietly and to earn their own living.
Brothers and sisters, do not be weary in doing what is
right. Take note of those who do not obey what we say in
this letter; have nothing to do with them, so that they may
be ashamed. Do not regard them as enemies, but warn
them as believers. Now may the Lord of peace himself
give you peace at all times in all ways. The Lord be with
all of you. I, Paul, write this greeting with my own hand.
This is the mark in every letter of mine; it is the way I
write. The grace of our Lord Jesus Christ be with all
of you.

*A Reading (Lesson) from the Gospel according to
Luke* [22:31–38]

Jesus said to Peter, "Simon, Simon, listen! Satan has
demanded to sift all of you like wheat, but I have prayed

for you that your own faith may not fail; and you, when once you have turned back, strengthen your brothers." And he said to him, "Lord, I am ready to go with you to prison and to death!" Jesus said, "I tell you, Peter, the cock will not crow this day, until you have denied three times that you know me." He said to them, "When I sent you out without a purse, bag, or sandals, did you lack anything?" They said, "No, not a thing." He said to them, "But now, the one who has a purse must take it, and likewise a bag. And the one who has no sword must sell his cloak and buy one. For I tell you, this scripture must be fulfilled in me, 'And he was counted among the lawless'; and indeed what is written about me is being fulfilled." They said, "Lord, look, here are two swords." He replied, "It is enough."

Week of 3 Advent

Sunday

Psalm 63:1–8(9–11) [page 670]
Psalm 98 [page 727] ❖ *Psalm 103* [page 733]

A Reading (Lesson) from the Book of Isaiah [13:6–13]

Wail, for the day of the LORD is near; it will come like destruction from the Almighty! Therefore all hands will be feeble, and every human heart will melt, and they will be dismayed. Pangs and agony will seize them; they will be in anguish like a woman in labor. They will look aghast at one another; their faces will be aflame. See, the day of the Lord comes, cruel, with wrath and fierce anger, to make the earth a desolation, and to destroy its sinners from it. For the stars of the heavens and their constellations will not give their light; the sun will be dark at its rising, and the moon will not shed its light. I will punish the world for its evil, and the wicked for their iniquity; I will put an end to the pride of the arrogant, and lay low the insolence of tyrants. I will make mortals more rare than fine gold, and humans than the gold of Ophir. Therefore I will make the heavens tremble, and the earth will be shaken out of its place, at the wrath of the Lord of hosts in the day of his fierce anger.

A Reading (Lesson) from the Letter to the Hebrews [12:18–29]

You have not come to something that can be touched, a blazing fire, and darkness, and gloom, and a tempest, and the sound of a trumpet, and a voice whose words made the hearers beg that not another word be spoken to them. (For they could not endure the order that was given, "If even an animal touches the mountain, it shall be stoned to death." Indeed, so terrifying was the sight that Moses said, "I tremble with fear.") But you have come to Mount Zion and to the city of the living God, the heavenly Jerusalem, and to innumerable angels in festal gathering, and to the assembly of the firstborn who are enrolled in heaven, and to God the judge of all, and to the spirits of the righteous made perfect, and to Jesus, the mediator of a new covenant, and to the sprinkled blood that speaks a better word than the blood of Abel. See that you do not refuse the one who is speaking; for if they did not escape when they refused the one who warned them on earth, how much less will we escape if we reject the one who warns from heaven! At that time his voice shook the earth; but now he has promised, "Yet once more I will shake not only the earth but also the heaven." This phrase, "Yet once more," indicates the removal of what is shaken—that is, created things—so that what cannot be shaken may remain. Therefore, since we are receiving a kingdom that cannot be shaken, let us give thanks, by which we offer to God an acceptable worship with reverence and awe; for indeed our God is a consuming fire.

A Reading (Lesson) from the Gospel according to John [3:22–30]

After speaking with Nicodemus, Jesus and his disciples went into the Judean countryside, and he spent some time there with them and baptized. John also was baptizing at Aenon near Salim because water was abundant there; and people kept coming and were being baptized—John, of course, had not yet been thrown into prison. Now a discussion about purification arose between John's disciples and a Jew. They came to John and said to him, "Rabbi, the one who was with you across the Jordan, to whom you testified, here he is baptizing, and all are going to him." John answered, "No one can receive anything except what has been given from heaven. You yourselves are my witnesses that I said, 'I am not the Messiah, but I have been sent ahead of him.' He who has the bride is the bridegroom. The friend of the bridegroom, who stands and hears him, rejoices greatly at the bridegroom's voice. For this reason my joy has been fulfilled. He must increase, but I must decrease."

Monday

Psalm 41 [page 641],   Psalm 52 [page 657]   ❖
Psalm 44 [page 645]

A Reading (Lesson) from the Book of Isaiah [8:16—9:1]

Bind up the testimony, seal the teaching among my disciples.
I will wait for the LORD, who is hiding his face from the
house of Jacob, and I will hope in him. See, I and the
children whom the LORD has given me are signs and
portents in Israel from the LORD of hosts, who dwells on
Mount Zion. Now if people say to you, "Consult the ghosts
and the familiar spirits that chirp and mutter; should not a
people consult their gods, the dead on behalf of the living,
for teaching and for instruction?", surely, those who speak
like this will have no dawn! They will pass through the land,
greatly distressed and hungry; when they are hungry, they
will be enraged and will curse their king and their gods.
They will turn their faces upward, or they will look to the
earth, but will see only distress and darkness, the gloom of
anguish; and they will be thrust into thick darkness. But
there will be no gloom for those who were in anguish. In the
former time he brought into contempt the land of Zebulun
and the land of Naphtali, but in the latter time he will make
glorious the way of the sea, the land beyond the Jordan,
Galilee of the nations.

*A Reading (Lesson) from the Second Letter of
Peter* [1:1–11]

Simeon Peter, a servant and apostle of Jesus Christ, to
those who have received a faith as precious as ours
through the righteousness of our God and Savior Jesus
Christ: May grace and peace be yours in abundance in the

knowledge of God and of Jesus our Lord. His divine power has given us everything needed for life and godliness, through the knowledge of him who called us by his own glory and goodness. Thus he has given us, through these things, his precious and very great promises, so that through them you may escape from the corruption that is in the world because of lust, and may become participants of the divine nature. For this very reason, you must make every effort to support your faith with goodness, and goodness with knowledge, and knowledge with self-control, and self-control with endurance, and endurance with godliness, and godliness with mutual affection, and mutual affection with love. For if these things are yours and are increasing among you, they keep you from being ineffective and unfruitful in the knowledge of our Lord Jesus Christ. For anyone who lacks these things is nearsighted and blind, and is forgetful of the cleansing of past sins. Therefore, brothers and sisters, be all the more eager to confirm your call and election, for if you do this, you will never stumble. For in this way, entry into the eternal kingdom of our Lord and Savior Jesus Christ will be richly provided for you.

A Reading (Lesson) from the Gospel according to Luke [22:39-53]

Jesus came out of the upper room, and went, as was his custom, to the Mount of Olives; and the disciples followed him. When he reached the place, he said to them, "Pray that you may not come into the time of trial." Then he withdrew from them about a stone's throw, knelt down, and prayed, "Father, if you are willing, remove this cup from me; yet, not my will but yours be done." Then an angel from heaven appeared to him and gave him strength.

In his anguish he prayed more earnestly, and his sweat became like great drops of blood falling down on the ground. When he got up from prayer, he came to the disciples and found them sleeping because of grief, and he said to them, "Why are you sleeping? Get up and pray that you may not come into the time of trial." While he was still speaking, suddenly a crowd came, and the one called Judas, one of the twelve, was leading them. He approached Jesus to kiss him; but Jesus said to him, "Judas, is it with a kiss that you are betraying the Son of Man?" When those who were around him saw what was coming, they asked, "Lord, should we strike with the sword?" Then one of them struck the slave of the high priest and cut off his right ear. But Jesus said, "No more of this!" And he touched his ear and healed him. Then Jesus said to the chief priests, the officers of the temple police, and the elders who had come for him, "Have you come out with swords and clubs as if I were a bandit? When I was with you day after day in the temple, you did not lay hands on me. But this is your hour, and the power of darkness!"

Tuesday

Psalm 45 [page 647]   ❖   *Psalm 47* [page 650], *Psalm 48* [page 651]

A Reading (Lesson) from the Book of Isaiah [9:1–7]

There will be no gloom for those who are in anguish. In the former time he brought into contempt the land of Zebulun and the land of Naphtali, but in the latter time he will make glorious the way of the sea, the land beyond the Jordan, Galilee of the nations. The people who walked in darkness have seen a great light; those who lived in a land of deep darkness—on them light has shined. You have multiplied the nation, you have increased its joy; they rejoice before you as with joy at the harvest, as people exult when dividing plunder. For the yoke of their burden, and the bar across their shoulders, the rod of their oppressor, you have broken as on the day of Midian. For all the boots of the tramping warriors and all the garments rolled in blood shall be burned as fuel for the fire. For a child has been born for us, a son given to us; authority rests upon his shoulders; and he is named Wonderful Counselor, Mighty God, Everlasting Father, Prince of Peace. His authority shall grow continually, and there shall be endless peace for the throne of David and his kingdom. He will establish and uphold it with justice and with righteousness from this time onward and forevermore. The zeal of the LORD of hosts will do this.

A Reading (Lesson) from the Second Letter of Peter [1:12–21]

I intend to keep on reminding you of these things, though you know them already and are established in the truth that has come to you. I think it right, as long as I am in this body, to refresh your memory, since I know that my death will come soon, as indeed our Lord Jesus Christ has made clear to me. And I will make every effort so that after my departure you may be able at any time to recall these things. For we did not follow cleverly devised myths when we made known to you the power and coming of our Lord Jesus Christ, but we had been eyewitnesses of his majesty. For he received honor and glory from God the Father when that voice was conveyed to him by the Majestic Glory, saying, "This is my Son, my Beloved, with whom I am well pleased." We ourselves heard this voice come from heaven, while we were with him on the holy mountain. So we have the prophetic message more fully confirmed. You will do well to be attentive to this as to a lamp shining in a dark place, until the day dawns and the morning star rises in your hearts. First of all you must understand this, that no prophecy of scripture is a matter of one's own interpretation, because no prophecy ever came by human will, but men and women moved by the Holy Spirit spoke from God.

A Reading (Lesson) from the Gospel according to Luke [22:54–69]

The crowd then seized Jesus and led him away, bringing him into the high priest's house. But Peter was following at a distance. When they had kindled a fire in the middle of the courtyard and sat down together, Peter sat among them. Then a servant-girl, seeing him in the firelight, stared at him and said, "This man also was with him." But he denied it, saying, "Woman, I do not know him." A little later someone else, on seeing him, said, "You also are one of them." But Peter said, "Man, I am not!" Then about an hour later still another kept insisting, "Surely this man also was with him; for he is a Galilean." But Peter said, "Man, I do not know what you are talking about!" At that moment, while he was still speaking, the cock crowed. The Lord turned and looked at Peter. Then Peter remembered the word of the Lord, how he had said to him, "Before the cock crows today, you will deny me three times." And he went out and wept bitterly. Now the men who were holding Jesus began to mock him and beat him; they also blindfolded him and kept asking him, "Prophesy! Who is it that struck you?" They kept heaping many other insults on him. When day came, the assembly of the elders of the people, both chief priests and scribes, gathered together, and they brought him to their council. They said, "If you are the Messiah, tell us." He replied, "If I tell you, you will not believe; and if I question you, you will not answer. But from now on the Son of Man will be seated at the right hand of the power of God."

Wednesday

Psalm 119:49–72 [page 767] ❖
Psalm 49 [page 652],   *(Psalm 53* [page 658])

A Reading (Lesson) from the Book of Isaiah [9:8–17]

The Lord sent a word against Jacob, and it fell on Israel; and all the people knew it—Ephraim and the inhabitants of Samaria—but in pride and arrogance of heart they said: "The bricks have fallen, but we will build with dressed stones; the sycamores have been cut down, but we will put cedars in their place." So the LORD raised adversaries against them, and stirred up their enemies, the Arameans on the east and the Philistines on the west, and they devoured Israel with open mouth. For all this his anger has not turned away; his hand is stretched out still. The people did not turn to him who struck them, or seek the LORD of hosts. So the LORD cut off from Israel head and tail, palm branch and reed in one day—elders and dignitaries are the head, and prophets who teach lies are the tail; for those who led this people led them astray, and those who were led by them were left in confusion. That is why the Lord did not have pity on their young people, or compassion on their orphans and widows; for everyone was godless and an evildoer, and every mouth spoke folly. For all this his anger has not turned away, his hand is stretched out still.

A Reading (Lesson) from the Second Letter of Peter [2:1–10a]

False prophets also arose among the people, just as there will be false teachers among you, who will secretly bring in destructive opinions. They will even deny the Master who bought them—bringing swift destruction on themselves. Even so, many will follow their licentious ways, and because of these teachers the way of truth will be maligned. And in their greed they will exploit you with deceptive words. Their condemnation, pronounced against them long ago, has not been idle, and their destruction is not asleep. For if God did not spare the angels when they sinned, but cast them into hell and committed them to chains of deepest darkness to be kept until the judgment; and if he did not spare the ancient world, even though he saved Noah, a herald of righteousness, with seven others, when he brought a flood on a world of the ungodly; and if by turning the cities of Sodom and Gomorrah to ashes he condemned them to extinction and made them an example of what is coming to the ungodly; and if he rescued Lot, a righteous man greatly distressed by the licentiousness of the lawless (for that righteous man, living among them day after day, was tormented in his righteous soul by their lawless deeds that he saw and heard), then the Lord knows how to rescue the godly from trial, and to keep the unrighteous under punishment until the day of judgment—especially those who indulge their flesh in depraved lust, and who despise authority.

A Reading (Lesson) from the Gospel according to Mark [1:1–8]

The beginning of the good news of Jesus Christ, the Son of God. As it is written in the prophet Isaiah, "See, I am

sending my messenger ahead of you, who will prepare
your way; the voice of one crying out in the wilderness:
'Prepare the way of the Lord, make his paths straight.' "
John the baptizer appeared in the wilderness, proclaiming
a baptism of repentance for the forgiveness of sins. And
people from the whole Judean countryside and all the
people of Jerusalem were going out to him, and were
baptized by him in the river Jordan, confessing their sins.
Now John was clothed with camel's hair, with a leather
belt around his waist, and he ate locusts and wild honey.
He proclaimed, "The one who is more powerful than I is
coming after me; I am not worthy to stoop down and
untie the thong of his sandals. I have baptized you with
water; but he will baptize you with the Holy Spirit."

Thursday

Psalm 50 [page 654]   ❖   *(Psalm 59* [page 665],
Psalm 60 [page 667])   or   *Psalm 33* [page 626]

A Reading (Lesson) from the Book of Isaiah [9:18—10:4]

Wickedness burned like a fire, consuming briers and thorns;
it kindled the thickets of the forest, and they swirled upward
in a column of smoke. Through the wrath of the LORD of
hosts the land was burned, and the people became like fuel
for the fire; no one spared another. They gorged on the
right, but still were hungry, and they devoured on the left,
but were not satisfied; they devoured the flesh of their own
kindred; Manasseh devoured Ephraim, and Ephraim
Manasseh, and together they were against Judah. For all
this his anger has not turned away; his hand is stretched out
still. Ah, you who make iniquitous decrees, who write
oppressive statutes, to turn aside the needy from justice and

to rob the poor of my people of their right, that widows may be your spoil, and that you may make the orphans your prey! What will you do on the day of punishment, in the calamity that will come from far away? To whom will you flee for help, and where will you leave your wealth, so as not to crouch among the prisoners or fall among the slain? For all this his anger has not turned away; his hand is stretched out still.

A Reading (Lesson) from the Second Letter of Peter [2:10b–16]

Bold and willful, they are not afraid to slander the glorious ones, whereas angels, though greater in might and power, do not bring against them a slanderous judgment from the Lord. These people, however, are like irrational animals, mere creatures of instinct, born to be caught and killed. They slander what they do not understand, and when those creatures are destroyed, they also will be destroyed, suffering the penalty for doing wrong. They count it a pleasure to revel in the daytime. They are blots and blemishes, reveling in their dissipation while they feast with you. They have eyes full of adultery, insatiable for sin. They entice unsteady souls. They have hearts trained in greed. Accursed children! They have left the straight road and have gone astray, following the road of Balaam son of Bosor, who loved the wages of doing wrong, but was rebuked for his own transgression; a speechless donkey spoke with a human voice and restrained the prophet's madness.

*A Reading (Lesson) from the Gospel according to
Matthew* [3:1–12]

In those days John the Baptist appeared in the wilderness
of Judea, proclaiming, "Repent, for the kingdom of
heaven has come near." This is the one of whom the
prophet Isaiah spoke when he said, "The voice of one
crying out in the wilderness: 'Prepare the way of the Lord,
make his paths straight.' " Now John wore clothing of
camel's hair with a leather belt around his waist, and his
food was locusts and wild honey. Then the people of
Jerusalem and all Judea were going out to him, and all the
region along the Jordan, and they were baptized by him in
the river Jordan, confessing their sins. But when he saw
many Pharisees and Sadducees coming for baptism, he said
to them, "You brood of vipers! Who warned you to flee
from the wrath to come? Bear fruit worthy of repentance.
Do not presume to say to yourselves, 'We have Abraham
as our ancestor'; for I tell you, God is able from these
stones to raise up children to Abraham. Even now the ax
is lying at the root of the trees; every tree therefore that
does not bear good fruit is cut down and thrown into the
fire. I baptize you with water for repentance, but one who
is more powerful than I is coming after me; I am not
worthy to carry his sandals. He will baptize you with the
Holy Spirit and fire. His winnowing fork is in his hand,
and he will clear his threshing floor and will gather his
wheat into the granary; but the chaff he will burn with
unquenchable fire."

Friday

Psalm 40 [page 640],   *Psalm 54* [page 659]   ❖
Psalm 51 [page 656]

A Reading (Lesson) from the Book of Isaiah [10:5-19]

Ah, Assyria, the rod of my anger, the club in their hands is
my fury! Against a godless nation I send him, and against
the people of my wrath I command him, to take spoil and
seize plunder, and to tread them down like the mire of the
streets. But this is not what he intends, nor does he have this
in mind; but it is in his heart to destroy, and to cut off
nations not a few. For he says: "Are not my commanders all
kings? Is not Calno like Carchemish? Is not Hamath like
Arpad? Is not Samaria like Damascus? As my hand has
reached to the kingdoms of the idols whose images were
greater than those of Jerusalem and Samaria, shall I not do
to Jerusalem and her idols what I have done to Samaria and
her images?" When the Lord has finished all his work on
Mount Zion and on Jerusalem, he will punish the arrogant
boasting of the king of Assyria and his haughty pride. For he
says: "By the strength of my hand I have done it, and by my
wisdom, for I have understanding; I have removed the
boundaries of peoples, and have plundered their treasures;
like a bull I have brought down those who sat on thrones.
My hand has found, like a nest, the wealth of the peoples;
and as one gathers eggs that have been forsaken, so I have
gathered all the earth; and there was none that moved a
wing, or opened its mouth, or chirped." Shall the ax vaunt
itself over the one who wields it, or the saw magnify itself
against the one who handles it? As if a rod should raise the
one who lifts it up, or as if a staff should lift the one who is
not wood! Therefore the Sovereign, the LORD of hosts, will
send wasting sickness among his stout warriors, and under
his glory a burning will be kindled, like the burning of fire.
The light of Israel will become a fire, and his Holy One a
flame; and it will burn and devour his thorns and briers in
one day. The glory of his forest and his fruitful land the

LORD will destroy, both soul and body, and it will be as when an invalid wastes away. The remnant of the trees of his forest will be so few that a child can write them down.

A Reading (Lesson) from the Second Letter of Peter [2:17–22]

These are waterless springs and mists driven by a storm; for them the deepest darkness has been reserved. For they speak bombastic nonsense, and with licentious desires of the flesh they entice people who have just escaped from those who live in error. They promise them freedom, but they themselves are slaves of corruption; for people are slaves to whatever masters them. For if, after they have escaped the defilements of the world through the knowledge of our Lord and Savior Jesus Christ, they are again entangled in them and overpowered, the last state has become worse for them than the first. For it would have been better for them never to have known the way of righteousness than, after knowing it, to turn back from the holy commandment that was passed on to them. It has happened to them according to the true proverb, "The dog turns back to its own vomit," and, "The sow is washed only to wallow in the mud."

A Reading (Lesson) from the Gospel according to Matthew [11:2–15]

When John heard in prison what the Messiah was doing, he sent word by his disciples and said to him, "Are you the one who is to come, or are we to wait for another?" Jesus answered them, "Go and tell John what you hear and see: the blind receive their sight, the lame walk, the lepers are cleansed, the deaf hear, the dead are raised, and the poor have good news brought to them. And blessed is anyone who takes no offense at me." As they went away, Jesus began to speak to the crowds about John: "What did you go out into the wilderness to look at? A reed shaken by the wind? What then did you go out to see? Someone dressed in soft robes? Look, those who wear soft robes are in royal palaces. What then did you go out to see? A prophet? Yes, I tell you, and more than a prophet. This is the one about whom it is written, 'See, I am sending my messenger ahead of you, who will prepare your way before you.' Truly I tell you, among those born of women no one has arisen greater than John the Baptist; yet the least in the kingdom of heaven is greater than he. From the days of John the Baptist until now the kingdom of heaven has suffered violence, and the violent take it by force. For all the prophets and the law prophesied until John came; and if you are willing to accept it, he is Elijah who is to come. Let anyone with ears listen!"

Saturday

Psalm 55 [page 660] ❖ *Psalm 138* [page 793], *Psalm 139:1–17(18–23)* [page 794]

A Reading (Lesson) from the Book of Isaiah [10:20–27]

On that day the remnant of Israel and the survivors of the house of Jacob will no more lean on the one who struck them, but will lean on the LORD, the Holy One of Israel, in truth. A remnant will return, the remnant of Jacob, to the mighty God. For though your people Israel were like the sand of the sea, only a remnant of them will return. Destruction is decreed, overflowing with righteousness. For the Lord GOD of hosts will make a full end, as decreed, in all the earth. Therefore thus says the Lord GOD of hosts: O my people, who live in Zion, do not be afraid of the

Assyrians when they beat you with a rod and lift up their staff against you as the Egyptians did. For in a very little while my indignation will come to an end, and my anger will be directed to their destruction. The LORD of hosts will wield a whip against them, as when he struck Midian at the rock of Oreb; his staff will be over the sea, and he will lift it as he did in Egypt. On that day his burden will be removed from your shoulder, and his yoke will be destroyed from your neck.

A Reading (Lesson) from the Letter of Jude [17–25]

You, beloved, must remember the predictions of the apostles of our Lord Jesus Christ; for they said to you, "In the last time there will be scoffers, indulging their own ungodly lusts." It is these wordly people, devoid of the Spirit, who are causing divisions. But you, beloved, build yourselves up on your most holy faith; pray in the Holy Spirit; keep yourselves in the love of God; look forward to the mercy of our Lord Jesus Christ that leads to eternal life. And have mercy on some who are wavering; save others by snatching them out of the fire; and have mercy on still others with fear, hating even the tunic defiled by their bodies. Now to him who is able to keep you from falling, and to make you stand without blemish in the presence of his glory with rejoicing, to the only God our Savior, through Jesus Christ our Lord, be glory, majesty, power, and authority, before all time and now and forever. Amen.

A Reading (Lesson) from the Gospel according to Luke [3:1–9]

In the fifteenth year of the reign of Emperor Tiberius, when Pontius Pilate was governor of Judea, and Herod was ruler of Galilee, and his brother Philip ruler of the

region of Ituraea and Trachonitis, and Lysanias ruler of
Abilene, during the high priesthood of Annas and
Caiaphas, the word of God came to John son of
Zechariah in the wilderness. He went into all the region
around the Jordan, proclaiming a baptism of repentance
for the forgiveness of sins, as it is written in the book of
the words of the prophet Isaiah, "The voice of one crying
out in the wilderness: 'Prepare the way of the Lord, make
his paths straight. Every valley shall be filled, and every
mountain and hill shall be made low, and the crooked
shall be made straight, and the rough ways made smooth;
and all flesh shall see the salvation of God.' " John said to
the crowds that came out to be baptized by him, "You
brood of vipers! Who warned you to flee from the wrath
to come? Bear fruits worthy of repentance. Do not begin
to say to yourselves, 'We have Abraham as our ancestor';
for I tell you, God is able from these stones to raise up
children to Abraham. Even now the ax is lying at the root
of the trees; every tree therefore that does not bear good
fruit is cut down and thrown into the fire."

Week of 4 Advent

Sunday

Psalm 24 [page 613], *Psalm 29* [page 620] ❖
Psalm 8 [page 592], *Psalm 84* [page 707]

A Reading (Lesson) from the Book of Isaiah [42:1–12]

Here is my servant, whom I uphold, my chosen, in whom my soul delights; I have put my spirit upon him; he will bring forth justice to the nations. He will not cry or lift up his voice, or make it heard in the street; a bruised reed he will not break, and a dimly burning wick he will not quench; he will faithfully bring forth justice. He will not grow faint or be crushed until he has established justice in the earth; and the coastlands wait for his teaching. Thus says God, the LORD, who created the heavens and stretched them out, who spread out the earth and what comes from it, who gives breath to the people upon it and spirit to those who walk in it: I am the LORD, I have called you in righteousness, I have taken you by the hand and kept you; I have given you as a covenant to the people, a light to the nations, to open the eyes that are blind, to bring out the prisoners from the dungeon, from the prison those who sit in darkness. I am the LORD, that is my name; my glory I give to no other, nor my praise to idols. See, the former things have come to pass, and new things I now declare; before they spring forth, I tell you of them. Sing to the LORD a new song, his praise from the end of the earth! Let the sea roar and all that fills it, the coastlands and their inhabitants. Let the desert and its towns lift up their voice, the villages that Kedar inhabits; let the inhabitants of Sela sing for joy, let them shout from the tops of the mountains. Let them give glory to the LORD, and declare his praise in the coastlands.

A Reading (Lesson) from the Letter of Paul to the Ephesians [6:10–20]

Be strong in the Lord and in the strength of his power. Put on the whole armor of God, so that you may be able to stand against the wiles of the devil. For our struggle is not against enemies of blood and flesh, but against the rulers, against the authorities, against the cosmic powers of this present darkness, against the spiritual forces of evil in the heavenly places. Therefore take up the whole armor of God, so that you may be able to withstand on that evil day, and having done everything, to stand firm. Stand therefore, and fasten the belt of truth around your waist, and put on the breastplate of righteousness. As shoes for your feet put on whatever will make you ready to proclaim the gospel of peace. With all of these, take the shield of faith, with which you will be able to quench all the flaming arrows of the evil one. Take the helmet of salvation, and the sword of the Spirit, which is the word of God. Pray in the Spirit at all times in every prayer and supplication. To that end keep alert and always persevere in supplication for all the saints. Pray also for me, so that when I speak, a message may be given to me to make known with boldness the mystery of the gospel, for which I am an ambassador in chains. Pray that I may declare it boldly, as I must speak.

A Reading (Lesson) from the Gospel according to John [3:16–21]

Jesus said to Nicodemus, "God so loved the world that he gave his only Son, so that everyone who believes in him may not perish but may have eternal life. Indeed, God did not send the Son into the world to condemn the world, but in order that the world might be saved through him. Those who believe in him are not condemned; but those who do not believe are condemned already, because they have not believed in the name of the only Son of God. And this is the judgment, that the light has come into the world, and people loved darkness rather than light because their deeds were evil. For all who do evil hate the light and do not come to the light, so that their deeds may not be exposed. But those who do what is true come to the light, so that it may be clearly seen that their deeds have been done in God."

Monday

Psalm 61 [page 668],   *Psalm 62* [page 669]   ❖
Psalm 112 [page 755],   *Psalm 115* [page 757]

A Reading (Lesson) from the Book of Isaiah [11:1–9]

A shoot shall come out from the stump of Jesse, and a branch shall grow out of his roots. The spirit of the LORD shall rest on him, the spirit of wisdom and understanding, the spirit of counsel and might, the spirit of knowledge and the fear of the LORD. His delight shall be in the fear of the LORD. He shall not judge by what his eyes see, or decide by what his ears hear; but with righteousness he shall judge the poor, and decide with equity for the meek of the earth; he shall strike the earth with the rod of his mouth, and with the breath of his lips he shall kill the wicked. Righteousness shall be the belt around his waist, and faithfulness the belt around his loins. The wolf shall live with the lamb, the leopard shall lie down with the kid, the calf and the lion and the fatling together, and a little child shall lead them. The cow and the bear shall graze, their young shall lie down together; and the lion shall eat straw like the ox. The nursing child shall play over the hole of the asp, and the weaned child shall put its hand on the adder's den. They will not hurt or destroy on all my holy mountain; for the earth will be full of the knowledge of the LORD as the waters cover the sea.

A Reading (Lesson) from the Revelation to John [20:1–10]

I saw an angel coming down from heaven, holding in his
hand the key to the bottomless pit and a great chain. He
seized the dragon, that ancient serpent, who is the Devil
and Satan, and bound him for a thousand years, and
threw him into the pit, and locked and sealed it over him,
so that he would deceive the nations no more, until the
thousand years were ended. After that he must be let out
for a little while. Then I saw thrones, and those seated on
them were given authority to judge. I also saw the souls of
those who had been beheaded for their testimony to Jesus
and for the word of God. They had not worshiped the
beast or its image and had not received its mark on their
foreheads or their hands. They came to life and reigned
with Christ a thousand years. (The rest of the dead did
not come to life until the thousand years were ended.)
This is the first resurrection. Blessed and holy are those
who share in the first resurrection. Over these the second
death has no power, but they will be priests of God and of
Christ, and they will reign with him a thousand years.
When the thousand years are ended, Satan will be released
from his prison and will come out to deceive the nations
at the four corners of the earth, Gog and Magog, in order
to gather them for battle; they are as numerous as the
sands of the sea. They marched up over the breadth of the
earth and surrounded the camp of the saints and the
beloved city. And fire came down from heaven and
consumed them. And the devil who had deceived them
was thrown into the lake of fire and sulfur, where the
beast and the false prophet were, and they will be
tormented day and night forever and ever.

A Reading (Lesson) from the Gospel according to John [5:30–47]

Jesus said to the Jews, "I can do nothing on my own. As I hear, I judge; and my judgment is just, because I seek to do not my own will but the will of him who sent me. If I testify about myself, my testimony is not true. There is another who testifies on my behalf, and I know that his testimony to me is true. You sent messengers to John, and he testified to the truth. Not that I accept such human testimony, but I say these things so that you may be saved. He was a burning and shining lamp, and you were willing to rejoice for a while in his light. But I have a testimony greater than John's. The works that the Father has given me to complete, the very works that I am doing, testify on my behalf that the Father has sent me. And the Father who sent me has himself testified on my behalf. You have never heard his voice or seen his form, and you do not have his word abiding in you, because you do not believe him whom he has sent. You search the scriptures because you think that in them you have eternal life; and it is they that testify on my behalf. Yet you refuse to come to me to have life. I do not accept glory from human beings. But I know that you do not have the love of God in you. I have come in my Father's name, and you do not accept me; if another comes in his own name, you will accept him. How can you believe when you accept glory from one another and do not seek the glory that comes from the one who alone is God? Do not think that I will accuse you before the Father; your accuser is Moses, on whom you have set your hope. If you believed Moses, you would believe me, for he wrote about me. But if you do not believe what he wrote, how will you believe what I say?"

Tuesday

Psalm 66 [page 673],   *Psalm 67* [page 675]   ❖
Psalm 116 [page 759],   *Psalm 117* [page 760]

A Reading (Lesson) from the Book of Isaiah [11:10–16]

On that day the root of Jesse shall stand as a signal to the peoples; the nations shall inquire of him, and his dwelling shall be glorious. On that day the Lord will extend his hand yet a second time to recover the remnant that is left of his people, from Assyria, from Egypt, from Pathros, from Ethiopia, from Elam, from Shinar, from Hamath, and from the coastlands of the sea. He will raise a signal for the nations, and will assemble the outcasts of Israel, and gather the dispersed of Judah from the four corners of the earth. The jealousy of Ephraim shall depart, the hostility of Judah shall be cut off; Ephraim shall not be jealous of Judah, and Judah shall not be hostile towards Ephraim. But they shall swoop down on the backs of the Philistines in the west, together they shall plunder the people of the east. They shall put forth their hand against Edom and Moab, and the Ammonites shall obey them. And the LORD will utterly destroy the tongue of the sea of Egypt; and will wave his hand over the River with his scorching wind; and will split it into seven channels, and make a way to cross on foot; so there shall be a highway from Assyria for the remnant that is left of his people, as there was for Israel when they came up from the land of Egypt.

A Reading (Lesson) from the Revelation to John [20:11—21:8]

Then I saw a great white throne and the one who sat on it; the earth and the heaven fled from his presence, and no place was found for them. And I saw the dead, great and small, standing before the throne, and books were opened. Also another book was opened, the book of life. And the dead were judged according to their works, as recorded in the books. And the sea gave up the dead that were in it, Death and Hades gave up the dead that were in them, and all were judged according to what they had done. Then Death and Hades were thrown into the lake of fire. This is the second death, the lake of fire; and anyone whose name was not found written in the book of life was thrown into the lake of fire. Then I saw a new heaven and a new earth; for the first heaven and the first earth had passed away, and the sea was no more. And I saw the holy city, the new Jerusalem, coming down out of heaven from God, prepared as a bride adorned for her husband. And I heard a loud voice from the throne saying, "See, the home of God is among mortals. He will dwell with them as their God; they will be his peoples, and God himself will be with them; he will wipe every tear from their eyes. Death will be no more; mourning and crying and pain will be no more, for the first things have passed away." And the one who was seated on the throne said, "See, I am making all things new." Also he said, "Write this, for these words are trustworthy and true." Then he said to me, "It is done! I am the Alpha and the Omega, the beginning and the end. To the thirsty I will give water as a gift from the spring of the water of life. Those who conquer will inherit these things, and I will be their God and they will be my children. But as for the cowardly, the faithless, the polluted, the murderers, the fornicators, the sorcerers, the idolaters, and all liars, their place will be in the lake that burns with fire and sulfur, which is the second death."

A Reading (Lesson) from the Gospel according to Luke [1:5-25]

In the days of King Herod of Judea, there was a priest named Zechariah, who belonged to the priestly order of Abijah. His wife was a descendant of Aaron, and her name was Elizabeth. Both of them were righteous before God, living blamelessly according to all the commandments and regulations of the Lord. But they had no children, because Elizabeth was barren, and both were getting on in years. Once when he was serving as priest before God and his section was on duty, he was chosen by lot, according to the custom of the priesthood, to enter the sanctuary of the Lord and offer incense. Now at the time of the incense offering, the whole assembly of the people was praying outside. Then there appeared to him an angel of the Lord, standing at the right side of the altar of incense. When Zechariah saw him, he was terrified; and fear overwhelmed him. But the angel said to him, "Do not be afraid, Zechariah, for your prayer has been heard. Your wife Elizabeth will bear you a son, and you will name him John. You will have joy and gladness, and many will rejoice at his birth, for he will be great in the sight of the Lord. He must never drink wine or strong drink; even before his birth he will be filled with the Holy Spirit. He will turn many of the people of Israel to the Lord their God. With the spirit and power of Elijah he will go before him, to turn the hearts of parents to their children, and the disobedient to the wisdom of the righteous, to make ready a people prepared for the Lord." Zechariah said to the angel, "How will I know that this is so? For I am an old man, and my wife is getting on in years." The angel replied, "I am Gabriel. I stand in the presence of God, and I have been sent to speak to you and to bring you this good news. But now, because you did not believe my words, which will be fulfilled in their time, you will become mute, unable to speak, until the day these things occur." Meanwhile the people were waiting for Zechariah, and wondered at his delay in the sanctuary. When he did come out, he could not speak to them, and they realized that he had seen a vision in the sanctuary. He kept motioning to them and remained unable to speak. When his time of service was ended, he went to his home. After those days his wife Elizabeth conceived, and for five months she remained in seclusion. She said, "This is what the Lord has done for me when he looked favorably on me and took away the disgrace I have endured among my people."

Wednesday

Psalm 72 [page 685] ❖ *Psalm 111* [page 754],
Psalm 113 [page 756]

A Reading (Lesson) from the Book of Isaiah [28:9–22]

"Whom will he teach knowledge, and to whom will he explain the message? Those who are weaned from milk, those taken from the breast? For it is precept upon precept, precept upon precept, line upon line, line upon line, here a little, there a little." Truly, with stammering lip and with alien tongue he will speak to this people, to whom he has said, "This is rest; give rest to the weary; and this is repose"; yet they would not hear. Therefore the word of the LORD will be to them, "Precept upon precept, precept upon precept, line upon line, line upon line, here a little, there a little;" in order that they may go, and fall backward, and be broken, and snared, and taken. Therefore hear the word of the LORD, you scoffers who rule this people in Jerusalem. Because you have said, "We have made a covenant with death, and with Sheol we have an agreement; when the overwhelming scourge passes through it will not come to us; for we have made lies our refuge, and in falsehood we have taken shelter"; therefore thus says the Lord GOD, See, I am laying in Zion a foundation stone, a tested stone, a precious cornerstone, a sure foundation: "One who trusts will not panic." And I will make justice the line, and righteousness the plummet; hail will sweep away the refuge of lies, and waters will overwhelm the shelter. Then your covenant with death will be annulled, and your agreement with Sheol will not stand; when the overwhelming scourge passes through you will be beaten down by it. As often as it passes through, it will take you; for morning by morning it will pass through, by day and by night; and it will be sheer terror to understand the message. For the bed is too short to stretch oneself on it, and the covering too narrow to wrap oneself in it. For the LORD will rise up as on Mount Perazim, he will rage as in the valley of Gibeon to do his deed!—strange is his deed! and to work his work—alien is his work! Now therefore do not scoff, or your bonds will be made stronger; for I have heard a decree of destruction from the Lord GOD of hosts upon the whole land.

A Reading (Lesson) from the Revelation to John [21:9–21]

Then one of the seven angels who had the seven bowls full of the seven last plagues came and said to me, "Come, I will show you the bride, the wife of the Lamb." And in the spirit he carried me away to a great, high mountain and showed me the holy city Jerusalem coming down out of heaven from God. It has the glory of God and a radiance like a very rare jewel, like jasper, clear as crystal.

It has a great, high wall with twelve gates, and at the gates twelve angels, and on the gates are inscribed the names of the twelve tribes of the Israelites; on the east three gates, on the north three gates, on the south three gates, and on the west three gates. And the wall of the city has twelve foundations, and on them are the twelve names of the twelve apostles of the Lamb. The angel who talked to me had a measuring rod of gold to measure the city and its gates and walls. The city lies foursquare, its length the same as its width; and he measured the city with his rod, fifteen hundred miles; its length and width and height are equal. He also measured its wall, one hundred forty-four cubits by human measurement, which the angel was using. The wall is built of jasper, while the city is pure gold, clear as glass. The foundations of the wall of the city are adorned with every jewel; the first was jasper, the second sapphire, the third agate, the fourth emerald, the fifth onyx, the sixth carnelian, the seventh chrysolite, the eighth beryl, the ninth topaz, the tenth chrysoprase, the eleventh jacinth, the twelfth amethyst. And the twelve gates are twelve pearls, each of the gates is a single pearl, and the street of the city is pure gold, transparent as glass.

A Reading (Lesson) from the Gospel according to Luke [1:26–38]

In the sixth month the angel Gabriel was sent by God to a town in Galilee called Nazareth, to a virgin engaged to a man whose name was Joseph, of the house of David. The virgin's name was Mary. And he came to her and said, "Greetings, favored one! The Lord is with you." But she was much perplexed by his words and pondered what sort of greeting this might be. The angel said to her, "Do not be afraid, Mary, for you have found favor with God. And now, you will conceive in your womb and bear a son, and you will name him Jesus. He will be great, and will be called the Son of the Most High, and the Lord God will give to him the throne of his ancestor David. He will reign over the house of Jacob forever, and of his kingdom there will be no end." Mary said to the angel, "How can this be, since I am a virgin?" The angel said to her, "The Holy Spirit will come upon you, and the power of the Most High will overshadow you; therefore the child to be born will be holy; he will be called Son of God. And now, your relative Elizabeth in her old age has also conceived a son; and this is the sixth month for her who was said to be barren. For nothing will be impossible with God." Then Mary said, "Here am I, the servant of the Lord; let it be with me according to your word." Then the angel departed from her.

Thursday

Psalm 80 [page 702] ❖ *Psalm 146* [page 803], *Psalm 147* [page 804]

A Reading (Lesson) from the Book of Isaiah [29:13–24]

The Lord said: Because these people draw near with their mouths and honor me with their lips, while their hearts are far from me, and their worship of me is a human commandment learned by rote; so I will again do amazing things with this people, shocking and amazing. The wisdom of their wise shall perish, and the discernment of the discerning shall be hidden. Ha! You who hide a plan too deep for the LORD, whose deeds are in the dark, and who say, "Who sees us? Who knows us?" You turn things upside down! Shall the potter be regarded as the clay? Shall the thing made say of its maker, "He did not make me"; or the thing formed say of the one who formed it, "He has no understanding"? Shall not Lebanon in a very little while become a fruitful field, and the fruitful field be regarded as a forest? On that day the deaf shall hear the words of a scroll, and out of their gloom and darkness the eyes of the blind shall see. The meek shall obtain fresh joy in the LORD, and the neediest people shall exult in the Holy One of Israel. For the tyrant shall be no more, and the scoffer shall cease to be; all those alert to do evil shall be cut off—those who cause a person to lose a lawsuit, who set a trap for the arbiter in the gate, and without grounds deny justice to the one in the right. Therefore thus says the LORD, who redeemed Abraham, concerning the house of Jacob: No longer shall Jacob be ashamed, no longer shall his face grow pale. For when he sees his children, the work of my hands, in his midst, they will sanctify my name; they will sanctify the Holy One of Jacob, and will stand in awe of the God of Israel. And those who err in spirit will come to understanding, and those who grumble will accept instruction.

A Reading (Lesson) from the Revelation to John [21:22—22:5]

I saw no temple in the city, for its temple is the Lord God the Almighty and the Lamb. And the city has no need of sun or moon to shine on it, for the glory of God is its light, and its lamp is the Lamb. The nations will walk by its light, and the kings of the earth will bring their glory into it. Its gates will never be shut by day—and there will be no night there. People will bring into it the glory and the honor of the nations. But nothing unclean will enter it, nor anyone who practices abomination or falsehood, but only those who are written in the Lamb's book of life. Then the angel showed me the river of the water of life, bright as crystal, flowing from the throne of God and of the Lamb through the middle of the street of the city. On either side of the river is the tree of life with its twelve kinds of fruit, producing its fruit each month; and the leaves of the tree are for the healing of the nations. Nothing accursed will be found there any more. But the throne of God and of the Lamb will be in it, and his servants will worship him; they will see his face, and his name will be on their foreheads. And there will be no more night; they need no light of lamp or sun, for the Lord God will be their light, and they will reign forever and ever.

A Reading (Lesson) from the Gospel according to Luke [1:39–48a(48b–56)]

In those days Mary set out and went with haste to a Judean town in the hill country, where she entered the house of Zechariah and greeted Elizabeth. When Elizabeth heard Mary's greeting, the child leaped in her womb. And Elizabeth was filled with the Holy Spirit and exclaimed with a loud cry, "Blessed are you among women, and blessed is the fruit of your womb. And why has this happened to me, that the mother of my Lord comes to me? For as soon as I heard the sound of your greeting, the child in my womb leaped for joy. And blessed is she who believed that there would be a fulfillment of what was spoken to her by the Lord." And Mary said, "My soul magnifies the Lord, and my spirit rejoices in God my Savior, for he has looked with favor on the lowliness of his servant."

"Surely, from now on all generations will call me blessed; for the Mighty One has done great things for me, and holy is his name. His mercy is for those who fear him from generation to generation. He has shown strength with his arm; he has scattered the proud in the thoughts of their hearts. He has brought down the powerful from their thrones, and lifted up the lowly; he has filled the hungry with good things, and sent the rich away empty. He has helped his servant Israel, in remembrance of his mercy, according to the promise he made to our ancestors, to Abraham and to his descendants forever." And Mary remained with her about three months and then returned to her home.

Friday

Psalm 93 [page 722], *Psalm 96* [page 725] ❖
Psalm 148 [page 805], *Psalm 150* [page 807]

A Reading (Lesson) from the Book of Isaiah [33:17–22]

Your eyes will see the king in his beauty; they will behold a land that stretches far away. Your mind will muse on the terror: "Where is the one who counted? Where is the one who weighed the tribute? Where is the one who counted the towers?" No longer will you see the insolent people, the people of an obscure speech that you cannot comprehend, stammering in a language that you cannot understand. Look on Zion, the city of our appointed festivals! Your eyes will see Jerusalem, a quiet habitation, an immovable tent, whose stakes will never be pulled up, and none of whose ropes will be broken. But there the LORD in majesty will be for us a place of broad rivers and streams, where no galley with oars can go, nor stately ship can pass. For the LORD is our judge, the LORD is our ruler, the LORD is our king; he will save us.

A Reading (Lesson) from the Revelation to John [22:6–11,18–20]

The angel said to me, "These words are trustworthy and true, for the Lord, the God of the spirits of the prophets, has sent his angel to show his servants what must soon take place." "See, I am coming soon! Blessed is the one who keeps the words of the prophecy of this book." I, John, am the one who heard and saw these things. And when I heard and saw them, I fell down to worship at the feet of the angel who showed them to me; but he said to me, "You must not do that! I am a fellow servant with you and your comrades the prophets, and with those who keep the words of this book. Worship God!" And he said to me, "Do not seal up the words of the prophecy of this book, for the time is near. Let the evildoer still do evil, and the filthy still be filthy, and the righteous still do right, and the holy still be holy." I warn everyone who hears the words of the prophecy of this book: if anyone adds to them, God will add to that person the plagues described in this book; if anyone takes away from the words of the book of this prophecy, God will take away that person's share in the tree of life and in the holy city, which are described in this book. The one who testifies to these things says, "Surely I am coming soon." Amen. Come, Lord Jesus!

A Reading (Lesson) from the Gospel according to Luke [1:57–66]

Now the time came for Elizabeth to give birth, and she bore a son. Her neighbors and relatives heard that the Lord had shown his great mercy to her, and they rejoiced with her. On the eighth day they came to circumcise the child, and they were going to name him Zechariah after his father. But his mother said, "No; he is to be called John." They said to her, "None of your relatives has this name." Then they began motioning to his father to find out what name he wanted to give him. He asked for a writing tablet and wrote, "His name is John." And all of them were amazed. Immediately his mouth was opened and his tongue freed, and he began to speak, praising God. Fear came over all their neighbors, and all these things were talked about throughout the entire hill country of Judea. All who heard them pondered them and said, "What then will this child become?" For, indeed, the hand of the Lord was with him.

December 24

MORNING PRAYER

Psalm 45 [page 647],   *Psalm 46* [page 649]

A Reading (Lesson) from the Book of Isaiah [35:1–10]

The wilderness and the dry land shall be glad, the desert shall rejoice and blossom; like the crocus it shall blossom abundantly, and rejoice with joy and singing. The glory of Lebanon shall be given to it, the majesty of Carmel and Sharon. They shall see the glory of the LORD, the majesty of our God. Strengthen the weak hands, and make firm the feeble knees. Say to those who are of a fearful heart, "Be strong, do not fear! Here is your God. He will come with vengeance, with terrible recompense. He will come and save you." Then the eyes of the blind shall be opened, and the ears of the deaf unstopped; then the lame shall leap like a deer, and the tongue of the speechless sing for joy. For waters shall break forth in the wilderness, and streams in the desert; the burning sand shall become a pool, and the thirsty ground springs of water; the haunt of jackals shall become a swamp, the grass shall become reeds and rushes. A highway shall be there, and it shall be called the Holy Way; the unclean shall not travel on it, but it shall be for God's people; no traveler, not even fools, shall go astray. No lion shall be there, nor shall any ravenous beast come up on it; they shall not be found there, but the redeemed shall walk there. And the ransomed of the LORD shall return, and come to Zion with singing; everlasting joy shall be upon their heads; they shall obtain joy and gladness, and sorrow and sighing shall flee away.

A Reading (Lesson) from the Revelation to John [22:12–17,21]

"See, I am coming soon; my reward is with me, to repay according to everyone's work. I am the Alpha and the Omega, the first and the last, the beginning and the end." Blessed are those who wash their robes, so that they will have the right to the tree of life and may enter the city by the gates. Outside are the dogs and sorcerers and fornicators and murderers and idolaters, and everyone who loves and practices falsehood. "It is I, Jesus, who sent my angel to you with this testimony for the churches. I am the root and the descendant of David, the bright morning star." The Spirit and the bride say, "Come." And let everyone who hears say, "Come." And let everyone who is thirsty come. Let anyone who wishes take the water of life as a gift. The grace of the Lord Jesus be with all the saints. Amen.

A Reading (Lesson) from the Gospel according to Luke [1:67–80]

John's father Zechariah was filled with the Holy Spirit, and spoke this prophecy: "Blessed be the Lord God of Israel, for he has looked favorably on his people and redeemed them. He has raised up a mighty savior for us in the house of his servant David, as he spoke through the mouth of his holy prophets from of old, that we would be saved from our enemies and from the hand of all who hate us. Thus he has shown the mercy promised to our ancestors, and has remembered his holy covenant, the oath that he swore to our ancestor Abraham, to grant us that we, being rescued from the hands of our enemies, might serve him without fear, in holiness and righteousness before him all our days. And you, child, will be called the prophet of the Most High; for you will go before the Lord to prepare his ways, to give knowledge of salvation to his people by the forgiveness of their sins. By the tender mercy of our God, the dawn from on high will break upon us, to give light to those who sit in darkness and in the shadow of death, to guide our feet into the way of peace." The child grew and became strong in spirit, and he was in the wilderness until the day he appeared publicly to Israel.

Christmas Eve

EVENING PRAYER

Psalm 89:1–29 [page 713]

A Reading (Lesson) from the Book of Isaiah [59:15b–21]

The LORD saw it, and it displeased him that there was no justice. He saw that there was no one, and was appalled that there was no one to intervene; so his own arm brought him victory, and his righteousness upheld him. He put on righteousness like a breastplate, and a helmet of salvation on his head; he put on garments of vengeance for clothing, and wrapped himself in fury as in a mantle. According to their deeds, so will he repay; wrath to his adversaries, requital to his enemies; to the coastlands he will render requital. So those in the west shall fear the name of the LORD, and those in the east, his glory; for he will come like a pent-up stream that the wind of the LORD drives on. And he will come to Zion as Redeemer, to those in Jacob who turn from transgression, says the LORD. And as for me, this is my covenant with them, says the LORD: my spirit that is upon you, and my words that I have put in your mouth, shall not depart out of your mouth, or out of the mouths of your children, or out of the mouths of your children's children, says the LORD, from now on and forever.

A Reading (Lesson) from the Letter of Paul to the Philippians [2:5–11]

Let the same mind be in you that was in Christ Jesus, who, though he was in the form of God, did not regard equality with God as something to be exploited, but emptied himself, taking the form of a slave, being born in human likeness. And being found in human form, he humbled himself and became obedient to the point of death—even death on a cross. Therefore God also highly exalted him and gave him the name that is above every name, so that at the name of Jesus every knee should bend, in heaven and on earth and under the earth, and every tongue should confess that Jesus Christ is Lord, to the glory of God the Father.

Christmas Day and Following

Christmas Day

Psalm 2 [page 586], *Psalm 85* [page 708] ❖
Psalm 110:1–5(6–7) [page 753], *Psalm 132* [page 785]

A Reading (Lesson) from the Book of Zechariah [2:10–13]

Sing and rejoice, O daughter Zion! For lo, I will come and
dwell in your midst, says the LORD. Many nations shall join
themsleves to the LORD on that day, and shall be my people;
and I will dwell in your midst. And you shall know that the
LORD of hosts has sent me to you. The LORD will inherit
Judah as his portion in the holy land, and will again choose
Jerusalem. Be silent, all people, before the LORD; for he has
roused himself from his holy dwelling.

A Reading (Lesson) from the First Letter of John [4:7–16]

Beloved, let us love one another, because love is from
God; everyone who loves is born of God and knows God.
Whoever does not love does not know God, for God is
love. God's love was revealed among us in this way: God
sent his only Son into the world so that we might live
through him. In this is love, not that we loved God but
that he loved us and sent his Son to be the atoning
sacrifice for our sins. Beloved, since God loved us so
much, we also ought to love one another. No one has ever
seen God; if we love one another, God lives in us, and his
love is perfected in us. By this we know that we abide in
him and he in us, because he has given us of his Spirit.
And we have seen and do testify that the Father has sent
his Son as the Savior of the world. God abides in those

who confess that Jesus is the Son of God, and they abide in God. So we have known and believe the love that God has for us. God is love, and those who abide in love abide in God, and God abides in them.

A Reading (Lesson) from the Gospel according to John [3:31–36]

The one who comes from above is above all; the one who is of the earth belongs to the earth and speaks about earthly things. The one who comes from heaven is above all. He testifies to what he has seen and heard, yet no one accepts his testimony. Whoever has accepted his testimony has certified this, that God is true. He whom God has sent speaks the words of God, for he gives the Spirit without measure. The Father loves the Son and has placed all things in his hands. Whoever believes in the Son has eternal life; whoever disobeys the Son will not see life, but must endure God's wrath.

First Sunday after Christmas

Psalm 93 [page 722],   *Psalm 96* [page 725]   ❖
Psalm 34 [page 627]

A Reading (Lesson) from the Book of Isaiah [62:6–7,10–12]

Upon your walls, O Jerusalem, I have posted sentinels; all day and all night they shall never be silent. You who remind the LORD, take no rest, and give him no rest until he establishes Jerusalem and makes it renowned throughout the earth. Go through, go through the gates, prepare the way for the people; build up, build up the highway, clear it of stones, lift up an ensign over the peoples. The LORD has proclaimed to the end of the earth: Say to daughter Zion, "See, your salvation comes; his reward is with him, and his recompense before him." They shall be called, "The Holy People, The Redeemed of the LORD"; and you shall be called, "Sought Out, A City Not Forsaken."

A Reading (Lesson) from the Letter to the Hebrews [2:10–18]

It was fitting that God, for whom and through whom all things exist, in bringing many children to glory, should make the pioneer of their salvation perfect through sufferings. For the one who sanctifies and those who are sanctified all have one Father. For this reason Jesus is not ashamed to call them brothers and sisters, saying, "I will proclaim your name to my brothers and sisters, in the midst of the congregation I will praise you." And again, "I will put my trust in him." And again, "Here am I and the children whom God has given me." Since, therefore, the children share flesh and blood, he himself likewise shared the same things, so that through death he might destroy the one who has the power of death, that is, the devil, and free those who all their lives were held in slavery by the fear of death. For it is clear that he did not come to help angels, but the descendants of Abraham. Therefore he had to become like his brothers and sisters in every respect, so that he might be a merciful and faithful high priest in the service of God, to make a sacrifice of atonement for the sins of the people. Because he himself was tested by what he suffered, he is able to help those who are being tested.

A Reading (Lesson) from the Gospel according to Matthew [1:18–25]

Now the birth of Jesus the Messiah took place in this way. When his mother Mary had been engaged to Joseph, but before they lived together, she was found to be with child from the Holy Spirit. Her husband Joseph, being a righteous man and unwilling to expose her to public disgrace, planned to dismiss her quietly. But just when he had resolved to do this, an angel of the Lord appeared to him in a dream and said, "Joseph, son of David, do not be afraid to take Mary as your wife, for the child conceived in her is from the Holy Spirit. She will bear a son, and you are to name him Jesus, for he will save his people from their sins." All this took place to fulfill what had been spoken by the Lord through the prophet: "Look, the virgin shall conceive and bear a son, and they shall name him Emmanuel," which means, "God is with us." When Joseph awoke from sleep, he did as the angel of the Lord commanded him; he took her as his wife, but had no marital relations with her until she had borne a son; and he named him Jesus.

December 29

Psalm 18:1–20 [page 602]   ❖   *Psalm 18:21–50* [page 604]*

A Reading (Lesson) from the Book of Isaiah [12:1–6]

You will say in that day: I will give thanks to you, O Lord, for though you were angry with me, your anger turned away, and you comforted me. Surely God is my salvation; I will trust, and will not be afraid, for the Lord God is my

---

* *If today is Saturday, use Psalms 23 [page 612] and 27 [page 617] at Evening Prayer.*

strength and my might; he has become my salvation. With joy you will draw water from the wells of salvation. And you will say in that day: Give thanks to the LORD, call on his name; make known his deeds among the nations; proclaim that his name is exalted. Sing praises to the LORD, for he has done gloriously; let this be known in all the earth. Shout aloud and sing for joy, O royal Zion, for great in your midst is the Holy One of Israel.

A Reading (Lesson) from the Revelation to John [1:1–8]

The Revelation of Jesus Christ, which God gave him to show his servants what must soon take place; he made it known by sending his angel to his servant John, who testified to the word of God and to the testimony of Jesus Christ, even to all that he saw. Blessed is the one who reads aloud the words of the prophecy, and blessed are those who hear and who keep what is written in it; for the time is near. John to the seven churches that are in Asia: Grace to you and peace from him who is and who was and who is to come, and from the seven spirits who are before his throne, and from Jesus Christ, the faithful witness, the firstborn of the dead, and the ruler of the kings of the earth. To him who loves us and freed us from our sins by his blood, and made us to be a kingdom, priests serving his God and Father, to him be glory and dominion forever and ever. Amen. Look! He is coming with the clouds; every eye will see him, even those who pierced him; and on his account all the tribes of the earth will wail. So it is to be. Amen. "I am the Alpha and the Omega," says the Lord God, who is and who was and who is to come, the Almighty.

A Reading (Lesson) from the Gospel according to John [7:37–52]

On the last day of the festival, the great day, while Jesus was standing there, he cried out, "Let anyone who is thirsty come to me, and let the one who believes in me drink. As the scripture has said, 'Out of the believer's heart shall flow rivers of living water.'" Now he said this about the Spirit, which believers in him were to receive; for as yet there was no Spirit, because Jesus was not yet glorified. When they heard these words, some in the crowd said, "This is really the prophet." Others said, "This is the Messiah." But some asked, "Surely the Messiah does not come from Galilee, does he? Has not the scripture said that the Messiah is descended from David and comes from Bethlehem, the village where David lived?" So there was a division in the crowd because of him. Some of them wanted to arrest him, but no one laid hands on him. Then the temple police went back to the chief priests and Pharisees, who asked them, "Why did you not arrest him?" The police answered, "Never has anyone spoken like this!" Then the Pharisees replied, "Surely you have not been deceived too, have you? Has any one of the authorities or of the Pharisees believed in him? But this crowd, which does not know the law—they are accursed." Nicodemus, who had gone to Jesus before, and who was one of them, asked, "Our law does not judge people without first giving them a hearing to find out what they are doing, does it?" They replied, "Surely you are not also from Galilee, are you? Search and you will see that no prophet is to arise from Galilee."

December 30

Psalm 20 [page 608],   *Psalm 21:1–7(8–14)* [page 608]   ❖
Psalm 23 [page 612],   *Psalm 27* [page 617]

A Reading (Lesson) from the Book of Isaiah [25:1–9]

O LORD, you are my God; I will exalt you, I will praise your
name; for you have done wonderful things, plans formed of
old, faithful and sure. For you have made the city a heap,
the fortified city a ruin; the palace of aliens is a city no more,
it will never be rebuilt. Therefore strong peoples will glorify
you; cities of ruthless nations will fear you. For you have
been a refuge to the poor, a refuge to the needy in their
distress, a shelter from the rainstorm and a shade from the
heat. When the blast of the ruthless was like a winter
rainstorm, the noise of aliens like heat in a dry place, you
subdued the heat with the shade of clouds; the song of the
ruthless was stilled. On this mountain the LORD of hosts
will make for all peoples a feast of rich food, a feast of
well-aged wines, of rich food filled with marrow, of
well-aged wines strained clear. And he will destroy on this
mountain the shroud that is cast over all peoples, the sheet
that is spread over all nations; he will swallow up death
forever. Then the Lord GOD will wipe away the tears from
all faces, and the disgrace of his people he will take away
from all the earth, for the LORD has spoken. It will be said
on that day, Lo, this is our God; we have waited for him, so
that he might save us. This is the LORD for whom we have
waited; let us be glad and rejoice in his salvation.

A Reading (Lesson) from the Revelation to John [1:9–20]

I John, your brother, who share with you in Jesus the
persecution and the kingdom and the patient endurance,

was on the island called Patmos because of the word of God and the testimony of Jesus. I was in the spirit on the Lord's day, and I heard behind me a loud voice like a trumpet saying, "Write in a book what you see and send it to the seven churches, to Ephesus, to Smyrna, to Pergamum, to Thyatira, to Sardis, to Philadelphia, and to Laodicea." Then I turned to see whose voice it was that spoke to me, and on turning I saw seven golden lampstands, and in the midst of the lampstands I saw one like the Son of Man, clothed with a long robe and with a golden sash across his chest. His head and his hair were white as white wool, white as snow; his eyes were like a flame of fire, his feet were like burnished bronze, refined as in a furnace, and his voice was like the sound of many waters. In his right hand he held seven stars, and from his mouth came a sharp, two-edged sword, and his face was like the sun shining with full force. When I saw him, I fell at his feet as though dead. But he placed his right hand on me, saying, "Do not be afraid; I am the first and the last, and the living one. I was dead, and see, I am alive forever and ever; and I have the keys of Death and of Hades. Now write what you have seen, what is, and what is to take place after this. As for the mystery of the seven stars that you saw in my right hand, and the seven golden lampstands: the seven stars are the angels of the seven churches, and the seven lampstands are the seven churches."

John 7:53—8:11 [page 28 above]

December 31

Psalm 46 [page 649], *Psalm 48* [page 651]

A Reading (Lesson) from the Book of Isaiah [26:1–9]

On that day this song will be sung in the land of Judah: We have a strong city; he sets up victory like walls and bulwarks. Open the gates, so that the righteous nation that keeps faith may enter in. Those of steadfast mind you keep in peace—in peace because they trust in you. Trust in the LORD forever, for in the LORD GOD you have an everlasting rock. For he has brought low the inhabitants of the height; the lofty city he lays low. He lays it low to the ground, casts it to the dust. The foot tramples it, the feet of the poor, the steps of the needy. The way of the righteous is level; O Just One, you make smooth the path of the righteous. In the path of your judgments, O LORD, we wait for you; your name and your renown are the soul's desire. My soul yearns for you in the night, my spirit within me earnestly seeks you. For when your judgments are in the earth, the inhabitants of the world learn righteousness.

A Reading (Lesson) from the Second Letter of Paul to the Corinthians [5:16—6:2]

From now on, therefore, we regard no one from a human point of view; even though we once knew Christ from a human point of view, we know him no longer in that way. So if anyone is in Christ, there is a new creation: everything old has passed away; see, everything has become new! All this is from God, who reconciled us to himself through Christ, and has given us the ministry of reconciliation; that is, in Christ God was reconciling the world to himself, not counting their trespasses against them, and entrusting the message of reconciliation to us. So we are ambassadors for Christ, since God is making his appeal through us; we entreat you on behalf of Christ, be reconciled to God. For our sake he made him to be sin who knew no sin, so that in him we might become the righteousness of God. As we work together with him, we urge you also not to accept the grace of God in vain. For he says, "At an acceptable time I have listened to you, and on a day of salvation I have helped you." See, now is the acceptable time; see, now is the day of salvation!

A Reading (Lesson) from the Gospel according to John [8:12–19]

Again Jesus spoke to them, saying, "I am the light of the world. Whoever follows me will never walk in darkness but will have the light of life." Then the Pharisees said to him, "You are testifying on your own behalf; your testimony is not valid." Jesus answered, "Even if I testify on my own behalf, my testimony is valid because I know where I have come from and where I am going, but you do not know where I come from or where I am going. You judge by human standards; I judge no one. Yet even if I do judge, my judgment is valid; for it is not I alone who judge, but I and the Father who sent me. In your law it is written that the testimony of two witnesses is valid. I testify on my own behalf, and the Father who sent me testifies on my behalf." Then they said to him, "Where is your Father?" Jesus answered, "You know neither me nor my Father. If you knew me, you would know my Father also."

Eve of Holy Name

_____

Psalm 90 [page 717]

A Reading (Lesson) from the Book of Isaiah [65:15b–25]

The Lord GOD will call his servants by a different name. Then whoever invokes a blessing in the land shall bless by the God of faithfulness, and whoever takes an oath in the land shall swear by the God of faithfulness; because the former troubles are forgotten and are hidden from my sight. For I am about to create new heavens and a new earth; the former things shall not be remembered or come to mind. But be glad and rejoice forever in what I am creating; for I am about to create Jerusalem as a joy, and its people as a delight. I will rejoice in Jerusalem, and delight in my people; no more shall the sound of weeping be heard in it, or the cry of distress. No more shall there be in it an infant that lives but a few days, or an old person who does not live out a lifetime; for one who dies at a hundred years will be considered a youth, and one who falls short of a hundred will be considered accursed. They shall build houses and inhabit them; they shall plant vineyards and eat their fruit. They shall not build and another inhabit; they shall not plant and another eat; for like the days of a tree shall the days of my people be, and my chosen shall long enjoy the work of their hands. They shall not labor in vain, or bear children for calamity; for they shall be offspring blessed by the LORD—and their descendants as well. Before they call I will answer, while they are yet speaking I will hear. The wolf and the lamb shall feed together, the lion shall eat straw like the ox; but the serpent—its food shall be dust! They shall not hurt or destroy on all my holy mountain, says the LORD.

A Reading (Lesson) from the Revelation to John [21:1–6]

Then I saw a new heaven and a new earth; for the first heaven and the first earth had passed away, and the sea was no more. And I saw the holy city, the new Jerusalem, coming down out of heaven from God, prepared as a bride adorned for her husband. And I heard a loud voice from the throne saying, "See, the home of God is among mortals. He will dwell with them as their God; they will be his peoples, and God himself will be with them; he will wipe every tear from their eyes. Death will be no more; mourning and crying and pain will be no more, for the first things have passed away." And the one who was seated on the throne said, "See, I am making all things new." Also he said, "Write this, for these words are trustworthy and true." Then he said to me, "It is done! I am the Alpha and the Omega, the beginning and the end. To the thirsty I will give water as a gift from the spring of the water of life."

Holy Name

Psalm 103 [page 733] ❖ *Psalm 148* [page 805]

A Reading (Lesson) from the Book of Genesis [17:1–12a,15–16]

When Abram was ninety-nine years old, the LORD appeared to Abram, and said to him, "I am God Almighty; walk before me, and be blameless. And I will make my covenant between me and you, and will make you exceedingly numerous." Then Abram fell on his face; and God said to him, "As for me, this is my covenant with you: You shall be the ancestor of a multitude of nations. No longer shall your name be Abram, but your name shall be Abraham; for I have made you the ancestor of a multitude of nations. I will make you exceedingly fruitful; and I will make nations of you, and kings shall come from you. I will establish my covenant between me and you, and your offspring after you throughout their generations, for an everlasting covenant, to be God to you and to your offspring after you. And I will give to you, and to your offspring after you, the land where you are now an alien, all the land of Canaan, for a perpetual holding; and I will be their God." God said to Abraham, As for you, you shall keep my covenant, you and your offspring after you throughout their generations. This is my covenant, which you shall keep, between me and you and your offspring after you: Every male among you shall be circumcised. You shall circumcise the flesh of your foreskins, and it shall be a sign of the covenant between me and you. Throughout your generations every male among you shall be circumcised when he is eight days old." God said to Abraham, "As for Sarai your wife, you shall not call her Sarai, but Sarah shall be her name. I will bless her, and moreover I will give you a son by her. I will bless her, and she shall give rise to nations; kings of peoples shall come from her."

A Reading (Lesson) from the Letter of Paul to the Colossians [2:6–12]

As you therefore have received Christ Jesus the Lord, continue to live your lives in him, rooted and built up in him and established in the faith, just as you were taught, abounding in thanksgiving. See to it that no one takes you captive through philosophy and empty deceit, according to human tradition, according to the elemental spirits of the universe, and not according to Christ. For in him the whole fullness of deity dwells bodily, and you have come to fullness in him, who is the head of every ruler and authority. In him also you were circumcised with a spiritual circumcision, by putting off the body of the flesh in the circumcision of Christ; when you were buried with him in baptism, you were also raised with him through faith in the power of God, who raised him from the dead.

A Reading (Lesson) from the Gospel according to John [16:23b–30]

Jesus said to the disciples, "Very truly, I tell you, if you ask anything of the Father in my name, he will give it to you. Until now you have not asked for anything in my name. Ask and you will receive, so that your joy may be complete. I have said these things to you in figures of speech. The hour is coming when I will no longer speak to you in figures, but will tell you plainly of the Father. On that day you will ask in my name. I do not say to you that I will ask the Father on your behalf; for the Father himself loves you, because you have loved me and have believed that I came from God. I came from the Father and have come into the world; again, I am leaving the world and am going to the Father." His disciples said, "Yes, now you are speaking plainly, not in any figure of speech! Now we know that you know all things, and do not need to have anyone question you; by this we believe that you came from God."

Second Sunday after Christmas

Psalm 66 [page 673], *Psalm 67* [page 675] ❖
Psalm 145 [page 801]

*A Reading (Lesson) from the Book of
Ecclesiasticus* [3:3–9,14–17]

Those who honor their father atone for sins, and those who
respect their mother are like those who lay up treasure.
Those who honor their father will have joy in their own
children, and when they pray they will be heard. Those who
respect their father will have long life, and those who honor
their mother obey the Lord; they will serve their parents as
their masters. Honor your father by word and deed, that his
blessing may come upon you. For a father's blessing
strengthens the houses of the children, but a mother's curse
uproots their foundations. For kindness to a father will not
be forgotten, and will be credited to you against your sins;
in the day of your distress it will be remembered in your
favor; like frost in fair weather, your sins will melt away.
Whoever forsakes a father is like a blasphemer, and
whoever angers a mother is cursed by the Lord. My child,
perform your tasks with humility; then you will be loved by
those whom God accepts.

A Reading (Lesson) from the First Letter of John [2:12–17]

I am writing to you, little children, because your sins are
forgiven on account of his name. I am writing to you,
fathers, because you know him who is from the beginning.
I am writing to you, young people, because you have
conquered the evil one. I write to you, children, because
you know the Father. I write to you, fathers, because you
know him who is from the beginning. I write to you,
young people, because you are strong and the word of
God abides in you, and you have overcome the evil one.
Do not love the world or the things in the world. The love
of the Father is not in those who love the world; for all
that is in the world—the desire of the flesh, the desire of

the eyes, the pride in riches—comes not from the Father but from the world. And the world and its desire are passing away, but those who do the will of God live forever.

A Reading (Lesson) from the Gospel according to John [6:41–47]

The Jews began to complain about him because he said, "I am the bread that came down from heaven." They were saying, "Is not this Jesus, the son of Joseph, whose father and mother we know? How can he now say, 'I have come down from heaven'?" Jesus answered them, "Do not complain among yourselves. No one can come to me unless drawn by the Father who sent me; and I will raise that person up on the last day. It is written in the prophets, 'And they shall all be taught by God.' Everyone who has heard and learned from the Father comes to me. Not that anyone has seen the Father except the one who is from God; he has seen the Father. Very truly, I tell you, whoever believes has eternal life."

January 2

Psalm 34 [page 627]   ❖   *Psalm 33* [page 626]

A Reading (Lesson) from the Book of Genesis [12:1–7]

The LORD said to Abram, "Go from your country and your kindred and your father's house to the land that I will show you. I will make of you a great nation, and I will bless you, and make your name great, so that you will be a blessing. I will bless those who bless you, and the one who curses you I will curse; and in you all the families of the earth shall be blessed." So Abram went, as the LORD had told him; and

ot went with him. Abram was seventy-five years old when
e departed from Haran. Abram took his wife Sarai and his
brother's son Lot, and all the possessions that they had
gathered, and the persons whom they had acquired in
Haran; and they set forth to go to the land of Canaan.
When they had come to the land of Canaan, Abram passed
through the land to the place at Shechem, to the oak of
Moreh. At that time the Canaanites were in the land. Then
the LORD appeared to Abram, and said, "To your offspring
will give this land." So he built there an altar to the LORD,
who had appeared to him.

Reading (Lesson) from the Letter to the
Hebrews [11:1–12]

Faith is the assurance of things hoped for, the conviction
of things not seen. Indeed, by faith our ancestors received
approval. By faith we understand that the worlds were
prepared by the word of God, so that what is seen was
made from things that are not visible. By faith Abel
offered to God a more acceptable sacrifice than Cain's.
Through this he received approval as righteous, God
himself giving approval to his gifts; he died, but through
his faith he still speaks. By faith Enoch was taken so that
he did not experience death; and "he was not found,
because God had taken him." For it was attested before he
was taken away that "he had pleased God." And without
faith it is impossible to please God, for whoever would
approach him must believe that he exists and that he
rewards those who seek him. By faith Noah, warned by
God about events as yet unseen, respected the warning and
built an ark to save his household; by this he condemned
the world and became an heir to the righteousness that is
in accordance with faith. By faith Abraham obeyed when

he was called to set out for a place that he was to receive as an inheritance; and he set out, not knowing where he was going. By faith he stayed for a time in the land he had been promised, as in a foreign land, living in tents, as did Isaac and Jacob, who were heirs with him of the same promise. For he looked forward to the city that has foundations, whose architect and builder is God. By faith he received power of procreation, even though he was too old—and Sarah herself was barren—because he considered him faithful who had promised. Therefore from one person, and this one as good as dead, descendants were born, "as many as the stars of heaven and as the innumerable grains of sand by the seashore."

A Reading (Lesson) from the Gospel according to John [6:35–42,48–51]

Jesus said to the Jews, "I am the bread of life. Whoever comes to me will never be hungry, and whoever believes me will never be thirsty. But I said to you that you have seen me and yet do not believe. Everything that the Father gives me will come to me, and anyone who comes to me will never drive away; for I have come down from heaven not to do my own will, but the will of him who sent me. And this is the will of him who sent me, that I should lose nothing of all that he has given me, but raise it up on the last day. This is indeed the will of my Father, that all who see the Son and believe in him may have eternal life; and I will raise them up on the last day." Then the Jews began to complain about him because he said, "I am the bread that came down from heaven." They were saying, "Is not this Jesus, the son of Joseph, whose father and mother we know? How can he now say, 'I have come down from heaven'?" Jesus answered them, "I am the bread of life.

Your ancestors ate the manna in the wilderness, and they died. This is the bread that comes down from heaven, so that one may eat of it and not die. I am the living bread that came down from heaven. Whoever eats of this bread will live forever; and the bread that I will give for the life of the world is my flesh."

January 3

Psalm 68 [page 676] ❖ *Psalm 72* [page 685]*

A Reading (Lesson) from the Book of Genesis [28:10–22]

Jacob left Beer-sheba and went toward Haran. He came to a certain place and stayed there for the night, because the sun had set. Taking one of the stones of the place, he put it under his head and lay down in that place. And he dreamed that there was a ladder set up on the earth, the top of it reaching to heaven; and the angels of God were ascending and descending on it. And the LORD stood beside him and said, "I am the LORD, the God of Abraham your father and the God of Isaac; the land on which you lie I will give to you and to your offspring; and your offspring shall be like the dust of the earth, and you shall spread abroad to the west and to the east and to the north and to the south; and all the families of the earth shall be blessed in you and in your offspring. Know that I am with you and will keep you wherever you go, and will bring you back to this land; for I will not leave you until I have done what I have promised you." Then Jacob woke from his sleep and said, "Surely the LORD is in this place—and I did not know it!" And he was afraid, and said, "How awesome is this place! This is none

* *today is Saturday, use Psalm 136 [page 789] at Evening Prayer.*

other than the house of God, and this is the gate of heaven." So Jacob rose early in the morning, and he took the stone that he had put under his head and set it up for a pillar and poured oil on the top of it. He called that place Bethel; but the name of the city was Luz at the first. Then Jacob made a vow, saying, "If God will be with me, and will keep me in this way that I go, and will give me bread to eat and clothing to wear, so that I come again to my father's house in peace, then the LORD shall be my God, and this stone, which I have set up for a pillar, shall be God's house; and of all that you give me I will surely give one tenth to you."

A Reading (Lesson) from the Letter to the Hebrews [11:13–22]

All of the descendants of Abraham died in faith without having received the promises, but from a distance they saw and greeted them. They confessed that they were strangers and foreigners on the earth, for people who speak in this way make it clear that they are seeking a homeland. If they had been thinking of the land that they had left behind, they would have had opportunity to return. But as it is, they desire a better country, that is, a heavenly one. Therefore God is not ashamed to be called their God; indeed, he has prepared a city for them. By faith Abraham, when put to the test, offered up Isaac. He who had received the promises was ready to offer up his only son, of whom he had been told, "It is through Isaac that descendants shall be named for you." He considered the fact that God is able even to raise someone from the dead—and figuratively speaking, he did receive him back. By faith Isaac invoked blessings for the future on Jacob and Esau. By faith Jacob, when dying, blessed each of the sons of Joseph, "bowing in worship over the top of his staff." By faith Joseph, at the end of his life, made mention of the exodus of the Israelites and gave instructions about his burial.

A Reading (Lesson) from the Gospel according to John [10:7–17]

Jesus said, "Very truly, I tell you, I am the gate for the sheep. All who came before me are thieves and bandits; but the sheep did not listen to them. I am the gate. Whoever enters by me will be saved, and will come in and go out and find pasture. The thief comes only to steal and kill and destroy. I came that they may have life, and have it abundantly. I am the good shepherd. The good shepherd lays down his life for the sheep. The hired hand, who is not the shepherd and does not own the sheep, sees the wolf coming and leaves the sheep and runs away—and the wolf snatches them and scatters them. The hired hand runs away because a hired hand does not care for the sheep. I am the good shepherd. I know my own and my own know me, just as the Father knows me and I know the Father. And I lay down my life for the sheep. I have other sheep that do not belong to this fold. I must bring them also, and they will listen to my voice. So there will be one flock, one shepherd. For this reason the Father loves me, because I lay down my life in order to take it up again."

January 4

Psalm 85 [page 708],   *Psalm 87* [page 711]   ❖
Psalm 89:1–29 [page 713]*

If today is Saturday, use Psalm 136 [page 789] at Evening Prayer.

A Reading (Lesson) from the Book of Exodus [3:1–12]

Moses was keeping the flock of his father-in-law Jethro, the priest of Midian; he led his flock beyond the wilderness, and came to Horeb, the mountain of God. There the angel of the LORD appeared to him in a flame of fire out of a bush; he looked, and the bush was blazing, yet it was not consumed. Then Moses said, "I must turn aside and look at this great sight, and see why the bush is not burned up." When the LORD saw that he had turned aside to see, God called to him out of the bush, "Moses, Moses!" And he said, "Here I am." Then he said, "Come no closer! Remove the sandals from your feet, for the place on which you are standing is holy ground." He said further, "I am the God of your father, the God of Abraham, the God of Isaac, and the God of Jacob." And Moses hid his face, for he was afraid to look at God. Then the LORD said, "I have observed the misery of my people who are in Egypt; I have heard their cry on account of their taskmasters. Indeed, I know their sufferings and I have come down to deliver them from the Egyptians, and to bring them up and out of that land to a good and broad land, a land flowing with milk and honey, to the country of the Canaanites, the Hittites, the Amorites, the Perizzites, the Hivites, and the Jebusites. The cry of the Israelites has now come to me; I have also seen how the Egyptians oppress them. So come, I will send you to Pharaoh to bring my people, the Israelites, out of Egypt." But Moses said to God, "Who am I that I should go to Pharaoh, and bring the Israelites out of Egypt?" He said, "I will be with you; and this shall be the sign for you that it is I who sent you: when you have brought the people out of Egypt, you shall worship God on this mountain."

A Reading (Lesson) from the Letter to the Hebrews [11:23–31]

By faith Moses was hidden by his parents for three months after his birth, because they saw that the child was beautiful; and they were not afraid of the king's edict. By faith Moses, when he was grown up, refused to be called a son of pharaoh's daughter, choosing rather to share ill-treatment with the people of God than to enjoy the fleeting pleasures of sin. He considered abuse suffered for the Christ to be greater wealth than the treasures of Egypt, for he was looking ahead to the reward. By faith he left Egypt, unafraid of the king's anger; for he persevered as though he saw him who is invisible. By faith he kept the Passover and the sprinkling of blood, so that the destroyer of the firstborn would not touch the firstborn of Israel. By faith the people passed through the Red Sea as if it were dry land, but when the Egyptians attempted to do so they were drowned. By faith the walls of Jericho fell after they had been encircled for seven days. By faith Rahab the prostitute did not perish with those who were disobedient, because she had received the spies in peace.

A Reading (Lesson) from the Gospel according to John [14:6–14]

Jesus said to Thomas, "I am the way, and the truth, and the life. No one comes to the Father except through me. If you know me, you will know my Father also. From now on you do know him and have seen him." Philip said to him, "Lord, show us the Father, and we will be satisfied." Jesus said to him, "Have I been with you all this time, Philip, and you still do not know me? Whoever has seen me has seen the Father. How can you say, 'Show us the Father'? Do you not believe that I am in the Father and

the Father is in me? The words that I say to you I do not
speak on my own; but the Father who dwells in me does
his works. Believe me that I am in the Father and the
Father is in me; but if you do not, then believe me because
of the works themselves. Very truly, I tell you, the one
who believes in me will also do the works that I do and,
in fact, will do greater works than these, because I am
going to the Father. I will do whatever you ask in my
name, so that the Father may be glorified in the Son. If in
my name you ask me for anything, I will do it."

January 5

MORNING PRAYER

Psalm 2 [page 586], *Psalm 110:1–5(6–7)* [page 753]

A Reading (Lesson) from the Book of Joshua [1:1–9]

After the death of Moses the servant of the LORD, the LORD
spoke to Joshua son of Nun, Moses' assistant, saying, "My
servant Moses is dead. Now proceed to cross the Jordan,
you and all this people, into the land that I am giving to
them, to the Israelites. Every place that the sole of your foot
will tread upon I have given to you, as I promised to Moses.
From the wilderness and the Lebanon as far as the great
river, the river Euphrates, all the land of the Hittites, to the
Great Sea in the west shall be your territory. No one shall be
able to stand against you all the days of your life. As I was
with Moses, so I will be with you; I will not fail you or
forsake you. Be strong and courageous; for you shall put
this people in possession of the land that I swore to their
ancestors to give them. Only be strong and very courageous,
being careful to act in accordance with all the law that my

servant Moses commanded you; do not turn from it to the right hand or to the left, so that you may be successful wherever you go. This book of the law shall not depart out of your mouth; you shall meditate on it day and night, so that you may be careful to act in accordance with all that is written in it. For then you shall make your way prosperous, and then you shall be successful. I hereby command you: Be strong and courageous; do not be frightened or dismayed, for the LORD your God is with you wherever you go."

A Reading (Lesson) from the Letter to the Hebrews [11:32—12:2]

What more should I say? For time would fail me to tell of Gideon, Barak, Samson, Jephthah, of David and Samuel and the prophets—who through faith conquered kingdoms, administered justice, obtained promises, shut the mouths of lions, quenched raging fire, escaped the edge of the sword, won strength out of weakness, became mighty in war, put foreign armies to flight. Women received their dead by resurrection. Others were tortured, refusing to accept release, in order to obtain a better resurrection. Others suffered mocking and flogging, and even chains and imprisonment. They were stoned to death, they were sawn in two, they were killed by the sword; they went about in skins of sheep and goats, destitute, persecuted, tormented—of whom the world was not worthy. They wandered in deserts and mountains, and in caves and holes in the ground. Yet all these, though they were commended for their faith, did not receive what was promised, since God had provided something better so that they would not, apart from us, be made perfect. Therefore, since we are surrounded by so great a cloud of witnesses, let us also lay aside every weight and the sin that clings so closely, and let us run with perseverance the race that is set before us, looking to Jesus the pioneer and perfecter of our faith, who for the sake of the joy that was set before him endured the cross, disregarding its shame, and has taken his seat at the right hand of the throne of God.

A Reading (Lesson) from the Gospel according to John [15:1–16]

Jesus said to the disciples, "I am the true vine, and my Father is the vinegrower. He removes every branch in me that bears no fruit. Every branch that bears fruit he prunes to make it bear more fruit. You have already been cleansed by the word that I have spoken to you. Abide in me as I abide in you. Just as the branch cannot bear fruit by itself unless it abides in the vine, neither can you unless you abide in me. I am the vine, you are the branches. Those who abide in me and I in them bear much fruit, because apart from me you can do nothing. Whoever does not abide in me is thrown away like a branch and withers; such branches are gathered, thrown into the fire, and burned. If you abide in me, and my words abide in you, ask for whatever you wish, and it will be done for you. My Father is glorified by this, that you bear much fruit and become my disciples. As the Father has loved me, so I have loved you; abide in my love. If you keep my commandments, you will abide in my love, just as I have kept my Father's commandments and abide in his love. I have said these things to you so that my joy may be in you, and that your joy may be complete. This is my commandment, that you love one another as I have loved you. No one has greater love than this, to lay down one's life for one's friends. You are my friends if you do what I command you. I do not call you servants any longer, because the servant does not know what the master is doing; but I have called you friends, because I have made known to you everything that I have heard from my Father. You did not choose me but I chose you. And I appointed you to go and bear fruit, fruit that will last, so that the Father will give you whatever you ask him in my name."

Eve of Epiphany

EVENING PRAYER

Psalm 29 [page 620], *Psalm 98* [page 727]

A Reading (Lesson) from the Book of Isaiah [66:18–23]

Thus says the LORD: "I know their works and their thoughts, and I am coming to gather all nations and tongues; and they shall come and shall see my glory, and I will set a sign among them. From them I will send survivors to the nations, to Tarshish, Put, and Lud—which draw the bow—to Tubal and Javan, to the coastlands far away that have not heard of my fame or seen my glory; and they shall declare my glory among the nations. They shall bring all your kindred from all the nations as an offering to the LORD, on horses, and in chariots, and in litters, and on mules, and on dromedaries, to my holy mountain Jerusalem, says the LORD, just as the Israelites bring a grain offering in a clean vessel to the house of the LORD. And I will also take some of them as priests and as Levites, says the LORD. For as the new heavens and the new earth, which I will make, shall remain before me, says the LORD; so shall your descendants and your name remain. From new moon to new moon, and from sabbath to sabbath, all flesh shall come to worship before me, says the LORD.

A Reading (Lesson) from the Letter of Paul to the Romans [15:7–13]

Welcome one another, therefore, just as Christ has welcomed you, for the glory of God. For I tell you that Christ has become a servant of the circumcised on behalf of the truth of God in order that he might confirm the promises given to the patriarchs, and in order that the Gentiles might glorify God for his mercy. As it is written, "Therefore I will confess you among the Gentiles, and sing praises to your name"; and again he says, "Rejoice, O Gentiles, with his people"; and again, "Praise the Lord, all you Gentiles, and let all the peoples praise him"; and again Isaiah says, "The root of Jesse shall come, the one who rises to rule the Gentiles; in him the Gentiles shall hope." May the God of hope fill you with all joy and peace in believing, so that you may abound in hope by the power of the Holy Spirit.

The Epiphany and Following

Epiphany

Psalm 46 [page 649],   *Psalm 97* [page 726]   ❖
Psalm 96 [page 725],   *Psalm 100* [page 729]

A Reading (Lesson) from the Book of Isaiah [52:7–10]

How beautiful upon the mountains are the feet of the messenger who announces peace, who brings good news, who announces salvation, who says to Zion, "Your God reigns." Listen! Your sentinels lift up their voices, together they sing for joy; for in plain sight they see the return of the Lord to Zion. Break forth together into singing, you ruins of Jerusalem; for the Lord has comforted his people, he has redeemed Jerusalem. The Lord has bared his holy arm before the eyes of all the nations; and all the ends of the earth shall see the salvation of our God.

A Reading (Lesson) from the Revelation to John [21:22–27]

I saw no temple in the city, for its temple is the Lord God the Almighty and the Lamb. And the city has no need of sun or moon to shine on it, for the glory of God is its light, and its lamp is the Lamb. The nations will walk by its light, and the kings of the earth will bring their glory into it. Its gates will never be shut by day—and there will be no night there. People will bring into it the glory and the honor of the nations. But nothing unclean will enter it, nor anyone who practices abomination or falsehood, but only those who are written in the Lamb's book of life.

A Reading (Lesson) from the Gospel according to Matthew [12:14–21]

The Pharisees went out and conspired against Jesus, how to destroy him. When Jesus became aware of this, he departed. Many crowds followed him, and he cured all of them, and he ordered them not to make him known. This was to fulfill what had been spoken through the prophet Isaiah: "Here is my servant, whom I have chosen, my beloved, with whom my soul is well pleased. I will put my Spirit upon him, and he will proclaim justice to the Gentiles. He will not wrangle or cry aloud, nor will anyone hear his voice in the streets. He will not break a bruised reed or quench a smoldering wick until he brings justice to victory. And in his name the Gentiles will hope.''

January 7*

Psalm 103 [page 733] ❖ *Psalm 114* [page 756], *Psalm 115* [page 757]

A Reading (Lesson) from the Book of Isaiah [52:3–6]

Thus says the LORD: You were sold for nothing, and you shall be redeemed without money. For thus says the Lord GOD: Long ago, my people went down into Egypt to reside there as aliens; the Assyrian, too, has oppressed them without cause. Now therefore what am I doing here, says the LORD, seeing that my people are taken away without cause? Their rulers howl, says the LORD, and continually, all day long, my name is despised. Therefore my people shall know my name; therefore in that day they shall know that it is I who speak; here am I.

A Reading (Lesson) from the Revelation to John [2:1–7]

One like the Son of Man said to me, "To the angel of the church in Ephesus write: These are the words of him who holds the seven stars in his right hand, who walks among the seven golden lampstands: I know your works, your toil and your patient endurance. I know that you cannot

---

* *The Psalms and Readings for the dated days after the Epiphany are used only until the following Saturday evening.*

tolerate evildoers; you have tested those who claim to be apostles but are not, and have found them to be false. I also know that you are enduring patiently and bearing up for the sake of my name, and that you have not grown weary. But I have this against you, that you have abandoned the love you had at first. Remember then from what you have fallen; repent, and do the works you did at first. If not, I will come to you and remove your lampstand from its place, unless you repent. Yet this is to your credit: you hate the works of the Nicolaitans, which I also hate. Let anyone who has an ear listen to what the Spirit is saying to the churches. To everyone who conquers, I will give permission to eat from the tree of life that is in the paradise of God."

A Reading (Lesson) from the Gospel according to John [2:1–11]

On the third day there was a wedding in Cana of Galilee, and the mother of Jesus was there. Jesus and his disciples had also been invited to the wedding. When the wine gave out, the mother of Jesus said to him, "They have no wine." And Jesus said to her, "Woman, what concern is that to you and to me? My hour has not yet come." His mother said to the servants, "Do whatever he tells you." Now standing there were six stone water jars for the Jewish rites of purification, each holding twenty or thirty gallons. Jesus said to them, "Fill the jars with water." And they filled them up to the brim. He said to them, "Now draw some out, and take it to the chief steward." So they took it. When the steward tasted the water that had become wine, and did not know where it came from (though the servants who had drawn the water knew), the steward called the bridegroom and said to him, "Everyone serves the good wine first, and then the inferior wine after the guests have become drunk. But you have kept the good wine until now." Jesus did this, the first of his signs, in Cana of Galilee, and revealed his glory; and his disciples believed in him.

January 8

Psalm 117 [page 760],   *Psalm 118* [page 760]   ❖
Psalm 112 [page 755],   *Psalm 113* [page 756]

A Reading (Lesson) from the Book of Isaiah [59:15–21]

Truth is lacking, and whoever turns from evil is despoiled. The LORD saw it, and it displeased him that there was no justice. He saw that there was no one, and was appalled that there was no one to intervene; so his own arm brought him victory, and his righteousness upheld him. He put on righteousness like a breastplate, and a helmet of salvation on his head; he put on garments of vengeance for clothing, and wrapped himself in fury as in a mantle. According to their deeds, so will he repay; wrath to his adversaries, requital to his enemies; to the coastlands he will render requital. So those in the west shall fear the name of the LORD, and those in the east, his glory; for he will come like a pent-up stream that the wind of the LORD drives on. And he will come to Zion as Redeemer, to those in Jacob who turn from transgression, says the LORD. And as for me, this is my covenant with them, says the LORD: my spirit that is upon you, and my words that I have put in your mouth, shall not depart out of your mouth, or out of the mouths of your children, or out of the mouths of your children's children, says the LORD, from now on and forever.

A Reading (Lesson) from the Revelation to John [2:8–17]

One like the Son of Man said to me, "To the angel of the
church in Smyrna write: These are the words of the first
and the last, who was dead and came to life: I know your
affliction and your poverty, even though you are rich. I
know the slander on the part of those who say that they
are Jews and are not, but are a synagogue of Satan. Do
not fear what you are about to suffer. Beware, the devil is
about to throw some of you into prison so that you may
be tested, and for ten days you will have affliction. Be
faithful until death, and I will give you the crown of life.
Let anyone who has an ear listen to what the Spirit is
saying to the churches. Whoever conquers will not be
harmed by the second death. And to the angel of the
church in Pergamum write: These are the words of him
who has the sharp two-edged sword: I know where you
are living, where Satan's throne is. Yet you are holding
fast to my name, and you did not deny your faith in me
even in the days of Antipas my witness, my faithful one,
who was killed among you, where Satan lives. But I have
a few things against you: you have some there who hold
to the teaching of Balaam, who taught Balak to put a
stumbling block before the people of Israel, so that they
would eat food sacrificed to idols and practice fornication.
So you also have some who hold to the teaching of the
Nicolaitans. Repent then. If not, I will come to you soon
and make war against them with the sword of my mouth.
Let anyone who has an ear listen to what the Spirit is
saying to the churches. To everyone who conquers I will
give some of the hidden manna, and I will give a white
stone, and on the white stone is written a new name that
no one knows except the one who receives it."

A Reading (Lesson) from the Gospel according to John [4:46–54]

Then Jesus came again to Cana in Galilee where he had changed the water into wine. Now there was a royal official whose son lay ill in Capernaum. When he heard that Jesus had come from Judea to Galilee, he went and begged him to come down and heal his son, for he was at the point of death. Then Jesus said to him, "Unless you see signs and wonders you will not believe." The official said to him. "Sir, come down before my little boy dies." Jesus said to him, "Go; your son will live." The man believed the word that Jesus spoke to him and started on his way. As he was going down, his slaves met him and told him that his child was alive. So he asked them the hour when he began to recover, and they said to him, "Yesterday at one in the afternoon the fever left him." The father realized that this was the hour when Jesus had said to him, "Your son will live." So he himself believed, along with his whole household. Now this was the second sign that Jesus did after coming from Judea to Galilee.

January 9

Psalm 121 [page 779],   *Psalm 122* [page 779],
Psalm 123 [page 780] ❖ *Psalm 131* [page 785],
Psalm 132 [page 785]

A Reading (Lesson) from the Book of Isaiah [63:1–5]

"Who is this that comes from Edom, from Bozrah in garments stained crimson? Who is this so splendidly robed, marching in his great might?" "It is I, announcing vindication, mighty to save." "Why are your robes red, and your garments like theirs who tread the winepress?" "I have trodden the winepress alone, and from the peoples no one was with me; I trod them in my anger and trampled them in my wrath; their juice spattered on my garments, and stained all my robes. For the day of vengeance was in my heart, and the year for my redeeming work had come. I looked, but there was no helper; I stared, but there was no one to sustain me; so my own arm brought me victory, and my wrath sustained me."

A Reading (Lesson) from the Revelation to John [2:18–29]

One like the Son of Man said to me, "To the angel of the church in Thyatira write: These are the words of the Son of God, who has eyes like a flame of fire, and whose feet are like burnished bronze: I know your works—your love, faith, service, and patient endurance. I know that your last works are greater than the first. But I have this against you: you tolerate that woman Jezebel, who calls herself a prophet and is teaching and beguiling my servants to practice fornication and to eat food sacrificed to idols. I gave her time to repent, but she refuses to repent of her fornication. Beware, I am throwing her on a bed, and those who commit adultery with her I am throwing into great distress, unless they repent of her doings; and I will strike her children dead. And all the churches will know that I am the one who searches minds and hearts, and I will give to each of you as your works deserve. But to the rest of you in Thyatira, who do not hold this teaching, who have not learned what some call 'the deep things of Satan,' to you I say, I do not lay on you any other burden; only hold fast to what you have until I come. To everyone who conquers and continues to do my works to the end, I will give authority over the nations; to rule them with an iron rod, as when clay pots are shattered—even as I also received authority from my Father. To the one who conquers I will also give the morning star. Let anyone who has an ear listen to what the Spirit is saying to the churches."

A Reading (Lesson) from the Gospel according to John [5:1–15]

After this there was a festival of the Jews, and Jesus went up to Jerusalem. Now in Jerusalem by the Sheep Gate there is a pool, called in Hebrew Beth-zatha, which has five porticoes. In these lay many invalids—blind, lame, and paralyzed. One man was there who had been ill for thirty-eight years. When Jesus saw him lying there and knew that he had been there a long time, he said to him, "Do you want to be made well?" The sick man answered him, "Sir, I have no one to put me into the pool when the water is stirred up; and while I am making my way, someone else steps down ahead of me." Jesus said to him, "Stand up, take your mat and walk." At once the man was made well, and he took up his mat and began to walk. Now that day was a sabbath. So the Jews said to the man who had been cured, "It is the sabbath; it is not lawful for you to carry your mat." But he answered them, "The man who made me well said to me, 'Take up your mat and walk.'" They asked him, "Who is the man who said to you, 'Take it up and walk'?" Now the man who had been healed did not know who it was, for Jesus had disappeared in the crowd that was there. Later Jesus found him in the temple and said to him, "See, you have been made well! Do not sin any more, so that nothing worse happens to you." The man went away and told the Jews that it was Jesus who had made him well.

Psalm 138 [page 793],
Psalm 139:1–17(18–23) [page 794]   ❖
Psalm 147 [page 804]

A Reading (Lesson) from the Book of Isaiah [65:1–9]

I was ready to be sought out by those who did not ask, to be found by those who did not seek me. I said, "Here I am, here I am," to a nation that did not call on my name. I held out my hands all day long to a rebellious people, who walk in a way that is not good, following their own devices; a people who provoke me to my face continually, sacrificing in gardens and offering incense on bricks; who sit inside tombs, and spend the night in secret places; who eat swine's flesh, with broth of abominable things in their vessels; who say, "Keep to yourself, do not come near me, for I am too holy for you." These are a smoke in my nostrils, a fire that burns all day long. See, it is written before me: I will not keep silent, but I will repay; I will indeed repay into their laps their iniquities and their ancestors' iniquities together, says the Lord; because they offered incense on the mountains and reviled me on the hills, I will measure into their laps full payment for their actions. Thus says the Lord: As the wine is found in the cluster, and they say, Do not destroy it, for there is a blessing in it," so I will do for my servants' sake, and not destroy them all. I will bring forth descendants from Jacob, and from Judah inheritors of my mountains; my chosen shall inherit it, and my servants shall settle there.

A Reading (Lesson) from the Revelation to John [3:1-6]

One like the Son of Man said to me, "To the angel of the
church in Sardis write: These are the words of him who
has the seven spirits of God and the seven stars: I know
your works; you have a name of being alive, but you are
dead. Wake up, and strengthen what remains and is on the
point of death, for I have not found your works perfect in
the sight of my God. Remember then what you received
and heard; obey it, and repent. If you do not wake up, I
will come like a thief, and you will not know at what
hour I will come to you. Yet you have still a few persons
in Sardis who have not soiled their clothes; they will walk
with me, dressed in white, for they are worthy. If you
conquer, you will be clothed like them in white robes, and
I will not blot your name out of the book of life; I will
confess your name before my Father and before his angels.
Let anyone who has an ear listen to what the Spirit is
saying to the churches."

*A Reading (Lesson) from the Gospel according to
John* [6:1-14]

Jesus went to the other side of the Sea of Galilee, also
called the Sea of Tiberias. A large crowd kept following
him, because they saw the signs that he was doing for the
sick. Jesus went up the mountain and sat down there with
his disciples. Now the Passover, the festival of the Jews,
was near. When he looked up and saw a large crowd
coming toward him, Jesus said to Philip, "Where are we
to buy bread for these people to eat?" He said this to test
him, for he himself knew what he was going to do. Philip
answered him, "Six months' wages would not buy enough
bread for each of them to get a little." One of his
disciples, Andrew, Simon Peter's brother, said to him,

There is a boy here who has five barley loaves and two fish. But what are they among so many people?" Jesus said, "Make the people sit down." Now there was a great deal of grass in the place; so they sat down, about five thousand in all. Then Jesus took the loaves, and when he had given thanks, he distributed them to those who were seated; so also the fish, as much as they wanted. When they were satisfied, he told his disciples, "Gather up the fragments left over, so that nothing may be lost." So they gathered them up, and from the fragments of the five barley loaves, left by those who had eaten, they filled twelve baskets. When the people saw the sign that he had done, they began to say, "This is indeed the prophet who is to come into the world."

January 11

Psalm 148 [page 805],   *Psalm 150* [page 807]   ❖
Psalm 91 [page 719],   *Psalm 92* [page 720]

A Reading (Lesson) from the Book of Isaiah [65:13–16]

Thus says the Lord GOD: My servants shall eat, but you shall be hungry; my servants shall drink, but you shall be thirsty; my servants shall rejoice, but you shall be put to shame; my servants shall sing for gladness of heart, but you shall cry out for pain of heart, and shall wail for anguish of spirit. You shall leave your name to my chosen to use as a curse, and the Lord GOD will put you to death; but to his servants he will give a different name. Then whoever invokes a blessing in the land shall bless by the God of faithfulness, and whoever takes an oath in the land shall swear by the God of faithfulness; because the former troubles are forgotten and are hidden from my sight.

A Reading (Lesson) from the Revelation to John [3:7–13]

One like the Son of Man said to me, "To the angel of the church in Philadelphia write: These are the words of the holy one, the true one, who has the key of David, who opens and no one will shut, who shuts and no one opens: I know your works. Look, I have set before you an open door, which no one is able to shut. I know that you have but little power, and yet you have kept my word and have not denied my name. I will make those of the synagogue of Satan who say that they are Jews and are not, but are lying—I will make them come and bow down before your feet, and they will learn that I have loved you. Because you have kept my word of patient endurance, I will keep you from the hour of trial that is coming on the whole world to test the inhabitants of the earth. I am coming soon; hold fast to what you have, so that no one may seize your crown. If you conquer, I will make you a pillar in the temple of my God; you will never go out of it. I will write on you the name of my God, and the name of the city of my God, the new Jerusalem that comes down from my God out of heaven, and my own new name. Let anyone who has an ear listen to what the Spirit is saying to the churches."

A Reading (Lesson) from the Gospel according to John [6:15–27]

When Jesus realized that they were about to come and take him by force to make him king, he withdrew again to the mountain by himself. When evening came, his disciples went down to the sea, got into a boat, and started across the sea to Capernaum. It was now dark, and Jesus had not yet come to them. The sea became rough because a strong wind was blowing. When they had rowed about hree or four miles, they saw Jesus walking on the sea and oming near the boat, and they were terrified. But he said o them, "It is I; do not be afraid." Then they wanted to ake him into the boat, and immediately the boat reached he land toward which they were going. The next day the rowd that had stayed on the other side of the sea saw hat there had been only one boat there. They also saw hat Jesus had not got into the boat with his disciples, but hat his disciples had gone away alone. Then some boats rom Tiberias came near the place where they had eaten he bread after the Lord had given thanks. So when the rowd saw that neither Jesus nor his disciples were there, hey themselves got into the boats and went to Capernaum ooking for Jesus. When they found him on the other side of the sea, they said to him, "Rabbi, when did you come here?" Jesus answered them, "Very truly, I tell you, you are looking for me, not because you saw signs, but because you ate your fill of the loaves. Do not work for he food that perishes, but for the food that endures for eternal life, which the Son of Man will give you. For it is on him that God the Father has set his seal."

January 12

MORNING PRAYER

salm 98 [page 727],   *Psalm 99* [page 728],
Psalm 100 [page 729])

A Reading (Lesson) from the Book of Isaiah [66:1–2,22–23]

Thus says the LORD: Heaven is my throne and the earth is my footstool; what is the house that you would build for me, and what is my resting place? All these things my hand has made, and so all these things are mine, says the LORD. But this is the one to whom I will look, to the humble and contrite in spirit, who trembles at my word. For as the new heavens and the new earth, which I will make, shall remain before me, says the LORD; so shall your descendants and your name remain. From new moon to new moon, and from sabbath to sabbath, all flesh shall come to worship before me, says the LORD.

A Reading (Lesson) from the Revelation to John [3:14–22]

One like the Son of Man said to me, "To the angel of the church in Laodicea write: The words of the Amen, the faithful and true witness, the origin of God's creation: I know your works; you are neither cold nor hot. I wish that you were either cold or hot. So, because you are lukewarm, and neither cold nor hot, I am about to spit you out of my mouth. For you say, 'I am rich, I have prospered, and I need nothing.' You do not realize that you are wretched, pitiable, poor, blind, and naked. Therefore I counsel you to buy from me gold refined by fire so that you may be rich; and white robes to clothe you and to keep the shame of your nakedness from being seen; and salve to anoint your eyes so that you may see. I reprove and discipline those whom I love. Be earnest, therefore, and repent. Listen! I am standing at the door, knocking; if you hear my voice and open the door, I will come in to you and eat with you, and you with me. To the one who conquers I will give a place with me on my throne, just as I myself conquered and sat down with my Father on his throne. Let anyone who has an ear listen to what the Spirit is saying to the churches."

A Reading (Lesson) from the Gospel according to
John [9:1–12, 35–38]

As Jesus walked along, he saw a man blind from birth. His disciples asked him, "Rabbi, who sinned, this man or his parents, that he was born blind?" Jesus answered, Neither this man nor his parents sinned; he was born blind so that God's works might be revealed in him. We must work the works of him who sent me while it is day; night is coming when no one can work. As long as I am in the world, I am the light of the world." When he had said this, he spat on the ground and made mud with the saliva and spread the mud on the man's eyes, saying to him, Go, wash in the pool of Siloam" (which means Sent). Then he went and washed and came back able to see. The neighbors and those who had seen him before as a beggar began to ask, "Is this not the man who used to sit and beg?" Some were saying, "It is he." Others were saying, No, but it is someone like him." He kept saying, "I am the man." But they kept asking him, "Then how were your eyes opened?" He answered, "The man called Jesus made mud, spread it on my eyes, and said to me, 'Go to Siloam and wash.' Then I went and washed and received my sight." They said to him, "Where is he?" He said, I do not know." Jesus heard that they had driven him out, and when he found him, he said, "Do you believe in the Son of Man?" He answered, "And who is he, sir? Tell me, so that I may believe in him." Jesus said to him, "You have seen him, and the one speaking with you is he." He said, "Lord, I believe." And he worshiped him.

Eve of 1 Epiphany

Psalm 104 [page 735]

A Reading (Lesson) from the Book of Isaiah [61:1–9]

The spirit of the Lord God is upon me, because the Lord has anointed me; he has sent me to bring good news to the oppressed, to bind up the brokenhearted, to proclaim liberty to the captives, and release to the prisoners; to proclaim the year of the Lord's favor, and the day of vengeance of our God; to comfort all who mourn; to provide for those who mourn in Zion—to give them a garland instead of ashes, the oil of gladness instead of mourning, the mantle of praise instead of a faint spirit. They will be called oaks of righteousness, the planting of the Lord, to display his glory. They shall build up the ancient ruins, they shall raise up the former devastations; they shall repair the ruined cities, the devastations of many generations. Strangers shall stand and feed your flocks, foreigners shall till your land and dress your vines; but you shall be called priests of the Lord, you shall be named ministers of our God; you shall enjoy the wealth of the nations, and in their riches you shall glory. Because their shame was double, and dishonor was proclaimed as their lot, therefore they shall possess a double portion; everlasting joy shall be theirs. For I the Lord love justice, I hate robbery and wrongdoing; I will faithfully give them their recompense, and I will make an everlasting covenant with them. Their descendants shall be known among the nations, and their offspring among the peoples; all who see them shall acknowledge that they are a people whom the Lord has blessed.

A Reading (Lesson) from the Letter of Paul to the Galatians [3:23–29; 4:4–7]

Now before faith came, we were imprisoned and guarded under the law until faith would be revealed. Therefore the law was our disciplinarian until Christ came, so that we might be justified by faith. But now that faith has come, we are no longer subject to a disciplinarian, for in Christ Jesus you are all children of God through faith. As many of you as were baptized into Christ have clothed yourselves with Christ. There is no longer Jew or Greek, there is no longer slave or free, there is no longer male and female; for all of you are one in Christ Jesus. And if you belong to Christ, then you are Abraham's offspring, heirs according to the promise. When the fullness of time had come, God has sent his Son, born of a woman, born under the law, in order to redeem those who were under the law, so that we might receive adoption as children. And because you are children, God has sent the Spirit of his Son into our hearts, crying "Abba! Father!" So you are no longer a slave but a child, and if a child then also an heir, through God.

Week of 1 Epiphany

Sunday

Psalm 146 [page 803], *Psalm 147* [page 804] ❖
Psalm 111 [page 754], *Psalm 112* [page 755],
Psalm 113 [page 756]

A Reading from the Book of Isaiah [40:1–11]

Comfort, O comfort my people, says your God. Speak
tenderly to Jerusalem, and cry to her that she has served her
term, that her penalty is paid, that she has received from the
LORD's hand double for all her sins. A voice cries out: "In
the wilderness prepare the way of the LORD, make straight
in the desert a highway for our God. Every valley shall be
lifted up, and every mountain and hill be made low; the
uneven ground shall become level, and the rough places a
plain. Then the glory of the LORD shall be revealed, and all
people shall see it together, for the mouth of the LORD has
spoken." A voice says, "Cry out!" And I said, "What shall I
cry?" All people are grass, their constancy is like the flower
of the field. The grass withers, the flower fades, when the
breath of the LORD blows upon it; surely the people are
grass. The grass withers, the flower fades; but the word of
our God will stand forever. Get you up to a high mountain,
O Zion, herald of good tidings; lift up your voice with
strength, O Jerusalem, herald of good tidings, lift it up, do
not fear; say to the cities of Judah, "Here is your God!" See,
the Lord GOD comes with might, and his arm rules for him;
his reward is with him, and his recompense before him. He
will feed his flock like a shepherd; he will gather the lambs
in his arms, and carry them in his bosom, and gently lead
the mother sheep.

*A Reading (Lesson) from the Letter to the
Hebrews* [1:1–12]

Long ago God spoke to our ancestors in many and various
ways by the prophets, but in these last days he has spoken
to us by a Son, whom he appointed heir of all things,
through whom he also created the worlds. He is the
reflection of God's glory and the exact imprint of God's

very being, and he sustains all things by his powerful word. When he had made purification for sins, he sat down at the right hand of the Majesty on high, having become as much superior to angels as the name he has inherited is more excellent than theirs. For to which of the angels did God ever say, "You are my Son; today I have begotten you"? Or again, "I will be his Father, and he will be my Son"? And again, when he brings the firstborn into the world, he says, "Let all God's angels worship him." Of the angels he says, "He makes his angels winds, and his servants flames of fire." But of the Son he says, "Your throne, O God, is forever and ever, and the righteous scepter is the scepter of your kingdom. You have loved righteousness and hated wickedness; therefore God, your God, has anointed you with the oil of gladness beyond your companions." And, "In the beginning, Lord, you founded the earth, and the heavens are the work of your hands; they will perish, but you remain; they will all wear out like clothing; like a cloak you will roll them up, and like clothing they will be changed. But you are the same, and your years will never end."

A Reading (Lesson) from the Gospel according to John [1:1–7,19–20,29–34]

In the beginning was the Word, and the Word was with God, and the Word was God. He was in the beginning with God. All things came into being through him, and without him not one thing came into being. What has come into being in him was life, and the life was the light of all people. The light shines in the darkness, and the darkness did not overcome it. There was a man sent from God, whose name was John. He came as a witness to testify to the light, so that all might believe through him.

This is the testimony given by John when the Jews sent priests and Levites from Jerusalem to ask him, "Who are you?" He confessed and did not deny it, but confessed, "I am not the Messiah." The next day he saw Jesus coming toward him and declared, "Here is the Lamb of God who takes away the sin of the world! This is he of whom I said, 'After me comes a man who ranks ahead of me because he was before me.' I myself did not know him; but I came baptizing with water for this reason, that he might be revealed to Israel." And John testified, "I saw the Spirit descending from heaven like a dove, and it remained on him. I myself did not know him, but the one who sent me to baptize with water said to me, 'He on whom you see the Spirit descend and remain is the one who baptizes with the Holy Spirit.' And I myself have seen and have testified that this is the Son of God."

Monday

Psalm 1 [page 585], *Psalm 2* [page 586], *Psalm 3* [page 587] ❖ *Psalm 4* [page 587], *Psalm 7* [page 590]

A Reading (Lesson) from the Book of Isaiah [40:12–23]

Who has measured the waters in the hollow of his hand and marked off the heavens with a span, enclosed the dust of the earth in a measure, and weighed the mountains in scales and the hills in a balance? Who has directed the spirit of the LORD, or as his counselor has instructed him? Whom did he consult for his enlightenment, and who taught him the path of justice? Who taught him knowledge, and showed him the way of understanding? Even the nations are like a drop from a bucket, and are accounted as dust on the scales; see, he takes up the isles like fine dust. Lebanon would not provide fuel enough, nor are its animals enough for a burnt offering. All the nations are as nothing before him; they are accounted by him as less than nothing and emptiness. To whom then will you liken God, or what likeness compare with him? An idol?—A workman casts it, and a goldsmith overlays it with gold, and casts for it silver chains. As a gift one chooses mulberry wood—wood that will not rot—then seeks out a skilled artisan to set up an image that will not topple. Have you not known? Have you not heard? Has it not been told you from the beginning? Have you not understood from the foundations of the earth? It is he who sits above the circle of the earth, and its inhabitants are like grasshoppers; who stretches out the heavens like a curtain, and spreads them like a tent to live in; who brings princes to naught, and makes the rulers of the earth as nothing.

A Reading (Lesson) from the Letter of Paul to the Ephesians [1:1-14]

Paul, an apostle of Christ Jesus by the will of God, to the saints who are in Ephesus and are faithful in Christ Jesus: Grace to you and peace from God our Father and the Lord Jesus Christ. Blessed be the God and Father of our Lord Jesus Christ, who has blessed us in Christ with every spiritual blessing in the heavenly places, just as he chose us in Christ before the foundation of the world to be holy and blameless before him in love. He destined us for adoption as his children through Jesus Christ, according to the good pleasure of his will, to the praise of his glorious grace that he freely bestowed on us in the Beloved. In him we have redemption through his blood, the forgiveness of our trespasses, according to the riches of his grace that he lavished on us. With all wisdom and insight he has made known to us the mystery of his will, according to his good pleasure that he set forth in Christ, as a plan for the fullness of time, to gather up all things in him, things in heaven and things on earth. In Christ we have also obtained an inheritance, having been destined according to the purpose of him who accomplishes all things according to his counsel and will, so that we, who were the first to set our hope on Christ, might live for the praise of his glory. In him you also, when you had heard the word of truth, the gospel of your salvation, and had believed in him, were marked with the seal of the promised Holy Spirit; this is the pledge of our inheritance toward redemption as God's own people, to the praise of his glory.

A Reading (Lesson) from the Gospel according to Mark [1:1–13]

The beginning of the good news of Jesus Christ, the Son of God. As it is written in the prophet Isaiah, "See, I am sending my messenger ahead of you, who will prepare your way; the voice of one crying out in the wilderness: 'Prepare the way of the Lord, make his paths straight,' " John the baptizer appeared in the wilderness, proclaiming a baptism of repentance for the forgiveness of sins. And people from the whole Judean countryside and all the people of Jerusalem were going out to him, and were baptized by him in the river Jordan, confessing their sins. Now John was clothed with camel's hair, with a leather belt around his waist, and he ate locusts and wild honey. He proclaimed, "The one who is more powerful than I is coming after me; I am not worthy to stoop down and untie the thong of his sandals. I have baptized you with water; but he will baptize you with the Holy Spirit." In those days Jesus came from Nazareth of Galilee and was baptized by John in the Jordan. And just as he was coming up out of the water, he saw the heavens torn apart and the Spirit descending like a dove on him. And a voice came from heaven, "You are my Son, the Beloved; with you I am well pleased." And the Spirit immediately drove him out into the wilderness. He was in the wilderness forty days, tempted by Satan; and he was with the wild beasts; and the angels waited on him.

Tuesday

Psalm 5 [page 588],   *Psalm 6* [page 589] ❖
Psalm 10 [page 594],   *Psalm 11* [page 596]

A Reading (Lesson) from the Book of Isaiah [40:25–31]

To whom then will you compare me, or who is my equal? says the Holy One. Lift up your eyes on high and see: Who created these? He who brings out their host and numbers them, calling them all by name; because he is great in strength, mighty in power, not one is missing. Why do you say, O Jacob, and speak, O Israel, "My way is hidden from the LORD, and my right is disregarded by my God"? Have you not known? Have you not heard? The LORD is the everlasting God, the Creator of the ends of the earth. He does not faint or grow weary; his understanding is unsearchable. He gives power to the faint, and strengthens the powerless. Even youths will faint and be weary, and the young will fall exhausted; but those who wait for the LORD shall renew their strength, they shall mount up with wings like eagles, they shall run and not be weary, they shall walk and not faint.

A Reading (Lesson) from the Letter of Paul to the Ephesians [1:15–23]

I have heard of your faith in the Lord Jesus and your love toward all the saints, and for this reason I do not cease to give thanks for you as I remember you in my prayers. I pray that the God of our Lord Jesus Christ, the Father of glory, may give you a spirit of wisdom and revelation as you come to know him, so that, with the eyes of your heart enlightened, you may know what is the hope to which he has called you, what are the riches of his glorious inheritance among the saints, and what is the immeasurable greatness of his power for us who believe, according to the working of his great power. God put this power to work in Christ when he raised him from the dead and seated him at his right hand in the heavenly places, far above all rule and authority and power and dominion, and above every name that is named, not only in this age but also in the age to come. And he has put all things under his feet and has made him the head over all things for the church, which is his body, the fullness of him who fills all in all.

A Reading (Lesson) from the Gospel according to Mark [1:14–28]

Now after John was arrested, Jesus came to Galilee, proclaiming the good news of God, and saying, "The time is fulfilled, and the kingdom of God has come near; repent, and believe in the good news." As Jesus passed along the Sea of Galilee, he saw Simon and his brother Andrew casting a net into the sea—for they were fishermen. And Jesus said to them, "Follow me and I will make you fish for people." And immediately they left their nets and followed him. As he went a little farther, he saw

James son of Zebedee and his brother John, who were in their boat mending the nets. Immediately he called them; and they left their father Zebedee in the boat with the hired men, and followed him. They went to Capernaum; and when the sabbath came, he entered the synagogue and taught. They were astounded at his teaching, for he taught them as one having authority, and not as the scribes. Just then there was in their synagogue a man with an unclean spirit, and he cried out, "What have you to do with us, Jesus of Nazareth? Have you come to destroy us? I know who you are, the Holy One of God." But Jesus rebuked him, saying, "Be silent, and come out of him!" And the unclean spirit, convulsing him and crying with a loud voice, came out of him. They were all amazed, and they kept on asking one another, "What is this? A new teaching—with authority! He commands even the unclean spirits, and they obey him." At once his fame began to spread throughout the surrounding region of Galilee.

Wednesday

Psalm 119:1–24 [page 763] ❖ *Psalm 12* [page 597], *Psalm 13* [page 597], *Psalm 14* [page 598]

A Reading (Lesson) from the Book of Isaiah [41:1–16]

Listen to me in silence, O coastlands; let the peoples renew their strength; let them approach, then let them speak; let us together draw near for judgment. Who has roused a victor from the east, summoned him to his service? He delivers up nations to him, and tramples kings under foot; he makes them like dust with his sword, like driven stubble with his bow. He pursues them and passes on safely, scarcely touching the path with his feet. Who has performed and done this, calling the generations from the beginning? I, the LORD, am first, and will be with the last. The coastlands have seen and are afraid, the ends of the earth tremble; they have drawn near and come. Each one helps the other, saying to one another, "Take courage!" The artisan encourages the goldsmith, and the one who smooths with the hammer encourages the one who strikes the anvil, saying of the soldering, "It is good"; and they fasten it with nails so that it cannot be moved. But you, Israel, my servant, Jacob, whom I have chosen, the offspring of Abraham, my friend; you whom I took from the ends of the earth, and called from its farthest corners, saying to you, "You are my servant, I have chosen you and not cast you off"; do not fear, for I am with you, do not be afraid, for I am your God; I will strengthen you, I will help you, I will uphold you with my victorious right hand. Yes, all who are incensed against you shall be ashamed and disgraced; those who strive against you shall be as nothing and shall perish. You shall seek those who contend with you, but you shall not find them; those who war against you shall be as nothing at all. For I, the LORD your God, hold your right hand; it is I who say to you, "Do not fear, I will help you." Do not fear, you worm Jacob, you insect Israel! I will help you, says the LORD; your Redeemer is the Holy One of Israel. Now, I will make of you a threshing sledge, sharp, new, and having teeth; you shall thresh the mountains and crush them, and you shall make the hills like chaff. You shall winnow them and the wind shall carry them away, and the tempest shall scatter them. Then you shall rejoice in the LORD; in the Holy One of Israel you shall glory.

A Reading (Lesson) from the Letter of Paul to the Ephesians [2:1–10]

You were dead through the trespasses and sins in which you once lived, following the course of this world, following the ruler of the power of the air, the spirit that is now at work among those who are disobedient. All of us once lived among them in the passions of our flesh, following the desires of flesh and senses, and we were by nature children of wrath, like everyone else. But God, who is rich in mercy, out of the great love with which he loved us even when we were dead through our trespasses, made us alive together with Christ—by grace you have been saved—and raised us up with him and seated us with him in the heavenly places in Christ Jesus, so that in the ages to come he might show the immeasurable riches of his grace in kindness toward us in Christ Jesus. For by grace you have been saved through faith, and this is not your own doing; it is the gift of God—not the result of works, so that no one may boast. For we are what he has made us, created in Christ Jesus for good works, which God prepared beforehand to be our way of life.

A Reading (Lesson) from the Gospel according to Mark [1:29–45]

As soon as Jesus left the synagogue, they entered the house of Simon and Andrew, with James and John. Now Simon's mother-in-law was in bed with a fever, and they told him about her at once. He came and took her by the hand and lifted her up. Then the fever left her, and she began to serve them. That evening, at sundown, they brought to him all who were sick or possessed with demons. And the whole city was gathered around the door. And he cured many who were sick with various diseases, and cast out many demons; and he would not permit the demons to speak, because they knew him. In the morning, while it was still very dark, he got up and went out to a deserted place, and there he prayed. And Simon and his companions hunted for him. When they found him, they said to him, "Everyone is searching for you." He answered, "Let us go on to the neighboring towns, so that I may proclaim the message there also; for that is what I came out to do." And he went throughout Galilee, proclaiming the message in their synagogues and casting out demons. A leper came to him begging him, and kneeling he said to him, "If you choose, you can make me clean." Moved with pity, Jesus stretched out his hand and touched him, and said to him, "I do choose. Be made clean!" Immediately the leprosy left him, and he was made clean. After sternly warning him he sent him away at once, saying to him, "See that you say nothing to anyone; but go, show yourself to the priest, and offer for your cleansing what Moses commanded, as a testimony to them." But he went out and began to proclaim it freely, and to spread the word, so that Jesus could no longer go into a town openly, but stayed out in the country; and people came to him from every quarter.

Thursday

Psalm 18:1–20 [page 602]   ❖   *Psalm 18:21–50* [page 604]

A Reading (Lesson) from the Book of Isaiah [41:17–29]

When the poor and needy seek water, and there is none, and their tongue is parched with thirst, I the LORD will answer them, I the God of Israel will not forsake them. I will open rivers on the bare heights, and fountains in the midst of the valleys; I will make the wilderness a pool of water, and the dry land springs of water. I will put in the wilderness the cedar, the acacia, the myrtle, and the olive; I will set in the desert the cypress, the plane and the pine together, so that all may see and know, all may consider and understand, that the hand of the LORD has done this, the Holy One of Israel has created it. Set forth your case, says the LORD; bring your proofs, says the King of Jacob. Let them bring them, and tell us what is to happen. Tell us the former things, what they are, so that we may consider them, and that we may know their outcome; or declare to us the things to come. Tell us what is to come hereafter, that we may know that you are gods; do good, or do harm, that we may be afraid and terrified. You, indeed, are nothing and your work is nothing at all; whoever chooses you is an abomination. I stirred up one from the north, and he has come, from the rising of the sun he was summoned by name. He shall trample on rulers as on mortar, as the potter treads clay. Who declared it from the beginning, so that we might know, and beforehand, so that we might say, "He is right"? There was no one who declared it, none who proclaimed, none who heard your words. I first have declared it to Zion, and I give to Jerusalem a herald of good tidings. But when I look there is no one; among these there is no counselor who, when I ask, gives an answer. No, they are all a delusion; their works are nothing; their images are empty wind.

A Reading (Lesson) from the Letter of Paul to the Ephesians [2:11–22]

So then, remember that at one time you Gentiles by birth, called "the uncircumcision" by those who are called "the circumcision"—a physical circumcision made in the flesh by human hands—remember that you were at that time without Christ, being aliens from the commonwealth of Israel, and strangers to the covenants of promise, having no hope and without God in the world. But now in Christ Jesus you who once were far off have been brought near by the blood of Christ. For he is our peace; in his flesh he has made both groups into one and has broken down the dividing wall, that is, the hostility between us. He has abolished the law with its commandments and ordinances, that he might create in himself one new humanity in place of the two, thus making peace, and might reconcile both groups to God in one body through the cross, thus putting to death that hostility through it. So he came and proclaimed peace to you who were far off and peace to those who were near; for through him both of us have access in one Spirit to the Father. So then you are no longer strangers and aliens, but you are citizens with the saints and also members of the household of God, built upon the foundation of the apostles and prophets, with Christ Jesus himself as the cornerstone. In him the whole structure is joined together and grows into a holy temple in the Lord; in whom you also are built together spiritually into a dwelling place for God.

A Reading (Lesson) from the Gospel according to Mark [2:1–12]

When Jesus returned to Capernaum after some days, it was reported that he was at home. So many gathered around that there was no longer room for them, not even in front of the door; and he was speaking the word to them. Then some people came, bringing to him a paralyzed man, carried by four of them. And when they could not bring him to Jesus because of the crowd, they removed the roof above him; and after having dug through it, they let down the mat on which the paralytic lay. When Jesus saw their faith, he said to the paralytic, "Son, your sins are forgiven." Now some of the scribes were sitting there, questioning in their hearts, "Why does this fellow speak in this way? It is blasphemy! Who can forgive sins but God alone?" At once Jesus perceived in his spirit that they were discussing these questions among themselves; and he said to them, "Why do you raise such questions in your hearts? Which is easier, to say to the paralytic, 'Your sins are forgiven,' or to say, 'Stand up and take your mat and walk'? But so that you may know that the Son of Man has authority on earth to forgive sins"—he said to the paralytic—"I say to you, stand up, take your mat and go to your home." And he stood up, and immediately took the mat and went out before all of them; so that they were all amazed and glorified God, saying, "We have never seen anything like this!"

Friday

Psalm 16 [page 599], *Psalm 17* [page 600] ❖
Psalm 22 [page 610]

A Reading (Lesson) from the Book of Isaiah [42:(1–9)10–17]

Here is my servant, whom I uphold, my chosen, in whom my soul delights; I have put my spirit upon him; he will bring forth justice to the nations. He will not cry or lift up his voice, or make it heard in the street; a bruised reed he will not break, and a dimly burning wick he will not quench; he will faithfully bring forth justice. He will not grow faint or be crushed until he has established justice in the earth; and the coastlands wait for his teaching. Thus says God, the LORD, who created the heavens and stretched them out, who spread out the earth and what comes from it, who gives breath to the people upon it and spirit to those who walk in it: I am the LORD, I have called you in righteousness, I have taken you by the hand and kept you; I have given you as a covenant to the people, a light to the nations, to open the eyes that are blind, to bring out the prisoners from the dungeon, from the prison those who sit in darkness. I am the LORD, that is my name; my glory I give to no other, nor my praise to idols. See, the former things have come to pass, and new things I now declare; before they spring forth, I tell you of them.

Sing to the LORD a new song, his praise from the end of the earth! Let the sea roar and all that fills it, the coastlands and their inhabitants. Let the desert and its towns lift up their voice, the villages that Kedar inhabits; let the inhabitants of Sela sing for joy, let them shout from the tops of the mountains. Let them give glory to the LORD, and declare his praise in the coastlands. The LORD goes forth like a soldier, like a warrior he stirs up his fury; he cries out, he shouts aloud, he shows himself mighty against his foes. For a long time I have held my peace, I have kept still and restrained myself; now I will cry out like a woman in labor, I will gasp and pant. I will lay waste mountains and hills, and dry up all their herbage; I will turn the rivers into islands, and dry up the pools. I will lead the blind by a road they do not know, by paths they have not known I will guide them. I will turn the darkness before them into light, the rough places into level ground. These are the things I will do, and I will not forsake them. They shall be turned back and utterly put to shame—those who trust in carved images, who say to cast images, "You are our gods."

A Reading (Lesson) from the Letter of Paul to the Ephesians [3:1–13]

This is the reason that I Paul am a prisoner for Christ Jesus for the sake of you Gentiles—for surely you have already heard of the commission of God's grace that was given me for you, and how the mystery was made known to me by revelation, as I wrote above in a few words, a reading of which will enable you to perceive my understanding of the mystery of Christ. In former generations this mystery was not made known to humankind, as it has now been revealed to his holy apostles and prophets by the Spirit: that is, the Gentiles have become fellow heirs, members of the same body, and sharers in the promise in Christ Jesus through the gospel. Of this gospel I have become a servant according to the gift of God's grace that was given me by the working of his power. Although I am the very least of all the saints, this grace was given to me to bring to the Gentiles the news of the boundless riches of Christ, and to make everyone see what is the plan of the mystery hidden for ages in God who created all things; so that through the church the wisdom of God in its rich variety might now be made known to the rulers and authorities in the heavenly places. This was in accordance with the eternal purpose that he has carried out in Christ Jesus our Lord, in whom we have access to God in boldness and confidence through faith in him. I pray therefore that you may not lose heart over my sufferings for you; they are your glory.

A Reading (Lesson) from the Gospel according to Mark [2:13–22]

Jesus went out again beside the sea; the whole crowd gathered around him, and he taught them. As he was walking along, he saw Levi son of Alphaeus sitting at the tax booth, and he said to him, "Follow me." And he got up and followed him. And as he sat at dinner in Levi's house, many tax collectors and sinners were also sitting with Jesus and his disciples—for there were many who followed him. When the scribes of the Pharisees saw that he was eating with sinners and tax collectors, they said to his disciples, "Why does he eat with tax collectors and sinners?" When Jesus heard this, he said to them, "Those who are well have no need of a physician, but those who are sick; I have come to call not the righteous but sinners." Now John's disciples and the Pharisees were fasting; and people came and said to him, "Why do John's disciples and the disciples of the Pharisees fast, but your disciples do not fast?" Jesus said to them, "The wedding guests cannot fast while the bridegroom is with them, can they? As long as they have the bridegroom with them, they cannot fast. The days will come when the bridegroom is taken away from them, and then they will fast on that day. No one sews a piece of unshrunk cloth on an old cloak; otherwise, the patch pulls away from it, the new from the old, and a worse tear is made. And no one puts new wine into old wineskins; otherwise, the wine will burst the skins, and the wine is lost, and so are the skins; but one puts new wine into fresh wineskins."

Saturday

Psalm 20 [page 608], *Psalm 21:1–7(8–14)* [page 608] ❖
Psalm 110:1–5(6–7) [page 753], *Psalm 116* [page 759],
Psalm 117 [page 760]

A Reading (Lesson) from the Book of Isaiah [43:1–13]

Thus says the LORD, he who created you, O Jacob, he who
formed you, O Israel: Do not fear, for I have redeemed you;
I have called you by name, you are mine. When you pass
through the waters, I will be with you; and through the
rivers, they shall not overwhelm you; when you walk
through fire you shall not be burned, and the flame shall not
consume you. For I am the LORD your God, the Holy One
of Israel, your Savior. I give Egypt as your ransom, Ethiopia
and Seba in exchange for you. Because you are precious in
my sight, and honored, and I love you, I give people in
return for you, nations in exchange for your life. Do not
fear, for I am with you; I will bring your offspring from the
east, and from the west I will gather you; I will say to the
north, "Give them up," and to the south, "Do not withhold;
bring my sons from far away and my daughters from the
end of the earth—everyone who is called by my name,
whom I created for my glory, whom I formed and made."
Bring forth the people who are blind, yet have eyes, who are
deaf, yet have ears! Let all the nations gather together, and
let the peoples assemble. Who among them declared this,
and foretold to us the former things? Let them bring their
witnesses to justify them, and let them hear and say, "It is
true." You are my witnesses, says the LORD, and my servant
whom I have chosen, so that you may know and believe me
and understand that I am he. Before me no god was formed,
nor shall there be any after me. I, I am the LORD, and
besides me there is no savior. I declared and saved and

proclaimed, when there was no strange god among you; and you are my witnesses, says the LORD. I am God, and also henceforth I am He; there is no one who can deliver from my hand; I work and who can hinder it?

A Reading (Lesson) from the Letter of Paul to the Ephesians [3:14-21]

For this reason I bow my knees before the Father, from whom every family in heaven and on earth takes its name. I pray that, according to the riches of his glory, he may grant that you may be strengthened in your inner being with power through his Spirit, and that Christ may dwell in your hearts through faith, as you are being rooted and grounded in love. I pray that you may have the power to comprehend, with all the saints, what is the breadth and length and height and depth, and to know the love of Christ that surpasses knowledge, so that you may be filled with all the fullness of God. Now to him who by the power at work within us is able to accomplish abundantly far more than all we can ask or imagine, to him be glory in the church and in Christ Jesus to all generations, forever and ever. Amen.

A Reading (Lesson) from the Gospel according to Mark [2:23—3:6]

One sabbath Jesus was going through the grainfields; and as they made their way his disciples began to pluck heads of grain. The Pharisees said to him, "Look, why are they doing what is not lawful on the sabbath?" And he said to them, "Have you never read what David did when he and his companions were hungry and in need of food? He entered the house of God, when Abiathar was high priest, and ate the bread of the Presence, which it is not lawful for any but the priests to eat, and he gave some to his companions." Then he said to them, "The sabbath was made for humankind, and not humankind for the sabbath; so the Son of Man is lord even of the sabbath." Again he entered the synagogue, and a man was there who had a withered hand. They watched him to see whether he would cure him on the sabbath, so that they might accuse him. And he said to the man who had the withered hand, "Come forward." Then he said to them, "Is it lawful to do good or to do harm on the sabbath, to save life or to kill?" But they were silent. He looked around at them with anger; he was grieved at their hardness of heart and said to the man, "Stretch out your hand." He stretched it out, and his hand was restored. The Pharisees went out and immediately conspired with the Herodians against him, how to destroy him.

Week of 2 Epiphany

Sunday

Psalm 148 [page 805],   *Psalm 149* [page 807],
Psalm 150 [page 807]   ❖   *Psalm 114* [page 756],
Psalm 115 [page 757]

A Reading (Lesson) from the Book of Isaiah [43:14—44:5]

Thus says the Lord, your Redeemer, the Holy One of Israel: For your sake I will send to Babylon and break down all the bars, and the shouting of the Chaldeans will be turned to lamentation. I am the LORD, your Holy One, the Creator of

Israel, your King. Thus says the LORD, who makes a way in the sea, a path in the mighty waters, who brings out chariot and horse, army and warrior; they lie down, they cannot rise, they are extinguished, quenched like a wick: Do not remember the former things, or consider the things of old. I am about to do a new thing; now it springs forth, do you not perceive it? I will make a way in the wilderness and rivers in the desert. The wild animals will honor me, the jackals and the ostriches; for I give water in the wilderness, rivers in the desert, to give drink to my chosen people, the people whom I formed for myself so that they might declare my praise. Yet you did not call upon me, O Jacob; but you have been weary of me, O Israel! You have not brought me your sheep for burnt offerings, or honored me with your sacrifices. I have not burdened you with offerings, or wearied you with frankincense. You have not bought me sweet cane with money, or satisfied me with the fat of your sacrifices. But you have burdened me with your sins; you have wearied me with your iniquities. I, I am He who blots out your transgressions for my own sake, and I will not remember your sins. Accuse me, let us go to trial; set forth your case, so that you may be proved right. Your first ancestor sinned, and your interpreters transgressed against me. Therefore I profaned the princes of the sanctuary, I delivered Jacob to utter destruction, and Israel to reviling. But now hear, O Jacob my servant, Israel whom I have chosen! Thus says the LORD who made you, who formed you in the womb and will help you: Do not fear, O Jacob my servant, Jeshurun whom I have chosen. For I will pour water on the thirsty land, and streams on the dry ground; I will pour my spirit upon your descendants, and my blessing on your offspring. They shall spring up like a green tamarisk, like willows by flowing streams. This one will say,

I am the LORD's," another will be called by the name of Jacob, yet another will write on the hand, "The LORD's," and adopt the name of Israel.

A Reading (Lesson) from the Letter to the Hebrews [6:17—7:10]

When God desired to show even more clearly to the heirs of the promise the unchangeable character of his purpose, he guaranteed it by an oath, so that through two unchangeable things, in which it is impossible that God would prove false, we who have taken refuge might be strongly encouraged to seize the hope set before us. We have this hope, a sure and steadfast anchor of the soul, a hope that enters the inner shrine behind the curtain, where Jesus, a forerunner on our behalf, has entered, having become a high priest forever according to the order of Melchizedek. This "King Melchizedek of Salem, priest of the Most High God, met Abraham as he was returning from defeating the kings and blessed him"; and to him Abraham apportioned 'one-tenth of everything." His name, in the first place, means "king of righteousness"; next he is also king of Salem, that is, "king of peace." Without father, without mother, without genealogy, having neither beginning of days nor end of life, but resembling the Son of God, he remains a priest forever. See how great he is! Even Abraham the patriarch gave him a tenth of the spoils. And those descendants of Levi who receive the priestly office have a commandment in the law to collect tithes from the people, that is, from their kindred, though these also are descended from Abraham. But this man, who does not belong to their ancestry, collected tithes from Abraham and blessed him who had received the promises. It is beyond dispute that the inferior is blessed by the superior. In the one case, tithes are received by those who are mortal; in the other, by one of whom it is testified that he lives. One might even say that Levi himself, who receives tithes, paid tithes through Abraham, for he was still in the loins of his ancestor when Melchizedek met him.

A Reading (Lesson) from the Gospel according to John [4:27–42]

Just then the disciples of Jesus came. They were astonished that he was speaking with a woman, but no one said, "What do you want?" or, "Why are you speaking with her?" Then the woman left her water jar and went back to the city. She said to the people, "Come and see a man who told me everything I have ever done! He cannot be the Messiah, can he?" They left the city and were on their way to him. Meanwhile the disciples were urging him, "Rabbi, eat something." But he said to them, "I have food to eat that you do not know about." So the disciples said to one another, "Surely no one has brought him something to eat?" Jesus said to them, "My food is to do the will of him who sent me and to complete his work. Do you not say, 'Four months more, then comes the harvest'? But I tell you, look around you, and see how the fields are ripe for harvesting. The reaper is already receiving wages and is gathering fruit for eternal life, so that sower and reaper may rejoice together. For here the saying holds true, 'One sows and another reaps.' I sent you to reap that for which you did not labor. Others have labored, and you have entered into their labor." Many Samaritans from that city believed in him because of the woman's testimony, "He told me everything I have ever done." So when the Samaritans came to him, they asked him to stay with them; and he stayed there two days. And many more believed because of his word. They said to the woman, "It is no longer because of what you said that we believe, for we have heard for ourselves, and we know that this is truly the Savior of the world."

Monday

Psalm 25 [page 614]   ❖   *Psalm 9* [page 593],
Psalm 15 [page 599]

A Reading (Lesson) from the Book of Isaiah [44:6–8,21–23]

Thus says the LORD, the King of Israel, and his Redeemer, the LORD of hosts: I am the first and I am the last; besides me there is no god. Who is like me? Let them proclaim it, let them declare and set it forth before me. Who has announced from of old the things to come? Let them tell us what is yet to be. Do not fear, or be afraid; have I not told you from of old and declared it? You are my witnesses! Is there any god besides me? There is no other rock; I know not one. Remember these things, O Jacob, and Israel, for you are my servant; I formed you, you are my servant; O Israel, you will not be forgotten by me. I have swept away your transgressions like a cloud, and your sins like mist; return to me, for I have redeemed you. Sing, O heavens, for the LORD has done it; shout, O depths of the earth; break forth into singing, O mountains, O forest, and every tree in it! For the LORD has redeemed Jacob, and will be glorified in Israel.

A Reading (Lesson) from the Letter of Paul to the Ephesians [4:1–16]

I therefore, the prisoner in the Lord, beg you to lead a life worthy of the calling to which you have been called, with all humility and gentleness, with patience, bearing with one another in love, making every effort to maintain the unity of the Spirit in the bond of peace. There is one body and one Spirit, just as you were called to the one hope of your calling, one Lord, one faith, one baptism, one God and Father of all, who is above all and through all and in all. But each of us was given grace according to the measure of Christ's gift. Therefore it is said, "When he ascended on high he made captivity itself a captive; he gave gifts to his people." (When it says, "He ascended," what does it mean but that he had also descended into the lower parts of the earth? He who descended is the same one who ascended far above all the heavens, so that he might fill all things.) The gifts he gave were that some would be apostles, some prophets, some evangelists, some pastors and teachers, to equip the saints for the work of ministry, for building up the body of Christ, until all of us come to the unity of the faith and of the knowledge of the Son of God, to maturity, to the measure of the full stature of Christ. We must no longer be children, tossed to and fro and blown about by every wind of doctrine, by people's trickery, by their craftiness in deceitful scheming. But speaking the truth in love, we must grow up in every way into him who is the head, into Christ, from whom the whole body, joined and knit together by every ligament with which it is equipped, as each part is working properly, promotes the body's growth in building itself up in love.

A Reading (Lesson) from the Gospel according to Mark [3:7–19a]

Jesus departed with his disciples to the sea, and a great multitude from Galilee followed him; hearing all that he was doing, they came to him in great numbers from Judea, Jerusalem, Idumea, beyond the Jordan, and the region around Tyre and Sidon. He told his disciples to have a boat ready for him because of the crowd, so that they would not crush him; for he had cured many, so that all who had diseases pressed upon him to touch him. Whenever the unclean spirits saw him, they fell down before him and shouted, "You are the Son of God!" But he sternly ordered them not to make him known. He went up the mountain and called to him those whom he wanted, and they came to him. And he appointed twelve, whom he also named apostles, to be with him, and to be sent out to proclaim the message, and to have authority to cast out demons. So he appointed the twelve: Simon (to whom he gave the name Peter); James son of Zebedee and John the brother of James (to whom he gave the name Boanerges, that is, Sons of Thunder); and Andrew, and Philip, and Bartholomew, and Matthew, and Thomas, and James son of Alphaeus, and Thaddaeus, and Simon the Cananaean, and Judas Iscariot, who betrayed him.

Tuesday

Psalm 26 [page 616],   *Psalm 28* [page 619]   ❖
Psalm 36 [page 632],   *Psalm 39* [page 638]

A Reading (Lesson) from the Book of Isaiah [44:9–20]

All who make idols are nothing, and the things they delight in do not profit; their witnesses neither see nor know. And so they will be put to shame. Who would fashion a god or cast an image that can do no good? Look, all its devotees shall be put to shame; the artisans too are merely human. Let them all assemble, let them stand up; they shall be terrified, they shall all be put to shame. The ironsmith fashions it and works it over the coals, shaping it with hammers, and forging it with his strong arm; he becomes hungry and his strength fails, he drinks no water and is faint. The carpenter stretches a line, marks it out with a stylus, fashions it with planes, and marks it with a compass; he makes it in human form, with human beauty, to be set up in a shrine. He cuts down cedars or chooses a holm tree or an oak and lets it grow strong among the trees of the forest. He plants a cedar and the rain nourishes it. Then it can be used as fuel. Part of it he takes and warms himself; he kindles a fire and bakes bread. Then he makes a god and worships it, makes it a carved image and bows down before it. Half of it he burns in the fire; over this half he roasts meat, eats it and is satisfied. He also warms himself and says, "Ah, I am warm, I can feel the fire!" The rest of it he makes into a god, his idol, bows down to it and worships it; he prays to it and says, "Save me, for you are my god!" They do not know, nor do they comprehend; for their eyes are shut, so that they cannot see, and their minds as well, so that they cannot understand. No one considers, nor is there knowledge or discernment to say, "Half of it I burned in the fire; I also baked bread on its coals, I roasted meat and have eaten. Now shall I make the rest of it an abomination? Shall I fall down before a block of wood?" He feeds on ashes; a deluded mind has led him astray, and he cannot save himself or say, "Is not this thing in my right hand a fraud?"

A Reading (Lesson) from the Letter of Paul to the Ephesians [4:17–32]

Now this I affirm and insist on in the Lord: you must no longer live as the Gentiles live, in the futility of their minds. They are darkened in their understanding, alienated from the life of God because of their ignorance and hardness of heart. They have lost all sensitivity and have abandoned themselves to licentiousness, greedy to practice every kind of impurity. That is not the way you learned Christ! For surely you have heard about him and were taught in him, as truth is in Jesus. You were taught to put away your former way of life, your old self, corrupt and deluded by its lusts, and to be renewed in the spirit of your minds, and to clothe yourselves with the new self, created according to the likeness of God in true righteousness and holiness. So then, putting away falsehood, let all of us speak the truth to our neighbors, for we are members of one another. Be angry but do not sin; do not let the sun go down on your anger, and do not make room for the devil. Thieves must give up stealing; rather let them labor and work honestly with their own hands, so as to have something to share with the needy. Let no evil talk come out of your mouths, but only what is useful for building up, as there is need, so that your words may give grace to those who hear. And do not grieve the Holy Spirit of God, with which you were marked with a seal for the day of redemption. Put away from you all bitterness and wrath and anger and wrangling and slander, together with all malice, and be kind to one another, tenderhearted, forgiving one another, as God in Christ has forgiven you.

A Reading (Lesson) from the Gospel according to Mark [3:19b–35]

Jesus went home; and the crowd came together again, so that they could not even eat. When his family heard it, they went out to restrain him, for people were saying, "He has gone out of his mind." And the scribes who came down from Jerusalem said, "He has Beelzebul, and by the ruler of the demons he casts out demons." And he called them to him, and spoke to them in parables, "How can Satan cast out Satan? If a kingdom is divided against itself, that kingdom cannot stand. And if a house is divided against itself, that house will not be able to stand. And if Satan has risen up against himself and is divided, he cannot stand, but his end has come. But no one can enter a strong man's house and plunder his property without first tying up the strong man; then indeed the house can be plundered. Truly I tell you, people will be forgiven for their sins and whatever blasphemies they utter; but whoever blasphemes against the Holy Spirit can never have forgiveness, but is guilty of an eternal sin"—for they had said, "He has an unclean spirit." Then his mother and his brothers came; and standing outside, they sent to him and called him. A crowd was sitting around him; and they said to him, "Your mother and your brothers and sisters are outside, asking for you." And he replied, "Who are my mother and my brothers?" And looking at those who sat around him, he said, "Here are my mother and my brothers! Whoever does the will of God is my brother and sister and mother."

Wednesday

Psalm 38 [page 636]   ❖   *Psalm 119:25–48* [page 765]

A Reading (Lesson) from the Book of Isaiah [44:24—45:7]

Thus says the LORD, your Redeemer, who formed you in the womb: I am the LORD, who made all things, who alone stretched out the heavens, who by myself spread out the earth; who frustrates the omens of liars, and makes fools of diviners; who turns back the wise, and makes their knowledge foolish; who confirms the word of his servant, and fulfills the prediction of his messengers; who says of Jerusalem, "It shall be inhabited," and of the cities of Judah, "They shall be rebuilt, and I will raise up their ruins"; who says to the deep, "Be dry—I will dry up your rivers"; who says of Cyrus, "He is my shepherd, and he shall carry out all my purpose"; and who says of Jerusalem, It shall be rebuilt," and of the temple, "Your foundation shall be laid." Thus says the LORD to his anointed, to Cyrus, whose right hand I have grasped to subdue nations before him and strip kings of their robes, to open doors before him—and the gates shall not be closed: I will go before you and level the mountains, I will break in pieces the doors of bronze and cut through the bars of iron, I will give you the treasures of darkness and riches hidden in secret places, so that you may know that it is I, the LORD, the God of Israel, who call you by your name. For the sake of my servant Jacob, and Israel my chosen, I call you by your name, I surname you, though you do not know me. I am the LORD, and there is no other; besides me there is no god. I arm you, though you do not know me, so that they may know, from the rising of the sun and from the west, that there is no one besides me; I am the LORD, and there is no other. I form light and create darkness, I make weal and create woe; I the LORD do all these things.

A Reading (Lesson) from the Letter of Paul to the Ephesians [5:1–14]

Be imitators of God, as beloved children, and live in love, as Christ loved us and gave himself up for us, a fragrant offering and sacrifice to God. But fornication and impurity of any kind, or greed, must not even be mentioned among you, as is proper among saints. Entirely out of place is obscene, silly, and vulgar talk; but instead, let there be thanksgiving. Be sure of this, that no fornicator or impure person, or one who is greedy (that is, an idolater), has any inheritance in the kingdom of Christ and of God. Let no one deceive you with empty words, for because of these things the wrath of God comes on those who are disobedient. Therefore do not be associated with them. For once you were darkness, but now in the Lord you are light. Live as children of light—for the fruit of the light is found in all that is good and right and true. Try to find out what is pleasing to the Lord. Take no part in the unfruitful works of darkness, but instead expose them. For it is shameful even to mention what such people do secretly; but everything exposed by the light becomes visible, for everything that becomes visible is light. Therefore it says, "Sleeper, awake! Rise from the dead, and Christ will shine on you."

A Reading (Lesson) from the Gospel according to Mark [4:1–20]

Again Jesus began to teach beside the sea. Such a very large crowd gathered around him that he got into a boat on the sea and sat there, while the whole crowd was beside the sea on the land. He began to teach them many things in parables, and in his teaching he said to them: "Listen! A sower went out to sow. And as he sowed, some

seed fell on the path, and the birds came and ate it up.
Other seed fell on rocky ground, where it did not have
much soil, and it sprang up quickly, since it had no depth
of soil. And when the sun rose, it was scorched; and since
it had no root, it withered away. Other seed fell among
thorns, and the thorns grew up and choked it, and it
yielded no grain. Other seed fell into good soil and
brought forth grain, growing up and increasing and
yielding thirty and sixty and a hundredfold." And he said,
"Let anyone with ears to hear listen!" When he was alone,
those who were around him along with the twelve asked
him about the parables. And he said to them, "To you has
been given the secret of the kingdom of God, but for those
outside, everything comes in parables; in order that 'they
may indeed look, but not perceive, and may indeed listen,
but not understand; so that they may not turn again and
be forgiven.'" And he said to them, "Do you not
understand this parable? Then how will you understand all
the parables? The sower sows the word. These are the
ones on the path where the word is sown: when they hear,
Satan immediately comes and takes away the word that is
sown in them. And these are the ones sown on rocky
ground: when they hear the word, they immediately
receive it with joy. But they have no root, and endure only
for a while; then, when trouble or persecution arises on
account of the word, immediately they fall away. And
others are those sown among the thorns: these are the
ones who hear the word, but the cares of the world, and
the lure of wealth, and the desire for other things come in
and choke the word, and it yields nothing. And these are
the ones sown on the good soil: they hear the word and
accept it and bear fruit, thirty and sixty and a
hundredfold."

Thursday

Psalm 37:1–18 [page 633]   ❖   *Psalm 37:19–42* [page 634]

A Reading (Lesson) from the Book of Isaiah [45:5–17]

Thus says the LORD to his anointed, to Cyrus, I am the
LORD, and there is no other; besides me there is no god. I
arm you, though you do not know me, so that they may
know, from the rising of the sun and from the west, that
there is no one besides me; I am the LORD, and there is no
other. I form light and create darkness, I make weal and
create woe; I the LORD do all these things. Shower, O
heavens, from above, and let the skies rain down
righteousness; let the earth open, that salvation may spring
up, and let it cause righteousness to sprout up also; I the
LORD have created it. Woe to you who strive with your
Maker, earthen vessels with the potter! Does the clay say to
the one who fashions it, "What are you making"? or "Your
work has no handles"? Woe to anyone who says to a father,
"What are you begetting?" or to a woman, "With what are
you in labor?" Thus says the LORD, the Holy One of Israel,
and its Maker: Will you question me about my children, or
command me concerning the work of my hands? I made the
earth, and created humankind upon it; it was my hands that
stretched out the heavens, and I commanded all their host. I
have aroused Cyrus in righteousness, and I will make all his
paths straight; he shall build my city and set my exiles free,
not for price or reward, says the LORD of hosts. Thus says
the LORD: The wealth of Egypt and the merchandise of
Ethiopia, and the Sabeans, tall of stature, shall come over to
you and be yours, they shall follow you; they shall come
over in chains and bow down to you. They will make
supplication to you, saying, "God is with you alone, and
there is no other; there is no god besides him." Truly, you

are a God who hides himself, O God of Israel, the Savior. All of them are put to shame and confounded, the makers of idols go in confusion together. But Israel is saved by the LORD with everlasting salvation; you shall not be put to shame or confounded to all eternity.

A Reading (Lesson) from the Letter of Paul to the Ephesians [5:15–33]

Be careful then how you live, not as unwise people but as wise, making the most of the time, because the days are evil. So do not be foolish, but understand what the will of the Lord is. Do not get drunk with wine, for that is debauchery; but be filled with the Spirit, as you sing psalms and hymns and spiritual songs among yourselves, singing and making melody to the Lord in your hearts, giving thanks to God the Father at all times and for everything in the name of our Lord Jesus Christ. Be subject to one another out of reverence for Christ. Wives, be subject to your husbands as you are to the Lord. For the husband is the head of the wife just as Christ is the head of the church, the body of which he is the Savior. Just as the church is subject to Christ, so also wives ought to be, in everything, to their husbands. Husbands, love your wives, just as Christ loved the church and gave himself up for her, in order to make her holy by cleansing her with the washing of water by the word, so as to present the church to himself in splendor, without a spot or wrinkle or anything of the kind—yes, so that she may be holy and without blemish. In the same way, husbands should love their wives as they do their own bodies. He who loves his wife loves himself. For no one ever hates his own body, but he nourishes and tenderly cares for it, just as Christ does for the church, because we are members of his body. "For this reason a man will leave his father and mother and be joined to his wife, and the two will become one flesh." This is a great mystery, and I am applying it to Christ and the church. Each of you, however, should love his wife as himself, and a wife should respect her husband.

A Reading (Lesson) from the Gospel according to Mark [4:21–34]

Jesus said to them, "Is a lamp brought in to be put under the bushel basket, or under the bed, and not on the lampstand? For there is nothing hidden, except to be disclosed; nor is anything secret, except to come to light. Let anyone with ears to hear listen!" And he said to them, "Pay attention to what you hear; the measure you give will be the measure you get, and still more will be given you. For to those who have, more will be given; and from those who have nothing, even what they have will be taken away." He also said, "The kingdom of God is as if someone would scatter seed on the ground, and would sleep and rise night and day, and the seed would sprout and grow, he does not know how. The earth produces of itself, first the stalk, then the head, then the full grain in the head. But when the grain is ripe, at once he goes in with his sickle, because the harvest has come." He also said, "With what can we compare the kingdom of God, or what parable will we use for it? It is like a mustard seed, which, when sown upon the ground, is the smallest of all the seeds on earth; yet when it is sown it grows up and becomes the greatest of all shrubs, and puts forth large branches, so that the birds of the air can make nests in its shade." With many such parables he spoke the word to them, as they were able to hear it; he did not speak to them except in parables, but he explained everything in private to his disciples.

Friday

Psalm 31 [page 622]   ❖   *Psalm 35* [page 629]

A Reading (Lesson) from the Book of Isaiah [45:18–25]

For thus says the LORD, who created the heavens (he is God!), who formed the earth and made it (he established it; he did not create it a chaos, he formed it to be inhabited!): I am the LORD, and there is no other. I did not speak in secret, in a land of darkness; I did not say to the offspring of Jacob, "Seek me in chaos." I the LORD speak the truth, I declare what is right. Assemble yourselves and come together, draw near, you survivors of the nations! They have no knowledge—those who carry about their wooden idols, and keep on praying to a god that cannot save. Declare and present your case; let them take counsel together! Who told this long ago? Who declared it of old? Was it not I, the LORD? There is no other god besides me, a righteous God and a Savior; there is no one besides me. Turn to me and be saved, all the ends of the earth! For I am God, and there is no other. By myself I have sworn, from my mouth has gone forth in righteousness a word that shall not return: "To me every knee shall bow, every tongue shall swear." Only in the LORD, it shall be said of me, are righteousness and strength; all who were incensed against him shall come to him and be ashamed. In the LORD all the offspring of Israel shall triumph and glory.

A Reading (Lesson) from the Letter of Paul to the Ephesians [6:1–9]

Children, obey your parents in the Lord, for this is right. "Honor your father and mother"—this is the first commandment with a promise: "so that it may be well with you and you may live long on the earth." And, fathers, do not provoke your children to anger, but bring them up in the discipline and instruction of the Lord. Slaves, obey your earthly masters with fear and trembling, in singleness of heart, as you obey Christ; not only while being watched, and in order to please them, but as slaves of Christ, doing the will of God from the heart. Render service with enthusiasm, as to the Lord and not to men and women, knowing that whatever good we do, we will receive the same again from the Lord, whether we are slaves or free. And, masters, do the same to them. Stop threatening them, for you know that both of you have the same Master in heaven, and with him there is no partiality.

A Reading (Lesson) from the Gospel according to Mark [4:35–41]

On that day, when evening had come, Jesus said to them, "Let us go across to the other side." And leaving the crowd behind, they took him with them in the boat, just as he was. Other boats were with him. A great windstorm arose and the waves beat into the boat, so that the boat was already being swamped. But he was in the stern, asleep on the cushion; and they woke him up and said to him, "Teacher, do you not care that we are perishing?" He woke up and rebuked the wind, and said to the sea, "Peace! Be still!" Then the wind ceased, and there was a dead calm. He said to them, "Why are you afraid? Have you still no faith?" And they were filled with great awe and said to one another, "Who then is this, that even the wind and the sea obey him?"

Saturday

Psalm 30 [page 621],   *Psalm 32* [page 624]   ❖
Psalm 42 [page 643],   *Psalm 43* [page 644]

A Reading (Lesson) from the Book of Isaiah [46:1–13]

Bel bows down, Nebo stoops, their idols are on beasts and cattle; these things you carry are loaded as burdens on weary animals. They stoop, they bow down together; they cannot save the burden, but themselves go into captivity. Listen to me, O house of Jacob, all the remnant of the house of Israel, who have been borne by me from your birth, carried from the womb; even to your old age I am he, even when you turn gray, I will carry you. I have made, and I will bear; I will carry and will save. To whom will you liken me and make me equal, and compare me, as though we were alike? Those who lavish gold from the purse, and weigh out silver in the scales—they hire a goldsmith, who makes it into a god; then they fall down and worship! They lift it to their shoulders, they carry it, they set it in its place, and it stands there; it cannot move from its place. If one cries out to it, it does not answer or save anyone from trouble. Remember this and consider, recall it to mind, you transgressors, remember the former things of old; for I am God, and there is no other; I am God, and there is no one like me, declaring the end from the beginning and from ancient times things not yet done, saying, "My purpose shall stand, and I will fulfill my intention," calling a bird of prey from the east, the man for my purpose from a far country. I have spoken, and I will bring it to pass; I have planned, and I will do it. Listen to me, you stubborn of heart, you who are far from deliverance: I bring near my deliverance, it is not far off, and my salvation will not tarry; I will put salvation in Zion, for Israel my glory.

A Reading (Lesson) from the Letter of Paul to the Ephesians [6:10–24]

Be strong in the Lord and in the strength of his power. Put on the whole armor of God, so that you may be able to stand against the wiles of the devil. For our struggle is not against enemies of blood and flesh, but against the rulers, against the authorities, against the cosmic powers of this present darkness, against the spiritual forces of evil in the heavenly places. Therefore take up the whole armor of God, so that you may be able to withstand on that evil day, and having done everything, to stand firm. Stand therefore, and fasten the belt of truth around your waist, and put on the breastplate of righteousness. As shoes for your feet put on whatever will make you ready to proclaim the gospel of peace. With all of these, take the shield of faith, with which you will be able to quench all the flaming arrows of the evil one. Take the helmet of salvation, and the sword of the Spirit, which is the word of God. Pray in the Spirit at all times in every prayer and supplication. To that end keep alert and always persevere in supplication for all the saints. Pray also for me, so that when I speak, a message may be given to me to make known with boldness the mystery of the gospel, for which I am an ambassador in chains. Pray that I may declare it boldly, as I must speak. So that you also may know how I am and what I am doing, Tychicus will tell you everything. He is a dear brother and a faithful minister in the Lord. I am sending him to you for this very purpose, to let you know how we are, and to encourage your hearts. Peace be to the whole community, and love with faith, from God the Father and the Lord Jesus Christ. Grace be with all who have an undying love for our Lord Jesus Christ.

A Reading (Lesson) from the Gospel according to Mark [5:1–20]

Jesus and his disciples came to the other side of the sea, to the country of the Gerasenes. And when he had stepped out of the boat, immediately a man out of the tombs with an unclean spirit met him. He lived among the tombs; and no one could restrain him any more, even with a chain; for he had often been restrained with shackles and chains, but the chains he wrenched apart, and the shackles he broke in pieces; and no one had the strength to subdue him. Night and day among the tombs and on the mountains he was always howling and bruising himself with stones. When he saw Jesus from a distance, he ran and bowed down before him; and he shouted at the top of his voice, "What have you to do with me, Jesus, Son of the Most High God? I adjure you by God, do not torment me." For he had said to him, "Come out of the man, you unclean spirit!" Then Jesus asked him, "What is your name?" He replied, "My name is Legion; for we are many." He begged him earnestly not to send them out of the country. Now there on the hillside a great herd of swine was feeding; and the unclean spirits begged him, "Send us into the swine; let us enter them." So he gave them permission. And the unclean spirits came out and entered the swine; and the herd, numbering about two thousand, rushed down the steep bank into the sea, and were drowned in the sea. The swineherds ran off and told it in the city and in the country. Then people came to see what it was that had happened. They came to Jesus and saw the demoniac sitting there, clothed and in his right mind, the very man who had had the legion; and they were afraid. Those who had seen what had happened to the demoniac and to the swine reported it. Then they began to beg Jesus to leave their neighborhood. As he was getting into the boat, the man who had been possessed by demons begged him that he might be with him. But Jesus refused, and said to him, "Go home to your friends, and tell them how much the Lord has done for you, and what mercy he has shown you." And he went away and began to proclaim in the Decapolis how much Jesus had done for him; and everyone was amazed.

Week of 3 Epiphany

Sunday

Psalm 63:1–8(9–11) [page 670],
Psalm 98 [page 727]   ❖   *Psalm 103* [page 733]

A Reading (Lesson) from the Book of Isaiah [47:1–15]

Come down and sit in the dust, virgin daughter Babylon! Sit on the ground without a throne, daughter Chaldea! For you shall no more be called tender and delicate. Take the millstones and grind meal, remove your veil, strip off your robe, uncover your legs, pass through the rivers. Your nakedness shall be uncovered, and your shame shall be seen. I will take vengeance, and I will spare no one. Our Redeemer—the LORD of hosts is his name—is the Holy One of Israel. Sit in silence, and go into darkness, daughter Chaldea! For you shall no more be called the mistress of kingdoms. I was angry with my people, I profaned my heritage; I gave them into your hand, you showed them no mercy; on the aged you made your yoke exceedingly heavy.

You said, "I shall be mistress forever," so that you did not lay these things to heart or remember their end. Now therefore hear this, you lover of pleasures, who sit securely, who say in your heart, "I am, and there is no one besides me; I shall not sit as a widow or know the loss of children"—both these things shall come upon you in a moment, in one day: the loss of children and widowhood shall come upon you in full measure, in spite of your many sorceries and the great power of your enchantments. You felt secure in your wickedness; you said, "No one sees me." Your wisdom and your knowledge led you astray, and you said in your heart, "I am, and there is no one besides me." But evil shall come upon you, which you cannot charm away; disaster shall fall upon you, which you will not be able to ward off; and ruin shall come on you suddenly, of which you know nothing. Stand fast in your enchantments and your many sorceries, with which you have labored from your youth; perhaps you may be able to succeed, perhaps you may inspire terror. You are wearied with your many consultations; let those who study the heavens stand up and save you, those who gaze at the stars, and at each new moon predict what shall befall you. See, they are like stubble, the fire consumes them; they cannot deliver themselves from the power of the flame. No coal for warming oneself is this, no fire to sit before! Such to you are those with whom you have labored, who have trafficked with you from your youth; they all wander about in their own paths; there is no one to save you.

A Reading (Lesson) from the Letter to the Hebrews [10:19–31]

Therefore, my friends, since we have confidence to enter the sanctuary by the blood of Jesus, by the new and living way that he opened for us through the curtain (that is, through his flesh), and since we have a great priest over the house of God, let us approach with a true heart in full assurance of faith, with our hearts sprinkled clean from an evil conscience and our bodies washed with pure water. Let us hold fast to the confession of our hope without wavering, for he who has promised is faithful. And let us consider how to provoke one another to love and good deeds, not neglecting to meet together, as is the habit of some, but encouraging one another, and all the more as you see the Day approaching. For if we willfully persist in sin after having received the knowledge of the truth, there no longer remains a sacrifice for sins, but a fearful prospect of judgment, and a fury of fire that will consume the adversaries. Anyone who has violated the law of Moses dies without mercy "on the testimony of two or three witnesses." How much worse punishment do you think will be deserved by those who have spurned the Son of God, profaned the blood of the covenant by which they were sanctified, and outraged the Spirit of grace? For we know the one who said, "Vengeance is mine, I will repay." And again, "The Lord will judge his people." It is a fearful thing to fall into the hands of the living God.

A Reading (Lesson) from the Gospel according to John [5:2–18]

Now in Jerusalem by the Sheep Gate there is a pool, called in Hebrew Beth-zatha, which has five porticoes. In these lay many invalids—blind, lame, and paralyzed. One man was there who had been ill for thirty-eight years. When Jesus saw him lying there and knew that he had been there a long time, he said to him, "Do you want to be made well?" The sick man answered him, "Sir, I have no one to put me into the pool when the water is stirred up; and while I am making my way, someone else steps down ahead of me." Jesus said to him, "Stand up, take your mat and walk." At once the man was made well, and he took up his mat and began to walk. Now that day was a sabbath. So the Jews said to the man who had been cured, "It is the sabbath; it is not lawful for you to carry your mat." But he answered them, "The man who made me well said to me, 'Take up your mat and walk.' " They asked him, "Who is the man who said to you, 'Take it up and walk'?" Now the man who had been healed did not know who it was, for Jesus had disappeared in the crowd that was there. Later Jesus found him in the temple and said to him, "See, you have been made well! Do not sin any more, so that nothing worse happens to you." The man went away and told the Jews that it was Jesus who had made him well. Therefore the Jews started persecuting Jesus, because he was doing such things on the sabbath. But Jesus answered them, "My Father is still working, and I also am working." For this reason the Jews were seeking all the more to kill him, because he was not only breaking the sabbath, but was also calling God his own Father, thereby making himself equal to God.

Monday

Psalm 41 [page 641],   *Psalm 52* [page 657]   ❖
Psalm 44 [page 645]

A Reading (Lesson) from the Book of Isaiah [48:1–11]

Hear this, O house of Jacob, who are called by the name of Israel, and who came forth from the loins of Judah; who swear by the name of the LORD, and invoke the God of

Israel, but not in truth or right. For they call themselves after the holy city, and lean on the God of Israel; the LORD of hosts is his name. The former things I declared long ago, they went out from my mouth and I made them known; then suddenly I did them and they came to pass. Because I know that you are obstinate, and your neck is an iron sinew and your forehead brass, I declared them to you from long ago, before they came to pass I announced them to you, so that you would not say, "My idol did them, my carved image and my cast image commanded them." You have heard; now see all this; and will you not declare it? From this time forward I make you hear new things, hidden things that you have not known. They are created now, not long ago; before today you have never heard of them, so that you could not say, "I already knew them." You have never heard, you have never known, from of old your ear has not been opened. For I knew that you would deal very treacherously, and that from birth you were called a rebel. For my name's sake I defer my anger, for the sake of my praise I restrain it for you, so that I may not cut you off. See, I have refined you, but not like silver; I have tested you in the furnace of adversity. For my own sake, for my own sake, I do it, for why should my name be profaned? My glory I will not give to another.

A Reading (Lesson) from the Letter of Paul to the Galatians [1:1–17]

Paul an apostle—sent neither by human commission nor from human authorities, but through Jesus Christ and God the Father, who raised him from the dead—and all the members of God's family who are with me, to the churches of Galatia: Grace to you and peace from God our Father and the Lord Jesus Christ, who gave himself for our sins to set us free from the present evil age, according to the will of our God and Father, to whom be the glory forever and ever. Amen. I am astonished that you are so quickly deserting the one who called you in the grace of Christ and are turning to a different gospel—not that there is another gospel, but there are some who are confusing you and want to pervert the gospel of Christ. But even if we or an angel from heaven should proclaim to you a gospel contrary to what we proclaimed to you, let that one be accursed! As we have said before, so now I repeat, if anyone proclaims to you a gospel contrary to what you received, let that one be accursed! Am I now seeking human approval, or God's approval? Or am I trying to please people? If I were still pleasing people, I would not be a servant of Christ. For I want you to know, brothers and sisters, that the gospel that was proclaimed by me is not of human origin; for I did not receive it from a human source, nor was I taught it, but I received it through a revelation of Jesus Christ. You have heard, no doubt, of my earlier life in Judaism. I was violently persecuting the church of God and was trying to destroy it. I advanced in Judaism beyond many among my people of the same age, for I was far more zealous for the traditions of my ancestors. But when God, who had set me apart before I was born and called me through his grace, was pleased to reveal his Son to me, so that I might proclaim him among the Gentiles, I did not confer with any human being, nor did I go up to Jerusalem to those who were already apostles before me, but I went away at once into Arabia, and afterwards I returned to Damascus.

A Reading (Lesson) from the Gospel according to Mark [5:21–43]

When Jesus had crossed again in the boat to the other side, a great crowd gathered around him; and he was by the sea. Then one of the leaders of the synagogue named Jairus came and, when he saw him, fell at his feet and begged him repeatedly, "My little daughter is at the point of death. Come and lay your hands on her, so that she may be made well, and live." So he went with him. And a large crowd followed him and pressed in on him. Now there was a woman who had been suffering from hemorrhages for twelve years. She had endured much under many physicians, and had spent all that she had; and she was no better, but rather grew worse. She had heard about Jesus, and came up behind him in the crowd and touched his cloak, for she said, "If I but touch his clothes, I will be made well." Immediately her hemorrhage stopped; and she felt in her body that she was healed of her disease. Immediately aware that power had gone forth from him, Jesus turned about in the crowd and said, "Who touched my clothes?" And his disciples said to him, "You see the crowd pressing in on you; how can you say, 'Who touched me?'" He looked all around to see who had done it. But the woman, knowing what had happened to her, came in fear and trembling, fell down before him, and told him the whole truth. He said to her, "Daughter, your faith has made you well; go in peace, and be healed of your disease." While he was still speaking, some people came from the leader's house to say, "Your daughter is dead. Why trouble the teacher any further?" But overhearing what they said, Jesus said to the leader of the synagogue, "Do not fear, only believe." He allowed no one to follow him except Peter, James, and John, the brother of James. When they came to the house of the leader of the synagogue, he saw a commotion, people weeping and wailing loudly. When he had entered, he said to them, "Why do you make a commotion and weep? The child is not dead but sleeping." And they laughed at him. Then he put them all outside, and took the child's father and mother and those who were with him, and went in where the child was. He took her by the hand and said to her, "Talitha cum," which means, "Little girl, get up!" And immediately the girl got up and began to walk about (she was twelve years of age). At this they were overcome with amazement. He strictly ordered them that no one should know this, and told them to give her something to eat.

Tuesday

Psalm 45 [page 647] ❖ *Psalm 47* [page 650],
Psalm 48 [page 651]

A Reading (Lesson) from the Book of Isaiah [48:12–21]

Listen to me, O Jacob, and Israel, whom I called: I am He; I am the first, and I am the last. My hand laid the foundation of the earth, and my right hand spread out the heavens; when I summon them, they stand at attention. Assemble, all of you, and hear! Who among them has declared these things? The LORD loves him; he shall perform his purpose on Babylon, and his arm shall be against the Chaldeans. I, even I, have spoken and called him, I have brought him, and he will prosper in his way. Draw near to me, hear this! From the beginning I have not spoken in secret, from the time it came to be I have been there. And now the Lord GOD has sent me and his spirit. Thus says the LORD, your Redeemer, the Holy One of Israel: I am the LORD your God, who teaches you for your own good, who leads you in the way you should go. O that you had paid attention to my commandments! Then your prosperity would have been like a river, and your success like the waves of the sea; your offspring would have been like the sand, and your descendants like its grains; their name would never be cut off or destroyed from before me. Go out from Babylon, flee from Chaldea, declare this with a shout of joy, proclaim it, send it forth to the end of the earth; say, "The LORD has redeemed his servant Jacob!" They did not thirst when he led them through the deserts; he made water flow for them from the rock; he split open the rock and the water gushed out.

A Reading (Lesson) from the Letter of Paul to the Galatians [1:18—2:10]

Then after three years I did go up to Jerusalem to visit Cephas and stayed with him fifteen days; but I did not see any other apostle except James the Lord's brother. In what I am writing to you, before God, I do not lie! Then I went into the regions of Syria and Cilicia and I was still unknown by sight to the churches of Judea that are in Christ, they only heard it said, "The one who formerly was persecuting us is now proclaiming the faith he once tried to destroy." And they glorified God because of me. Then after fourteen years I went up again to Jerusalem with Barnabas, taking Titus along with me. I went up in response to a revelation. Then I laid before them (though only in a private meeting with the acknowledged leaders) the gospel that I proclaim among the Gentiles, in order to make sure that I was not running, or had not run, in vain. But even Titus, who was with me, was not compelled to be circumcised, though he was a Greek. But because of false believers secretly brought in, who slipped in to spy on the freedom we have in Christ Jesus, so that they might enslave us—we did not submit to them even for a moment, so that the truth of the gospel might always remain with you. And from those who were supposed to be acknowledged leaders (what they actually were makes no difference to me; God shows no partiality)—those leaders contributed nothing to me. On the contrary, when they saw that I had been entrusted with the gospel for the uncircumcised, just as Peter had been entrusted with the gospel for the circumcised (for he who worked through Peter making him an apostle to the circumcised also worked through me in sending me to the Gentiles), and when James and Cephas and John, who were acknowledged pillars, recognized the grace that had been given to me, they gave to Barnabas and me the right hand of fellowship, agreeing that we should go to the Gentiles and they to the circumcised. They asked only one thing, that we remember the poor, which was actually what I was eager to do.

A Reading (Lesson) from the Gospel according to Mark [6:1–13]

Jesus left that place and came to his hometown, and his disciples followed him. On the sabbath he began to teach in the synagogue, and many who heard him were astounded. They said, "Where did this man get all this? What is this wisdom that has been given to him? What deeds of power are being done by his hands! Is not this the carpenter, the son of Mary and brother of James and Joses and Judas and Simon, and are not his sisters here with us?" And they took offense at him. Then Jesus said to them, "Prophets are not without honor, except in their hometown, and among their own kin, and in their own house." And he could do no deed of power there, except that he laid his hands on a few sick people and cured them. And he was amazed at their unbelief. Then he went about among the villages teaching. He called the twelve and began to send them out two by two, and gave them authority over the unclean spirits. He ordered them to take nothing for their journey except a staff; no bread, no bag, no money in their belts; but to wear sandals and not to put on two tunics. He said to them, "Wherever you enter a house, stay there until you leave the place. If any place will not welcome you and they refuse to hear you, as you leave, shake off the dust that is on your feet as a testimony against them." So they went out and proclaimed that all should repent. They cast out many demons, and anointed with oil many who were sick and cured them.

Wednesday

Psalm 119:49–72 [page 767] ❖
Psalm 49 [page 652], *(Psalm 53* [page 658])

A Reading (Lesson) from the Book of Isaiah [49:1–12]

Listen to me, O coastlands, pay attention, you peoples from far away! The LORD called me before I was born, while I was in my mother's womb he named me. He made my mouth like a sharp sword, in the shadow of his hand he hid me; he made me a polished arrow, in his quiver he hid me away. And he said to me, "You are my servant, Israel, in whom I will be glorified." But I said, "I have labored in vain, I have spent my strength for nothing and vanity; yet surely my cause is with the LORD, and my reward with my

God." And now the LORD says, who formed me in the womb to be his servant, to bring Jacob back to him, and that Israel might be gathered to him, for I am honored in the sight of the LORD, and my God has become my strength—he says, "It is too light a thing that you should be my servant to raise up the tribes of Jacob and to restore the survivors of Israel; I will give you as a light to the nations, that my salvation may reach to the end of the earth." Thus says the LORD, the Redeemer of Israel and his Holy One, to one deeply despised, abhorred by the nations, the slave of rulers, "Kings shall see and stand up, princes, and they shall prostrate themselves, because of the LORD, who is faithful, the Holy One of Israel, who has chosen you." Thus says the LORD: In a time of favor I have answered you, on a day of salvation I have helped you; I have kept you and given you as a covenant to the people, to establish the land, to apportion the desolate heritages; saying to the prisoners, "Come out," to those who are in darkness, "Show yourselves." They shall feed along the ways, on all the bare heights shall be their pasture; they shall not hunger or thirst, neither scorching wind nor sun shall strike them down, for he who has pity on them will lead them, and by springs of water will guide them. And I will turn all my mountains into a road, and my highways shall be raised up. Lo, these shall come from far away, and lo, these from the north and from the west, and these from the land of Syene.

A Reading (Lesson) from the Letter of Paul to the Galatians [2:11–21]

When Cephas came to Antioch, I opposed him to his face, because he stood self-condemned; for until certain people came from James, he used to eat with the Gentiles. But after they came, he drew back and kept himself separate for fear of the circumcision faction. And the other Jews joined him in this hypocrisy, so that even Barnabas was led astray by their hypocrisy. But when I saw that they were not acting consistently with the truth of the gospel, I said to Cephas before them all, "If you, though a Jew, live like a Gentile and not like a Jew, how can you compel the Gentiles to live like Jews?" We ourselves are Jews by birth and not Gentile sinners; yet we know that a person is justified not by the works of the law but through faith in Jesus Christ. And we have come to believe in Christ Jesus, so that we might be justified by faith in Christ, and not by doing the works of the law, because no one will be justified by the works of the law. But if, in our effort to be justified in Christ, we ourselves have been found to be sinners, is Christ then a servant of sin? Certainly not! But if I build up again the very things that I once tore down, then I demonstrate that I am a transgressor. For through the law I died to the law, so that I might live to God. I have been crucified with Christ; and it is no longer I who live, but it is Christ who lives in me. And the life I now live in the flesh I live by faith in the Son of God, who loved me and gave himself for me. I do not nullify the grace of God; for if justification comes through the law, then Christ died for nothing.

A Reading (Lesson) from the Gospel according to Mark [6:13–29]

The disciples cast out many demons, and anointed with oil many who were sick and cured them. King Herod heard of it, for Jesus' name had become known. Some were saying, "John the baptizer has been raised from the dead; and for this reason these powers are at work in him." But others said, "It is Elijah." And others said, "It is a prophet, like one of the prophets of old." But when Herod heard of it, he said, "John, whom I beheaded, has been raised." For Herod himself had sent men who arrested John, bound him, and put him in prison on account of Herodias, his brother Philip's wife, because Herod had married her. For John had been telling Herod, "It is not lawful for you to have your brother's wife." And Herodias had a grudge against him, and wanted to kill him. But she could not, for Herod feared John, knowing that he was a righteous and holy man, and he protected him. When he heard him, he was greatly perplexed; and yet he liked to listen to him. But an opportunity came when Herod on his birthday gave a banquet for his courtiers and officers and for the leaders of Galilee. When his daughter Herodias came in and danced, she pleased Herod and his guests; and the king said to the girl, "Ask me for whatever you wish, and I will give it." And he solemnly swore to her, "Whatever you ask me, I will give you, even half of my kingdom." She went out and said to her mother, "What should I ask for?" She replied, "The head of John the baptizer." Immediately she rushed back to the king and requested, "I want you to give me at once the head of John the Baptist on a platter." The king was deeply grieved; yet out of regard for his oaths and for the guests, he did not want to refuse her. Immediately the king sent a soldier of the guard with orders to bring John's head. He went and beheaded him in the prison, brought his head on a platter, and gave it to the girl. Then the girl gave it to her mother. When his disciples heard about it, they came and took his body, and laid it in a tomb.

Thursday

Psalm 50 [page 654]   ❖   (*Psalm 59* [page 665],
Psalm 60 [page 667])   or   *Psalm 118* [page 760]

A Reading (Lesson) from the Book of Isaiah [49:13–23]

Sing for joy, O heavens, and exult, O earth; break forth, O
mountains, into singing! For the LORD has comforted his
people, and will have compassion on his suffering ones. But
Zion said, "The LORD has forsaken me, my Lord has
forgotten me." Can a woman forget her nursing child, or
show no compassion for the child of her womb? Even these
may forget, yet I will not forget you. See, I have inscribed
you on the palms of my hands; your walls are continually
before me. Your builders outdo your destroyers, and those
who laid you waste go away from you. Lift up your eyes all
around and see; they all gather, they come to you. As I live,
says the LORD, you shall put all of them on like an
ornament, and like a bride you shall bind them on. Surely
your waste and your desolate places and your devastated
land—surely now you will be too crowded for your
inhabitants, and those who swallowed you up will be far
away. The children born in the time of your bereavement
will yet say in your hearing: "The place is too crowded for
me; make room for me to settle." Then you will say in your
heart, "Who has borne me these? I was bereaved and
barren, exiled and put away—so who has reared these? I
was left all alone—where then have these come from?"
Thus says the Lord GOD: I will soon lift up my hand to the
nations, and raise my signal to the peoples; and they shall
bring your sons in their bosom, and your daughters shall be
carried on their shoulders. Kings shall be your foster fathers,
and their queens your nursing mothers. With their faces to

the ground they shall bow down to you, and lick the dust of your feet. Then you will know that I am the LORD; those who wait for me shall not be put to shame.

A Reading (Lesson) from the Letter of Paul to the Galatians [3:1–14]

You foolish Galatians! Who has bewitched you? It was before your eyes that Jesus Christ was publicly exhibited as crucified! The only thing I want to learn from you is this: Did you receive the Spirit by doing the works of the law or by believing what you heard? Are you so foolish? Having started with the Spirit, are you now ending with the flesh? Did you experience so much for nothing?—if it really was for nothing. Well then, does God supply you with the Spirit and work miracles among you by your doing the works of the law, or by your believing what you heard? Just as Abraham "believed God, and it was reckoned to him as righteousness," so, you see, those who believe are the descendants of Abraham. And the scripture, foreseeing that God would justify the Gentiles by faith, declared the gospel beforehand to Abraham, saying, "All the Gentiles shall be blessed in you." For this reason, those who believe are blessed with Abraham who believed. For all who rely on the works of the law are under a curse; for it is written, "Cursed is everyone who does not observe and obey all the things written in the book of the law." Now it is evident that no one is justified before God by the law; for "The one who is righteous will live by faith." But the law does not rest on faith; on the contrary, "Whoever does the works of the law will live by them." Christ redeemed us from the curse of the law by becoming a curse for us—for it is written, "Cursed is everyone who hangs on a tree"—in order that in Christ Jesus the blessing of Abraham might come to the Gentiles, so that we might receive the promise of the Spirit through faith.

A Reading (Lesson) from the Gospel according to Mark [6:30–46]

The apostles gathered around Jesus, and told him all that they had done and taught. He said to them, "Come away to a deserted place all by yourselves and rest a while." For many were coming and going, and they had no leisure even to eat. And they went away in the boat to a deserted place by themselves. Now many saw them going and recognized them, and they hurried there on foot from all the towns and arrived ahead of them. As he went ashore, he saw a great crowd; and he had compassion for them, because they were like sheep without a shepherd; and he began to teach them many things. When it grew late, his disciples came to him and said, "This is a deserted place, and the hour is now very late; send them away so that they may go into the surrounding country and villages and buy something for themselves to eat." But he answered them, "You give them something to eat." They said to him, "Are we to go and buy two hundred denarii worth of bread, and give it to them to eat?" And he said to them, "How many loaves have you? Go and see." When they had found out, they said, "Five, and two fish." Then he ordered them to get all the people to sit down in groups on the green grass. So they sat down in groups of hundreds and of fifties. Taking the five loaves and the two fish, he looked up to heaven, and blessed and broke the loaves, and gave them to his disciples to set before the people; and he divided the two fish among them all. And all ate and were filled; and they took up twelve baskets full of broken pieces and of the fish. Those who had eaten the loaves numbered five thousand men. Immediately he made his disciples get into the boat and go on ahead to the other side, to Bethsaida, while he dismissed the crowd. After saying farewell to them, he went up on the mountain to pray.

Friday

Psalm 40 [page 640],   *Psalm 54* [page 659]   ❖
Psalm 51 [page 656]

A Reading (Lesson) from the Book of Isaiah [50:1–11]

Thus says the LORD: Where is your mother's bill of divorce with which I put her away? Or which of my creditors is it to whom I have sold you? No, because of your sins you were sold, and for your transgressions your mother was put away. Why was no one there when I came? Why did no one answer when I called? Is my hand shortened, that it cannot redeem? Or have I no power to deliver? By my rebuke I dry up the sea, I make the rivers a desert; their fish stink for lack of water, and die of thirst. I clothe the heavens with blackness, and make sackcloth their covering. The Lord GOD has given me the tongue of a teacher, that I may know how to sustain the weary with a word. Morning by morning he wakens—wakens my ear to listen as those who are taught. The Lord GOD has opened my ear, and I was not rebellious, I did not turn backward. I gave my back to those who struck me, and my cheeks to those who pulled out the beard; I did not hide my face from insult and spitting. The Lord GOD helps me; therefore I have not been disgraced; therefore I have set my face like flint, and I know that I shall not be put to shame; he who vindicates me is near. Who will contend with me? Let us stand up together. Who are my adversaries? Let them confront me. It is the Lord GOD who helps me; who will declare me guilty? All of them will wear out like a garment; the moth will eat them up. Who among you fears the LORD and obeys the voice of his servant, who walks in darkness and has no light, yet trusts in the name of the LORD and relies upon his God? But all of you are kindlers of fire, lighters of firebrands. Walk in the flame of your fire, and among the brands that you have kindled! This is what you shall have from my hand: you shall lie down in torment.

A Reading (Lesson) from the Letter of Paul to the Galatians [3:15–22]

Brothers and sisters, I give an example from daily life: once a person's will has been ratified, no one adds to it or annuls it. Now the promises were made to Abraham and to his offspring; it does not say, "And to offsprings," as of many; but it says, "And to your offspring," that is, to one person, who is Christ. My point is this: the law, which came four hundred thirty years later, does not annul a covenant previously ratified by God, so as to nullify the promise. For if the inheritance comes from the law, it no longer comes from the promise; but God granted it to Abraham through the promise. Why then the law? It was added because of transgressions, until the offspring would come to whom the promise had been made; and it was ordained through angels by a mediator. Now a mediator involves more than one party; but God is one. Is the law then opposed to the promises of God? Certainly not! For if a law had been given that could make alive, then righteousness would indeed come through the law. But the scripture has imprisoned all things under the power of sin, so that what was promised through faith in Jesus Christ might be given to those who believe.

A Reading (Lesson) from the Gospel according to Mark [6:47–56]

When evening came, the boat was out on the sea, and he was alone on the land. When he saw that they were straining at the oars against an adverse wind, he came towards them early in the morning, walking on the sea. He intended to pass them by. But when they saw him walking on the sea, they thought it was a ghost and cried out; for they all saw him and were terrified. But immediately he spoke to them and said, "Take heart, it is I; do not be afraid." Then he got into the boat with them and the wind ceased. And they were utterly astounded, for they did not understand about the loaves, but their hearts were hardened. When they had crossed over, they came to land at Gennesaret and moored the boat. When they got out of the boat, people at once recognized him, and rushed about that whole region and began to bring the sick on mats to wherever they heard he was. And wherever he went, into villages or cities or farms, they laid the sick in the marketplaces, and begged him that they might touch even the fringe of his cloak; and all who touched it were healed.

Saturday

Psalm 55 [page 660] ❖ *Psalm 138* [page 793], *Psalm 139:1–17(18–23)* [page 794]

A Reading (Lesson) from the Book of Isaiah [51:1–8]

Listen to me, you that pursue righteousness, you that seek
the LORD. Look to the rock from which you were hewn, and
to the quarry from which you were dug. Look to Abraham
your father and to Sarah who bore you; for he was but one
when I called him, but I blessed him and made him many.
For the LORD will comfort Zion; he will comfort all her
waste places, and will make her wilderness like Eden, her
desert like the garden of the LORD; joy and gladness will be
found in her, thanksgiving and the voice of song. Listen to
me, my people, and give heed to me, my nation; for a
teaching will go out from me, and my justice for a light to
the peoples. I will bring near my deliverance swiftly, my
salvation has gone out and my arms will rule the peoples;
the coastlands wait for me, and for my arm they hope. Lift
up your eyes to the heavens, and look at the earth beneath;
for the heavens will vanish like smoke, the earth will wear
out like a garment, and those who live on it will die like
gnats; but my salvation will be forever, and my deliverance
will never be ended. Listen to me, you who know
righteousness, you people who have my teaching in your
hearts; do not fear the reproach of others, and do not be
dismayed when they revile you. For the moth will eat them
up like a garment, and the worm will eat them like wool;
but my deliverance will be forever, and my salvation to all
generations.

*A Reading (Lesson) from the Letter of Paul to the
Galatians* [3:23–29]

Now before faith came, we were imprisoned and guarded
under the law until faith would be revealed. Therefore the
law was our disciplinarian until Christ came, so that we
might be justified by faith. But now that faith has come,

we are no longer subject to a disciplinarian, for in Christ Jesus you are all children of God through faith. As many of you as were baptized into Christ have clothed yourselves with Christ. There is no longer Jew or Greek, there is no longer slave or free, there is no longer male and female; for all of you are one in Christ Jesus. And if you belong to Christ, then you are Abraham's offspring, heirs according to the promise.

A Reading (Lesson) from the Gospel according to Mark [7:1–23]

Now when the Pharisees and some of the scribes who had come from Jerusalem gathered around him, they noticed that some of his disciples were eating with defiled hands, that is, without washing them. (For the Pharisees, and all the Jews, do not eat unless they thoroughly wash their hands, thus observing the tradition of the elders; and they do not eat anything from the market unless they wash it; and there are also many other traditions that they observe, the washing of cups, pots, and bronze kettles.) So the Pharisees and the scribes asked him, "Why do your disciples not live according to the tradition of the elders, but eat with defiled hands?" He said to them, "Isaiah prophesied rightly about you hypocrites, as it is written, 'This people honors me with their lips, but their hearts are far from me; in vain do they worship me, teaching human precepts as doctrines.' You abandon the commandment of God and hold to human tradition." Then he said to them, "You have a fine way of rejecting the commandment of God in order to keep your tradition! For Moses said, 'Honor your father and your mother'; and, 'Whoever speaks evil of father or mother must surely die.' But you say that if anyone tells father or mother, 'Whatever support you might have had from me is Corban' (that is, an offering to God)—then you no longer permit doing anything for a father or mother, thus making void the word of God through your tradition that you have handed on. And you do many things like this." Then he called the crowd again and said to them, "Listen to me, all of you, and understand: there is nothing outside a person that by going in can defile, but the things that come out are what defile." When he had left the crowd and entered the house, his disciples asked him about the parable. He said to them, "Then do you also fail to understand? Do you not see that whatever goes into a person from outside cannot defile, since it enters, not the heart but the stomach, and goes out into the sewer?" (Thus he declared all foods clean.) And he said, "It is what comes out of a person that defiles. For it is from within, from the human heart, that evil intentions come: fornication, theft, murder, adultery, avarice, wickedness, deceit, licentiousness, envy, slander, pride, folly. All these evil things come from within, and they defile a person."

Week of 4 Epiphany

Sunday

Psalm 24 [page 613],   *Psalm 29* [page 620]   ❖
Psalm 8 [page 592],   *Psalm 84* [page 707]

A Reading (Lesson) from the Book of Isaiah [51:9–16]

Awake, awake, put on strength, O arm of the LORD!
Awake, as in days of old, the generations of long ago! Was it
not you who cut Rahab in pieces, who pierced the dragon?
Was it not you who dried up the sea, the waters of the great
deep; who made the depths of the sea a way for the
redeemed to cross over? So the ransomed of the LORD shall
return, and come to Zion with singing; everlasting joy shall
be upon their heads; they shall obtain joy and gladness, and
sorrow and sighing shall flee away. I, I am he who comforts
you; why then are you afraid of a mere mortal who must
die, a human being who fades like grass? You have forgotten
the LORD, your Maker, who stretched out the heavens and
laid the foundations of the earth. You fear continually all
day long because of the fury of the oppressor, who is bent
on destruction. But where is the fury of the oppressor? The
oppressed shall speedily be released; they shall not die and
go down to the Pit, nor shall they lack bread. For I am the
LORD your God, who stirs up the sea so that its waves
roar—the LORD of hosts is his name. I have put my words in
your mouth, and hidden you in the shadow of my hand,
stretching out the heavens and laying the foundations of the
earth, and saying to Zion, "You are my people."

*A Reading (Lesson) from the Letter to the
Hebrews* [11:8–16]

By faith Abraham obeyed when he was called to set out
for a place that he was to receive as an inheritance; and he
set out, not knowing where he was going. By faith he
stayed for a time in the land he had been promised, as in a
foreign land, living in tents, as did Isaac and Jacob, who
were heirs with him of the same promise. For he looked
forward to the city that has foundations, whose architect

and builder is God. By faith he received power of procreation, even though he was too old—and Sarah herself was barren—because he considered him faithful who had promised. Therefore from one person, and this one as good as dead, descendants were born, "as many as the stars of heaven and as the innumerable grains of sand by the seashore." All of these died in faith without having received the promises, but from a distance they saw and greeted them. They confessed that they were strangers and foreigners on the earth, for people who speak in this way make it clear that they are seeking a homeland. If they had been thinking of the land that they had left behind, they would have had opportunity to return. But as it is, they desire a better country, that is, a heavenly one. Therefore God is not ashamed to be called their God; indeed, he has prepared a city for them.

A Reading (Lesson) from the Gospel according to John [7:14-31]

About the middle of the festival of Booths Jesus went up into the temple and began to teach. The Jews were astonished at it, saying, "How does this man have such learning, when he has never been taught?" Then Jesus answered them, "My teaching is not mine but his who sent me. Anyone who resolves to do the will of God will know whether the teaching is from God or whether I am speaking on my own. Those who speak on their own seek their own glory; but the one who seeks the glory of him who sent him is true, and there is nothing false in him. Did not Moses give you the law? Yet none of you keeps the law. Why are you looking for an opportunity to kill me?" The crowd answered, "You have a demon! Who is trying to kill you?" Jesus answered them, "I performed ne work, and all of you are astonished. Moses gave you circumcision (it is, of course, not from Moses, but from the patriarchs), and you circumcise a man on the sabbath. If a man receives circumcision on the sabbath in order that the law of Moses may not be broken, are you angry with me because I healed a man's whole body on the sabbath? Do not judge by appearances, but judge with right judgment." Now some of the people of Jerusalem were saying, "Is not this the man whom they are trying to kill? And here he is, speaking openly, but they say nothing to him! Can it be that the authorities really know that this is the Messiah? Yet we know where this man is from; but when the Messiah comes, no one will know where he is from." Then Jesus cried out as he was teaching in the temple, "You know me, and you know where I am from. I have not come on my own. But the one who sent me is true, and you do not know him. I know him, because I am from him, and he sent me." Then they tried to arrest him, but no one laid hands on him, because his hour had not yet come. Yet many in the crowd believed in him and were saying, "When the Messiah comes, will he do more signs than this man has done?"

Monday

Psalm 56 [page 662],   Psalm 57 [page 663],
Psalm 58 [page 664])   ❖   Psalm 64 [page 671],
Psalm 65 [page 672]

A *Reading (Lesson) from the Book of Isaiah* [51:17–23]

Rouse yourself, rouse yourself! Stand up, O Jerusalem, you who have drunk at the hand of the LORD the cup of his wrath, who have drunk to the dregs the bowl of staggering.

There is no one to guide her among all the children she has borne; there is no one to take her by the hand among all the children she has brought up. These two things have befallen you—who will grieve with you?—devastation and destruction, famine and sword—who will comfort you? Your children have fainted, they lie at the head of every street like an antelope in a net; they are full of the wrath of the LORD, the rebuke of your God. Therefore hear this, you who are wounded, who are drunk, but not with wine: Thus says your Sovereign, the LORD, your God who pleads the cause of his people: See, I have taken from your hand the cup of staggering; you shall drink no more from the bowl of my wrath. And I will put it into the hand of your tormentors, who have said to you, "Bow down, that we may walk on you"; and you have made your back like the ground and like the street for them to walk on.

A Reading (Lesson) from the Letter of Paul to the Galatians [4:1–11]

My point is this: heirs, as long as they are minors, are no better than slaves, though they are the owners of all the property; but they remain under guardians and trustees until the date set by the father. So with us; while we were minors, we were enslaved to the elemental spirits of the world. But when the fullness of time had come, God sent his Son, born of a woman, born under the law, in order to redeem those who were under the law, so that we might receive adoption as children. And because you are children, God has sent the Spirit of his Son into our hearts, crying, "Abba! Father!" So you are no longer a slave but a child, and if a child then also an heir, through God. Formerly, when you did not know God, you were enslaved to beings that by nature are not gods. Now, however, that you have come to know God, or rather to be known by God, how can you turn back again to the weak and beggarly elemental spirits? How can you want to be enslaved to them again? You are observing special days, and months, and seasons, and years. I am afraid that my work for you may have been wasted.

A Reading (Lesson) from the Gospel according to Mark [7:24–37]

From there Jesus set out and went away to the region of Tyre. He entered a house and did not want anyone to know he was there. Yet he could not escape notice, but a woman whose little daughter had an unclean spirit immediately heard about him, and she came and bowed down at his feet. Now the woman was a Gentile, of Syrophoenician origin. She begged him to cast the demon out of her daughter. He said to her, "Let the children be fed first, for it is not fair to take the children's food and throw it to the dogs." But she answered him, "Sir, even the dogs under the table eat the children's crumbs." Then he said to her, "For saying that, you may go—the demon has left your daughter." So she went home, found the child lying on the bed, and the demon gone. Then he returned from the region of Tyre, and went by way of Sidon towards the Sea of Galilee, in the region of the Decapolis. They brought to him a deaf man who had an impediment in his speech; and they begged him to lay his hand on him. He took him aside in private, away from the crowd, and put his fingers into his ears, and he spat and touched his tongue. Then looking up to heaven, he sighed and said to him, "Ephphatha," that is, "Be opened." And immediately his ears were opened, his tongue was released, and he spoke plainly. Then Jesus ordered them to tell no one; but the more he ordered them, the more zealously they proclaimed it. They were astounded beyond measure, saying, "He has done everything well; he even makes the deaf to hear and the mute to speak."

Tuesday

Psalm 61 [page 668], *Psalm 62* [page 669] ❖
Psalm 68:1–20(21–23)24–36 [page 676]

A Reading (Lesson) from the Book of Isaiah [52:1–12]

Awake, awake, put on your strength, O Zion! Put on your beautiful garments, O Jerusalem, the holy city; for the uncircumcised and the unclean shall enter you no more. Shake yourself from the dust, rise up, O captive Jerusalem; loose the bonds from your neck, O captive daughter Zion! For thus says the LORD: You were sold for nothing, and you shall be redeemed without money. For thus says the Lord GOD: Long ago, my people went down into Egypt to reside there as aliens; the Assyrian, too, has oppressed them without cause. Now therefore what am I doing here, says the LORD, seeing that my people are taken away without cause? Their rulers howl, says the LORD, and continually, all day long, my name is despised. Therefore my people shall know my name; therefore in that day they shall know that it is I who speak; here am I. How beautiful upon the mountains are the feet of the messenger who announces peace, who brings good news, who announces salvation, who says to Zion, "Your God reigns." Listen! Your sentinels lift up their voices, together they sing for joy; for in plain sight they see the return of the LORD to Zion. Break forth together into singing, you ruins of Jerusalem; for the LORD has comforted his people, he has redeemed Jerusalem.

The LORD has bared his holy arm before the eyes of all the nations; and all the ends of the earth shall see the salvation of our God. Depart, depart, go out from there! Touch no unclean thing; go out from the midst of it, purify yourselves, you who carry the vessels of the LORD. For you shall not go out in haste, and you shall not go in flight; for the LORD will go before you, and the God of Israel will be your rear guard.

A Reading (Lesson) from the Letter of Paul to the Galatians [4:12–20]

Friends, I beg you, become as I am, for I also have become as you are. You have done me no wrong. You know that it was because of a physical infirmity that I first announced the gospel to you; though my condition put you to the test, you did not scorn or despise me, but welcomed me as an angel of God, as Christ Jesus. What has become of the good will you felt? For I testify that, had it been possible, you would have torn out your eyes and given them to me. Have I now become your enemy by telling you the truth? They make much of you, but for no good purpose; they want to exclude you, so that you may make much of them. It is good to be made much of for a good purpose at all times, and not only when I am present with you. My little children, for whom I am again in the pain of childbirth until Christ is formed in you, I wish I were present with you now and could change my tone, for I am perplexed about you.

A Reading (Lesson) from the Gospel according to Mark [8:1–10]

In those days when there was again a great crowd without anything to eat, he called his disciples and said to them, "I have compassion for the crowd, because they have been with me now for three days and have nothing to eat. If I send them away hungry to their homes, they will faint on the way—and some of them have come from a great distance." His disciples replied, "How can one feed these people with bread here in the desert?" He asked them, "How many loaves do you have?" They said, "Seven." Then he ordered the crowd to sit down on the ground; and he took the seven loaves, and after giving thanks he broke them and gave them to his disciples to distribute; and they distributed them to the crowd. They had also a few small fish; and after blessing them, he ordered that these too should be distributed. They ate and were filled; and they took up the broken pieces left over, seven baskets full. Now there were about four thousand people. And he sent them away. And immediately he got into the boat with his disciples and went to the district of Dalmanutha.

Wednesday

Psalm 72 [page 685]   ❖   *Psalm 119:73–96* [page 769]

*A Reading (Lesson) from the Book of
Isaiah* [54:1–10(11–17)]

Sing, O barren one who did not bear; burst into song and shout, you who have not been in labor! For the children of the desolate woman will be more than the children of her that is married, says the LORD. Enlarge the site of your tent, and let the curtains of your habitations be stretched out; do not hold back; lengthen your cords and strengthen your stakes. For you will spread out to the right and to the left, and your descendants will possess the nations and will settle the desolate towns. Do not fear, for you will not be ashamed; do not be discouraged, for you will not suffer disgrace; for you will forget the shame of your youth, and the disgrace of your widowhood you will remember no more. For your Maker is your husband, the LORD of hosts is his name; the Holy One of Israel is your Redeemer, the God of the whole earth he is called. For the LORD has called you like a wife forsaken and grieved in spirit, like the wife of a man's youth when she is cast off, says your God. For a brief moment I abandoned you, but with great compassion I will gather you. In overflowing wrath for a moment I hid my face from you, but with everlasting love I will have compassion on you, says the LORD, your Redeemer. This is like the days of Noah to me: Just as I swore that the waters of Noah would never again go over the earth, so I have sworn that I will not be angry with you and will not rebuke you. For the mountains may depart and the hills be removed, but my steadfast love shall not depart from you, and my covenant of peace shall not be removed, says the LORD, who has compassion on you.

O afflicted one, storm-tossed, and not comforted, I am about to set your stones in antimony, and lay your foundations with sapphires. I will make your pinnacles of rubies, your gates of jewels, and all your wall of precious stones. All your children shall be taught by the LORD, and great shall be the prosperity of your children. In righteousness you shall be established; you shall be far from oppression, for you shall not fear; and from terror, for it shall not come near you. If anyone stirs up strife, it is not from me; whoever stirs up strife with you shall fall because of you. See it is I who have created the smith who blows the fire of coals, and produces a weapon fit for its purpose; I have also created the ravager to destroy. No weapon that is fashioned against you shall prosper, and you shall confute every tongue that rises against you in judgment. This is the heritage of the servants of the LORD and their vindication from me, says the LORD.

A Reading (Lesson) from the Letter of Paul to the Galatians [4:21–31]

Tell me, you who desire to be subject to the law, will you not listen to the law? For it is written that Abraham had two sons, one by a slave woman and the other by a free woman. One, the child of the slave, was born according to the flesh; the other, the child of the free woman, was born through the promise. Now this is an allegory: these women are two covenants. One woman, in fact, is Hagar, from Mount Sinai, bearing children for slavery. Now Hagar is Mount Sinai in Arabia and corresponds to the present Jerusalem, for she is in slavery with her children. But the other woman corresponds to the Jerusalem above; she is free, and she is our mother. For it is written, "Rejoice, you childless one, you who bear no children, burst into song and shout, you who endure no birth pangs; for the children of the desolate woman are more numerous than the children of the one who is married." Now you, my friends, are children of the promise, like Isaac. But just as at that time the child who was born according to the flesh persecuted the child who was born according to the Spirit, so it is now also. But what does the scripture say? "Drive out the slave and her child; for the child of the slave will not share the inheritance with the child of the free woman." So then, friends, we are children, not of the slave but of the free woman.

*A Reading (Lesson) from the Gospel according to
Mark* [8:11–26]

The Pharisees came and began to argue with Jesus, asking him for a sign from heaven, to test him. And he sighed deeply in his spirit and said, "Why does this generation ask for a sign? Truly I tell you, no sign will be given to this generation." And he left them, and getting into the boat again, he went across to the other side. Now the disciples had forgotten to bring any bread; and they had only one loaf with them in the boat. And he cautioned them, saying, "Watch out—beware of the yeast of the Pharisees and the yeast of Herod." They said to one another, "It is because we have no bread." And becoming aware of it, Jesus said to them, "Why are you talking about having no bread? Do you still not perceive or understand? Are your hearts hardened? Do you have eyes, and fail to see? Do you have ears, and fail to hear? And do you not remember? When I broke the five loaves for the five thousand, how many baskets full of broken pieces did you collect?" They said to him, "Twelve." "And the seven for the four thousand, how many baskets full of broken pieces did you collect?" And they said to him, "Seven." Then he said to them, "Do you not yet understand?" They came to Bethsaida. Some people brought a blind man to him and begged him to touch him. He took the blind man by the hand and led him out of the village; and when he had put saliva on his eyes and laid his hands on him, he asked him, "Can you see anything?" And the man looked up and said, "I can see people, but they look like trees, walking." Then Jesus laid his hands on his eyes again; and he looked intently and his sight was restored, and he saw everything clearly. Then he sent him away to his home, saying, "Do not even go into the village."

Thursday

(Psalm 70 [page 682]), *Psalm 71* [page 683] ❖
Psalm 74 [page 689]

A Reading (Lesson) from the Book of Isaiah [55:1–13]

Ho, everyone who thirsts, come to the waters; and you that
have no money, come, buy and eat! Come, buy wine and
milk without money and without price. Why do you spend
your money for that which is not bread, and your labor for
that which does not satisfy? Listen carefully to me, and eat
what is good, and delight yourselves in rich food. Incline
your ear, and come to me; listen, so that you may live. I will
make with you an everlasting covenant, my steadfast, sure
love for David. See, I made him a witness to the peoples, a
leader and commander for the peoples. See, you shall call
nations that you do not know, and nations that do not
know you shall run to you, because of the LORD your God,
the Holy One of Israel, for he has glorified you. Seek the
LORD while he may be found, call upon him while he is
near; let the wicked forsake their way, and the unrighteous
their thoughts; let them return to the LORD, that he may
have mercy on them, and to our God, for he will abundantly
pardon. For my thoughts are not your thoughts, nor are
your ways my ways, says the LORD. For as the heavens are
higher than the earth, so are my ways higher than your ways
and my thoughts than your thoughts. For as the rain and the
snow come down from heaven, and do not return there until
they have watered the earth, making it bring forth and
sprout, giving seed to the sower and bread to the eater, so
shall my word be that goes out from my mouth; it shall not
return to me empty, but it shall accomplish that which I
purpose, and succeed in the thing for which I sent it. For
you shall go out in joy, and be led back in peace; the

mountains and the hills before you shall burst into song, and all the trees of the field shall clap their hands. Instead of the thorn shall come up the cypress; instead of the brier shall come up the myrtle; and it shall be to the LORD for a memorial, for an everlasting sign that shall not be cut off.

A Reading (Lesson) from the Letter of Paul to the Galatians [5:1–15]

For freedom Christ has set us free. Stand firm, therefore, and do not submit again to a yoke of slavery. Listen! I, Paul, am telling you that if you let yourselves be circumcised, Christ will be of no benefit to you. Once again I testify to every man who lets himself be circumcised that he is obliged to obey the entire law. You who want to be justified by the law have cut yourselves off from Christ; you have fallen away from grace. For through the Spirit, by faith, we eagerly wait for the hope of righteousness. For in Christ Jesus neither circumcision nor uncircumcision counts for anything; the only thing that counts is faith working through love. You were running well; who prevented you from obeying the truth? Such persuasion does not come from the one who calls you. A little yeast leavens the whole batch of dough. I am confident about you in the Lord that you will not think otherwise. But whoever it is that is confusing you will pay the penalty. But my friends, why am I still being persecuted if I am still preaching circumcision? In that case the offense of the cross has been removed. I wish those who unsettle you would castrate themselves! For you were called to freedom, brothers and sisters; only do not use your freedom as an opportunity for self-indulgence, but through love become slaves to one another. For the whole law is summed up in a single commandment, "You shall love your neighbor as yourself." If, however, you bite and devour one another, take care that you are not consumed by one another.

A Reading (Lesson) from the Gospel according to Mark [8:27—9:1]

Jesus went on with his disciples to the village of Caesarea Philippi; and on the way he asked his disciples, "Who do people say that I am?" And they answered him, "John the Baptist; and others, Elijah; and still others, one of the prophets." He asked them, "But who do you say that I am?" Peter answered him, "You are the Messiah." And he sternly ordered them not to tell anyone about him. Then he began to teach them that the Son of Man must undergo great suffering, and be rejected by the elders, the chief priests, and the scribes, and be killed, and after three days rise again. He said all this quite openly. And Peter took him aside and began to rebuke him. But turning and looking at his disciples, he rebuked Peter and said, "Get behind me, Satan! For you are setting your mind not on divine things but on human things." He called the crowd with his disciples, and said to them, "If any want to become my followers, let them deny themselves and take up their cross and follow me. For those who want to save their life will lose it, and those who lose their life for my sake, and for the sake of the gospel, will save it. For what will it profit them to gain the whole world and forfeit their life? Indeed, what can they give in return for their life? Those who are ashamed of me and of my words in this adulterous and sinful generation, of them the Son of Man will also be ashamed when he comes in the glory of his Father with the holy angels." And he said to them,

"Truly I tell you, there are some standing here who will not taste death until they see that the kingdom of God has come with power."

Friday

Psalm 69:1–23(24–30)31–38 [page 679]   ❖
Psalm 73 [page 687]

A Reading (Lesson) from the Book of Isaiah [56:1–8]

Thus says the LORD: Maintain justice, and do what is right, for soon my salvation will come, and my deliverance be revealed. Happy is the mortal who does this, the one who holds fast, who keeps the sabbath, not profaning it, and refrains from doing any evil. Do not let the foreigner joined to the LORD say, "The LORD will surely separate me from his people"; and do not let the eunuch say, "I am just a dry tree." For thus says the LORD: To the eunuchs who keep my sabbaths, who choose the things that please me and hold fast my covenant, I will give, in my house and within my walls, a monument and a name better than sons and daughters; I will give them an everlasting name that shall not be cut off. And the foreigners who join themselves to the LORD, to minister to him, to love the name of the LORD, and to be his servants, all who keep the sabbath, and do not profane it, and hold fast my covenant—these I will bring to my holy mountain, and make them joyful in my house of prayer; their burnt offerings and their sacrifices will be accepted on my altar; for my house shall be called a house of prayer for all peoples. Thus says the Lord GOD, who gathers the outcasts of Israel, I will gather others to them besides those already gathered.

A Reading (Lesson) from the Letter of Paul to the Galatians [5:16–24]

Live by the Spirit, I say, and do not gratify the desires of the flesh. For what the flesh desires is opposed to the Spirit, and what the Spirit desires is opposed to the flesh; for these are opposed to each other, to prevent you from doing what you want. But if you are led by the Spirit, you are not subject to the law. Now the works of the flesh are obvious: fornication, impurity, licentiousness, idolatry, sorcery, enmities, strife, jealousy, anger, quarrels, dissensions, factions, envy, drunkenness, carousing, and things like these. I am warning you, as I warned you before: those who do such things will not inherit the kingdom of God. By contrast, the fruit of the Spirit is love, joy, peace, patience, kindness, generosity, faithfulness, gentleness, and self-control. There is no law against such things. And those who belong to Christ Jesus have crucified the flesh with its passions and desires.

A Reading (Lesson) from the Gospel according to Mark [9:2–13]

Six days later, Jesus took with him Peter and James and John, and led them up a high mountain apart, by themselves. And he was transfigured before them, and his clothes became dazzling white, such as no one on earth could bleach them. And there appeared to them Elijah with Moses, who were talking with Jesus. Then Peter said to Jesus, "Rabbi, it is good for us to be here; let us make three dwellings, one for you, one for Moses, and one for Elijah." He did not know what to say, for they were terrified. Then a cloud overshadowed them, and from the cloud there came a voice, "This is my Son, the Beloved; listen to him!" Suddenly when they looked around, they saw no one with them any more, but only Jesus. As they were coming down the mountain, he ordered them to tell no one about what they had seen, until after the Son of Man had risen from the dead. So they kept the matter to themselves, questioning what this rising from the dead could mean. Then they asked him, "Why do the scribes say that Elijah must come first?" He said to them, "Elijah is indeed coming first to restore all things. How then is it written about the Son of Man, that he is to go through many sufferings and be treated with contempt? But I tell you that Elijah has come, and they did to him whatever they pleased, as it is written about him."

Saturday

Psalm 75 [page 691],   *Psalm* 76 [page 692] ❖
Psalm 23 [page 612],   *Psalm* 27 [page 617]

A Reading (Lesson) from the Book of Isaiah [57:3–13]

Come here, you children of a sorceress, you offspring of an adulterer and a whore. Whom are you mocking? Against whom do you open your mouth wide and stick out your tongue? Are you not children of transgression, the offspring of deceit—you that burn with lust among the oaks, under every green tree; you that slaughter your children in the valleys, under the clefts of the rocks? Among the smooth stones of the valley is your portion; they, they, are your lot; to them you have poured out a drink offering, you have brought a grain offering. Shall I be appeased for these things? Upon a high and lofty mountain you have set your bed, and there you went up to offer sacrifice. Behind the door and the doorpost you have set up your symbol; for, in deserting me, you have uncovered your bed, you have gone up to it, you have made it wide; and you have made a bargain for yourself with them, you have loved their bed, you have gazed on their nakedness. You journeyed to Molech with oil, and multiplied your perfumes; you sent your envoys far away, and sent down even to Sheol. You grew weary from your many wanderings, but you did not say, "It is useless." You found your desire rekindled, and so you did not weaken. Whom did you dread and fear so that you lied, and did not remember me or give me a thought? Have I not kept silent and closed my eyes, and so you do not fear me? I will concede your righteousness and your works, but they will not help you. When you cry out, let your collection of idols deliver you! The wind will carry them off, a breath will take them away. But whoever takes refuge in me shall possess the land and inherit my holy mountain.

A Reading (Lesson) from the Letter of Paul to the Galatians [5:25—6:10]

If we live by the Spirit, let us also be guided by the Spirit. Let us not become conceited, competing against one another, envying one another. My friends, if anyone is detected in a transgression, you who have received the Spirit should restore such a one in a spirit of gentleness. Take care that you yourselves are not tempted. Bear one another's burdens, and in this way you will fulfill the law of Christ. For if those who are nothing think they are something, they deceive themselves. All must test their own work; then that work, rather than their neighbor's work, will become a cause for pride. For all must carry their own loads. Those who are taught the word must share in all good things with their teacher. Do not be deceived; God is not mocked, for you reap whatever you sow. If you sow to your own flesh, you will reap corruption from the flesh; but if you sow to the Spirit, you will reap eternal life from the Spirit. So let us not grow weary in doing what is right, for we will reap at harvest time, if we do not give up. So then, whenever we have an opportunity, let us work for the good of all, and especially for those of the family of faith.

A Reading (Lesson) from the Gospel according to Mark [9:14–29]

When Jesus, Peter, and John came to the disciples, they saw a great crowd around them, and some scribes arguing with them. When the whole crowd saw Jesus, they were immediately overcome with awe, and they ran forward to greet him. He asked them, "What are you arguing about with them?" Someone from the crowd answered him, "Teacher, I brought you my son; he has a spirit that makes him unable to speak; and whenever it seizes him, it dashes him down; and he foams and grinds his teeth and becomes rigid; and I asked your disciples to cast it out, but they could not do so." He answered them, "You faithless generation, how much longer must I be among you? How much longer must I put up with you? Bring him to me." And they brought the boy to him. When the spirit saw him, immediately it convulsed the boy, and he fell on the ground and rolled about, foaming at the mouth. Jesus asked the father, "How long has this been happening to him?" And he said, "From childhood. It has often cast him into the fire and into the water, to destroy him; but if you are able to do anything, have pity on us and help us." Jesus said to him, "If you are able!—All things can be done for the one who believes." Immediately the father of the child cried out, "I believe; help my unbelief!" When Jesus saw that a crowd came running together, he rebuked the unclean spirit, saying to it, "You spirit that keeps this boy from speaking and hearing, I command you, come out of him, and never enter him again!" After crying out and convulsing him terribly, it came out, and the boy was like a corpse, so that most of them said, "He is dead." But Jesus took him by the hand and lifted him up, and he was able to stand. When he had entered the house, his disciples asked him privately, "Why could we not cast it out?" He said to them, "This kind can come out only through prayer."

Week of 5 Epiphany

Sunday

Psalm 93 [page 722],   *Psalm 96* [page 725]   ❖
Psalm 34 [page 627]

A Reading (Lesson) from the Book of Isaiah [57:14–21]

It shall be said, "Build up, build up, prepare the way, remove every obstruction from my people's way." For thus says the high and lofty one who inhabits eternity, whose name is Holy: I dwell in the high and holy place, and also with those who are contrite and humble in spirit, to revive the spirit of the humble, and to revive the heart of the contrite. For I will not continually accuse, nor will I always be angry; for then the spirits would grow faint before me, even the souls that I have made. Because of their wicked covetousness I was angry; I struck them, I hid and was angry; but they kept turning back to their own ways. I have seen their ways, but I will heal them; I will lead them and repay them with comfort, creating for their mourners the fruit of the lips. Peace, peace, to the far and the near, says the LORD; and I will heal them. But the wicked are like the tossing sea that cannot keep still; its waters toss up mire and mud. There is no peace, says my God, for the wicked.

A Reading (Lesson) from the Letter to the Hebrews [12:1–6]

Since we are surrounded by so great a cloud of witnesses, let us also lay aside every weight and the sin that clings so closely, and let us run with perseverance the race that is set before us, looking to Jesus the pioneer and perfecter of our faith, who for the sake of the joy that was set before him endured the cross, disregarding its shame, and has taken his seat at the right hand of the throne of God. Consider him who endured such hostility against himself from sinners, so that you may not grow weary or lose heart. In your struggle against sin you have not yet resisted to the point of shedding your blood. And you have forgotten the exhortation that addresses you as children—"My child, do not regard lightly the discipline of the Lord, or lose heart when you are punished by him; for the Lord disciplines those whom he loves, and chastises every child whom he accepts."

A Reading (Lesson) from the Gospel according to John [7:37–46]

On the last day of the festival of Booths, the great day, while Jesus was standing there, he cried out, "Let anyone who is thirsty come to me, and let the one who believes in me drink. As the scripture has said, 'Out of the believer's heart shall flow rivers of living water.' " Now he said this about the Spirit, which believers in him were to receive; for as yet there was no Spirit, because Jesus was not yet glorified. When they heard these words, some in the crowd said, "This is really the prophet." Others said, "This is the Messiah." But some asked, "Surely the Messiah does not come from Galilee, does he? Has not the scripture said that the Messiah is descended from David and comes from Bethlehem, the village where David lived?" So there was a division in the crowd because of him. Some of them wanted to arrest him, but no one laid hands on him. Then the temple police went back to the chief priests and Pharisees, who asked them, "Why did you not arrest him?" The police answered, "Never has anyone spoken like this!"

Monday

Psalm 80 [page 702] ❖ *Psalm 77* [page 693], (*Psalm 79* [page 701])

A Reading (Lesson) from the Book of Isaiah [58:1–12]

Shout out, do not hold back! Lift up your voice like a trumpet! Announce to my people their rebellion, to the house of Jacob their sins. Yet day after day they seek me and delight to know my ways, as if they were a nation that practiced righteousness and did not forsake the ordinance of their God; they ask of me righteous judgments, they delight to draw near to God. "Why do we fast, but you do not see? Why humble ourselves, but you do not notice?" Look, you serve your own interest on your fast day, and oppress all your workers. Look, you fast only to quarrel and to fight and to strike with a wicked fist. Such fasting as you do today will not make your voice heard on high. Is such the fast that I choose, a day to humble oneself? Is it to bow down the head like a bulrush, and to lie in sackcloth and ashes? Will you call this a fast, a day acceptable to the LORD? Is not this the fast that I choose: to loose the bonds of injustice, to undo the thongs of the yoke, to let the oppressed go free, and to break every yoke? Is it not to share your bread with the hungry, and bring the homeless poor into your house; when you see the naked, to cover them, and not to hide yourself from your own kin? Then your light shall break forth like the dawn, and your healing shall spring up quickly; your vindicator shall go before you, the glory of the LORD shall be your rear guard. Then you shall call, and the LORD will answer; you shall cry for help, and he will say, Here I am. If you remove the yoke from among you, the pointing of the finger, the speaking of evil, if you offer your food to the hungry and satisfy the needs of the afflicted, then your light shall rise in the darkness and your gloom be like the noonday. The LORD will guide you continually, and satisfy your needs in parched places, and make your bones strong; and you shall be like a watered garden, like a spring of water, whose waters never fail. Your ancient ruins shall be rebuilt; you shall raise up the foundations of many generations; you shall be called the repairer of the breach, the restorer of streets to live in.

A Reading (Lesson) from the Letter of Paul to the Galatians [6:11–18]

See what large letters I make when I am writing in my own hand! It is those who want to make a good showing in the flesh that try to compel you to be circumcised—only that they may not be persecuted for the cross of Christ. Even the circumcised do not themselves obey the law, but they want you to be circumcised so that they may boast about your flesh. May I never boast of anything except the cross of our Lord Jesus Christ, by which the world has been crucified to me, and I to the world. For neither circumcision nor uncircumcision is anything; but a new creation is everything! As for those who will follow this rule—peace be upon them, and mercy, and upon the Israel of God. From now on, let no one make trouble for me; for I carry the marks of Jesus branded on my body. May the grace of our Lord Jesus Christ be with your spirit, brothers and sisters. Amen.

A Reading (Lesson) from the Gospel according to Mark [9:30-41]

Jesus and his disciples went on from there and passed through Galilee. He did not want anyone to know it; for he was teaching his disciples, saying to them, "The Son of Man is to be betrayed into human hands, and they will kill him, and three days after being killed, he will rise again." But they did not understand what he was saying and were afraid to ask him. Then they came to Capernaum; and when he was in the house he asked them, "What were you arguing about on the way?" But they were silent, for on the way they had argued with one another who was the greatest. He sat down, called the twelve, and said to them, "Whoever wants to be first must be last of all and servant of all." Then he took a little child and put it among them; and taking it in his arms, he said to them, "Whoever welcomes one such child in my name welcomes me, and whoever welcomes me welcomes not me but the one who sent me." John said to him, "Teacher, we saw someone casting out demons in your name, and we tried to stop him, because he was not following us." But Jesus said, "Do not stop him; for no one who does a deed of power in my name will be able soon afterward to speak evil of me. Whoever is not against us is for us. For truly I tell you, whoever gives you a cup of water to drink because you bear the name of Christ will by no means lose the reward."

Tuesday

Psalm 78:1–39 [page 694]   ❖   *Psalm 78:40–72* [page 698]

A Reading (Lesson) from the Book of Isaiah [59:1–15a]

See, the LORD's hand is not too short to save, nor his ear too dull to hear. Rather, your iniquities have been barriers between you and your God, and your sins have hidden his face from you so that he does not hear. For your hands are defiled with blood, and your fingers with iniquity; your lips have spoken lies, your tongue mutters wickedness. No one brings suit justly, no one goes to law honestly; they rely on empty pleas, they speak lies, conceiving mischief and begetting iniquity. They hatch adders' eggs, and weave the spider's web; whoever eats their eggs dies, and the crushed egg hatches out a viper. Their webs cannot serve as clothing; they cannot cover themselves with what they make. Their works are works of iniquity, and deeds of violence are in their hands. Their feet run to evil, and they rush to shed innocent blood; their thoughts are thoughts of iniquity, desolation and destruction are in their highways. The way of peace they do not know, and there is no justice in their paths. Their roads they have made crooked; no one who walks in them knows peace. Therefore justice is far from us, and righteousness does not reach us; we wait for light, and lo! there is darkness; and for brightness, but we walk in gloom. We grope like the blind along a wall, groping like those who have no eyes; we stumble at noon as in the twilight, among the vigorous as though we were dead. We all growl like bears; like doves we moan mournfully. We wait for justice, but there is none; for salvation, but it is far from us. For our transgressions before you are many, and our sins testify against us. Our transgressions indeed are with us, and we know our iniquities: transgressing, and denying the LORD, and turning away from following our God, talking oppression and revolt, conceiving lying words and uttering them from the heart. Justice is turned back, and righteousness stands at a distance; for truth stumbles in the public square, and uprightness cannot enter. Truth is lacking, and whoever turns from evil is despoiled.

A Reading (Lesson) from the Second Letter of Paul to Timothy [1:1–14]

Paul, an apostle of Christ Jesus by the will of God, for the sake of the promise of life that is in Christ Jesus, to Timothy, my beloved child: Grace, mercy, and peace from God the Father and Christ Jesus our Lord. I am grateful to God—whom I worship with a clear conscience, as my ancestors did—when I remember you constantly in my prayers night and day. Recalling your tears, I long to see you so that I may be filled with joy. I am reminded of your sincere faith, a faith that lived first in your grandmother Lois and your mother Eunice and now, I am sure, lives in you. For this reason I remind you to rekindle the gift of God that is within you through the laying on of my hands; for God did not give us a spirit of cowardice, but rather a spirit of power and of love and of self-discipline. Do not be ashamed, then, of the testimony about our Lord or of me his prisoner, but join with me in suffering for the gospel, relying on the power of God, who saved us and called us with a holy calling, not according to our works, but according to his own purpose and grace. This grace was given to us in Christ Jesus before the ages began, but it has now been revealed through the appearing of our Savior Christ Jesus, who abolished death and brought life and immortality to light through the gospel. For this gospel I was appointed a herald and an apostle and a teacher, and for this reason I suffer as I do. But I am not ashamed, for I know the one in whom I have put my trust, and I am sure that he is able to guard until that day what I have entrusted to him. Hold to the standard of sound teaching that you have heard from me, in the faith and love that are in Christ Jesus. Guard the good treasure entrusted to you, with the help of the Holy Spirit living in us.

A Reading (Lesson) from the Gospel according to Mark [9:42–50]

Jesus said, "If any of you put a stumbling block before one of these little ones who believe in me, it would be better for you if a great millstone were hung around your neck and you were thrown into the sea. If your hand causes you to stumble, cut it off; it is better for you to enter life maimed than to have two hands and to go to hell, to the unquenchable fire. And if your foot causes you to stumble, cut it off; it is better for you to enter life lame than to have two feet and to be thrown into hell. And if your eye causes you to stumble, tear it out; it is better for you to enter the kingdom of God with one eye than to have two eyes and to be thrown into hell, where their worm never dies, and the fire is never quenched. For everyone will be salted with fire. Salt is good; but if salt has lost its saltiness, how can you season it? Have salt in yourselves, and be at peace with one another."

Wednesday

Psalm 119:97–120 [page 771]   ❖   *Psalm 81* [page 704],
Psalm 82 [page 705]

Isaiah 59:15b–21 [page 73 above]

*A Reading (Lesson) from the Second Letter of Paul to
Timothy* [1:15—2:13]

You are aware that all who are in Asia have turned away
from me, including Phygelus and Hermogenes. May the
Lord grant mercy to the household of Onesiphorus,
because he often refreshed me and was not ashamed of my
chain; when he arrived in Rome, he eagerly searched for
me and found me—may the Lord grant that he will find
mercy from the Lord on that day! And you know very
well how much service he rendered in Ephesus. You then,
my child, be strong in the grace that is in Christ Jesus;
and what you have heard from me through many
witnesses entrust to faithful people who will be able to
teach others as well. Share in suffering like a good soldier
of Christ Jesus. No one serving in the army gets entangled
in everyday affairs; the soldier's aim is to please the
enlisting officer. And in the case of an athlete, no one is
crowned without competing according to the rules. It is
the farmer who does the work who ought to have the first
share of the crops. Think over what I say, for the Lord
will give you understanding in all things. Remember Jesus
Christ, raised from the dead, a descendant of David—that
is my gospel, for which I suffer hardship, even to the point
of being chained like a criminal. But the word of God is
not chained. Therefore I endure everything for the sake of
the elect, so that they may also obtain the salvation that is
in Christ Jesus, with eternal glory. The saying is sure: If
we have died with him, we will also live with him; if we

endure, we will also reign with him; if we deny him, he will also deny us; if we are faithless, he remains faithful—for he cannot deny himself.

A Reading (Lesson) from the Gospel according to Mark [10:1–16]

He left that place and went to the region of Judea and beyond the Jordan. And crowds again gathered around him; and, as was his custom, he again taught them. Some Pharisees came, and to test him they asked, "Is it lawful for a man to divorce his wife?" He answered them, "What did Moses command you?" They said, "Moses allowed a man to write a certificate of dismissal and to divorce her." But Jesus said to them, "Because of your hardness of heart he wrote this commandment for you. But from the beginning of creation, 'God made them male and female.' 'For this reason a man shall leave his father and mother and be joined to his wife, and the two shall become one flesh.' So they are no longer two, but one flesh. Therefore what God has joined together, let no one separate." Then in the house the disciples asked him again about this matter. He said to them, "Whoever divorces his wife and marries another commits adultery against her; and if she divorces her husband and marries another, she commits adultery." People were bringing little children to him in order that he might touch them; and the disciples spoke sternly to them. But when Jesus saw this, he was indignant and said to them, "Let the little children come to me; do not stop them; for it is to such as these that the kingdom of God belongs. Truly I tell you, whoever does not receive the kingdom of God as a little child will never enter it." And he took them up in his arms, laid his hands on them, and blessed them.

Thursday

(*Psalm 83* [page 706]) or *Psalm 146* [page 803],
Psalm 147 [page 804] ❖ *Psalm 85* [page 708],
Psalm 86 [page 709]

A Reading (Lesson) from the Book of Isaiah [60:1–17]

Arise, shine; for your light has come, and the glory of the
LORD has risen upon you. For darkness shall cover the
earth, and thick darkness the peoples; but the LORD will
arise upon you, and his glory will appear over you. Nations
shall come to your light, and kings to the brightness of your
dawn. Lift up your eyes and look around; they all gather
together, they come to you; your sons shall come from far
away, and your daughters shall be carried on their nurses'
arms. Then you shall see and be radiant; your heart shall
thrill and rejoice, because the abundance of the sea shall be
brought to you, the wealth of the nations shall come to you.
A multitude of camels shall cover you, the young camels of
Midian and Ephah; all those from Sheba shall come. They
shall bring gold and frankincense, and shall proclaim the
praise of the LORD. All the flocks of Kedar shall be gathered
to you, the rams of Nebaioth shall minister to you; they
shall be acceptable on my altar, and I will glorify my
glorious house. Who are these that fly like a cloud, and like
doves to their windows? For the coastlands shall wait for
me, the ships of Tarshish first, to bring your children from
far away, their silver and gold with them, for the name of
the LORD your God, and for the Holy One of Israel, because
he has glorified you. Foreigners shall build up your walls,
and their kings shall minister to you; for in my wrath I
struck you down, but in my favor I have had mercy on you.
Your gates shall always be open; day and night they shall
not be shut, so that nations shall bring you their wealth,

with their kings led in procession. For the nation and kingdom that will not serve you shall perish; those nations shall be utterly laid waste. The glory of Lebanon shall come to you, the cypress, the plane, and the pine, to beautify the place of my sanctuary; and I will glorify where my feet rest. The descendants of those who oppressed you shall come bending low to you, and all who despised you shall bow down at your feet; they shall call you the City of the LORD, the Zion of the Holy One of Israel. Whereas you have been forsaken and hated, with no one passing through, I will make you majestic forever, a joy from age to age. You shall suck the milk of nations, you shall suck the breasts of kings; and you shall know that I, the LORD, am your Savior and your Redeemer, the Mighty One of Jacob. Instead of bronze I will bring gold, instead of iron I will bring silver; instead of wood, bronze, instead of stones, iron. I will appoint Peace as your overseer and Righteousness as your taskmaster.

A Reading (Lesson) from the Second Letter of Paul to Timothy [2:14–26]

Remind them of this, and warn them before God that they are to avoid wrangling over words, which does no good but only ruins those who are listening. Do your best to present yourself to God as one approved by him, a worker who has no need to be ashamed, rightly explaining the word of truth. Avoid profane chatter, for it will lead people into more and more impiety, and their talk will spread like gangrene. Among them are Hymenaeus and Philetus, who have swerved from the truth by claiming that the resurrection has already taken place. They are upsetting the faith of some. But God's firm foundation stands, bearing this inscription: "The Lord knows those who are his," and, "Let everyone who calls on the name of the Lord turn away from wickedness." In a large house there are utensils not only of gold and silver but also of wood and clay, some for special use, some for ordinary. All who cleanse themselves of the things I have mentioned will become special utensils, dedicated and useful to the owner of the house, ready for every good work. Shun youthful passions and pursue righteousness, faith, love, and peace, along with those who call on the Lord from a pure heart. Have nothing to do with stupid and senseless controversies; you know that they breed quarrels. And the Lord's servant must not be quarrelsome but kindly to everyone, an apt teacher, patient, correcting opponents with gentleness. God may perhaps grant that they will repent and come to know the truth, and that they may escape from the snare of the devil, having been held captive by him to do his will.

A Reading (Lesson) from the Gospel according to Mark [10:17–31]

As Jesus was setting out on his journey, a man ran up and knelt before him, and asked him, "Good Teacher, what must I do to inherit eternal life?" Jesus said to him, "Why do you call me good? No one is good but God alone. You know the commandments: 'You shall not murder; You shall not commit adultery; You shall not steal; You shall not bear false witness; You shall not defraud; Honor your father and mother.'" He said to him, "Teacher, I have kept all these since my youth." Jesus, looking at him, loved him and said, "You lack one thing; go, sell what you own, and give the money to the poor, and you will have treasure in heaven; then come, follow me." When he heard this, he was shocked and went away grieving, for he had many possessions. Then Jesus looked around and said to his disciples, "How hard it will be for those who have wealth to enter the kingdom of God!" And the disciples were perplexed at these words. But Jesus said to them again, "Children, how hard it is to enter the kingdom of God! It is easier for a camel to go through the eye of a needle than for someone who is rich to enter the kingdom of God." They were greatly astounded and said to one another, "Then who can be saved?" Jesus looked at them and said, "For mortals it is impossible, but not for God; for God all things are possible." Peter began to say to him, "Look, we have left everything and followed you." Jesus said, "Truly I tell you, there is no one who has left house or brothers or sisters or mother or father or children or fields, for my sake and for the sake of the good news, who will not receive a hundredfold now in this age—houses, brothers and sisters, mothers and children, and fields, with persecutions—and in the age to come eternal life. But many who are first will be last, and the last will be first."

Friday

Psalm 88 [page 712] ❖ *Psalm 91* [page 719],
Psalm 92 [page 720]

Isaiah 61:1–9 [page 118 above]

A Reading (Lesson) from the Second Letter of Paul to Timothy [3:1–17]

You must understand this, that in the last days distressing times will come. For people will be lovers of themselves, lovers of money, boasters, arrogant, abusive, disobedient to their parents, ungrateful, unholy, inhuman, implacable, slanderers, profligates, brutes, haters of good, treacherous, reckless, swollen with conceit, lovers of pleasure rather than lovers of God, holding to the outward form of godliness but denying its power. Avoid them! For among them are those who make their way into households and captivate silly women, overwhelmed by their sins and swayed by all kinds of desires, who are always being instructed and can never arrive at a knowledge of the truth. As Jannes and Jambres opposed Moses, so these people, of corrupt mind and counterfeit faith, also oppose the truth. But they will not make much progress, because, as in the case of those two men, their folly will become plain to everyone. Now you have observed my teaching, my conduct, my aim in life, my faith, my patience, my love, my steadfastness, my persecutions and suffering the things that happened to me in Antioch, Iconium, and Lystra. What persecutions I endured! Yet the Lord rescued me from all of them. Indeed, all who want to live a godly life in Christ Jesus will be persecuted. But wicked people and impostors will go from bad to worse, deceiving others and being deceived. But as for you, continue in what you have learned and firmly believed, knowing from whom you learned it, and how from childhood you have known the sacred writings that are able to instruct you for salvation through faith in Christ Jesus. All scripture is inspired by God and is useful for teaching, for reproof, for correction, and for training in righteousness, so that everyone who belongs to God may be proficient, equipped for every good work.

A Reading (Lesson) from the Gospel according to Mark [10:32–45]

Jesus and his disciples were on the road, going up to Jerusalem, and Jesus was walking ahead of them; they were amazed, and those who followed were afraid. He took the twelve aside again and began to tell them what was to happen to him, saying, "See, we are going up to Jerusalem, and the Son of Man will be handed over to the chief priests and the scribes, and they will condemn him to death; then they will hand him over to the Gentiles; they will mock him, and spit upon him, and flog him, and kill him; and after three days he will rise again." James and John, the sons of Zebedee, came forward to him and said to him, "Teacher, we want you to do for us whatever we ask of you." And he said to them, "What is it you want me to do for you?" And they said to him, "Grant us to sit, one at your right hand and one at your left, in your glory." But Jesus said to them, "You do not know what you are asking. Are you able to drink the cup that I drink, or be baptized with the baptism that I am baptized with?" They replied, "We are able." Then Jesus said to them, 'The cup that I drink you will drink; and with the baptism with which I am baptized, you will be baptized; but to sit at my right hand or at my left is not mine to grant, but it is for those for whom it has been prepared." When the ten heard this, they began to be angry with James and John. So Jesus called them and said to them, "You know that among the Gentiles those whom they recognize as their rulers lord it over them, and their great ones are tyrants over them. But it is not so among you; but whoever wishes to become great among you must be your servant, and whoever wishes to be first among you must be slave of all. For the Son of Man came not to be served but to serve, and to give his life a ransom for many."

Saturday

Psalm 87 [page 711], *Psalm 90* [page 717] ❖
Psalm 136 [page 789]

A Reading (Lesson) from the Book of Isaiah [61:10—62:5]

I will greatly rejoice in the LORD, my whole being shall exult in my God; for he has clothed me with the garments of salvation, he has covered me with the robe of righteousness, as a bridegroom decks himself with a garland, and as a bride adorns herself with her jewels. For as the earth brings forth its shoots, and as a garden causes what is sown in it to spring up, so the Lord GOD will cause righteousness and praise to spring up before all the nations. For Zion's sake I will not keep silent, and for Jerusalem's sake I will not rest, until her vindication shines out like the dawn, and her salvation like a burning torch. The nations shall see your vindication, and all the kings your glory; and you shall be called by a new name that the mouth of the LORD will give. You shall be a crown of beauty in the hand of the LORD, and a royal diadem in the hand of your God. You shall no more be termed Forsaken, and your land shall no more be termed Desolate; but you shall be called My Delight Is in Her, and your land Married; for the LORD delights in you, and your land shall be married. For as a young man marries a young woman, so shall your builder marry you, and as the bridegroom rejoices over the bride, so shall your God rejoice over you.

A Reading (Lesson) from the Second Letter of Paul to Timothy [4:1–8]

In the presence of God and of Christ Jesus, who is to judge the living and the dead, and in view of his appearing and his kingdom, I solemnly urge you: proclaim the message; be persistent whether the time is favorable or unfavorable; convince, rebuke, and encourage, with the utmost patience in teaching. For the time is coming when people will not put up with sound doctrine, but having itching ears, they will accumulate for themselves teachers to suit their own desires, and will turn away from listening to the truth and wander away to myths. As for you, always be sober, endure suffering, do the work of an evangelist, carry out your ministry fully. As for me, I am already being poured out as a libation, and the time of my departure has come. I have fought the good fight, I have finished the race, I have kept the faith. From now on there is reserved for me the crown of righteousness, which the Lord, the righteous judge, will give me on that day, and not only to me but also to all who have longed for his appearing.

A Reading (Lesson) from the Gospel according to Mark [10:46–52]

Jesus and his disciples came to Jericho. As he and his disciples and a large crowd were leaving Jericho, Bartimaeus son of Timaeus, a blind beggar, was sitting by the roadside. When he heard that it was Jesus of Nazareth, he began to shout out and say, "Jesus, Son of David, have mercy on me!" Many sternly ordered him to be quiet, but he cried out even more loudly, "Son of David, have mercy on me!" Jesus stood still and said, "Call him here." And they called the blind man, saying to him, "Take heart; get up, he is calling you." So throwing off his cloak, he sprang up and came to Jesus. Then Jesus said to him, "What do you want me to do for you?" The blind man said to him, "My teacher, let me see again." Jesus said to him, "Go; your faith has made you well." Immediately he regained his sight and followed him on the way.

Week of 6 Epiphany

Sunday

Psalm 66 [page 673], *Psalm 67* [page 675] ❖
Psalm 19 [page 606], *Psalm 46* [page 649]

A Reading (Lesson) from the Book of Isaiah [62:6–12]

Upon your walls, O Jerusalem, I have posted sentinels; all day and all night they shall never be silent. You who remind the LORD, take no rest, and give him no rest until he establishes Jerusalem and makes it renowned throughout the earth. The LORD has sworn by his right hand and by his mighty arm: I will not again give your grain to be food for your enemies, and foreigners shall not drink the wine for which you have labored; but those who garner it shall eat it and praise the LORD, and those who gather it shall drink it in my holy courts. Go through, go through the gates, prepare the way for the people; build up, build up the highway, clear it of stones, lift up an ensign over the peoples. The LORD has proclaimed to the end of the earth: Say to daughter Zion, "See, your salvation comes; his reward is with him, and his recompense before him." They shall be called, "The Holy People, The Redeemed of the LORD"; and you shall be called, "Sought Out, A City Not Forsaken."

A Reading (Lesson) from the First Letter of John [2:3–11]

Now by this we may be sure that we know him, if we obey his commandments. Whoever says, "I have come to know him," but does not obey his commandments, is a liar, and in such a person the truth does not exist; but whoever obeys his word, truly in this person the love of God has reached perfection. By this we may be sure that we are in him: whoever says, "I abide in him," ought to walk just as he walked. Beloved, I am writing you no new commandment, but an old commandment that you have had from the beginning; the old commandment is the word that you have heard. Yet I am writing you a new commandment that is true in him and in you, because the darkness is passing away and the true light is already shining. Whoever says, "I am in the light," while hating a brother or sister, is still in the darkness. Whoever loves a brother or sister lives in the light, and in such a person there is no cause for stumbling. But whoever hates another believer is in the darkness, walks in the darkness, and does not know the way to go, because the darkness has brought on blindness.

John 8:12–19 [page 84 above]

Monday

Psalm 89:1–18 [page 713] ❖ *Psalm 89:19–52* [page 715]

A Reading (Lesson) from the Book of Isaiah [63:1–6]

"Who is this that comes from Edom, from Bozrah in garments stained crimson? Who is this so splendidly robed, marching in his great might?" "It is I, announcing vindication, mighty to save." "Why are your robes red, and your garments like theirs who tread the winepress?" "I have trodden the winepress alone, and from the peoples no one was with me; I trod them in my anger and trampled them in my wrath; their juice spattered on my garments, and stained all my robes. For the day of vengeance was in my heart, and the year for my redeeming work had come. I looked, but there was no helper; I stared, but there was no one to sustain me; so my own arm brought me victory, and my wrath sustained me. I trampled down peoples in my anger, I crushed them in my wrath, and I poured out their lifeblood on the earth."

A Reading (Lesson) from the First Letter of Paul to Timothy [1:1–17]

Paul, an apostle of Christ Jesus by the command of God our Savior and of Christ Jesus our hope, to Timothy, my loyal child in the faith: Grace, mercy, and peace from God the Father and Christ Jesus our Lord. I urge you, as I did when I was on my way to Macedonia, to remain in Ephesus so that you may instruct certain people not to teach any different doctrine, and not to occupy themselves with myths and endless genealogies that promote speculations rather than the divine training that is known by faith. But the aim of such instruction is love that comes from a pure heart, a good conscience, and sincere faith. Some people have deviated from these and turned to meaningless talk, desiring to be teachers of the law, without understanding either what they are saying or the things about which they make assertions. Now we know that the law is good, if one uses it legitimately. This means understanding that the law is laid down not for the innocent but for the lawless and disobedient, for the godless and sinful, for the unholy and profane, for those who kill their father or mother, for murderers, fornicators, sodomites, slave traders, liars, perjurers, and whatever else is contrary to the sound teaching that conforms to the glorious gospel of the blessed God, which he entrusted to me. I am grateful to Christ Jesus our Lord, who has strengthened me, because he judged me faithful and appointed me to his service, even though I was formerly a blasphemer, a persecutor, and a man of violence. But I received mercy because I had acted ignorantly in unbelief, and the grace of our Lord overflowed for me with the faith and love that are in Christ Jesus. The saying is sure and worthy of full acceptance, that Christ Jesus came into the world to save sinners—of whom I am the foremost. But for that very reason I received mercy, so that in me, as the foremost, Jesus Christ might display the utmost patience, making me an example to those who would come to believe in him for eternal life. To the King of the ages, immortal, invisible, the only God, be honor and glory forever and ever. Amen.

A Reading (Lesson) from the Gospel according to Mark [11:1–11]

When they were approaching Jerusalem, at Bethphage and Bethany, near the Mount of Olives, he sent two of his disciples and said to them, "Go into the village ahead of you, and immediately as you enter it, you will find tied there a colt that has never been ridden; untie it and bring it. If anyone says to you, 'Why are you doing this?' just say this, 'The Lord needs it and will send it back here immediately.' " They went away and found a colt tied near a door, outside in the street. As they were untying it, some of the bystanders said to them, "What are you doing, untying the colt?" They told them what Jesus had said; and they allowed them to take it. Then they brought the colt to Jesus and threw their cloaks on it; and he sat on it. Many people spread their cloaks on the road, and others spread leafy branches that they had cut in the fields. Then those who went ahead and those who followed were shouting, "Hosanna! Blessed is the one who comes in the name of the Lord! Blessed is the coming kingdom of our ancestor David! Hosanna in the highest heaven!" Then he entered Jerusalem and went into the temple; and when he had looked around at everything, as it was already late, he went out to Bethany with the twelve.

Tuesday

Psalm 97 [page 726], *Psalm 99* [page 728], *(Psalm 100* [page 729]) ❖ *Psalm 94* [page 722], *(Psalm 95* [page 724])

A Reading (Lesson) from the Book of Isaiah [63:7–14]

I will recount the gracious deeds of the LORD, the praiseworthy acts of the LORD, because of all that the LORD has done for us, and the great favor to the house of Israel that he has shown them according to his mercy, according to the abundance of his steadfast love. For he said, "Surely they are my people, children who will not deal falsely"; and he became their savior in all their distress. It was no messenger or angel but his presence that saved them; in his love and in his pity he redeemed them; he lifted them up and carried them all the days of old. But they rebelled and grieved his holy spirit; therefore he became their enemy; he himself fought against them. Then they remembered the days of old, of Moses his servant. Where is the one who brought them up out of the sea with the shepherds of his flock? Where is the one who put within them his holy spirit, who caused his glorious arm to march at the right hand of Moses, who divided the waters before them to make for himself an everlasting name, who led them through the depths? Like a horse in the desert, they did not stumble. Like cattle that go down into the valley, the spirit of the LORD gave them rest. Thus you led your people, to make for yourself a glorious name.

A Reading (Lesson) from the First Letter of Paul to Timothy [1:18—2:8]

I am giving you these instructions, Timothy, my child, in accordance with the prophecies made earlier about you, so that by following them you may fight the good fight, having faith and a good conscience. By rejecting conscience, certain persons have suffered shipwreck in the faith; among them are Hymenaeus and Alexander, whom I have turned over to Satan, so that they may learn not to blaspheme. First of all, then, I urge that supplications, prayers, intercessions, and thanksgivings be made for everyone, for kings and all who are in high positions, so that we may lead a quiet and peaceable life in all godliness and dignity. This is right and is acceptable in the sight of God our Savior, who desires everyone to be saved and to come to the knowledge of the truth. For there is one God; there is also one mediator between God and humankind, Christ Jesus, himself human, who gave himself a ransom for all—this was attested at the right time. For this I was appointed a herald and an apostle (I am telling the truth, I am not lying), a teacher of the Gentiles in faith and truth. I desire then, that in every place the men should pray, lifting up holy hands without anger or argument.

A Reading (Lesson) from the Gospel according to Mark [11:12–26]

On the following day, when they came from Bethany, Jesus was hungry. Seeing in the distance a fig tree in leaf, he went to see whether perhaps he would find anything on it. When he came to it, he found nothing but leaves, for it was not the season for figs. He said to it, "May no one ever eat fruit from you again." And his disciples heard it. Then they came to Jerusalem. And he entered the temple and began to drive out those who were selling and those who were buying in the temple, and he overturned the tables of the money changers and the seats of those who sold doves; and he would not allow anyone to carry anything through the temple. He was teaching and saying, "Is it not written, 'My house shall be called a house of prayer for all the nations'? But you have made it a den of robbers." And when the chief priests and the scribes heard it, they kept looking for a way to kill him; for they were afraid of him, because the whole crowd was spellbound by his teaching. And when evening came, Jesus and his disciples went out of the city. In the morning as they passed by, they saw the fig tree withered away to its roots. Then Peter remembered and said to him, "Rabbi, look! The fig tree that you cursed has withered." Jesus answered them, "Have faith in God. Truly I tell you, if you say to this mountain, 'Be taken up and thrown into the sea,' and if you do not doubt in your heart, but believe that what you say will come to pass, it will be done for you. So I tell you, whatever you ask for in prayer, believe that you have received it, and it will be yours. Whenever you stand praying, forgive, if you have anything against anyone; so that your Father in heaven may also forgive you your trespasses."

Wednesday

Psalm 101 [page 730], *Psalm 109:1–4(5–19)20–30* [page 750] ❖ *Psalm 119:121–144* [page 773]

A Reading (Lesson) from the Book of Isaiah [63:15—64:9]

Look down from heaven and see, from your holy and glorious habitation. Where are your zeal and your might? The yearning of your heart and your compassion? They are withheld from me. For you are our father, though Abraham does not know us and Israel does not acknowledge us; you, O LORD, are our father; our Redeemer from of old is your name. Why, O LORD, do you make us stray from your ways and harden our heart, so that we do not fear you? Turn back for the sake of your servants, for the sake of the tribes that are your heritage. Your holy people took possession for a little while; but now our adversaries have trampled down your sanctuary. We have long been like those whom you do not rule, like those not called by your name. O that you would tear open the heavens and come down, so that the mountains would quake at your presence—as when fire kindles brushwood and the fire causes water to boil—to make your name known to your adversaries, so that the nations might tremble at your presence! When you did awesome deeds that we did not expect, you came down, the mountains quaked at your presence. From ages past no one has heard, no ear has perceived, no eye has seen any God besides you, who works for those who wait for him. You meet those who gladly do right, those who remember you in your ways. But you were angry, and we sinned; because you hid yourself we transgressed. We have all become like one who is unclean, and all our righteous deeds are like a filthy cloth. We all fade like a leaf, and our iniquities, like the wind, take us away. There is no one who calls on your name, or attempts to take hold of you; for you have hidden your face from us, and have delivered us into the hand of our iniquity. Yet, O LORD, you are our Father; we are the clay, and you are our potter; we are all the work of your hand. Do not be exceedingly angry, O LORD, and do not remember iniquity forever. Now consider, we are all your people.

A Reading (Lesson) from the First Letter of Paul to Timothy [3:1–16]

The saying is sure: whoever aspires to the office of bishop desires a noble task. Now a bishop must be above reproach, married only once, temperate, sensible, respectable, hospitable, an apt teacher, not a drunkard, not violent but gentle, not quarrelsome, and not a lover of money. He must manage his own household well, keeping his children submissive and respectful in every way—for if someone does not know how to manage his own household, how can he take care of God's church? He must not be a recent convert, or he may be puffed up with conceit and fall into the condemnation of the devil. Moreover, he must be well thought of by outsiders, so that he may not fall into disgrace and the snare of the devil. Deacons likewise must be serious, not double-tongued, not indulging in much wine, not greedy for money; they must hold fast to the mystery of the faith with a clear conscience. And let them first be tested; then, if they prove themselves blameless, let them serve as deacons. Women likewise must be serious, not slanderers, but temperate, faithful in all things. Let deacons be married only once, and let them manage their children and their households well; for those who serve well as deacons gain a good standing for themselves and great boldness in the faith that is in Christ Jesus. I hope to come to you soon, but I am writing these instructions to you so that, if I am delayed, you may know how one ought to behave in the household of God, which is the church of the living God, the pillar and bulwark of the truth. Without any doubt, the mystery of our religion is great: He was revealed in flesh, vindicated in spirit, seen by angels, proclaimed among Gentiles, believed in throughout the world, taken up in glory.

A Reading (Lesson) from the Gospel according to Mark [11:27–12:12]

Again they came to Jerusalem. As Jesus was walking in the temple, the chief priests, the scribes, and the elders came to him and said, "By what authority are you doing these things? Who gave you this authority to do them?" Jesus said to them, "I will ask you one question; answer me, and I will tell you by what authority I do these things. Did the baptism of John come from heaven, or was it of human origin? Answer me." They argued with one another, "If we say, 'From heaven,' he will say, 'Why then did you not believe him?' But shall we say, 'Of human origin'?"—they were afraid of the crowd, for all regarded John as truly a prophet. So they answered Jesus, "We do not know." And Jesus said to them, "Neither will I tell you by what authority I am doing these things." Then Jesus began to speak to them in parables. "A man planted a vineyard, put a fence around it, dug a pit for the wine press, and built a watchtower; then he leased it to tenants and went to another country. When the season came, he sent a slave to the tenants to collect from them his share of the produce of the vineyard. But they seized him, and beat him, and sent him away empty-handed. And again he sent another slave to them; this one they beat over the head and insulted. Then he sent another, and that one they killed. And so it was with many others; some they beat, and others they killed. He had still one other, a beloved son. Finally he sent him to them, saying, 'They will respect my son.' But those tenants said to one another, 'This is the heir; come, let us kill him, and the inheritance will be ours.' So they seized him, killed him, and threw him out of the vineyard. What then will the owner of the vineyard do? He will come and destroy the tenants and give the vineyard to others. Have you not read this scripture: 'The stone that the builders rejected has become the cornerstone; this was the Lord's doing, and it is amazing in our eyes'?" When they realized that he had told this parable against them, they wanted to arrest him, but they feared the crowd. So they left him and went away.

Thursday

Psalm 105:1–22 [page 738] ❖ *Psalm 105:23–45* [page 739]

A Reading (Lesson) from the Book of Isaiah [65:1–12]

I was ready to be sought out by those who did not ask, to be found by those who did not seek me. I said, "Here I am, here I am," to a nation that did not call on my name. I held out my hands all day long to a rebellious people, who walk in a way that is not good, following their own devices; a people who provoke me to my face continually, sacrificing in gardens and offering incense on bricks; who sit inside tombs, and spend the night in secret places; who eat swine's flesh, with broth of abominable things in their vessels; who say, "Keep to yourself, do not come near me, for I am too holy for you." These are a smoke in my nostrils, a fire that burns all day long. See, it is written before me: I will not keep silent, but I will repay; I will indeed repay into their laps their iniquities and their ancestors' iniquities together, says the LORD; because they offered incense on the mountains and reviled me on the hills, I will measure into their laps full payment for their actions. Thus says the LORD: As the wine is found in the cluster, and they say, "Do not destroy it, for there is a blessing in it," so I will do for my servants' sake, and not destroy them all. I will bring forth descendants from Jacob, and from Judah inheritors of my mountains; my chosen shall inherit it, and my servants shall settle there. Sharon shall become a pasture for flocks, and the Valley of Achor a place for herds to lie down, for my people who have sought me. But you who forsake the LORD, who forget my holy mountain, who set a table for Fortune and fill cups of mixed wine for Destiny; I will destine you to the sword, and all of you shall bow down to the slaughter; because, when I called, you did not answer, when I spoke, you did not listen, but you did what was evil in my sight, and chose what I did not delight in.

A Reading (Lesson) from the First Letter of Paul to Timothy [4:1-16]

Now the Spirit expressly says that in later times some will renounce the faith by paying attention to deceitful spirits and teachings of demons, through the hypocrisy of liars whose consciences are seared with a hot iron. They forbid marriage and demand abstinence from foods, which God created to be received with thanksgiving by those who believe and know the truth. For everything created by God is good, and nothing is to be rejected, provided it is received with thanksgiving; for it is sanctified by God's word and by prayer. If you put these instructions before the brothers and sisters, you will be a good servant of Christ Jesus, nourished on the words of the faith and of the sound teaching that you have followed. Have nothing to do with profane myths and old wives' tales. Train yourself in godliness, for, while physical training is of some value, godliness is valuable in every way, holding promise for both the present life and the life to come. The saying is sure and worthy of full acceptance. For to this end we toil and struggle, because we have our hope set on the living God, who is the Savior of all people, especially of those who believe. These are the things you must insist on and teach. Let no one despise your youth, but set the believers an example in speech and conduct, in love, in faith, in purity. Until I arrive, give attention to the public reading of scripture, to exhorting, to teaching. Do not neglect the gift that is in you, which was given to you through prophecy with the laying on of hands by the council of elders. Put these things into practice, devote yourself to them, so that all may see your progress. Pay close attention to yourself and to your teaching; continue in these things, for in doing this you will save both yourself and your hearers.

*A Reading (Lesson) from the Gospel according to
Mark* [12:13–27]

The chief priests and the scribes and the elders sent to
Jesus some of the Pharisees and some of the Herodians, to
trap him in what he said. And they came and said to him,
"Teacher, we know that you are sincere, and show
deference to no one; for you do not regard people with
partiality, but teach the way of God in accordance with
truth. Is it lawful to pay taxes to the emperor, or not?
Should we pay them, or should we not?" But knowing
their hypocrisy, he said to them, "Why are you putting me
to the test? Bring me a denarius and let me see it." And
they brought one. Then he said to them, "Whose head is
this, and whose title?" They answered, "The emperor's."
Jesus said to them, "Give to the emperor the things that
are the emperor's, and to God the things that are God's."
And they were utterly amazed at him. Some Sadducees,
who say there is no resurrection, came to him and asked
him a question, saying, "Teacher, Moses wrote for us that
'if a man's brother dies, leaving a wife but no child, the
man shall marry the widow and raise up children for his
brother.' There were seven brothers; the first married and,
when he died, left no children; and the second married her
and died, leaving no children; and the third likewise; none
of the seven left children. Last of all the woman herself
died. In the resurrection whose wife will she be? For the
seven had married her." Jesus said to them, "Is not this
the reason you are wrong, that you know neither the
scriptures nor the power of God? For when they rise from
the dead, they neither marry nor are given in marriage,
but are like angels in heaven. And as for the dead being
raised, have you not read in the book of Moses, in the
story about the bush, how God said to him, 'I am the God

of Abraham, the God of Isaac, and the God of Jacob'? He is God not of the dead, but of the living; you are quite wrong."

Friday

Psalm 102 [page 731]   ❖   *Psalm 107:1–32* [page 746]

A Reading (Lesson) from the Book of Isaiah [65:17–25]

For I am about to create new heavens and a new earth; the former things shall not be remembered or come to mind. But be glad and rejoice forever in what I am creating; for I am about to create Jerusalem as a joy, and its people as a delight. I will rejoice in Jerusalem, and delight in my people; no more shall the sound of weeping be heard in it, or the cry of distress. No more shall there be in it an infant that lives but a few days, or an old person who does not live out a lifetime; for one who dies at a hundred years will be considered a youth, and one who falls short of a hundred will be considered accursed. They shall build houses and inhabit them; they shall plant vineyards and eat their fruit. They shall not build and another inhabit; they shall not plant and another eat; for like the days of a tree shall the days of my people be, and my chosen shall long enjoy the work of their hands. They shall not labor in vain, or bear children for calamity; for they shall be offspring blessed by the LORD—and their descendants as well. Before they call I will answer, while they are yet speaking I will hear. The wolf and the lamb shall feed together, the lion shall eat straw like the ox; but the serpent—its food shall be dust! They shall not hurt or destroy on all my holy mountain, says the LORD.

A Reading (Lesson) from the First Letter of Paul to Timothy [5:17–22(23–25)]

Let the elders who rule well be considered worthy of double honor, especially those who labor in preaching and teaching; for the scripture says, "You shall not muzzle an ox while it is treading out the grain," and, "The laborer deserves to be paid." Never accept any accusation against an elder except on the evidence of two or three witnesses. As for those who persist in sin, rebuke them in the presence of all, so that the rest also may stand in fear. In the presence of God and of Christ Jesus and of the elect angels, I warn you to keep these instructions without prejudice, doing nothing on the basis of partiality. Do not ordain anyone hastily, and do not participate in the sins of others; keep yourself pure.

> No longer drink only water, but take a little wine for the sake of your stomach and your frequent ailments. The sins of some people are conspicuous and precede them to judgment, while the sins of others follow them there. So also good works are conspicuous; and even when they are not, they cannot remain hidden.

A Reading (Lesson) from the Gospel according to Mark [12:28–34]

One of the scribes came near and heard them disputing with one another, and seeing that Jesus answered them well, he asked him, "Which commandment is the first of all?" Jesus answered, "The first is, 'Hear, O Israel: the Lord our God, the Lord is one; you shall love the Lord your God with all your heart, and with all your soul, and with all your mind, and with all your strength.' The second is this, 'You shall love your neighbor as yourself.'

There is no other commandment greater than these." Then the scribe said to him, "You are right, Teacher; you have truly said that 'he is one, and besides him there is no other'; and 'to love him with all the heart, and with all the understanding, and with all the strength', and 'to love one's neighbor as oneself,'—this is much more important than all whole burnt offerings and sacrifices." When Jesus saw that he answered wisely, he said to him, "You are not far from the kingdom of God." After that no one dared to ask him any question.

Saturday

Psalm 107:33–43 [page 748],
Psalm 108:1–6(7–13) [page 749] ❖ *Psalm 33* [page 626]

A Reading (Lesson) from the Book of Isaiah [66:1–6]

Thus says the LORD: Heaven is my throne and the earth is my footstool; what is the house that you would build for me, and what is my resting place? All these things my hand has made, and so all these things are mine, says the LORD. But this is the one to whom I will look, to the humble and contrite in spirit, who trembles at my word. Whoever slaughters an ox is like one who kills a human being; whoever sacrifices a lamb, like one who breaks a dog's neck; whoever presents a grain offering, like one who offers swine's blood; whoever makes a memorial offering of frankincense, like one who blesses an idol. These have chosen their own ways, and in their abominations they take delight; I also will choose to mock them, and bring upon them what they fear; because, when I called, no one answered, when I spoke, they did not listen; but they did what was evil in my sight, and chose what did not please me. Hear the word of the LORD, you who tremble at his word: Your own people who hate you and reject you for my name's sake have said, "Let the LORD be glorified, so that we may see your joy"; but it is they who shall be put to shame. Listen, an uproar from the city! A voice from the temple! The voice of the LORD, dealing retribution to his enemies!

A Reading (Lesson) from the First Letter of Paul to Timothy [6:6–21]

There is great gain in godliness combined with contentment; for we brought nothing into the world, so that we can take nothing out of it; but if we have food and clothing, we will be content with these. But those who want to be rich fall into temptation and are trapped by many senseless and harmful desires that plunge people into ruin and destruction. For the love of money is a root of all kinds of evil, and in their eagerness to be rich some have wandered away from the faith and pierced themselves with many pains. But as for you, man of God, shun all this; pursue righteousness, godliness, faith, love, endurance, gentleness. Fight the good fight of the faith; take hold of the eternal life, to which you were called and for which you made the good confession in the presence of many witnesses. In the presence of God, who gives life to all things, and of Christ Jesus, who in his testimony before Pontius Pilate made the good confession, I charge you to keep the commandment without spot or blame until the manifestation of our Lord Jesus Christ, which he will bring about at the right time—he who is the blessed and only Sovereign, the King of kings and Lord of lords. It is he alone who has immortality and dwells in unapproachable light, whom no one has ever seen or can see; to him be honor and eternal dominion. Amen. As for those who in the present age are rich, command them not to be haughty, or to set their hopes on the uncertainty of riches, but rather on God who richly provides us with everything for our enjoyment. They are to do good, to be rich in good works, generous, and ready to share, thus storing up for themselves the treasure of a good foundation for the future, so that they may take hold of the life that really is life. Timothy, guard what has been entrusted to you. Avoid the profane chatter and contradictions of what is falsely called knowledge; by professing it some have missed the mark as regards the faith. Grace be with you.

A Reading (Lesson) from the Gospel according to Mark [12:35–44]

While Jesus was teaching in the temple, he said, "How can the scribes say that the Messiah is the son of David? David himself, by the Holy Spirit, declared, 'The Lord said to my Lord, "Sit at my right hand, until I put your enemies under your feet." ' David himself calls him Lord; so how can he be his son?" And the large crowd was listening to him with delight. As he taught, he said, "Beware of the scribes, who like to walk around in long robes, and to be greeted with respect in the marketplaces, and to have the best seats in the synagogues and places of honor at banquets! They devour widows' houses and for the sake of appearance say long prayers. They will receive the greater condemnation." He sat down opposite the treasury, and watched the crowd putting money into the treasury. Many rich people put in large sums. A poor widow came and put in two small copper coins, which are worth a penny. Then he called his disciples and said to them, "Truly I tell you, this poor widow has put in more than all those who are contributing to the treasury. For all of them have contributed out of their abundance; but she out of her poverty has put in everything she had, all she had to live on."

Week of 7 Epiphany

Sunday

Psalm 118 [page 760] ❖ *Psalm 145* [page 801]

A Reading (Lesson) from the Book of Isaiah [66:7–14]

Thus says the LORD: Before she was in labor she gave birth; before her pain came upon her she delivered a son. Who has heard of such a thing? Who has seen such things? Shall a land be born in one day? Shall a nation be delivered in one moment? Yet as soon as Zion was in labor she delivered her children. Shall I open the womb and not deliver? says the LORD; shall I, the one who delivers, shut the womb? says your God. Rejoice with Jerusalem, and be glad for her, all you who love her; rejoice with her in joy, all you who mourn over her—that you may nurse and be satisfied from her consoling breast; that you may drink deeply with delight from her glorious bosom. For thus says the LORD: I will extend prosperity to her like a river, and the wealth of the nations like an overflowing stream; and you shall nurse and be carried on her arm, and dandled on her knees. As a mother comforts her child, so I will comfort you; you shall be comforted in Jerusalem. You shall see, and your heart shall rejoice; your bodies shall flourish like the grass; and it shall be known that the hand of the LORD is with his servants, and his indignation is against his enemies.

A Reading (Lesson) from the First Letter of John [3:4–10]

Everyone who commits sin is guilty of lawlessness; sin is lawlessness. You know that he was revealed to take away sins, and in him there is no sin. No one who abides in him sins; no one who sins has either seen him or known him. Little children, let no one deceive you. Everyone who does what is right is righteous, just as he is righteous. Everyone who commits sin is a child of the devil; for the devil has been sinning from the beginning. The Son of God was revealed for this purpose, to destroy the works of the devil. Those who have been born of God do not sin, because God's seed abides in them; they cannot sin, because they have been born of God. The children of God and the children of the devil are revealed in this way: all who do not do what is right are not from God, nor are those who do not love their brothers and sisters.

A Reading (Lesson) from the Gospel according to John [10:7–16]

Again Jesus said to the Pharisees, "Very truly, I tell you, I am the gate for the sheep. All who came before me are thieves and bandits; but the sheep did not listen to them. I am the gate. Whoever enters by me will be saved, and will come in and go out and find pasture. The thief comes only to steal and kill and destroy. I came that they may have life, and have it abundantly. I am the good shepherd. The good shepherd lays down his life for the sheep. The hired hand, who is not the shepherd and does not own the sheep, sees the wolf coming and leaves the sheep and runs away—and the wolf snatches them and scatters them. The hired hand runs away because a hired hand does not care for the sheep. I am the good shepherd. I know my own and my own know me, just as the Father knows me and I know the Father. And I lay down my life for the sheep. I have other sheep that do not belong to this fold. I must bring them also, and they will listen to my voice. So there will be one flock, one shepherd."

Monday

Psalm 106:1–18 [page 741]   ∴   *Psalm 106:19–48* [page 743]

A Reading (Lesson) from the Book of Ruth [1:1–14]

In the days when the judges ruled, there was a famine in the land, and a certain man of Bethlehem in Judah went to live in the country of Moab, he and his wife and two sons. The name of the man was Elimelech and the name of his wife Naomi, and the names of his two sons were Mahlon and Chilion; they were Ephrathites from Bethlehem in Judah. They went into the country of Moab and remained there. But Elimelech, the husband of Naomi, died, and she was left with her two sons. These took Moabite wives; the name of the one was Orpah and the name of the other Ruth. When they had lived there about ten years, both Mahlon and Chilion also died, so that the woman was left without her two sons and her husband. Then she started to return with her daughters-in-law from the country of Moab, for she had heard in the country of Moab that the LORD had considered his people and given them food. So she set out from the place where she had been living, she and her two daughters-in-law, and they went on their way to go back to the land of Judah. But Naomi said to her two daughters-in-law, "Go back each of you to your mother's house. May the LORD deal kindly with you, as you have dealt with the dead and with me. The LORD grant that you may find security, each of you in the house of your husband." Then she kissed them, and they wept aloud. They said to her, "No, we will return with you to your people." But Naomi said, "Turn back, my daughters, why will you go with me? Do I still have sons in my womb that they may become your husbands? Turn back, my daughters, go your way, for I am too old to have a husband. Even if I thought there was hope for me, even if I should have a husband tonight and bear sons, would you then wait until they were grown? Would you then refrain from marrying? No, my daughters, it has been far more bitter for me than for you, because the hand of the LORD has turned against me." Then they wept aloud again. Orpah kissed her mother-in-law, but Ruth clung to her.

A Reading (Lesson) from the Second Letter of Paul to the Corinthians [1:1–11]

Paul, an apostle of Christ Jesus by the will of God, and Timothy our brother, to the church of God that is in Corinth, including all the saints throughout Achaia: Grace to you and peace from God our Father and the Lord Jesus Christ. Blessed be the God and Father of our Lord Jesus Christ, the Father of mercies and the God of all consolation, who consoles us in all our affliction, so that we may be able to console those who are in any affliction with the consolation with which we ourselves are consoled by God. For just as the sufferings of Christ are abundant for us, so also our consolation is abundant through Christ. If we are being afflicted, it is for your consolation and salvation; if we are being consoled, it is for your consolation, which you experience when you patiently endure the same sufferings that we are also suffering. Our hope for you is unshaken; for we know that as you share in our sufferings, so also you share in our consolation. We do not want you to be unaware, brothers and sisters, of the affliction we experienced in Asia; for we were so utterly, unbearably crushed that we despaired of life itself. Indeed, we felt that we had received the sentence of death so that we would rely not on ourselves but on God who raises the dead. He who rescued us from so deadly a peril will continue to rescue us; on him we have set our hope that he will rescue us again, as you also join in helping us by your prayers, so that many will give thanks on our behalf for the blessing granted us through the prayers of many.

A Reading (Lesson) from the Gospel according to Matthew [5:1–12]

When Jesus saw the crowds, he went up the mountain; and after he sat down, his disciples came to him. Then he began to speak, and taught them, saying: "Blessed are the poor in spirit, for theirs is the kingdom of heaven. Blessed are those who mourn, for they will be comforted. Blessed are the meek, for they will inherit the earth. Blessed are those who hunger and thirst for righteousness, for they will be filled. Blessed are the merciful, for they will receive mercy. Blessed are the pure in heart, for they will see God. Blessed are the peacemakers, for they will be called children of God. Blessed are those who are persecuted for righteousness' sake, for theirs is the kingdom of heaven. Blessed are you when people revile you and persecute you and utter all kinds of evil against you falsely on my account. Rejoice and be glad, for your reward is great in heaven, for in the same way they persecuted the prophets who were before you."

Tuesday

(Psalm 120 [page 778]), *Psalm 121* [page 779],
Psalm 122 [page 779], *Psalm 123* [page 780] ❖
Psalm 124 [page 781], *Psalm 125* [page 781],
Psalm 126 [page 782], *(Psalm 127* [page 782])

A Reading (Lesson) from the Book of Ruth [1:15–22]

Naomi said to Ruth, "See, your sister-in-law has gone back to her people and to her gods; return after your sister-in-law." But Ruth said, "Do not press me to leave you or to turn back from following you! Where you go, I will go; Where you lodge, I will lodge; your people shall be my people, and your God my God. Where you die, I will die—there will I be buried. May the Lord do thus and so to me, and more as well, if even death parts me from you!" When Naomi saw that she was determined to go with her, she said no more to her. So the two of them went on until they came to Bethlehem. When they came to Bethlehem, the whole town was stirred because of them; and the women said, "Is this Naomi?" She said to them, "Call me no longer Naomi, call me Mara, for the Almighty has dealt bitterly with me. I went away full, but the Lord has brought me back empty; why call me Naomi when the Lord has dealt harshly with me, and the Almighty has brought calamity upon me?" So Naomi returned together with Ruth the Moabite, her daughter-in-law, who came back with her from the country of Moab. They came to Bethlehem at the beginning of the barley harvest.

A Reading (Lesson) from the Second Letter of Paul to the Corinthians [1:12–22]

Indeed, this is our boast, the testimony of our conscience: we have behaved in the world with frankness and godly sincerity, not by earthly wisdom but by the grace of God—and all the more toward you. For we write you nothing other than what you can read and also understand; I hope you will understand until the end—as you have already understood us in part—that on the day of the Lord Jesus we are your boast even as you are our boast. Since I was sure of this, I wanted to come to you first, so that you might have a double favor; I wanted to visit you on my way to Macedonia, and to come back to you from Macedonia and have you send me on to Judea. Was I vacillating when I wanted to do this? Do I make my plans according to ordinary human standards, ready to say "Yes, yes" and "No, no" at the same time? As surely as God is faithful, our word to you has not been "Yes and No." For the Son of God, Jesus Christ, whom we proclaimed among you, Silvanus and Timothy and I, was not "Yes and No"; but in him it is always "Yes." For in him every one of God's promises is a "Yes." For this reason it is through him that we say the "Amen," to the glory of God. But it is God who establishes us with you in Christ and has anointed us, by putting his seal on us and giving us his Spirit in our hearts as a first installment.

A Reading (Lesson) from the Gospel according to Matthew [5:13–20]

Jesus opened his mouth and taught his disciples, saying, "You are the salt of the earth; but if salt has lost its taste, how can its saltiness be restored? It is no longer good for anything, but is thrown out and trampled under foot. You are the light of the world. A city built on a hill cannot be hid. No one after lighting a lamp puts it under the bushel basket, but on the lampstand, and it gives light to all in the house. In the same way, let your light shine before others, so that they may see your good works and give glory to your Father in heaven. Do not think that I have come to abolish the law or the prophets; I have come not to abolish but to fulfill. For truly I tell you, until heaven and earth pass away, not one letter, not one stroke of a letter, will pass from the law until all is accomplished. Therefore, whoever breaks one of the least of these commandments, and teaches others to do the same, will be called least in the kingdom of heaven; but whoever does them and teaches them will be called great in the kingdom of heaven. For I tell you, unless your righteousness exceeds that of the scribes and Pharisees, you will never enter the kingdom of heaven."

Wednesday

Psalm 119:145–176 [page 775] ❖ *Psalm 128* [page 783], *Psalm 129* [page 784], *Psalm 130* [page 784]

A Reading (Lesson) from the Book of Ruth [2:1–13]

Now Naomi had a kinsman on her husband's side, a prominent rich man, of the family of Elimelech, whose name was Boaz. And Ruth the Moabite said to Naomi, "Let me go to the field and glean among the ears of grain, behind someone in whose sight I may find favor." She said to her, "Go, my daughter." So she went. She came and gleaned in the field behind the reapers. As it happened, she came to the part of the field belonging to Boaz, who was of the family of Elimelech. Just then Boaz came from Bethlehem. He said to the reapers, "The LORD be with you." They answered, "The LORD bless you." Then Boaz said to his servant who was in charge of the reapers, "To whom does this young woman belong?" The servant who was in charge of the reapers answered, "She is the Moabite who came back with Naomi from the country of Moab. She said, 'Please, let me glean and gather among the sheaves behind the reapers.' So she came, and she has been on her feet from early this morning until now, without resting even for a moment." Then Boaz said to Ruth, "Now listen, my daughter, do not go to glean in another field or leave this one, but keep close to my young women. Keep your eyes on the field that is being reaped, and follow behind them. I have ordered the young men not to bother you. If you get thirsty, go to the vessels and drink from what the young men have drawn." Then she fell prostrate, with her face to the ground, and said to him, "Why have I found favor in your sight, that you should take notice of me, when I am a foreigner?" But Boaz answered her, "All that you have done for your mother-in-law since the death of your husband has been fully told me, and how you left your father and mother and your native land and came to a people that you did not know before. May the LORD reward you for your deeds, and may you have a full reward from the LORD, the God of Israel, under whose wings you have come for refuge!" Then she said, "May I continue to find favor in your sight, my lord, for you have comforted me and spoken kindly to your servant, even though I am not one of your servants."

A Reading (Lesson) from the Second Letter of Paul to the Corinthians [1:23—2:17]

I call on God as witness against me: it was to spare you that I did not come again to Corinth. I do not mean to imply that we lord it over your faith; rather, we are workers with you for your joy, because you stand firm in the faith. So I made up my mind not to make you another painful visit. For if I cause you pain, who is there to make me glad but the one whom I have pained? And I wrote as I did, so that when I came, I might not suffer pain from those who should have made me rejoice; for I am confident about all of you, that my joy would be the joy of all of you. For I wrote you out of much distress and anguish of heart and with many tears, not to cause you pain, but to let you know the abundant love that I have for you. But if anyone has caused pain, he has caused it not to me, but to some extent—not to exaggerate it—to all of you. This punishment by the majority is enough for such a person; so now instead you should forgive and console him, so that he may not be overwhelmed by excessive sorrow. So I urge you to reaffirm your love for him. I wrote for this reason: to test you and to know whether you are obedient in everything. Anyone whom you forgive, I also forgive. What I have forgiven, if I have forgiven anything, has been for your sake in the presence of Christ. And we do this so that we may not be outwitted by Satan; for we are not ignorant of his designs. When I came to Troas to proclaim the good news of Christ, a door was opened for me in the Lord; but my mind could not rest because I did not find my brother Titus there. So I said farewell to them and went on to Macedonia. But thanks be to God, who in Christ always leads us in triumphal procession, and through us spreads in every place the fragrance that comes from knowing him. For we are the aroma of Christ to God among those who are being saved and among those who are perishing; to the one a fragrance from death to death, to the other a fragrance from life to life. Who is sufficient for these things? For we are not peddlers of God's word like so many; but in Christ we speak as persons of sincerity, as persons sent from God and standing in his presence.

A Reading (Lesson) from the Gospel according to Matthew [5:21–26]

Jesus opened his mouth and taught his disciples, saying: You have heard that it was said to those of ancient times, You shall not murder'; and 'whoever murders shall be liable to judgment.' But I say to you that if you are angry with a brother or sister, you will be liable to judgment; and if you insult a brother or sister, you will be liable to the council; and if you say, 'You fool,' you will be liable to the hell of fire. So when you are offering your gift at the altar, if you remember that your brother or sister has something against you, leave your gift there before the altar and go; first be reconciled to your brother or sister, and then come and offer your gift. Come to terms quickly with your accuser while you are on the way to court with him, or your accuser may hand you over to the judge, and the judge to the guard, and you will be thrown into prison. Truly I tell you, you will never get out until you have paid the last penny."

Thursday

Psalm 131 [page 785], *Psalm 132* [page 785], *(Psalm 133* [page 787]) ❖ *Psalm 134* [page 787], *Psalm 135* [page 788]

A Reading (Lesson) from the Book of Ruth [2:14–23]

At mealtime Boaz said to Ruth, "Come here, and eat some of this bread, and dip your morsel in the sour wine." So she sat beside the reapers, and he heaped up for her some parched grain. She ate until she was satisfied, and she had some left over. When she got up to glean, Boaz instructed his young men, "Let her glean even among the standing sheaves, and do not reproach her. You must also pull out some handfuls for her from the bundles, and leave them for her to glean, and do not rebuke her." So she gleaned in the field until evening. Then she beat out what she had gleaned, and it was about an ephah of barley. She picked it up and came into the town, and her mother-in-law saw how much she had gleaned. Then she took out and gave her what was left over after she herself had been satisfied. Her mother-in-law said to her, "Where did you glean today? And where have you worked? Blessed be the man who took notice of you." So she told her mother-in-law with whom she had worked, and said, "The name of the man with whom I worked today is Boaz." Then Naomi said to her daughter-in-law, "Blessed be he by the Lord, whose kindness has not forsaken the living or the dead!" Naomi also said to her, "The man is a relative of ours, one of our nearest kin." Then Ruth the Moabite said, "He even said to me, 'Stay close by my servants, until they have finished all my harvest.' " Naomi said to Ruth, her daughter-in-law, "It is better, my daughter, that you go out with his young women, otherwise you might be bothered in another field." So she stayed close to the young women of Boaz, gleaning until the end of the barley and wheat harvests; and she lived with her mother-in-law.

*A Reading (Lesson) from the Second Letter of Paul to the
Corinthians* [3:1–18]

Are we beginning to commend ourselves again? Surely we
do not need, as some do, letters of recommendation to
you or from you, do we? You yourselves are our letter,
written on our hearts, to be known and read by all; and
you show that you are a letter of Christ, prepared by us,
written not with ink but with the Spirit of the living God,
not on tablets of stone but on tablets of human hearts.
Such is the confidence that we have through Christ toward
God. Not that we are competent of ourselves to claim
anything as coming from us; our competence is from God,
who has made us competent to be ministers of a new
covenant, not of letter but of spirit; for the letter kills, but
the Spirit gives life. Now if the ministry of death, chiseled
in letters on stone tablets, came in glory so that the people
of Israel could not gaze at Moses' face because of the
glory of his face, a glory now set aside, how much more
will the ministry of the Spirit come in glory? For if there
was glory in the ministry of condemnation, much more
does the ministry of justification abound in glory! Indeed,
what once had glory has lost its glory because of the
greater glory; for if what was set aside came through
glory, much more has the permanent come in glory! Since,
then, we have such a hope, we act with great boldness,
not like Moses, who put a veil over his face to keep the
people of Israel from gazing at the end of the glory that
was being set aside. But their minds were hardened.
Indeed, to this very day, when they hear the reading of the
old covenant, that same veil is still there, since only in
Christ is it set aside. Indeed, to this very day whenever
Moses is read, a veil lies over their minds; but when one
turns to the Lord, the veil is removed. Now the Lord is

the Spirit, and where the Spirit of the Lord is, there is freedom. And all of us, with unveiled faces, seeing the glory of the Lord as though reflected in a mirror, are being transformed into the same image from one degree of glory to another; for this comes from the Lord, the Spirit.

A Reading (Lesson) from the Gospel according to Matthew [5:27–37]

Jesus opened his mouth and taught his disciples, saying: "You have heard that it was said, 'You shall not commit adultery.' But I say to you that everyone who looks at a woman with lust has already committed adultery with her in his heart. If your right eye causes you to sin, tear it out and throw it away; it is better for you to lose one of your members than for your whole body to be thrown into hell. And if your right hand causes you to sin, cut it off and throw it away; it is better for you to lose one of your members than for your whole body to go into hell. "It was also said, 'Whoever divorces his wife, let him give her a certificate of divorce.' But I say to you that anyone who divorces his wife, except on the ground of unchastity, causes her to commit adultery; and whoever marries a divorced woman commits adultery. Again, you have heard that it was said to those of ancient times, 'You shall not swear falsely, but carry out the vows you have made to the Lord.' But I say to you, Do not swear at all, either by heaven, for it is the throne of God, or by the earth, for it is the city of the great King. And do not swear by your head, for you cannot make one hair white or black. Let your word be 'Yes, Yes' or 'No, No'; anything more than this comes from the evil one."

Friday

Psalm 140 [page 796], *Psalm 142* [page 798] ❖
Psalm 141 [page 797], *Psalm 143:1–11(12)* [page 798]

A Reading (Lesson) from the Book of Ruth [3:1–18]

Naomi her mother-in-law said to Ruth, "My daughter, I need to seek some security for you, so that it may be well with you. Now here is our kinsman Boaz, with whose young women you have been working. See, he is winnowing barley tonight at the threshing floor. Now wash and anoint yourself, and put on your best clothes and go down to the threshing floor; but do not make yourself known to the man until he has finished eating and drinking. When he lies down, observe the place where he lies; then, go and uncover his feet and lie down; and he will tell you what to do." She said to her, "All that you tell me I will do." So she went down to the threshing floor and did just as her mother-in-law had instructed her. When Boaz had eaten and drunk, and he was in a contented mood, he went to lie down at the end of the heap of grain. Then she came stealthily and uncovered his feet, and lay down. At midnight the man was startled, and turned over, and there, lying at his feet, was a woman! He said, "Who are you?" And she answered, "I am Ruth, your servant; spread your cloak over your servant, for you are next-of-kin." He said, "May you be blessed by the LORD, my daughter; this last instance of your loyalty is better than the first; you have not gone after young men, whether poor or rich. And now, my daughter, do not be afraid, I will do for you all that you ask, for all the assembly of my people know that you are a worthy woman. But now, though it is true that I am a near kinsman, there is another kinsman more closely related than I. Remain this night, and in the morning, if he will act as next-of-kin for you, good; let him do it. If he is not willing to act as next-of-kin for you, then, as the LORD lives, I will act as next-of-kin for you. Lie down until the morning." So she lay at his feet until morning, but got up before one person could recognize another; for he said, "It must not be known that the woman came to the threshing floor." Then he said, "Bring the cloak you are wearing and hold it out." So she held it, and he measured out six measures of barley, and put it on her back; then he went into the city. She came to her mother-in-law, who said, "How did things go with you, my daughter?" Then she told her all that the man had done for her, saying, "He gave me these six measures of barley, for he said, 'Do not go back to your mother-in-law empty-handed.' " She replied, "Wait, my daughter, until you learn how the matter turns out, for the man will not rest, but will settle the matter today."

A Reading (Lesson) from the Second Letter of Paul to the Corinthians [4:1–12]

Since it is by God's mercy that we are engaged in this ministry, we do not lose heart. We have renounced the shameful things that one hides; we refuse to practice cunning or to falsify God's word; but by the open statement of the truth we commend ourselves to the conscience of everyone in the sight of God. And even if our gospel is veiled, it is veiled to those who are perishing. In their case the god of this world has blinded the minds of the unbelievers, to keep them from seeing the light of the gospel of the glory of Christ, who is the image of God. For we do not proclaim ourselves; we proclaim Jesus Christ as Lord and ourselves as your slaves for Jesus' sake. For it is the God who said, "Let light shine out of

darkness," who has shone in our hearts to give the light of
the knowledge of the glory of God in the face of Jesus
Christ. But we have this treasure in clay jars, so that it
may be made clear that this extraordinary power belongs
to God and does not come from us. We are afflicted in
every way, but not crushed; perplexed, but not driven to
despair; persecuted, but not forsaken; struck down, but
not destroyed; always carrying in the body the death of
Jesus, so that the life of Jesus may also be made visible in
our bodies. For while we live, we are always being given
up to death for Jesus' sake, so that the life of Jesus may
be made visible in our mortal flesh. So death is at work in
us, but life in you.

*A Reading (Lesson) from the Gospel according to
Matthew* [5:38–48]

Jesus opened his mouth and taught his disciples, saying:
"You have heard that it was said, 'An eye for an eye and a
tooth for a tooth.' But I say to you, Do not resist an
evildoer. But if anyone strikes you on the right cheek, turn
the other also; and if anyone wants to sue you and take
your coat, give your cloak as well; and if anyone forces
you to go one mile, go also the second mile. Give to
everyone who begs from you, and do not refuse anyone
who wants to borrow from you. You have heard that it
was said, 'You shall love your neighbor and hate your
enemy.' But I say to you, Love your enemies and pray for
those who persecute you, so that you may be children of
your Father in heaven; for he makes his sun rise on the
evil and on the good, and sends rain on the righteous and
on the unrighteous. For if you love those who love you,
what reward do you have? Do not even the tax collectors

do the same? And if you greet only your brothers and sisters, what more are you doing than others? Do not even the Gentiles do the same? Be perfect, therefore, as your heavenly Father is perfect."

Saturday

Psalm 137:1–6(7–9) [page 792],
Psalm 144 [page 800] ❖ *Psalm 104* [page 735]

A Reading (Lesson) from the Book of Ruth [4:1–17]

No sooner had Boaz gone up to the gate and sat down there than the next-of-kin, of whom Boaz had spoken, came passing by. So Boaz said, "Come over, friend; sit down here." And he went over and sat down. Then Boaz took ten men of the elders of the city, and said, "Sit down here"; so they sat down. He then said to the next-of-kin, "Naomi, who has come back from the country of Moab, is selling the parcel of land that belonged to our kinsman Elimelech. So I thought I would tell you of it, and say: Buy it in the presence of those sitting here, and in the presence of the elders of my people. If you will redeem it, redeem it; but if you will not, tell me, so that I may know; for there is no one prior to you to redeem it, and I come after you." So he said, "I will redeem it." Then Boaz said, "The day you acquire the field from the hand of Naomi, you are also acquiring Ruth the Moabite, the widow of the dead man, to maintain the dead man's name on his inheritance." At this, the next-of-kin said, "I cannot redeem it for myself without damaging my own inheritance. Take my right of redemption yourself, for I cannot redeem it." Now this was the custom in former times in Israel concerning redeeming and exchanging: to confirm a transaction, the one took off a sandal and gave it to the other; this was the manner of attesting in Israel. So when the next-of-kin said to Boaz, "Acquire it for yourself," he took off his sandal. Then Boaz said to the elders and all the people, "Today you are witnesses that I have acquired from the hand of Naomi all that belonged to Elimelech and all that belonged to Chilion and Mahlon. I have also acquired Ruth the Moabite, the wife of Mahlon, to be my wife, to maintain the dead man's name on his inheritance, in order that the name of the dead may not be cut off from his kindred and from the gate of his native place; today you are witnesses." Then all the people who were at the gate, along with the elders, said, "We are witnesses. May the LORD make the woman who is coming into your house like Rachel and Leah, who together built up the house of Israel. May you produce children in Ephrathah and bestow a name in Bethlehem; and, through the children that the LORD will give you by this young woman, may your house be like the house of Perez, whom Tamar bore to Judah." So Boaz took Ruth and she became his wife. When they came together, the LORD made her conceive, and she bore a son. Then the women said to Naomi, "Blessed be the LORD, who has not left you this day without next-of-kin; and may his name be renowned in Israel! He shall be to you a restorer of life and a nourisher of your old age; for your daughter-in-law who loves you, who is more to you than seven sons, has borne him." Then Naomi took the child and laid him in her bosom, and became his nurse. The women of the neighborhood gave him a name, saying, "A son has been born to Naomi." They named him Obed; he became the father of Jesse, the father of David.

A Reading (Lesson) from the Second Letter of Paul to the Corinthians [4:13—5:10]

Just as we have the same spirit of faith that is in accordance with scripture—"I believed, and so I spoke"—we also believe, and so we speak, because we know that the one who raised the Lord Jesus will raise us also with Jesus, and will bring us with you into his presence. Yes, everything is for your sake, so that grace, as it extends to more and more people, may increase thanksgiving, to the glory of God. So we do not lose heart. Even though our outer nature is wasting away, our inner nature is being renewed day by day. For this slight momentary affliction is preparing us for an eternal weight of glory beyond all measure, because we look not at what can be seen but at what cannot be seen; for what can be seen is temporary, but what cannot be seen is eternal. For we know that if the earthly tent we live in is destroyed, we have a building from God, a house not made with hands, eternal in the heavens. For in this tent we groan, longing to be clothed with our heavenly dwelling—if indeed, when we have taken it off we will not be found naked. For while we are still in this tent, we groan under our burden, because we wish not to be unclothed but to be further clothed, so that what is mortal may be swallowed up by life. He who has prepared us for this very thing is God, who has given us the Spirit as a guarantee. So we are always confident; even though we know that while we are at home in the body we are away from the Lord—for we walk by faith, not by sight. Yes, we do have confidence, and we would rather be away from the body and at home with the Lord. So whether we are at home or away, we make it our aim to please him. For all of us must appear before the judgment seat of

Christ, so that each may receive recompense for what has been done in the body, whether good or evil.

A Reading (Lesson) from the Gospel according to Matthew [6:1–6]

Jesus opened his mouth and taught his disciples, saying: "Beware of practicing your piety before others in order to be seen by them; for then you have no reward from your Father in heaven. So whenever you give alms, do not sound a trumpet before you, as the hypocrites do in the synagogues and in the streets, so that they may be praised by others. Truly I tell you, they have received their reward. But when you give alms, do not let your left hand know what your right hand is doing, so that your alms may be done in secret; and your Father who sees in secret will reward you. And whenever you pray, do not be like the hypocrites; for they love to stand and pray in the synagogues and at the street corners, so that they may be seen by others. Truly I tell you, they have received their reward. But whenever you pray, go into your room and shut the door and pray to your Father who is in secret; and your Father who sees in secret will reward you."

Week of 8 Epiphany

Sunday

Psalm 146 [page 803],   *Psalm 147* [page 804]   ❖
Psalm 111 [page 754],   *Psalm 112* [page 755],
Psalm 113 [page 756]

A Reading (Lesson) from the Book of Deuteronomy [4:1–9]

Moses undertook to explain the law, saying, "And now, O
Israel, give heed to the statutes and ordinances that I am
teaching you to observe, so that you may live to enter and
occupy the land that the LORD, the God of your ancestors, is
giving you. You must neither add anything to what I
command you nor take away anything from it, but keep the
commandments of the LORD your God with which I am
charging you. You have seen for yourselves what the LORD
did with regard to the Baal of Peor—how the LORD your
God destroyed from among you everyone who followed the
Baal of Peor, while those of you who held fast to the LORD
your God are all live today. See, just as the LORD my God
has charged me, I now teach you statutes and ordinances for
you to observe in the land that you are about to enter and
occupy. You must observe them diligently, for this will
show your wisdom and discernment to the peoples, who,
when they hear all these statutes, will say, 'Surely this great
nation is a wise and discerning people!' For what other great
nation has a god so near to it as the LORD our God is
whenever we call to him? And what other great nation has
statutes and ordinances as just as this entire law that I am
setting before you today? But take care and watch
yourselves closely, so as neither to forget the things that
your eyes have seen nor to let them slip from your mind all
the days of your life; make them known to your children
and your children's children."

2 Timothy 4:1–8 [page 219 above]

*A Reading (Lesson) from the Gospel according to
John* [12:1–8]

Six days before the Passover Jesus came to Bethany, the
home of Lazarus, whom he had raised from the dead.

There they gave a dinner for him. Martha served, and Lazarus was one of those at the table with him. Mary took a pound of costly perfume made of pure nard, anointed Jesus' feet, and wiped them with her hair. The house was filled with the fragrance of the perfume. But Judas Iscariot, one of his disciples (the one who was about to betray him), said, "Why was this perfume not sold for three hundred denarii and the money given to the poor?" (He said this not because he cared about the poor, but because he was a thief; he kept the common purse and used to steal what was put into it.) Jesus said, "Leave her alone. She bought it so that she might keep it for the day of my burial. You always have the poor with you, but you do not always have me."

Monday

Psalm 1 [page 585],   *Psalm 2* [page 586],
Psalm 3 [page 587]   ❖   *Psalm 4* [page 587],
Psalm 7 [page 590]

A Reading (Lesson) from the Book of Deuteronomy [4:9–14]

Moses undertook to explain the law as follows: Take care and watch yourselves closely, so as neither to forget the things that your eyes have seen nor to let them slip from your mind all the days of your life; make them known to your children and your children's children—how you once stood before the LORD your God at Horeb, when the LORD said to me, "Assemble the people for me, and I will let them hear my words, so that they may learn to fear me as long as they live on the earth, and may teach their children so"; you approached and stood at the foot of the mountain while the mountain was blazing up to the very heavens, shrouded in dark clouds. Then the LORD spoke to you out of the fire. You heard the sound of words but saw no form; there was only a voice. He declared to you his covenant, which he charged you to observe, that is, the ten commandments; and he wrote them on two stone tablets. And the LORD charged me at that time to teach you statutes and ordinances for you to observe in the land that you are about to cross into and occupy.

A Reading (Lesson) from the Second Letter of Paul to the Corinthians [10:1–18]

I myself, Paul, appeal to you by the meekness and gentleness of Christ—I who am humble when face to face with you, but bold toward you when I am away!—I ask that when I am present I need not show boldness by daring to oppose those who think we are acting according to human standards. Indeed, we live as human beings, but we do not wage war according to human standards; for the weapons of our warfare are not merely human, but they have divine power to destroy strongholds. We destroy arguments and every proud obstacle raised up against the knowledge of God, and we take every thought captive to obey Christ. We are ready to punish every disobedience when your obedience is complete. Look at what is before your eyes. If you are confident that you belong to Christ, remind yourself of this, that just as you belong to Christ, so also do we. Now, even if I boast a little too much of our authority, which the Lord gave for building you up and not for tearing you down, I will not be ashamed of it. I do not want to seem as though I am trying to frighten you with my letters. For they say, "His letters are weighty and strong, but his bodily presence is weak, and his speech contemptible." Let such people understand that what we say by letter when absent, we will also do when present.

We do not dare to classify or compare ourselves with some of those who commend themselves. But when they measure themselves by one another, and compare themselves with one another, they do not show good sense. We, however, will not boast beyond limits, but will keep within the field that God has assigned to us, to reach out even as far as you. For we were not overstepping our limits when we reached you; we were the first to come all the way to you with the good news of Christ. We do not boast beyond limits, that is, in the labors of others; but our hope is that, as your faith increases, our sphere of action among you may be greatly enlarged, so that we may proclaim the good news in lands beyond you, without boasting of work already done in someone else's sphere of action. "Let the one who boasts, boast in the Lord." For it is not those who commend themselves that are approved, but those whom the Lord commends.

A Reading (Lesson) from the Gospel according to Matthew [6:7–15]

Jesus began to teach, saying: "When you are praying, do not heap up empty phrases as the Gentiles do; for they think that they will be heard because of their many words. Do not be like them, for your Father knows what you need before you ask him. Pray then in this way: Our Father in heaven, hallowed be your name. Your kingdom come. Your will be done, on earth as it is in heaven. Give us this day our daily bread. And forgive us our debts, as we also have forgiven our debtors. And do not bring us to the time of trial, but rescue us from the evil one. For if you forgive others their trespasses, your heavenly Father will also forgive you; but if you do not forgive others, neither will your Father forgive your trespasses."

Tuesday

Psalm 5 [page 588],   *Psalm 6* [page 589]   ❖
Psalm 10 [page 594],   *Psalm 11* [page 596]

*A Reading (Lesson) from the Book of
Deuteronomy* [4:15–24]

Moses undertook to explain the law as follows: Since you
saw no form when the LORD spoke to you at Horeb out of
the fire, take care and watch yourselves closely, so that you
do not act corruptly by making an idol for yourselves, in the
form of any figure—the likeness of male or female, the
likeness of any animal that is on the earth, the likeness of
any winged bird that flies in the air, the likeness of anything
that creeps on the ground, the likeness of any fish that is in
the water under the earth. And when you look up to the
heavens and see the sun, the moon, and the stars, all the
host of heaven, do not be led astray and bow down to them
and serve them, things that the LORD your God has allotted
to all the peoples everywhere under heaven. But the LORD
has taken you and brought you out of the iron-smelter, out
of Egypt, to become a people of his very own possession, as
you are now. The LORD was angry with me because of you,
and he vowed that I should not cross the Jordan and that I
should not enter the good land that the LORD your God is
giving for your possession. For I am going to die in this land
without crossing over the Jordan, but you are going to cross
over to take possession of that good land. So be careful not
to forget the covenant that the LORD your God made with
you, and not to make for yourselves an idol in the form of
anything that the LORD your God has forbidden you. For
the LORD your God is a devouring fire, a jealous God.

*A Reading (Lesson) from the Second Letter of Paul to the
Corinthians* [11:1–21a]

I wish you would bear with me in a little foolishness. Do
bear with me! I feel a divine jealousy for you, for I
promised you in marriage to one husband, to present you
as a chaste virgin to Christ. But I am afraid that as the
serpent deceived Eve by its cunning, your thoughts will be
led astray from a sincere and pure devotion to Christ. For
if someone comes and proclaims another Jesus than the
one we proclaimed, or if you receive a different spirit from
the one you received, or a different gospel from the one
you accepted, you submit to it readily enough. I think that
I am not in the least inferior to these super-apostles. I may
be untrained in speech, but not in knowledge; certainly in
every way and in all things we have made this evident to
you. Did I commit a sin by humbling myself so that you
might be exalted, because I proclaimed God's good news
to you free of charge? I robbed other churches by
accepting support from them in order to serve you. And
when I was with you and was in need, I did not burden
anyone, for my needs were supplied by the friends who
came from Macedonia. So I refrained and will continue to
refrain from burdening you in any way. As the truth of
Christ is in me, this boast of mine will not be silenced in
the regions of Achaia. And why? Because I do not love
you? God knows I do! And what I do I will also continue
to do, in order to deny an opportunity to those who want
an opportunity to be recognized as our equals in what
they boast about. For such boasters are false apostles,
deceitful workers, disguising themselves as apostles of
Christ. And no wonder! Even Satan disguises himself as an
angel of light. So it is not strange if his ministers also
disguise themselves as ministers of righteousness. Their

end will match their deeds. I repeat, let no one think that I am a fool; but if you do, then accept me as a fool, so that I too may boast a little. What I am saying in regard to this boastful confidence, I am saying not with the Lord's authority, but as a fool; since many boast according to human standards, I will also boast. For you gladly put up with fools, being wise yourselves! For you put up with it when someone makes slaves of you, or preys upon you, or takes advantage of you, or puts on airs, or gives you a slap in the face. To my shame, I must say, we were too weak for that!

A Reading (Lesson) from the Gospel according to Matthew [6:16–23]

Jesus began to teach, saying: "Whenever you fast, do not look dismal, like the hypocrites, for they disfigure their faces so as to show others that they are fasting. Truly I tell you, they have received their reward. But when you fast, put oil on your head and wash your face, so that your fasting may be seen not by others but by your Father who is in secret; and your Father who sees in secret will reward you. Do not store up for yourselves treasures on earth, where moth and rust consume and where thieves break in and steal; but store up for yourselves treasures in heaven, where neither moth nor rust consumes and where thieves do not break in and steal. For where your treasure is, there your heart will be also. The eye is the lamp of the body. So, if your eye is healthy, your whole body will be full of light; but if your eye is unhealthy, your whole body will be full of darkness. If then the light in you is darkness, how great is the darkness!"

Wednesday

Psalm 119:1–24 [page 763] ❖ *Psalm 12* [page 597],
Psalm 13 [page 597],   *Psalm 14* [page 598]

*A Reading (Lesson) from the Book of
Deuteronomy* [4:25–31]

Moses undertook to explain the law, saying, When you have
had children and children's children, and become
complacent in the land, if you act corruptly by making an
idol in the form of anything, thus doing what is evil in the
sight of the LORD your God, and provoking him to anger, I
call heaven and earth to witness against you today that you
will soon utterly perish from the land that you are crossing
the Jordan to occupy; you will not live long on it, but will
be utterly destroyed. The LORD will scatter you among the
peoples; only a few of you will be left among the nations
where the LORD will lead you. There you will serve other
gods made by human hands, objects of wood and stone that
neither see, nor hear, nor eat, nor smell. From there you will
seek the LORD your God, and you will find him if you search
after him with all your heart and soul. In your distress,
when all these things have happened to you in time to come,
you will return to the LORD your God and heed him.
Because the LORD your God is a merciful God, he will
neither abandon you nor destroy you; he will not forget the
covenant with your ancestors that he swore to them.

*A Reading (Lesson) from the Second Letter of Paul to the
Corinthians* [11:21b–33]

Whatever anyone dares to boast of—I am speaking as a
fool—I also dare to boast of that. Are they Hebrews? So
am I. Are they Israelites? So am I. Are they descendants of

Abraham? So am I. Are they ministers of Christ? I am talking like a madman—I am a better one: with far greater labors, far more imprisonments, with countless floggings, and often near death. Five times I have received from the Jews the forty lashes minus one. Three times I was beaten with rods. Once I received a stoning. Three times I was shipwrecked; for a night and a day I was adrift at sea; on frequent journeys, in danger from rivers, danger from bandits, danger from my own people, danger from Gentiles, danger in the city, danger in the wilderness, danger at sea, danger from false brothers and sisters; in toil and hardship, through many a sleepless night, hungry and thirsty, often without food, cold and naked. And, besides other things, I am under daily pressure because of my anxiety for all the churches. Who is weak, and I am not weak? Who is made to stumble, and I am not indignant? If I must boast, I will boast of the things that show my weakness. The God and Father of the Lord Jesus (blessed be he forever!) knows that I do not lie. In Damascus, the governor under King Aretas guarded the city of Damascus in order to seize me, but I was let down in a basket through a window in the wall, and escaped from his hands.

A Reading (Lesson) from the Gospel according to Matthew [6:24–34]

Jesus opened his mouth and taught his disciples, saying: "No one can serve two masters; for a slave will either hate the one and love the other, or be devoted to the one and despise the other. You cannot serve God and wealth. Therefore I tell you, do not worry about your life, what you will eat or what you will drink, or about your body, what you will wear. Is not life more than food, and the body more than clothing? Look at the birds of the air; they neither sow nor reap nor gather into barns, and yet your heavenly Father feeds them. Are you not of more value than they? And can any of you by worrying add a single hour to your span of life? And why do you worry about clothing? Consider the lilies of the field, how they grow; they neither toil nor spin, yet I tell you, even Solomon in all his glory was not clothed like one of these. But if God so clothes the grass of the field, which is alive today and tomorrow is thrown into the oven, will he not much more clothe you—you of little faith? Therefore do not worry, saying, 'What will we eat?' or 'What will we drink?' or 'What will we wear?' For it is the Gentiles who strive for all these things; and indeed your heavenly Father knows that you need all these things. But strive first for the kingdom of God and his righteousness, and all these things will be given to you as well. So do not worry about tomorrow, for tomorrow will bring worries of its own. Today's trouble is enough for today."

Thursday

Psalm 18:1–20 [page 602] ❖ *Psalm 18:21–50* [page 604]

A Reading (Lesson) from the Book of Deuteronomy [4:32–40]

Moses undertook to explain the law, saying, Ask now about former ages, long before your own, ever since the day that God created human beings on the earth; ask from one end of heaven to the other: has anything so great as this ever happened or has its like ever been heard of? Has any people ever heard the voice of a god speaking out of a fire, as you have heard, and lived? Or has any god ever attempted to go and take a nation for himself from the midst of another nation, by trials, by signs and wonders, by war, by a mighty hand and an outstretched arm, and by terrifying displays of power, as the LORD your God did for you in Egypt before your very eyes? To you it was shown so that you would acknowledge that the LORD is God; there is no other besides him. From heaven he made you hear his voice to discipline you. On earth he showed you his great fire, while you heard his words coming out of the fire. And because he loved your ancestors, he chose their descendants after them. He brought you out of Egypt with his own presence, by his great power, driving out before you nations greater and mightier than yourselves, to bring you in, giving you their land for a possession, as it is still today. So acknowledge today and take to heart that the LORD is God in heaven above and on the earth beneath; there is no other. Keep his statutes and his commandments, which I am commanding you today for your own well-being and that of your descendants after you, so that you may long remain in the land that the LORD your God is giving you for all time.

A Reading (Lesson) from the Second Letter of Paul to the Corinthians [12:1–10]

It is necessary to boast; nothing is to be gained by it, but I will go on to visions and revelations of the Lord. I know a person in Christ who fourteen years ago was caught up to the third heaven—whether in the body or out of the body I do not know; God knows. And I know that such a person—whether in the body or out of the body I do not know; God knows—was caught up into Paradise and heard things that are not to be told, that no mortal is permitted to repeat. On behalf of such a one I will boast, but on my own behalf I will not boast, except of my weaknesses. But if I wish to boast, I will not be a fool, for I will be speaking the truth. But I refrain from it, so that no one may think better of me than what is seen in me or heard from me, even considering the exceptional character of the revelations. Therefore, to keep me from being too elated, a thorn was given me in the flesh, a messenger of Satan to torment me, to keep me from being too elated. Three times I appealed to the LORD about this, that it would leave me, but he said to me, "My grace is sufficient for you, for power is made perfect in weakness." So, I will boast all the more gladly of my weaknesses, so that the power of Christ may dwell in me. Therefore I am content with weaknesses, insults, hardships, persecutions, and calamities for the sake of Christ; for whenever I am weak, then I am strong.

A Reading (Lesson) from the Gospel according to Matthew [7:1–12]

Jesus began to teach, saying: "Do not judge, so that you may not be judged. For with the judgment you make you will be judged, and the measure you give will be the measure you get. Why do you see the speck in your neighbor's eye, but do not notice the log in your own eye? Or how can you say to your neighbor, Let me take the speck out of your eye, while the log is in your own eye? You hypocrite, first take the log out of your own eye, and then you will see clearly to take the speck out of your neighbor's eye. Do not give what is holy to dogs; and do not throw your pearls before swine, or they will trample them under foot and turn and maul you. Ask, and it will be given you; search, and you will find; knock, and the door will be opened for you. For everyone who asks receives, and everyone who searches finds, and for everyone who knocks, the door will be opened. Is there anyone among you who, if your child asks for bread, will give a stone? Or if the child asks for a fish, will give a snake? If you then, who are evil, know how to give good gifts to your children, how much more will your Father in heaven give good things to those who ask him! In everything do to others as you would have them do to you; for this is the law and the prophets."

Friday

Psalm 16 [page 599],   *Psalm 17* [page 600]   ❖
Psalm 22 [page 610]

A Reading (Lesson) from the Book of Deuteronomy [5:1–22]

Moses convened all Israel, and said to them: Hear, O Israel, the statutes and ordinances that I am addressing to you today; you shall learn them and observe them diligently. The LORD our God made a covenant with us at Horeb. Not with our ancestors did the LORD make this covenant, but with us, who are all of us here alive today. The LORD spoke with you face to face at the mountain, out of the fire. (At that time I was standing between the LORD and you to declare to you the words of the LORD; for you were afraid because of the fire and did not go up the mountain.) And he said: I am the LORD your God, who brought you out of the land of Egypt, out of the house of slavery; you shall have no other gods before me. You shall not make for yourself an idol, whether in the form of anything that is in heaven above, or that is on the earth beneath, or that is in the water under the earth. You shall not bow down to them or worship them; for I the LORD your God am a jealous God, punishing children for the iniquity of parents, to the third and fourth generation of those who reject me, but showing steadfast love to the thousandth generation of those who love me and keep my commandments. You shall not make wrongful use of the name of the LORD your God, for the LORD will not acquit anyone who misuses his name. Observe the sabbath day and keep it holy, as the LORD your God commanded you. Six days you shall labor and do all your work. But the seventh day is a sabbath to the LORD your God; you shall not do any work—you, or your son or your daughter, or your male or female slave, or your ox or your donkey, or any of your livestock, or the resident alien in your towns, so that your male and female slave may rest as well as you. Remember that you were a slave in the land of Egypt, and the LORD your God brought you out from there with a mighty hand and an outstretched arm; therefore the LORD your God commanded you to keep the sabbath day. Honor your father and your mother, as the LORD your God commanded you, so that your days may be long and that it may go well with you in the land that the LORD your God is giving you. You shall not murder. Neither shall you commit adultery. Neither shall you steal. Neither shall you bear false witness against your neighbor. Neither shall you covet your neighbor's wife. Neither shall you desire your neighbor's house, or field, or male or female slave, or ox, or donkey, or anything that belongs to your neighbor. These words the LORD spoke with a loud voice to your whole assembly at the mountain, out of the fire, the cloud, and the thick darkness, and he added no more. He wrote them on two stone tablets, and gave them to me.

A Reading (Lesson) from the Second Letter of Paul to the Corinthians [12:11–21]

I have been a fool! You forced me to it. Indeed you should have been the ones commending me, for I am not at all inferior to these super-apostles, even though I am nothing. The signs of a true apostle were performed among you with utmost patience, signs and wonders and mighty works. How have you been worse off than the other churches, except that I myself did not burden you? Forgive me this wrong! Here I am, ready to come to you this third time. And I will not be a burden, because I do not want what is yours but you; for children ought not to lay up for their parents, but parents for their children. I will most gladly spend and be spent for you. If I love you more, am I to be loved less? Let it be assumed that I did not burden you. Nevertheless (you say) since I was crafty, I took you in by deceit. Did I take advantage of you through any of those whom I sent to you? I urged Titus to go, and sent the brother with him. Titus did not take advantage of you, did he? Did we not conduct ourselves with the same spirit? Did we not take the same steps? Have you been thinking all along that we have been defending ourselves before you? We are speaking in Christ before God. Everything we do, beloved, is for the sake of building you up. For I fear that when I come, I may find you not as I wish, and that you may find me not as you wish; I fear that there may perhaps be quarreling, jealousy, anger, selfishness, slander, gossip, conceit, and disorder. I fear that when I come again, my God may humble me before you, and that I may have to mourn over many who previously sinned and have not repented of the impurity, sexual immorality, and licentiousness that they have practiced.

A Reading (Lesson) from the Gospel according to Matthew [7:13–21]

Jesus began to teach, saying: "Enter through the narrow gate; for the gate is wide and the road is easy that leads to destruction, and there are many who take it. For the gate is narrow and the road is hard that leads to life, and there are few who find it. Beware of false prophets, who come to you in sheep's clothing but inwardly are ravenous wolves. You will know them by their fruits. Are grapes gathered from thorns, or figs from thistles? In the same way, every good tree bears good fruit, but the bad tree bears bad fruit. A good tree cannot bear bad fruit, nor can a bad tree bear good fruit. Every tree that does not bear good fruit is cut down and thrown into the fire. Thus you will know them by their fruits. Not everyone who says to me, 'Lord, Lord,' will enter the kingdom of heaven, but only the one who does the will of my Father in heaven."

Saturday

Psalm 20 [page 608],   *Psalm 21:1–7(8–14)* [page 608]   ❖
Psalm 110:1–5(6–7) [page 753],   *Psalm 116* [page 759],
Psalm 117 [page 760]

A Reading (Lesson) from the Book of Deuteronomy [5:22–33]

Moses convened all Israel, and said to them: These words the LORD spoke with a loud voice to your whole assembly at the mountain, out of the fire, the cloud, and the thick darkness, and he added no more. He wrote them on two stone tablets, and gave them to me. When you heard the voice out of the darkness, while the mountain was burning with fire, you approached me, all the heads of your tribes and your elders; and you said, "Look, the LORD our God has shown us his glory and greatness, and we have heard his voice out of the fire. Today we have seen that God may speak to someone and the person may still live. So now why should we die? For this great fire will consume us; if we hear the voice of the LORD our God any longer, we shall die. For who is there of all flesh that has heard the voice of the living God speaking out of fire, as we have, and remained alive? Go near, you yourself, and hear all that the LORD our God will say. Then tell us everything that the LORD our God tells you, and we will listen and do it." The Lord heard your words when you spoke to me, and the LORD said to me: "I have heard the words of this people, which they have spoken to you; they are right in all that they have spoken. If only they had such a mind as this, to fear me and to keep all my commandments always, so that it might go well with them and with their children forever! Go say to them, 'Return to your tents.' But you, stand here by me, and I will tell you all the commandments, the statutes and the ordinances, that you shall teach them, so that they may do them in the land that I am giving them to possess." You must therefore be careful to do as the LORD your God has commanded you; you shall not turn to the right or to the left. You must follow exactly the path that the LORD your God has commanded you, so that you may live, and that it may go well with you, and that you may live long in the land that you are to possess.

A Reading (Lesson) from the Second Letter of Paul to the Corinthians [13:1-14]

This is the third time I am coming to you. "Any charge must be sustained by the evidence of two or three witnesses." I warned those who sinned previously and all the others, and I warn them now while absent, as I did when present on my second visit, that if I come again, I will not be lenient—since you desire proof that Christ is speaking in me. He is not weak in dealing with you, but is powerful in you. For he was crucified in weakness, but lives by the power of God. For we are weak in him, but in dealing with you we will live with him by the power of God. Examine yourselves to see whether you are living in the faith. Test yourselves. Do you not realize that Jesus Christ is in you?—unless, indeed, you fail to meet the test! I hope you will find out that we have not failed. But we pray to God that you may not do anything wrong—not that we may appear to have met the test, but that you may do what is right, though we may seem to have failed. For we cannot do anything against the truth, but only for the truth. For we rejoice when we are weak and you are strong. This is what we pray for, that you may become perfect. So I write these things while I am away from you, so that when I come, I may not have to be severe in using the authority that the Lord has given me for building up and not for tearing down. Finally, brothers and sisters, farewell. Put things in order, listen to my appeal, agree with one another, live in peace; and the God of love and peace will be with you. Greet one another with a holy kiss. All the saints greet you. The grace of the Lord Jesus Christ, the love of God, and the communion of the Holy Spirit be with all of you.

A Reading (Lesson) from the Gospel according to Matthew [7:22–29]

Jesus opened his mouth and taught his disciples, saying: 'On that day many will say to me, 'Lord, Lord, did we not prophesy in your name, and cast out demons in your name, and do many deeds of power in your name?' Then I will declare to them, 'I never knew you; go away from me, you evil-doers.' Everyone then who hears these words of mine and acts on them will be like a wise man who built his house on rock. The rain fell, the floods came, and the winds blew and beat on that house, but it did not fall, because it had been founded on rock. And everyone who hears these words of mine and does not act on them will be like a foolish man who built his house on sand. The rain fell, and the floods came, and the winds blew and beat against that house, and it fell—and great was its fall!" Now when Jesus had finished saying these things, the crowds were astounded at his teaching, for he taught them as one having authority, and not as their scribes.

Week of Last Epiphany

Sunday

Psalm 148 [page 805],   *Psalm 149* [page 807],
Psalm 150 [page 807]   ❖   *Psalm 114* [page 756],
Psalm 115 [page 757]

A Reading (Lesson) from the Book of Deuteronomy [6:1–9]

Moses convened all Israel, and said to them: This is the commandment—the statutes and the ordinances—that the LORD your God charged me to teach you to observe in the land that you are about to cross into and occupy, so that you and your children and your children's children, may fear the LORD your God all the days of your life, and keep all his decrees and his commandments that I am commanding you, so that your days may be long. Hear therefore, O Israel, and observe them diligently, so that it may go well with you, and so that you may multiply greatly in a land flowing with milk and honey, as the LORD, the God of your ancestors, has promised you. Hear, O Israel: The LORD is our God, the LORD alone. You shall love the LORD your God with all your heart, and with all your soul, and with all your might. Keep these words that I am commanding you today in your heart. Recite them to your children and talk about them when you are at home and when you are away, when you lie down and when you rise. Bind them as a sign on your hand, fix them as an emblem on your forehead, and write them on the doorposts of your house and on your gates.

Hebrews 12:18–29 [page 38 above]

A Reading (Lesson) from the Gospel according to John [12:24–32]

Jesus answered Andrew and Philip, "Very truly, I tell you, unless a grain of wheat falls into the earth and dies, it remains just a single grain; but if it dies, it bears much fruit. Those who love their life lose it, and those who hate their life in this world will keep it for eternal life. Whoever serves me must follow me, and where I am, there will my servant be also. Whoever serves me, the Father will honor. Now my soul is troubled. And what should I say—'Father, save me from this hour'? No, it is for this reason that I have come to this hour. Father, glorify your name." Then a voice came from heaven, "I have glorified it, and I will glorify it again." The crowd standing there heard it and said that it was thunder. Others said, "An angel has spoken to him." Jesus answered, "This voice has come for your sake, not for mine. Now is the judgment of this world; now the ruler of this world will be driven out. And I, when I am lifted up from the earth, will draw all people to myself."

Monday

Psalm 25 [page 614] ❖ *Psalm 9* [page 593],
Psalm 15 [page 599]

A Reading (Lesson) from the Book of Deuteronomy [6:10–15]

Moses convened all Israel, and said to them: When the LORD your God has brought you into the land that he swore to your ancestors, to Abraham, to Isaac, and to Jacob, to give you—a land with fine, large cities that you did not build, houses filled with all sorts of goods that you did not fill, hewn cisterns that you did not hew, vineyards and olive groves that you did not plant—and when you have eaten your fill, take care that you do not forget the LORD, who brought you out of the land of Egypt, out of the house of slavery. The LORD your God you shall fear; him you shall serve, and by his name alone you shall swear. Do not follow other gods, any of the gods of the peoples who are all around you, because the LORD your God, who is present with you, is a jealous God. The anger of the LORD your God would be kindled against you and he would destroy you from the face of the earth.

A Reading (Lesson) from the Letter to the Hebrews [1:1–14]

Long ago God spoke to our ancestors in many and various ways by the prophets, but in these last days he has spoken to us by a Son, whom he appointed heir of all things, through whom he also created the worlds. He is the reflection of God's glory and the exact imprint of God's very being, and he sustains all things by his powerful word. When he had made purification for sins, he sat down at the right hand of the Majesty on high, having become as much superior to angels as the name he has inherited is more excellent than theirs. For to which of the angels did God ever say, "You are my Son; today I have begotten you"? Or again, "I will be his Father, and he will be my Son"? And again, when he brings the firstborn into the world, he says, "Let all God's angels worship him." Of the angels he says, "He makes his angels winds, and his servants flames of fire." But of the Son he says, "Your throne, O God, is forever and ever, and the righteous scepter is the scepter of your kingdom. You have loved righteousness and hated wickedness; therefore God, your God, has anointed you with the oil of gladness beyond your companions." And, "In the beginning, Lord, you founded the earth, and the heavens are the work of your hands; they will perish, but you remain; they will all wear out like clothing; like a cloak you will roll them up, and like clothing they will be changed. But you are the same, and your years will never end." But to which of the angels has he ever said, "Sit at my right hand until I make your enemies a footstool for your feet"? Are not all angels spirits in the divine service, sent to serve for the sake of those who are to inherit salvation?

A Reading (Lesson) from the Gospel according to John [1:1–18]

In the beginning was the Word, and the Word was with God, and the Word was God. He was in the beginning with God. All things came into being through him, and without him not one thing came into being. What has come into being in him was life, and the life was the light of all people. The light shines in the darkness, and the darkness did not overcome it. There was a man sent from God, whose name was John. He came as a witness to testify to the light, so that all might believe through him. He himself was not the light, but he came to testify to the light. The true light, which enlightens everyone, was coming into the world. He was in the world, and the world came into being through him; yet the world did not know him. He came to what was his own, and his own people did not accept him. But to all who received him, who believed in his name, he gave power to become children of God, who were born, not of blood or of the will of the flesh or of the will of man, but of God. And the Word became flesh and lived among us, and we have seen his glory, the glory as of a father's only son, full of grace and truth. (John testified to him and cried out, "This was he of whom I said, 'He who comes after me ranks ahead of me because he was before me.' ") From his fullness we have all received, grace upon grace. The law indeed was given through Moses; grace and truth came through Jesus Christ. No one has ever seen God. It is God the only Son, who is close to the Father's heart, who has made him known.

Tuesday

Psalm 26 [page 616],   Psalm 28 [page 619] ❖
Psalm 36 [page 632],   Psalm 39 [page 638]

*A Reading (Lesson) from the Book of
Deuteronomy* [6:16–25]

Moses convened all Israel and said to them: Do not put the
LORD your God to the test, as you tested him at Massah.
You must diligently keep the commandments of the LORD
your God, and his decrees, and his statutes that he has
commanded you. Do what is right and good in the sight of
the LORD, so that it may go well with you, and so that you
may go in and occupy the good land that the LORD swore to
your ancestors to give you, thrusting out all your enemies
from before you, as the LORD has promised. When your
children ask you in time to come, "What is the meaning of
the decrees and the statutes and the ordinances that the
LORD our God has commanded you?" then you shall say to
your children, "We were Pharaoh's slaves in Egypt, but the
LORD brought us out of Egypt with a mighty hand. The
LORD displayed before our eyes great and awesome signs
and wonders against Egypt, against Pharaoh and all his
household. He brought us out from there in order to bring
us in, to give us the land that he promised on oath to our
ancestors. Then the LORD commanded us to observe all
these statutes, to fear the LORD our God, for our lasting
good, so as to keep us alive, as is now the case. If we
diligently observe this entire commandment before the LORD
our God, as he has commanded us, we will be in the right."

*A Reading (Lesson) from the Letter to the
Hebrews* [2:1–10]

We must pay greater attention to what we have heard, so
that we do not drift away from it. For if the message
declared through angels was valid, and every transgression
or disobedience received a just penalty, how can we escape
if we neglect so great a salvation? It was declared at first
through the Lord, and it was attested to us by those who
heard him, while God added his testimony by signs and
wonders and various miracles, and by gifts of the Holy
Spirit, distributed according to his will. Now God did not
subject the coming world, about which we are speaking,
to angels. But someone has testified somewhere, "What are
human beings that you are mindful of them, or mortals,
that you care for them? You have made them for a little
while lower than the angels; you have crowned them with
glory and honor, subjecting all things under their feet."
Now in subjecting all things to them, God left nothing
outside their control. As it is, we do not yet see everything
in subjection to them, but we do see Jesus, who for a little
while was made lower than the angels, now crowned with
glory and honor because of the suffering of death, so that
by the grace of God he might taste death for everyone. It
was fitting that God, for whom and through whom all
things exist, in bringing many children to glory, should
make the pioneer of their salvation perfect through
sufferings.

*A Reading (Lesson) from the Gospel according to
John* [1:19–28]

This is the testimony given by John when the Jews sent
priests and Levites from Jerusalem to ask him, "Who are
you?" He confessed and did not deny it, but confessed,

'I am not the Messiah." And they asked him, "What then? Are you Elijah?" He said, "I am not." "Are you the prophet?" He answered, "No." Then they said to him, 'Who are you? Let us have an answer for those who sent us. What do you say about yourself?" He said, "I am the voice of one crying out in the wilderness, 'Make straight the way of the Lord,' " as the prophet Isaiah said. Now they had been sent from the Pharisees. They asked him, 'Why then are you baptizing if you are neither the Messiah, nor Elijah, nor the prophet?" John answered them, "I baptize with water. Among you stands one whom you do not know, the one who is coming after me; I am not worthy to untie the thong of his sandal." This took place in Bethany across the Jordan where John was baptizing.

Ash Wednesday

*Psalm 95** [page 724] & *Psalm 32* [page 624],
Psalm 143 [page 798] ❖ *Psalm 102* [page 731],
Psalm 130 [page 784]

A Reading (Lesson) from the Book of Jonah [3:1—4:11]

The word of the LORD came to Jonah a second time, saying, 'Get up, go to Nineveh, that great city, and proclaim to it the message that I tell you." So Jonah set out and went to Nineveh, according to the word of the LORD. Now Nineveh was an exceedingly large city, a three days' walk across. Jonah began to go into the city, going a day's walk. And he cried out, "Forty days more, and Nineveh shall be overthrown!" And the people of Nineveh believed God; they

For the Invitatory

proclaimed a fast, and everyone, great and small, put on sackcloth. When the news reached the king of Nineveh, he rose from his throne, removed his robe, covered himself with sackcloth, and sat in ashes. Then he had a proclamation made in Nineveh: "By the decree of the king and his nobles: No human being or animal, no herd or flock, shall taste anything. They shall not feed, nor shall they drink water. Human beings and animals shall be covered with sackcloth, and they shall cry mightily to God. All shall turn from their evil ways and from the violence that is in their hands. Who knows? God may relent and change his mind; he may turn from his fierce anger, so that we do not perish." When God saw what they did, how they turned from their evil ways, God changed his mind about the calamity that he had said he would bring upon them; and he did not do it. But this was very displeasing to Jonah, and he became angry. He prayed to the LORD and said, "O LORD! Is not this what I said while I was still in my own country? That is why I fled to Tarshish at the beginning; for I knew that you are a gracious God and merciful, slow to anger, and abounding in steadfast love, and ready to relent from punishing. And now, O LORD, please take my life from me, for it is better for me to die than to live." And the LORD said, "Is it right for you to be angry?" Then Jonah went out of the city and sat down east of the city, and made a booth for himself there. He sat under it in the shade, waiting to see what would become of the city. The LORD God appointed a bush, and made it come up over Jonah, to give shade over his head, to save him from his discomfort; so Jonah was very happy about the bush. But when dawn came up the next day, God appointed a worm that attacked the bush, so that it withered. When the sun rose, God prepared a sultry east wind, and the sun beat down on the head of Jonah so that he was faint and asked that he might die. He said, "It is better for me to die than to live." But God said to Jonah, "Is it right for you to be angry about the bush?" And he said, "Yes, angry enough to die." Then the LORD said, "You are concerned about the bush, for which you did not labor and which you did not grow; it came into being in a night and perished in a night. And should I not be concerned about Nineveh, that great city, in which there are more than a hundred and twenty thousand persons who do not know their right hand from their left, and also many animals?"

A Reading (Lesson) from the Letter to the Hebrews [12:1–14]

Therefore, since we are surrounded by so great a cloud of witnesses, let us also lay aside every weight and the sin that clings so closely, and let us run with perseverance the race that is set before us, looking to Jesus the pioneer and perfecter of our faith, who for the sake of the joy that was set before him endured the cross, disregarding its shame, and has taken his seat at the right hand of the throne of God. Consider him who endured such hostility against himself from sinners, so that you may not grow weary or lose heart. In your struggle against sin you have not yet resisted to the point of shedding your blood. And you have forgotten the exhortation that addresses you as children—"My child, do not regard lightly the discipline of the Lord, or lose heart when you are punished by him; for the Lord disciplines those whom he loves, and chastises every child whom he accepts." Endure trials for the sake of discipline. God is treating you as children; for what child is there whom a parent does not discipline? If you do not have that discipline in which all children share, then you are illegitimate and not his children. Moreover, we had human parents to discipline us, and we respected them. Should we not be even more willing to be subject to the Father of spirits and live? For they disciplined us for a short time as seemed best to them, but he disciplines us for our good, in order that we may share his holiness. Now, discipline always seems painful rather than pleasant at the time, but later it yields the peaceful fruit of righteousness to those who have been trained by it. Therefore lift your drooping hands and strengthen your weak knees, and make straight paths for your feet, so that what is lame may not be put out of joint, but rather be healed. Pursue peace with everyone, and the holiness without which no one will see the Lord.

A Reading (Lesson) from the Gospel according to Luke [18:9–14]

Jesus told this parable to some who trusted in themselves that they were righteous and regarded others with contempt: "Two men went up to the temple to pray, one a Pharisee and the other a tax collector. The Pharisee, standing by himself, was praying thus, 'God, I thank you that I am not like other people: thieves, rogues, adulterers, or even like this tax collector. I fast twice a week; I give a tenth of all my income.' But the tax collector, standing far off, would not even look up to heaven, but was beating his breast and saying, 'God, be merciful to me, a sinner!' I tell you, this man went down to his home justified rather than the other; for all who exalt themselves will be humbled, but all who humble themselves will be exalted."

Thursday

Psalm 37:1–18 [page 633]   ❖   *Psalm 37:19–42* [page 634]

A Reading (Lesson) from the Book of
Deuteronomy [7:6–11]

Moses convened all Israel, and said to them: You are a
people holy to the LORD your God; the LORD your God has
chosen you out of all the peoples on earth to be his people,
his treasured possession. It was not because you were more
numerous than any other people that the LORD set his heart
on you and chose you—for you were the fewest of all
peoples. It was because the LORD loved you and kept the
oath that he swore to your ancestors, that the LORD has
brought you out with a mighty hand, and redeemed you
from the house of slavery, from the hand of Pharaoh king of
Egypt. Know therefore that the LORD your God is God, the
faithful God who maintains covenant loyalty with those
who love him and keep his commandments, to a thousand
generations, and who repays in their own person those who
reject him. He does not delay but repays in their own person
those who reject him. Therefore, observe diligently the
commandment—the statutes, and the ordinances—that I am
commanding you today.

A Reading (Lesson) from the Letter of Paul to
Titus [1:1–16]

Paul, a servant of God and an apostle of Jesus Christ, for
the sake of the faith of God's elect and the knowledge of
the truth that is in accordance with godliness, in the hope
of eternal life that God, who never lies, promised before
the ages began—in due time he revealed his word through
the proclamation with which I have been entrusted by the
command of God our Savior, to Titus, my loyal child in
the faith we share: Grace and peace from God the Father
and Christ Jesus our Savior. I left you behind in Crete for
this reason, so that you should put in order what

remained to be done, and should appoint elders in every town, as I directed you: someone who is blameless, married only once, whose children are believers, not accused of debauchery and not rebellious. For a bishop, as God's steward, must be blameless; he must not be arrogant or quick-tempered or addicted to wine or violent or greedy for gain; but he must be hospitable, a lover of goodness, prudent, upright, devout, and self-controlled. He must have a firm grasp of the word that is trustworthy in accordance with the teaching, so that he may be able both to preach with sound doctrine and to refute those who contradict it. There are also many rebellious people, idle talkers and deceivers, especially those of the circumcision; they must be silenced, since they are upsetting whole families by teaching for sordid gain what it is not right to teach. It was one of them, their very own prophet, who said, "Cretans are always liars, vicious brutes, lazy gluttons." That testimony is true. For this reason rebuke them sharply, so that they may become sound in the faith, not paying attention to Jewish myths or to commandments of those who reject the truth. To the pure all things are pure, but to the corrupt and unbelieving nothing is pure. Their very minds and consciences are corrupted. They profess to know God, but they deny him by their actions. They are detestable, disobedient, unfit for any good work.

A Reading (Lesson) from the Gospel according to John [1:29–34]

The next day John saw Jesus coming toward him and declared, "Here is the Lamb of God who takes away the sin of the world! This is he of whom I said, 'After me comes a man who ranks ahead of me because he was before me.' I myself did not know him; but I came baptizing with water for this reason, that he might be revealed to Israel." And John testified, "I saw the Spirit descending from heaven like a dove, and it remained on him. I myself did not know him, but the one who sent me to baptize with water said to me, 'He on whom you see the Spirit descend and remain is the one who baptizes with the Holy Spirit.' And I myself have seen and have testified that this is the Son of God."

Friday

Psalm 95* [page 724] & *Psalm 31* [page 622] ❖
Psalm 35 [page 629]

A Reading (Lesson) from the Book of Deuteronomy [7:12–16]

Moses convened all Israel, and said to them: If you heed these ordinances, by diligently observing them, the LORD your God will maintain with you the covenant loyalty that he swore to your ancestors; he will love you, bless you, and multiply you; he will bless the fruit of your womb and the fruit of your ground, your grain and your wine and your oil, the increase of your cattle and the issue of your flock, in the land that he swore to your ancestors to give you. You shall be the most blessed of peoples, with neither sterility nor barrenness among you or your livestock. The LORD will turn away from you every illness; all the dread diseases of Egypt that you experienced, he will not inflict on you, but he will lay them on all who hate you. You shall devour all the peoples that the LORD your God is giving over to you, showing them no pity; you shall not serve their gods, for that would be a snare to you.

For the Invitatory

As for you, teach what is consistent with sound doctrine. Tell the older men to be temperate, serious, prudent, and sound in faith, in love, and in endurance. Likewise, tell the older women to be reverent in behavior, not to be slanderers or slaves to drink; they are to teach what is good, so that they may encourage the young women to love their husbands, to love their children, to be self-controlled, chaste, good managers of the household, kind, being submissive to their husbands, so that the word of God may not be discredited. Likewise, urge the younger men to be self-controlled. Show yourself in all respects a model of good works, and in your teaching show integrity, gravity, and sound speech that cannot be censured; then any opponent will be put to shame, having nothing evil to say of us. Tell slaves to be submissive to their masters and to give satisfaction in every respect; they are not to talk back, not to pilfer, but to show complete and perfect fidelity, so that in everything they may be an ornament to the doctrine of God our Savior. For the grace of God has appeared, bringing salvation to all, training us to renounce impiety and worldly passions, and in the present age to live lives that are self-controlled, upright, and godly, while we wait for the blessed hope and the manifestation of the glory of our great God and Savior, Jesus Christ. He it is who gave himself for us that he might redeem us from all iniquity and purify for himself a people of his own who are zealous for good deeds. Declare these things; exhort and reprove with all authority. Let no one look down on you.

A Reading (Lesson) from the Gospel according to John [1:35-42]

The next day John again was standing with two of his disciples, and as he watched Jesus walk by, he exclaimed, "Look, here is the Lamb of God!" The two disciples heard him say this, and they followed Jesus. When Jesus turned and saw them following, he said to them, "What are you looking for?" They said to him, "Rabbi" (which translated means Teacher), "where are you staying?" He said to them, "Come and see." They came and saw where he was staying, and they remained with him that day. It was about four o'clock in the afternoon. One of the two who heard John speak and followed him was Andrew, Simon Peter's brother. He first found his brother Simon and said to him, "We have found the Messiah" (which is translated Anointed). He brought Simon to Jesus, who looked at him and said, "You are Simon son of John. You are to be called Cephas" (which is translated Peter).

Saturday

Psalm 30 [page 621], *Psalm 32* [page 624] ❖
Psalm 42 [page 643], *Psalm 43* [page 644]

A Reading (Lesson) from the Book of Deuteronomy [7:17-26]

Moses convened all Israel, and said to them: If you say to yourself, "These nations are more numerous than I; how can I dispossess them?" do not be afraid of them. Just remember what the LORD your God did to Pharaoh and to all Egypt, the great trials that your eyes saw, the signs and wonders, the mighty hand and the outstretched arm by which the LORD your God brought you out. The LORD your

God will do the same to all the peoples of whom you are afraid. Moreover, the LORD your God will send the pestilence against them, until even the survivors and the fugitives are destroyed. Have no dread of them, for the LORD your God, who is present with you, is a great and awesome God. The LORD your God will clear away these nations before you little by little; you will not be able to make a quick end of them, otherwise the wild animals would become too numerous for you. But the LORD your God will give them over to you, and throw them into great panic, until they are destroyed. He will hand their kings over to you and you shall blot out their name from under heaven; no one will be able to stand against you, until you have destroyed them. The images of their gods you shall burn with fire. Do not covet the silver or the gold that is on them and take it for yourself, because you could be ensnared by it; for it is abhorrent to the LORD your God. Do not bring an abhorrent thing into your house, or you will be set apart for destruction like it. You must utterly detest and abhor it, for it is set apart for destruction.

A Reading (Lesson) from the Letter of Paul to Titus [3:1–15]

Remind them to be subject to rulers and authorities, to be obedient, to be ready for every good work, to speak evil of no one, to avoid quarreling, to be gentle, and to show every courtesy to everyone. For we ourselves were once foolish, disobedient, led astray, slaves to various passions and pleasures, passing our days in malice and envy, despicable, hating one another. But when the goodness and loving kindness of God our Savior appeared, he saved us, not because of any works of righteousness that we had done, but according to his mercy, through the water of rebirth and renewal by the Holy Spirit. This Spirit he poured out on us richly through Jesus Christ our Savior, so that, having been justified by his grace, we might become heirs according to the hope of eternal life. The saying is sure. I desire that you insist on these things, so that those who have come to believe in God may be careful to devote themselves to good works; these things are excellent and profitable to everyone. But avoid stupid controversies, genealogies, dissensions, and quarrels about the law, for they are unprofitable and worthless. After a first and second admonition, have nothing more to do with anyone who causes divisions, since you know that such a person is perverted and sinful, being self-condemned. When I send Artemas to you, or Tychicus, do your best to come to me at Nicopolis, for I have decided to spend the winter there. Make every effort to send Zenas the lawyer and Apollos on their way, and see that they lack nothing. And let people learn to devote themselves to good works in order to meet urgent needs, so that they may not be unproductive. All who are with me send greetings to you. Greet those who love us in the faith. Grace be with all of you.

A Reading (Lesson) from the Gospel according to John [1:43–51]

The next day Jesus decided to go to Galilee. He found Philip and said to him, "Follow me." Now Philip was from Bethsaida, the city of Andrew and Peter. Philip found Nathanael and said to him, "We have found him about whom Moses in the law and also the prophets wrote, Jesus son of Joseph from Nazareth." Nathanael said to him, "Can anything good come out of Nazareth?" Philip said to him, "Come and see." When Jesus saw Nathanael coming toward him, he said of him, "Here is truly an Israelite in whom there is no deceit!" Nathanael asked him, "Where did you get to know me?" Jesus answered, "I saw you under the fig tree before Philip called you." Nathanael replied, "Rabbi, you are the Son of God! You are the King of Israel!" Jesus answered, "Do you believe because I told you that I saw you under the fig tree? You will see greater things than these." And he said to him, "Very truly, I tell you, you will see heaven opened and the angels of God ascending and descending upon the Son of Man."

Week of 1 Lent

Sunday

Psalm 63:1–8(9–11) [page 670],
Psalm 98 [page 727]   ❖   *Psalm 103* [page 733]

A Reading (Lesson) from the Book of Deuteronomy [8:1–10]

Moses convened all Israel, and said to them: This entire commandment that I command you today you must diligently observe, so that you may live and increase, and go in and occupy the land that the LORD promised on oath to your ancestors. Remember the long way that the LORD your God has led you these forty years in the wilderness, in order to humble you, testing you to know what was in your heart, whether or not you would keep his commandments. He humbled you by letting you hunger, then by feeding you with manna, with which neither you nor your ancestors were acquainted, in order to make you understand that one does not live by bread alone, but by every word that comes from the mouth of the LORD. The clothes on your back did not wear out and your feet did not swell these forty years. Know then in your heart that as a parent disciplines a child so the LORD your God disciplines you. Therefore keep the commandments of the LORD your God, by walking in his ways and by fearing him. For the LORD your God is bringing you into a good land, a land with flowing streams, with springs and underground waters welling up in valleys and hills, a land of wheat and barley, of vines and fig trees and pomegranates, a land of olive trees and honey, a land where you may eat bread without scarcity, where you will lack nothing, a land whose stones are iron and from whose hills you may mine copper. You shall eat your fill and bless the LORD your God for the good land that he has given you.

A Reading (Lesson) from the First Letter of Paul to the Corinthians [1:17–31]

Christ did not send me to baptize but to proclaim the gospel, and not with eloquent wisdom, so that the cross of Christ might not be emptied of its power. For the message about the cross is foolishness to those who are perishing, but to us who are being saved it is the power of God. For it is written, "I will destroy the wisdom of the wise, and the discernment of the discerning I will thwart." Where is the one who is wise? Where is the scribe? Where is the debater of this age? Has not God made foolish the wisdom of the world? For since, in the wisdom of God, the world did not know God through wisdom, God decided, through the foolishness of our proclamation, to save those who believe. For Jews demand signs and Greeks desire wisdom, but we proclaim Christ crucified, a stumbling block to Jews and foolishness to Gentiles, but to those who are the called, both Jews and Greeks, Christ the power of God and the wisdom of God. For God's foolishness is wiser than human wisdom, and God's weakness is stronger than human strength. Consider your own call, brothers and sisters: not many of you were wise by human standards, not many were powerful, not many were of noble birth. But God chose what is foolish in the world to shame the wise; God chose what is weak in the world to shame the strong; God chose what is low and despised in the world, things that are not, to reduce to nothing things that are, so that no one might boast in the presence of God. He is the source of your life in Christ Jesus, who became for us wisdom from God, and righteousness and sanctification and redemption, in order that, as it is written, "Let the one who boasts, boast in the Lord."

A Reading (Lesson) from the Gospel according to Mark [2:18–22]

John's disciples and the Pharisees were fasting; and people came and said to Jesus, "Why do John's disciples and the disciples of the Pharisees fast, but your disciples do not fast?" Jesus said to them, "The wedding guests cannot fast while the bridegroom is with them, can they? As long as they have the bridegroom with them, they cannot fast. The days will come when the bridegroom is taken away from them, and then they will fast on that day. No one sews a piece of unshrunk cloth on an old cloak; otherwise, the patch pulls away from it, the new from the old, and a worse tear is made. And no one puts new wine into old wineskins; otherwise, the wine will burst the skins, and the wine is lost, and so are the skins; but one puts new wine into fresh wineskins.''

Monday

Psalm 41 [page 641], *Psalm 52* [page 657] ❖
Psalm 44 [page 645]

A Reading (Lesson) from the Book of Deuteronomy [8:11–20]

Moses convened all Israel, and said to them: Take care that you do not forget the LORD your God, by failing to keep his commandments, his ordinances, and his statutes, which I am commanding you today. When you have eaten your fill and have built fine houses and live in them, and when your herds and flocks have multiplied, and your silver and gold is multiplied, and all that you have is multiplied, then do not exalt yourself, forgetting the LORD your God, who brought you out of the land of Egypt, out of the house of slavery, who led you through the great and terrible wilderness, an arid wasteland with poisonous snakes and scorpions. He made water flow for you from flint rock, and fed you in the wilderness with manna that your ancestors did not know, to humble you and to test you, and in the end to do you good. Do not say to yourself, "My power and the might of my own hand have gotten me this wealth." But remember the LORD your God, for it is he who gives you power to get wealth, so that he may confirm his covenant that he swore to your ancestors, as he is doing today. If you do forget the LORD your God and follow other gods to serve and worship them, I solemnly warn you today that you shall surely perish. Like the nations that the LORD is destroying before you, so shall you perish, because you would not obey the voice of the LORD your God.

A Reading (Lesson) from the Letter to the Hebrews [2:11–18]

The one who sanctifies and those who are sanctified all have one Father. For this reason Jesus is not ashamed to call them brothers and sisters, saying, "I will proclaim your name to my brothers and sisters, in the midst of the congregation I will praise you." And again, "I will put my trust in him." And again, "Here am I and the children whom God has given me." Since, therefore, the children share flesh and blood, he himself likewise shared the same things, so that through death he might destroy the one who has the power of death, that is, the devil, and free those who all their lives were held in slavery by the fear of death. For it is clear that he did not come to help angels, but the descendants of Abraham. Therefore he had to become like his brothers and sisters in every respect, so that he might be a merciful and faithful high priest in the service of God, to make a sacrifice of atonement for the sins of the people. Because he himself was tested by what he suffered, he is able to help those who are being tested.

A Reading (Lesson) from the Gospel according to John [2:1–12]

On the third day there was a wedding in Cana of Galilee, and the mother of Jesus was there. Jesus and his disciples had also been invited to the wedding. When the wine gave out, the mother of Jesus said to him, "They have no wine." And Jesus said to her, "Woman, what concern is that to you and to me? My hour has not yet come." His mother said to the servants, "Do whatever he tells you." Now standing there were six stone water jars for the Jewish rites of purification, each holding twenty or thirty gallons. Jesus said to them, "Fill the jars with water." And they filled them up to the brim. He said to them, "Now draw some out, and take it to the chief steward." So they took it. When the steward tasted the water that had become wine, and did not know where it came from (though the servants who had drawn the water knew), the steward called the bridegroom and said to him, "Everyone serves the good wine first, and then the inferior wine after the guests have become drunk. But you have kept the good wine until now." Jesus did this, the first of his signs, in Cana of Galilee, and revealed his glory; and his disciples believed in him. After this he went down to Capernaum with his mother, his brothers, and his disciples; and they remained there a few days.

Tuesday

Psalm 45 [page 647] ❖ *Psalm 47* [page 650],
Psalm 48 [page 651]

A Reading (Lesson) from the Book of Deuteronomy [9:4-12]

Moses convened all Israel, and said to them: When the LORD your God thrusts them out before you, do not say to yourself, "It is because of my righteousness that the LORD has brought me in to occupy this land"; it is rather because of the wickedness of these nations that the LORD is dispossessing them before you. It is not because of your righteousness or the uprightness of your heart that you are going in to occupy their land; but because of the wickedness of these nations the LORD your God is dispossessing them before you, in order to fulfill the promise that the LORD made on oath to your ancestors, to Abraham, to Isaac, and to Jacob. Know, then, that the LORD your God is not giving you this good land to occupy because of your righteousness; for you are a stubborn people. Remember and do not forget how you provoked the LORD your God to wrath in the wilderness; you have been rebellious against the LORD from the day you came out of the land of Egypt until you came to this place. Even at Horeb you provoked the LORD to wrath, and the LORD was so angry with you that he was ready to destroy you. When I went up the mountain to receive the stone tablets, the tablets of the covenant that the LORD made with you, I remained on the mountain forty days and forty nights; I neither ate bread nor drank water. And the LORD gave me the two stone tablets written with the finger of God; on them were all the words that the LORD had spoken to you at the mountain out of the fire on the day of the assembly. At the end of forty days and forty nights the LORD gave me the two stone tablets, the tablets of the covenant. Then the LORD said to me, "Get up, go down quickly from here, for your people whom you have brought from Egypt have acted corruptly. They have been quick to turn from the way that I commanded them; they have cast an image for themselves."

A Reading (Lesson) from the Letter to the Hebrews [3:1–11]

Therefore, brothers and sisters, holy partners in a heavenly calling, consider that Jesus, the apostle and high priest of our confession, was faithful to the one who appointed him, just as Moses also "was faithful in all God's house." Yet Jesus is worthy of more glory than Moses, just as the builder of a house has more honor than the house itself. (For every house is built by someone, but the builder of all things is God.) Now Moses was faithful in all God's house as a servant, to testify to the things that would be spoken later. Christ, however, was faithful over God's house as a son, and we are his house if we hold firm the confidence and the pride that belong to hope. Therefore, as the Holy Spirit says, "Today, if you hear his voice, do not harden your hearts as in the rebellion, as on the day of testing in the wilderness, where your ancestors put me to the test, though they had seen my works for forty years. Therefore I was angry with that generation, and I said, 'They always go astray in their hearts, and they have not known my ways.' As in my anger I swore, 'They will not enter my rest.' "

A Reading (Lesson) from the Gospel according to John [2:13–22]

The Passover of the Jews was near, and Jesus went up to Jerusalem. In the temple he found people selling cattle, sheep, and doves, and the money changers seated at their tables. Making a whip of cords, he drove all of them out of the temple, both the sheep and the cattle. He also poured out the coins of the money changers and overturned their tables. He told those who were selling the doves, "Take these things out of here! Stop making my Father's house a marketplace!" His disciples remembered that it was written, "Zeal for your house will consume me." The Jews then said to him, "What sign can you show us for doing this?" Jesus answered them, "Destroy this temple, and in three days I will raise it up." The Jews then said, "This temple has been under construction for forty-six years, and will you raise it up in three days?" But

he was speaking of the temple of his body. After he was
raised from the dead, his disciples remembered that he had
said this; and they believed the scripture and the word that
Jesus had spoken.

Wednesday

Psalm 119:49–72 [page 767] ❖ *Psalm 49* [page 652],
(Psalm 53 [page 658])

*A Reading (Lesson) from the Book of
Deuteronomy* [9:13–21]

Moses convened all Israel, and said to them: Furthermore
the Lord said to me, "I have seen that this people is indeed
a stubborn people. Let me alone that I may destroy them
and blot out their name from under heaven; and I will make
of you a nation mightier and more numerous than they." So
I turned and went down from the mountain, while the
mountain was ablaze; the two tablets of the covenant were
in my two hands. Then I saw that you had indeed sinned
against the Lord your God, by casting for yourselves an
image of a calf; you had been quick to turn from the way
that the Lord had commanded you. So I took hold of the
two tablets and flung them from my two hands, smashing
them before your eyes. Then I lay prostrate before the Lord
as before, forty days and forty nights; I neither ate bread nor
drank water, because of all the sin you had committed,
provoking the Lord by doing what was evil in his sight. For
I was afraid that the anger that the Lord bore against you
was so fierce that he would destroy you. But the Lord
listened to me that time also. The Lord was so angry with
Aaron that he was ready to destroy him, but I interceded
also on behalf of Aaron at that same time. Then I took the

sinful thing you had made, the calf, and burned it with fire and crushed it, grinding it thoroughly, until it was reduced to dust; and I threw the dust of it into the stream that runs down the mountain.

A Reading (Lesson) from the Letter to the
Hebrews [3:12–19]

Take care, brothers and sisters, that none of you may have an evil, unbelieving heart that turns away from the living God. But exhort one another every day, as long as it is called "today," so that none of you may be hardened by the deceitfulness of sin. For we have become partners of Christ, if only we hold our first confidence firm to the end. As it is said, "Today, if you hear his voice, do not harden your hearts as in the rebellion." Now who were they who heard and yet were rebellious? Was it not all those who left Egypt under the leadership of Moses? But with whom was he angry forty years? Was it not those who sinned, whose bodies fell in the wilderness? And to whom did he swear that they would not enter his rest, if not to those who were disobedient? So we see that they were unable to enter because of unbelief.

A Reading (Lesson) from the Gospel according to
John [2:23—3:15]

When Jesus was in Jerusalem during the Passover festival, many believed in his name because they saw the signs that he was doing. But Jesus on his part would not entrust himself to them, because he knew all people and needed no one to testify about anyone; for he himself knew what was in everyone. Now there was a Pharisee named Nicodemus, a leader of the Jews. He came to Jesus by night and said to him, "Rabbi, we know that you are a teacher who has come from God; for no one can do these signs that you do apart from the presence of God." Jesus answered him, "Very truly, I tell you, no one can see the kingdom of God without being born from above." Nicodemus said to him, "How can anyone be born after having grown old? Can one enter a second time into the mother's womb and be born?" Jesus answered, Very truly, I tell you, no one can enter the kingdom of God without being born of water and Spirit. What is born of the flesh is flesh, and what is born of the Spirit is spirit. Do not be astonished that I said to you, 'You must be born from above.' The wind blows where it chooses, and you hear the sound of it, but you do not know where it comes from or where it goes. So it is with everyone who is born of the Spirit." Nicodemus said to him, "How can these things be?" Jesus answered him, "Are you a teacher of Israel, and yet you do not understand these things? Very truly, I tell you, we speak of what we know and testify to what we have seen; yet you do not receive our testimony. If I have told you about earthly things and you do not believe, how can you believe if I tell you about heavenly things? No one has ascended into heaven except the one who descended from heaven, the Son of Man. And just as Moses lifted up the serpent in the wilderness, so must the Son of Man be lifted up, that whoever believes in him may have eternal life."

Thursday

Psalm 50 [page 654]   ❖   *(Psalm 59* [page 665], *Psalm 60* [page 667])   or   *Psalm 19* [page 606], *Psalm 46* [page 649]

A Reading (Lesson) from the Book of
Deuteronomy [9:23—10:5]

Moses convened all Israel, and said to them: When the
LORD sent you from Kadesh-barnea, saying, "Go up and
occupy the land that I have given you," you rebelled against
the command of the LORD your God, neither trusting him
nor obeying him. You have been rebellious against the LORD
as long as he has known you. Throughout the forty days
and forty nights that I lay prostrate before the LORD when
the LORD intended to destroy you, I prayed to the LORD and
said, "Lord GOD, do not destroy the people who are your
very own possession, whom you redeemed in your
greatness, whom you brought out of Egypt with a mighty
hand. Remember your servants, Abraham, Isaac, and Jacob;
pay no attention to the stubbornness of this people, their
wickedness and their sin, otherwise the land from which you
have brought us might say, 'Because the LORD was not able
to bring them into the land that he promised them, and
because he hated them, he has brought them out to let them
die in the wilderness.' For they are the people of your very
own possession, whom you brought out by your great
power and by your outstretched arm." At that time the
LORD said to me, "Carve out two tablets of stone like the
former ones, and come up to me on the mountain, and make
an ark of wood. I will write on the tablets the words that
were on the former tablets, which you smashed, and you
shall put them in the ark." So I made an ark of acacia wood,
cut two tablets of stone like the former ones, and went up
the mountain with the two tablets in my hand. Then he
wrote on the tablets the same words as before, the ten
commandments that the LORD had spoken to you on the
mountain out of the fire on the day of the assembly; and the
LORD gave them to me. So I turned and came down from

the mountain, and put the tablets in the ark that I had made; and there they are, as the LORD commanded me.

A Reading (Lesson) from the Letter to the
Hebrews [4:1–10]

While the promise of entering his rest is still open, let us take care that none of you should seem to have failed to reach it. For indeed the good news came to us just as to them; but the message they heard did not benefit them, because they were not united by faith with those who listened. For we who have believed enter that rest, just as God has said, "As in my anger I swore, 'They shall not enter my rest,'" though his works were finished at the foundation of the world. For in one place it speaks about the seventh day as follows, "And God rested on the seventh day from all his works." And again in this place it says, "They shall not enter my rest." Since therefore it remains open for some to enter it, and those who formerly received the good news failed to enter because of disobedience, again he sets a certain day—"today"— saying through David much later, in the words already quoted, "Today, if you hear his voice, do not harden your hearts." For if Joshua had given them rest, God would not speak later about another day. So then, a sabbath rest still remains for the people of God; for those who enter God's rest also cease from their labors as God did from his.

John 3:16–21 [page 56 above]

Friday

*Psalm 95** [page 724] & *Psalm 40* [page 640],
Psalm 54 [page 659] ❖ *Psalm 51* [page 656]

*A Reading (Lesson) from the Book of
Deuteronomy* [10:12–22]

Moses convened all Israel, and said to them: So now, O
Israel, what does the LORD your God require of you? Only
to fear the LORD your God, to walk in all his ways, to love
him, to serve the LORD your God with all your heart and
with all your soul, and to keep the commandments of the
LORD your God and his decrees that I am commanding you
today, for your own well-being. Although heaven and the
heaven of heavens belong to the LORD your God, the earth
with all that is in it, yet the LORD set his heart in love on
your ancestors alone and chose you, their descendants after
them, out of all the peoples, as it is today. Circumcise, then,
the foreskin of your heart, and do not be stubborn any
longer. For the LORD your God is God of gods and Lord of
lords, the great God, mighty and awesome, who is not
partial and takes no bribe, who executes justice for the
orphan and the widow, and who loves the strangers,
providing them food and clothing. You shall also love the
stranger, for you were strangers in the land of Egypt. You
shall fear the LORD your God; him alone you shall worship;
to him you shall hold fast, and by his name you shall swear.
He is your praise; he is your God, who has done for you
these great and awesome things that your own eyes have
seen. Your ancestors went down to Egypt seventy persons;
and now the LORD your God has made you as numerous as
the stars in heaven.

* *For the Invitatory*

A Reading (Lesson) from the Letter to the
Hebrews [4:11–16]

Let us make every effort to enter that rest, so that no one
may fall through such disobedience as theirs. Indeed, the
word of God is living and active, sharper than any
two-edged sword, piercing until it divides soul from spirit,
joints from marrow; it is able to judge the thoughts and
intentions of the heart. And before him no creature is
hidden, but all are naked and laid bare to the eyes of the
one to whom we must render an account. Since, then, we
have a great high priest who has passed through the
heavens, Jesus, the Son of God, let us hold fast to our
confession. For we do not have a high priest who is
unable to sympathize with our weaknesses, but we have
one who in every respect has been tested as we are, yet
without sin. Let us therefore approach the throne of grace
with boldness, so that we may receive mercy and find
grace to help in time of need.

A Reading (Lesson) from the Gospel according to
John [3:22–36]

Jesus and his disciples went into the Judean countryside,
and he spent some time there with them and baptized.
John also was baptizing at Aenon near Salim because
water was abundant there; and people kept coming and
were being baptized—John, of course, had not yet been
thrown into prison. Now a discussion about purification
arose between John's disciples and a Jew. They came to
John and said to him, "Rabbi, the one who was with you
across the Jordan, to whom you testified, here he is
baptizing, and all are going to him." John answered, "No
one can receive anything except what has been given from
heaven. You yourselves are my witnesses that I said, 'I am

not the Messiah, but I have been sent ahead of him.' He who has the bride is the bridegroom. The friend of the bridegroom, who stands and hears him, rejoices greatly at the bridegroom's voice. For this reason my joy has been fulfilled. He must increase, but I must decrease." The one who comes from above is above all; the one who is of the earth belongs to the earth and speaks about earthly things. The one who comes from heaven is above all. He testifies to what he has seen and heard, yet no one accepts his testimony. Whoever has accepted his testimony has certified this, that God is true. He whom God has sent speaks the words of God, for he gives the Spirit without measure. The Father loves the Son and has placed all things in his hands. Whoever believes in the Son has eternal life; whoever disobeys the Son will not see life, but must endure God's wrath.

Saturday

Psalm 55 [page 660] ❖ *Psalm 138* [page 793], *Psalm 139:1–17(18–23)* [page 794]

A Reading (Lesson) from the Book of Deuteronomy [11:18–28]

Moses convened all Israel, and said to them: You shall put these words of mine in your heart and soul, and you shall bind them as a sign on your hand, and fix them as an emblem on your forehead. Teach them to your children, talking about them when you are at home and when you are away, when you lie down and when you rise. Write them on the doorposts of your house and on your gates, so that your days and the days of your children may be multiplied in the land that the LORD swore to your ancestors to give them, as long as the heavens are above the earth. If you will diligently observe this entire commandment that I am commanding you, loving the LORD your God, walking in all his ways, and holding fast to him, then the LORD will drive out all these nations before you, and you will dispossess nations larger and mightier than yourselves. Every place on which you set foot shall be yours; your territory shall extend from the wilderness to the Lebanon and from the River, the river Euphrates, to the Western Sea. No one will be able to stand against you; the LORD your God will put the fear and dread of you on all the land on which you set foot, as he promised you. See, I am setting before you today a blessing and a curse: the blessing, if you obey the commandments of the LORD your God that I am commanding you today; and the curse, if you do not obey the commandments of the LORD your God, but turn from the way that I am commanding you today, to follow other gods that you have not known.

A Reading (Lesson) from the Letter to the Hebrews [5:1–10]

Every high priest chosen from among mortals is put in charge of things pertaining to God on their behalf, to offer gifts and sacrifices for sins. He is able to deal gently with the ignorant and wayward, since he himself is subject to weakness; and because of this he must offer sacrifice for his own sins as well as for those of the people. And one does not presume to take this honor, but takes it only when called by God, just as Aaron was. So also Christ did not glorify himself in becoming a high priest, but was appointed by the one who said to him, "You are my Son, today I have begotten you"; as he says also in another place, "You are a priest forever, according to the order of Melchizedek." In the days of his flesh, Jesus offered up prayers and supplications, with loud cries and tears, to the one who was able to save him from death, and he was heard because of his reverent submission. Although he was a Son, he learned obedience through what he suffered; and having been made perfect, he became the source of eternal salvation for all who obey him, having been designated by God a high priest according to the order of Melchizedek.

A Reading (Lesson) from the Gospel according to John [4:1–26]

Now when Jesus learned that the Pharisees had heard, "Jesus is making and baptizing more disciples than John"—although it was not Jesus himself but his disciples who baptized—he left Judea and started back to Galilee. But he had to go through Samaria. So he came to a Samaritan city called Sychar, near the plot of ground that Jacob had given to his son Joseph. Jacob's well was there, and Jesus, tired out by his journey, was sitting by the well. It was about noon. A Samaritan woman came to draw water, and Jesus said to her, "Give me a drink." (His disciples had gone to the city to buy food.) The Samaritan woman said to him, "How is it that you, a Jew, ask a drink of me, a woman of Samaria?" (Jews do not share things in common with Samaritans.) Jesus answered her, "If you knew the gift of God, and who it is that is saying to you, 'Give me a drink,' you would have asked him, and he would have given you living water." The woman said to him, "Sir, you have no bucket, and the well is deep. Where do you get that living water? Are you greater than our ancestor Jacob, who gave us the well, and with his sons and his flocks drank from it?" Jesus said to her, "Everyone who drinks of this water will be thirsty again, but those who drink of the water that I will give them will never be thirsty. The water that I will give will become in them a spring of water gushing up to eternal life." The woman said to him, "Sir, give me this water, so that I may never be thirsty or have to keep coming here to draw water." Jesus said to her, "Go, call your husband, and come back." The woman answered him, "I have no husband." Jesus said to her, "You are right in saying, 'I have no husband'; for you have had five husbands, and the one you have now is not your husband. What you have said is true!" The woman said to him, "Sir, I see that you are a prophet. Our ancestors worshiped on this mountain, but you say that the place where people must worship is in Jerusalem." Jesus said to her, "Woman, believe me, the hour is coming when you will worship the Father neither on this mountain nor in Jerusalem. You worship what you do not know; we worship what we know, for salvation is from the Jews. But the hour is coming, and is now here, when the true worshipers will worship the Father in spirit and truth, for the Father seeks such as these to worship him. God is spirit, and those who worship him must worship in spirit and truth." The woman said to him, "I know that Messiah is coming" (who is called Christ). "When he comes, he will proclaim all things to us." Jesus said to her, "I am he, the one who is speaking to you."

Week of 2 Lent

Sunday

Psalm 24 [page 613], *Psalm 29* [page 620] ❖
Psalm 8 [page 592], *Psalm 84* [page 707]

A Reading (Lesson) from the Book of Jeremiah [1:1–10]

The words of Jeremiah son of Hilkiah, of the priests who were in Anathoth in the land of Benjamin, to whom the word of the LORD came in the days of King Josiah son of Amon of Judah, in the thirteenth year of his reign. It came also in the days of King Jehoiakim son of Josiah of Judah, and until the end of the eleventh year of King Zedekiah son of Josiah of Judah, until the captivity of Jerusalem in the fifth month. Now the word of the LORD came to me saying, "Before I formed you in the womb I knew you, and before you were born I consecrated you; I appointed you a prophet to the nations." Then I said, "Ah, Lord GOD! Truly I do not know how to speak, for I am only a boy." But the LORD said to me, "Do not say, 'I am only a boy'; for you shall go to all to whom I send you, and you shall speak whatever I command you. Do not be afraid of them, for I am with you to deliver you, says the LORD." Then the LORD put out his hand and touched my mouth; and the LORD said to me, "Now I have put my words in your mouth. See, today I appoint you over nations and over kingdoms, to pluck up and to pull down, to destroy and to overthrow, to build and to plant."

A Reading (Lesson) from the First Letter of Paul to the Corinthians [3:11-23]

No one can lay any foundation other than the one that has been laid; that foundation is Jesus Christ. Now if anyone builds on the foundation with gold, silver, precious stones, wood, hay, straw—the work of each builder will become visible, for the Day will disclose it, because it will be revealed with fire, and the fire will test what sort of work each has done. If what has been built on the foundation survives, the builder will receive a reward. If the work is burned up, the builder will suffer loss; the builder will be saved, but only as through fire. Do you not know that you are God's temple and that God's Spirit dwells in you? If anyone destroys God's temple, God will destroy that person. For God's temple is holy, and you are that temple. Do not deceive yourselves. If you think that you are wise in this age, you should become fools so that you may become wise. For the wisdom of this world is foolishness with God. For it is written, "He catches the wise in their craftiness," and again, "The Lord knows the thoughts of the wise, that they are futile." So let no one boast about human leaders. For all things are yours, whether Paul or Apollos or Cephas or the world or life or death or the present or the future—all belong to you, and you belong to Christ, and Christ belongs to God.

A Reading (Lesson) from the Gospel according to Mark [3:31-4:9]

Jesus' mother and his brothers came; and standing outside, they sent to him and called him. A crowd was sitting around him; and they said to him, "Your mother and your brothers and sisters are outside, asking for you." And he replied, "Who are my mother and my brothers?" And looking at those who sat around him, he said, "Here are my mother and my brothers! Whoever does the will of God is my brother and sister and mother." Again he began to teach beside the sea. Such a very large crowd gathered around him that he got into a boat on the sea and sat there, while the whole crowd was beside the sea on the land. He began to teach them many things in parables, and in his teaching he said to them: "Listen! A sower went out to sow. And as he sowed, some seed fell on the path, and the birds came and ate it up. Other seed fell on rocky ground, where it did not have much soil, and it sprang up quickly, since it had no depth of soil. And when the sun rose, it was scorched; and since it had no root, it withered away. Other seed fell among thorns, and the thorns grew up and choked it, and it yielded no grain. Other seed fell into good soil and brought forth grain, growing up and increasing and yielding thirty and sixty and a hundredfold." And he said, "Let anyone with ears to hear listen!"

Monday

Psalm 56 [page 662], *Psalm 57* [page 663], *(Psalm 58* [page 664]) ❖ *Psalm 64* [page 671], *Psalm 65* [page 672]

A Reading (Lesson) from the Book of Jeremiah [1:11–19]

The word of the LORD came to me, saying, "Jeremiah, what do you see?" And I said, "I see a branch of an almond tree." Then the LORD said to me, "You have seen well, for I am watching over my word to perform it." The word of the LORD came to me a second time, saying, "What do you see?" And I said, "I see a boiling pot, tilted away from the north." Then the LORD said to me: Out of the north disaster shall break out on all the inhabitants of the land. For now I am calling all the tribes of the kingdoms of the north, says the LORD; and they shall come and all of them shall set their thrones at the entrance of the gates of Jerusalem, against all its surrounding walls and against all the cities of Judah. And I will utter my judgments against them, for all their wickedness in forsaking me; they have made offerings to other gods, and worshiped the works of their own hands. But you, gird up your loins; stand up and tell them everything that I command you. Do not break down before them, or I will break you before them. And I for my part have made you today a fortified city, an iron pillar, and a bronze wall, against the whole land—against the kings of Judah, its princes, its priests, and the people of the land. They will fight against you; but they shall not prevail against you, for I am with you, says the LORD, to deliver you.

A Reading (Lesson) from the Letter of Paul to the Romans [1:1–15]

Paul, a servant of Jesus Christ, called to be an apostle, set apart for the gospel of God, which he promised beforehand through his prophets in the holy scriptures, the gospel concerning his Son, who was descended from David according to the flesh and was declared to be Son of God with power according to the spirit of holiness by resurrection from the dead, Jesus Christ our Lord, through whom we have received grace and apostleship to bring about the obedience of faith among all the Gentiles for the sake of his name, including yourselves who are called to belong to Jesus Christ, to all God's beloved in Rome, who are called to be saints: Grace to you and peace from God our Father and the Lord Jesus Christ. First, I thank my God through Jesus Christ for all of you, because your faith is proclaimed throughout the world. For God, whom I serve with my spirit by announcing the gospel of his Son, is my witness that without ceasing I remember you always in my prayers, asking that by God's will I may somehow at last succeed in coming to you. For I am longing to see you so that I may share with you some spiritual gift to strengthen you—or rather so that we may be mutually encouraged by each other's faith, both yours and mine. I want you to know, brothers and sisters, that I have often intended to come to you (but thus far have been prevented), in order that I may reap some harvest among you as I have among the rest of the Gentiles. I am a debtor both to Greeks and to barbarians, both to the wise and to the foolish—hence my eagerness to proclaim the gospel to you also who are in Rome.

John 4:27–42 [page 142 above]

Tuesday

Psalm 61 [page 668], *Psalm 62* [page 669] ❖
Psalm 68:1–20(21–23)24–36 [page 676]

A Reading (Lesson) from the Book of Jeremiah [2:1–13]

The word of the LORD came to me, saying: Go and proclaim in the hearing of Jerusalem, Thus says the LORD: I remember the devotion of your youth, your love as a bride, how you followed me in the wilderness, in a land not sown. Israel was holy to the LORD, the first fruits of his harvest. All who ate of it were held guilty; disaster came upon them, says the LORD. Hear the word of the LORD, O house of

Jacob, and all the families of the house of Israel. Thus says the LORD: What wrong did your ancestors find in me that they went far from me, and went after worthless things, and became worthless themselves? They did not say, "Where is the LORD who brought us up from the land of Egypt, who led us in the wilderness, in a land of deserts and pits, in a land of drought and deep darkness, in a land that no one passes through, where no one lives?" I brought you into a plentiful land to eat its fruits and its good things. But when you entered you defiled my land, and made my heritage an abomination. The priests did not say, "Where is the LORD?" Those who handle the law did not know me; the rulers transgressed against me; the prophets prophesied by Baal, and went after things that do not profit. Therefore once more I accuse you, says the LORD, and I accuse your children's children. Cross to the coasts of Cyprus and look, send to Kedar and examine with care; see if there has ever been such a thing. Has a nation changed its gods, even though they are no gods? But my people have changed their glory for something that does not profit. Be appalled, O heavens, at this, be shocked, be utterly desolate, says the LORD, for my people have committed two evils: they have forsaken me, the fountain of living water, and dug out cisterns for themselves, cracked cisterns that can hold no water.

A Reading (Lesson) from the Letter of Paul to the Romans [1:16–25]

For I am not ashamed of the gospel; it is the power of God for salvation to everyone who has faith, to the Jew first and also to the Greek. For in it the righteousness of God is revealed through faith for faith; as it is written, "The one who is righteous will live by faith." For the wrath of God is revealed from heaven against all ungodliness and wickedness of those who by their wickedness suppress the truth. For what can be known about God is plain to them, because God has shown it to them. Ever since the creation of the world his eternal power and divine nature, invisible though they are, have been understood and seen through the things he has made. So they are without excuse; for though they knew God, they did not honor him as God or give thanks to him, but they became futile in their thinking, and their senseless minds were darkened. Claiming to be wise, they became fools; and they exchanged the glory of the immortal God for images resembling a mortal human being or birds or four-footed animals or reptiles. Therefore God gave them up in the lusts of their hearts to impurity, to the degrading of their bodies among themselves, because they exchanged the truth about God for a lie and worshiped and served the creature rather than the Creator, who is blessed forever! Amen.

A Reading (Lesson) from the Gospel according to John [4:43–54]

After two days in Samaria Jesus went from that place to Galilee (for Jesus himself had testified that a prophet has no honor in the prophet's own country). When he came to Galilee, the Galileans welcomed him, since they had seen all that he had done in Jerusalem at the festival; for they too had gone to the festival. Then he came again to Cana in Galilee where he had changed the water into wine. Now there was a royal official whose son lay ill in Capernaum. When he heard that Jesus had come from Judea to Galilee, he went and begged him to come down and heal his son, for he was at the point of death. Then

Jesus said to him, "Unless you see signs and wonders you will not believe." The official said to him, "Sir, come down before my little boy dies." Jesus said to him, "Go; your son will live." The man believed the word that Jesus spoke to him and started on his way. As he was going down, his slaves met him and told him that his child was alive. So he asked them the hour when he began to recover, and they said to him, "Yesterday at one in the afternoon the fever left him." The father realized that this was the hour when Jesus had said to him, "Your son will live." So he himself believed, along with his whole household. Now this was the second sign that Jesus did after coming from Judea to Galilee.

Wednesday

Psalm 72 [page 685] ❖ *Psalm 119:73–96* [page 769]

A Reading (Lesson) from the Book of Jeremiah [3:6–18]

The LORD said to me in the days of King Josiah: Have you seen what she did, that faithless one, Israel, how she went up on every high hill and under every green tree, and played the whore there? And I thought, "After she has done all this she will return to me"; but she did not return, and her false sister Judah saw it. She saw that for all the adulteries of that faithless one, Israel, I had sent her away with a decree of divorce; yet her false sister Judah did not fear, but she too went and played the whore. Because she took her whoredom so lightly, she polluted the land, committing adultery with stone and tree. Yet for all this her false sister Judah did not return to me with her whole heart, but only in pretense, says the LORD. Then the LORD said to me: Faithless Israel has shown herself less guilty than false Judah. Go, and proclaim these words toward the north, and say: Return, faithless Israel, says the LORD. I will not look on you in anger, for I am merciful, says the LORD; I will not be angry forever. Only acknowledge your guilt, that you have rebelled against the LORD your God, and scattered your favors among strangers under every green tree, and have not obeyed my voice, says the LORD. Return, O faithless children, says the LORD, for I am your master; I will take you, one from a city and two from a family, and I will bring you to Zion. I will give you shepherds after my own heart, who will feed you with knowledge and understanding. And when you have multiplied and increased in the land, in those days, says the LORD, they shall no longer say, "The ark of the covenant of the LORD." It shall not come to mind, or be remembered, or missed; nor shall another one be made. At that time Jerusalem shall be called the throne of the LORD, and all nations shall gather to it, to the presence of the LORD in Jerusalem, and they shall no longer stubbornly follow their own evil will. In those days the house of Judah shall join the house of Israel, and together they shall come from the land of the north to the land that I gave your ancestors for a heritage.

A Reading (Lesson) from the Letter of Paul to the Romans [1:28—2:11]

Since they did not see fit to acknowledge God, God gave them up to a debased mind and to things that should not be done. They were filled with every kind of wickedness, evil, covetousness, malice. Full of envy, murder, strife, deceit, craftiness, they are gossips, slanderers, God-haters, insolent, haughty, boastful, inventors of evil, rebellious toward parents, foolish, faithless, heartless, ruthless. They know God's decree, that those who practice such things deserve to die—yet they not only do them but even applaud others who practice them. Therefore you have no excuse, whoever you are, when you judge others; for in passing judgment on another you condemn yourself, because you, the judge, are doing the very same things. You say, "We know that God's judgment on those who do such things is in accordance with truth." Do you imagine, whoever you are, that when you judge those who do such things and yet do them yourself, you will escape the judgment of God? Or do you despise the riches of his kindness and forbearance and patience? Do you not realize that God's kindness is meant to lead you to repentance? But by your hard and impenitent heart you are storing up wrath for yourself on the day of wrath, when God's righteous judgment will be revealed. For he will repay according to each one's deeds: to those who by patiently doing good seek for glory and honor and immortality, he will give eternal life; while for those who are self-seeking and who obey not the truth but wickedness, there will be wrath and fury. There will be anguish and distress for everyone who does evil, the Jew first and also the Greek, but glory and honor and peace for everyone who does good, the Jew first and also the Greek. For God shows no partiality.

A Reading (Lesson) from the Gospel according to John [5:1–18]

After the second sign in Cana there was a festival of the Jews, and Jesus went up to Jerusalem. Now in Jerusalem by the Sheep Gate there is a pool, called in Hebrew Beth-zatha, which has five porticoes. In these lay many invalids—blind, lame, and paralyzed. One man was there who had been ill for thirty-eight years. When Jesus saw him lying there and knew that he had been there a long time, he said to him, "Do you want to be made well?" The sick man answered him, "Sir, I have no one to put me into the pool when the water is stirred up; and while I am making my way, someone else steps down ahead of me." Jesus said to him, "Stand up, take your mat and walk." At once the man was made well, and he took up his mat and began to walk. Now that day was a sabbath. So the Jews said to the man who had been cured, "It is the sabbath; it is not lawful for you to carry your mat." But he answered them, "The man who made me well said to me, 'Take up your mat and walk.' " They asked him, "Who is the man who said to you, 'Take it up and walk'?" Now the man who had been healed did not know who it was, for Jesus had disappeared in the crowd that was there. Later Jesus found him in the temple and said to him, "See, you have been made well! Do not sin any more, so that nothing worse happens to you." The man went away and told the Jews that it was Jesus who had made him well. Therefore the Jews started persecuting Jesus, because he was doing such things on the sabbath. But Jesus answered them, "My Father is still working, and I also am working." For this reason the Jews were seeking all the more to kill him, because he was not only breaking the sabbath, but was also calling God his own Father, thereby making himself equal to God.

Thursday

(Psalm 70 [page 682]),   *Psalm 71* [page 683]   ❖
Psalm 74 [page 689]

*A Reading (Lesson) from the Book of
Jeremiah* [4:9–10,19–28]

On that day, says the LORD, courage shall fail the king and
the officials; the priests shall be appalled and the prophets
astounded. Then I said, "Ah, Lord GOD, how utterly you
have deceived this people and Jerusalem, saying, 'It shall be
well with you,' even while the sword is at the throat!" My
anguish, my anguish! I writhe in pain! Oh, the walls of my
heart! My heart is beating wildly; I cannot keep silent; for I
hear the sound of the trumpet, the alarm of war. Disaster
overtakes disaster, the whole land is laid waste. Suddenly
my tents are destroyed, my curtains in a moment. How long
must I see the standard, and hear the sound of the trumpet?
"For my people are foolish, they do not know me; they are
stupid children, they have no understanding. They are
skilled in doing evil, but do not know how to do good." I
looked on the earth, and lo, it was waste and void; and to
the heavens, and they had no light. I looked on the
mountains, and lo, they were quaking, and all the hills
moved to and fro. I looked, and lo, there was no one at all,
and all the birds of the air had fled. I looked, and lo, the
fruitful land was a desert, and all its cities were laid in ruins
before the LORD, before his fierce anger. For thus says the
LORD: The whole land shall be a desolation; yet I will not
make a full end. Because of this the earth shall mourn, and
the heavens above grow black; for I have spoken, I have
purposed; I have not relented nor will I turn back.

*A Reading (Lesson) from the Letter of Paul to the
Romans* [2:12–24]

All who have sinned apart from the law will also perish
apart from the law, and all who have sinned under the
law will be judged by the law. For it is not the hearers of

the law who are righteous in God's sight, but the doers of the law who will be justified. When Gentiles, who do not possess the law, do instinctively what the law requires, these, though not having the law, are a law to themselves. They show that what the law requires is written on their hearts, to which their own conscience also bears witness; and their conflicting thoughts will accuse or perhaps excuse them on the day when, according to my gospel, God, through Jesus Christ, will judge the secret thoughts of all. But if you call yourself a Jew and rely on the law and boast of your relation to God and know his will and determine what is best because you are instructed in the law, and if you are sure that you are a guide to the blind, a light to those who are in darkness, a corrector of the foolish, a teacher of children, having in the law the embodiment of knowledge and truth, you, then, that teach others, will you not teach yourself? While you preach against stealing, do you steal? You that forbid adultery, do you commit adultery? You that abhor idols, do you rob temples? You that boast in the law, do you dishonor God by breaking the law? For, as it is written, "The name of God is blasphemed among the Gentiles because of you."

A Reading (Lesson) from the Gospel according to John [5:19–29]

Jesus said to the Jews, "Very truly, I tell you, the Son can do nothing on his own, but only what he sees the Father doing; for whatever the Father does, the Son does likewise. The Father loves the Son and shows him all that he himself is doing; and he will show him greater works than these, so that you will be astonished. Indeed, just as the Father raises the dead and gives them life, so also the Son gives life to whomever he wishes. The Father judges no one but has given all judgment to the Son, so that all may honor the Son just as they honor the Father. Anyone who does not honor the Son does not honor the Father who sent him. Very truly, I tell you, anyone who hears my word and believes him who sent me has eternal life, and does not come under judgment, but has passed from death to life. Very truly, I tell you, the hour is coming, and is now here, when the dead will hear the voice of the Son of God, and those who hear will live. For just as the Father has life in himself, so he has granted the Son also to have life in himself; and he has given him authority to execute judgment, because he is the Son of Man. Do not be astonished at this; for the hour is coming when all who are in their graves will hear his voice and will come out—those who have done good, to the resurrection of life, and those who have done evil, to the resurrection of condemnation."

Friday

*Psalm 95** [page 724] &
Psalm 69:1–23(24–30)31–38 [page 679]   ❖
Psalm 73 [page 687]

A Reading (Lesson) from the Book of Jeremiah [5:1–9]

Run to and fro through the streets of Jerusalem, look around and take note! Search its squares and see if you can find one person who acts justly and seeks truth—so that I may pardon Jerusalem. Although they say, "As the LORD lives," yet they swear falsely. O LORD, do your eyes not look

---

* *For the Invitatory*

for truth? You have struck them, but they felt no anguish; you have consumed them, but they refused to take correction. They have made their faces harder than rock; they have refused to turn back. Then I said, "These are only the poor, they have no sense; for they do not know the way of the LORD, the law of their God. Let me go to the rich and speak to them; surely they know the way of the LORD, the law of their God." But they all alike had broken the yoke, they had burst the bonds. Therefore a lion from the forest shall kill them, a wolf from the desert shall destroy them. A leopard is watching against their cities; everyone who goes out of them shall be torn in pieces—because their transgressions are many, their apostasies are great. How can I pardon you? Your children have forsaken me, and have sworn by those who are no gods. When I fed them to the full, they committed adultery and trooped to the houses of prostitutes. They were well-fed lusty stallions, each neighing for his neighbor's wife. Shall I not punish them for these things? says the LORD; and shall I not bring retribution on a nation such as this?

A Reading (Lesson) from the Letter of Paul to the Romans [2:25—3:18]

Circumcision indeed is of value if you obey the law; but if you break the law, your circumcision has become uncircumcision. So, if those who are uncircumcised keep the requirements of the law, will not their uncircumcision be regarded as circumcision? Then those who are physically uncircumcised but keep the law will condemn you that have the written code and circumcision but break the law. For a person is not a Jew who is one outwardly, nor is true circumcision something external and physical.

Rather, a person is a Jew who is one inwardly, and real circumcision is a matter of the heart—it is spiritual and not literal. Such a person receives praise not from others but from God. Then what advantage has the Jew? Or what is the value of circumcision? Much, in every way. For in the first place the Jews were entrusted with the oracles of God. What if some were unfaithful? Will their faithlessness nullify the faithfulness of God? By no means! Although everyone is a liar, let God be proved true, as it is written, "So that you may be justified in your words, and prevail in your judging." But if our injustice serves to confirm the justice of God, what should we say? That God is unjust to inflict wrath on us? (I speak in a human way.) By no means! For then how could God judge the world? But if through my falsehood God's truthfulness abounds to his glory, why am I still being condemned as a sinner? And why not say (as some people slander us by saying that we say), "Let us do evil so that good may come"? Their condemnation is deserved! What then? Are we any better off? No, not at all; for we have already charged that all, both Jews and Greeks, are under the power of sin, as it is written: "There is no one who is righteous, not even one; there is no one who has understanding, there is no one who seeks God. All have turned aside, together they have become worthless; there is no one who shows kindness, there is not even one." "Their throats are opened graves; they use their tongues to deceive." "The venom of vipers is under their lips." "Their mouths are full of cursing and bitterness." "Their feet are swift to shed blood; ruin and misery are in their paths, and the way of peace they have not known." "There is no fear of God before their eyes."

John 5:30–47 [page 59 above]

Saturday

Psalm 75 [page 691],   *Psalm 76* [page 692]   ❖
Psalm 23 [page 612],   *Psalm 27* [page 617]

A Reading (Lesson) from the Book of Jeremiah [5:20–31]

Declare this in the house of Jacob, proclaim it in Judah:
Hear this, O foolish and senseless people, who have eyes,
but do not see, who have ears, but do not hear. Do you not
fear me? says the LORD; Do you not tremble before me? I
placed the sand as a boundary for the sea, a perpetual
barrier that it cannot pass; though the waves toss, they
cannot prevail, though they roar, they cannot pass over it.
But this people has a stubborn and rebellious heart; they
have turned aside and gone away. They do not say in their
hearts, "Let us fear the LORD our God, who gives the rain in
its season, the autumn rain and the spring rain, and keeps
for us the weeks appointed for the harvest." Your iniquities
have turned these away, and your sins have deprived you of
good. For scoundrels are found among my people; they take
over the goods of others. Like fowlers they set a trap; they
catch human beings. Like a cage full of birds, their houses
are full of treachery; therefore they have become great and
rich, they have grown fat and sleek. They know no limits in
deeds of wickedness; they do not judge with justice the
cause of the orphan, to make it prosper, and they do not
defend the rights of the needy. Shall I not punish them for
these things? says the LORD, and shall I not bring retribution
on a nation such as this? An appalling and horrible thing has
happened in the land: the prophets prophesy falsely, and the

priests rule as the prophets direct; my people love to have it so, but what will you do when the end comes?

A Reading (Lesson) from the Letter of Paul to the Romans [3:19–31]

We know that whatever the law says, it speaks to those who are under the law, so that every mouth may be silenced, and the whole world may be held accountable to God. For "no human being will be justified in his sight" by deeds prescribed by the law, for through the law comes the knowledge of sin. But now, apart from law, the righteousness of God has been disclosed, and is attested by the law and the prophets, the righteousness of God through faith in Jesus Christ for all who believe. For there is no distinction, since all have sinned and fall short of the glory of God; they are now justified by his grace as a gift, through the redemption that is in Christ Jesus, whom God put forward as a sacrifice of atonement by his blood, effective through faith. He did this to show his righteousness, because in his divine forbearance he had passed over the sins previously committed; it was to prove at the present time that he himself is righteous and that he justifies the one who has faith in Jesus. Then what becomes of boasting? It is excluded. By what law? By that of works? No, but by the law of faith. For we hold that a person is justified by faith apart from works prescribed by the law. Or is God the God of Jews only? Is he not the God of Gentiles also? Yes, of Gentiles also, since God is one; and he will justify the circumcised on the ground of faith and the uncircumcised through that same faith. Do we then overthrow the law by this faith? By no means! On the contrary, we uphold the law.

A Reading (Lesson) from the Gospel according to
John [7:1–13]

Jesus went about in Galilee. He did not wish to go about
in Judea because the Jews were looking for an opportunity
to kill him. Now the Jewish festival of Booths was near.
So his brothers said to him, "Leave here and go to Judea
so that your disciples also may see the works you are
doing; for no one who wants to be widely known acts in
secret. If you do these things, show yourself to the world."
(For not even his brothers believed in him.) Jesus said to
them, "My time has not yet come, but your time is always
here. The world cannot hate you, but it hates me because
I testify against it that its works are evil. Go to the festival
yourselves. I am not going to this festival, for my time has
not yet fully come." After saying this, he remained in
Galilee. But after his brothers had gone to the festival,
then he also went, not publicly but as it were in secret.
The Jews were looking for him at the festival and saying,
"Where is he?" And there was considerable complaining
about him among the crowds. While some were saying,
"He is a good man," others were saying, "No, he is
deceiving the crowd." Yet no one would speak openly
about him for fear of the Jews.

Week of 3 Lent

Sunday

Psalm 93 [page 722],   *Psalm 96* [page 725]   ❖
Psalm 34 [page 627]

A Reading (Lesson) from the Book of Jeremiah [6:9–15]

Thus says the LORD of hosts: Glean thoroughly as a vine the remnant of Israel; like a grape-gatherer, pass your hand again over its branches. To whom shall I speak and give warning, that they may hear? See, their ears are closed, they cannot listen. The word of the LORD is to them an object of scorn; they take no pleasure in it. But I am full of the wrath of the LORD; I am weary of holding it in. Pour it out on the children in the street, and on the gatherings of young men as well; both husband and wife shall be taken, the old folk and the very aged. Their houses shall be turned over to others, their fields and wives together; for I will stretch out my hand against the inhabitants of the land, says the LORD. For from the least to the greatest of them, everyone is greedy for unjust gain; and from prophet to priest, everyone deals falsely. They have treated the wound of my people carelessly, saying, "Peace, peace," when there is no peace. They acted shamefully, they committed abomination; yet they were not ashamed, they did not know how to blush. Therefore they shall fall among those who fall; at the time that I punish them, they shall be overthrown, says the LORD.

A Reading (Lesson) from the First Letter of Paul to the Corinthians [6:12–20]

"All things are lawful for me," but not all things are beneficial. "All things are lawful for me," but I will not be dominated by anything. "Food is meant for the stomach and the stomach for food," and God will destroy both one and the other. The body is meant not for fornication but for the Lord, and the Lord for the body. And God raised the Lord and will also raise us by his power. Do you not know that your bodies are members of Christ? Should I therefore take the members of Christ and make them members of a prostitute? Never! Do you not know that whoever is united to a prostitute becomes one body with her? For it is said, "The two shall be one flesh." But anyone united to the Lord becomes one spirit with him. Shun fornication! Every sin that a person commits is outside the body; but the fornicator sins against the body itself. Or do you not know that your body is a temple of the Holy Spirit within you, which you have from God, and that you are not your own? For you were bought with a price; therefore glorify God in your body.

Mark 5:1–20 [page 159 above]

Monday

Psalm 80 [page 702]   ❖   *Psalm 77* [page 693], *(Psalm 79* [page 701])

A Reading (Lesson) from the Book of Jeremiah [7:1–15]

The word that came to Jeremiah from the LORD: Stand in the gate of the LORD's house, and proclaim there this word, and say, Hear the word of the LORD, all you people of Judah, you that enter these gates to worship the LORD. Thus says the LORD of hosts, the God of Israel: Amend your ways and your doings, and let me dwell with you in this place. Do not trust in these deceptive words: "This is the temple of the LORD, the temple of the LORD, the temple of the LORD." For if you truly amend your ways and your doings, if you truly act justly one with another, if you do not oppress the alien, the orphan, and the widow, or shed innocent blood in this place, and if you do not go after other gods to your own hurt, then I will dwell with you in this place, in the land that I gave of old to your ancestors forever and ever. Here you are, trusting in deceptive words to no avail. Will you steal, murder, commit adultery, swear falsely, make offerings to Baal, and go after other gods that you have not known, and then come and stand before me in this house, which is called by my name, and say, "We are safe!"—only to go on doing all these abominations? Has this house, which is called by my name, become a den of robbers in your sight? You know, I too am watching, says the LORD. Go now to my place that was in Shiloh, where I made my name dwell at first, and see what I did to it for the wickedness of my people Israel. And now, because you have done all these things, says the LORD, and when I spoke to you persistently, you did not listen, and when I called you, you did not answer, therefore I will do to the house that is called by my name, in which you trust, and to the place that I gave to you and to your ancestors, just what I did to Shiloh. And I will cast you out of my sight, just as I cast out all your kinsfolk, all the offspring of Ephraim.

A Reading (Lesson) from the Letter of Paul to the Romans [4:1–12]

What then are we to say was gained by Abraham, our ancestor according to the flesh? For if Abraham was justified by works, he has something to boast about, but not before God. For what does the scripture say? "Abraham believed God, and it was reckoned to him as righteousness." Now to one who works, wages are not reckoned as a gift but as something due. But to one who without works trusts him who justifies the ungodly, such faith is reckoned as righteousness. So also David speaks of the blessedness of those to whom God reckons righteousness apart from works: "Blessed are those whose iniquities are forgiven and whose sins are covered; blessed is the one against whom the Lord will not reckon sin." Is this blessedness, then, pronounced only on the circumcised, or also on the uncircumcised? We say, "Faith was reckoned to Abraham as righteousness." How then was it reckoned to him? Was it before or after he had been circumcised? It was not after, but before he was circumcised. He received the sign of circumcision as a seal of the righteousness that he had by faith while he was still uncircumcised. The purpose was to make him the ancestor of all who believe without being circumcised and who thus have righteousness reckoned to them, and likewise the ancestor of the circumcised who are not only circumcised but who also follow the example of the faith that our ancestor Abraham had before he was circumcised.

A Reading (Lesson) from the Gospel according to John [7:14–36]

About the middle of the festival Jesus went up into the temple and began to teach. The Jews were astonished at it, saying, "How does this man have such learning, when he has never been taught?" Then Jesus answered them, "My teaching is not mine but his who sent me. Anyone who resolves to do the will of God will know whether the teaching is from God or whether I am speaking on my own. Those who speak on their own seek their own glory; but the one who seeks the glory of him who sent him is true, and there is nothing false in him. Did not Moses give you the law? Yet none of you keeps the law. Why are you looking for an opportunity to kill me?" The crowd answered, "You have a demon! Who is trying to kill you?" Jesus answered them, "I performed one work, and all of you are astonished. Moses gave you circumcision (it is, of course, not from Moses, but from the patriarchs), and you circumcise a man on the sabbath. If a man receives circumcision on the sabbath in order that the law of Moses may not be broken, are you angry with me because I healed a man's whole body on the sabbath? Do not judge by appearances, but judge with right judgment." Now some of the people of Jerusalem were saying, "Is not this the man whom they are trying to kill? And here he is, speaking openly, but they say nothing to him! Can it be that the authorities really know that this is the Messiah? Yet we know where this man is from; but when the Messiah comes, no one will know where he is from." Then Jesus cried out as he was teaching in the temple, "You know me, and you know where I am from. I have not come on my own. But the one who sent me is true, and you do not know him. I know him, because I am from him, and he sent me." Then they tried to arrest him, but no one laid hands on him, because his hour had not yet come. Yet many in the crowd believed in him and were saying, "When the Messiah comes, will he do more signs than this man has done?" The Pharisees heard the crowd muttering such things about him, and the chief priests and Pharisees sent temple police to arrest him. Jesus then said, "I will be with you a little while longer, and then I am going to him who sent me. You will search for me, but you will not find me; and where I am, you cannot come." The Jews said to one another, "Where does this man intend to go that we will not find him? Does he intend to go to the Dispersion among the Greeks and teach the Greeks? What does he mean by saying, 'You will search for me and you will not find me' and 'Where I am, you cannot come'?"

Tuesday

Psalm 78:1–39 [page 694]   ❖   *Psalm 78:40–72* [page 698]

A Reading (Lesson) from the Book of Jeremiah [7:21–34]

Thus says the LORD of hosts, the God of Israel: Add your burnt offerings to your sacrifices, and eat the flesh. For in the day that I brought your ancestors out of the land of Egypt, I did not speak to them or command them concerning burnt offerings and sacrifices. But this command I gave them, "Obey my voice, and I will be your God, and you shall be my people; and walk only in the way that I command you, so that it may be well with you." Yet they did not obey or incline their ear, but, in the stubbornness of their evil will, they walked in their own counsels, and looked backward rather than forward. From the day that your ancestors came out of the land of Egypt until this day, I have persistently sent all my servants the prophets to them, day after day; yet they did not listen to me, or pay attention, but they stiffened their necks. They did worse than their ancestors did. So you shall speak all these words to them, but they will not listen to you. You shall call to them, but they will not answer you. You shall say to them: This is the nation that did not obey the voice of the LORD their God, and did not accept discipline; truth has perished; it is cut off from their lips. Cut off your hair and throw it away; raise a lamentation on the bare heights, for the LORD has rejected and forsaken the generation that provoked his wrath. For the people of Judah have done evil in my sight, says the LORD; they have set their abominations in the house that is called by my name, defiling it. And they go on building the high place of Topheth, which is in the valley of the son of Hinnom, to burn their sons and their daughters in the fire—which I did not command, nor did it come into my mind. Therefore, the days are surely coming, says the LORD, when it will no more be called Topheth, or the valley of the son of Hinnom, but the valley of Slaughter: for they will bury in Topheth until there is no more room. The corpses of this people will be food for the birds of the air, and for the animals of the earth; and no one will frighten them away. And I will bring to an end the sound of mirth and gladness, the voice of the bride and bridegroom in the cities of Judah and in the streets of Jerusalem; for the land shall become a waste.

A Reading (Lesson) from the Letter of Paul to the Romans [4:13–25]

The promise that he would inherit the world did not come to Abraham or to his descendants through the law but through the righteousness of faith. If it is the adherents of the law who are to be the heirs, faith is null and the promise is void. For the law brings wrath; but where there is no law, neither is there violation. For this reason it depends on faith, in order that the promise may rest on grace and be guaranteed to all his descendants, not only to the adherents of the law but also to those who share the faith of Abraham (for he is the father of all of us, as it is written, "I have made you the father of many nations")—in the presence of the God in whom he believed, who gives life to the dead and calls into existence the things that do not exist. Hoping against hope, he believed that he would become "the father of many nations," according to what was said, "So numerous shall your descendants be." He did not weaken in faith when he considered his own body, which was already as good as dead (for he was about a hundred years old), or when he considered the barrenness of Sarah's womb. No distrust made him waver concerning the promise of God, but he grew strong in his faith as he gave glory to God, being fully convinced that God was able to do what he had promised. Therefore his faith "was reckoned to him as righteousness." Now the words, "it was reckoned to him," were written not for his sake alone, but for ours also. It will be reckoned to us who believe in him who raised Jesus our Lord from the dead, who was handed over to death for our trespasses and was raised for our justification.

John 7:37–52 [page 80 above]

Wednesday

Psalm 119:97–120 [page 771] ❖ *Psalm 81* [page 704], *Psalm 82* [page 705]

A Reading (Lesson) from the Book of Jeremiah [8:18—9:6]

My joy is gone, grief is upon me, my heart is sick. Hark, the cry of my poor people from far and wide in the land: "Is the LORD not in Zion? Is her King not in her?" ("Why have they provoked me to anger with their images, with their foreign idols?") "The harvest is past, the summer is ended, and we are not saved." For the hurt of my poor people I am hurt, I mourn, and dismay has taken hold of me. Is there no balm in Gilead? Is there no physician there? Why then has the health of my poor people not been restored? O that my head were a spring of water, and my eyes a fountain of tears, so that I might weep day and night for the slain of my poor people! O that I had in the desert a traveler's lodging place, that I might leave my people and go away from them! For they are all adulterers, a band of traitors. They bend their tongues like bows; they have grown strong in the land for falsehood, and not for truth; for they proceed from evil to evil, and they do not know me, says the LORD. Beware of your neighbors, and put no trust in any of your kin; for all your kin are supplanters, and every neighbor goes around like a slanderer. They all deceive their neighbors, and no one speaks the truth; they have taught their tongues to speak lies; they commit iniquity and are too weary to repent. Oppression upon oppression, deceit upon deceit! They refuse to know me, says the LORD.

A Reading (Lesson) from the Letter of Paul to the Romans [5:1–11]

Since we are justified by faith, we have peace with God through our Lord Jesus Christ, through whom we have obtained access to this grace in which we stand; and we boast in our hope of sharing the glory of God. And not only that, but we also boast in our sufferings, knowing that suffering produces endurance, and endurance produces character, and character produces hope, and hope does not disappoint us, because God's love has been poured into our hearts through the Holy Spirit that has been given to us. For while we were still weak, at the right time Christ died for the ungodly. Indeed, rarely will anyone die for a righteous person—though perhaps for a good person someone might actually dare to die. But God proves his love for us in that while we still were sinners Christ died for us. Much more surely then, now that we have been justified by his blood, will we be saved through him from the wrath of God. For if while we were enemies, we were reconciled to God through the death of his Son, much more surely, having been reconciled, will we be saved by his life. But more than that, we even boast in God through our Lord Jesus Christ, through whom we have now received reconciliation.

A Reading (Lesson) from the Gospel according to John [8:12–20]

Again Jesus spoke to the crowd, saying, "I am the light of the world. Whoever follows me will never walk in darkness but will have the light of life." Then the Pharisees said to him, "You are testifying on your own behalf; your testimony is not valid." Jesus answered, "Even if I testify on my own behalf, my testimony is valid because I know where I have come from and where I am going, but you do not know where I come from or where I am going. You judge by human standards; I judge no one. Yet even if I do judge, my judgment is valid; for it is not I alone who judge, but I and the Father who sent me. In your law it is written that the testimony of two witnesses is valid. I testify on my own behalf, and the Father who sent me testifies on my behalf." Then they said to him, "Where is your Father?" Jesus answered, "You know neither me nor my Father. If you knew me, you would know my Father also." He spoke these words while he was teaching in the treasury of the temple, but no one arrested him, because his hour had not yet come.

Thursday

(Psalm 83 [page 706]) or Psalm 42 [page 643], Psalm 43 [page 644] ❖ Psalm 85 [page 708], Psalm 86 [page 709]

A Reading (Lesson) from the Book of Jeremiah [10:11–24]

Thus shall you say to them: The gods who did not make the heavens and the earth shall perish from the earth and from under the heavens. It is the LORD who made the earth by his power, who established the world by his wisdom, and by his understanding stretched out the heavens. When he utters his voice, there is a tumult of waters in the heavens, and he makes the mist rise from the ends of the earth. He makes lightnings for the rain, and he brings out the wind from his storehouses. Everyone is stupid and without knowledge; goldsmiths are all put to shame by their idols; for their images are false, and there is no breath in them. They are worthless, a work of delusion; at the time of their punishment they shall perish. Not like these is the LORD, the portion of Jacob, for he is the one who formed all things, and Israel is the tribe of his inheritance; the LORD of hosts is his name. Gather up your bundle from the ground, O you who live under siege! For thus says the LORD: I am going to sling out the inhabitants of the land at this time, and I will bring distress on them, so that they shall feel it. Woe is me because of my hurt! My wound is severe. But I said, "Truly this is my punishment, and I must bear it." My tent is destroyed, and all my cords are broken; my children have gone from me, and they are no more; there is no one to spread my tent again, and to set up my curtains. For the shepherds are stupid, and do not inquire of the LORD; therefore they have not prospered, and all their flock is scattered. Hear, a noise! Listen, it is coming—a great commotion from the land of the north to make the cities of Judah a desolation, a lair of jackals. I know, O LORD, that the way of human beings is not in their control, that mortals as they walk cannot direct their steps. Correct me, O LORD, but in just measure; not in your anger, or you will bring me to nothing.

A Reading (Lesson) from the Letter of Paul to the Romans [5:12–21]

Just as sin came into the world through one man, and death came through sin, and so death spread to all because all have sinned—sin was indeed in the world before the law, but sin is not reckoned when there is no law. Yet death exercised dominion from Adam to Moses, even over those whose sins were not like the transgression of Adam, who is a type of the one who was to come. But the free gift is not like the trespass. For if the many died through the one man's trespass, much more surely have the grace of God and the free gift in the grace of the one man, Jesus Christ, abounded for the many. And the free gift is not like the effect of the one man's sin. For the judgment following one trespass brought condemnation, but the free gift following many trespasses brings justification. If, because of the one man's trespass, death exercised dominion through that one, much more surely will those who receive the abundance of grace and the free gift of righteousness exercise dominion in life through the one man, Jesus Christ. Therefore just as one man's trespass led to condemnation for all, so one man's act of righteousness leads to justification and life for all. For just as by the one man's disobedience the many were made sinners, so by the one man's obedience the many will be made righteous. But law came in, with the result that the trespass multiplied; but where sin increased, grace abounded all the more, so that, just as sin exercised dominion in death, so grace might also exercise dominion through justification leading to eternal life through Jesus Christ our Lord.

A Reading (Lesson) from the Gospel according to John [8:21–32]

Again Jesus said to the crowd, "I am going away, and you will search for me, but you will die in your sin. Where I am going, you cannot come." Then the Jews said, "Is he going to kill himself? Is that what he means by saying, 'Where I am going, you cannot come'?" He said to them, "You are from below, I am from above; you are of this world, I am not of this world. I told you that you would die in your sins, for you will die in your sins unless you believe that I am he." They said to him, "Who are you?" Jesus said to them, "Why do I speak to you at all? I have much to say about you and much to condemn; but the one who sent me is true, and I declare to the world what I have heard from him." They did not understand that he was speaking to them about the Father. So Jesus said, "When you have lifted up the Son of Man, then you will realize that I am he, and that I do nothing on my own, but I speak these things as the Father instructed me. And the one who sent me is with me; he has not left me alone, for I always do what is pleasing to him." As he was saying these things, many believed in him. Then Jesus said to the Jews who had believed in him, "If you continue in my word, you are truly my disciples; and you will know the truth, and the truth will make you free."

Friday

Psalm 95* [page 724]   &   *Psalm 88* [page 712]   ❖
Psalm 91 [page 719],   *Psalm 92* [page 720]

A Reading (Lesson) from the Book of Jeremiah [11:1–8, 14–20]

The word that came to Jeremiah from the Lord: Hear the words of this covenant, and speak to the people of Judah and the inhabitants of Jerusalem. You shall say to them, Thus says the Lord, the God of Israel: Cursed be anyone who does not heed the words of this covenant, which I commanded your ancestors when I brought them out of the land of Egypt, from the iron-smelter, saying, Listen to my voice, and do all that I command you. So shall you be my people, and I will be your God, that I may perform the oath that I swore to your ancestors, to give them a land flowing with milk and honey, as at this day. Then I answered, "So be it, Lord." And the Lord said to me: Proclaim all these words in the cities of Judah, and in the streets of Jerusalem: Hear the words of this covenant and do them. For I solemnly warned your ancestors when I brought them up out of the land of Egypt, warning them persistently, even to this day, saying, Obey my voice. Yet they did not obey or incline their ear, but everyone walked in the stubbornness of an evil will. So I brought upon them all the words of this covenant, which I commanded them to do, but they did not. As for you, do not pray for this people, or lift up a cry or prayer on their behalf, for I will not listen when they call to me in the time of their trouble. What right has my beloved in my house, when she has done vile deeds? Can vows and sacrificial flesh avert your doom? Can you then exult? The Lord once called you, "A green olive tree, fair with goodly fruit"; but with the roar of a great tempest he will set fire to it, and its branches will be consumed. The Lord of hosts, who planted you, has pronounced evil against you, because

---

For the Invitatory

of the evil that the house of Israel and the house of Judah have done, provoking me to anger by making offerings to Baal. It was the LORD who made it known to me, and I knew; then you showed me their evil deeds. But I was like a gentle lamb led to the slaughter. And I did not know it was against me that they devised schemes, saying, "Let us destroy the tree with its fruit, let us cut him off from the land of the living, so that his name will no longer be remembered!" But you, O LORD of hosts, who judge righteously, who try the heart and the mind, let me see your retribution upon them, for to you I have committed my cause.

A Reading (Lesson) from the Letter of Paul to the Romans [6:1–11]

What then are we to say? Should we continue in sin in order that grace may abound? By no means! How can we who died to sin go on living in it? Do you not know that all of us who have been baptized into Christ Jesus were baptized into his death? Therefore we have been buried with him by baptism into death, so that, just as Christ was raised from the dead by the glory of the Father, so we too might walk in newness of life. For if we have been united with him in a death like his, we will certainly be united with him in a resurrection like his. We know that our old self was crucified with him so that the body of sin might be destroyed, and we might no longer be enslaved to sin. For whoever has died is freed from sin. But if we have died with Christ, we believe that we will also live with him. We know that Christ, being raised from the dead, will never die again; death no longer has dominion over him. The death he died, he died to sin, once for all; but the life he lives, he lives to God. So you also must consider yourselves dead to sin and alive to God in Christ Jesus.

A Reading (Lesson) from the Gospel according to John [8:33–47]

The Jews answered Jesus, "We are descendants of Abraham and have never been slaves to anyone. What do you mean by saying, 'You will be made free'?" Jesus answered them, "Very truly, I tell you, everyone who commits sin is a slave to sin. The slave does not have a permanent place in the household; the son has a place there forever. So if the Son makes you free, you will be free indeed. I know that you are descendants of Abraham; yet you look for an opportunity to kill me, because there is no place in you for my word. I declare what I have seen in the Father's presence; as for you, you should do what you have heard from the Father." They answered him, "Abraham is our father." Jesus said to them, "If you were Abraham's children, you would be doing what Abraham did, but now you are trying to kill me, a man who has told you the truth that I heard from God. This is not what Abraham did. You are indeed doing what your father does." They said to him, "We are not illegitimate children; we have one father, God himself." Jesus said to them, "If God were your Father, you would love me, for I came from God and now I am here. I did not come on my own, but he sent me. Why do you not understand what I say? It is because you cannot accept my word. You are from your father the devil, and you choose to do your father's desires. He was a murderer from the beginning and does not stand in the truth, because there is no truth in him. When he lies, he speaks according to his own nature, for he is a liar and the father of lies. But because I tell the truth, you do not believe me. Which of you convicts me of sin? If I tell the truth, why do you not believe me? Whoever is from God hears the words of God. The reason you do not hear them is that you are not from God."

Saturday

Psalm 87 [page 711],   *Psalm 90* [page 717]   ❖
Psalm 136 [page 789]

A Reading (Lesson) from the Book of Jeremiah [13:1–11]

Thus said the LORD to me, "Go and buy yourself a linen
loincloth, and put it on your loins, but do not dip it in
water." So I bought a loincloth according to the word of the
LORD, and put it on my loins. And the word of the LORD
came to me a second time, saying, "Take the loincloth that
you bought and are wearing, and go now to the Euphrates,
and hide it there in a cleft of the rock." So I went, and hid it
by the Euphrates, as the LORD commanded me. And after
many days the LORD said to me, "Go now to the Euphrates,
and take from there the loincloth that I commanded you to
hide there." Then I went to the Euphrates, and dug, and I
took the loincloth from the place where I had hidden it. But
now the loincloth was ruined; it was good for nothing. Then
the word of the LORD came to me: Thus says the LORD: Just
so I will ruin the pride of Judah and the great pride of
Jerusalem. This evil people, who refuse to hear my words,
who stubbornly follow their own will and have gone after
other gods to serve them and worship them, shall be like this
loincloth, which is good for nothing. For as the loincloth
clings to one's loins, so I made the whole house of Israel and
the whole house of Judah cling to me, says the LORD, in
order that they might be for me a people, a name, a praise,
and a glory. But they would not listen.

*A Reading (Lesson) from the Letter of Paul to the
Romans* [6:12–23]

Do not let sin exercise dominion in your mortal bodies, to
make you obey their passions. No longer present your

members to sin as instruments of wickedness, but present yourselves to God as those who have been brought from death to life, and present your members to God as instruments of righteousness. For sin will have no dominion over you, since you are not under law but under grace. What then? Should we sin because we are not under law but under grace? By no means! Do you not know that if you present yourselves to anyone as obedient slaves, you are slaves of the one whom you obey, either of sin, which leads to death, or of obedience, which leads to righteousness? But thanks be to God that you, having once been slaves of sin, have become obedient from the heart to the form of teaching to which you were entrusted, and that you, having been set free from sin, have become slaves of righteousness. I am speaking in human terms because of your natural limitations. For just as you once presented your members as slaves to impurity and to greater and greater iniquity, so now present your members as slaves to righteousness for sanctification. When you were slaves of sin, you were free in regard to righteousness. So what advantage did you then get from the things of which you now are ashamed? The end of those things is death. But now that you have been freed from sin and enslaved to God, the advantage you get is sanctification. The end is eternal life. For the wages of sin is death, but the free gift of God is eternal life in Christ Jesus our Lord.

A Reading (Lesson) from the Gospel according to John [8:47–59]

Jesus said to the Jews, "Whoever is from God hears the words of God. The reason you do not hear them is that you are not from God." The Jews answered him, "Are we not right in saying that you are a Samaritan and have a demon?" Jesus answered, "I do not have a demon; but I honor my Father, and you dishonor me. Yet I do not seek my own glory; there is one who seeks it and he is the judge. Very truly, I tell you, whoever keeps my word will never see death." The Jews said to him, "Now we know that you have a demon. Abraham died, and so did the prophets; yet you say, 'Whoever keeps my word will never taste death.' Are you greater than our father Abraham, who died? The prophets also died. Who do you claim to be?" Jesus answered, "If I glorify myself, my glory is nothing. It is my Father who glorifies me, he of whom you say, 'He is our God,' though you do not know him. But I know him; if I would say that I do not know him, I would be a liar like you. But I do know him and I keep his word. Your ancestor Abraham rejoiced that he would see my day; he saw it and was glad." Then the Jews said to him, "You are not yet fifty years old, and have you seen Abraham?" Jesus said to them, "Very truly, I tell you, before Abraham was, I am." So they picked up stones to throw at him, but Jesus hid himself and went out of the temple.

Week of 4 Lent

Sunday

Psalm 66 [page 673],   *Psalm 67* [page 675]   ❖
Psalm 19 [page 606],   *Psalm 46* [page 649]

A Reading (Lesson) from the Book of Jeremiah   [14:1–9,17–22]

The word of the LORD that came to Jeremiah concerning the drought: Judah mourns and her gates languish; they lie in gloom on the ground, and the cry of Jerusalem goes up. Her nobles send their servants for water; they come to the cisterns, they find no water, they return with their vessels empty. They are ashamed and dismayed and cover their heads, because the ground is cracked. Because there has been no rain on the land the farmers are dismayed; they cover their heads. Even the doe in the field forsakes her newborn fawn because there is no grass. The wild asses stand on the bare heights, they pant for air like jackals; their eyes fail because there is no herbage. Although our iniquities testify against us, act, O LORD, for your name's sake; our apostasies indeed are many, and we have sinned against you. O hope of Israel, its savior in time of trouble, why should you be like a stranger in the land, like a traveler turning aside for the night? Why should you be like someone confused, like a mighty warrior who cannot give help? Yet you, O LORD, are in the midst of us, and we are called by your name; do not forsake us! You shall say to them this word: Let my eyes run down with tears night and day, and let them not cease, for the virgin daughter—my people—is struck down with a crushing blow, with a very grievous wound. If I go out into the field, look—those killed by the sword! And if I enter the city, look—those sick with famine! For both prophet and priest ply their trade throughout the land, and have no knowledge. Have you completely rejected Judah? Does your heart loathe Zion? Why have you struck us down so that there is no healing for us? We look for peace, but find no good; for a time of healing, but there is terror instead. We acknowledge our wickedness, O LORD, the iniquity of our ancestors, for we have sinned against you. Do not spurn us, for your name's sake; do not dishonor your glorious throne; remember and do not break your covenant with us. Can any idols of the nations bring rain? Or can the heavens give showers? Is it not you, O LORD our God? We set our hope on you, for it is you who do all this.

A Reading (Lesson) from the Letter of Paul to the Galatians [4:21—5:1]

Tell me, you who desire to be subject to the law, will you not listen to the law? For it is written that Abraham had two sons, one by a slave woman and the other by a free woman. One, the child of the slave, was born according to the flesh; the other, the child of the free woman, was born through the promise. Now this is an allegory: these women are two covenants. One woman, in fact, is Hagar, from Mount Sinai, bearing children for slavery. Now Hagar is Mount Sinai in Arabia and corresponds to the present Jerusalem, for she is in slavery with her children. But the other woman corresponds to the Jerusalem above; she is free, and she is our mother. For it is written, "Rejoice, you childless one, you who bear no children, burst into song and shout, you who endure no birth pangs; for the children of the desolate woman are more numerous than the children of the one who is married." Now you, my friends, are children of the promise, like Isaac. But just as at that time the child who was born according to the flesh persecuted the child who was born according to the Spirit, so it is now also. But what does the scripture say? "Drive out the slave and her child; for the child of the slave will not share the inheritance with the child of the free woman." So then, friends, we are children, not of the slave but of the free woman. For freedom Christ has set us free. Stand firm, therefore, and do not submit again to a yoke of slavery.

A Reading (Lesson) from the Gospel according to Mark [8:11–21]

The Pharisees came and began to argue with Jesus, asking him for a sign from heaven, to test him. And he sighed deeply in his spirit and said, "Why does this generation ask for a sign? Truly I tell you, no sign will be given to this generation." And he left them, and getting into the boat again, he went across to the other side. Now the disciples had forgotten to bring any bread; and they had only one loaf with them in the boat. And he cautioned them, saying, "Watch out—beware of the yeast of the Pharisees and the yeast of Herod." They said to one another, "It is because we have no bread." And becoming aware of it, Jesus said to them, "Why are you talking about having no bread? Do you still not perceive or understand? Are your hearts hardened? Do you have eyes, and fail to see? Do you have ears, and fail to hear? And do you not remember? When I broke the five loaves for the five thousand, how many baskets full of broken pieces did you collect?" They said to him, "Twelve." "And the seven for the four thousand, how many baskets full of broken pieces did you collect?" And they said to him, "Seven." Then he said to them, "Do you not yet understand?"

Monday

Psalm 89:1–18 [page 713]   ❖   *Psalm 89:19–52* [page 715]

A Reading (Lesson) from the Book of Jeremiah [16:10–21]

The word of the LORD came to me: When you tell this people all these words, and they say to you, "Why has the LORD pronounced all this great evil against us? What is our iniquity? What is the sin that we have committed against the

Lord our God?" then you shall say to them: It is because your ancestors have forsaken me, says the Lord, and have gone after other gods and have served and worshiped them, and have forsaken me and have not kept my law; and because you have behaved worse than your ancestors, for here you are, every one of you, following your stubborn evil will, refusing to listen to me. Therefore I will hurl you out of this land into a land that neither you nor your ancestors have known, and there you shall serve other gods day and night, for I will show you no favor. Therefore, the days are surely coming, says the Lord, when it shall no longer be said, "As the Lord lives who brought the people of Israel up out of the land of Egypt," but "As the Lord lives who brought the people of Israel up out of the land of the north and out of all the lands where he had driven them." For I will bring them back to their own land that I gave to their ancestors. I am now sending for many fishermen, says the Lord, and they shall catch them; and afterward I will send for many hunters, and they shall hunt them from every mountain and every hill, and out of the clefts of the rocks. For my eyes are on all their ways; they are not hidden from my presence, nor is their iniquity concealed from my sight. And I will doubly repay their iniquity and their sin, because they have polluted my land with the carcasses of their detestable idols, and have filled my inheritance with their abominations. O Lord, my strength and my stronghold, my refuge in the day of trouble, to you shall the nations come from the ends of the earth and say: Our ancestors have inherited nothing but lies, worthless things in which there is no profit. Can mortals make for themselves gods? Such are no gods! "Therefore I am surely going to teach them, this time I am going to teach them my power and my might, and they shall know that my name is the Lord."

A Reading (Lesson) from the Letter of Paul to the Romans [7:1–12]

Do you not know, brothers and sisters—for I am speaking to those who know the law—that the law is binding on a person only during that person's lifetime? Thus a married woman is bound by the law to her husband as long as he lives; but if her husband dies, she is discharged from the law concerning the husband. Accordingly, she will be called an adulteress if she lives with another man while her husband is alive. But if her husband dies, she is free from that law, and if she marries another man, she is not an adulteress. In the same way, my friends, you have died to the law through the body of Christ, so that you may belong to another, to him who has been raised from the dead in order that we may bear fruit for God. While we were living in the flesh, our sinful passions, aroused by the law, were at work in our members to bear fruit for death. But now we are discharged from the law, dead to that which held us captive, so that we are slaves not under the old written code but in the new life of the Spirit. What then should we say? That the law is sin? By no means! Yet, if it had not been for the law, I would not have known sin. I would not have known what it is to covet if the law had not said, "You shall not covet." But sin, seizing an opportunity in the commandment, produced in me all kinds of covetousness. Apart from the law sin lies dead. I was once alive apart from the law, but when the commandment came, sin revived and I died, and the very commandment that promised life proved to be death to me. For sin, seizing an opportunity in the commandment, deceived me and through it killed me. So the law is holy, and the commandment is holy and just and good.

A Reading (Lesson) from the Gospel according to John [6:1–15]

After this Jesus went to the other side of the Sea of Galilee, also called the Sea of Tiberias. A large crowd kept following him, because they saw the signs that he was doing for the sick. Jesus went up the mountain and sat down there with his disciples. Now the Passover, the festival of the Jews, was near. When he looked up and saw a large crowd coming toward him, Jesus said to Philip, "Where are we to buy bread for these people to eat?" He said this to test him, for he himself knew what he was going to do. Philip answered him, "Six months' wages would not buy enough bread for each of them to get a little." One of his disciples, Andrew, Simon Peter's brother, said to him, "There is a boy here who has five barley loaves and two fish. But what are they among so many people?" Jesus said, "Make the people sit down." Now there was a great deal of grass in the place; so they sat down, about five thousand in all. Then Jesus took the loaves, and when he had given thanks, he distributed them to those who were seated; so also the fish, as much as they wanted. When they were satisfied, he told his disciples, "Gather up the fragments left over, so that nothing may be lost." So they gathered them up, and from the fragments of the five barley loaves, left by those who had eaten, they filled twelve baskets. When the people saw the sign that he had done, they began to say, "This is indeed the prophet who is to come into the world." When Jesus realized that they were about to come and take him by force to make him king, he withdrew again to the mountain by himself.

Tuesday

Psalm 97 [page 726], *Psalm 99* [page 728],
(Psalm 100 [page 729]) ❖ *Psalm 94* [page 722],
(Psalm 95 [page 724])

A Reading (Lesson) from the Book of Jeremiah [17:19–27]

Thus said the LORD to me: Go and stand in the People's
Gate, by which the kings of Judah enter and by which they
go out, and in all the gates of Jerusalem, and say to them:
Hear the word of the LORD, you kings of Judah, and all
Judah, and all the inhabitants of Jerusalem, who enter by
these gates. Thus says the LORD: For the sake of your lives,
take care that you do not bear a burden on the sabbath day
or bring it in by the gates of Jerusalem. And do not carry a
burden out of your houses on the sabbath or do any work,
but keep the sabbath day holy, as I commanded your
ancestors. Yet they did not listen or incline their ear; they
stiffened their necks and would not hear or receive
instruction. But if you listen to me, says the LORD, and bring
in no burden by the gates of this city on the sabbath day, but
keep the sabbath day holy and do not work on it, then there
shall enter by the gates of this city kings who sit on the
throne of David, riding in chariots and on horses, they and
their officials, the people of Judah and the inhabitants of
Jerusalem; and this city shall be inhabited forever. And
people shall come from the towns of Judah and the places
around Jerusalem, from the land of Benjamin, from the
Shephelah, from the hill country, and from the Negeb,
bringing burnt offerings and sacrifices, grain offerings and
frankincense, and bringing thank offerings to the house of
the LORD. But if you do not listen to me, to keep the sabbath
day holy, and to carry in no burden through the gates of

Jerusalem on the sabbath day, then I will kindle a fire in its gates; it shall devour the palaces of Jerusalem and shall not be quenched.

A Reading (Lesson) from the Letter of Paul to the Romans [7:13–25]

Did what is good, then, bring death to me? By no means! It was sin, working death in me through what is good, in order that sin might be shown to be sin, and through the commandment might become sinful beyond measure. For we know that the law is spiritual; but I am of the flesh, sold into slavery under sin. I do not understand my own actions. For I do not do what I want, but I do the very thing I hate. Now if I do what I do not want, I agree that the law is good. But in fact it is no longer I that do it, but sin that dwells within me. For I know that nothing good dwells within me, that is, in my flesh. I can will what is right, but I cannot do it. For I do not do the good I want, but the evil I do not want is what I do. Now if I do what I do not want, it is no longer I that do it, but sin that dwells within me. So I find it to be a law that when I want to do what is good, evil lies close at hand. For I delight in the law of God in my inmost self, but I see in my members another law at war with the law of my mind, making me captive to the law of sin that dwells in my members. Wretched man that I am! Who will rescue me from this body of death? Thanks be to God through Jesus Christ our Lord! So then, with my mind I am a slave to the law of God, but with my flesh I am a slave to the law of sin.

John 6:15–27 [page 114 above]

Wednesday

Psalm 101 [page 730],
Psalm 109:1–4(5–19)20–30 [page 750] ❖
Psalm 119:121–144 [page 773]

A Reading (Lesson) from the Book of Jeremiah [18:1–11]

The word that came to Jeremiah from the LORD: "Come, go down to the potter's house, and there I will let you hear my words." So I went down to the potter's house, and there he was working at his wheel. The vessel he was making of clay was spoiled in the potter's hand, and he reworked it into another vessel, as seemed good to him. Then the word of the LORD came to me: Can I not do with you, O house of Israel, just as this potter has done? says the LORD. Just like the clay in the potter's hand, so are you in my hand, O house of Israel. At one moment I may declare concerning a nation or a kingdom, that I will pluck up and break down and destroy it, but if that nation, concerning which I have spoken, turns from its evil, I will change my mind about the disaster that I intended to bring on it. And at another moment I may declare concerning a nation or a kingdom that I will build and plant it, but if it does evil in my sight, not listening to my voice, then I will change my mind about the good that I had intended to do to it. Now, therefore, say to the people of Judah and the inhabitants of Jerusalem: Thus says the LORD: Look, I am a potter shaping evil against you and devising a plan against you. Turn now, all of you from your evil way, and amend your ways and your doings.

*A Reading (Lesson) from the Letter of Paul to the
Romans* [8:1–11]

There is therefore now no condemnation for those who
are in Christ Jesus. For the law of the Spirit of life in
Christ Jesus has set you free from the law of sin and of
death. For God has done what the law, weakened by the
flesh, could not do: by sending his own Son in the likeness
of sinful flesh, and to deal with sin, he condemned sin in
the flesh, so that the just requirement of the law might be
fulfilled in us, who walk not according to the flesh but
according to the Spirit. For those who live according to
the flesh set their minds on the things of the flesh, but
those who live according to the Spirit set their minds on
the things of the Spirit. To set the mind on the flesh is
death, but to set the mind on the Spirit is life and peace.
For this reason the mind that is set on the flesh is hostile
to God; it does not submit to God's law—indeed it
cannot, and those who are in the flesh cannot please God.
But you are not in the flesh; you are in the Spirit, since the
Spirit of God dwells in you. Anyone who does not have
the Spirit of Christ does not belong to him. But if Christ is
in you, though the body is dead because of sin, the Spirit
is life because of righteousness. If the Spirit of him who
raised Jesus from the dead dwells in you, he who raised
Christ from the dead will give life to your mortal bodies
also through his Spirit that dwells in you.

*A Reading (Lesson) from the Gospel according to
John* [6:27–40]

Jesus said to the people, "Do not work for the food that
perishes, but for the food that endures for eternal life,
which the Son of Man will give you. For it is on him that
God the Father has set his seal." Then they said to him,

"What must we do to perform the works of God?" Jesus answered them, "This is the work of God, that you believe in him whom he has sent." So they said to him, "What sign are you going to give us then, so that we may see it and believe you? What work are you performing? Our ancestors ate the manna in the wilderness; as it is written, 'He gave them bread from heaven to eat.' " Then Jesus said to them, "Very truly, I tell you, it was not Moses who gave you the bread from heaven, but it is my Father who gives you the true bread from heaven. For the bread of God is that which comes down from heaven and gives life to the world." They said to him, "Sir, give us this bread always." Jesus said to them, "I am the bread of life. Whoever comes to me will never be hungry, and whoever believes in me will never be thirsty. But I said to you that you have seen me and yet do not believe. Everything that the Father gives me will come to me, and anyone who comes to me I will never drive away; for I have come down from heaven, not to do my own will, but the will of him who sent me. And this is the will of him who sent me, that I should lose nothing of all that he has given me, but raise it up on the last day. This is indeed the will of my Father, that all who see the Son and believe in him may have eternal life; and I will raise them up on the last day."

Thursday

Psalm 69:1–23(24–30)31–38 [page 679] ❖
Psalm 73 [page 687]

A Reading (Lesson) from the Book of Jeremiah [22:13–23]

Woe to him who builds his house by unrighteousness, and his upper rooms by injustice; who makes his neighbors work for nothing, and does not give them their wages; who says, "I will build myself a spacious house with large upper rooms," and who cuts out windows for it, paneling it with cedar, and painting it with vermilion. Are you a king because you compete in cedar? Did not your father eat and drink and do justice and righteousness? Then it was well with him. He judged the cause of the poor and needy; then it was well. Is not this to know me? says the LORD. But your eyes and heart are only on your dishonest gain, for shedding innocent blood, and for practicing oppression and violence. Therefore thus says the LORD concerning King Jehoiakim son of Josiah of Judah: They shall not lament for him, saying, "Alas, my brother!" or "Alas, sister!" They shall not lament for him, saying, "Alas, lord!" or "Alas, his majesty!" With the burial of a donkey he shall be buried—dragged off and thrown out beyond the gates of Jerusalem. Go up to Lebanon, and cry out, and lift up your voice in Bashan; cry out from Abarim, for all your lovers are crushed. I spoke to you in your prosperity, but you said, "I will not listen." This has been your way from your youth, for you have not obeyed my voice. The wind shall shepherd all your shepherds, and your lovers shall go into captivity; then you will be ashamed and dismayed because of all your wickedness. O inhabitant of Lebanon, nested among the cedars, how you will groan when pangs come upon you, pain as of a woman in labor!

A Reading (Lesson) from the Letter of Paul to the Romans [8:12–27]

Brothers and sisters, we are debtors, not to the flesh, to live according to the flesh—for if you live according to the flesh, you will die; but if by the Spirit you put to death the deeds of the body, you will live. For all who are led by the Spirit of God are children of God. For you did not receive a spirit of slavery to fall back into fear, but you have received a spirit of adoption. When we cry, "Abba! Father!" it is that very Spirit bearing witness with our spirit that we are children of God, and if children, then heirs, heirs of God and joint heirs with Christ—if, in fact, we suffer with him so that we may also be glorified with him. I consider that the sufferings of this present time are not worth comparing with the glory about to be revealed to us. For the creation waits with eager longing for the revealing of the children of God; for the creation was subjected to futility, not of its own will but by the will of the one who subjected it, in hope that the creation itself will be set free from its bondage to decay and will obtain the freedom of the glory of the children of God. We know that the whole creation has been groaning in labor pains until now; and not only the creation, but we ourselves, who have the first fruits of the Spirit, groan inwardly while we wait for adoption, the redemption of our bodies. For in hope we were saved. Now hope that is seen is not hope. For who hopes for what is seen? But if we hope for what we do not see, we wait for it with patience. Likewise the Spirit helps us in our weakness; for we do not know how to pray as we ought, but that very Spirit intercedes with sighs too deep for words. And God, who searches the heart, knows what is the mind of the Spirit, because the Spirit intercedes for the saints according to the will of God.

A Reading (Lesson) from the Gospel according to John [6:41–51]

The Jews began to complain about Jesus because he said, "I am the bread that came down from heaven." They were saying, "Is not this Jesus, the son of Joseph, whose father and mother we know? How can he now say, 'I have come down from heaven'?" Jesus answered them, "Do not complain among yourselves. No one can come to me unless drawn by the Father who sent me; and I will raise that person up on the last day. It is written in the prophets, 'And they shall all be taught by God.' Everyone who has heard and learned from the Father comes to me. Not that anyone has seen the Father except the one who is from God; he has seen the Father. Very truly, I tell you, whoever believes has eternal life. I am the bread of life. Your ancestors ate the manna in the wilderness, and they died. This is the bread that comes down from heaven, so that one may eat of it and not die. I am the living bread that came down from heaven. Whoever eats of this bread will live forever; and the bread that I will give for the life of the world is my flesh."

Friday

Psalm 95* [page 724] & *Psalm 102* [page 731] ❖
Psalm 107:1–32 [page 746]

A Reading (Lesson) from the Book of Jeremiah [23:1–8]

Woe to the shepherds who destroy and scatter the sheep of my pasture! says the LORD. Therefore thus says the LORD, the God of Israel, concerning the shepherds who shepherd

---

* *For the Invitatory*

my people: It is you who have scattered my flock, and have driven them away, and you have not attended to them. So I will attend to you for your evil doings, says the LORD. Then I myself will gather the remnant of my flock out of all the lands where I have driven them, and I will bring them back to their fold, and they shall be fruitful and multiply. I will raise up shepherds over them who will shepherd them, and they shall not fear any longer, or be dismayed, nor shall any be missing, says the LORD. The days are surely coming, says the LORD, when I will raise up for David a righteous Branch, and he shall reign as king and deal wisely, and shall execute justice and righteousness in the land. In his days Judah will be saved and Israel will live in safety. And this is the name by which he will be called: "The LORD is our righteousness." Therefore, the days are surely coming, says the LORD, when it shall no longer be said, "As the LORD lives who brought the people of Israel up out of the land of Egypt," but "As the LORD lives who brought out and led the offspring of the house of Israel out of the land of the north and out of all the lands where he had driven them." Then they shall live in their own land.

A Reading (Lesson) from the Letter of Paul to the Romans [8:28–39]

We know that all things work together for good for those who love God, who are called according to his purpose. For those whom he foreknew he also predestined to be conformed to the image of his Son, in order that he might be the firstborn within a large family. And those whom he predestined he also called; and those whom he called he also justified; and those whom he justified he also glorified. What then are we to say about these things? If God is for us, who is against us? He who did not withhold his own Son, but gave him up for all of us, will he not with him also give us everything else? Who will bring any charge against God's elect? It is God who justifies. Who is to condemn? It is Christ Jesus, who died, yes, who was raised, who is at the right hand of God, who indeed intercedes for us. Who will separate us from the love of Christ? Will hardship, or distress, or persecution, or famine, or nakedness, or peril, or sword? As it is written, "For your sake we are being killed all day long; we are accounted as sheep to be slaughtered." No, in all these things we are more than conquerors through him who loved us. For I am convinced that neither death, nor life, nor angels, nor rulers, nor things present, nor things to come, nor powers, nor height, nor depth, nor anything else in all creation, will be able to separate us from the love of God in Christ Jesus our Lord.

A Reading (Lesson) from the Gospel according to John [6:52–59]

The Jews disputed among themselves, saying, "How can this man give us his flesh to eat?" So Jesus said to them, "Very truly, I tell you, unless you eat the flesh of the Son of Man and drink his blood, you have no life in you. Those who eat my flesh and drink my blood have eternal life, and I will raise them up on the last day; for my flesh is true food and my blood is true drink. Those who eat my flesh and drink my blood abide in me, and I in them. Just as the living Father sent me, and I live because of the Father, so whoever eats me will live because of me. This is the bread that came down from heaven, not like that which your ancestors ate, and they died. But the one who eats this bread will live forever." He said these things while he was teaching in the synagogue at Capernaum.

Saturday

Psalm 107:33–43 [page 748],
Psalm 108:1–6(7–13) [page 749] ❖ *Psalm 33* [page 626]

A Reading (Lesson) from the Book of Jeremiah [23:9–15]

Concerning the prophets: My heart is crushed within me, all my bones shake; I have become like a drunkard, like one overcome by wine, because of the LORD and because of his holy words. For the land is full of adulterers; because of the curse the land mourns, and the pastures of the wilderness are dried up. Their course has been evil, and their might is not right. Both prophet and priest are ungodly; even in my house I have found their wickedness, says the LORD. Therefore their way shall be to them like slippery paths in the darkness, into which they shall be driven and fall; for I will bring disaster upon them in the year of their punishment, says the LORD. In the prophets of Samaria I saw a disgusting thing: they prophesied by Baal and led my people Israel astray. But in the prophets of Jerusalem I have seen a more shocking thing: they commit adultery and walk in lies; they strengthen the hands of evildoers, so that no one turns from wickedness; all of them have become like Sodom to me, and its inhabitants like Gomorrah. Therefore thus says the LORD of hosts concerning the prophets: "I am going to make them eat wormwood, and give them poisoned water to drink; for from the prophets of Jerusalem ungodliness has spread throughout the land."

A Reading (Lesson) from the Letter of Paul to the Romans [9:1–18]

I am speaking the truth in Christ—I am not lying; my conscience confirms it by the Holy Spirit—I have great sorrow and unceasing anguish in my heart. For I could wish that I myself were accursed and cut off from Christ for the sake of my own people, my kindred according to the flesh. They are Israelites, and to them belong the adoption, the glory, the covenants, the giving of the law, the worship, and the promises; to them belong the patriarchs, and from them, according to the flesh, comes the Messiah, who is over all, God blessed forever. Amen. It is not as though the word of God had failed. For not all Israelites truly belong to Israel, and not all of Abraham's children are his true descendants; but "It is through Isaac that descendants shall be named for you." This means that it is not the children of the flesh who are the children of God, but the children of the promise are counted as descendants. For this is what the promise said, "About this time I will return and Sarah shall have a son." Nor is that all; something similar happened to Rebecca when she had conceived children by one husband, our ancestor Isaac. Even before they had been born or had done anything good or bad (so that God's purpose of election might continue, not by works but by his call) she was told, "The elder shall serve the younger." As it is written, "I have loved Jacob, but I have hated Esau." What then are we to say? Is there injustice on God's part? By no means! For he says to Moses, "I will have mercy on whom I have mercy, and I will have compassion on whom I have compassion." So it depends not on human will or exertion, but on God who shows mercy. For the scripture says to Pharaoh, "I have raised you up for the very purpose of showing my power in you, so that my name may be proclaimed in all the earth." So then he has mercy on whomever he chooses, and he hardens the heart of whomever he chooses.

A Reading (Lesson) from the Gospel according to John [6:60–71]

When many of Jesus' disciples heard him say, "Whoever eats of this bread will live forever," they said, "This teaching is difficult; who can accept it?" But Jesus, being aware that his disciples were complaining about it, said to them, "Does this offend you? Then what if you were to see the Son of Man ascending to where he was before? It is the spirit that gives life; the flesh is useless. The words that I have spoken to you are spirit and life. But among you there are some who do not believe." For Jesus knew from the first who were the ones that did not believe, and who was the one that would betray him. And he said, "For this reason I have told you that no one can come to me unless it is granted by the Father." Because of this many of his disciples turned back and no longer went about with him. So Jesus asked the twelve, "Do you also wish to go away?" Simon Peter answered him, "Lord, to whom can we go? You have the words of eternal life. We have come to believe and know that you are the Holy One of God." Jesus answered them, "Did I not choose you, the twelve? Yet one of you is a devil." He was speaking of Judas son of Simon Iscariot, for he, though one of the twelve, was going to betray him.

Week of 5 Lent

Sunday

Psalm 118 [page 760]   ❖   *Psalm 145* [page 801]

A Reading (Lesson) from the Book of Jeremiah [23:16–32]

Thus says the LORD of hosts: Do not listen to the words of
the prophets who prophesy to you; they are deluding you.
They speak visions of their own minds, not from the mouth
of the LORD. They keep saying to those who despise the
word of the LORD, "It shall be well with you"; and to all
who stubbornly follow their own stubborn hearts, they say,
"No calamity shall come upon you." For who has stood in
the council of the LORD so as to see and to hear his word?
Who has given heed to his word so as to proclaim it? Look,
the storm of the LORD! Wrath has gone forth, a whirling
tempest; it will burst upon the head of the wicked. The
anger of the LORD will not turn back until he has executed
and accomplished the intents of his mind. In the latter days
you will understand it clearly. I did not send the prophets,
yet they ran; I did not speak to them, yet they prophesied.
But if they had stood in my council, then they would have
proclaimed my words to my people, and they would have
turned them from their evil way, and from the evil of their
doings. Am I a God near by, says the LORD, and not a God
far off? Who can hide in secret places so that I cannot see
them? says the LORD. Do I not fill heaven and earth? says
the LORD. I have heard what the prophets have said who
prophesy lies in my name, saying, "I have dreamed, I have
dreamed!" How long? Will the hearts of the prophets ever
turn back—those who prophesy lies, and who prophesy the

deceit of their own heart? They plan to make my people forget my name by their dreams that they tell one another, just as their ancestors forgot my name for Baal. Let the prophet who has a dream tell the dream, but let the one who has my word speak my word faithfully. What has straw in common with wheat? says the LORD. Is not my word like fire, says the LORD, and like a hammer that breaks a rock in pieces? See, therefore, I am against the prophets, says the LORD, who steal my words from one another. See, I am against the prophets, says the LORD, who use their own tongues and say, "Says the LORD." See, I am against those who prophesy lying dreams, says the LORD, and who tell them, and who lead my people astray by their lies and their recklessness, when I did not send them or appoint them; so they do not profit this people at all, says the LORD.

A Reading (Lesson) from the First Letter of Paul to the Corinthians [9:19–27]

Though I am free with respect to all, I have made myself a slave to all, so that I might win more of them. To the Jews I became as a Jew, in order to win Jews. To those under the law I became as one under the law (though I myself am not under the law) so that I might win those under the law. To those outside the law I became as one outside the law (though I am not free from God's law but am under Christ's law) so that I might win those outside the law. To the weak I became weak, so that I might win the weak. I have become all things to all people, that I might by all means save some. I do it all for the sake of the gospel, so that I may share in its blessings. Do you not know that in a race the runners all compete, but only one receives the prize? Run in such a way that you may win it. Athletes exercise self-control in all things; they do it to receive a perishable wreath, but we an imperishable one. So I do not run aimlessly, nor do I box as though beating the air; but I punish my body and enslave it, so that after proclaiming to others I myself should not be disqualified.

A Reading (Lesson) from the Gospel according to Mark [8:31—9:1]

Jesus began to teach his disciples that the Son of Man must undergo great suffering, and be rejected by the elders, the chief priests, and the scribes, and be killed, and after three days rise again. He said all this quite openly. And Peter took him aside and began to rebuke him. But turning and looking at his disciples, he rebuked Peter and said, "Get behind me, Satan! For you are setting your mind not on divine things but on human things." He called the crowd with his disciples, and said to them, "If any want to become my followers, let them deny themselves and take up their cross and follow me. For those who want to save their life will lose it, and those who lose their life for my sake, and for the sake of the gospel, will save it. For what will it profit them to gain the whole world and forfeit their life? Indeed, what can they give in return for their life? Those who are ashamed of me and of my words in this adulterous and sinful generation, of them the Son of Man will also be ashamed when he comes in the glory of his Father with the holy angels." And he said to them, "Truly I tell you, there are some standing here who will not taste death until they see that the kingdom of God has come with power."

Monday

Psalm 31 [page 622] ❖ *Psalm 35* [page 629]

A Reading (Lesson) from the Book of Jeremiah [24:1–10]

The LORD showed me two baskets of figs placed before the temple of the LORD. This was after King Nebuchadrezzar of Babylon had taken into exile from Jerusalem King Jeconiah son of Jehoiakim of Judah, together with the officials of Judah, the artisans, and the smiths, and had brought them to Babylon. One basket had very good figs, like first-ripe figs, but the other basket had very bad figs, so bad that they could not be eaten. And the LORD said to me, "What do you see, Jeremiah?" I said, "Figs, the good figs very good, and the bad figs very bad, so bad that they cannot be eaten." Then the word of the LORD came to me: Thus says the LORD, the God of Israel: Like these good figs, so I will regard as good the exiles from Judah, whom I have sent away from this place to the land of the Chaldeans. I will set my eyes upon them for good, and I will bring them back to this land. I will build them up, and not tear them down; I will plant them, and not pluck them up. I will give them a heart to know that I am the LORD; and they shall be my people and I will be their God, for they shall return to me with their whole heart. But thus says the LORD: Like the bad figs that are so bad they cannot be eaten, so will I treat King Zedekiah of Judah, his officials, the remnant of Jerusalem who remain in this land, and those who live in the land of Egypt. I will make them a horror, an evil thing, to all the kingdoms of the earth—a disgrace, a byword, a taunt, and a curse in all the places where I shall drive them. And I will send sword, famine, and pestilence upon them, until they are utterly destroyed from the land that I gave to them and their ancestors.

*A Reading (Lesson) from the Letter of Paul to the
Romans* [9:19–33]

You will say to me then, "Why then does he still find
fault? For who can resist his will?" But who indeed are
you, a human being, to argue with God? Will what is
molded say to the one who molds it, "Why have you
made me like this?" Has the potter no right over the clay,
to make out of the same lump one object for special use
and another for ordinary use? What if God, desiring to
show his wrath and to make known his power, has
endured with much patience the objects of wrath that are
made for destruction; and what if he has done so in order
to make known the riches of his glory for the objects of
mercy, which he has prepared beforehand for
glory—including us whom he has called, not from the
Jews only but also from the Gentiles? As indeed he says in
Hosea, "Those who were not my people I will call 'my
people,' and her who was not beloved I will call
'beloved.' " "And in the very place where it was said to
them, 'You are not my people,' there they shall be called
children of the living God." And Isaiah cries out
concerning Israel, "Though the number of the children of
Israel were like the sand of the sea, only a remnant of
them will be saved; for the Lord will execute his sentence
on the earth quickly and decisively." And as Isaiah
predicted, "If the Lord of hosts had not left survivors to
us, we would have fared like Sodom and been made like
Gomorrah." What then are we to say? Gentiles, who did
not strive for righteousness, have attained it, that is,
righteousness through faith; but Israel, who did strive for
the righteousness that is based on the law, did not succeed
in fulfilling that law. Why not? Because they did not strive
for it on the basis of faith, but as if it were based on

works. They have stumbled over the stumbling stone, as it is written, "See, I am laying in Zion a stone that will make people stumble, a rock that will make them fall, and whoever believes in him will not be put to shame."

A Reading (Lesson) from the Gospel according to John [9:1–17]

As he walked along, Jesus saw a man blind from birth. His disciples asked him, "Rabbi, who sinned, this man or his parents, that he was born blind?" Jesus answered, "Neither this man nor his parents sinned; he was born blind so that God's works might be revealed in him. We must work the works of him who sent me while it is day; night is coming when no one can work. As long as I am in the world, I am the light of the world." When he had said this, he spat on the ground and made mud with the saliva and spread the mud on the man's eyes, saying to him, "Go, wash in the pool of Siloam" (which means Sent). Then he went and washed and came back able to see. The neighbors and those who had seen him before as a beggar began to ask, "Is this not the man who used to sit and beg?" Some were saying, "It is he." Others were saying, "No, but it is someone like him." He kept saying, "I am the man." But they kept asking him, "Then how were your eyes opened?" He answered, "The man called Jesus made mud, spread it on my eyes, and said to me, 'Go to Siloam and wash.' Then I went and washed and received my sight." They said to him, "Where is he?" He said, "I do not know." They brought to the Pharisees the man who had formerly been blind. Now it was a sabbath day when Jesus made the mud and opened his eyes. Then the Pharisees also began to ask him how he had received his sight. He said to them, "He put mud on my eyes. Then I washed, and now I see." Some of the Pharisees said, "This man is not from God, for he does not observe the sabbath." But others said, "How can a man who is a sinner perform such signs?" And they were divided. So they said again to the blind man, "What do you say about him? It was your eyes he opened." He said, "He is a prophet."

Tuesday

(Psalm 120 [page 778]),   *Psalm 121* [page 779],
Psalm 122 [page 779],   *Psalm 123* [page 780] ❖
Psalm 124 [page 781],   *Psalm 125* [page 781],
Psalm 126 [page 782],   *(Psalm 127* [page 782])

A Reading (Lesson) from the Book of Jeremiah [25:8–17]

Thus says the LORD of hosts: Because you have not obeyed my words, I am going to send for all the tribes of the north, says the LORD, even for King Nebuchadrezzar of Babylon, my servant, and I will bring them against this land and its inhabitants, and against all these nations around; I will utterly destroy them, and make them an object of horror and of hissing, and an everlasting disgrace. And I will banish from them the sound of mirth and the sound of gladness, the voice of the bridegroom and the voice of the bride, the sound of the millstones and the light of the lamp. This whole land shall become a ruin and a waste, and these nations shall serve the king of Babylon seventy years. Then after seventy years are completed, I will punish the king of Babylon and that nation, the land of the Chaldeans, for their iniquity, says the LORD, making the land an everlasting waste. I will bring upon that land all the words that I have uttered against it, everything written in this book, which

Jeremiah prophesied against all the nations. For many nations and great kings shall make slaves of them also; and I will repay them according to their deeds and the work of their hands. For thus the LORD, the God of Israel, said to me: Take from my hand this cup of the wine of wrath, and make all the nations to whom I send you drink it. They shall drink and stagger and go out of their minds because of the sword that I am sending among them. So I took the cup from the LORD's hand, and made all the nations to whom the LORD sent me drink it.

A Reading (Lesson) from the Letter of Paul to the Romans [10:1–13]

Brothers and sisters, my heart's desire and prayer to God for them is that they may be saved. I can testify that they have a zeal for God, but it is not enlightened. For, being ignorant of the righteousness that comes from God, and seeking to establish their own, they have not submitted to God's righteousness. For Christ is the end of the law so that there may be righteousness for everyone who believes. Moses writes concerning the righteousness that comes from the law, that "the person who does these things will live by them." But the righteousness that comes from faith says, "Do not say in your heart, 'Who will ascend into heaven?'" (that is, to bring Christ down) "or 'Who will descend into the abyss?'" (that is, to bring Christ up from the dead). But what does it say? "The word is near you, on your lips and in your heart" (that is, the word of faith that we proclaim); because if you confess with your lips that Jesus is Lord and believe in your heart that God raised him from the dead, you will be saved. For one believes with the heart and so is justified, and one confesses with the mouth and so is saved. The scripture says, "No one who believes in him will be put to shame." For there is no distinction between Jew and Greek; the same Lord is Lord of all and is generous to all who call on him. For, "Everyone who calls on the name of the Lord shall be saved."

A Reading (Lesson) from the Gospel according to John [9:18–41]

The Jews did not believe that the man had been blind and had received his sight until they called the parents of the man who had received his sight and asked them, "Is this your son, who you say was born blind? How then does he now see?" His parents answered, "We know that this is our son, and that he was born blind; but we do not know how it is that now he sees, nor do we know who opened his eyes. Ask him; he is of age. He will speak for himself." His parents said this because they were afraid of the Jews; for the Jews had already agreed that anyone who confessed Jesus to be the Messiah would be put out of the synagogue. Therefore his parents said, "He is of age; ask him." So for the second time they called the man who had been blind, and they said to him, "Give glory to God! We know that this man is a sinner." He answered, "I do not know whether he is a sinner. One thing I do know, that though I was blind, now I see." They said to him, "What did he do to you? How did he open your eyes?" He answered them, "I have told you already, and you would not listen. Why do you want to hear it again? Do you also want to become his disciples?" Then they reviled him, saying, "You are his disciple, but we are disciples of Moses. We know that God has spoken to Moses, but as for this man, we do not know where he comes from." The man answered, "Here is an astonishing thing! You do not know where he comes from, and yet he opened my eyes. We know that God does not listen to sinners, but he does listen to one who worships him and obeys his will. Never since the world began has it been heard that anyone opened the eyes of a person born blind. If this man were not from God, he could do nothing." They answered him, "You were born entirely in sins, and are you trying to teach us?" And they drove him out. Jesus heard that they had driven him out, and when he found him, he said, "Do you believe in the Son of Man?" He answered, "And who is he, sir? Tell me, so that I may believe in him." Jesus said to him, "You have seen him, and the one speaking with you is he." He said, "Lord, I believe." And he worshiped him. Jesus said, "I came into this world for judgment so that those who do not see may see, and those who do see may become blind." Some of the Pharisees near him heard this and said to him, "Surely we are not blind, are we?" Jesus said to them, "If you were blind, you would not have sin. But now that you say, 'We see,' your sin remains."

Wednesday

Psalm 119:145–176 [page 775]   ❖   *Psalm 128* [page 783],
Psalm 129 [page 784],   *Psalm 130* [page 784]

A Reading (Lesson) from the Book of Jeremiah [25:30–38]

You, therefore, shall prophesy against them all these words, and say to them: The LORD will roar from on high, and from his holy habitation utter his voice; he will roar mightily against his fold, and shout, like those who tread grapes, against all the inhabitants of the earth. The clamor will resound to the ends of the earth, for the LORD has an indictment against the nations; he is entering into judgment with all flesh, and the guilty he will put to the sword, says the LORD. Thus says the LORD of hosts: See, disaster is spreading from nation to nation, and a great tempest is stirring from the farthest parts of the earth! Those slain by the LORD on that day shall extend from one end of the earth to the other. They shall not be lamented, or gathered, or buried; they shall become dung on the surface of the ground. Wail, you shepherds, and cry out; roll in ashes, you lords of the flock, for the days of your slaughter have come—and your dispersions, and you shall fall like a choice vessel. Flight shall fail the shepherds, and there shall be no escape for the lords of the flock. Hark! the cry of the shepherds, and the wail of the lords of the flock! For the LORD is despoiling their pasture, and the peaceful folds are devastated, because of the fierce anger of the LORD. Like a lion he has left his covert; for their land has become a waste because of the cruel sword, and because of his fierce anger.

A Reading (Lesson) from the Letter of Paul to the Romans [10:14–21]

How are they to call on one in whom they have not believed? And how are they to believe in one of whom they have never heard? And how are they to hear without someone to proclaim him? And how are they to proclaim him unless they are sent? As it is written, "How beautiful are the feet of those who bring good news!" But not all have obeyed the good news; for Isaiah says, "Lord, who has believed our message?" So faith comes from what is heard, and what is heard comes through the word of Christ. But I ask, have they not heard? Indeed they have; for "Their voice has gone out to all the earth, and their words to the ends of the world." Again I ask, did Israel not understand? First Moses says, "I will make you jealous of those who are not a nation; with a foolish nation I will make you angry." Then Isaiah is so bold as to say, "I have been found by those who did not seek me; I have shown myself to those who did not ask for me." But of Israel he says, "All day long I have held out my hands to a disobedient and contrary people."

A Reading (Lesson) from the Gospel according to John [10:1–18]

Jesus said to the crowd, "Very truly, I tell you, anyone who does not enter the sheepfold by the gate but climbs in by another way is a thief and a bandit. The one who enters by the gate is the shepherd of the sheep. The gatekeeper opens the gate for him, and the sheep hear his voice. He calls his own sheep by name and leads them out. When he has brought out all his own, he goes ahead of them, and the sheep follow him because they know his voice. They will not follow a stranger, but they will run from him because they do not know the voice of strangers." Jesus used this figure of speech with them, but they did not understand what he was saying to them. So again Jesus said to them, "Very truly, I tell you, I am the gate for the sheep. All who came before me are thieves and bandits; but the sheep did not listen to them. I am the gate. Whoever enters by me will be saved, and will come in and go out and find pasture. The thief comes only to steal and kill and destroy. I came that they may have life, and have it abundantly. I am the good shepherd. The good shepherd lays down his life for the sheep. The hired hand, who is not the shepherd and does not own the sheep, sees the wolf coming and leaves the sheep and runs away—and the wolf snatches them and scatters them. The hired hand runs away because a hired hand does not care for the sheep. I am the good shepherd. I know my own and my own know me, just as the Father knows me and I know the Father. And I lay down my life for the sheep. I have other sheep that do not belong to this fold. I must bring them also, and they will listen to my voice. So there will be one flock, one shepherd. For this reason the Father loves me, because I lay down my life in order to take it up again. No one takes it from me, but I lay it down of my own accord. I have power to lay it down, and I have power to take it up again. I have received this command from my Father."

Thursday

Psalm 131 [page 785], *Psalm 132* [page 785],
(Psalm 133 [page 787]) ❖ *Psalm 140* [page 796],
Psalm 142 [page 798]

A Reading (Lesson) from the Book of Jeremiah [26:1–16]

At the beginning of the reign of King Jehoiakim son of Josiah of Judah, this word came from the LORD: Thus says the LORD: Stand in the court of the LORD's house, and speak to all the cities of Judah that come to worship in the house of the LORD; speak to them all the words that I command you; do not hold back a word. It may be that they will listen, all of them, and will turn from their evil way, that I may change my mind about the disaster that I intend to bring on them because of their evil doings. You shall say to them: Thus says the LORD: If you will not listen to me, to walk in my law that I have set before you, and to heed the words of my servants the prophets whom I send to you urgently—though you have not heeded—then I will make this house like Shiloh, and I will make this city a curse for all the nations of the earth. The priests and the prophets and all the people heard Jeremiah speaking these words in the house of the LORD. And when Jeremiah had finished speaking all that the LORD had commanded him to speak to all the people, then the priests and the prophets and all the people laid hold of him, saying, "You shall die! Why have you prophesied in the name of the LORD, saying, 'This house shall be like Shiloh, and this city shall be desolate, without inhabitant'?" And all the people gathered around Jeremiah in the house of the LORD. When the officials of Judah heard these things, they came up from the king's house to the house of the LORD and took their seat in the entry of the New Gate of the house of the LORD. Then the priests and the prophets said to the officials and to all the people, "This man deserves the sentence of death because he has prophesied against this city, as you have heard with your own ears." Then Jeremiah spoke to all the officials and all the people, saying, "It is the LORD who sent me to prophesy against this house and this city all the words you have heard. Now therefore amend your ways and your doings, and obey the voice of the LORD your God, and the LORD will change his mind about the disaster that he has pronounced against you. But as for me, here I am in your hands. Do with me as seems good and right to you. Only know for certain that if you put me to death, you will be bringing innocent blood upon yourselves and upon this city and its inhabitants, for in truth the LORD sent me to you to speak all these words in your ears." Then the officials and all the people said to the priests and the prophets, "This man does not deserve the sentence of death, for he has spoken to us in the name of the LORD our God."

*A Reading (Lesson) from the Letter of Paul to the
Romans* [11:1–12]

I ask, then, has God rejected his people? By no means! I
myself am an Israelite, a descendant of Abraham, a
member of the tribe of Benjamin. God has not rejected his
people whom he foreknew. Do you not know what the
scripture says of Elijah, how he pleads with God against
Israel? "Lord, they have killed your prophets, they have
demolished your altars; I alone am left, and they are
seeking my life." But what is the divine reply to him?
"I have kept for myself seven thousand who have not
bowed the knee to Baal." So too at the present time there
is a remnant, chosen by grace. But if it is by grace, it is no
longer on the basis of works, otherwise grace would no
longer be grace. What then? Israel failed to obtain what it
was seeking. The elect obtained it, but the rest were
hardened, as it is written, "God gave them a sluggish
spirit, eyes that would not see and ears that would not
hear, down to this very day." And David says, "Let their
table become a snare and a trap, a stumbling block and a
retribution for them; let their eyes be darkened so that
they cannot see, and keep their backs forever bent." So I
ask, have they stumbled so as to fall? By no means! But
through their stumbling salvation has come to the
Gentiles, so as to make Israel jealous. Now if their
stumbling means riches for the world, and if their defeat
means riches for Gentiles, how much more will their full
inclusion mean!

*A Reading (Lesson) from the Gospel according to
John* [10:19–42]

Again the Jews were divided because of Jesus' words.
Many of them were saying, "He has a demon and is out

of his mind. Why listen to him?" Others were saying, "These are not the words of one who has a demon. Can a demon open the eyes of the blind?" At that time the festival of the Dedication took place in Jerusalem. It was winter, and Jesus was walking in the temple, in the portico of Solomon. So the Jews gathered around him and said to him, "How long will you keep us in suspense? If you are the Messiah, tell us plainly." Jesus answered, "I have told you, and you do not believe. The works that I do in my Father's name testify to me; but you do not believe, because you do not belong to my sheep. My sheep hear my voice. I know them, and they follow me. I give them eternal life, and they will never perish. No one will snatch them out of my hand. What my Father has given me is greater than all else, and no one can snatch it out of the Father's hand. The Father and I are one." The Jews took up stones again to stone him. Jesus replied, "I have shown you many good works from the Father. For which of these are you going to stone me?" The Jews answered, "It is not for a good work that we are going to stone you, but for blasphemy, because you, though only a human being, are making yourself God." Jesus answered, "Is it not written in your law, 'I said, you are gods'? If those to whom the word of God came were called 'gods'—and the scripture cannot be annulled—can you say that the one whom the Father has sanctified and sent into the world is blaspheming because I said, 'I am God's Son'? If I am not doing the works of my Father, then do not believe me. But if I do them, even though you do not believe me, believe the works, so that you may know and understand that the Father is in me and I am in the Father." Then they tried to arrest him again, but he escaped from their hands. He went away again across the Jordan to the place where John had been baptizing earlier, and he remained there.

Many came to him, and they were saying, "John performed no sign, but everything that John said about this man was true." And many believed in him there.

Friday

Psalm 95* [page 724] & *Psalm 22* [page 610] ❖
Psalm 141 [page 797], *Psalm 143:1–11(12)* [page 798]

A Reading (Lesson) from the Book of Jeremiah [29:1,4–13]

These are the words of the letter that the prophet Jeremiah sent from Jerusalem to the remaining elders among the exiles, and to the priests, the prophets, and all the people, whom Nebuchadnezzar had taken into exile from Jerusalem to Babylon. Thus says the LORD of hosts, the God of Israel, to all the exiles whom I have sent into exile from Jerusalem to Babylon: Build houses and live in them; plant gardens and eat what they produce. Take wives and have sons and daughters; take wives for your sons, and give your daughters in marriage, that they may bear sons and daughters; multiply there, and do not decrease. But seek the welfare of the city where I have sent you into exile, and pray to the LORD on its behalf, for in its welfare you will find your welfare. For thus says the LORD of hosts, the God of Israel: Do not let the prophets and the diviners who are among you deceive you, and do not listen to the dreams that they dream, for it is a lie that they are prophesying to you in my name; I did not send them, says the LORD. For thus says the LORD: Only when Babylon's seventy years are completed will I visit you, and I will fulfill to you my promise and bring

---

* *For the Invitatory*

you back to this place. For surely I know the plans I have for you, says the LORD, plans for your welfare and not for harm, to give you a future with hope. Then when you call upon me and come and pray to me, I will hear you. When you search for me, you will find me; if you seek me with all your heart.

A Reading (Lesson) from the Letter of Paul to the Romans [11:13–24]

Now I am speaking to you Gentiles. Inasmuch then as I am an apostle to the Gentiles, I glorify my ministry in order to make my own people jealous, and thus save some of them. For if their rejection is the reconciliation of the world, what will their acceptance be but life from the dead! If the part of the dough offered as first fruits is holy, then the whole batch is holy; and if the root is holy, then the branches also are holy. But if some of the branches were broken off, and you, a wild olive shoot, were grafted in their place to share the rich root of the olive tree, do not boast over the branches. If you do boast, remember that it is not you that support the root, but the root that supports you. You will say, "Branches were broken off so that I might be grafted in." That is true. They were broken off because of their unbelief, but you stand only through faith. So do not become proud, but stand in awe. For if God did not spare the natural branches, perhaps he will not spare you. Note then the kindness and the severity of God: severity toward those who have fallen, but God's kindness toward you, provided you continue in his kindness; otherwise you also will be cut off. And even those of Israel, if they do not persist in unbelief, will be grafted in, for God has the power to graft them in again.

For if you have been cut from what is by nature a wild olive tree and grafted, contrary to nature, into a cultivated olive tree, how much more will these natural branches be grafted back into their own olive tree.

A Reading (Lesson) from the Gospel according to John [11:1–27]

Now a certain man was ill, Lazarus of Bethany, the village of Mary and her sister Martha. Mary was the one who anointed the Lord with perfume and wiped his feet with her hair; her brother Lazarus was ill. So the sisters sent a message to Jesus, "Lord, he whom you love is ill." But when Jesus heard it, he said, "This illness does not lead to death; rather it is for God's glory, so that the Son of God may be glorified through it." Accordingly, though Jesus loved Martha and her sister and Lazarus, after having heard that Lazarus was ill, he stayed two days longer in the place where he was. Then after this he said to the disciples, "Let us go to Judea again." The disciples said to him, "Rabbi, the Jews were just now trying to stone you, and are you going there again?" Jesus answered, "Are there not twelve hours of daylight? Those who walk during the day do not stumble, because they see the light of this world. But those who walk at night stumble, because the light is not in them." After saying this, he told them, "Our friend Lazarus has fallen asleep, but I am going there to awaken him." The disciples said to him, "Lord, if he has fallen asleep, he will be all right." Jesus, however, had been speaking about his death, but they thought that he was referring merely to sleep. Then Jesus told them plainly, "Lazarus is dead. For your sake I am glad I was not there, so that you may believe. But let us go to him." Thomas, who was called the Twin, said to his fellow disciples, "Let us also go, that we may die with him." When Jesus arrived, he found that Lazarus had already been in the tomb four days. Now Bethany was near Jerusalem, some two miles away, and many of the Jews had come to Martha and Mary to console them about their brother. When Martha heard that Jesus was coming, she went and met him, while Mary stayed at home. Martha said to Jesus, "Lord, if you had been here, my brother would not have died. But even now I know that God will give you whatever you ask of him." Jesus said to her, "Your brother will rise again." Martha said to him, "I know that he will rise again in the resurrection on the last day." Jesus said to her, "I am the resurrection and the life. Those who believe in me, even though they die, will live, and everyone who lives and believes in me will never die. Do you believe this?" She said to him, "Yes, Lord, I believe that you are the Messiah, the Son of God, the one coming into the world."

or this

A Reading (Lesson) from the Gospel according to John [12:1–10]

Six days before the Passover Jesus came to Bethany, the home of Lazarus, whom he had raised from the dead. There they gave a dinner for him. Martha served, and Lazarus was one of those at the table with him. Mary took a pound of costly perfume made of pure nard, anointed Jesus' feet, and wiped them with her hair. The house was filled with the fragrance of the perfume. But Judas Iscariot, one of his disciples (the one who was about to betray him), said, "Why was this perfume not sold for three hundred denarii and the money given to the poor?"

(He said this not because he cared about the poor, but because he was a thief; he kept the common purse and used to steal what was put into it.) Jesus said, "Leave her alone. She bought it so that she might keep it for the day of my burial. You always have the poor with you, but you do not always have me." When the great crowd of the Jews learned that he was there, they came not only because of Jesus but also to see Lazarus, whom he had raised from the dead. So the chief priests planned to put Lazarus to death as well.

Saturday

Psalm 137:1–6(7–9) [page 792],   *Psalm 144* [page 800] ❖ *Psalm 42* [page 643],   *Psalm 43* [page 644]

A Reading (Lesson) from the Book of Jeremiah [31:27–34]

The days are surely coming, says the LORD, when I will sow the house of Israel and the house of Judah with the seed of humans and the seed of animals. And just as I have watched over them to pluck up and break down, to overthrow, destroy, and bring evil, so I will watch over them to build and to plant, says the LORD. In those days they shall no longer say: "The parents have eaten sour grapes, and the children's teeth are set on edge." But all shall die for their own sins; the teeth of everyone who eats sour grapes shall be set on edge. The days are surely coming, says the LORD, when I will make a new covenant with the house of Israel and the house of Judah. It will not be like the covenant that I made with their ancestors when I took them by the hand to bring them out of the land of Egypt—a covenant that they broke, though I was their husband, says the LORD. But this is the covenant that I will make with the house of Israel after those days, says the LORD: I will put my law within them, and I will write it on their hearts; and I will be their God, and they shall be my people. No longer shall they teach one another, or say to each other, "Know the LORD," for they shall all know me, from the least of them to the greatest, says the LORD; for I will forgive their iniquity, and remember their sin no more.

A Reading (Lesson) from the Letter of Paul to the Romans [11:25–36]

So that you may not claim to be wiser than you are, brothers and sisters, I want you to understand this mystery: a hardening has come upon part of Israel, until the full number of the Gentiles has come in. And so all Israel will be saved; as it is written, "Out of Zion will come the Deliverer; he will banish ungodliness from Jacob." "And this is my covenant with them, when I take away their sins." As regards the gospel they are enemies of God for your sake; but as regards election they are beloved, for the sake of their ancestors; for the gifts and the calling of God are irrevocable. Just as you were once disobedient to God but have now received mercy because of their disobedience, so they have now been disobedient in order that, by the mercy shown to you, they too may now receive mercy. For God has imprisoned all in disobedience so that he may be merciful to all. O the depth of the riches and wisdom and knowledge of God! How unsearchable are his judgments and how inscrutable his ways! "For who has known the mind of the Lord? Or who has been his counselor?" "Or who has given a gift to him, to receive a gift in return?" For from him and through him and to him are all things. To him be the glory forever. Amen.

A Reading (Lesson) from the Gospel according to John [11:28–44]

When Martha had said this, she went back and called her sister Mary, and told her privately, "The Teacher is here and is calling for you." And when she heard it, she got up quickly and went to him. Now Jesus had not yet come to the village, but was still at the place where Martha had met him. The Jews who were with her in the house, consoling her, saw Mary get up quickly and go out. They followed her because they thought that she was going to the tomb to weep there. When Mary came where Jesus was and saw him, she knelt at his feet and said to him, "Lord, if you had been here, my brother would not have died." When Jesus saw her weeping, and the Jews who came with her also weeping, he was greatly disturbed in spirit and deeply moved. He said, "Where have you laid him?" They said to him, "Lord, come and see." Jesus began to weep. So the Jews said, "See how he loved him!" But some of them said, "Could not he who opened the eyes of the blind man have kept this man from dying?" Then Jesus, again greatly disturbed, came to the tomb. It was a cave, and a stone was lying against it. Jesus said, "Take away the stone." Martha, the sister of the dead man, said to him, "Lord, already there is a stench because he has been dead four days." Jesus said to her, "Did I not tell you that if you believed, you would see the glory of God?" So they took away the stone. And Jesus looked upward and said, "Father, I thank you for having heard me. I knew that you always hear me, but I have said this for the sake of the crowd standing here, so that they may believe that you sent me." When he had said this, he cried with a loud voice, "Lazarus, come out!" The dead man came out, his hands and feet bound with strips of cloth, and his face wrapped in a cloth. Jesus said to them, "Unbind him, and let him go."

or this

A Reading (Lesson) from the Gospel according to John [12:37–50]

Although Jesus had performed so many signs in their presence, they did not believe in him. This was to fulfill the word spoken by the prophet Isaiah: "Lord, who has believed our message, and to whom has the arm of the Lord been revealed?" And so they could not believe, because Isaiah also said, "He has blinded their eyes and hardened their heart, so that they might not look with their eyes, and understand with their heart and turn—and I would heal them." Isaiah said this because he saw his glory and spoke about him. Nevertheless many, even of the authorities, believed in him. But because of the Pharisees they did not confess it, for fear that they would be put out of the synagogue; for they loved human glory more than the glory that comes from God. Then Jesus cried aloud: "Whoever believes in me believes not in me but in him who sent me. And whoever sees me sees him who sent me. I have come as light into the world, so that everyone who believes in me should not remain in the darkness. I do not judge anyone who hears my words and does not keep them, for I came not to judge the world, but to save the world. The one who rejects me and does not receive my word has a judge; on the last day the word that I have spoken will serve as judge, for I have not spoken on my own, but the Father who sent me has himself given me a commandment about what to say and what to speak. And I know that his commandment is eternal life. What I speak, therefore, I speak just as the Father has told me."

Holy Week

Palm Sunday

Psalm 24 [page 613], *Psalm 29* [page 620] ❖
Psalm 103 [page 733]

A Reading (Lesson) from the Book of Zechariah [9:9–12]*

Rejoice greatly, O daughter Zion! Shout aloud, O daughter Jerusalem! Lo, your king comes to you; triumphant and victorious is he, humble and riding on a donkey, on a colt, the foal of a donkey. He will cut off the chariot from Ephraim and the war horse from Jerusalem; and the battle bow shall be cut off, and he shall command peace to the nations; his dominion shall be from sea to sea, and from the River to the ends of the earth. As for you also, because of the blood of my covenant with you, I will set your prisoners free from the waterless pit. Return to your stronghold, O prisoners of hope; today I declare that I will restore to you double.

* *Intended for use in the morning*

A Reading (Lesson) from the First Letter of Paul to Timothy [6:12–16]*

Fight the good fight of the faith; take hold of the eternal life, to which you were called and for which you made the good confession in the presence of many witnesses. In the presence of God, who gives life to all things, and of Christ Jesus, who in his testimony before Pontius Pilate made the good confession, I charge you to keep the commandment without spot or blame until the manifestation of our Lord Jesus Christ, which he will bring about at the right time—he who is the blessed and only Sovereign, the King of kings and Lord of lords. It is he alone who has immortality and dwells in unapproachable light, whom no one has ever seen or can see; to him be honor and eternal dominion. Amen.

A Reading (Lesson) from the Book of Zechariah [12:9–11;13:1, 7–9]†

Thus says the Lord: On that day I will seek to destroy all the nations that come against Jerusalem. And I will pour out a spirit of compassion and supplication on the house of David and the inhabitants of Jerusalem, so that, when they look on the one whom they have pierced, they shall mourn for him as one mourns for an only child, and weep bitterly over him, as one weeps over a firstborn. On that day the mourning in Jerusalem will be as great as the mourning for Hadad-rimmon in the plain of Megiddo. On that day a fountain shall be opened for the house of David and the inhabitants of Jerusalem, to cleanse them from sin and impurity. "Awake, O sword, against my shepherd,

* *Intended for use in the morning*

† *Intended for use in the evening*

against the man who is my associate," says the LORD of hosts. Strike the shepherd, that the sheep may be scattered; I will turn my hand against the little ones. In the whole land, says the LORD, two-thirds shall be cut off and perish, and one-third shall be left alive. And I will put this third into the fire, refine them as one refines silver, and test them as gold is tested. They will call on my name, and I will answer them. I will say, "They are my people"; and they will say, "The LORD is our God."

A Reading (Lesson) from the Gospel according to Matthew [21:12–17]*

Jesus entered the temple and drove out all who were selling and buying in the temple, and he overturned the tables of the money changers and the seats of those who sold doves. He said to them, "It is written, 'My house shall be called a house of prayer'; but you are making it a den of robbers." The blind and the lame came to him in the temple, and he cured them. But when the chief priests and the scribes saw the amazing things that he did, and heard the children crying out in the temple, "Hosanna to the Son of David," they became angry and said to him, "Do you hear what these are saying?" Jesus said to them, "Yes; have you never read, 'Out of the mouths of infants and nursing babies you have prepared praise for yourself'?" He left them, went out of the city to Bethany, and spent the night there.

---

* *Intended for use in the evening*

Monday

Psalm 51:1–18(19–20) [page 656] ❖
Psalm 69:1–23 [page 679]

A Reading (Lesson) from the Book of Jeremiah [12:1–16]

You will be in the right, O LORD, when I lay charges against you; but let me put my case to you. Why does the way of the guilty prosper? Why do all who are treacherous thrive? You plant them, and they take root; they grow and bring forth fruit; you are near in their mouths yet far from their hearts. But you, O LORD, know me; You see me and test me—my heart is with you. Pull them out like sheep for the slaughter, and set them apart for the day of slaughter. How long will the land mourn, and the grass of every field wither? For the wickedness of those who live in it the animals and the birds are swept away, and because people said, "He is blind to our ways." If you have raced with foot-runners and they have wearied you, how will you compete with horses? And if in a safe land you fall down, how will you fare in the thickets of the Jordan? For even your kinsfolk and your own family, even they have dealt treacherously with you; they are in full cry after you; do not believe them, though they speak friendly words to you. I have forsaken my house, I have abandoned my heritage; I have given the beloved of my heart into the hands of her enemies. My heritage has become to me like a lion in the forest; she has lifted up her voice against me—therefore I hate her. Is the hyena greedy for my heritage at my command? Are the birds of prey all around her? Go, assemble all the wild animals; bring them to devour her. Many shepherds have destroyed my vineyard, they have trampled down my portion, they have made my pleasant portion a desolate wilderness. They have made it a desolation; desolate, it mourns to me. The whole land is made desolate, but no one lays it to heart. Upon all the bare heights in the desert spoilers have come; for the sword of the Lord devours from one end of the land to the other; no one shall be safe. They have sown wheat and have reaped thorns, they have tired themselves out but profit nothing. They shall be ashamed of their harvests because of the fierce anger of the LORD. Thus says the LORD concerning all my evil neighbors who touch the heritage that I have given my people Israel to inherit: I am about to pluck them up from their land, and I will pluck up the house of Judah from among them. And after I have plucked them up, I will again have compassion on them, and I will bring them again to their heritage and to their land, every one of them. And then, if they will diligently learn the ways of my people, to swear by my name, "As the LORD lives," as they taught my people to swear by Baal, then they shall be built up in the midst of my people.

A Reading (Lesson) from the Letter of Paul to the Philippians [3:1–14]

Finally, my brothers and sisters, rejoice in the Lord. To write the same things to you is not troublesome to me, and for you it is a safeguard. Beware of the dogs, beware of the evil workers, beware of those who mutilate the flesh! For it is we who are the circumcision, who worship in the Spirit of God and boast in Christ Jesus and have no confidence in the flesh—even though I, too, have reason for confidence in the flesh. If anyone else has reason to be confident in the flesh, I have more: circumcised on the eighth day, a member of the people of Israel, of the tribe of Benjamin, a Hebrew born of Hebrews; as to the law, a Pharisee; as to zeal, a persecutor of the church; as to righteousness under the law, blameless. Yet whatever gains

I had, these I have come to regard as loss because of Christ. More than that, I regard everything as loss because of the surpassing value of knowing Christ Jesus my Lord. For his sake I have suffered the loss of all things, and I regard them as rubbish, in order that I may gain Christ and be found in him, not having a righteousness of my own that comes from the law, but one that comes through faith in Christ, the righteousness from God based on faith. I want to know Christ and the power of his resurrection and the sharing of his sufferings by becoming like him in his death, if somehow I may attain the resurrection from the dead. Not that I have already obtained this or have already reached the goal, but I press on to make it my own, because Christ Jesus has made me his own. Beloved, I do not consider that I have made it my own, but this one thing I do: forgetting what lies behind and straining forward to what lies ahead, I press on toward the goal for the prize of the heavenly call of God in Christ Jesus.

A Reading (Lesson) from the Gospel according to John [12:9–19]

When the great crowd of the Jews learned that he was there, they came not only because of Jesus but also to see Lazarus, whom he had raised from the dead. So the chief priests planned to put Lazarus to death as well, since it was on account of him that many of the Jews were deserting and were believing in Jesus. The next day the great crowd that had come to the festival heard that Jesus was coming to Jerusalem. So they took branches of palm trees and went out to meet him, shouting, "Hosanna! Blessed is the one who comes in the name of the Lord—the King of Israel!" Jesus found a young donkey and sat on it; as it is written: "Do not be afraid, daughter of Zion. Look, your king is coming, sitting on a donkey's colt!" His disciples did not understand these things at first; but when Jesus was glorified, then they remembered that these things had been written of him and had been done to him. So the crowd that had been with him when he called Lazarus out of the tomb and raised him from the dead continued to testify. It was also because they heard that he had performed this sign that the crowd went to meet him. The Pharisees then said to one another, "You see, you can do nothing. Look, the world has gone after him!"

Tuesday

Psalm 6 [page 589],   *Psalm 12* [page 597] ❖
Psalm 94 [page 722]

A Reading (Lesson) from the Book of Jeremiah [15:10–21]

Woe is me, my mother, that you ever bore me, a man of strife and contention to the whole land! I have not lent, nor have I borrowed, yet all of them curse me. The LORD said: Surely I have intervened in your life for good, surely I have imposed enemies on you in a time of trouble and in a time of distress. Can iron and bronze break iron from the north? Your wealth and your treasures I will give as plunder, without price, for all your sins, throughout all your territory. I will make you serve your enemies in a land that you do not know, for in my anger a fire is kindled that shall burn forever. O LORD, you know; remember me and visit me, and bring down retribution for me on my persecutors. In your forbearance do not take me away; know that on your account I suffer insult. Your words were found, and I ate them, and your words became to me a joy and the delight of my heart; for I am called by your name, O Lord, God of hosts. I did not sit in the company of merrymakers, nor did I rejoice; under the weight of your hand I sat alone, for you had filled me with indignation. Why is my pain unceasing, my wound incurable, refusing to be healed? Truly, you are to me like a deceitful brook, like waters that fail. Therefore thus says the Lord: If you turn back, I will take you back, and you shall stand before me. If you utter what is precious, and not what is worthless, you shall serve as my mouth. It is they who will turn to you, not you who will turn to them. And I will make you to this people a fortified wall of bronze; they will fight against you, but they shall not prevail over you, for I am with you to save you and deliver you, says the Lord. I will deliver you out of the hand of the wicked, and redeem you from the grasp of the ruthless.

A Reading (Lesson) from the Letter of Paul to the Philippians [3:15–21]

Let those of us then who are mature be of the same mind; and if you think differently about anything, this too God will reveal to you. Only let us hold fast to what we have attained. Brothers and sisters, join in imitating me, and observe those who live according to the example you have in us. For many live as enemies of the cross of Christ; I have often told you of them, and now I tell you even with tears. Their end is destruction; their god is the belly; and their glory is in their shame; their minds are set on earthly things. But our citizenship is in heaven, and it is from there that we are expecting a Savior, the Lord Jesus Christ. He will transform the body of our humiliation that it may be conformed to the body of his glory, by the power that also enables him to make all things subject to himself.

A Reading (Lesson) from the Gospel according to John [12:20–26]

Among those who went up to worship at the festival were some Greeks. They came to Philip, who was from Bethsaida in Galilee, and said to him, "Sir, we wish to see Jesus." Philip went and told Andrew; then Andrew and Philip went and told Jesus. Jesus answered them, "The hour has come for the Son of Man to be glorified. Very truly, I tell you, unless a grain of wheat falls into the earth and dies, it remains just a single grain; but if it dies, it bears much fruit. Those who love their life lose it, and those who hate their life in this world will keep it for eternal life. Whoever serves me must follow me, and where I am, there will my servant be also. Whoever serves me, the Father will honor."

Wednesday

Psalm 55 [page 660]   ❖   *Psalm 74* [page 689]

A Reading (Lesson] from the Book of Jeremiah [17:5–10,14–17]

Thus says the LORD: Cursed are those who trust in mere mortals and make mere flesh their strength, whose hearts turn away from the LORD. They shall be like a shrub in the desert, and shall not see when relief comes. They shall live in the parched places of the wilderness, in an uninhabited salt land. Blessed are those who trust in the LORD, whose trust is the LORD. They shall be like a tree planted by water, sending out its roots by the stream. It shall not fear when heat comes, and its leaves shall stay green; in the year of drought it is not anxious, and it does not cease to bear fruit. The heart is devious above all else; it is perverse—who can understand it? I the LORD test the mind and search the heart, to give to all according to their ways, according to the fruit of their doings. Heal me, O LORD, and I shall be healed; save me, and I shall be saved; for you are my praise. See how they say to me, "Where is the word of the LORD? Let it come!" But I have not run away from being a shepherd in your service, nor have I desired the fatal day. You know what came from my lips; it was before your face. Do not become a terror to me; you are my refuge in the day of disaster.

A Reading (Lesson) from the Letter of Paul to the Philippians [4:1–13]

My brothers and sisters, whom I love and long for, my joy and crown, stand firm in the Lord in this way, my beloved. I urge Euodia and I urge Syntyche to be of the same mind in the Lord. Yes, and I ask you also, my loyal companion, help these women, for they have struggled beside me in the work of the gospel, together with Clement and the rest of my co-workers, whose names are in the book of life. Rejoice in the Lord always; again I will say, Rejoice. Let your gentleness be known to everyone. The Lord is near. Do not worry about anything, but in everything by prayer and supplication with thanksgiving let your requests be made known to God. And the peace of God, which surpasses all understanding, will guard your hearts and your minds in Christ Jesus. Finally, beloved, whatever is true, whatever is honorable, whatever is just, whatever is pure, whatever is pleasing, whatever is commendable, if there is any excellence and if there is anything worthy of praise, think about these things. Keep on doing the things that you have learned and received and heard and seen in me, and the God of peace will be with you. I rejoice in the Lord greatly that now at last you have revived your concern for me; indeed, you were concerned for me, but had no opportunity to show it. Not that I am referring to being in need; for I have learned to be content with whatever I have. I know what it is to have little, and I know what it is to have plenty. In any and all circumstances I have learned the secret of being well-fed and of going hungry, of having plenty and of being in need. I can do all things through him who strengthens me.

A Reading (Lesson) from the Gospel according to John [12:27–36]

Jesus said, "Now my soul is troubled. And what should I say—'Father, save me from this hour'? No, it is for this reason that I have come to this hour. Father, glorify your name." Then a voice came from heaven, "I have glorified it, and I will glorify it again." The crowd standing there heard it and said that it was thunder. Others said. "An angel has spoken to him." Jesus answered, "This voice has come for your sake, not for mine. Now is the judgment of this world; now the ruler of this world will be driven out. And I, when I am lifted up from the earth, will draw all people to myself." He said this to indicate the kind of death he was to die. The crowd answered him, "We have heard from the law that the Messiah remains forever. How can you say that the Son of Man must be lifted up? Who is this Son of Man?" Jesus said to them, "The light is with you for a little longer. Walk while you have the light, so that the darkness may not overtake you. If you walk in the darkness, you do not know where you are going. While you have the light, believe in the light, so that you may become children of light." After Jesus had said this, he departed and hid from them.

Maundy Thursday

Psalm 102 [page 731] ❖ *Psalm 142* [page 798],
Psalm 143 [page 798]

A Reading (Lesson) from the Book of Jeremiah [20:7–11]

O LORD, you have enticed me, and I was enticed; you have overpowered me, and you have prevailed. I have become a laughingstock all day long; everyone mocks me. For whenever I speak, I must cry out, I must shout, "Violence and destruction!" For the word of the LORD has become for me a reproach and derision all day long. If I say, "I will not mention him, or speak any more in his name," then within me there is something like a burning fire shut up in my bones; I am weary with holding it in, and I cannot. For I hear many whispering: "Terror is all around! Denounce him! Let us denounce him!" All my close friends are watching for me to stumble. "Perhaps he can be enticed, and we can prevail against him, and take our revenge on him." But the LORD is with me like a dread warrior; therefore my persecutors will stumble, and they will not prevail. They will be greatly shamed, for they will not succeed. Their eternal dishonor will never be forgotten.

A Reading (Lesson) from the First Letter of Paul to the Corinthians [10:14–17,11:27–32]

My dear friends, flee from the worship of idols. I speak as to sensible people; judge for yourselves what I say. The cup of blessing that we bless, is it not a sharing in the blood of Christ? The bread that we break, is it not a sharing in the body of Christ? Because there is one bread, we who are many are one body, for we all partake of the one bread. Whoever, therefore, eats the bread or drinks the cup of the Lord in an unworthy manner will be answerable for the body and blood of the Lord. Examine yourselves, and only then eat of the bread and drink of the cup. For all who eat and drink without discerning the body, eat and drink judgment against themselves. For this reason many of you are weak and ill, and some have died. But if we judged ourselves, we would not be judged. But when we are judged by the Lord, we are disciplined so that we may not be condemned along with the world.

A Reading (Lesson) from the Gospel according to John [17:1–11(12–26)]

After Jesus had spoken, he looked up to heaven and said, "Father, the hour has come; glorify your Son so that the Son may glorify you, since you have given him authority over all people, to give eternal life to all whom you have given him. And this is eternal life, that they may know you, the only true God, and Jesus Christ whom you have sent. I glorified you on earth by finishing the work that you gave me to do. So now, Father, glorify me in your own presence with the glory that I had in your presence before the world existed. I have made your name known to those whom you gave me from the world. They were yours, and you gave them to me, and they have kept your word. Now they know that everything you have given me is from you; for the words that you gave to me I have given to them, and they have received them and know in truth that I came from you; and they have believed that you sent me. I am asking on their behalf; I am not asking on behalf of the world, but on behalf of those whom you gave me, because they are yours. All mine are yours, and yours are mine; and I have been glorified in them. And now I am no longer in the world, but they are in the world, and I am coming to you. Holy Father, protect them in your name that you have given me, so that they may be one, as we are one."

"While I was with them, I protected them in your name that you have given me. I guarded them, and not one of them was lost except the one destined to be lost, so that the scripture might be fulfilled. But now I am coming to you, and I speak these things in the world so that they may have my joy made complete in themselves. I have given them your word, and the world has hated them because they do not belong to the world, just as I do not belong to the world. I am not asking you to take them out of the world, but I ask you to protect them from the evil one. They do not belong to the world, just as I do not belong to the world. Sanctify them in the truth; your word is truth. As you have sent me into the world, so I have sent them into the world. And for their sakes I sanctify myself, so that they also may be sanctified in truth. I ask not only on behalf of these, but also on behalf of those who will believe in me through their word, that they may all be one. As you, Father, are in me and I am in you, may they also be in us, so that the world may believe that you have sent me. The glory that you have given me I have given them, so that they may be one, as we are one, I in them and you in me, that they may become completely one, so that the world may know that you have sent me and have loved them even as you have loved me. Father, I desire that those also, whom you have given me, may be with me where I am, to see my glory, which you have given me because you loved me before the foundation of the world. Righteous Father, the world does not know you, but I know you; and these know that you have sent me. I made your name known to them, and I will make it known, so that the love with which you have loved me may be in them, and I in them."

Good Friday

Psalm 95* [page 724] & *Psalm 22* [page 610] ❖
Psalm 40:1–14(15–19) [page 640], *Psalm 54* [page 659]

A Reading (Lesson) from the Book of Wisdom
[1:16—2:1,12–22]

The ungodly by their words and deeds summoned death; considering him a friend, they pined away and made a covenant with him, because they are fit to belong to his company. For they reasoned unsoundly, saying to themselves, "Short and sorrowful is our life, and there is no remedy when a life comes to its end, and no one has been known to return from Hades. Let us lie in wait for the righteous man, because he is inconvenient to us and opposes our actions; he reproaches us for sins against the law, and accuses us of sins against our training. He professes to have knowledge of God, and calls himself a child of the Lord. He

---

* *For the Invitatory*

became to us a reproof of our thoughts; the very sight of him is a burden to us, because his manner of life is unlike that of others, and his ways are strange. We are considered by him as something base, and he avoids our ways as unclean; he calls the last end of the righteous happy, and boasts that God is his father. Let us see if his words are true, and let us test what will happen at the end of his life; for if the righteous man is God's child, he will help him, and will deliver him from the hand of his adversaries. Let us test him with insult and torture, so that we may find out how gentle he is, and make trial of his forbearance. Let us condemn him to a shameful death, for, according to what he says, he will be protected." Thus they reasoned, but they were led astray, for their wickedness blinded them, and they did not know the secret purposes of God, nor hoped for the wages of holiness, nor discerned the prize for blameless souls.

or this

A Reading (Lesson) from the Book of Genesis [22:1–14]

God tested Abraham. He said to him, "Abraham!" And he said, "Here I am." He said, "Take your son, your only son Isaac, whom you love, and go to the land of Moriah, and offer him there as a burnt offering on one of the mountains that I shall show you." So Abraham rose early in the morning, saddled his donkey, and took two of his young men with him, and his son Isaac; he cut the wood for the burnt offering, and set out and went to the place in the distance that God had shown him. On the third day Abraham looked up and saw the place far away. Then Abraham said to his young men, "Stay here with the donkey; the boy and I will go over there; we will worship, and then we will come back to you." Abraham took the wood of the burnt offering and laid it on his son Isaac, and he himself carried the fire and the knife. So the two of them walked on together. Isaac said to his father Abraham, "Father!" And he said, "Here I am, my son." He said, "The fire and the wood are here, but where is the lamb for a burnt offering?" Abraham said, "God himself will provide the lamb for a burnt offering, my son." So the two of them walked on together. When they came to the place that God had shown him, Abraham built an altar there and laid the wood in order. He bound his son Isaac, and laid him on the altar, on top of the wood. Then Abraham reached out his hand and took the knife to kill his son. But the angel of the LORD called to him from heaven, and said, "Abraham, Abraham!" And he said, "Here I am." He said, "Do not lay your hand on the boy or do anything to him; for now I know that you fear God, since you have not withheld your son, your only son, from me." And Abraham looked up and saw a ram, caught in a thicket by its horns. Abraham went and took the ram and offered it up as a burnt offering instead of his son. So Abraham called that place "The LORD will provide"; as it is said to this day, "On the mount of the LORD it shall be provided."

A Reading (Lesson) from the First Letter of Peter [1:10–20]

Concerning salvation, the prophets who prophesied of the grace that was to be yours made careful search and inquiry, inquiring about the person or time that the Spirit of Christ within them indicated when it testified in advance to the sufferings destined for Christ and the subsequent glory. It was revealed to them that they were serving not themselves but you, in regard to the things that have now been announced to you through those who brought you good news by the Holy Spirit sent from heaven—things into which angels long to look! Therefore prepare your minds for action; discipline yourselves; set all your hope on the grace that Jesus Christ will bring you when he is revealed. Like obedient children, do not be conformed to the desires that you formerly had in ignorance. Instead, as he who called you is holy, be holy yourselves in all your conduct; for it is written, "You shall be holy, for I am holy." If you invoke as Father the one who judges all people impartially according to their deeds, live in reverent fear during the time of your exile. You know that you were ransomed from the futile ways inherited from your ancestors, not with perishable things like silver or gold, but with the precious blood of Christ, like that of a lamb without defect or blemish. He was destined before the foundation of the world, but was revealed at the end of the ages for your sake.

A Reading (Lesson) from the Gospel according to John [13:36–38]*

Simon Peter said to Jesus, "Lord, where are you going?" Jesus answered, "Where I am going, you cannot follow me now; but you will follow afterward." Peter said to him, "Lord, why can I not follow you now? I will lay down my life for you." Jesus answered, "Will you lay down your life for me? Very truly, I tell you, before the cock crows, you will have denied me three times."

Intended for use in the morning

A Reading (Lesson) from the Gospel according to John [19:38–42]*

Joseph of Arimathea, who was a disciple of Jesus, though a secret one because of his fear of the Jews, asked Pilate to let him take away the body of Jesus. Pilate gave him permission; so he came and removed his body. Nicodemus, who had at first come to Jesus by night, also came, bringing a mixture of myrrh and aloes, weighing about a hundred pounds. They took the body of Jesus and wrapped it with the spices in linen cloths, according to the burial custom of the Jews. Now there was a garden in the place where he was crucified, and in the garden there was a new tomb in which no one had ever been laid. And so, because it was the Jewish day of Preparation, and the tomb was nearby, they laid Jesus there.

Holy Saturday

Psalm 95† [page 724]   &   *Psalm 88* [page 712]   ❖
Psalm 27 [page 617]

A Reading (Lesson) from the Book of Job [19:21–27a]

Job answered Bildad the Shuhite: "Have pity on me, have pity on me, O you my friends, for the hand of God has touched me! Why do you, like God, pursue me, never satisfied with my flesh? O that my words were written down! O that they were inscribed in a book! O that with an iron pen and with lead they were engraved on a rock forever! For I know that my Redeemer lives, and that at the

* *Intended for use in the evening*

† *For the Invitatory*

last he will stand upon the earth; and after my skin has been thus destroyed, then in my flesh I shall see God, whom I shall see on my side, and my eyes shall behold, and not another."

A Reading (Lesson) from the Letter to the Hebrews [4:1–16]*

While the promise of entering his rest is still open, let us take care that none of you should seem to have failed to reach it. For indeed the good news came to us just as to them; but the message they heard did not benefit them, because they were not united by faith with those who listened. For we who have believed enter that rest, just as God has said, "As in my anger I swore, 'They shall not enter my rest,'" though his works were finished at the foundation of the world. For in one place it speaks about the seventh day as follows, "And God rested on the seventh day from all his works." And again in this place it says, "They shall not enter my rest." Since therefore it remains open for some to enter it, and those who formerly received the good news failed to enter because of disobedience, again he sets a certain day—"today"— saying through David much later, in the words already quoted, "Today, if you hear his voice, do not harden your hearts." For if Joshua had given them rest, God would not speak later about another day. So then, a sabbath rest still remains for the people of God; for those who enter God's rest also cease from their labors as God did from his. Let us therefore make every effort to enter that rest, so that no one may fall through such disobedience as theirs. Indeed, the word of God is living and active, sharper than any

* Intended for use in the morning

two-edged sword, piercing until it divides soul from spirit, joints from marrow; it is able to judge the thoughts and intentions of the heart. And before him no creature is hidden, but all are naked and laid bare to the eyes of the one to whom we must render an account. Since, then, we have a great high priest who has passed through the heavens, Jesus, the Son of God, let us hold fast to our confession. For we do not have a high priest who is unable to sympathize with our weaknesses, but we have one who in every respect has been tested as we are, yet without sin. Let us therefore approach the throne of grace with boldness, so that we may receive mercy and find grace to help in time of need.

Romans 8:1–11 [page 362 above]*

Easter Week

Easter Day

Psalm 148 [page 805], *Psalm 149* [page 807], *Psalm 150* [page 807] ❖ *Psalm 113* [page 756], *Psalm 114* [page 756] or *Psalm 118* [page 760]

A Reading (Lesson) from the Book of Exodus [12:1–14]†

The Lord said to Moses and Aaron in the land of Egypt: This month shall mark for you the beginning of months; it shall be the first month of the year for you. Tell the whole

---

* *Intended for use in the evening*

† *Intended for use in the morning*

congregation of Israel that on the tenth of this month they are to take a lamb for each family, a lamb for each household. If a household is too small for a whole lamb, it shall join its closest neighbor in obtaining one; the lamb shall be divided in proportion to the number of people who eat of it. Your lamb shall be without blemish, a year-old male; you may take it from the sheep or from the goats. You shall keep it until the fourteenth day of this month; then the whole assembled congregation of Israel shall slaughter it at twilight. They shall take some of the blood and put it on the two doorposts and the lintel of the houses in which they eat it. They shall eat the lamb that same night; they shall eat it roasted over the fire with unleavened bread and bitter herbs. Do not eat any of it raw or boiled in water, but roasted over the fire, with its head, legs, and inner organs. You shall let none of it remain until the morning; anything that remains until the morning you shall burn. This is how you shall eat it: your loins girded, your sandals on your feet, and your staff in your hand; and you shall eat it hurriedly. It is the passover of the LORD. For I will pass through the land of Egypt that night, and I will strike down every firstborn in the land of Egypt, both human beings and animals; on all the gods of Egypt I will execute judgments: I am the LORD. The blood shall be a sign for you on the houses where you live: when I see the blood, I will pass over you, and no plague shall destroy you when I strike the land of Egypt. This day shall be a day of remembrance for you. You shall celebrate it as a festival to the LORD; throughout your generations you shall observe it as a perpetual ordinance.

John 1:1–18 [page 282 above]*

---

* *Intended for use in the morning*

A Reading (Lesson) from the Book of Isaiah [51:9–11]*

Awake, awake, put on strength, O arm of the LORD! Awake, as in days of old, the generations of long ago! Was it not you who cut Rahab in pieces, who pierced the dragon? Was it not you who dried up the sea, the waters of the great deep; who made the depths of the sea a way for the redeemed to cross over? So the ransomed of the LORD shall return, and come to Zion with singing; everlasting joy shall be upon their heads; they shall obtain joy and gladness, and sorrow and sighing shall flee away.

A Reading (Lesson) from the Gospel according to Luke [24:13–35]*

Now on that same day two of Jesus' followers were going to a village called Emmaus, about seven miles from Jerusalem, and talking with each other about all these things that had happened. While they were talking and discussing, Jesus himself came near and went with them, but their eyes were kept from recognizing him. And he said to them, "What are you discussing with each other while you walk along?" They stood still, looking sad. Then one of them, whose name was Cleopas, answered him, "Are you the only stranger in Jerusalem who does not know the things that have taken place there in these days?" He asked them, "What things?" They replied, "The things about Jesus of Nazareth, who was a prophet mighty in deed and word before God and all the people, and how our chief priests and leaders handed him over to be condemned to death and crucified him. But we had hoped that he was the one to redeem Israel. Yes, and besides all this, it is now the third day since these things

* *Intended for use in the evening*

took place. Moreover, some women of our group astounded us. They were at the tomb early this morning, and when they did not find his body there, they came back and told us that they had indeed seen a vision of angels who said that he was alive. Some of those who were with us went to the tomb and found it just as the women had said; but they did not see him." Then he said to them, "Oh, how foolish you are, and how slow of heart to believe all that the prophets have declared! Was it not necessary that the Messiah should suffer these things and then enter into his glory?" Then beginning with Moses and all the prophets, he interpreted to them the things about himself in all the scriptures. As they came near the village to which they were going, he walked ahead as if he were going on. But they urged him strongly, saying, "Stay with us, because it is almost evening and the day is now nearly over." So he went in to stay with them. When he was at the table with them, he took bread, blessed and broke it, and gave it to them. Then their eyes were opened, and they recognized him; and he vanished from their sight. They said to each other, "Were not our hearts burning within us while he was talking to us on the road, while he was opening the scriptures to us?" That same hour they got up and returned to Jerusalem; and they found the eleven and their companions gathered together. They were saying, "The Lord has risen indeed, and he has appeared to Simon!" Then they told what had happened on the road, and how he had been made known to them in the breaking of the bread.

or this

A Reading (Lesson) from the Gospel according to John [20:19–23]*

When it was evening on that day, the first day of the week, and the doors of the house where the disciples had met were locked for fear of the Jews, Jesus came and stood among them and said, "Peace be with you." After he said this, he showed them his hands and his side. Then the disciples rejoiced when they saw the Lord. Jesus said to them again, "Peace be with you. As the Father has sent me, so I send you." When he had said this, he breathed on them and said to them, "Receive the Holy Spirit. If you forgive the sins of any, they are forgiven them; if you retain the sins of any, they are retained."

Monday

Psalm 93 [page 722],   *Psalm 98* [page 727]   ❖
Psalm 66 [page 673]

A Reading (Lesson) from the Book of Jonah [2:1–9]

Jonah prayed to the Lord his God from the belly of the fish, saying, "I called to the LORD out of my distress, and he answered me; out of the belly of Sheol I cried, and you heard my voice. You cast me into the deep, into the heart of the seas, and the flood surrounded me; all your waves and your billows passed over me. Then I said, 'I am driven away from your sight; how shall I look again upon your holy temple?' The waters closed in over me; the deep surrounded me; weeds were wrapped around my head at the roots of the mountains. I went down to the land whose bars closed upon me forever; yet you brought up my life from the Pit, O LORD

---

* *Intended for use in the evening*

my God. As my life was ebbing away, I remembered the
LORD; and my prayer came to you, into your holy temple.
Those who worship vain idols forsake their true loyalty. But
I with the voice of thanksgiving will sacrifice to you; what I
have vowed I will pay. Deliverance belongs to the LORD!"

A Reading (Lesson) from the Acts of the Apostles
[2:14, 22–32]*

Peter, standing with the eleven, raised his voice and
addressed them, "Men of Judea and all who live in
Jerusalem, let this be known to you, and listen to what I
say. You that are Israelites, listen to what I have to say:
Jesus of Nazareth, a man attested to you by God with
deeds of power, wonders, and signs that God did through
him among you, as you yourselves know—this man,
handed over to you according to the definite plan and
foreknowledge of God, you crucified and killed by the
hands of those outside the law. But God raised him up,
having freed him from death, because it was impossible
for him to be held in its power. For David says concerning
him, 'I saw the Lord always before me, for he is at my
right hand so that I will not be shaken; therefore my heart
was glad, and my tongue rejoiced; moreover my flesh will
live in hope. For you will not abandon my soul to Hades,
or let your Holy One experience corruption. You have
made known to me the ways of life; you will make me full
of gladness with your presence.' Fellow Israelites, I may
say to you confidently of our ancestor David that he both
died and was buried, and his tomb is with us to this day.
Since he was a prophet, he knew that God had sworn with
an oath to him that he would put one of his descendants

---

* *Duplicates the First Lesson at the Eucharist. Readings from Year Two may be substituted.*

on his throne. Foreseeing this, David spoke of the resurrection of the Messiah, saying, 'He was not abandoned to Hades, nor did his flesh experience corruption.' This Jesus God raised up, and of that all of us are witnesses."

A Reading (Lesson) from the Gospel according to John [14:1–14]

Jesus said to the disciples, "Do not let your hearts be troubled. Believe in God, believe also in me. In my Father's house there are many dwelling places. If it were not so, would I have told you that I go to prepare a place for you? And if I go and prepare a place for you, I will come again and will take you to myself, so that where I am, there you may be also. And you know the way to the place where I am going." Thomas said to him, "Lord, we do not know where you are going. How can we know the way?" Jesus said to him, "I am the way, and the truth, and the life. No one comes to the Father except through me. If you know me, you will know my Father also. From now on you do know him and have seen him." Philip said to him, "Lord, show us the Father, and we will be satisfied." Jesus said to him, "Have I been with you all this time, Philip, and you still do not know me? Whoever has seen me has seen the Father. How can you say, 'Show us the Father'? Do you not believe that I am in the Father and the Father is in me? The words that I say to you I do not speak on my own; but the Father who dwells in me does his works. Believe me that I am in the Father and the Father is in me; but if you do not, then believe me because of the works themselves. Very truly, I tell you, the one who believes in me will also do the works that I do and, in fact, will do greater works than these, because I am going to the Father. I will do whatever you ask in my name, so that the Father may be glorified in the Son. If in my name you ask me for anything, I will do it."

Tuesday

Psalm 103 [page 733] ❖ *Psalm 111* [page 754], *Psalm 114* [page 756]

A Reading (Lesson) from the Book of Isaiah [30:18–21]

The LORD waits to be gracious to you; therefore he will rise up to show mercy to you. For the LORD is a God of justice; blessed are all those who wait for him. Truly, O people in Zion, inhabitants of Jerusalem, you shall weep no more. He will surely be gracious to you at the sound of your cry; when he hears it, he will answer you. Though the Lord may give you the bread of adversity and the water of affliction, yet your Teacher will not hide himself any more, but your eyes shall see your Teacher. And when you turn to the right or when you turn to the left, your ears shall hear a word behind you, saying, "This is the way; walk in it."

A Reading (Lesson) from the Acts of the Apostles [2:36–41(42–47)]*

Peter, standing with the eleven, raised his voice and addressed them, "Let the entire house of Israel know with certainty that God has made him both Lord and Messiah, this Jesus whom you crucified." Now when they heard this, they were cut to the heart and said to Peter and to the other apostles, "Brothers, what should we do?" Peter

---

* *Duplicates the First Lesson at the Eucharist. Readings from Year Two may be substituted.*

said to them, "Repent, and be baptized every one of you in the name of Jesus Christ so that your sins may be forgiven; and you will receive the gift of the Holy Spirit. For the promise is for you, for your children, and for all who are far away, everyone whom the Lord our God calls to him." And he testified with many other arguments and exhorted them, saying, "Save yourselves from this corrupt generation."

So those who welcomed his message were baptized, and that day about three thousand persons were added. They devoted themselves to the apostles' teaching and fellowship, to the breaking of bread and the prayers. Awe came upon everyone, because many wonders and signs were being done by the apostles. All who believed were together and had all things in common; they would sell their possessions and goods and distribute the proceeds to all, as any had need. Day by day, as they spent much time together in the temple, they broke bread at home and ate their food with glad and generous hearts, praising God and having the goodwill of all the people. And day by day the Lord added to their number those who were being saved.

A Reading (Lesson) from the Gospel according to John [14:15–31]

Jesus said to Philip and the disciples, "If you love me, you will keep my commandments. And I will ask the Father, and he will give you another Advocate, to be with you forever. This is the Spirit of truth, whom the world cannot receive, because it neither sees him nor knows him. You know him, because he abides with you, and he will be in you. I will not leave you orphaned; I am coming to you.

In a little while the world will no longer see me, but you will see me; because I live, you also will live. On that day you will know that I am in my Father, and you in me, and I in you. They who have my commandments and keep them are those who love me; and those who love me will be loved by my Father, and I will love them and reveal myself to them." Judas (not Iscariot) said to him, "Lord, how is it that you will reveal yourself to us, and not to the world?" Jesus answered him, "Those who love me will keep my word, and my Father will love them, and we will come to them and make our home with them. Whoever does not love me does not keep my words; and the word that you hear is not mine, but is from the Father who sent me. I have said these things to you while I am still with you. But the Advocate, the Holy Spirit, whom the Father will send in my name, will teach you everything, and remind you of all that I have said to you. Peace I leave with you; my peace I give to you. I do not give to you as the world gives. Do not let your hearts be troubled, and do not let them be afraid. You heard me say to you, 'I am going away, and I am coming to you.' If you loved me, you would rejoice that I am going to the Father, because the Father is greater than I. And now I have told you this before it occurs, so that when it does occur, you may believe. I will no longer talk much with you, for the ruler of this world is coming. He has no power over me; but I do as the Father has commanded me, so that the world may know that I love the Father. Rise, let us be on our way."

Wednesday

Psalm 97 [page 726],   *Psalm 99* [page 728]   ❖
Psalm 115 [page 757]

A Reading (Lesson) from the Book of Micah [7:7–15]

As for me, I will look to the LORD, I will wait for the God of
my salvation; my God will hear me. Do not rejoice over me,
O my enemy; when I fall, I shall rise; when I sit in darkness,
the LORD will be a light to me. I must bear the indignation
of the LORD, because I have sinned against him, until he
takes my side and executes judgment for me. He will bring
me out to the light; I shall see his vindication. Then my
enemy will see, and shame will cover her who said to me,
"Where is the LORD your God?" My eyes will see her
downfall; now she will be trodden down like the mire of the
streets. A day for the building of your walls! In that day the
boundary shall be far extended. In that day they will come
to you from Assyria to Egypt, and from Egypt to the River,
from sea to sea and from mountain to mountain. But the
earth will be desolate because of its inhabitants, for the fruit
of their doings. Shepherd your people with your staff, the
flock that belongs to you, which lives alone in a forest in the
midst of a garden land; let them feed in Bashan and Gilead
as in the days of old. As in the days when you came out of
the land of Egypt, show us marvelous things.

A Reading (Lesson) from the Acts of the Apostles [3:1–10]*

One day Peter and John were going up to the temple at
the hour of prayer, at three o'clock in the afternoon. And
a man lame from birth was being carried in. People would
lay him daily at the gate of the temple called the Beautiful
Gate so that he could ask for alms from those entering the
temple. When he saw Peter and John about to go into the
temple, he asked them for alms. Peter looked intently at

---

* *Duplicates the First Lesson at the Eucharist. Readings from Year Two may be substituted.*

him, as did John, and said, "Look at us." And he fixed his attention on them, expecting to receive something from them. But Peter said, "I have no silver or gold, but what I have I give you; in the name of Jesus Christ of Nazareth, stand up and walk." And he took him by the right hand and raised him up; and immediately his feet and ankles were made strong. Jumping up, he stood and began to walk, and he entered the temple with them, walking and leaping and praising God. All the people saw him walking and praising God, and they recognized him as the one who used to sit and ask for alms at the Beautiful Gate of the temple; and they were filled with wonder and amazement at what had happened to him.

A Reading (Lesson) from the Gospel according to John [15:1–11]

Jesus said to his disciples, "I am the true vine, and my Father is the vinegrower. He removes every branch in me that bears no fruit. Every branch that bears fruit he prunes to make it bear more fruit. You have already been cleansed by the word that I have spoken to you. Abide in me as I abide in you. Just as the branch cannot bear fruit by itself unless it abides in the vine, neither can you unless you abide in me. I am the vine, you are the branches. Those who abide in me and I in them bear much fruit, because apart from me you can do nothing. Whoever does not abide in me is thrown away like a branch and withers; such branches are gathered, thrown into the fire, and burned. If you abide in me, and my words abide in you, ask for whatever you wish, and it will be done for you. My Father is glorified by this, that you bear much fruit and become my disciples. As the Father has loved me, so I have loved you; abide in my love. If you keep my commandments, you will abide in my love, just as I have kept my Father's commandments and abide in his love. I have said these things to you so that my joy may be in you, and that your joy may be complete."

Thursday

Psalm 146 [page 803], *Psalm 147* [page 804]   ❖
Psalm 148 [page 805], *Psalm 149* [page 807]

A Reading (Lesson) from the Book of Ezekiel [37:1–14]

The hand of the LORD came upon me, and he brought me out by the spirit of the LORD and set me down in the middle of a valley; it was full of bones. He led me all around them; there were very many lying in the valley, and they were very dry. He said to me, "Mortal, can these bones live?" I answered, "O Lord GOD, you know." Then he said to me, "Prophesy to these bones, and say to them: O dry bones, hear the word of the LORD. Thus says the Lord GOD to these bones: I will cause breath to enter you, and you shall live. I will lay sinews on you, and will cause flesh to come upon you, and cover you with skin, and put breath in you, and you shall live; and you shall know that I am the LORD." So I prophesied as I had been commanded; and as I prophesied, suddenly there was a noise, a rattling, and the bones came together, bone to its bone. I looked, and there were sinews on them, and flesh had come upon them, and skin had covered them; but there was no breath in them. Then he said to me, "Prophesy to the breath, prophesy, mortal, and say to the breath: Thus says the Lord GOD: Come from the four winds, O breath, and breathe upon these slain, that they may live." I prophesied as he commanded me, and the breath came into them, and they lived, and stood on their feet, a vast multitude. Then he said to me, "Mortal, these bones are the whole house of Israel. They say, 'Our bones are dried up, and our hope is lost; we are cut off completely.' Therefore prophesy, and say to them, Thus says the Lord GOD: I am going to open your graves, and bring you up from your graves, O my people; and I will bring you back to the land of Israel. And you shall know that I am the LORD, when I open your graves, and bring you up from your graves, O my people. I will put my spirit within you, and you shall live, and I will place you on your own soil; then you shall know that I, the LORD, have spoken and will act, says the LORD."

A Reading (Lesson) from the Acts of the Apostles [3:11–26]*

While the lame man who had been cured clung to Peter and John, all the people ran together to them in the portico called Solomon's Portico, utterly astonished. When Peter saw it, he addressed the people, "You Israelites, why do you wonder at this, or why do you stare at us, as though by our own power or piety we had made him walk? The God of Abraham, the God of Isaac, and the God of Jacob, the God of our ancestors has glorified his servant Jesus, whom you handed over and rejected in the presence of Pilate, though he had decided to release him. But you rejected the Holy and Righteous One and asked to have a murderer given to you, and you killed the Author of life, whom God raised from the dead. To this we are witnesses. And by faith in his name, his name itself has made this man strong, whom you see and know; and the faith that is through Jesus has given him this perfect

* Duplicates the First Lesson at the Eucharist. Readings from Year Two may be substituted.

health in the presence of all of you. And now, friends, I know that you acted in ignorance, as did also your rulers. In this way God fulfilled what he had foretold through all the prophets, that his Messiah would suffer. Repent therefore, and turn to God so that your sins may be wiped out, so that times of refreshing may come from the presence of the Lord, and that he may send the Messiah appointed for you, that is, Jesus, who must remain in heaven until the time of universal restoration that God announced long ago through his holy prophets. Moses said, 'The Lord your God will raise up for you from your own people a prophet like me. You must listen to whatever he tells you. And it will be that everyone who does not listen to that prophet will be utterly rooted out of the people.' And all the prophets, as many as have spoken, from Samuel and those after him, also predicted these days. You are the descendants of the prophets and of the covenant that God gave to your ancestors, saying to Abraham, 'And in your descendants all the families of the earth shall be blessed.' When God raised up his servant, he sent him first to you, to bless you by turning each of you from your wicked ways."

A Reading (Lesson) from the Gospel according to John [15:12–27]

Jesus said to his disciples, "This is my commandment, that you love one another as I have loved you. No one has greater love than this, to lay down one's life for one's friends. You are my friends if you do what I command you. I do not call you servants any longer, because the servant does not know what the master is doing; but I have called you friends, because I have made known to you everything that I have heard from my Father. You did not choose me but I chose you. And I appointed you to go and bear fruit, fruit that will last, so that the Father will give you whatever you ask him in my name. I am giving you these commands so that you may love one another. If the world hates you, be aware that it hated me before it hated you. If you belonged to the world, the world would love you as its own. Because you do not belong to the world, but I have chosen you out of the world—therefore the world hates you. Remember the word that I said to you. 'Servants are not greater than their master.' If they persecuted me, they will persecute you; if they kept my word, they will keep yours also. But they will do all these things to you on account of my name, because they do not know him who sent me. If I had not come and spoken to them, they would not have sin; but now they have no excuse for their sin. Whoever hates me hates my Father also. If I had not done among them the works that no one else did, they would not have sin. But now they have seen and hated both me and my Father. It was to fulfill the word that is written in their law, 'They hated me without a cause.' When the Advocate comes, whom I will send to you from the Father, the Spirit of truth who comes from the Father, he will testify on my behalf. You also are to testify because you have been with me from the beginning."

Friday

Psalm 136 [page 789]   ❖   *Psalm 118* [page 760]

A Reading (Lesson) from the Book of Daniel [12:1–4,13]

The vision of one in human form said to me, "At that time Michael, the great prince, the protector of your people,

shall arise. There shall be a time of anguish, such as has
never occurred since nations first came into existence. But at
that time your people shall be delivered, everyone who is
found written in the book. Many of those who sleep in the
dust of the earth shall awake, some to everlasting life, and
some to shame and everlasting contempt. Those who are
wise shall shine like the brightness of the sky, and those who
lead many to righteousness, like the stars forever and ever.
But you, Daniel, keep the words secret and the book sealed
until the time of the end. Many shall be running back and
forth, and evil shall increase. But you, go your way, and
rest; you shall rise for your reward at the end of the days."

A Reading (Lesson) from the Acts of the Apostles [4:1–12]*

While Peter and John were speaking to the people, the
priests, the captain of the temple, and the Sadducees came
to them, much annoyed because they were teaching the
people and proclaiming that in Jesus there is the
resurrection of the dead. So they arrested them and put
them in custody until the next day, for it was already
evening. But many of those who heard the word believed;
and they numbered about five thousand. The next day
their rulers, elders, and scribes assembled in Jerusalem,
with Annas the high priest, Caiaphas, John, and
Alexander, and all who were of the high-priestly family.
When they had made the prisoners stand in their midst,
they inquired, "By what power or by what name did you
do this?" Then Peter, filled with the Holy Spirit, said to
them, "Rulers of the people and elders, if we are
questioned today because of a good deed done to someone
who was sick and are asked how this man has been

* Duplicates the First Lesson at the Eucharist. Readings from Year Two may be substituted.

healed, let it be known to all of you, and to all the people of Israel, that this man is standing before you in good health by the name of Jesus Christ of Nazareth, whom you crucified, whom God raised from the dead. This Jesus is 'the stone that was rejected by you, the builders; it has become the cornerstone.' There is salvation in no one else, for there is no other name under heaven given among mortals by which we must be saved."

A Reading (Lesson) from the Gospel according to John [16:1–15]

Jesus said to his disciples, "I have said these things to you to keep you from stumbling. They will put you out of the synagogues. Indeed, an hour is coming when those who kill you will think that by doing so they are offering worship to God. And they will do this because they have not known the Father or me. But I have said these things to you so that when their hour comes you may remember that I told you about them. I did not say these things to you from the beginning, because I was with you. But now I am going to him who sent me; yet none of you asks me, 'Where are you going?' But because I have said these things to you, sorrow has filled your hearts. Nevertheless I tell you the truth: it is to your advantage that I go away, for if I do not go away, the Advocate will not come to you; but if I go, I will send him to you. And when he comes, he will prove the world wrong about sin and righteousness and judgment: about sin, because they do not believe in me; about righteousness, because I am going to the Father and you will see me no longer; about judgment, because the ruler of this world has been condemned. I still have many things to say to you, but you cannot bear them now. When the Spirit of truth comes, he will guide you into all the truth; for he will not speak on his own, but will speak whatever he hears, and he will declare to you the things that are to come. He will glorify me, because he will take what is mine and declare it to you. All that the Father has is mine. For this reason I said that he will take what is mine and declare it to you."

Saturday

Psalm 145 [page 801] ❖ *Psalm 104* [page 735]

Isaiah 25:1–9 [page 81 above]

A Reading (Lesson) from the Acts of the Apostles [4:13–21(22–31)]*

When the rulers, elders, and scribes saw the boldness of Peter and John and realized that they were uneducated and ordinary men, they were amazed and recognized them as companions of Jesus. When they saw the man who had been cured standing beside them, they had nothing to say in opposition. So they ordered them to leave the council while they discussed the matter with one another. They said, "What will we do with them? For it is obvious to all who live in Jerusalem that a notable sign has been done through them; we cannot deny it. But to keep it from spreading further among the people, let us warn them to speak no more to anyone in this name." So they called them and ordered them not to speak or teach at all in the name of Jesus. But Peter and John answered them, "Whether it is right in God's sight to listen to you rather than to God, you must judge; for we cannot keep from speaking about what we have seen and heard." After

---

* *Duplicates the First Lesson at the Eucharist. Readings from Year Two may be substituted.*

threatening them again, they let them go, finding no way to punish them because of the people, for all of them praised God for what had happened.

For the man on whom this sign of healing had been performed was more than forty years old. After they were released, they went to their friends and reported what the chief priests and the elders had said to them. When they heard it, they raised their voices together to God and said, "Sovereign Lord, who made the heaven and the earth, the sea, and everything in them, it is you who said by the Holy Spirit through our ancestor David, your servant: 'Why did the Gentiles rage, and the peoples imagine vain things? The kings of the earth took their stand, and the rulers have gathered together against the Lord and against his Messiah.' For in this city, in fact, both Herod and Pontius Pilate, with the Gentiles and the peoples of Israel, gathered together against your holy servant Jesus, whom you anointed, to do whatever your hand and your plan had predestined to take place. And now, Lord, look at their threats, and grant to your servants to speak your word with all boldness, while you stretch out your hand to heal, and signs and wonders are performed through the name of your holy servant Jesus." When they had prayed, the place in which they were gathered together was shaken; and they were all filled with the Holy Spirit and spoke the word of God with boldness.

A Reading (Lesson) from the Gospel according to John [16:16–33]

Jesus said to his disciples, "A little while, and you will no longer see me, and again a little while, and you will see me." Then some of his disciples said to one another,

"What does he mean by saying to us, 'A little while, and you will no longer see me, and again a little while, and you will see me'; and 'Because I am going to the Father'?" They said, "What does he mean by this 'a little while'? We do not know what he is talking about." Jesus knew that they wanted to ask him, so he said to them, "Are you discussing among yourselves what I meant when I said, 'A little while, and you will no longer see me, and again a little while, and you will see me'? Very truly I tell you, you will weep and mourn, but the world will rejoice; you will have pain, but your pain will turn into joy. When a woman is in labor, she has pain, because her hour has come. But when her child is born, she no longer remembers the anguish because of the joy of having brought a human being into the world. So you have pain now; but I will see you again, and your hearts will rejoice, and no one will take your joy from you. On that day you will ask nothing of me. Very truly, I tell you, if you ask anything of the Father in my name, he will give it to you. Until now you have not asked for anything in my name. Ask and you will receive, so that your joy may be complete. I have said these things to you in figures of speech. The hour is coming when I will no longer speak to you in figures, but will tell you plainly of the Father. On that day you will ask in my name. I do not say to you that I will ask the Father on your behalf; for the Father himself loves you, because you have loved me and have believed that I came from God. I came from the Father and have come into the world; again, I am leaving the world and am going to the Father." His disciples said, "Yes, now you are speaking plainly, not in any figure of speech! Now we know that you know all things, and do not need to have anyone question you; by this we believe that you came from God." Jesus answered them, "Do you now believe? The hour is coming, indeed it has come, when you will be scattered, each one to his home, and you will leave me alone. Yet I am not alone because the Father is with me. I have said this to you, so that in me you may have peace. In the world you face persecution. But take courage; I have conquered the world!"

Week of 2 Easter

Sunday

Psalm 146 [page 803], *Psalm 147* [page 804] ❖
Psalm 111 [page 754], *Psalm 112* [page 755],
Psalm 113 [page 756]

A Reading (Lesson) from the Book of Isaiah [43:8–13]

Bring forth the people who are blind, yet have eyes, who are deaf, yet have ears! Let all the nations gather together, and let the peoples assemble. Who among them declared this, and foretold to us the former things? Let them bring their witnesses to justify them, and let them hear and say, "It is true." You are my witnesses, says the LORD, and my servant whom I have chosen, so that you may know and believe me and understand that I am he. Before me no god was formed, nor shall there be any after me. I, I am the LORD, and besides me there is no savior. I declared and saved and proclaimed, when there was no strange god among you; and you are my witnesses, says the LORD. I am God, and also henceforth I am He; there is no one who can deliver from my hand; I work and who can hinder it?

A Reading (Lesson) from the First Letter of Peter [2:2–10]

Like newborn infants, long for the pure, spiritual milk, so
that by it you may grow into salvation—if indeed you
have tasted that the Lord is good. Come to him, a living
stone, though rejected by mortals yet chosen and precious
in God's sight, and like living stones, let yourselves be
built into a spiritual house, to be a holy priesthood, to
offer spiritual sacrifices acceptable to God through Jesus
Christ. For it stands in scripture: "See, I am laying in Zion
a stone, a cornerstone chosen and precious; and whoever
believes in him will not be put to shame." To you then
who believe, he is precious; but for those who do not
believe, "The stone that the builders rejected has become
the very head of the corner," and "A stone that makes
them stumble, and a rock that makes them fall." They
stumble because they disobey the word, as they were
destined to do. But you are a chosen race, a royal
priesthood, a holy nation, God's own people, in order that
you may proclaim the mighty acts of him who called you
out of darkness into his marvelous light. Once you were
not a people, but now you are God's people; once you had
not received mercy, but now you have received mercy.

*A Reading (Lesson) from the Gospel according to
John* [14:1–7]

Jesus said to Peter and the disciples, "Do not let your
hearts be troubled. Believe in God, believe also in me. In
my Father's house there are many dwelling places. If it
were not so, would I have told you that I go to prepare a
place for you? And if I go and prepare a place for you, I
will come again and will take you to myself, so that where
I am, there you may be also. And you know the way to
the place where I am going." Thomas said to him, "Lord,

we do not know where you are going. How can we know the way?" Jesus said to him, "I am the way, and the truth, and the life. No one comes to the Father except through me. If you know me, you will know my Father also. From now on you do know him and have seen him."

Monday

Psalm 1 [page 585], *Psalm 2* [page 586], *Psalm 3* [page 587] ❖ *Psalm 4* [page 587], *Psalm 7* [page 590]

A Reading (Lesson) from the Book of Daniel [1:1–21]

In the third year of the reign of King Jehoiakim of Judah, King Nebuchadnezzar of Babylon came to Jerusalem and besieged it. The Lord let King Jehoiakim of Judah fall into his power, as well as some of the vessels of the house of God. These he brought to the land of Shinar, and placed the vessels in the treasury of his gods. Then the king commanded his palace master Ashpenaz to bring some of the Israelites of the royal family and of the nobility, young men without physical defect and handsome, versed in every branch of wisdom, endowed with knowledge and insight, and competent to serve in the king's palace; they were to be taught the literature and language of the Chaldeans. The king assigned them a daily portion of the royal rations of food and wine. They were to be educated for three years, so that at the end of that time they could be stationed in the king's court. Among them were Daniel, Hananiah, Mishael, and Azariah, from the tribe of Judah. The palace master gave them other names: Daniel he called Belteshazzar, Hananiah he called Shadrach, Mishael he called Meshach, and Azariah he called Abednego. But Daniel resolved that he would not defile himself with the royal rations of food and wine; so he asked the palace master to allow him not to defile himself. Now God allowed Daniel to receive favor and compassion from the palace master. The palace master said to Daniel, "I am afraid of my lord the king; he has appointed your food and your drink. If he should see you in poorer condition than the other young men of your own age, you would endanger my head with the king." Then Daniel asked the guard whom the palace master had appointed over Daniel, Hananiah, Mishael, and Azariah: "Please test your servants for ten days. Let us be given vegetables to eat and water to drink. You can then compare our appearance with the appearance of the young men who eat the royal rations, and deal with your servants according to what you observe." So he agreed to this proposal and tested them for ten days. At the end of ten days it was observed that they appeared better and fatter than all the young men who had been eating the royal rations. So the guard continued to withdraw their royal rations and the wine they were to drink, and gave them vegetables. To these four young men God gave knowledge and skill in every aspect of literature and wisdom. Daniel also had insight into all visions and dreams. At the end of the time that the king had set for them to be brought in, the palace master brought them into the presence of Nebuchadnezzar, and the king spoke with them. And among them all, no one was found to compare with Daniel, Hananiah, Mishael, and Azariah; therefore they were stationed in the king's court. In every matter of wisdom and understanding concerning which the king inquired of them, he found them ten times better than all the magicians and enchanters in his whole kingdom. And Daniel continued there until the first year of King Cyrus.

A Reading (Lesson) from the First Letter of John [1:1–10]

We declare to you what was from the beginning, what we have heard, what we have seen with our eyes, what we have looked at and touched with our hands, concerning the word of life—this life was revealed, and we have seen it and testify to it, and declare to you the eternal life that was with the Father and was revealed to us—we declare to you what we have seen and heard so that you also may have fellowship with us; and truly our fellowship is with the Father and with his Son Jesus Christ. We are writing these things so that our joy may be complete. This is the message we have heard from him and proclaim to you, that God is light and in him there is no darkness at all. If we say that we have fellowship with him while we are walking in darkness, we lie and do not do what is true; but if we walk in the light as he himself is in the light, we have fellowship with one another, and the blood of Jesus his Son cleanses us from all sin. If we say that we have no sin, we deceive ourselves, and the truth is not in us. If we confess our sins, he who is faithful and just will forgive us our sins and cleanse us from all unrighteousness. If we say that we have not sinned, we make him a liar, and his word is not in us.

A Reading (Lesson) from the Gospel according to John [17:1–11]

After Jesus had spoken these words, he looked up to heaven and said, "Father, the hour has come; glorify your Son so that the Son may glorify you, since you have given him authority over all people, to give eternal life to all whom you have given him. And this is eternal life, that they may know you, the only true God, and Jesus Christ whom you have sent. I glorified you on earth by finishing the work that you gave me to do. So now, Father, glorify me in your own presence with the glory that I had in your presence before the world existed. I have made your name known to those whom you gave me from the world. They were yours, and you gave them to me, and they have kept your word. Now they know that everything you have given me is from you; for the words that you gave to me I have given to them, and they have received them and know in truth that I came from you; and they have believed that you sent me. I am asking on their behalf; I am not asking on behalf of the world, but on behalf of those whom you gave me, because they are yours. All mine are yours, and yours are mine; and I have been glorified in them. And now I am no longer in the world, but they are in the world, and I am coming to you. Holy Father, protect them in your name that you have given me, so that they may be one, as we are one."

Tuesday

Psalm 5 [page 588], *Psalm 6* [page 589] ❖
Psalm 10 [page 594], *Psalm 11* [page 596]

A Reading (Lesson) from the Book of Daniel [2:1–16]

In the second year of Nebuchadnezzar's reign, Nebuchadnezzar dreamed such dreams that his spirit was troubled and his sleep left him. So the king commanded that the magicians, the enchanters, the sorcerers, and the Chaldeans be summoned to tell the king his dreams. When they came in and stood before the king, he said to them, "I have had such a dream that my spirit is troubled by the desire to understand it." The Chaldeans said to the king (in Aramaic), "O king, live forever! Tell your servants the dream, and we will reveal the interpretation." The king answered the Chaldeans, "This is a public decree: if you do not tell me both the dream and its interpretation, you shall be torn limb from limb, and your houses shall be laid in ruins. But if you do tell me the dream and its interpretation, you shall receive from me gifts and rewards and great honor. Therefore tell me the dream and its interpretation." They answered a second time, "Let the king first tell his servants the dream, then we can give its interpretation." The king answered, "I know with certainty that you are trying to gain time, because you see I have firmly decreed: if you do not tell me the dream, there is but one verdict for you. You have agreed to speak lying and misleading words to me until things take a turn. Therefore, tell me the dream, and I shall know that you can give me its interpretation." The Chaldeans answered the king, "There is no one on earth who can reveal what the king demands! In fact no king, however great and powerful, has ever asked such a thing of any magician or enchanter or Chaldean. The thing that the king is asking is too difficult, and no one can reveal it to the king except the gods, whose dwelling is not with mortals." Because of this the king flew into a violent rage and commanded that all the wise men of Babylon be destroyed. The decree was issued, and the wise men were about to be executed; and they looked for Daniel and his companions, to execute them. Then Daniel responded with prudence and discretion to Arioch, the king's chief executioner, who had gone out to execute the wise men of Babylon; he asked Arioch, the royal official, "Why is the decree of the king so urgent?" Arioch then explained the matter to Daniel. So Daniel went in and requested that the king give him time and he would tell the king the interpretation.

A Reading (Lesson) from the First Letter of John [2:1–11]

My little children, I am writing these things to you so that
you may not sin. But if anyone does sin, we have an
advocate with the Father, Jesus Christ the righteous; and
he is the atoning sacrifice for our sins, and not for ours
only but also for the sins of the whole world. Now by this
we may be sure that we know him, if we obey his
commandments. Whoever says, "I have come to know
him," but does not obey his commandments, is a liar, and
in such a person the truth does not exist; but whoever
obeys his word, truly in this person the love of God has
reached perfection. By this we may be sure that we are in
him: whoever says, "I abide in him," ought to walk just as
he walked. Beloved, I am writing you no new
commandment, but an old commandment that you have
had from the beginning; the old commandment is the
word that you have heard. Yet I am writing you a new
commandment that is true in him and in you, because the
darkness is passing away and the true light is already
shining. Whoever says, "I am in the light," while hating a
brother or sister, is still in the darkness. Whoever loves a
brother or sister lives in the light, and in such a person
there is no cause for stumbling. But whoever hates another
believer is in the darkness, walks in the darkness, and does
not know the way to go, because the darkness has brought
on blindness.

*A Reading (Lesson) from the Gospel according to
John* [17:12–19]

Jesus looked up to heaven and said, "While I was with
them, I protected them in your name that you have given
me. I guarded them, and not one of them was lost except
the one destined to be lost, so that the scripture might be

fulfilled. But now I am coming to you, and I speak these things in the world so that they may have my joy made complete in themselves. I have given them your word, and the world has hated them because they do not belong to the world, just as I do not belong to the world. I am not asking you to take them out of the world, but I ask you to protect them from the evil one. They do not belong to the world, just as I do not belong to the world. Sanctify them in the truth; your word is truth. As you have sent me into the world, so I have sent them into the world. And for their sakes I sanctify myself, so that they also may be sanctified in truth."

Wednesday

Psalm 119:1–24 [page 763] ❖ *Psalm 12* [page 597], *Psalm 13* [page 597], *Psalm 14* [page 598]

A Reading (Lesson) from the Book of Daniel [2:17–30]

Daniel went to his home and informed his companions, Hananiah, Mishael, and Azariah, and told them to seek mercy from the God of heaven concerning this mystery, so that Daniel and his companions with the rest of the wise men of Babylon might not perish. Then the mystery was revealed to Daniel in a vision of the night, and Daniel blessed the God of heaven. Daniel said: "Blessed be the name of God from age to age, for wisdom and power are his. He changes times and seasons, deposes kings and sets up kings; he gives wisdom to the wise and knowledge to those who have understanding. He reveals deep and hidden things; he knows what is in the darkness, and light dwells with him. To you, O God of my ancestors, I give thanks and praise, for you have given me wisdom and power, and have now revealed to me what we asked of you, for you have revealed to us what the king ordered." Therefore Daniel went to Arioch, whom the king had appointed to destroy the wise men of Babylon, and said to him, "Do not destroy the wise men of Babylon; bring me in before the king, and I will give the king the interpretation." Then Arioch quickly brought Daniel before the king and said to him: "I have found among the exiles from Judah a man who can tell the king the interpretation." The king said to Daniel, whose name was Belteshazzar, "Are you able to tell me the dream that I have seen and its interpretation?" Daniel answered the king, "No wise men, enchanters, magicians, or diviners can show to the king the mystery that the king is asking, but there is a God in heaven who reveals mysteries, and he has disclosed to King Nebuchadnezzar what will happen at the end of days. Your dream and the visions of your head as you lay in bed were these: To you, O king, as you lay in bed, came thoughts of what would be hereafter, and the revealer of mysteries disclosed to you what is to be. But as for me, this mystery has not been revealed to me because of any wisdom that I have more than any other living being, but in order that the interpretation may be known to the king and that you may understand the thoughts of your mind."

1 John 2:12–17 [page 89 above]

A Reading (Lesson) from the Gospel according to John [17:20–26]

Jesus looked up to heaven and said, "I ask not only on behalf of these, but also on behalf of those who will believe in me through their word, that they may all be one. As you, Father, are in me and I am in you, may they also be in us, so that the world may believe that you have sent me. The glory that you have given me I have given them, so that they may be one, as we are one, I in them and you in me, that they may become completely one, so that the world may know that you have sent me and have loved them even as you have loved me. Father, I desire that those also, whom you have given me, may be with me where I am, to see my glory, which you have given me because you loved me before the foundation of the world. Righteous Father, the world does not know you, but I know you; and these know that you have sent me. I made your name known to them, and I will make it known, so that the love with which you have loved me may be in them, and I in them."

Thursday

Psalm 18:1–20 [page 602] ❖ *Psalm 18:21–50* [page 604]

A Reading (Lesson) from the Book of Daniel [2:31–49]

Daniel answered the king, "You were looking, O king, and lo! there was a great statue. This statue was huge, its brilliance extraordinary; it was standing before you, and its appearance was frightening. The head of that statue was of fine gold, its chest and arms of silver, its middle and thighs of bronze, its legs of iron, its feet partly of iron and partly of clay. As you looked on, a stone was cut out, not by human hands, and it struck the statue on its feet of iron and clay and broke them in pieces. Then the iron, the clay, the bronze, the silver, and the gold, were all broken in pieces and became like the chaff of the summer threshing floors; and the wind carried them away, so that not a trace of them could be found. But the stone that struck the statue became a great mountain and filled the whole earth. This was the dream; now we will tell the king its interpretation. You, O king, the king of kings—to whom the God of heaven has given the kingdom, the power, the might, and the glory, into whose hand he has given human beings, wherever they live, the wild animals of the field, and the birds of the air, and whom he has established as ruler over them all—you are the head of gold. After you shall arise another kingdom inferior to yours, and yet a third kingdom of bronze, which shall rule over the whole earth. And there shall be a fourth kingdom, strong as iron; just as iron crushes and smashes everything, it shall crush and shatter all these. As you saw the feet and toes partly of potter's clay and partly of iron, it shall be a divided kingdom; but some of the strength of iron shall be in it, as you saw the iron mixed with the clay. As the toes of the feet were part iron and part clay, so the kingdom shall be partly strong and partly brittle. As you saw the iron mixed with clay, so will they mix with one another in marriage, but they will not hold together, just as iron does not mix with clay. And in the days of those kings the God of heaven will set up a kingdom that shall never be destroyed, nor shall this kingdom be left to another people. It shall crush all these kingdoms and bring them to an end, and it shall stand forever; just as you saw that a stone was cut from the mountain not by hands, and that it crushed the iron, the bronze, the clay, the silver, and the gold. The great God has informed the king what shall be hereafter. The dream is certain, and its interpretation trustworthy." Then King Nebuchadnezzar fell on his face, worshiped Daniel, and commanded that a grain offering and incense be offered to him. The king said to Daniel, "Truly, your God is God of gods and Lord of kings and a revealer of mysteries, for you have been able to reveal this mystery!" Then the king promoted Daniel, gave him many great gifts, and made him ruler over the whole province of Babylon and chief prefect over all the wise men of Babylon. Daniel made a request of the king, and he appointed Shadrach, Meshach, and Abednego over the affairs of the province of Babylon. But Daniel remained at the king's court.

A Reading (Lesson) from the First Letter of John [2:18–29]

Children, it is the last hour! As you have heard that antichrist is coming, so now many antichrists have come. From this we know that it is the last hour. They went out from us, but they did not belong to us; for if they had belonged to us, they would have remained with us. But by going out they made it plain that none of them belongs to us. But you have been anointed by the Holy One, and all of you have knowledge. I write to you, not because you do not know the truth, but because you know it, and you know that no lie comes from the truth. Who is the liar but the one who denies that Jesus is the Christ? This is the antichrist, the one who denies the Father and the Son. No one who denies the Son has the Father; everyone who confesses the Son has the Father also. Let what you heard from the beginning abide in you. If what you heard from the beginning abides in you, then you will abide in the Son and in the Father. And this is what he has promised us, eternal life. I write these things to you concerning those who would deceive you. As for you, the anointing that you received from him abides in you, and so you do not need anyone to teach you. But as his anointing teaches you about all things, and is true and is not a lie, and just as it has taught you, abide in him. And now, little children, abide in him, so that when he is revealed we may have confidence and not be put to shame before him at his coming. If you know that he is righteous, you may be sure that everyone who does right has been born of him.

A Reading (Lesson) from the Gospel according to Luke [3:1–14]

In the fifteenth year of the reign of Emperor Tiberius, when Pontius Pilate was governor of Judea, and Herod was ruler of Galilee, and his brother Philip ruler of the region of Ituraea and Trachonitis, and Lysanias ruler of Abilene, during the high priesthood of Annas and Caiaphas, the word of God came to John son of Zechariah in the wilderness. He went into all the region around the Jordan, proclaiming a baptism of repentance for the forgiveness of sins, as it is written in the book of the words of the prophet Isaiah, "The voice of one crying out in the wilderness: 'Prepare the way of the Lord, make his paths straight. Every valley shall be filled, and every mountain and hill shall be made low, and the crooked shall be made straight, and the rough ways made smooth; and all flesh shall see the salvation of God.' " John said to the crowds that came out to be baptized by him, "You brood of vipers! Who warned you to flee from the wrath to come? Bear fruits worthy of repentance. Do not begin to say to yourselves, 'We have Abraham as our ancestor'; for I tell you, God is able from these stones to raise up children to Abraham. Even now the ax is lying at the root of the trees; every tree therefore that does not bear good fruit is cut down and thrown into the fire." And the crowds asked him, "What then should we do?" In reply he said to them, "Whoever has two coats must share with anyone who has none; and whoever has food must do likewise." Even tax collectors came to be baptized, and they asked him, "Teacher, what should we do?" He said to them, "Collect no more than the amount prescribed for you." Soldiers also asked him, "And we, what should we do?" He said to them, "Do not extort money from anyone by threats or false accusation, and be satisfied with your wages."

Friday

Psalm 16 [page 599], *Psalm 17* [page 600] ❖
Psalm 134 [page 787], *Psalm 135* [page 788]

A Reading (Lesson) from the Book of Daniel [3:1–18]

King Nebuchadnezzar made a golden statue whose height was sixty cubits and whose width was six cubits; he set it up on the plain of Dura in the province of Babylon. Then King Nebuchadnezzar sent for the satraps, the prefects, and the governors, the counselors, the treasurers, the justices, the magistrates, and all the officials of the provinces to assemble and come to the dedication of the statue that King Nebuchadnezzar had set up. So the satraps, the prefects, and the governors, the counselors, the treasurers, the justices, the magistrates, and all the officials of the provinces, assembled for the dedication of the statue that King Nebuchadnezzar had set up. When they were standing before the statue that Nebuchadnezzar had set up, the herald proclaimed aloud, "You are commanded, O peoples, nations, and languages, that when you hear the sound of the horn, pipe, lyre, trigon, harp, drum, and entire musical ensemble, you are to fall down and worship the golden statue that King Nebuchadnezzar has set up. Whoever does not fall down and worship shall immediately be thrown into a furnace of blazing fire." Therefore, as soon as all the peoples heard the sound of the horn, pipe, lyre, trigon, harp, drum, and entire musical ensemble, all the peoples, nations, and languages fell down and worshiped the golden statue that King Nebuchadnezzar had set up. Accordingly, at this time certain Chaldeans came forward and denounced the Jews. They said to King Nebuchadnezzar, "O king, live forever! You, O king, have made a decree, that everyone who hears the sound of the horn, pipe, lyre, trigon, harp, drum, and entire musical ensemble, shall fall down and worship the golden statue, and whoever does not fall down and worship shall be thrown into a furnace of blazing fire. There are certain Jews whom you have appointed over the affairs of the province of Babylon: Shadrach, Meshach, and Abednego. These pay no heed to you, O King. They do not serve your gods and they do not worship the golden statue that you have set up." Then Nebuchadnezzar in furious rage commanded that Shadrach, Meshach, and Abednego be brought in; so they brought those men before the king. Nebuchadnezzar said to them, "Is it true, O Shadrach, Meshach, and Abednego, that you do not serve my gods and you do not worship the golden statue that I have set up? Now if you are ready when you hear the sound of the horn, pipe, lyre, trigon, harp, drum, and entire musical ensemble to fall down and worship the statue that I have made, well and good. But if you do not worship, you shall immediately be thrown into a furnace of blazing fire, and who is the god that will deliver you out of my hands?" Shadrach, Meshach, and Abednego answered the king, "O Nebuchadnezzar, we have no need to present a defense to you in this matter. If our God whom we serve is able to deliver us from the furnace of blazing fire and out of your hand, O king, let him deliver us. But if not, be it known to you, O king, that we will not serve your gods and we will not worship the golden statue that you have set up."

A Reading (Lesson) from the First Letter of John [3:1–10]

See what love the Father has given us, that we should be
called children of God; and that is what we are. The
reason the world does not know us is that it did not know
him. Beloved, we are God's children now; what we will be
has not yet been revealed. What we do know is this: when
he is revealed, we will be like him, for we will see him as
he is. And all who have this hope in him purify
themselves, just as he is pure. Everyone who commits sin
is guilty of lawlessness; sin is lawlessness. You know that
he was revealed to take away sins, and in him there is no
sin. No one who abides in him sins; no one who sins has
either seen him or known him. Little children, let no one
deceive you. Everyone who does what is right is righteous,
just as he is righteous. Everyone who commits sin is a
child of the devil; for the devil has been sinning from the
beginning. The Son of God was revealed for this purpose,
to destroy the works of the devil. Those who have been
born of God do not sin, because God's seed abides in
them; they cannot sin, because they have been born of
God. The children of God and the children of the devil are
revealed in this way: all who do not do what is right are
not from God, nor are those who do not love their
brothers and sisters.

*A Reading (Lesson) from the Gospel according to
Luke* [3:15–22]

As the people were filled with expectation, and all were
questioning in their hearts concerning John, whether he
might be the Messiah, John answered all of them by
saying, "I baptize you with water; but one who is more
powerful than I is coming; I am not worthy to untie the
thong of his sandals. He will baptize you with the Holy

Spirit and fire. His winnowing fork is in his hand, to clear
his threshing floor and to gather the wheat into his
granary; but the chaff he will burn with unquenchable
fire." So, with many other exhortations, he proclaimed the
good news to the people. But Herod the ruler, who had
been rebuked by him because of Herodias, his brother's
wife, and because of all the evil things that Herod had
done, added to them all by shutting up John in prison.
Now when all the people were baptized, and when Jesus
also had been baptized and was praying, the heaven was
opened, and the Holy Spirit descended upon him in bodily
form like a dove. And a voice came from heaven, "You
are my Son, the Beloved; with you I am well pleased."

Saturday

Psalm 20 [page 608], *Psalm 21:1–7(8–14)* [page 608] ❖
Psalm 110:1–5(6–7) [page 753], *Psalm 116* [page 759],
Psalm 117 [page 760]

A Reading (Lesson) from the Book of Daniel [3:19–30]

Then Nebuchadnezzar was so filled with rage against
Shadrach, Meshach, and Abednego that his face was
distorted. He ordered the furnace heated up seven times
more than was customary, and ordered some of the
strongest guards in his army to bind Shadrach, Meshach,
and Abednego and to throw them into the furnace of
blazing fire. So the men were bound, still wearing their
tunics, their trousers, their hats, and their other garments,
and they were thrown into the furnace of blazing fire.
Because the king's command was urgent and the furnace
was so overheated, the raging flames killed the men who
lifted Shadrach, Meshach, and Abednego. But the three

men, Shadrach, Meshach, and Abednego, fell down, bound, into the furnace of blazing fire. Then King Nebuchadnezzar was astonished and rose up quickly. He said to his counselors, "Was it not three men that we threw bound into the fire?" They answered the king, "True, O king." He replied, "But I see four men unbound, walking in the middle of the fire, and they are not hurt; and the fourth has the appearance of a god." Nebuchadnezzar then approached the door of the furnace of blazing fire and said, "Shadrach, Meshach, and Abednego, servants of the Most High God, come out! Come here!" So Shadrach, Meshach, and Abednego came out from the fire. And the satraps, the prefects, the governors, and the king's counselors gathered together and saw that the fire had not had any power over the bodies of those men; the hair of their heads was not singed, their tunics were not harmed, and not even the smell of fire came from them. Nebuchadnezzar said, "Blessed be the God of Shadrach, Meshach, and Abednego, who has sent his angel and delivered his servants who trusted in him. They disobeyed the king's command and yielded up their bodies rather than serve and worship any god except their own God. Therefore I make a decree: Any people, nation, or language that utters blasphemy against the God of Shadrach, Meshach, and Abednego shall be torn limb from limb, and their houses laid in ruins; for there is no other god who is able to deliver in this way." Then the king promoted Shadrach, Meshach, and Abednego in the province of Babylon.

A Reading (Lesson) from the First Letter of John [3:11–18]

This is the message you have heard from the beginning, that we should love one another. We must not be like Cain who was from the evil one and murdered his brother. And why did he murder him? Because his own deeds were evil and his brother's righteous. Do not be astonished, brothers and sisters, that the world hates you. We know that we have passed from death to life because we love one another. Whoever does not love abides in death. All who hate a brother or sister are murderers, and you know that murderers do not have eternal life abiding in them. We know love by this, that he laid down his life for us—and we ought to lay down our lives for one another. How does God's love abide in anyone who has the world's goods and sees a brother or sister in need and yet refuses help? Little children, let us love, not in word or speech, but in truth and action.

A Reading (Lesson) from the Gospel according to Luke [4:1–13]

Jesus, full of the Holy Spirit, returned from the Jordan and was led by the Spirit in the wilderness, where for forty days he was tempted by the devil. He ate nothing at all during those days, and when they were over, he was famished. The devil said to him, "If you are the Son of God, command this stone to become a loaf of bread." Jesus answered him, "It is written, 'One does not live by bread alone.' " Then the devil led him up and showed him in an instant all the kingdoms of the world. And the devil said to him, "To you I will give their glory and all this authority; for it has been given over to me, and I give it to anyone I please. If you, then, will worship me, it will all be yours." Jesus answered him, "It is written, 'Worship the Lord your God, and serve only him.' " Then the devil took him to Jerusalem, and placed him on the pinnacle of the temple, saying to him, "If you are the Son of God, throw yourself down from here, for it is written, 'He will command his angels concerning you, to protect you,' and 'On their hands they will bear you up, so that you will not dash your foot against a stone.' " Jesus answered him, "It is said, 'Do not put the Lord your God to the test.' " When the devil had finished every test, he departed from him until an opportune time.

Week of 3 Easter

Sunday

Psalm 148 [page 805]   *Psalm 149* [page 807],
Psalm 150 [page 807]   ❖   *Psalm 114* [page 756],
Psalm 115 [page 757]

A Reading (Lesson) from the Book of Daniel [4:1–18]

King Nebuchadnezzar to all peoples, nations, and languages that live throughout the earth: May you have abundant prosperity! The signs and wonders that the Most High God has worked for me I am pleased to recount. How great are his signs, how mighty his wonders! His kingdom is an everlasting kingdom, and his sovereignty is from generation to generation. I, Nebuchadnezzar, was living at ease in my home and prospering in my palace. I saw a dream that frightened me; my fantasies in bed and the visions of my head terrified me. So I made a decree that all the wise men of Babylon should be brought before me, in order that they might tell me the interpretation of the dream. Then the magicians, the enchanters, the Chaldeans, and the diviners came in, and I told them the dream, but they could not tell me its interpretation. At last Daniel came in before me—he who was named Belteshazzar after the name of my god, and who is endowed with a spirit of the holy gods—and I told him the dream: "O Belteshazzar, chief of the magicians, I know that you are endowed with a spirit of the holy gods and that no mystery is too difficult for you. Hear the dream that I saw; tell me its interpretation. Upon my bed this is what I saw; there was a tree at the center of the earth, and its height was great. The tree grew great and strong, its top reached to heaven, and it was visible to the ends of the whole earth. Its foliage was beautiful, its fruit abundant, and it provided food for all. The animals of the field found shade under it, the birds of the air nested in its branches, and from it all living beings were fed. I continued looking, in the visions of my head as I lay in bed, and there was a holy watcher, coming down from heaven. He cried aloud and said: 'Cut down the tree and chop off its branches, strip off its foliage and scatter its fruit. Let the animals flee from beneath it and the birds from its branches. But leave its stump and roots in the ground, with a band of iron and bronze, in the tender grass of the field. Let him be bathed with the dew of heaven, and let his lot be with the animals of the field in the grass of the earth. Let his mind be changed from that of a human, and let the mind of an animal be given to him. And let seven times pass over him. The sentence is rendered by decree of the watchers, the decision is given by order of the holy ones, in order that all who live may know that the Most High is sovereign over the kingdom of mortals; he gives it to whom he will and sets over it the lowliest of human beings.' This is the dream that I, King Nebuchadnezzar, saw. Now you, Belteshazzar, declare the interpretation, since all the wise men of my kingdom are unable to tell me the interpretation. You are able, however, for you are endowed with a spirit of the holy gods."

A Reading (Lesson) from the First Letter of Peter [4:7–11]

The end of all things is near; therefore be serious and discipline yourselves for the sake of your prayers. Above all, maintain constant love for one another, for love covers a multitude of sins. Be hospitable to one another without complaining. Like good stewards of the manifold grace of God, serve one another with whatever gift each of you has received. Whoever speaks must do so as one speaking the very words of God; whoever serves must do so with the strength that God supplies, so that God may be glorified in all things through Jesus Christ. To him belong the glory and the power forever and ever. Amen.

A Reading (Lesson) from the Gospel according to John [21:15–25]

When they had finished breakfast, Jesus said to Simon Peter, "Simon son of John, do you love me more than these?" He said to him, "Yes, Lord; you know that I love you." Jesus said to him, "Feed my lambs." A second time he said to him, "Simon son of John, do you love me?" He said to him, "Yes, Lord; you know that I love you." Jesus said to him, "Tend my sheep." He said to him the third time, "Simon son of John, do you love me?" Peter felt hurt because he said to him the third time, "Do you love me?" And he said to him, "Lord, you know everything; you know that I love you." Jesus said to him, "Feed my sheep. Very truly, I tell you, when you were younger, you used to fasten your own belt and to go wherever you wished. But when you grow old, you will stretch out your hands, and someone else will fasten a belt around you and take you where you do not wish to go." (He said this to indicate the kind of death by which he would glorify God.) After this he said to him, "Follow me." Peter turned and saw the disciple whom Jesus loved following them; he was the one who had reclined next to Jesus at the supper and had said, "Lord, who is it that is going to betray you?" When Peter saw him, he said to Jesus, "Lord, what about him?" Jesus said to him, "If it is my will that he remain until I come, what is that to you? Follow me!" So the rumor spread in the community that this disciple would not die. Yet Jesus did not say to him that he would not die, but, "If it is my will that he remain until I come, what is that to you?" This is the disciple who is testifying to these things and has written them, and we know that his testimony is true. But there are also many other things that Jesus did; if every one of them were written down, I suppose that the world itself could not contain the books that would be written.

Monday

Psalm 25 [page 614] ❖ *Psalm 9* [page 593], *Psalm 15* [page 599]

A Reading (Lesson) from the Book of Daniel [4:19–27]

Then Daniel, who was called Belteshazzar, was severely distressed for a while. His thoughts terrified him. The king said, "Belteshazzar, do not let the dream or the interpretation terrify you." Belteshazzar answered, "My lord, may the dream be for those who hate you, and its interpretation for your enemies! The tree that you saw, which grew great and strong, so that its top reached to heaven and was visible to the end of the whole earth, whose foliage was beautiful and its fruit abundant, and which provided food for all, under which animals of the field lived, and in whose branches the birds of the air had nests—it is you, O king! You have grown great and strong. Your greatness has increased and reaches to heaven, and your sovereignty to the ends of the earth. And whereas the king saw a holy watcher coming down from heaven and saying, 'Cut down the tree and destroy it, but leave its stump and roots in the ground, with a band of iron and bronze, in the grass of the field; and let him be bathed with the dew of heaven, and let his lot be with the animals of the field, until seven times pass over him'—this is the interpretation, O king, and it is a decree of the Most High that has come upon my lord the king: You shall be driven away from human society, and your dwelling shall be with the wild animals. You shall be made to eat grass like oxen, you shall be bathed with the dew of heaven, and seven times shall pass over you, until you have learned that the Most High has sovereignty over the kingdom of mortals, and gives it to whom he will. As it was commanded to leave the stump and roots of the tree, your kingdom shall be re-established for you from the time that you learn that Heaven is sovereign. Therefore, O king, may my counsel be acceptable to you: atone for your sins with righteousness, and your iniquities with mercy to the oppressed, so that your prosperity may be prolonged."

A Reading (Lesson) from the First Letter of John [3:19—4:6]

By this we will know that we are from the truth and will reassure our hearts before him whenever our hearts condemn us; for God is greater than our hearts, and he knows everything. Beloved, if our hearts do not condemn us, we have boldness before God; and we receive from him whatever we ask, because we obey his commandments and do what pleases him. And this is his commandment, that we should believe in the name of his Son Jesus Christ and love one another, just as he has commanded us. All who obey his commandments abide in him, and he abides in them. And by this we know that he abides in us, by the Spirit that he has given us. Beloved, do not believe every spirit, but test the spirits to see whether they are from God; for many false prophets have gone out into the world. By this you know the Spirit of God: every spirit that confesses that Jesus Christ has come in the flesh is from God, and every spirit that does not confess Jesus is not from God. And this is the spirit of the antichrist, of which you have heard that it is coming; and now it is already in the world. Little children, you are from God, and have conquered them; for the one who is in you is greater than the one who is in the world. They are from the world; therefore what they say is from the world, and the world listens to them. We are from God. Whoever knows God listens to us, and whoever is not from God does not listen to us. From this we know the spirit of truth and the spirit of error.

A Reading (Lesson) from the Gospel according to Luke [4:14–30]

Jesus, filled with the power of the Spirit, returned to Galilee, and a report about him spread through all the surrounding country. He began to teach in their synagogues and was praised by everyone. When he came to Nazareth, where he had been brought up, he went to the synagogue on the sabbath day, as was his custom. He stood up to read, and the scroll of the prophet Isaiah was given to him. He unrolled the scroll and found the place where it was written: "The Spirit of the Lord is upon me, because he has anointed me to bring good news to the poor. He has sent me to proclaim release to the captives and recovery of sight to the blind, to let the oppressed go free, to proclaim the year of the Lord's favor." And he rolled up the scroll, gave it back to the attendant, and sat down. The eyes of all in the synagogue were fixed on him. Then he began to say to them, "Today this scripture has been fulfilled in your hearing." All spoke well of him and were amazed at the gracious words that came from his mouth. They said, "Is not this Joseph's son?" He said to them, "Doubtless you will quote to me this proverb, 'Doctor, cure yourself!' And you will say, 'Do here also in your hometown the things that we have heard you did at Capernaum.'" And he said, "Truly I tell you, no prophet is accepted in the prophet's hometown. But the truth is, there were many widows in Israel in the time of Elijah, when the heaven was shut up three years and six months, and there was a severe famine over all the land; yet Elijah was sent to none of them except to a widow at Zarephath in Sidon. There were also many lepers in Israel in the time of the prophet Elisha, and none of them was cleansed except Naaman the Syrian." When they heard this, all in the synagogue were filled with rage. They got up, drove him out of the town, and led him to the brow of the hill on which their town was built, so that they might hurl him off the cliff. But he passed through the midst of them and went on his way.

Tuesday

Psalm 26 [page 616], *Psalm 28* [page 619] ❖
Psalm 36 [page 632], *Psalm 39* [page 638]

A Reading (Lesson) from the Book of Daniel [4:28–37]

All this came upon King Nebuchadnezzar. At the end of twelve months he was walking on the roof of the royal palace of Babylon, and the king said, "Is this not magnificent Babylon, which I have built as a royal capital by my mighty power and for my glorious majesty?" While the words were still in the king's mouth, a voice came from heaven: "O King Nebuchadnezzar, to you it is declared: The kingdom has departed from you! You shall be driven away from human society, and your dwelling shall be with the animals of the field. You shall be made to eat grass like oxen, and seven times shall pass over you, until you have learned that the Most High has sovereignty over the kingdom of mortals and gives it to whom he will." Immediately the sentence was fulfilled against Nebuchadnezzar. He was driven away from human society, ate grass like oxen, and his body was bathed with the dew of heaven, until his hair grew as long as eagles' feathers and his nails became like birds' claws. When that period was over, I, Nebuchadnezzar, lifted my eyes to heaven, and my reason returned to me. I blessed the Most High, and praised and honored the one who lives forever. For his sovereignty is an everlasting sovereignty, and his kingdom endures from generation to generation. All the inhabitants of the earth are accounted as nothing, and he does what he wills with the host of heaven and the inhabitants of the earth. There is no one who can stay his hand or say to him, "What are you doing?" At that time my reason returned to me; and my majesty and splendor were restored to me for the glory of my kingdom. My counselors and my lords sought me out, I was re-established over my kingdom, and still more greatness was added to me. Now I, Nebuchadnezzar, praise and extol and honor the King of heaven, for all his works are truth, and his ways are justice, and he is able to bring low those who walk in pride.

A Reading (Lesson) from the First Letter of John [4:7–21]

Beloved, let us love one another, because love is from God; everyone who loves is born of God and knows God. Whoever does not love does not know God, for God is love. God's love was revealed among us in this way: God sent his only Son into the world so that we might live through him. In this is love, not that we loved God but that he loved us and sent his Son to be the atoning sacrifice for our sins. Beloved, since God loved us so much, we also ought to love one another. No one has ever seen God; if we love one another, God lives in us, and his love is perfected in us. By this we know that we abide in him and he in us, because he has given us of his Spirit. And we have seen and do testify that the Father has sent his Son as the Savior of the world. God abides in those who confess that Jesus is the Son of God, and they abide in God. So we have known and believe the love that God has for us. God is love, and those who abide in love abide in God, and God abides in them. Love has been perfected among us in this: that we may have boldness on the day of judgment, because as he is, so are we in this world. There is no fear in love, but perfect love casts out fear; for fear has to do with punishment, and whoever fears has not reached perfection in love. We love because he first loved us. Those who say, "I love God," and hate their brothers or sisters, are liars; for those who do not love a brother or sister whom they have seen, cannot love God whom they have not seen. The commandment we have from him is this: those who love God must love their brothers and sisters also.

A Reading (Lesson) from the Gospel according to Luke [4:31–37]

Jesus went down to Capernaum, a city in Galilee, and was teaching them on the sabbath. They were astounded at his teaching, because he spoke with authority. In the synagogue there was a man who had the spirit of an unclean demon, and he cried out with a loud voice, "Let us alone! What have you to do with us, Jesus of Nazareth? Have you come to destroy us? I know who you are, the Holy One of God." But Jesus rebuked him, saying, "Be silent, and come out of him!" When the demon had thrown him down before them, he came out of him without having done him any harm. They were all amazed and kept saying to one another, "What kind of utterance is this? For with authority and power he commands the unclean spirits, and out they come!" And a report about him began to reach every place in the region.

Wednesday

Psalm 38 [page 636] ❖ *Psalm 119:25–48* [page 765]

A Reading (Lesson) from the Book of Daniel [5:1–12]

King Belshazzar made a great festival for a thousand of his lords, and he was drinking wine in the presence of the thousand. Under the influence of the wine, Belshazzar commanded that they bring in the vessels of gold and silver that his father Nebuchadnezzar had taken out of the temple in Jerusalem, so that the king and his lords, his wives, and his concubines might drink from them. So they brought in the vessels of gold and silver that had been taken out of the temple, the house of God in Jerusalem, and the king and his lords, his wives, and his concubines drank from them. They drank the wine and praised the gods of gold and silver, bronze, iron, wood, and stone. Immediately the fingers of a human hand appeared and began writing on the plaster of the wall of the royal palace, next to the lampstand. The king was watching the hand as it wrote. Then the king's face turned pale, and his thoughts terrified him. His limbs gave way, and his knees knocked together. The king cried aloud to bring in the enchanters, the Chaldeans, and the diviners; and the king said to the wise men of Babylon, "Whoever can read this writing and tell me its interpretation shall be clothed in purple, have a chain of gold around his neck, and rank third in the kingdom." Then all the king's wise men came in, but they could not read the writing or tell the king the interpretation. Then King Belshazzar became greatly terrified and his face turned pale, and his lords were perplexed. The queen, when she heard the discussion of the king and his lords, came into the banqueting hall. The queen said, "O king, live forever! Do not let your thoughts terrify you or your face grow pale. There is a man in your kingdom who is endowed with a spirit of the holy gods. In the days of your father he was found to have enlightenment, understanding, and wisdom like the wisdom of the gods. Your father, King Nebuchadnezzar, made him chief of the magicians, enchanters, Chaldeans, and diviners, because an excellent spirit, knowledge, and understanding to interpret dreams, explain riddles, and solve problems were found in this Daniel, whom the king named Belteshazzar. Now let Daniel be called, and he will give the interpretation."

A Reading (Lesson) from the First Letter of John [5:1–12]

Everyone who believes that Jesus is the Christ has been born of God, and everyone who loves the parent loves the child. By this we know that we love the children of God, when we love God and obey his commandments. For the love of God is this, that we obey his commandments. And his commandments are not burdensome, for whatever is born of God conquers the world. And this is the victory that conquers the world, our faith. Who is it that conquers the world but the one who believes that Jesus is the Son of God? This is the one who came by water and blood, Jesus Christ, not with the water only but with the water and the blood. And the Spirit is the one that testifies, for the Spirit is the truth. There are three that testify: the Spirit and the water and the blood, and these three agree. If we receive human testimony, the testimony of God is greater; for this is the testimony of God that he has testified to his Son. Those who believe in the Son of God have the testimony in their hearts. Those who do not believe in God have made him a liar by not believing in the testimony that God has given concerning his Son. And this is the testimony: God gave us eternal life, and this life is in his Son. Whoever has the Son has life; whoever does not have the Son of God does not have life.

A Reading (Lesson) from the Gospel according to Luke [4:38–44]

After leaving the synagogue Jesus entered Simon's house. Now Simon's mother-in-law was suffering from a high fever, and they asked him about her. Then he stood over her and rebuked the fever, and it left her. Immediately she got up and began to serve them. As the sun was setting, all those who had any who were sick with various kinds of diseases brought them to him; and he laid his hands on each of them and cured them. Demons also came out of many, shouting, "You are the Son of God!" But he rebuked them and would not allow them to speak, because they knew that he was the Messiah. At daybreak he departed and went into a deserted place. And the crowds were looking for him; and when they reached him, they wanted to prevent him from leaving them. But he said to them, "I must proclaim the good news of the kingdom of God to the other cities also; for I was sent for this purpose." So he continued proclaiming the message in the synagogues of Judea.

Thursday

Psalm 37:1–18 [page 633] ❖ *Psalm 37:19–42* [page 634]

A Reading (Lesson) from the Book of Daniel [5:13–30]

Then Daniel was brought in before the king. The king said to Daniel, "So you are Daniel, one of the exiles of Judah, whom my father the king brought from Judah? I have heard of you that a spirit of the gods is in you, and that enlightenment, understanding, and excellent wisdom are found in you. Now the wise men, the enchanters, have been brought in before me to read this writing and tell me its interpretation, but they were not able to give the interpretation of the matter. But I have heard that you can give interpretations and solve problems. Now if you are able to read the writing and tell me its interpretation, you shall be clothed in purple, have a chain of gold around your neck, and rank third in the kingdom." Then Daniel answered in the presence of the king, "Let your gifts be for yourself, or give your rewards to someone else! Nevertheless I will read

the writing to the king and let him know the interpretation.
O king, the Most High God gave your father
Nebuchadnezzar kingship, greatness, glory, and majesty.
And because of the greatness that he gave him, all peoples,
nations, and languages trembled and feared before him. He
killed those he wanted to kill, kept alive those he wanted to
keep alive, honored those he wanted to honor, and degraded
those he wanted to degrade. But when his heart was lifted
up and his spirit was hardened so that he acted proudly, he
was deposed from his kingly throne, and his glory was
stripped from him. He was driven from human society, and
his mind was made like that of an animal. His dwelling was
with the wild asses, he was fed grass like oxen, and his body
was bathed with the dew of heaven, until he learned that the
Most High God has sovereignty over the kingdom of
mortals, and sets over it whomever he will. And you,
Belshazzar his son, have not humbled your heart, even
though you knew all this! You have exalted yourself against
the Lord of heaven! The vessels of his temple have been
brought in before you, and you and your lords, your wives
and your concubines have been drinking wine from them.
You have praised the gods of silver and gold, of bronze,
iron, wood, and stone, which do not see or hear or know;
but the God in whose power is your very breath, and to
whom belong all your ways, you have not honored. "So
from his presence the hand was sent and this writing was
inscribed. And this is the writing that was inscribed: MENE,
MENE, TEKEL, and PARSIN. This is the interpretation of the
matter: MENE, God has numbered the days of your kingdom
and brought it to an end; TEKEL, you have been weighed on
the scales and found wanting; PERES, your kingdom is
divided and given to the Medes and Persians." Then
Belshazzar gave the command, and Daniel was clothed in
purple, a chain of gold was put around his neck, and a

proclamation was made concerning him that he should rank third in the kingdom. That very night Belshazzar, the Chaldean king, was killed. And Darius the Mede received the kingdom, being about sixty-two years old.

A Reading (Lesson) from the First Letter of John [5:13–20(21)]

I write these things to you who believe in the name of the Son of God, so that you may know that you have eternal life. And this is the boldness we have in him, that if we ask anything according to his will, he hears us. And if we know that he hears us in whatever we ask, we know that we have obtained the requests made of him. If you see your brother or sister committing what is not a mortal sin, you will ask, and God will give life to such a one—to those whose sin is not mortal. There is sin that is mortal; I do not say that you should pray about that. All wrongdoing is sin, but there is sin that is not mortal. We know that those who are born of God do not sin, but the one who was born of God protects them, and the evil one does not touch them. We know that we are God's children, and that the whole world lies under the power of the evil one. And we know that the Son of God has come and has given us understanding so that we may know him who is true; and we are in him who is true, in his Son Jesus Christ. He is the true God and eternal life.

| Little children, keep yourselves from idols.

A Reading (Lesson) from the Gospel according to Luke [5:1–11]

Once while Jesus was standing beside the lake of Gennesaret, and the crowd was pressing in on him to hear the word of God, he saw two boats there at the shore of the lake; the fishermen had gone out of them and were washing their nets. He got into one of the boats, the one belonging to Simon, and asked him to put out a little way from the shore. Then he sat down and taught the crowds from the boat. When he had finished speaking, he said to Simon, "Put out into the deep water and let down your nets for a catch." Simon answered, "Master, we have worked all night long but have caught nothing. Yet if you say so, I will let down the nets." When they had done this, they caught so many fish that their nets were beginning to break. So they signaled their partners in the other boat to come and help them. And they came and filled both boats, so that they began to sink. But when Simon Peter saw it, he fell down at Jesus' knees, saying, "Go away from me, Lord, for I am a sinful man!" For he and all who were with him were amazed at the catch of fish that they had taken; and so also were James and John, sons of Zebedee, who were partners with Simon. Then Jesus said to Simon, "Do not be afraid; from now on you will be catching people." When they had brought their boats to shore, they left everything and followed him.

Friday

Psalm 105:1–22 [page 738]   ❖   *Psalm 105:23–45* [page 739]

A Reading (Lesson) from the Book of Daniel [6:1–15]

It pleased Darius to set over the kingdom one hundred twenty satraps, stationed throughout the whole kingdom, and over them three presidents, including Daniel; to these the satraps gave account, so that the king might suffer no loss. Soon Daniel distinguished himself above all the other presidents and satraps because an excellent spirit was in him, and the king planned to appoint him over the whole kingdom. So the presidents and the satraps tried to find grounds for complaint against Daniel in connection with the kingdom. But they could find no grounds for complaint or any corruption, because he was faithful, and no negligence or corruption could be found in him. The men said, "We shall not find any ground for complaint against this Daniel unless we find it in connection with the law of his God." So the presidents and satraps conspired and came to the king and said to him, "O King Darius, live forever! All the presidents of the kingdom, the prefects and the satraps, the counselors and the governors are agreed that the king should establish an ordinance and enforce an interdict, that whoever prays to anyone, divine or human, for thirty days, except to you, O king, shall be thrown into a den of lions. Now, O king, establish the interdict and sign the document, so that it cannot be changed, according to the law of the Medes and the Persians, which cannot be revoked." Therefore King Darius signed the document and interdict. Although Daniel knew that the document had been signed, he continued to go to his house, which had windows in its upper room open toward Jerusalem, and to get down on his knees three times a day to pray to his God and praise him, just as he had done previously. The conspirators came and found Daniel praying and seeking mercy before his God. Then they approached the king and said concerning the interdict, "O king! Did you not sign an interdict, that anyone who prays to anyone, divine or human, within thirty days except to you, O king, shall be thrown into a den of lions?" The king answered, "The thing stands fast, according to the law of the Medes and Persians, which cannot be revoked." Then they responded to the king, "Daniel, one of the exiles from Judah, pays no attention to you, O king, or to the interdict you have signed, but he is saying his prayers three times a day." When the king heard the charge, he was very much distressed. He was determined to save Daniel, and until the sun went down he made every effort to rescue him. Then the conspirators came to the king and said to him, "Know, O king, that it is a law of the Medes and Persians that no interdict or ordinance that the king establishes can be changed."

A Reading (Lesson) from the Second Letter of John [1–13]

The elder to the elect lady and her children, whom I love in the truth, and not only I but also all who know the truth, because of the truth that abides in us and will be with us forever: Grace, mercy, and peace will be with us from God the Father and from Jesus Christ, the Father's Son, in truth and love. I was overjoyed to find some of your children walking in the truth, just as we have been commanded by the Father. But now, dear lady, I ask you, not as though I were writing you a new commandment, but one we have had from the beginning, let us love one another. And this is love, that we walk according to his commandments; this is the commandment just as you have heard it from the beginning—you must walk in it. Many deceivers have gone out into the world, those who do not confess that Jesus Christ has come in the flesh; any such person is the deceiver and the antichrist! Be on your guard, so that you do not lose what we have worked for, but may receive a full reward. Everyone who does not abide in the teaching of Christ, but goes beyond it, does not have God; whoever abides in the teaching has both the Father and the Son. Do not receive into the house or welcome anyone who comes to you and does not bring this teaching; for to welcome is to participate in the evil deeds of such a person. Although I have much to write to you, I would rather not use paper and ink; instead I hope to come to you and talk with you face to face, so that our joy may be complete. The children of your elect sister send you their greetings.

A Reading (Lesson) from the Gospel according to Luke [5:12–26]

Once, when Jesus was in one of the cities, there was a man covered with leprosy. When he saw Jesus, he bowed with his face to the ground and begged him, "Lord, if you choose, you can make me clean." Then Jesus stretched out his hand, touched him, and said, "I do choose. Be made clean." Immediately the leprosy left him. And he ordered him to tell no one. "Go," he said, "and show yourself to the priest, and, as Moses commanded, make an offering for your cleansing, for a testimony to them." But now more than ever the word about Jesus spread abroad; many crowds would gather to hear him and to be cured of their diseases. But he would withdraw to deserted places and pray. One day, while he was teaching, Pharisees and teachers of the law were sitting near by (they had come from every village of Galilee and Judea and from Jerusalem); and the power of the Lord was with him to heal. Just then some men came, carrying a paralyzed man on a bed. They were trying to bring him in and lay him before Jesus; but finding no way to bring him in because of the crowd, they went up on the roof and let him down with his bed through the tiles into the middle of the crowd in front of Jesus. When he saw their faith, he said, "Friend, your sins are forgiven you." Then the scribes and the Pharisees began to question. "Who is this who is speaking blasphemies? Who can forgive sins but God alone?" When Jesus perceived their questionings, he answered them, "Why do you raise such questions in your hearts? Which is easier, to say, 'Your sins are forgiven you,' or to say, 'Stand up and walk'? But so that you may know that the Son of Man has authority on earth to forgive sins"—he said to the one who was paralyzed—"I say to you, stand up and take your bed and go to your home." Immediately he stood up before them, took what he had been lying on, and went to his home, glorifying God. Amazement seized all of them, and they glorified God and were filled with awe, saying, "We have seen strange things today."

Saturday

Psalm 30 [page 621],   *Psalm 32* [page 624]   ❖
Psalm 42 [page 643],   *Psalm 43* [page 644]

A Reading (Lesson) from the Book of Daniel [6:16–28]

Then the king gave the command, and Daniel was brought and thrown into the den of lions. The king said to Daniel, "May your God, whom you faithfully serve, deliver you!" A stone was brought and laid on the mouth of the den, and the king sealed it with his own signet and with the signet of his lords, so that nothing might be changed concerning Daniel. Then the king went to his palace and spent the night fasting; no food was brought to him, and sleep fled from him. Then, at break of day, the king got up and hurried to the den of lions. When he came near the den where Daniel was, he cried out anxiously to Daniel, "O Daniel, servant of the living God, has your God whom you faithfully serve been able to deliver you from the lions?" Daniel then said to the king, "O king, live forever! My God sent his angel and shut the lions' mouths so that they would not hurt me, because I was found blameless before him; and also before you, O king, I have done no wrong." Then the king was exceedingly glad and commanded that Daniel be taken up out of the den. So Daniel was taken up out of the den, and no kind of harm was found on him, because he had trusted in his God. The king gave a command, and those who had accused Daniel were brought and thrown into the den of lions—they, their children, and their wives. Before they reached the bottom of the den the lions overpowered them and broke all their bones in pieces. Then King Darius wrote to all peoples and nations of every language throughout the whole world: "May you have abundant prosperity! I make a decree, that in all my royal dominion people should tremble and fear before the God of Daniel: For he is the living God, enduring forever. His kingdom shall never be destroyed, and his dominion has no end. He delivers and rescues, he works signs and wonders in heaven and on earth; for he has saved Daniel from the power of the lions." So this Daniel prospered during the reign of Darius and the reign of Cyrus the Persian.

A Reading (Lesson) from the Third Letter of John [1–15]

The elder to the beloved Gaius, whom I love in truth. Beloved, I pray that all may go well with you and that you may be in good health, just as it is well with your soul. I was overjoyed when some of the friends arrived and testified to your faithfulness to the truth, namely how you walk in the truth. I have no greater joy than this, to hear that my children are walking in the truth. Beloved, you do faithfully whatever you do for the friends, even though they are strangers to you; they have testified to your love before the church. You will do well to send them on in a manner worthy of God; for they began their journey for the sake of Christ, accepting no support from non-believers. Therefore we ought to support such people, so that we may become co-workers with the truth. I have written something to the church; but Diotrephes, who likes to put himself first, does not acknowledge our authority. So if I come, I will call attention to what he is doing in spreading false charges against us. And not content with those charges, he refuses to welcome the friends, and even prevents those who want to do so and expels them from the church. Beloved, do not imitate what is evil but imitate what is good. Whoever does good is from God; whoever does evil has not seen God. Everyone has testified favorably about Demetrius, and so has the truth itself. We also testify for him, and you know that our testimony is true. I have much to write to you, but I would rather not write with pen and ink; instead I hope to see you soon, and we will talk together face to face. Peace to you. The friends send you their greetings. Greet the friends there, each by name.

A Reading (Lesson) from the Gospel according to Luke [5:27–39]

After this Jesus went out and saw a tax collector named Levi, sitting at the tax booth; and he said to him, "Follow me." And he got up, left everything, and followed him. Then Levi gave a great banquet for him in his house; and there was a large crowd of tax collectors and others sitting at the table with them. The Pharisees and their scribes were complaining to his disciples, saying, "Why do you eat and drink with tax collectors and sinners?" Jesus answered, "Those who are well have no need of a physician, but those who are sick; I have come to call not the righteous but sinners to repentance." Then they said to him, "John's disciples, like the disciples of the Pharisees, frequently fast and pray, but your disciples eat and drink." Jesus said to them, "You cannot make wedding guests fast while the bridegroom is with them, can you? The days will come when the bridegroom will be taken away from them, and then they will fast in those days." He also told them a parable: "No one tears a piece from a new garment and sews it on an old garment; otherwise the new will be torn, and the piece from the new will not match the old. And no one puts new wine into old wineskins; otherwise the new wine will burst the skins and will be spilled, and the skins will be destroyed. But new wine must be put into fresh wineskins. And no one after drinking old wine desires new wine, but says, 'The old is good.' "

Week of 4 Easter

Sunday

Psalm 63:1–8(9–11) [page 670], *Psalm 98* [page 727] ∵
Psalm 103 [page 733]

A Reading (Lesson) from the Book of Wisdom [1:1–15]

Love righteousness, you rulers of the earth, think of the Lord in goodness and seek him with sincerity of heart; because he is found by those who do not put him to the test, and manifests himself to those who do not distrust him. For perverse thoughts separate people from God, and when his power is tested, it exposes the foolish; because wisdom will

not enter a deceitful soul, or dwell in a body enslaved to sin.
For a holy and disciplined spirit will flee from deceit, and
will leave foolish thoughts behind, and will be ashamed at
the approach of unrighteousness. For wisdom is a kindly
spirit, but will not free blasphemers from the guilt of their
words; because God is witness of their inmost feelings, and
a true observer of their hearts, and a hearer of their tongues.
Because the spirit of the Lord has filled the world, and that
which holds all things together knows what is said,
therefore those who utter unrighteous things will not escape
notice, and justice, when it punishes, will not pass them by.
For inquiry will be made into the counsels of the ungodly,
and a report of their words will come to the Lord, to convict
them of their lawless deeds; because a jealous ear hears all
things, and the sound of grumbling does not go unheard.
Beware then of useless grumbling, and keep your tongue
from slander; because no secret word is without result, and
a lying mouth destroys the soul. Do not invite death by the
error of your life, or bring on destruction by the works of
your hands; because God did not make death, and he does
not delight in the death of the living. For he created all
things so that they might exist; the generative forces of the
world are wholesome, and there is no destructive poison in
them, and the dominion of Hades is not on earth. For
righteousness is immortal.

A Reading (Lesson) from the First Letter of Peter [5:1–11]

Now as an elder myself and a witness of the sufferings of
Christ, as well as one who shares in the glory to be
revealed, I exhort the elders among you to tend the flock
of God that is in your charge, exercising the oversight, not
under compulsion but willingly, as God would have you
do it—not for sordid gain but eagerly. Do not lord it over

those in your charge, but be examples to the flock. And when the chief shepherd appears, you will win the crown of glory that never fades away. In the same way, you who are younger must accept the authority of the elders. And all of you must clothe yourselves with humility in your dealings with one another, for "God opposes the proud, but gives grace to the humble." Humble yourselves therefore under the mighty hand of God, so that he may exalt you in due time. Cast all your anxiety on him, because he cares for you. Discipline yourselves, keep alert. Like a roaring lion your adversary the devil prowls around, looking for someone to devour. Resist him, steadfast in your faith, for you know that your brothers and sisters in all the world are undergoing the same kinds of suffering. And after you have suffered for a little while, the God of all grace, who has called you to his eternal glory in Christ, will himself restore, support, strengthen, and establish you. To him be the power forever and ever. Amen.

A Reading (Lesson) from the Gospel according to Matthew [7:15–29]

Jesus taught his disciples, saying: "Beware of false prophets, who come to you in sheep's clothing but inwardly are ravenous wolves. You will know them by their fruits. Are grapes gathered from thorns, or figs from thistles? In the same way, every good tree bears good fruit, but the bad tree bears bad fruit. A good tree cannot bear bad fruit, nor can a bad tree bear good fruit. Every tree that does not bear good fruit is cut down and thrown into the fire. Thus you will know them by their fruits. Not everyone who says to me, 'Lord, Lord,' will enter the kingdom of heaven, but only the one who does the will of my Father in heaven. On that day many will say to me, 'Lord, Lord, did we not prophesy in your name, and cast out demons in your name, and do many deeds of power in your name?' Then I will declare to them, 'I never knew you; go away from me, you evildoers.' Everyone then who hears these words of mine and acts on them will be like a wise man who built his house on rock. The rain fell, the floods came, and the winds blew and beat on that house, but it did not fall, because it had been founded on rock. And everyone who hears these words of mine and does not act on them will be like a foolish man who built his house on sand. The rain fell, and the floods came, and the winds blew and beat against that house, and it fell—and great was its fall!" Now when Jesus had finished saying these things, the crowds were astounded at his teaching, for he taught them as one having authority, and not as their scribes.

Monday

Psalm 41 [page 641], *Psalm 52* [page 657] ❖
Psalm 44 [page 645]

A Reading (Lesson) from the Book of Wisdom [1:16—2:11, 21–24]

The ungodly by their words and deeds summoned death; considering him a friend, they pined away and made a covenant with him, because they are fit to belong to his company. For they reasoned unsoundly, saying to themselves, "Short and sorrowful is our life, and there is no remedy when a life comes to its end, and no one has been known to return from Hades. For we were born by mere chance, and hereafter we shall be as though we had never been, for the breath in our nostrils is smoke, and reason is a spark kindled by the beating of our hearts; when it is extinguished, the body will turn to ashes, and the spirit will dissolve like empty air. Our name will be forgotten in time, and no one will remember our works; our life will pass away like the traces of a cloud, and be scattered like mist that is chased by the rays of the sun and overcome by its heat. For our allotted time is the passing of a shadow, and there is no return from our death, because it is sealed up and no one turns back. Come, therefore, let us enjoy the good things that exist, and make use of the creation to the full as in youth. Let us take our fill of costly wine and perfumes, and let no flower of spring pass us by. Let us crown ourselves with rosebuds before they wither. Let none of us fail to share in our revelry; everywhere let us leave signs of enjoyment, because this is our portion, and this our lot. Let us oppress the righteous poor man; let us not spare the widow or regard the gray hairs of the aged. But let our might be our law of right, for what is weak proves itself to be useless." Thus they reasoned, but they were led astray, for their wickedness blinded them, and they did not know the secret purposes of God, nor hoped for the wages of holiness, nor discerned the prize for blameless souls; for God created us for incorruption, and made us in the image of his own eternity, but through the devil's envy death entered the world, and those who belong to his company experience it.

A Reading (Lesson) from the Letter of Paul to the Colossians [1:1–14]

Paul, an apostle of Christ Jesus by the will of God, and Timothy our brother, to the saints and faithful brothers and sisters in Christ in Colossae: Grace to you and peace from God our Father. In our prayers for you we always thank God, the Father of our Lord Jesus Christ, for we have heard of your faith in Christ Jesus and of the love that you have for all the saints, because of the hope laid up for you in heaven. You have heard of this hope before in the word of the truth, the gospel that has come to you. Just as it is bearing fruit and growing in the whole world, so it has been bearing fruit among yourselves from the day you heard it and truly comprehended the grace of God. This you learned from Epaphras, our beloved fellow servant. He is a faithful minister of Christ on your behalf, and he has made known to us your love in the Spirit. For this reason, since the day we heard it, we have not ceased praying for you and asking that you may be filled with the knowledge of God's will in all spiritual wisdom and understanding, so that you may lead lives worthy of the Lord, fully pleasing to him, as you bear fruit in every good work and as you grow in the knowledge of God. May you be made strong with all the strength that comes from his glorious power, and may you be prepared to endure everything with patience, while joyfully giving thanks to the Father, who has enabled you to share in the inheritance of the saints in the light. He has rescued us from the power of darkness and transferred us into the kingdom of his beloved Son, in whom we have redemption, the forgiveness of sins.

A Reading (Lesson) from the Gospel according to Luke [6:1-11]

One sabbath while Jesus was going through the grainfields, his disciples plucked some heads of grain, rubbed them in their hands, and ate them. But some of the Pharisees said, "Why are you doing what is not lawful on the sabbath?" Jesus answered, "Have you not read what David did when he and his companions were hungry? He entered the house of God and took and ate the bread of the Presence, which it is not lawful for any but the priests to eat, and gave some to his companions." Then he said to them, "The Son of Man is lord of the sabbath." On another sabbath he entered the synagogue and taught, and there was a man there whose right hand was withered. The scribes and the Pharisees watched him to see whether he would cure on the sabbath, so that they might find an accusation against him. Even though he knew what they were thinking, he said to the man who had the withered hand, "Come and stand here." He got up and stood there. Then Jesus said to them, "I ask you, is it lawful to do good or to do harm on the sabbath, to save life or to destroy it?" After looking around at all of them, he said to him, "Stretch out your hand." He did so, and his hand was restored. But they were filled with fury and discussed with one another what they might do to Jesus.

Tuesday

Psalm 45 [page 647] ❖ *Psalm 47* [page 650],
Psalm 48 [page 651]

A Reading (Lesson) from the Book of Wisdom [3:1–9]

The souls of the righteous are in the hand of God, and no torment will ever touch them. In the eyes of the foolish they seemed to have died, and their departure was thought to be a disaster, and their going from us to be their destruction; but they are at peace. For though in the sight of others they were punished, their hope is full of immortality. Having been disciplined a little, they will receive great good, because

God tested them and found them worthy of himself; like gold in the furnace he tried them, and like a sacrificial burnt offering he accepted them. In the time of their visitation they will shine forth, and will run like sparks through the stubble. They will govern nations and rule over peoples, and the Lord will reign over them forever. Those who trust in him will understand truth, and the faithful will abide with him in love, because grace and mercy are upon his holy ones, and he watches over his elect.

A Reading (Lesson) from the Letter of Paul to the Colossians [1:15–23]

Christ is the image of the invisible God, the firstborn of all creation; for in him all things in heaven and on earth were created, things visible and invisible, whether thrones or dominions or rulers or powers—all things have been created through him and for him. He himself is before all things, and in him all things hold together. He is the head of the body, the church; he is the beginning, the firstborn from the dead, so that he might come to have first place in everything. For in him all the fullness of God was pleased to dwell, and through him God was pleased to reconcile to himself all things, whether on earth or in heaven, by making peace through the blood of his cross. And you who were once estranged and hostile in mind, doing evil deeds, he has now reconciled in his fleshly body through death, so as to present you holy and blameless and irreproachable before him—provided that you continue securely established and steadfast in the faith, without shifting from the hope promised by the gospel that you heard, which has been proclaimed to every creature under heaven. I, Paul, became a servant of this gospel.

*A Reading (Lesson) from the Gospel according to
Luke* [6:12–26]

Now during those days Jesus went out to the mountain to
pray; and he spent the night in prayer to God. And when
day came, he called his disciples and chose twelve of them,
whom he also named apostles: Simon, whom he named
Peter, and his brother Andrew, and James, and John, and
Philip, and Bartholomew, and Matthew, and Thomas, and
James son of Alphaeus, and Simon, who was called the
Zealot, and Judas son of James, and Judas Iscariot, who
became a traitor. He came down with them and stood on
a level place, with a great crowd of his disciples and a
great multitude of people from all Judea, Jerusalem, and
the coast of Tyre and Sidon. They had come to hear him
and to be healed of their diseases; and those who were
troubled with unclean spirits were cured. And all in the
crowd were trying to touch him, for power came out from
him and healed all of them. Then he looked up at his
disciples and said: "Blessed are you who are poor, for
yours is the kingdom of God. Blessed are you who are
hungry now, for you will be filled. Blessed are you who
weep now, for you will laugh. Blessed are you when
people hate you, and when they exclude you, revile you,
and defame you on account of the Son of Man. Rejoice in
that day and leap for joy, for surely your reward is great
in heaven; for that is what their ancestors did to the
prophets. But woe to you who are rich, for you have
received your consolation. Woe to you who are full now,
for you will be hungry. Woe to you who are laughing
now, for you will mourn and weep. Woe to you when all
speak well of you, for that is what their ancestors did to
the false prophets."

Wednesday

Psalm 119:49–72 [page 767] ❖ *Psalm 49* [page 652],
(Psalm 53 [page 658])

A Reading (Lesson) from the Book of Wisdom [4:16—5:8]

The righteous who have died will condemn the ungodly
who are living, and youth that is quickly perfected will
condemn the prolonged old age of the unrighteous. For they
will see the end of the wise, and will not understand what
the Lord purposed for them, and for what he kept them
safe. The unrighteous will see, and will have contempt for
them, but the Lord will laugh them to scorn. After this they
will become dishonored corpses, and an outrage among the
dead forever; because he will dash them speechless to the
ground, and shake them from the foundations; they will be
left utterly dry and barren, and they will suffer anguish, and
the memory of them will perish. They will come with dread
when their sins are reckoned up, and their lawless deeds will
convict them to their face. Then the righteous will stand
with great confidence in the presence of those who have
oppressed them and those who make light of their labors.
When the unrighteous see them, they will be shaken with
dreadful fear, and they will be amazed at the unexpected
salvation of the righteous. They will speak to one another in
repentance, and in anguish of spirit they will groan, and say,
"These are persons whom we once held in derision and made
a byword of reproach—fools that we were! We thought that
their lives were madness and that their end was without
honor. Why have they been numbered among the children
of God? And why is their lot among the saints? So it was we
who strayed from the way of truth, and the light of
righteousness did not shine on us, and the sun did not rise
upon us. We took our fill of the paths of lawlessness and

destruction, and we journeyed through trackless deserts, but the way of the Lord we have not known. What has our arrogance profited us? And what good has our boasted wealth brought us?"

A Reading (Lesson) from the Letter of Paul to the Colossians [1:24—2:7]

I am now rejoicing in my sufferings for your sake, and in my flesh I am completing what is lacking in Christ's afflictions for the sake of his body, that is, the church. I became its servant according to God's commission that was given to me for you, to make the word of God fully known, the mystery that has been hidden throughout the ages and generations but has now been revealed to his saints. To them God chose to make known how great among the Gentiles are the riches of the glory of this mystery, which is Christ in you, the hope of glory. It is he whom we proclaim, warning everyone and teaching everyone in all wisdom, so that we may present everyone mature in Christ. For this I toil and struggle with all the energy that he powerfully inspires within me. For I want you to know how much I am struggling for you, and for those in Laodicea, and for all who have not seen me face to face. I want their hearts to be encouraged and united in love, so that they may have all the riches of assured understanding and have the knowledge of God's mystery, that is, Christ himself, in whom are hidden all the treasures of wisdom and knowledge. I am saying this so that no one may deceive you with plausible arguments. For though I am absent in body, yet I am with you in spirit, and I rejoice to see your morale and the firmness of your faith in Christ. As you therefore have received Christ Jesus, the Lord, continue to live your lives in him, rooted and built up in him and established in the faith, just as you were taught, abounding in thanksgiving.

A Reading (Lesson) from the Gospel according to Luke [6:27–38]

Jesus looked up at his disciples, and said: "I say to you that listen, Love your enemies, do good to those who hate you, bless those who curse you, pray for those who abuse you. If anyone strikes you on the cheek, offer the other also; and from anyone who takes away your coat do not withhold even your shirt. Give to everyone who begs from you; and if anyone takes away your goods, do not ask for them again. Do to others as you would have them do to you. If you love those who love you, what credit is that to you? For even sinners love those who love them. If you do good to those who do good to you, what credit is that to you? For even sinners do the same. If you lend to those from whom you hope to receive, what credit is that to you? Even sinners lend to sinners, to receive as much again. But love your enemies, do good, and lend, expecting nothing in return. Your reward will be great, and you will be children of the Most High; for he is kind to the ungrateful and the wicked. Be merciful, just as your Father is merciful. Do not judge, and you will not be judged; do not condemn, and you will not be condemned. Forgive, and you will be forgiven; give, and it will be given to you. A good measure, pressed down, shaken together, running over, will be put into your lap; for the measure you give will be the measure you get back."

Thursday

Psalm 50 [page 654] ❖ (*Psalm 59* [page 665],
Psalm 60 [page 667]) or *Psalm 114* [page 756],
Psalm 115 [page 757]

A Reading (Lesson) from the Book of Wisdom [5:9–23]

The unrighteous will say in their repentance, "All those
things have vanished like a shadow, and like a rumor that
passes by; like a ship that sails through the billowy water,
and when it has passed no trace can be found, no track of its
keel in the waves; or as, when a bird flies through the air, no
evidence of its passage is found; the light air, lashed by the
beat of its pinions and pierced by the force of its rushing
flight, is traversed by the movement of its wings, and
afterward no sign of its coming is found there; or as, when
an arrow is shot at a target, the air, thus divided, comes
together at once, so that no one knows its pathway. So we
also, as soon as we were born, ceased to be, and we had no
sign of virtue to show, but were consumed in our
wickedness." Because the hope of the ungodly is like
thistledown carried by the wind, and like a light frost driven
away by a storm; it is dispersed like smoke before the wind,
and it passes like the remembrance of a guest who stays but
a day. But the righteous live forever, and their reward is
with the Lord; the Most High takes care of them. Therefore
they will receive a glorious crown and a beautiful diadem
from the hand of the Lord, because with his right hand he
will cover them, and with his arm he will shield them. The
Lord will take his zeal as his whole armor, and will arm all
creation to repel his enemies; he will put on righteousness as
a breastplate, and wear impartial justice as a helmet; he will
take holiness as an invincible shield, and sharpen stern
wrath for a sword, and creation will join with him to fight

against his frenzied foes. Shafts of lightning will fly with true aim, and will leap from the clouds to the target, as from a well-drawn bow, and hailstones full of wrath will be hurled as from a catapult; the water of the sea will rage against them, and rivers will relentlessly overwhelm them; a mighty wind will rise against them, and like a tempest it will winnow them away. Lawlessness will lay waste the whole earth, and evildoing will overturn the thrones of rulers.

A Reading (Lesson) from the Letter of Paul to the Colossians [2:8–23]

See to it that no one takes you captive through philosophy and empty deceit, according to human tradition, according to the elemental spirits of the universe, and not according to Christ. For in him the whole fullness of deity dwells bodily, and you have come to fullness in him, who is the head of every ruler and authority. In him also you were circumcised with a spiritual circumcision, by putting off the body of the flesh in the circumcision of Christ; when you were buried with him in baptism, you were also raised with him through faith in the power of God, who raised him from the dead. And when you were dead in trespasses and the uncircumcision of your flesh, God made you alive together with him, when he forgave us all our trespasses, erasing the record that stood against us with its legal demands. He set this aside, nailing it to the cross. He disarmed the rulers and authorities and made a public example of them, triumphing over them in it. Therefore do not let anyone condemn you in matters of food and drink or of observing festivals, new moons, or sabbaths. These are only a shadow of what is to come, but the substance belongs to Christ. Do not let anyone disqualify you, insisting on self-abasement and worship of angels, dwelling on visions, puffed up without cause by a human way of thinking, and not holding fast to the head, from whom the whole body, nourished and held together by its ligaments and sinews, grows with a growth that is from God. If with Christ you died to the elemental spirits of the universe, why do you live as if you still belonged to the world? Why do you submit to regulations, "Do not handle, Do not taste, Do not touch"? All these regulations refer to things that perish with use; they are simply human commands and teachings. These have indeed an appearance of wisdom in promoting self-imposed piety, humility, and severe treatment of the body, but they are of no value in checking self-indulgence.

A Reading (Lesson) from the Gospel according to
Luke [6:39–49]

Jesus told his disciples a parable: "Can a blind person guide a blind person? Will not both fall into a pit? A disciple is not above the teacher, but everyone who is fully qualified will be like the teacher. Why do you see the speck in your neighbor's eye, but do not notice the log in your own eye? Or how can you say to your neighbor, 'Friend, let me take out the speck in your eye,' when you yourself do not see the log in your own eye? You hypocrite, first take the log out of your own eye, and then you will see clearly to take the speck out of your neighbor's eye. No good tree bears bad fruit, nor again does a bad tree bear good fruit; for each tree is known by its own fruit. Figs are not gathered from thorns, nor are grapes picked from a bramble bush. The good person out of the good treasure of the heart produces good, and the evil person out of evil treasure produces evil; for it is out of the abundance of the heart that the mouth speaks. Why do you call me, 'Lord, Lord,' and do not do what I tell you? I will show you what someone is like who comes to me, hears my words, and acts on them. That one is like a man building a house, who dug deeply and laid the foundation on rock; when a flood arose, the river burst against that house but could not shake it, because it had been well built. But the one who hears and does not act is like a man who built a house on the ground without a foundation. When the river burst against it, immediately it fell, and great was the ruin of that house."

Friday

Psalm 40 [page 640],   *Psalm 54* [page 659]   ❖
Psalm 51 [page 656]

A Reading (Lesson) from the Book of Wisdom [6:12–23]

Wisdom is radiant and unfading, and she is easily discerned by those who love her, and is found by those who seek her. She hastens to make herself known to those who desire her. One who rises early to seek her will have no difficulty, for she will be found sitting at the gate. To fix one's thought on her is perfect understanding, and one who is vigilant on her account will soon be free from care, because she goes about seeking those worthy of her, and she graciously appears to them in their paths, and meets them in every thought. The beginning of wisdom is the most sincere desire for instruction, and concern for instruction is love of her, and love of her is the keeping of her laws, and giving heed to her laws is assurance of immortality, and immortality brings one near to God; so the desire for wisdom leads to a kingdom. Therefore if you delight in thrones and scepters, O monarchs over the peoples, honor wisdom, so that you may reign forever. I will tell you what wisdom is and how she came to be, and I will hide no secrets from you, but I will trace her course from the beginning of creation, and make knowledge of her clear, and I will not pass by the truth; nor will I travel in the company of sickly envy, for envy does not associate with wisdom.

A Reading (Lesson) from the Letter of Paul to the Colossians [3:1–11]

If you have been raised with Christ, seek the things that are above, where Christ is, seated at the right hand of God. Set your minds on things that are above, not on things that are on earth, for you have died, and your life is hidden with Christ in God. When Christ who is your life is revealed, then you also will be revealed with him in glory. Put to death, therefore, whatever in you is earthly: fornication, impurity, passion, evil desire, and greed (which is idolatry). On account of these the wrath of God is coming on those who are disobedient. These are the ways you also once followed, when you were living that life. But now you must get rid of all such things—anger, wrath, malice, slander, and abusive language from your mouth. Do not lie to one another, seeing that you have stripped off the old self with its practices and have clothed yourselves with the new self, which is being renewed in knowledge according to the image of its creator. In that renewal there is no longer Greek and Jew, circumcised and uncircumcised, barbarian, Scythian, slave and free; but Christ is all and in all!

A Reading (Lesson) from the Gospel according to Luke [7:1–17]

After Jesus had finished all his sayings in the hearing of the people, he entered Capernaum. A centurion there had a slave whom he valued highly, and who was ill and close to death. When he heard about Jesus, he sent some Jewish elders to him, asking him to come and heal his slave. When they came to Jesus they appealed to him earnestly, saying, "He is worthy of having you do this for him, for he loves our people, and it is he who built our synagogue for us." And Jesus went with them, but when he was not far from the house, the centurion sent friends to say to him, "Lord, do not trouble yourself, for I am not worthy to have you come under my roof; therefore I did not presume to come to you. But only speak the word, and let my servant be healed. For I also am a man set under authority, with soldiers under me; and I say to one, 'Go,' and he goes, and to another, 'Come,' and he comes, and to my slave, 'Do this,' and the slave does it." When Jesus heard this he was amazed at him, and turning to the crowd that followed him, he said, "I tell you, not even in Israel have I found such faith." When those who had been sent returned to the house, they found the slave in good health. Soon afterwards he went to a town called Nain, and his disciples and a large crowd went with him. As he approached the gate of the town, a man who had died was being carried out. He was his mother's only son, and she was a widow; and with her was a large crowd from the town. When the Lord saw her, he had compassion for her and said to her, "Do not weep." Then he came forward and touched the bier, and the bearers stood still. And he said, "Young man, I say to you, rise!" The dead man sat up and began to speak, and Jesus gave him to his mother. Fear seized all of them; and they glorified God, saying, "A great prophet has risen among us!" and "God has looked favorably on his people!" This word about him spread throughout Judea and all the surrounding country.

Saturday

Psalm 55 [page 660] ❖ *Psalm 138* [page 793],
Psalm 139:1–17(18–23) [page 794]

A Reading (Lesson) from the Book of Wisdom [7:1–14]

I also am mortal, like everyone else, a descendant of the
first-formed child of earth; and in the womb of a mother I
was molded into flesh, within the period of ten months,
compacted with blood, from the seed of a man and the
pleasure of marriage. And when I was born, I began to
breathe the common air, and fell upon the kindred earth; my
first sound was a cry, as is true of all. I was nursed with care
in swaddling clothes. For no king has had a different
beginning of existence; there is for all one entrance into life,
and one way out. Therefore I pray, and understanding was
given me; I called on God, and the spirit of wisdom came to
me. I preferred her to scepters and thrones, and I accounted
wealth as nothing in comparison with her. Neither did I
liken to her any priceless gem, because all gold is but a little
sand in her sight, and silver will be accounted as clay before
her. I loved her more than health and beauty, and I chose to
have her rather than light, because her radiance never
ceases. All good things came to me along with her, and in
her hands uncounted wealth. I rejoiced in them all, because
wisdom leads them; but I did not know that she was their
mother. I learned without guile and I impart without
grudging; I do not hide her wealth, for it is an unfailing
treasure for mortals; those who get it obtain friendship with
God, commended for the gifts that come from instruction.

*A Reading (Lesson) from the Letter of Paul to the
Colossians* [3:12–17]

As God's chosen ones, holy and beloved, clothe yourselves
with compassion, kindness, humility, meekness, and
patience. Bear with one another and, if anyone has a
complaint against another, forgive each other; just as the
Lord has forgiven you, so you also must forgive. Above
all, clothe yourselves with love, which binds everything
together in perfect harmony. And let the peace of Christ
rule in your hearts, to which indeed you were called in the
one body. And be thankful. Let the word of Christ dwell
in you richly; teach and admonish one another in all
wisdom; and with gratitude in your hearts sing psalms,
hymns, and spiritual songs to God. And whatever you do,
in word or deed, do everything in the name of the Lord
Jesus, giving thanks to God the Father through him.

*A Reading (Lesson) from the Gospel according to
Luke* [7:18–28(29–30)31–35]

The disciples of John reported all these things to him. So
John summoned two of his disciples and sent them to the
Lord to ask, "Are you the one who is to come, or are we
to wait for another?" When the men had come to him,
they said, "John the Baptist has sent us to you to ask,
'Are you the one who is to come, or are we to wait for
another?'" Jesus had just then cured many people of
diseases, plagues, and evil spirits, and had given sight to
many who were blind. And he answered them, "Go and
tell John what you have seen and heard: the blind receive
their sight, the lame walk, the lepers are cleansed, the deaf
hear, the dead are raised, the poor have good news
brought to them. And blessed is anyone who takes no

offense at me." When John's messengers had gone, Jesus began to speak to the crowds about John: "What did you go out into the wilderness to look at? A reed shaken by the wind? What then did you go out to see? Someone dressed in soft robes? Look, those who put on fine clothing and live in luxury are in royal palaces. What then did you go out to see? A prophet? Yes, I tell you, and more than a prophet. This is the one about whom it is written, 'See, I am sending my messenger ahead of you, who will prepare your way before you.' I tell you, among those born of women no one is greater than John; yet the least in the kingdom of God is greater than he."

(And all the people who heard this, including the tax collectors, acknowledged the justice of God, because they had been baptized with John's baptism. But by refusing to be baptized by him, the Pharisees and the lawyers rejected God's purpose for themselves.)

"To what then will I compare the people of this generation, and what are they like? They are like children sitting in the marketplace and calling to one another, 'We played the flute for you, and you did not dance; we wailed, and you did not weep.' For John the Baptist has come eating no bread and drinking no wine, and you say, 'He has a demon'; the Son of Man has come eating and drinking, and you say, 'Look, a glutton and a drunkard, a friend of tax collectors and sinners!' Nevertheless, wisdom is vindicated by all her children."

Week of 5 Easter

Sunday

Psalm 24 [page 613],   *Psalm 29* [page 620]   ❖
Psalm 8 [page 592],   *Psalm 84* [page 707]

A Reading (Lesson) from the Book of Wisdom [7:22—8:1]

Wisdom, the fashioner of all things, taught me. There is in
her a spirit that is intelligent, holy, unique, manifold, subtle,
mobile, clear, unpolluted, distinct, invulnerable, loving the
good, keen, irresistible, beneficent, humane, steadfast, sure,
free from anxiety, all-powerful, overseeing all, and
penetrating through all spirits that are intelligent, pure, and
altogether subtle. For wisdom is more mobile than any
motion; because of her pureness she pervades and penetrates
all things. For she is a breath of the power of God, and a
pure emanation of the glory of the Almighty; therefore
nothing defiled gains entrance into her. For she is a
reflection of eternal light, a spotless mirror of the working
of God, and an image of his goodness. Although she is but
one, she can do all things, and while remaining in herself,
she renews all things; in every generation she passes into
holy souls and makes them friends of God, and prophets;
for God loves nothing so much as the person who lives with
wisdom. She is more beautiful than the sun, and excels every
constellation of the stars. Compared with the light she is
found to be superior, for it is succeeded by the night, but
against wisdom evil does not prevail. She reaches mightily
from one end of the earth to the other, and she orders all
things well.

A Reading (Lesson) from the Second Letter of Paul to the Thessalonians [2:13–17]

We must always give thanks to God for you, brothers and sisters beloved by the Lord, because God chose you as the first fruits for salvation through sanctification by the Spirit and through belief in the truth. For this purpose he called you through our proclamation of the good news, so that you may obtain the glory of our Lord Jesus Christ. So then, brothers and sisters, stand firm and hold fast to the traditions that you were taught by us, either by word of mouth or by our letter. Now may our Lord Jesus Christ himself and God our Father, who loved us and through grace gave us eternal comfort and good hope, comfort your hearts and strengthen them in every good work and word.

A Reading (Lesson) from the Gospel according to Matthew [7:7–14]

Jesus taught his disciples, saying: "Ask, and it will be given you; search, and you will find; knock, and the door will be opened for you. For everyone who asks receives, and everyone who searches finds, and for everyone who knocks, the door will be opened. Is there anyone among you who, if your child asks for bread, will give a stone? Or if the child asks for a fish, will give a snake? If you then, who are evil, know how to give good gifts to your children, how much more will your Father in heaven give good things to those who ask him! In everything do to others as you would have them do to you; for this is the law and the prophets. Enter through the narrow gate; for the gate is wide and the road is easy that leads to destruction, and there are many who take it. For the gate is narrow and the road is hard that leads to life, and there are few who find it."

Monday

Psalm 56 [page 662], *Psalm 57* [page 663],
(Psalm 58 [page 664]) ❖ *Psalm 64* [page 671],
Psalm 65 [page 672]

A Reading (Lesson) from the Book of Wisdom [9:1,7–18]

I appealed to the Lord and said, "O God of my ancestors
and Lord of mercy, who have made all things by your word,
you have chosen me to be king of your people and to be
judge over your sons and daughters. You have given
command to build a temple on your holy mountain, and an
altar in the city of your habitation, a copy of the holy tent
that you prepared from the beginning. With you is wisdom,
she who knows your works and was present when you made
the world; she understand what is pleasing in your sight and
what is right according to your commandments. Send her
forth from the holy heavens, and from the throne of your
glory send her, that she may labor at my side, and that I
may learn what is pleasing to you. For she knows and
understands all things, and she will guide me wisely in my
actions and guard with her glory. Then my works will be
acceptable, and I shall judge your people justly, and shall be
worthy of the throne of my father. For who can learn the
counsel of God? Or who can discern what the Lord wills?
For the reasoning of mortals is worthless, and our designs
are likely to fail; for a perishable body weighs down the
soul, and this earthy tent burdens the thoughtful mind. We
can hardly guess at what is on earth, and what is at hand we
find with labor; but who has traced out what is in the
heavens? Who has learned your counsel, unless you have
given wisdom and sent your holy spirit from on high? And
thus the paths of those on earth were set right, and people
were taught what pleases you, and were saved by wisdom."

A Reading (Lesson) from the Letter of Paul to the
Colossians [(3:18—4:1)2–18]

Wives, be subject to your husbands, as is fitting in the
Lord. Husbands, love your wives and never treat them
harshly. Children, obey your parents in everything, for
this is your acceptable duty in the Lord. Fathers, do not
provoke your children, or they may lose heart. Slaves,
obey your earthly masters in everything, not only while
being watched and in order to please them, but
wholeheartedly, fearing the Lord. Whatever your task,
put yourselves into it, as done for the Lord and not for
your masters, since you know that from the Lord you
will receive the inheritance as your reward; you serve
the Lord Christ. For the wrongdoer will be paid back
for whatever wrong has been done, and there is no
partiality. Masters, treat your slaves justly and fairly,
for you know that you also have a Master in heaven.

Devote yourselves to prayer, keeping alert in it with
thanksgiving. At the same time pray for us as well that
God will open to us a door for the word, that we may
declare the mystery of Christ, for which I am in prison, so
that I may reveal it clearly, as I should. Conduct
yourselves wisely toward outsiders, making the most of
the time. Let your speech always be gracious, seasoned
with salt, so that you may know how you ought to answer
everyone. Tychicus will tell you all the news about me; he
is a beloved brother, a faithful minister, and a fellow
servant in the Lord. I have sent him to you for this very
purpose, so that you may know how we are and that he
may encourage your hearts; he is coming with Onesimus,
the faithful and beloved brother, who is one of you. They
will tell you about everything here. Aristarchus my fellow

prisoner greets you, as does Mark the cousin of Barnabas, concerning whom you have received instructions—if he comes to you, welcome him. And Jesus who is called Justus greets you. These are the only ones of the circumcision among my co-workers for the kingdom of God, and they have been a comfort to me. Epaphras, who is one of you, a servant of Christ Jesus, greets you. He is always wrestling in his prayers on your behalf, so that you may stand mature and fully assured in everything that God wills. For I testify for him that he has worked hard for you and for those in Laodicea and in Hierapolis. Luke, the beloved physician, and Demas greet you. Give my greetings to the brothers and sisters in Laodicea, and to Nympha and the church in her house. And when this letter has been read among you, have it read also in the church of the Laodiceans; and see that you read also the letter from Laodicea. And say to Archippus, "See that you complete the task that you have received in the Lord." I, Paul, write this greeting with my own hand. Remember my chains. Grace be with you.

A Reading (Lesson) from the Gospel according to Luke [7:36–50]

One of the Pharisees asked Jesus to eat with him, and he went into the Pharisee's house and took his place at the table. And a woman in the city, who was a sinner, having learned that he was eating in the Pharisee's house, brought an alabaster jar of ointment. She stood behind him at his feet, weeping, and began to bathe his feet with her tears and to dry them with her hair. Then she continued kissing his feet and anointing them with the ointment. Now when the Pharisee who had invited him saw it, he said to himself, "If this man were a prophet, he would have known who and what kind of woman this is who is touching him—that she is a sinner." Jesus spoke up and said to him, "Simon, I have something to say to you." "Teacher," he replied, "speak." "A certain creditor had two debtors; one owed five hundred denarii, and the other fifty. When they could not pay, he canceled the debts for both of them. Now which of them will love him more?" Simon answered, "I suppose the one for whom he canceled the greater debt." And Jesus said to him, "You have judged rightly." Then turning toward the woman, he said to Simon, "Do you see this woman? I entered your house; you gave me no water for my feet, but she has bathed my feet with her tears and dried them with her hair. You gave me no kiss, but from the time I came in she has not stopped kissing my feet. You did not anoint my head with oil, but she has anointed my feet with ointment. Therefore, I tell you, her sins, which were many, have been forgiven; hence she has shown great love. But the one to whom little is forgiven, loves little." Then he said to her, "Your sins are forgiven." But those who were at the table with him began to say among themselves, "Who is this who even forgives sins?" And he said to the woman, "Your faith has saved you; go in peace."

Tuesday

Psalm 61 [page 668],   *Psalm 62* [page 669]   ❖
Psalm 68:1–20(21–23)24–36 [page 676]

A Reading (Lesson) from the Book of Wisdom [10:1–4(5–12)13–21]

Wisdom protected the first-formed father of the world, when he alone had been created; she delivered him from his transgression, and gave him strength to rule all things. But when an unrighteous man departed from her in his anger, he perished because in rage he killed his brother. When the earth was flooded because of him, wisdom again saved it, steering the righteous man by a paltry piece of wood.

Wisdom also, when the nations in wicked agreement had been put to confusion, recognized the righteous man and preserved him blameless before God, and kept him strong in the face of his compassion for his child. Wisdom rescued a righteous man when the ungodly were perishing; he escaped the fire that descended on the Five Cities. Evidence of their wickedness still remains: a continually smoking wasteland, plants bearing fruit that does not ripen, and a pillar of salt standing as a monument to an unbelieving soul. For because they passed wisdom by, they not only were hindered from recognizing the good, but also left for humankind a reminder of their folly, so that their failures could never go unnoticed. Wisdom rescued from troubles those who served her. When a righteous man fled from his brother's wrath, she guided him on straight paths; she showed him the kingdom of God, and gave him knowledge of holy things; she prospered him in his labors, and increased the fruit of his toil. When his oppressors were covetous, she stood by him and made him rich. She protected him from his enemies, and kept him safe from those who lay in wait for him; in his arduous contest she gave him the victory, so that he might learn that godliness is more powerful than anything else.

When a righteous man was sold, wisdom did not desert him, but delivered him from sin. She descended with him into the dungeon, and when he was in prison she did not leave him, until she brought him the scepter of a kingdom and authority over his masters. Those who accused him she showed to be false, and she gave him everlasting honor. A holy people and blameless race wisdom delivered from a nation of oppressors. She entered the soul of a servant of the Lord, and withstood dread kings with wonders and signs. She gave to holy people the reward of their labors; she guided them along a marvelous way, and became a shelter to them by day, and a starry flame through the night. She brought them over the Red Sea, and led them through deep waters; but she drowned their enemies, and cast them up from the depth of the sea. Therefore the righteous plundered the ungodly; they sang hymns, O Lord, to your holy name, and praised with one accord your defending hand; for wisdom opened the mouths of those who were mute, and made the tongues of infants speak clearly.

A Reading (Lesson) from the Letter of Paul to the Romans [12:1–21]

I appeal to you therefore, brothers and sisters, by the mercies of God, to present your bodies as a living sacrifice, holy and acceptable to God, which is your spiritual worship. Do not be conformed to this world, but be transformed by the renewing of your minds, so that you may discern what is the will of God—what is good and acceptable and perfect. For by the grace given to me I say to everyone among you not to think of yourself more highly than you ought to think, but to think with sober judgment, each according to the measure of faith that God has assigned. For as in one body we have many members, and not all the members have the same function, so we, who are many, are one body in Christ, and individually we are members one of another. We have gifts that differ according to the grace given to us: prophecy, in proportion to faith; ministry, in ministering; the teacher, in teaching; the exhorter, in exhortation; the giver, in generosity; the leader, in diligence; the compassionate, in cheerfulness. Let love be genuine; hate what is evil, hold fast to what is good; love one another with mutual affection; outdo one another in showing honor. Do not lag in zeal, be ardent in spirit, serve the Lord. Rejoice in hope, be patient in suffering, persevere in prayer. Contribute to the needs of the saints; extend hospitality to strangers. Bless those who persecute you; bless and do not curse them. Rejoice with those who rejoice, weep with those who weep. Live in harmony with one another; do not be haughty, but associate with the lowly; do not claim to be wiser than you are. Do not repay anyone evil for evil, but take thought for what is noble in the sight of all. If it is possible, so far as it depends on you, live peaceably with all. Beloved, never avenge yourselves, but leave room for the wrath of God; for it is written, "Vengeance is mine, I will repay, says the Lord." No, "if your enemies are hungry, feed them; if they are thirsty, give them something to drink; for by doing this you will heap burning coals on their heads." Do not be overcome by evil, but overcome evil with good.

A Reading (Lesson) from the Gospel according to Luke [8:1-15]

Soon afterwards Jesus went on through cities and villages, proclaiming and bringing the good news of the kingdom of God. The twelve were with him, as well as some women who had been cured of evil spirits and infirmities:

Mary, called Magdalene, from whom seven demons had gone out, and Joanna, the wife of Herod's steward Chuza, and Susanna, and many others, who provided for them out of their resources. When a great crowd gathered and people from town after town came to him, he said in a parable: "A sower sent out to sow his seed; and as he sowed, some fell on the path and was trampled on, and the birds of the air ate it up. Some fell on the rock; and as it grew up, it withered for lack of moisture. Some fell among thorns, and the thorns grew with it and choked it. Some fell into good soil, and when it grew, it produced a hundredfold." As he said this, he called out, "Let anyone with ears to hear listen!" Then his disciples asked him what this parable meant. He said, "To you it has been given to know the secrets of the kingdom of God; but to others I speak in parables, so that 'looking they may not perceive, and listening they may not understand.' Now the parable is this: The seed is the word of God. The ones on the path are those who have heard; then the devil comes and takes away the word from their hearts, so that they may not believe and be saved. The ones on the rock are those who, when they hear the word, receive it with joy. But these have no root; they believe only for a while and in a time of testing fall away. As for what fell among the thorns, these are the ones who hear; but as they go on their way, they are choked by the cares and riches and pleasures of life, and their fruit does not mature. But as for that in the good soil, these are the ones who, when they hear the word, hold it fast in an honest and good heart, and bear fruit with patient endurance."

Wednesday

Psalm 72 [page 685]   ❖   *Psalm 119:73–96* [page 769]

A Reading (Lesson) from the Book of Wisdom [13:1–9]

For all people who were ignorant of God were foolish by
nature; and they were unable from the good things that are
seen to know the one who exists, nor did they recognize the
artisan while paying heed to his works; but they supposed
that either fire or wind or swift air, or the circle of the stars,
or turbulent water, or the luminaries of heaven were the
gods that rule the world. If through delight in the beauty of
these things people assumed them to be gods, let them know
how much better than these is their Lord, for the author of
beauty created them. And if people were amazed at their
power and working, let them perceive from them how much
more powerful is the one who formed them. For from the
greatness and beauty of created things comes a
corresponding perception of their Creator. Yet these people
are little to be blamed, for perhaps they go astray while
seeking God and desiring to find him. For while they live
among his works, they keep searching, and they trust in
what they see, because the things that are seen are beautiful.
Yet again, not even they are to be excused; for if they had
the power to know so much that they could investigate the
world, how did they fail to find sooner the Lord of these
things?

*A Reading (Lesson) from the Letter of Paul to the
Romans* [13:1–14]

Let every person be subject to the governing authorities;
for there is no authority except from God, and those
authorities that exist have been instituted by God.

Therefore whoever resists authority resists what God has appointed, and those who resist will incur judgment. For rulers are not a terror to good conduct, but to bad. Do you wish to have no fear of the authority? Then do what is good, and you will receive its approval; for it is God's servant for your good. But if you do what is wrong, you should be afraid, for the authority does not bear the sword in vain! It is the servant of God to execute wrath on the wrongdoer. Therefore one must be subject, not only because of wrath but also because of conscience. For the same reason you also pay taxes, for the authorities are God's servants, busy with this very thing. Pay to all what is due them—taxes to whom taxes are due, revenue to whom revenue is due, respect to whom respect is due, honor to whom honor is due. Owe no one anything, except to love one another; for the one who loves another has fulfilled the law. The commandments, "You shall not commit adultery; You shall not murder; You shall not steal; You shall not covet"; and any other commandment, are summed up in this word, "Love your neighbor as yourself." Love does no wrong to a neighbor; therefore, love is the fulfilling of the law. Besides this, you know what time it is, how it is now the moment for you to wake from sleep. For salvation is nearer to us now than when we became believers; the night is far gone, the day is near. Let us then lay aside the works of darkness and put on the armor of light; let us live honorably as in the day, not in reveling and drunkenness, not in debauchery and licentiousness, not in quarreling and jealousy. Instead, put on the Lord Jesus Christ, and make no provision for the flesh, to gratify its desires.

A Reading (Lesson) from the Gospel according to
Luke [8:16–25]

Jesus said to his disciples, "No one after lighting a lamp
hides it under a jar, or puts it under a bed, but puts it on
a lampstand, so that those who enter may see the light.
For nothing is hidden that will not be disclosed, nor is
anything secret that will not become known and come to
light. Then pay attention to how you listen; for to those
who have, more will be given; and from those who do not
have, even what they seem to have will be taken away."
Then his mother and his brothers came to him, but they
could not reach him because of the crowd. And he was
told, "Your mother and your brothers are standing
outside, wanting to see you." But he said to them, "My
mother and my brothers are those who hear the word of
God and do it." One day he got into a boat with his
disciples, and he said to them, "Let us go across to the
other side of the lake." So they put out, and while they
were sailing he fell asleep. A windstorm swept down on
the lake, and the boat was filling with water, and they
were in danger. They went to him and woke him up,
shouting, "Master, Master, we are perishing!" And he
woke up and rebuked the wind and the raging waves; they
ceased, and there was a calm. He said to them, "Where is
your faith?" They were afraid and amazed, and said to
one another, "Who then is this, that he commands even
the winds and the water, and they obey him?"

Thursday

(Psalm 70 [page 682]),   *Psalm 71* [page 683]   ❖
Psalm 74 [page 689]

A Reading (Lesson) from the Book of
Wisdom [14:27—15:3]

The worship of idols not to be named is the beginning and
cause and end of every evil. For their worshipers either rave
in exultation, or prophesy lies, or live unrighteously, or
readily commit perjury; for because they trust in lifeless
idols they swear wicked oaths and expect to suffer no harm.
But just penalties will overtake them on two counts; because
they thought wrongly about God in devoting themselves to
idols, and because in deceit they swore unrighteously
through contempt for holiness. For it is not the power of the
things by which people swear, but the just penalty for those
who sin, that always pursues the transgression of the
unrighteous. But you, our God, are kind and true, patient,
and ruling all things in mercy. For even if we sin we are
yours, knowing your power; but we will not sin, because we
know that you acknowledge us as yours. For to know you is
complete righteousness, and to know your power is the root
of immortality.

A Reading (Lesson) from the Letter of Paul to the
Romans [14:1–12]

Welcome those who are weak in faith, but not for the
purpose of quarreling over opinions. Some believe in
eating anything, while the weak eat only vegetables. Those
who eat must not despise those who abstain, and those
who abstain must not pass judgment on those who eat; for
God has welcomed them. Who are you to pass judgment
on servants of another? It is before their own lord that
they stand or fall. And they will be upheld, for the Lord is
able to make them stand. Some judge one day to be better
than another, while others judge all days to be alike. Let
all be fully convinced in their own minds. Those who

observe the day, observe it in honor of the Lord. Also those who eat, eat in honor of the Lord, since they give thanks to God; while those who abstain, abstain in honor of the Lord and give thanks to God. We do not live to ourselves, and we do not die to ourselves. If we live, we live to the Lord, and if we die, we die to the Lord; so then, whether we live or whether we die, we are the Lord's. For to this end Christ died and lived again, so that he might be Lord of both the dead and the living. Why do you pass judgment on your brother or sister? Or you, why do you despise your brother or sister? For we will all stand before the judgment seat of God. For it is written, "As I live, says the Lord, every knee shall bow to me, and every tongue shall give praise to God." So then, each of us will be accountable to God.

A Reading (Lesson) from the Gospel according to Luke [8:26–39]

Jesus and his disciples arrived at the country of the Gerasenes, which is opposite Galilee. As he stepped out on land, a man of the city who had demons met him. For a long time he had worn no clothes, and he did not live in a house, but in the tombs. When he saw Jesus, he fell down before him and shouted at the top of his voice, "What have you to do with me, Jesus, Son of the Most High God? I beg you, do not torment me"—for Jesus had commanded the unclean spirit to come out of the man. (For many times it had seized him; he was kept under guard and bound with chains and shackles, but he would break the bonds and be driven by the demon into the wilds.) Jesus then asked him, "What is your name?" He said, "Legion"; for many demons had entered him. They begged him not to order them to go back into the abyss.

Now there on the hillside a large herd of swine was feeding; and the demons begged Jesus to let them enter these. So he gave them permission. Then the demons came out of the man and entered the swine, and the herd rushed down the steep bank into the lake and was drowned. When the swineherds saw what had happened, they ran off and told it in the city and in the country. Then people came out to see what had happened, and when they came to Jesus, they found the man from whom the demons had gone sitting at the feet of Jesus, clothed and in his right mind. And they were afraid. Those who had seen it told them how the one who had been possessed by demons had been healed. Then all the people of the surrounding country of the Gerasenes asked Jesus to leave them; for they were seized with great fear. So he got into the boat and returned. The man from whom the demons had gone begged that he might be with him; but Jesus sent him away, saying, "Return to your home, and declare how much God has done for you." So he went away, proclaiming throughout the city how much Jesus had done for him.

Friday

Psalm 106:1–18 [page 741] ❖ *Psalm 106:19–48* [page 743]

A Reading (Lesson) from the Book of Wisdom [16:15—17:1]

To escape from your hand is impossible; for the ungodly, refusing to know you, were flogged by the strength of your arm, pursued by unusual rains and hail and relentless storms, and utterly consumed by fire. For—most incredible of all—in water, which quenches all things, the fire had still greater effect, for the universe defends the righteous. At one time the flame was restrained, so that it might not consume the creatures sent against the ungodly, but that seeing this they might know that they were being pursued by the judgment of God; and at another time even in the midst of water it burned more intensely than fire, to destroy the crops of the unrighteous land. Instead of these things you gave your people food of angels, and without their toil you supplied them from heaven with bread ready to eat, providing every pleasure and suited to every taste. For your sustenance manifested your sweetness toward your children; and the bread, ministering to the desire of the one who took it, was changed to suit everyone's liking. Snow and ice withstood fire without melting, so that they might know that the crops of their enemies were being destroyed by the fire that blazed in the hail and flashed in the showers of rain; whereas the fire, in order that the righteous might be fed, even forgot its native power. For creation, serving you who made it, exerts itself to punish the unrighteous, and in kindness relaxes on behalf of those who trust in you. Therefore at that time also, changed into all forms, it served your all-nourishing bounty, according to the desire of those who had need, so that your children, whom you loved, O Lord, might learn that it is not the production of crops that feeds humankind but that your word sustains those who trust in you. For what was not destroyed by fire was melted when simply warmed by a fleeting ray of the sun, to make it known that one must rise before the sun to give you thanks, and must pray to you at the dawning of the light; for the hope of an ungrateful person will melt like wintry frost, and flow away like waste water. Great are your judgments and hard to describe; therefore uninstructed souls have gone astray.

A Reading (Lesson) from the Letter of Paul to the Romans [14:13–23]

Let us no longer pass judgment on one another, but resolve instead never to put a stumbling block or hindrance in the way of another. I know and am persuaded in the Lord Jesus that nothing is unclean in itself; but it is unclean for anyone who thinks it unclean. If your brother or sister is being injured by what you eat, you are no longer walking in love. Do not let what you eat cause the ruin of one for whom Christ died. So do not let your good be spoken of as evil. For the kingdom of God is not food and drink but righteousness and peace and joy in the Holy Spirit. The one who thus serves Christ is acceptable to God and has human approval. Let us then pursue what makes for peace and for mutual upbuilding. Do not, for the sake of food, destroy the work of God. Everything is indeed clean, but it is wrong for you to make others fall by what you eat; it is good not to eat meat or drink wine or do anything that makes your brother or sister stumble. The faith that you have, have as your own conviction before God. Blessed are those who have no reason to condemn themselves because of what they approve. But those who have doubts are condemned if they eat, because they do not act from faith; for whatever does not proceed from faith is sin.

A Reading (Lesson) from the Gospel According to Luke [8:40–56]

When Jesus returned, the crowd welcomed him, for they were all waiting for him. Just then there came a man named Jairus, a leader of the synagogue. He fell at Jesus' feet and begged him to come to his house, for he had an only daughter, about twelve years old, who was dying. As he went, the crowds pressed in on him. Now there was a woman who had been suffering from hemorrhages for twelve years; and though she had spent all she had on physicians, no one could cure her. She came up behind him and touched the fringe of his clothes, and immediately her hemorrhage stopped. Then Jesus asked, "Who touched me?" When all denied it, Peter said, "Master, the crowds surround you and press in on you." But Jesus said, "Someone touched me; for I noticed that power had gone out from me." When the woman saw that she could not remain hidden, she came trembling; and falling down before him, she declared in the presence of all the people why she had touched him, and how she had been immediately healed. He said to her, "Daughter, your faith has made you well; go in peace." While he was still speaking, someone came from the leader's house to say, "Your daughter is dead; do not trouble the teacher any longer." When Jesus heard this, he replied, "Do not fear. Only believe, and she will be saved." When he came to the house, he did not allow anyone to enter with him, except Peter, John, and James, and the child's father and mother. They were all weeping and wailing for her; but he said, "Do not weep; for she is not dead but sleeping." And they laughed at him, knowing that she was dead. But he took her by the hand and called out, "Child, get up!" Her spirit returned, and she got up at once. Then he directed them to give her something to eat. Her parents were astounded; but he ordered them to tell no one what had happened.

Saturday

Psalm 75 [page 691], *Psalm 76* [page 692] ❖
Psalm 23 [page 612], *Psalm 27* [page 617]

A Reading (Lesson) from the Book of Wisdom [19:1–8, 18–22]

The ungodly were assailed to the end by pitiless anger,
for God knew in advance even their future actions: how,
though they themselves had permitted your people to depart
and hastily sent them out, they would change their minds
and pursue them. For while they were still engaged in
mourning, and were lamenting at the graves of their dead,
they reached another foolish decision, and pursued as
fugitives those whom they had begged and compelled to
leave. For the fate they deserved drew them on to this end,
and made them forget what had happened, in order that
they might fill up the punishment that their torments still
lacked, and that your people might experience an incredible
journey, but they themselves might meet a strange death.
For the whole creation in its nature was fashioned anew,
complying with your commands, so that your children
might be kept unharmed. The cloud was seen
overshadowing the camp, and dry land emerging where
water had stood before, an unhindered way out of the Red
Sea, and a grassy plain out of the raging waves, where those
protected by your hand passed through as one nation, after
gazing on marvelous wonders. For the elements changed
place with one another, as on a harp the notes vary the
nature of the rhythm, while each note remains the same.
This may be clearly inferred from the sight of what took
place. For land animals were transformed into water
creatures, and creatures that swim moved over to the land.
Fire even in water retained its normal power, and water
forgot its fire-quenching nature. Flames, on the contrary,
failed to consume the flesh of perishable creatures that
walked among them, nor did they melt the crystalline,
quick-melting kind of heavenly food. For in everything, O

Lord, you have exalted and glorified your people, and you have not neglected to help them at all times and in all places.

A Reading (Lesson) from the Letter of Paul to the Romans [15:1–13]

We who are strong ought to put up with the failings of the weak, and not to please ourselves. Each of us must please our neighbor for the good purpose of building up the neighbor. For Christ did not please himself; but, as it is written, "The insults of those who insult you have fallen on me." For whatever was written in former days was written for our instruction, so that by steadfastness and by the encouragement of the scriptures we might have hope. May the God of steadfastness and encouragement grant you to live in harmony with one another, in accordance with Christ Jesus, so that together you may with one voice glorify the God and Father of our Lord Jesus Christ. Welcome one another, therefore, just as Christ has welcomed you, for the glory of God. For I tell you that Christ has become a servant of the circumcised on behalf of the truth of God in order that he might confirm the promises given to the patriarchs, and in order that the Gentiles might glorify God for his mercy. As it is written, "Therefore I will confess you among the Gentiles, and sing praises to your name"; and again he says, "Rejoice, O Gentiles, with his people"; and again, "Praise the Lord, all you Gentiles, and let all the peoples praise him"; and again Isaiah says, "The root of Jesse shall come, the one who rises to rule the Gentiles; in him the Gentiles shall hope." May the God of hope fill you with all joy and peace in believing, so that you may abound in hope by the power of the Holy Spirit.

A Reading (Lesson) from the Gospel according to
Luke [9:1–17]

Jesus called the twelve together and gave them power and
authority over all demons and to cure diseases, and he
sent them out to proclaim the kingdom of God and to
heal. He said to them, "Take nothing for your journey, no
staff, nor bag, nor bread, nor money—not even an extra
tunic. Whatever house you enter, stay there, and leave
from there. Wherever they do not welcome you, as you
are leaving that town shake the dust off your feet as a
testimony against them." They departed and went through
the villages, bringing the good news and curing diseases
everywhere. Now Herod the ruler heard about all that had
taken place, and he was perplexed, because it was said by
some that John had been raised from the dead, by some
that Elijah had appeared, and by others that one of the
ancient prophets had arisen. Herod said, "John I
beheaded; but who is this about whom I hear such
things?" And he tried to see him. On their return the
apostles told Jesus all they had done. He took them with
him and withdrew privately to a city called Bethsaida.
When the crowds found out about it, they followed him;
and he welcomed them, and spoke to them about the
kingdom of God, and healed those who needed to be
cured. The day was drawing to a close, and the twelve
came to him and said, "Send the crowd away, so that they
may go into the surrounding villages and countryside, to
lodge and get provisions; for we are here in a deserted
place." But he said to them, "You give them something to
eat." They said, "We have no more than five loaves and
two fishes—unless we are to go and buy food for all these
people." For there were about five thousand men. And he
said to his disciples, "Make them sit down in groups of

about fifty each." They did so and made them all sit down. And taking the five loaves and the two fish, he looked up to heaven, and blessed and broke them, and gave them to the disciples to set before the crowd. And all ate and were filled. What was left over was gathered up, twelve baskets of broken pieces.

Week of 6 Easter

Sunday

Psalm 93 [page 722],   *Psalm 96* [page 725]   ❖
Psalm 34 [page 627]

A Reading (Lesson) from the Book of Ecclesiasticus [43:1-12, 27-32]

The pride of the higher realms is the clear vault of the sky, as glorious to behold as the sight of the heavens. The sun, when it appears, proclaims as it rises what a marvelous instrument it is, the work of the Most High. At noon it parches the land, and who can withstand its burning heat? A man tending a furnace works in burning heat, but three times as hot is the sun scorching the mountains; it breathes out fiery vapors, and its bright rays blind the eyes. Great is the Lord who made it; at his orders it hurries on its course. It is the moon that marks the changing seasons, governing the times, their everlasting sign. From the moon comes the sign for festal days, a light that wanes when it completes its course. The new moon, as its name suggests, renews itself; how marvelous it is in this change, a beacon to the hosts on high, shining in the vault of the heavens! The glory of the stars is the beauty of heaven, a glittering array in the heights of the Lord. On the orders of the Holy One they stand in their appointed places; they never relax in their watches. Look at the rainbow, and praise him who made it; it is exceedingly beautiful in its brightness. It encircles the sky with its glorious arc; the hands of the Most High have stretched it out. We could say more but could never say enough; let the final word be: "He is the all." Where can we find the strength to praise him? For he is greater than all his works. Awesome is the Lord and very great, and marvelous is his power. Glorify the Lord and exalt him as much as you can, for he surpasses even that. When you exalt him, summon all your strength, and do not grow weary, for you cannot praise him enough. Who has seen him and can describe him? Or who can extol him as he is? Many things greater than these lie hidden, for I have seen but few of his works.

A Reading (Lesson) from the First Letter of Paul to Timothy [3:14—4:5]

I hope to come to you soon, but I am writing these instructions to you so that, if I am delayed, you may know how one ought to behave in the household of God, which is the church of the living God, the pillar and bulwark of the truth. Without any doubt, the mystery of our religion is great: He was revealed in flesh, vindicated in spirit, seen by angels, proclaimed among Gentiles, believed in throughout the world, taken up in glory. Now the Spirit expressly says that in later times some will renounce the faith by paying attention to deceitful spirits and teachings of demons, through the hypocrisy of liars whose consciences are seared with a hot iron. They forbid marriage and demand abstinence from foods, which God created to be received with thanksgiving by those who believe and know the truth. For everything created by God is good, and nothing is to be rejected, provided it is received with thanksgiving; for it is sanctified by God's word and by prayer.

A Reading (Lesson) from the Gospel according to Matthew [13:24–34a]

Jesus put before them another parable: "The kingdom of heaven may be compared to someone who sowed good seed in his field; but while everybody was asleep, an enemy came and sowed weeds among the wheat, and then went away. So when the plants came up and bore grain, then the weeds appeared as well. And the slaves of the householder came and said to him, 'Master, did you not sow good seed in your field? Where, then, did these weeds come from?' He answered, 'An enemy has done this.' The slaves said to him, 'Then do you want us to go and gather them?' But he replied, 'No; for in gathering the weeds you would uproot the wheat along with them. Let both of them grow together until the harvest; and at harvest time I will tell the reapers, Collect the weeds first and bind them in bundles to be burned, but gather the wheat into my barn.'" He put before them another parable: "The kingdom of heaven is like a mustard seed that someone took and sowed in his field; it is the smallest of all the seeds, but when it has grown it is the greatest of shrubs and becomes a tree, so that the birds of the air come and make nests in its branches." He told them another parable: "The kingdom of heaven is like yeast that a woman took and mixed in with three measures of flour until all of it was leavened." Jesus told the crowds all these things in parables.

Monday

Psalm 80 [page 702] ❖ *Psalm 77* [page 693],
(Psalm 79 [page 701])

Deuteronomy 8:1–10 [page 296 above]

A Reading (Lesson) from the Letter of James [1:1–15]

James, a servant of God and of the Lord Jesus Christ, to
the twelve tribes in the Dispersion: Greetings. My brothers
and sisters, whenever you face trials of any kind, consider
it nothing but joy, because you know that the testing of
your faith produces endurance; and let endurance have its
full effect, so that you may be mature and complete,
lacking in nothing. If any of you is lacking in wisdom, ask
God, who gives to all generously and ungrudgingly, and it
will be given you. But ask in faith, never doubting, for the
one who doubts is like a wave of the sea, driven and
tossed by the wind; for the doubter, being double-minded
and unstable in every way, must not expect to receive
anything from the Lord. Let the believer who is lowly
boast in being raised up, and the rich in being brought
low, because the rich will disappear like a flower in the
field. For the sun rises with its scorching heat and withers
the field; its flower falls, and its beauty perishes. It is the
same way with the rich; in the midst of a busy life, they
will wither away. Blessed is anyone who endures
temptation. Such a one has stood the test and will receive
the crown of life that the Lord has promised to those who
love him. No one, when tempted, should say, "I am being
tempted by God"; for God cannot be tempted by evil and
he himself tempts no one. But one is tempted by one's
own desire, being lured and enticed by it; then, when that
desire has conceived, it gives birth to sin, and that sin,
when it is fully grown, gives birth to death.

*A Reading (Lesson) from the Gospel according to
Luke* [9:18–27]

Once when Jesus was praying alone, with only the
disciples near him, he asked them, "Who do the crowds
say that I am?" They answered, "John the Baptist; but
others, Elijah; and still others, that one of the ancient
prophets has arisen." He said to them, "But who do you
say that I am?" Peter answered, "The Messiah of God."
He sternly ordered and commanded them not to tell
anyone, saying, "The Son of Man must undergo great
suffering, and be rejected by the elders, chief priests, and
scribes, and be killed, and on the third day be raised."
Then he said to them all, "If any want to become my
followers, let them deny themselves and take up their cross
daily and follow me. For those who want to save their life
will lose it, and those who lose their life for my sake will
save it. What does it profit them if they gain the whole
world, but lose or forfeit themselves? Those who are
ashamed of me and of my words, of them the Son of Man
will be ashamed when he comes in his glory and the glory
of the Father and of the holy angels. But truly I tell you,
there are some standing here who will not taste death
before they see the kingdom of God."

Tuesday

Psalm 78:1–39 [page 694]   ❖   *Psalm 78: 40–72* [page 698]

Deuteronomy 8:11–20 [page 299 above]

A Reading (Lesson) from the Letter of James [1:16–27]

Do not be deceived, my beloved. Every generous act of
giving, with every perfect gift, is from above, coming

down from the Father of lights, with whom there is no variation or shadow due to change. In fulfillment of his own purpose he gave us birth by the word of truth, so that we would become a kind of first fruits of his creatures. You must understand this, my beloved: let everyone be quick to listen, slow to speak, slow to anger; for your anger does not produce God's righteousness. Therefore rid yourselves of all sordidness and rank growth of wickedness, and welcome with meekness the implanted word that has the power to save your souls. But be doers of the word, and not merely hearers who deceive themselves. For if any are hearers of the word and not doers, they are like those who look at themselves in a mirror; for they look at themselves and, on going away, immediately forget what they were like. But those who look into the perfect law, the law of liberty, and persevere, being not hearers who forget but doers who act—they will be blessed in their doing. If any think they are religious, and do not bridle their tongues but deceive their hearts, their religion is worthless. Religion that is pure and undefiled before God, the Father, is this: to care for orphans and widows in their distress, and to keep oneself unstained by the world.

A Reading (Lesson) from the Gospel according to Luke [11:1–13]

Jesus was praying in a certain place, and after he had finished, one of his disciples said to him, "Lord, teach us to pray, as John taught his disciples." He said to them, "When you pray, say: Father, hallowed be your name. Your kingdom come. Give us each day our daily bread. And forgive us our sins, for we ourselves forgive everyone indebted to us. And do not bring us to the time of trial."

And he said to them, "Suppose one of you has a friend, and you go to him at midnight and say to him, 'Friend, lend me three loaves of bread; for a friend of mine has arrived, and I have nothing to set before him.' And he answers from within, 'Do not bother me; the door has already been locked, and my children are with me in bed; I cannot get up and give you anything.' I tell you, even though he will not get up and give him anything because he is his friend, at least because of his persistence he will get up and give him whatever he needs. So I say to you, Ask, and it will be given you; search, and you will find; knock, and the door will be opened for you. For everyone who asks receives, and everyone who searches finds, and for everyone who knocks, the door will be opened. Is there anyone among you who, if your child asks for a fish, will give a snake instead of a fish? Or if the child asks for an egg, will give a scorpion? If you then, who are evil, know how to give good gifts to your children, how much more will the heavenly Father give the Holy Spirit to those who ask him!"

Wednesday

MORNING PRAYER

Psalm 119:97–120 [page 771]

A Reading (Lesson) from the Book of Baruch [3:24–37]

O Israel, how great is the house of God, how vast the territory that he possesses! It is great and has no bounds; it is high and immeasurable. The giants were born there, who were famous of old, great in stature, expert in war. God did not choose them, or give them the way to knowledge; so they perished because they had no wisdom, they perished through their folly. Who has gone up into heaven, and taken her, and brought her down from the clouds? Who has gone over the sea, and found her, and will buy her for pure gold? No one knows the way to her, or is concerned about the path to her. But the one who knows all things knows her, he found her by his understanding. The one who prepared the earth for all time filled it with four-footed creatures; the one who sends forth the light, and it goes; he called it, and it obeyed him, trembling; the stars shone in their watches, and were glad; he called them, and they said, "Here we are!" They shone with gladness for him who made them. This is our God; no other can be compared to him. He found the whole way to knowledge, and gave her to his servant Jacob and to Israel, whom he loved. Afterward she appeared on earth and lived with humankind.

A Reading (Lesson) from the Letter of James [5:13–18]

Are any among you suffering? They should pray. Are any cheerful? They should sing songs of praise. Are any among you sick? They should call for the elders of the church and have them pray over them, anointing them with oil in the name of the Lord. The prayer of faith will save the sick, and the Lord will raise them up; and anyone who has committed sins will be forgiven. Therefore confess your sins to one another, and pray for one another so that you may be healed. The prayer of the righteous is powerful and effective. Elijah was a human being like us, and he prayed fervently that it might not rain, and for three years and six months it did not rain on the earth. Then he prayed again, and the heaven gave rain and the earth yielded its harvest.

A Reading (Lesson) from the Gospel according to Luke [12:22–31]

Jesus said to his disciples, "I tell you, do not worry about your life, what you will eat, or about your body, what you will wear. For life is more than food, and the body more than clothing. Consider the ravens: they neither sow nor reap, they have neither storehouse nor barn, and yet God feeds them. Of how much more value are you than the birds! And can any of you by worrying add a single hour to your span of life? If then you are not able to do so small a thing as that, why do you worry about the rest? Consider the lilies, how they grow: they neither toil nor spin; yet I tell you, even Solomon in all his glory was not clothed like one of these. But if God so clothes the grass of the field, which is alive today and tomorrow is thrown into the oven, how much more will he clothe you—you of little faith! And do not keep striving for what you are to eat and what you are to drink, and do not keep worrying. For it is the nations of the world that strive after all these things, and your Father knows that you need them. Instead, strive for his kingdom; and these things will be given to you as well."

Eve of Ascension

EVENING PRAYER

Psalm 68:1–20 [page 676]

A Reading (Lesson) from the Second Book of the Kings [2:1–15]

Now when the LORD was about to take Elijah up to heaven by a whirlwind, Elijah and Elisha were on their way from

Gilgal. Elijah said to Elisha, "Stay here; for the LORD has sent me as far as Bethel." But Elisha said, "As the LORD lives, and as you yourself live, I will not leave you." So they went down to Bethel. The company of prophets who were in Bethel came out to Elisha, and said to him, "Do you know that today the LORD will take your master away from you?" And he said, "Yes, I know; keep silent." Elijah said to him, "Elisha, stay here; for the LORD has sent me to Jericho." But he said, "As the LORD lives, and as you yourself live, I will not leave you." So they came to Jericho. The company of prophets who were at Jericho drew near to Elisha, and said to him, "Do you know that today the LORD will take your master away from you?" And he answered, "Yes, I know; be silent." Then Elijah said to him, "Stay here; for the LORD has sent me to the Jordan." But he said, "As the LORD lives, and as you yourself live, I will not leave you." So the two of them went on. Fifty men of the company of prophets also went, and stood at some distance from them, as they both were standing by the Jordan. Then Elijah took his mantle and rolled it up, and struck the water; the water was parted to the one side and to the other, until the two of them crossed on dry ground. When they had crossed, Elijah said to Elisha, "Tell me what I may do for you before I am taken from you." Elisha said, "Please let me inherit a double share of your spirit." He responded, "You have asked a hard thing; yet, if you see me as I am being taken from you, it will be granted you; if not, it will not." As they continued walking and talking, a chariot of fire and horses of fire separated the two of them, and Elijah ascended in a whirlwind into heaven. Elisha kept watching and crying out, "Father, father! The chariots of Israel and its horsemen!" But when he could no longer see him, he grasped his own clothes and tore them in two pieces. He picked up the mantle of Elijah that had fallen from him, and went back and stood on the bank of the Jordan. He took the mantle of Elijah that had fallen from him, and struck the water, saying, "Where is the Lord, the God of Elijah?" When he had struck the water, the water was parted to the one side and to the other, and Elisha went over. When the company of prophets who were at Jericho saw him at a distance, they declared, "The spirit of Elijah rests on Elisha." They came to meet him and bowed to the ground before him.

A Reading (Lesson) from the Revelation to John [5:1–14]

I saw in the right hand of the one seated on the throne a scroll written on the inside and on the back, sealed with seven seals; and I saw a mighty angel proclaiming with a loud voice, "Who is worthy to open the scroll and break its seals?" And no one in heaven or on earth or under the earth was able to open the scroll or to look into it. And I began to weep bitterly because no one was found worthy to open the scroll or to look into it. Then one of the elders said to me, "Do not weep. See, the Lion of the tribe of Judah, the Root of David, has conquered, so that he can open the scroll and its seven seals." Then I saw between the throne and the four living creatures and among the elders a Lamb standing as if it had been slaughtered, having seven horns and seven eyes, which are the seven spirits of God sent out into all the earth. He went and took the scroll from the right hand of the one who was seated on the throne. When he had taken the scroll, the four living creatures and the twenty-four elders fell before the Lamb, each holding a harp and golden bowls full of incense, which are the prayers of the saints. They sing a new song: "You are worthy to take the scroll and to open its seals, for you were slaughtered and by your blood you ransomed for God saints from every tribe and language and people and nation; you have made them to be a kingdom and priests serving our God, and they will reign on earth." Then I looked, and I heard the voice of many angels surrounding the throne and the living creatures and the elders; they numbered myriads of myriads and thousands of thousands, singing with full voice, "Worthy is the Lamb that was slaughtered to receive power and wealth and wisdom and might and honor and glory and blessing!" Then I heard every creature in heaven and on earth and under the earth and in the sea, and all that is in them, singing, "To the one seated on the throne and to the Lamb be blessing and honor and glory and might forever and ever!" And the four living creatures said, "Amen!" And the elders fell down and worshiped.

Ascension Day

Psalm 8 [page 592],   *Psalm 47* [page 650]   ❖
Psalm 24 [page 613],   *Psalm 96* [page 725]

A Reading (Lesson) from the Book of Ezekiel [1:1–14, 24–28b]

In the thirtieth year, in the fourth month, on the fifth day of the month, as I was among the exiles by the river Chebar, the heavens were opened, and I saw visions of God. On the fifth day of the month (it was the fifth year of the exile of King Jehoiachin), the word of the LORD came to the priest Ezekiel son of Buzi, in the land of the Chaldeans by the river Chebar; and the hand of the LORD was on him there. As I looked, a stormy wind came out of the north: a great cloud with brightness around it and fire flashing forth continually, and in the middle of the fire, something like gleaming amber. In the middle of it was something like four living creatures. This was their appearance: they were of human form. Each had four faces, and each of them had four wings. Their legs were straight, and the soles of their feet were like the sole of a calf's foot; and they sparkled like burnished bronze. Under their wings on their four sides they had human hands. And the four had their faces and their wings thus: their wings touched one another; each of them moved straight ahead, without turning as they moved. As for the appearance of their faces: the four had the face of a human being, the face of a lion on the right side, the face of an ox on the left side, and the face of an eagle; such were their faces. Their wings were spread out above; each creature had two wings, each of which touched the wing of another, while two covered their bodies. Each moved straight ahead; wherever the spirit would go, they went, without turning as they went. In the middle of the living creatures there was something that looked like burning coals of fire, like torches moving to and fro among the living creatures; the fire was bright, and lightning issued from the fire. The living creatures darted to and fro, like a flash of lightning. When they moved, I heard the sound of their wings like the sound of mighty waters, like the thunder of the Almighty, a sound of tumult like the sound of an army; when they stopped, they let down their wings. And there came a voice from above the dome over their heads; when they stopped, they let down their wings. And above the dome over their heads there was something like a throne, in appearance like sapphire; and seated above the likeness of a throne was something that seemed like a human form. Upward from what appeared like the loins I saw something like gleaming amber, something that looked like fire enclosed all around; and downward from what looked like the loins I saw something that looked like fire, and there was a splendor all around. Like the bow in a cloud on a rainy day, such was the appearance of the splendor all around. This was the appearance of the likeness of the glory of the LORD.

A Reading (Lesson) from the Letter to the Hebrews [2:5–18]

God did not subject the coming world, about which we are speaking, to angels. But someone has testified somewhere, "What are human beings that you are mindful of them, or mortals, that you care for them? You have made them for a little while lower than the angels; you have crowned them with glory and honor, subjecting all things under their feet." Now in subjecting all things to them, God left nothing outside their control. As it is, we do not yet see everything in subjection to them, but we do see Jesus, who for a little while was made lower than the angels, now crowned with glory and honor because of the suffering of death, so that by the grace of God he might taste death for everyone. It was fitting that God, for whom and through whom all things exist, in bringing many children to glory, should make the pioneer of their salvation perfect through sufferings. For the one who sanctifies and those who are sanctified all have one Father. For this reason Jesus is not ashamed to call them brothers and sisters, saying, "I will proclaim your name to my brothers and sisters, in the midst of the congregation I will praise you." And again, "I will put my trust in him." And again, "Here am I and the children whom God has given me." Since, therefore, the children share flesh and blood, he himself likewise shared the same things, so that through death he might destroy the one who has the power of death, that is, the devil, and free those who all their lives were held in slavery by the fear of death. For it is clear that he did not come to help angels, but the descendants of Abraham. Therefore he had to become like his brothers and sisters in every respect, so that he might be a merciful and faithful high priest in the service of God, to make a sacrifice of atonement for the sins of the people. Because he himself was tested by what he suffered, he is able to help those who are being tested.

A Reading (Lesson) from the Gospel according to Matthew [28:16–20]

The eleven disciples went to Galilee, to the mountain to which Jesus had directed them. When they saw him, they worshiped him; but some doubted. And Jesus came and said to them, "All authority in heaven and on earth has been given to me. Go therefore and make disciples of all nations, baptizing them in the name of the Father and of the Son and of the Holy Spirit, and teaching them to obey everything that I have commanded you. And remember, I am with you always, to the end of the age."

Friday

Psalm 85 [page 708], *Psalm 86* [page 709] ❖
Psalm 91 [page 719], *Psalm 92* [page 720]

A Reading (Lesson) from the Book of Ezekiel [1:28—3:3]

Like the bow in a cloud on a rainy day, such was the appearance of the splendor all around. This was the appearance of the likeness of the glory of the LORD. When I saw it, I fell on my face, and I heard the voice of someone speaking. He said to me: O mortal, stand up on your feet, and I will speak with you. And when he spoke to me, a spirit entered into me and set me on my feet; and I heard him speaking to me. He said to me, Mortal, I am sending you to the people of Israel, to a nation of rebels who have rebelled against me; they and their ancestors have transgressed against me to this very day. The descendants are impudent and stubborn. I am sending you to them, and you shall say to them, "Thus says the Lord GOD." Whether they hear or refuse to hear (for they are a rebellious house), they shall know that there has been a prophet among them. And you, O mortal, do not be afraid of them, and do not be afraid of their words, though briers and thorns surround you and you live among scorpions; do not be afraid of their words, and do not be dismayed at their looks, for they are a rebellious house. You shall speak my words to them, whether they hear or refuse to hear; for they are a rebellious house. But you, mortal, hear what I say to you; do not be rebellious like that rebellious house; open your mouth and eat what I give you. I looked, and a hand was stretched out to me, and a written scroll was in it. He spread it before me; it had writing on the front and on the back, and written on it were words of lamentation and mourning and woe. He said to me, O mortal, eat what is offered to you; eat this scroll, and go, speak to the house of Israel. So I opened my mouth, and he gave me the scroll to eat. He said to me, Mortal, eat this scroll that I give you and fill your stomach with it. Then I ate it; and in my mouth it was as sweet as honey.

A Reading (Lesson) from the Letter to the Hebrews [4:14—5:6]

Since, then, we have a great high priest who has passed through the heavens, Jesus, the Son of God, let us hold fast to our confession. For we do not have a high priest

who is unable to sympathize with our weaknesses, but we
have one who in every respect has been tested as we are,
yet without sin. Let us therefore approach the throne of
grace with boldness, so that we may receive mercy and
find grace to help in time of need. Every high priest chosen
from among mortals is put in charge of things pertaining
to God on their behalf, to offer gifts and sacrifices for sins.
He is able to deal gently with the ignorant and wayward,
since he himself is subject to weakness; and because of this
he must offer sacrifice for his own sins as well as for those
of the people. And one does not presume to take this
honor, but takes it only when called by God, just as
Aaron was. So also Christ did not glorify himself in
becoming a high priest, but was appointed by the one who
said to him, "You are my Son, today I have begotten
you"; as he says also in another place, "You are a priest
forever, according to the order of Melchizedek."

A Reading (Lesson) from the Gospel according to
Luke [9:28–36]

Jesus took with him Peter and John and James, and went
up on the mountain to pray. And while he was praying,
the appearance of his face changed, and his clothes became
dazzling white. Suddenly they saw two men, Moses and
Elijah, talking to him. They appeared in glory and were
speaking of his departure, which he was about to
accomplish at Jerusalem. Now Peter and his companions
were weighed down with sleep; but since they had stayed
awake, they saw his glory and the two men who stood
with him. Just as they were leaving him, Peter said to
Jesus, "Master, it is good for us to be here; let us make
three dwellings, one for you, one for Moses, and one for
Elijah"—not knowing what he said. While he was saying

this, a cloud came and overshadowed them; and they were terrified as they entered the cloud. Then from the cloud came a voice that said, "This is my Son, my Chosen; listen to him!" When the voice had spoken, Jesus was found alone. And they kept silent and in those days told no one any of the things they had seen.

Saturday

Psalm 87 [page 711],   *Psalm 90* [page 717]   ❖
Psalm 136 [page 789]

A Reading (Lesson) from the Book of Ezekiel [3:4–17]

A voice said to me: Mortal, go to the house of Israel and speak my very words to them. For you are not sent to a people of obscure speech and difficult language, but to the house of Israel—not to many peoples of obscure speech and difficult language, whose words you cannot understand. Surely, if I sent you to them, they would listen to you. But the house of Israel will not listen to you, for they are not willing to listen to me; because all the house of Israel have a hard forehead and a stubborn heart. See, I have made your face hard against their faces, and your forehead hard against their foreheads. Like the hardest stone, harder than flint, I have made your forehead; do not fear them or be dismayed at their looks, for they are a rebellious house. He said to me: Mortal, all my words that I shall speak to you receive in your heart and hear with your ears; then go to the exiles, to your people, and speak to them. Say to them, "Thus says the Lord GOD"; whether they hear or refuse to hear. Then the spirit lifted me up, and as the glory of the LORD rose from its place, I heard behind me the sound of loud rumbling; it was the sound of the wings of the living creatures brushing against one another, and the sound of the wheels beside them, that sounded like a loud rumbling. The spirit lifted me up and bore me away; I went in bitterness in the heat of my spirit, the hand of the LORD being strong upon me. I came to the exiles at Tel-abib, who lived by the river Chebar. And I sat there among them, stunned, for seven days. At the end of seven days, the word of the LORD came to me: Mortal, I have made you a sentinel for the house of Israel; whenever you hear a word from my mouth, you shall give them warning from me.

A Reading (Lesson) from the Letter to the Hebrews [5:7–14]

In the days of his flesh, Jesus offered up prayers and supplications, with loud cries and tears, to the one who was able to save him from death, and he was heard because of his reverent submission. Although he was a Son, he learned obedience through what he suffered; and having been made perfect, he became the source of eternal salvation for all who obey him, having been designated by God a high priest according to the order of Melchizedek. About this we have much to say that is hard to explain, since you have become dull in understanding. For though by this time you ought to be teachers, you need someone to teach you again the basic elements of the oracles of God. You need milk, not solid food; for everyone who lives on milk, being still an infant, is unskilled in the word of righteousness. But solid food is for the mature, for those whose faculties have been trained by practice to distinguish good from evil.

A Reading (Lesson) from the Gospel according to Luke [9:37–50]

On the next day, when Jesus, with Peter and John and James, had come down from the mountain, a great crowd met him. Just then a man from the crowd shouted, "Teacher, I beg you to look at my son; he is my only child. Suddenly a spirit seizes him, and all at once he shrieks. It convulses him until he foams at the mouth; it mauls him and will scarcely leave him. I begged your disciples to cast it out, but they could not." Jesus answered, "You faithless and perverse generation, how much longer must I be with you and bear with you? Bring your son here." While he was coming, the demon dashed him to the ground in convulsions. But Jesus rebuked the unclean spirit, healed the boy, and gave him back to his father. And all were astounded at the greatness of God. While everyone was amazed at all that he was doing, he said to his disciples, "Let these words sink into your ears: The Son of Man is going to be betrayed into human hands." But they did not understand this saying; its meaning was concealed from them, so that they could not perceive it. And they were afraid to ask him about this saying. An argument arose among them as to which one of them was the greatest. But Jesus, aware of their inner thoughts, took a little child and put it by his side, and said to them, "Whoever welcomes this child in my name welcomes me, and whoever welcomes me welcomes the one who sent me; for the least among all of you is the greatest." John answered, "Master, we saw someone casting out demons in your name, and we tried to stop him, because he does not follow with us." But Jesus said to him, "Do not stop him; for whoever is not against you is for you."

Week of 7 Easter

Sunday

Psalm 66 [page 673],   *Psalm 67* [page 675]   ❖
Psalm 19 [page 606],   *Psalm 46* [page 649]

A Reading (Lesson) from the Book of Ezekiel [3:16–27]

At the end of seven days, the word of the LORD came to me:
Mortal, I have made you a sentinel for the house of Israel;
whenever you hear a word from my mouth, you shall give
them warning from me. If I say to the wicked, "You shall
surely die," and you give them no warning, or speak to
warn the wicked from their wicked way, in order to save
their life, those wicked persons shall die for their iniquity;
but their blood I will require at your hand. But if you warn
the wicked, and they do not turn from their wickedness, or
from their wicked way, they shall die for their iniquity; but
you will have saved your life. Again, if the righteous turn
from their righteousness and commit iniquity, and I lay a
stumbling block before them, they shall die; because you
have not warned them, they shall die for their sin, and their
righteous deeds that they have done shall not be
remembered; but their blood I will require at your hand. If,
however, you warn the righteous not to sin, and they do not
sin, they shall surely live, because they took warning; and
you will have saved your life. Then the hand of the LORD
was upon me there; and he said to me, Rise up, go out into
the valley, and there I will speak with you. So I rose up and
went out into the valley; and the glory of the LORD stood
there, like the glory that I had seen by the river Chebar; and
I fell on my face. The spirit entered into me, and set me on

my feet; and he spoke with me and said to me: Go, shut yourself inside your house. As for you, mortal, cords shall be placed on you, and you shall be bound with them, so that you cannot go out among the people; and I will make your tongue cling to the roof of your mouth, so that you shall be speechless and unable to reprove them; for they are a rebellious house. But when I speak with you, I will open your mouth, and you shall say to them, "Thus says the Lord GOD"; let those who will hear, hear; and let those who refuse to hear, refuse; for they are a rebellious house.

Ephesians 2:1–10 [page 129 above]

A Reading (Lesson) from the Gospel according to Matthew [10:24–33,40–42]

Jesus sent out the twelve, charging them, "A disciple is not above the teacher, nor a slave above the master; it is enough for the disciple to be like the teacher, and the slave like the master. If they have called the master of the house Beelzebul, how much more will they malign those of his household! So have no fear of them; for nothing is covered up that will not be uncovered, and nothing secret that will not become known. What I say to you in the dark, tell in the light; and what you hear whispered, proclaim from the housetops. Do not fear those who kill the body but cannot kill the soul; rather fear him who can destroy both soul and body in hell. Are not two sparrows sold for a penny? Yet not one of them will fall to the ground apart from your Father. And even the hairs of your head are all counted. So do not be afraid; you are of more value than many sparrows. Everyone therefore who acknowledges me before others, I also will acknowledge before my Father in heaven; but whoever denies me before others, I also will deny before my Father in heaven. Whoever welcomes you welcomes me, and whoever welcomes me welcomes the one who sent me. Whoever welcomes a prophet in the name of a prophet will receive a prophet's reward; and whoever welcomes a righteous person in the name of a righteous person will receive the reward of the righteous; and whoever gives even a cup of cold water to one of these little ones in the name of a disciple—truly I tell you, none of these will lose their reward."

Monday

Psalm 89:1–18 [page 713]   ❖   *Psalm 89:19–52* [page 715]

A Reading (Lesson) from the Book of Ezekiel [4:1–17]

The spirit spoke with me and said to me: You, O mortal, take a brick and set it before you. On it portray a city, Jerusalem; and put siegeworks against it, and build a siege wall against it, and cast up a ramp against it; set camps also against it, and plant battering rams against it all around. Then take an iron plate and place it as an iron wall between you and the city; set your face toward it, and let it be in a state of siege, and press the siege against it. This is a sign for the house of Israel. Then lie on your left side, and place the punishment of the house of Israel upon it; you shall bear their punishment for the number of the days that you lie there. For I assign to you a number of days, three hundred ninety days, equal to the number of the years of their punishment; and so you shall bear the punishment of the house of Israel. When you have completed these, you shall lie down a second time, but on your right side, and bear the punishment of the house of Judah; forty days I assign you, one day for each year. You shall set your face toward the siege of Jerusalem, and with your arm bared you shall prophesy against it. See, I am putting cords on you so that you cannot turn from one side to the other until you have completed the days of your siege. And you, take wheat and barley, beans and lentils, millet and spelt; put them into one vessel, and make bread for yourself. During the number of days that you lie on your side, three hundred ninety days, you shall eat it. The food that you eat shall be twenty shekels a day by weight; at fixed times you shall eat it. And you shall drink water by measure, one-sixth of a hin; at fixed times you shall drink. You shall eat it as a barleycake, baking it in their sight on human dung. The LORD said, "Thus shall the people of Israel eat their bread, unclean, among the nations to which I will drive them." Then I said, "Ah Lord GOD! I have never defiled myself; from my youth up until now I have never eaten what died of itself or was torn by animals, nor has carrion flesh come into my mouth." Then he said to me, "See, I will let you have cow's dung instead of human dung, on which you may prepare your bread." Then he said to me, Mortal, I am going to break the staff of bread in Jerusalem; they shall eat bread by weight and with fearfulness; and they shall drink water by measure and in dismay. Lacking bread and water, they will look at one another in dismay, and waste away under their punishment.

A Reading (Lesson) from the Letter to the Hebrews [6:1–12]

Let us go on toward perfection, leaving behind the basic teaching about Christ, and not laying again the foundation: repentance from dead works and faith toward God, instruction about baptisms, laying on of hands, resurrection of the dead, and eternal judgment. And we will do this, if God permits. For it is impossible to restore again to repentance those who have once been enlightened, and have tasted the heavenly gift, and have shared in the Holy Spirit, and have tasted the goodness of the word of God and the powers of the age to come, and then have fallen away, since on their own they are crucifying again the Son of God and are holding him up to contempt. Ground that drinks up the rain falling on it repeatedly, and that produces a crop useful to those for whom it is cultivated, receives a blessing from God. But if it produces thorns and thistles, it is worthless and on the verge of being cursed; its end is to be burned over. Even though we speak in this way, beloved, we are confident of better things in your case, things that belong to salvation. For God is not unjust; he will not overlook your work and the love that you showed for his sake in serving the saints, as you still do. And we want each one of you to show the same diligence so as to realize the full assurance of hope to the very end, so that you may not become sluggish, but imitators of those who through faith and patience inherit the promises.

A Reading (Lesson) from the Gospel according to Luke [9:51–62]

When the days drew near for him to be taken up, Jesus set his face to go to Jerusalem. And he sent messengers ahead of him. On their way they entered a village of the Samaritans to make ready for him; but they did not receive him, because his face was set toward Jerusalem. When his disciples James and John saw it, they said, "Lord, do you want us to command fire to come down from heaven and consume them?" But he turned and rebuked them. Then they went on to another village. As they were going along the road, someone said to him, "I will follow you wherever you go." And Jesus said to him, "Foxes have holes, and birds of the air have nests; but the Son of Man has nowhere to lay his head." To another he said, "Follow me." But he said, "Lord, first let me go and bury my father." But Jesus said to him, "Let the dead bury their own dead; but as for you, go and proclaim the kingdom of God." Another said, "I will follow you, Lord; but let me first say farewell to those at my home." Jesus said to him, "No one who puts a hand to the plow and looks back is fit for the kingdom of God."

Tuesday

Psalm 97 [page 726], *Psalm 99* [page 728], *(Psalm 100* [page 729]) ❖ *Psalm 94* [page 722], *(Psalm 95* [page 724])

A Reading (Lesson) from the Book of Ezekiel [7:10–15, 23b–27]

The word of the LORD came to me: See, the day! See, it comes! Your doom has gone out. The rod has blossomed, pride has budded. Violence has grown into a rod of wickedness. None of them shall remain, not their abundance, not their wealth; no pre-eminence among them. The time has come, the day draws near; let not the buyer rejoice, nor the seller mourn, for wrath is upon all their multitude. For the sellers shall not return to what has been sold as long as they remain alive. For the vision concerns all their multitude; it shall not be revoked. Because of their iniquity, they cannot maintain their lives. They have blown the horn and made everything ready; but no one goes to battle, for my wrath is upon all their multitude. The sword is outside, pestilence and famine are inside; those in the field die by the sword; those in the city—famine and pestilence devour them. For the land is full of bloody crimes; the city is full of violence. I will bring the worst of the nations to take possession of their houses. I will put an end to the arrogance of the strong, and their holy places shall be profaned. When anguish comes, they will seek peace, but there shall be none. Disaster comes upon disaster, rumor follows rumor; they shall keep seeking a vision from the prophet; instruction shall perish from the priest, and counsel from the elders. The king shall mourn, the prince shall be wrapped in despair, and the hands of the people of the land shall tremble. According to their way I will deal with them; according to their own judgments I will judge them. And they shall know that I am the LORD.

A Reading (Lesson) from the Letter to the Hebrews [6:13–20]

When God made a promise to Abraham, because he had no one greater by whom to swear, he swore by himself, saying, "I will surely bless you and multiply you." And thus Abraham, having patiently endured, obtained the promise. Human beings, of course, swear by someone greater than themselves, and an oath given as confirmation puts an end to all dispute. In the same way, when God desired to show even more clearly to the heirs of the promise the unchangeable character of his purpose, he guaranteed it by an oath, so that through two unchangeable things, in which it is impossible that God would prove false, we who have taken refuge might be strongly encouraged to seize the hope set before us. We have this hope, a sure and steadfast anchor of the soul, a hope that enters the inner shrine behind the curtain, where Jesus, a forerunner on our behalf, has entered, having become a high priest forever according to the order of Melchizedek.

A Reading (Lesson) from the Gospel according to Luke [10:1–17]

After this the Lord appointed seventy others and sent them on ahead of him in pairs to every town and place where he himself intended to go. He said to them, "The harvest is plentiful, but the laborers are few; therefore ask the Lord of the harvest to send out laborers into his harvest. Go on your way. See, I am sending you out like lambs into the midst of wolves. Carry no purse, no bag, no sandals; and greet no one on the road. Whatever house you enter, first say, 'Peace to this house!' And if anyone is there who shares in peace, your peace will rest on that person; but if not, it will return to you. Remain in the same house, eating and drinking whatever they provide, for the laborer deserves to be paid. Do not move about from house to house. Whenever you enter a town and its people welcome you, eat what is set before you; cure the sick who are there, and say to them, 'The kingdom of God has come near to you.' But whenever you enter a town and they do not welcome you, go out into its streets and say, 'Even the dust of your town that clings to our feet, we wipe off in protest against you. Yet know this: the kingdom of God has come near.' I tell you, on that day it will be more tolerable for Sodom than for that town. Woe to you, Chorazin! Woe to you, Bethsaida! For if the deeds of power done in you had been done in Tyre and Sidon, they would have repented long ago, sitting in sackcloth and ashes. But at the judgment it will be more tolerable for Tyre and Sidon than for you. And you, Capernaum, will you be exalted to heaven? No, you will be brought down to Hades. Whoever listens to you listens to me, and whoever rejects you rejects me, and whoever rejects me rejects the one who sent me." The seventy returned with joy, saying, "Lord, in your name even the demons submit to us!"

Wednesday

Psalm 101 [page 730], *Psalm 109:1–4(5–19)20–30* [page 750] ❖ *Psalm 119:121–144* [page 773]

A Reading (Lesson) from the Book of Ezekiel [11:14–25]

The word of the LORD came to me: Mortal, your kinsfolk, your own kin, your fellow exiles, the whole house of Israel, all of them, are those of whom the inhabitants of Jerusalem have said, "They have gone far from the LORD; to us this land is given for a possession." Therefore say: Thus says the Lord GOD: Though I removed them far away among the nations, and though I scattered them among the countries, yet I have been a sanctuary to them for a little while in the countries where they have gone. Therefore say: Thus says the Lord GOD: I will gather you from the peoples, and assemble you out of the countries where you have been scattered, and I will give you the land of Israel. When they come there, they will remove from it all its detestable things and all its abominations. I will give them one heart, and put a new spirit within them; I will remove the heart of stone from their flesh and give them a heart of flesh, so that they may follow my statutes and keep my ordinances and obey them. Then they shall be my people, and I will be their God. But as for those whose heart goes after their detestable things and their abominations, I will bring their deeds upon their own heads, says the Lord GOD. Then the cherubim lifted up their wings, with the wheels beside them; and the glory of the God of Israel was above them. And the glory of the LORD ascended from the middle of the city, and stopped on the mountain east of the city. The spirit lifted me up and brought me in a vision by the spirit of God into Chaldea, to the exiles. Then the vision that I had seen left me. And I told the exiles all the things that the LORD had shown me.

A Reading (Lesson) from the Letter to the Hebrews [7:1–17]

This "King Melchizedek of Salem, priest of the Most High God, met Abraham as he was returning from defeating the kings and blessed him"; and to him Abraham apportioned "one-tenth of everything." His name, in the first place, means "king of righteousness"; next he is also king of Salem, that is, "king of peace." Without father, without mother, without genealogy, having neither beginning of days nor end of life, but resembling the Son of God, he remains a priest forever. See how great he is! Even Abraham the patriarch gave him a tenth of the spoils. And those descendants of Levi who receive the priestly office have a commandment in the law to collect tithes from the people, that is, from their kindred, though these also are descended from Abraham. But this man, who does not belong to their ancestry, collected tithes from Abraham and blessed him who had received the promises. It is beyond dispute that the inferior is blessed by the superior. In the one case, tithes are received by those who are mortal; in the other, by one of whom it is testified that he lives. One might even say that Levi himself, who receives tithes, paid tithes through Abraham, for he was still in the

loins of his ancestor when Melchizedek met him. Now if
perfection had been attainable through the levitical
priesthood—for the people received the law under this
priesthood—what further need would there have been to
speak of another priest arising according to the order of
Melchizedek, rather than one according to the order of
Aaron? For when there is a change in the priesthood, there
is necessarily a change in the law as well. Now the one of
whom these things are spoken belonged to another tribe,
from which no one has ever served at the altar. For it is
evident that our Lord was descended from Judah, and in
connection with that tribe Moses said nothing about
priests. It is even more obvious when another priest arises,
resembling Melchizedek, one who has become a priest, not
through a legal requirement concerning physical descent,
but through the power of an indestructible life. For it is
attested of him, "You are a priest forever, according to the
order of Melchizedek."

*A Reading (Lesson) from the Gospel according to
Luke* [10:17–24]

The seventy returned with joy, saying, "Lord, in your
name even the demons submit to us!" He said to them,
"I watched Satan fall from heaven like a flash of lightning.
See, I have given you authority to tread on snakes and
scorpions, and over all the power of the enemy; and
nothing will hurt you. Nevertheless, do not rejoice at this,
that the spirits submit to you, but rejoice that your names
are written in heaven." At that same hour Jesus rejoiced in
the Holy Spirit and said, "I thank you, Father, Lord of
heaven and earth, because you have hidden these things
from the wise and the intelligent and have revealed them
to infants; yes, Father, for such was your gracious will. All

things have been handed over to me by my Father; and no one knows who the Son is except the Father, or who the Father is except the Son and anyone to whom the Son chooses to reveal him." Then turning to the disciples, Jesus said to them privately, "Blessed are the eyes that see what you see! For I tell you that many prophets and kings desired to see what you see, but did not see it, and to hear what you hear, but did not hear it."

Thursday

Psalm 105:1–22 [page 738] ❖ *Psalm 105:23–45* [page 739]

A Reading (Lesson) from the Book of Ezekiel [18:1–4, 19–32]

The word of the LORD came to me: What do you mean by repeating this proverb concerning the land of Israel, "The parents have eaten sour grapes, and the children's teeth are set on edge"? As I live, says the Lord GOD, this proverb shall no more be used by you in Israel. Know that all lives are mine; the life of the parent as well as the life of the child is mine: it is only the person who sins that shall die. Yet you say, "Why should not the son suffer for the iniquity of the father?" When the son has done what is lawful and right, and has been careful to observe all my statutes, he shall surely live. The person who sins shall die. A child shall not suffer for the iniquity of a parent, nor a parent suffer for the iniquity of a child; the righteousness of the righteous shall be his own, and the wickedness of the wicked shall be his own. But if the wicked turn away from all their sins that they have committed and keep all my statutes and do what is lawful and right, they shall surely live; they shall not die. None of the transgressions that they have committed shall be remembered against them; for the righteousness that they have done they shall live. Have I any pleasure in the death of the wicked, says the Lord God, and not rather that they should turn from their ways and live? But when the righteous turn away from their righteousness and commit iniquity and do the same abominable things that the wicked do, shall they live? None of the righteous deeds that they have done shall be remembered; for the treachery of which they are guilty and the sin they have committed, they shall die. Yet you say, "The way of the Lord is unfair." Hear now, O house of Israel: Is my way unfair? Is it not your ways that are unfair? When the righteous turn away from their righteousness and commit iniquity, they shall die for it; for the iniquity that they have committed they shall die. Again, when the wicked turn away from the wickedness they have committed and do what is lawful and right, they shall save their life. Because they considered and turned away from all the transgressions that they had committed, they shall surely live; they shall not die. Yet the house of Israel says, "The way of the Lord is unfair." O house of Israel, are my ways unfair? Is it not your ways that are unfair? Therefore I will judge you, O house of Israel, all of you according to your ways, says the Lord God. Repent and turn from all your transgressions; otherwise iniquity will be your ruin. Cast away from you all the transgressions that you have committed against me, and get yourselves a new heart and a new spirit! Why will you die, O house of Israel? For I have no pleasure in the death of anyone, says the Lord God. Turn, then, and live.

A Reading (Lesson) from the Letter to the Hebrews [7:18–28]

There is, on the one hand, the abrogation of an earlier commandment because it was weak and ineffectual (for the law made nothing perfect); there is, on the other hand, the introduction of a better hope, through which we approach God. This was confirmed with an oath; for others who became priests took their office without an oath, but this one became a priest with an oath, because of the one who said to him, "The Lord has sworn and will not change his mind. 'You are a priest forever' "—accordingly Jesus has also become the guarantee of a better covenant. Furthermore, the former priests were many in number, because they were prevented by death from continuing in office; but he holds his priesthood permanently, because he continues forever. Consequently he is able for all time to save those who approach God through him, since he always lives to make intercession for them. For it was fitting that we should have such a high priest, holy, blameless, undefiled, separated from sinners, and exalted above the heavens. Unlike the other high priests, he has no need to offer sacrifices day after day, first for his own sins, and then for those of the people; this he did once for all when he offered himself. For the law appoints as high priests those who are subject to weakness, but the word of the oath, which came later than the law, appoints a Son who has been made perfect forever.

A Reading (Lesson) from the Gospel according to Luke [10:25–37]

A lawyer stood up to test Jesus. "Teacher," he said, "what must I do to inherit eternal life?" He said to him, "What is written in the law? What do you read there?" He answered, "You shall love the Lord your God with all your heart, and with all your soul, and with all your strength, and with all your mind; and your neighbor as yourself." And he said to him, "You have given the right answer; do this, and you will live." But wanting to justify himself, he asked Jesus, "And who is my neighbor?" Jesus replied, "A man was going down from Jerusalem to Jericho, and fell into the hands of robbers, who stripped him, beat him, and went away, leaving him half dead. Now by chance a priest was going down that road; and when he saw him, he passed by on the other side. So likewise a Levite, when he came to the place and saw him, passed by on the other side. But a Samaritan while traveling came near him; and when he saw him, he was moved with pity. He went to him and bandaged his wounds, having poured oil and wine on them. Then he put him on his own animal, brought him to an inn, and took care of him. The next day he took out two denarii, gave them to the innkeeper, and said, 'Take care of him; and when I come back, I will repay you whatever more you spend.' Which of these three, do you think, was a neighbor to the man who fell into the hands of the robbers?" He said, "The one who showed him mercy." Jesus said to him, "Go and do likewise."

Friday

Psalm 102 [page 731] ❖ *Psalm 107:1–32* [page 746]

A Reading (Lesson) from the Book of Ezekiel [34:17–31]

As for you, my flock, thus says the Lord GOD: I shall judge between sheep and sheep, between rams and goats: Is it not enough for you to feed on the good pasture, but you must tread down with your feet the rest of your pasture? When you drink of clear water, must you foul the rest with your feet? And must my sheep eat what you have trodden with your feet, and drink what you have fouled with your feet?

Therefore, thus says the Lord GOD to them: I myself will judge between the fat sheep and the lean sheep. Because you pushed with flank and shoulder, and butted at all the weak animals with your horns until you scattered them far and wide, I will save my flock, and they shall no longer be ravaged; and I will judge between sheep and sheep. I will set up over them one shepherd, my servant David, and he shall feed them: he shall feed them and be their shepherd. And I, the LORD, will be their God, and my servant David shall be prince among them; I, the LORD, have spoken. I will make with them a covenant of peace and banish wild animals from the land, so that they may live in the wild and sleep in the woods securely. I will make them and the region around my hill a blessing; and I will send down the showers in their season; they shall be showers of blessing. The trees of the field shall yield their fruit, and the earth shall yield its increase. They shall be secure on their soil; and they shall know that I am the LORD, when I break the bars of their yoke, and save them from the hands of those who enslaved them. They shall no more be plunder for the nations, nor shall the animals of the land devour them; they shall live in safety, and no one shall make them afraid. I will provide for them a splendid vegetation so that they shall no more be consumed with hunger in the land, and no longer suffer the insults of the nations. They shall know that I, the LORD their God, am with them, and that they, the house of Israel, are my people, says the Lord GOD. You are my sheep, the sheep of my pasture and I am your God, says the Lord GOD.

A Reading (Lesson) from the Letter to the Hebrews [8:1–13]

Now the main point in what we are saying is this: we have such a high priest, one who is seated at the right hand of the throne of the Majesty in the heavens, a minister in the sanctuary and the true tent that the Lord, and not any mortal, has set up. For every high priest is appointed to offer gifts and sacrifices; hence it is necessary for this priest also to have something to offer. Now if he were on earth, he would not be a priest at all, since there are priests who offer gifts according to the law. They offer worship in a sanctuary that is a sketch and shadow of the heavenly one; for Moses, when he was about to erect the tent, was warned, "See that you make everything according to the pattern that was shown you on the mountain." But Jesus has now obtained a more excellent ministry, and to that degree he is the mediator of a better covenant, which has been enacted through better promises. For if that first covenant had been faultless, there would have been no need to look for a second one. God finds fault with them when he says: "The days are surely coming, says the Lord, when I will establish a new covenant with the house of Israel and with the house of Judah; not like the covenant that I made with their ancestors, on the day when I took them by the hand to lead them out of the land of Egypt; for they did not continue in my covenant, and so I had no concern for them, says the Lord. This is the covenant that I will make with the house of Israel after those days, says the Lord: I will put my laws in their minds, and write them on their hearts, and I will be their God, and they shall be my people. And they shall not teach one another or say to each other, 'Know the Lord,' for they shall all know me, from the least of them to the greatest. For I will be merciful toward their iniquities, and I will remember their sins no more." In speaking of "a new covenant," he has made the first one obsolete. And what is obsolete and growing old will soon disappear.

A Reading (Lesson) from the Gospel according to
Luke [10:38–42]

Now as they went on their way, Jesus entered a certain village, where a woman named Martha welcomed him into her home. She had a sister named Mary, who sat at the Lord's feet and listened to what he was saying. But Martha was distracted by her many tasks; so she came to him and asked, "Lord, do you not care that my sister has left me to do all the work by myself? Tell her then to help me." But the Lord answered her, "Martha, Martha, you are worried and distracted by many things; there is need of only one thing. Mary has chosen the better part, which will not be taken away from her."

Saturday

MORNING PRAYER

Psalm 107:33–43 [page 748],
Psalm 108:1–6(7–13) [page 749]

A Reading (Lesson) from the Book of Ezekiel [43:1–12]

A man, whose appearance was like bronze, brought me to the gate, the gate facing east. And there, the glory of the God of Israel was coming from the east; the sound was like the sound of mighty waters; and the earth shone with his glory. The vision I saw was like the vision that I had seen when he came to destroy the city, and like the vision that I had seen by the river Chebar; and I fell upon my face. As the glory of the LORD entered the temple by the gate facing east, the spirit lifted me up, and brought me into the inner court; and the glory of the LORD filled the temple. While the man was standing beside me, I heard someone speaking to me out of the temple. He said to me: Mortal, this is the place of my throne and the place for the soles of my feet, where I will reside among the people of Israel forever. The house of Israel shall no more defile my holy name, neither they nor their kings, by their whoring, and by the corpses of their kings at their death. When they placed their threshold by my threshold and their doorposts beside my doorposts, with only a wall between me and them, they were defiling my holy name by their abominations that they committed; therefore I have consumed them in my anger. Now let them put away their idolatry and the corpses of their kings far from me, and I will reside among them forever. As for you, mortal, describe the temple to the house of Israel, and let them measure the pattern; and let them be ashamed of their iniquities. When they are ashamed of all that they have done, make known to them the plan of the temple, its arrangement, its exits and its entrances, and its whole form—all its ordinances and its entire plan and all its laws; and write it down in their sight, so that they may observe and follow the entire plan and all its ordinances. This is the law of the temple: the whole territory on the top of the mountain all around shall be most holy. This is the law of the temple.

A Reading (Lesson) from the Letter to the Hebrews [9:1–14]

Now even the first covenant had regulations for worship and an earthly sanctuary. For a tent was constructed, the first one, in which were the lampstand, the table, and the bread of the Presence; this is called the Holy Place. Behind the second curtain was a tent called the Holy of Holies. In it stood the golden altar of incense and the ark of the covenant overlaid on all sides with gold, in which there were a golden urn holding the manna, and Aaron's rod that budded, and the tablets of the covenant; above it were the cherubim of glory overshadowing the mercy seat. Of these things we cannot speak now in detail. Such preparations having been made, the priests go continually into the first tent to carry out their ritual duties; but only the high priest goes into the second, and he but once a year, and not without taking the blood that he offers for himself and for the sins committed unintentionally by the people. By this the Holy Spirit indicates that the way into the sanctuary has not yet been disclosed as long as the first tent is still standing. This is a symbol of the present time, during which gifts and sacrifices are offered that cannot perfect the conscience of the worshiper, but deal only with food and drink and various baptisms, regulations for the body imposed until the time comes to set things right. But when Christ came as a high priest of the good things that have come, then through the greater and perfect tent (not made with hands, that is, not of this creation), he entered once for all into the Holy Place, not with the blood of goats and calves, but with his own blood, thus obtaining eternal redemption. For if the blood of goats and bulls, with the sprinkling of the ashes of a heifer, sanctifies those who have been defiled so that their flesh is purified, how much more will the blood of Christ, who through the eternal Spirit offered himself without blemish to God, purify our conscience from dead works to worship the living God!

A Reading (Lesson) from the Gospel according to Luke [11:14–23]

Jesus was casting out a demon that was mute; when the demon had gone out, the one who had been mute spoke, and the crowds were amazed. But some of them said,

"He casts out demons by Beelzebul, the ruler of the demons." Others, to test him, kept demanding from him a sign from heaven. But he knew what they were thinking and said to them, "Every kingdom divided against itself becomes a desert, and house falls on house. If Satan also is divided against himself, how will his kingdom stand?—for you say that I cast out the demons by Beelzebul. Now if I cast out the demons by Beelzebul, by whom do your exorcists cast them out? Therefore they will be your judges. But if it is by the finger of God that I cast out the demons, then the kingdom of God has come to you. When a strong man, fully armed, guards his castle, his property is safe. But when one stronger than he attacks him and overpowers him, he takes away his armor in which he trusted and divides his plunder. Whoever is not with me is against me, and whoever does not gather with me scatters."

Eve of Pentecost

EVENING PRAYER

Psalm 33 [page 626]

A Reading (Lesson) from the Book of Exodus [19:3–8a, 16–20]

Moses went up to God; the LORD called to him from the mountain, saying, "Thus you shall say to the house of Jacob, and tell the Israelites: You have seen what I did to the Egyptians, and how I bore you on eagles' wings and brought you to myself. Now therefore, if you obey my voice and keep my covenant, you shall be my treasured possession out of all the peoples. Indeed, the whole earth is mine, but you shall be for me a priestly kingdom and a holy nation. These are the words that you shall speak to the Israelites." So Moses came, summoned the elders of the people, and set before them all these words that the LORD had commanded him. The people all answered as one: "Everything that the LORD has spoken we will do." On the morning of the third day there was thunder and lightning, as well as a thick cloud on the mountain, and a blast of a trumpet so loud that all the people who were in the camp trembled. Moses brought the people out of the camp to meet God. They took their stand at the foot of the mountain. Now Mount Sinai was wrapped in smoke, because the LORD had descended upon it in fire; the smoke went up like the smoke of a kiln, while the whole mountain shook violently. As the blast of the trumpet grew louder and louder, Moses would speak and God would answer him in thunder. When the LORD descended upon Mount Sinai, to the top of the mountain, the Lord summoned Moses to the top of the mountain, and Moses went up.

A Reading (Lesson) from the First Letter of Peter [2:4–10]

Come to the Lord, a living stone, though rejected by mortals yet chosen and precious in God's sight, and like living stones, let yourselves be built into a spiritual house, to be a holy priesthood, to offer spiritual sacrifices acceptable to God through Jesus Christ. For it stands in scripture: "See, I am laying in Zion a stone, a cornerstone chosen and precious; and whoever believes in him will not be put to shame." To you then who believe, he is precious; but for those who do not believe, "The stone that the builders rejected has become the very head of the corner," and "A stone that makes them stumble, and a rock that makes them fall." They stumble because they disobey the word, as they were destined to do. But you are a chosen race, a royal priesthood, a holy nation, God's own people in order that you may proclaim the mighty acts of him who called you out of darkness into his marvelous light. Once you were not a people, but now you are God's people; once you had not received mercy, but now you have received mercy.

The Day of Pentecost

Psalm 118 [page 760]   ❖   *Psalm 145* [page 801]

Isaiah 11:1–9 [page 57 above]

A Reading (Lesson) from the First Letter of Paul to the Corinthians [2:1–13]

When I came to you, brothers and sisters, I did not come proclaiming the mystery of God to you in lofty words or wisdom. For I decided to know nothing among you except Jesus Christ, and him crucified. And I came to you in weakness and in fear and in much trembling. My speech and my proclamation were not with plausible words of wisdom, but with a demonstration of the Spirit and of power, so that your faith might rest not on human wisdom but on the power of God. Yet among the mature we do speak wisdom, though it is not a wisdom of this age or of the rulers of this age, who are doomed to perish. But we speak God's wisdom, secret and hidden, which God decreed before the ages for our glory. None of the rulers of this age understood this; for if they had, they would not have crucified the Lord of glory. But, as it is written, "What no eye has seen, nor ear heard, nor the human heart conceived, what God has prepared for those who love him"—these things God has revealed to us through the Spirit; for the Spirit searches everything, even the depths of God. For what human being knows what is truly human except the human spirit that is within? So also no one comprehends what is truly God's except the Spirit of God. Now we have received not the spirit of the world, but the Spirit that is from God, so that we may understand the gifts bestowed on us by God. And we speak of these things in words not taught by human wisdom but taught by the Spirit, interpreting spiritual things to those who are spiritual.

A Reading (Lesson) from the Gospel according to John [14:21–29]

Jesus said to Philip, "They who have my commandments and keep them are those who love me; and those who love me will be loved by my Father, and I will love them and reveal myself to them." Judas (not Iscariot) said to him, "Lord, how is it that you will reveal yourself to us, and not to the world?" Jesus answered him, "Those who love me will keep my word, and my Father will love them, and we will come to them and make our home with them. Whoever does not love me does not keep my words; and the word that you hear is not mine, but is from the Father who sent me. I have said these things to you while I am still with you. But the Advocate, the Holy Spirit, whom the Father will send in my name, will teach you everything, and remind you of all that I have said to you. Peace I leave with you; my peace I give to you. I do not give to you as the world gives. Do not let your hearts be troubled, and do not let them be afraid. You heard me say to you, 'I am going away, and I am coming to you.' If you loved me, you would rejoice that I am going to the Father,

because the Father is greater than I. And now I have told
you this before it occurs, so that when it does occur, you
may believe."

*On the weekdays which follow, the Readings are taken from the
numbered Proper (one through six) which corresponds most closely to
the date of Pentecost.*

Eve of Trinity Sunday

EVENING PRAYER

Psalm 104 [page 735]

*A Reading (Lesson) from the Book of
Ecclesiasticus* [42:15–25]

I will now call to mind the works of the Lord, and will
declare what I have seen. By the word of the Lord his works
are made; and all his creatures do his will. The sun looks
down on everything with its light, and the work of the Lord
is full of his glory. The Lord has not empowered even his
holy ones to recount all his marvelous works, which the
Lord the Almighty has established so that the universe may
stand firm in his glory. He searches out the abyss and the
human heart; he understands their innermost secrets. For
the Most High knows all that may be known; he sees from
of old the things that are to come. He discloses what has
been and what is to be, and he reveals the traces of hidden
things. No thought escapes him, and nothing is hidden from
him. He has set in order the splendors of his wisdom; he is
from all eternity one and the same. Nothing can be added or
taken away, and he needs no one to be his counselor. How
desirable are all his works, and how sparkling they are to

see! All these things live and remain forever; each creature is preserved to meet a particular need. All things come in pairs, one opposite the other, and he has made nothing incomplete. Each supplements the virtues of the other. Who could ever tire of seeing his glory?

Ephesians 3:14–21 [page 138 above]

Trinity Sunday

Psalm 146 [page 803],   *Psalm 147* [page 804]   ❖
Psalm 111 [page 754],   *Psalm 112* [page 755],
Psalm 113 [page 756]

A Reading (Lesson) from the Book of
Ecclesiasticus [43:1–12(27–33)]

The pride of the higher realms is the clear vault of the sky, as glorious to behold as the sight of the heavens. The sun, when it appears, proclaims as it rises what a marvelous instrument it is, the work of the Most High. At noon it parches the land, and who can withstand its burning heat? A man tending a furnace works in burning heat, but three times as hot is the sun scorching the mountains; it breathes out fiery vapors, and its bright rays blind the eyes. Great is the Lord who made it; at his orders it hurries on its course. It is the moon that marks the changing seasons, governing the times, their everlasting signs. From the moon comes the sign for festal days, a light that wanes when it completes its course. The new moon, as its name suggests, renews itself; how marvelous it is in this change, a beacon to the hosts on high, shining in the vault of the heavens! The glory of the stars is the beauty of heaven, a glittering array in the heights of the Lord. On the orders of the Holy One they stand in their appointed places; they never relax in their watches. Look at the rainbow, and praise him who made it; it is exceedingly beautiful in its brightness. It encircles the sky with its glorious arc; the hands of the Most High have stretched it out.

> We could say more but could never say enough; let the final word be: "He is the all." Where can we find the strength to praise him? For he is greater than all his works. Awesome is the Lord and very great, and marvelous is his power. Glorify the Lord and exalt him as much as you can, for he surpasses even that. When you exalt him, summon all your strength, and do not grow weary, for you cannot praise him enough. Who has seen him and can describe him? Or who can extol him as he is? Many things greater than these lie hidden, for I have seen but few of his works. For the Lord has made all things, and to the godly he has given wisdom.

Ephesians 4:1–16 [page 144 above]

John 1:1–18 [page 282 above]

On the weekdays which follow, the Readings are taken from the numbered Proper (two through seven) which corresponds most closely to the date of Trinity Sunday.

The Season after Pentecost

Proper 1 *Week of the Sunday closest to May 11*

Monday

Psalm 106:1–18 [page 741] ❖ *Psalm 106:19–48* [page 743]

A Reading (Lesson) from the Book of Isaiah [63:7–14]

I will recount the gracious deeds of the LORD, the praiseworthy acts of the LORD, because of all that the LORD has done for us, and the great favor to the house of Israel that he has shown them according to his mercy, according to the abundance of his steadfast love. For he said, "Surely they are my people, children who will not deal falsely"; and he became their savior in all their distress. It was no messenger or angel but his presence that saved them; in his love and in his pity he redeemed them; he lifted them up and carried them all the days of old. But they rebelled and grieved his holy spirit; therefore he became their enemy; he himself fought against them. Then they remembered the days of old, of Moses his servant. Where is the one who brought them up out of the sea with the shepherds of his flock? Where is the one who put within them his holy spirit, who caused his glorious arm to march at the right hand of Moses, who divided the waters before them to make for himself an everlasting name, who led them through the depths? Like a horse in the desert, they did not stumble. Like cattle that go down into the valley, the spirit of the LORD gave them rest. Thus you led your people, to make for yourself a glorious name.

A Reading (Lesson) from the Second Letter of Paul to Timothy [1:1–14]

Paul, an apostle of Christ Jesus by the will of God, for the sake of the promise of life that is in Christ Jesus, to Timothy, my beloved child: Grace, mercy, and peace from God the Father and Christ Jesus our Lord. I am grateful to God—whom I worship with a clear conscience, as my ancestors did—when I remember you constantly in my prayers night and day. Recalling your tears, I long to see you so that I may be filled with joy. I am reminded of your sincere faith, a faith that lived first in your grandmother Lois and your mother Eunice and now, I am sure, lives in you. For this reason I remind you to rekindle the gift of God that is within you through the laying on of my hands; for God did not give us a spirit of cowardice, but rather a spirit of power and of love and of self-discipline. Do not be ashamed, then, of the testimony about our Lord or of me his prisoner, but join with me in suffering for the gospel, relying on the power of God, who saved us and called us with a holy calling, not according to our works but according to his own purpose and grace. This grace was given to us in Christ Jesus before the ages began, but it has now been revealed through the appearing of our Savior Christ Jesus, who abolished death and brought life and immortality to light through the gospel. For this gospel I was appointed a herald and an apostle and a teacher, and for this reason I suffer as I do. But I am not ashamed, for I know the one in whom I have put my trust, and I am sure that he is able to guard until that day what I have entrusted to him. Hold to the standard of sound teaching that you have heard from me, in the faith and love that are in Christ Jesus. Guard the good treasure entrusted to you, with the help of the Holy Spirit living in us.

A Reading (Lesson) from the Gospel according to
Luke [11:24–36]

Jesus, knowing their thoughts, said to them, "When the unclean spirit has gone out of a person, it wanders through waterless regions looking for a resting place, but not finding any, it says, 'I will return to my house from which I came.' When it comes, it finds it swept and put in order. Then it goes and brings seven other spirits more evil than itself, and they enter and live there; and the last state of that person is worse than the first." While he was saying this, a woman in the crowd raised her voice and said to him, "Blessed is the womb that bore you and the breasts that nursed you!" But he said, "Blessed rather are those who hear the word of God and obey it!" When the crowds were increasing, he began to say, "This generation is an evil generation; it asks for a sign, but no sign will be given to it except the sign of Jonah. For just as Jonah became a sign to the people of Nineveh, so the Son of Man will be to this generation. The queen of the South will rise at the judgment with the people of this generation and condemn them, because she came from the ends of the earth to listen to the wisdom of Solomon, and see, something greater than Solomon is here! The people of Nineveh will rise up at the judgment with this generation and condemn it, because they repented at the proclamation of Jonah, and see, something greater than Jonah is here! No one after lighting a lamp puts it in a cellar, but on the lampstand so that those who enter may see the light. Your eye is the lamp of your body. If your eye is healthy, your whole body is full of light; but if it is not healthy, your body is full of darkness. Therefore consider whether the light in you is not darkness. If then your whole body is full of light, with no part of it in darkness, it will be as full of light as when a lamp gives you light with its rays."

Tuesday

(Psalm 120 [page 778]),   *Psalm 121* [page 779],
Psalm 122 [page 779],   *Psalm 123* [page 780]   ❖
Psalm 124 [page 781],   *Psalm 125* [page 781],
Psalm 126 [page 782],   *(Psalm 127* [page 782])

A Reading (Lesson) from the Book of Isaiah [63:15—64:9]

Look down from heaven and see, from your holy and glorious habitation. Where are your zeal and your might? The yearning of your heart and your compassion? They are withheld from me. For you are our father, though Abraham does not know us and Israel does not acknowledge us; you, O Lord, are our father; our Redeemer from of old is your name. Why, O Lord, do you make us stray from your ways and harden our heart, so that we do not fear you? Turn back for the sake of your servants, for the sake of the tribes that are your heritage. Your holy people took possession for a little while; but now our adversaries have trampled down your sanctuary. We have long been like those whom you do not rule, like those not called by your name. O that you would tear open the heavens and come down, so that the mountains would quake at your presence—as when fire kindles brushwood and the fire causes water to boil—to make your name known to your adversaries, so that the nations might tremble at your presence! When you did awesome deeds that we did not expect, you came down, the mountains quaked at your presence. From ages past no one has heard, no ear has perceived, no eye has seen any God besides you, who works for those who wait for him. You meet those who gladly do right, those who remember you in your ways. But you were angry, and we sinned; because you hid yourself we transgressed. We have all become like one who is unclean, and all our righteous deeds are like a filthy cloth. We all fade like a leaf, and our iniquities, like the wind, take us away. There is no one who calls on your name, or attempts to take hold of you; for you have hidden your face from us, and have delivered us into the hand of our iniquity. Yet, O LORD, you are our Father; we are the clay, and you are our potter; we are all the work of your hand. Do not be exceedingly angry, O LORD, and do not remember iniquity forever. Now consider, we are all your people.

A Reading (Lesson) from the Second Letter of Paul to Timothy [1:15—2:13]

You are aware that all who are in Asia have turned away from me, including Phygelus and Hermogenes. May the Lord grant mercy to the household of Onesiphorus, because he often refreshed me and was not ashamed of my chain; when he arrived in Rome, he eagerly searched for me and found me—may the Lord grant that he will find mercy from the Lord on that day! And you know very well how much service he rendered in Ephesus. You then, my child, be strong in the grace that is in Christ Jesus; and what you have heard from me through many witnesses entrust to faithful people who will be able to teach others as well. Share in suffering like a good soldier of Christ Jesus. No one serving in the army gets entangled in everyday affairs; the soldier's aim is to please the enlisting officer. And in the case of an athlete, no one is crowned without competing according to the rules. It is the farmer who does the work who ought to have the first share of the crops. Think over what I say, for the Lord will give you understanding in all things. Remember Jesus Christ, raised from the dead, a descendant of David—that is my gospel, for which I suffer hardship, even to the point of being chained like a criminal. But the word of God is not chained. Therefore I endure everything for the sake of the elect, so that they may also obtain the salvation that is in Christ Jesus, with eternal glory. The saying is sure: If we have died with him, we will also live with him; if we endure, we will also reign with him; if we deny him, he will also deny us; if we are faithless, he remains faithful—for he cannot deny himself.

A Reading (Lesson) from the Gospel according to Luke [11:37–52]

While Jesus was speaking, a Pharisee invited him to dine with him; so he went in and took his place at the table. The Pharisee was amazed to see that he did not first wash before dinner. Then the Lord said to him, "Now you Pharisees clean the outside of the cup and of the dish, but inside you are full of greed and wickedness. You fools! Did not the one who made the outside make the inside also? So give for alms those things that are within; and see, everything will be clean for you. But woe to you Pharisees! For you tithe mint and rue and herbs of all kinds, and neglect justice and the love of God; it is these you ought to have practiced, without neglecting the others. Woe to you Pharisees! For you love to have the seat of honor in the synagogues and to be greeted with respect in the marketplaces. Woe to you! For you are like unmarked graves, and people walk over them without realizing it." One of the lawyers answered him, "Teacher, when you say these things, you insult us too." And he said, "Woe also to you lawyers! For you load people with burdens hard to bear, and you yourselves do not lift a finger to ease them. Woe to you! For you build the tombs of the prophets whom your ancestors killed. So you are witnesses and approve of the deeds of your ancestors; for they killed them, and you build their tombs. Therefore also the Wisdom of God said, 'I will send them prophets and apostles, some of whom they will kill and persecute,' so that this generation may be charged with the blood of all the prophets shed since the foundation of the world, from the blood of Abel to the blood of Zechariah, who perished between the altar and the sanctuary. Yes, I tell you, it will be charged against this generation. Woe to you lawyers! For you have taken away the key of knowledge; you did not enter yourselves, and you hindered those who were entering."

Wednesday

Psalm 119:145–176 [page 775] ❖ *Psalm 128* [page 783], *Psalm 129* [page 784], *Psalm 130* [page 784]

A Reading (Lesson) from the Book of Isaiah [65:1–12]

I was ready to be sought out by those who did not ask, to be found by those who did not seek me. I said, "Here I am, here I am," to a nation that did not call on my name. I held out my hands all day long to a rebellious people, who walk in a way that is not good, following their own devices; a people who provoke me to my face continually, sacrificing in gardens and offering incense on bricks; who sit inside tombs, and spend the night in secret places; who eat swine's flesh, with broth of abominable things in their vessels; who say, "Keep to yourself, do not come near me, for I am too holy for you." These are a smoke in my nostrils, a fire that burns all day long. See, it is written before me: I will not keep silent, but I will repay; I will indeed repay into their laps their iniquities and their ancestors' iniquities together, says the LORD; because they offered incense on the mountains and reviled me on the hills, I will measure into their laps full payment for their actions. Thus says the LORD: As the wine is found in the cluster, and they say, "Do not destroy it, for there is a blessing in it," so I will do for my servants' sake, and not destroy them all. I will bring forth descendants from Jacob, and from Judah inheritors of my mountains; my chosen shall inherit it, and my servants shall settle there. Sharon shall become a pasture for flocks, and the Valley of Anchor a place for herds to lie down, for my people who have sought me. But you who forsake the LORD, who forget my holy mountain, who set a table for Fortune and fill cups of mixed wine for Destiny; I will destine you to the sword, and all of you shall bow down to the slaughter; because, when I called, you did not answer, when I spoke, you did not listen, but you did what was evil in my sight, and chose what I did not delight in.

A Reading (Lesson) from the Second Letter of Paul to Timothy [2:14–26]

Remind them of this, and warn them before God that they are to avoid wrangling over words, which does no good but only ruins those who are listening. Do your best to present yourself to God as one approved by him, a worker who has no need to be ashamed, rightly explaining the word of truth. Avoid profane chatter, for it will lead people into more and more impiety, and their talk will spread like gangrene. Among them are Hymenaeus and Philetus, who have swerved from the truth by claiming that the resurrection has already taken place. They are upsetting the faith of some. But God's firm foundation stands, bearing this inscription: "The Lord knows those who are his," and, "Let everyone who calls on the name of the Lord turn away from wickedness." In a large house there are utensils not only of gold and silver but also of wood and clay, some for special use, some for ordinary. All who cleanse themselves of the things I have mentioned will become special utensils, dedicated and useful to the owner of the house, ready for every good work. Shun youthful passions and pursue righteousness, faith, love, and peace, along with those who call on the Lord from a pure heart. Have nothing to do with stupid and senseless controversies; you know that they breed quarrels. And the Lord's servant must not be quarrelsome but kindly to everyone, an apt teacher, patient, correcting opponents with gentleness. God may perhaps grant that they will repent and come to know the truth, and that they may escape from the snare of the devil, having been held captive by him to do his will.

A Reading (Lesson) from the Gospel according to Luke [11:53—12:12]

When Jesus went outside, the scribes and the Pharisees began to be very hostile toward him and to cross-examine him about many things, lying in wait for him, to catch him in something he might say. Meanwhile, when the crowd gathered by the thousands, so that they trampled on one another, he began to speak first to his disciples, "Beware of the yeast of the Pharisees, that is, their hypocrisy. Nothing is covered up that will not be uncovered, and nothing secret that will not become known. Therefore whatever you have said in the dark will be heard in the light, and what you have whispered behind closed doors will be proclaimed from the housetops. I tell you, my friends, do not fear those who kill the body, and after that can do nothing more. But I will warn you whom to fear: fear him who, after he has killed, has authority to cast into hell. Yes, I tell you, fear him! Are not five sparrows sold for two pennies? Yet not one of them is forgotten in God's sight. But even the hairs of your head are all counted. Do not be afraid; you are of more value than many sparrows. And I tell you, everyone who acknowledges me before others, the Son of Man also will acknowledge before the angels of God; but whoever denies me before others will be denied before the angels of God. And everyone who speaks a word against the Son of Man will be forgiven; but whoever blasphemes against the Holy Spirit will not be forgiven. When they bring you before the synagogues, the rulers, and the authorities, do not worry about how you are to defend yourselves or what you are to say; for the Holy Spirit will teach you at that very hour what you ought to say."

Thursday

Psalm 131 [page 785], *Psalm 132* [page 785], *(Psalm 133* [page 787]) ❖ *Psalm 134* [page 787], *Psalm 135* [page 788]

A Reading (Lesson) from the Book of Isaiah [65:17–25]

I am about to create new heavens and a new earth; the former things shall not be remembered or come to mind. But be glad and rejoice forever in what I am creating; for I am about to create Jerusalem as a joy, and its people as a delight. I will rejoice in Jerusalem, and delight in my people; no more shall the sound of weeping be heard in it, or the cry of distress. No more shall there be in it an infant that lives but a few days, or an old person who does not live out a lifetime; for one who dies at a hundred years will be considered a youth, and one who falls short of a hundred will be considered accursed. They shall build houses and inhabit them; they shall plant vineyards and eat their fruit. They shall not build and another inhabit; they shall not plant and another eat; for like the days of a tree shall the days of my people be, and my chosen shall long enjoy the work of their hands. They shall not labor in vain, or bear children for calamity; for they shall be offspring blessed by the LORD—and their descendants as well. Before they call I will answer, while they are yet speaking I will hear. The wolf and the lamb shall feed together, the lion shall eat straw like the ox; but the serpent—its food shall be dust! They shall not hurt or destroy on all my holy mountain, says the LORD.

A Reading (Lesson) from the Second Letter of Paul to Timothy [3:1-17]

You must understand this, that in the last days distressing times will come. For people will be lovers of themselves, lovers of money, boasters, arrogant, abusive, disobedient to their parents, ungrateful, unholy, inhuman, implacable, slanderers, profligates, brutes, haters of good, treacherous, reckless, swollen with conceit, lovers of pleasure rather than lovers of God, holding to the outward form of godliness but denying its power. Avoid them! For among them are those who make their way into households and captivate silly women, overwhelmed by their sins and swayed by all kinds of desires, who are always being instructed and can never arrive at a knowledge of the truth. As Jannes and Jambres opposed Moses, so these people, of corrupt mind and counterfeit faith, also oppose the truth. But they will not make much progress, because, as in the case of those two men, their folly will become plain to everyone. Now you have observed my teaching, my conduct, my aim in life, my faith, my patience, my love, my steadfastness, my persecutions, and my suffering the things that happened to me in Antioch, Iconium, and Lystra. What persecutions I endured! Yet the Lord rescued me from all of them. Indeed, all who want to live a godly life in Christ Jesus will be persecuted. But wicked people and impostors will go from bad to worse, deceiving others and being deceived. But as for you, continue in what you have learned and firmly believed, knowing from whom you learned it, and how from childhood you have known the sacred writings that are able to instruct you for salvation through faith in Christ Jesus. All scripture is inspired by God and is useful for teaching, for reproof, for correction, and for training in righteousness, so that everyone who belongs to God may be proficient, equipped for every good work.

A Reading (Lesson) from the Gospel according to Luke [12:13–31]

Someone in the crowd said to Jesus, "Teacher, tell my brother to divide the family inheritance with me." But he said to him, "Friend, who set me to be a judge or arbitrator over you?" And he said to them, "Take care! Be on your guard against all kinds of greed; for one's life does not consist in the abundance of possessions." Then he told them a parable: "The land of a rich man produced abundantly. And he thought to himself, 'What should I do, for I have no place to store my crops?' Then he said, 'I will do this: I will pull down my barns and build larger ones, and there I will store all my grain and my goods. And I will say to my soul, 'Soul, you have ample goods laid up for many years; relax, eat, drink, be merry.' But

God said to him, 'You fool! This very night your life is being demanded of you. And the things you have prepared, whose will they be?' So it is with those who store up treasures for themselves but are not rich toward God." He said to his disciples, "Therefore I tell you, do not worry about your life, what you will eat, or about your body, what you will wear. For life is more than food, and the body more than clothing. Consider the ravens: they neither sow nor reap, they have neither storehouse nor barn, and yet God feeds them. Of how much more value are you than the birds! And can any of you by worrying add a single hour to your span of life? If then you are not able to do so small a thing as that, why do you worry about the rest? Consider the lilies, how they grow: they neither toil nor spin; yet I tell you, even Solomon in all his glory was not clothed like one of these. But if God so clothes the grass of the field, which is alive today and tomorrow is thrown into the oven, how much more will he clothe you—you of little faith! And do not keep striving for what you are to eat and what you are to drink, and do not keep worrying. For it is the nations of the world that strive after all these things, and your Father knows that you need them. Instead, strive for his kingdom, and these things will be given to you as well."

Friday

Psalm 140 [page 796], *Psalm 142* [page 798] ❖
Psalm 141 [page 797], *Psalm 143:1–11(12)* [page 798]

A Reading (Lesson) from the Book of Isaiah [66:1–6]

Thus says the LORD: Heaven is my throne and the earth is
my footstool; what is the house that you would build for
me, and what is my resting place? All these things my hand
has made, and so all these things are mine, says the LORD.
But this is the one to whom I will look, to the humble and
contrite in spirit, who trembles at my word. Whoever
slaughters an ox is like one who kills a human being;
whoever sacrifices a lamb, like one who breaks a dog's neck;
whoever presents a grain offering, like one who offers
swine's blood; whoever makes a memorial offering of
frankincense, like one who blesses an idol. These have
chosen their own ways, and in their abominations they take
delight; I also will choose to mock them, and bring upon
them what they fear; because, when I called, no one
answered, when I spoke, they did not listen; but they did
what was evil in my sight, and chose what did not please
me. Hear the word of the LORD, you who tremble at his
word: Your own people who hate you and reject you for my
name's sake have said, "Let the LORD be glorified, so that
we may see your joy"; but it is they who shall be put to
shame. Listen, an uproar from the city! A voice from the
temple! The voice of the LORD, dealing retribution to his
enemies!

*A Reading (Lesson) from the Second Letter of Paul to
Timothy* [4:1–8]

In the presence of God and of Christ Jesus, who is to
judge the living and the dead, and in view of his appearing
and his kingdom, I solemnly urge you: proclaim the
message; be persistent whether the time is favorable or
unfavorable; convince, rebuke, and encourage, with the
utmost patience in teaching. For the time is coming when

people will not put up with sound doctrine, but having itching ears, they will accumulate for themselves teachers to suit their own desires, and will turn away from listening to the truth and wander away to myths. As for you, always be sober, endure suffering, do the work of an evangelist, carry out your ministry fully. As for me, I am already being poured out as a libation, and the time of my departure has come. I have fought the good fight, I have finished the race, I have kept the faith. From now on there is reserved for me the crown of righteousness, which the Lord, the righteous judge, will give me on that day, and not only to me but also to all who have loved his appearing.

A Reading (Lesson) from the Gospel according to Luke [12:32–48]

Jesus said to his disciples, "Do not be afraid, little flock, for it is your Father's good pleasure to give you the kingdom. Sell your possessions, and give alms. Make purses for yourselves that do not wear out, an unfailing treasure in heaven, where no thief comes near and no moth destroys. For where your treasure is, there your heart will be also. "Be dressed for action and have your lamps lit; be like those who are waiting for their master to return from the wedding banquet, so that they may open the door for him as soon as he comes and knocks. Blessed are those slaves whom the master finds alert when he comes; truly I tell you, he will fasten his belt and have them sit down to eat, and he will come and serve them. If he comes during the middle of the night, or near dawn, and finds them so, blessed are those slaves. But know this: if the owner of the house had known at what hour the thief was coming, he would not have let his house be broken into. You also must be ready, for the Son of Man is coming at an unexpected hour." Peter said, "Lord, are you telling this parable for us or for everyone?" And the Lord said, "Who then is the faithful and prudent manager whom his master will put in charge of his slaves, to give their allowance of food at the proper time? Blessed is that slave whom his master will find at work when he arrives. Truly I tell you, he will put that one in charge of all his possessions. But if that slave says to himself, 'My master is delayed in coming,' and if he begins to beat the other slaves, men and women, and to eat and drink and get drunk, the master of that slave will come on a day when he does not expect him and at an hour that he does not know, and will cut him in pieces, and put him with the unfaithful. That slave who knew what his master wanted, but did not prepare himself or do what was wanted, will receive a severe beating. But the one who did not know and did what deserved a beating will receive a light beating. From everyone to whom much has been given, much will be required; and from the one to whom much has been entrusted, even more will be demanded."

Saturday

Psalm 137:1–6(7–9) [page 792],
Psalm 144 [page 800]   ❖   *Psalm 104* [page 735]

A Reading (Lesson) from the Book of Isaiah [66:7–14]

Hear the word of the LORD: "Before she was in labor she gave birth; before her pain came upon her she delivered a son. Who has heard of such a thing? Who has seen such things? Shall a land be born in one day? Shall a nation be delivered in one moment? Yet as soon as Zion was in labor she delivered her children. Shall I open the womb and not deliver? says the LORD; shall I, the one who delivers, shut the womb? says your God. Rejoice with Jerusalem, and be glad for her, all you who love her; rejoice with her in joy, all you who mourn over her—that you may nurse and be satisfied from her consoling breast; that you may drink deeply with delight from her glorious bosom. For thus says the LORD: I will extend prosperity to her like a river, and the wealth of the nations like an overflowing stream; and you shall nurse and be carried on her arm, and dandled on her knees. As a mother comforts her child, so I will comfort you; you shall be comforted in Jerusalem. You shall see, and your heart shall rejoice; your bodies shall flourish like the grass; and it shall be known that the hand of the LORD is with his servants, and his indignation is against his enemies.

A Reading (Lesson) from the Second Letter of Paul to Timothy [4:9–22]

Do your best to come to me soon, for Demas, in love with this present world, has deserted me and gone to Thessalonica; Crescens has gone to Galatia, Titus to Dalmatia. Only Luke is with me. Get Mark and bring him with you, for he is useful in my ministry. I have sent Tychicus to Ephesus. When you come, bring the cloak that I left with Carpus at Troas, also the books, and above all the parchments. Alexander the coppersmith did me great harm; the Lord will pay him back for his deeds. You also must beware of him, for he strongly opposed our message. At my first defense no one came to my support, but all deserted me. May it not be counted against them! But the Lord stood by me and gave me strength, so that through me the message might be fully proclaimed and all the Gentiles might hear it. So I was rescued from the lion's mouth. The Lord will rescue me from every evil attack and save me for his heavenly kingdom. To him be the glory forever and ever. Amen. Greet Prisca and Aquila, and the household of Onesiphorus. Erastus remained in Corinth; Trophimus I left ill in Miletus. Do your best to come before winter. Eubulus sends greetings to you, as do Pudens and Linus and Claudia and all the brothers and sisters. The Lord be with your spirit. Grace be with you.

A Reading (Lesson) from the Gospel according to Luke [12:49–59]

Jesus said to his disciples, "I came to bring fire to the earth, and how I wish it were already kindled! I have a baptism with which to be baptized, and what stress I am under until it is completed! Do you think that I have come to bring peace to the earth? No, I tell you, but rather division! From now on five in one household will be divided, three against two and two against three; they will be divided: father against son and son against father, mother against daughter and daughter against mother, mother-in-law against her daughter-in-law and daughter-in-law against mother-in-law." He also said to the crowds, "When you see a cloud rising in the west, you immediately say, 'It is going to rain'; and so it happens. And when you see the south wind blowing, you say, 'There will be scorching heat'; and it happens. You hypocrites! You know how to interpret the appearance of earth and sky, but why do you not know how to interpret the present time? And why do you not judge for yourselves what is right? Thus, when you go with your accuser before a magistrate, on the way make an effort to settle the case, or you may be dragged before the judge, and the judge hand you over to the officer, and the officer throw you in prison. I tell you, you will never get out until you have paid the very last penny."

Proper 2 *Week of the Sunday closest to May 18*

Monday

Psalm 1 [page 585], *Psalm 2* [page 586],
Psalm 3 [page 587] ❖ *Psalm 4* [page 587],
Psalm 7 [page 590]

A Reading (Lesson) from the Book of Ruth [1:1–18]

In the days when the judges ruled, there was a famine in the land, and a certain man of Bethlehem in Judah went to live in the country of Moab, he and his wife and two sons. The name of the man was Elimelech and the name of his wife Naomi, and the names of his two sons were Mahlon and Chilion; they were Ephrathites from Bethlehem in Judah. They went into the country of Moab and remained there. But Elimelech, the husband of Naomi, died, and she was left with her two sons. These took Moabite wives; the name of the one was Orpah and the name of the other Ruth. When they had lived there about ten years, both Mahlon and Chilion also died, so that the woman was left without her two sons and her husband. Then she started to return with her daughters-in-law from the country of Moab, for she had heard in the country of Moab that the LORD had considered his people and given them food. So she set out from the place where she had been living, she and her two daughters-in-law, and they went on their way to go back to the land of Judah. But Naomi said to her two daughters-in-law, "Go back each of you to your mother's house. May the LORD deal kindly with you, as you have dealt with the dead and with me. The LORD grant that you may find security, each of you in the house of your husband." Then she kissed them, and they wept aloud. They said to her, "No, we will return with you to your people." But Naomi said, "Turn back, my daughters, why will you go with me? Do I still have sons in my womb that they may become your husbands? Turn back, my daughters, go your way, for I am too old to have a husband. Even if I thought there was hope for me, even if I should have a husband tonight and bear sons, would you then wait until they were grown? Would you then refrain from marrying? No, my daughters, it has been far more bitter for me than for you, because the hand of the LORD has turned against me." Then they wept aloud again. Orpah kissed her mother-in-law, but Ruth clung to her. So she said, "See, your sister-in-law has gone back to her people and to her gods; return after your sister-in-law." But Ruth said, "Do not press me to leave you or to turn back from following you! Where you go, I will go; where you lodge, I will lodge; your people shall be my people, and your God my God. Where you die, I will die—there will I be buried. May the LORD do thus and so to me, and more as well, if even death parts me from you!" When Naomi saw that she was determined to go with her, she said no more to her.

A Reading (Lesson) from the First Letter of Paul to Timothy [1:1–17]

Paul, an apostle of Christ Jesus by the command of God our Savior and of Christ Jesus our hope, to Timothy, my loyal child in the faith: Grace, mercy, and peace from God the Father and Christ Jesus our Lord. I urge you, as I did when I was on my way to Macedonia, to remain in Ephesus so that you may instruct certain people not to teach any different doctrine, and not to occupy themselves with myths and endless genealogies that promote speculations rather than the divine training that is known by faith. But the aim of such instruction is love that comes from a pure heart, a good conscience, and sincere faith. Some people have deviated from these and turned to meaningless talk, desiring to be teachers of the law, without understanding either what they are saying or the things about which they make assertions. Now we know that the law is good, if one uses it legitimately. This means understanding that the law is laid down not for the innocent but for the lawless and disobedient, for the godless and sinful, for the unholy and profane, for those who kill their father or mother, for murderers, fornicators, sodomites, slave traders, liars, perjurers, and whatever else is contrary to the sound teaching that conforms to the glorious gospel of the blessed God, which he entrusted to me. I am grateful to Christ Jesus our Lord, who has strengthened me, because he judged me faithful and appointed me to his service, even though I was formerly a blasphemer, a persecutor, and a man of violence. But I received mercy because I had acted ignorantly in unbelief, and the grace of our Lord overflowed for me with the faith and love that are in Christ Jesus. The saying is sure and worthy of full acceptance, that Christ Jesus came into the world to save sinners—of whom I am the foremost. But for that very reason I received mercy, so that in me, as the foremost, Jesus Christ might display the utmost patience, making me an example to those who would come to believe in him for eternal life. To the King of the ages, immortal, invisible, the only God, be honor and glory forever and ever. Amen.

A Reading (Lesson) from the Gospel according to Luke [13:1–9]

At that very time there were some present who told him about the Galileans whose blood Pilate had mingled with their sacrifices. He asked them, "Do you think that because these Galileans suffered in this way they were worse sinners than all other Galileans? No, I tell you; but unless you repent, you will all perish as they did. Or those eighteen who were killed when the tower of Siloam fell on them—do you think that they were worse offenders than all the others living in Jerusalem? No, I tell you; but unless you repent, you will all perish just as they did." Then he told this parable: "A man had a fig tree planted in his vineyard; and he came looking for fruit on it and found none. So he said to the gardener, 'See here! For three years I have come looking for fruit on this fig tree, and still I find none. Cut it down! Why should it be wasting the soil?' He replied, 'Sir, let it alone for one more year, until I dig around it and put manure on it. If it bears fruit next year, well and good; but if not, you can cut it down.' "

Tuesday

Psalm 5 [page 588],   *Psalm 6* [page 589] ❖
Psalm 10 [page 594],   *Psalm 11* [page 596]

A Reading (Lesson) from the Book of Ruth [1:19—2:13]

Naomi and Ruth went on until they came to Bethlehem. When they came to Bethlehem, the whole town was stirred because of them; and the women said, "Is this Naomi?" She said to them, "Call me no longer Naomi, call me Mara, for the Almighty has dealt bitterly with me. I went away full, but the LORD has brought me back empty; why call me Naomi when the LORD has dealt harshly with me, and the Almighty has brought calamity upon me?" So Naomi returned together with Ruth the Moabite, her daughter-in-law, who came back with her from the country of Moab. They came to Bethlehem at the beginning of the barley harvest. Now Naomi had a kinsman on her husband's side, a prominent rich man, of the family of Elimelech, whose name was Boaz. And Ruth the Moabite said to Naomi, "Let me go to the field and glean among the ears of grain, behind someone in whose sight I may find favor." She said to her, "Go, my daughter." So she went. She came and gleaned in the field behind the reapers. As it happened, she came to the part of the field belonging to Boaz, who was of the family of Elimelech. Just then Boaz came from Bethlehem. He said to the reapers, "The LORD be with you." They answered, "The LORD bless you." then Boaz said to his servant who was in charge of the reapers, "To whom does this young woman belong?" The servant who was in charge of the reapers answered, "She is the Moabite who came back with Naomi from the country of Moab. She said, 'Please, let me glean and gather among the sheaves behind the reapers.' So she came, and she has been on her feet from early this morning until now, without resting even for a moment." Then Boaz said to Ruth, "Now listen, my daughter, do not go to glean in another field or leave this one, but keep close to my young women. Keep your eyes on the field that is being reaped, and follow behind them. I have ordered the young men not to bother you. If you get thirsty, go to the vessels and drink from what the young men have drawn." Then she fell prostrate, with her face to the ground, and said to him, "Why have I found favor in your sight, that you should take notice of me, when I am a foreigner?" But Boaz answered her, "All that you have done for your mother-in-law since the death of your husband has been fully told me, and how you left your father and mother and your native land and came to a people that you did not know before. May the LORD reward you for your deeds, and may you have a full reward from the LORD, the God of Israel, under whose wings you have come for refuge!" Then she said, "May I continue to find favor in your sight, my lord, for you have comforted me and spoken kindly to your servant, even though I am not one of your servants."

A Reading (Lesson) from the First Letter of Paul to Timothy [1:18—2:8]

I am giving you these instructions, Timothy, my child, in accordance with the prophecies made earlier about you, so that by following them you may fight the good fight, having faith and a good conscience. By rejecting conscience, certain persons have suffered shipwreck in the faith; among them are Hymenaeus and Alexander, whom I have turned over to Satan, so that they may learn not to blaspheme. First of all, then, I urge that supplications, prayers, intercessions, and thanksgivings be made for everyone, for kings and all who are in high positions, so that we may lead a quiet and peaceable life in all godliness and dignity. This is right and is acceptable in the sight of God our Savior, who desires everyone to be saved and to come to the knowledge of the truth. For there is one God; there is also one mediator between God and humankind, Christ Jesus, himself human, who gave himself a ransom for all—this was attested at the right time. For this I was appointed a herald and an apostle (I am telling the truth, I am not lying), a teacher of the Gentiles in faith and truth. I desire, then, that in every place the men should pray, lifting up holy hands without anger or argument.

A Reading (Lesson) from the Gospel according to Luke
[13:10–17]

Jesus was teaching in one of the synagogues on the
sabbath. And just then there appeared a woman with a
spirit that had crippled her for eighteen years. She was
bent over and was quite unable to stand up straight. When
Jesus saw her, he called her over and said, "Woman, you
are set free from your ailment." When he laid his hands
on her, immediately she stood up straight and began
praising God. But the leader of the synagogue, indignant
because Jesus had cured on the sabbath, kept saying to the
crowd, "There are six days on which work ought to be
done; come on those days, and be cured, and not on the
sabbath day." But the Lord answered him and said, "You
hypocrites! Does not each of you on the sabbath untie his
ox or his donkey from the manger, and lead it away to
give it water? And ought not this woman, a daughter of
Abraham whom Satan bound for eighteen long years, be
set free from this bondage on the sabbath day?" When he
said this, all his opponents were put to shame; and the
entire crowd was rejoicing at all the wonderful things that
he was doing.

Wednesday

Psalm 119:1–24 [page 763]   ❖   *Psalm 12* [page 597],
Psalm 13 [page 597],   *Psalm 14* [page 598]

A Reading (Lesson) from the Book of Ruth [2:14–23]

At mealtime Boaz said to Ruth, "Come here, and eat some
of this bread, and dip your morsel in the sour wine." So she
sat beside the reapers, and he heaped up for her some
parched grain. She ate until she was satisfied, and she had

some left over. When she got up to glean, Boaz instructed his young men, "Let her glean even among the standing sheaves, and do not reproach her. You must also pull out some handfuls for her from the bundles, and leave them for her to glean, and do not rebuke her." So she gleaned in the field until evening. Then she beat out what she had gleaned, and it was about an ephah of barley. She picked it up and came into the town, and her mother-in-law saw how much she had gleaned. Then she took out and gave her what was left over after she herself had been satisfied. Her mother-in-law said to her, "Where did you glean today? And where have you worked? Blessed be the man who took notice of you." So she told her mother-in-law with whom she had worked, and said, "The name of the man with whom I worked today is Boaz." Then Naomi said to her daughter-in-law, "Blessed be he by the LORD, whose kindness has not forsaken the living or the dead!" Naomi also said to her, "The name is a relative of ours, one of our nearest kin." Then Ruth the Moabite said, "He even said to me, 'Stay close by my servants, until they have finished all my harvest.'" Naomi said to Ruth, her daughter-in-law, "It is better, my daughter, that you go out with his young women, otherwise you might be bothered in another field." So she stayed close to the young women of Boaz, gleaning until the end of the barley and wheat harvests; and she lived with her mother-in-law.

A Reading (Lesson) from the First Letter of Paul to Timothy [3:1–16]

The saying is sure: whoever aspires to the office of bishop desires a noble task. Now a bishop must be above reproach, married only once, temperate, sensible, respectable, hospitable, an apt teacher, not a drunkard, not violent but gentle, not quarrelsome, and not a lover of money. He must manage his own household well, keeping his children submissive and respectful in every way—for if someone does not know how to manage his own household, how can he take care of God's church? He must not be a recent convert, or he may be puffed up with conceit and fall into the condemnation of the devil. Moreover, he must be well thought of by outsiders, so that he may not fall into disgrace and the snare of the devil. Deacons likewise must be serious, not double-tongued, not indulging in much wine, not greedy for money; they must hold fast to the mystery of the faith with a clear conscience. And let them first be tested; then, if they prove themselves blameless, let them serve as deacons. Women likewise must be serious, not slanderers, but temperate, faithful in all things. Let deacons be married only once, and let them manage their children and their households well; for those who serve well as deacons gain a good standing for themselves and great boldness in the faith that is in Christ Jesus. I hope to come to you soon, but I am writing these instructions to you so that, if I am delayed, you may know how one ought to behave in the household of God, which is the church of the living God, the pillar and bulwark of the truth. Without any doubt, the mystery of our religion is great: He was revealed in flesh, vindicated in spirit, seen by angels, proclaimed among Gentiles, believed in throughout the world, taken up in glory.

A Reading (Lesson) from the Gospel according to Luke [13:18–30]

Jesus said, "What is the kingdom of God like? And to what should I compare it? It is like a mustard seed that someone took and sowed in the garden; it grew and became a tree, and the birds of the air made nests in its branches." And again he said, "To what should I compare the kingdom of God? It is like yeast that a woman took and mixed in with three measures of flour until all of it was leavened." Jesus went through one town and village after another, teaching as he made his way to Jerusalem. Someone asked him, "Lord, will only a few be saved?" He said to them, "Strive to enter through the narrow door; for many, I tell you, will try to enter and will not be able. When once the owner of the house has got up and shut the door, and you begin to stand outside and to knock at the door, saying, 'Lord, open to us,' then in reply he will say to you, 'I do not know where you come from.' Then you will begin to say, 'We ate and drank with you, and you taught in our streets.' But he will say, 'I do not know where you come from; go away from me, all you evildoers!' There will be weeping and gnashing of teeth when you see Abraham and Isaac and Jacob and all the prophets in the kingdom of God, and you yourselves thrown out. Then people will come from east and west, from north and south, and will eat in the kingdom of God. Indeed, some are last who will be first, and some are first who will be last."

Thursday

Psalm 18:1–20 [page 602] ❖ *Psalm 18:21–50* [page 604]

A Reading (Lesson) from the Book of Ruth [3:1–18]

Naomi her mother-in-law said to Ruth "My daughter, I need to seek some security for you, so that it may be well with you. Now here is our kinsman Boaz, with whose young women you have been working. See, he is winnowing barley tonight at the threshing floor. Now wash and anoint yourself, and put on your best clothes and go down to the threshing floor; but do not make yourself known to the man until he has finished eating and drinking. When he lies down, observe the place where he lies; then, go and uncover his feet and lie down; and he will tell you what to do." She said to her, "All that you tell me I will do." So she went down to the threshing floor and did just as her mother-in-law had instructed her. When Boaz had eaten and drunk, and he was in a contented mood, he went to lie down at the end of the heap of grain. Then she came stealthily and uncovered his feet, and lay down. At midnight the man was startled, and turned over, and there, lying at his feet, was a woman! He said, "Who are you?" And she answered, "I am Ruth, your servant; spread your cloak over your servant, for you are next-of-kin." He said, "May you be blessed by the LORD, my daughter; this last instance of your loyalty is better than the first; you have not gone after young men, whether poor or rich. And now, my daughter, do not be afraid, I will do for you all that you ask, for all the assembly of my people know that you are a worthy woman. But now, though it is true that I am a near kinsman, there is another kinsman more closely related than I. Remain this night, and in the morning, if he will act as next-of-kin for you, good; let him do it. If he is not willing to act as next-of-kin for you, then, as the LORD lives, I will act as next-of-kin for you. Lie down until the morning." So she lay at his feet until morning, but got up before one person could recognize another; for he said, "It must not be known that the woman came to the threshing floor." Then he said, "Bring the cloak you are wearing and hold it out." So she held it, and he measured out six measures of barley, and put it on her back; then he went into the city. She came to her mother-in-law, who said, "How did things go with you, my daughter?" Then she told her all that the man had done for her, saying, "He gave me these six measures of barley, for he said, 'Do not go back to your mother-in-law empty-handed.' " She replied, "Wait, my daughter, until you learn how the matter turns out, for the man will not rest, but will settle the matter today."

A Reading (Lesson) from the First Letter of Paul to Timothy [4:1–16]

Now the Spirit expressly says that in later times some will renounce the faith by paying attention to deceitful spirits and teachings of demons, through the hypocrisy of liars whose consciences are seared with a hot iron. They forbid marriage and demand abstinence from foods, which God created to be received with thanksgiving by those who believe and know the truth. For everything created by God is good, and nothing is to be rejected, provided it is received with thanksgiving; for it is sanctified by God's word and by prayer. If you put these instructions before the brothers and sisters, you will be a good servant of Christ Jesus, nourished on the words of the faith and of the sound teaching that you have followed. Have nothing to do with profane myths and old wives' tales. Train yourself in godliness, for, while physical training is of some value, godliness is valuable in every way, holding promise for both the present life and the life to come. The saying is sure and worthy of full acceptance. For to this end we toil and struggle, because we have our hope set on the living God, who is the Savior of all people, especially of those who believe. These are the things you must insist on and teach. Let no one despise your youth, but set the believers an example in speech and conduct, in love, in faith, in purity. Until I arrive, give attention to the public reading of scripture, to exhorting, to teaching. Do not neglect the gift that is in you, which was given to you through prophecy with the laying on of hands by the council of elders. Put these things into practice, devote yourself to them, so that all may see your progress. Pay close attention to yourself and to your teaching; continue in these things, for in doing this you will save both yourself and your hearers.

A Reading (Lesson) from the Gospel according to Luke [13:31–35]

At that very hour some Pharisees came and said to Jesus, "Get away from here, for Herod wants to kill you." He said to them, "Go and tell that fox for me, 'Listen, I am casting out demons and performing cures today and tomorrow, and on the third day I finish my work. Yet today, tomorrow, and the next day I must be on my way, because it is impossible for a prophet to be killed outside of Jerusalem.' Jerusalem, Jerusalem, the city that kills the prophets and stones those who are sent to it! How often have I desired to gather your children together as a hen gathers her brood under her wings, and you were not willing! See, your house is left to you. And I tell you, you will not see me until the time comes when you say, 'Blessed is the one who comes in the name of the Lord.' "

Friday

Psalm 16 [page 599],
Psalm 17 [page 600] ❖ *Psalm 22* [page 610]

A Reading (Lesson) from the Book of Ruth [4:1–17]

No sooner had Boaz gone up to the gate and sat down there
than the next-of-kin, of whom Boaz had spoken, came
passing by. So Boaz said, "Come over, friend; sit down
here." And he went over and sat down. Then Boaz took ten
men of the elders of the city, and said, "Sit down here"; so
they sat down. He then said to the next-of-kin, "Naomi,
who has come back from the country of Moab, is selling the
parcel of land that belonged to our kinsman Elimelech. So I
thought I would tell you of it, and say: Buy it in the presence
of those sitting here, and in the presence of the elders of my
people. If you will redeem it, redeem it; but if you will not,
tell me, so that I may know; for there is no one prior to you
to redeem it, and I come after you." So he said, "I will
redeem it." Then Boaz said, "The day you acquire the field
from the hand of Naomi, you are also acquiring Ruth the
Moabite, the widow of the dead man, to maintain the dead
man's name on his inheritance." At this, the next-of-kin
said, "I cannot redeem it for myself without damaging my
own inheritance. Take my right of redemption yourself, for
I cannot redeem it." Now this was the custom in former
times in Israel concerning redeeming and exchanging: to
confirm a transaction, the one took off a sandal and gave it
to the other; this was the manner of attesting in Israel. So
when the next-of-kin said to Boaz, "Acquire it for yourself,"
he took off his sandal. Then Boaz said to the elders and all
the people, "Today you are witnesses that I have acquired
from the hand of Naomi all that belonged to Elimelech and
all that belonged to Chilion and Mahlon. I have also
acquired Ruth the Moabite, the wife of Mahlon, to be my
wife, to maintain the dead man's name on his inheritance, in
order that the name of the dead may not be cut off from his
kindred and from the gate of his native place; today you are

witnesses." Then all the people who were at the gate, along with the elders, said, "We are witnesses. May the LORD make the woman who is coming into your house like Rachel and Leah, who together built up the house of Israel. May you produce children in Ephrathah and bestow a name in Bethlehem; and, through the children that the LORD will give you by this young woman, may your house be like the house of Perez, whom Tamar bore to Judah." So Boaz took Ruth and she became his wife. When they came together, the LORD made her conceive, and she bore a son. Then the women said to Naomi, "Blessed be the LORD, who has not left you this day without next-of-kin; and may his name be renowned in Israel! He shall be to you a restorer of life and a nourisher of your old age; for your daughter-in-law who loves you, who is more to you than seven sons, has borne him." Then Naomi took the child and laid him in her bosom, and became his nurse. The women of the neighborhood gave him a name, saying, "A son has been born to Naomi." They named him Obed; he became the father of Jesse, the father of David.

A Reading (Lesson) from the First Letter of Paul to Timothy [5:17–22 (23–25)]

Let the elders who rule well be considered worthy of double honor, especially those who labor in preaching and teaching; for the scripture says, "You shall not muzzle an ox while it is treading out the grain," and, "The laborer deserves to be paid." Never accept any accusation against an elder except on the evidence of two or three witnesses. As for those who persist in sin, rebuke them in the presence of all, so that the rest also may stand in fear. In the presence of God and of Christ Jesus and of the elect angels, I warn you to keep these instructions without prejudice, doing nothing on the basis of partiality. Do not ordain anyone hastily, and do not participate in the sins of others; keep yourself pure.

> No longer drink only water, but take a little wine for the sake of your stomach and your frequent ailments. The sins of some people are conspicuous and precede them to judgment, while the sins of others follow them there. So also good works are conspicuous; and even when they are not, they cannot remain hidden.

A Reading (Lesson) from the Gospel according to Luke [14:1–11]

On one occasion when Jesus was going to the house of a leader of the Pharisees to eat a meal on the sabbath, they were watching him closely. Just then, in front of him, there was a man who had dropsy. And Jesus asked the lawyers and Pharisees, "Is it lawful to cure people on the sabbath, or not?" But they were silent. So Jesus took him and healed him, and sent him away. Then he said to them, "If one of you has a child or an ox that has fallen into a well, will you not immediately pull it out on a sabbath day?" And they could not reply to this. When he noticed how the guests chose the places of honor, he told them a parable. "When you are invited by someone to a wedding banquet, do not sit down at the place of honor, in case someone more distinguished than you has been invited by your host; and the host who invited both of you may come and say to you, 'Give this person your place,' and then in disgrace you would start to take the lowest place. But when you are invited, go and sit down at the lowest place, so that when your host comes, he may say to you, 'Friend, move up higher'; then you will be honored in the presence of all who sit at the table with you. For all who exalt themselves will be humbled, and those who humble themselves will be exalted."

Saturday

Psalm 20 [page 608], *Psalm 21:1–7(8–14)* [page 608] ❖
Psalm 110:1–5(6–7) [page 753], *Psalm 116* [page 759],
Psalm 117 [page 760]

A Reading (Lesson) from the Book of Deuteronomy [1:1–8]

These are the words that Moses spoke to all Israel beyond the Jordan—in the wilderness, on the plain opposite Suph, between Paran and Tophel, Laban, Hazeroth, and Di-zahab. (By the way of Mount Seir it takes eleven days to reach Kadesh-barnea from Horeb.) In the fortieth year, on the first day of the eleventh month, Moses spoke to the Israelites just as the LORD had commanded him to speak to them. This was after he had defeated King Sihon of the Amorites, who reigned in Heshbon, and King Og of Bashan, who reigned in Ashtaroth and in Edrei. Beyond the Jordan in the land of Moab, Moses undertook to expound this law as follows: The LORD our God spoke to us at Horeb, saying, "You have stayed long enough at this mountain. Resume your journey, and go into the hill country of the Amorites as well as into the neighboring regions—the Arabah, the hill country, the Shephelah, the Negeb, and the seacoast—the land of the Canaanites and the Lebanon, as far as the great river, the river Euphrates. See, I have set the land before you; go in and take possession of the land that I swore to your ancestors, to Abraham, to Isaac, and to Jacob, to give to them and to their descendants after them."

A Reading (Lesson) from the First Letter of Paul to Timothy [6:6–21]

There is great gain in godliness combined with contentment; for we brought nothing into the world, so that we can take nothing out of it; but if we have food and clothing, we will be content with these. But those who want to be rich fall into temptation and are trapped by many senseless and harmful desires that plunge people into ruin and destruction. For the love of money is a root of all kinds of evil, and in their eagerness to be rich some have wandered away from the faith and pierced themselves with many pains. But as for you, man of God, shun all this; pursue righteousness, godliness, faith, love, endurance, gentleness. Fight the good fight of the faith; take hold of the eternal life, to which you were called and for which you made the good confession in the presence of many witnesses. In the presence of God, who gives life to all things, and of Christ Jesus, who in his testimony before Pontius Pilate made the good confession, I charge you to keep the commandment without spot or blame until the manifestation of our Lord Jesus Christ, which he will bring about at the right time—he who is the blessed and only Sovereign, the King of kings and Lord of lords. It is he alone who has immortality and dwells in unapproachable light, whom no one has ever seen or can see; to him be honor and eternal dominion. Amen. As for those who in the present age are rich, command them not to be haughty, or to set their hopes on the uncertainty of riches, but rather on God who richly provides us with everything for our enjoyment. They are to do good, to be rich in good works, generous, and ready to share, thus storing up for themselves the treasure of a good foundation for the future, so that they may take hold of the life that really is life. Timothy, guard what has been entrusted to you. Avoid the profane chatter and contradictions of what is falsely called knowledge; by professing it some have missed the mark as regards the faith. Grace be with you.

A Reading (Lesson) from the Gospel according to Luke [14:12–24]

Jesus said also to the man who had invited him, "When you give a luncheon or a dinner, do not invite your friends or your brothers or your relatives or rich neighbors, in case they may invite you in return, and you would be repaid. But when you give a banquet, invite the poor, the crippled, the lame, and the blind. And you will be blessed, because they cannot repay you, for you will be repaid at the resurrection of the righteous." One of the dinner guests, on hearing this, said to him, "Blessed is the one who will eat bread in the kingdom of God!" Then Jesus said to him, "Someone gave a great dinner and invited many. At the time for the dinner he sent his slave to say to those who had been invited, 'Come: for everything is ready now.' But they all alike began to make excuses. The first said to him, 'I have bought a piece of land, and I must go out and see it; please accept my regrets.' Another said, 'I have bought five yoke of oxen, and I am going to try them out; please accept my regrets.' Another said, 'I have just been married, and therefore I cannot come.' So the slave returned and reported this to his master. Then the owner of the house became angry and said to his slave, 'Go out at once into the streets and lanes of the town and bring in the poor, the crippled, the blind, and the lame.' And the slave said, 'Sir, what you ordered has been done, and there is still room.' Then the master said to the slave, 'Go out into the roads and lanes, and compel people to come in, so that my house may be filled. For I tell you, none of those who were invited will taste my dinner.' "

Proper 3   *Week of the Sunday closest to May 25*

Sunday

Psalm 148 [page 805],   *Psalm 149* [page 807],
Psalm 150 [page 807]   ❖   *Psalm 114* [page 756],
Psalm 115 [page 757]

A Reading (Lesson) from the Book of Deuteronomy [4:1–9]

Moses undertook to explain the law, saying, "So now, Israel, give heed to the statutes and ordinances that I am teaching you to observe, so that you may live to enter and occupy the land that the LORD, the God of your ancestors, is giving you. You must neither add anything to what I command you nor take away anything from it, but keep the commandments of the LORD your God with which I am charging you. You have seen for yourselves what the LORD did with regard to the Baal of Peor—how the LORD your God destroyed from among you everyone who followed the Baal of Peor, while those of you who held fast to the LORD your God are all alive today. See, just as the LORD my God has charged me, I now teach you statues and ordinances for you to observe in the land that you are about to enter and occupy. You must observe them diligently, for this will show your wisdom and discernment to the peoples, who, when they hear all these statutes, will say, "Surely this great nation is a wise and discerning people!" For what other great nation has a god so near to it as the LORD our God is whenever we call to him? And what other great nation has statutes and ordinances as just as this entire law that I am setting before you today? But take care and watch yourselves closely, so as neither to forget the things that your eyes have seen nor to let them slip from your mind all the days of your life; make them known to your children and your children's children."

A Reading (Lesson) from the Revelation to John
[7:1–4, 9–17]

After this I saw four angels standing at the four corners of the earth, holding back the four winds of the earth so that no wind could blow on earth or sea or against any tree. I saw another angel ascending from the rising of the sun, having the seal of the living God, and he called with a loud voice to the four angels who had been given power to damage earth and sea, saying, "Do not damage the earth or the sea or the trees, until we have marked the servants of our God with a seal on their foreheads." And I heard the number of those who were sealed, one hundred forty-four thousand, sealed out of every tribe of the people of Israel. After this I looked, and there was a great multitude that no one could count, from every nation, from all tribes and peoples and languages, standing before the throne and before the Lamb, robed in white, with palm branches in their hands. They cried out in a loud voice, saying, "Salvation belongs to our God who is seated on the throne, and to the Lamb!" And all the angels stood around the throne and around the elders and the four living creatures, and they fell on their faces before the throne and worshiped God, singing, "Amen! Blessing and glory and wisdom and thanksgiving and honor and power and might be to our God forever and ever! Amen." Then one of the elders addressed me, saying, "Who are these, robed in white, and where have they come from?" I said to him, "Sir, you are the one that knows." Then he said to me, "These are they who have come out of the great ordeal; they have washed their robes and made them white in the blood of the Lamb. For this reason they are before the throne of God, and worship him day and night within his temple, and the one who is seated on the throne will shelter them. They will hunger no more, and thirst no more; the sun will not strike them, nor any scorching heat; for the Lamb at the center of the throne will be their shepherd, and he will guide them to springs of the water of life, and God will wipe away every tear from their eyes."

A Reading (Lesson) from the Gospel according to Matthew [12:33–45]

After healing the blind and dumb demoniac, Jesus said to the people, "Either make the tree good, and its fruit good; or make the tree bad, and its fruit bad; for the tree is known by its fruit. You brood of vipers! How can you speak good things, when you are evil? For out of the abundance of the heart the mouth speaks. The good person brings good things out of a good treasure, and the evil person brings evil things out of an evil treasure. I tell you, on the day of judgment you will have to give an account for every careless word you utter; for by your words you will be justified, and by your words you will be condemned." Then some of the scribes and Pharisees said to him, "Teacher, we wish to see a sign from you." But he answered them, "An evil and adulterous generation asks for a sign, but no sign will be given to it except the sign of the prophet Jonah. For just as Jonah was three days and three nights in the belly of the sea monster, so for three days and three nights the Son of Man will be in the heart of the earth. The people of Nineveh will rise up at the judgment with this generation and condemn it, because they repented at the proclamation of Jonah, and see, something greater than Jonah is here! The queen of the South will rise up at the judgment with this generation and condemn it, because she came from the ends of the earth to listen to the wisdom of Solomon, and see, something greater than Solomon is here! When the unclean spirit has gone out of a person, it wanders through waterless regions looking for a resting place, but it finds none. Then it says, 'I will return to my house from which I came.' When it comes, it finds it empty, swept, and put in order. Then it goes and brings along seven other spirits more evil than itself, and they enter and live there; and the last state of that person is worse than the first. So will it be also with this evil generation."

Monday

Psalm 25 [page 614] ❖ *Psalm 9* [page 593],
Psalm 15 [page 599]

A Reading (Lesson) from the Book of Deuteronomy [4:9–14]

Moses undertook to explain the law, saying, "Only take care and watch yourselves closely, so as neither to forget the things that your eyes have seen nor to let them slip from your mind all the days of your life; make them known to your children and your children's children—how you once stood before the LORD your God at Horeb, when the LORD said to me, 'Assemble the people for me, and I will let them hear my words, so that they may learn to fear me as long as they live on the earth, and may teach their children so'; you approached and stood at the foot of the mountain while the mountain was blazing up to the very heavens, shrouded in dark clouds. Then the LORD spoke to you out of the fire. You heard the sound of words but saw no form; there was only a voice. He declared to you his covenant, which he charged you to observe, that is, the ten commandments; and he wrote them on two stone tablets. And the LORD charged me at that time to teach you statutes and ordinances for you to observe in the land that you are about to cross into and occupy."

A Reading (Lesson) from the Second Letter of Paul to the Corinthians [1:1–11]

Paul, an apostle of Christ Jesus by the will of God, and Timothy our brother, to the church of God that is in Corinth, including all the saints throughout Achaia: Grace to you and peace from God our Father and the Lord Jesus Christ. Blessed be the God and Father of our Lord Jesus Christ, the Father of mercies and the God of all consolation, who consoles us in all our affliction, so that we may be able to console those who are in any affliction with the consolation with which we ourselves are consoled by God. For just as the sufferings of Christ are abundant for us, so also our consolation is abundant through Christ. If we are being afflicted, it is for your consolation and salvation; if we are being consoled, it is for your consolation, which you experience when you patiently endure the same sufferings that we are also suffering. Our hope for you is unshaken; for we know that as you share in our sufferings, so also you share in our consolation. We do not want you to be unaware, brothers and sisters, of the affliction we experienced in Asia; for we were so utterly, unbearably crushed that we despaired of life itself. Indeed, we felt that we had received the sentence of death so that we would rely not on ourselves but on God who raises the dead. He who rescued us from so deadly a peril will continue to rescue us; on him we have set our hope that he will rescue us again, as you also join in helping us by your prayers, so that many will give thanks on our behalf for the blessing granted us through the prayers of many.

A Reading (Lesson) from the Gospel according to Luke
[14:25–35]

Now large crowds were traveling with Jesus; and he turned and said to them, "Whoever comes to me and does not hate father and mother, wife and children, brothers and sisters, yes, and even life itself, cannot be my disciple. Whoever does not carry the cross and follow me cannot be my disciple. For which of you, intending to build a tower, does not first sit down and estimate the cost, to see whether he has enough to complete it? Otherwise, when he has laid a foundation and is not able to finish, all who see it will begin to ridicule him, saying, 'This fellow began to build and was not able to finish.' Or what king, going out to wage war against another king, will not sit down first and consider whether he is able with ten thousand to oppose the one who comes against him with twenty thousand? If he cannot, then, while the other is still far away, he sends a delegation and asks for the terms of peace. So therefore, none of you can become my disciple if you do not give up all your possessions. Salt is good; but if salt has lost its taste, how can its saltiness be restored?

It is fit neither for the soil nor for the manure pile; they throw it away. Let anyone with ears to hear listen!''

Tuesday

Psalm 26 [page 616],   *Psalm 28* [page 619]   ❖
Psalm 36 [page 632],   *Psalm 39* [page 638]

A Reading (Lesson) from the Book of Deuteronomy
[4:15–24]

Moses undertook to explain the law, saying, "Since you saw no form when the LORD spoke to you at Horeb out of the fire, take care and watch yourselves closely, so that you do not act corruptly by making an idol for yourselves, in the form of any figure—the likeness of male or female, the likeness of any animal that is on the earth, the likeness of any winged bird that flies in the air, the likeness of anything that creeps on the ground, the likeness of any fish that is in the water under the earth. And when you look up to the heavens and see the sun, the moon, and the stars, all the host of heaven, do not be led astray and bow down to them and serve them, things that the LORD your God has allotted to all the peoples everywhere under heaven. But the LORD has taken you and brought you out of the iron-smelter, out of Egypt, to become a people of his very own possession, as you are now. The LORD was angry with me because of you, and he vowed that I should not cross the Jordan and that I should not enter the good land that the LORD your God is giving for your possession. For I am going to die in this land without crossing over the Jordan, but you are going to cross over to take possession of that good land. So be careful not to forget the covenant that the LORD your God made with you, and not to make for yourselves an idol in the form of anything that the LORD your God has forbidden you. For the LORD your God is a devouring fire, a jealous God."

A Reading (Lesson) from the Second Letter of Paul to the Corinthians [1:12–22]

This is our boast, the testimony of our conscience: we have behaved in the world with frankness and godly sincerity, not by earthly wisdom but by the grace of God—and all the more toward you. For we write you nothing other than what you can read and also understand; I hope you will understand until the end—as you have already understood us in part—that on the day of the Lord Jesus we are your boast even as you are our boast. Since I was sure of this, I wanted to come to you first, so that you might have a double favor; I wanted to visit you on my way to Macedonia, and to come back to you from Macedonia and have you send me on to Judea. Was I vacillating when I wanted to do this? Do I make my plans according to ordinary human standards, ready to say "Yes, yes" and "No, no" at the same time? As surely as God is faithful, our word to you has not been "Yes and No." For the Son of God, Jesus Christ, whom we proclaimed among you, Silvanus and Timothy and I, was not "Yes and No"; but in him it is always "Yes." For in him every one of God's promises is a "Yes." For this reason it is through him that we say the "Amen," to the glory of God. But it is God who establishes us with you in Christ and has anointed us, by putting his seal on us and giving us his Spirit in our hearts as a first installment.

A Reading (Lesson) from the Gospel according to Luke [15:1–10]

Now all the tax collectors and sinners were coming near to listen to Jesus. And the Pharisees and the scribes were grumbling and saying, "This fellow welcomes sinners and eats with them." So he told them this parable: "Which one of you, having a hundred sheep and losing one of them, does not leave the ninety-nine in the wilderness and go after the one that is lost until he finds it? When he has found it, he lays it on his shoulders and rejoices. And when he comes home, he calls together his friends and neighbors, saying to them, 'Rejoice with me, for I have found my sheep that was lost.' Just so, I tell you, there will be more joy in heaven over one sinner who repents than over ninety-nine righteous persons who need no repentance. Or what woman having ten silver coins, if she loses one of them, does not light a lamp, sweep the house, and search carefully until she finds it? When she has found it, she calls together her friends and neighbors, saying, 'Rejoice with me, for I have found the coin that I had lost.' Just so, I tell you, there is joy in the presence of the angels of God over one sinner who repents."

Wednesday

Psalm 38 [page 636]   ❖   *Psalm 119:25–48* [page 765]

A Reading (Lesson) from the Book of Deuteronomy [4:25–31]

Moses undertook to explain the law, saying, "When you have had children and children's children, and become complacent in the land, if you act corruptly by making an idol in the form of anything, thus doing what is evil in the

sight of the LORD your God, and provoking him to anger, I
call heaven and earth to witness against you today that you
will soon utterly perish from the land that you are crossing
the Jordan to occupy; you will not live long on it, but will
be utterly destroyed. The LORD will scatter you among the
peoples; only a few of you will be left among the nations
where the LORD will lead you. There you will serve other
gods made by human hands, objects of wood and stone that
neither see, nor hear, nor eat, nor smell. From there you will
seek the LORD your God, and you will find him if you search
after him with all your heart and soul. In your distress,
when all these things have happened to you in time to come,
you will return to the LORD your God and heed him.
Because the LORD your God is a merciful God, he will
neither abandon you nor destroy you; he will not forget the
covenant with your ancestors that he swore to them."

*A Reading (Lesson) from the Second Letter of Paul to the
Corinthians* [1:23—2:17]

I call on God as witness against me: it was to spare you
that I did not come again to Corinth. I do not mean to
imply that we lord it over your faith; rather, we are
workers with you for your joy, because you stand firm in
the faith. So I made up my mind not to make you another
painful visit. For if I cause you pain, who is there to make
me glad but the one whom I have pained? And I wrote as
I did, so that when I came, I might not suffer pain from
those who should have made me rejoice; for I am
confident about all of you, that my joy would be the joy
of all of you. For I wrote you out of much distress and
anguish of heart and with many tears, not to cause you
pain, but to let you know the abundant love that I have
for you. But if anyone has caused pain, he has caused it

not to me, but to some extent—not to exaggerate it—to all of you. This punishment by the majority is enough for such a person; so now instead you should forgive and console him, so that he may not be overwhelmed by excessive sorrow. So I urge you to reaffirm your love for him. I wrote for this reason: to test you and to know whether you are obedient in everything. Anyone whom you forgive, I also forgive. What I have forgiven, if I have forgiven anything, has been for your sake in the presence of Christ. And we do this so that we may not be outwitted by Satan; for we are not ignorant of his designs. When I came to Troas to proclaim the good news of Christ, a door was opened for me in the Lord; but my mind could not rest because I did not find my brother Titus there. So I said farewell to them and went on to Macedonia. But thanks be to God, who in Christ always leads us in triumphal procession, and through us spreads in every place the fragrance that comes from knowing him. For we are the aroma of Christ to God among those who are being saved and among those who are perishing; to the one a fragrance from death to death, to the other a fragrance from life to life. Who is sufficient for these things? For we are not peddlers of God's word like so many; but in Christ we speak as persons of sincerity, as persons sent from God and standing in his presence.

A Reading (Lesson) from the Gospel according to Luke [15:1–2, 11–32]

All the tax collectors and sinners were coming near to listen to Jesus. And the Pharisees and the scribes were grumbling and saying, "This fellow welcomes sinners and eats with them." Then Jesus said, 'There was a man who had two sons. The younger of them said to his father,

'Father, give me the share of the property that will belong to me.' So he divided his property between them. A few days later the younger son gathered all he had and traveled to a distant country, and there he squandered his property in dissolute living. When he had spent everything, a severe famine took place throughout that country, and he began to be in need. So he went and hired himself out to one of the citizens of that country, who sent him to his fields to feed the pigs. He would gladly have filled himself with the pods that the pigs were eating; and no one gave him anything. But when he came to himself he said, 'How many of my father's hired hands have bread enough and to spare, but here I am dying of hunger! I will get up and go to my father, and I will say to him, "Father, I have sinned against heaven and before you; I am no longer worthy to be called your son; treat me like one of your hired hands."' So he set off and went to his father. But while he was still far off, his father saw him and was filled with compassion; he ran and put his arms around him and kissed him. Then the son said to him, 'Father, I have sinned against heaven and before you; I am no longer worthy to be called your son.' But the father said to his slaves, 'Quickly, bring out a robe—the best one—and put it on him; put a ring on his finger and sandals on his feet. And get the fatted calf and kill it, and let us eat and celebrate; for this son of mine was dead and is alive again; he was lost and is found!' And they began to celebrate. Now his elder son was in the field; and when he came and approached the house, he heard music and dancing. He called one of the slaves and asked what was going on. He replied, 'Your brother has come, and your father has killed the fatted calf, because he has got him back safe and sound.' Then he became angry and refused to go in. His father came out and began to plead with him. But he answered his father, 'Listen! For all these years I have been working like a slave for you, and I have never disobeyed your command; yet you have never given me even a young goat so that I might celebrate with my friends. But when this son of yours came back, who has devoured your property with prostitutes, you killed the fatted calf for him!' Then the father said to him, 'Son, you are always with me, and all that is mine is yours. But we had to celebrate and rejoice, because this brother of yours was dead and has come to life; he was lost and has been found.' "

Thursday

Psalm 37:1–18 [page 633] ❖ *Psalm 37:19–42* [page 634]

A Reading (Lesson) from the Book of Deuteronomy [4:32–40]

Moses undertook to explain the law, saying, "Ask now about former ages, long before your own, ever since the day that God created human beings on the earth; ask from one end of heaven to the other: has anything so great as this ever happened or has its like ever been heard of? Has any people ever heard the voice of a god speaking out of a fire, as you have heard, and lived? Or has any god ever attempted to go and take a nation for himself from the midst of another nation, by trials, by signs and wonders, by war, by a mighty hand and an outstretched arm, and by terrifying displays of power, as the LORD your God did for you in Egypt before your very eyes? To you it was shown so that you would acknowledge that the LORD is God; there is no other besides him. From heaven he made you hear his voice to discipline you. On earth he showed you his great fire, while you heard his words coming out of the fire. And because he loved your ancestors, he chose their descendants after them. He brought you out of Egypt with his own presence, by his great power, driving out before you nations greater and mightier than yourselves, to bring you in, giving you their land for a possession, as it is still today. So acknowledge today and take to heart that the LORD is God in heaven above and on the earth beneath; there is no other. Keep his statutes and his commandments, which I am commanding you today for your own well-being and that of your descendants after you, so that you may long remain in the land that the LORD your God is giving you for all time."

A Reading (Lesson) from the Second Letter of Paul to the Corinthians [3:1–18]

Are we beginning to commend ourselves again? Surely we do not need, as some do, letters of recommendation to you or from you, do we? You yourselves are our letter, written on our hearts, to be known and read by all; and you show that you are a letter of Christ, prepared by us, written not with ink but with the Spirit of the living God, not on tablets of stone but on tablets of human hearts. Such is the confidence that we have through Christ toward God. Not that we are competent of ourselves to claim anything as coming from us; our competence is from God, who has made us competent to be ministers of a new covenant, not of letter but of spirit; for the letter kills, but the Spirit gives life. Now if the ministry of death, chiseled in letters on stone tablets, came in glory so that the people of Israel could not gaze at Moses' face because of the glory of his face, a glory now set aside, how much more will the ministry of the Spirit come in glory? For if there was glory in the ministry of condemnation, much more does the ministry of justification abound in glory! Indeed, what once had glory has lost its glory because of the greater glory; for if what was set aside came through glory, much more has the permanent come in glory! Since, then, we have such a hope, we act with great boldness, not like Moses, who put a veil over his face to keep the people of Israel from gazing at the end of the glory that was being set aside. But their minds were hardened. Indeed, to this very day, when they hear the reading of the old covenant, that same veil is still there, since only in Christ is it set aside. Indeed, to this very day whenever Moses is read, a veil lies over their minds; but when one turns to the Lord, the veil is removed. Now the Lord is the Spirit, and where the Spirit of the Lord is, there is freedom. And all of us, with unveiled faces, seeing the glory of the Lord as though reflected in a mirror, are being transformed into the same image from one degree of glory to another; for this comes from the Lord, the Spirit.

A Reading (Lesson) from the Gospel according to Luke [16:1–9]

Jesus said to the disciples, "There was a rich man who had a manager, and charges were brought to him that this man was squandering his property. So he summoned him and said to him, 'What is this that I hear about you? Give me an accounting of your management, because you cannot be my manager any longer.' Then the manager said to himself, 'What will I do, now that my master is taking the position away from me? I am not strong enough to dig, and I am ashamed to beg. I have decided what to do so that, when I am dismissed as manager, people may welcome me into their homes.' So, summoning his master's debtors one by one, he asked the first, 'How much do you owe my master?' He answered, 'A hundred jugs of olive oil.' He said to him, 'Take your bill, sit down quickly, and make it fifty.' Then he asked another, 'And how much do you owe?' He replied, 'A hundred containers of wheat.' He said to him, 'Take your bill and make it eighty.' And his master commended the dishonest manager because he had acted shrewdly; for the children of this age are more shrewd in dealing with their own generation than are the children of light. And I tell you, make friends for yourselves by means of dishonest wealth so that when it is gone, they may welcome you into the eternal homes.''

Friday

Psalm 31 [page 622]   ❖   *Psalm 35* [page 629]

A Reading (Lesson) from the Book of Deuteronomy [5:1–22]

Moses convened all Israel, and said to them: "Hear, O Israel, the statutes and ordinances that I am addressing to you today; you shall learn them and observe them diligently. The LORD our God made a covenant with us at Horeb. Not with our ancestors did the LORD make this covenant, but with us, who are all of us here alive today. The LORD spoke with you face to face at the mountain, out of the fire. (At that time I was standing between the LORD and you to declare to you the words of the LORD; for you were afraid because of the fire and did not go up the mountain.) And he said: I am the LORD your God, who brought you out of the land of Egypt, out of the house of slavery; you shall have no other gods before me. You shall not make for yourself an idol, whether in the form of anything that is in heaven above, or that is on the earth beneath, or that is in the water under the earth. You shall not bow down to them or worship them; for I the LORD your God am a jealous God, punishing children for the iniquity of parents, to the third and fourth generation of those who reject me, but showing steadfast love to the thousandth generation of those who love me and keep my commandments. You shall not make wrongful use of the name of the LORD your God, for the LORD will not acquit anyone who misuses his name. Observe the sabbath day and keep it holy, as the LORD your God commanded you. Six days you shall labor and do all your work. But the seventh day is a sabbath to the LORD your God; you shall not do any work—you, or your son or your daughter, or your male or female slave, or your ox or your donkey, or any of your livestock, or the resident alien in your towns, so that your male and female slave may rest as well as you. Remember that you were a slave in the land of Egypt, and the LORD your God brought you out from there with a mighty hand and an outstretched arm; therefore the LORD your God commanded you to keep the sabbath day. Honor your father and your mother, as the LORD your God commanded you, so that your days may be long and that it may go well with you in the land that the LORD your God is giving you. You shall not murder. Neither shall you commit adultery. Neither shall you steal. Neither shall you bear false witness against your neighbor. Neither shall you covet your neighbor's wife. Neither shall you desire your neighbor's house, or field, or male or female slave, or ox, or donkey, or anything that belongs to your neighbor. These words the LORD spoke with a loud voice to your whole assembly at the mountain, out of the fire, the cloud, and the thick darkness, and he added no more. He wrote them on two stone tablets, and gave them to me."

A Reading (Lesson) from the Second Letter of Paul to the Corinthians [4:1–12]

Since it is by God's mercy that we are engaged in this ministry, we do not lose heart. We have renounced the shameful things that one hides; we refuse to practice cunning or to falsify God's word; but by the open statement of the truth we commend ourselves to the conscience of everyone in the sight of God. And even if our gospel is veiled, it is veiled to those who are perishing. In their case the god of this world has blinded the minds of the unbelievers, to keep them from seeing the light of the gospel of the glory of Christ, who is the image of God. For we do not proclaim ourselves; we proclaim Jesus Christ as Lord and ourselves as your slaves for Jesus' sake. For it is the God who said, "Let light shine out of darkness," who has shone in our hearts to give the light of the knowledge of the glory of God in the face of Jesus Christ. But we have this treasure in clay jars, so that it may be made clear that this extraordinary power belongs to God and does not come from us. We are afflicted in every way, but not crushed; perplexed, but not driven to despair; persecuted, but not forsaken; struck down, but not destroyed; always carrying in the body the death of Jesus, so that the life of Jesus may also be made visible in our bodies. For while we live, we are always being given up to death for Jesus' sake, so that the life of Jesus may be made visible in our mortal flesh. So death is at work in us, but life in you.

A Reading (Lesson) from the Gospel according to Luke [16:10–17(18)]

Jesus said to the disciples, "Whoever is faithful in a very little is faithful also in much; and whoever is dishonest in a very little is dishonest also in much. If then you have not been faithful with the dishonest wealth, who will entrust to you the true riches? And if you have not been faithful with what belongs to another, who will give you what is your own? No slave can serve two masters; for a slave will either hate the one and love the other, or be devoted to the one and despise the other. You cannot serve God and wealth." The Pharisees, who were lovers of money, heard all this, and they ridiculed him. So he said to them, "You are those who justify yourselves in the sight of others; but God knows your hearts; for what is prized by human beings is an abomination in the sight of God. The law and the prophets were in effect until John came; since then the good news of the kingdom of God is proclaimed, and everyone tries to enter it by force. But it is easier for heaven and earth to pass away, than for one stroke of a letter in the law to be dropped."

"Anyone who divorces his wife and marries another commits adultery, and whoever marries a woman divorced from her husband commits adultery."

Saturday

Psalm 30 [page 621], *Psalm 32* [page 624] ❖
Psalm 42 [page 643], *Psalm 43* [page 644]

A Reading (Lesson) from the Book of Deuteronomy
[5:22–33]

Moses summoned all Israel, and said to them, "These words the LORD spoke with a loud voice to your whole assembly at the mountain, out of the fire, the cloud, and the thick darkness, and he added no more. He wrote them on two stone tablets, and gave them to me. When you heard the voice out of the darkness, while the mountain was burning with fire, you approached me, all the heads of your tribes and your elders; and you said, 'Look, the LORD our God has shown us his glory and greatness, and we have heard his voice out of the fire. Today we have seen that God may speak to someone and the person may still live. So now why should we die? For this great fire will consume us; if we hear the voice of the LORD our God any longer, we shall die. For who is there of all flesh that has heard the voice of the living God speaking out of fire, as we have, and remained alive? Go near, you yourself, and hear all that the LORD our God will say. Then tell us everything that the LORD our God tells you, and we will listen and do it.' The LORD heard your words when you spoke to me, and the LORD said to me: 'I have heard the words of this people, which they have spoken to you; they are right in all that they have spoken. If only they had such a mind as this, to fear me and to keep all my commandments always, so that it might go well with them and with their children forever! Go say to them, "Return to your tents." But you, stand here by me, and I will tell you all the commandments, the statutes and the ordinances, that you shall teach them, so that they may do them in the land that I am giving them to possess.' You must therefore be careful to do as the LORD your God has commanded you; you shall not turn to the right or to the left. You must follow exactly the path that the LORD your God has commanded you, so that you may live, and that it may go well with you, and that you may live long in the land that you are to possess."

A Reading (Lesson) from the Second Letter of Paul to the Corinthians [4:13—5:10]

Just as we have the same spirit of faith that is in accordance with scripture—"I believed, and so I spoke"— we also believe, and so we speak, because we know that the one who raised the Lord Jesus will raise us also with Jesus, and will bring us with you into his presence. Yes, everything is for your sake, so that grace, as it extends to more and more people, may increase thanksgiving, to the glory of God. So we do not lose heart. Even though our outer nature is wasting away, our inner nature is being renewed day by day. For this slight momentary affliction is preparing us for an eternal weight of glory beyond all measure, because we look not at what can be seen but at what cannot be seen; for what can be seen is temporary, but what cannot be seen is eternal. For we know that if the earthly tent we live in is destroyed, we have a building from God, a house not made with hands, eternal in the heavens. For in this tent we groan, longing to be clothed with our heavenly dwelling—if indeed, when we have taken it off we will not be found naked. For while we are still in this tent, we groan under our burden, because we wish not to be unclothed but to be further clothed, so that what is mortal may be swallowed up by life. He who has prepared us for this very thing is God, who has given us the Spirit as a guarantee. So we are always confident; even though we know that while we are at home in the body we are away from the Lord—for we walk by faith, not by sight. Yes, we do have confidence, and we would rather be away from the body and at home with the Lord. So whether we are at home or away, we make it our aim to please him. For all of us must appear before the judgment seat of Christ, so that each may receive recompense for what has been done in the body, whether good or evil.

A Reading (Lesson) from the Gospel according to Luke
[16:19–31]

Jesus said to the disciples, "There was a rich man who
was dressed in purple and fine linen and who feasted
sumptuously every day. And at his gate lay a poor man
named Lazarus, covered with sores, who longed to satisfy
his hunger with what fell from the rich man's table; even
the dogs would come and lick his sores. The poor man
died and was carried away by the angels to be with
Abraham. The rich man also died and was buried. In
Hades, where he was being tormented, he looked up and
saw Abraham far away with Lazarus by his side. He called
out, 'Father Abraham, have mercy on me, and send
Lazarus to dip the tip of his finger in water and cool my
tongue; for I am in agony in these flames.' But Abraham
said, 'Child, remember that during your lifetime you
received your good things, and Lazarus in like manner evil
things; but now he is comforted here, and you are in
agony. Besides all this, between you and us a great chasm
has been fixed, so that those who might want to pass from
here to you cannot do so, and no one can cross from there
to us.' He said, 'Then, father, I beg you to send him to my
father's house—for I have five brothers—that he may
warn them, so that they will not also come into this place
of torment.' Abraham replied, 'They have Moses and the
prophets; they should listen to them.' He said, 'No, father
Abraham; but if someone goes to them from the dead,
they will repent.' He said to him, 'If they do not listen to
Moses and the prophets, neither will they be convinced
even if someone rises from the dead.' "

Proper 4   *Week of the Sunday closest to June 1*

Sunday

Psalm 63:1–8(9–11) [page 670],   *Psalm 98* [page 727]   ❖
Psalm 103 [page 733]

A Reading (Lesson) from the Book of Deuteronomy
[11:1–12]

Moses summoned all Israel, and said to them, "You shall
love the LORD your God, and keep his charge, his decrees,
his ordinances, and his commandments always. Remember
today that it was not your children (who have not known or
seen the discipline of the LORD your God), but it is you who
must acknowledge his greatness, his mighty hand and his
outstretched arm, his signs and his deeds that he did in
Egypt to Pharaoh, the king of Egypt, and to all his land;
what he did to the Egyptian army, to their horses and
chariots, how he made the water of the Red Sea flow over
them as they pursued you, so that the LORD has destroyed
them to this day; what he did to you in the wilderness, until
you came to this place; and what he did to Dathan and
Abiram, sons of Eliab son of Reuben, how in the midst of all
Israel the earth opened its mouth and swallowed them up,
along with their households, their tents, and every living
being in their company; for it is your own eyes that have
seen every great deed that the LORD did. Keep, then, this
entire commandment that I am commanding you today, so
that you may have strength to go in and occupy the land
that you are crossing over to occupy, and so that you may
live long in the land that the LORD swore to your ancestors
to give them and to their descendants, a land flowing with
milk and honey. For the land that you are about to enter to

occupy is not like the land of Egypt, from which you have come, where you sow your seed and irrigate by foot like a vegetable garden. But the land that you are crossing over to occupy is a land of hills and valleys, watered by rain from the sky, a land that the LORD your God looks after. The eyes of the LORD your God are always on it, from the beginning of the year to the end of the year."

A Reading (Lesson) from the Revelation to John [10:1–11]

I saw another mighty angel coming down from heaven, wrapped in a cloud, with a rainbow over his head; his face was like the sun, and his legs like pillars of fire. He held a little scroll open in his hand. Setting his right foot on the sea and his left foot on the land, he gave a great shout, like a lion roaring. And when he shouted, the seven thunders sounded. And when the seven thunders had sounded, I was about to write, but I heard a voice from heaven saying, "Seal up what the seven thunders have said, and do not write it down." Then the angel whom I saw standing on the sea and the land raised his right hand to heaven and swore by him who lives forever and ever, who created heaven and what is in it, the earth and what is in it, and the sea and what is in it: "There will be no more delay, but in the days when the seventh angel is to blow his trumpet, the mystery of God will be fulfilled, as he announced to his servants the prophets." Then the voice that I had heard from heaven spoke to me again, saying, "Go, take the scroll that is open in the hand of the angel who is standing on the sea and on the land." So I went to the angel and told him to give me the little scroll; and he said to me, "Take it, and eat; it will be bitter to your stomach, but sweet as honey in your mouth." So I took the little scroll from the hand of the angel and ate it;

it was sweet as honey in my mouth, but when I had eaten it, my stomach was made bitter. Then they said to me, "You must prophesy again about many peoples and nations and languages and kings."

A Reading (Lesson) from the Gospel according to Matthew [13:44–58]

Jesus said to his disciples, "The kingdom of heaven is like treasure hidden in a field, which someone found and hid; then in his joy he goes and sells all that he has and buys that field. Again, the kingdom of heaven is like a merchant in search of fine pearls; on finding one pearl of great value, he went and sold all that he had and bought it. Again, the kingdom of heaven is like a net that was thrown into the sea and caught fish of every kind; when it was full, they drew it ashore, sat down, and put the good into baskets but threw out the bad. So it will be at the end of the age. The angels will come out and separate the evil from the righteous and throw them into the furnace of fire, where there will be weeping and gnashing of teeth. Have you understood all this?" They answered, "Yes." And he said to them, "Therefore every scribe who has been trained for the kingdom of heaven is like the master of a household who brings out of his treasure what is new and what is old." When Jesus had finished these parables, he left that place. He came to his hometown and began to teach the people in their synagogue, so that they were astounded and said, "Where did this man get this wisdom and these deeds of power? Is not this the carpenter's son? Is not his mother called Mary? And are not his brothers James and Joseph and Simon and Judas? And are not all his sisters with us? Where then did this man get all this?" And they took offense at him. But Jesus said to them,

"Prophets are not without honor except in their own country and in their own house." And he did not do many deeds of power there, because of their unbelief.

Monday

Psalm 41 [page 641],   *Psalm 52* [page 657]   ❖
Psalm 44 [page 645]

A Reading (Lesson) from the Book of Deuteronomy [11:13–19]

Moses summoned all Israel, and said to them, "If you will only heed my every commandment that I am commanding you today—loving the LORD your God, and serving him with all your heart and with all your soul—then he will give the rain for your land in its season, the early rain and the later rain, and you will gather in your grain, your wine, and your oil; and he will give grass in your fields for your livestock, and you will eat your fill. Take care, or you will be seduced into turning away, serving other gods and worshiping them, for then the anger of the LORD will be kindled against you and he will shut up the heavens, so that there will be no rain and the land will yield no fruit; then you will perish quickly off the good land that the LORD is giving you. You shall put these words of mine in your heart and soul, and you shall bind them as a sign on your hand, and fix them as an emblem on your forehead. Teach them to your children, talking about them when you are at home and when you are away, when you lie down and when you rise."

A Reading (Lesson) from the Second Letter of Paul to the Corinthians [5:11—6:2]

Knowing the fear of the Lord, we try to persuade others; but we ourselves are well known to God, and I hope that we are also well known to your consciences. We are not commending ourselves to you again, but giving you an opportunity to boast about us, so that you may be able to answer those who boast in outward appearance and not in the heart. For if we are beside ourselves, it is for God; if we are in our right mind, it is for you. For the love of Christ urges us on, because we are convinced that one has died for all; therefore all have died. And he died for all, so that those who live might live no longer for themselves, but for him who died and was raised for them. From now on, therefore, we regard no one from a human point of view; even though we once knew Christ from a human point of view, we know him no longer in that way. So if anyone is in Christ, there is a new creation: everything old has passed away; see, everything has become new! All this is from God, who reconciled us to himself through Christ, and has given us the ministry of reconciliation; that is, in Christ God was reconciling the world to himself, not counting their trespasses against them, and entrusting the message of reconciliation to us. So we are ambassadors for Christ, since God is making his appeal through us; we entreat you on behalf of Christ, be reconciled to God. For our sake he made him to be sin who knew no sin, so that in him we might become the righteousness of God. As we work together with him, we urge you also not to accept the grace of God in vain. For he says, "At an acceptable time I have listened to you, and on a day of salvation I have helped you." See, now is the acceptable time; see, now is the day of salvation!

A Reading (Lesson) from the Gospel according to Luke
[17:1–10]

Jesus said to his disciples, "Occasions for stumbling are
bound to come, but woe to anyone by whom they come!
It would be better for you if a millstone were hung around
your neck and you were thrown into the sea than for you
to cause one of these little ones to stumble. Be on your
guard! If another disciple sins, you must rebuke the
offender, and if there is repentance, you must forgive. And
if the same person sins against you seven times a day, and
turns back to you seven times and says, 'I repent,' you
must forgive." The apostles said to the Lord, "Increase
our faith!" The Lord replied, "If you had faith the size of
a mustard seed, you could say to this mulberry tree, 'Be
uprooted and planted in the sea,' and it would obey you.
Who among you would say to your slave who has just
come in from plowing or tending sheep in the field, 'Come
here at once and take your place at the table'? Would you
not rather say to him, 'Prepare supper for me, put on your
apron and serve me while I eat and drink; later you may
eat and drink'? Do you thank the slave for doing what
was commanded? So you also, when you have done all
that you were ordered to do, say, 'We are worthless
slaves; we have done only what we ought to have done!'"

Tuesday

Psalm 45 [page 647]   ❖   *Psalm 47* [page 650],
Psalm 48 [page 651]

A Reading (Lesson) from the Book of Deuteronomy
[12:1–12]

Moses summoned all Israel, and said to them, "These are
the statutes and ordinances that you must diligently observe

in the land that the Lord, the God of your ancestors, has given you to occupy all the days that you live on the earth. You must demolish completely all the places where the nations whom you are about to dispossess served their gods, on the mountain heights, on the hills, and under every leafy tree. Break down their altars, smash their pillars, burn their sacred poles with fire, and hew down the idols of their gods, and thus blot out their name from their places. You shall not worship the Lord your God in such ways. But you shall seek the place that the Lord your God will choose out of all your tribes as his habitation to put his name there. You shall go there, bringing there your burnt offerings and your sacrifices, your tithes and your donations, your votive gifts, your freewill offerings, and the firstlings of your herds and flocks. And you shall eat there in the presence of the Lord your God, you and your households together, rejoicing in all the undertakings in which the Lord your God has blessed you. You shall not act as we are acting here today, all of us according to our own desires, for you have not yet come into the rest and the possession that the Lord your God is giving you. When you cross over the Jordan and live in the land that the Lord your God is allotting to you, and when he gives you rest from your enemies all around so that you live in safety, then you shall bring everything that I command you to the place that the Lord your God will choose as a dwelling for his name: your burnt offerings and your sacrifices, your tithes and your donations, and all your choice votive gifts that you vow to the Lord. And you shall rejoice before the Lord your God, you together with your sons and your daughters, your male and female slaves, and the Levites who reside in your towns (since they have no allotment or inheritance with you)."

A Reading (Lesson) from the Second Letter of Paul to the Corinthians [6:3–13(14—7:1)]

We are putting no obstacle in anyone's way, so that no fault may be found with our ministry, but as servants of God we have commended ourselves in every way; through great endurance, in afflictions, hardships, calamities, beatings, imprisonments, riots, labors, sleepless nights, hunger; by purity, knowledge, patience, kindness, holiness of spirit, genuine love, truthful speech, and the power of God; with the weapons of righteousness for the right hand and for the left; in honor and dishonor, in ill repute and good repute. We are treated as impostors, and yet are true; as unknown, and yet are well known; as dying, and see—we are alive; as punished, and yet not killed; as sorrowful, yet always rejoicing; as poor, yet making many rich; as having nothing, and yet possessing everything. We have spoken frankly to you Corinthians; our heart is wide open to you. There is no restriction in our affections, but only in yours. In return—I speak as to children—open wide your hearts also.

Do not be mismatched with unbelievers. For what partnership is there between righteousness and lawlessness? Or what fellowship is there between light and darkness? What agreement does Christ have with Belair? Or what does a believer share with an unbeliever? What agreement has the temple of God with idols? For we are the temple of the living God; as God said, "I will live in them and walk among them, and I will be their God, and they shall be my people. Therefore come out from them, and be separate from them, says the Lord, and touch nothing unclean; then I will welcome you, and I will be your father, and you shall be my sons and daughters, says the Lord Almighty." Since we have these promises, beloved, let us cleanse ourselves from every defilement of body and of spirit, making holiness perfect in the fear of God.

A Reading (Lesson) from the Gospel according to Luke [17:11–19]

On the way to Jerusalem Jesus was going through the region between Samaria and Galilee. As he entered a village, ten lepers approached him. Keeping their distance, they called out, saying, "Jesus, Master, have mercy on us!" When he saw them, he said to them, "Go and show yourselves to the priests." And as they went, they were made clean. Then one of them, when he saw that he was healed, turned back, praising God with a loud voice. He prostrated himself at Jesus' feet and thanked him. And he was a Samaritan. Then Jesus asked, "Were not ten made clean? But the other nine, where are they? Was none of them found to return and give praise to God except this foreigner?" Then he said to him, "Get up and go on your way; your faith has made you well."

Wednesday

Psalm 119:49–72 [page 767]   ❖   *Psalm 49* [page 652], *(Psalm 53* [page 658])

A Reading (Lesson) from the Book of Deuteronomy [13:1–11]

Moses summoned all Israel, and said to them, "If prophets or those who divine by dreams appear among you and promise you omens or portents, and the omens or the portents declared by them take place, and they say, 'Let us follow other gods' (whom you have not known) 'and let us serve them,' you must not heed the words of those prophets or those who divine by dreams; for the LORD your God is testing you, to know whether you indeed love the LORD your God with all your heart and soul. The LORD your God you shall follow, him alone you shall fear, his commandments you shall keep, his voice you shall obey, him you shall serve, and to him you shall hold fast. But those prophets or those who divine by dreams shall be put to death for having spoken treason against the LORD your God—who brought you out of the land of Egypt and redeemed you from the house of slavery—to turn you from the way in which the LORD your God commanded you to walk. So you shall purge the evil from your midst. If anyone secretly entices you—even if it is your brother, your father's son or your mother's son, or your own son or daughter, or the wife you embrace, or your most intimate friend—saying, 'Let us go worship other gods,' whom neither you nor your ancestors have known, any of the gods of the peoples that are around you, whether near you or far away from you, from one end of the earth to the other, you must not yield to or heed any such persons. Show them no pity or compassion and do not shield them. But you shall surely kill them; your own hand shall be first against them to execute them, and afterwards the hand of all the people. Stone them to death for trying to turn you away from the LORD your God, who brought you out of the land of Egypt, out of the house of slavery. Then all Israel shall hear and be afraid, and never again do any such wickedness."

A Reading (Lesson) from the Second Letter of Paul to the Corinthians [7:2–16]

Make room in your hearts for us; we have wronged no one, we have corrupted no one, we have taken advantage of no one. I do not say this to condemn you, for I said before that you are in our hearts, to die together and to live together. I often boast about you; I have great pride in you; I am filled with consolation; I am overjoyed in all our affliction. For even when we came into Macedonia, our bodies had no rest, but we were afflicted in every way—disputes without and fears within. But God, who consoles the downcast, consoled us by the arrival of Titus, and not only by his coming, but also by the consolation with which he was consoled about you, as he told us of your longing, your mourning, your zeal for me, so that I rejoiced still more. For even if I made you sorry with my letter, I do not regret it (though I did regret it, for I see that I grieved you with that letter, though only briefly). Now I rejoice, not because you were grieved, but because your grief led to repentance; for you felt a godly grief, so that you were not harmed in any way by us. For godly grief produces a repentance that leads to salvation and brings no regret, but worldly grief produces death. For see what earnestness this godly grief has produced in you, what eagerness to clear yourselves, what indignation, what alarm, what longing, what zeal, what punishment! At every point you have proved yourselves guiltless in the matter. So although I wrote to you, it was not on account of the one who did the wrong, nor on account of the one who was wronged, but in order that your zeal for us might be made known to you before God. In this we find comfort. In addition to our own consolation, we rejoiced still more at the joy of Titus, because his mind has been set at rest by all of you. For if I have been somewhat boastful about you to him, I was not disgraced; but just as everything we said to you was true, so our boasting to Titus has proved true as well. And his heart goes out all the more to you, as he remembers the obedience of all of

you, and how you welcomed him with fear and trembling.
I rejoice, because I have complete confidence in you.

A Reading (Lesson) from the Gospel according to Luke
[17:20–37]

Once Jesus was asked by the Pharisees when the kingdom
of God was coming, and he answered, "The kingdom of
God is not coming with things that can be observed; nor
will they say, 'Look, here it is!' or 'There it is!' For, in
fact, the kingdom of God is among you." Then he said to
the disciples, "The days are coming when you will long to
see one of the days of the Son of Man, and you will not
see it. They will say to you, 'Look there!' or 'Look here!'
Do not go, do not set off in pursuit. For as the lightning
flashes and lights up the sky from one side to the other, so
will the Son of Man be in his day. But first he must
endure much suffering and be rejected by this generation.
Just as it was in the days of Noah, so too it will be in the
days of the Son of Man. They were eating and drinking,
and marrying and being given in marriage, until the day
Noah entered the ark, and the flood came and destroyed
all of them. Likewise, just as it was in the days of Lot:
they were eating and drinking, buying and selling, planting
and building, but on the day that Lot left Sodom, it rained
fire and sulfur from heaven and destroyed all of them—
it will be like that on the day that the Son of Man is
revealed. On that day, anyone on the housetop who has
belongings in the house must not come down to take them
away; and likewise anyone in the field must not turn back.
Remember Lot's wife. Those who try to make their life
secure will lose it, but those who lose their life will keep
it. I tell you, on that night there will be two in one bed;

one will be taken and the other left. There will be two women grinding meal together; one will be taken and the other left." Then they asked him, "Where, Lord?" He said to them, "Where the corpse is, there the vultures will gather."

Thursday

Psalm 50 [page 654]   ❖   (*Psalm 59* [page 665],
Psalm 60 [page 667]) or *Psalm 8* [page 592],
Psalm 84 [page 707]

A Reading (Lesson) from the Book of Deuteronomy
[16:18–20; 17:14–20]

Moses summoned all Israel, and said to them, "You shall appoint judges and officials throughout your tribes, in all your towns that the LORD your God is giving you, and they shall render just decisions for the people. You must not distort justice; you must not show partiality; and you must not accept bribes, for a bribe blinds the eyes of the wise and subverts the cause of those who are in the right. Justice, and only justice, you shall pursue, so that you may live and occupy the land that the LORD your God is giving you. When you have come into the land that the LORD your God is giving you, and have taken possession of it and settled in it, and you say, 'I will set a king over me, like all the nations that are around me,' you may indeed set over you a king whom the LORD your God will choose. One of your own community you may set as king over you; you are not permitted to put a foreigner over you, who is not of your own community. Even so, he must not acquire many horses for himself, or return the people to Egypt in order to acquire more horses, since the LORD has said to you, 'You must never return that way again.' And he must not acquire many wives for himself, or else his heart will turn away; also silver and gold he must not acquire in great quantity for himself. When he has taken the throne of his kingdom, he shall have a copy of this law written for him in the presence of the levitical priests. It shall remain with him and he shall read in it all the days of his life, so that he may learn to fear the Lord his God, diligently observing all the words of this law and these statutes, neither exalting himself above other members of the community nor turning aside from the commandment, either to the right or to the left, so that he and his descendants may reign long over his kingdom in Israel."

A Reading (Lesson) from the Second Letter of Paul to the Corinthians [8:1–16]

We want you to know, brothers and sisters, about the grace of God that has been granted to the churches of Macedonia; for during a severe ordeal of affliction, their abundant joy and their extreme poverty have overflowed in a wealth of generosity on their part. For, as I can testify, they voluntarily gave according to their means, and even beyond their means, begging us earnestly for the privilege of sharing in this ministry to the saints—and this, not merely as we expected; they gave themselves first to the Lord and, by the will of God, to us, so that we might urge Titus that, as he had already made a beginning, so he should also complete this generous undertaking among you. Now as you excel in everything—in faith, in speech, in knowledge, in utmost eagerness, and in our love for you—so we want you to excel also in this generous undertaking. I do not say this as a command, but I am testing the genuineness of your love against the earnestness of others. For you know the generous act of our Lord Jesus Christ, that though he was rich, yet for your sakes he became poor, so that by his poverty you might become rich. And in this matter I am giving my advice: it is appropriate for you who began last year not only to do something but even to desire to do something—now finish doing it, so that your eagerness may be matched by completing it according to your means. For if the eagerness is there, the gift is acceptable according to what one has—not according to what one does not have. I do not mean that there should be relief for others and pressure on you, but it is a question of a fair balance between your present abundance and their need, so that their abundance may be for your need, in order that there may be a fair balance. As it is written, "The one who had much did not have too much, and the one who had little did not have too little." But thanks be to God who put in the heart of Titus the same eagerness for you that I myself have.

A Reading (Lesson) from the Gospel according to Luke
[18:1–8]

Jesus told the disciples a parable about their need to pray always and not to lose heart. He said, "In a certain city there was a judge who neither feared God nor had respect for people. In that city there was a widow who kept coming to him and saying, 'Grant me justice against my opponent.' For a while he refused; but later he said to himself, 'Though I have no fear of God and no respect for anyone, yet because this widow keeps bothering me, I will grant her justice, so that she may not wear me out by continually coming.'" And the Lord said, "Listen to what the unjust judge says. And will not God grant justice to his chosen ones who cry to him day and night? Will he delay long in helping them? I tell you, he will quickly grant justice to them. And yet, when the Son of Man comes, will he find faith on earth?"

Friday

Psalm 40 [page 640], *Psalm 54* [page 659] ❖
Psalm 51 [page 656]

A Reading (Lesson) from the Book of Deuteronomy [26:1–11]

Moses summoned all Israel, and said to them: "When you have come into the land that the LORD your God is giving you as an inheritance to possess, and you possess it, and settle in it, you shall take some of the first of all the fruit of the ground, which you harvest from the land that the LORD your God is giving you, and you shall put it in a basket and go to the place that the LORD your God will choose as a dwelling for his name. You shall go to the priest who is in office at that time, and say to him, 'Today I declare to the LORD your God that I have come into the land that the LORD swore to our ancestors to give us.' When the priest takes the basket from your hand and sets it down before the altar of the LORD your God, you shall make this response before the LORD your God: 'A wandering Aramean was my ancestor; he went down into Egypt and lived there as an alien, few in number, and there he became a great nation, mighty and populous. When the Egyptians treated us harshly and afflicted us, by imposing hard labor on us, we cried to the LORD, the God of our ancestors; the LORD heard our voice and saw our affliction, our toil, and our oppression. The LORD brought us out of Egypt with a mighty hand and an outstretched arm, with a terrifying display of power, and with signs and wonders; and he brought us into this place and gave us this land, a land flowing with milk and honey. So now I bring the first of the fruit of the ground that you, O LORD, have given me.' You shall set it down before the LORD your God and bow down before the LORD your God. Then you, together with the Levites and the aliens who reside among you, shall celebrate with all the bounty that the LORD your God has given to you and to your house."

A Reading (Lesson) from the Second Letter of Paul to the Corinthians [8:16–24]

Thanks be to God who put in the heart of Titus the same eagerness for you that I myself have. For he not only accepted our appeal, but since he is more eager than ever, he is going to you of his own accord. With him we are sending the brother who is famous among all the churches for his proclaiming the good news; and not only that, but he has also been appointed by the churches to travel with us while we are administering this generous undertaking for the glory of the Lord himself and to show our goodwill. We intend that no one should blame us about this generous gift that we are administering, for we intend to do what is right not only in the Lord's sight but also in the sight of others. And with them we are sending our brother whom we have often tested and found eager in many matters, but who is now more eager than ever because of his great confidence in you. As for Titus, he is my partner and co-worker in your service; as for our brothers, they are messengers of the churches, the glory of Christ. Therefore openly before the churches, show them the proof of your love and of our reason for boasting about you.

A Reading (Lesson) from the Gospel according to Luke
[18:9–14]

Jesus also told this parable to some who trusted in themselves that they were righteous and regarded others with contempt: "Two men went up to the temple to pray, one a Pharisee and the other a tax collector. The Pharisee, standing by himself, was praying thus, 'God, I thank you that I am not like other people: thieves, rogues, adulterers, or even like this tax collector. I fast twice a week; I give a tenth of all my income.' But the tax collector, standing far off, would not even look up to heaven, but was beating his breast and saying, 'God, be merciful to me, a sinner!' I tell you, this man went down to his home justified rather than the other; for all who exalt themselves will be humbled, but all who humble themselves will be exalted."

Saturday

Psalm 55 [page 660] ❖ *Psalm 138* [page 793],
Psalm 139:1–17(18–23) [page 794]

A Reading (Lesson) from the Book of Deuteronomy
[29:2–15]

Moses summoned all Israel and said to them: "You have seen all that the LORD did before your eyes in the land of Egypt, to Pharaoh, and to all his servants and to all his land, the great trials that your eyes saw, the signs, and those great wonders. But to this day the LORD has not given you a mind to understand, or eyes to see, or ears to hear. I have led you forty years in the wilderness. The clothes on your back have not worn out, and the sandals on your feet have not worn out; you have not eaten bread, and you have not drunk wine or strong drink—so that you may know that I am the LORD your God. When you came to this place, King Sihon of

Heshbon and King Og of Bashan came out against us for battle, but we defeated them. We took their land and gave it as an inheritance to the Reubenites, the Gadites, and the half-tribe of Manasseh. Therefore diligently observe the words of this covenant, in order that you may succeed in everything that you do. You stand assembled today, all of you, before the LORD your God—the leaders of your tribes, your elders, and your officials, all the men of Israel, your children, your women, and the aliens who are in your camp, both those who cut your wood and those who draw your water—to enter into the covenant of the LORD your God, sworn by an oath, which the LORD your God is making with you today; in order that he may establish you today as his people, and that he may be your God, as he promised you and as he swore to your ancestors, to Abraham, to Isaac, and to Jacob. I am making this covenant, sworn by an oath, not only with you who stand here with us today before the LORD our God, but also with those who are not here with us today."

A Reading (Lesson) from the Second Letter of Paul to the Corinthians [9:1–15]

Now it is not necessary for me to write you about the ministry to the saints, for I know your eagerness, which is the subject of my boasting about you to the people of Macedonia, saying that Achaia has been ready since last year; and your zeal has stirred up most of them. But I am sending the brothers in order that our boasting about you may not prove to have been empty in this case, so that you may be ready, as I said you would be; otherwise, if some Macedonians come with me and find that you are not ready, we would be humiliated—to say nothing of you—in this undertaking. So I thought it necessary to urge the brothers to go on ahead to you, and arrange in advance for this bountiful gift that you have promised, so that it may be ready as a voluntary gift and not as an extortion. The point is this: the one who sows sparingly will also reap sparingly, and the one who sows bountifully will also reap bountifully. Each of you must give as you have made up your mind, not reluctantly or under compulsion, for God loves a cheerful giver. And God is able to provide you with every blessing in abundance, so that by always having enough of everything, you may share abundantly in every good work. As it is written, "He scatters abroad, he gives to the poor; his righteousness endures forever." He who supplies seed to the sower and bread for food will supply and multiply your seed for sowing and increase the harvest of your righteousness. You will be enriched in every way for your great generosity, which will produce thanksgiving to God through us; for the rendering of this ministry not only supplies the needs of the saints but also overflows with many thanksgivings to God. Through the testing of this ministry you glorify God by your obedience to the confession of the gospel of Christ and by the generosity of your sharing with them and with all others, while they long for you and pray for you because of the surpassing grace of God that he has given you. Thanks be to God for his indescribable gift!

A Reading (Lesson) from the Gospel according to Luke
[18:15–30]

People were bringing even infants to him that he might touch them; and when the disciples saw it, they sternly ordered them not to do it. But Jesus called for them and said, "Let the little children come to me, and do not stop them; for it is to such as these that the kingdom of God belongs. Truly I tell you, whoever does not receive the kingdom of God as a little child will never enter it." A certain ruler asked him, "Good Teacher, what must I do to inherit eternal life?" Jesus said to him, "Why do you call me good? No one is good but God alone. You know the commandments: 'You shall not commit adultery; You shall not murder; You shall not steal; You shall not bear false witness; Honor your father and mother.' " He replied, "I have kept all these since my youth." When Jesus heard this, he said to him, "There is still one thing lacking. Sell all that you own and distribute the money to the poor, and you will have treasure in heaven; then come, follow me." But when he heard this, he became sad; for he was very rich. Jesus looked at him and said, "How hard it is for those who have wealth to enter the kingdom of God! Indeed, it is easier for a camel to go through the eye of a needle than for someone who is rich to enter the kingdom of God." Those who heard it said, "Then who can be saved?" He replied, "What is impossible for mortals is possible for God." Then Peter said, "Look, we have left our homes and followed you." And he said to them, "Truly I tell you, there is no one who has left house or wife or brothers or parents or children, for the sake of the kingdom of God, who will not get back very much more in this age, and in the age to come eternal life."

Proper 5   *Week of the Sunday closest to June 8*

Sunday

Psalm 24 [page 613],   *Psalm 29* [page 620]   ❖
Psalm 8 [page 592],   *Psalm 84* [page 707]

A Reading (Lesson) from the Book of Deuteronomy
[29:16–29]

Moses summoned all Israel and said to them: "You know how we lived in the land of Egypt, and how we came through the midst of the nations through which you passed. You have seen their detestable things, the filthy idols of wood and stone, of silver and gold, that were among them. It may be that there is among you a man or woman, or a family or tribe, whose heart is already turning away from the LORD our God to serve the gods of those nations. It may be that there is among you a root sprouting poisonous and bitter growth. All who hear the words of this oath and bless themselves, thinking in their hearts, 'We are safe even though we go our own stubborn ways' (thus bringing disaster on moist and dry alike)—the LORD will be unwilling to pardon them, for the LORD's anger and passion will smoke against them. All the curses written in this book will descend on them, and the LORD will blot out their names from under heaven. The LORD will single them out from all the tribes of Israel for calamity, in accordance with all the curses of the covenant written in this book of the law. The next generation, your children who rise up after you, as well as the foreigner who comes from a distant country, will see the devastation of that land and the afflictions with which the LORD has afflicted it—all its soil burned out by sulfur and salt, nothing planted, nothing sprouting, unable to support any vegetation, like the destruction of Sodom and Gomorrah, Admah and Zeboiim, which the LORD destroyed in his fierce anger—they and indeed all the nations will wonder, 'Why has the LORD done thus to this land? What caused this great display of anger?' They will conclude, "It is because they abandoned the covenant of the LORD, the God of their ancestors, which he made with them when he brought them out of the land of Egypt. They turned and served other gods, worshiping them, gods whom they had not known and whom he had not allotted to them; so the anger of the LORD was kindled against that land, bringing on it every curse written in this book. The LORD uprooted them from their land in anger, fury, and great wrath, and cast them into another land, as is now the case. The secret things belong to the LORD our God, but the revealed things belong to us and to our children forever, to observe all the words of this law."

A Reading (Lesson) from the Revelation to John [12:1–12]

A great portent appeared in heaven: a woman clothed with the sun, with the moon under her feet, and on her head a crown of twelve stars. She was pregnant and was crying out in birthpangs, in the agony of giving birth. Then another portent appeared in heaven: a great red dragon, with seven heads and ten horns, and seven diadems on his heads. His tail swept down a third of the stars of heaven and threw them to the earth. Then the dragon stood before the woman who was about to bear a child, so that he might devour her child as soon as it was born. And she gave birth to a son, a male child, who is to rule all the nations with a rod of iron. But her child was snatched away and taken to God and to his throne; and the woman fled into the wilderness, where she has a place prepared by God, so that there she can be nourished for one thousand two hundred sixty days. And war broke out in heaven; Michael and his angels fought against the dragon. The dragon and his angels fought back, but they were defeated, and there was no longer any place for them in heaven. The great dragon was thrown down, that ancient serpent, who is called the Devil and Satan, the deceiver of the whole world—he was thrown down to the earth, and his angels were thrown down with him. Then I heard a loud voice in heaven, proclaiming, "Now have come the salvation and the power and the kingdom of our God and the authority of his Messiah, for the accuser of our comrades has been thrown down, who accuses them day and night before our God. But they have conquered him by the blood of the Lamb and by the word of their testimony, for they did not cling to life even in the face of death. Rejoice then, you heavens and those who dwell in them! But woe to the earth and the sea, for the devil has come down to you with great wrath, because he knows that his time is short!"

A Reading (Lesson) from the Gospel according to Matthew [15:29–39]

Jesus went on from the district of Tyre and Sidon and passed along the Sea of Galilee, and he went up the mountain, where he sat down. Great crowds came to him, bringing with them the lame, the maimed, the blind, the mute, and many others. They put them at his feet, and he cured them, so that the crowd was amazed when they saw the mute speaking, the maimed whole, the lame walking, and the blind seeing. And they praised the God of Israel. Then Jesus called his disciples to him and said, "I have compassion for the crowd, because they have been with me now for three days and have nothing to eat; and I do not want to send them away hungry, for they might faint on the way." The disciples said to him, "Where are we to get enough bread in the desert to feed so great a crowd?" Jesus asked them, "How many loaves have you?" They said, "Seven, and a few small fish." Then ordering the crowd to sit down on the ground, he took the seven loaves and the fish; and after giving thanks he broke them and gave them to the disciples, and the disciples gave them to the crowds. And all of them ate and were filled; and they took up the broken pieces left over, seven baskets full. Those who had eaten were four thousand men, besides women and children. After sending away the crowds, he got into the boat and went to the region of Magadan.

Monday

Psalm 56 [page 662], *Psalm 57* [page 663], ·
(Psalm 58 [page 664]) ❖ *Psalm 64* [page 671],
Psalm 65 [page 672]

A Reading (Lesson) from the Book of Deuteronomy
[30:1–10]

Moses summoned all Israel and said to them: "When all these things have happened to you, the blessings and the curses that I have set before you, if you call them to mind among all the nations where the LORD your God has driven you, and return to the LORD your God, and you and your children obey him with all your heart and with all your soul, just as I am commanding you today, then the LORD your God will restore your fortunes and have compassion on you, gathering you again from all the peoples among whom the LORD your God has scattered you. Even if you are exiled to the ends of the world, from there the LORD your God will gather you, and from there he will bring you back. The LORD your God will bring you into the land that your ancestors possessed, and you will possess it; he will make you more prosperous and numerous than your ancestors. Moreover, the LORD your God will circumcise your heart and the heart of your descendants, so that you will love the

LORD your God with all your heart and with all your soul, in order that you may live. The LORD your God will put all these curses on your enemies and on the adversaries who took advantage of you. Then you shall again obey the LORD, observing all his commandments that I am commanding you today, and the LORD your God will make you abundantly prosperous in all your undertakings, in the fruit of your body, in the fruit of your livestock, and in the fruit of your soil. For the LORD will again take delight in prospering you, just as he delighted in prospering your ancestors, when you obey the LORD your God by observing his commandments and decrees that are written in this book of the law, because you turn to the LORD your God with all your heart and with all your soul."

A Reading (Lesson) from the Second Letter of Paul to the Corinthians [10:1–18]

I myself, Paul, appeal to you by the meekness and gentleness of Christ—I who am humble when face to face with you, but bold toward you when I am away!—I ask that when I am present I need not show boldness by daring to oppose those who think we are acting according to human standards. Indeed, we live as human beings, but we do not wage war according to human standards; for the weapons of our warfare are not merely human, but they have divine power to destroy strongholds. We destroy arguments and every proud obstacle raised up against the knowledge of God, and we take every thought captive to obey Christ. We are ready to punish every disobedience when your obedience is complete. Look at what is before your eyes. If you are confident that you belong to Christ, remind yourself of this, that just as you belong to Christ, so also do we. Now, even if I boast a little too much of our authority, which the Lord gave for building you up and not for tearing you down, I will not be ashamed of it. I do not want to seem as though I am trying to frighten you with my letters. For they say, "His letters are weighty and strong, but his bodily presence is weak, and his speech contemptible." Let such people understand that what we say by letter when absent, we will also do when present. We do not dare to classify or compare ourselves with some of those who commend themselves. But when they measure themselves by one another, and compare themselves with one another, they do not show good sense. We, however, will not boast beyond limits, but will keep within the field that God has assigned to us, to reach out even as far as you. For we were not overstepping our limits when we reached you; we were the first to come all the way to you with the good news of Christ. We do not boast beyond limits, that is, in the labors of others; but our hope is that, as your faith increases, our sphere of action among you may be greatly enlarged, so that we may proclaim the good news in lands beyond you, without boasting of work already done in someone else's sphere of action. "Let the one who boasts, boast in the Lord." For it is not those who commend themselves that are approved, but those whom the Lord commends.

A Reading (Lesson) from the Gospel according to Luke [18:31–43]

Taking the twelve aside, Jesus said to them, "See, we are going up to Jerusalem, and everything that is written about the Son of Man by the prophets will be accomplished. For he will be handed over to the Gentiles; and he will be mocked and insulted and spat upon. After they have flogged him, they will kill him, and on the third day he will rise again." But they understood nothing about all these things; in fact, what he said was hidden from them, and they did not grasp what was said. As he approached Jericho, a blind man was sitting by the roadside begging. When he heard a crowd going by, he asked what was happening. They told him, "Jesus of Nazareth is passing by." Then he shouted, "Jesus, Son of David, have mercy on me!" Those who were in front sternly ordered him to be quiet; but he shouted even more loudly, "Son of David, have mercy on me!" Jesus stood still and ordered the man to be brought to him; and when he came near, he asked him, "What do you want me to do for you?" He said, "Lord, let me see again." Jesus said to him, "Receive your sight; your faith has saved you." Immediately he regained his sight and followed him, glorifying God; and all the people, when they saw it, praised God.

Tuesday

Psalm 61 [page 668], *Psalm 62* [page 669] ❖
Psalm 68:1–20(21–23)24–36 [page 676]

A Reading (Lesson) from the Book of Deuteronomy
[30:11–20]

Moses summoned all Israel and said to them: "Surely, this commandment that I am commanding you today is not too hard for you, nor is it too far away. It is not in heaven, that you should say, 'Who will go up to heaven for us, and get it for us so that we may hear it and observe it?' Neither is it beyond the sea, that you should say, 'Who will cross to the other side of the sea for us, and get it for us so that we may hear it and observe it?' No, the word is very near to you; it is in your mouth and in your heart for you to observe. See, I have set before you today life and prosperity, death and adversity. If you obey the commandments of the LORD your God that I am commanding you today, by loving the LORD your God, walking in his ways, and observing his commandments, decrees, and ordinances, then you shall live and become numerous, and the LORD your God will bless you in the land that you are entering to possess. But if your heart turns away and you do not hear, but are led astray to bow down to other gods and serve them, I declare to you today that you shall perish; you shall not live long in the land that you are crossing the Jordan to enter and possess. I call heaven and earth to witness against you today that I have set before you life and death, blessings and curses. Choose life so that you and your descendants may live, loving the LORD your God, obeying him, and holding fast to him; for that means life to you and length of days, so that you may live in the land that the LORD swore to give to your ancestors, to Abraham, to Isaac, and to Jacob."

A Reading (Lesson) from the Second Letter of Paul to the Corinthians [11:1–21a]

I wish you would bear with me in a little foolishness. Do bear with me! I feel a divine jealousy for you, for I promised you in marriage to one husband, to present you as a chaste virgin to Christ. But I am afraid that as the serpent deceived Eve by its cunning, your thoughts will be led astray from a sincere and pure devotion to Christ. For if someone comes and proclaims another Jesus than the one we proclaimed, or if you receive a different spirit from the one you received, or a different gospel from the one you accepted, you submit to it readily enough. I think that I am not in the least inferior to these super-apostles. I may be untrained in speech, but not in knowledge; certainly in every way and in all things we have made this evident to you. Did I commit a sin by humbling myself so that you might be exalted, because I proclaimed God's good news to you free of charge? I robbed other churches by accepting support from them in order to serve you. And when I was with you and was in need, I did not burden anyone, for my needs were supplied by the friends who came from Macedonia. So I refrained and will continue to refrain from burdening you in any way. As the truth of Christ is in me, this boast of mine will not be silenced in the regions of Achaia. And why? Because I do not love you? God knows I do! And what I do I will also continue to do, in order to deny an opportunity to those who want an opportunity to be recognized as our equals in what they boast about. For such boasters are false apostles, deceitful workers, disguising themselves as apostles of Christ. And no wonder! Even Satan disguises himself as an angel of light. So it is not strange if his ministers also disguise themselves as ministers of righteousness. Their end will match their deeds. I repeat, let no one think that I am a fool; but if you do, then accept me as a fool, so that I too may boast a little. What I am saying in regard to this boastful confidence, I am saying not with the Lord's authority, but as a fool; since many boast according to human standards, I will also boast. For you gladly put up with fools, being wise yourselves! For you put up with it when someone makes slaves of you, or preys upon you, or takes advantage of you, or puts on airs, or gives you a slap in the face. To my shame, I must say, we were too weak for that!

A Reading (Lesson) from the Gospel according to Luke
[19:1–10]

Jesus entered Jericho and was passing through it. A man
was there named Zacchaeus; he was a chief tax collector
and was rich. He was trying to see who Jesus was, but on
account of the crowd he could not, because he was short
in stature. So he ran ahead and climbed a sycamore tree to
see him, because he was going to pass that way. When
Jesus came to the place, he looked up and said to him,
"Zacchaeus, hurry and come down; for I must stay at your
house today." So he hurried down and was happy to
welcome him. All who saw it began to grumble and said,
"He has gone to be the guest of one who is a sinner."
Zacchaeus stood there and said to the Lord, "Look, half
of my possessions, Lord, I will give to the poor; and if I
have defrauded anyone of anything, I will pay back four
times as much." Then Jesus said to him, "Today salvation
has come to this house, because he too is a son of
Abraham. For the Son of Man came to seek out and to
save the lost."

Wednesday

Psalm 72 [page 685]   ❖   *Psalm 119:73–96* [page 769]

A Reading (Lesson) from the Book of Deuteronomy
[31:30—32:14]

Moses recited the words of this song, to the very end, in the
hearing of the whole assembly of Israel: "Give ear, O
heavens, and I will speak; let the earth hear the words of my
mouth. May my teaching drop like the rain, my speech
condense like the dew; like gentle rain on grass, like showers
on new growth. For I will proclaim the name of the LORD;

ascribe greatness to our God! The Rock, his work is perfect, and all his ways are just. A faithful God, without deceit, just and upright is he; yet his degenerate children have dealt falsely with him, a perverse and crooked generation. Do you thus repay the LORD, O foolish and senseless people? Is not he your father, who created you, who made you and established you? Remember the days of old, consider the years long past; ask your father, and he will inform you; your elders, and they will tell you. When the Most High apportioned the nations, when he divided humankind, he fixed the boundaries of the peoples according to the number of the gods; the LORD's own portion was his people, Jacob his allotted share. He sustained him in a desert land, in a howling wilderness waste; he shielded him, cared for him, guarded him as the apple of his eye. As an eagle stirs up its nest, and hovers over its young; as it spreads its wings, takes them up, and bears them aloft on its pinions, the LORD alone guided him; no foreign god was with him. He set him atop the heights of the land, and fed him with produce of the field; he nursed him with honey from the crags, with oil from flinty rock; curds from the herd, and milk from the flock, with fat of lambs and rams; Bashan bulls and goats, together with the choicest wheat—you drank fine wine from the blood of grapes."

A Reading (Lesson) from the Second Letter of Paul to the Corinthians [11:21b–33]

Whatever anyone dares to boast of—I am speaking as a fool—I also dare to boast of that. Are they Hebrews? So am I. Are they Israelites? So am I. Are they descendants of Abraham? So am I. Are they ministers of Christ? I am talking like a madman—I am a better one: with far greater labors, far more imprisonments, with countless floggings, and often near death. Five times I have received from the Jews the forty lashes minus one. Three times I was beaten with rods. Once I received a stoning. Three times I was shipwrecked; for a night and a day I was adrift at sea; on frequent journeys, in danger from rivers, danger from bandits, danger from my own people, danger from Gentiles, danger in the city, danger in the wilderness, danger at sea, danger from false brothers and sisters; in toil and hardship, through many a sleepless night, hungry and thirsty, often without food, cold and naked. And, besides other things, I am under daily pressure because of my anxiety for all the churches. Who is weak, and I am not weak? Who is made to stumble, and I am not indignant? If I must boast, I will boast of the things that show my weakness. The God and Father of the Lord Jesus (blessed be he forever!) knows that I do not lie. In Damascus, the governor under King Aretas guarded the city of Damascus in order to seize me, but I was let down in a basket through a window in the wall, and escaped from his hands.

A Reading (Lesson) from the Gospel according to Luke
[19:11–27]

As they were listening to this, Jesus went on to tell a parable, because he was near Jerusalem, and because they supposed that the kingdom of God was to appear immediately. So he said, "A nobleman went to a distant country to get royal power for himself and then return. He summoned ten of his slaves, and gave them ten pounds, and said to them, 'Do business with these until I come back.' But the citizens of his country hated him and sent a delegation after him, saying, 'We do not want this man to rule over us.' When he returned, having received royal power, he ordered these slaves, to whom he had given the money, to be summoned so that he might find out what they had gained by trading. The first came forward and said, 'Lord, your pound has made ten more pounds.' He said to him, 'Well done, good slave! Because you have been trustworthy in a very small thing, take charge of ten cities.' Then the second came, saying, 'Lord, your pound has made five pounds.' He said to him, 'And you, rule over five cities.' Then the other came, saying, 'Lord, here is your pound. I wrapped it up in a piece of cloth, for I was afraid of you, because you are a harsh man; you take what you did not deposit, and reap what you did not sow.' He said to him, 'I will judge you by your own words, you wicked slave! You knew, did you, that I was a harsh man, taking what I did not deposit and reaping what I did not sow? Why then did you not put my money into the bank? Then when I returned, I could have collected it with interest.' He said to the bystanders, 'Take the pound from him and give it to the one who has ten pounds.' (And they said to him, 'Lord, he has ten pounds!') 'I tell you, to all those who have, more will be given; but from those who have nothing, even what they have will be taken away. But as for these enemies of mine who did not want me to be king over them—bring them here and slaughter them in my presence.' "

Thursday

(Psalm 70 [page 682]),
Psalm 71 [page 683] ❖ *Psalm 74* [page 689]

A Reading (Lesson) from the Book of Ecclesiasticus
[44:19—45:5]

Abraham was the great father of a multitude of nations, and no one has been found like him in glory. He kept the law of the Most High, and entered into a covenant with him; he certified the covenant in his flesh, and when he was tested he proved faithful. Therefore the Lord assured him with an oath that the nations would be blessed through his offspring; that he would make him as numerous as the dust of the earth, and exalt his offspring like the stars, and give them an inheritance from sea to sea and from the Euphrates to the ends of the earth. To Isaac also he gave the same assurance for the sake of his father Abraham. The blessing of all people and the covenant he made to rest on the head of Jacob; he acknowledged him with his blessings, and gave him his inheritance; he divided his portions, and distributed them among twelve tribes. From his descendants the Lord brought forth a godly man, who found favor in the sight of all and was beloved by God and people, Moses, whose memory is blessed. He made him equal in glory to the holy ones, and made him great, to the terror of his enemies. By his words he performed swift miracles; the Lord glorified him in the presence of kings. He gave him commandments for his people, and revealed to him his glory. For his faithfulness and meekness he consecrated him, choosing him out of all humankind. He allowed him to hear his voice, and led him into the dark cloud, and gave him the commandments face to face, the law of life and knowledge, so that he might teach Jacob the covenant, and Israel his decrees.

A Reading (Lesson) from the Second Letter of Paul to the Corinthians [12:1–10]

It is necessary to boast; nothing is to be gained by it, but I will go on to visions and revelations of the Lord. I know a person in Christ who fourteen years ago was caught up to the third heaven—whether in the body or out of the body I do not know; God knows. And I know that such a person—whether in the body or out of the body I do not know; God knows—was caught up into Paradise and heard things that are not to be told, that no mortal is permitted to repeat. On behalf of such a one I will boast, but on my own behalf I will not boast, except of my weaknesses. But if I wish to boast, I will not be a fool, for I will be speaking the truth. But I refrain from it, so that no one may think better of me than what is seen in me or heard from me, even considering the exceptional character of the revelations. Therefore, to keep me from being too elated, a thorn was given me in the flesh, a messenger of Satan to torment me, to keep me from being too elated. Three times I appealed to the Lord about this, that it would leave me, but he said to me, "My grace is sufficient for you, for power is made perfect in weakness." So, I will boast all the more gladly of my weaknesses, so that the power of Christ may dwell in me. Therefore I am content with weaknesses, insults, hardships, persecutions, and calamities for the sake of Christ; for whenever I am weak, then I am strong.

A Reading (Lesson) from the Gospel according to Luke [19:28–40]

After he had said this, Jesus went on ahead, going up to Jerusalem. When he had come near Bethphage and Bethany, at the place called the Mount of Olives, he sent two of the disciples, saying, "Go into the village ahead of you, and as you enter it you will find tied there a colt that has never been ridden. Untie it and bring it here. If anyone asks you, 'Why are you untying it?' just say this, 'The Lord needs it.' " So those who were sent departed and found it as he had told them. As they were untying the colt, its owners asked them, "Why are you untying the colt?" They said, "The Lord needs it." Then they brought it to Jesus; and after throwing their cloaks on the colt, they set Jesus on it. As he rode along, people kept spreading their cloaks on the road. As he was now approaching the path down from the Mount of Olives, the whole multitude of the disciples began to praise God joyfully with a loud voice for all the deeds of power that they had seen, saying, "Blessed is the king who comes in the name of the Lord! Peace in heaven, and glory in the highest heaven!" Some of the Pharisees in the crowd said to him, "Teacher, order your disciples to stop." He answered, "I tell you, if these were silent, the stones would shout out."

Friday

Psalm 69:1–23(24–30)31–38 [page 679] ❖
Psalm 73 [page 687]

A Reading (Lesson) from the Book of Ecclesiasticus [45:6–16]

He exalted Aaron, a holy man like Moses who was his brother, of the tribe of Levi. He made an everlasting covenant with him, and gave him the priesthood of the people. He blessed him with stateliness, and put a glorious robe on him. He clothed him in perfect splendor, and strengthened him with the symbols of authority, the linen undergarments, the long robe, and the ephod. And he encircled him with pomegranates, with many golden bells all around, to send forth a sound as he walked, to make their ringing heard in the temple as a reminder to his people; with the sacred vestment, of gold and violet and purple, the work of an embroiderer; with the oracle of judgment, Urim and Thummim; with twisted crimson, the work of an artisan; with precious stones engraved like seals, in a setting of gold, the work of a jeweler, to commemorate in engraved letters each of the tribes of Israel; with a gold crown upon his turban, inscribed like a seal with "Holiness," a distinction to be prized, the work of an expert, a delight to the eyes, richly adorned. Before him such beautiful things did not exist. No outsider ever put them on, but only his sons and his descendants in perpetuity. His sacrifices shall be wholly burned twice every day continually. Moses ordained him, and anointed him with holy oil; it was an everlasting covenant for him and for his descendants as long as the heavens endure, to minister to the Lord and serve as priest and bless his people in his name. He chose him out of all the living to offer sacrifice to the Lord, incense and a pleasing odor as a memorial portion, to make atonement for the people.

A Reading (Lesson) from the Second Letter of Paul to the Corinthians [12:11–21]

I have been a fool! You forced me to it. Indeed you should have been the ones commending me, for I am not at all inferior to these super-apostles, even though I am nothing. The signs of a true apostle were performed among you with utmost patience, signs and wonders and mighty works. How have you been worse off than the other churches, except that I myself did not burden you? Forgive me this wrong! Here I am, ready to come to you this third time. And I will not be a burden, because I do not want what is yours but you; for children ought not to lay up for their parents, but parents for their children. I will most gladly spend and be spent for you. If I love you more, am I to be loved less? Let it be assumed that I did not burden you. Nevertheless (you say) since I was crafty, I took you in by deceit. Did I take advantage of you through any of those whom I sent to you? I urged Titus to go, and sent the brother with him. Titus did not take advantage of you, did he? Did we not conduct ourselves with the same spirit? Did we not take the same steps? Have you been thinking all along that we have been defending ourselves before you? We are speaking in Christ before God. Everything we do, beloved, is for the sake of building you up. For I fear that when I come, I may find you not as I wish, and that you may find me not as you wish; I fear that there may perhaps be quarreling, jealousy, anger, selfishness, slander, gossip, conceit, and disorder. I fear that when I come again, my God may humble me before you, and that I may have to mourn over many who previously sinned and have not repented of the impurity, sexual immorality, and licentiousness that they have practiced.

A Reading (Lesson) from the Gospel according to Luke [19:41–48]

As Jesus came near and saw Jerusalem, he wept over it, saying, "If you, even you, had only recognized on this day the things that make for peace! But now they are hidden from your eyes. Indeed, the days will come upon you, when your enemies will set up ramparts around you and surround you, and hem you in on every side. They will crush you to the ground, you and your children within you, and they will not leave within you one stone upon another; because you did not recognize the time of your visitation from God." Then he entered the temple and began to drive out those who were selling things there; and he said, "It is written, 'My house shall be a house of prayer'; but you have made it a den of robbers." Every day he was teaching in the temple. The chief priests, the scribes, and the leaders of the people kept looking for a way to kill him; but they did not find anything they could do, for all the people were spellbound by what they heard.

Saturday

Psalm 75 [page 691], *Psalm 76* [page 692] ❖
Psalm 23 [page 612], *Psalm 27* [page 617]

A Reading (Lesson) from the Book of Ecclesiasticus [46:1–10]

Joshua son of Nun was mighty in war, and was the successor of Moses in the prophetic office. He became, as his name implies, a great savior of God's elect, to take vengeance on the enemies that rose against them, so that he might give Israel its inheritance. How glorious he was when he lifted his hands and brandished his sword against the cities! Who before him ever stood so firm? For he waged the wars of the Lord. Was it not through him that the sun stood still and one day become as long as two? He called upon the Most High, the Mighty One, when enemies pressed him on every side, and the great Lord answered him with hailstones of mighty power. He overwhelmed that nation in battle, and on the slope he destroyed his opponents, so that the nations might know his armament, that he was fighting in the sight of the Lord; for he was a devoted follower of the Mighty One. And in the days of Moses he proved his loyalty, he and Caleb son of Jephunneh: they opposed the congregation, restrained the people from sin, and stilled their wicked grumbling. And these two alone were spared out of six hundred thousand infantry, to lead the people into their inheritance, the land flowing with milk and honey. The Lord gave Caleb strength, which remained with him in his old age, so that he went up to the hill country, and his children obtained it for an inheritance, so that all the Israelites might see how good it is to follow the Lord.

2 Corinthians 13:1–14 [page 276 above]

A Reading (Lesson) from the Gospel according to Luke [20:1–8]

One day, as Jesus was teaching the people in the temple and telling the good news, the chief priests and the scribes came with the elders and said to him, "Tell us, by what authority are you doing these things? Who is it who gave you this authority?" He answered them, "I will also ask you a question, and you tell me: Did the baptism of John come from heaven, or was it of human origin?" They discussed it with one another, saying, "If we say, 'From heaven,' he will say, 'Why did you not believe him?' But if we say, 'Of human origin,' all the people will stone us; for they are convinced that John was a prophet." So they answered that they did not know where it came from. Then Jesus said to them, "Neither will I tell you by what authority I am doing these things."

Proper 6 *Week of the Sunday closest to June 15*

Sunday

Psalm 93 [page 722], *Psalm 96* [page 725] ❖
Psalm 34 [page 627]

A Reading (Lesson) from the Book of Ecclesiasticus
[46:11–20]

The judges also, with their respective names, whose hearts
did not fall into idolatry and who did not turn away from
the Lord—may their memory be blessed! May their bones
send forth new life from where they lie, and may the names
of those who have been honored live again in their children!
Samuel was beloved by his Lord; a prophet of the Lord, he
established the kingdom and anointed rulers over his people.
By the law of the Lord he judged the congregation, and the
Lord watched over Jacob. By his faithfulness he was proved
to be a prophet, and by his words he became known as a
trustworthy seer. He called upon the Lord, the Mighty One,
when his enemies pressed him on every side, and he offered
in sacrifice a suckling lamb. Then the Lord thundered from
heaven, and made his voice heard with a mighty sound; he
subdued the leaders of the enemy and all the rulers of the
Philistines. Before the time of his eternal sleep, Samuel bore
witness before the Lord and his anointed: "No property, not
so much as a pair of shoes, have I taken from anyone!" And
no one accused him. Even after he had fallen asleep, he
prophesied and made known to the king his death, and
lifted up his voice from the ground in prophecy, to blot out
the wickedness of the people.

A Reading (Lesson) from the Revelation to John [15:1–8]

I saw another portent in heaven, great and amazing: seven angels with seven plagues, which are the last, for with them the wrath of God is ended. And I saw what appeared to be a sea of glass mixed with fire, and those who had conquered the beast and its image and the number of its name, standing beside the sea of glass with harps of God in their hands. And they sing the song of Moses, the servant of God, and the song of the Lamb: "Great and amazing are your deeds, Lord God the Almighty! Just and true are your ways, King of the nations! Lord, who will not fear and glorify your name? For you alone are holy. All nations will come and worship before you, for your judgments have been revealed." After this I looked, and the temple of the tent of witness in heaven was opened, and out of the temple came the seven angels with the seven plagues, robed in pure bright linen, with golden sashes across their chests. Then one of the four living creatures gave the seven angels seven golden bowls full of the wrath of God, who lives forever and ever; and the temple was filled with smoke from the glory of God and from his power, and no one could enter the temple until the seven plagues of the seven angels were ended.

A Reading (Lesson) from the Gospel according to Matthew [18:1–14]

The disciples came to Jesus and asked, "Who is the greatest in the kingdom of heaven?" He called a child, whom he put among them, and said, "Truly I tell you, unless you change and become like children, you will never enter the kingdom of heaven. Whoever becomes humble like this child is the greatest in the kingdom of heaven. Whoever welcomes one such child in my name welcomes me. If any of you put a stumbling block before one of these little ones who believe in me, it would be better for you if a great millstone were fastened around your neck and you were drowned in the depth of the sea. Woe to the world because of stumbling blocks! Occasions for stumbling are bound to come, but woe to the one by whom the stumbling block comes! If your hand or your foot causes you to stumble, cut it off and throw it away; it is better for you to enter life maimed or lame than to have two hands or two feet and to be thrown into the eternal fire. And if your eye causes you to stumble, tear it out and throw it away; it is better for you to enter life with one eye than to have two eyes and to be thrown into the hell of fire. Take care that you do not despise one of these little ones; for, I tell you, in heaven their angels continually see the face of my Father in heaven. What do you think? If a shepherd has a hundred sheep, and one of them has gone astray, does he not leave the ninety-nine on the mountains and go in search of the one that went astray? And if he finds it, truly I tell you, he rejoices over it more than over the ninety-nine that never went astray. So it is not the will of your Father in heaven that one of these little ones should be lost."

Monday

Psalm 80 [page 702] ❖ *Psalm 77* [page 693], *(Psalm 79* [page 701])

A Reading (Lesson) from the First Book of Samuel [1:1–20]

There was a certain man of Ramathaim, a Zuphite from the hill country of Ephraim, whose name was Elkanah son of Jeroham son of Elihu son of Tohu son of Zuph, an Ephraimite. He had two wives; the name of the one was Hannah, and the name of the other Peninnah. Peninnah had children, but Hannah had no children. Now this man used to go up year by year from his town to worship and to sacrifice to the LORD of hosts at Shiloh, where the two sons of Eli, Hophni and Phinehas, were priests of the LORD. On the day when Elkanah sacrificed, he would give portions to his wife Peninnah and to all her sons and daughters; but to Hannah he gave a double portion, because he loved her, though the LORD had closed her womb. Her rival used to provoke her severely, to irritate her, because the LORD had closed her womb. So it went on year by year; as often as she went up to the house of the LORD, she used to provoke her. Therefore Hannah wept and would not eat. Her husband Elkanah said to her, "Hannah, why do you weep? Why do you not eat? Why is your heart sad? Am I not more to you than ten sons?" After they had eaten and drunk at Shiloh, Hannah rose and presented herself before the LORD. Now Eli the priest was sitting on the seat beside the doorpost of the temple of the LORD. She was deeply distressed and prayed to the LORD, and wept bitterly. She made this vow: "O LORD of hosts, if only you will look on the misery of your servant, and remember me, and not forget your servant, but will give to your servant a male child, then I will set him before you as a nazirite until the day of his death. He shall drink neither wine nor intoxicants, and no razor shall touch his head." As she continued praying before the LORD, Eli observed her mouth. Hannah was praying silently; only her lips moved, but her voice was not heard; therefore Eli thought she was drunk. So Eli said to her, "How long will you make a drunken spectacle of yourself? Put away your wine." But Hannah answered, "No, my lord, I am a woman deeply troubled; I have drunk neither wine nor strong drink, but I have been pouring out my soul before the LORD. Do not regard your servant as a worthless woman, for I have been speaking out of my great anxiety and vexation all this time." Then Eli answered, "Go in peace; the God of Israel grant the petition you have made to him." And she said, "Let your servant find favor in your sight." Then the woman went to her quarters, ate and drank with her husband, and her countenance was sad no longer. They rose early in the morning and worshiped before the LORD; then they went back to their house at Ramah. Elkanah knew his wife Hannah, and the LORD remembered her. In due time Hannah conceived and bore a son. She named him Samuel, for she said, "I have asked him of the LORD."

A Reading (Lesson) from the Acts of the Apostles [1:1–14]

In the first book, Theophilus, I wrote about all that Jesus did and taught from the beginning until the day when he was taken up to heaven, after giving instructions through the Holy Spirit to the apostles whom he had chosen. After his suffering he presented himself alive to them by many convincing proofs, appearing to them during forty days and speaking about the kingdom of God. While staying with them, he ordered them not to leave Jerusalem, but to wait there for the promise of the Father. "This," he said, "is what you have heard from me; for John baptized with water, but you will be baptized with the Holy Spirit not many days from now." So when they had come together, they asked him, "Lord, is this the time when you will restore the kingdom to Israel?" He replied, "It is not for you to know the times or periods that the Father has set by his own authority. But you will receive power when the Holy Spirit has come upon you; and you will be my witnesses in Jerusalem, in all Judea and Samaria, and to the ends of the earth." When he had said this, as they were watching, he was lifted up, and a cloud took him out of their sight. While he was going and they were gazing up toward heaven, suddenly two men in white robes stood by them. They said, "Men of Galilee, why do you stand looking up toward heaven? This Jesus, who has been taken up from you into heaven, will come in the same way as you saw him go into heaven." Then they returned to Jerusalem from the mount called Olivet, which is near Jerusalem, a sabbath day's journey away. When they had entered the city, they went to the room upstairs where they were staying, Peter, and John, and James, and Andrew, Philip and Thomas, Bartholomew and Matthew, James son of Alphaeus, and Simon the Zealot, and Judas son of James. All these were constantly devoting themselves to prayer, together with certain women, including Mary the mother of Jesus, as well as his brothers.

A Reading (Lesson) from the Gospel according to Luke [20:9–19]

Jesus began to tell the people this parable: "A man planted a vineyard, and leased it to tenants, and went to another country for a long time. When the season came, he sent a slave to the tenants in order that they might give him his share of the produce of the vineyard; but the tenants beat him and sent him away empty-handed. Next he sent another slave; that one also they beat and insulted and sent away empty-handed. And he sent still a third;

this one also they wounded and threw out. Then the owner of the vineyard said, 'What shall I do? I will send my beloved son; perhaps they will respect him.' But when the tenants saw him, they discussed it among themselves and said, 'This is the heir; let us kill him so that the inheritance may be ours.' So they threw him out of the vineyard and killed him. What then will the owner of the vineyard do to them? He will come and destroy those tenants and give the vineyard to others." When they heard this, they said, "Heaven forbid!" But he looked at them and said, "What then does this text mean: 'The stone that the builders rejected has become the cornerstone'? Everyone who falls on that stone will be broken to pieces; and it will crush anyone on whom it falls." When the scribes and chief priests realized that he had told this parable against them, they wanted to lay hands on him at that very hour, but they feared the people.

Tuesday

Psalm 78:1–39 [page 694] ❖ *Psalm 78:40–72* [page 698]

A Reading (Lesson) from the First Book of Samuel
[1:21—2:11]

The man Elkanah and all his household went up to offer to the LORD the yearly sacrifice, and to pay his vow. But Hannah did not go up, for she said to her husband, "As soon as the child is weaned, I will bring him, that he may appear in the presence of the LORD, and remain there forever; I will offer him as a nazirite for all time." Her husband Elkanah said to her, "Do what seems best to you, wait until you have weaned him; only—may the LORD establish his word." So the woman remained and nursed her son, until she weaned him. When she had weaned him, she took him up with her, along with a three-year-old bull, an ephah of flour, and a skin of wine. She brought him to the house of the LORD at Shiloh; and the child was young. Then they slaughtered the bull, and they brought the child to Eli. And she said, "Oh, my lord! As you live, my lord, I am the woman who was standing here in your presence, praying to the LORD. For this child I prayed; and the LORD has granted me the petition that I made to him. Therefore I have lent him to the LORD; as long as he lives, he is given to the LORD." She left him there for the LORD. Hannah prayed and said, "My heart exults in the LORD; my strength is exalted in my God. My mouth derides my enemies, because I rejoice in my victory. There is no Holy One like the LORD, no one besides you; there is no Rock like our God. Talk no more so very proudly, let not arrogance come from your mouth; for the LORD is a God of knowledge, and by him actions are weighed. The bows of the mighty are broken, but the feeble gird on strength. Those who were full have hired themselves out for bread, but those who were hungry are fat with spoil. The barren has borne seven, but she who has many children is forlorn. The LORD kills and brings to life; he brings down to Sheol and raises up. The LORD makes poor and makes rich; he brings low, he also exalts. He raises up the poor from the dust; he lifts the needy from the ash heap, to make them sit with princes and inherit a seat of honor. For the pillars of the earth are the LORD's, and on them he has set the world. He will guard the feet of his faithful ones, but the wicked shall be cut off in darkness; for not by might does one prevail. The LORD! His adversaries shall be shattered; the Most High will thunder in heaven. The LORD will judge the ends of the earth; he will give strength to his king, and exalt the power of his anointed." Then Elkanah went home to Ramah, while the boy remained to minister to the LORD, in the presence of the priest Eli.

A Reading (Lesson) from the Acts of the Apostles [1:15–26]

In those days Peter stood up among the believers (together
the crowd numbered about one hundred twenty persons)
and said, "Friends, the scripture had to be fulfilled, which
the Holy Spirit through David foretold concerning Judas,
who became a guide for those who arrested Jesus—for he
was numbered among us and was allotted his share in this
ministry." (Now this man acquired a field with the reward
of his wickedness; and falling headlong, he burst open in
the middle and all his bowels gushed out. This became
known to all the residents of Jerusalem, so that the field
was called in their language Hakeldama, that is, Field of
Blood.) "For it is written in the book of Psalms, 'Let his
homestead become desolate, and let there be no one to live
in it'; and 'Let another take his position of overseer.' So
one of the men who have accompanied us during all the
time that the Lord Jesus went in and out among us,
beginning from the baptism of John until the day when he
was taken up from us—one of these must become a
witness with us to his resurrection." So they proposed
two, Joseph called Barsabbas, who was also known as
Justus, and Matthias. Then they prayed and said, "Lord,
you know everyone's heart. Show us which one of these
two you have chosen to take the place in this ministry and
apostleship from which Judas turned aside to go to his
own place." And they cast lots for them, and the lot fell
on Matthias; and he was added to the eleven apostles.

A Reading (Lesson) from the Gospel according to Luke
[20:19–26]

When the scribes and chief priests realized that Jesus had
told this parable against them, they wanted to lay hands
on him at that very hour, but they feared the people. So
they watched him and sent spies who pretended to be

honest, in order to trap him by what he said, so as to hand him over to the jurisdiction and authority of the governor. So they asked him, "Teacher, we know that you are right in what you say and teach, and you show deference to no one, but teach the way of God in accordance with truth. Is it lawful for us to pay taxes to the emperor, or not?" But he perceived their craftiness and said to them, "Show me a denarius. Whose head and whose title does it bear?" They said, "The emperor's." He said to them, "Then give to the emperor the things that are the emperor's, and to God the things that are God's." And they were not able in the presence of the people to trap him by what he said; and being amazed by his answer, they became silent.

Wednesday

Psalm 119:97–120 [page 771] ❖ *Psalm 81* [page 704], *Psalm 82* [page 705]

A Reading (Lesson) from the First Book of Samuel [2:12–26]

Now the sons of Eli were scoundrels; they had no regard for the LORD or for the duties of the priests to the people. When anyone offered sacrifice, the priest's servant would come, while the meat was boiling, with a three-pronged fork in his hand, and he would thrust it into the pan, or kettle, or caldron, or pot; all that the fork brought up the priest would take for himself. This is what they did at Shiloh to all the Israelites who came there. Moreover, before the fat was burned, the priest's servant would come and say to the one who was sacrificing, "Give meat for the priest to roast; for he will not accept boiled meat from you, but only raw." And if the man said to him, "Let them burn the fat first, and then take whatever you wish," he would say, "No, you must give it now; if not, I will take it by force." Thus the sin of the young men was very great in the sight of the LORD; for they treated the offerings of the LORD with contempt. Samuel was ministering before the LORD, a boy wearing a linen ephod. His mother used to make for him a little robe and take it to him each year, when she went up with her husband to offer the yearly sacrifice. Then Eli would bless Elkanah and his wife, and say, "May the LORD repay you with children by this woman for the gift that she made to the LORD"; and then they would return to their home. And the LORD took note of Hannah; she conceived and bore three sons and two daughters. And the boy Samuel grew up in the presence of the LORD. Now Eli was very old. He heard all that his sons were doing to all Israel, and how they lay with the women who served at the entrance to the tent of meeting. He said to them, "Why do you do such things? For I hear of your evil dealings from all these people. No, my sons; it is not a good report that I hear the people of the LORD spreading abroad. If one person sins against another, someone can intercede for the sinner with the LORD; but if someone sins against the LORD, who can make intercession?" But they would not listen to the voice of their father; for it was the will of the LORD to kill them. Now the boy Samuel continued to grow both in stature and in favor with the LORD and with the people.

A Reading (Lesson) from the Acts of the Apostles [2:1–21]

When the day of Pentecost had come, they were all together in one place. And suddenly from heaven there came a sound like the rush of a violent wind, and it filled the entire house where they were sitting. Divided tongues, as of fire, appeared among them, and a tongue rested on each of them. All of them were filled with the Holy Spirit and began to speak in other languages, as the Spirit gave them ability. Now there were devout Jews from every nation under heaven living in Jerusalem. And at this sound the crowd gathered and was bewildered, because each one heard them speaking in the native language of each. Amazed and astonished, they asked, "Are not all these who are speaking Galileans? And how is it that we hear, each of us, in our own native language? Parthians, Medes, Elamites, and residents of Mesopotamia, Judea and Cappadocia, Pontus and Asia, Phrygia and Pamphylia, Egypt and the parts of Libya belonging to Cyrene, and visitors from Rome, both Jews and proselytes, Cretans and Arabs—in our own languages we hear them speaking about God's deeds of power." All were amazed and perplexed, saying to one another, "What does this mean?" But others sneered and said, "They are filled with new wine." But Peter, standing with the eleven, raised his voice and addressed them, "Men of Judea and all who live in Jerusalem, let this be known to you, and listen to what I say. Indeed, these are not drunk, as you suppose, for it is only nine o'clock in the morning. No, this is what was spoken through the prophet Joel: 'In the last days it will be, God declares, that I will pour out my Spirit upon all flesh, and your sons and your daughters shall prophesy, and your young men shall see visions, and your old men shall dream dreams. Even upon my slaves, both men and women, in those days I will pour out my Spirit; and they shall prophesy. And I will show portents in the heaven above and signs on the earth below, blood, and fire, and smoky mist. The sun shall be turned to darkness and the moon to blood, before the coming of the Lord's great and glorious day. Then everyone who calls on the name of the Lord shall be saved."

A Reading (Lesson) from the Gospel according to Luke
[20:27–40]

Some Sadducees, those who say there is no resurrection, came to Jesus and asked him a question, "Teacher, Moses wrote for us that if a man's brother dies, leaving a wife but no children, the man shall marry the widow and raise up children for his brother. Now there were seven brothers; the first married, and died childless; then the second and the third married her, and so in the same way all seven died childless. Finally the woman also died. In the resurrection, therefore, whose wife will the woman be? For the seven had married her." Jesus said to them, "Those who belong to this age marry and are given in marriage; but those who are considered worthy of a place in that age and in the resurrection from the dead neither marry nor are given in marriage. Indeed they cannot die anymore, because they are like angels and are children of God, being children of the resurrection. And the fact that the dead are raised Moses himself showed, in the story about the bush, where he speaks of the Lord as the God of Abraham, the God of Isaac, and the God of Jacob. Now he is God not of the dead, but of the living; for to him all of them are alive." Then some of the scribes answered, "Teacher, you have spoken well." For they no longer dared to ask him another question.

Thursday

(Psalm 83 [page 706]) or *Psalm 34* [page 627] ❖
Psalm 85 [page 708], *Psalm 86* [page 709]

A Reading (Lesson) from the First Book of Samuel [2:27–36]

A man of God came to Eli and said to him, "Thus the LORD has said, 'I revealed myself to the family of your ancestor in Egypt when they were slaves to the house of Pharaoh. I chose him out of all the tribes of Israel to be my priest, to go up to my altar, to offer incense, to wear an ephod before me; and I gave to the family of your ancestor all my offerings by fire from the people of Israel. Why then look with greedy eye at my sacrifices and my offerings that I commanded, and honor your sons more than me by fattening yourselves on the choicest parts of every offering of my people Israel?' Therefore the LORD the God of Israel declares: 'I promised that your family and the family of your ancestor should go in and out before me forever'; but now the LORD declares: 'Far be it from me; for those who honor me I will honor, and those who despise me shall be treated with contempt. See, a time is coming when I will cut off your strength and the strength of your ancestor's family, so that no one in your family will live to old age. Then in distress you will look with greedy eye on all the prosperity that shall be bestowed upon Israel; and no one in your family shall ever live to old age. The only one of you whom I shall not cut off from my altar shall be spared to weep out his eyes and grieve his heart; all the members of your household shall die by the sword. The fate of your two sons, Hophni and Phinehas, shall be the sign to you—both of them shall die on the same day. I will raise up for myself a faithful priest, who shall do according to what is in my heart and in my mind. I will build him a sure house, and he shall go in and out before my anointed one forever. Everyone who is left in your family shall come to implore him for a piece of silver or a loaf of bread, and shall say, Please put me in one of the priest's places, that I may eat a morsel of bread.' "

A Reading (Lesson) from the Acts of the Apostles [2:22–36]

Peter, standing with the eleven, lifted up his voice and addressed them, "You that are Israelites, listen to what I have to say: Jesus of Nazareth, a man attested to you by God with deeds of power, wonders, and signs that God did through him among you, as you yourselves know—this man, handed over to you according to the definite plan and foreknowledge of God, you crucified and killed by the hands of those outside the law. But God raised him up, having freed him from death, because it was impossible for him to be held in its power. For David says concerning him, 'I saw the Lord always before me, for he is at my right hand so that I will not be shaken; therefore my heart was glad, and my tongue rejoiced; moreover my flesh will live in hope. For you will not abandon my soul to Hades, or let your Holy One experience corruption. You have made known to me the ways of life; you will make me full of gladness with your presence.' Fellow Israelites, I may say to you confidently of our ancestor David that he both died and was buried, and his tomb is with us to this day. Since he was a prophet, he knew that God had sworn with an oath to him that he would put one of his descendants on his throne. Foreseeing this, David spoke of the resurrection of the Messiah, saying, 'He was not abandoned to Hades, nor did his flesh experience corruption.' This Jesus God raised up, and of that all of us are witnesses. Being therefore exalted at the right hand of God, and having received from the Father the promise of the Holy Spirit, he has poured out this that you both see and hear. For David did not ascend into the heavens, but he himself says, 'The Lord said to my Lord, "Sit at my right hand, until I make your enemies your footstool." ' Therefore let the entire house of Israel know with certainty that God has made him both Lord and Messiah, this Jesus whom you crucified."

A Reading (Lesson) from the Gospel according to Luke [20:41—21:4]

Jesus said to the Sadducees, "How can they say that the Messiah is David's son? For David himself says in the book of Psalms, 'The Lord said to my Lord, "Sit at my right hand, until I make your enemies your footstool." ' David thus calls him Lord; so how can he be his son?" In the hearing of all the people he said to the disciples, "Beware of the scribes, who like to walk around in long robes, and love to be greeted with respect in the marketplaces, and to have the best seats in the synagogues and places of honor at banquets. They devour widows' houses and for the sake of appearance say long prayers. They will receive the greater condemnation." He looked up and saw rich people putting their gifts into the treasury; he also saw a poor widow put in two small copper coins. He said, "Truly I tell you, this poor widow has put in more than all of them; for all of them have contributed out of their abundance, but she out of her poverty has put in all she had to live on."

Friday

Psalm 88 [page 712]   ❖   *Psalm 91* [page 719],
Psalm 92 [page 720]

A Reading (Lesson) from the First Book of Samuel [3:1–21]

Now the boy Samuel was ministering to the LORD under Eli. The word of the LORD was rare in those days; visions were not widespread. At that time Eli, whose eyesight had begun to grow dim so that he could not see, was lying down in his room; the lamp of God had not yet gone out, and Samuel was lying down in the temple of the LORD, where the ark of God was. Then the LORD called, "Samuel! Samuel!" and he said, "Here I am!" and ran to Eli, and said, "Here I am, for you called me." But he said, "I did not call; lie down again." So he went and lay down. The LORD called again, "Samuel!" Samuel got up and went to Eli, and said, "Here I am, for you called me." But he said, "I did not call, my son; lie down again." Now Samuel did not yet know the LORD, and the word of the LORD had not yet been revealed to him. The LORD called Samuel again, a third time. And he got up and went to Eli, and said, "Here I am, for you called me." Then Eli perceived that the LORD was calling the boy. Therefore Eli said to Samuel, "Go, lie down; and if he calls you, you shall say, 'Speak, LORD, for your servant is listening.' " So Samuel went and lay down in his place. Now the LORD came and stood there, calling as before, "Samuel! Samuel!" And Samuel said, "Speak, for your servant is listening." Then the LORD said to Samuel, "See, I am about to do something in Israel that will make both ears of anyone who hears of it tingle. On that day I will fulfill against Eli all that I have spoken concerning his house, from beginning to end. For I have told him that I am about to punish his house forever, for the iniquity that he knew, because his sons were blaspheming God, and he did not restrain them. Therefore I swear to the house of Eli that the iniquity of Eli's house shall not be expiated by sacrifice or offering forever." Samuel lay there until morning; then he opened the doors of the house of the LORD. Samuel was afraid to tell the vision to Eli. But Eli called Samuel and said, "Samuel, my son." He said, "Here I am." Eli said, "What was it that he told you? Do not hide it from me. May God do so to you and more also, if

you hide anything from me of all that he told you." So
Samuel told him everything and hid nothing from him. Then
he said, "It is the LORD; let him do what seems good to
him." As Samuel grew up, the LORD was with him and let
none of his words fall to the ground. And all Israel from
Dan to Beer-sheba knew that Samuel was a trustworthy
prophet of the LORD. The LORD continued to appear at
Shiloh, for the LORD revealed himself to Samuel at Shiloh by
the word of the LORD.

A Reading (Lesson) from the Acts of the Apostles [2:37–47]

When the people heard Peter's words they were cut to the
heart and said to Peter and to the other apostles,
"Brothers, what should we do?" Peter said to them,
"Repent, and be baptized every one of you in the name of
Jesus Christ so that your sins may be forgiven; and you
will receive the gift of the Holy Spirit. For the promise is
for you, for your children, and for all who are far away,
everyone whom the Lord our God calls to him." And he
testified with many other arguments and exhorted them,
saying, "Save yourselves from this corrupt generation." So
those who welcomed his message were baptized, and that
day about three thousand persons were added. They
devoted themselves to the apostles' teaching and
fellowship, to the breaking of bread and the prayers. Awe
came upon everyone, because many wonders and signs
were being done by the apostles. All who believed were
together and had all things in common; they would sell
their possessions and goods and distribute the proceeds to
all, as any had need. Day by day, as they spent much time
together in the temple, they broke bread at home and ate
their food with glad and generous hearts, praising God

and having the goodwill of all the people. And day by day the Lord added to their number those who were being saved.

A Reading (Lesson) from the Gospel according to Luke [21:5–19]

When some were speaking about the temple, how it was adorned with beautiful stones and gifts dedicated to God, Jesus said, "As for these things that you see, the days will come when not one stone will be left upon another; all will be thrown down." They asked him, "Teacher, when will this be, and what will be the sign that this is about to take place?" And he said, "Beware that you are not led astray; for many will come in my name and say, 'I am he!' and, 'The time is near!' Do not go after them. When you hear of wars and insurrections, do not be terrified; for these things must take place first, but the end will not follow immediately." Then he said to them, "Nation will rise against nation, and kingdom against kingdom; there will be great earthquakes, and in various places famines and plagues; and there will be dreadful portents and great signs from heaven. But before all this occurs, they will arrest you and persecute you; they will hand you over to synagogues and prisons, and you will be brought before kings and governors because of my name. This will give you an opportunity to testify. So make up your minds not to prepare your defense in advance; for I will give you words and a wisdom that none of your opponents will be able to withstand or contradict. You will be betrayed even by parents and brothers, by relatives and friends; and they will put some of you to death. You will be hated by all because of my name. But not a hair of your head will perish. By your endurance you will gain your souls."

Saturday

Psalm 87 [page 711],   *Psalm 90* [page 717] ❖
Psalm 136 [page 789]

A Reading (Lesson) from the First Book of Samuel [4:1b–11]

In those days the Philistines mustered for war against Israel,
and Israel went out to battle against them; they encamped at
Ebenezer, and the Philistines encamped at Aphek. The
Philistines drew up in line against Israel, and when the battle
was joined, Israel was defeated by the Philistines, who killed
about four thousand men on the field of battle. When the
troops came to the camp, the elders of Israel said, "Why has
the Lord put us to rout today before the Philistines? Let us
bring the ark of the covenant of the Lord here from Shiloh,
so that he may come among us and save us from the power
of our enemies." So the people sent to Shiloh, and brought
from there the ark of the covenant of the Lord of hosts,
who is enthroned on the cherubim. The two sons of Eli,
Hophni and Phinehas, were there with the ark of the
covenant of God. When the ark of the covenant of the Lord
came into the camp, all Israel gave a mighty shout, so that
the earth resounded. When the Philistines heard the noise
of the shouting, they said, "What does this great shouting in
the camp of the Hebrews mean?" When they learned that
the ark of the Lord had come to the camp, the Philistines
were afraid; for they said, "Gods have come into the camp."
They also said, "Woe to us! For nothing like this has
happened before. Woe to us! Who can deliver us from the
power of these mighty gods? These are the gods who struck
the Egyptians with every sort of plague in the wilderness.
Take courage, and be men, O Philistines, in order not to
become slaves to the Hebrews as they have been to you; be
men and fight." So the Philistines fought; Israel was

defeated, and they fled, everyone to his home. There was a very great slaughter, for there fell of Israel thirty thousand foot soldiers. The ark of God was captured; and the two sons of Eli, Hophni and Phinehas, died.

A Reading (Lesson) from the Acts of the Apostles
[4:32—5:11]

Now the whole group of those who believed were of one heart and soul, and no one claimed private ownership of any possessions, but everything they owned was held in common. With great power the apostles gave their testimony to the resurrection of the Lord Jesus, and great grace was upon them all. There was not a needy person among them, for as many as owned lands or houses sold them and brought the proceeds of what was sold. They laid it at the apostles' feet, and it was distributed to each as any had need. There was a Levite, a native of Cyprus, Joseph, to whom the apostles gave the name Barnabas (which means "son of encouragement"). He sold a field that belonged to him, then brought the money, and laid it at the apostles' feet. But a man named Ananias, with the consent of his wife Sapphira, sold a piece of property; with his wife's knowledge, he kept back some of the proceeds, and brought only a part and laid it at the apostles' feet. "Ananias," Peter asked, "why has Satan filled your heart to lie to the Holy Spirit and to keep back part of the proceeds of the land? While it remained unsold, did it not remain your own? And after it was sold, were not the proceeds at your disposal? How is it that you have contrived this deed in your heart? You did not lie to us but to God!" Now when Ananias heard these words, he fell down and died. And great fear seized all who heard of it. The young men came and wrapped up his body, then carried him out and buried him. After an interval of about three hours his wife came in, not knowing what had happened. Peter said to her, "Tell me whether you and your husband sold the land for such and such a price." And she said, "Yes, that was the price." Then Peter said to her, "How is it that you have agreed together to put the Spirit of the Lord to the test? Look, the feet of those who have buried your husband are at the door, and they will carry you out." Immediately she fell down at his feet and died. When the young men came in they found her dead, so they carried her out and buried her beside her husband. And great fear seized the whole church and all who heard of these things.

A Reading (Lesson) from the Gospel according to Luke
[21:20–28]

Jesus said, "When you see Jerusalem surrounded by armies, then know that its desolation has come near. Then those in Judea must flee to the mountains, and those inside the city must leave it, and those out in the country must not enter it; for these are days of vengeance, as a fulfillment of all that is written. Woe to those who are pregnant and to those who are nursing infants in those days! For there will be great distress on the earth and wrath against this people; they will fall by the edge of the sword and be taken away as captives among all nations; and Jerusalem will be trampled on by the Gentiles, until the times of the Gentiles are fulfilled. There will be signs in the sun, the moon, and the stars, and on the earth distress among nations confused by the roaring of the sea and the waves. People will faint from fear and foreboding of what is coming upon the world, for the powers of the heavens will be shaken. Then they will see 'the Son of

Man coming in a cloud' with power and great glory. Now when these things begin to take place, stand up and raise your heads, because your redemption is drawing near."

Proper 7   *Week of the Sunday closest to June 22*

Sunday

Psalm 66 [page 673],   *Psalm 67* [page 675] ❖
Psalm 19 [page 606],   *Psalm 46* [page 649]

A Reading (Lesson) from the First Book of Samuel [4:12–22]

A man of Benjamin ran from the battle line, and came to Shiloh the same day, with his clothes torn and with earth upon his head. When he arrived, Eli was sitting upon his seat by the road watching, for his heart trembled for the ark of God. When the man came into the city and told the news, all the city cried out. When Eli heard the sound of the outcry, he said, "What is this uproar?" Then the man came quickly and told Eli. Now Eli was ninety-eight years old and his eyes were set, so that he could not see. The man said to Eli, "I have just come from the battle; I fled from the battle today." He said, "How did it go, my son?" The messenger replied, "Israel has fled before the Philistines, and there has also been a great slaughter among the troops; your two sons also, Hophni and Phinehas, are dead, and the ark of God has been captured." When he mentioned the ark of God, Eli fell over backward from his seat by the side of the gate; and his neck was broken and he died, for he was an old man, and heavy. He had judged Israel forty years. Now his daughter-in-law, the wife of Phinehas, was pregnant, about to give birth. When she heard the news that the ark of God was captured, and that her father-in-law and her husband were dead, she bowed and gave birth; for her labor pains overwhelmed her. As she was about to die, the women attending her said to her, "Do not be afraid, for you have borne a son." But she did not answer or give heed. She named the child Ichabod, meaning, "The glory has departed from Israel," because the ark of God had been captured and because of her father-in-law and her husband. She said, "The glory has departed from Israel, for the ark of God has been captured."

A Reading (Lesson) from the Letter of James [1:1–18]

James, a servant of God and of the Lord Jesus Christ, to the twelve tribes in the Dispersion: Greetings. My brothers and sisters, whenever you face trials of any kind, consider it nothing but joy, because you know that the testing of your faith produces endurance; and let endurance have its full effect, so that you may be mature and complete, lacking in nothing. If any of you is lacking in wisdom, ask God, who gives to all generously and ungrudgingly, and it will be given you. But ask in faith, never doubting, for the one who doubts is like a wave of the sea, driven and tossed by the wind; for the doubter, being double-minded and unstable in every way, must not expect to receive anything from the Lord. Let the believer who is lowly boast in being raised up, and the rich in being brought low, because the rich will disappear like a flower in the field. For the sun rises with its scorching heat and withers the field; its flower falls, and its beauty perishes. It is the same way with the rich; in the midst of a busy life, they will wither away. Blessed is anyone who endures temptation. Such a one has stood the test and will receive the crown of life that the Lord has promised to those who love him. No one, when tempted, should say, "I am being tempted by God"; for God cannot be tempted by evil and he himself tempts no one. But one is tempted by one's own desire, being lured and enticed by it; then, when that desire has conceived, it gives birth to sin, and that sin, when it is fully grown, gives birth to death. Do not be deceived, my beloved. Every generous act of giving, with every perfect gift, is from above, coming down from the Father of lights, with whom there is no variation or shadow due to change. In fulfillment of his own purpose he gave us birth by the word of truth, so that we would become a kind of first fruits of his creatures.

A Reading (Lesson) from the Gospel according to Matthew [19:23–30]

Jesus said to his disciples, "Truly I tell you, it will be hard for a rich person to enter the kingdom of heaven. Again I tell you, it is easier for a camel to go through the eye of a needle than for someone who is rich to enter the kingdom of God." When the disciples heard this, they were greatly astounded and said, "Then who can be saved?" But Jesus looked at them and said, "For mortals it is impossible, but for God all things are possible." Then Peter said in reply, "Look, we have left everything and followed you. What then will we have?" Jesus said to them, "Truly I tell you, at the renewal of all things, when the Son of Man is seated on the throne of his glory, you who have followed me will also sit on twelve thrones, judging the twelve tribes of Israel. And everyone who has left houses or brothers or sisters or father or mother or children or fields, for my name's sake, will receive a hundredfold, and will inherit eternal life. But many who are first will be last, and the last will be first."

Monday

Psalm 89:1–18 [page 713] ❖ *Psalm 89:19–52* [page 715]

A Reading (Lesson) from the First Book of Samuel [5:1–12]

When the Philistines captured the ark of God, they brought it from Ebenezer to Ashdod; then the Philistines took the ark of God and brought it into the house of Dagon and placed it beside Dagon. When the people of Ashdod rose early the next day, there was Dagon, fallen on his face to the ground before the ark of the LORD. So they took Dagon and put him back in his place. But when they rose early on the next morning, Dagon had fallen on his face to the ground before the ark of the LORD, and the head of Dagon and both his hands were lying cut off upon the threshold; only the trunk of Dagon was left to him. This is why the priests of Dagon and all who enter the house of Dagon do not step on the threshold of Dagon in Ashdod to this day. The hand of the LORD was heavy upon the people of Ashdod, and he terrified and struck them with tumors, both in Ashdod and in its territory. And when the inhabitants of Ashdod saw how things were, they said, "The ark of the God of Israel must not remain with us; for his hand is heavy on us and on our god Dagon." So they sent and gathered together all the lords of the Philistines, and said, "What shall we do with the ark of the God of Israel?" The inhabitants of Gath replied, "Let the ark of God be moved on to us." So they moved the ark of the God of Israel to Gath. But after they had brought it to Gath, the hand of the LORD was against the city, causing a very great panic; he struck the inhabitants of the city, both young and old, so that tumors broke out on them. So they sent the ark of the God of Israel to Ekron. But when the ark of God came to Ekron, the people of Ekron cried out, "Why have they brought around to us the ark of the God of Israel to kill us and our people?" They sent therefore and gathered together all the lords of the Philistines, and said, "Send away the ark of the God of Israel, and let it return to its own place, that it may not kill us and our people." For there was a deathly panic throughout the whole city. The hand of God was very heavy there; those who did not die were stricken with tumors, and the cry of the city went up to heaven.

A Reading (Lesson) from the Acts of the Apostles [5:12–26]

Now many signs and wonders were done among the people through the apostles. And they were all together in Solomon's Portico. None of the rest dared to join them, but the people held them in high esteem. Yet more than ever believers were added to the Lord, great numbers of both men and women, so that they even carried out the sick into the streets, and laid them on cots and mats, in order that Peter's shadow might fall on some of them as he came by. A great number of people would also gather from the towns around Jerusalem, bringing the sick and those tormented by unclean spirits, and they were all cured. Then the high priest took action; he and all who were with him (that is, the sect of the Sadducees), being filled with jealousy, arrested the apostles and put them in the public prison. But during the night an angel of the Lord opened the prison doors, brought them out, and said, "Go, stand in the temple and tell the people the whole message about this life." When they heard this, they entered the temple at daybreak and went on with their teaching. When the high priest and those with him arrived, they called together the council and the whole body of the elders of Israel, and sent to the prison to have them brought. But when the temple police went there, they did not find them in the prison; so they returned and reported, "We found the prison securely locked and the guards standing at the doors, but when we opened them, we found no one inside." Now when the captain of the temple and the chief priests heard these words, they were perplexed about them, wondering what might be going on. Then someone arrived and announced, "Look, the men whom you put in prison are standing in the temple and teaching the people!" Then the captain went with the temple police and brought them, but without violence, for they were afraid of being stoned by the people.

A Reading (Lesson) from the Gospel according to Luke [21:29–36]

Jesus told them a parable: "Look at the fig tree and all the trees; as soon as they sprout leaves you can see for yourselves and know that summer is already near. So also, when you see these things taking place, you know that the kingdom of God is near. Truly I tell you, this generation will not pass away until all things have taken place. Heaven and earth will pass away, but my words will not pass away. Be on guard so that your hearts are not weighed down with dissipation and drunkenness and the worries of this life, and that day catch you unexpectedly, like a trap. For it will come upon all who live on the face of the whole earth. Be alert at all times, praying that you may have the strength to escape all these things that will take place, and to stand before the Son of Man."

Tuesday

Psalm 97 [page 726], *Psalm 99* [page 728], *(Psalm 100* [page 729]) ❖ *Psalm 94* [page 722], *(Psalm 95* [page 724])

A Reading (Lesson) from the First Book of Samuel [6:1–16]

The ark of the LORD was in the country of the Philistines seven months. Then the Philistines called for the priests and the diviners and said, "What shall we do with the ark of the LORD? Tell us what we should send with it to its place." They said, "If you send away the ark of the God of Israel, do not send it empty, but by all means return him a guilt offering. Then you will be healed and will be ransomed; will not his hand then turn from you?" And they said, "What is the guilt offering that we shall return to him?" They answered, "Five gold tumors and five gold mice, according to the number of the lords of the Philistines; for the same plague was upon all of you and upon your lords. So you must make images of your tumors and images of your mice that ravage the land, and give glory to the God of Israel; perhaps he will lighten his hand on you and your gods and your land. Why should you harden your hearts as the Egyptians and Pharaoh hardened their hearts? After he had made fools of them, did they not let the people go, and they departed? Now then, get ready a new cart and two milch cows that have never borne a yoke, and yoke the cows to the cart, but take their calves home, away from them. Take the ark of the LORD and place it on the cart, and put in a box at its side the figures of gold, which you are returning to him as a guilt offering. Then send it off, and let it go its way. And watch; if it goes up on the way to its own land, to Beth-shemesh, then it is he who has done us this great harm; but if not, then we shall know that it is not his hand that struck us; it happened to us by chance." The men did so; they took two milch cows and yoked them to the cart, and shut up their calves at home. They put the ark of the LORD on the cart, and the box with the gold mice and the images of their tumors. The cows went straight in the direction of Beth-shemesh along one highway, lowing as they went; they turned neither to the right nor to the left, and the lords of the Philistines went after them as far as the border of Beth-shemesh. Now the people of Beth-shemesh were reaping their wheat harvest in the valley. When they looked up and saw the ark, they went with rejoicing to meet it. The cart came into the field of Joshua of Beth-shemesh, and stopped there. A large stone was there; so they split up the wood of the cart and offered the cows as a burnt offering to the LORD. The Levites took down the ark of the LORD and the box that was beside it, in which were the gold objects, and set them upon the large stone. Then the people of Beth-shemesh offered burnt offerings and presented sacrifices on that day to the LORD. When the five lords of the Philistines saw it, they returned that day to Ekron.

A Reading (Lesson) from the Acts of the Apostles [5:27–42]

When the Sadducees had brought the apostles, they had them stand before the council. The high priest questioned them, saying, "We gave you strict orders not to teach in this name, yet here you have filled Jerusalem with your teaching and you are determined to bring this man's blood on us." But Peter and the apostles answered, "We must obey God rather than any human authority. The God of our ancestors raised up Jesus, whom you had killed by hanging him on a tree. God exalted him at his right hand as Leader and Savior that he might give repentance to Israel and forgiveness of sins. And we are witnesses to these things, and so is the Holy Spirit whom God has given to those who obey him." When they heard this, they were enraged and wanted to kill them. But a Pharisee in the council named Gamaliel, a teacher of the law, respected by all the people, stood up and ordered the men to be put outside for a short time. Then he said to them,

"Fellow Israelites, consider carefully what you propose to do to these men. For some time ago Theudas rose up, claiming to be somebody, and a number of men, about four hundred, joined him; but he was killed, and all who followed him were dispersed and disappeared. After him Judas the Galilean rose up at the time of the census and got people to follow him; he also perished, and all who followed him were scattered. So in the present case, I tell you, keep away from these men and let them alone; because if this plan or this undertaking is of human origin, it will fail; but if it is of God, you will not be able to overthrow them—in that case you may even be found fighting against God!" They were convinced by him, and when they had called in the apostles, they had them flogged. Then they ordered them not to speak in the name of Jesus, and let them go. As they left the council, they rejoiced that they were considered worthy to suffer dishonor for the sake of the name. And every day in the temple and at home they did not cease to teach and proclaim Jesus as the Messiah.

A Reading (Lesson) from the Gospel according to Luke [21:37—22:13]

Every day Jesus was teaching in the temple, and at night he would go out and spend the night on the Mount of Olives, as it was called. And all the people would get up early in the morning to listen to him in the temple. Now the festival of Unleavened Bread, which is called the Passover, was near. The chief priests and the scribes were looking for a way to put Jesus to death, for they were afraid of the people. Then Satan entered into Judas called Iscariot, who was one of the twelve; he went away and conferred with the chief priests and officers of the temple police about how he might betray him to them. They were greatly pleased and agreed to give him money. So he consented and began to look for an opportunity to betray him to them when no crowd was present. Then came the day of Unleavened Bread, on which the Passover lamb had to be sacrificed. So Jesus sent Peter and John, saying, "Go and prepare the Passover meal for us that we may eat it." They asked him, "Where do you want us to make preparations for it?" "Listen," he said to them, "when you have entered the city, a man carrying a jar of water will meet you; follow him into the house he enters and say to the owner of the house, 'The teacher asks you, "Where is the guest room, where I may eat the Passover with my disciples?"' He will show you a large room upstairs, already furnished. Make preparations for us there." So they went and found everything as he had told them; and they prepared the Passover meal.

Wednesday

Psalm 101 [page 730], *Psalm 109:1–4(5–19)20–30* [page 750] ❖ *Psalm 119:121–144* [page 773]

A Reading (Lesson) from the First Book of Samuel [7:2–17]

From the day that the ark was lodged at Kiriath-jearim, a long time passed, some twenty years, and all the house of Israel lamented after the LORD. Then Samuel said to all the house of Israel, "If you are returning to the LORD with all your heart, then put away the foreign gods and the Astartes from among you. Direct your heart to the LORD, and serve him only, and he will deliver you out of the hand of the Philistines." So Israel put away the Baals and the Astartes, and they served the LORD only. Then Samuel said, "Gather

all Israel at Mizpah, and I will pray to the LORD for you."
So they gathered at Mizpah, and drew water and poured it
out before the LORD. They fasted that day, and said, "We
have sinned against the LORD." And Samuel judged the
people of Israel at Mizpah. When the Philistines heard that
the people of Israel had gathered at Mizpah, the lords of the
Philistines went up against Israel. And when the people of
Israel heard of it they were afraid of the Philistines. The
people of Israel said to Samuel, "Do not cease to cry out to
the LORD our God for us, and pray that he may save us from
the hand of the Philistines." So Samuel took a sucking lamb
and offered it as a whole burnt offering to the LORD; Samuel
cried out to the LORD for Israel, and the LORD answered
him. As Samuel was offering up the burnt offering, the
Philistines drew near to attack Israel; but the LORD
thundered with a mighty voice that day against the
Philistines and threw them into confusion; and they were
routed before Israel. And the men of Israel went out of
Mizpah and pursued the Philistines, and struck them down
as far as beyond Beth-car. Then Samuel took a stone and set
it up between Mizpah and Jeshanah, and named it Ebenezer;
for he said, "Thus far the LORD has helped us." So the
Philistines were subdued and did not again enter the
territory of Israel; the hand of the LORD was against the
Philistines all the days of Samuel. The towns that the
Philistines had taken from Israel were restored to Israel,
from Ekron to Gath; and Israel recovered their territory
from the hand of the Philistines. There was peace also
between Israel and the Amorites. Samuel judged Israel all
the days of his life. He went on a circuit year by year to
Bethel, Gilgal, and Mizpah; and he judged Israel in all these
places. Then he would come back to Ramah, for his home
was there; he administered justice there to Israel, and built
there an altar to the LORD.

A Reading (Lesson) from the Acts of the Apostles [6:1–15]

Now during those days, when the disciples were increasing
in number, the Hellenists complained against the Hebrews
because their widows were being neglected in the daily
distribution of food. And the twelve called together the
whole community of the disciples and said, "It is not right
that we should neglect the word of God in order to wait
on tables. Therefore, friends, select from among yourselves
seven men of good standing, full of the Spirit and of
wisdom, whom we may appoint to this task, while we, for
our part, will devote ourselves to prayer and to serving the
word." What they said pleased the whole community, and
they chose Stephen, a man full of faith and the Holy
Spirit, together with Philip, Prochorus, Nicanor, Timon,
Parmenas, and Nicolaus, a proselyte of Antioch. They had
these men stand before the apostles, who prayed and laid
their hands on them. The word of God continued to
spread; the number of the disciples increased greatly in
Jerusalem, and a great many of the priests became
obedient to the faith. Stephen, full of grace and power, did
great wonders and signs among the people. Then some of
those who belonged to the synagogue of the Freedmen (as
it was called), Cyrenians, Alexandrians, and others of
those from Cilicia and Asia, stood up and argued with
Stephen. But they could not withstand the wisdom and the
Spirit with which he spoke. Then they secretly instigated
some men to say, "We have heard him speak blasphemous
words against Moses and God." They stirred up the
people as well as the elders and the scribes; then they
suddenly confronted him, seized him, and brought him
before the council. They set up false witnesses who said,
"This man never stops saying things against this holy place
and the law; for we have heard him say that this Jesus of

Nazareth will destroy this place and will change the customs that Moses handed on to us." And all who sat in the council looked intently at him, and they saw that his face was like the face of an angel.

A Reading (Lesson) from the Gospel according to Luke [22:14–23]

When the hour of the Passover came, Jesus took his place at the table, and the apostles with him. He said to them, "I have eagerly desired to eat this Passover with you before I suffer; for I tell you, I will not eat it until it is fulfilled in the kingdom of God." Then he took a cup, and after giving thanks he said, "Take this and divide it among yourselves; for I tell you that from now on I will not drink of the fruit of the vine until the kingdom of God comes." Then he took a loaf of bread, and when he had given thanks, he broke it and gave it to them, saying, "This is my body, which is given for you. Do this in remembrance of me." And he did the same with the cup after supper, saying, "This cup that is poured out for you is the new covenant in my blood. But see, the one who betrays me is with me, and his hand is on the table. For the Son of Man is going as it has been determined, but woe to that one by whom he is betrayed!" Then they began to ask one another, which one of them it could be who would do this.

Thursday

Psalm 105:1–22 [page 738] ❖ *Psalm 105:23–45* [page 739]

A Reading (Lesson) from the First Book of Samuel [8:1–22]

When Samuel became old, he made his sons judges over Israel. The name of his firstborn son was Joel, and the name of his second, Abijah; they were judges in Beer-sheba. Yet his sons did not follow in his ways, but turned aside after gain; they took bribes and perverted justice. Then all the elders of Israel gathered together and came to Samuel at Ramah, and said to him, "You are old and your sons do not follow in your ways; appoint for us, then, a king to govern us, like other nations." But the thing displeased Samuel when they said, "Give us a king to govern us." Samuel prayed to the LORD, and the LORD said to Samuel, "Listen to the voice of the people in all that they say to you; for they have not rejected you, but they have rejected me from being king over them. Just as they have done to me, from the day I brought them up out of Egypt to this day, forsaking me and serving other gods, so also they are doing to you. Now then, listen to their voice; only—you shall solemnly warn them, and show them the ways of the king who shall reign over them." So Samuel reported all the words of the LORD to the people who were asking him for a king. He said, "These will be the ways of the king who will reign over you: he will take your sons and appoint them to his chariots and to be his horsemen, and to run before his chariots; and he will appoint for himself commanders of thousands and commanders of fifties, and some to plow his ground and to reap his harvest, and to make his implements of war and the equipment of his chariots. He will take your daughters to be perfumers and cooks and bakers. He will take the best of your fields and vineyards and olive orchards and give them to his courtiers. He will take one-tenth of your grain and of your vineyards and give it to his officers and his courtiers. He will take your male and female slaves, and the best of your cattle and donkeys, and put them to his work. He will take one-tenth of your flocks, and you shall be his slaves. And in that day you will cry out because of your king, whom you have chosen for yourselves; but the LORD will not answer you in that day." But the people refused to listen to the voice of Samuel; they said, "No! but we are determined to have a king over us, so that we also may be like other nations, and that our king may govern us and go out before us and fight our battles." When Samuel had heard all the words of the people, he repeated them in the ears of the LORD. The LORD said to Samuel, "Listen to their voice and set a king over them." Samuel then said to the people of Israel, "Each of you return home."

A Reading (Lesson) from the Acts of the Apostles
[6:15—7:16]

All who sat in the council looked intently at Stephen, and they saw that his face was like the face of an angel. Then the high priest asked him, "Are these things so?" And Stephen replied: "Brothers and fathers, listen to me. The God of glory appeared to our ancestor Abraham when he was in Mesopotamia, before he lived in Haran, and said to him, 'Leave your country and your relatives and go to the land that I will show you.' Then he left the country of the Chaldeans and settled in Haran. After his father died, God had him move from there to this country in which you are now living. He did not give him any of it as a heritage, not even a foot's length, but promised to give it to him as his possession and to his descendants after him, even though he had no child. And God spoke in these terms, that his descendants would be resident aliens in a country belonging to others, who would enslave them and mistreat them during four hundred years. 'But I will judge the nation that they serve,' said God, 'and after that they shall come out and worship me in this place.' Then he gave him the covenant of circumcision. And so Abraham became the father of Isaac and circumcised him on the eighth day; and Isaac became the father of Jacob, and Jacob of the twelve patriarchs. The patriarchs, jealous of Joseph, sold him into Egypt; but God was with him, and rescued him from all his afflictions, and enabled him to win favor and to show wisdom when he stood before Pharaoh, king of Egypt, who appointed him ruler over Egypt and over all his household. Now there came a famine throughout Egypt and Canaan, and great suffering, and our ancestors could find no food. But when Jacob heard that there was grain in Egypt, he sent our ancestors there on their first visit. On the second visit Joseph made himself known to his brothers, and Joseph's family became known to Pharaoh. Then Joseph sent and invited his father Jacob and all his relatives to come to him, seventy-five in all; so Jacob went down to Egypt. He himself died there as well as our ancestors, and their bodies were brought back to Shechem and laid in the tomb that Abraham had bought for a sum of silver from the sons of Hamor in Shechem."

A Reading (Lesson) from the Gospel according to Luke [22:24–30]

A dispute also arose among the disciples, as to which one of them was to be regarded as the greatest. But he said to them, "The kings of the Gentiles lord it over them; and those in authority over them are called benefactors. But not so with you; rather the greatest among you must become like the youngest, and the leader like one who serves. For who is greater, the one who is at the table or the one who serves? Is it not the one at the table? But I am among you as one who serves. You are those who have stood by me in my trials; and I confer on you, just as my Father has conferred on me, a kingdom, so that you may eat and drink at my table in my kingdom, and you will sit on thrones judging the twelve tribes of Israel."

Friday

Psalm 102 [page 731] ❖ *Psalm 107:1–32* [page 746]

A Reading (Lesson) from the First Book of Samuel [9:1–14]

There was a man of Benjamin whose name was Kish son of Abiel son of Zeror son of Becorath son of Aphiah, a Benjaminite, a man of wealth. He had a son whose name was Saul, a handsome young man. There was not a man among the people of Israel more handsome than he; he stood head and shoulders above everyone else. Now the donkeys of Kish, Saul's father, had strayed. So Kish said to his son Saul, "Take one of the boys with you; go and look for the donkeys." He passed through the hill country of Ephraim and passed through the land of Shalishah, but they did not find them. And they passed through the land of Shaalim, but they were not there. Then he passed through the land of Benjamin, but they did not find them. When they came to the land of Zuph, Saul said to the boy who was with him, "Let us turn back, or my father will stop worrying about the donkeys and worry about us." But he said to him, "There is a man of God in this town; he is a man held in honor. Whatever he says always comes true. Let us go there now; perhaps he will tell us about the journey on which we have set out." Then Saul replied to the boy, "But if we go, what can we bring the man? For the bread in our sacks is gone, and there is no present to bring to the man of God. What have we?" The boy answered Saul again, "Here, I have with me a quarter shekel of silver; I will give it to the man of God, to tell us our way." (Formerly in Israel, anyone who went to inquire of God would say, "Come, let us go to the seer"; for the one who is now called a prophet was formerly called a seer.) Saul said to the boy, "Good; come, let us go." So they went to the town where the man of God was. As they went up the hill to the town, they met some girls coming out to draw water, and said to them, "Is the seer here?" They answered, "Yes, there he is just ahead of you. Hurry; he has come just now to the town, because the people have a sacrifice today at the shrine. As soon as you enter the town, you will find him, before he goes up to the shrine to eat. For the people will not eat until he comes, since he must bless the sacrifice; afterward those eat who are invited. Now go up, for you will meet him immediately." So they went up to the town. As they were entering the town, they saw Samuel coming out toward them on his way up to the shrine.

A Reading (Lesson) from the Acts of the Apostles [7:17–29]

Stephen said, "As the time drew near for the fulfillment of the promise that God had made to Abraham, our people in Egypt increased and multiplied until another king who had not known Joseph ruled over Egypt. He dealt craftily with our race and forced our ancestors to abandon their infants so that they would die. At this time Moses was born, and he was beautiful before God. For three months he was brought up in his father's house; and when he was abandoned, Pharaoh's daughter adopted him and brought him up as her own son. So Moses was instructed in all the wisdom of the Egyptians and was powerful in his words and deeds. When he was forty years old, it came into his heart to visit his relatives, the Israelites. When he saw one of them being wronged, he defended the oppressed man and avenged him by striking down the Egyptian. He supposed that his kinsfolk would understand that God through him was rescuing them, but they did not understand. The next day he came to some of them as they were quarreling and tried to reconcile them, saying, 'Men, you are brothers; why do you wrong each other?' But the man who was wronging his neighbor pushed Moses aside, saying, 'Who made you a ruler and a judge over us? Do you want to kill me as you killed the Egyptian yesterday?' When he heard this, Moses fled and became a resident alien in the land of Midian. There he became the father of two sons."

A Reading (Lesson) from the Gospel according to Luke
[22:31–38]

Jesus said, "Simon, Simon, listen! Satan has demanded to sift all of you like wheat, but I have prayed for you that your own faith may not fail; and you, when once you have turned back, strengthen your brothers." And he said to him, "Lord, I am ready to go with you to prison and to death!" Jesus said, "I tell you, Peter, the cock will not crow this day, until you have denied three times that you know me." He said to them, "When I sent you out without a purse, bag, or sandals, did you lack anything?" They said, "No, not a thing." He said to them, "But now, the one who has a purse must take it, and likewise a bag. And the one who has no sword must sell his cloak and buy one. For I tell you, this scripture must be fulfilled in me, 'And he was counted among the lawless'; and indeed what is written about me is being fulfilled." They said, "Lord, look, here are two swords." He replied, "It is enough."

Saturday

Psalm 107:33–43 [page 748],
Psalm 108:1–6(7–13) [page 749]   ❖   *Psalm 33* [page 626]

A Reading (Lesson) from the First Book of Samuel
[9:15—10:1]

Now the day before Saul came, the LORD had revealed to Samuel: "Tomorrow about this time I will send to you a man from the land of Benjamin, and you shall anoint him to be ruler over my people Israel. He shall save my people from the hand of the Philistines; for I have seen the suffering of my people, because their outcry has come to me." When Samuel saw Saul, the LORD told him, "Here is the man of whom I spoke to you. He it is who shall rule over my people." Then Saul approached Samuel inside the gate, and said, "Tell me, please, where is the house of the seer?" Samuel answered Saul, "I am the seer; go up before me to the shrine, for today you shall eat with me, and in the morning I will let you go and will tell you all that is on your mind. As for your donkeys that were lost three days ago, give no further thought to them, for they have been found. And on whom is all Israel's desire fixed, if not on you and on all your ancestral house?" Saul answered, "I am only a Benjaminite, from the least of the tribes of Israel, and my family is the humblest of all the families of the tribe of Benjamin. Why then have you spoken to me in this way?" Then Samuel took Saul and his servant-boy and brought them into the hall, and gave them a place at the head of those who had been invited, of whom there were about thirty. And Samuel said to the cook, "Bring the portion I gave you, the one I asked you to put aside." The cook took up the thigh and what went with it and set them before Saul. Samuel said, "See, what was kept is set before you. Eat; for it is set before you at the appointed time, so that you might eat with the guests." So Saul ate with Samuel that day. When they came down from the shrine into the town, a bed was spread for Saul on the roof, and he lay down to sleep. Then at the break of dawn Samuel called to Saul upon the roof, "Get up, so that I may send you on your way." Saul got up, and both he and Samuel went out into the street. As they were going down to the outskirts of the town, Samuel said to Saul, "Tell the boy to go on before us, and when he has passed on, stop here yourself for a while, that I may make known to you the word of God." Samuel took a vial of oil and poured it on his head, and kissed him; he said, "The LORD has anointed you ruler over his people Israel. You shall reign over the people of the LORD and you will save them from the hand of their enemies all around. Now this shall be the sign to you that the LORD has anointed you ruler over his heritage."

A Reading (Lesson) from the Acts of the Apostles [7:30–43]

Stephen said, "Now when forty years had passed, an angel appeared to Moses in the wilderness of Mount Sinai, in the flame of a burning bush. When Moses saw it, he was amazed at the sight; and as he approached to look, there came the voice of the Lord: 'I am the God of your ancestors, the God of Abraham, Isaac, and Jacob.' Moses began to tremble and did not dare to look. Then the Lord said to him, 'Take off the sandals from your feet, for the place where you are standing is holy ground. I have surely seen the mistreatment of my people who are in Egypt and have heard their groaning, and I have come down to rescue them. Come now, I will send you to Egypt.' It was this Moses whom they rejected when they said, 'Who made you a ruler and a judge?' and whom God now sent as both ruler and liberator through the angel who appeared to him in the bush. He led them out, having performed wonders and signs in Egypt, at the Red Sea, and in the wilderness for forty years. This is the Moses who said to the Israelites, 'God will raise up a prophet for you from your own people as he raised me up.' He is the one who was in the congregation in the wilderness with the angel who spoke to him at Mount Sinai, and with our ancestors; and he received living oracles to give to us. Our ancestors were unwilling to obey him; instead, they pushed him aside, and in their hearts they turned back to Egypt, saying to Aaron, 'Make gods for us who will lead the way for us; as for this Moses who led us out from the land of Egypt, we do not know what has happened to him.' At that time they made a calf, offered a sacrifice to the idol, and reveled in the works of their hands. But God turned away from them and handed them over to worship the host of heaven, as it is written in the book of the prophets: 'Did you offer to me slain victims and sacrifices forty years in the wilderness, O house of Israel? No; you took along the tent of Moloch, and the star of your god Rephan, the images that you made to worship; so I will remove you beyond Babylon.' "

A Reading (Lesson) from the Gospel according to Luke
[22:39–51]

Jesus came out and went, as was his custom, to the Mount of Olives; and the disciples followed him. When he reached the place, he said to them, "Pray that you may not come into the time of trial." Then he withdrew from them about a stone's throw, knelt down, and prayed, "Father, if you are willing, remove this cup from me; yet, not my will but yours be done." Then an angel from heaven appeared to him and gave him strength. In his anguish he prayed more earnestly, and his sweat became like great drops of blood falling down on the ground. When he got up from prayer, he came to the disciples and found them sleeping because of grief, and he said to them, "Why are you sleeping? Get up and pray that you may not come into the time of trial." While he was still speaking, suddenly a crowd came, and the one called Judas, one of the twelve, was leading them. He approached Jesus to kiss him; but Jesus said to him, "Judas, is it with a kiss that you are betraying the Son of Man?" When those who were around him saw what was coming, they asked, "Lord, should we strike with the sword?" Then one of them struck the slave of the high priest and cut off his right ear. But Jesus said, "No more of this!" And he touched his ear and healed him.

Proper 8 *Week of the Sunday closest to June 29*

Sunday

Psalm 118 [page 760] ❖ *Psalm 145* [page 801]

A Reading (Lesson) from the First Book of Samuel [10:1–16]

Samuel took a vial of oil and poured it on Saul's head, and kissed him; he said, "The LORD has anointed you ruler over his people Israel. You shall reign over the people of the LORD and you will save them from the hand of their enemies all around. Now this shall be the sign to you that the LORD has anointed you ruler over his heritage: When you depart from me today you will meet two men by Rachel's tomb in the territory of Benjamin at Zelzah; they will say to you, 'The donkeys that you went to seek are found, and now your father has stopped worrying about them and is worrying about you, saying: What shall I do about my son?' Then you shall go on from there further and come to the oak of Tabor; three men going up to God at Bethel will meet you there, one carrying three kids, another carrying three loaves of bread, and another carrying a skin of wine. They will greet you and give you two loaves of bread, which you shall accept from them. After that you shall come to Gibeath-elohim, at the place where the Philistine garrison is; there, as you come to the town, you will meet a band of prophets coming down from the shrine with harp, tambourine, flute, and lyre playing in front of them; they will be in a prophetic frenzy. Then the spirit of the LORD will possess you, and you will be in a prophetic frenzy along with them and be turned into a different person. Now when these signs meet you, do whatever you see fit to do, for God is with you. And you shall go down to Gilgal ahead of me; then I will come down to you to present burnt offerings and offer sacrifices of well-being. Seven days you shall wait, until I come to you and show you what you shall do." As he turned away to leave Samuel, God gave him another heart; and all these signs were fulfilled that day. When they were going from there to Gibeah, a band of prophets met him;

and the spirit of God possessed him, and he fell into a prophetic frenzy along with them. When all who knew him before saw how he prophesied with the prophets, the people said to one another, "What has come over the son of Kish? Is Saul also among the prophets?" A man of the place answered, "And who is their father?" Therefore it became a proverb, "Is Saul also among the prophets?" When his prophetic frenzy had ended, he went home. Saul's uncle said to him and to the boy, "Where did you go?" And he replied, "To seek the donkeys; and when we saw they were not to be found, we went to Samuel." Saul's uncle said, "Tell me what Samuel said to you." Saul said to his uncle, "He told us that the donkeys had been found." But about the matter of the kingship, of which Samuel had spoken, he did not tell him anything.

A Reading (Lesson) from the Letter of Paul to the Romans [4:13–25]

The promise that he would inherit the world did not come to Abraham or to his descendants through the law but through the righteousness of faith. If it is the adherents of the law who are to be the heirs, faith is null and the promise is void. For the law brings wrath; but where there is no law, neither is there violation. For this reason it depends on faith, in order that the promise may rest on grace and be guaranteed to all his descendants, not only to the adherents of the law but also to those who share the faith of Abraham (for he is the father of all of us, as it is written, "I have made you the father of many nations")— in the presence of the God in whom he believed, who gives life to the dead and calls into existence the things that do not exist. Hoping against hope, he believed that he would become "the father of many nations," according to

what was said, "So numerous shall your descendants be."
He did not weaken in faith when he considered his own
body, which was already as good as dead (for he was
about a hundred years old), or when he considered the
barrenness of Sarah's womb. No distrust made him waver
concerning the promise of God, but he grew strong in his
faith as he gave glory to God, being fully convinced that
God was able to do what he had promised. Therefore his
faith "was reckoned to him as righteousness." Now the
words, "it was reckoned to him," were written not for his
sake alone, but for ours also. It will be reckoned to us
who believe in him who raised Jesus our Lord from the
dead, who was handed over to death for our trespasses
and was raised for our justification.

A Reading (Lesson) from the Gospel according to Matthew
[21:23–32]

When Jesus entered the temple, the chief priests and the
elders of the people came to him as he was teaching, and
said, "By what authority are you doing these things, and
who gave you this authority?" Jesus said to them, "I will
also ask you one question; if you tell me the answer, then
I will also tell you by what authority I do these things.
Did the baptism of John come from heaven, or was it of
human origin?" And they argued with one another, "If we
say, 'From heaven,' he will say to us, 'Why then did you
not believe him?' But if we say, 'Of human origin,' we are
afraid of the crowd; for all regard John as a prophet." So
they answered Jesus, "We do not know." And he said to
them, "Neither will I tell you by what authority I am
doing these things. What do you think? A man had two
sons; he went to the first and said, 'Son, go and work in
the vineyard today.' He answered, 'I will not'; but later he

changed his mind and went. The father went to the second and said the same; and he answered, 'I go, sir'; but he did not go. Which of the two did the will of his father?" They said, "The first." Jesus said to them, "Truly I tell you, the tax collectors and the prostitutes are going into the kingdom of God ahead of you. For John came to you in the way of righteousness and you did not believe him, but the tax collectors and the prostitutes believed him; and even after you saw it, you did not change your minds and believe him."

Monday

Psalm 106:1–18 [page 741] ❖ *Psalm 106:19–48* [page 743]

A Reading (Lesson) from the First Book of Samuel [10:17–27]

Samuel summoned the people to the LORD at Mizpah and said to them, "Thus says the LORD, the God of Israel, 'I brought up Israel out of Egypt, and I rescued you from the hand of the Egyptians and from the hand of all the kingdoms that were oppressing you.' But today you have rejected your God, who saves you from all your calamities and your distresses; and you have said, 'No! but set a king over us.' Now therefore present yourselves before the LORD by your tribes and by your clans." Then Samuel brought all the tribes of Israel near, and the tribe of Benjamin was taken by lot. He brought the tribe of Benjamin near by its families, and the family of the Matrites was taken by lot. Finally he brought the family of the Matrites near man by man, and Saul the son of Kish was taken by lot. But when they sought him, he could not be found. So they inquired again of the LORD, "Did the man come here?" and the LORD said, "See, he has hidden himself among the baggage." Then they ran and brought him from there. When he took his stand among the people, he was head and shoulders taller than any of them. Samuel said to all the people, "Do you see the one whom the LORD has chosen? There is no one like him among all the people." And all the people shouted, "Long live the king!" Samuel told the people the rights and duties of the kingship; and he wrote them in a book and laid it up before the LORD. Then Samuel sent all the people back to their homes. Saul also went to his home at Gibeah, and with him went warriors whose hearts God had touched. But some worthless fellows said, "How can this man save us?" They despised him and brought him no present. But he held his peace.

A Reading (Lesson) from the Acts of the Apostles
[7:44—8:1a]

Stephen said, "Our ancestors had the tent of testimony in the wilderness, as God directed when he spoke to Moses, ordering him to make it according to the pattern he had seen. Our ancestors in turn brought it in with Joshua when they dispossessed the nations that God drove out before our ancestors. And it was there until the time of David, who found favor with God and asked that he might find a dwelling place for the house of Jacob. But it was Solomon who built a house for him. Yet the Most High does not dwell in houses made with human hands; as the prophet says, 'Heaven is my throne, and the earth is my footstool. What kind of house will you build for me, says the Lord, or what is the place of my rest? Did not my hand make all these things?' You stiff-necked people, uncircumcised in heart and ears, you are forever opposing the Holy Spirit, just as your ancestors used to do. Which of the prophets did your ancestors not persecute? They killed those who foretold the coming of the Righteous One, and now you have become his betrayers and murderers. You are the ones that received the law as ordained by angels, and yet you have not kept it." When they heard these things, they became enraged and ground their teeth at Stephen. But filled with the Holy Spirit, he gazed into heaven and saw the glory of God and Jesus standing at the right hand of God. "Look," he said, "I see the heavens opened and the Son of Man standing at the right hand of God!" But they covered their ears, and with a loud shout all rushed together against him. Then they dragged him out of the city and began to stone him; and the witnesses laid their coats at the feet of a young man named Saul. While they were stoning Stephen, he prayed, "Lord Jesus, receive my spirit." Then he knelt down and cried out in a loud voice, "Lord, do not hold this sin against them." When he had said this, he died. And Saul approved of their killing him.

A Reading (Lesson) from the Gospel according to Luke
[22:52–62]

Jesus said to the chief priests, the officers of the temple police, and the elders who had come for him, "Have you come out with swords and clubs as if I were a bandit? When I was with you day after day in the temple, you did not lay hands on me. But this is your hour, and the power of darkness!" Then they seized him and led him away, bringing him into the high priest's house. But Peter was following at a distance. When they had kindled a fire in the middle of the courtyard and sat down together, Peter sat among them. Then a servant-girl, seeing him in the firelight, stared at him and said, "This man also was with him." But he denied it, saying, "Woman, I do not know him." A little later someone else, on seeing him, said, "You also are one of them." But Peter said, "Man, I am not!" Then about an hour later still another kept insisting, "Surely this man also was with him; for he is a Galilean." But Peter said, "Man, I do not know what you are talking about!" At that moment, while he was still speaking, the cock crowed. The Lord turned and looked at Peter. Then Peter remembered the word of the Lord, how he had said to him, "Before the cock crows today, you will deny me three times." And he went out and wept bitterly.

Tuesday

(Psalm 120 [page 778]),   *Psalm 121* [page 779],
Psalm 122 [page 779],   *Psalm 123* [page 780] ❖
Psalm 124 [page 781],   *Psalm 125* [page 781],
Psalm 126 [page 782],   *(Psalm 127* [page 782])

A Reading (Lesson) from the First Book of Samuel [11:1–15]

Nahash the Ammonite went up and besieged Jabesh-gilead; and all the men of Jabesh said to Nahash, "Make a treaty with us, and we will serve you." But Nahash the Ammonite said to them, "On this condition I will make a treaty with you, namely that I gouge out everyone's right eye, and thus put disgrace upon all Israel." The elders of Jabesh said to him, "Give us seven days' respite that we may send messengers through all the territory of Israel. Then, if there is no one to save us, we will give ourselves up to you." When the messengers came to Gibeah of Saul, they reported the matter in the hearing of the people; and all the people wept aloud. Now Saul was coming from the field behind the oxen; and Saul said, "What is the matter with the people, that they are weeping?" So they told him the message from the inhabitants of Jabesh. And the spirit of God came upon Saul in power when he heard these words, and his anger was greatly kindled. He took a yoke of oxen, and cut them in pieces and sent them throughout all the territory of Israel by messengers, saying, "Whoever does not come out after Saul and Samuel, so shall it be done to his oxen!" Then the dread of the LORD fell upon the people, and they came out as one. When he mustered them at Bezek, those from Israel were three hundred thousand, and those from Judah seventy thousand. They said to the messengers who had come, "Thus shall you say to the inhabitants of Jabesh-gilead: 'Tomorrow, by the time the sun is hot, you shall have deliverance.' " When the messengers came and told the inhabitants of Jabesh, they rejoiced. So the inhabitants of Jabesh said, "Tomorrow we will give ourselves up to you, and you may do to us whatever seems good to you." The next day Saul put the people in three companies. At the morning watch they came into the camp and cut down the Ammonites until the heat of the day; and those who survived were scattered, so that no two of them were left together. The people said to Samuel, "Who is it that said, 'Shall Saul reign over us?' Give them to us so that we may put them to death." But Saul said, "No one shall be put to death this day, for today the LORD has brought deliverance to Israel." Samuel said to the people, "Come, let us go to Gilgal and there renew the kingship." So all the people went to Gilgal, and there they made Saul king before the LORD in Gilgal. There they sacrificed offerings of well-being before the LORD, and there Saul and all the Israelites rejoiced greatly.

A Reading (Lesson) from the Acts of the Apostles [8:1–13]

Saul was consenting to Stephen's death. That day a severe
persecution began against the church in Jerusalem, and all
except the apostles were scattered throughout the
countryside of Judea and Samaria. Devout men buried
Stephen and made loud lamentation over him. But Saul
was ravaging the church by entering house after house;
dragging off both men and women, he committed them to
prison. Now those who were scattered went from place to
place, proclaiming the word. Philip went down to the city
of Samaria and proclaimed the Messiah to them. The
crowds with one accord listened eagerly to what was said
by Philip, hearing and seeing the signs that he did, for
unclean spirits, crying with loud shrieks, came out of
many who were possessed; and many others who were
paralyzed or lame were cured. So there was great joy in
that city. Now a certain man named Simon had previously
practiced magic in the city and amazed the people of
Samaria, saying that he was someone great. All of them,
from the least to the greatest, listened to him eagerly,
saying, "This man is the power of God that is called
Great." And they listened eagerly to him because for a
long time he had amazed them with his magic. But when
they believed Philip, who was proclaiming the good news
about the kingdom of God and the name of Jesus Christ,
they were baptized, both men and women. Even Simon
himself believed. After being baptized, he stayed constantly
with Philip and was amazed when he saw the signs and
great miracles that took place.

A Reading (Lesson) from the Gospel according to Luke
[22:63–71]

The men who were holding Jesus began to mock him and
beat him; they also blindfolded him and kept asking him,

"Prophesy! Who is it that struck you?" They kept heaping many other insults on him. When day came, the assembly of the elders of the people, both chief priests and scribes, gathered together, and they brought him to their council. They said, "If you are the Messiah, tell us." He replied, "If I tell you, you will not believe; and if I question you, you will not answer. But from now on the Son of Man will be seated at the right hand of the power of God." All of them asked, "Are you, then, the Son of God?" He said to them, "You say that I am." Then they said, "What further testimony do we need? We have heard it ourselves from his own lips!"

Wednesday

Psalm 119:145–176 [page 775] ❖ *Psalm 128* [page 783], *Psalm 129* [page 784], *Psalm 130* [page 784]

A Reading (Lesson) from the First Book of Samuel [12:1–6, 16–25]

Samuel said to all Israel, "I have listened to you in all that you have said to me, and have set a king over you. See, it is the king who leads you now; I am old and gray, but my sons are with you. I have led you from my youth until this day. Here I am; testify against me before the LORD and before his anointed. Whose ox have I taken? Or whose donkey have I taken? Or whom have I defrauded? Whom have I oppressed? Or from whose hand have I taken a bribe to blind my eyes with it? Testify against me and I will restore it to you." They said, "You have not defrauded us or oppressed us or taken anything from the hand of anyone." He said to them, "The LORD is witness against you, and his anointed is witness this day, that you have not found anything in my hand." And they said, "He is witness." Samuel said to the people,

"The LORD is witness, who appointed Moses and Aaron and brought your ancestors up out of the land of Egypt. Now therefore take your stand and see this great thing that the LORD will do before your eyes. Is it not the wheat harvest today? I will call upon the LORD, that he may send thunder and rain; and you shall know and see that the wickedness that you have done in the sight of the LORD is great in demanding a king for yourselves." So Samuel called upon the LORD, and the LORD sent thunder and rain that day; and all the people greatly feared the LORD and Samuel. All the people said to Samuel, "Pray to the LORD your God for your servants, so that we may not die; for we have added to all our sins the evil of demanding a king for ourselves." And Samuel said to the people, "Do not be afraid; you have done all this evil, yet do not turn aside from following the LORD, but serve the LORD with all your heart; and do not turn aside after useless things that cannot profit or save, for they are useless. For the LORD will not cast away his people, for his great name's sake, because it has pleased the LORD to make you a people for himself. Moreover as for me, far be it from me that I should sin against the LORD by ceasing to pray for you; and I will instruct you in the good and the right way. Only fear the LORD, and serve him faithfully with all your heart; for consider what great things he has done for you. But if you still do wickedly, you shall be swept away, both you and your king."

A Reading (Lesson) from the Acts of the Apostles [8:14–25]

When the apostles at Jerusalem heard that Samaria had accepted the word of God, they sent Peter and John to them. The two went down and prayed for them that they might receive the Holy Spirit (for as yet the Spirit had not come upon any of them; they had only been baptized in the name of the Lord Jesus). Then Peter and John laid their hands on them, and they received the Holy Spirit. Now when Simon saw that the Spirit was given through the laying on the apostles' hands, he offered them money, saying, "Give me also this power so that anyone on whom I lay my hands may receive the Holy Spirit." But Peter said to him, "May your silver perish with you, because you thought you could obtain God's gift with money! You have no part or share in this, for your heart is not right before God. Repent therefore of this wickedness of yours, and pray to the Lord that, if possible, the intent of your heart may be forgiven you. For I see that you are in the gall of bitterness and the chains of wickedness." Simon answered, "Pray for me to the Lord, that nothing of what you have said may happen to me." Now after Peter and John had testified and spoken the word of the Lord, they returned to Jerusalem, proclaiming the good news to many villages of the Samaritans.

A Reading (Lesson) from the Gospel according to Luke [23:1–12]

The assembly rose as a body and brought Jesus before Pilate. They began to accuse him, saying, "We found this man perverting our nation, forbidding us to pay taxes to the emperor, and saying that he himself is the Messiah, a king." Then Pilate asked him, "Are you the king of the Jews?" He answered, "You say so." Then Pilate said to the chief priests and the crowds, "I find no basis for an accusation against this man." But they were insistent and said, "He stirs up the people by teaching throughout all Judea, from Galilee where he began even to this place." When Pilate heard this, he asked whether the man was a Galilean. And when he learned that he was under Herod's jurisdiction, he sent him off to Herod, who was himself in Jerusalem at that time. When Herod saw Jesus, he was very glad, for he had been wanting to see him for a long time, because he had heard about him and was hoping to see him perform some sign. He questioned him at some length, but Jesus gave him no answer. The chief priests and the scribes stood by, vehemently accusing him. Even Herod with his soldiers treated him with contempt and mocked him; then he put an elegant robe on him, and sent him back to Pilate. That same day Herod and Pilate became friends with each other; before this they had been enemies.

Thursday

Psalm 131 [page 785], *Psalm 132* [page 785],
(Psalm 133 [page 787]) ❖ *Psalm 134* [page 787],
Psalm 135 [page 788]

A Reading (Lesson) from the First Book of Samuel [13:5–18]

The Philistines mustered to fight with Israel, thirty thousand chariots, and six thousand horsemen, and troops like the sand on the seashore in multitude; they came up and encamped at Michmash, to the east of Beth-aven. When the Israelites saw that they were in distress (for the troops were hard pressed), the people hid themselves in caves and in holes and in rocks and in tombs and in cisterns. Some Hebrews crossed the Jordan to the land of Gad and Gilead. Saul was still at Gilgal, and all the people followed him trembling. He waited seven days, the time appointed by Samuel; but Samuel did not come to Gilgal, and the people began to slip away from Saul. So Saul said, "Bring the burnt offering here to me, and the offerings of well-being." And he offered the burnt offering. As soon as he had finished offering the burnt offering, Samuel arrived; and Saul went out to meet him and salute him. Samuel said, "What have you done?" Saul replied, "When I saw that the people were slipping away from me, and that you did not come within the days appointed, and that the Philistines were mustering at Michmash, I said, 'Now the Philistines will come down upon me at Gilgal, and I have not entreated the favor of the LORD'; so I forced myself, and offered the burnt offering." Samuel said to Saul, "You have done foolishly; you have not kept the commandment of the LORD your God, which he commanded you. The LORD would have established your kingdom over Israel forever, but now your kingdom will not continue; the LORD has sought out a man after his own heart; and the LORD has appointed him to be ruler over his people, because you have not kept what the LORD commanded you." And Samuel left and went on his way from Gilgal. The rest of the people followed Saul to join the army; they went up from Gilgal toward Gibeah of Benjamin. Saul counted the people who were present with him, about six hundred men. Saul, his son Jonathan, and the people who were present with them stayed in Geba of Benjamin; but the Philistines encamped at Michmash. And raiders came out of the camp of the Philistines in three companies; one company turned toward Ophrah, to the land of Shual, another company turned toward Beth-horon, and another company turned toward the mountain that looks down upon the valley of Zeboim toward the wilderness.

A Reading (Lesson) from the Acts of the Apostles [8:26–40]

An angel of the Lord said to Philip, "Get up and go toward the south to the road that goes down from

Jerusalem to Gaza." (This is a wilderness road.) So he got up and went. Now there was an Ethiopian eunuch, a court official of the Candace, queen of the Ethiopians, in charge of her entire treasury. He had come to Jerusalem to worship and was returning home; seated in his chariot, he was reading the prophet Isaiah. Then the Spirit said to Philip, "Go over to this chariot and join it." So Philip ran up to it and heard him reading the prophet Isaiah. He asked, "Do you understand what you are reading?" He replied, "How can I, unless someone guides me?" And he invited Philip to get in and sit beside him. Now the passage of the scripture that he was reading was this: "Like a sheep he was led to the slaughter, and like a lamb silent before its shearer, so he does not open his mouth. In his humiliation justice was denied him. Who can describe his generation? For his life is taken away from the earth." The eunuch asked Philip, "About whom, may I ask you, does the prophet say this, about himself or about someone else?" Then Philip began to speak, and starting with this scripture, he proclaimed to him the good news about Jesus. As they were going along the road, they came to some water; and the eunuch said, "Look, here is water! What is to prevent me from being baptized?" He commanded the chariot to stop, and both of them, Philip and the eunuch, went down into the water, and Philip baptized him. When they came up out of the water, the Spirit of the Lord snatched Philip away; the eunuch saw him no more, and went on his way rejoicing. But Philip found himself at Azotus, and as he was passing through the region, he proclaimed the good news to all the towns until he came to Caesarea.

A Reading (Lesson) from the Gospel according to Luke
[23:13–25]

Pilate called together the chief priests, the leaders, and the people, and said to them, "You brought me this man as one who was perverting the people; and here I have examined him in your presence and have not found this man guilty of any of your charges against him. Neither has Herod, for he sent him back to us. Indeed, he has done nothing to deserve death. I will therefore have him flogged and release him." Then they all shouted out together, "Away with this fellow! Release Barabbas for us!" (This was a man who had been put in prison for an insurrection that had taken place in the city, and for murder.) Pilate, wanting to release Jesus, addressed them again; but they kept shouting, "Crucify, crucify him!" A third time he said to them, "Why, what evil has he done? I have found in him no ground for the sentence of death; I will therefore have him flogged and then release him." But they kept urgently demanding with loud shouts that he should be crucified; and their voices prevailed. So Pilate gave his verdict that their demand should be granted. He released the man they asked for, the one who had been put in prison for insurrection and murder, and he handed Jesus over as they wished.

Friday

Psalm 140 [page 796],   *Psalm 142* [page 798]   ❖
Psalm 141 [page 797],   *Psalm 143:1–11(12)* [page 798]

A Reading (Lesson) from the First Book of Samuel
[13:19—14:15]

There was no smith to be found throughout all the land of Israel; for the Philistines said, "The Hebrews must not make swords or spears for themselves"; so all the Israelites went down to the Philistines to sharpen their plowshares, mattocks, axes, or sickles. The charge was two-thirds of a shekel for the plowshares and for the mattocks; and one-third of a shekel for sharpening the axes and for setting the goads. So on the day of the battle neither sword nor spear was to be found in the possession of any of the people with Saul and Jonathan; but Saul and his son Jonathan had them. Now a garrison of the Philistines had gone out to the pass of Michmash. One day Jonathan son of Saul said to the young man who carried his armor, "Come, let us go over to the Philistine garrison on the other side." But he did not tell his father. Saul was staying in the outskirts of Gibeah under the pomegranate tree that is at Migron; the troops that were with him were about six hundred men, along with Ahijah son of Ahitub, Ichabod's brother, son of Phinehas son of Eli, the priest of the LORD in Shiloh, carrying an ephod. Now the people did not know that Jonathan had gone. In the pass, by which Jonathan tried to go over to the Philistine garrison, there was a rocky crag on one side and a rocky crag on the other; the name of the one was Bozez, and the name of the other Seneh. One crag rose on the north in front of Michmash, and the other on the south in front of Geba. Jonathan said to the young man who carried his armor, "Come, let us go over to the garrison of these uncircumcised; it may be that the LORD will act for us; for nothing can hinder the LORD from saving by many or by few." His armor-bearer said to him, "Do all that your mind inclines to. I am with you; as your mind is, so is mine." Then Jonathan said, "Now we will cross over to those men and will show ourselves to them. If they say to us, 'Wait until we come to you,' then we will stand still in our place, and we will not go up to them. But if they say, 'Come up to us,' then we will go up; for the LORD has given them into our hand. That will be the sign for us." So both of them showed themselves to the garrison of the Philistines; and the Philistines said, "Look, Hebrews are coming out of the holes where they have hidden themselves." The men of the garrison hailed Jonathan and his armor-bearer, saying, "Come up to us, and we will show you something." Jonathan said to his armor-bearer, "Come up after me; for the LORD has given them into the hand of Israel." Then Jonathan climbed up on his hands and feet, with his armor-bearer following after him. The Philistines fell before Jonathan, and his armor-bearer, coming after him, killed them. In that first slaughter Jonathan and his armor-bearer killed about twenty men within an area about half a furrow long in an acre of land. There was a panic in the camp, in the field, and among all the people; the garrison and even the raiders trembled; the earth quaked; and it became a very great panic.

A Reading (Lesson) from the Acts of the Apostles [9:1–9]

Saul, still breathing threats and murder against the disciples of the Lord, went to the high priest and asked him for letters to the synagogues at Damascus, so that if he found any who belonged to the Way, men or women, he might bring them bound to Jerusalem. Now as he was going along and approaching Damascus, suddenly a light from heaven flashed around him. He fell to the ground and heard a voice saying to him, "Saul, Saul, why do you persecute me?" He asked, "Who are you, Lord?" The reply came, "I am Jesus, whom you are persecuting. But get up and enter the city, and you will be told what you are to do." The men who were traveling with him stood speechless because they heard the voice but saw no one. Saul got up from the ground, and though his eyes were open, he could see nothing; so they led him by the hand and brought him into Damascus. For three days he was without sight, and neither ate nor drank.

A Reading (Lesson) from the Gospel according to Luke [23:26–31]

As they led Jesus away, they seized a man, Simon of Cyrene, who was coming from the country, and they laid the cross on him, and made him carry it behind Jesus. A great number of the people followed him, and among them were women who were beating their breasts and wailing for him. But Jesus turned to them and said, "Daughters of Jerusalem, do not weep for me, but weep for yourselves and for your children. For the days are surely coming when they will say, 'Blessed are the barren, and the wombs that never bore, and the breasts that never nursed.' Then they will begin to say to the mountains, 'Fall on us'; and to the hills, 'Cover us.' For if they do this when the wood is green, what will happen when it is dry?"

Saturday

Psalm 137:1–6(7–9) [page 792],
Psalm 144 [page 800] ❖ *Psalm 104* [page 735]

A Reading (Lesson) from the First Book of Samuel [14:16–30]

Saul's lookouts in Gibeah of Benjamin were watching as the multitude was surging back and forth. Then Saul said to the troops that were with him, "Call the roll and see who has gone from us." When they had called the roll, Jonathan and his armor-bearer were not there. Saul said to Ahijah, "Bring the ark of God here." For at that time the ark of God went with the Israelites. While Saul was talking to the priest, the tumult in the camp of the Philistines increased more and more; and Saul said to the priest, "Withdraw your hand." Then Saul and all the people who were with him rallied and went into the battle; and every sword was against the other, so that there was very great confusion. Now the Hebrews who previously had been with the Philistines and had gone up with them into the camp turned and joined the Israelites who were with Saul and Jonathan. Likewise, when all the Israelites who had gone into hiding in the hill country of Ephraim heard that the Philistines were fleeing, they too followed closely after them in the battle. So the LORD gave Israel the victory that day. The battle passed beyond Beth-aven, and the troops with Saul numbered altogether about ten thousand men. The battle spread out over the hill country of Ephraim. Now Saul committed a very rash act on that day. He had laid an oath on the troops, saying, "Cursed be anyone who eats food before it is evening and I have been avenged on my enemies." So none of the troops tasted food. All the troops came upon a honeycomb; and there was honey on the ground. When the troops came upon the honeycomb, the honey was dripping out; but they did not put their hands to their mouths, for they feared the oath. But Jonathan had not heard his father charge the troops with the oath; so he extended the staff that was in his hand, and dipped the tip of it in the honeycomb, and put his hand to his mouth; and his eyes brightened. Then one of the soldiers said, "Your father strictly charged the troops with an oath, saying, 'Cursed be anyone who eats food this day.' And so the troops are faint." Then Jonathan said, "My father has troubled the land; see how my eyes have brightened because I tasted a little of this honey. How much better if today the troops had eaten freely of the spoil taken from their enemies; for now the slaughter among the Philistines has not been great."

A Reading (Lesson) from the Acts of the Apostles [9:10–19a]

There was a disciple at Damascus named Ananias. The Lord said to him in a vision, "Ananias." He answered, "Here I am, Lord." The Lord said to him, "Get up and go to the street called Straight, and at the house of Judas look for a man of Tarsus named Saul. At this moment he is praying, and he has seen in a vision a man named Ananias come in and lay his hands on him so that he might regain his sight." But Ananias answered, "Lord, I have heard from many about this man, how much evil he has done to your saints in Jerusalem; and here he has authority from the chief priests to bind all who invoke your name." But the Lord said to him, "Go, for he is an instrument whom I have chosen to bring my name before Gentiles and kings and before the people of Israel; I myself will show him how much he must suffer for the sake of my name." So Ananias went and entered the house. He laid his hands on Saul and said, "Brother Saul, the Lord Jesus, who appeared to you on your way here, has sent me so that you may regain your sight and be filled with the Holy Spirit." And immediately something like scales fell from his eyes, and his sight was restored. Then he got up and was baptized, and after taking some food, he regained his strength.

A Reading (Lesson) from the Gospel according to Luke
[23:32–43]

Two others also, who were criminals, were led away to be
put to death with him. When they came to the place that
is called The Skull, they crucified Jesus there with the
criminals, one on his right and one on his left. Then Jesus
said, "Father, forgive them; for they do not know what
they are doing." And they cast lots to divide his clothing.
And the people stood by, watching; but the leaders scoffed
at him, saying, "He saved others; let him save himself if
he is the Messiah of God, his chosen one!" The soldiers
also mocked him, coming up and offering him sour wine,
and saying, "If you are the King of the Jews, save
yourself!" There was also an inscription over him, "This is
the King of the Jews." One of the criminals who were
hanged there kept deriding him and saying, "Are you not
the Messiah? Save yourself and us!" But the other rebuked
him, saying, "Do you not fear God, since you are under
the same sentence of condemnation? And we indeed have
been condemned justly, for we are getting what we deserve
for our deeds, but this man has done nothing wrong."
Then he said, "Jesus, remember me when you come into
your kingdom." He replied, "Truly I tell you, today you
will be with me in Paradise."

Proper 9 *Week of the Sunday closest to July 6*

Sunday

Psalm 146 [page 803], *Psalm 147* [page 804] ❖
Psalm 111 [page 754], *Psalm 112* [page 755],
Psalm 113 [page 756]

A Reading (Lesson) from the First Book of Samuel
[14:36–45]

Saul said, "Let us go down after the Philistines by night and despoil them until the morning light; let us not leave one of them." They said, "Do whatever seems good to you." But the priest said, "Let us draw near to God here." So Saul inquired of God, "Shall I go down after the Philistines? Will you give them into the hand of Israel?" But he did not answer him that day. Saul said, "Come here, all you leaders of the people; and let us find out how this sin has arisen today. For as the LORD lives who saves Israel, even if it is in my son Jonathan, he shall surely die!" But there was no one among all the people who answered him. He said to all Israel, "You shall be on one side, and I and my son Jonathan will be on the other side." The people said to Saul, "Do what seems good to you." Then Saul said, "O LORD God of Israel, why have you not answered your servant today? If this guilt is in me or in my son Jonathan, O LORD God of Israel, give Urim; but if this guilt is in your people Israel, give Thummim." And Jonathan and Saul were indicated by the lot, but the people were cleared. Then Saul said, "Cast the lot between me and my son Jonathan." And Jonathan was taken. Then Saul said to Jonathan, "Tell me what you have done." Jonathan told him, "I tasted a little honey with the tip of the staff that was in my hand; here I am, I will die." Saul said, "God do so to me and more also; you shall surely die, Jonathan!" Then the people said to Saul, "Shall Jonathan die, who has accomplished this great victory in Israel? Far from it! As the LORD lives, not one hair of his head shall fall to the ground; for he has worked with God today." So the people ransomed Jonathan, and he did not die.

A Reading (Lesson) from the Letter of Paul to the Romans
[5:1–11]

Therefore, since we are justified by faith, we have peace
with God through our Lord Jesus Christ, through whom
we have obtained access to this grace in which we stand;
and we boast in our hope of sharing the glory of God.
And not only that, but we also boast in our sufferings,
knowing that suffering produces endurance, and endurance
produces character, and character produces hope, and
hope does not disappoint us, because God's love has been
poured into our hearts through the Holy Spirit that has
been given to us. For while we were still weak, at the right
time Christ died for the ungodly. Indeed, rarely will
anyone die for a righteous person—though perhaps for a
good person someone might actually dare to die. But God
proves his love for us in that while we still were sinners
Christ died for us. Much more surely then, now that we
have been justified by his blood, will we be saved through
him from the wrath of God. For if while we were enemies,
we were reconciled to God through the death of his Son,
much more surely, having been reconciled, will we be
saved by his life. But more than that, we even boast in
God through our Lord Jesus Christ, through whom we
have now received reconciliation.

A Reading (Lesson) from the Gospel according to Matthew
[22:1–14]

Once more Jesus spoke to them in parables, saying: "The
kingdom of heaven may be compared to a king who gave
a wedding banquet for his son. He sent his slaves to call
those who had been invited to the wedding banquet, but
they would not come. Again he sent other slaves, saying,
'Tell those who have been invited: Look, I have prepared

my dinner, my oxen and my fat calves have been slaughtered, and everything is ready; come to the wedding banquet.' But they made light of it and went away, one to his farm, another to his business, while the rest seized his slaves, mistreated them, and killed them. The king was enraged. He sent his troops, destroyed those murderers, and burned their city. Then he said to his slaves, 'The wedding is ready, but those invited were not worthy. Go therefore into the main streets, and invite everyone you find to the wedding banquet.' Those slaves went out into the streets and gathered all whom they found, both good and bad; so the wedding hall was filled with guests. But when the king came in to see the guests, he noticed a man there who was not wearing a wedding robe, and he said to him, 'Friend, how did you get in here without a wedding robe?' And he was speechless. Then the king said to the attendants, 'Bind him hand and foot, and throw him into the outer darkness, where there will be weeping and gnashing of teeth.' For many are called, but few are chosen.''

Monday

Psalm 1 [page 585], *Psalm 2* [page 586], *Psalm 3* [page 587] ❖ *Psalm 4* [page 587], *Psalm 7* [page 590]

A Reading (Lesson) from the First Book of Samuel [15:1–3, 7–23]

Samuel said to Saul, "The LORD sent me to anoint you king over his people Israel; now therefore listen to the words of the LORD. Thus says the LORD of hosts, 'I will punish the Amalekites for what they did in opposing the Israelites when they came up out of Egypt. Now go and attack Amalek, and utterly destroy all that they have; do not spare them, but kill both man and woman, child and infant, ox and sheep, camel and donkey.' " Saul defeated the Amalekites, from Havilah as far as Shur, which is east of Egypt. He took King Agag of the Amalekites alive, but utterly destroyed all the people with the edge of the sword. Saul and the people spared Agag, and the best of the sheep and of the cattle and of the fatlings, and the lambs, and all that was valuable, and would not utterly destroy them; all that was despised and worthless they utterly destroyed. The word of the LORD came to Samuel: "I regret that I made Saul king, for he has turned back from following me, and has not carried out my commands." Samuel was angry; and he cried out to the LORD all night. Samuel rose early in the morning to meet Saul, and Samuel was told, "Saul went to Carmel, where he set up a monument for himself, and on returning he passed on down to Gilgal." When Samuel came to Saul, Saul said to him, "May you be blessed by the LORD; I have carried out the command of the LORD." But Samuel said, "What then is this bleating of sheep in my ears, and the lowing of cattle that I hear?" Saul said, "They have brought them from the Amalekites; for the people spared the best of the sheep and the cattle, to sacrifice to the LORD your God; but the rest we have utterly destroyed." Then Samuel said to Saul, "Stop! I will tell you what the LORD said to me last night." He replied, "Speak." Samuel said, "Though you are little in your own eyes, are you not the head of the tribes of Israel? The LORD anointed you king over Israel. And the LORD sent you on a mission, and said, 'Go, utterly destroy the sinners, the Amalekites, and fight against them until they are consumed.' Why then did you not obey the voice of the LORD? Why did you swoop down on the spoil, and do what was evil in the sight of the LORD?" Saul said to Samuel,

"I have obeyed the voice of the LORD, I have gone on the mission on which the LORD sent me, I have brought Agag the king of Amalek, and I have utterly destroyed the Amalekites. But from the spoil the people took sheep and cattle, the best of the things devoted to destruction, to sacrifice to the LORD your God in Gilgal." And Samuel said, "Has the LORD as great delight in burnt offerings and sacrifices, as in obeying the voice of the LORD? Surely, to obey is better than sacrifice, and to heed than the fat of rams. For rebellion is no less a sin than divination, and stubbornness is like iniquity and idolatry. Because you have rejected the word of the LORD, he has also rejected you from being king."

A Reading (Lesson) from the Acts of the Apostles [9:19b–31]

For several days Saul was with the disciples at Damascus, and immediately he began to proclaim Jesus in the synagogues, saying, "He is the Son of God." All who heard him were amazed and said, "Is not this the man who made havoc in Jerusalem among those who invoked this name? And has he not come here for the purpose of bringing them bound before the chief priests?" Saul became increasingly more powerful and confounded the Jews who lived in Damascus by proving that Jesus was the Messiah. After some time had passed, the Jews plotted to kill him, but their plot became known to Saul. They were watching the gates day and night so that they might kill him; but his disciples took him by night and let him down through an opening in the wall, lowering him in a basket. When he had come to Jerusalem, he attempted to join the disciples; and they were all afraid of him, for they did not believe that he was a disciple. But Barnabas took him, brought him to the apostles, and described for them how on the road he had seen the Lord, who had spoken to him, and how in Damascus he had spoken boldly in the name of Jesus. So he went in and out among them in Jerusalem, speaking boldly in the name of the Lord. He spoke and argued with the Hellenists; but they were attempting to kill him. When the believers learned of it, they brought him down to Caesarea and sent him off to Tarsus. Meanwhile the church throughout Judea, Galilee, and Samaria had peace and was built up. Living in the fear of the Lord and in the comfort of the Holy Spirit, it increased in numbers.

A Reading (Lesson) from the Gospel according to Luke
[23:44–56a]

It was now about noon, and darkness came over the whole land until three in the afternoon, while the sun's light failed; and the curtain of the temple was torn in two. Then Jesus, crying with a loud voice, said, "Father, into your hands I commend my spirit." Having said this, he breathed his last. When the centurion saw what had taken place, he praised God and said, "Certainly this man was innocent." And when all the crowds who had gathered there for this spectacle saw what had taken place, they returned home, beating their breasts. But all his acquaintances, including the women who had followed him from Galilee, stood at a distance, watching these things. Now there was a good and righteous man named Joseph, who, though a member of the council, had not agreed to their plan and action. He came from the Jewish town of Arimathea, and he was waiting expectantly for the kingdom of God. This man went to Pilate and asked for the body of Jesus. Then he took it down, wrapped it in a linen cloth, and laid it in a rock-hewn tomb where no one had ever been laid. It was the day of Preparation, and the sabbath was beginning. The women who had come with him from Galilee followed, and they saw the tomb and how his body was laid. Then they returned, and prepared spices and ointments.

Tuesday

Psalm 5 [page 588], *Psalm 6* [page 589] ❖
Psalm 10 [page 594], *Psalm 11* [page 596]

A Reading (Lesson) from the First Book of Samuel
[15:24–35]

Saul said to Samuel, "I have sinned; for I have transgressed the commandment of the LORD and your words, because I feared the people and obeyed their voice. Now therefore, I pray, pardon my sin, and return with me, so that I may worship the LORD." Samuel said to Saul, "I will not return with you; for you have rejected the word of the LORD, and the LORD has rejected you from being king over Israel." As Samuel turned to go away, Saul caught hold of the hem of his robe, and it tore. And Samuel said to him, "The LORD has torn the kingdom of Israel from you this very day, and has given it to a neighbor of yours, who is better than you. Moreover the Glory of Israel will not recant or change his mind; for he is not a mortal, that he should change his mind." Then Saul said, "I have sinned; yet honor me now before the elders of my people and before Israel, and return with me, so that I may worship the LORD your God." So Samuel turned back after Saul; and Saul worshiped the LORD. Then Samuel said, "Bring Agag king of the Amalekites here to me." And Agag came to him haltingly.

Agag said, "Surely this is the bitterness of death." But Samuel said, "As your sword has made women childless, so your mother shall be childless among women." And Samuel hewed Agag in pieces before the LORD in Gilgal. Then Samuel went to Ramah; and Saul went up to his house in Gibeah of Saul. Samuel did not see Saul again until the day of his death, but Samuel grieved over Saul. And the LORD was sorry that he had made Saul king over Israel.

A Reading (Lesson) from the Acts of the Apostles [9:32–43]

As Peter went here and there among all the believers, he came down also to the saints living in Lydda. There he found a man named Aeneas, who had been bedridden for eight years, for he was paralyzed. Peter said to him, "Aeneas, Jesus Christ heals you; get up and make your bed!" And immediately he got up. And all the residents of Lydda and Sharon saw him and turned to the Lord. Now in Joppa there was a disciple whose name was Tabitha, which in Greek is Dorcas. She was devoted to good works and acts of charity. At that time she became ill and died. When they had washed her, they laid her in a room upstairs. Since Lydda was near Joppa, the disciples, who heard that Peter was there, sent two men to him with the request, "Please come to us without delay." So Peter got up and went with them; and when he arrived, they took him to the room upstairs. All the widows stood beside him, weeping and showing tunics and other clothing that Dorcas had made while she was with them. Peter put all of them outside, and then he knelt down and prayed. He turned to the body and said, "Tabitha, get up." Then she opened her eyes, and seeing Peter, she sat up. He gave her his hand and helped her up. Then calling the saints and widows, he showed her to be alive. This became known throughout Joppa, and many believed in the Lord. Meanwhile he stayed in Joppa for some time with a certain Simon, a tanner.

A Reading (Lesson) from the Gospel according to Luke [23:56b—24:11]

On the sabbath the women rested according to the commandment. But on the first day of the week, at early dawn, they came to the tomb, taking the spices that they had prepared. They found the stone rolled away from the tomb, but when they went in, they did not find the body. While they were perplexed about this, suddenly two men in dazzling clothes stood beside them. The women were terrified and bowed their faces to the ground, but the men said to them, "Why do you look for the living among the dead? He is not here, but has risen. Remember how he told you, while he was still in Galilee, that the Son of Man must be handed over to sinners, and be crucified, and on the third day rise again." Then they remembered his words, and returning from the tomb, they told all this to the eleven and to all the rest. Now it was Mary Magdalene, Joanna, Mary the mother of James, and the other women with them who told this to the apostles. But these words seemed to them an idle tale, and they did not believe them.

Wednesday

Psalm 119:1–24 [page 763] ❖ *Psalm 12* [page 597], *Psalm 13* [page 597], *Psalm 14* [page 598]

A Reading (Lesson) from the First Book of Samuel [16:1–13]

The LORD said to Samuel, "How long will you grieve over Saul? I have rejected him from being king over Israel. Fill your horn with oil and set out; I will send you to Jesse the Bethlehemite, for I have provided for myself a king among his sons." Samuel said, "How can I go? If Saul hears of it, he will kill me." And the LORD said, "Take a heifer with you, and say, 'I have come to sacrifice to the LORD.' Invite Jesse to the sacrifice, and I will show you what you shall do; and you shall anoint for me the one whom I name to you." Samuel did what the LORD commanded, and came to Bethlehem. The elders of the city came to meet him trembling, and said, "Do you come peaceably?" He said, "Peaceably; I have come to sacrifice to the LORD; sanctify yourselves and come with me to the sacrifice." And he sanctified Jesse and his sons and invited them to the sacrifice. When they came, he looked on Eliab and thought. "Surely the LORD's anointed is now before the LORD." But the LORD said to Samuel, "Do not look on his appearance or on the height of his stature, because I have rejected him; for the LORD does not see as mortals see; they look on the outward appearance, but the LORD looks on the heart." Then Jesse called Abinadab, and made him pass before Samuel. He said, "Neither has the LORD chosen this one." Then Jesse made Shammah pass by. And he said, "Neither has the LORD chosen this one." Jesse made seven of his sons pass before Samuel, and Samuel said to Jesse, "The LORD has not chosen any of these." Samuel said to Jesse, "Are all your sons here?" And he said, "There remains yet the youngest, but he is keeping the sheep." And Samuel said to Jesse, "Send and bring him; for we will not sit down until he comes here." He sent and brought him in. Now he was ruddy, and had beautiful eyes, and was handsome. The

LORD said, "Rise and anoint him; for this is the one." Then Samuel took the horn of oil, and anointed him in the presence of his brothers; and the spirit of the LORD came mightily upon David from that day forward. Samuel then set out and went to Ramah.

A Reading (Lesson) from the Acts of the Apostles [10:1–16]

In Caesarea there was a man named Cornelius, a centurion of the Italian Cohort, as it was called. He was a devout man who feared God with all his household; he gave alms generously to the people and prayed constantly to God. One afternoon at about three o'clock he had a vision in which he clearly saw an angel of God coming in and saying to him, "Cornelius." He stared at him in terror and said, "What is it, Lord?" He answered, "Your prayers and your alms have ascended as a memorial before God. Now send men to Joppa for a certain Simon who is called Peter; he is lodging with Simon, a tanner, whose house is by the seaside." When the angel who spoke to him had left, he called two of his slaves and a devout soldier from the ranks of those who served him, and after telling them everything, he sent them to Joppa. About noon the next day, as they were on their journey and approaching the city, Peter went up on the roof to pray. He became hungry and wanted something to eat; and while it was being prepared, he fell into a trance. He saw the heaven opened and something like a large sheet coming down, being lowered to the ground by its four corners. In it were all kinds of four-footed creatures and reptiles and birds of the air. Then he heard a voice saying, "Get up, Peter; kill and eat." But Peter said, "By no means, Lord; for I have never eaten anything that is profane or unclean." The voice said to him again, a second time, "What God has made clean, you must not call profane." This happened three times, and the thing was suddenly taken up to heaven.

A Reading (Lesson) from the Gospel according to Luke [24:13–35]

Now on that same day two of the disciples were going to a village called Emmaus, about seven miles from Jerusalem, and talking with each other about all these things that had happened. While they were talking and discussing, Jesus himself came near and went with them, but their eyes were kept from recognizing him. And he said to them, "What are you discussing with each other while you walk along?" They stood still, looking sad. Then one of them, whose name was Cleopas, answered him, "Are you the only stranger in Jerusalem who does not know the things that have taken place there in these days?" He asked them, "What things?" They replied, "The things about Jesus of Nazareth, who was a prophet mighty in deed and word before God and all the people, and how our chief priests and leaders handed him over to be condemned to death and crucified him. But we had hoped that he was the one to redeem Israel. Yes, and besides all this, it is now the third day since these things took place. Moreover, some women of our group astounded us. They were at the tomb early this morning, and when they did not find his body there, they came back and told us that they had indeed seen a vision of angels who said that he was alive. Some of those who were with us went to the tomb and found it just as the women had said; but they did not see him." Then he said to them, "Oh, how foolish you are, and how slow of heart to believe all that the prophets have declared! Was it not necessary that the Messiah should suffer these things and then enter into his glory?" Then beginning with Moses and all the prophets, he interpreted to them the things about himself in all the scriptures. As they came near the village to which they were going, he walked ahead as if he were going on. But they urged him strongly, saying, "Stay with us, because it is almost evening and the day is now nearly over." So he went in to stay with them. When he was at the table with them, he took bread, blessed and broke it, and gave it to them. Then their eyes were opened, and they recognized him; and he vanished from their sight. They said to each other, "Were not our hearts burning within us while he was talking to us on the road, while he was opening the scriptures to us?" That same hour they got up and returned to Jerusalem; and they found the eleven and their companions gathered together. They were saying, "The Lord has risen indeed, and he has appeared to Simon!" Then they told what had happened on the road, and how he had been made known to them in the breaking of the bread.

Thursday

Psalm 18:1–20 [page 602]   ❖   *Psalm 18:21–50* [page 604]

A Reading (Lesson) from the First Book of Samuel
[16:14—17:11]

The spirit of the LORD departed from Saul, and an evil spirit from the LORD tormented him. And Saul's servants said to him, "See now, an evil spirit from God is tormenting you. Let our lord now command the servants who attend you to look for someone who is skillful in playing the lyre; and when the evil spirit from God is upon you, he will play it, and you will feel better." So Saul said to his servants,

"Provide for me someone who can play well, and bring him to me." One of the young men answered, "I have seen a son of Jesse the Bethlehemite who is skillful in playing, a man of valor, a warrior, prudent in speech, and a man of good presence; and the LORD is with him." So Saul sent messengers to Jesse, and said, "Send me your son David who is with the sheep." Jesse took a donkey loaded with bread, a skin of wine, and a kid, and sent them by his son David to Saul. And David came to Saul, and entered his service. Saul loved him greatly, and he became his armor-bearer. Saul sent to Jesse, saying, "Let David remain in my service, for he has found favor in my sight." And whenever the evil spirit from God came upon Saul, David took the lyre and played it with his hand, and Saul would be relieved and feel better, and the evil spirit would depart from him. Now the Philistines gathered their armies for battle; they were gathered at Socoh, which belongs to Judah, and encamped between Socoh and Azekah, in Ephes-dammim. Saul and the Israelites gathered and encamped in the valley of Elah, and formed ranks against the Philistines. The Philistines stood on the mountain on the one side, and Israel stood on the mountain on the other side, with a valley between them. And there came out from the camp of the Philistines a champion named Goliath, of Gath, whose height was six cubits and a span. He had a helmet of bronze on his head, and he was armed with a coat of mail; the weight of the coat was five thousand shekels of bronze. He had greaves of bronze on his legs and a javelin of bronze slung between his shoulders. The shaft of his spear was like a weaver's beam, and his spear's head weighed six hundred shekels of iron; and his shield-bearer went before him. He stood and shouted to the ranks of Israel, "Why have you come out to draw up for battle? Am I not a Philistine, and are you not servants of Saul? Choose a man for yourselves, and let him come down to me. If he is able to fight with me and kill me, then we will be your servants; but if I prevail against him and kill him, then you shall be our servants and serve us." And the Philistine said, "Today I defy the ranks of Israel! Give me a man, that we may fight together." When Saul and all Israel heard these words of the Philistine, they were dismayed and greatly afraid.

A Reading (Lesson) from the Acts of the Apostles [10:17–33]

While Peter was greatly puzzled about what to make of the vision that he had seen, suddenly the men sent by Cornelius appeared. They were asking for Simon's house and were standing by the gate. They called out to ask whether Simon, who was called Peter, was staying there. While Peter was still thinking about the vision, the Spirit said to him, "Look, three men are searching for you. Now get up, go down, and go with them without hesitation; for I have sent them." So Peter went down to the men and said, "I am the one you are looking for; what is the reason for your coming?" They answered, "Cornelius, a centurion, an upright and God-fearing man, who is well spoken of by the whole Jewish nation, was directed by a holy angel to send for you to come to his house and to hear what you have to say." So Peter invited them in and gave them lodging. The next day he got up and went with them, and some of the believers from Joppa accompanied him. The following day they came to Caesarea. Cornelius was expecting them and had called together his relatives and close friends. On Peter's arrival Cornelius met him, and falling at his feet, worshiped him. But Peter made him get up, saying, 'Stand up; I am only a mortal." And as he talked with him, he went in and found that many had assembled; and he said to them, "You yourselves know that it is unlawful for a Jew to associate with or to visit a Gentile; but God has shown me that I should not call anyone profane or unclean. So when I was sent for, I came without objection. Now may I ask why you sent for me?" Cornelius replied, "Four days ago at this very hour, at three o'clock, I was praying in my house when suddenly a man in dazzling clothes stood before me. He said, 'Cornelius, your prayer has been heard and your alms have been remembered before God. Send therefore to Joppa and ask for Simon, who is called Peter; he is staying in the home of Simon, a tanner, by the sea.' Therefore I sent for you immediately, and you have been kind enough to come. So now all of us are here in the presence of God to listen to all that the Lord has commanded you to say."

A Reading (Lesson) from the Gospel according to Luke
[24:36–53]

As the disciples were talking about what happened on the road, Jesus himself stood among them and said to them, "Peace be with you." They were startled and terrified, and thought that they were seeing a ghost. He said to them, "Why are you frightened, and why do doubts arise in your hearts? Look at my hands and my feet; see that it is I myself. Touch me and see; for a ghost does not have flesh and bones as you see that I have." And when he had said this, he showed them his hands and his feet. While in their joy they were disbelieving and still wondering, he said to them, "Have you anything here to eat?" They gave him a piece of broiled fish, and he took it and ate in their presence. Then he said to them, "These are my words that I spoke to you while I was still with you—that everything written about me in the law of Moses, the prophets, and the psalms must be fulfilled." Then he opened their minds to understand the scriptures, and he said to them, "Thus it is written, that the Messiah is to suffer and to rise from the dead on the third day, and that repentance and forgiveness of sins is to be proclaimed in his name to all nations, beginning from Jerusalem. You are witnesses of these things. And see, I am sending upon you what my Father promised; so stay here in the city until you have been clothed with power from on high." Then he led them out as far as Bethany, and, lifting up his hands, he blessed them. While he was blessing them, he withdrew from them and was carried up into heaven. And they worshiped him, and returned to Jerusalem with great joy; and they were continually in the temple blessing God.

Friday

Psalm 16 [page 599],   *Psalm 17* [page 600]   ❖
Psalm 22 [page 610]

A Reading (Lesson) from the First Book of Samuel
[17:17–30]

Jesse said to his son David, "Take for your brothers an ephah of this parched grain and these ten loaves, and carry them quickly to the camp to your brothers; also take these ten cheeses to the commander of their thousand. See how your brothers fare, and bring some token from them." Now Saul, and they, and all the men of Israel, were in the valley of Elah, fighting with the Philistines. David rose early in the morning, left the sheep with a keeper, took the provisions, and went as Jesse had commanded him. He came to the encampment as the army was going forth to the battle line, shouting the war cry. Israel and the Philistines drew up for battle, army against army. David left the things in charge of the keeper of the baggage, ran to the ranks, and went and greeted his brothers. As he talked with them, the champion, the Philistine of Gath, Goliath by name, came up out of the ranks of the Philistines, and spoke the same words as before. And David heard him. All the Israelites, when they saw the man, fled from him and were very much afraid. The Israelites said, "Have you seen this man who has come up? Surely he has come up to defy Israel. The king will greatly enrich the man who kills him, and will give him his daughter and make his family free in Israel." David said to the men who stood by him, "What shall be done for the man who kills this Philistine, and takes away the reproach from Israel? For who is this uncircumcised Philistine that he should defy the armies of the living God?" The people answered him in the same way, "So shall it be done for the man who kills him." His eldest brother Eliab heard him talking to the men; and Eliab's anger was kindled against David. He said, "Why have you come down? With whom have you left those few sheep in the wilderness? I know your presumption and the evil of your heart; for you have come down just to see the battle." David said, "What have I done now? It was only a question." He turned away from him toward another and spoke in the same way; and the people answered him again as before.

A Reading (Lesson) from the Acts of the Apostles [10:34–48]

Peter began to speak to them: "I truly understand that God shows no partiality, but in every nation anyone who fears him and does what is right is acceptable to him. You know the message he sent to the people of Israel, preaching peace by Jesus Christ—he is Lord of all. That message spread throughout Judea, beginning in Galilee after the baptism that John announced: how God anointed

Jesus of Nazareth with the Holy Spirit and with power; how he went about doing good and healing all who were oppressed by the devil, for God was with him. We are witnesses to all that he did both in Judea and in Jerusalem. They put him to death by hanging him on a tree; but God raised him on the third day and allowed him to appear, not to all the people but to us who were chosen by God as witnesses, and who ate and drank with him after he rose from the dead. He commanded us to preach to the people and to testify that he is the one ordained by God as judge of the living and the dead. All the prophets testify about him that everyone who believes in him receives forgiveness of sins through his name." While Peter was still speaking, the Holy Spirit fell upon all who heard the word. The circumcised believers who had come with Peter were astounded that the gift of the Holy Spirit had been poured out even on the Gentiles, for they heard them speaking in tongues and extolling God. Then Peter said, "Can anyone withhold the water for baptizing these people who have received the Holy Spirit just as we have?" So he ordered them to be baptized in the name of Jesus Christ. Then they invited him to stay for several days.

A Reading (Lesson) from the Gospel according to Mark [1:1–13]

The beginning of the good news of Jesus Christ, the Son of God. As it is written in the prophet Isaiah, "See, I am sending my messenger ahead of you, who will prepare your way; the voice of one crying out in the wilderness: 'Prepare the way of the Lord, make his paths straight,' " John the baptizer appeared in the wilderness, proclaiming a baptism of repentance for the forgiveness of sins. And people from the whole Judean countryside and all the people of Jerusalem were going out to him, and were baptized by him in the river Jordan, confessing their sins. Now John was clothed with camel's hair, with a leather belt around his waist, and he ate locusts and wild honey. He proclaimed, "The one who is more powerful than I is coming after me; I am not worthy to stoop down and untie the thong of his sandals. I have baptized you with water; but he will baptize you with the Holy Spirit." In those days Jesus came from Nazareth of Galilee and was baptized by John in the Jordan. And just as he was coming up out of the water, he saw the heavens torn apart and the Spirit descending like a dove on him. And a voice came from heaven, "You are my Son, the Beloved; with you I am well pleased." And the Spirit immediately drove him out into the wilderness. He was in the wilderness forty days, tempted by Satan; and he was with the wild beasts; and the angels waited on him.

Saturday

Psalm 20 [page 608],   *Psalm 21:1–7(8–14)* [page 608]   ❖
Psalm 110:1–5(6–7) [page 753],   *Psalm 116* [page 759],
Psalm 117 [page 760]

A Reading (Lesson) from the First Book of Samuel
[17:31–49]

When the words that David spoke were heard, they repeated them before Saul; and he sent for him. David said to Saul, "Let no one's heart fail because of him; your servant will go and fight with this Philistine." Saul said to David, "You are not able to go against this Philistine to fight with him; for you are just a boy, and he has been a warrior from his youth." But David said to Saul, "Your servant used to keep sheep for his father; and whenever a lion or a bear came, and took a lamb from the flock, I went after it and struck it down, rescuing the lamb from its mouth; and if it turned against me, I would catch it by the jaw, strike it down, and kill it. Your servant has killed both lions and bears; and this uncircumcised Philistine shall be like one of them, since he has defied the armies of the living God." David said, "The LORD, who saved me from the paw of the lion and from the paw of the bear, will save me from the hand of this Philistine." So Saul said to David, "Go, and may the LORD be with you!" Saul clothed David with his armor; he put a bronze helmet on his head and clothed him with a coat of mail. David strapped Saul's sword over the armor, and he tried in vain to walk, for he was not used to them. Then David said to Saul, "I cannot walk with these; for I am not used to them." So David removed them. Then he took his staff in his hand, and chose five smooth stones from the wadi, and put them in his shepherd's bag, in the pouch; his sling was in his hand, and he drew near to the Philistine. The Philistine came on and drew near to David, with his shield-bearer in front of him. When the Philistine looked and saw David, he disdained him, for he was only a youth, ruddy and handsome in appearance. The Philistine said to David, "Am I a dog, that you come to me with sticks?" And the Philistine cursed David by his gods. The Philistine said to David, "Come to me, and I will give your flesh to the birds of the air and to the wild animals of the field." But David said to the Philistine, "You come to me with sword and spear and javelin; but I come to you in the name of the LORD of hosts, the God of the armies of Israel, whom you have defied. This very day the LORD will deliver you into my hand, and I will strike you down and cut off your head; and I will give the dead bodies of the Philistine army this very day to the birds of the air and to the wild animals of the earth, so that all the earth may know that there is a God in Israel, and that all this assembly may know that the LORD does not save by sword and spear; for the battle is the LORD's and he will give you into our hand." When the Philistine drew nearer to meet David, David ran quickly toward the battle line to meet the Philistine. David put his hand in his bag, took out a stone, slung it, and struck the Philistine on his forehead; the stone sank into his forehead, and he fell face down on the ground.

A Reading (Lesson) from the Acts of the Apostles [11:1–18]

The apostles and the believers who were in Judea heard that the Gentiles had also accepted the word of God. So when Peter went up to Jerusalem, the circumcised believers criticized him, saying, "Why did you go to uncircumcised men and eat with them?" Then Peter began to explain it to them, step by step, saying, "I was in the city of Joppa praying, and in a trance I saw a vision. There was something like a large sheet coming down from heaven, being lowered by its four corners; and it came close to me. As I looked at it closely I saw four-footed animals, beasts of prey, reptiles, and birds of the air. I also heard a voice saying to me, 'Get up, Peter; kill and eat.' But I replied, 'By no means, Lord; for nothing profane or unclean has ever entered my mouth.' But a second time the voice answered from heaven, 'What God has made clean, you must not call profane.' This happened three times; then everything was pulled up again to heaven. At that very moment three men, sent to me from Caesarea, arrived at the house where we were. The Spirit told me to go with them and not to make a distinction between them and us. These six brothers also accompanied me, and we entered the man's house. He told us how he had seen the angel standing in his house and saying, 'Send to Joppa and bring Simon, who is called Peter; he will give you a message by which you and your entire household will be saved.' And as I began to speak, the Holy Spirit fell upon them just as it had upon us at the beginning. And I remembered the word of the Lord, how he had said, 'John baptized with water, but you will be baptized with the Holy Spirit.' If then God gave them the same gift that he gave us when we believed in the Lord Jesus Christ, who was I that I could hinder God?" When they heard this, they were silenced. And they praised God, saying, "Then God has given even to the Gentiles the repentance that leads to life."

A Reading (Lesson) from the Gospel according to Mark
[1:14–28]

After John was arrested, Jesus came to Galilee, proclaiming the good news of God, and saying, "The time is fulfilled, and the kingdom of God has come near; repent, and believe in the good news." As Jesus passed along the Sea of Galilee, he saw Simon and his brother Andrew casting a net into the sea—for they were fishermen. And Jesus said to them, "Follow me and I will make you fish for people." And immediately they left their nets and followed him. As he went a little farther, he saw James son of Zebedee and his brother John, who were in their boat mending the nets. Immediately he called them; and they left their father Zebedee in the boat with the hired men, and followed him. They went to Capernaum; and when the sabbath came, he entered the synagogue and taught. They were astounded at his teaching, for he taught them as one having authority, and not as the scribes. Just then there was in their synagogue a man with an unclean spirit, and he cried out, "What have you to do with us, Jesus of Nazareth? Have you come to destroy us? I know who you are, the Holy One of God." But Jesus rebuked him, saying, "Be silent, and come out of him!" And the unclean spirit, convulsing him and crying out with a loud voice, came out of him. They were all amazed, and they kept on asking one another, "What is this? A new teaching—with authority! He commands even the unclean spirits, and they obey him." At once his fame began to spread throughout the surrounding region of Galilee.

Proper 10 *Week of the Sunday closest to July 13*

Sunday

Psalm 148 [page 805], *Psalm 149* [page 807],
Psalm 150 [page 807] ❖ *Psalm 114* [page 756],
Psalm 115 [page 757]

A Reading (Lesson) from the First Book of Samuel
[17:50—18:4]

David prevailed over the Philistine with a sling and a stone, striking down the Philistine and killing him; there was no sword in David's hand. Then David ran and stood over the Philistine; he grasped his sword, drew it out of its sheath, and killed him; then he cut off his head with it. When the Philistines saw that their champion was dead, they fled. The troops of Israel and Judah rose up with a shout and pursued the Philistines as far as Gath and the gates of Ekron, so that the wounded Philistines fell on the way from Shaaraim as far as Gath and Ekron. The Israelites came back from chasing the Philistines, and they plundered their camp.

David took the head of the Philistine and brought it to
Jerusalem; but he put his armor in his tent. When Saul saw
David go out against the Philistine, he said to Abner, the
commander of the army, "Abner, whose son is this young
man?" Abner said, "As your soul lives, O king, I do not
know." The king said, "Inquire whose son the stripling is."
On David's return from killing the Philistine, Abner took
him and brought him before Saul, with the head of the
Philistine in his hand. Saul said to him, "Whose son are you,
young man?" And David answered, "I am the son of your
servant Jesse the Bethlehemite." When David had finished
speaking to Saul, the soul of Jonathan was bound to the
soul of David, and Jonathan loved him as his own soul. Saul
took him that day and would not let him return to his
father's house. Then Jonathan made a covenant with David,
because he loved him as his own soul. Jonathan stripped
himself of the robe that he was wearing, and gave it to
David, and his armor, and even his sword and his bow and
his belt.

A Reading (Lesson) from the Letter of Paul to the Romans
[10:4–17]

Christ is the end of the law so that there may be
righteousness for everyone who believes. Moses writes
concerning the righteousness that comes from the law, that
"the person who does these things will live by them." But
the righteousness that comes from faith says, "Do not say
in your heart, 'Who will ascend into heaven?' " (that is, to
bring Christ down) "or 'Who will descend into the
abyss?' " (that is, to bring Christ up from the dead). But
what does it say? "The word is near you, on your lips and
in your heart" (that is, the word of faith that we
proclaim); because if you confess with your lips that Jesus

is Lord and believe in your heart that God raised him from the dead, you will be saved. For one believes with the heart and so is justified, and one confesses with the mouth and so is saved. The scripture says, "No one who believes in him will be put to shame." For there is no distinction between Jew and Greek; the same Lord is Lord of all and is generous to all who call on him. For, "Everyone who calls on the name of the Lord shall be saved." But how are they to call on one in whom they have not believed? And how are they to believe in one of whom they have never heard? And how are they to hear without someone to proclaim him? And how are they to proclaim him unless they are sent? As it is written, "How beautiful are the feet of those who bring good news!" But not all have obeyed the good news; for Isaiah says, "Lord, who has believed our message?" So faith comes from what is heard, and what is heard comes through the word of Christ.

A Reading (Lesson) from the Gospel according to Matthew [23:29–39]

Jesus said to the crowds and to his disciples, "Woe to you, scribes and Pharisees, hypocrites! For you build the tombs of the prophets and decorate the graves of the righteous, and you say, 'If we had lived in the days of our ancestors, we would not have taken part with them in shedding the blood of the prophets.' Thus you testify against yourselves that you are descendants of those who murdered the prophets. Fill up, then, the measure of your ancestors. You snakes, you brood of vipers! How can you escape being sentenced to hell? Therefore I send you prophets, sages, and scribes, some of whom you will kill and crucify, and some you will flog in your synagogues and pursue from

town to town, so that upon you may come all the
righteous blood shed on earth, from the blood of righteous
Abel to the blood of Zechariah son of Barachiah, whom
you murdered between the sanctuary and the altar. Truly I
tell you, all this will come upon this generation. Jerusalem,
Jerusalem, the city that kills the prophets and stones those
who are sent to it! How often have I desired to gather
your children together as a hen gathers her brood under
her wings, and you were not willing! See, your house is
left to you, desolate. For I tell you, you will not see me
again until you say, 'Blessed is the one who comes in the
name of the Lord.' "

Monday

Psalm 25 [page 614] ❖ *Psalm 9* [page 593],
Psalm 15 [page 599]

A Reading (Lesson) from the First Book of Samuel
[18:5–16, 27b–30]

David went out and was successful wherever Saul sent him;
as a result, Saul set him over the army. And all the people,
even the servants of Saul, approved. As they were coming
home, when David returned from killing the Philistine, the
women came out of all the towns of Israel, singing and
dancing, to meet King Saul, with tambourines, with songs of
joy, and with musical instruments. And the women sang to
one another as they made merry, "Saul has killed his
thousands, and David his ten thousands." Saul was very
angry, for this saying displeased him. He said, "They have
ascribed to David ten thousands, and to me they have
ascribed thousands; what more can he have but the
kingdom?" So Saul eyed David from that day on. The next

day an evil spirit from God rushed upon Saul, and he raved within his house, while David was playing the lyre, as he did day by day. Saul had his spear in his hand; and Saul threw the spear, for he thought, "I will pin David to the wall." But David eluded him twice. Saul was afraid of David, because the LORD was with him but had departed from Saul. So Saul removed him from his presence, and made him a commander of a thousand; and David marched out and came in, leading the army. David had success in all his undertakings; for the LORD was with him. When Saul saw that he had great success, he stood in awe of him. But all Israel and Judah loved David; for it was he who marched out and came in leading them. Saul gave him his daughter Michal as a wife. But when Saul realized that the LORD was with David, and that Saul's daughter Michal loved him, Saul was still more afraid of David. So Saul was David's enemy from that time forward. Then the commanders of the Philistines came out to battle; and as often as they came out, David had more success than all the servants of Saul, so that his fame became very great.

A Reading (Lesson) from the Acts of the Apostles [11:19–30]

Those who were scattered because of the persecution that took place over Stephen traveled as far as Phoenicia, Cyprus, and Antioch, and they spoke the word to no one except Jews. But among them were some men of Cyprus and Cyrene who, on coming to Antioch, spoke to the Hellenists also, proclaiming the Lord Jesus. The hand of the Lord was with them, and a great number became believers and turned to the Lord. News of this came to the ears of the church in Jerusalem, and they sent Barnabas to Antioch. When he came and saw the grace of God, he rejoiced, and he exhorted them all to remain faithful to the Lord with steadfast devotion; for he was a good man, full of the Holy Spirit and of faith. And a great many people were brought to the Lord. Then Barnabas went to Tarsus to look for Saul, and when he had found him, he brought him to Antioch. So it was that for an entire year they met with the church and taught a great many people, and it was in Antioch that the disciples were first called "Christians." At that time prophets came down from Jerusalem to Antioch. One of them named Agabus stood up and predicted by the Spirit that there would be a severe famine over all the world; and this took place during the reign of Claudius. The disciples determined that according to their ability, each would send relief to the believers living in Judea; this they did, sending it to the elders by Barnabas and Saul.

A Reading (Lesson) from the Gospel according to Mark [1:29–45]

Immediately Jesus left the synagogue, and entered the house of Simon and Andrew, with James and John. Now Simon's mother-in-law was in bed with a fever, and they told him about her at once. He came and took her by the hand and lifted her up. Then the fever left her, and she began to serve them. That evening, at sundown, they brought to him all who were sick or possessed with demons. And the whole city was gathered around the door. And he cured many who were sick with various diseases, and cast out many demons; and he would not permit the demons to speak, because they knew him. In the morning, while it was still very dark, he got up and went out to a deserted place, and there he prayed. And Simon and his companions hunted for him. When they found him, they said to him, "Everyone is searching for you." He answered, "Let us go on to the neighboring towns, so that I may proclaim the message there also; for that is what I came out to do." And he went throughout Galilee, proclaiming the message in their synagogues and casting out demons. A leper came to him begging him, and kneeling he said to him, "If you choose, you can make me clean." Moved with pity, Jesus stretched out his hand and touched him, and said to him, "I do choose. Be made clean!" Immediately the leprosy left him, and he was made clean. After sternly warning him he sent him away at once, saying to him, "See that you say nothing to anyone; but go, show yourself to the priest, and offer for your cleansing what Moses commanded, as a testimony to them." But he went out and began to proclaim it freely, and to spread the word, so that Jesus could no longer go into a town openly, but stayed out in the country; and people came to him from every quarter.

Tuesday

Psalm 26 [page 616],   *Psalm 28* [page 619]   ❖
Psalm 36 [page 632],   *Psalm 39* [page 638]

A Reading (Lesson) from the First Book of Samuel [19:1–18]

Saul spoke with his son Jonathan and with all his servants about killing David. But Saul's son Jonathan took great delight in David. Jonathan told David, "My father Saul is trying to kill you; therefore be on guard tomorrow morning; stay in a secret place and hide yourself. I will go out and stand beside my father in the field where you are, and I will speak to my father about you; if I learn anything I will tell you." Jonathan spoke well of David to his father Saul, saying to him, "The king should not sin against his servant

David, because he has not sinned against you, and because his deeds have been of good service to you; for he took his life in his hand when he attacked the Philistine, and the LORD brought about a great victory for all Israel. You saw it, and rejoiced; why then will you sin against an innocent person by killing David without cause?" Saul heeded the voice of Jonathan; Saul swore, "As the LORD lives, he shall not be put to death." So Jonathan called David and related all these things to him. Jonathan then brought David to Saul, and he was in his presence as before. Again there was war, and David went out to fight the Philistines. He launched a heavy attack on them, so that they fled before him. Then an evil spirit from the LORD came upon Saul, as he sat in his house with his spear in his hand, while David was playing music. Saul sought to pin David to the wall with the spear; but he eluded Saul, so that he struck the spear into the wall. David fled and escaped that night. Saul sent messengers to David's house to keep watch over him, planning to kill him in the morning, David's wife Michal told him, "If you do not save your life tonight, tomorrow you will be killed." So Michal let David down through the window; he fled away and escaped. Michal took an idol and laid it on the bed; she put a net of goats' hair on its head, and covered it with the clothes. When Saul sent messengers to take David, she said, "He is sick." Then Saul sent the messengers to see David for themselves. He said, "Bring him up to me in the bed, that I may kill him." When the messengers came in, the idol was in the bed, with the covering of goats' hair on its head. Saul said to Michal, "Why have you deceived me like this, and let my enemy go, so that he has escaped?" Michal answered Saul, "He said to me, 'Let me go; why should I kill you?' " Now David fled and escaped; he came to Samuel at Ramah, and told him all that Saul had done to him. He and Samuel went and settled at Naioth.

A Reading (Lesson) from the Acts of the Apostles [12:1–17]

About that time King Herod laid violent hands upon some
who belonged to the church. He had James, the brother of
John, killed with the sword. After he saw that it pleased
the Jews, he proceeded to arrest Peter also. (This was
during the festival of Unleavened Bread.) When he had
seized him, he put him in prison and handed him over to
four squads of soldiers to guard him, intending to bring
him out to the people after the Passover. While Peter was
kept in prison, the church prayed fervently to God for
him. The very night before Herod was going to bring him
out, Peter, bound with two chains, was sleeping between
two soldiers, while guards in front of the door were
keeping watch over the prison. Suddenly an angel of the
Lord appeared and a light shone in the cell. He tapped
Peter on the side and woke him, saying, "Get up quickly."
And the chains fell off his wrists. The angel said to him,
"Fasten your belt and put on your sandals." He did so.
Then he said to him, "Wrap your cloak around you and
follow me." Peter went out and followed him; he did not
realize that what was happening with the angel's help was
real; he thought he was seeing a vision. After they had
passed the first and the second guard, they came before the
iron gate leading into the city. It opened for them of its
own accord, and they went outside and walked along a
lane, when suddenly the angel left him. Then Peter came
to himself and said, "Now I am sure that the Lord has
sent his angel and rescued me from the hands of Herod
and from all that the Jewish people were expecting." As
soon as he realized this, he went to the house of Mary, the
mother of John whose other name was Mark, where many
had gathered and were praying. When he knocked at the
outer gate, a maid named Rhoda came to answer. On
recognizing Peter's voice, she was so overjoyed that,

instead of opening the gate, she ran in and announced that Peter was standing at the gate. They said to her, "You are out of your mind!" But she insisted that it was so. They said, "It is his angel." Meanwhile Peter continued knocking; and when they opened the gate, they saw him and were amazed. He motioned to them with his hand to be silent, and described for them how the Lord had brought him out of the prison. And he added, "Tell this to James and to the believers." Then he left and went to another place.

A Reading (Lesson) from the Gospel according to Mark [2:1–12]

When Jesus returned to Capernaum after some days, it was reported that he was at home. So many gathered around that there was no longer room for them, not even in front of the door; and he was speaking the word to them. Then some people came, bringing to him a paralyzed man, carried by four of them. And when they could not bring him to Jesus because of the crowd, they removed the roof above him; and after having dug through it, they let down the mat on which the paralytic lay. When Jesus saw their faith, he said to the paralytic, "Son, your sins are forgiven." Now some of the scribes were sitting there, questioning in their hearts, "Why does this fellow speak in this way? It is blasphemy! Who can forgive sins but God alone?" At once Jesus perceived in his spirit that they were discussing these questions among themselves; and he said to them, "Why do you raise such questions in your hearts? Which is easier, to say to the paralytic, 'Your sins are forgiven,' or to say, 'Stand up and take your mat and walk'? But so that you may know that the Son of Man has authority on earth to forgive sins"—he said to the paralytic—"I say to you, stand up, take your mat and go to your home." And he stood up, and immediately took the mat and went out before all of them; so that they were all amazed and glorified God, saying, "We have never seen anything like this!"

Wednesday

Psalm 38 [page 636] ❖ *Psalm 119:25–48* [page 765]

A Reading (Lesson) from the First Book of Samuel [20:1–23]

David fled from Naioth in Ramah. He came before Jonathan and said, "What have I done? What is my guilt? And what is my sin against your father that he is trying to take my life?" He said to him, "Far from it! You shall not die. My father does nothing either great or small without disclosing it to me; and why should my father hide this from me? Never!" But David also swore, "Your father knows well that you like me; and he thinks, 'Do not let Jonathan know this, or he will be grieved.' But truly, as the LORD lives and as you yourself live, there is but a step between me and death." Then Jonathan said to David, "Whatever you say, I will do for you." David said to Jonathan, "Tomorrow is the new moon, and I should not fail to sit with the king at the meal; but let me go, so that I may hide in the field until the third evening. If your father misses me at all, then say, 'David earnestly asked leave of me to run to Bethlehem his city; for there is a yearly sacrifice there for all the family.' If he says, 'Good!' it will be well with your servant; but if he is angry, then know that evil has been determined by him. Therefore deal kindly with your servant, for you have brought your servant into a sacred covenant with you. But if there is guilt in me, kill me yourself; why should you bring me to your father?" Jonathan said, "Far be it from you! If I knew that it was decided by my father that evil should come upon you, would I not tell you?" Then David said to Jonathan, "Who will tell me if your father answers you harshly?" Jonathan replied to David, "Come, let us go out into the field." So they both went out into the field. Jonathan said to David, "By the LORD, the God of Israel! When I have sounded out my father, about this time tomorrow, or on the third day, if he is well disposed toward David, shall I not then send and disclose it to you? But if my father intends to do you harm, the LORD do so to Jonathan, and more also, if I do not disclose it to you, and send you away, so that you may go in safety. May the LORD be with you, as he has been with my father. If I am still alive, show me the faithful love of the LORD; but if I die, never cut off your faithful love from my house, even if the LORD were to cut off every one of the enemies of David from the face of the earth." Thus Jonathan made a covenant with the house of David, saying, "May the LORD seek out the enemies of David." Jonathan made David swear again by his love for him; for he loved him as he loved his own life. Jonathan said to him, "Tomorrow is the new moon; you will be missed, because your place will be empty. On the day after tomorrow, you shall go a long way down; go to the place where you hid yourself earlier, and remain beside the stone there. I will shoot three arrows to the side of it, as though I shot at a mark. Then I will send the boy, saying, 'Go, find the arrows.' If I say to the boy, 'Look, the arrows are on this side of you, collect them,' then you are to come, for, as the LORD lives, it is safe for you and there is no danger. But if I say to the young man, 'Look, the arrows are beyond you,' then go; for the LORD has sent you away. As for the matter about which you and I have spoken, the LORD is witness between you and me forever."

A Reading (Lesson) from the Acts of the Apostles [12:18–25]

When morning came, there was no small commotion among the soldiers over what had become of Peter. When Herod had searched for him and could not find him, he examined the guards and ordered them to be put to death. Then Peter went down from Judea to Caesarea and stayed there. Now Herod was angry with the people of Tyre and Sidon. So they came to him in a body; and after winning over Blastus, the king's chamberlain, they asked for a reconciliation, because their country depended on the king's country for food. On an appointed day Herod put on his royal robes, took his seat on the platform, and delivered a public address to them. The people kept shouting, "The voice of a god, and not of a mortal!" And immediately, because he had not given the glory to God, an angel of the Lord struck him down, and he was eaten by worms and died. But the word of God continued to advance and gain adherents. Then after completing their mission Barnabas and Saul returned to Jerusalem and brought with them John, whose other name was Mark.

A Reading (Lesson) from the Gospel according to Mark [2:13–22]

Jesus went out again beside the sea; the whole crowd gathered around him, and he taught them. As he was walking along, he saw Levi son of Alphaeus sitting at the tax booth, and he said to him, "Follow me." And he got up and followed him. And as he sat at dinner in Levi's house, many tax collectors and sinners were also sitting with Jesus and his disciples—for there were many who followed him. When the scribes of the Pharisees saw that he was eating with sinners and tax collectors, they said to his disciples, "Why does he eat with tax collectors and sinners?" When Jesus heard this, he said to them, "Those who are well have no need of a physician, but those who are sick; I have come to call not the righteous but sinners." Now John's disciples and the Pharisees were fasting; and people came and said to him, "Why do John's disciples and the disciples of the Pharisees fast, but your disciples do not fast?" Jesus said to them, "The wedding guests cannot fast while the bridegroom is with them, can they? As long as they have the bridegroom with them, they cannot fast. The days will come when the bridegroom is taken away from them, and then they will fast on that day. No one sews a piece of unshrunk cloth on an old cloak; otherwise, the patch pulls away from it, the new from the old, and a worse tear is made. And no one puts new wine into old wineskins; otherwise, the wine will burst the skins, and the wine is lost, and so are the skins; but one puts new wine into fresh wineskins."

Thursday

Psalm 37:1–18 [page 633]   ❖   *Psalm 37:19–42* [page 634]

A Reading (Lesson) from the First Book of Samuel
[20:24–42]

David hid himself in the field. When the new moon came, the king sat at the feast to eat. The king sat upon his seat, as at other times, upon the seat by the wall. Jonathan stood, while Abner sat by Saul's side; but David's place was empty. Saul did not say anything that day; for he thought, "Something has befallen him; he is not clean, surely he is not clean." But on the second day, the day after the new moon, David's place was empty. And Saul said to his son Jonathan, "Why has the son of Jesse not come to the feast, either yesterday or today?" Jonathan answered Saul, "David earnestly asked leave of me to go to Bethlehem; he said, 'Let me go; for our family is holding a sacrifice in the city, and my brother has commanded me to be there. So now, if I have found favor in your sight, let me get away, and see my brothers.' For this reason he has not come to the king's table." Then Saul's anger was kindled against Jonathan. He said to him, "You son of a perverse, rebellious woman! Do I not know that you have chosen the son of Jesse to your own shame, and to the shame of your mother's nakedness? For as long as the son of Jesse lives upon the earth, neither you nor your kingdom shall be established. Now send and bring him to me, for he shall surely die." Then Jonathan answered his father Saul, "Why should he be put to death? What has he done?" But Saul threw his spear at him to strike him; so Jonathan knew that it was the decision of his father to put David to death. Jonathan rose from the table in fierce anger and ate no food on the second day of the month, for he was grieved for David, and because his father had disgraced him. In the morning Jonathan went out into the field to the appointment with David, and with him was a little boy. He said to the boy, "Run and find the arrows that I shoot." As the boy ran, he shot an arrow beyond him. When the boy came to the place where Jonathan's arrow had fallen, Jonathan called after the boy and said, "Is the arrow not beyond you?" Jonathan called after the boy, "Hurry, be quick, do not linger." So Jonathan's boy gathered up the arrows and came to his master. But the boy knew nothing; only Jonathan and David knew the arrangement. Jonathan gave his weapons to the boy and said to him, "Go and carry them to the city." As soon as the boy had gone, David rose from beside the stone heap and prostrated himself with his face to the ground. He bowed three times, and they kissed each other, and wept with each other; David wept the more.

Then Jonathan said to David, "Go in peace, since both of us have sworn in the name of the Lord, saying, 'The Lord shall be between me and you, and between my descendants and your descendants, forever.'" He got up and left; and Jonathan went into the city.

A Reading (Lesson) from the Acts of the Apostles [13:1–12]

Now in the church at Antioch there were prophets and teachers: Barnabas, Simeon who was called Niger, Lucius of Cyrene, Manaen a member of the court of Herod the ruler, and Saul. While they were worshiping the Lord and fasting, the Holy Spirit said, "Set apart for me Barnabas and Saul for the work to which I have called them." Then after fasting and praying they laid their hands on them and sent them off. So, being sent out by the Holy Spirit, they went down to Seleucia; and from there they sailed to Cyprus. When they arrived at Salamis, they proclaimed the word of God in the synagogues of the Jews. And they had John also to assist them. When they had gone through the whole island as far as Paphos, they met a certain magician, a Jewish false prophet, named Bar-Jesus. He was with the proconsul, Sergius Paulus, an intelligent man, who summoned Barnabas and Saul and wanted to hear the word of God. But the magician Elymas (for that is the translation of his name) opposed them and tried to turn the proconsul away from the faith. But Saul, also known as Paul, filled with the Holy Spirit, looked intently at him and said, "You son of the devil, you enemy of all righteousness, full of all deceit and villainy, will you not stop making crooked the straight paths of the Lord? And now listen—the hand of the Lord is against you, and you will be blind for a while, unable to see the sun." Immediately mist and darkness came over him, and he went about groping for someone to lead him by the hand. When the proconsul saw what had happened, he believed, for he was astonished at the teaching about the Lord.

A Reading (Lesson) from the Gospel according to Mark
[2:23—3:6]

One sabbath Jesus was going through the grainfields; and as they made their way his disciples began to pluck heads of grain. The Pharisees said to him, "Look, why are they doing what is not lawful on the sabbath?" And he said to them, "Have you never read what David did when he and his companions were hungry and in need of food? He entered the house of God, when Abiathar was high priest, and ate the bread of the Presence, which it is not lawful for any but the priests to eat, and he gave some to his companions." Then he said to them, "The sabbath was made for humankind, and not humankind for the sabbath; so the Son of Man is lord even of the sabbath." Again he entered the synagogue, and a man was there who had a withered hand. They watched him to see whether he would cure him on the sabbath, so that they might accuse him. And he said to the man who had the withered hand, "Come forward." Then he said to them, "Is it lawful to do good or to do harm on the sabbath, to save life or to kill?" But they were silent. He looked around at them with anger; he was grieved at their hardness of heart and said to the man, "Stretch out your hand." He stretched it out, and his hand was restored. The Pharisees went out and immediately conspired with the Herodians against him, how to destroy him.

Friday

Psalm 31 [page 622] ❖ *Psalm 35* [page 629]

A Reading (Lesson) from the First Book of Samuel [21:1–15]

David came to Nob to the priest Ahimelech. Ahimelech came trembling to meet David, and said to him, "Why are you alone, and no one with you?" David said to the priest Ahimelech, "The king has charged me with a matter, and said to me, 'No one must know anything of the matter about which I send you, and with which I have charged you.' I have made an appointment with the young men for such and such a place. Now then, what have you at hand? Give me five loaves of bread, or whatever is here." The priest answered David, "I have no ordinary bread at hand, only holy bread—provided that the young men have kept themselves from women." David answered the priest, "Indeed women have been kept from us as always when I go on an expedition; the vessels of the young men are holy even when it is a common journey; how much more today will their vessels be holy?" So the priest gave him the holy bread; for there was no bread there except the bread of the Presence, which is removed from before the LORD, to be replaced by hot bread on the day it is taken away. Now a certain man of the servants of Saul was there that day, detained before the LORD; his name was Doeg the Edomite, the chief of Saul's shepherds. David said to Ahimelech, "Is there no spear or sword here with you? I did not bring my sword or my weapons with me, because the king's business required haste." The priest said, "The sword of Goliath the Philistine, whom you killed in the valley of Elah, is here wrapped in a cloth behind the ephod; if you will take that, take it, for there is none here except that one." David said, "There is none like it; give it to me." David rose and fled that day from Saul; he went to King Achish of Gath. The servants of Achish said to him, "Is this not David the king of the land? Did they not sing to one another of him in dances, 'Saul has killed his thousands, and David his ten thousands'?" David took these words to heart and was very much afraid of King Achish of Gath. So he changed his behavior before them; he pretended to be mad when in their presence. He scratched marks on the doors of the gate, and let his spittle run down his beard. Achish said to his servants, "Look, you see the man is mad; why then have you brought him to me? Do I lack madmen, that you have brought this fellow to play the madman in my presence? Shall this fellow come into my house?"

A Reading (Lesson) from the Acts of the Apostles [13:13–25]

Paul and his companions set sail from Paphos and came to Perga in Pamphylia. John, however, left them and returned to Jerusalem; but they went on from Perga and came to Antioch in Pisidia. And on the sabbath day they went into the synagogue and sat down. After the reading of the law and the prophets, the officials of the synagogue sent them a message, saying, "Brothers, if you have any word of exhortation for the people, give it." So Paul stood up and with a gesture began to speak: "You Israelites, and others who fear God, listen. The God of this people Israel chose our ancestors and made the people great during their stay in the land of Egypt, and with uplifted arm he led them out of it. For about forty years he put up with them in the wilderness. After he had destroyed seven nations in the land of Canaan, he gave them their land as an inheritance for about four hundred fifty years. After that he gave them judges until the time of the prophet Samuel. Then they asked for a king; and God gave them Saul son of Kish, a man of the tribe of Benjamin, who reigned for forty years. When he had removed him, he made David their king. In his testimony about him, he said, 'I have found David, son of Jesse, to be a man after my heart, who will carry out all my wishes.' Of this man's posterity God has brought to Israel a Savior, Jesus, as he promised; before his coming John had already proclaimed a baptism of repentance to all the people of Israel. And as John was finishing his work, he said, 'What do you suppose that I am? I am not he. No, but one is coming after me; I am not worthy to untie the thong of the sandals on his feet.' "

A Reading (Lesson) from the Gospel according to Mark [3:7-19a]

Jesus departed with his disciples to the sea, and a great multitude from Galilee followed him; hearing all that he was doing, they came to him in great numbers from Judea, Jerusalem, Idumea, beyond the Jordan, and the region around Tyre and Sidon. He told his disciples to have a boat ready for him because of the crowd, so that they would not crush him; for he had cured many, so that all who had diseases pressed upon him to touch him. Whenever the unclean spirits saw him, they fell down before him and shouted, "You are the Son of God!" But he sternly ordered them not to make him known. He went up the mountain and called to him those whom he wanted, and they came to him. And he appointed twelve, whom he also named apostles, to be with him, and to be sent out to proclaim the message, and to have authority to cast out demons. So he appointed the twelve: Simon (to whom he gave the name Peter); James son of Zebedee and John the brother of James (to whom he gave the name Boanerges, that is, Sons of Thunder); and Andrew, and

Philip, and Bartholomew, and Matthew, and Thomas, and James son of Alphaeus, and Thaddaeus, and Simon the Cananaean, and Judas Iscariot, who betrayed him.

Saturday

Psalm 30 [page 621], *Psalm 32* [page 624] ❖
Psalm 42 [page 643], *Psalm 43* [page 644]

A Reading (Lesson) from the First Book of Samuel [22:1–23]

David left there and escaped to the cave of Adullam; when his brothers and all his father's house heard of it, they went down there to him. Everyone who was in distress, and everyone who was in debt, and everyone who was discontented gathered to him; and he became captain over them. Those who were with him numbered about four hundred. David went from there to Mizpeh of Moab. He said to the king of Moab, "Please let my father and mother come to you, until I know what God will do for me." He left them with the king of Moab, and they stayed with him all the time that David was in the stronghold. Then the prophet Gad said to David, "Do not remain in the stronghold; leave, and go into the land of Judah." So David left, and went into the forest of Hereth. Saul heard that David and those who were with him had been located. Saul was sitting at Gibeah, under the tamarisk tree on the height, with his spear in his hand, and all his servants were standing around him. Saul said to his servants who stood around him, "Hear now, you Benjaminites; will the son of Jesse give every one of you fields and vineyards, will he make you all commanders of thousands and commanders of hundreds? Is that why all of you have conspired against me? No one discloses to me when my son makes a league with the son of

Jesse, none of you is sorry for me or discloses to me that my son has stirred up my servant against me, to lie in wait, as he is doing today." Doeg the Edomite, who was in charge of Saul's servants, answered, "I saw the son of Jesse coming to Nob, to Ahimelech son of Ahitub; he inquired of the LORD for him, gave him provisions, and gave him the sword of Goliath the Philistine." The king sent for the priest Ahimelech son of Ahitub and for all his father's house, the priests who were at Nob; and all of them came to the king. Saul said, "Listen now, son of Ahitub." He answered, "Here I am, my lord." Saul said to him, "Why have you conspired against me, you and the son of Jesse, by giving him bread and a sword, and by inquiring of God for him, so that he has risen against me, to lie in wait, as he is doing today?" Then Ahimelech answered the king, "Who among all your servants is so faithful as David? He is the king's son-in-law, and is quick to do your bidding, and is honored in your house. Is today the first time that I have inquired of God for him? By no means! Do not let the king impute anything to his servant or to any member of my father's house; for your servant has known nothing of all this, much or little." The king said, "You shall surely die, Ahimelech, you and all your father's house." The king said to the guard who stood around him, "Turn and kill the priests of the LORD, because their hand also is with David; they knew that he fled, and did not disclose it to me." But the servants of the king would not raise their hand to attack the priests of the LORD. Then the king said to Doeg, "You, Doeg, turn and attack the priests." Doeg the Edomite turned and attacked the priests; on that day he killed eighty-five who wore the linen ephod. Nob, the city of the priests, he put to the sword; men and women, children and infants, oxen, donkeys, and sheep, he put to the sword. But one of the sons of Ahimelech son of Ahitub, named Abiathar, escaped and fled after David. Abiathar told David that Saul had killed the priests of the LORD. David said to Abiathar, "I knew on that day, when Doeg the Edomite was there, that he would surely tell Saul. I am responsible for the lives of all your father's house. Stay with me, and do not be afraid; for the one who seeks my life seeks your life; you will be safe with me."

A Reading (Lesson) from the Acts of the Apostles [13:26–43]

Paul said, "My brothers, you descendants of Abraham's family, and others who fear God, to us the message of this salvation has been sent. Because the residents of Jerusalem and their leaders did not recognize him or understand the words of the prophets that are read every sabbath, they fulfilled those words by condemning him. Even though they found no cause for a sentence of death, they asked Pilate to have him killed. When they had carried out everything that was written about him, they took him down from the tree and laid him in a tomb. But God raised him from the dead; and for many days he appeared to those who came up with him from Galilee to Jerusalem, and they are now his witnesses to the people. And we bring you the good news that what God promised to our ancestors he has fulfilled for us, their children, by raising Jesus; as also it is written in the second psalm, 'You are my Son; today I have begotten you.' As to his raising him from the dead, no more to return to corruption, he has spoken in this way, 'I will give you the holy promises made to David.' Therefore he has also said in another psalm, 'You will not let your Holy One experience corruption.' For David, after he had served the purpose of God in his own generation, died, was laid beside his ancestors, and experienced corruption; but he whom God raised up experienced no corruption. Let it be known to you therefore, my brothers, that through this man forgiveness of sins is proclaimed to you; by this Jesus everyone who believes is set free from all those sins from which you could not be freed by the law of Moses. Beware, therefore, that what the prophets said does not happen to you: 'Look, you scoffers! Be amazed and perish, for in your days I am doing a work, a work that you will never believe, even if someone tells you.' " As Paul and Barnabas were going out, the people urged them to speak about these things again the next sabbath. When the meeting of the synagogue broke up, many Jews and devout converts to Judaism followed Paul and Barnabas, who spoke to them and urged them to continue in the grace of God.

A Reading (Lesson) from the Gospel according to Mark
[3:19b–35]

Jesus went home; and the crowd came together again, so that they could not even eat. When his family heard it, they went out to restrain him, for people were saying, "He has gone out of his mind." And the scribes who came down from Jerusalem said, "He has Beelzebul, and by the ruler of the demons he casts out demons." And he called them to him, and spoke to them in parables, "How can Satan cast out Satan? If a kingdom is divided against itself, that kingdom cannot stand. And if a house is divided against itself, that house will not be able to stand. And if Satan has risen up against himself and is divided, he cannot stand, but his end has come. But no one can enter a strong man's house and plunder his property without first tying up the strong man; then indeed the house can be plundered. Truly I tell you, people will be forgiven for their sins and whatever blasphemies they utter; but whoever blasphemes against the Holy Spirit can never have forgiveness, but is guilty of an eternal sin"—for they had said, "He has an unclean spirit." Then his mother and his brothers came; and standing outside, they sent to him and called him. A crowd was sitting around him; and they said to him, "Your mother and your brothers and sisters are outside, asking for you." And he replied, "Who are my mother and my brothers?" And looking at those who sat around him, he said, "Here are my mother and my brothers! Whoever does the will of God is my brother and sister and mother."

Proper 11 *Week of the Sunday closest to July 20*

Sunday

Psalm 63:1–8 (9–11) [page 670],
Psalm 98 [page 727] ❖ *Psalm 103* [page 733]

A Reading (Lesson) from the First Book of Samuel [23:7–18]

It was told Saul that David had come to Keilah. And Saul said, "God has given him into my hand; for he has shut himself in by entering a town that has gates and bars." Saul summoned all the people to war, to go down to Keilah, to besiege David and his men. When David learned that Saul was plotting evil against him, he said to the priest Abiathar, "Bring the ephod here." David said, "O LORD, the God of Israel, your servant has heard that Saul seeks to come to Keilah, to destroy the city on my account. And now, will Saul come down as your servant has heard? O LORD, the God of Israel, I beseech you, tell your servant." The LORD said, "He will come down." Then David said, "Will the men of Keilah surrender me and my men into the hand of Saul?" The LORD said, "They will surrender you." Then David and his men, who were about six hundred, set out and left Keilah; they wandered wherever they could go. When Saul was told that David had escaped from Keilah, he gave up the expedition. David remained in the strongholds in the wilderness, in the hill country of the Wilderness of Ziph. Saul sought him every day, but the LORD did not give him into his hand. David was in the Wilderness of Ziph at Horesh when he learned that Saul had come out to seek his life. Saul's son Jonathan set out and came to David at Horesh; there he strengthened his hand through the LORD. He said to him, "Do not be afraid; for the hand of my father Saul shall not find you; you shall be king over Israel, and I shall be second to you; my father Saul also knows that this is so." Then the two of them made a covenant before the LORD; David remained at Horesh, and Jonathan went home.

A Reading (Lesson) from the Letter of Paul to the Romans [11:33—12:2]

O the depth of the riches and wisdom and knowledge of God! How unsearchable are his judgments and how inscrutable his ways! "For who has known the mind of the Lord? Or who has been his counselor?" "Or who has given a gift to him, to receive a gift in return?" For from him and through him and to him are all things. To him be the glory forever. Amen. I appeal to you therefore, brothers and sisters, by the mercies of God, to present your bodies as a living sacrifice, holy and acceptable to God, which is your spiritual worship. Do not be conformed to this world, but be transformed by the renewing of your minds, so that you may discern what is the will of God—what is good and acceptable and perfect.

A Reading (Lesson) from the Gospel according to Matthew [25:14–30]

Jesus answered the disciples, "It will be as if a man, going on a journey, summoned his slaves and entrusted his property to them; to one he gave five talents, to another two, to another one, to each according to his ability. Then he went away. The one who had received the five talents went off at once and traded with them, and made five more talents. In the same way, the one who had the two talents made two more talents. But the one who had received the one talent went off and dug a hole in the ground and hid his master's money. After a long time the master of those slaves came and settled accounts with them. Then the one who had received the five talents came forward, bringing five more talents, saying, 'Master, you handed over to me five talents; see, I have made five more talents.' His master said to him, 'Well done, good and trustworthy slave; you have been trustworthy in a few things, I will put you in charge of many things; enter into the joy of your master.' And the one with the two talents also came forward, saying, 'Master, you handed over to me two talents; see, I have made two more talents.' His master said to him, 'Well done, good and trustworthy slave; you have been trustworthy in a few things, I will put you in charge of many things; enter into the joy of your master.' Then the one who had received the one talent also came forward, saying, 'Master, I knew that you were a harsh man, reaping where you did not sow, and gathering where you did not scatter seed; so I was afraid, and I went and hid your talent in the ground. Here you have what is yours.' But his master replied, 'You wicked and lazy slave! You knew, did you, that I reap where I did not sow, and gather where I did not scatter? Then you ought to have invested my money with the bankers, and on my return I would have received what was my own with interest. So take the talent from him, and give it to the one with the ten talents. For to all those who have, more will be given, and they will have an abundance; but from those who have nothing, even what they have will be taken away. As for this worthless slave, throw him into the outer darkness, where there will be weeping and gnashing of teeth.' "

Monday

Psalm 41 [page 641],   *Psalm 52* [page 657]   ❖
Psalm 44 [page 645]

A Reading (Lesson) from the First Book of Samuel   [24:1–22]

When Saul returned from following the Philistines, he was told, "David is in the wilderness of En-gedi." Then Saul took three thousand chosen men out of all Israel, and went to look for David and his men in the direction of the Rocks of the Wild Goats. He came to the sheepfolds beside the road, where there was a cave; and Saul went in to relieve himself. Now David and his men were sitting in the innermost parts of the cave. The men of David said to him, "Here is the day of which the LORD said to you, 'I will give your enemy into your hand, and you shall do to him as it seems good to you.' " Then David went and stealthily cut off a corner of Saul's cloak. Afterward David was stricken to the heart because he had cut off a corner of Saul's cloak. He said to his men, "The LORD forbid that I should do this

thing to my lord, the LORD's anointed, to raise my hand
against him; for he is the LORD's anointed." So David
scolded his men severely and did not permit them to attack
Saul. Then Saul got up and left the cave, and went on his
way. Afterwards David also rose up and went out of the
cave and called after Saul, "My lord the king!" When Saul
looked behind him, David bowed with his face to the
ground, and did obeisance. David said to Saul, "Why do
you listen to the words of those who say, 'David seeks to do
you harm'? This very day your eyes have seen how the LORD
gave you into my hand in the cave; and some urged me to
kill you, but I spared you. I said, 'I will not raise my hand
against my lord; for he is the LORD's anointed.' See, my
father, see the corner of your cloak in my hand; for by the
fact that I cut off the corner of your cloak, and did not kill
you, you may know for certain that there is no wrong or
treason in my hands. I have not sinned against you, though
you are hunting me to take my life. May the LORD judge
between me and you! May the LORD avenge me on you; but
my hand shall not be against you. As the ancient proverb
says, 'Out of the wicked comes forth wickedness'; but my
hand shall not be against you. Against whom has the king of
Israel come out? Whom do you pursue? A dead dog? A
single flea? May the LORD therefore be judge, and give
sentence between me and you. May he see to it, and plead
my cause, and vindicate me against you." When David had
finished speaking these words to Saul, Saul said, "Is this
your voice, my son David?" Saul lifted up his voice and
wept. He said to David, "You are more righteous than I; for
you have repaid me good, whereas I have repaid you evil.
Today you have explained how you have dealt well with
me, in that you did not kill me when the LORD put me into
your hands. For who has ever found an enemy, and sent the
enemy safely away? So may the LORD reward you with good

for what you have done to me this day. Now I know that you shall surely be king, and that the kingdom of Israel shall be established in your hand. Swear to me therefore by the LORD that you will not cut off my descendants after me, and that you will not wipe out my name from my father's house." So David swore this to Saul. Then Saul went home; but David and his men went up to the stronghold.

A Reading (Lesson) from the Acts of the Apostles [13:44–52]

The next sabbath almost the whole city gathered to hear the word of the Lord. But when the Jews saw the crowds, they were filled with jealousy; and blaspheming, they contradicted what was spoken by Paul. Then both Paul and Barnabas spoke out boldly, saying, "It was necessary that the word of God should be spoken first to you. Since you reject it and judge yourselves to be unworthy of eternal life, we are now turning to the Gentiles. For so the Lord has commanded us, saying, 'I have set you to be a light for the Gentiles, so that you may bring salvation to the ends of the earth.' " When the Gentiles heard this, they were glad and praised the word of the Lord; and as many as had been destined for eternal life became believers. Thus the word of the Lord spread throughout the region. But the Jews incited the devout women of high standing and the leading men of the city, and stirred up persecution against Paul and Barnabas, and drove them out of their region. So they shook the dust off their feet in protest against them, and went to Iconium. And the disciples were filled with joy and with the Holy Spirit.

A Reading (Lesson) from the Gospel according to Mark
[4:1-20]

Again Jesus began to teach beside the sea. Such a very
large crowd gathered around him that he got into a boat
on the sea and sat there, while the whole crowd was
beside the sea on the land. He began to teach them many
things in parables, and in his teaching he said to them:
"Listen! A sower went out to sow. And as he sowed, some
seed fell on the path, and the birds came and ate it up.
Other seed fell on rocky ground, where it did not have
much soil, and it sprang up quickly, since it had no depth
of soil. And when the sun rose, it was scorched; and since
it had no root, it withered away. Other seed fell among
thorns, and the thorns grew up and choked it, and it
yielded no grain. Other seed fell into good soil and
brought forth grain, growing up and increasing and
yielding thirty and sixty and a hundredfold." And he said,
Let anyone with ears to hear listen!" When he was alone,
those who were around him along with the twelve asked
him about the parables. And he said to them, "To you has
been given the secret of the kingdom of God, but for those
outside, everything comes in parables; in order that 'they
may indeed look, but not perceive, and may indeed listen,
but not understand; so that they may not turn again and
be forgiven.' " And he said to them, "Do you not
understand this parable? Then how will you understand all
the parables? The sower sows the word. These are the
ones on the path where the word is sown: when they hear,
Satan immediately comes and takes away the word that is
sown in them. And these are the ones sown on rocky
ground: when they hear the word, they immediately
receive it with joy. But they have no root, and endure only
for a while; then, when trouble or persecution arises on

account of the word, immediately they fall away. And others are those sown among the thorns: these are the ones who hear the word, but the cares of the world, and the lure of wealth, and the desire for other things come in and choke the word, and it yields nothing. And these are the ones sown on the good soil: they hear the word and accept it and bear fruit, thirty and sixty and a hundredfold."

Tuesday

Psalm 45 [page 647] ❖ *Psalm 47* [page 650], *Psalm 48* [page 651]

A Reading (Lesson) from the First Book of Samuel [25:1–22]

Samuel died; and all Israel assembled and mourned for him. They buried him at his home in Ramah. Then David got up and went down to the wilderness of Paran. There was a man in Maon, whose property was in Carmel. The man was very rich; he had three thousand sheep and a thousand goats. He was shearing his sheep in Carmel. Now the name of the man was Nabal, and the name of his wife Abigail. The woman was clever and beautiful, but the man was surly and mean; he was a Calebite. David heard in the wilderness that Nabal was shearing his sheep. So David sent ten young men; and David said to the young men, "Go up to Carmel, and go to Nabal, and greet him in my name. Thus you shall salute him: 'Peace be to you, and peace be to your house, and peace be to all that you have. I hear that you have shearers; now your shepherds have been with us, and we did them no harm, and they missed nothing, all the time they were in Carmel. Ask your young men, and they will tell you. Therefore let my young men find favor in your sight; for we have come on a feast day. Please give whatever you have at hand to your servants and to your son David.' " When David's young men came, they said all this to Nabal in the name of David; and then they waited. But Nabal answered David's servants, "Who is David? Who is the son of Jesse? There are many servants today who are breaking away from their masters. Shall I take my bread and my water and the meat that I have butchered for my shearers, and give it to men who come from I do not know where?" So David's young men turned away, and came back and told him all this. David said to his men, "Every man strap on his sword!" And every one of them strapped on his sword; David also strapped on his sword; and about four hundred men went up after David, while two hundred remained with the baggage. But one of the young men told Abigail, Nabal's wife, "David sent messengers out of the wilderness to salute our master; and he shouted insults at them. Yet the men were very good to us, and we suffered no harm, and we never missed anything when we were in the fields, as long as we were with them; they were a wall to us both by night and by day, all the while we were with them keeping the sheep. Now therefore know this and consider what you should do; for evil has been decided against our master and against all his house; he is so ill-natured that no one can speak to him." Then Abigail hurried and took two hundred loaves, two skins of wine, five sheep ready dressed, five measures of parched grain, one hundred clusters of raisins, and two hundred cakes of figs. She loaded them on donkeys and said to her young men, "Go on ahead of me; I am coming after you." But she did not tell her husband Nabal. As she rode on the donkey and came down under cover of the mountain, David and his men came down toward her; and she met them. Now David had said, "Surely it was in vain that I protected all that this fellow has in the wilderness, so that nothing was missed of all that belonged to him; but he has returned me evil for good. God do so to David and more also, if by morning I leave so much as one male of all who belong to him."

A Reading (Lesson) from the Acts of the Apostles [14:1–18]

At Iconium Paul and Barnabas entered together into the Jewish synagogue, and spoke in such a way that a great number of both Jews and Greeks became believers. But the unbelieving Jews stirred up the Gentiles and poisoned their minds against the brothers. So they remained for a long time, speaking boldly for the Lord, who testified to the word of his grace by granting signs and wonders to be done through them. But the residents of the city were divided; some sided with the Jews, and some with the apostles. And when an attempt was made by both Gentiles and Jews, with their rulers, to mistreat them and to stone them, the apostles learned of it and fled to Lystra and Derbe, cities of Lycaonia, and to the surrounding country; and there they continued proclaiming the good news. In Lystra there was a man sitting who could not use his feet and had never walked, for he had been crippled from birth. He listened to Paul as he was speaking. And Paul, looking at him intently and seeing that he had faith to be healed, said in a loud voice, "Stand upright on your feet." And the man sprang up and began to walk. When the crowds saw what Paul had done, they shouted in the Lycaonian language, "The gods have come down to us in human form!" Barnabas they called Zeus, and Paul they called Hermes, because he was the chief speaker. The priest of Zeus, whose temple was just outside the city, brought oxen and garlands to the gates; he and the crowds wanted to offer sacrifice. When the apostles Barnabas and

Paul heard of it, they tore their clothes and rushed out into the crowd shouting, "Friends, why are you doing this? We are mortals just like you, and we bring you good news, that you should turn from these worthless things to the living God, who made the heaven and the earth and the sea and all that is in them. In past generations he allowed all the nations to follow their own ways; yet he has not left himself without a witness in doing good—giving you rains from heaven and fruitful seasons, and filling you with food and your hearts with joy." Even with these words, they scarcely restrained the crowds from offering sacrifice to them.

A Reading (Lesson) from the Gospel according to Mark [4:21–34]

Jesus said to those who were about him with the twelve, "Is a lamp brought in to be put under the bushel basket, or under the bed, and not on the lampstand? For there is nothing hidden, except to be disclosed; nor is anything secret, except to come to light. Let anyone with ears to hear listen!" And he said to them, "Pay attention to what you hear; the measure you give will be the measure you get, and still more will be given you. For to those who have, more will be given; and from those who have nothing, even what they have will be taken away." He also said, "The kingdom of God is as if someone would scatter seed on the ground, and would sleep and rise night and day, and the seed would sprout and grow, he does not know how. The earth produces of itself, first the stalk, then the head, then the full grain in the head. But when the grain is ripe, at once he goes in with his sickle, because the harvest has come." He also said, "With what can we compare the kingdom of God, or what parable will we use for it? It is like a mustard seed, which, when sown upon the ground, is the smallest of all the seeds on earth; yet when it is sown it grows up and becomes the greatest of all shrubs, and puts forth large branches, so that the birds of the air can make nests in its shade." With many such parables he spoke the word to them, as they were able to hear it; he did not speak to them except in parables, but he explained everything in private to his disciples.

Wednesday

Psalm 119:49–72 [page 767]   ❖   *Psalm 49* [page 652], *(Psalm 53* [page 658])

A Reading (Lesson) from the First Book of Samuel [25:23–44]

When Abigail saw David, she hurried and alighted from the donkey, fell before David on her face, bowing to the ground. She fell at his feet and said, "Upon me alone, my lord, be the guilt; please let your servant speak in your ears, and hear the words of your servant. My lord, do not take seriously this ill-natured fellow, Nabal; for as his name is, so is he; Nabal is his name, and folly is with him; but I, your servant, did not see the young men of my lord, whom you sent. Now then, my lord, as the LORD lives, and as you yourself live, since the LORD has restrained you from bloodguilt and from taking vengeance with your own hand, now let your enemies and those who seek to do evil to my lord be like Nabal. And now let this present that your servant has brought to my lord be given to the young men who follow my lord. Please forgive the trespass of your servant; for the LORD will certainly make my lord a sure house, because my lord is fighting the battles of the LORD; and evil shall not be found in you so long as you live. If anyone should rise up to pursue you and to seek your life, the life of my lord shall be bound in the bundle of the living under the care of the LORD your God; but the lives of your enemies he shall sling out as from the hollow of a sling. When the LORD has done to my lord according to all the good that he has spoken concerning you, and has appointed you prince over Israel, my lord shall have no cause of grief, or pangs of conscience, for having shed blood without cause or for having saved himself. And when the LORD has dealt well with my lord, then remember your servant." David said to Abigail, "Blessed be the LORD, the God of Israel, who sent you to meet me today! Blessed be your good sense, and blessed be you, who have kept me today from bloodguilt and from avenging myself by my own hand! For as surely as the LORD the God of Israel lives, who has restrained me from hurting you, unless you had hurried and come to meet me, truly by morning there would not have been left to Nabal so much as one male." Then David received from her hand what she had brought him; he said to her, "Go up to your house in peace; see, I have heeded your voice, and I have granted your petition." Abigail came to Nabal; he was holding a feast in his house, like the feast of a king. Nabal's heart was merry within him, for he was very drunk; so she told him nothing at all until the morning light. In the morning, when the wine had gone out of Nabal, his wife told him these things, and his heart died within him; he became like a stone. About ten days later the LORD struck Nabal, and he died. When David heard that Nabal was dead, he said, "Blessed be the LORD who has judged the case of Nabal's insult to me, and has kept back his servant from evil; the LORD has returned the evil-doing of Nabal upon his own head." Then David sent and wooed Abigail, to make her his wife. When David's servants came to

Abigail at Carmel, they said to her, "David has sent us to you to take you to him as his wife." She rose and bowed down, with her face to the ground, and said, "Your servant is a slave to wash the feet of the servants of my lord." Abigail got up hurriedly and rode away on a donkey; her five maids attended her. She went after the messengers of David and became his wife. David also married Ahinoam of Jezreel; both of them became his wives. Saul had given his daughter Michal, David's wife, to Palti son of Laish, who was from Gallim.

A Reading (Lesson) from the Acts of the Apostles [14:19–28]

Jews came to Lystra from Antioch and Iconium; and won over the crowds. Then they stoned Paul and dragged him out of the city, supposing that he was dead. But when the disciples surrounded him, he got up and went into the city. The next day he went on with Barnabas to Derbe. After they had proclaimed the good news to that city and had made many disciples, they returned to Lystra, then on to Iconium and Antioch. There they strengthened the souls of the disciples and encouraged them to continue in the faith, saying, "It is through many persecutions that we must enter the kingdom of God." And after they had appointed elders for them in each church, with prayer and fasting they entrusted them to the Lord in whom they had come to believe. Then they passed through Pisidia and came to Pamphylia. When they had spoken the word in Perga, they went down to Attalia. From there they sailed back to Antioch, where they had been commended to the grace of God for the work that they had completed. When they arrived, they called the church together and related all that God had done with them, and how he had opened a door of faith for the Gentiles. And they stayed there with the disciples for some time.

A Reading (Lesson) from the Gospel according to Mark [4:35–41]

On that day, when evening had come, Jesus said to them, "Let us go across to the other side." And leaving the crowd behind, they took him with them in the boat, just as he was. Other boats were with him. A great windstorm arose, and the waves beat into the boat, so that the boat was already being swamped. But he was in the stern, asleep on the cushion; and they woke him up and said to him, "Teacher, do you not care that we are perishing?" He woke up and rebuked the wind, and said to the sea, "Peace! Be still!" Then the wind ceased, and there was a dead calm. He said to them, "Why are you afraid? Have you still no faith?" And they were filled with great awe and said to one another, "Who then is this, that even the wind and the sea obey him?"

Thursday

Psalm 50 [page 654] ❖ (*Psalm 59* [page 665],
Psalm 60 [page 667]) or *Psalm 66* [page 673],
Psalm 67 [page 675]

A Reading (Lesson) from the First Book of Samuel [28:3–20]

Samuel had died, and all Israel had mourned for him and buried him in Ramah, his own city. Saul had expelled the mediums and the wizards from the land. The Philistines assembled, and came and encamped at Shunem. Saul gathered all Israel, and they encamped at Gilboa. When Saul saw the army of the Philistines, he was afraid, and his heart trembled greatly. When Saul inquired of the LORD, the LORD did not answer him, not by dreams, or by Urim, or by prophets. Then Saul said to his servants, "Seek out for me a woman who is a medium, so that I may go to her and inquire of her." His servants said to him, "There is a medium at Endor." So Saul disguised himself and put on other clothes and went there, he and two men with him. They came to the woman by night. And he said, "Consult a spirit for me, and bring up for me the one whom I name to you." The woman said to him, "Surely you know what Saul has done, how he has cut off the mediums and the wizards from the land. Why then are you laying a snare for my life to bring about my death?" But Saul swore to her by the LORD, "As the LORD lives, no punishment shall come upon you for this thing." Then the woman said, "Whom shall I bring up for you?" He answered, "Bring up Samuel for me." When the woman saw Samuel, she cried out with a loud voice; and the woman said to Saul, "Why have you deceived me? You are Saul!" The king said to her, "Have no fear; what do you see?" The woman said to Saul, "I see a divine being coming up out of the ground." He said to her, "What is his appearance?" She said, "An old man is coming up; he is wrapped in a robe." So Saul knew that it was Samuel, and he bowed with his face to the ground, and did obeisance. Then Samuel said to Saul, "Why have you disturbed me by bringing me up?" Saul answered, "I am in great distress, for the Philistines are warring against me, and God has turned away from me and answers me no more, either by prophets or by dreams; so I have summoned you to tell me what I should do." Samuel said, "Why then do you ask me, since the LORD has turned from you and become your enemy? The LORD has done to you just as he spoke by me; for the

LORD has torn the kingdom out of your hand, and given it to your neighbor, David. Because you did not obey the voice of the LORD, and did not carry out his fierce wrath against Amalek, therefore the LORD has done this thing to you today. Moreover the LORD will give Israel along with you into the hands of the Philistines; and tomorrow you and your sons shall be with me; the LORD will also give the army of Israel into the hands of the Philistines." Immediately Saul fell full length on the ground, filled with fear because of the words of Samuel; and there was no strength in him, for he had eaten nothing all day and all night.

A Reading (Lesson) from the Acts of the Apostles [15:1–11]

Certain individuals came down from Judea and were teaching the brothers, "Unless you are circumcised according to the custom of Moses, you cannot be saved." And after Paul and Barnabas had no small dissension and debate with them, Paul and Barnabas and some of the others were appointed to go up to Jerusalem to discuss this question with the apostles and the elders. So they were sent on their way by the church, and as they passed through both Phoenicia and Samaria, they reported the conversion of the Gentiles, and brought great joy to all the believers. When they came to Jerusalem, they were welcomed by the church and the apostles and the elders, and they reported all that God had done with them. But some believers who belonged to the sect of the Pharisees stood up and said, "It is necessary for them to be circumcised and ordered to keep the law of Moses." The apostles and the elders met together to consider this matter. After there had been much debate, Peter stood up and said to them, "My brothers, you know that in the early days God made a choice among you, that I should be the one through whom the Gentiles would hear the message of the good news and become believers. And God, who knows the human heart, testified to them by giving them the Holy Spirit, just as he did to us; and in cleansing their hearts by faith he has made no distinction between them and us. Now therefore why are you putting God to the test by placing on the neck of the disciples a yoke that neither our ancestors nor we have been able to bear? On the contrary, we believe that we will be saved through the grace of the Lord Jesus, just as they will."

A Reading (Lesson) from the Gospel according to Mark [5:1–20]

Jesus and the disciples came to the other side of the sea, to the country of the Gerasenes. And when he had stepped out of the boat, immediately a man out of the tombs with an unclean spirit met him. He lived among the tombs; and no one could restrain him any more, even with a chain; for he had often been restrained with shackles and chains, but the chains he wrenched apart, and the shackles he broke in pieces; and no one had the strength to subdue him. Night and day among the tombs and on the mountains he was always howling and bruising himself with stones. When he saw Jesus from a distance, he ran and bowed down before him; and he shouted at the top of his voice, "What have you to do with me, Jesus, Son of the Most High God? I adjure you by God, do not torment me." For he had said to him, "Come out of the man, you unclean spirit!" Then Jesus asked him, "What is your name?" He replied, "My name is Legion; for we are many." He begged him earnestly not to send them out of the country. Now there on the hillside a great herd of swine was feeding; and the unclean spirits begged him,

"Send us into the swine; let us enter them." So he gave them permission. And the unclean spirits came out and entered the swine; and the herd, numbering about two thousand, rushed down the steep bank into the sea, and were drowned in the sea. The swineherds ran off and told it in the city and in the country. Then people came to see what it was that had happened. They came to Jesus and saw the demoniac sitting there, clothed and in his right mind, the very man who had had the legion; and they were afraid. Those who had seen what had happened to the demoniac and to the swine reported it. Then they began to beg Jesus to leave their neighborhood. As he was getting into the boat, the man who had been possessed by demons begged him that he might be with him. But Jesus refused, and said to him, "Go home to your friends, and tell them how much the Lord has done for you, and what mercy he has shown you." And he went away and began to proclaim in the Decapolis how much Jesus had done for him; and everyone was amazed.

Friday

Psalm 40 [page 640],   *Psalm 54* [page 659]   ❖
Psalm 51 [page 656]

A Reading (Lesson) from the First Book of Samuel [31:1–13]

The Philistines fought against Israel; and the men of Israel fled before the Philistines, and many fell on Mount Gilboa. The Philistines overtook Saul and his sons; and the Philistines killed Jonathan and Abinadab and Malchishua, the sons of Saul. The battle pressed hard upon Saul; the archers found him, and he was badly wounded by them. Then Saul said to his armor-bearer, "Draw your sword and thrust me through with it, so that these uncircumcised may not come and thrust me through, and make sport of me." But his armor-bearer was unwilling; for he was terrified. So Saul took his own sword and fell upon it. When his armor-bearer saw that Saul was dead, he also fell upon his sword and died with him. So Saul and his three sons and his armor-bearer and all his men died together on the same day. When the men of Israel who were on the other side of the valley and those beyond the Jordan saw that the men of Israel had fled and that Saul and his sons were dead, they forsook their towns and fled; and the Philistines came and occupied them. The next day, when the Philistines came to strip the dead, they found Saul and his three sons fallen on Mount Gilboa. They cut off his head, stripped off his armor, and sent messengers throughout the land of the Philistines to carry the good news to the houses of their idols and to the people. They put his armor in the temple of Astarte; and they fastened his body to the wall of Beth-shan. But when the inhabitants of Jabesh-gilead heard what the Philistines had done to Saul, all the valiant men set out, traveled all night long, and took the body of Saul and the bodies of his sons from the wall of Beth-shan. They came to Jabesh and burned them there. Then they took their bones and buried them under the tamarisk tree in Jabesh, and fasted seven days.

A Reading (Lesson) from the Acts of the Apostles [15:12–21]

The whole assembly kept silence, and listened to Barnabas and Paul as they told of all the signs and wonders that God had done through them among the Gentiles. After they finished speaking, James replied, "My brothers, listen to me. Simeon has related how God first looked favorably on the Gentiles, to take from among them a people for his name. This agrees with the words of the prophets, as it is written, 'After this I will return, and I will rebuild the dwelling of David, which has fallen; from its ruins I will rebuild it, and I will set it up, so that all other peoples may seek the Lord—even all the Gentiles over whom my name has been called. Thus says the Lord, who has been making these things known from long ago.' Therefore I have reached the decision that we should not trouble those Gentiles who are turning to God, but we should write to them to abstain only from things polluted by idols and from fornication and from whatever has been strangled and from blood. For in every city, for generations past, Moses has had those who proclaim him, for he has been read aloud every sabbath in the synagogues."

A Reading (Lesson) from the Gospel according to Mark [5:21–43]

When Jesus had crossed again in the boat to the other side, a great crowd gathered around him; and he was by the sea. Then one of the leaders of the synagogue named Jairus came and, when he saw him, fell at his feet and begged him repeatedly, "My little daughter is at the point of death. Come and lay your hands on her, so that she may be made well, and live." So he went with him. And a large crowd followed him and pressed in on him. Now there was a woman who had been suffering from hemorrhages for twelve years. She had endured much under many physicians, and had spent all that she had; and she was no better, but rather grew worse. She had heard about Jesus, and came up behind him in the crowd and touched his cloak, for she said, "If I but touch his clothes, I will be made well." Immediately her hemorrhage stopped; and she felt in her body that she was healed of her disease. Immediately aware that power had gone forth from him, Jesus turned about in the crowd and said, "Who touched my clothes?" And his disciples said to him, "You see the crowd pressing in on you; how can you say, 'Who touched me?'" He looked all around to see who had done it. But the woman, knowing what had happened to her, came in fear and trembling, fell down before him, and told him the whole truth. He said to her, "Daughter, your faith has made you well; go in peace, and be healed of your disease." While he was still speaking, some people came from the leader's house to say, "Your daughter is dead. Why trouble the teacher any further?" But overhearing what they said, Jesus said to the leader of the synagogue, "Do not fear, only believe." He allowed no one to follow him except Peter, James, and John, the brother of James. When they came to the house of the leader of the synagogue, he saw a commotion, people weeping and wailing loudly. When he had entered, he said to them, "Why do you make a commotion and weep? The child is not dead but sleeping." And they laughed at him. Then he put them all outside, and took the child's father and mother and those who were with him, and went in where the child was. He took her by the hand and said to her, "Talitha cum," which means, "Little girl, get up!" And immediately the girl got up and began to walk about (she was twelve years of age). At this they were overcome with amazement. He strictly ordered them that no one should know this, and told them to give her something to eat.

Saturday

Psalm 55 [page 660] ❖ *Psalm 138* [page 793],
Psalm 139:1–17(18–23) [page 794]

A Reading (Lesson) from the Second Book of Samuel
[1:1–16]

After the death of Saul, when David had returned from
defeating the Amalekites, David remained two days in
Ziklag. On the third day, a man came from Saul's camp,
with his clothes torn and dirt on his head. When he came to
David, he fell to the ground and did obeisance. David said
to him, "Where have you come from?" He said to him,
"I have escaped from the camp of Israel." David said to him,
"How did things go? Tell me!" He answered, "The army fled
from the battle, but also many of the army fell and died; and
Saul and his son Jonathan also died." Then David asked the
young man who was reporting to him, "How do you know
that Saul and his son Jonathan died?" The young man
reporting to him said, "I happened to be on Mount Gilboa;
and there was Saul leaning on his spear, while the chariots
and the horsemen drew close to him. When he looked
behind him, he saw me, and called to me. I answered, 'Here
sir.' And he said to me, 'Who are you?' I answered him,
'I am an Amalekite.' He said to me, 'Come, stand over me
and kill me; for convulsions have seized me, and yet my life
still lingers.' So I stood over him, and killed him, for I knew
that he could not live after he had fallen. I took the crown
that was on his head and the armlet that was on his arm,
and I have brought them here to my lord." Then David took
hold of his clothes and tore them; and all the men who were
with him did the same. They mourned and wept, and fasted
until evening for Saul and for his son Jonathan, and for the
army of the LORD and for the house of Israel, because they

had fallen by the sword. David said to the young man who had reported to him, "Where do you come from?" He answered, "I am the son of a resident alien, and Amalekite." David said to him, "Were you not afraid to lift your hand to destroy the LORD's anointed?" Then David called one of the young men and said, "Come here and strike him down." So he struck him down and he died. David said to him, "Your blood be on your head; for your own mouth has testified against you, saying, 'I have killed the LORD's anointed.' "

A Reading (Lesson) from the Acts of the Apostles [15:22–35]

The apostles and the elders, with the consent of the whole church, decided to choose men from among their members and to send them to Antioch with Paul and Barnabas. They sent Judas called Barsabbas, and Silas, leaders among the brothers, with the following letter: "The brothers, both the apostles and the elders, to the believers of Gentile origin in Antioch and Syria and Cilicia, greetings. Since we have heard that certain persons who have gone out from us, though with no instructions from us, have said things to disturb you and have unsettled your minds, we have decided unanimously to choose representatives and send them to you, along with our beloved Barnabas and Paul, who have risked their lives for the sake of our Lord Jesus Christ. We have therefore sent Judas and Silas, who themselves will tell you the same things by word of mouth. For it has seemed good to the Holy Spirit and to us to impose on you no further burden than these essentials: that you abstain from what has been sacrificed to idols and from blood and from what is strangled and from fornication. If you keep yourselves from these, you will do well. Farewell." So they were sent off and went down to Antioch. When they gathered the congregation together, they delivered the letter. When its members read it, they rejoiced at the exhortation. Judas and Silas, who were themselves prophets, said much to encourage and strengthen the believers. After they had been there for some time, they were sent off in peace by the believers to those who had sent them. But Paul and Barnabas remained in Antioch, and there, with many others, they taught and proclaimed the word of the Lord.

A Reading (Lesson) from the Gospel according to Mark [6:1–13]

Jesus left that place and came to his hometown, and his disciples followed him. On the sabbath he began to teach in the synagogue, and many who heard him were astounded. They said, "Where did this man get all this? What is this wisdom that has been given to him? What deeds of power are being done by his hands! Is not this the carpenter, the son of Mary and brother of James and Joses and Judas and Simon, and are not his sisters here with us?" And they took offense at him. Then Jesus said to them, "Prophets are not without honor, except in their hometown, and among their own kin, and in their own house." And he could do no deed of power there, except that he laid his hands on a few sick people and cured them. And he was amazed at their unbelief. Then he went about among the villages teaching. He called the twelve and began to send them out two by two, and gave them authority over the unclean spirits. He ordered them to take nothing for their journey except a staff; no bread, no bag, no money in their belts; but to wear sandals and not to put on two tunics. He said to them, "Wherever you enter a house, stay there until you leave the place. If any place will not welcome you and they refuse to hear you, as you leave, shake off the dust that is on your feet as a testimony against them." So they went out and proclaimed that all should repent. They cast out many demons, and anointed with oil many who were sick and cured them.

Proper 12 *Week of the Sunday closest to July 27*

Sunday

Psalm 24 [page 613], *Psalm 29* [page 620] ❖
Psalm 8 [page 592], *Psalm 84* [page 707]

A Reading (Lesson) from the Second Book of Samuel [1:17–27]

David intoned this lamentation over Saul and his son Jonathan. (He ordered that The Song of the Bow be taught to the people of Judah; it is written in the Book of Jashar.) He said: Your glory, O Israel, lies slain upon your high places! How the mighty have fallen! Tell it not in Gath, proclaim it not in the streets of Ashkelon; or the daughters of the Philistines will rejoice, the daughters of the uncircumcised will exult. You mountains of Gilboa, let there be no dew or rain upon you, nor bounteous fields! For there the shield of the mighty was defiled, the shield of Saul, anointed with oil no more. From the blood of the slain, from the fat of the mighty, the bow of Jonathan did not turn back, nor the sword of Saul return empty. Saul and Jonathan, beloved and lovely! In life and in death they were not divided; they were swifter than eagles, they were stronger than lions. O daughters of Israel, weep over Saul, who clothed you with crimson, in luxury, who put ornaments of gold on your apparel. How the mighty have fallen in the midst of the battle! Jonathan lies slain upon your high places. I am distressed for you, my brother Jonathan; greatly beloved were you to me; your love to me was wonderful, passing the love of women. How the mighty have fallen, and the weapons of war perished!

A Reading (Lesson) from the Letter of Paul to the Romans
[12:9–21]

Let love be genuine; hate what is evil, hold fast to what is good; love one another with mutual affection; outdo one another in showing honor. Do not lag in zeal, be ardent in spirit, serve the Lord. Rejoice in hope, be patient in suffering, persevere in prayer. Contribute to the needs of the saints; extend hospitality to strangers. Bless those who persecute you; bless and do not curse them. Rejoice with those who rejoice, weep with those who weep. Live in harmony with one another; do not be haughty, but associate with the lowly; do not claim to be wiser than you are. Do not repay anyone evil for evil, but take thought for what is noble in the sight of all. If it is possible, so far as it depends on you, live peaceably with all. Beloved, never avenge yourselves, but leave room for the wrath of God; for it is written, "Vengeance is mine, I will repay, says the Lord." No, "if your enemies are hungry, feed them; if they are thirsty, give them something to drink; for by doing this you will heap burning coals on their heads." Do not be overcome by evil, but overcome evil with good.

A Reading (Lesson) from the Gospel according to Matthew
[25:31–46]

Jesus said to the disciples, "When the Son of Man comes in his glory, and all the angels with him, then he will sit on the throne of his glory. All the nations will be gathered before him, and he will separate people one from another as a shepherd separates the sheep from the goats, and he will put the sheep at his right hand and the goats at the left. Then the king will say to those at his right hand, 'Come, you that are blessed by my Father, inherit the kingdom prepared for you from the foundation of the world; for I was hungry and you gave me food, I was thirsty and you gave me something to drink, I was a stranger and you welcomed me, I was naked and you gave me clothing, I was sick and you took care of me, I was in prison and you visited me.' Then the righteous will answer him, 'Lord, when was it that we saw you hungry and gave you food, or thirsty and gave you something to drink? And when was it that we saw you a stranger and welcomed you, or naked and gave you clothing? And when was it that we saw you sick or in prison and visited you?' And the king will answer them, 'Truly I tell you, just as you did it to one of the least of these who are members of my family, you did it to me.' Then he will say to those at his left hand, 'You that are accursed, depart from me into the eternal fire prepared for the devil and his angels; for I was hungry and you gave me no food, I was thirsty and you gave me nothing to drink, I was a stranger and you did not welcome me, naked and you did not give me clothing, sick and in prison and you did not visit me.' Then they also will answer, 'Lord, when was it that we saw you hungry or thirsty or a stranger or naked or sick or in prison, and did not take care of you?' Then he will answer them, 'Truly I tell you, just as you did not do it to one of the least of these, you did not do it to me.' And these will go away into eternal punishment, but the righteous into eternal life."

Monday

Psalm 56 [page 662],   Psalm 57 [page 663],
(Psalm 58 [page 664]) ❖ Psalm 64 [page 671],
Psalm 65 [page 672]

A Reading (Lesson) from the Second Book of Samuel
[2:1–11]

David inquired of the LORD, "Shall I go up into any of the cities of Judah?" The LORD said to him, "Go up." David said, "To which shall I go up?" He said, "To Hebron." So David went up there, along with his two wives, Ahinoam of Jezreel, and Abigail the widow of Nabal of Carmel. David brought up the men who were with him, every one with his household; and they settled in the towns of Hebron. Then the people of Judah came, and there they anointed David king over the house of Judah. When they told David, "It was the people of Jabesh-gilead who buried Saul," David sent messengers to the people of Jabesh-gilead, and said to them, "May you be blessed by the LORD, because you showed this loyalty to Saul your lord, and buried him! Now may the LORD show steadfast love and faithfulness to you! And I too will reward you because you have done this thing. Therefore let your hands be strong, and be valiant for Saul your lord is dead, and the house of Judah has anointed me king over them." But Abner son of Ner, commander of Saul's army, had taken Ishbaal son of Saul and brought him over to Mahanaim. He made him king over Gilead, the Ashurites, Jezreel, Ephraim, Benjamin, and over all Israel. Ishbaal, Saul's son, was forty years old when he began to reign over Israel, and he reigned two years. But the house of Judah followed David. The time that David was king in Hebron over the house of Judah was seven years and six months.

A Reading (Lesson) from the Acts of the Apostles
[15:36—16:5]

After some days Paul said to Barnabas, "Come, let us return and visit the believers in every city where we proclaimed the word of the Lord and see how they are doing." Barnabas wanted to take with them John called Mark. But Paul decided not to take with them one who had deserted them in Pamphylia and had not accompanied them in the work. The disagreement became so sharp that they parted company; Barnabas took Mark with him and sailed away to Cyprus. But Paul chose Silas and set out, the believers commending him to the grace of the Lord. He went through Syria and Cilicia, strengthening the churches. Paul went on also to Derbe and to Lystra, where there was a disciple named Timothy, the son of a Jewish woman who was a believer; but his father was a Greek. He was well spoken of by the believers in Lystra and Iconium. Paul wanted Timothy to accompany him; and he took him and had him circumcised because of the Jews who were in those places, for they all knew that his father was a Greek. As they went from town to town, they delivered to them for observance the decisions that had been reached by the apostles and elders who were in Jerusalem. So the churches were strengthened in the faith and increased in numbers daily.

A Reading (Lesson) from the Gospel according to Mark
[6:14–29]

King Herod heard of Jesus' preaching and his miraculous deeds, for Jesus' name had become known. Some were saying, "John the baptizer has been raised from the dead; and for this reason these powers are at work in him." But others said, "It is Elijah." And others said, "It is a prophet, like one of the prophets of old." But when Herod heard of it, he said, "John, whom I beheaded, has been raised." For Herod himself had sent men who arrested John, bound him, and put him in prison on account of Herodias, his brother Philip's wife, because Herod had married her. For John had been telling Herod, "It is not lawful for you to have your brother's wife." And Herodias had a grudge against him, and wanted to kill him. But she could not, for Herod feared John, knowing that he was a righteous and holy man, and he protected him. When he heard him, he was greatly perplexed; and yet he liked to listen to him. But an opportunity came when Herod on his birthday gave a banquet for his courtiers and officers and for the leaders of Galilee. When his daughter Herodias came in and danced, she pleased Herod and his guests; and the king said to the girl, "Ask me for whatever you wish, and I will give it." And he solemnly swore to her, "Whatever you ask me, I will give you, even half of my kingdom." She went out and said to her mother, "What should I ask for?" She replied, "The head of John the baptizer." Immediately she rushed back to the king and requested, "I want you to give me at once the head of John the Baptist on a platter." The king was deeply grieved; yet out of regard for his oaths and for the guests, he did not want to refuse her. Immediately the king sent a soldier of the guard with orders to bring John's head. He went and beheaded him in the prison, brought his head on a platter, and gave it to the girl. Then the girl gave it to her mother. When his disciples heard about it, they came and took his body, and laid it in a tomb.

Tuesday

Psalm 61 [page 668],   *Psalm 62* [page 669]   ❖
Psalm 68:1–20(21–23)24–36 [page 676]

A Reading (Lesson) from the Second Book of Samuel
[3:6–21]

While there was war between the house of Saul and the
house of David, Abner was making himself strong in the
house of Saul. Now Saul had a concubine whose name was
Rizpah daughter of Aiah. And Ishbaal said to Abner, "Why
have you gone in to my father's concubine?" The words of
Ishbaal made Abner very angry; he said, "Am I a dog's head
for Judah? Today I keep showing loyalty to the house of
your father Saul, to his brothers, and to his friends, and
have not given you into the hand of David; and yet you
charge me now with a crime concerning this woman. So
may God do to Abner and so may he add to it! For just what
the LORD has sworn to David, that will I accomplish for
him, to transfer the kingdom from the house of Saul, and set
up the throne of David over Israel and over Judah, from
Dan to Beer-sheba." And Ishbaal could not answer Abner
another word, because he feared him. Abner sent
messengers to David at Hebron, saying, "To whom does the
land belong? Make your covenant with me, and I will give
you my support to bring all Israel over to you." He said,
"Good; I will make a covenant with you. But one thing I
require of you: you shall never appear in my presence unless
you bring Saul's daughter Michal when you come to see
me." Then David sent messengers to Saul's son Ishbaal,
saying, "Give me my wife Michal, to whom I became
engaged at the price of one hundred foreskins of the
Philistines." Ishbaal sent and took her from her husband
Paltiel the son of Laish. But her husband went with her,

weeping as he walked behind her all the way to Bahurim. Then Abner said to him, "Go back home!" So he went back. Abner sent word to the elders of Israel, saying, "For some time past you have been seeking David as king over you. Now then bring it about; for the LORD has promised David: Through my servant David I will save my people Israel from the hand of the Philistines, and from all their enemies." Abner also spoke directly to the Benjaminites; then Abner went to tell David at Hebron all that Israel and the whole house of Benjamin were ready to do. When Abner came with twenty men to David at Hebron, David made a feast for Abner and the men who were with him. Abner said to David, "Let me go and rally all Israel to my lord the king, in order that they may make a covenant with you, and that you may reign over all that your heart desires." So David dismissed Abner, and he went away in peace.

A Reading (Lesson) from the Acts of the Apostles [16:6–15]

Paul and Timothy went through the region of Phrygia and Galatia, having been forbidden by the Holy Spirit to speak the word in Asia. When they had come opposite Mysia, they attempted to go into Bithynia, but the Spirit of Jesus did not allow them; so, passing by Mysia, they went down to Troas. During the night Paul had a vision: there stood a man of Macedonia pleading with him and saying, "Come over to Macedonia and help us." When he had seen the vision, we immediately tried to cross over to Macedonia, being convinced that God had called us to proclaim the good news to them. We set sail from Troas and took a straight course to Samothrace, the following day to Neapolis, and from there to Philippi, which is a leading city of the district of Macedonia and a Roman colony. We remained in this city for some days. On the sabbath day we went outside the gate by the river, where we supposed there was a place of prayer; and we sat down and spoke to the women who had gathered there. A certain woman named Lydia, a worshiper of God, was listening to us; she was from the city of Thyatira and a dealer in purple cloth. The Lord opened her heart to listen eagerly to what was said by Paul. When she and her household were baptized, she urged us, saying, "If you have judged me to be faithful to the Lord, come and stay at my home." And she prevailed upon us.

A Reading (Lesson) from the Gospel according to Mark [6:30–46]

The apostles gathered around Jesus, and told him all that they had done and taught. He said to them, "Come away to a deserted place all by yourselves and rest a while." For many were coming and going, and they had no leisure even to eat. And they went away in the boat to a deserted place by themselves. Now many saw them going and recognized them, and they hurried there on foot from all the towns and arrived ahead of them. As he went ashore, he saw a great crowd; and he had compassion for them, because they were like sheep without a shepherd; and he began to teach them many things. When it grew late, his disciples came to him and said, "This is a deserted place, and the hour is now very late; send them away so that they may go into the surrounding country and villages and buy something for themselves to eat." But he answered them, "You give them something to eat." They said to him, "Are we to go and buy two hundred denarii worth of bread, and give it to them to eat?" And he said to them, "How many loaves have you? Go and see." When they had found out, they said, "Five, and two fish." Then he ordered them to get all the people to sit down in groups on the green grass. So they sat down in groups of hundreds and of fifties. Taking the five loaves and the two fish, he looked up to heaven, and blessed and broke the loaves, and gave them to his disciples to set before the people; and he divided the two fish among them all. And all ate and were filled; and they took up twelve baskets full of broken pieces and of the fish. Those who had eaten the loaves numbered five thousand men. Immediately he made his disciples get into the boat and go on ahead to the other side, to Bethsaida, while he dismissed the crowd. After saying farewell to them, he went up on the mountain to pray.

Wednesday

Psalm 72 [page 685] ❖ *Psalm 119:73–96* [page 769]

A Reading (Lesson) from the Second Book of Samuel
[3:22–39]

Just as David sent Abner away the servants of David arrived with Joab from a raid, bringing much spoil with them. But Abner was not with David at Hebron, for David had dismissed him, and he had gone away in peace. When Joab and all the army that was with him came, it was told Joab, "Abner son of Ner came to the king, and he has dismissed him, and he has gone away in peace." Then Joab went to the king and said, "What have you done? Abner came to you; why did you dismiss him, so that he got away? You know that Abner son of Ner came to deceive you, and to learn your comings and goings and to learn all that you are doing." When Joab came out from David's presence, he sent messengers after Abner, and they brought him back from the cistern of Sirah; but David did not know about it. When Abner returned to Hebron, Joab took him aside in the gateway to speak with him privately, and there he stabbed him in the stomach. So he died for shedding the blood of Asahel, Joab's brother. Afterward, when David heard of it, he said, "I and my kingdom are forever guiltless before the LORD for the blood of Abner son of Ner. May the guilt fall on the head of Joab, and on all his father's house; and may the house of Joab never be without one who has a discharge, or who is leprous, or who holds a spindle, or who falls by the sword, or who lacks food!" So Joab and his brother Abishai murdered Abner because he had killed their brother Asahel in the battle at Gibeon. Then David said to Joab and to all the people who were with him, "Tear your clothes, and put on sackcloth, and mourn over Abner." And King David followed the bier. They buried Abner at Hebron. The king lifted up his voice and wept at the grave of Abner, and all the people wept. The king lamented for Abner, saying, "Should Abner die as a fool dies? Your hands were not bound, your feet were not fettered; as one falls before the wicked you have fallen." And all the people wept over him again. Then all the people came to persuade David to eat something while it was still day; but David swore, saying, "So may God do to me, and more, if I taste bread or anything else before the sun goes down!" All the people took notice of it, and it pleased them; just as everything the king did pleased all the people. So all the people and all Israel understood that day that the king had no part in the killing of Abner son of Ner. And the king said to his servants, "Do you not know that a prince and a great man has fallen this day in Israel? Today I am powerless, even though anointed king; these men, the sons of Zeruiah, are too violent for me. The LORD pay back the one who does wickedly in accordance with his wickedness!"

A Reading (Lesson) from the Acts of the Apostles [16:16–24]

One day, as we were going to the place of prayer, we met a slave girl who had a spirit of divination and brought her owners a great deal of money by fortune-telling. While she followed Paul and us, she would cry out, "These men are slaves of the Most High God, who proclaim to you a way of salvation." She kept doing this for many days. But Paul, very much annoyed, turned and said to the spirit, "I order you in the name of Jesus Christ to come out of her." And it came out that very hour. But when her owners saw that their hope of making money was gone, they seized Paul and Silas and dragged them into the marketplace before the authorities. When they had brought them before the magistrates, they said, "These men are disturbing our city; they are Jews and are advocating customs that are not lawful for us as Romans to adopt or observe." The crowd joined in attacking them, and the magistrates had them stripped of their clothing and ordered them to be beaten with rods. After they had given them a severe flogging, they threw them into prison and ordered the jailer to keep them securely. Following these instructions, he put them in the innermost cell and fastened their feet in the stocks.

A Reading (Lesson) from the Gospel according to Mark [6:47–56]

When evening came, the boat was out on the sea, and Jesus was alone on the land. When he saw that they were straining at the oars against an adverse wind, he came towards them early in the morning, walking on the sea. He intended to pass them by. But when they saw him walking on the sea, they thought it was a ghost and cried out; for they all saw him and were terrified. But immediately he spoke to them and said, "Take heart, it is

I; do not be afraid." Then he got into the boat with them and the wind ceased. And they were utterly astounded, for they did not understand about the loaves, but their hearts were hardened. When they had crossed over, they came to land at Gennesaret and moored the boat. When they got out of the boat, people at once recognized him, and rushed about that whole region and began to bring the sick on mats to wherever they heard he was. And wherever he went, into villages or cities or farms, they laid the sick in the marketplaces, and begged him that they might touch even the fringe of his cloak; and all who touched it were healed.

Thursday

(Psalm 70 [page 682]),   *Psalm 71* [page 683]   ❖
Psalm 74 [page 689]

A Reading (Lesson) from the Second Book of Samuel
[4:1–12]

When Saul's son Ishbaal heard that Abner had died at Hebron, his courage failed, and all Israel was dismayed. Saul's son had two captains of raiding bands; the name of the one was Baanah, and the name of the other Rechab. They were sons of Rimmon a Benjaminite from Beeroth— for Beeroth is considered to belong to Benjamin. (Now the people of Beeroth had fled to Gittaim and are there as resident aliens to this day). Saul's son Jonathan had a son who was crippled in his feet. He was five years old when the news about Saul and Jonathan came from Jezreel. His nurse picked him up and fled; and, in her haste to flee, it happened that he fell and became lame. His name was Mephibosheth. Now the sons of Rimmon the Beerothite,

Rechab and Baanah, set out, and about the heat of the day they came to the house of Ishbaal, while he was taking his noonday rest. They came inside the house as though to take wheat, and they struck him in the stomach; then Rechab and his brother Baanah escaped. Now they had come into the house while he was lying on his couch in his bedchamber; they attacked him, killed him, and beheaded him. Then they took his head and traveled by way of the Arabah all night long. They brought the head of Ishbaal to David at Hebron and said to the king, "Here is the head of Ishbaal, son of Saul, your enemy, who sought your life; the LORD has avenged my lord the king this day on Saul and on his offspring." David answered Rechab and his brother Baanah, the sons of Rimmon the Beerothite, "As the LORD lives, who has redeemed my life out of every adversity, when the one who told me, 'See, Saul is dead,' thought he was bringing good news, I seized him and killed him at Ziklag—this was the reward I gave him for his news. How much more then, when wicked men have killed a righteous man on his bed in his own house! And now shall I not require his blood at your hand, and destroy you from the earth?" So David commanded the young men, and they killed them; they cut off their hands and feet, and hung their bodies beside the pool at Hebron. But the head of Ishbaal they took and buried in the tomb of Abner at Hebron.

A Reading (Lesson) from the Acts of the Apostles [16:25–40]

About midnight Paul and Silas were praying and singing hymns to God, and the prisoners were listening to them. Suddenly there was an earthquake, so violent that the foundations of the prison were shaken; and immediately all the doors were opened and everyone's chains were unfastened. When the jailer woke up and saw the prison doors wide open, he drew his sword and was about to kill himself, since he supposed that the prisoners had escaped. But Paul shouted in a loud voice, "Do not harm yourself, for we are all here." The jailer called for lights, and rushing in, he fell down trembling before Paul and Silas. Then he brought them outside and said, "Sirs, what must I do to be saved?" They answered, "Believe on the Lord Jesus, and you will be saved, you and your household." They spoke the word of the Lord to him and to all who were in his house. At the same hour of the night he took them and washed their wounds; then he and his entire family were baptized without delay. He brought them up into the house and set food before them; and he and his entire household rejoiced that he had become a believer in God. When morning came, the magistrates sent the police, saying, "Let those men go." And the jailer reported the message to Paul, saying, "The magistrates sent word to let you go; therefore come out now and go in peace." But Paul replied, "They have beaten us in public, uncondemned, men who are Roman citizens, and have thrown us into prison; and now are they going to discharge us in secret? Certainly not! Let them come and take us out themselves." The police reported these words to the magistrates, and they were afraid when they heard that they were Roman citizens; so they came and apologized to them. And they took them out and asked them to leave the city. After leaving the prison they went to Lydia's home; and when they had seen and encouraged the brothers and sisters there, they departed.

A Reading (Lesson) from the Gospel according to Mark
[7:1–23]

Now when the Pharisees and some of the scribes who had come from Jerusalem gathered around Jesus, they noticed that some of his disciples were eating with defiled hands, that is, without washing them. (For the Pharisees, and all the Jews, do not eat unless they thoroughly wash their hands, thus observing the tradition of the elders; and they do not eat anything from the market unless they wash it; and there are also many other traditions that they observe, the washing of cups, pots, and bronze kettles.) So the Pharisees and the scribes asked him, "Why do your disciples not live according to the tradition of the elders, but eat with defiled hands?" He said to them, "Isaiah prophesied rightly about you hypocrites, as it is written, 'This people honors me with their lips, but their hearts are far from me; in vain do they worship me, teaching human precepts as doctrines.' You abandon the commandment of God and hold to human tradition." Then he said to them, "You have a fine way of rejecting the commandment of God in order to keep your tradition! For Moses said, 'Honor your father and your mother'; and, 'Whoever speaks evil of father or mother must surely die.' But you say that if anyone tells father or mother, 'Whatever support you might have had from me is Corban' (that is, an offering to God)—then you no longer permit doing anything for a father or mother, thus making void the word of God through your tradition that you have handed on. And you do many things like this." Then he called the crowd again and said to them, "Listen to me, all of you, and understand: there is nothing outside a person that by going in can defile, but the things that come out are what defile." When he had left the crowd and entered the house, his disciples asked him about the parable. He said to them, "Then do you also fail to understand? Do you not see that whatever goes into a person from outside cannot defile, since it enters, not the heart but the stomach, and goes out into the sewer?" (Thus he declared all foods clean.) And he said, "It is what comes out of a person that defiles. For it is from within, from the human heart, that evil intentions come: fornication, theft, murder, adultery, avarice, wickedness, deceit, licentiousness, envy, slander, pride, folly. All these evil things come from within, and they defile a person."

Friday

Psalm 69:1–23(24–30)31–38 [page 679] ❖
Psalm 73 [page 687]

A Reading (Lesson) from the Second Book of Samuel
[5:1–12]

All the tribes of Israel came to David at Hebron, and said, "Look, we are your bone and flesh. For some time, while Saul was king over us, it was you who led out Israel and brought it in. The LORD said to you: It is you who shall be shepherd of my people Israel, you who shall be ruler over Israel." So all the elders of Israel came to the king at Hebron; and King David made a covenant with them at Hebron before the LORD, and they anointed David king over Israel. David was thirty years old when he began to reign, and he reigned forty years. At Hebron he reigned over Judah seven years and six months; and at Jerusalem he reigned over all Israel and Judah thirty-three years. The king and his men marched to Jerusalem against the Jebusites, the inhabitants of the land, who said to David, "You will not come in here, even the blind and the lame will turn you back"—thinking, "David cannot come in here." Nevertheless David took the stronghold of Zion, which is now the city of David. David had said on that day, "Whoever would strike down the Jebusites, let him get up the water shaft to attack the lame and the blind, those whom David hates." Therefore it is said, "The blind and the lame shall not come into the house." David occupied the stronghold, and named it the city of David. David built the city all around from the Millo inward. And David became greater and greater, for the LORD, the God of hosts, was with him. King Hiram of Tyre sent messengers to David, along with cedar trees, and carpenters and masons who built David a house. David then perceived that the LORD had established him king over Israel, and that he had exalted his kingdom for the sake of his people Israel.

A Reading (Lesson) from the Acts of the Apostles [17:1–15]

After Paul and Silas had passed through Amphipolis and Apollonia, they came to Thessalonica, where there was a synagogue of the Jews. And Paul went in, as was his custom, and on three sabbath days argued with them from the scriptures, explaining and proving that it was necessary for the Messiah to suffer and to rise from the dead, and saying, "This is the Messiah, Jesus whom I am proclaiming to you." Some of them were persuaded and joined Paul and Silas, as did a great many of the devout Greeks and not a few of the leading women. But the Jews became jealous, and with the help of some ruffians in the marketplaces they formed a mob and set the city in an uproar. While they were searching for Paul and Silas to bring them out to the assembly, they attacked Jason's house. When they could not find them, they dragged Jason and some believers before the city authorities, shouting, "These people who have been turning the world upside down have come here also, and Jason has entertained them as guests. They are all acting contrary to the decrees of the emperor, saying that there is another king named Jesus." The people and the city officials were disturbed when they heard this, and after they had taken bail from Jason and the others, they let them go. That very night the believers sent Paul and Silas off to Beroea; and when they arrived, they went to the Jewish synagogue. These Jews were more receptive than those in Thessalonica, for they welcomed the message very eagerly and examined the scriptures every day to see whether these things were so. Many of them therefore believed, including not a few Greek women and men of high standing. But when the Jews of Thessalonica learned that the word of God had been proclaimed by Paul in Beroea as well, they came there too, to stir up and incite the crowds. Then the believers immediately sent Paul away to the coast, but Silas and Timothy remained behind. Those who conducted Paul brought him as far as Athens; and after receiving instructions to have Silas and Timothy join him as soon as possible, they left him.

A Reading (Lesson) from the Gospel according to Mark [7:24–37]

From there Jesus set out and went away to the region of Tyre. He entered a house and did not want anyone to know he was there. Yet he could not escape notice, but a woman whose little daughter had an unclean spirit immediately heard about him, and she came and bowed down at his feet. Now the woman was a Gentile, of Syrophoenician origin. She begged him to cast the demon out of her daughter. He said to her, "Let the children be fed first, for it is not fair to take the children's food and throw it to the dogs." But she answered him, "Sir, even the dogs under the table eat the children's crumbs." Then he said to her, "For saying that, you may go—the demon has left your daughter." So she went home, found the child lying on the bed, and the demon gone. Then he returned from the region of Tyre, and went by way of Sidon towards the Sea of Galilee, in the region of the Decapolis. They brought to him a deaf man who had an impediment in his speech; and they begged him to lay his hand on him. He took him aside in private, away from the crowd, and put his fingers into his ears, and he spat and touched his tongue. Then looking up to heaven, he sighed and said to him, "Ephphatha," that is, "Be opened." And immediately his ears were opened, his tongue was released, and he spoke plainly. Then Jesus ordered them to tell no one; but the more he ordered them, the more zealously they proclaimed it. They were astounded beyond measure, saying, "He has done everything well; he even makes the deaf to hear and the mute to speak."

Saturday

Psalm 75 [page 691], *Psalm 76* [page 692] ❖
Psalm 23 [page 612], *Psalm 27* [page 617]

A Reading (Lesson) from the Second Book of Samuel [5:22—6:11]

Once again the Philistines came up, and were spread out in the valley of Rephaim. When David inquired of the LORD, he said, "You shall not go up; go around to their rear, and come upon them opposite the balsam trees. When you hear the sound of marching in the tops of the balsam trees, then be on the alert; for then the LORD has gone out before you to strike down the army of the Philistines." David did just as the LORD had commanded him; and he struck down the Philistines from Geba all the way to Gezer. David again gathered all the chosen men of Israel, thirty thousand. David and all the people with him set out and went from Baale-judah, to bring up from there the ark of God, which is called by the name of the LORD of hosts who is enthroned on the cherubim. They carried the ark of God on a new cart, and brought it out of the house of Abinadab, which was on the hill. Uzzah and Ahio, the sons of Abinadab, were driving the new cart with the ark of God; and Ahio went in front of the ark. David and all the house of Israel were dancing before the LORD with all their might, with songs and lyres and harps and tambourines and castanets and cymbals. When they came to the threshing floor of Nacon, Uzzah reached out his hand to the ark of God and took hold of it, for the oxen shook it. The anger of the LORD was kindled against Uzzah; and God struck him there because he reached out his hand to the ark; and he died there beside the ark of God. David was angry because the LORD had burst forth with an outburst upon Uzzah; so that place is called Perez-uzzah, to this day. David was afraid of the LORD that day; he said, "How can the ark of the LORD come into my care?" So David was unwilling to take the ark of the LORD into his care in the city of David; instead David took it to the house of Obed-edom the Gittite. The ark of the LORD remained in the house of Obed-edom the Gittite three months; and the LORD blessed Obed-edom and all his household.

A Reading (Lesson) from the Acts of the Apostles [17:16–34]

While Paul was waiting for Silas and Timothy at Athens, he was deeply distressed to see that the city was full of idols. So he argued in the synagogue with the Jews and the devout persons, and also in the marketplace every day with those who happened to be there. Also some Epicurean and Stoic philosophers debated with him. Some said, "What does this babbler want to say?" Others said, "He seems to be a proclaimer of foreign divinities." (This was because he was telling the good news about Jesus and the resurrection.) So they took him and brought him to the Areopagus and asked him, "May we know what this new teaching is that you are presenting? It sounds rather strange to us, so we would like to know what it means." Now all the Athenians and the foreigners living there would spend their time in nothing but telling or hearing something new. Then Paul stood in front of the Areopagus and said, "Athenians, I see how extremely religious you are in every way. For as I went through the city and looked carefully at the objects of your worship, I found among them an altar with the inscription, 'To an unknown god.' What therefore you worship as unknown, this I proclaim to you. The God who made the world and everything in it, he who is Lord of heaven and earth, does not live in shrines made by human hands, nor is he served by human hands, as though he needed anything, since he himself gives to all mortals life and breath and all things. From one ancestor he made all nations to inhabit the whole earth, and he allotted the times of their existence and the boundaries of the places where they would live, so that they would search for God and perhaps grope for him and find him—though indeed he is not far from each one of us. For 'In him we live and move and have our being';

as even some of your own poets have said, 'For we too are his offspring.' Since we are God's offspring, we ought not to think that the deity is like gold, or silver, or stone, an image formed by the art and imagination of mortals. While God has overlooked the times of human ignorance, now he commands all people everywhere to repent, because he has fixed a day on which he will have the world judged in righteousness by a man whom he has appointed, and of this he has given assurance to all by raising him from the dead." When they heard of the resurrection of the dead, some scoffed; but others said, "We will hear you again about this." At that point Paul left them. But some of them joined him and became believers, including Dionysius the Areopagite and a woman named Damaris, and others with them.

A Reading (Lesson) from the Gospel according to Mark [8:1–10]

In those days when there was again a great crowd without anything to eat, Jesus called his disciples and said to them, "I have compassion for the crowd, because they have been with me now for three days and have nothing to eat. If I send them away hungry to their homes, they will faint on the way—and some of them have come from a great distance." His disciples replied, "How can one feed these people with bread here in the desert?" He asked them, "How many loaves do you have?" They said, "Seven." Then he ordered the crowd to sit down on the ground; and he took the seven loaves, and after giving thanks he broke them and gave them to his disciples to distribute; and they distributed them to the crowd. They had also a few small fish; and after blessing them, he ordered that these too should be distributed. They ate and were filled; and they took up the broken pieces left over, seven baskets full. Now there were about four thousand people. And he sent them away. And immediately he got into the boat with his disciples and went to the district of Dalmanutha.

Proper 13   *Week of the Sunday closest to August 3*

Sunday

Psalm 93 [page 722],   *Psalm 96* [page 725] ❖
Psalm 34 [page 627]

A Reading (Lesson) from the Second Book of Samuel
[6:12–23]

It was told King David, "The LORD has blessed the household of Obed-edom and all that belongs to him, because of the ark of God." So David went and brought up the ark of God from the house of Obed-edom to the city of David with rejoicing; and when those who bore the ark of the LORD had gone six paces, he sacrificed an ox and a fatling. David danced before the LORD with all his might; David was girded with a linen ephod. So David and all the house of Israel brought up the ark of the LORD with shouting, and with the sound of the trumpet. As the ark of the LORD came into the city of David, Michal daughter of Saul looked out of the window, and saw King David leaping and dancing before the LORD; and she despised him in her heart. They brought in the ark of the LORD, and set it in its place, inside the tent that David had pitched for it; and David offered burnt offerings and offerings of well-being before the LORD. When David had finished offering the burnt offerings and the offerings of well-being, he blessed the people in the name of the Lord of hosts, and distributed food among all the people, the whole multitude of Israel, both men and women, to each a cake of bread, a portion of meat, and a cake of raisins. Then all the people went back to their homes. David returned to bless his household. But Michal the daughter of Saul came out to meet David, and said, "How the king of Israel honored himself today, uncovering himself today before the eyes of his servants' maids, as any vulgar fellow might shamelessly uncover himself!" David said to Michal, "It was before the Lord, who chose me in place of your father and all his household, to appoint me as prince over Israel, the people of the Lord, that I have danced before the Lord. I will make myself yet more contemptible than this, and I will be abased in my own eyes; but by the maids of whom you have spoken, by them I shall be held in honor." And Michal the daughter of Saul had no child to the day of her death.

A Reading (Lesson) from the Letter of Paul to the Romans [14:7–12]

We do not live to ourselves, and we do not die to ourselves. If we live, we live to the Lord, and if we die, we die to the Lord; so then, whether we live or whether we die, we are the Lord's. For to this end Christ died and lived again, so that he might be Lord of both the dead and the living. Why do you pass judgment on your brother or sister? Or you, why do you despise your brother or sister? For we will all stand before the judgment seat of God. For it is written, "As I live, says the Lord, every knee shall bow to me, and every tongue shall give praise to God." So then, each of us will be accountable to God.

A Reading (Lesson) from the Gospel according to John
[1:43–51]

The next day Jesus decided to go to Galilee. He found
Philip and said to him, "Follow me." Now Philip was
from Bethsaida, the city of Andrew and Peter. Philip found
Nathanael and said to him, "We have found him about
whom Moses in the law and also the prophets wrote,
Jesus son of Joseph from Nazareth." Nathanael said to
him, "Can anything good come out of Nazareth?" Philip
said to him, "Come and see." When Jesus saw Nathanael
coming toward him, he said of him, "Here is truly an
Israelite in whom there is no deceit!" Nathanael asked
him, "Where did you get to know me?" Jesus answered,
"I saw you under the fig tree before Philip called you."
Nathanael replied, "Rabbi, you are the Son of God! You
are the King of Israel!" Jesus answered, "Do you believe
because I told you that I saw you under the fig tree? You
will see greater things than these." And he said to him,
"Very truly, I tell you, you will see heaven opened and
the angels of God ascending and descending upon the Son
of Man."

Monday

Psalm 80 [page 702] ❖ *Psalm 77* [page 693],
(Psalm 79 [page 701])

A Reading (Lesson) from the Second Book of Samuel
[7:1–17]

When the king was settled in his house, and the LORD had
given him rest from all his enemies around him, the king
said to the prophet Nathan, "See now, I am living in a house
of cedar, but the ark of God stays in a tent." Nathan said to

the king, "Go, do all that you have in mind; for the LORD is with you." But that same night the word of the LORD came to Nathan: Go and tell my servant David: Thus says the LORD: Are you the one to build me a house to live in? I have not lived in a house since the day I brought up the people of Israel from Egypt to this day, but I have been moving about in a tent and a tabernacle. Wherever I have moved about among all the people of Israel, did I ever speak a word with any of the tribal leaders of Israel, whom I commanded to shepherd my people Israel, saying, "Why have you not built me a house of cedar?" Now therefore thus you shall say to my servant David: Thus says the LORD of hosts: I took you from the pasture, from following the sheep to be prince over my people Israel; and I have been with you wherever you went, and have cut off all your enemies from before you; and I will make for you a great name, like the name of the great ones of the earth. And I will appoint a place for my people Israel and will plant them, so that they may live in their own place, and be disturbed no more; and evildoers shall afflict them no more, as formerly, from the time that I appointed judges over my people Israel; and I will give you rest from all your enemies. Moreover the LORD declares to you that the LORD will make you a house. When your days are fulfilled and you lie down with your ancestors, I will raise up your offspring after you, who shall come forth from your body, and I will establish his kingdom. He shall build a house for my name, and I will establish the throne of his kingdom forever. I will be a father to him, and he shall be a son to me. When he commits iniquity, I will punish him with a rod such as mortals use, with blows inflicted by human beings. But I will not take my steadfast love from him, as I took it from Saul, whom I put away from before you. Your house and your kingdom shall be made sure forever before me; your throne shall be established forever. In accordance with all these words and with all this vision, Nathan spoke to David.

A Reading (Lesson) from the Acts of the Apostles [18:1–11]

Paul left Athens and went to Corinth. There he found a Jew named Aquila, a native of Pontus, who had recently come from Italy with his wife Priscilla, because Claudius had ordered all Jews to leave Rome. Paul went to see them, and, because he was of the same trade, he stayed with them, and they worked together—by trade they were tentmakers. Every sabbath he would argue in the synagogue and would try to convince Jews and Greeks. When Silas and Timothy arrived from Macedonia, Paul was occupied with proclaiming the word, testifying to the Jews that the Messiah was Jesus. When they opposed and reviled him, in protest he shook the dust from his clothes and said to them, "Your blood be on your own heads! I am innocent. From now on I will go to the Gentiles." Then he left the synagogue and went to the house of a man named Titius Justus, a worshiper of God; his house was next door to the synagogue. Crispus, the official of the synagogue, became a believer in the Lord, together with all his household; and many of the Corinthians who heard Paul became believers and were baptized. One night the Lord said to Paul in a vision, "Do not be afraid, but speak and do not be silent; for I am with you, and no one will lay a hand on you to harm you, for there are many in this city who are my people." He stayed there a year and six months, teaching the word of God among them.

A Reading (Lesson) from the Gospel according to Mark
[8:11–21]

The Pharisees came and began to argue with Jesus, asking
him for a sign from heaven, to test him. And he sighed
deeply in his spirit and said, "Why does this generation
ask for a sign? Truly I tell you, no sign will be given to
this generation." And he left them, and getting into the
boat again, he went across to the other side. Now the
disciples had forgotten to bring any bread; and they had
only one loaf with them in the boat. And he cautioned
them, saying, "Watch out—beware of the yeast of the
Pharisees and the yeast of Herod." They said to one
another, "It is because we have no bread." And becoming
aware of it, Jesus said to them, "Why are you talking
about having no bread? Do you still not perceive or
understand? Are your hearts hardened? Do you have eyes,
and fail to see? Do you have ears, and fail to hear? And
do you not remember? When I broke the five loaves for
the five thousand, how many baskets full of broken pieces
did you collect?" They said to him, "Twelve." "And the
seven for the four thousand, how many baskets full of
broken pieces did you collect?" And they said to him,
"Seven." Then he said to them, "Do you not yet
understand?"

Tuesday

Psalm 78:1–39 [page 694] ❖ *Psalm 78:40–72* [page 698]

A Reading (Lesson) from the Second Book of Samuel
[7:18–29]

King David went in and sat before the LORD, and said,
"Who am I, O Lord GOD, and what is my house, that you

have brought me thus far? And yet this was a small thing in your eyes, O Lord GOD; you have spoken also of your servant's house for a great while to come. May this be instruction for the people, O Lord GOD! And what more can David say to you? For you know your servant, O Lord GOD! Because of your promise, and according to your own heart, you have wrought all this greatness, so that your servant may know it. Therefore you are great, O LORD God; for there is no one like you, and there is no God besides you, according to all that we have heard with our ears. Who is like your people, like Israel? Is there another nation on earth whose God went to redeem it as a people, and to make a name for himself, doing great and awesome things for them, by driving out before his people nations and their gods? And you established your people Israel for yourself to be your people forever; and you, O LORD, became their God. And now, O LORD God, as for the word that you have spoken concerning your servant and concerning his house, confirm it forever; do as you have promised. Thus your name will be magnified forever in the saying, 'The LORD of hosts is God over Israel'; and the house of your servant David will be established before you. For you, O LORD of hosts, the God of Israel, have made this revelation to your servant, saying, 'I will build you a house'; therefore your servant has found courage to pray this prayer to you. And now, O Lord GOD, you are God, and your words are true, and you have promised this good thing to your servant; now therefore may it please you to bless the house of your servant, so that it may continue forever before you; for you, O Lord GOD, have spoken, and with your blessing shall the house of your servant be blessed forever."

A Reading (Lesson) from the Acts of the Apostles [18:12–28]

When Gallio was proconsul of Achaia, the Jews made a united attack on Paul and brought him before the tribunal. They said, "This man is persuading people to worship God in ways that are contrary to the law." Just as Paul was about to speak, Gallio said to the Jews, "If it were a matter of crime or serious villainy, I would be justified in accepting the complaint of you Jews; but since it is a matter of questions about words and names and your own law, see to it yourselves; I do not wish to be a judge of these matters." And he dismissed them from the tribunal. Then all of them seized Sosthenes, the official of the synagogue, and beat him in front of the tribunal. But Gallio paid no attention to any of these things. After staying there for a considerable time, Paul said farewell to the believers and sailed for Syria, accompanied by Priscilla and Aquila. At Cenchreae he had his hair cut, for he was under a vow. When they reached Ephesus, he left them there, but first he himself went into the synagogue and had a discussion with the Jews. When they asked him to stay longer, he declined; but on taking leave of them, he said, "I will return to you, if God wills." Then he set sail from Ephesus. When he had landed at Caesarea, he went up to Jerusalem and greeted the church, and then went down to Antioch. After spending some time there he departed and went from place to place through the region of Galatia and Phrygia, strengthening all the disciples. Now there came to Ephesus a Jew named Apollos, a native of Alexandria. He was an eloquent man, well-versed in the scriptures. He had been instructed in the Way of the Lord; and he spoke with burning enthusiasm and taught accurately the things concerning Jesus, though he knew only the baptism of John. He began to speak boldly in the synagogue; but when Priscilla and Aquila heard him, they took him aside and explained the Way of God to him more accurately. And when he wished to cross over to Achaia, the believers encouraged him and wrote to the disciples to welcome him. On his arrival he greatly helped those who through grace had become believers, for he powerfully refuted the Jews in public, showing by the scriptures that the Messiah is Jesus.

A Reading (Lesson) from the Gospel according to Mark [8:22–33]

Jesus and the disciples came to Bethsaida. Some people brought a blind man to him and begged him to touch him. He took the blind man by the hand and led him out of the village; and when he had put saliva on his eyes and laid his hands on him, he asked him, "Can you see anything?" And the man looked up and said, "I can see people, but they look like trees, walking." Then Jesus laid his hands on his eyes again; and he looked intently and his sight was restored, and he saw everything clearly. Then he sent him away to his home, saying, "Do not even go into the village." Jesus went on with his disciples to the villages of Caesarea Philippi; and on the way he asked his disciples, "Who do people say that I am?" And they answered him, "John the Baptist; and others, Elijah; and still others, one of the prophets." He asked them, "But who do you say that I am?" Peter answered him, "You are the Messiah." And he sternly ordered them not to tell anyone about him. Then he began to teach them that the Son of Man must undergo great suffering, and be rejected by the elders, the chief priests, and the scribes, and be killed, and after three days rise again. He said all this quite openly. And Peter took him aside and began to rebuke him. But turning and looking at his disciples, he rebuked Peter and said, "Get behind me, Satan! For you are setting your mind not on divine things but on human things."

Wednesday

Psalm 119:97–120 [page 771] ❖ *Psalm 81* [page 704], *Psalm 82* [page 705]

A Reading (Lesson) from the Second Book of Samuel [9:1–13]

David asked, "Is there still anyone left of the house of Saul to whom I may show kindness for Jonathan's sake?" Now there was a servant of the house of Saul whose name was Ziba, and he was summoned to David. The king said to him, "Are you Ziba?" And he said, "At your service!" The king said, "Is there anyone remaining of the house of Saul to whom I may show the kindness of God?" Ziba said to the king, "There remains a son of Jonathan; he is crippled in his feet." The king said to him, "Where is he?" Ziba said to the king, "He is in the house of Machir son of Ammiel, at Lo-debar." Then King David sent and brought him from the house of Machir son of Ammiel, at Lo-debar. Mephibosheth son of Jonathan son of Saul came to David, and fell on his face and did obeisance. David said, "Mephibosheth!" He answered, "I am your servant." David said to him, "Do not be afraid, for I will show you kindness for the sake of your father Jonathan; I will restore to you all the land of your grandfather Saul, and you yourself shall eat at my table always." He did obeisance and said, "What is your servant, that you should look upon a dead dog such as I?" Then the king summoned Saul's servant Ziba, and said to him, "All that belonged to Saul and to all his house I have given to your master's grandson. You and your sons and your servants shall till the land for him, and shall bring in the produce, so that your master's grandson may have food to eat; but your master's grandson Mephibosheth shall always eat at my table." Now Ziba had fifteen sons and twenty servants. Then Ziba said to the king, "According to all that my lord the king commands his servant, so your servant will do." Mephibosheth ate at David's table, like one of the king's sons. Mephibosheth had a young son whose name was Mica. And all who lived in Ziba's house became Mephibosheth's servants. Mephibosheth lived in Jerusalem, for he always ate at the king's table. Now he was lame in both his feet.

A Reading (Lesson) from the Acts of the Apostles [19:1–10]

While Apollos was in Corinth, Paul passed through the interior regions and came to Ephesus, where he found some disciples. He said to them, "Did you receive the Holy Spirit when you became believers?" They replied, "No, we have not even heard that there is a Holy Spirit." Then he said, "Into what then were you baptized?" They answered, "Into John's baptism." Paul said, "John baptized with the baptism of repentance, telling the people to believe in the one who was to come after him, that is, in Jesus." On hearing this, they were baptized in the name of the Lord Jesus. When Paul had laid his hands on them, the Holy Spirit came upon them, and they spoke in tongues and prophesied—altogether there were about twelve of them. He entered the synagogue and for three months spoke out boldly, and argued persuasively about the kingdom of God. When some stubbornly refused to believe and spoke evil of the Way before the congregation, he left them, taking the disciples with him, and argued daily in the lecture hall of Tyrannus. This continued for two years, so that all the residents of Asia, both Jews and Greeks, heard the word of the Lord.

A Reading (Lesson) from the Gospel according to Mark [8:34—9:1]

Jesus called the crowd with his disciples, and said to them, "If any want to become my followers, let them deny themselves and take up their cross and follow me. For those who want to save their life will lose it, and those who lose their life for my sake, and for the sake of the gospel, will save it. For what will it profit them to gain the whole world and forfeit their life? Indeed, what can they give in return for their life? Those who are ashamed of me and of my words in this adulterous and sinful generation, of them the Son of Man will also be ashamed when he comes in the glory of his Father with the holy angels." And he said to them, "Truly I tell you, there are some standing here who will not taste death until they see that the kingdom of God has come with power."

Thursday

(*Psalm 83* [page 706]) or *Psalm 145* [page 801] ❖
Psalm 85 [page 708], *Psalm 86* [page 709]

A Reading (Lesson) from the Second Book of Samuel [11:1–27]

In the spring of the year, the time when kings go out to battle, David sent Joab with his officers and all Israel with him; they ravaged the Ammonites, and besieged Rabbah. But David remained at Jerusalem. It happened, late one afternoon, when David rose from his couch and was walking about on the roof of the king's house, that he saw from the roof a woman bathing; the woman was very beautiful. David sent someone to inquire about the woman. It was reported, "This is Bathsheba daughter of Eliam, the wife of Uriah the Hittite." So David sent messengers to get her, and she came to him, and he lay with her. (Now she was purifying herself after her period.) Then she returned to her house. The woman conceived; and she sent and told David, "I am pregnant." So David sent word to Joab, "Send me Uriah the Hittite." And Joab sent Uriah to David. When Uriah came to him, David asked how Joab and the people fared, and how the war was going. Then David said to Uriah, "Go down to your house, and wash your feet." Uriah went out of the king's house, and there followed him a present from the king. But Uriah slept at the entrance of the king's house with all the servants of his lord, and did not go down to his house. When they told David, "Uriah did not go down to his house," David said to Uriah, "You have just come from a journey. Why did you not go down to your house?" Uriah said to David, "The ark and Israel and Judah remain in booths; and my lord Joab and the servants of my lord are camping in the open field; shall I then go to my house, to eat and to drink, and to lie with my wife? As you live, and as your soul lives, I will not do such a thing." Then David said to Uriah, "Remain here today also, and tomorrow I will send you back." So Uriah remained in Jerusalem that day. On the next day, David invited him to eat and drink in his presence and made him drunk; and in the evening he went out to lie on his couch with the servants of his lord, but he did not go down to his house. In the morning David wrote a letter to Joab, and sent it by the hand of Uriah. In the letter he wrote, "Set Uriah in the forefront of the hardest fighting, and then draw back from him, so that he may be struck down and die." As Joab was besieging the city, he assigned Uriah to the place where he knew there were valiant warriors. The men of the city came out and fought with Joab; and some of the servants of David among the people fell. Uriah the Hittite was killed as well. Then Joab sent and told David all the news about the fighting; and he instructed the messenger, "When you have finished telling the king all the news about the fighting, then, if the king's anger rises, and if he says to you, 'Why did you go so near the city to fight? Did you not know that they would shoot from the wall? Who killed Abimelech son of Jerubbaal? Did not a woman throw an upper millstone on him from the wall, so that he died at Thebez? Why did you go so near the wall?' then you shall say, 'Your servant Uriah the Hittite is dead too.' " So the messenger went, and came and told David all that Joab had sent him to tell. The messenger said to David, "The men gained an advantage over us, and came out against us in the field; but we drove them back to the entrance of the gate. Then the archers shot at your servants from the wall; some of the king's servants are dead; and your servant Uriah the Hittite is dead also." David said to the messenger, "Thus you shall say to Joab, 'Do not let this matter trouble you, for the sword devours now one and now another; press your attack on the city, and overthrow it.' And encourage him." When the wife of Uriah heard that her husband was dead, she made lamentation for him. When the mourning was over, David sent and brought her to his house, and she became his wife, and bore him a son.

A Reading (Lesson) from the Acts of the Apostles [19:11–20]

God did extraordinary miracles through Paul, so that when the handkerchiefs or aprons that had touched his skin were brought to the sick, their diseases left them, and the evil spirits came out of them. Then some itinerant Jewish exorcists tried to use the name of the Lord Jesus over those who had evil spirits, saying, "I adjure you by the Jesus whom Paul proclaims." Seven sons of a Jewish high priest named Sceva were doing this. But the evil spirit said to them in reply, "Jesus I know, and Paul I know; but who are you?" Then the man with the evil spirit leaped on them, mastered them all, and so overpowered them that they fled out of the house naked and wounded. When this became known to all residents of Ephesus, both Jews and Greeks, everyone was awestruck; and the name of the Lord Jesus was praised. Also many of those who became believers confessed and disclosed their practices. A number of those who practiced magic collected their books and burned them publicly; when the value of these books was calculated, it was found to come to fifty thousand silver coins. So the word of the Lord grew mightily and prevailed.

A Reading (Lesson) from the Gospel according to Mark [9:2–13]

Six days later, Jesus took with him Peter and James and John, and led them up a high mountain apart, by themselves. And he was transfigured before them, and his clothes became dazzling white, such as no one on earth could bleach them. And there appeared to them Elijah with Moses, who were talking with Jesus. Then Peter said to Jesus, "Rabbi, it is good for us to be here; let us make three dwellings, one for you, one for Moses, and one for Elijah." He did not know what to say, for they were terrified. Then a cloud overshadowed them, and from the cloud there came a voice, "This is my Son, the Beloved; listen to him!" Suddenly when they looked around, they saw no one with them any more, but only Jesus. As they were coming down the mountain, he ordered them to tell no one about what they had seen, until after the Son of Man had risen from the dead. So they kept the matter to themselves, questioning what this rising from the dead could mean. Then they asked him, "Why do the scribes say that Elijah must come first?" He said to them, "Elijah is indeed coming first to restore all things. How then is it written about the Son of Man, that he is to go through many sufferings and be treated with contempt? But I tell you that Elijah has come, and they did to him whatever they pleased, as it is written about him."

Friday

Psalm 88 [page 712] ❖ *Psalm 91* [page 719],
Psalm 92 [page 720]

A Reading (Lesson) from the Second Book of Samuel
[12:1–14]

The LORD sent Nathan to David. He came to him, and said to him, "There were two men in a certain city, the one rich and the other poor. The rich man had very many flocks and herds; but the poor man had nothing but one little ewe lamb, which he had bought. He brought it up, and it grew up with him and with his children; it used to eat of his meager fare, and drink from his cup, and lie in his bosom, and it was like a daughter to him. Now there came a traveler to the rich man, and he was loath to take one of his own flock or herd to prepare for the wayfarer who had come to him, but he took the poor man's lamb, and prepared that for the guest who had come to him." Then David's anger was greatly kindled against the man. He said to Nathan, "As the LORD lives, the man who has done this deserves to die; he shall restore the lamb fourfold, because he did this thing, and because he had no pity." Nathan said to David, "You are the man! Thus says the LORD, the God of Israel: I anointed you king over Israel, and I rescued you from the hand of Saul; I gave you your master's house, and your master's wives into your bosom, and gave you the house of Israel and of Judah; and if that had been too little, I would have added as much more. Why have you despised the word of the LORD, to do what is evil in his sight? You have struck down Uriah the Hittite with the sword, and have taken his wife to be your wife, and have killed him with the sword of the Ammonites. Now therefore the sword shall never depart from your house, for you have despised me, and have taken the wife of Uriah the Hittite to be your wife. Thus says the LORD: I will raise up trouble against you from within your own house; and I will take your wives before your eyes, and give them to your neighbor, and he shall lie with your wives in the sight of this very sun. For you did it secretly; but I will do this thing before all Israel, and before the sun." David said to Nathan, "I have sinned against the LORD." Nathan said to David, "Now the LORD has put away your sin; you shall not die. Nevertheless, because by this deed you have utterly scorned the LORD, the child that is born to you shall die."

A Reading (Lesson) from the Acts of the Apostles [19:21–41]

After these things had been accomplished, Paul resolved in the Spirit to go through Macedonia and Achaia, and then to go on to Jerusalem. He said, "After I have gone there, I must also see Rome." So he sent two of his helpers, Timothy and Erastus, to Macedonia, while he himself stayed for some time longer in Asia. About that time no little disturbance broke out concerning the Way. A man named Demetrius, a silversmith who made silver shrines of Artemis, brought no little business to the artisans. These he gathered together, with the workers of the same trade, and said, "Men, you know that we get our wealth from this business. You also see and hear that not only in Ephesus but in almost the whole of Asia this Paul has persuaded and drawn away a considerable number of people by saying that gods made with hands are not gods. And there is danger not only that this trade of ours may come into disrepute but also that the temple of the great goddess Artemis will be scorned, and she will be deprived of her majesty that brought all Asia and the world to worship her." When they heard this, they were enraged and shouted, "Great is Artemis of the Ephesians!" The city was filled with the confusion; and people rushed together to the theater, dragging with them Gaius and Aristarchus, Macedonians who were Paul's travel companions. Paul wished to go into the crowd, but the disciples would not let him; even some officials of the province of Asia, who were friendly to him, sent him a message urging him not to venture into the theater. Meanwhile, some were shouting one thing, some another; for the assembly was in confusion, and most of them did not know why they had come together. Some of the crowd gave instructions to Alexander, whom the Jews had pushed forward. And Alexander motioned for silence and tried to make a defense before the people. But when they recognized that he was a Jew, for about two hours all of them shouted in unison, "Great is Artemis of the Ephesians!" But when the town clerk had quieted the crowd, he said, "Citizens of Ephesus, who is there that does not know that the city of the Ephesians is the temple keeper of the great Artemis and of the statue that fell from heaven? Since these things cannot be denied, you ought to be quiet and do nothing rash. You have brought these men here who are neither temple robbers nor blasphemers of our goddess. If therefore Demetrius and the artisans with him have a complaint against anyone, the courts are open, and there are proconsuls; let them bring charges there against one another. If there is anything further you want to know, it must be settled in the regular assembly. For we are in danger of being charged with rioting today, since there is no cause that we can give to justify this commotion." When he had said this, he dismissed the assembly.

A Reading (Lesson) from the Gospel according to Mark [9:14-29]

When Jesus, with Peter and James and John, came to the disciples, they saw a great crowd around them, and some scribes arguing with them. When the whole crowd saw him, they were immediately overcome with awe, and they ran forward to greet him. He asked them, "What are you arguing about with them?" Someone from the crowd answered him, "Teacher, I brought you my son; he has a spirit that makes him unable to speak; and whenever it seizes him, it dashes him down; and he foams and grinds his teeth and becomes rigid; and I asked your disciples to cast it out, but they could not do so." He answered them, "You faithless generation, how much longer must I be among you? How much longer must I put up with you? Bring him to me." And they brought the boy to him. When the spirit saw him, immediately it convulsed the boy, and he fell on the ground and rolled about, foaming at the mouth. Jesus asked the father, "How long has this been happening to him?" And he said, "From childhood.

It has often cast him into the fire and into the water, to destroy him; but if you are able to do anything, have pity on us and help us." Jesus said to him, "If you are able!—All things can be done for the one who believes." Immediately the father of the child cried out, "I believe; help my unbelief!" When Jesus saw that a crowd came running together, he rebuked the unclean spirit, saying to it, "You spirit that keeps this boy from speaking and hearing, I command you, come out of him, and never enter him again!" After crying out and convulsing him terribly, it came out, and the boy was like a corpse, so that most of them said, "He is dead." But Jesus took him by the hand and lifted him up, and he was able to stand. When he had entered the house, his disciples asked him privately, "Why could we not cast it out?" He said to them, "This kind can come out only through prayer."

Saturday

Psalm 87 [page 711],   *Psalm 90* [page 717]   ❖
Psalm 136 [page 789]

A Reading (Lesson) from the Second Book of Samuel [12:15–31]

Nathan went to his house. The LORD struck the child that Uriah's wife bore to David, and it became very ill. David therefore pleaded with God for the child; David fasted, and went in and lay all night on the ground. The elders of his house stood beside him, urging him to rise from the ground; but he would not, nor did he eat food with them. On the seventh day the child died. And the servants of David were afraid to tell him that the child was dead; for they said, "While the child was still alive, we spoke to him, and he did not listen to us; how then can we tell him the child is dead?

He may do himself some harm." But when David saw that his servants were whispering together, he perceived that the child was dead; and David said to his servants, "Is the child dead?" They said, "He is dead." Then David rose from the ground, washed, anointed himself, and changed his clothes. He went into the house of the LORD, and worshiped; he then went to his own house; and when he asked, they set food before him and he ate. Then his servants said to him, "What is this thing that you have done? You fasted and wept for the child while it was alive; but when the child died, you rose and ate food." He said, "While the child was still alive, I fasted and wept; for I said, 'Who knows? The LORD may be gracious to me, and the child may live.' But now he is dead; why should I fast? Can I bring him back again? I shall go to him, but he will not return to me." Then David consoled his wife Bathsheba, and went to her, and lay with her; and she bore a son, and he named him Solomon. The LORD loved him, and sent a message by the prophet Nathan; so he named him Jedidiah, because of the LORD. Now Joab fought against Rabbah of the Ammonites, and took the royal city. Joab sent messengers to David, and said, "I have fought against Rabbah; moreover, I have taken the water city. Now, then, gather the rest of the people together, and encamp against the city, and take it; or I myself will take the city, and it will be called by my name." So David gathered all the people together and went to Rabbah, and fought against it and took it. He took the crown of Milcom from his head; the weight of it was a talent of gold, and in it was a precious stone; and it was placed on David's head. He also brought forth the spoil of the city, a very great amount. He brought out the people who were in it, and set them to work with saws and iron picks and iron axes, or sent them to the brickworks. Thus he did to all the cities of the Ammonites. Then David and all the people returned to Jerusalem.

A Reading (Lesson) from the Acts of the Apostles [20:1–16]

After the uproar had ceased, Paul sent for the disciples; and after encouraging them and saying farewell, he left for Macedonia. When he had gone through those regions and had given the believers much encouragement, he came to Greece, where he stayed for three months. He was about to set sail for Syria when a plot was made against him by the Jews, and so he decided to return through Macedonia. He was accompanied by Sopater son of Pyrrhus from Beroea, by Aristarchus and Secundus from Thessalonica, by Gaius from Derbe, and by Timothy, as well as by Tychicus and Trophimus from Asia. They went ahead and were waiting for us in Troas; but we sailed from Philippi after the days of Unleavened Bread, and in five days we joined them in Troas, where we stayed for seven days. On the first day of the week, when we met to break bread, Paul was holding a discussion with them; since he intended to leave the next day, he continued speaking until midnight. There were many lamps in the room upstairs where we were meeting. A young man named Eutychus, who was sitting in the window, began to sink off into a deep sleep while Paul talked still longer. Overcome by sleep, he fell to the ground three floors below and was picked up dead. But Paul went down, and bending over him took him in his arms, and said, "Do not be alarmed, for his life is in him." Then Paul went upstairs, and after he had broken bread and eaten, he continued to converse with them until dawn; then he left. Meanwhile they had taken the boy away alive and were not a little comforted. We went ahead to the ship and set sail for Assos, intending to take Paul on board there; for he had made this arrangement, intending to go by land himself. When he met us in Assos, we took him on board and went to Mitylene. We sailed from there, and on the following day we arrived opposite Chios. The next day we touched at Samos, and the day after that we came to Miletus. For Paul had decided to sail past Ephesus, so that he might not have to spend time in Asia, he was eager to be in Jerusalem, if possible, on the day of Pentecost.

A Reading (Lesson) from the Gospel according to Mark
[9:30–41]

Jesus and the disciples went on from there and passed through Galilee. He did not want anyone to know it; for he was teaching his disciples, saying to them, "The Son of Man is to be betrayed into human hands, and they will kill him, and three days after being killed, he will rise again." But they did not understand what he was saying and were afraid to ask him. Then they came to Capernaum; and when he was in the house he asked them, "What were you arguing about on the way?" But they were silent, for on the way they had argued with one another who was the greatest. He sat down, called the twelve, and said to them, "Whoever wants to be first must be last of all and servant of all." Then he took a little child and put it among them; and taking it in his arms, he said to them, "Whoever welcomes one such child in my name welcomes me, and whoever welcomes me welcomes not me but the one who sent me." John said to him, "Teacher, we saw someone casting out demons in your name, and we tried to stop him, because he was not following us." But Jesus said, "Do not stop him; for no one who does a deed of power in my name will be able soon afterward to speak evil of me. Whoever is not against us is for us. For truly I tell you, whoever gives you a cup of water to drink because you bear the name of Christ will by no means lose the reward."

Proper 14   *Week of the Sunday closest to August 10*

Sunday

Psalm 66 [page 673],   *Psalm 67* [page 675]   ❖
Psalm 19 [page 606],   *Psalm 46* [page 649]

A Reading (Lesson) from the Second Book of Samuel
[13:1–22]

David's son Absalom had a beautiful sister whose name was
Tamar; and David's son Amnon fell in love with her.
Amnon was so tormented that he made himself ill because
of his sister Tamar, for she was a virgin and it seemed
impossible to Amnon to do anything to her. But Amnon had
a friend whose name was Jonadab, the son of David's
brother Shimeah; and Jonadab was a very crafty man. He
said to him, "O son of the king, why are you so haggard
morning after morning? Will you not tell me?" Amnon said
to him, "I love Tamar, my brother Absalom's sister."
Jonadab said to him, "Lie down on your bed, and pretend
to be ill; and when your father comes to see you, say to him,
'Let my sister Tamar come and give me something to eat,
and prepare the food in my sight, so that I may see it and eat
it from her hand.' " So Amnon lay down, and pretended to
be ill; and when the king came to see him, Amnon said to
the king, "Please let my sister Tamar come and make a
couple of cakes in my sight, so that I may eat from her
hand." Then David sent home to Tamar, saying, "Go to
your brother Amnon's house, and prepare food for him." So
Tamar went to her brother Amnon's house, where he was
lying down. She took dough, kneaded it, made cakes in his
sight, and baked the cakes. Then she took the pan and set
them out before him, but he refused to eat. Amnon said,
"Send out everyone from me." So everyone went out from

him. Then Amnon said to Tamar, "Bring the food into the chamber, so that I may eat from your hand." So Tamar took the cakes she had made, and brought them into the chamber to Amnon her brother. But when she brought them near him to eat, he took hold of her, and said to her, "Come, lie with me, my sister." She answered him, "No, my brother, do not force me; for such a thing is not done in Israel; do not do anything so vile! As for me, where could I carry my shame? And as for you, you would be as one of the scoundrels in Israel. Now therefore, I beg you, speak to the king; for he will not withhold me from you." But he would not listen to her; and being stronger than she, he forced her and lay with her. Then Amnon was seized with a very great loathing for her; indeed, his loathing was even greater than the lust he had felt for her. Amnon said to her, "Get out!" But she said to him, "No, my brother; for this wrong in sending me away is greater than the other that you did to me." But he would not listen to her. He called the young man who served him and said, "Put this woman out of my presence, and bolt the door after her." (Now she was wearing a long robe with sleeves; for this is how the virgin daughters of the king were clothed in earlier times.) So his servant put her out, and bolted the door after her. But Tamar put ashes on her head, and tore the long robe that she was wearing; she put her hand on her head, and went away, crying aloud as she went. Her brother Absalom said to her, "Has Amnon your brother been with you? Be quiet for now, my sister; he is your brother; do not take this to heart." So Tamar remained, a desolate woman, in her brother Absalom's house. When King David heard of all these things, he became very angry, but he would not punish his son Amnon, because he loved him, for he was his firstborn. But Absalom spoke to Amnon neither good nor bad; for Absalom hated Amnon, because he had raped his sister Tamar.

A Reading (Lesson) from the Letter of Paul to the Romans
[15:1–13]

We who are strong ought to put up with the failings of
the weak, and not to please ourselves. Each of us must
please our neighbor for the good purpose of building up
the neighbor. For Christ did not please himself; but, as it
is written, "The insults of those who insult you have fallen
on me." For whatever was written in former days was
written for our instruction, so that by steadfastness and by
the encouragement of the scriptures we might have hope.
May the God of steadfastness and encouragement grant
you to live in harmony with one another, in accordance
with Christ Jesus, so that together you may with one voice
glorify the God and Father of our Lord Jesus Christ.
Welcome one another, therefore, just as Christ has
welcomed you, for the glory of God. For I tell you that
Christ has become a servant of the circumcised on behalf
of the truth of God in order that he might confirm the
promises given to the patriarchs, and in order that the
Gentiles might glorify God for his mercy. As it is written,
"Therefore I will confess you among the Gentiles, and sing
praises to your name"; and again he says, "Rejoice, O
Gentiles, with his people"; and again, "Praise the Lord, all
you Gentiles, and let all the peoples praise him"; and
again Isaiah says, "The root of Jesse shall come, the one
who rises to rule the Gentiles; in him the Gentiles shall
hope." May the God of hope fill you with all joy and
peace in believing, so that you may abound in hope by the
power of the Holy Spirit.

A Reading (Lesson) from the Gospel according to John
[3:22–36]

Jesus and his disciples went into the Judean countryside, and he spent some time there with them and baptized. John also was baptizing at Aenon near Salim because water was abundant there; and people kept coming and were being baptized—John, of course, had not yet been thrown into prison. Now a discussion about purification arose between John's disciples and a Jew. They came to John and said to him, "Rabbi, the one who was with you across the Jordan, to whom you testified, here he is baptizing, and all are going to him." John answered, "No one can receive anything except what has been given from heaven. You yourselves are my witnesses that I said, 'I am not the Messiah, but I have been sent ahead of him.' He who has the bride is the bridegroom. The friend of the bridegroom, who stands and hears him, rejoices greatly at the bridegroom's voice. For this reason my joy has been fulfilled. He must increase, but I must decrease." The one who comes from above is above all; the one who is of the earth belongs to the earth and speaks about earthly things. The one who comes from heaven is above all. He testifies to what he has seen and heard, yet no one accepts his testimony. Whoever has accepted his testimony has certified this, that God is true. He whom God has sent speaks the words of God, for he gives the Spirit without measure. The Father loves the Son and has placed all things in his hands. Whoever believes in the Son has eternal life; whoever disobeys the Son will not see life, but must endure God's wrath.

Monday

Psalm 89:1–18 [page 713] ❖ *Psalm 89:19–52* [page 715]

A Reading (Lesson) from the Second Book of Samuel
[13:23–39]

After two full years Absalom had sheepshearers at
Baal-hazor, which is near Ephraim, and Absalom invited all
the king's sons. Absalom came to the king, and said, "Your
servant has sheepshearers; will the king and his servants
please go with your servant?" But the king said to Absalom,
"No, my son, let us not all go, or else we will be burdensome
to you." He pressed him, but he would not go but gave him
his blessing. Then Absalom said, "If not, please let my
brother Amnon go with us." The king said to him, "Why
should he go with you?" But Absalom pressed him until he
let Amnon and all the king's sons go with him. Absalom
made a feast like a king's feast. Then Absalom commanded
his servants, "Watch when Amnon's heart is merry with
wine, and when I say to you, 'Strike Amnon,' then kill him.
Do not be afraid; have I not myself commanded you? Be
courageous and valiant." So the servants of Absalom did to
Amnon as Absalom had commanded. Then all the king's
sons rose, and each mounted his mule and fled. While they
were on the way, the report came to David that Absalom
had killed all the king's sons, and not one of them was left.
The king rose, tore his garments, and lay on the ground; and
all his servants who were standing by tore their garments.
But Jonadab, the son of David's brother Shimeah, said,
"Let not my lord suppose that they have killed all the young
men the king's sons; Amnon alone is dead. This has been
determined by Absalom from the day Amnon raped his
sister Tamar. Now therefore, do not let my lord the king
take it to heart, as if all the king's sons were dead; for

Amnon alone is dead." But Absalom fled. When the young man who kept watch looked up, he saw many people coming from the Horonaim road by the side of the mountain. Jonadab said to the king, "See, the king's sons have come; as your servant said, so it has come about." As soon as he had finished speaking, the king's sons arrived, and raised their voices and wept; and the king and all his servants also wept very bitterly. But Absalom fled, and went to Talmai son of Ammihud, king of Geshur. David mourned for his son day after day. Absalom, having fled to Geshur, stayed there three years. And the heart of the king went out, yearning for Absalom; for he was now consoled over the death of Amnon.

A Reading (Lesson) from the Acts of the Apostles [20:17–38]

From Miletus Paul sent a message to Ephesus, asking the elders of the church to meet him. When they came to him, he said to them: "You yourselves know how I lived among you the entire time from the first day that I set foot in Asia, serving the Lord with all humility and with tears, enduring the trials that came to me through the plots of the Jews. I did not shrink from doing anything helpful, proclaiming the message to you and teaching you publicly and from house to house, as I testified to both Jews and Greeks about repentance toward God and faith toward our Lord Jesus. And now, as a captive to the Spirit, I am on my way to Jerusalem, not knowing what will happen to me there, except that the Holy Spirit testifies to me in every city that imprisonment and persecutions are waiting for me. But I do not count my life of any value to myself, if only I may finish my course and the ministry that I received from the Lord Jesus, to testify to the good news of God's grace. And now I know that none of you, among whom I have gone about proclaiming the kingdom, will ever see my face again. Therefore I declare to you this day that I am not responsible for the blood of any of you, for I did not shrink from declaring to you the whole purpose of God. Keep watch over yourselves and over all the flock, of which the Holy Spirit has made you overseers, to shepherd the church of God that he obtained with the blood of his own Son. I know that after I have gone, savage wolves will come in among you, not sparing the flock. Some even from your own group will come distorting the truth in order to entice the disciples to follow them. Therefore be alert, remembering that for three years I did not cease night or day to warn everyone with tears. And now I commend you to God and to the message of his grace, a message that is able to build you up and to give you the inheritance among all who are sanctified. I coveted no one's silver or gold or clothing. You know for yourselves that I worked with my own hands to support myself and my companions. In all this I have given you an example that by such work we must support the weak, remembering the words of the Lord Jesus, for he himself said, 'It is more blessed to give than to receive.' " When he had finished speaking, he knelt down with them all and prayed. There was much weeping among them all; they embraced Paul and kissed him, grieving especially because of what he had said, that they would not see him again. Then they brought him to the ship.

A Reading (Lesson) from the Gospel according to Mark [9:42–50]

Jesus said, "If any of you put a stumbling block before one of these little ones who believe in me, it would be better for you if a great millstone were hung around your neck and you were thrown into the sea. If your hand causes you to stumble, cut it off; it is better for you to enter life maimed than to have two hands and to go to hell, to the unquenchable fire. And if your foot causes you to stumble, cut it off; it is better for you to enter life lame than to have two feet and to be thrown into hell. And if your eye causes you to stumble, tear it out; it is better for you to enter the kingdom of God with one eye than to have two eyes and to be thrown into hell, where their worm never dies, and the fire is never quenched. For everyone will be salted with fire. Salt is good; but if salt has lost its saltiness, how can you season it? Have salt in yourselves, and be at peace with one another."

Tuesday

Psalm 97 [page 726], *Psalm 99* [page 728], *(Psalm 100* [page 729]) ❖ *Psalm 94* [page 722], *(Psalm 95* [page 724])

A Reading (Lesson) from the Second Book of Samuel [14:1–20]

Joab son of Zeruiah perceived that the king's mind was on Absalom. Joab sent to Tekoa and brought from there a wise woman. He said to her, "Pretend to be a mourner; put on mourning garments, do not anoint yourself with oil, but behave like a woman who has been mourning many days for the dead. Go to the king and speak to him as follows." And Joab put the words into her mouth. When the woman of Tekoa came to the king, she fell on her face to the ground and did obeisance, and said, "Help, O king!" The king asked her, "What is your trouble?" She answered, "Alas, I am a widow; my husband is dead. Your servant had two sons, and they fought with one another in the field; there was no one to part them, and one struck the other and killed him. Now the whole family has risen against your servant. They say, 'Give up the man who struck his brother, so that we may kill him for the life of his brother whom he murdered, even if we destroy the heir as well.' Thus they would quench my one remaining ember, and leave to my husband neither name nor remnant on the face of the earth." Then the king said to the woman, "Go to your house, and I will give orders concerning you." The woman of Tekoa said to the king, "On me be the guilt, my lord the king, and on my father's house; let the king and his throne be guiltless." The king said, "If anyone says anything to you, bring him to me, and he shall never touch you again." Then she said, "Please, may the king keep the LORD your God in mind, so that the avenger of blood may kill no more, and my son not be destroyed." He said, "As the LORD lives, not one hair of your son shall fall to the ground." Then the woman said, "Please let your servant speak a word to my lord the king." He said, "Speak." The woman said, "Why then have you planned such a thing against the people of God? For in giving this decision the king convicts himself, inasmuch as the king does not bring his banished one home again. We must all die; we are like water spilled on the ground, which cannot be gathered up. But God will not take away a life; he will devise plans so as not to keep an outcast banished forever from his presence. Now I have come to say this to my lord the king because the people have made me afraid; your servant thought, 'I will speak to the king; it may be that the king will perform the request of his servant. For the king will hear, and deliver his servant from the hand of the man who would cut both me and my son off from the heritage of God.' Your servant thought, 'The word of my

lord the king will set me at rest'; for my lord the king is like
the angel of God, discerning good and evil. The LORD your
God be with you!" Then the king answered the woman,
"Do not withhold from me anything I ask you." The woman
said, "Let my lord the king speak." The king said, "Is the
hand of Joab with you in all this?" The woman answered
and said, "As surely as you live, my lord the king, one
cannot turn right or left from anything that my lord the king
has said. For it was your servant Joab who commanded me;
it was he who put all these words into the mouth of your
servant. In order to change the course of affairs your servant
Joab did this. But my lord has wisdom like the wisdom of
the angel of God to know all things that are on the earth."

A Reading (Lesson) from the Acts of the Apostles [21:1–14]

When we had parted from them and set sail, we came by
a straight course to Cos, and the next day to Rhodes, and
from there to Patara. When we found a ship bound for
Phoenicia, we went on board and set sail. We came in
sight of Cyprus; and leaving it on our left, we sailed to
Syria and landed at Tyre, because the ship was to unload
its cargo there. We looked up the disciples and stayed
there for seven days. Through the Spirit they told Paul not
to go on to Jerusalem. When our days there were ended,
we left and proceeded on our journey; and all of them,
with wives and children, escorted us outside the city.
There we knelt down on the beach and prayed and said
farewell to one another. Then we went on board the ship,
and they returned home. When we had finished the voyage
from Tyre, we arrived at Ptolemais; and we greeted the
believers and stayed with them for one day. The next day
we left and came to Caesarea; and we went into the house
of Philip the evangelist, one of the seven, and stayed with

him. He had four unmarried daughters who had the gift of prophecy. While we were staying there for several days, a prophet named Agabus came down from Judea. He came to us and took Paul's belt, bound his own feet and hands with it, and said, "Thus says the Holy Spirit, 'This is the way the Jews in Jerusalem will bind the man who owns this belt and will hand him over to the Gentiles.' " When we heard this, we and the people there urged him not to go up to Jerusalem. Then Paul answered, "What are you doing, weeping and breaking my heart? For I am ready not only to be bound but even to die in Jerusalem for the name of the Lord Jesus." Since he would not be persuaded, we remained silent except to say, "The Lord's will be done."

A Reading (Lesson) from the Gospel according to Mark [10:1–16]

Jesus left that place and went to the region of Judea and beyond the Jordan. And crowds again gathered around him; and, as was his custom, he again taught them. Some Pharisees came, and to test him they asked, "Is it lawful for a man to divorce his wife?" He answered them, "What did Moses command you?" They said, "Moses allowed a man to write a certificate of dismissal and to divorce her." But Jesus said to them, "Because of your hardness of heart he wrote this commandment for you. But from the beginning of creation, 'God made them male and female.' 'For this reason a man shall leave his father and mother and be joined to his wife, and the two shall become one flesh.' So they are no longer two, but one flesh. Therefore what God has joined together, let no one separate." Then in the house the disciples asked him again about this matter. He said to them, "Whoever divorces his wife and marries another commits adultery against her; and if she divorces her husband and marries another, she commits adultery." People were bringing little children to him in order that he might touch them; and the disciples spoke sternly to them. But when Jesus saw this, he was indignant and said to them, "Let the little children come to me; do not stop them; for it is to such as these that the kingdom of God belongs. Truly I tell you, whoever does not receive the kingdom of God as a little child will never enter it." And he took them up in his arms, laid his hands on them, and blessed them.

Wednesday

Psalm 101 [page 730],
Psalm 109:1–4(5–19)20–30 [page 750] ❖
Psalm 119:121–144 [page 773]

A Reading (Lesson) from the Second Book of Samuel
[14:21–33]

The king said to Joab, "Very well, I grant this; go, bring back the young man Absalom." Joab prostrated himself with his face to the ground and did obeisance, and blessed the king; and Joab said, "Today your servant knows that I have found favor in your sight, my lord the king, in that the king has granted the request of his servant." So Joab set off, went to Geshur, and brought Absalom to Jerusalem. The king said, "Let him go to his own house; he is not to come into my presence." So Absalom went to his own house, and did not come into the king's presence. Now in all Israel there was no one to be praised so much for his beauty as Absalom; from the sole of his foot to the crown of his head there was no blemish in him. When he cut the hair of his head (for at the end of every year he used to cut it; when it was heavy on him, he cut it), he weighed the hair of his head, two hundred shekels by the king's weight. There were born to Absalom three sons, and one daughter whose name was Tamar; she was a beautiful woman. So Absalom lived two full years in Jerusalem, without coming into the king's presence. Then Absalom sent for Joab to send him to the king; but Joab would not come to him. He sent a second time, but Joab would not come. Then he said to his servants, "Look, Joab's field is next to mine, and he has barley there; go and set it on fire." So Absalom's servants set the field on fire. Then Joab rose and went to Absalom at his house, and said to him, "Why have your servants set my field on fire?" Absalom answered Joab, "Look, I sent word to you: Come here, that I may send you to the king with the question, 'Why have I come from Geshur? It would be better for me to be there still.' Now let me go into the king's presence; if there is guilt in me, let him kill me!" Then Joab went to the king and told him; and he summoned Absalom. So he came to the king and prostrated himself with his face to the ground before the king; and the king kissed Absalom.

A Reading (Lesson) from the Acts of the Apostles [21:15-26]

After these days we got ready and started to go up to Jerusalem. Some of the disciples from Caesarea also came along and brought us to the house of Mnason of Cyprus, an early disciple, with whom we were to stay. When we arrived in Jerusalem, the brothers welcomed us warmly. The next day Paul went with us to visit James; and all the elders were present. After greeting them, he related one by one the things that God had done among the Gentiles through his ministry. When they heard it, they praised God. Then they said to him, "You see, brother, how many thousands of believers there are among the Jews, and they are all zealous for the law. They have been told about you that you teach all the Jews living among the Gentiles to forsake Moses, and that you tell them not to circumcise their children or observe the customs. What then is to be done? They will certainly hear that you have come. So do what we tell you. We have four men who are under a vow. Join these men, go through the rite of purification with them, and pay for the shaving of their heads. Thus all will know that there is nothing in what they have been told about you, but that you yourself observe and guard the law. But as for the Gentiles who have become believers, we have sent a letter with our judgment that they should abstain from what has been sacrificed to idols and from blood and from what is strangled and from fornication." Then Paul took the men, and the next day, having purified himself, he entered the temple with them, making public the completion of the days of purification when the sacrifice would be made for each of them.

A Reading (Lesson) from the Gospel according to Mark [10:17–31]

As Jesus was setting out on a journey, a man ran up and knelt before him, and asked him, "Good Teacher, what must I do to inherit eternal life?" Jesus said to him, "Why do you call me good? No one is good but God alone. You know the commandments: 'You shall not murder; You shall not commit adultery; You shall not steal; You shall not bear false witness; You shall not defraud; Honor your father and mother.' " He said to him, "Teacher, I have kept all these since my youth." Jesus, looking at him, loved him and said, "You lack one thing; go, sell what you own, and give the money to the poor, and you will have treasure in heaven; then come, follow me." When he heard this, he was shocked and went away grieving, for he had many possessions. Then Jesus looked around and said to his disciples, "How hard it will be for those who have wealth to enter the kingdom of God!" And the disciples were perplexed at these words. But Jesus said to them again, "Children, how hard it is to enter the kingdom of God! It is easier for a camel to go through the eye of a needle than for someone who is rich to enter the kingdom of God." They were greatly astounded and said to one another, "Then who can be saved?" Jesus looked at them and said, "For mortals it is impossible, but not for God; for God all things are possible." Peter began to say to him, "Look, we have left everything and followed you." Jesus said, "Truly I tell you, there is no one who has left house or brothers or sisters or mother or father or children or fields, for my sake and for the sake of the good news, who will not receive a hundredfold now in this age—houses, brothers and sisters, mothers and children, and fields with persecutions—and in the age to come eternal life. But many who are first will be last, and the last will be first."

Thursday

Psalm 105:1–22 [page 738]   ❖   *Psalm 105:23–45* [page 739]

A Reading (Lesson) from the Second Book of Samuel [15:1–18]

After this Absalom got himself a chariot and horses, and fifty men to run ahead of him. Absalom used to rise early and stand beside the road into the gate; and when anyone brought a suit before the king for judgment, Absalom would call out and say, "From what city are you?" When the person said, "Your servant is of such and such a tribe in Israel," Absalom would say, "See, your claims are good and right; but there is no one deputed by the king to hear you." Absalom said moreover, "If only I were judge in the land! Then all who had a suit or cause might come to me, and I would give them justice." Whenever people came near to do obeisance to him, he would put out his hand and take hold of them, and kiss them. Thus Absalom did to every Israelite who came to the king for judgment; so Absalom stole the hearts of the people of Israel. At the end of four years Absalom said to the king, "Please let me go to Hebron and pay the vow that I have made to the LORD. For your servant made a vow while I lived at Geshur in Aram: If the LORD will indeed bring me back to Jerusalem, then I will worship the LORD in Hebron." The king said to him, "Go in peace." So he got up, and went to Hebron. But Absalom sent secret messengers throughout all the tribes of Israel, saying, "As soon as you hear the sound of the trumpet, then shout: Absalom has become king at Hebron!" Two hundred men from Jerusalem went with Absalom; they were invited guests, and they went in their innocence, knowing nothing of the matter. While Absalom was offering the sacrifices, he sent for Ahithophel the Gilonite, David's counselor, from his city Giloh. The conspiracy grew in strength, and the people with Absalom kept increasing. A messenger came to David, saying, "The hearts of the Israelites have gone after Absalom." Then David said to all his officials who were with him at Jerusalem, "Get up! Let us flee, or there will be no escape for us from Absalom. Hurry, or he will soon overtake us, and bring disaster down upon us, and attack the city with the edge of the sword." The king's officials said to the king, "Your servants are ready to do whatever our lord the king decides." So the king left, followed by all his household, except ten concubines whom he left behind to look after the house. The king left, followed by all the people; and they stopped at the last house. All his officials passed by him; and all the Cherethites, and all the Pelethites, and all the six hundred Gittites who had followed him from Gath, passed on before the king.

A Reading (Lesson) from the Acts of the Apostles [21:27–36]

When the seven days of purification were almost completed, the Jews from Asia, who had seen Paul in the temple, stirred up the whole crowd. They seized him, shouting, "Fellow Israelites, help! This is the man who is teaching everyone everywhere against our people, our law, and this place; more than that, he has actually brought Greeks into the temple and has defiled this holy place." For they had previously seen Trophimus the Ephesian with him in the city, and they supposed that Paul had brought him into the temple. Then all the city was aroused, and the people rushed together. They seized Paul and dragged him out of the temple, and immediately the doors were shut. While they were trying to kill him, word came to the tribune of the cohort that all Jerusalem was in an uproar. Immediately he took soldiers and centurions and ran down to them. When they saw the tribune and the soldiers, they stopped beating Paul. Then the tribune came, arrested him, and ordered him to be bound with two chains; he inquired who he was and what he had done. Some in the crowd shouted one thing, some another; and as he could not learn the facts because of the uproar, he ordered him to be brought into the barracks. When Paul came to the steps, the violence of the mob was so great that he had to be carried by the soldiers. The crowd that followed kept shouting, "Away with him!"

A Reading (Lesson) from the Gospel according to Mark
[10:32–45]

Jesus and the disciples were on the road, going up to
Jerusalem, and Jesus was walking ahead of them; they
were amazed, and those who followed were afraid. He
took the twelve aside again and began to tell them what
was to happen to him, saying, "See, we are going up to
Jerusalem, and the Son of Man will be handed over to the
chief priests and the scribes, and they will condemn him to
death; then they will hand him over to the Gentiles; then
they will mock him, and spit upon him, and flog him, and
kill him; and after three days he will rise again." James
and John, the sons of Zebedee, came forward to him and
said to him, "Teacher, we want you to do for us whatever
we ask of you." And he said to them, "What is it you
want me to do for you?" And they said to him, "Grant us
to sit, one at your right hand and one at your left, in your
glory." But Jesus said to them, "You do not know what
you are asking. Are you able to drink the cup that I drink,
or be baptized with the baptism that I am baptized with?"
They replied, "We are able." Then Jesus said to them,
"The cup that I drink you will drink; and with the baptism
with which I am baptized, you will be baptized; but to sit
at my right hand or at my left is not mine to grant, but it
is for those for whom it has been prepared." When the ten
heard this, they began to be angry with James and John.
So Jesus called them and said to them, "You know that
among the Gentiles those whom they recognize as their
rulers lord it over them, and their great ones are tyrants
over them. But it is not so among you; but whoever
wishes to become great among you must be your servant,
and whoever wishes to be first among you must be slave
of all. For the Son of Man came not to be served but to
serve, and to give his life a ransom for many."

Friday

Psalm 102 [page 731] ❖ *Psalm 107:1–32* [page 746]

A Reading (Lesson) from the Second Book of Samuel
[15:19–37]

The king said to Ittai the Gittite, "Why are you also coming
with us? Go back, and stay with the king; for you are a
foreigner, and also an exile from your home. You came only
yesterday, and shall I today make you wander about with
us, while I go wherever I can? Go back, and take your
kinsfolk with you; and may the LORD show steadfast love
and faithfulness to you." But Ittai answered the king, "As
the LORD lives, and as my lord the king lives, wherever my
lord the king may be, whether for death or for life, there
also your servant will be." David said to Ittai, "Go then,
march on." So Ittai the Gittite marched on, with all his men
and all the little ones who were with him. The whole
country wept aloud as all the people passed by; the king
crossed the Wadi Kidron, and all the people moved on
toward the wilderness. Abiathar came up, and Zadok also,
with all the Levites, carrying the ark of the covenant of God.
They set down the ark of God, until the people had all
passed out of the city. Then the king said to Zadok, "Carry
the ark of God back into the city. If I find favor in the eyes
of the LORD, he will bring me back and let me see both it
and the place where it stays. But if he says, 'I take no
pleasure in you,' here I am, let him do to me what seems
good to him." The king also said to the priest Zadok,
"Look, go back to the city in peace, you and Abiathar, with
your two sons, Ahimaaz your son, and Jonathan son of
Abiathar. See, I will wait at the fords of the wilderness until
word comes from you to inform me." So Zadok and
Abiathar carried the ark of God back to Jerusalem, and they

remained there. But David went up the ascent of the Mount of Olives, weeping as he went, with his head covered and walking barefoot; and all the people who were with him covered their heads and went up, weeping as they went. David was told that Ahithophel was among the conspirators with Absalom. And David said, "O LORD, I pray you, turn the counsel of Ahithophel into foolishness." When David came to the summit, where God was worshiped, Hushai the Archite came to meet him with his coat torn and earth on his head. David said to him, "If you go on with me, you will be a burden to me. But if you return to the city and say to Absalom, 'I will be your servant, O king; as I have been your father's servant in time past, so now I will be your servant,' then you will defeat for me the counsel of Ahithophel. The priests Zadok and Abiathar will be with you there. So whatever you hear from the king's house, tell it to the priests Zadok and Abiathar. Their two sons are with them there, Zadok's son Ahimaaz and Abiathar's son Jonathan; and by them you shall report to me everything you hear." So Hushai, David's friend, came into the city, just as Absalom was entering Jerusalem.

A Reading (Lesson) from the Acts of the Apostles
[21:37—22:16]

Just as Paul was about to be brought into the barracks, he said to the tribune, "May I say something to you?" The tribune replied, "Do you know Greek? Then you are not the Egyptian who recently stirred up a revolt and led the four thousand assassins out into the wilderness?" Paul replied, "I am a Jew, from Tarsus in Cilicia, a citizen of an important city; I beg you, let me speak to the people." When he had given him permission, Paul stood on the steps and motioned to the people for silence; and when there was a great hush, he addressed them in the Hebrew language, saying: "Brothers and fathers, listen to the defense that I now make before you." When they heard him addressing them in Hebrew, they became even more quiet. Then he said: "I am a Jew, born in Tarsus in Cilicia, but brought up in this city at the feet of Gamaliel, educated strictly according to our ancestral law, being zealous for God, just as all of you are today. I persecuted this Way up to the point of death by binding both men and women and putting them in prison, as the high priest and the whole council of elders can testify about me. From them I also received letters to the brothers in Damascus, and I went there in order to bind those who were there and to bring them back to Jerusalem for punishment. While I was on my way and approaching Damascus, about noon a great light from heaven suddenly shone about me. I fell to the ground and heard a voice saying to me, 'Saul, Saul, why are you persecuting me?' I answered, 'Who are you, Lord?' Then he said to me, 'I am Jesus of Nazareth whom you are persecuting.' Now those who were with me saw the light but did not hear the voice of the one who was speaking to me. I asked, 'What am I to do, Lord?' The Lord said to me, 'Get up and go to Damascus; there you will be told everything that has been assigned to you to do.' Since I could not see because of the brightness of that light, those who were with me took my hand and led me to Damascus. A certain Ananias, who was a devout man according to the law and well spoken of by all the Jews living there, came to me; and standing beside me, he said, 'Brother Saul, regain your sight!' In that very hour I regained my sight and saw him. Then he said, 'The God of our ancestors has chosen you to know his will, to see the Righteous One and to hear his own voice; for you will be his witness to all the world of what you have seen and heard. And now why do you delay? Get up, be baptized, and have your sins washed away, calling on his name.' "

A Reading (Lesson) from the Gospel according to Mark [10:46–52]

They came to Jericho. As Jesus and his disciples and a large crowd were leaving Jericho, Bartimaeus son of Timaeus, a blind beggar, was sitting by the roadside. When he heard that it was Jesus of Nazareth, he began to shout out and say, "Jesus, Son of David, have mercy on me!" Many sternly ordered him to be quiet, but he cried out even more loudly, "Son of David, have mercy on me!" Jesus stood still and said, "Call him here." And they called the blind man, saying to him, "Take heart; get up, he is calling you." So throwing off his cloak, he sprang up and came to Jesus. Then Jesus said to him, "What do you want me to do for you?" The blind man said to him, "My teacher, let me see again." Jesus said to him, "Go; your faith has made you well." Immediately he regained his sight and followed him on the way.

Saturday

Psalm 107:33–43 [page 748],
Psalm 108:1–6(7–13) [page 749] ❖ *Psalm 33* [page 626]

A Reading (Lesson) from the Second Book of Samuel [16:1–23]

When David had passed a little beyond the summit, Ziba the servant of Mephibosheth met him, with a couple of donkeys saddled, carrying two hundred loaves of bread, one hundred bunches of raisins, one hundred of summer fruits, and one skin of wine. The king said to Ziba, "Why have you brought these?" Ziba answered, "The donkeys are for the king's household to ride, the bread and summer fruit for the young men to eat, and the wine is for those to drink who faint in the wilderness." The king said, "And where is your master's son?" Ziba said to the king, "He remains in Jerusalem; for he said, 'Today the house of Israel will give me back my grandfather's kingdom.'" Then the king said to Ziba, "All that belonged to Mephibosheth is now yours." Ziba said, "I do obeisance; let me find favor in your sight, my lord the king." When King David came to Bahurim, a man of the family of the house of Saul came out whose name was Shimei son of Gera; he came out cursing. He threw stones at David and at all the servants of King David; now all the people and all the warriors were on his right and on his left. Shimei shouted while he cursed, "Out! Out! Murderer! Scoundrel! The LORD has avenged on all of you the blood of the house of Saul, in whose place you have reigned; and the LORD has given the kingdom into the hand of your son Absalom. See, disaster has overtaken you; for you are a man of blood." Then Abishai son of Zeruiah said to the king, "Why should this dead dog curse my lord the king? Let me go over and take off his head." But the king said, "What have I to do with you, you sons of Zeruiah? If he is cursing because the LORD has said to him, 'Curse David,' who then shall say, 'Why have you done so?'" David said to Abishai and to all his servants, "My own son seeks my life; how much more now may this Benjaminite! Let him alone, and let him curse; for the LORD has bidden him. It may be that the LORD will look on my distress, and the LORD will repay me with good for this cursing of me today." So David and his men went on the road, while Shimei went along on the hillside opposite him and cursed as he went, throwing stones and flinging dust at him. The king and all the people who were with him arrived weary at the Jordan; and there he refreshed himself. Now Absalom and all the Israelites came to Jerusalem; Ahithophel was with him. When Hushai the Archite, David's friend, came to Absalom, Hushai said to Absalom, "Long live the king! Long live the king!" Absalom said to Hushai, "Is this your loyalty to your friend? Why did you not go with your friend?" Hushai said to Absalom, "No; but the one whom the LORD and this people and all the Israelites have chosen, his I will be, and with him I will remain. Moreover, whom should I serve? Should it not be his son? Just as I have served your father, so I will serve you." Then Absalom said to Ahithophel, "Give us your counsel; what shall we do?" Ahithophel said to Absalom, "Go in to your father's concubines, the ones he has left to look after the house; and all Israel will hear that you have made yourself odious to your father, and the hands of all who are with you will be strengthened." So they pitched a tent for Absalom upon the roof; and Absalom went in to his father's concubines in the sight of all Israel. Now in those days the counsel that Ahithophel gave was as if one consulted the oracle of God; so all the counsel of Ahithophel was esteemed, both by David and by Absalom.

A Reading (Lesson) from the Acts of the Apostles [22:17–29]

Paul spoke to the people in the Hebrew language, saying, "After I had returned to Jerusalem and while I was praying in the temple, I fell into a trance and saw Jesus saying to me, 'Hurry and get out of Jerusalem quickly, because they will not accept your testimony about me.' And I said, 'Lord, they themselves know that in every synagogue I imprisoned and beat those who believed in you. And while the blood of your witness Stephen was shed, I myself was standing by, approving and keeping the coats of those who killed him.' Then he said to me, 'Go, for I will send you far away to the Gentiles.' " Up to this point they listened to him, but then they shouted, "Away with such a fellow from the earth! For he should not be allowed to live." And while they were shouting, throwing off their cloaks, and tossing dust into the air, the tribune directed that he was to be brought into the barracks, and ordered him to be examined by flogging, to find out the reason for this outcry against him. But when they had tied him up with thongs, Paul said to the centurion who was standing by, "Is it legal for you to flog a Roman citizen who is uncondemned?" When the centurion heard that, he went to the tribune and said to him, "What are you about to do? This man is a Roman citizen." The tribune came and asked Paul, "Tell me, are you a Roman citizen?" And he said, "Yes." The tribune answered, "It cost me a large sum of money to get my citizenship." Paul said, "But I was born a citizen." Immediately those who were about to examine him drew back from him; and the tribune also was afraid, for he realized that Paul was a Roman citizen and that he had bound him.

A Reading (Lesson) from the Gospel according to Mark [11:1–11]

When they were approaching Jerusalem, at Bethphage and Bethany, near the Mount of Olives, he sent two of his disciples and said to them, "Go into the village ahead of you, and immediately as you enter it, you will find tied there a colt that has never been ridden; untie it and bring it. If anyone says to you, 'Why are you doing this?' just say this, 'The Lord needs it and will send it back here immediately.' " They went away and found a colt tied near a door, outside in the street. As they were untying it, some of the bystanders said to them, "What are you doing, untying the colt?" They told them what Jesus had said; and they allowed them to take it. Then they brought the colt to Jesus and threw their cloaks on it; and he sat on it. Many people spread their cloaks on the road, and others spread leafy branches that they had cut in the fields. Then those who went ahead and those who followed were shouting, "Hosanna! Blessed is the one who comes in the name of the Lord! Blessed is the coming kingdom of our ancestor David! Hosanna in the highest heaven!" Then he entered Jerusalem and went into the temple; and when he had looked around at everything, as it was already late, he went out to Bethany with the twelve.

Proper 15   *Week of the Sunday closest to August 17*

Sunday

Psalm 118 [page 760]   ❖   *Psalm 145* [page 801]

A Reading (Lesson) from the Second Book of Samuel [17:1–23]

Ahithophel said to Absalom, "Let me choose twelve thousand men, and I will set out and pursue David tonight. I will come upon him while he is weary and discouraged, and throw him into a panic; and all the people who are with him will flee. I will strike down only the king, and I will bring all the people back to you as a bride comes home to her husband. You seek the life of only one man, and all the people will be at peace." The advice pleased Absalom and all the elders of Israel. Then Absalom said, "Call Hushai the Archite also, and let us hear too what he has to say." When

Hushai came to Absalom, Absalom said to him, "This is what Ahithophel has said; shall we do as he advises? If not, you tell us." Then Hushai said to Absalom, "This time the counsel that Ahithophel has given is not good." Hushai continued, "You know that your father and his men are warriors, and that they are enraged, like a bear robbed of her cubs in the field. Besides, your father is expert in war; he will not spend the night with the troops. Even now he has hidden himself in one of the pits, or in some other place. And when some of our troops fall at the first attack, whoever hears it will say, 'There has been a slaughter among the troops who follow Absalom.' Then even the valiant warrior, whose heart is like the heart of a lion, will utterly melt with fear; for all Israel knows that your father is a warrior, and that those who are with him are valiant warriors. But my counsel is that all Israel be gathered to you, from Dan to Beer-sheba, like the sand by the sea for multitude, and that you go to battle in person. So we shall come upon him in whatever place he may be found, and we shall light on him as the dew falls on the ground; and he will not survive, nor will any of those with him. If he withdraws into a city, then all Israel will bring ropes to that city, and we shall drag it into the valley, until not even a pebble is to be found there." Absalom and all the men of Israel said, "The counsel of Hushai the Archite is better than the counsel of Ahithophel." For the LORD had ordained to defeat the good counsel of Ahithophel, so that the LORD might bring ruin on Absalom. Then Hushai said to the priests Zadok and Abiathar, "Thus and so did Ahithophel counsel Absalom and the elders of Israel; and thus and so I have counseled. Therefore send quickly and tell David, 'Do not lodge tonight at the fords of the wilderness, but by all means cross over; otherwise the king and all the people who are with him will be swallowed up.' " Jonathan and Ahimaaz were waiting at En-rogel; a servant girl used to go and tell them, and they would go and tell King David; for they could not risk being seen entering the city. But a boy saw them, and told Absalom; so both of them went away quickly, and came to the house of a man at Bahurim, who had a well in his courtyard; and they went down into it. The man's wife took a covering, stretched it over the well's mouth, and spread out grain on it; and nothing was known of it. When Absalom's servants came to the woman at the house, they said, "Where are Ahimaaz and Jonathan?" The woman said to them, "They have crossed over the brook of water." And when they had searched and could not find them, they returned to Jerusalem. After they had gone, the men came up out of the well, and went and told King David. They said to David, "Go and cross the water quickly; for thus and so has Ahithophel counseled against you." So David and all the people who were with him set out and crossed the Jordan; by daybreak not one was left who had not crossed the Jordan. When Ahithophel saw that his counsel was not followed, he saddled his donkey and went off home to his own city. He set his house in order, and hanged himself; he died and was buried in the tomb of his father.

A Reading (Lesson) from the Letter of Paul to the Galatians [3:6–14]

Just as Abraham "believed God, and it was reckoned to him as righteousness," so, you see, those who believe are the descendants of Abraham. And the scripture, foreseeing that God would justify the Gentiles by faith, declared the gospel beforehand to Abraham, saying, "All the Gentiles shall be blessed in you." For this reason, those who believe are blessed with Abraham who believed. For all who rely on the works of the law are under a curse; for it is written, "Cursed is everyone who does not observe and obey all the things written in the book of the law." Now it is evident that no one is justified before God by the law; for "The one who is righteous will live by faith." But the law does not rest on faith; on the contrary, "Whoever does the works of the law will live by them." Christ redeemed us from the curse of the law by becoming a curse for us—for it is written, "Cursed is everyone who hangs on a tree"—in order that in Christ Jesus the blessing of Abraham might come to the Gentiles, so that we might receive the promise of the Spirit through faith.

A Reading (Lesson) from the Gospel according to John
[5:30–47]

Jesus said to the Jews, "I can do nothing on my own. As I hear, I judge; and my judgment is just, because I seek to do not my own will but the will of him who sent me. If I testify about myself, my testimony is not true. There is another who testifies on my behalf, and I know that his testimony to me is true. You sent messengers to John, and he testified to the truth. Not that I accept such human testimony, but I say these things so that you may be saved. He was a burning and shining lamp, and you were willing to rejoice for a while in his light. But I have a testimony greater than John's. The works that the Father has given me to complete, the very works that I am doing, testify on my behalf that the Father has sent me. And the Father who sent me has himself testified on my behalf. You have never heard his voice or seen his form, and you do not have his word abiding in you, because you do not believe him whom he has sent. You search the scriptures because you think that in them you have eternal life; and it is they that testify on my behalf. Yet you refuse to come to me to have life. I do not accept glory from human beings. But I know that you do not have the love of God in you. I have come in my Father's name, and you do not accept me; if another comes in his own name, you will accept him. How can you believe when you accept glory from one another and do not seek the glory that comes from the one who alone is God? Do not think that I will accuse you before the Father; your accuser is Moses, on whom you have set your hope. If you believed Moses, you would believe me, for he wrote about me. But if you do not believe what he wrote, how will you believe what I say?"

Monday

Psalm 106:1–18 [page 741]   ❖   *Psalm 106:19–48* [page 743]

A Reading (Lesson) from the Second Book of Samuel [17:24—18:8]

David came to Mahanaim, while Absalom crossed the Jordan with all the men of Israel. Now Absalom had set Amasa over the army in the place of Joab. Amasa was the son of a man named Ithra the Ishmaelite, who had married Abigal daughter of Nahash, sister of Zeruiah, Joab's mother. The Israelites and Absalom encamped in the land of Gilead. When David came to Mahanaim, Shobi son of Nahash from Rabbah of the Ammonites, and Machir son of Ammiel from Lo-debar, and Barzillai the Gileadite from Rogelim, brought beds, basins, and earthen vessels, wheat, barley, meal, parched grain, beans and lentils, honey and curds, sheep, and cheese from the herd, for David and the people with him to eat; for they said, "The troops are hungry and weary and thirsty in the wilderness." Then

David mustered the men who were with him, and set over them commanders of thousands and commanders of hundreds. And David divided the army into three groups: one third under the command of Joab, one third under the command of Abishai son of Zeruiah, Joab's brother, and one third under the command of Ittai the Gittite. The king said to the men, "I myself will also go out with you." But the men said, "You shall not go out. For if we flee, they will not care about us. If half of us die, they will not care about us. But you are worth ten thousand of us; therefore it is better that you send us help from the city." The king said to them, "Whatever seems best to you I will do." So the king stood at the side of the gate, while all the army marched out by hundreds and by thousands. The king ordered Joab and Abishai and Ittai, saying, "Deal gently for my sake with the young man Absalom." And all the people heard when the king gave orders to all the commanders concerning Absalom. So the army went out into the field against Israel; and the battle was fought in the forest of Ephraim. The men of Israel were defeated there by the servants of David, and the slaughter there was great on that day, twenty thousand men. The battle spread over the face of all the country; and the forest claimed more victims that day than the sword.

A Reading (Lesson) from the Acts of the Apostles
[22:30—23:11]

Since the tribune wanted to find out what Paul was being accused of by the Jews, the next day he released him and ordered the chief priests and the entire council to meet. He brought Paul down and had him stand before them. While Paul was looking intently at the council he said, "Brothers, up to this day I have lived my life with a clear conscience before God." Then the high priest Ananias ordered those standing near him to strike him on the mouth. At this Paul said to him, "God will strike you, you whitewashed wall! Are you sitting there to judge me according to the law, and yet in violation of the law you order me to be struck?" Those standing nearby said, "Do you dare to insult God's high priest?" And Paul said, "I did not realize, brothers, that he was high priest; for it is written, 'You shall not speak evil of a leader of your people.'" When Paul noticed that some were Sadducees and others were Pharisees, he called out in the council, "Brothers, I am a Pharisee, a son of Pharisees. I am on trial concerning the hope of the resurrection of the dead." When he said this, a dissension began between the Pharisees and the Sadducees, and the assembly was divided. (The Sadducees say that there is no resurrection, or angel, or spirit; but the Pharisees acknowledge all three.) Then a great clamor arose, and certain scribes of the Pharisees' group stood up and contended, "We find nothing wrong with this man. What if a spirit or an angel has spoken to him?" When the dissension became violent, the tribune, fearing that they would tear Paul to pieces, ordered the soldiers to go down, take him by force, and bring him into the barracks. That night the Lord stood near him and said, "Keep up your courage! For just as you have testified for me in Jerusalem, so you must bear witness also in Rome."

A Reading (Lesson) from the Gospel according to Mark [11:12–26]

On the following day, when they came from Bethany, Jesus was hungry. Seeing in the distance a fig tree in leaf, he went to see whether perhaps he would find anything on it. When he came to it, he found nothing but leaves, for it was not the season for figs. He said to it, "May no one

ever eat fruit from you again." And his disciples heard it.
Then they came to Jerusalem. And he entered the temple
and began to drive out those who were selling and those
who were buying in the temple, and he overturned the
tables of the money changers and the seats of those who
sold doves; and he would not allow anyone to carry
anything through the temple. He was teaching and saying,
"Is it not written, 'My house shall be called a house of
prayer for all the nations'? But you have made it a den of
robbers." And when the chief priests and the scribes heard
it, they kept looking for a way to kill him; for they were
afraid of him, because the whole crowd was spellbound by
his teaching. And when evening came, Jesus and his
disciples went out of the city. In the morning as they
passed by, they saw the fig tree withered away to its roots.
Then Peter remembered and said to him, "Rabbi, look!
The fig tree that you cursed has withered." Jesus answered
them, "Have faith in God. Truly I tell you, if you say to
this mountain, 'Be taken up and thrown into the sea,' and
if you do not doubt in your heart, but believe that what
you say will come to pass, it will be done for you. So I tell
you, whatever you ask for in prayer, believe that you have
received it, and it will be yours. Whenever you stand
praying, forgive, if you have anything against anyone; so
that your Father in heaven may also forgive you your
trespasses. But if you do not forgive, neither will your
Father in heaven forgive your trespasses."

Tuesday

(*Psalm 120* [page 778]),   *Psalm 121* [page 779],
Psalm 122 [page 779],   *Psalm 123* [page 780]   ❖
Psalm 124 [page 781],   *Psalm 125* [page 781],
Psalm 126 [page 782],   (*Psalm 127* [page 782])

A Reading (Lesson) from the Second Book of Samuel
[18:9–18]

Absalom happened to meet the servants of David. Absalom
was riding on his mule, and the mule went under the thick
branches of a great oak. His head caught fast in the oak,
and he was left hanging between heaven and earth, while the
mule that was under him went on. A man saw it, and told
Joab, "I saw Absalom hanging in an oak." Joab said to the
man who told him, "What, you saw him! Why then did you
not strike him there to the ground? I would have been glad
to give you ten pieces of silver and a belt." But the man said
to Joab, "Even if I felt in my hand the weight of a thousand
pieces of silver, I would not raise my hand against the king's
son; for in our hearing the king commanded you and
Abishai and Ittai, saying: For my sake protect the young
man Absalom! On the other hand, if I had dealt
treacherously against his life (and there is nothing hidden
from the king), then you yourself would have stood aloof."
Joab said, "I will not waste time like this with you." He
took three spears in his hand, and thrust them into the heart
of Absalom, while he was still alive in the oak. And ten
young men, Joab's armorbearers, surrounded Absalom and
struck him, and killed him. Then Joab sounded the trumpet,
and the troops came back from pursuing Israel, for Joab
restrained the troops. They took Absalom, threw him into a
great pit in the forest, and raised over him a very great heap
of stones. Meanwhile all the Israelites fled to their homes.
Now Absalom in his lifetime had taken and set up for
himself a pillar that is in the King's Valley, for he said, "I
have no son to keep my name in remembrance"; he called
the pillar by his own name. It is called Absalom's
Monument to this day.

A Reading (Lesson) from the Acts of the Apostles [23:12–24]

In the morning the Jews joined in a conspiracy and bound themselves by an oath neither to eat nor drink until they had killed Paul. There were more than forty who joined in this conspiracy. They went to the chief priests and elders and said, "We have strictly bound ourselves by an oath to taste no food until we have killed Paul. Now then, you and the council must notify the tribune to bring him down to you, on the pretext that you want to make a more thorough examination of his case. And we are ready to do away with him before he arrives." Now the son of Paul's sister heard about the ambush; so he went and gained entrance to the barracks and told Paul. Paul called one of the centurions and said, "Take this young man to the tribune, for he has something to report to him." So he took him, brought him to the tribune, and said, "The prisoner Paul called me and asked me to bring this young man to you; he has something to tell you." The tribune took him by the hand, drew him aside privately, and asked, "What is it that you have to report to me?" He answered, "The Jews have agreed to ask you to bring Paul down to the council tomorrow, as though they were going to inquire more thoroughly into his case. But do not be persuaded by them, for more than forty of their men are lying in ambush for him. They have bound themselves by an oath neither to eat nor drink until they kill him. They are ready now and are waiting for your consent." So the tribune dismissed the young man, ordering him, "Tell no one that you have informed me of this." Then he summoned two of the centurions and said, "Get ready to leave by nine o'clock tonight for Caesarea with two hundred soldiers, seventy horsemen, and two hundred spearmen. Also provide mounts for Paul to ride, and take him safely to Felix the governor."

A Reading (Lesson) from the Gospel according to Mark
[11:27—12:12]

Jesus and the disciples came again to Jerusalem. As he was walking in the temple, the chief priests, the scribes, and the elders came to him and said, "By what authority are you doing these things? Who gave you this authority to do them?" Jesus said to them, "I will ask you one question; answer me, and I will tell you by what authority I do these things. Did the baptism of John come from heaven, or was it of human origin? Answer me." They argued with one another, "If we say, 'From heaven,' he will say, 'Why then did you not believe him?' But shall we say, 'Of human origin'?"—they were afraid of the crowd, for all regarded John as truly a prophet. So they answered Jesus, "We do not know." And Jesus said to them, "Neither will I tell you by what authority I am doing these things." Then he began to speak to them in parables. "A man planted a vineyard, put a fence around it, dug a pit for the wine press, and built a watchtower; then he leased it to tenants and went to another country. When the season came, he sent a slave to the tenants to collect from them his share of the produce of the vineyard. But they seized him, and beat him, and sent him away empty-handed. And again he sent another slave to them; this one they beat over the head and insulted. Then he sent another, and that one they killed. And so it was with many others; some they beat, and others they killed. He had still one other, a beloved son. Finally he sent him to them, saying, 'They will respect my son.' But those tenants said to one another, 'This is the heir; come, let us kill him, and the inheritance will be ours.' So they seized him, killed him, and threw him out of the vineyard. What then will the owner of the vineyard do? He will come and destroy the tenants and give the vineyard to others. Have you not read this scripture: 'The stone that the builders rejected has become the cornerstone; this was the Lord's doing, and it is amazing in our eyes'?" When they realized that he had told this parable against them, they wanted to arrest him, but they feared the crowd. So they left him and went away.

Wednesday

Psalm 119:145–176 [page 775] ❖ *Psalm 128* [page 783], *Psalm 129* [page 784], *Psalm 130* [page 784]

A Reading (Lesson) from the Second Book of Samuel [18:19–33]

Ahimaaz son of Zadok said, "Let me run, and carry tidings to the king that the LORD has delivered him from the power of his enemies." Joab said to him, "You are not to carry tidings today; you may carry tidings another day, but today you shall not do so, because the king's son is dead." Then Joab said to a Cushite, "Go, tell the king what you have seen." The Cushite bowed before Joab, and ran. Then Ahimaaz son of Zadok said again to Joab, "Come what may, let me also run after the Cushite." And Joab said, "Why will you run, my son, seeing that you have no reward for the tidings?" "Come what may," he said, "I will run." So he said to him, "Run." Then Ahimaaz ran by the way of the Plain, and outran the Cushite. Now David was sitting between the two gates. The sentinel went up to the roof of the gate by the wall, and when he looked up, he saw a man running alone. The sentinel shouted and told the king. The king said, "If he is alone, there are tidings in his mouth." He kept coming, and drew near. Then the sentinel saw another man running; and the sentinel called to the gatekeeper and said, "See, another man running alone!" The king said, "He also is bringing tidings." The sentinel said, "I think the running of the first one is like the running of Ahimaaz son of Zadok." The king said, "He is a good man, and comes with good tidings." Then Ahimaaz cried out to the king, "All is well!" He prostrated himself before the king with his face to the ground, and said, "Blessed be the LORD your God, who has delivered up the men who raised their hand against my lord the king." The king said, "Is it well with the young man Absalom?" Ahimaaz answered. "When Joab sent your servant, I saw a great tumult, but I do not know what it was." The king said, "Turn aside, and stand here." So he turned aside, and stood still. Then the Cushite came; and the Cushite said, "Good tidings for my lord the king! For the LORD has vindicated you this day, delivering you from the power of all who rose up against you." The king said to the Cushite, "Is it well with the young man Absalom?" The Cushite answered, "May the enemies of my lord the king, and all who rise up to do you harm, be like that young man." The king was deeply moved, and went up to the chamber over the gate, and wept; and as he went, he said, "O my son Absalom, my son, my son Absalom! Would I had died instead of you, O Absalom, my son, my son!"

A Reading (Lesson) from the Acts of the Apostles [23:23–35]

The tribune called two of the centurions and said, "Get ready to leave by nine o'clock tonight for Caesarea with two hundred soldiers, seventy horsemen, and two hundred spearmen. Also provide mounts for Paul to ride, and take him safely to Felix the governor." He wrote a letter to this effect: "Claudius Lysias to his Excellency the governor Felix, greetings. This man was seized by the Jews and was about to be killed by them, but when I had learned that he was a Roman citizen, I came with the guard and rescued him. Since I wanted to know the charge for which they accused him, I had him brought to their council. I found that he was accused concerning questions of their law, but was charged with nothing deserving death or imprisonment. When I was informed that there would be a plot against the man, I sent him to you at once, ordering his accusers also to state before you what they have against him." So the soldiers, according to their instructions, took Paul and brought him during the night to Antipatris. The next day they let the horsemen go on with him, while they returned to the barracks. When they came to Caesarea and delivered the letter to the governor, they presented Paul also before him. On reading the letter, he asked what province he belonged to, and when he learned that he was from Cilicia, he said, "I will give you a hearing when your accusers arrive." Then he ordered that he be kept under guard in Herod's headquarters.

A Reading (Lesson) from the Gospel according to Mark
[12:13–27]

They sent to Jesus some of the Pharisees and some of the Herodians to trap him in what he said. And they came and said to him, "Teacher, we know that you are sincere, and show deference to no one; for you do not regard people with partiality, but teach the way of God in accordance with truth. Is it lawful to pay taxes to the emperor, or not? Should we pay them, or should we not?" But knowing their hypocrisy, he said to them, "Why are you putting me to the test? Bring me a denarius and let me see it." And they brought one. Then he said to them, "Whose head is this, and whose title?" They answered, "The emperor's." Jesus said to them, "Give to the emperor the things that are the emperor's, and to God the things that are God's." And they were utterly amazed at him. Some Sadducees, who say there is no resurrection, came to him and asked him a question, saying, "Teacher, Moses wrote for us that 'if a man's brother dies, leaving a wife but no child, the man shall marry the widow and raise up children for his brother.' There were seven brothers; the first married and, when he died, left no children; and the second married her and died, leaving no children; and the third likewise; none of the seven left children. Last of all the woman herself died. In the resurrection whose wife will she be? For the seven had married her." Jesus said to them, "Is not this the reason you are wrong, that you know neither the scriptures nor the power of God? For when they rise from the dead, they neither marry nor are given in marriage, but are like angels in heaven. And as for the dead being raised, have you not read in the book of Moses, in the story about the bush, how God said to him, 'I am the God of Abraham, the God of Isaac, and the God of Jacob'? He is God not of the dead, but of the living; you are quite wrong."

Thursday

Psalm 131 [page 785],   *Psalm 132* [page 785],
(Psalm 133 [page 787])   ❖   *Psalm 134* [page 787],
Psalm 135 [page 788]

A Reading (Lesson) from the Second Book of Samuel
[19:1–23]

It was told Joab, "The king is weeping and mourning for Absalom." So the victory that day was turned into mourning for all the troops; for the troops heard that day,

"The king is grieving for his son." The troops stole into the city that day as soldiers steal in who are ashamed when they flee in battle. The king covered his face, and the king cried with a loud voice, "O my son Absalom, O Absalom, my son, my son!" Then Joab came into the house to the king, and said, "Today you have covered with shame the faces of all your officers who have saved your life today, and the lives of your sons and your daughters, and the lives of your wives and your concubines, for love of those who hate you and for hatred of those who love you. You have made it clear today that commanders and officers are nothing to you; for I perceive that if Absalom were alive and all of us were dead today, then you would be pleased. So go out at once and speak kindly to your servants; for I swear by the LORD, if you do not go, not a man will stay with you this night; and this will be worse for you than any disaster that has come upon you from your youth until now." Then the king got up and took his seat in the gate. The troops were all told, "See, the king is sitting in the gate"; and all the troops came before the king. Meanwhile, all the Israelites had fled to their homes. All the people were disputing throughout all the tribes of Israel, saying, "The king delivered us from the hand of our enemies, and saved us from the hand of the Philistines; and now he has fled out of the land because of Absalom. But Absalom, whom we anointed over us, is dead in battle. Now therefore why do you say nothing about bringing the king back?" King David sent this message to the priests Zadok and Abiathar, "Say to the elders of Judah, 'Why should you be the last to bring the king back to his house? The talk of all Israel has come to the king. You are my kin, you are my bone and my flesh; why then should you be the last to bring back the king?' And say to Amasa, 'Are you not my bone and my flesh? So may God do to me, and more, if you are not the commander of my army from now on, in place of Joab.' " Amasa swayed the hearts of all the people of Judah as one, and they sent word to the king, "Return, both you and all your servants." So the king came back to the Jordan; and Judah came to Gilgal to meet the king and to bring him over the Jordan. Shimei son of Gera, the Benjaminite, from Bahurim, hurried to come down with the people of Judah to meet King David; with him were a thousand people from Benjamin. And Ziba, the servant of the house of Saul, with his fifteen sons and his twenty servants, rushed down to the Jordan ahead of the king, while the crossing was taking place, to bring over the king's household, and to do his pleasure. Shimei son of Gera fell down before the king, as he was about to cross the Jordan, and said to the king, "May my lord not hold me guilty or remember how your servant did wrong on the day my lord the king left Jerusalem; may the king not bear it in mind. For your servant knows that I have sinned; therefore, see, I have come this day, the first of all the house of Joseph to come down to meet my lord the king." Abishai son of Zeruiah answered, "Shall not Shimei be put to death for this, because he cursed the LORD's anointed?" But David said, "What have I to do with you, you sons of Zeruiah, that you should today become an adversary to me? Shall anyone be put to death in Israel this day? For do I not know that I am this day king over Israel?" The king said to Shimei, "You shall not die." And the king gave him his oath.

A Reading (Lesson) from the Acts of the Apostles [24:1–23]

Five days later the high priest Ananias came down with some elders and an attorney, a certain Tertullus, and they reported their case against Paul to the governor. When Paul had been summoned, Tertullus began to accuse him, saying: "Your Excellency, because of you we have long enjoyed peace, and reforms have been made for this people because of your foresight. We welcome this in every way and everywhere with utmost gratitude. But, to detain you no further, I beg you to hear us briefly with your customary graciousness. We have, in fact, found this man a pestilent fellow, an agitator among all the Jews throughout the world, and a ringleader of the sect of the Nazarenes. He even tried to profane the temple, and so we seized him. By examining him yourself you will be able to learn from him concerning everything of which we accuse him." The Jews also joined in the charge by asserting that all this was true. When the governor motioned to him to speak, Paul replied: "I cheerfully make my defense, knowing that for many years you have been a judge over this nation. As you can find out, it is not more than twelve days since I went up to worship in Jerusalem. They did not find me disputing with anyone in the temple or stirring up a crowd either in the synagogues or throughout the city. Neither can they prove to you the charge that they now bring against me. But this I admit to you, that according to the Way, which they call a sect, I worship the God of our ancestors, believing everything laid down according to the law or written in the prophets. I have a hope in God—a hope that they themselves also accept—that there will be a resurrection of both the righteous and the unrighteous. Therefore I do my best always to have a clear conscience toward God and all people. Now after some years I came to bring alms to my nation and to offer sacrifices. While I was doing this, they found me in the temple, completing the rite of purification, without any crowd or disturbance. But there were some Jews from Asia—they ought to be here before you to make an accusation, if they have anything against me. Or let these men here tell what crime they had found when I stood before the council, unless it was this one sentence that I called out while standing before them, 'It is about the resurrection of the dead that I am on trial before you today.' " But Felix, who was rather well informed about the Way, adjourned the hearing with the comment, "When Lysias the tribune comes down, I will decide your case." Then he ordered the centurion to keep him in custody, but to let him have some liberty and not to prevent any of his friends from taking care of his needs.

A Reading (Lesson) from the Gospel according to Mark [12:28–34]

One of the scribes came near and heard them disputing with one another, and seeing that Jesus answered them well, he asked him, "Which commandment is the first of all?" Jesus answered, "The first is, 'Hear, O Israel: the Lord our God, the Lord is one; you shall love the Lord your God with all your heart, and with all your soul, and with all your mind, and with all your strength.' The second is this, 'You shall love your neighbor as yourself.' There is no other commandment greater than these." Then the scribe said to him, "You are right, Teacher; you have truly said that 'he is one, and besides him there is no other'; and 'to love him with all the heart, and with all the understanding, and with all the strength,' and 'to love one's neighbor as oneself,'—this is much more important than all whole burnt offerings and sacrifices." When Jesus saw that he answered wisely, he said to him, "You are not far from the kingdom of God." After that no one dared to ask him any question.

Friday

Psalm 140 [page 796], *Psalm 142* [page 798] ❖
Psalm 141 [page 797], *Psalm 143:1–11(12)* [page 798]

A Reading (Lesson) from the Second Book of Samuel
[19:24–43]

Mephibosheth grandson of Saul came down to meet the
king; he had not taken care of his feet, or trimmed his beard,
or washed his clothes, from the day the king left until the
day he came back in safety. When he came from Jerusalem
to meet the king, the king said to him, "Why did you not go
with me, Mephibosheth?" He answered, "My lord, O king,
my servant deceived me; for your servant said to him,
'Saddle a donkey for me, so that I may ride on it and go with
the king.' For your servant is lame. He has slandered your
servant to my lord the king. But my lord the king is like the
angel of God; do therefore what seems good to you. For all
my father's house were doomed to death before my lord the
king; but you set your servant among those who eat at your
table. What further right have I, then, to appeal to the
king?" The king said to him, "Why speak any more of your
affairs? I have decided: you and Ziba shall divide the land."
Mephibosheth said to the king, "Let him take it all, since
my lord the king has arrived home safely." Now Barzillai
the Gileadite had come down from Rogelim; he went on
with the king to the Jordan, to escort him over the Jordan.
Barzillai was a very aged man, eighty years old. He had
provided the king with food while he stayed at Mahanaim,
for he was a very wealthy man. The king said to Barzillai,
"Come over with me, and I will provide for you in Jerusalem
at my side." But Barzillai said to the king, "How many
years have I still to live, that I should go up with the king to
Jerusalem? Today I am eighty years old; can I discern what

is pleasant and what is not? Can your servant taste what he eats or what he drinks? Can I still listen to the voice of singing men and singing women? Why then should your servant be an added burden to my lord the king? Your servant will go a little way over the Jordan with the king. Why should the king recompense me with such a reward? Please let your servant return, so that I may die in my own town, near the graves of my father and my mother. But here is your servant Chimham; let him go over with my lord the king; and do for him whatever seems good to you." The king answered, "Chimham shall go over with me, and I will do for him whatever seems good to you; and all that you desire of me I will do for you." Then all the people crossed over the Jordan, and the king crossed over; the king kissed Barzillai and blessed him, and he returned to his own home. The king went on to Gilgal, and Chimham went on with him; all the people of Judah, and also half the people of Israel, brought the king on his way. Then all the people of Israel came to the king, and said to him, "Why have our kindred the people of Judah stolen you away, and brought the king and his household over the Jordan, and all David's men with him?" All the people of Judah answered the people of Israel, "Because the king is near of kin to us. Why then are you angry over this matter? Have we eaten at all at the king's expense? Or has he given us any gift?" But the people of Israel answered the people of Judah, "We have ten shares in the king, and in David also we have more than you. Why then did you despise us? Were we not the first to speak of bringing back our king?" But the words of the people of Judah were fiercer than the words of the people of Israel.

A Reading (Lesson) from the Acts of the Apostles
[24:24—25:12]

Some days later when Felix came with his wife Drusilla,
who was Jewish, he sent for Paul and heard him speak
concerning faith in Christ Jesus. And as he discussed
justice, self-control, and the coming judgment, Felix
became frightened and said, "Go away for the present;
when I have an opportunity, I will send for you." At the
same time he hoped that money would be given him by
Paul, and for that reason he used to send for him very
often and converse with him. After two years had passed,
Felix was succeeded by Porcius Festus; and since he
wanted to grant the Jews a favor, Felix left Paul in prison.
Three days after Festus had arrived in the province, he
went up from Caesarea to Jerusalem where the chief
priests and the leaders of the Jews gave him a report
against Paul. They appealed to him and requested, as a
favor to them against Paul, to have him transferred to
Jerusalem. They were, in fact, planning an ambush to kill
him along the way. Festus replied that Paul was being kept
at Caesarea, and that he himself intended to go there
shortly. "So," he said, "let those of you who have the
authority come down with me, and if there is anything
wrong about the man, let them accuse him." After he had
stayed among them not more than eight or ten days, he
went down to Caesarea; the next day he took his seat on
the tribunal and ordered Paul to be brought. When he
arrived, the Jews who had gone down from Jerusalem
surrounded him, bringing many serious charges against
him, which they could not prove. Paul said in his defense,
"I have in no way committed an offense against the law of
the Jews, or against the temple, or against the emperor."
But Festus, wishing to do the Jews a favor, asked Paul,

"Do you wish to go up to Jerusalem and be tried there before me on these charges?" Paul said, "I am appealing to the emperor's tribunal; this is where I should be tried. I have done no wrong to the Jews, as you very well know. Now if I am in the wrong and have committed something for which I deserve to die, I am not trying to escape death; but if there is nothing to their charges against me, no one can turn me over to them. I appeal to the emperor." Then Festus, after he had conferred with his council, replied, "You have appealed to the emperor; to the emperor you will go."

A Reading (Lesson) from the Gospel according to Mark [12:35-44]

While Jesus was teaching in the temple, he said, "How can the scribes say that the Messiah is the son of David? David himself, by the Holy Spirit, declared, 'The Lord said to my Lord, "Sit at my right hand, until I put your enemies under your feet." ' David himself calls him Lord; so how can he be his son?" And the large crowd was listening to him with delight. As he taught, he said, "Beware of the scribes, who like to walk around in long robes, and to be greeted with respect in the marketplaces, and to have the best seats in the synagogues and places of honor at banquets! They devour widows' houses and for the sake of appearance say long prayers. They will receive the greater condemnation." He sat down opposite the treasury, and watched the crowd putting money into the treasury. Many rich people put in large sums. A poor widow came and put in two small copper coins, which are worth a penny. Then he called his disciples and said to them, "Truly I tell you, this poor widow has put in more than all those who are contributing to the treasury. For all of them have contributed out of their abundance; but she out of her poverty has put in everything she had, all she had to live on."

Saturday

Psalm 137:1–6(7–9) [page 792],
Psalm 144 [page 800] ❖ *Psalm 104* [page 735]

A Reading (Lesson) from the Second Book of Samuel [23:1–7, 13–17]

Now these are the last words of David: "The oracle of David, son of Jesse, the oracle of the man whom God exalted, the anointed of the God of Jacob, the favorite of the Strong One of Israel: The spirit of the LORD speaks through me, his word is upon my tongue. The God of Israel has spoken, the Rock of Israel has said to me: One who rules over people justly, ruling in the fear of God, is like the light of morning, like the sun rising on a cloudless morning, gleaming from the rain on the grassy land. Is not my house like this with God? For he has made with me an everlasting covenant, ordered in all things and secure. Will he not cause to prosper all my help and my desire? But the godless are all like thorns that are thrown away; for they cannot be picked up with the hand; to touch them one uses an iron bar or the shaft of a spear. And they are entirely consumed in fire on the spot." Towards the beginning of harvest three of the thirty chiefs went down to join David at the cave of Adullam, while a band of Philistines was encamped in the valley of Rephaim. David was then in the stronghold; and the garrison of the Philistines was then at Bethlehem. David said longingly, "O that someone would give me water to drink from the well of Bethlehem that is by the gate!" Then the three warriors broke through the camp of the Philistines, drew water from the well of Bethlehem that was by the gate, and brought it to David. But he would not drink of it; he poured it out to the LORD, for he said, "The LORD forbid that I should do this. Can I drink the blood of the men who went at the risk of their lives?" Therefore he would not drink it. The three warriors did these things.

A Reading (Lesson) from the Acts of the Apostles [25:13–27]

After several days had passed, King Agrippa and Bernice arrived at Caesarea to welcome Festus. Since they were staying there several days, Festus laid Paul's case before the king, saying, "There is a man here who was left in prison by Felix. When I was in Jerusalem, the chief priests and the elders of the Jews informed me about him and asked for a sentence against him. I told them that it was not the custom of the Romans to hand over anyone before the accused had met the accusers face to face and had been given an opportunity to make a defense against the charge. So when they met here, I lost no time, but on the next day took my seat on the tribunal and ordered the man to be brought. When the accusers stood up, they did not charge him with any of the crimes that I was expecting. Instead they had certain points of disagreement with him about their own religion and about a certain Jesus, who had died, but whom Paul asserted to be alive. Since I was at a loss how to investigate these questions, I asked whether he wished to go to Jerusalem and be tried there on these charges. But when Paul had appealed to be kept in custody for the decision of his Imperial Majesty, I ordered him to be held until I could send him to the emperor." Agrippa said to Festus, "I would like to hear the man myself." "Tomorrow," he said, "you will hear him." So on the next day Agrippa and Bernice came with great pomp, and they entered the audience hall with the military tribunes and the prominent men of the city. Then Festus gave the order and Paul was brought in. And Festus said, "King Agrippa and all here present with us, you see this man about whom the whole Jewish community petitioned me, both in Jerusalem and here, shouting that he ought not to live any longer. But I found that he had done nothing deserving death; and when he appealed to his Imperial Majesty, I decided to send him. But I have nothing definite to write to our sovereign about him. Therefore I have brought him before all of you, and especially before you, King Agrippa, so that, after we have examined him, I may have something to write—for it seems to me unreasonable to send a prisoner without indicating the charges against him."

A Reading (Lesson) from the Gospel according to Mark [13:1–13]

As Jesus came out of the temple, one of his disciples said to him, "Look, Teacher, what large stones and what large buildings!" Then Jesus asked him, "Do you see these great buildings? Not one stone will be left here upon another; all will be thrown down." When he was sitting on the Mount of Olives opposite the temple, Peter, James, John, and Andrew asked him privately, "Tell us, when will this be, and what will be the sign that all these things are about to be accomplished?" Then Jesus began to say to them, "Beware that no one leads you astray. Many will come in my name and say, 'I am he!' and they will lead many astray. When you hear of wars and rumors of wars, do not be alarmed; this must take place, but the end is still to come. For nation will rise against nation, and kingdom against kingdom; there will be earthquakes in various places; there will be famines. This is but the beginning of the birthpangs. As for yourselves, beware; for they will hand you over to councils; and you will be beaten in synagogues; and you will stand before governors and kings because of me, as a testimony to them. And the good news must first be proclaimed to all nations. When they bring you to trial and hand you over, do not worry beforehand about what you are to say; but say whatever is given you at that time, for it is not you who speak, but the Holy Spirit. Brother will betray brother to death, and a father his child, and children will rise against parents and have them put to death; and you will be hated by all because of my name. But the one who endures to the end will be saved."

Proper 16   *Week of the Sunday closest to August 24*

Sunday

Psalm 146 [page 803],   *Psalm 147* [page 804]   ❖
Psalm 111 [page 754],   *Psalm 112* [page 755],
Psalm 113 [page 756]

A Reading (Lesson) from the Second Book of Samuel [24:1–2, 10–25]

Again the anger of the LORD was kindled against Israel, and he incited David against them, saying, "Go, count the people of Israel and Judah." So the king said to Joab and the commanders of the army, who were with him, "Go through all the tribes of Israel, from Dan to Beer-sheba, and take a census of the people, so that I may know how many there are." But afterward, David was stricken to the heart because he had numbered the people. David said to the LORD, "I have sinned greatly in what I have done. But now, O LORD, I pray you, take away the guilt of your servant; for I have done very foolishly." When David rose in the morning, the word of the LORD came to the prophet Gad, David's seer, saying, "Go and say to David: Thus says the LORD: Three things I offer you; choose one of them, and I will do it to you." So Gad came to David and told him; he asked him, "Shall three years of famine come to you on your land? Or will you flee three months before your foes while they pursue you? Or shall there be three days' pestilence in your land? Now consider, and decide what answer I shall return to the one who sent me." Then David said to Gad, "I am in great distress; let us fall into the hand of the LORD, for his mercy is great; but let me not fall into human hands." So the LORD sent a pestilence on Israel from that morning until the appointed time; and seventy thousand of the people died, from Dan to Beer-sheba. But when the angel stretched out his hand toward Jerusalem to destroy it, the LORD relented concerning the evil, and said to the angel who was bringing destruction among the people, "It is enough; now stay your hand." The angel of the LORD was then by the threshing floor of Araunah the Jebusite. When David saw the angel who was destroying the people, he said to the LORD, "I alone have sinned, and I alone have done wickedly; but these sheep, what have they done? Let your hand, I pray, be against me and against my father's house." That day Gad came to David and said to him, "Go up and erect an altar to the LORD on the threshing floor of Araunah the Jebusite." Following Gad's instructions, David went up, as the LORD had commanded. When Araunah looked down, he saw the king and his servants coming toward him; and Araunah went out and prostrated himself before the king with his face to the ground. Araunah said, "Why has my lord the king come to his servant?" David said, "To buy the threshing floor from you in order to build an altar to the LORD, so that the plague may be averted from the people." Then Araunah said to David, "Let my lord the king take and offer up what seems good to him; here are the oxen for the burnt offering, and the threshing sledges and the yokes of the oxen for the wood. All this, O king, Araunah gives to the king." And Araunah said to the king, "May the LORD your God respond favorably to you." But the king said to Araunah, "No, but I will buy them from you for a price; I will not offer burnt offerings to the LORD my God that cost me nothing." So David bought the threshing floor and the oxen for fifty shekels of silver. David built there an altar to the LORD, and offered burnt offerings and offerings of well-being. So the LORD answered his supplication for the land, and the plague was averted from Israel.

A Reading (Lesson) from the Letter of Paul to the Galatians [3:23—4:7]

Before faith came, we were imprisoned and guarded under the law until faith would be revealed. Therefore the law was our disciplinarian until Christ came, so that we might be justified by faith. But now that faith has come, we are no longer subject to a disciplinarian, for in Christ Jesus you are all children of God through faith. As many of you as were baptized into Christ have clothed yourselves with Christ. There is no longer Jew or Greek, there is no longer slave or free, there is no longer male and female; for all of you are one in Christ Jesus. And if you belong to Christ, then you are Abraham's offspring, heirs according to the promise. My point is this: heirs, as long as they are minors, are no better than slaves, though they are the owners of all the property; but they remain under guardians and trustees until the date set by the father. So with us; while we were minors, we were enslaved to the elemental spirits of the world. But when the fullness of time had come, God sent his Son, born of a woman, born under the law, in order to redeem those who were under the law, so that we might receive adoption as children. And because you are children, God has sent the Spirit of his Son into our hearts, crying, "Abba! Father!" So you are no longer a slave but a child, and if a child then also an heir, through God.

A Reading (Lesson) from the Gospel according to John
[8:12–20]

Jesus spoke to them, saying, "I am the light of the world. Whoever follows me will never walk in darkness but will have the light of life." Then the Pharisees said to him, "You are testifying on your own behalf; your testimony is not valid." Jesus answered, "Even if I testify on my own behalf, my testimony is valid because I know where I have come from and where I am going, but you do not know where I come from or where I am going. You judge by human standards; I judge no one. Yet even if I do judge, my judgment is valid; for it is not I alone who judge, but I and the Father who sent me. In your law it is written that the testimony of two witnesses is valid. I testify on my own behalf, and the Father who sent me testifies on my behalf." Then they said to him, "Where is your Father?" Jesus answered, "You know neither me nor my Father. If you knew me, you would know my Father also." He spoke these words while he was teaching in the treasury of the temple, but no one arrested him, because his hour had not yet come.

Monday

Psalm 1 [page 585],   *Psalm 2* [page 586],
Psalm 3 [page 587]   ❖   *Psalm 4* [page 587],
Psalm 7 [page 590]

A Reading (Lesson) from the First Book of the Kings
[1:5–31]

Adonijah son of Haggith exalted himself, saying, "I will be
king"; he prepared for himself chariots and horsemen, and
fifty men to run before him. His father had never at any time
displeased him by asking, "Why have you done thus and
so?" He was also a very handsome man, and he was born
next after Absalom. He conferred with Joab son of Zeruiah
and with the priest Abiathar, and they supported Adonijah.
But the priest Zadok, and Benaiah son of Jehoiada, and the
prophet Nathan, and Shimei, and Rei, and David's own
warriors did not side with Adonijah. Adonijah sacrificed
sheep, oxen, and fatted cattle by the stone Zoheleth, which
is beside En-rogel, and he invited all his brothers, the king's
sons, and all the royal officials of Judah, but he did not
invite the prophet Nathan or Benaiah or the warriors or his
brother Solomon. Then Nathan said to Bathsheba,
Solomon's mother, "Have you not heard that Adonijah son
of Haggith has become king and our lord David does not
know it? Now therefore come, let me give you advice, so
that you may save your own life and the life of your son
Solomon. Go in at once to King David, and say to him,
'Did you not, my lord the king, swear to your servant,
saying: Your son Solomon shall succeed me as king, and he
shall sit on my throne? Why then is Adonijah king?' Then
while you are still there speaking with the king, I will come
in after you and confirm your words." So Bathsheba went to
the king in his room. The king was very old; Abishag the

Shunammite was attending the king. Bathsheba bowed and did obeisance to the king, and the king said, "What do you wish?" She said to him, "My lord, you swore to your servant by the LORD your God, saying: Your son Solomon shall succeed me as king, and he shall sit on my throne. But now suddenly Adonijah has become king, though you, my lord the king, do not know it. He has sacrificed oxen, fatted cattle, and sheep in abundance, and has invited all the children of the king, the priest Abiathar, and Joab the commander of the army; but your servant Solomon he has not invited. But you, my lord the king—the eyes of all Israel are on you to tell them who shall sit on the throne of my lord the king after him. Otherwise it will come to pass, when my lord the king sleeps with his ancestors, that my son Solomon and I will be counted offenders." While she was still speaking with the king, the prophet Nathan came in. The king was told, "Here is the prophet Nathan." When he came in before the king, he did obeisance to the king, with his face to the ground. Nathan said, "My lord the king, have you said, 'Adonijah shall succeed me as king, and he shall sit on my throne'? For today he has gone down and has sacrificed oxen, fatted cattle, and sheep in abundance, and has invited all the king's children, Joab the commander of the army, and the priest Abiathar, who are now eating and drinking before him, and saying, 'Long live King Adonijah!' But he did not invite me, your servant, and the priest Zadok, and Benaiah son of Jehoiada, and your servant Solomon. Has this thing been brought about by my lord the king and you have not let your servants know who should sit on the throne of my lord the king after him?" King David answered, "Summon Bathsheba to me." So she came into the king's presence, and stood before the king. The king swore, saying, "As the LORD lives, who has saved my life from every adversity, as I swore to you by the LORD, the

God of Israel, 'Your son Solomon shall succeed me as king, and he shall sit on my throne in my place,' so will I do this day." Then Bathsheba bowed with her face to the ground, and did obeisance to the king, and said, "May my lord King David live forever!"

A Reading (Lesson) from the Acts of the Apostles [26:1–23]

Agrippa said to Paul, "You have permission to speak for yourself." Then Paul stretched out his hand and began to defend himself: "I consider myself fortunate that it is before you, King Agrippa, I am to make my defense today against all the accusations of the Jews, because you are especially familiar with all the customs and controversies of the Jews; therefore I beg of you to listen to me patiently. All the Jews know my way of life from my youth, a life spent from the beginning among my own people and in Jerusalem. They have known for a long time, if they are willing to testify, that I have belonged to the strictest sect of our religion and lived as a Pharisee. And now I stand here on trial on account of my hope in the promise made by God to our ancestors, a promise that our twelve tribes hope to attain, as they earnestly worship day and night. It is for this hope, your Excellency, that I am accused by Jews! Why is it thought incredible by any of you that God raises the dead? Indeed, I myself was convinced that I ought to do many things against the name of Jesus of Nazareth. And that is what I did in Jerusalem; with authority received from the chief priests, I not only locked up many of the saints in prison, but I also cast my vote against them when they were being condemned to death. By punishing them often in all the synagogues I tried to force them to blaspheme; and since I was so furiously enraged at them, I pursued them even to foreign cities. With this in mind, I was traveling to Damascus with the authority and commission of the chief priests, when at midday along the road, your Excellency, I saw a light from heaven, brighter than the sun, shining around me and my companions. When we had all fallen to the ground, I heard a voice saying to me in the Hebrew language, 'Saul, Saul, why are you persecuting me? It hurts you to kick against the goads.' I asked, 'Who are you, Lord?' The Lord answered, 'I am Jesus whom you are persecuting. But get up and stand on your feet; for I have appeared to you for this purpose, to appoint you to serve and testify to the things in which you have seen me and to those in which I will appear to you. I will rescue you from your people and from the Gentiles—to whom I am sending you to open their eyes so that they may turn from darkness to light and from the power of Satan to God, so that they may receive forgiveness of sins and a place among those who are sanctified by faith in me.' After that, King Agrippa, I was not disobedient to the heavenly vision, but declared first to those in Damascus, then in Jerusalem and throughout the countryside of Judea, and also to the Gentiles, that they should repent and turn to God and do deeds consistent with repentance. For this reason the Jews seized me in the temple and tried to kill me. To this day I have had help from God, and so I stand here, testifying to both small and great, saying nothing but what the prophets and Moses said would take place: that the Messiah must suffer, and that, by being the first to rise from the dead, he would proclaim light both to our people and to the Gentiles."

A Reading (Lesson) from the Gospel according to Mark
[13:14–27]

Jesus said, "When you see the desolating sacrilege set up where it ought not to be (let the reader understand), then those in Judea must flee to the mountains; the one on the housetop must not go down or enter the house to take anything away; the one in the field must not turn back to get a coat. Woe to those who are pregnant and to those who are nursing infants in those days! Pray that it may not be in winter. For in those days there will be suffering, such as has not been from the beginning of the creation that God created until now, no, and never will be. And if the Lord had not cut short those days, no one would be saved; but for the sake of the elect, whom he chose, he has cut short those days. And if anyone says to you at that time, 'Look! Here is the Messiah!' or 'Look! There he is!'—do not believe it. False messiahs and false prophets will appear and produce signs and omens, to lead astray, if possible, the elect. But be alert; I have already told you everything. But in those days, after that suffering, the sun will be darkened, and the moon will not give its light, and the stars will be falling from heaven, and the powers in the heavens will be shaken. Then they will see 'the Son of Man coming in clouds' with great power and glory. Then he will send out the angels, and gather his elect from the four winds, from the ends of the earth to the ends of heaven."

Tuesday

Psalm 5 [page 588], *Psalm 6* [page 589] ❖
Psalm 10 [page 594], *Psalm 11* [page 596]

A Reading (Lesson) from the First Book of the Kings
[1:38—2:4]

The priest Zadok, the prophet Nathan, and Benaiah son of
Jehoiada, and the Cherethites and the Pelethites, went down
and had Solomon ride on King David's mule, and led him to
Gihon. There the priest Zadok took the horn of oil from the
tent and anointed Solomon. Then they blew the trumpet,
and all the people said, "Long live King Solomon!" And all
the people went up following him, playing on pipes and
rejoicing with great joy, so that the earth quaked at their
noise. Adonijah and all the guests who were with him heard
it as they finished feasting. When Joab heard the sound of
the trumpet, he said, "Why is the city in an uproar?" While
he was still speaking, Jonathan son of the priest Abiathar
arrived. Adonijah said, "Come in, for you are a worthy man
and surely you bring good news." Jonathan answered
Adonijah, "No, for our lord King David has made Solomon
king; the king has sent with him the priest Zadok, the
prophet Nathan, and Benaiah son of Jehoiada, and the
Cherethites and the Pelethites; and they had him ride on the
king's mule; the priest Zadok and the prophet Nathan have
anointed him king at Gihon; and they have gone up from
there rejoicing, so that the city is in an uproar. This is the
noise that you heard. Solomon now sits on the royal throne.
Moreover the king's servants came to congratulate our lord
King David, saying, 'May God make the name of Solomon
more famous than yours, and make his throne greater than
your throne.' The king bowed in worship on the bed and
went on to pray thus, 'Blessed be the Lord, the God of
Israel, who today has granted one of my offspring to sit on
my throne and permitted me to witness it.' " Then all the
guests of Adonijah got up trembling and went their own
ways. Adonijah, fearing Solomon, got up and went to grasp

the horns of the altar. Solomon was informed, "Adonijah is afraid of King Solomon; see, he has laid hold of the horns of the altar, saying, 'Let King Solomon swear to me first that he will not kill his servant with the sword.' " So Solomon responded, "If he proves to be a worthy man, not one of his hairs shall fall to the ground; but if wickedness is found in him, he shall die." Then King Solomon sent to have him brought down from the altar. He came to do obeisance to King Solomon; and Solomon said to him, "Go home." When David's time to die drew near, he charged his son Solomon, saying: "I am about to go the way of all the earth. Be strong, be courageous, and keep the charge of the LORD your God, walking in his ways and keeping his statutes, his commandments, his ordinances, and his testimonies, as it is written in the law of Moses, so that you may prosper in all that you do and wherever you turn. Then the LORD will establish his word that he spoke concerning me: 'If your heirs take heed to their way, to walk before me in faithfulness with all their heart and with all their soul, there shall not fail you a successor on the throne of Israel.' "

A Reading (Lesson) from the Acts of the Apostles
[26:24—27:8]

While he was making this defense, Festus exclaimed, "You are out of your mind, Paul! Too much learning is driving you insane!" But Paul said, "I am not out of my mind, most excellent Festus, but I am speaking the sober truth. Indeed the king knows about these things, and to him I speak freely; for I am certain that none of these things has escaped his notice, for this was not done in a corner. King Agrippa, do you believe the prophets? I know that you believe." Agrippa said to Paul, "Are you so quickly persuading me to become a Christian?" Paul replied,

"Whether quickly or not, I pray to God that not only you but also all who are listening to me today might become such as I am—except for these chains." Then the king got up, and with him the governor and Bernice and those who had been seated with them; and as they were leaving, they said to one another, "This man is doing nothing to deserve death or imprisonment." Agrippa said to Festus, "This man could have been set free if he had not appealed to the emperor." When it was decided that we were to sail for Italy, they transferred Paul and some other prisoners to a centurion of the Augustan Cohort, named Julius. Embarking on a ship of Adramyttium that was about to set sail to the ports along the coast of Asia, we put to sea, accompanied by Aristarchus, a Macedonian from Thessalonica. The next day we put in at Sidon; and Julius treated Paul kindly, and allowed him to go to his friends to be cared for. Putting out to sea from there, we sailed under the lee of Cyprus, because the winds were against us. After we had sailed across the sea that is off Cilicia and Pamphylia, we came to Myra in Lycia. There the centurion found an Alexandrian ship bound for Italy and put us on board. We sailed slowly for a number of days and arrived with difficulty off Cnidus, and as the wind was against us, we sailed under the lee of Crete off Salmone. Sailing past it with difficulty, we came to a place called Fair Havens, near the city of Lasea.

A Reading (Lesson) from the Gospel according to Mark [13:28–37]

Jesus said, "From the fig tree learn its lesson: as soon as its branch becomes tender and puts forth its leaves, you know that summer is near. So also, when you see these things taking place, you know that he is near, at the very gates. Truly I tell you, this generation will not pass away until all these things have taken place. Heaven and earth will pass away, but my words will not pass away. But about that day or hour no one knows, neither the angels in heaven, nor the Son, but only the Father. Beware, keep alert; for you do not know when the time will come. It is like a man going on a journey, when he leaves home and puts his slaves in charge, each with his work, and commands the doorkeeper to be on the watch. Therefore, keep awake—for you do not know when the master of the house will come, in the evening, or at midnight, or at cockcrow, or at dawn, or else he may find you asleep when he comes suddenly. And what I say to you I say to all: Keep awake."

Wednesday

Psalm 119:1–24 [page 763] ❖ *Psalm 12* [page 597], *Psalm 13* [page 597], *Psalm 14* [page 598]

A Reading (Lesson) from the First Book of the Kings [3:1–15]

Solomon made a marriage alliance with Pharaoh king of Egypt; he took Pharaoh's daughter and brought her into the city of David, until he had finished building his own house and the house of the LORD and the wall around Jerusalem. The people were sacrificing at the high places, however, because no house had yet been built for the name of the LORD. Solomon loved the LORD, walking in the statutes of his father David; only, he sacrificed and offered incense at the high places. The king went to Gibeon to sacrifice there, for that was the principal high place; Solomon used to offer a thousand burnt offerings on that altar. At Gibeon the

LORD appeared to Solomon in a dream by night; and God said, "Ask what I should give you." And Solomon said, "You have shown great and steadfast love to your servant my father David, because he walked before you in faithfulness, in righteousness, and in uprightness of heart toward you; and you have kept for him this great and steadfast love, and have given him a son to sit on his throne today. And now, O LORD my God, you have made your servant king in place of my father David, although I am only a little child; I do not know how to go out or come in. And your servant is in the midst of the people whom you have chosen, a great people, so numerous they cannot be numbered or counted. Give your servant therefore an understanding mind to govern your people, able to discern between good and evil; for who can govern this your great people?" It pleased the Lord that Solomon had asked this. God said to him, "Because you have asked this, and have not asked for yourself long life or riches, or for the life of your enemies, but have asked for yourself understanding to discern what is right, I now do according to your word. Indeed I give you a wise and discerning mind; no one like you has been before you and no one like you shall arise after you. I give you also what you have not asked, both riches and honor all your life; no other king shall compare with you. If you will walk in my ways, keeping my statutes and my commandments, as your father David walked, then I will lengthen your life." Then Solomon awoke; it had been a dream. He came to Jerusalem where he stood before the ark of the covenant of the LORD. He offered up burnt offerings and offerings of well-being, and provided a feast for all his servants.

A Reading (Lesson) from the Acts of the Apostles [27:9–26]

Since much time had been lost and sailing was now
dangerous, because even the Fast had already gone by,
Paul advised them, saying, "Sirs, I can see that the voyage
will be with danger and much heavy loss, not only of the
cargo and the ship, but also of our lives." But the
centurion paid more attention to the pilot and to the
owner of the ship than to what Paul said. Since the harbor
was not suitable for spending the winter, the majority was
in favor of putting to sea from there, on the chance that
somehow they could reach Phoenix, where they could
spend the winter. It was a harbor of Crete, facing
southwest and northwest. When a moderate south wind
began to blow, they thought they could achieve their
purpose; so they weighed anchor and began to sail past
Crete, close to the shore. But soon a violent wind, called
the northeaster, rushed down from Crete. Since the ship
was caught and could not be turned head-on into the
wind, we gave way to it and were driven. By running
under the lee of a small island called Cauda we were
scarcely able to get the ship's boat under control. After
hoisting it up they took measures to undergird the ship;
then, fearing that they would run on the Syrtis, they
lowered the sea anchor and so were driven. We were being
pounded by the storm so violently that on the next day
they began to throw the cargo overboard, and on the third
day with their own hands they threw the ship's tackle
overboard. When neither sun nor stars appeared for many
days, and no small tempest raged, all hope of our being
saved was at last abandoned. Since they had been without
food for a long time, Paul then stood up among them and
said, "Men, you should have listened to me and not have
set sail from Crete and thereby avoided this damage and

loss. I urge you now to keep up your courage, for there will be no loss of life among you, but only of the ship. For last night there stood by me an angel of the God to whom I belong and whom I worship, and he said, 'Do not be afraid, Paul; you must stand before the emperor; and indeed, God has granted safety to all those who are sailing with you.' So keep up your courage, men, for I have faith in God that it will be exactly as I have been told. But we will have to run aground on some island."

A Reading (Lesson) from the Gospel according to Mark [14:1–11]

It was two days before the Passover and the festival of Unleavened Bread. The chief priests and the scribes were looking for a way to arrest Jesus by stealth and kill him; for they said, "Not during the festival, or there may be a riot among the people." While he was at Bethany in the house of Simon the leper, as he sat at the table, a woman came with an alabaster jar of very costly ointment of nard, and she broke open the jar and poured the ointment on his head. But some were there who said to one another in anger, "Why was the ointment wasted in this way? For this ointment could have been sold for more than three hundred denarii, and the money given to the poor." And they scolded her. But Jesus said, "Let her alone; why do you trouble her? She has performed a good service for me. For you always have the poor with you, and you can show kindness to them whenever you wish; but you will not always have me. She has done what she could; she has anointed my body beforehand for its burial. Truly I tell you, wherever the good news is proclaimed in the whole world, what she has done will be told in remembrance of her." Then Judas Iscariot, who was one of the twelve, went to the chief priests in order to betray him to them. When they heard it, they were greatly pleased, and promised to give him money. So he began to look for an opportunity to betray him.

Thursday

Psalm 18:1–20 [page 602] ❖ *Psalm 18:21–50* [page 604]

A Reading (Lesson) from the First Book of the Kings [3:16–28]

Two women who were prostitutes came to the king and stood before him. The one woman said, "Please, my lord, this woman and I live in the same house; and I gave birth while she was in the house. Then on the third day after I gave birth, this woman also gave birth. We were together; there was no one else with us in the house, only the two of us were in the house. Then this woman's son died in the night, because she lay on him. She got up in the middle of the night and took my son from beside me while your servant slept. She laid him at her breast, and laid her dead son at my breast. When I rose in the morning to nurse my son, I saw that he was dead; but when I looked at him closely in the morning, clearly it was not the son I had borne." But the other woman said, "No, the living son is mine, and the dead son is yours." The first said, "No, the dead son is yours, and the living son is mine." So they argued before the king. Then the king said, "The one says, 'This is my son that is alive, and your son is dead'; while the other says, 'Not so! Your son is dead, and my son is the living one.'" So the king said, "Bring me a sword," and they brought a sword before the king. The king said, "Divide the living boy in two; then give half to the one, and half to the other." But the woman whose son was alive said to the king—because compassion for her son burned within her—"Please, my lord, give her the living boy; certainly do not kill him!" The other said, "It shall be neither mine nor yours; divide it." Then the king responded: "Give the first woman the living boy; do not kill him. She is his mother." All Israel heard of the judgment that the king had rendered; and they stood in awe of the king, because they perceived that the wisdom of God was in him, to execute justice.

A Reading (Lesson) from the Acts of the Apostles [27:27-44]

When the fourteenth night had come, as we were drifting across the sea of Adria, about midnight the sailors suspected that they were nearing land. So they took soundings and found twenty fathoms; a little farther on they took soundings again and found fifteen fathoms. Fearing that we might run on the rocks, they let down four anchors from the stern and prayed for day to come. But when the sailors tried to escape from the ship and had lowered the boat into the sea, on the pretext of putting out anchors from the bow, Paul said to the centurion and the soldiers, "Unless these men stay in the ship, you cannot be saved." Then the soldiers cut away the ropes of the boat and set it adrift. Just before daybreak, Paul urged all of them to take some food, saying, "Today is the fourteenth day that you have been in suspense and remaining without food, having eaten nothing. Therefore I urge you to take some food, for it will help you survive; for none of you will lose a hair from your heads." After he had said this, he took bread; and giving thanks to God in the presence of all, he broke it and began to eat. Then all of them were encouraged and took food for themselves. (We were in all two hundred seventy-six persons in the

ship.) After they had satisfied their hunger, they lightened
the ship by throwing the wheat into the sea. In the
morning they did not recognize the land, but they noticed
a bay with a beach, on which they planned to run the ship
ashore, if they could. So they cast off the anchors and left
them in the sea. At the same time they loosened the ropes
that tied the steering-oars; then hoisting the foresail to the
wind, they made for the beach. But striking a reef, they
ran the ship aground; the bow stuck and remained
immovable, but the stern was being broken up by the
force of the waves. The soldiers' plan was to kill the
prisoners, so that none might swim away and escape; but
the centurion, wishing to save Paul, kept them from
carrying out their plan. He ordered those who could swim
to jump overboard first and make for the land, and the
rest to follow, some on planks and others on pieces of the
ship. And so it was that all were brought safely to land.

A Reading (Lesson) from the Gospel according to Mark
[14:12–26]

On the first day of Unleavened Bread, when the Passover
lamb is sacrificed, his disciples said to him, "Where do
you want us to go and make the preparations for you to
eat the Passover?" So he sent two of his disciples, saying
to them, "Go into the city, and a man carrying a jar of
water will meet you; follow him, and wherever he enters,
say to the owner of the house, 'The Teacher asks, Where
is my guest room where I may eat the Passover with my
disciples?' He will show you a large room upstairs,
furnished and ready. Make preparations for us there." So
the disciples set out and went to the city, and found
everything as he had told them; and they prepared the
Passover meal. When it was evening, he came with the

twelve. And when they had taken their places and were eating, Jesus said, "Truly I tell you, one of you will betray me, one who is eating with me." They began to be distressed and to say to him one after another, "Surely, not I?" He said to them, "It is one of the twelve, one who is dipping bread into the bowl with me. For the Son of Man goes as it is written of him, but woe to that one by whom the Son of Man is betrayed! It would have been better for that one not to have been born." While they were eating, he took a loaf of bread, and after blessing it he broke it, gave it to them, and said, "Take; this is my body." Then he took a cup, and after giving thanks he gave it to them, and all of them drank from it. He said to them, "This is my blood of the covenant, which is poured out for many. Truly I tell you, I will never again drink of the fruit of the vine until that day when I drink it new in the kingdom of God." When they had sung the hymn, they went out to the Mount of Olives.

Friday

Psalm 16 [page 599], *Psalm 17* [page 600] ❖
Psalm 22 [page 610]

A Reading (Lesson) from the First Book of the Kings
[5:1—6:1,7]

King Hiram of Tyre sent his servants to Solomon, when he heard that they had anointed him king in place of his father; for Hiram had always been a friend to David. Solomon sent word to Hiram, saying, "You know that my father David could not build a house for the name of the LORD his God because of the warfare with which his enemies surrounded him, until the LORD put them under the soles of his feet. But now the LORD my God has given me rest on every side; there is neither adversary nor misfortune. So I intend to build a house for the name of the LORD my God, as the LORD said to my father David, 'Your son, whom I will set on your throne in your place, shall build the house for my name.' Therefore command that cedars from the Lebanon be cut for me. My servants will join your servants, and I will give you whatever wages you set for your servants; for you know that there is no one among us who knows how to cut timber like the Sidonians." When Hiram heard the words of Solomon, he rejoiced greatly, and said, "Blessed be the LORD today, who has given to David a wise son to be over this great people." Hiram sent word to Solomon, "I have heard the message that you have sent to me; I will fulfill all your needs in the matter of cedar and cypress timber. My servants shall bring it down to the sea from the Lebanon; I will make it into rafts to go by sea to the place you indicate. I will have them broken up there for you to take away. And you shall meet my needs by providing food for my household." So Hiram supplied Solomon's every need for timber of cedar and cypress. Solomon in turn gave Hiram twenty thousand cors of wheat as food for his household, and twenty cors of fine oil. Solomon gave this to Hiram year by year. So the LORD gave Solomon wisdom, as he promised him. There was peace between Hiram and Solomon; and the two of them made a treaty. King Solomon conscripted forced labor out of all Israel; the levy numbered thirty thousand men. He sent them to the Lebanon, ten thousand a month in shifts; they would be a month in the Lebanon and two months at home; Adoniram was in charge of the forced labor. Solomon also had seventy thousand laborers and eighty thousand stonecutters in the hill country, besides Solomon's three thousand three hundred supervisors who were over the work, having charge of the people who did the work. At the king's command, they quarried out great, costly stones in order to lay the foundation of the house with dressed stones. So Solomon's builders and Hiram's builders and the Giblites did the stonecutting and prepared the timber and the stone to build the house. In the four hundred eightieth year after the Israelites came out of the land of Egypt, in the fourth year of Solomon's reign over Israel, in the month of Ziv, which is the second month, he began to build the house of the LORD. The house was built with stone finished at the quarry, so that neither hammer nor ax nor any tool of iron was heard in the temple while it was being built.

A Reading (Lesson) from the Acts of the Apostles [28:1–16]

After we had reached safety, we then learned that the island was called Malta. The natives showed us unusual kindness. Since it had begun to rain and was cold, they kindled a fire and welcomed all of us around it. Paul had gathered a bundle of brushwood and was putting it on the fire, when a viper, driven out by the heat, fastened itself on his hand. When the natives saw the creature hanging from his hand, they said to one another, "This man must be a murderer; though he has escaped from the sea, justice has not allowed him to live." He, however, shook off the creature into the fire and suffered no harm. They were expecting him to swell up or drop dead, but after they had waited a long time and saw that nothing unusual had happened to him, they changed their minds and began to say that he was a god. Now in the neighborhood of that place were lands belonging to the leading man of the island, named Publius, who received us and entertained us hospitably for three days. It so happened that the father of Publius lay sick in bed with fever and dysentery. Paul visited him and cured him by praying and putting his hands on him. After this happened, the rest of the people on the island who had diseases also came and were cured. They bestowed many honors on us, and when we were about to sail, they put on board all the provisions we needed. Three months later we set sail on a ship that had wintered at the island, an Alexandrian ship with the Twin Brothers as its figurehead. We put in at Syracuse and stayed there for three days; then we weighed anchor and came to Rhegium. After one day there a south wind sprang up, and on the second day we came to Puteoli. There we found believers and were invited to stay with them for seven days. And so we came to Rome. The believers from there, when they heard of us, came as far as the Forum of Appius and Three Taverns to meet us. On seeing them, Paul thanked God and took courage. When we came into Rome, Paul was allowed to live by himself, with the soldier who was guarding him.

A Reading (Lesson) from the Gospel according to Mark [14:27–42]

Jesus said to the disciples, "You will all become deserters; for it is written, 'I will strike the shepherd, and the sheep will be scattered.' But after I am raised up, I will go before you to Galilee." Peter said to him, "Even though all become deserters, I will not." Jesus said to him, "Truly I tell you, this day, this very night, before the cock crows twice, you will deny me three times." But he said vehemently, "Even though I must die with you, I will not deny you." And all of them said the same. They went to a place called Gethsemane; and he said to his disciples, "Sit here while I pray." He took with him Peter and James and John, and began to be distressed and agitated. And said to them, "I am deeply grieved, even to death; remain here, and keep awake." And going a little farther, he threw himself on the ground and prayed that, if it were possible, the hour might pass from him. He said, "Abba, Father, for you all things are possible; remove this cup from me; yet, not what I want, but what you want." He came and found them sleeping; and he said to Peter, "Simon, are you asleep? Could you not keep awake one hour? Keep awake and pray that you may not come into the time of trial; the spirit indeed is willing, but the flesh is weak." And again he went away and prayed, saying the same words. And once more he came and found them sleeping, for their eyes were very heavy; and they did not know what to say to him. He came a third time and said to them, "Are you still sleeping and taking your rest? Enough! The hour has come; the Son of Man is betrayed into the hands of sinners. Get up, let us be going. See, my betrayer is at hand."

Saturday

Psalm 20 [page 608], *Psalm 21:1–7(8–14)* [page 608]   ❖
Psalm 110:1–5(6–7) [page 753], *Psalm 116* [page 759],
Psalm 117 [page 760]

A Reading (Lesson) from the First Book of the Kings
[7:51—8:21]

All the work that King Solomon did on the house of the LORD was finished. Solomon brought in the things that his father David had dedicated, the silver, the gold, and the vessels, and stored them in the treasuries of the house of the LORD. Then Solomon assembled the elders of Israel and all the heads of the tribes, the leaders of the ancestral houses of the Israelites, before King Solomon in Jerusalem, to bring up the ark of the covenant of the LORD out of the city of David, which is Zion. All the people of Israel assembled to King Solomon at the festival in the month Ethanim, which is the seventh month. And all the elders of Israel came, and the priests carried the ark. So they brought up the ark of the LORD, the tent of meeting, and all the holy vessels that were in the tent; the priests and the Levites brought them up. King Solomon and all the congregation of Israel, who had assembled before him, were with him before the ark, sacrificing so many sheep and oxen that they could not be counted or numbered. Then the priests brought the ark of the covenant of the LORD to its place, in the inner sanctuary of the house, in the most holy place, underneath the wings of the cherubim. For the cherubim spread out their wings over the place of the ark, so that the cherubim made a covering above the ark and its poles. The poles were so long that the ends of the poles were seen from the holy place in front of the inner sanctuary; but they could not be seen from outside; they are there to this day. There was nothing in the ark except the two tablets of stone that Moses had placed there at Horeb, where the LORD made a covenant with the Israelites, when they came out of the land of Egypt. And when the priests came out of the holy place, a cloud filled the house of the LORD, so that the priests could not stand to minister because of the cloud; for the glory of the LORD filled the house of the LORD. Then Solomon said, "The LORD has said that he would dwell in thick darkness. I have built you an exalted house, a place for you to dwell in forever." Then the king turned around and blessed all the assembly of Israel, while all the assembly of Israel stood. He said, "Blessed be the LORD, the God of Israel, who with his hand has fulfilled what he promised with his mouth to my father David, saying, 'Since the day that I brought my people Israel out of Egypt, I have not chosen a city from any of the tribes of Israel in which to build a house, that my name might be there; but I chose David to be over my people Israel.' My father David had it in mind to build a house for the name of the LORD, the God of Israel. But the LORD said to my father David, 'You did well to consider building a house for my name; nevertheless you shall not build the house, but your son who shall be born to you shall build the house for my name.' Now the LORD has upheld the promise that he made; for I have risen in the place of my father David; I sit on the throne of Israel, as the LORD promised, and have built the house for the name of the LORD, the God of Israel. There I have provided a place for the ark, in which is the covenant of the LORD that he made with our ancestors when he brought them out of the land of Egypt."

A Reading (Lesson) from the Acts of the Apostles [28:17–31]

Three days later Paul called together the local leaders of the Jews. When they had assembled, he said to them, "Brothers, though I had done nothing against our people or the customs of our ancestors, yet I was arrested in Jerusalem and handed over to the Romans. When they had examined me, the Romans wanted to release me, because there was no reason for the death penalty in my case. But when the Jews objected, I was compelled to appeal to the emperor—even though I had no charge to bring against my nation. For this reason therefore I have asked to see you and speak with you, since it is for the sake of the hope of Israel that I am bound with this chain." They replied, "We have received no letters from Judea about you, and none of the brothers coming here has reported or spoken anything evil about you. But we would like to hear from you what you think, for with regard to this sect we know that everywhere it is spoken against." After they had set a day to meet with him, they came to him at his lodgings in great numbers. From morning until evening he explained the matter to them, testifying to the kingdom of God and trying to convince them about Jesus both from the law of Moses and from the prophets. Some were convinced by what he had said, while others refused to believe. So they disagreed with each other; and as they were leaving, Paul made one further statement: "The Holy Spirit was right in saying to your ancestors through the prophet Isaiah, 'Go to this people and say, You will indeed listen, but never understand, and you will indeed look, but never perceive. For this people's heart has grown dull, and their ears are hard of hearing, and they have shut their eyes; so that they might not look with their eyes, and listen with their ears, and understand with their heart and turn—and I would heal them.' Let it be known to you then that this salvation of God has been sent to the Gentiles; they will listen." He lived there two whole years at his own expense and welcomed all who came to him, proclaiming the kingdom of God and teaching about the Lord Jesus Christ with all boldness and without hindrance.

A Reading (Lesson) from the Gospel according to Mark [14:43–52]

Immediately, while Jesus was still speaking, Judas, one of the twelve, arrived; and with him there was a crowd with swords and clubs, from the chief priests, the scribes, and the elders. Now the betrayer had given them a sign, saying, "The one I will kiss is the man; arrest him and lead him away under guard." So when he came, he went up to him at once and said, "Rabbi!" and kissed him. Then they laid hands on him and arrested him. But one of those who stood near drew his sword and struck the slave of the high priest, cutting off his ear. Then Jesus said to them, "Have you come out with swords and clubs to arrest me as though I were a bandit? Day after day I was with you in the temple teaching, and you did not arrest me. But let the scriptures be fulfilled." All of them deserted him and fled. A certain young man was following him, wearing nothing but a linen cloth. They caught hold of him, but he left the linen cloth and ran off naked.

Proper 17 *Week of the Sunday closest to August 31*

Sunday

Psalm 148 [page 805], *Psalm 149* [page 807], *Psalm 150* [page 807] ❖ *Psalm 114* [page 756], *Psalm 115* [page 757]

A Reading (Lesson) from the First Book of the Kings [8:22–30(31–40)]

Solomon stood before the altar of the LORD in the presence of all the assembly of Israel, and spread out his hands to heaven. He said, "O LORD, God of Israel, there is no God like you in heaven above or on earth beneath, keeping covenant and steadfast love for your servants who walk before you with all their heart, the covenant that you kept for your servant my father David as you declared to him; you promised with your mouth and have this day fulfilled with your hand. Therefore, O LORD, God of Israel, keep for your servant my father David that which you promised him, saying, 'There shall never fail you a successor before me to sit on the throne of Israel, if only your children look to their way, to walk before me as you have walked before me.' Therefore, O God of Israel, let your word be confirmed, which you promised to your servant my father David. But will God indeed dwell on the earth? Even heaven and the highest heaven cannot contain you, much less this house that I have built! Regard your servant's prayer and his plea, O LORD my God, heeding the cry and the prayer that your servant prays to you today; that your eyes may be open night and day toward this house, the place of which you said, 'My name shall be there,' that you may heed the prayer that your servant prays toward this place. Hear the plea of your servant and of your people Israel when they pray toward this place; O hear in heaven your dwelling place; heed and forgive."

"If someone sins against a neighbor and is given an oath to swear, and comes and swears before your altar in this house, then hear in heaven, and act, and judge your servants, condemning the guilty by bringing their conduct on their own head, and vindicating the righteous by rewarding them according to their righteousness. When your people Israel, having sinned against you, are defeated before an enemy but turn again to you, confess your name, pray and plead with you in this house, then hear in heaven, forgive the sin of your people Israel, and bring them again to the land that you gave to their ancestors. When heaven is shut up and there is no rain because they have sinned against you, and then they pray toward this place, confess your name, and turn from their sin, because you punish them, then hear in heaven, and forgive the sin of your servants, your people Israel, when you teach them the good way in which they should walk; and grant rain on your land, which you have given to your people as an inheritance. If there is famine in the land, if there is plague, blight, mildew, locust, or caterpillar; if their enemy besieges them in any of their cities; whatever plague, whatever sickness there is; whatever prayer, whatever plea there is from any individual or from all your people Israel, all knowing the afflictions of their own hearts so that they stretch out their hands toward this house; then hear in heaven your dwelling place, forgive, act, and render to all whose hearts you know—according to all their ways, for only you know what is in every human heart—so that they may fear you all the days that they live in the land that you gave to our ancestors."

A Reading (Lesson) from the First Letter of Paul to Timothy [4:7b–16]

Train yourself in godliness, for, while physical training is of some value, godliness is valuable in every way, holding promise for both the present life and the life to come. The saying is sure and worthy of full acceptance. For to this end we toil and struggle, because we have our hope set on the living God, who is the Savior of all people, especially of those who believe. These are the things you must insist on and teach. Let no one despise your youth, but set the believers an example in speech and conduct, in love, in faith, in purity. Until I arrive, give attention to the public reading of scripture, to exhorting, to teaching. Do not neglect the gift that is in you, which was given to you through prophecy with the laying on of hands by the council of elders. Put these things into practice, devote yourself to them, so that all may see your progress. Pay close attention to yourself and to your teaching; continue in these things, for in doing this you will save both yourself and your hearers.

A Reading (Lesson) from the Gospel according to John [8:47–59]

Jesus said to the Jews, "Whoever is from God hears the words of God. The reason you do not hear them is that you are not from God." The Jews answered him, "Are we not right in saying that you are a Samaritan and have a demon?" Jesus answered, "I do not have a demon; but I honor my Father, and you dishonor me. Yet I do not seek my own glory; there is one who seeks it and he is the judge. Very truly, I tell you, whoever keeps my word will never see death." The Jews said to him, "Now we know that you have a demon. Abraham died, and so did the prophets; yet you say, 'Whoever keeps my word will never taste death.' Are you greater than our father Abraham, who died? The prophets also died. Who do you claim to be?" Jesus answered, "If I glorify myself, my glory is nothing. It is my Father who glorifies me, he of whom you say, 'He is our God,' though you do not know him. But I know him; if I would say that I do not know him, I would be a liar like you. But I do know him and I keep his word. Your ancestor Abraham rejoiced that he would see my day; he saw it and was glad." Then the Jews said to him, "You are not yet fifty years old, and have you seen Abraham?" Jesus said to them, "Very truly, I tell you, before Abraham was, I am." So they picked up stones to throw at him, but Jesus hid himself and went out of the temple.

Monday

Psalm 25 [page 614] ❖ *Psalm 9* [page 593],
Psalm 15 [page 599]

A Reading (Lesson) from the Second Book of Chronicles
[6:32—7:7]

Solomon knelt upon his knees in the presence of all the
assembly of Israel, and spread forth his hands toward
heaven, and said, "When foreigners, who are not of your
people Israel, come from a distant land because of your
great name, and your mighty hand, and your outstretched
arm, when they come and pray toward this house, may you
hear from heaven your dwelling place, and do whatever the
foreigners ask of you, in order that all the peoples of the
earth may know your name and fear you, as do your people
Israel, and that they may know that your name has been
invoked on this house that I have built. If your people go
out to battle against their enemies, by whatever way you
shall send them, and they pray to you toward this city that
you have chosen and the house that I have built for your
name, then hear from heaven their prayer and their plea,
and maintain their cause. If they sin against you—for there
is no one who does not sin—and you are angry with them
and give them to an enemy, so that they are carried away
captive to a land far or near; then if they come to their
senses in the land to which they have been taken captive,
and repent, and plead with you in the land of their captivity,
saying, 'We have sinned, and have done wrong; we have
acted wickedly'; if they repent with all their heart and soul
in the land of their captivity, to which they were taken
captive, and pray toward their land, which you gave to their
ancestors, the city that you have chosen, and the house that
I have built for your name, then hear from heaven your

dwelling place their prayer and their pleas, maintain their cause and forgive your people who have sinned against you. Now, O my God, let your eyes be open and your ears attentive to prayer from this place. Now rise up, O LORD God, and go to your resting place, you and the ark of your might. Let your priests, O LORD God, be clothed with salvation, and let your faithful rejoice in your goodness. O LORD God, do not reject your anointed one. Remember your steadfast love for your servant David." When Solomon had ended his prayer, fire came down from heaven and consumed the burnt offering and the sacrifices; and the glory of the LORD filled the temple. The priests could not enter the house of the LORD, because the glory of the LORD filled the LORD's house. When all the people of Israel saw the fire come down and the glory of the LORD on the temple, they bowed down on the pavement with their faces to the ground, and worshiped and gave thanks to the LORD, saying, "For he is good, for his steadfast love endures forever." Then the king and all the people offered sacrifice before the LORD. King Solomon offered as a sacrifice twenty-two thousand oxen and one hundred twenty thousand sheep. So the king and all the people dedicated the house of God. The priests stood at their posts; the Levites also, with the instruments for music to the LORD that King David had made for giving thanks to the LORD—for his steadfast love endures forever—whenever David offered praises by their ministry. Opposite them the priests sounded trumpets; and all Israel stood. Solomon consecrated the middle of the court that was in front of the house of the LORD; for there he offered the burnt offerings and the fat of the offerings of well-being because the bronze altar Solomon had made could not hold the burnt offering and the grain offering and the fat parts.

A Reading (Lesson) from the Letter of James [2:1–13]

My brothers and sisters, do you with your acts of
favoritism really believe in our glorious Lord Jesus Christ?
For if a person with gold rings and in fine clothes comes
into your assembly, and if a poor person in dirty clothes
also comes in, and if you take notice of the one wearing
the fine clothes and say, "Have a seat here, please," while
to the one who is poor you say, "Stand there," or, "Sit at
my feet," have you not made distinctions among
yourselves, and become judges with evil thoughts? Listen,
my beloved brothers and sisters. Has not God chosen the
poor in the world to be rich in faith and to be heirs of the
kingdom that he has promised to those who love him? But
you have dishonored the poor. Is it not the rich who
oppress you? Is it not they who drag you into court? Is it
not they who blaspheme the excellent name that was
invoked over you? You do well if you really fulfill the
royal law according to the scripture, "You shall love your
neighbor as yourself." But if you show partiality, you
commit sin and are convicted by the law as transgressors.
For whoever keeps the whole law but fails in one point
has become accountable for all of it. For the one who
said, "You shall not commit adultery," also said, "You
shall not murder." Now if you do not commit adultery
but if you murder, you have become a transgressor of the
law. So speak and so act as those who are to be judged by
the law of liberty. For judgment will be without mercy to
anyone who has shown no mercy; mercy triumphs over
judgment.

A Reading (Lesson) from the Gospel according to Mark
[14:53–65]

The crowd took Jesus to the high priest; and all the chief
priests, the elders, and the scribes were assembled. Peter
had followed him at a distance, right into the courtyard of
the high priest; and he was sitting with the guards,
warming himself at the fire. Now the chief priests and the
whole council were looking for testimony against Jesus to
put him to death; but they found none. For many gave
false testimony against him, and their testimony did not
agree. Some stood up and gave false testimony against
him, saying, "We heard him say, 'I will destroy this
temple that is made with hands, and in three days I will
build another, not made with hands.' " But even on this
point their testimony did not agree. Then the high priest
stood up before them and asked Jesus, "Have you no
answer? What is it that they testify against you?" But he
was silent and did not answer. Again the high priest asked
him, "Are you the Messiah, the Son of the Blessed One?"
Jesus said, "I am; and 'you will see the Son of Man seated
at the right hand of the Power,' and 'coming with the
clouds of heaven.' " Then the high priest tore his clothes
and said, "Why do we still need witnesses? You have
heard his blasphemy! What is your decision?" All of them
condemned him as deserving death. Some began to spit on
him, to blindfold him, and to strike him, saying to him,
"Prophesy!" The guards also took him over and beat him.

Tuesday

Psalm 26 [page 616],   *Psalm 28* [page 619]   ❖
Psalm 36 [page 632],   *Psalm 39* [page 638]

A Reading (Lesson) from the First Book of the Kings
[8:65—9:9]

Solomon held the festival at that time, and all Israel with
him—a great assembly, people from Lebohamath to the
Wadi of Egypt—before the LORD our God, seven days. On
the eighth day he sent the people away; and they blessed the
king, and went to their tents, joyful and in good spirits
because of all the goodness that the LORD had shown to his
servant David and to his people Israel. When Solomon had
finished building the house of the LORD and the king's house
and all that Solomon desired to build, the LORD appeared to
Solomon a second time, as he had appeared to him at
Gibeon. The LORD said to him, "I have heard your prayer
and your plea, which you made before me; I have
consecrated this house that you have built, and put my name
there forever; my eyes and my heart will be there for all
time. As for you, if you will walk before me, as David your
father walked, with integrity of heart and uprightness, doing
according to all that I have commanded you, and keeping
my statutes and my ordinances, then I will establish your
royal throne over Israel forever, as I promised your father
David, saying, 'There shall not fail you a successor on the
throne of Israel.' If you turn aside from following me, you
or your children, and do not keep my commandments and
my statutes that I have set before you, but go and serve
other gods and worship them, then I will cut Israel off from
the land that I have given them; and the house that I have
consecrated for my name I will cast out of my sight; and
Israel will become a proverb and a taunt among all peoples.
This house will become a heap of ruins; everyone passing by
it will be astonished, and will hiss; and they will say, 'Why
has the LORD done such a thing to this land and to this
house?' Then they will say, 'Because they have forsaken the

Lord their God, who brought their ancestors out of the land of Egypt, and embraced other gods, worshiping them and serving them; therefore the Lord has brought this disaster upon them.' "

A Reading (Lesson) from the Letter of James [2:14–26]

What good is it, my brothers and sisters, if you say you have faith but do not have works? Can faith save you? If a brother or sister is naked and lacks daily food, and one of you says to them, "Go in peace; keep warm and eat your fill," and yet you do not supply their bodily needs, what is the good of that? So faith by itself, if it has no works, is dead. But someone will say, "You have faith and I have works." Show me your faith apart from your works, and I by my works will show you my faith. You believe that God is one; you do well. Even the demons believe—and shudder. Do you want to be shown, you senseless person, that faith apart from works is barren? Was not our ancestor Abraham justified by works when he offered his son Isaac on the altar? You see that faith was active along with his works, and faith was brought to completion by the works. Thus the scripture was fulfilled that says, "Abraham believed God, and it was reckoned to him as righteousness," and he was called the friend of God. You see that a person is justified by works and not by faith alone. Likewise, was not Rahab the prostitute also justified by works when she welcomed the messengers and sent them out by another road? For just as the body without the spirit is dead, so faith without works is also dead.

A Reading (Lesson) from the Gospel according to Mark
[14:66–72]

While Peter was below in the courtyard, one of the servant-girls of the high priest came by. When she saw Peter warming himself, she stared at him and said, "You also were with Jesus, the man from Nazareth." But he denied it, saying, "I do not know or understand what you are talking about." And he went out into the forecourt. Then the cock crowed. And the servant-girl, on seeing him, began again to say to the bystanders, "This man is one of them." But again he denied it. Then after a little while the bystanders again said to Peter, "Certainly you are one of them; for you are a Galilean." But he began to curse, and he swore an oath, "I do not know this man you are talking about." At that moment the cock crowed for the second time. Then Peter remembered that Jesus had said to him, "Before the cock crows twice, you will deny me three times." And he broke down and wept.

Wednesday

Psalm 38 [page 636]   ∴   *Psalm 119:25–48* [page 765]

A Reading (Lesson) from the First Book of the Kings [9:24—10:13]

Pharaoh's daughter went up from the city of David to her own house that Solomon had built for her; then he built the Millo. Three times a year Solomon used to offer up burnt offerings and sacrifices of well-being on the altar that he built for the LORD, offering incense before the LORD. So he completed the house. King Solomon built a fleet of ships at Ezion-geber, which is near Eloth on the shore of the Red Sea, in the land of Edom. Hiram sent his servants with the fleet, sailors who were familiar with the sea, together with the servants of Solomon. They went to Ophir, and imported from there four hundred twenty talents of gold, which they delivered to King Solomon. When the queen of Sheba heard of the fame of Solomon, (fame due to the name of the LORD), she came to test him with hard questions. She came to Jerusalem with a very great retinue, with camels bearing spices, and very much gold, and precious stones; and when she came to Solomon, she told him all that was on her mind. Solomon answered all her questions; there was nothing hidden from the king that he could not explain to her. When the queen of Sheba had observed all the wisdom of Solomon, the house that he had built, the food of his table, the seating of his officials, and the attendance of his servants, their clothing, his valets, and his burnt offerings that he offered at the house of the LORD, there was no more spirit in her. So she said to the king, "The report was true that I heard in my own land of your accomplishments and of your wisdom, but I did not believe the reports until I came and my own eyes had seen it. Not even half had been told me; your wisdom and prosperity far surpass the report that I had heard. Happy are your wives! Happy are these your servants, who continually attend you and hear your wisdom! Blessed be the LORD your God, who has delighted in you and set you on the throne of Israel! Because the LORD loved Israel forever, he has made you king to execute justice and righteousness." Then she gave the king one hundred twenty talents of gold, a great quantity of spices, and precious stones; never again did spices come in such quantity as that which the queen of Sheba gave to King Solomon. Moreover, the fleet of Hiram, which carried gold from Ophir, brought from Ophir a great quantity of almug wood and precious stones. From the almug wood the king made supports for the house of the LORD, and for the king's house, lyres also and harps for the singers; no such almug wood has come or been seen to this day. Meanwhile King Solomon gave to the queen of Sheba every desire that she expressed, as well as what he gave her out of Solomon's royal bounty. Then she returned to her own land, with her servants.

A Reading (Lesson) from the Letter of James [3:1–12]

Not many of you should become teachers, my brothers and sisters, for you know that we who teach will be judged with greater strictness. For all of us make many mistakes. Anyone who makes no mistakes in speaking is perfect, able to keep the whole body in check with a bridle. If we put bits into the mouths of horses to make them obey us, we guide their whole bodies. Or look at ships: though they are so large that it takes strong winds to drive them, yet they are guided by a very small rudder wherever the will of the pilot directs. So also the tongue is a small member, yet it boasts of great exploits. How great a forest is set ablaze by a small fire! And the tongue is a fire. The tongue is placed among our members as a world of iniquity; it stains the whole body, sets on fire the cycle of nature, and is itself set on fire by hell. For every species of beast and bird, of reptile and sea creature, can be tamed and has been tamed by the human species, but no one can tame the tongue—a restless evil, full of deadly poison. With it we bless the Lord and Father, and with it we curse those who are made in the likeness of God. From the same mouth come blessing and cursing. My brothers and sisters, this ought not to be so. Does a spring pour forth from the same opening both fresh and brackish water? Can a fig tree, my brothers and sisters, yield olives, or a grapevine figs? No more can salt water yield fresh.

A Reading (Lesson) from the Gospel according to
Mark [15:1–11]

As soon as it was morning, the chief priests held a
consultation with the elders and scribes and the whole
council. They bound Jesus, led him away, and handed him
over to Pilate. Pilate asked him, "Are you the King of the
Jews?" He answered him, "You say so." Then the chief
priests accused him of many things. Pilate asked him
again, "Have you no answer? See how many charges they
bring against you." But Jesus made no further reply, so
that Pilate was amazed. Now at the festival he used to
release a prisoner for them, anyone for whom they asked.
Now a man called Barabbas was in prison with the rebels
who had committed murder during the insurrection. So the
crowd came and began to ask Pilate to do for them
according to his custom. Then he answered them, "Do
you want me to release for you the King of the Jews?" For
he realized that it was out of jealousy that the chief priests
had handed him over. But the chief priests stirred up the
crowd to have him release Barabbas for them instead.

Thursday

Psalm 37:1–18 [page 633]   ❖   *Psalm 37:19–42* [page 634]

A Reading (Lesson) from the First Book of the
Kings [11:1–13]

King Solomon loved many foreign women along with the
daughter of Pharaoh: Moabite, Ammonite, Edomite,
Sidonian, and Hittite women, from the nations concerning
which the LORD had said to the Israelites, "You shall not
enter into marriage with them, neither shall they with you;
for they will surely incline your heart to follow their gods";

Solomon clung to these in love. Among his wives were seven hundred princesses and three hundred concubines; and his wives turned away his heart. For when Solomon was old, his wives turned away his heart after other gods; and his heart was not true to the LORD his God, as was the heart of his father David. For Solomon followed Astarte the goddess of the Sidonians, and Milcom the abomination of the Ammonites. So Solomon did what was evil in the sight of the LORD, and did not completely follow the LORD, as his father David had done. Then Solomon built a high place for Chemosh the abomination of Moab, and for Molech the abomination of the Ammonites, on the mountain east of Jerusalem. He did the same for all his foreign wives, who offered incense and sacrificed to their gods. Then the LORD was angry with Solomon, because his heart had turned away from the LORD, the God of Israel, who had appeared to him twice, and had commanded him concerning this matter, that he should not follow other gods; but he did not observe what the LORD commanded. Therefore the LORD said to Solomon, "Since this has been your mind and you have not kept my covenant and my statutes that I have commanded you, I will surely tear the kingdom from you and give it to your servant. Yet for the sake of your father David I will not do it in your lifetime; I will tear it out of the hand of your son. I will not, however, tear away the entire kingdom; I will give one tribe to your son, for the sake of my servant David and for the sake of Jerusalem, which I have chosen."

A Reading (Lesson) from the Letter of James [3:13—4:12]

Who is wise and understanding among you? Show by your good life that your works are done with gentleness born of wisdom. But if you have bitter envy and selfish ambition in your hearts, do not be boastful and false to the truth. Such wisdom does not come down from above, but is earthly, unspiritual, devilish. For where there is envy and selfish ambition, there will also be disorder and wickedness of every kind. But the wisdom from above is first pure, then peaceable, gentle, willing to yield, full of mercy and good fruits, without a trace of partiality or hypocrisy. And a harvest of righteousness is sown in peace for those who make peace. Those conflicts and disputes among you, where do they come from? Do they not come from your cravings that are at war within you? You want something and do not have it; so you commit murder. And you covet something and cannot obtain it; so you engage in disputes and conflicts. You do not have, because you do not ask. You ask and do not receive, because you ask wrongly, in order to spend what you get on your pleasures. Adulterers! Do you not know that friendship with the world is enmity with God? Therefore whoever wishes to be a friend of the world becomes an enemy of God. Or do you suppose that it is for nothing that the scripture says, "God yearns jealously for the spirit that he has made to dwell in us"? But he gives all the more grace; therefore it says, "God opposes the proud, but gives grace to the humble." Submit yourselves therefore to God. Resist the devil, and he will flee from you. Draw near to God, and he will draw near to you. Cleanse your hands, you sinners, and purify your hearts, you double-minded. Lament and mourn and weep. Let your laughter be turned into mourning and your joy into dejection. Humble yourselves before the Lord, and he will exalt you. Do not speak evil against one another, brothers and sisters. Whoever speaks evil against another or judges another, speaks evil against the law and judges the law; but if you judge the law, you are not a doer of the law but a judge. There is one lawgiver and judge who is able to save and to destroy. So who, then, are you to judge your neighbor?

A Reading (Lesson) from the Gospel according to Mark [15:12–21]

Pilate spoke to the crowd again, "Then what do you wish me to do with the man you call the King of the Jews?" They shouted back, "Crucify him!" Pilate asked them, "Why, what evil has he done?" But they shouted all the more, "Crucify him!" So Pilate, wishing to satisfy the crowd, released Barabbas for them; and after flogging Jesus, he handed him over to be crucified. Then the soldiers led him into the courtyard of the palace (that is, the governor's headquarters); and they called together the whole cohort. And they clothed him in a purple cloak; and after twisting some thorns into a crown, they put it on him. And they began saluting him, "Hail, King of the Jews!" They struck his head with a reed, spat upon him, and knelt down in homage to him. After mocking him, they stripped him of the purple cloak and put his own clothes on him. Then they led him out to crucify him. They compelled a passer-by, who was coming in from the country, to carry his cross; it was Simon of Cyrene, the father of Alexander and Rufus.

Friday

Psalm 31 [page 622] ❖ *Psalm 35* [page 629]

A Reading (Lesson) from the First Book of the Kings [11:26–43]

Jeroboam son of Nebat, an Ephraimite of Zeredah, a servant of Solomon, whose mother's name was Zeruah, a widow, rebelled against the king. The following was the reason he rebelled against the king. Solomon built the Millo, and closed up the gap in the wall of the city of his father

David. The man Jeroboam was very able, and when Solomon saw that the young man was industrious he gave him charge over all the forced labor of the house of Joseph. About that time, when Jeroboam was leaving Jerusalem, the prophet Ahijah the Shilonite found him on the road. Ahijah had clothed himself with a new garment. The two of them were alone in the open country when Ahijah laid hold of the new garment he was wearing and tore it into twelve pieces. He then said to Jeroboam: Take for yourself ten pieces; for thus says the LORD, the God of Israel, "See, I am about to tear the kingdom from the hand of Solomon, and will give you ten tribes. One tribe will remain his, for the sake of my servant David and for the sake of Jerusalem, the city that I have chosen out of all the tribes of Israel. This is because he has forsaken me, worshiped Astarte the goddess of the Sidonians, Chemosh the god of Moab, and Milcom the god of the Ammonites, and has not walked in my ways, doing what is right in my sight and keeping my statutes and my ordinances, as his father David did. Nevertheless I will not take the whole kingdom away from him but will make him ruler all the days of his life, for the sake of my servant David whom I chose and who did keep my commandments and my statutes; but I will take the kingdom away from his son and give it to you—that is, the ten tribes. Yet to his son I will give one tribe, so that my servant David may always have a lamp before me in Jerusalem, the city where I have chosen to put my name. I will take you, and you shall reign over all that your soul desires; you shall be king over Israel. If you will listen to all that I command you, walk in my ways, and do what is right in my sight by keeping my statutes and my commandments, as David my servant did, I will be with you, and will build you an enduring house, as I built for David, and I will give Israel to you. For this reason I will punish the descendants of David, but not forever." Solomon sought therefore to kill Jeroboam; but Jeroboam promptly fled to Egypt, to King Shishak of Egypt, and remained in Egypt until the death of Solomon. Now the rest of the acts of Solomon, all that he did as well as his wisdom, are they not written in the Book of the Acts of Solomon? The time that Solomon reigned in Jerusalem over all Israel was forty years. Solomon slept with his ancestors and was buried in the city of his father David; and his son Rehoboam succeeded him.

A Reading (Lesson) from the Letter of James [4:13—5:6]

Come now, you who say, "Today or tomorrow we will go to such and such a town and spend a year there, doing business and making money." Yet you do not even know what tomorrow will bring. What is your life? For you are a mist that appears for a little while and then vanishes. Instead you ought to say, "If the Lord wishes, we will live and do this or that." As it is, you boast in your arrogance; all such boasting is evil. Anyone, then, who knows the right thing to do and fails to do it, commits sin. Come now, you rich people, weep and wail for the miseries that are coming to you. Your riches have rotted, and your clothes are moth-eaten. Your gold and silver have rusted, and their rust will be evidence against you, and it will eat your flesh like fire. You have laid up treasure for the last days. Listen! The wages of the laborers who mowed your fields, which you kept back by fraud, cry out, and the cries of the harvesters have reached the ears of the Lord of hosts. You have lived on the earth in luxury and in pleasure; you have fattened your hearts in a day of slaughter. You have condemned and murdered the righteous one, who does not resist you.

*A Reading (Lesson) from the Gospel according to
Mark* [15:22–32]

They brought Jesus to the place called Golgotha (which
means the place of a skull). And they offered him wine
mixed with myrrh; but he did not take it. And they
crucified him, and divided his clothes among them, casting
lots to decide what each should take. It was nine o'clock
in the morning when they crucified him. The inscription of
the charge against him read, "The King of the Jews." And
with him they crucified two bandits, one on his right and
one on his left. Those who passed by derided him, shaking
their heads and saying, "Aha! You who would destroy the
temple and build it in three days, save yourself, and come
down from the cross!" In the same way the chief priests,
along with the scribes, were also mocking him among
themselves and saying, "He saved others; he cannot save
himself. Let the Messiah, the King of Israel, come down
from the cross now, so that we may see and believe."
Those who were crucified with him also taunted him.

Saturday

Psalm 30 [page 621],   *Psalm 32* [page 624]   ❖
Psalm 42 [page 643],   *Psalm 43* [page 644]

*A Reading (Lesson) from the First Book of the
Kings* [12:1–20]

Rehoboam went to Shechem, for all Israel had come to
Shechem to make him king. When Jeroboam son of Nebat
heard of it (for he was still in Egypt, where he had fled from
King Solomon), then Jeroboam returned from Egypt. And
they sent and called him; and Jeroboam and all the assembly
of Israel came and said to Rehoboam, "Your father made

our yoke heavy. Now therefore lighten the hard service of your father and his heavy yoke that he placed on us, and we will serve you." He said to them, "Go away for three days, then come again to me." So the people went away. Then King Rehoboam took counsel with the older men who had attended his father Solomon while he was still alive, saying, "How do you advise me to answer this people?" They answered him, "If you will be a servant to this people today and serve them, and speak good words to them when you answer them, then they will be your servants forever." But he disregarded the advice that the older men gave him, and consulted with the young men who had grown up with him and now attended him. He said to them, "What do you advise that we answer this people who have said to me, 'Lighten the yoke that your father put on us'?" The young men who had grown up with him said to him, "Thus you should say to this people who spoke to you, 'Your father made our yoke heavy, but you must lighten it for us'; thus you should say to them, 'My little finger is thicker than my father's loins. Now, whereas my father laid on you a heavy yoke, I will add to your yoke. My father disciplined you with whips, but I will discipline you with scorpions.' " So Jeroboam and all the people came to Rehoboam the third day, as the king had said, "Come to me again the third day." The king answered the people harshly. He disregarded the advice that the older men had given him and spoke to them according to the advice of the young men, "My father made your yoke heavy, but I will add to your yoke; my father disciplined you with whips, but I will discipline you with scorpions." So the king did not listen to the people, because it was a turn of affairs brought about by the LORD that he might fulfill his word, which the LORD had spoken by Ahijah the Shilonite to Jeroboam son of Nebat. When all Israel saw that the king would not listen to them, the people answered the king, "What share do we have in David? We have no inheritance in the son of Jesse. To your tents, O Israel! Look now to your own house, O David." So Israel went away to their tents. But Rehoboam reigned over the Israelites who were living in the towns of Judah. When King Rehoboam sent Adoram, who was taskmaster over the forced labor, all Israel stoned him to death. King Rehoboam then hurriedly mounted his chariot to flee to Jerusalem. So Israel has been in rebellion against the house of David to this day. When all Israel heard that Jeroboam had returned, they sent and called him to the assembly and made him king over all Israel. There was no one who followed the house of David, except the tribe of Judah alone.

A Reading (Lesson) from the Letter of James [5:7–12,19–20]

Be patient, therefore, beloved, until the coming of the Lord. The farmer waits for the precious crop from the earth, being patient with it until it receives the early and the late rains. You also must be patient. Strengthen your hearts, for the coming of the Lord is near. Beloved, do not grumble against one another, so that you may not be judged. See, the Judge is standing at the doors! As an example of suffering and patience, beloved, take the prophets who spoke in the name of the Lord. Indeed we call blessed those who showed endurance. You have heard of the endurance of Job, and you have seen the purpose of the Lord, how the Lord is compassionate and merciful. Above all, my beloved, do not swear, either by heaven or by earth or by any other oath, but let your "Yes" be yes and your "No" be no, so that you may not fall under condemnation. My brothers and sisters, if anyone among you wanders from the truth and is brought back by another, you should know that whoever brings back a sinner from wandering will save the sinner's soul from death and will cover a multitude of sins.

A Reading (Lesson) from the Gospel according to Mark [15:33–39]

When it was noon, darkness came over the whole land until three in the afternoon. At three o'clock Jesus cried out with a loud voice, "Eloi, Eloi, lema sabachthani?" which means, "My God, my God, why have you forsaken me?" When some of the bystanders heard it, they said, "Listen, he is calling for Elijah." And someone ran, filled a sponge with sour wine, put it on a stick, and gave it to him to drink, saying, "Wait, let us see whether Elijah will come to take him down." Then Jesus gave a loud cry and breathed his last. And the curtain of the temple was torn in two, from top to bottom. Now when the centurion, who stood facing him, saw that in this way he breathed his last, he said, "Truly this man was God's Son!"

Proper 18   *Week of the Sunday closest to September 7*

Sunday

Psalm 63:1–8(9–11) [page 670],
Psalm 98 [page 727]   ❖   *Psalm 103* [page 733]

A Reading (Lesson) from the First Book of the Kings [12:21–33]

When Rehoboam came to Jerusalem, he assembled all the house of Judah and the tribe of Benjamin, one hundred eighty thousand chosen troops to fight against the house of Israel, to restore the kingdom to Rehoboam son of

Solomon. But the word of God came to Shemaiah the man of God: Say to King Rehoboam of Judah, son of Solomon, and to all the house of Judah and Benjamin, and to the rest of the people, "Thus says the LORD, You shall not go up or fight against your kindred the people of Israel. Let everyone go home, for this thing is from me." So they heeded the word of the LORD and went home again, according to the word of the LORD. Then Jeroboam built Shechem in the hill country of Ephraim, and resided there; he went out from there and built Penuel. Then Jeroboam said to himself, "Now the kingdom may well revert to the house of David. If this people continues to go up to offer sacrifices in the house of the LORD at Jerusalem, the heart of this people will turn again to their master, King Rehoboam of Judah; they will kill me and return to King Rehoboam of Judah." So the king took counsel, and made two calves of gold. He said to the people, "You have gone up to Jerusalem long enough. Here are your gods, O Israel, who brought you up out of the land of Egypt." He set one in Bethel, and the other he put in Dan. And this thing became a sin, for the people went to worship before the one at Bethel and before the other as far as Dan. He also made houses on high places, and appointed priests from among all the people, who were not Levites. Jeroboam appointed a festival on the fifteenth day of the eighth month like the festival that was in Judah, and he offered sacrifices on the altar; so he did in Bethel, sacrificing to the calves that he had made. And he placed in Bethel the priests of the high places that he had made. He went up to the altar that he had made in Bethel on the fifteenth day in the eighth month, in the month that he alone had devised; he appointed a festival for the people of Israel, and he went up to the altar to offer incense.

A Reading (Lesson) from the Acts of the Apostles [4:18–31]

The council called Peter and John and charged them not
to speak or teach at all in the name of Jesus. But Peter
and John answered them, "Whether it is right in God's
sight to listen to you rather than to God, you must judge;
for we cannot keep from speaking about what we have
seen and heard." After threatening them again, they let
them go, finding no way to punish them because of the
people, for all of them praised God for what had
happened. For the man on whom this sign of healing had
been performed was more than forty years old. After they
were released, they went to their friends and reported
what the chief priests and the elders had said to them.
When they heard it, they raised their voices together to
God and said, "Sovereign Lord, who made the heaven and
the earth, the sea, and everything in them, it is you who
said by the Holy Spirit through our ancestor David, your
servant: 'Why did the Gentiles rage, and the peoples
imagine vain things? The kings of the earth took their
stand, and the rulers have gathered together against the
Lord and against his Messiah.' For in this city, in fact,
both Herod and Pontius Pilate, with the Gentiles and the
peoples of Israel, gathered together against your holy
servant Jesus, whom you anointed, to do whatever your
hand and your plan had predestined to take place. And
now, Lord, look at their threats, and grant to your
servants to speak your word with all boldness, while you
stretch out your hand to heal, and signs and wonders are
performed through the name of your holy servant Jesus."
When they had prayed, the place in which they were
gathered together was shaken; and they were all filled with
the Holy Spirit and spoke the word of God with boldness.

A Reading (Lesson) from the Gospel according to John [10:31–42]

The Jews took up stones again to stone him. Jesus replied, "I have shown you many good works from the Father. For which of these are you going to stone me?" The Jews answered. "It is not for a good work that we are going to stone you, but for blasphemy, because you, though only a human being, are making yourself God." Jesus answered, "Is it not written in your law, 'I said, you are gods'? If those to whom the word of God came were called 'gods'— and the scripture cannot be annulled—can you say that the one whom the Father has sanctified and sent into the world is blaspheming because I said, 'I am God's Son'? If I am not doing the works of my Father, then do not believe me. But if I do them, even though you do not believe me, believe the works, so that you may know and understand that the Father is in me and I am in the Father." Then they tried to arrest him again, but he escaped from their hands. He went away again across the Jordan to the place where John had been baptizing earlier, and he remained there. Many came to him, and they were saying, "John performed no sign, but everything that John said about this man was true." And many believed in him there.

Monday

Psalm 41 [page 641], *Psalm 52* [page 657] ❖
Psalm 44 [page 645]

A Reading (Lesson) from the First Book of the Kings [13:1–10]

While Jeroboam was standing by the altar to offer incense, a man of God came out of Judah by the word of the LORD to

Bethel and proclaimed against the altar by the word of the LORD, and said, "O altar, altar, thus says the LORD: 'A son shall be born to the house of David, Josiah by name; and he shall sacrifice on you the priests of the high places who offer incense on you, and human bones shall be burned on you.' " He gave a sign the same day, saying, "This is the sign that the LORD has spoken: 'The altar shall be torn down, and the ashes that are on it shall be poured out.' " When the king heard what the man of God cried out against the altar at Bethel, Jeroboam stretched out his hand from the altar, saying, "Seize him!" But the hand that he stretched out against him withered so that he could not draw it back to himself. The altar also was torn down, and the ashes poured out from the altar, according to the sign that the man of God had given by the word of the LORD. The king said to the man of God, "Entreat now the favor of the LORD your God, and pray for me, so that my hand may be restored to me." So the man of God entreated the LORD; and the king's hand was restored to him, and became as it was before. Then the king said to the man of God, "Come home with me and dine, and I will give you a gift." But the man of God said to the king, "If you give me half your kingdom, I will not go in with you; nor will I eat food or drink water in this place. For thus I was commanded by the word of the LORD: You shall not eat food, or drink water, or return by the way that you came." So he went another way, and did not return by the way that he had come to Bethel.

A Reading (Lesson) from the Letter of Paul to the Philippians [1:1–11]

Paul and Timothy, servants of Christ Jesus, to all the saints in Christ Jesus who are in Philippi, with the bishops and deacons: Grace to you and peace from God our

Father and the Lord Jesus Christ. I thank my God every time I remember you, constantly praying with joy in every one of my prayers for all of you, because of your sharing in the gospel from the first day until now. I am confident of this, that the one who began a good work among you will bring it to completion by the day of Jesus Christ. It is right for me to think this way about all of you, because you hold me in your heart, for all of you share in God's grace with me, both in my imprisonment and in the defense and confirmation of the gospel. For God is my witness, how I long for all of you with the compassion of Christ Jesus. And this is my prayer, that your love may overflow more and more with knowledge and full insight to help you to determine what is best, so that in the day of Christ you may be pure and blameless, having produced the harvest of righteousness that comes through Jesus Christ for the glory and praise of God.

A Reading (Lesson) from the Gospel according to Mark [15:40–47]

There were also women looking on from a distance; among them were Mary Magdalene, and Mary the mother of James the younger and of Joses, and Salome. These used to follow him and provided for him when he was in Galilee; and there were many other women who had come up with him to Jerusalem. When evening had come, and since it was the day of Preparation, that is, the day before the sabbath, Joseph of Arimathea, a respected member of the council, who was also himself waiting expectantly for the kingdom of God, went boldly to Pilate and asked for the body of Jesus. Then Pilate wondered if he were already dead; and summoning the centurion, he asked him whether he had been dead for some time. When he learned from the centurion that he was dead, he granted the body to Joseph. Then Joseph bought a linen cloth, and taking down the body, wrapped it in the linen cloth, and laid it in a tomb that had been hewn out of the rock. He then rolled a stone against the door of the tomb. Mary Magdalene and Mary the mother of Joses saw where the body was laid.

Tuesday

Psalm 45 [page 647] ❖ *Psalm 47* [page 650], *Psalm 48* [page 651]

A Reading (Lesson) from the First Book of the Kings [16:23–34]

In the thirty-first year of King Asa of Judah, Omri began to reign over Israel; he reigned for twelve years, six of them in Tirzah. He bought the hill of Samaria from Shemer for two talents of silver; he fortified the hill, and called the city that he built, Samaria, after the name of Shemer, the owner of the hill. Omri did what was evil in the sight of the LORD; he did more evil than all who were before him. For he walked in all the way of Jeroboam son of Nebat, and in the sins that he caused Israel to commit, provoking the LORD, the God of Israel, to anger by their idols. Now the rest of the acts of Omri that he did, and the power that he showed, are they not written in the Book of the Annals of the Kings of Israel? Omri slept with his ancestors, and was buried in Samaria; his son Ahab succeeded him. In the thirty-eighth year of King Asa of Judah, Ahab son of Omri began to reign over Israel in Samaria twenty-two years. Ahab son of Omri did evil in the sight of the LORD more than all who were before him. And as if it had been a light thing for him to walk in

the sins of Jeroboam son of Nebat, he took as his wife
Jezebel daughter of King Ethbaal of the Sidonians, and went
and served Baal, and worshiped him. He erected an altar for
Baal in the house of Baal, which he built in Samaria. Ahab
also made a sacred pole. Ahab did more to provoke the
anger of the LORD, the God of Israel, than had all the kings
of Israel who were before him. In his days Hiel of Bethel
built Jericho; he laid its foundation at the cost of Abiram his
firstborn, and set up its gates at the cost of his youngest son
Segub, according to the word of the LORD, which he spoke
by Joshua son of Nun.

*A Reading (Lesson) from the Letter of Paul to the
Philippians* [1:12–30]

I want you to know, beloved, that what has happened to
me has actually helped to spread the gospel, so that it has
become known throughout the whole imperial guard and
to everyone else that my imprisonment is for Christ; and
most of the brothers and sisters, having been made
confident in the Lord by my imprisonment, dare to speak
the word with greater boldness and without fear. Some
proclaim Christ from envy and rivalry, but others from
goodwill. These proclaim Christ out of love, knowing that
I have been put here for the defense of the gospel; the
others proclaim Christ out of selfish ambition, not
sincerely but intending to increase my suffering in my
imprisonment. What does it matter? Just this, that Christ
is proclaimed in every way, whether out of false motives
or true; and in that I rejoice. Yes, and I will continue to
rejoice, for I know that through your prayers and the help
of the Spirit of Jesus Christ this will turn out for my
deliverance. It is my eager expectation and hope that I will
not be put to shame in any way, but that by my speaking

with all boldness, Christ will be exalted now as always in my body, whether by life or by death. For to me, living is Christ and dying is gain. If I am to live in the flesh, that means fruitful labor for me; and I do not know which I prefer. I am hard pressed between the two: my desire is to depart and be with Christ, for that is far better; but to remain in the flesh is more necessary for you. Since I am convinced of this, I know that I will remain and continue with all of you for your progress and joy in faith, so that I may share abundantly in your boasting in Christ Jesus when I come to you again. Only, live your life in a manner worthy of the gospel of Christ, so that, whether I come and see you or am absent and hear about you, I will know that you are standing firm in one spirit, striving side by side with one mind for the faith of the gospel, and are in no way intimidated by your opponents. For them this is evidence of their destruction, but of your salvation. And this is God's doing. For he has graciously granted you the privilege not only of believing in Christ, but of suffering for him as well—since you are having the same struggle that you saw I had and now hear that I still have.

A Reading (Lesson) from the Gospel according to Mark [16:1–8(9–20)]

When the sabbath was over, Mary Magdalene, and Mary the mother of James, and Salome bought spices, so that they might go and anoint him. And very early on the first day of the week, when the sun had risen, they went to the tomb. They had been saying to one another, "Who will roll away the stone for us from the entrance to the tomb?" When they looked up, they saw that the stone, which was very large, had already been rolled back. As they entered the tomb, they saw a young man, dressed in a white robe, sitting on the right side; and they were alarmed. But he said to them, "Do not be alarmed; you are looking for Jesus of Nazareth, who was crucified. He has been raised; he is not here. Look, there is the place they laid him. But go, tell his disciples and Peter that he is going ahead of you to Galilee; there you will see him, just as he told you." So they went out and fled from the tomb, for terror and amazement had seized them; and they said nothing to anyone, for they were afraid.

Now after he rose early on the first day of the week, he appeared first to Mary Magdalene, from whom he had cast out seven demons. She went out and told those who had been with him, while they were mourning and weeping. But when they heard that he was alive and had been seen by her, they would not believe it. After this he appeared in another form to two of them, as they were walking into the country. And they went back and told the rest, but they did not believe them. Later he appeared to the eleven themselves as they were sitting at the table; and he upbraided them for their lack of faith and stubbornness, because they had not believed those who saw him after he had risen. And he said to them, "Go into all the world and proclaim the good news to the whole creation. The one who believes and is baptized will be saved; but the one who does not believe will be condemned. And these signs will accompany those who believe: by using my name they will cast out demons; they will speak in new tongues; they will pick up snakes in their hands, and if they drink any deadly thing, it will not hurt them; they will lay their hands on the sick, and they will recover." So then the Lord Jesus, after he had spoken to them, was taken up into heaven and sat down at the right hand of

God. And they went out and proclaimed the good news everywhere, while the Lord worked with them and confirmed the message by the signs that accompanied it.

Wednesday

Psalm 119:49–72 [page 767]   ❖   Psalm 49 [page 652], (Psalm 53 [page 658])

A Reading (Lesson) from the First Book of the Kings [17:1–24]

Elijah the Tishbite, of Tishbe in Gilead, said to Ahab, "As the LORD the God of Israel lives, before whom I stand, there shall be neither dew nor rain these years, except by my word." The word of the LORD came to him, saying, "Go from here and turn eastward, and hide yourself by the Wadi Cherith, which is east of the Jordan. You shall drink from the Wadi, and I have commanded the ravens to feed you there." So he went and did according to the word of the LORD; he went and lived by the Wadi Cherith, which is east of the Jordan. The ravens brought him bread and meat in the morning, and bread and meat in the evening; and he drank from the wadi. But after a while the wadi dried up, because there was no rain in the land. Then the word of the LORD came to him, saying, "Go now to Zarephath, which belongs to Sidon, and live there; for I have commanded a widow there to feed you." So he set out and went to Zarephath. When he came to the gate of the town, a widow was there gathering sticks; he called to her and said, "Bring me a little water in a vessel, so that I may drink." As she was going to bring it, he called to her and said, "Bring me a morsel of bread in your hand." But she said, "As the LORD your God lives, I have nothing baked, only a handful of meal in a jar, and a little oil in a jug; I am now gathering a couple of sticks, so that I may go home and prepare it for myself and my son, that we may eat it, and die." Elijah said to her, "Do not be afraid; go and do as you have said; but first make me a little cake of it and bring it to me, and afterwards make something for yourself and your son. For thus says the LORD the God of Israel: The jar of meal will not be emptied and the jug of oil will not fail until the day that the LORD sends rain on the earth." She went and did as Elijah said, so that she as well as he and her household ate for many days. The jar of meal was not emptied, neither did the jug of oil fail, according to the word of the LORD that he spoke by Elijah. After this the son of the woman, the mistress of the house, became ill; his illness was so severe that there was no breath left in him. She then said to Elijah, "What have you against me, O man of God? You have come to me to bring my sin to remembrance, and to cause the death of my son!" But he said to her, "Give me your son." He took him from her bosom, carried him up into the upper chamber where he was lodging, and laid him on his own bed. He cried out to the LORD, "O LORD my God, have you brought calamity even upon the widow with whom I am staying, by killing her son?" Then he stretched himself upon the child three times, and cried out to the LORD, "O LORD my God, let this child's life come into him again." The LORD listened to the voice of Elijah; the life of the child came into him again, and he revived. Elijah took the child, brought him down from the upper chamber into the house, and gave him to his mother; then Elijah said, "See, your son is alive." So the woman said to Elijah, "Now I know that you are a man of God, and that the word of the LORD in your mouth is truth."

A Reading (Lesson) from the Letter of Paul to the Philippians [2:1–11]

If then there is any encouragement in Christ, any consolation from love, any sharing in the Spirit, any compassion and sympathy, make my joy complete: be of the same mind, having the same love, being in full accord and of one mind. Do nothing from selfish ambition or conceit, but in humility regard others as better than yourselves. Let each of you look not to your own interests, but to the interests of others. Let the same mind be in you that was in Christ Jesus, who, though he was in the form of God, did not regard equality with God as something to be exploited, but emptied himself, taking the form of a slave, being born in human likeness. And being found in human form, he humbled himself and became obedient to the point of death—even death on a cross. Therefore God also highly exalted him and gave him the name that is above every name, so that at the name of Jesus every knee should bend, in heaven and on earth and under the earth, and every tongue should confess that Jesus Christ is Lord, to the glory of God the Father.

A Reading (Lesson) from the Gospel according to Matthew [2:1–12]

In the time of King Herod, after Jesus was born in Bethlehem of Judea, wise men from the East came to Jerusalem, asking, "Where is the child who has been born king of the Jews? For we observed his star at its rising, and have come to pay him homage." When King Herod heard this, he was frightened, and all Jerusalem with him; and calling together all the chief priests and scribes of the people, he inquired of them where the Messiah was to be born. They told him, "In Bethlehem of Judea; for so it has been written by the prophet: 'And you, Bethlehem, in the land of Judah, are by no means least among the rulers of Judah; for from you shall come a ruler who is to shepherd my people Israel.' " Then Herod secretly called for the wise men and learned from them the exact time when the star had appeared. Then he sent them to Bethlehem, saying, "Go and search diligently for the child; and when you have found him, bring me word so that I may also go and pay him homage." When they had heard the king, they set out; and there, ahead of them, went the star that they had seen at its rising, until it stopped over the place where the child was. When they saw that the star had stopped, they were overwhelmed with joy. On entering the house, they saw the child with Mary his mother; and they knelt down and paid him homage. Then, opening their treasure chests, they offered him gifts of gold, frankincense, and myrrh. And having been warned in a dream not to return to Herod, they left for their own country by another road.

Thursday

Psalm 50 [page 654] ❖ *(Psalm 59* [page 665], *Psalm 60* [page 667]) or *Psalm 93* [page 722], *Psalm 96* [page 725]

A Reading (Lesson) from the First Book of the Kings [18:1–19]

After many days the word of the Lord came to Elijah, in the third year of the drought, saying, "Go, present yourself to Ahab; I will send rain on the earth." So Elijah went to present himself to Ahab. The famine was severe in Samaria. Ahab summoned Obadiah, who was in charge of the palace.

(Now Obadiah revered the LORD greatly; when Jezebel was killing off the prophets of the LORD, Obadiah took a hundred prophets, hid them fifty to a cave, and provided them with bread and water.) Then Ahab said to Obadiah, "Go through the land to all the springs of water and to all the wadis; perhaps we may find grass to keep the horses and mules alive, and not lose some of the animals." So they divided the land between them to pass through it; Ahab went in one direction by himself, and Obadiah went in another direction by himself. As Obadiah was on the way, Elijah met him; Obadiah recognized him, fell on his face, and said, "Is it you, my lord Elijah?" He answered him, "It is I. Go, tell your lord that Elijah is here." And he said, "How have I sinned, that you would hand your servant over to Ahab, to kill me? As the LORD your God lives, there is no nation or kingdom to which my lord has not sent to seek you; and when they would say, 'He is not here,' he would require an oath of the kingdom or nation, that they had not found you. But now you say, 'Go, tell your lord that Elijah is here.' As soon as I have gone from you, the spirit of the LORD will carry you I know not where; so, when I come and tell Ahab and he cannot find you, he will kill me, although I your servant have revered the LORD from my youth. Has it not been told my lord what I did when Jezebel killed the prophets of the LORD, how I hid a hundred of the LORD's prophets fifty to a cave, and provided them with bread and water? Yet now you say, 'Go, tell your lord that Elijah is here'; he will surely kill me." Elijah said, "As the LORD of hosts lives, before whom I stand, I will surely show myself to him today." So Obadiah went to meet Ahab, and told him; and Ahab went to meet Elijah. When Ahab saw Elijah, Ahab said to him, "Is it you, you troubler of Israel?" He answered, "I have not troubled Israel; but you have, and your father's house, because you have forsaken the commandments of the LORD and followed the Baals. Now therefore have all Israel assemble for me at Mount Carmel, with the four hundred fifty prophets of Baal and the four hundred prophets of Asherah, who eat at Jezebel's table."

A Reading (Lesson) from the Letter of Paul to the Philippians [2:12–30]

Therefore, my beloved, just as you have always obeyed me, not only in my presence, but much more now in my absence, work out your own salvation with fear and trembling; for it is God who is at work in you, enabling you both to will and to work for his good pleasure. Do all things without murmuring and arguing, so that you may be blameless and innocent, children of God without blemish in the midst of a crooked and perverse generation, in which you shine like stars in the world. It is by your holding fast to the word of life that I can boast on the day of Christ that I did not run in vain or labor in vain. But even if I am being poured out as a libation over the sacrifice and the offering of your faith, I am glad and rejoice with all of you—and in the same way you also must be glad and rejoice with me. I hope in the Lord Jesus to send Timothy to you soon, so that I may be cheered by news of you. I have no one like him who will be genuinely concerned for your welfare. All of them are seeking their own interests, not those of Jesus Christ. But Timothy's worth you know, how like a son with a father he has served with me in the work of the gospel. I hope therefore to send him as soon as I see how things go with me; and I trust in the Lord that I will also come soon. Still, I think it necessary to send to you Epaphroditus—my brother and co-worker and fellow soldier, your messenger and minister to my need; for he has been longing for all of you, and has been distressed because you heard that he was ill. He was indeed so ill that he nearly died. But God had mercy on him, and not only on him but on me also, so that I would not have one sorrow after another. I am the more eager to send him, therefore, in order that you may rejoice at seeing him again, and that I may be less anxious. Welcome him then in the Lord with all joy, and honor such people, because he came close to death for the work of Christ, risking his life to make up for those services that you could not give me.

A Reading (Lesson) from the Gospel according to Matthew [2:13–23]

After the wise men had left, an angel of the Lord appeared to Joseph in a dream and said, "Get up, take the child and his mother, and flee to Egypt, and remain there until I tell you; for Herod is about to search for the child, to destroy him." Then Joseph got up, took the child and his mother by night, and went to Egypt, and remained there until the death of Herod. This was to fulfill what had been spoken by the Lord through the prophet, "Out of Egypt I have called my son." When Herod saw that he had been tricked by the wise men, he was infuriated, and he sent and killed all the children in and around Bethlehem who were two years old or under, according to the time that he had learned from the wise men. Then was fulfilled what had been spoken through the prophet Jeremiah: "A voice was heard in Ramah, wailing and loud lamentation, Rachel weeping for her children; she refused to be consoled, because they are no more." When Herod died, an angel of the Lord suddenly appeared in a dream to Joseph in Egypt and said, "Get up, take the child and his mother, and go to the land of Israel, for those who were seeking the child's life are dead." Then Joseph got up, took the child and his mother, and went to the land of Israel. But when he heard that Archelaus was ruling over Judea in place of his father Herod, he was afraid to go there. And after being warned in a dream, he went away to the district of Galilee. There he made his home in a town called Nazareth, so that what had been spoken through the prophets might be fulfilled, "He will be called a Nazorean."

Friday

Psalm 40 [page 640],   *Psalm 54* [page 659]   ❖
Psalm 51 [page 656]

A Reading (Lesson) from the First Book of the Kings [18:20–40]

Ahab sent to all the Israelites, and assembled the prophets at Mount Carmel. Elijah then came near to all the people, and said, "How long will you go limping with two different opinions? If the LORD is God, follow him; but if Baal, then follow him." The people did not answer him a word. Then Elijah said to the people, "I, even I only, am left a prophet of the LORD; but Baal's prophets number four hundred fifty. Let two bulls be given to us; let them choose one bull for themselves, cut it in pieces, and lay it on the wood, but put no fire to it; I will prepare the other bull and lay it on the wood, but put no fire to it. Then you call on the name of your god and I will call on the name of the LORD; the god who answers by fire is indeed God." All the people answered, "Well spoken!" Then Elijah said to the prophets of Baal, "Choose for yourselves one bull and prepare it first, for you are many; then call on the name of your god, but put no fire to it." So they took the bull that was given them, prepared it, and called on the name of Baal from morning until noon, crying, "O Baal, answer us!" But there was no voice, and no answer. They limped about the altar that they had made. At noon Elijah mocked them, saying, "Cry aloud! Surely he is a god; either he is meditating, or he has wandered away, or he is on a journey, or perhaps he is asleep and must be awakened." Then they cried aloud and, as was their custom, they cut themselves with swords and lances until the blood gushed out over them. As midday passed, they raved on until the time of the offering of the oblation, but there was no voice, no answer, and no response. Then Elijah said to all the people, "Come closer to me"; and all the people came closer to him. First he repaired the altar of the LORD that had been thrown down; Elijah took twelve stones, according to the number of the tribes of the sons of Jacob, to whom the word of the LORD came, saying, "Israel shall be your name"; with the stones he built an altar in the name of the LORD. Then he made a trench around the altar, large enough to contain two measures of seed. Next he put the wood in order, cut the bull in pieces, and laid it on the wood. He said, "Fill four jars with water and pour it on the burnt offering and on the wood." Then he said, "Do it a second time"; and they did it a second time. Again he said, "Do it a third time"; and they did it a third time, so that the water ran all around the altar, and filled the trench also with water. At the time of the offering of the oblation, the prophet Elijah came near and said, "O LORD, God of Abraham, Isaac, and Israel, let it be known this day that you are God in Israel, that I am your servant, and that I have done all these things at your bidding. Answer me, O LORD, answer me, so that this people may know that you, O LORD, are God, and that you have turned their hearts back." Then the fire of the LORD fell and consumed the burnt offering, the wood, the stones, and the dust, and even licked up the water that was in the trench. When all the people saw it, they fell on their faces and said, "The LORD indeed is God; the LORD indeed is God." Elijah said to them, "Seize the prophets of Baal; do not let one of them escape." Then they seized them; and Elijah brought them down to the Wadi Kishon, and killed them there.

A Reading (Lesson) from the Letter of Paul to the Philippians [3:1–16]

Finally, my brothers and sisters, rejoice in the Lord. To write the same things to you is not troublesome to me, and for you it is a safeguard. Beware of the dogs, beware of the evil workers, beware of those who mutilate the flesh! For it is we who are the circumcision, who worship in the Spirit of God and boast in Christ Jesus and have no confidence in the flesh—even though I, too, have reason for confidence in the flesh. If anyone else has reason to be confident in the flesh, I have more: circumcised on the eighth day, a member of the people of Israel, of the tribe of Benjamin, a Hebrew born of Hebrews; as to the law, a Pharisee; as to zeal, a persecutor of the church; as to righteousness under the law, blameless. Yet whatever gains I had, these I have come to regard as loss because of Christ. More than that, I regard everything as loss because of the surpassing value of knowing Christ Jesus my Lord. For his sake I have suffered the loss of all things, and I regard them as rubbish, in order that I may gain Christ and be found in him, not having a righteousness of my own that comes from the law, but one that comes through faith in Christ, the righteousness from God based on faith. I want to know Christ and the power of his resurrection and the sharing of his sufferings by becoming like him in his death, if somehow I may attain the resurrection from the dead. Not that I have already obtained this or have already reached the goal; but I press on to make it my own, because Christ Jesus has made me his own. Beloved, I do not consider that I have made it my own; but this one thing I do: forgetting what lies behind and straining forward to what lies ahead, I press on toward the goal for the prize of the heavenly call of God in Christ Jesus. Let those of us then who are mature be of the same mind; and if you think differently about anything, this too God will reveal to you. Only let us hold fast to what we have attained.

A Reading (Lesson) from the Gospel according to Matthew [3:1–12]

In those days John the Baptist appeared in the wilderness of Judea, proclaiming, "Repent, for the kingdom of heaven has come near." This is the one of whom the prophet Isaiah spoke when he said, "The voice of one crying out in the wilderness: 'Prepare the way of the Lord, make his paths straight.' " Now John wore clothing of camel's hair with a leather belt around his waist, and his food was locusts and wild honey. Then the people of Jerusalem and all Judea were going out to him, and all the region along the Jordan, and they were baptized by him in the river Jordan, confessing their sins. But when he saw many Pharisees and Sadducees coming for baptism, he said to them, "You brood of vipers! Who warned you to flee from the wrath to come? Bear fruit worthy of repentance. Do not presume to say to yourselves, 'We have Abraham as our ancestor'; for I tell you, God is able from these stones to raise up children to Abraham. Even now the ax is lying at the root of the trees; every tree therefore that does not bear good fruit is cut down and thrown into the fire. I baptize you with water for repentance, but one who is more powerful than I is coming after me; I am not worthy to carry his sandals. He will baptize you with the Holy Spirit and fire. His winnowing fork is in his hand, and he will clear his threshing floor and will gather his wheat into the granary; but the chaff he will burn with unquenchable fire."

Saturday

Psalm 55 [page 660] ❖ *Psalm 138* [page 793], *Psalm 139:1–17(18–23)* [page 794]

A Reading (Lesson) from the First Book of the Kings [18:41—19:8]

Elijah said to Ahab, "Go up, eat and drink; for there is a sound of rushing rain." So Ahab went up to eat and to drink. Elijah went up to the top of Carmel; there he bowed himself down upon the earth and put his face between his knees. He said to his servant, "Go up now, look toward the sea." He went up and looked, and said, "There is nothing." Then he said, "Go again seven times." At the seventh time he said, "Look, a little cloud no bigger than a person's hand is rising out of the sea." Then he said, "Go say to Ahab, 'Harness your chariot and go down before the rain stops you.' " In a little while the heavens grew black with clouds and wind; there was a heavy rain. Ahab rode off and went to Jezreel. But the hand of the LORD was on Elijah; he girded up his loins and ran in front of Ahab to the entrance of Jezreel. Ahab told Jezebel all that Elijah had done, and how he had killed all the prophets with the sword. Then Jezebel sent a messenger to Elijah, saying, "So may the gods do to me, and more also, if I do not make your life like the life of one of them by this time tomorrow." Then he was afraid; he got up and fled for his life, and came to Beer-sheba, which belongs to Judah; he left his servant there. But he himself went a day's journey into the wilderness, and came and sat down under a solitary broom tree. He asked that he might die: "It is enough; now, O LORD, take away my life, for I am no better than my ancestors." Then he lay down under the broom tree and fell asleep. Suddenly an angel touched him and said to him, "Get up and eat." He looked, and there at his head was a cake baked on hot stones, and a jar of water. He ate and drank, and lay down again. The angel of the LORD came a second time, touched him, and said, "Get up and eat, otherwise the journey will be too much for you." He got up, and ate and drank; then he went in the strength of that food forty days and forty nights to Horeb the mount of God.

A Reading (Lesson) from the Letter of Paul to the Philippians [3:17—4:7]

Brothers and sisters, join in imitating me, and observe those who live according to the example you have in us. for many live as enemies of the cross of Christ; I have often told you of them, and now I tell you even with tears. Their end is destruction; their god is the belly; and their glory is in their shame; their minds are set on earthly things. But our citizenship is in heaven, and it is from there that we are expecting a Savior, the Lord Jesus Christ. He will transform the body of our humiliation that it may be conformed to the body of his glory, by the power that also enables him to make all things subject to himself. Therefore, my brothers and sisters, whom I love and long for, my joy and crown, stand firm in the Lord in this way, my beloved. I urge Euodia and I urge Syntyche to be of the same mind in the Lord. Yes, and I ask you also, my loyal companion, help these women, for they have struggled beside me in the work of the gospel, together with Clement and the rest of my co-workers, whose names are in the book of life. Rejoice in the Lord always; again I will say, Rejoice. Let your gentleness be known to everyone. The Lord is near. Do not worry about anything, but in everything by prayer and supplication with thanksgiving let your requests be made known to God. And the peace of God, which surpasses all understanding, will guard your hearts and your minds in Christ Jesus.

A Reading (Lesson) from the Gospel according to Matthew [3:13–17]

Jesus came from Galilee to John at the Jordan, to be baptized by him. John would have prevented him, saying, "I need to be baptized by you, and do you come to me?" But Jesus answered him, "Let it be so now; for it is proper for us in this way to fulfill all righteousness." Then he consented. And when Jesus had been baptized, just as he came up from the water, suddenly the heavens were opened to him and he saw the Spirit of God descending like a dove and alighting on him. And a voice from heaven said, "This is my Son, the Beloved, with whom I am well pleased."

Proper 19   *Week of the Sunday closest to September 14*

Sunday

Psalm 24 [page 613],   *Psalm 29* [page 620]   ❖
Psalm 8 [page 592],   *Psalm 84* [page 707]

A Reading (Lesson) from the First Book of the Kings [19:8–21]

Elijah got up, and ate and drank; then he went in the strength of that food forty days and forty nights to Horeb the mount of God. At that place he came to a cave, and spent the night there. Then the word of the LORD came to him, saying, "What are you doing here, Elijah?" He answered, "I have been very zealous for the LORD, the God of hosts; for the Israelites have forsaken your covenant, thrown down your altars, and killed your prophets with the sword. I alone am left, and they are seeking my life, to take it away." He said, "Go out and stand on the mountain before the LORD, for the LORD is about to pass by." Now there was a great wind, so strong that it was splitting mountains and breaking rocks in pieces before the LORD, but the LORD was not in the wind; and after the wind an earthquake, but the LORD was not in the earthquake; and after the earthquake a fire, but the LORD was not in the fire; and after the fire a sound of sheer silence. When Elijah heard it, he wrapped his face in his mantle and went out and stood at the entrance of the cave. Then there came a voice to him that said, "What are you doing here, Elijah?" He answered, "I have been very zealous for the LORD, the God of hosts; for the Israelites have forsaken your covenant, thrown down your altars, and killed your prophets with the sword. I alone am left, and they are seeking my life, to take it away." Then the LORD said to him, "Go, return on your way to the wilderness of Damascus; when you arrive, you shall anoint Hazael as king over Aram. Also you shall anoint Jehu son of Nimshi as king over Israel; and you shall anoint Elisha son of Shaphat of Abel-meholah as prophet in your place. Whoever escapes from the sword of Hazael, Jehu shall kill; and whoever escapes from the sword of Jehu, Elisha shall kill. Yet I will leave seven thousand in Israel, all the knees that have not bowed to Baal, and every mouth that has not kissed him." So he set out from there, and found Elisha son of Shaphat, who was plowing. There were twelve yoke of oxen ahead of him, and he was with the twelfth. Elijah passed by him and threw his mantle over him. He left the oxen, ran after Elijah, and said, "Let me kiss my father and my mother, and then I will follow you." Then Elijah said to him, "Go back again; for what have I done to you?" He returned from following him, took the yoke of oxen, and slaughtered them; using the equipment from the oxen, he boiled their flesh, and gave it to the people, and they ate. Then he set out and followed Elijah, and became his servant.

A Reading (Lesson) from the Acts of the Apostles [5:34–42]

A Pharisee in the council named Gamaliel, a teacher of the law, respected by all the people, stood up and ordered the apostles to be put outside for a short time. Then he said to them, "Fellow Israelites, consider carefully what you propose to do to these men. For some time ago Theudas rose up, claiming to be somebody, and a number of men, about four hundred, joined him; but he was killed, and all who followed him were dispersed and disappeared. After him Judas the Galilean rose up at the time of the census and got people to follow him; he also perished, and all who followed him were scattered. So in the present case, I tell you, keep away from these men and let them alone; because if this plan or this undertaking is of human origin, it will fail; but if it is of God, you will not be able to overthrow them—in that case you may even be found fighting against God!" They were convinced by him, and when they had called in the apostles, they had them flogged. Then they ordered them not to speak in the name of Jesus, and let them go. As they left the council, they rejoiced that they were considered worthy to suffer dishonor for the sake of the name. And every day in the temple and at home they did not cease to teach and proclaim Jesus as the Messiah.

A Reading (Lesson) from the Gospel according to John [11:45–57]

Many of the Jews who had come with Mary and had seen what Jesus did, believed in him. But some of them went to the Pharisees and told them what he had done. So the chief priests and the Pharisees called a meeting of the council, and said, "What are we to do? This man is performing many signs. If we let him go on like this, everyone will believe in him, and the Romans will come and destroy both our holy place and our nation." But one of them, Caiaphas, who was high priest that year, said to them, "You know nothing at all! You do not understand that it is better for you to have one man die for the people than to have the whole nation destroyed." He did not say this on his own, but being high priest that year he prophesied that Jesus was about to die for the nation, and not for the nation only, but to gather into one the dispersed children of God. So from that day on they planned to put him to death. Jesus therefore no longer walked about openly among the Jews, but went from there to a town called Ephraim in the region near the wilderness; and he remained there with the disciples. Now the Passover of the Jews was near, and many went up from the country to Jerusalem before the Passover to purify themselves. They were looking for Jesus and were asking one another as they stood in the temple, "What do you think? Surely he will not come to the festival, will he?" Now the chief priests and the Pharisees had given orders that anyone who knew where Jesus was should let them know, so that they might arrest him.

Monday

Psalm 56 [page 662], *Psalm* 57 [page 663], *(Psalm* 58 [page 664]) ❖ *Psalm* 64 [page 671], *Psalm* 65 [page 672]

A Reading (Lesson) from the First Book of the Kings [21:1–16]

Naboth the Jezreelite had a vineyard in Jezreel, beside the palace of King Ahab of Samaria. And Ahab said to Naboth, "Give me your vineyard, so that I may have it for a vegetable garden, because it is near my house; I will give you a better vineyard for it; or, if it seems good to you, I will give you its value in money." But Naboth said to Ahab, "The Lord forbid that I should give you my ancestral inheritance." Ahab went home resentful and sullen because of what Naboth the Jezreelite had said to him; for he had said, "I will not give you my ancestral inheritance." He lay down on his bed, turned away his face, and would not eat. His wife Jezebel came to him and said, "Why are you so depressed that you will not eat?" He said to her, "Because I spoke to

Naboth the Jezreelite and said to him, 'Give me your vineyard for money; or else, if you prefer, I will give you another vineyard for it'; but he answered, 'I will not give you my vineyard.' " His wife Jezebel said to him, "Do you now govern Israel? Get up, eat some food, and be cheerful; I will give you the vineyard of Naboth the Jezreelite." So she wrote letters in Ahab's name and sealed them with his seal; she sent the letters to the elders and the nobles who lived with Naboth in his city. She wrote in the letters, "Proclaim a fast, and seat Naboth at the head of the assembly; seat two scoundrels opposite him, and have them bring a charge against him, saying, 'You have cursed God and the king.' Then take him out, and stone him to death." The men of his city, the elders and the nobles who lived in his city, did as Jezebel had sent word to them. Just as it was written in the letters that she had sent to them, they proclaimed a fast and seated Naboth at the head of the assembly. The two scoundrels came in and sat opposite him; and the scoundrels brought a charge against Naboth, in the presence of the people, saying, "Naboth cursed God and the king." So they took him outside the city, and stoned him to death. Then they sent to Jezebel, saying, "Naboth has been stoned; he is dead." As soon as Jezebel heard that Naboth had been stoned and was dead, Jezebel said to Ahab, "Go, take possession of the vineyard of Naboth the Jezreelite, which he refused to give you for money; for Naboth is not alive, but dead." As soon as Ahab heard that Naboth was dead, Ahab set out to go down to the vineyard of Naboth the Jezreelite, to take possession of it.

A Reading (Lesson) from the First Letter of Paul to the Corinthians [1:1–19]

Paul, called to be an apostle of Christ Jesus by the will of God, and our brother Sosthenes, to the church of God that is in Corinth, to those who are sanctified in Christ Jesus, called to be saints, together with all those who in every place call on the name of our Lord Jesus Christ, both their Lord and ours: Grace to you and peace from God our Father and the Lord Jesus Christ. I give thanks to my God always for you because of the grace of God that has been given you in Christ Jesus, for in every way you have been enriched in him, in speech and knowledge of every kind—just as the testimony of Christ has been strengthened among you—so that you are not lacking in any spiritual gift as you wait for the revealing of our Lord Jesus Christ. He will also strengthen you to the end, so that you may be blameless on the day of our Lord Jesus Christ. God is faithful; by him you were called into the fellowship of his Son, Jesus Christ our Lord. Now I appeal to you, brothers and sisters, by the name of our Lord Jesus Christ, that all of you be in agreement and that there be no divisions among you, but that you be united in the same mind and the same purpose. For it has been reported to me by Chloe's people that there are quarrels among you, my brothers and sisters. What I mean is that each of you says, "I belong to Paul," or "I belong to Apollos," or "I belong to Cephas," or "I belong to Christ." Has Christ been divided? Was Paul crucified for you? Or were you baptized in the name of Paul? I thank God that I baptized none of you except Crispus and Gaius, so that no one can say that you were baptized in my name. (I did baptize also the household of Stephanas; beyond that, I do not know whether I baptized anyone else.) For Christ did not send me to baptize but to proclaim the gospel, and not with eloquent wisdom, so that the cross of Christ might not be emptied of its power. For the message about the cross is foolishness to those who are perishing, but to us who are being saved it is the power of God. For it is written, "I will destroy the wisdom of the wise, and the discernment of the discerning I will thwart."

A Reading (Lesson) from the Gospel according to Matthew [4:1–11]

Jesus was led up by the Spirit into the wilderness to be tempted by the devil. He fasted forty days and forty nights, and afterwards he was famished. The tempter came and said to him, "If you are the Son of God, command these stones to become loaves of bread." But he answered, "It is written, 'One does not live by bread alone, but by every word that comes from the mouth of God.'" Then the devil took him to the holy city and placed him on the pinnacle of the temple, saying to him, "If you are the Son of God, throw yourself down; for it is written, 'He will command his angels concerning you,' and 'On their hands they will bear you up, so that you will not dash your foot against a stone.'" Jesus said to him, "Again it is written, 'Do not put the Lord your God to the test.'" Again, the devil took him to a very high mountain and showed him all the kingdoms of the world and their splendor; and he said to him, "All these I will give you, if you will fall down, and worship me." Jesus said to him, "Away with you, Satan! for it is written, 'Worship the Lord your God, and serve only him.'" Then the devil left him, and suddenly angels came and waited on him.

Tuesday

Psalm 61 [page 668],   *Psalm 62* [page 669]   ❖
Psalm 68:1–20(21–23)24–36 [page 676]

A Reading (Lesson) from the First Book of the Kings [21:17–29]

The word of the LORD came to Elijah the Tishbite, saying: Go down to meet King Ahab of Israel, who rules in Samaria; he is now in the vineyard of Naboth, where he has gone to take possession. You shall say to him, "Thus says the LORD: Have you killed, and also taken possession?" You shall say to him, "Thus says the LORD: In the place where dogs licked up the blood of Naboth, dogs will also lick up your blood." Ahab said to Elijah, "Have you found me, O my enemy?" He answered, "I have found you. Because you have sold yourself to do what is evil in the sight of the LORD, I will bring disaster on you; I will consume you, and will cut off from Ahab every male, bond or free, in Israel; and I will make your house like the house of Jeroboam son of Nebat, and like the house of Baasha son of Ahijah, because you have provoked me to anger and have caused Israel to sin. Also concerning Jezebel the LORD said, 'The dogs shall eat Jezebel within the bounds of Jezreel.' Anyone belonging to Ahab who dies in the city the dogs shall eat; and anyone of his who dies in the open country the birds of the air shall eat." (Indeed, there was no one like Ahab, who sold himself to do what was evil in the sight of the LORD, urged on by his wife Jezebel. He acted most abominably in going after idols, as the Amorites had done, whom the LORD drove out before the Israelites.) When Ahab heard those words, he tore his clothes and put sackcloth over his bare flesh; he fasted, lay in the sackcloth, and went about dejectedly. Then the word of the LORD came to Elijah the

Tishbite: "Have you seen how Ahab has humbled himself before me? Because he has humbled himself before me, I will not bring the disaster in his days; but in his son's days I will bring the disaster on his house."

A Reading (Lesson) from the First Letter of Paul to the Corinthians [1:20–31]

Where is the one who is wise? Where is the scribe? Where is the debater of this age? Has not God made foolish the wisdom of the world? For since, in the wisdom of God, the world did not know God through wisdom, God decided, through the foolishness of our proclamation, to save those who believe. For Jews demand signs and Greeks desire wisdom, but we proclaim Christ crucified, a stumbling block to Jews and foolishness to Gentiles, but to those who are the called, both Jews and Greeks, Christ the power of God and the wisdom of God. For God's foolishness is wiser than human wisdom, and God's weakness is stronger than human strength. Consider your own call, brothers and sisters: not many of you were wise by human standards, not many were powerful, not many were of noble birth. But God chose what is foolish in the world to shame the wise; God chose what is weak in the world to shame the strong; God chose what is low and despised in the world, things that are not, to reduce to nothing things that are, so that no one might boast in the presence of God. He is the source of your life in Christ Jesus, who became for us wisdom from God, and righteousness and sanctification and redemption, in order that, as it is written, "Let the one who boasts, boast in the Lord."

*A Reading (Lesson) from the Gospel according to
Matthew* [4:12–17]

When Jesus heard that John had been arrested, he
withdrew to Galilee. He left Nazareth and made his home
in Capernaum by the sea, in the territory of Zebulun and
Naphtali, so that what had been spoken through the
prophet Isaiah might be fulfilled: "Land of Zebulun, land
of Naphtali, on the road by the sea, across the Jordan,
Galilee of the Gentiles—the people who sat in darkness
have seen a great light, and for those who sat in the region
and shadow of death light has dawned." From that time
Jesus began to proclaim, "Repent, for the kingdom of
heaven has come near."

Wednesday

Psalm 72 [page 685] ❖ *Psalm 119:73–96* [page 769]

*A Reading (Lesson) from the First Book of the
Kings* [22:1–28]

For three years Aram and Israel continued without war. But
in the third year King Jehoshaphat of Judah came down to
the king of Israel. The king of Israel said to his servants,
"Do you know that Ramoth-gilead belongs to us, yet we are
doing nothing to take it out of the hand of the king of
Aram?" He said to Jehoshaphat, "Will you go with me to
battle at Ramoth-gilead?" Jehoshaphat replied to the king of
Israel, "I am as you are; my people are your people, my
horses are your horses." But Jehoshaphat also said to the
king of Israel, "Inquire first for the word of the LORD."
Then the king of Israel gathered the prophets together,
about four hundred of them, and said to them, "Shall I go to
battle against Ramoth-gilead, or shall I refrain?" They said,

"Go up; for the LORD will give it into the hand of the king."
But Jehoshaphat said, "Is there no other prophet of the
LORD here of whom we may inquire?" The king of Israel
said to Jehoshaphat, "There is still one other by whom we
may inquire of the LORD, Micaiah son of Imlah; but I hate
him, for he never prophesies anything favorable about me,
but only disaster." Jehoshaphat said, "Let the king not say
such a thing." Then the king of Israel summoned an officer
and said, "Bring quickly Micaiah son of Imlah." Now the
king of Israel and King Jehoshaphat of Judah were sitting
on their thrones, arrayed in their robes, at the threshing
floor at the entrance of the gate of Samaria; and all the
prophets were prophesying before them. Zedekiah son of
Chenaanah made for himself horns of iron, and he said,
"Thus says the LORD: With these you shall gore the
Arameans until they are destroyed." All the prophets were
prophesying the same and saying, "Go up to Ramoth-gilead
and triumph; the LORD will give it into the hand of the
king." The messenger who had gone to summon Micaiah
said to him, "Look, the words of the prophets with one
accord are favorable to the king; let your word be like the
word of one of them, and speak favorably." But Micaiah
said, "As the LORD lives, whatever the LORD says to me,
that I will speak." When he had come to the king, the king
said to him, "Micaiah, shall we go to Ramoth-gilead to
battle, or shall we refrain?" He answered him, "Go up and
triumph; the LORD will give it into the hand of the king."
But the king said to him, "How many times must I make
you swear to tell me nothing but the truth in the name of the
LORD?" Then Micaiah said, "I saw all Israel scattered on
the mountains, like sheep that have no shepherd; and the
LORD said, 'These have no master; let each one go home in
peace.' " The king of Israel said to Jehoshaphat, "Did I not
tell you that he would not prophesy anything favorable

about me, but only disaster?" Then Micaiah said, "Therefore hear the word of the LORD: I saw the LORD sitting on his throne, with all the host of heaven standing beside him to the right and to the left of him. And the LORD said, 'Who will entice Ahab, so that he may go up and fall at Ramoth-gilead?' Then one said one thing, and another said another, until a spirit came forward and stood before the LORD, saying, 'I will entice him.' 'How?' the LORD asked him. He replied, 'I will go out and be a lying spirit in the mouth of all his prophets.' Then the LORD said, 'You are to entice him, and you shall succeed; go out and do it.' So you see, the LORD has put a lying spirit in the mouth of all these your prophets; the LORD has decreed disaster for you." Then Zedekiah son of Chenaanah came up to Micaiah, slapped him on the cheek, and said, "Which way did the spirit of the LORD pass from me to speak to you?" Micaiah replied, "You will find out on that day when you go in to hide in an inner chamber." The king of Israel then ordered, "Take Micaiah, and return him to Amon the governor of the city and to Joash the king's son, and say, 'Thus says the king: Put this fellow in prison, and feed him on reduced rations of bread and water until I come in peace.' " Micaiah said, "If you return in peace, the LORD has not spoken by me." And he said, "Hear, you peoples, all of you!"

1 Corinthians 2:1–13 [page 564 above]

A Reading (Lesson) from the Gospel according to Matthew [4:18–25]

As Jesus walked by the Sea of Galilee, he saw two brothers, Simon, who is called Peter, and Andrew his brother, casting a net into the sea—for they were fishermen. And he said to them, "Follow me, and I will make you fish for people." Immediately they left their nets and followed him. As he went from there, he saw two other brothers, James son of Zebedee and his brother John, in the boat with their father Zebedee, mending their nets, and he called them. Immediately they left the boat and their father, and followed him. Jesus went throughout Galilee, teaching in their synagogues and proclaiming the good news of the kingdom and curing every disease and every sickness among the people. So his fame spread throughout all Syria, and they brought to him all the sick, those who were afflicted with various diseases and pains, demoniacs, epileptics, and paralytics, and he cured them. And great crowds followed him from Galilee, the Decapolis, Jerusalem, Judea, and from beyond the Jordan.

Thursday

(Psalm 70 [page 682]), *Psalm 71* [page 683] ❖
Psalm 74 [page 689]

A Reading (Lesson) from the First Book of the Kings [22:29–45]

The king of Israel and King Jehoshaphat of Judah went up to Ramoth-gilead. The king of Israel said to Jehoshaphat, "I will disguise myself and go into battle, but you wear your robes." So the king of Israel disguised himself and went into battle. Now the king of Aram had commanded the thirty-two captains of his chariots, "Fight with no one small or great, but only with the king of Israel." When the captains of the chariots saw Jehoshaphat, they said, "It is surely the king of Israel." So they turned to fight against him; and Jehoshaphat cried out. When the captains of the chariots saw that it was not the king of Israel, they turned back from pursuing him. But a certain man drew his bow and unknowingly struck the king of Israel between the scale armor and the breastplate; so he said to the driver of his chariot, "Turn around, and carry me out of the battle, for I am wounded." The battle grew hot that day, and the king was propped up in his chariot facing the Arameans, until at evening he died; the blood from the wound had flowed into the bottom of the chariot. Then about sunset a shout went through the army, "Every man to his city, and every man to his country!" So the king died, and was brought to Samaria; they buried the king in Samaria. They washed the chariot by the pool of Samaria; the dogs licked up his blood, and the prostitutes washed themselves in it, according to the word of the LORD that he had spoken. Now the rest of the acts of Ahab, and all that he did, and the ivory house that he built, and all the cities that he built, are they not written in the Book of the Annals of the Kings of Israel? So Ahab slept with his ancestors; and his son Ahaziah succeeded him. Jehoshaphat son of Asa began to reign over Judah in the fourth year of King Ahab of Israel. Jehoshaphat was thirty-five years old when he began to reign, and he reigned twenty-five years in Jerusalem. His mother's name was Azubah daughter of Shilhi. He walked in all the way of his father Asa; he did not turn aside from it, doing what was right in the sight of the LORD; yet the high places were not taken away, and the people still sacrificed and offered incense on the high places. Jehoshaphat also made peace with the king of Israel. Now the rest of the acts of Jehoshaphat, and his power that he showed, and how he waged war, are they not written in the Book of the Annals of the Kings of Judah?

A Reading (Lesson) from the First Letter of Paul to the Corinthians [2:14—3:15]

Those who are unspiritual do not receive the gifts of God's Spirit, for they are foolishness to them, and they are unable to understand them because they are spiritually discerned. Those who are spiritual discern all things, and they are themselves subject to no one else's scrutiny. "For who has known the mind of the Lord so as to instruct him?" But we have the mind of Christ. And so, brothers and sisters, I could not speak to you as spiritual people, but rather as people of the flesh, as infants in Christ. I fed you with milk, not solid food, for you were not ready for solid food. Even now you are still not ready, for you are still of the flesh. For as long as there is jealousy and quarreling among you, are you not of the flesh, and behaving according to human inclinations? For when one says, "I belong to Paul," and another, "I belong to Apollos," are you not merely human? What then is Apollos? What is Paul? Servants through whom you came to believe, as the Lord assigned to each. I planted, Apollos watered, but God gave the growth. So neither the one who plants nor the one who waters is anything, but only God who gives the growth. The one who plants and the one who waters have a common purpose, and each will receive wages according to the labor of each. For we are God's servants, working together; you are God's field, God's building. According to the grace of God given to me, like a skilled master builder I laid a foundation, and someone else is building on it. Each builder must choose with care how to build on it. For no one can lay any foundation other than the one that has been laid; that foundation is Jesus Christ. Now if anyone builds on the foundation with gold, silver, precious stones, wood, hay, straw—the work of each builder will become visible, for the Day will disclose it, because it will be revealed with fire, and the fire will test what sort of work each has done. If what has been built on the foundation survives, the builder will receive a reward. If the work is burned up, the builder will suffer loss; the builder will be saved, but only as through fire.

A Reading (Lesson) from the Gospel according to Matthew [5:1–10]

When Jesus saw the crowds, he went up the mountain; and after he sat down, his disciples came to him. Then he began to speak, and taught them, saying: "Blessed are the poor in spirit, for theirs is the kingdom of heaven. Blessed are those who mourn, for they will be comforted. Blessed are the meek, for they will inherit the earth. Blessed are those who hunger and thirst for righteousness, for they will be filled. Blessed are the merciful, for they will receive mercy. Blessed are the pure in heart, for they will see God. Blessed are the peacemakers, for they will be called children of God. Blessed are those who are persecuted for righteousness' sake, for theirs is the kingdom of heaven."

Friday

Psalm 69:1–23(24–30)31–38 [page 679] ❖
Psalm 73 [page 687]

A Reading (Lesson) from the Second Book of the Kings [1:2–17]

Ahaziah had fallen through the lattice in his upper chamber in Samaria, and lay injured; so he sent messengers, telling them, "Go, inquire of Baal-zebub, the god of Ekron, whether I shall recover from this injury." But the angel of the LORD said to Elijah the Tishbite, "Get up, go to meet the messengers of the king of Samaria, and say to them, 'Is it because there is no God in Israel that you are going to inquire of Baal-zebub, the god of Ekron?' Now therefore thus says the LORD, 'You shall not leave the bed to which you have gone, but you shall surely die.' " So Elijah went. The messengers returned to the king, who said to them, "Why have you returned?" They answered him, "There came a man to meet us, who said to us, 'Go back to the king who sent you, and say to him: Thus says the LORD: Is it because there is no God in Israel that you are sending to inquire of Baal-zebub, the god of Ekron? Therefore you shall not leave the bed to which you have gone, but shall surely die.' " He said to them, "What sort of man was he who came to meet you and told you these things?" They answered him, "A hairy man, with a leather belt around his waist." He said, "It is Elijah the Tishbite." Then the king sent to him a captain of fifty with his fifty men. He went up to Elijah, who was sitting on the top of a hill, and said to him, "O man of God, the king says, 'Come down.' " But Elijah answered the captain of fifty, "If I am a man of God, let fire come down from heaven and consume you and your fifty." Then fire came down from heaven, and consumed him and his fifty. Again the king sent to him another captain of fifty with his fifty. He went up and said to him, "O man of God, this is the king's order: Come down quickly!" But Elijah answered them, "If I am a man of God, let fire come down from heaven and consume you and your fifty." Then the fire of God came down from heaven and consumed him and his fifty. Again the king sent the captain of a third fifty with his fifty. So the third captain of fifty went up, and came and fell on his knees before Elijah, and entreated him, "O man of God, please let my life, and the life of these fifty servants of

yours, be precious in your sight. Look, fire came down
from heaven and consumed the two former captains of fifty
men with their fifties; but now let my life be precious in
your sight." Then the angel of the LORD said to Elijah,
"Go down with him; do not be afraid of him." So he set out
and went down with him to the king, and said to him,
"Thus says the LORD: Because you have sent messengers to
inquire of Baal-zebub, the god of Ekron,—is it because there
is no God in Israel to inquire of his word?—therefore you
shall not leave the bed to which you have gone, but you
shall surely die." So he died according to the word of the
LORD that Elijah had spoken. His brother, Jehoram,
succeeded him as king in the second year of King Jehoram
son of Jehoshaphat of Judah, because Ahaziah had no son.

*A Reading (Lesson) from the First Letter of Paul to the
Corinthians* [3:16–23]

Do you not know that you are God's temple and that
God's Spirit dwells in you? If anyone destroys God's
temple, God will destroy that person. For God's temple is
holy, and you are that temple. Do not deceive yourselves.
If you think that you are wise in this age, you should
become fools so that you may become wise. For the
wisdom of this world is foolishness with God. For it is
written, "He catches the wise in their craftiness," and
again, "The Lord knows the thoughts of the wise, that
they are futile." So let no one boast about human leaders.
For all things are yours, whether Paul or Apollos or
Cephas or the world or life or death or the present or the
future—all belong to you, and you belong to Christ, and
Christ belongs to God.

A Reading (Lesson) from the Gospel according to Matthew [5:11–16]

Jesus opened his mouth and taught his disciples, saying, "Blessed are you when people revile you and persecute you and utter all kinds of evil against you falsely on my account. Rejoice and be glad, for your reward is great in heaven, for in the same way they persecuted the prophets who were before you. You are the salt of the earth; but if salt has lost its taste, how can its saltiness be restored? It is no longer good for anything, but is thrown out and trampled under foot. You are the light of the world. A city built on a hill cannot be hid. No one after lighting a lamp puts it under the bushel basket, but on the lampstand, and it gives light to all in the house. In the same way, let your light shine before others, so that they may see your good works and give glory to your Father in heaven."

Saturday

Psalm 75 [page 691],   *Psalm 76* [page 692]   ❖
Psalm 23 [page 612],   *Psalm 27* [page 617]

A Reading (Lesson) from the Second Book of the Kings [2:1–18]

When the LORD was about to take Elijah up to heaven by a whirlwind, Elijah and Elisha were on their way from Gilgal. Elijah said to Elisha, "Stay here; for the LORD has sent me as far as Bethel." But Elisha said, "As the LORD lives, and as you yourself live, I will not leave you." So they went down to Bethel. The company of prophets who were in Bethel came out to Elisha, and said to him, "Do you know that today the LORD will take your master away from you?" And he said, "Yes, I know; keep silent." Elijah said to him,

"Elisha, stay here; for the LORD has sent me to Jericho." But he said, "As the LORD lives, and as you yourself live, I will not leave you." So they came to Jericho. The company of prophets who were at Jericho drew near to Elisha, and said to him, "Do you know that today the LORD will take your master away from you?" And he answered, "Yes, I know; be silent." Then Elijah said to him, "Stay here; for the LORD has sent me to the Jordan." But he said, "As the LORD lives, and as you yourself live, I will not leave you." So the two of them went on. Fifty men of the company of prophets also went, and stood at some distance from them, as they both were standing by the Jordan. Then Elijah took his mantle and rolled it up, and struck the water; the water was parted to the one side and to the other, until the two of them crossed on dry ground. When they had crossed, Elijah said to Elisha, "Tell me what I may do for you, before I am taken from you." Elisha said, "Please let me inherit a double share of your spirit." He responded, "You have asked a hard thing; yet, if you see me as I am being taken from you, it will be granted you; if not, it will not." As they continued walking and talking, a chariot of fire and horses of fire separated the two of them, and Elijah ascended in a whirlwind into heaven. Elisha kept watching and crying out, "Father, father! The chariots of Israel and its horsemen!" But when he could no longer see him, he grasped his own clothes and tore them in two pieces. He picked up the mantle of Elijah that had fallen from him, and went back and stood on the bank of the Jordan. He took the mantle of Elijah that had fallen from him, and struck the water, saying, "Where is the LORD, the God of Elijah?" When he had struck the water, the water was parted to the one side and to the other, and Elisha went over. When the company of prophets who were at Jericho saw him at a distance, they declared, "The spirit of Elijah rests on Elisha." They came to meet him and bowed to the ground before him. They said to him, "See now, we have fifty strong men among your servants; please let them go and seek your master; it may be that the spirit of the LORD has caught him up and thrown him down on some mountain or into some valley." He responded, "No, do not send them." But when they urged him until he was ashamed, he said, "Send them." So they sent fifty men who searched for three days but did not find him. When they came back to him (he had remained at Jericho), he said to them, "Did I not say to you, Do not go?"

A Reading (Lesson) from the First Letter of Paul to the Corinthians [4:1–7]

Think of us in this way, as servants of Christ and stewards of God's mysteries. Moreover, it is required of stewards that they be found trustworthy. But with me it is a very small thing that I should be judged by you or by any human court. I do not even judge myself. I am not aware of anything against myself, but I am not thereby acquitted. It is the Lord who judges me. Therefore do not pronounce judgment before the time, before the Lord comes, who will bring to light the things now hidden in darkness and will disclose the purposes of the heart. Then each one will receive commendation from God. I have applied all this to Apollos and myself for your benefit, brothers and sisters, so that you may learn through us the meaning of the saying, "Nothing beyond what is written," so that none of you will be puffed up in favor of one against another. For who sees anything different in you? What do you have that you did not receive? And if you received it, why do you boast as if it were not a gift?

A Reading (Lesson) from the Gospel according to Matthew [5:17–20]

Jesus opened his mouth and taught his disciples, saying, "Do not think that I have come to abolish the law or the prophets; I have come not to abolish but to fulfill. For truly I tell you, until heaven and earth pass away, not one letter, not one stroke of a letter, will pass from the law until all is accomplished. Therefore, whoever breaks one of the least of these commandments, and teaches others to do the same, will be called least in the kingdom of heaven; but whoever does them and teaches them will be called great in the kingdom of heaven. For I tell you, unless your righteousness exceeds that of the scribes and Pharisees, you will never enter the kingdom of heaven."

Proper 20 *Week of the Sunday closest to September 21*

Sunday

Psalm 93 [page 722], *Psalm 96* [page 725] ❖
Psalm 34 [page 627]

A Reading (Lesson) from the Second Book of the Kings [4:8–37]

One day Elisha was passing through Shunem, where a wealthy woman lived, who urged him to have a meal. So whenever he passed that way, he would stop there for a meal. She said to her husband, "Look, I am sure that this man who regularly passes our way is a holy man of God. Let us make a small roof chamber with walls, and put there for him a bed, a table, a chair, and a lamp, so that he can stay there whenever he comes to us." One day when he came there, he went up to the chamber and lay down there. He said to his servant Gehazi, "Call the Shunammite woman." When he had called her, she stood before him. He said to him, "Say to her, Since you have taken all this trouble for us, what may be done for you? Would you have a word spoken on your behalf to the king or to the commander of the army?" She answered, "I live among my own people." He said, "What then may be done for her?" Gehazi answered, "Well, she has no son, and her husband is old." He said, "Call her." When he had called her, she stood at the door. He said, "At this season, in due time, you shall embrace a son." She replied, "No, my lord, O man of God; do not deceive your servant." The woman conceived and bore a son at that season, in due time, as Elisha had declared to her. When the child was older, he went out one day to his father among the reapers. He complained to his father, "Oh, my head, my head!" The father said to his servant, "Carry him to his mother." He carried him and brought him to his mother; the child sat on her lap until noon, and he died. She went up and laid him on the bed of the man of God, closed the door on him, and left. Then she called to her husband, and said, "Send me one of the servants and one of the donkeys, so that I may quickly go to the man of God and come back again." He said, "Why go to him today? It is neither new moon nor sabbath." She said, "It will be all right." Then she saddled the donkey and said to her servant, "Urge the animal on; do not hold back for me unless I tell you." So she set out, and came to the man of God at Mount Carmel. When the man of God saw her coming, he said to Gehazi his servant, "Look, there is the Shunammite woman; run at once to meet her, and say to her, Are you all right? Is your husband all right? Is the child all right?" She answered, "It is all right." When she came to the man of God at the mountain, she caught hold of his feet.

Gehazi approached to push her away. But the man of God said, "Let her alone, for she is in bitter distress; the LORD has hidden it from me and has not told me." Then she said, "Did I ask my lord for a son? Did I not say, Do not mislead me?" He said to Gehazi, "Gird up your loins, and take my staff in your hand, and go. If you meet anyone, give no greeting, and if anyone greets you, do not answer; and lay my staff on the face of the child." Then the mother of the child said, "As the LORD lives, and as you yourself live, I will not leave without you." So he rose up and followed her. Gehazi went on ahead and laid the staff on the face of the child, but there was no sound or sign of life. He came back to meet him and told him, "The child has not awakened." When Elisha came into the house, he saw the child lying dead on his bed. So he went in and closed the door on the two of them, and prayed to the LORD. Then he got up on the bed and lay upon the child, putting his mouth upon his mouth, his eyes upon his eyes, and his hands upon his hands; and while he lay bent over him, the flesh of the child became warm. He got down, walked once to and fro in the room, then got up again and bent over him; the child sneezed seven times, and the child opened his eyes. Elisha summoned Gehazi and said, "Call the Shunammite woman." So he called her. When she came to him, he said, "Take your son." She came and fell at his feet, bowing to the ground; then she took her son and left.

A Reading (Lesson) from the Acts of the Apostles [9:10–31]

There was a disciple in Damascus named Ananias. The Lord said to him in a vision, "Ananias." He answered, "Here I am, Lord." The Lord said to him, "Get up and go to the street called Straight, and at the house of Judas look for a man of Tarsus named Saul. At this moment he is praying, and he has seen in a vision a man named Ananias come in and lay his hands on him so that he might regain his sight." But Ananias answered, "Lord, I have heard from many about this man, how much evil he has done to your saints in Jerusalem; and here he has authority from the chief priests to bind all who invoke your name." But the Lord said to him, "Go, for he is an instrument whom I have chosen to bring my name before Gentiles and kings and before the people of Israel; I myself will show him how much he must suffer for the sake of my name." So Ananias went and entered the house. He laid his hands on Saul and said, "Brother Saul, the Lord Jesus, who appeared to you on your way here, has sent me so that you may regain your sight and be filled with the Holy Spirit." And immediately something like scales fell from his eyes, and his sight was restored. Then he got up and was baptized, and after taking some food, he regained his strength. For several days he was with the disciples in Damascus, and immediately he began to proclaim Jesus in the synagogues, saying, "He is the Son of God." All who heard him were amazed and said, "Is not this the man who made havoc in Jerusalem among those who invoked his name? And has he not come here for the purpose of bringing them bound before the chief priests?" Saul became increasingly more powerful and confounded the Jews who lived in Damascus by proving that Jesus was the Messiah. After some time had passed, the Jews plotted to kill him, but their plot became known to Saul. They were watching the gates day and night so that they might kill him; but his disciples took him by night and let him down through an opening in the wall, lowering him in a basket. When he had come to Jerusalem, he attempted to join the disciples; and they were all afraid of him, for they did not believe that he was a disciple. But Barnabas took him, brought him to the apostles, and described for them how on the road he had seen the Lord, who had spoken to him, and how in Damascus he had spoken boldly in the name of Jesus. So he went in and out among them in Jerusalem, speaking boldly in the name of the Lord. He spoke and argued with the Hellenists; but they were attempting to kill him. When the believers learned of it, they brought him down to Caesarea and sent him off to Tarsus. Meanwhile the church throughout Judea, Galilee, and Samaria had peace and was built up. Living in the fear of the Lord and in the comfort of the Holy Spirit, it increased in numbers.

A Reading (Lesson) from the Gospel according to Luke [3:7–18]

John the Baptist said to the crowds that came out to be baptized by him, "You brood of vipers! Who warned you to flee from the wrath to come? Bear fruits worthy of repentance. Do not begin to say to yourselves, 'We have Abraham as our ancestor'; for I tell you, God is able from these stones to raise up children to Abraham. Even now the ax is lying at the root of the trees; every tree therefore that does not bear good fruit is cut down and thrown into the fire." And the crowds asked him, "What then should we do?" In reply he said to them, "Whoever has two coats must share with anyone who has none; and whoever has food must do likewise." Even tax collectors came to be baptized, and they asked him, "Teacher, what should we do?" He said to them, "Collect no more than the amount prescribed for you." Soldiers also asked him, "And we, what should we do?" He said to them, "Do not extort money from anyone by threats or false accusation, and be satisfied with your wages." As the people were filled with expectation, and all were questioning in their hearts concerning John, whether he might be the Messiah, John answered all of them by saying, "I baptize you with water; but one who is more powerful than I is coming; I am not worthy to untie the thong of his sandals. He will baptize you with the Holy Spirit and fire. His winnowing fork is in his hand, to clear his threshing floor and to gather the wheat into his granary; but the chaff he will burn with unquenchable fire." So, with many other exhortations, he proclaimed the good news to the people.

Monday

Psalm 80 [page 702] ❖ *Psalm 77* [page 693], (*Psalm 79* [page 701])

A Reading (Lesson) from the Second Book of the Kings [5:1–19]

Naaman, commander of the army of the king of Aram, was a great man and in high favor with his master, because by him the LORD had given victory to Aram. The man, though a mighty warrior, suffered from leprosy. Now the Arameans on one of their raids had taken a young girl captive from the land of Israel, and she served Naaman's wife. She said to her mistress, "If only my lord were with the prophet who is in Samaria! He would cure him of his leprosy." So Naaman went in and told his lord just what the girl from the land of Israel had said. And the king of Aram said, "Go then, and I will send along a letter to the king of Israel." He went, taking with him ten talents of silver, six thousand shekels of gold, and ten sets of garments. He brought the letter to the king of Israel, which read, "When this letter reaches you, know that I have sent to you my servant Naaman, that you may cure him of his leprosy." When the king of Israel read the letter, he tore his clothes, and said, "Am I God, to give death or life, that this man sends word to me to cure a man of his leprosy? Just look and see how he is trying to pick a quarrel with me." But when Elisha the man of God heard that the king of Israel had torn his clothes, he sent a message to the king, "Why have you torn your clothes? Let him come to me, that he may learn that there is a prophet in Israel." So Naaman came with his horses and chariots, and halted at the entrance of Elisha's house. Elisha sent a messenger to him, saying, "Go, wash in the Jordan seven times, and your flesh shall be restored and you shall be clean." But Naaman became angry and went away, saying, "I thought that for me he would surely come out, and stand and call on the name of the LORD his God, and would wave his hand over the spot, and cure the leprosy! Are not Abana and Pharpar, the rivers of Damascus, better than all the waters of Israel? Could I not wash in them, and be clean?" He turned and went away in a rage. But his servants approached and said to him, "Father, if the prophet had commanded you to do something difficult, would you not have done it? How much more, when all he said to you was, 'Wash, and be clean'?" So he went down and immersed himself seven times in the Jordan, according to the word of the man of God; his flesh was restored like the flesh of a young boy, and he was clean. Then he returned to the man of God, he and all his company; he came and stood before him and said, "Now I know that there is no God in all the earth except in Israel; please accept a present from your servant." But he said, "As the LORD lives, whom I serve, I will accept nothing!" He urged him to accept, but he refused. Then Naaman said, "If not, please let two muleloads of earth be given to your servant; for your servant will no longer offer burnt offering or sacrifice to any god except the LORD. But may the LORD pardon your servant on one count: when my master goes into the house of Rimmon to worship there, leaning on my arm, and I bow down in the house of Rimmon, when I do bow down in the house of Rimmon, may the LORD pardon your servant on this one count." He said to him, "Go in peace."

A Reading (Lesson) from the First Letter of Paul to the Corinthians [4:8–21]

Already you have all you want! Already you have become rich! Quite apart from us you have become kings! Indeed, I wish that you had become kings, so that we might be kings with you! For I think that God has exhibited us apostles as last of all, as though sentenced to death, because we have become a spectacle to the world, to angels and to mortals. We are fools for the sake of Christ, but you are wise in Christ. We are weak, but you are strong. You are held in honor, but we in disrepute. To the present hour we are hungry and thirsty, we are poorly clothed and beaten and homeless, and we grow weary from the work of our own hands. When reviled, we bless; when persecuted, we endure; when slandered, we speak kindly. We have become like the rubbish of the world, the dregs of all things, to this very day. I am not writing this to make you ashamed, but to admonish you as my beloved children. For though you might have ten thousand guardians in Christ, you do not have many fathers. Indeed, in Christ Jesus I became your father through the gospel. I appeal to you, then, be imitators of me. For this reason I sent you Timothy, who is my beloved and faithful child in the LORD, to remind you of my ways in Christ Jesus, as I teach them everywhere in every church. But some of you, thinking that I am not coming to you, have become arrogant. But I will come to you soon, if the LORD wills, and I will find out not the talk of these arrogant people but their power. For the kingdom of God depends not on talk but on power. What would you prefer? Am I to come to you with a stick, or with love in a spirit of gentleness?

A Reading (Lesson) from the Gospel according to Matthew [5:21–26]

Jesus opened his mouth and taught his disciples, saying, "You have heard that it was said to those of ancient times, 'You shall not murder'; and 'whoever murders shall be liable to judgment.' But I say to you that if you are angry with a brother or sister, you will be liable to judgment; and if you insult a brother or sister, you will be liable to the council; and if you say, 'You fool,' you will be liable to the hell of fire. So when you are offering your gift at the altar, if you remember that your brother or sister has something against you, leave your gift there before the altar and go; first be reconciled to your brother or sister, and then come and offer your gift. Come to terms quickly with your accuser while you are on the way to court with him, or your accuser may hand you over to the judge, and the judge to the guard, and you will be thrown into prison. Truly I tell you, you will never get out until you have paid the last penny."

Tuesday

Psalm 78:1–39 [page 694]   ❖   *Psalm 78:40–72* [page 698]

A Reading (Lesson) from the Second Book of the Kings [5:19–27]

Elisha said to Naaman, "Go in peace." But when Naaman had gone from him a short distance, Gehazi, the servant of Elisha the man of God, thought, "My master has let that Aramean Naaman off too lightly by not accepting from him what he offered. As the LORD lives, I will run after him and get something out of him." So Gehazi went after Naaman. When Naaman saw someone running after him, he jumped down from the chariot to meet him and said, "Is everything all right?" He replied, "Yes, but my master has sent me to say, 'Two members of a company of prophets have just come to me from the hill country of Ephraim; please give them a talent of silver and two changes of clothing.'" Naaman said, "Please accept two talents." He urged him, and tied up two talents of silver in two bags, with two changes of clothing, and gave them to two of his servants, who carried them in front of Gehazi. When he came to the citadel, he took the bags from them, and stored them inside; he dismissed the men, and they left. He went in and stood before his master; and Elisha said to him, "Where have you been, Gehazi?" He answered, "Your servant has not gone anywhere at all." But he said to him, "Did I not go with you in spirit when someone left his chariot to meet you? Is this a time to accept money and to accept clothing, olive orchards and vineyards, sheep and oxen, and male and female slaves? Therefore the leprosy of Naaman shall cling to you, and to your descendants forever." So he left his presence leprous, as white as snow.

A Reading (Lesson) from the First Letter of Paul to the Corinthians [5:1–8]

It is actually reported that there is sexual immorality among you, and of a kind that is not found even among pagans; for a man is living with his father's wife. And you are arrogant! Should you not rather have mourned, so that he who has done this would have been removed from among you? For though absent in body, I am present in spirit; and as if present I have already pronounced judgment in the name of the Lord Jesus on the man who has done such a thing. When you are assembled, and my spirit is present with the power of our Lord Jesus, you are to hand this man over to Satan for the destruction of the flesh, so that his spirit may be saved in the day of the LORD. Your boasting is not a good thing. Do you not know that a little yeast leavens the whole batch of dough? Clean out the old yeast so that you may be a new batch, as you really are unleavened. For our paschal lamb, Christ, has been sacrificed. Therefore, let us celebrate the festival, not with the old yeast, the yeast of malice and evil, but with the unleavened bread of sincerity and truth.

A Reading (Lesson) from the Gospel according to Matthew [5:27–37]

Jesus opened his mouth and taught his disciples, saying, "You have heard that it was said, 'You shall not commit adultery.' But I say to you that everyone who looks at a woman with lust has already committed adultery with her in his heart. If your right eye causes you to sin, tear it out and throw it away; it is better for you to lose one of your members than for your whole body to be thrown into hell. And if your right hand causes you to sin, cut it off and throw it away; it is better for you to lose one of your members than for your whole body to go into hell. It was also said, 'Whoever divorces his wife, let him give her a certificate of divorce.' But I say to you that anyone who divorces his wife, except on the ground of unchastity, causes her to commit adultery; and whoever marries a divorced woman commits adultery. Again, you have heard that it was said to those of ancient times, 'You shall not swear falsely, but carry out the vows you have made to the LORD.' But I say to you, Do not swear at all, either by heaven, for it is the throne of God, or by the earth, for it is his footstool, or by Jerusalem, for it is the city of the great King. And do not swear by your head, for you cannot make one hair white or black. Let your word be 'Yes, Yes' or 'No, No'; anything more than this comes from the evil one."

Wednesday

Psalm 119:97–120 [page 771] ❖ *Psalm 81* [page 704], *Psalm 82* [page 705]

A Reading (Lesson) from the Second Book of the Kings [6:1–23]

The company of prophets said to Elisha, "As you see, the place where we live under your charge is too small for us. Let us go to the Jordan, and let us collect logs there, one for each of us, and build a place there for us to live." He answered, "Do so." Then one of them said, "Please come with your servants." And he answered, "I will." So he went with them. When they came to the Jordan, they cut down trees. But as one was felling a log, his ax head fell into the water; he cried out, "Alas, master! It was borrowed." Then the man of God said, "Where did it fall?" When he showed him the place, he cut off a stick, and threw it in there, and made the iron float. He said, "Pick it up." So he reached out his hand and took it. Once when the king of Aram was at war with Israel, he took counsel with his officers. He said, "At such and such a place shall be my camp." But the man of God sent word to the king of Israel, "Take care not to pass this place, because the Arameans are going down there." The king of Israel sent word to the place of which the man of God spoke. More than once or twice he warned such a place so that it was on the alert. The mind of the king of

Aram was greatly perturbed because of this; he called his officers and said to them, "Now tell me who among us sides with the king of Israel?" Then one of his officers said, "No one, my lord king. It is Elisha, the prophet in Israel, who tells the king of Israel the words that you speak in your bedchamber." He said, "Go and find where he is; I will send and seize him." He was told, "He is in Dothan." So he sent horses and chariots there and a great army; they came by night, and surrounded the city. When an attendant of the man of God rose early in the morning and went out, an army with horses and chariots was all around the city. His servant said, "Alas, master! What shall we do?" He replied, "Do not be afraid, for there are more with us than there are with them." Then Elisha prayed: "O LORD, please open his eyes that he may see." So the LORD opened the eyes of the servant, and he saw; the mountain was full of horses and chariots of fire all around Elisha. When the Arameans came down against him, Elisha prayed to the LORD, and said, "Strike this people, please, with blindness." So he struck them with blindness as Elisha had asked. Elisha said to them, "This is not the way, and this is not the city; follow me, and I will bring you to the man whom you seek." And he led them to Samaria. As soon as they entered Samaria, Elisha said, "O LORD, open the eyes of these men so that they may see." The LORD opened their eyes, and they saw that they were inside Samaria. When the king of Israel saw them he said to Elisha, "Father, shall I kill them? Shall I kill them?" He answered, "No! Did you capture with your sword and your bow those whom you want to kill? Set food and water before them so that they may eat and drink; and let them go to their master." So he prepared for them a great feast; after they ate and drank, he sent them on their way, and they went to their master. And the Arameans no longer came raiding into the land of Israel.

A Reading (Lesson) from the First Letter of Paul to the Corinthians [5:9—6:8]

I wrote to you in my letter not to associate with sexually immoral persons—not at all meaning the immoral of this world, or the greedy and robbers, or idolaters, since you would then need to go out of the world. But now I am writing to you not to associate with anyone who bears the name of brother or sister who is sexually immoral or greedy, or is an idolater, reviler, drunkard, or robber. Do not even eat with such a one. For what have I to do with judging those outside? Is it not those who are inside that you are to judge? God will judge those outside. "Drive out the wicked person from among you." When any of you has a grievance against another, do you dare to take it to court before the unrighteous, instead of taking it before the saints? Do you not know that the saints will judge the world? And if the world is to be judged by you, are you incompetent to try trivial cases? Do you not know that we are to judge angels—to say nothing of ordinary matters? If you have ordinary cases, then, do you appoint as judges those who have no standing in the church? I say this to your shame. Can it be that there is no one among you wise enough to decide between one believer and another, but a believer goes to court against a believer—and before unbelievers at that? In fact, to have lawsuits at all with one another is already a defeat for you. Why not rather be wronged? Why not rather be defrauded? But you yourselves wrong and defraud—and believers at that.

A Reading (Lesson) from the Gospel according to Matthew [5:38–48]

Jesus opened his mouth and taught his disciples, saying, "You have heard that it was said, 'An eye for an eye and a tooth for a tooth.' But I say to you, Do not resist an evildoer. But if anyone strikes you on the right cheek, turn the other also; and if anyone wants to sue you and take your coat, give your cloak as well; and if anyone forces you to go one mile, go also the second mile. Give to everyone who begs from you, and do not refuse anyone who wants to borrow from you. You have heard that it was said, 'You shall love your neighbor and hate your enemy.' But I say to you, Love your enemies and pray for those who persecute you, so that you may be children of your Father in heaven; for he makes his sun rise on the evil and on the good, and sends rain on the righteous and on the unrighteous. For if you love those who love you, what reward do you have? Do not even the tax collectors do the same? And if you greet only your brothers and sisters, what more are you doing than others? Do not even the Gentiles do the same? Be perfect, therefore, as your heavenly Father is perfect."

Thursday

(*Psalm 83* [page 706]) or *Psalm 116* [page 759], *Psalm 117* [page 760] ❖ *Psalm 85* [page 708], *Psalm 86* [page 709]

A Reading (Lesson) from the Second Book of the Kings [9:1–16]

The prophet Elisha called a member of the company of prophets and said to him, "Gird up your loins; take this flask of oil in your hand, and go to Ramoth-gilead. When you arrive, look there for Jehu son of Jehoshaphat, son of Nimshi; go in and get him to leave his companions, and take him into an inner chamber. Then take the flask of oil, pour it on his head, and say, 'Thus says the LORD: I anoint you king over Israel.' Then open the door and flee; do not linger." So the young man, the young prophet, went to Ramoth-gilead. He arrived while the commanders of the army were in council, and he announced, "I have a message for you, commander." "For which one of us?" asked Jehu. "For you, commander." So Jehu got up and went inside; the young man poured the oil on his head, saying to him, "Thus says the LORD the God of Israel: I anoint you king over the people of the LORD, over Israel. You shall strike down the house of your master Ahab, so that I may avenge on Jezebel the blood of my servants the prophets, and the blood of all the servants of the LORD. For the whole house of Ahab shall perish; I will cut off from Ahab every male, bond or free, in Israel. I will make the house of Ahab like the house of Jeroboam son of Nebat, and like the house of Baasha son of Ahijah. The dogs shall eat Jezebel in the territory of Jezreel, and no one shall bury her." Then he opened the door and fled. When Jehu came back to his master's officers, they said to him, "Is everything all right? Why did that madman come to you?" He answered them, "You know the sort and how they babble." They said, "Liar! Come on, tell us!" So he said, "This is just what he said to me: 'Thus says the LORD, I anoint you king over Israel.'" Then hurriedly they all took their cloaks and spread them for him on the bare steps; and they blew the trumpet, and proclaimed, "Jehu is king." Thus Jehu son of Jehoshaphat son of Nimshi conspired against Joram. Joram with all Israel had been on guard at Ramoth-gilead against King Hazael of Aram; but King Joram had returned to be healed in Jezreel of the wounds that the Arameans had inflicted on him, when he fought against King Hazael of Aram. So Jehu said, "If this is your wish, then let no one slip out of the city to go and tell the news in Jezreel." Then Jehu mounted his chariot and went to Jezreel, where Joram was lying ill. King Ahaziah of Judah had come down to visit Joram.

A Reading (Lesson) from the First Letter of Paul to the Corinthians [6:12–20]

"All things are lawful for me," but not all things are beneficial. "All things are lawful for me," but I will not be dominated by anything. "Food is meant for the stomach and the stomach for food, and God will destroy both one and the other. The body is meant not for fornication but for the Lord, and the Lord for the body. And God raised the Lord and will also raise us by his power. Do you not know that your bodies are members of Christ? Should I therefore take the members of Christ and make them members of a prostitute? Never! Do you not know that whoever is united to a prostitute becomes one body with her? For it is said, "The two shall be one flesh." But anyone united to the Lord becomes one spirit with him. Shun fornication! Every sin that a person commits is outside the body; but the fornicator sins against the body itself. Or do you not know that your body is a temple of the Holy Spirit within you, which you have from God, and that you are not your own? For you were bought with a price; therefore glorify God in your body.

A Reading (Lesson) from the Gospel according to Matthew [6:1–6, 16–18]

Jesus opened his mouth and taught his disciples, saying, "Beware of practicing your piety before others in order to be seen by them; for then you have no reward from your Father in heaven. So whenever you give alms, do not sound a trumpet before you, as the hypocrites do in the synagogues and in the streets, so that they may be praised by others. Truly I tell you, they have received their reward. But when you give alms, do not let your left hand know what your right hand is doing, so that your alms may be done in secret; and your Father who sees in secret will reward you. And whenever you pray, do not be like the hypocrites; for they love to stand and pray in the synagogues and at the street corners, so that they may be seen by others. Truly I tell you, they have received their reward. But whenever you pray, go into your room and shut the door and pray to your Father who is in secret; and your Father who sees in secret will reward you. And whenever you fast, do not look dismal, like the hypocrites, for they disfigure their faces so as to show others that they are fasting. Truly I tell you, they have received their reward. But when you fast, put oil on your head and wash your face, so that your fasting may be seen not by others but by your Father who is in secret; and your Father who sees in secret will reward you."

Friday

Psalm 88 [page 712] ❖ *Psalm 91* [page 719], *Psalm 92* [page 720]

A Reading (Lesson) from the Second Book of the Kings [9:17–37]

In Jezreel, the sentinel standing on the tower spied the company of Jehu arriving, and said, "I see a company." Joram said, "Take a horseman; send him to meet them, and let him say, 'Is it peace?'" So the horseman went to meet him; he said, "Thus says the king, 'Is it peace?'" Jehu responded, "What have you to do with peace? Fall in behind me." The sentinel reported, saying, "The messenger reached them, but he is not coming back." Then he sent out a second horseman, who came to them and said, "Thus says the king, 'Is it peace?' " Jehu answered, "What have you to do with peace? Fall in behind me." Again the sentinel reported, "He reached them, but he is not coming back. It looks like the driving of Jehu son of Nimshi; for he drives like a maniac." Joram said, "Get ready." And they got his chariot ready. Then King Joram of Israel and King Ahaziah of Judah set out, each in his chariot, and went to meet Jehu; they met him at the property of Naboth the Jezreelite. When Joram saw Jehu, he said, "Is it peace, Jehu?" He answered, "What peace can there be, so long as the many whoredoms and sorceries of your mother Jezebel continue?" Then Joram reined about and fled, saying to Ahaziah, "Treason, Ahaziah!" Jehu drew his bow with all his strength, and shot Joram between the shoulders, so that the arrow pierced his heart; and he sank in his chariot. Jehu said to his aide Bidkar, "Lift him out, and throw him on the plot of ground belonging to Naboth the Jezreelite; for remember, when you and I rode side by side behind his father Ahab how the Lord uttered this oracle against him: 'For the blood of Naboth and for the blood of his children that I saw yesterday, says the Lord, I swear I will repay you on this very plot of ground.' Now therefore lift him out and throw him on the plot of ground, in accordance with the word of the Lord." When King Ahaziah of Judah saw this, he fled in the direction of Beth-haggan. Jehu pursued him, saying, "Shoot him also!" And they shot him in the chariot at the ascent to Gur, which is by Ibleam. Then he fled to Megiddo, and died there. His officers carried him in a chariot to Jerusalem, and buried him in his tomb with his ancestors in the city of David. In the eleventh year of Joram son of Ahab,

Ahaziah began to reign over Judah. When Jehu came to Jezreel, Jezebel heard of it; she painted her eyes, and adorned her head, and looked out of the window. As Jehu entered the gate, she said, "Is it peace, Zimri, murderer of your master?" He looked up to the window and said, "Who is on my side? Who?" Two or three eunuchs looked out at him. He said, "Throw her down." So they threw her down; some of her blood spattered on the wall and on the horses, which trampled on her. Then he went in and ate and drank; he said, "See to that cursed woman and bury her; for she is a king's daughter." But when they went to bury her, they found no more of her than the skull and the feet and the palms of her hands. When they came back and told him, he said, "This is the word of the LORD, which he spoke by his servant Elijah the Tishbite, 'In the territory of Jezreel the dogs shall eat the flesh of Jezebel; the corpse of Jezebel shall be like dung on the field in the territory of Jezreel, so that no one can say, This is Jezebel.' "

A Reading (Lesson) from the First Letter of Paul to the Corinthians [7:1–9]

Now concerning the matters about which you wrote: "It is well for a man not to touch a woman." But because of cases of sexual immorality, each man should have his own wife and each woman her own husband. The husband should give to his wife her conjugal rights, and likewise the wife to her husband. For the wife does not have authority over her own body, but the husband does; likewise the husband does not have authority over his own body, but the wife does. Do not deprive one another except perhaps by agreement for a set time, to devote yourselves to prayer, and then come together again, so that Satan may not tempt you because of your lack of self-control. This I say by way of concession, not of command. I wish that all were as I myself am. But each has a particular gift from God, one having one kind and another a different kind. To the unmarried and the widows I say that it is well for them to remain unmarried as I am. But if they are not practicing self-control, they should marry. For it is better to marry than to be aflame with passion.

A Reading (Lesson) from the Gospel According to Matthew [6:7–15]

Jesus opened his mouth and taught his disciples, saying, "When you are praying, do not heap up empty phrases as the Gentiles do; for they think that they will be heard because of their many words. Do not be like them, for your Father knows what you need before you ask him. Pray then in this way: Our Father in heaven, hallowed be your name. Your kingdom come. Your will be done, on earth as it is in heaven. Give us this day our daily bread. And forgive us our debts, as we also have forgiven our debtors. And do not bring us to the time of trial, but rescue us from the evil one. For if you forgive others their trespasses, your heavenly Father will also forgive you; but if you do not forgive others, neither will your Father forgive your trespasses."

Saturday

Psalm 87 [page 711], *Psalm 90* [page 717] ❖
Psalm 136 [page 789]

A Reading (Lesson) from the Second Book of the Kings [11:1–20a]

When Athaliah, Ahaziah's mother, saw that her son was dead, she set about to destroy all the royal family. But

Jehosheba, King Joram's daughter, Ahaziah's sister, took Joash son of Ahaziah, and stole him away from among the king's children who were about to be killed; she put him and his nurse in a bedroom. Thus she hid him from Athaliah, so that he was not killed; he remained with her six years, hidden in the house of the LORD, while Athaliah reigned over the land. But in the seventh year Jehoiada summoned the captains of the Carites and of the guards and had them come to him in the house of the LORD. He made a covenant with them and put them under oath in the house of the LORD; then he showed them the king's son. He commanded them, "This is what you are to do: one-third of you, those who go off duty on the sabbath and guard the king's house (another third being at the gate Sur and a third at the gate behind the guards), shall guard the palace; and your two divisions that come on duty in force on the sabbath and guard the house of the LORD shall surround the king, each with weapons in hand; and whoever approaches the ranks is to be killed. Be with the king in his comings and goings." The captains did according to all that the priest Jehoiada commanded; each brought his men who were to go off duty on the sabbath, with those who were to come on duty on the sabbath, and came to the priest Jehoiada. The priest delivered to the captains the spears and shields that had been King David's, which were in the house of the LORD; the guards stood, every man with his weapons in his hand, from the south side of the house to the north side of the house, around the altar and the house, to guard the king on every side. Then he brought out the king's son, put the crown on him, and gave him the covenant; they proclaimed him king, and anointed him; they clapped their hands and shouted, "Long live the king!" When Athaliah heard the noise of the guard and of the people, she went into the house of the LORD to the people; when she looked, there was the king standing by the pillar, according to custom, with the captains and the trumpeters beside the king, and all the people of the land rejoicing and blowing trumpets. Athaliah tore her clothes and cried, "Treason! Treason!" Then the priest Jehoiada commanded the captains who were set over the army, "Bring her out between the ranks, and kill with the sword anyone who follows her." For the priest said, "Let her not be killed in the house of the LORD." So they laid hands on her; she went through the horses' entrance to the king's house, and there she was put to death. Jehoiada made a covenant between the LORD and the king and people, that they should be the LORD's people; also between the king and the people. Then all the people of the land went to the house of Baal, and tore it down; his altars and his images they broke in pieces, and they killed Mattan, the priest of Baal, before the altars. The priest posted guards over the house of the LORD. He took the captains, the Carites, the guards, and all the people of the land; then they brought the king down from the house of the LORD, marching through the gate of the guards to the king's house. He took his seat on the throne of the kings. So all the people of the land rejoiced.

A Reading (Lesson) from the First Letter of Paul to the Corinthians [7:10–24]

To the married I give this command—not I but the LORD— that the wife should not separate from her husband (but if she does separate, let her remain unmarried or else be reconciled to her husband), and that the husband should not divorce his wife. To the rest I say—I and not the Lord—that if any believer has a wife who is an unbeliever, and she consents to live with him, he should not divorce her. And if any woman has a husband who is an unbeliever, and he consents to live with her, she should not divorce him. For the unbelieving husband is made holy through his wife, and the unbelieving wife is made holy through her husband. Otherwise, your children would be unclean, but as it is, they are holy. But if the unbelieving partner separates, let it be so; in such a case the brother or sister is not bound. It is to peace that God has called you. Wife, for all you know, you might save your husband. Husband, for all you know, you might save your wife. However that may be, let each of you lead the life that the Lord has assigned, to which God called you. This is my rule in all the churches. Was anyone at the time of his call already circumcised? Let him not seek to remove the marks of circumcision. Was anyone at the time of his call uncircumcised? Let him not seek circumcision. Circumcision is nothing, and uncircumcision is nothing; but obeying the commandments of God is everything. Let each of you remain in the condition in which you were called. Were you a slave when called? Do not be concerned about it. Even if you can gain your freedom, make use of your present condition now more than ever. For whoever was called in the Lord as a slave is a freed person belonging to the Lord, just as whoever was free when called is a slave of Christ. You were bought with a price; do not become slaves of human masters. In whatever condition you were called, brothers and sisters, there remain with God.

A Reading (Lesson) from the Gospel according to Matthew [6:19-24]

Jesus opened his mouth and taught his disciples, saying, "Do not store up for yourselves treasures on earth, where moth and rust consume and where thieves break in and steal; but store up for yourselves treasures in heaven, where neither moth nor rust consumes and where thieves do not break in and steal. For where your treasure is, there your heart will be also. The eye is the lamp of the body. So, if your eye is healthy, your whole body will be full of light; but if your eye is unhealthy, your whole body will be full of darkness. If then the light in you is darkness, how great is the darkness! No one can serve two masters; for a slave will either hate the one and love the other, or be devoted to the one and despise the other. You cannot serve God and wealth."

Proper 21   *Week of the Sunday closest to September 28*

Sunday

Psalm 66 [page 673],   *Psalm 67* [page 675]   ❖
Psalm 19 [page 606],   *Psalm 46* [page 649]

A Reading (Lesson) from the Second Book of the Kings [17:1–18]

In the twelfth year of King Ahaz of Judah, Hoshea son of Elah began to reign in Samaria over Israel; he reigned nine years. He did what was evil in the sight of the LORD, yet not like the kings of Israel who were before him. King Shalmaneser of Assyria came up against him; Hoshea became his vassal, and paid him tribute. But the king of Assyria found treachery in Hoshea; for he had sent messengers to King So of Egypt, and offered no tribute to the king of Assyria, as he had done year by year; therefore the king of Assyria confined him and imprisoned him. Then the king of Assyria invaded all the land and came to

Samaria; for three years he besieged it. In the ninth year of Hoshea the king of Assyria captured Samaria; he carried the Israelites away to Assyria. He placed them in Halah, on the Habor, the river of Gozan, and in the cities of the Medes. This occurred because the people of Israel had sinned against the LORD their God, who had brought them up out of the land of Egypt from under the hand of Pharaoh king of Egypt. They had worshiped other gods and walked in the customs of the nations whom the LORD drove out before the people of Israel, and in the customs that the kings of Israel had introduced. The people of Israel secretly did things that were not right against the LORD their God. They built for themselves high places at all their towns, from watchtower to fortified city; they set up for themselves pillars and sacred poles on every high hill and under every green tree; there they made offerings on all the high places, as the nations did whom the LORD carried away before them. They did wicked things, provoking the LORD to anger; they served idols, of which the LORD had said to them, "You shall not do this." Yet the LORD warned Israel and Judah by every prophet and every seer, saying, "Turn from your evil ways and keep my commandments and my statutes, in accordance with all the law that I commanded your ancestors and that I sent to you by my servants the prophets." They would not listen but were stubborn, as their ancestors had been, who did not believe in the LORD their God. They despised his statutes, and his covenant that he made with their ancestors, and the warnings that he gave them. They went after false idols and became false; they followed the nations that were around them, concerning whom the LORD had commanded them that they should not do as they did. They rejected all the commandments of the LORD their God and made for themselves cast images of two calves; they made a sacred pole, worshiped all the host of heaven, and served Baal.

They made their sons and their daughters pass through fire; they used divination and augury; and they sold themselves to do evil in the sight of the LORD, provoking him to anger. Therefore the LORD was very angry with Israel and removed them out of his sight; none was left but the tribe of Judah alone.

A Reading (Lesson) from the Acts of the Apostles [9:36–43]

In Joppa there was a disciple whose name was Tabitha, which in Greek is Dorcas. She was devoted to good works and acts of charity. At that time she became ill and died. When they had washed her, they laid her in a room upstairs. Since Lydda was near Joppa, the disciples, who heard that Peter was there, sent two men to him with the request, "Please come to us without delay." So Peter got up and went with them; and when he arrived, they took him to the room upstairs. All the widows stood beside him, weeping and showing tunics and other clothing that Dorcas had made while she was with them. Peter put all of them outside, and then he knelt down and prayed. He turned to the body and said, "Tabitha, get up." Then she opened her eyes, and seeing Peter, she sat up. He gave her his hand and helped her up. Then calling the saints and widows, he showed her to be alive. This became known throughout Joppa, and many believed in the Lord. Meanwhile he stayed in Joppa for some time with a certain Simon, a tanner.

A Reading (Lesson) from the Gospel according to Luke [5:1–11]

While Jesus was standing beside the lake of Gennesaret, and the crowd was pressing in on him to hear the word of God, he saw two boats there at the shore of the lake; the fishermen had gone out of them and were washing their nets. He got into one of the boats, the one belonging to Simon, and asked him to put out a little way from the shore. Then he sat down and taught the crowds from the boat. When he had finished speaking, he said to Simon, "Put out into the deep water and let down your nets for a catch." Simon answered, "Master, we have worked all night long but have caught nothing. Yet if you say so, I will let down the nets." When they had done this, they caught so many fish that their nets were beginning to break. So they signaled their partners in the other boat to come and help them. And they came and filled both boats, so that they began to sink. But when Simon Peter saw it, he fell down at Jesus' knees, saying, "Go away from me, Lord, for I am a sinful man!" For he and all who were with him were amazed at the catch of fish that they had taken; and so also were James and John, sons of Zebedee, who were partners with Simon. Then Jesus said to Simon, "Do not be afraid; from now on you will be catching people." When they had brought their boats to shore, they left everything and followed him.

Monday

Psalm 89:1–18 [page 713] ❖ *Psalm 89:19–52* [page 715]

A Reading (Lesson) from the Second Book of the Kings [17:24–41]

The king of Assyria brought people from Babylon, Cuthah, Avva, Hamath, and Sepharvaim, and placed them in the cities of Samaria in place of the people of Israel; they took possession of Samaria, and settled in its cities. When they first settled there, they did not worship the LORD; therefore the LORD sent lions among them, which killed some of them. So the king of Assyria was told, "The nations that you have carried away and placed in the cities of Samaria do not know the law of the god of the land; therefore he has sent lions among them; they are killing them, because they do not know the law of the god of the land." Then the king of Assyria commanded, "Send there one of the priests whom you carried away from there; let him go and live there, and teach them the law of the god of the land." So one of the priests whom they had carried away from Samaria came and lived in Bethel; he taught them how they should worship the LORD. But every nation still made gods of its own and put them in the shrines of the high places that the people of Samaria had made, every nation in the cities in which they lived; the people of Babylon made Succoth-benoth, the people of Cuth made Nergal, the people of Hamath made Ashima; the Avvites made Nibhaz and Tartak; the Sepharvites burned their children in the fire to Adrammelech and Anammelech, the gods of Sepharvaim. They also worshiped the LORD and appointed from among themselves all sorts of people as priests of the high places, who sacrificed for them in the shrines of the high places. So they worshiped the LORD but also served their own gods, after the manner of the nations from among whom they had been carried away. To this day they continue to practice their former customs. They do not worship the LORD and they do not follow the statutes or the ordinances or the law or the commandment that the LORD commanded the children of Jacob, whom he named Israel. The LORD had made a covenant with them and commanded them, "You shall not worship other gods or bow yourselves to them or serve them or sacrifice to them, but you shall worship the LORD, who brought you out of the land of Egypt with great power and with an outstretched arm; you shall bow yourselves to him,

and to him you shall sacrifice. The statutes and the
ordinances and the law and the commandment that he
wrote for you, you shall always be careful to observe. You
shall not worship other gods; you shall not forget the
covenant that I have made with you. You shall not worship
other gods, but you shall worship the LORD your God; he
will deliver you out of the hand of all your enemies." They
would not listen, however, but they continued to practice
their former custom. So these nations worshiped the LORD,
but also served their carved images; to this day their
children and their children's children continue to do as their
ancestors did.

*A Reading (Lesson) from the First Letter of Paul to the
Corinthians* [7:25–31]

Concerning virgins, I have no command of the Lord, but I
give my opinion as one who by the Lord's mercy is
trustworthy. I think that, in view of the impending crisis,
it is well for you to remain as you are. Are you bound to
a wife? Do not seek to be free. Are you free from a wife?
Do not seek a wife. But if you marry, you do not sin, and
if a virgin marries, she does not sin. Yet those who marry
will experience distress in this life, and I would spare you
that. I mean, brothers and sisters, the appointed time has
grown short; from now on, let even those who have wives
be as though they had none, and those who mourn as
though they were not mourning, and those who rejoice as
though they were not rejoicing, and those who buy as
though they had no possessions, and those who deal with
the world as though they had no dealings with it. For the
present form of this world is passing away.

A Reading (Lesson) from the Gospel according to Matthew [6:25–34]

Jesus opened his mouth and taught his disciples, saying: "Therefore I tell you, do not worry about your life, what you will eat or what you will drink, or about your body, what you will wear. Is not life more than food, and the body more than clothing? Look at the birds of the air; they neither sow nor reap nor gather into barns, and yet your heavenly Father feeds them. Are you not of more value than they? And can any of you by worrying add a single hour to your span of life? And why do you worry about clothing? Consider the lilies of the field, how they grow; they neither toil nor spin, yet I tell you, even Solomon in all his glory was not clothed like one of these. But if God so clothes the grass of the field, which is alive today and tomorrow is thrown into the oven, will he not much more clothe you—you of little faith? Therefore do not worry, saying, 'What will we eat?' or 'What will we drink?' or 'What will we wear?' For it is the Gentiles who strive for all these things; and indeed your heavenly Father knows that you need all these things. But strive first for the kingdom of God and his righteousness, and all these things will be given to you as well. So do not worry about tomorrow, for tomorrow will bring worries of its own. Today's trouble is enough for today."

Tuesday

Psalm 97 [page 726], *Psalm 99* [page 728],
(Psalm 100 [page 729]) ❖ *Psalm 94* [page 722],
(Psalm 95 [page 724])

A Reading (Lesson) from the Second Book of Chronicles [29:1–3;30:1(2–9)10–27]

Hezekiah began to reign when he was twenty-five years old; he reigned twenty-nine years in Jerusalem. His mother's name was Abijah daughter of Zechariah. He did what was right in the sight of the LORD, just as his ancestor David had done. In the first year of his reign, in the first month, he opened the doors of the house of the LORD and repaired them. Hezekiah sent word to all Israel and Judah, and wrote letters also to Ephraim and Manasseh, that they should come to the house of the LORD at Jerusalem, to keep the passover to the LORD the God of Israel.

For the king and his officials and all the assembly in Jerusalem had taken counsel to keep the passover in the second month (for they could not keep it at its proper time because the priests had not sanctified themselves in sufficient number, nor had the people assembled in Jerusalem). The plan seemed right to the king and all the assembly. So they decreed to make a proclamation throughout all Israel, from Beer-sheba to Dan, that the people should come and keep the passover to the LORD the God of Israel, at Jerusalem; for they had not kept it in great numbers as prescribed. So couriers went throughout all Israel and Judah with letters from the king and his officials, as the king had commanded, saying, "O people of Israel, return to the LORD, the God of Abraham, Isaac, and Israel, so that he may turn again to the remnant of you who have escaped from the hand of the kings of Assyria. Do not be like your ancestors and your kindred, who were faithless to the LORD God of their ancestors, so that he made them a desolation, as you see. Do not now be stiff-necked as your ancestors were, but yield yourselves to the LORD

and come to his sanctuary, which he has sanctified
forever, and serve the LORD your God, so that his fierce
anger may turn away from you. For as you return to
the LORD, your kindred and your children will find
compassion with their captors, and return to this land.
For the LORD your God is gracious and merciful, and
will not turn away his face from you, if you return to
him."

So the couriers went from city to city through the country
of Ephraim and Manasseh, and as far as Zebulun; but
they laughed them to scorn, and mocked them. Only a few
from Asher, Manasseh, and Zebulun humbled themselves
and came to Jerusalem. The hand of God was also on
Judah to give them one heart to do what the king and the
officials commanded by the word of the LORD. Many
people came together in Jerusalem to keep the festival of
unleavened bread in the second month, a very large
assembly. They set to work and removed the altars that
were in Jerusalem, and all the altars for offering incense
they took away and threw into the Wadi Kidron. They
slaughtered the passover lamb on the fourteenth day of the
second month. The priests and the Levites were ashamed,
and they sanctified themselves and brought burnt offerings
into the house of the LORD. They took their accustomed
posts according to the law of Moses the man of God; the
priests dashed the blood that they received from the hands
of the Levites. For there were many in the assembly who
had not sanctified themselves; therefore the Levites had to
slaughter the passover lamb for everyone who was not
clean, to make it holy to the LORD. For a multitude of the
people, many of them from Ephraim, Manasseh, Issachar,
and Zebulun, had not cleansed themselves, yet they ate the
passover otherwise than as prescribed. But Hezekiah
prayed for them, saying, "The good LORD pardon all who

set their hearts to seek God, the LORD the God of their ancestors, even though not in accordance with the sanctuary's rules of cleanness." The LORD heard Hezekiah, and healed the people. The people of Israel who were present at Jerusalem kept the festival of unleavened bread seven days with great gladness; and the Levites and the priests praised the LORD day by day, accompanied by loud instruments for the LORD. Hezekiah spoke encouragingly to all the Levites who showed good skill in the service of the LORD. So the people ate the food of the festival for seven days, sacrificing offerings of well-being and giving thanks to the LORD the God of their ancestors. Then the whole assembly agreed together to keep the festival for another seven days; so they kept it for another seven days with gladness. For King Hezekiah of Judah gave the assembly a thousand bulls and seven thousand sheep for offerings, and the officials gave the assembly a thousand bulls and ten thousand sheep. The priests sanctified themselves in great numbers. The whole assembly of Judah, the priests and the Levites, and the whole assembly that came out of Israel, and the resident aliens who came out of the land of Israel, and the resident aliens who lived in Judah, rejoiced. There was great joy in Jerusalem, for since the time of Solomon son of King David of Israel there had been nothing like this in Jerusalem. Then the priests and the Levites stood up and blessed the people, and their voice was heard; their prayer came to his holy dwelling in heaven.

A Reading (Lesson) from the First Letter of Paul to the Corinthians [7:32–40]

I want you to be free from anxieties. The unmarried man is anxious about the affairs of the Lord, how to please the Lord; but the married man is anxious about the affairs of the world, how to please his wife, and his interests are divided. And the unmarried woman and the virgin are anxious about the affairs of the Lord, so that they may be holy in body and spirit; but the married woman is anxious about the affairs of the world, how to please her husband. I say this for your own benefit, not to put any restraint upon you, but to promote good order and unhindered devotion to the Lord. If anyone thinks that he is not behaving properly toward his fiancée, if his passions are strong, and so it has to be, let him marry as he wishes; it is no sin. Let them marry. But if someone stands firm in his resolve, being under no necessity but having his own desire under control, and has determined in his own mind to keep her as his fiancée, he will do well. So then, he who marries his fiancée does well; and he who refrains from marriage will do better. A wife is bound as long as her husband lives. But if the husband dies, she is free to marry anyone she wishes, only in the Lord. But in my judgment she is more blessed if she remains as she is. And I think that I too have the Spirit of God.

A Reading (Lesson) from the Gospel according to Matthew [7:1–12]

Jesus opened his mouth and taught his disciples, saying: "Do not judge, so that you may not be judged. For with the judgment you make you will be judged, and the measure you give will be the measure you get. Why do you see the speck in your neighbor's eye, but do not notice the log in your own eye? Or how can you say to your neighbor, 'Let me take the speck out of your eye,' while the log is in your own eye? You hypocrite, first take the log out of your own eye, and then you will see clearly to take the speck out of your neighbor's eye. Do not give what is holy to dogs; and do not throw your pearls before swine, or they will trample them under foot and turn and maul you. Ask, and it will be given to you; search, and you will find; knock, and the door will be opened for you. For everyone who asks receives, and everyone who searches finds, and for everyone who knocks, the door will be opened. Is there anyone among you who, if your child asks for bread, will give a stone? Or if the child asks for a fish, will give a snake? If you then, who are evil, know how to give good gifts to your children, how much more will your Father in heaven give good things to those who ask him! In everything do to others as you would have them do to you; for this is the law and the prophets."

Wednesday

Psalm 101 [page 730],
Psalm 109:1–4(5–19)20–30 [page 750] ❖
Psalm 119:121–144 [page 773]

A Reading (Lesson) from the Second Book of the Kings [18:9–25]

In the fourth year of King Hezekiah, which was the seventh year of King Hoshea son of Elah of Israel, King Shalmaneser of Assyria came up against Samaria, besieged it, and at the end of three years, took it. In the sixth year of Hezekiah, which was the ninth year of King Hoshea of Israel, Samaria was taken. The king of Assyria carried the Israelites away to Assyria, settled them in Halah, on the Habor, the river of Gozan, and in the cities of the Medes, because they did not obey the voice of the LORD their God but transgressed his covenant—all that Moses the servant of the LORD had commanded; they neither listened nor obeyed. In the fourteenth year of King Hezekiah, King Sennacherib of

Assyria came up against all the fortified cities of Judah and captured them. King Hezekiah of Judah sent to the king of Assyria at Lachish, saying, "I have done wrong; withdraw from me; whatever you impose on me I will bear." The king of Assyria demanded of King Hezekiah of Judah three hundred talents of silver and thirty talents of gold. Hezekiah gave him all the silver that was found in the house of the LORD and in the treasuries of the king's house. At that time Hezekiah stripped the gold from the doors of the temple of the LORD, and from the doorposts that King Hezekiah of Judah had overlaid and gave it to the king of Assyria. The king of Assyria sent the Tartan, the Rabsaris, and the Rabshakeh with a great army from Lachish to King Hezekiah at Jerusalem. They went up and came to Jerusalem. When they arrived, they came and stood by the conduit of the upper pool, which is on the highway to the Fuller's Field. When they called for the king, there came out to them Eliakim son of Hilkiah, who was in charge of the palace, and Shebnah the secretary, and Joah son of Asaph, the recorder. The Rabshakeh said to them, "Say to Hezekiah: Thus says the great king, the king of Assyria: On what do you base this confidence of yours? Do you think that mere words are strategy and power for war? On whom do you now rely, that you have rebelled against me? See, you are relying now on Egypt, that broken reed of a staff, which will pierce the hand of anyone who leans on it. Such is Pharaoh king of Egypt to all who rely on him. But if you say to me, 'We rely on the LORD our God,' is it not he whose high places and altars Hezekiah has removed, saying to Judah and to Jerusalem, 'You shall worship before this altar in Jerusalem'? Come now, make a wager with my master the king of Assyria: I will give you two thousand horses, if you are able on your part to set riders on them. How then can you repulse a single captain among the least of my master's servants, when you rely on Egypt for chariots and for horsemen? Moreover, is it without the LORD that I have come up against this place to destroy it? The LORD said to me, Go up against this land, and destroy it."

A Reading (Lesson) from the First Letter of Paul to the Corinthians [8:1-13]

Now concerning food sacrificed to idols: we know that "all of us possess knowledge." Knowledge puffs up, but love builds up. Anyone who claims to know something does not yet have the necessary knowledge; but anyone who loves God is known by him. Hence, as to the eating of food offered to idols, we know that "no idol in the world really exists," and that "there is no God but one." Indeed, even though there may be so-called gods in heaven or on earth—as in fact there are many gods and many lords—yet for us there is one God, the Father, from whom are all things and for whom we exist, and one Lord, Jesus Christ, through whom are all things and through whom we exist. It is not everyone, however, who has this knowledge. Since some have become so accustomed to idols until now, they still think of the food they eat as food offered to an idol; and their conscience, being weak, is defiled. "Food will not bring us close to God." We are no worse off if we do not eat, and no better off if we do. But take care that this liberty of yours does not somehow become a stumbling block to the weak. For if others see you, who possess knowledge, eating in the temple of an idol, might they not, since their conscience is weak, be encouraged to the point of eating food sacrificed to idols? So by your knowledge those weak believers for whom Christ died are destroyed. But when you thus sin against members of your family, and wound their conscience when it is weak, you sin against Christ. Therefore, if food is a cause of their falling, I will never eat meat, so that I may not cause one of them to fall.

A Reading (Lesson) from the Gospel according to Matthew [7:13–21]

Jesus opened his mouth and taught his disciples, saying: "Enter through the narrow gate; for the gate is wide and the road is easy that leads to destruction, and there are many who take it. For the gate is narrow and the road is hard that leads to life, and there are few who find it. Beware of false prophets, who come to you in sheep's clothing but inwardly are ravenous wolves. You will know them by their fruits. Are grapes gathered from thorns, or figs from thistles? In the same way, every good tree bears good fruit, but the bad tree bears bad fruit. A good tree cannot bear bad fruit, nor can a bad tree bear good fruit. Every tree that does not bear good fruit is cut down and thrown into the fire. Thus you will know them by their fruits. Not everyone who says to me, 'Lord, Lord,' will enter the kingdom of heaven, but only the one who does the will of my Father in heaven."

Thursday

Psalm 105:1–22 [page 738]   ❖   *Psalm 105:23–45* [page 739]

A Reading (Lesson) from the Second Book of the Kings [18:28–37]

The Rabshakeh stood and called out in a loud voice in the language of Judah, "Hear the word of the great king, the king of Assyria! Thus says the king: 'Do not let Hezekiah deceive you, for he will not be able to deliver you out of my hand. Do not let Hezekiah make you rely on the Lord by saying, The Lord will surely deliver us, and this city will not be given into the hand of the king of Assyria.' Do not listen to Hezekiah; for thus says the king of Assyria: 'Make your peace with me and come out to me; then every one of you will eat from your own vine and your own fig tree, and drink water from your own cistern, until I come and take you away to a land like your own land, a land of grain and wine, a land of bread and vineyards, a land of olive oil and honey, that you may live and not die. Do not listen to Hezekiah when he misleads you by saying, The Lord will deliver us. Has any of the gods of the nations ever delivered its land out of the hand of the king of Assyria? Where are the gods of Hamath and Arpad? Where are the gods of Sepharvaim, Hena, and Ivvah? Have they delivered Samaria out of my hand? Who among all the gods of the countries have delivered their countries out of my hand, that the Lord should deliver Jerusalem out of my hand?' " But the people were silent and answered him not a word, for the king's command was, "Do not answer him." Then Eliakim son of Hilkiah, who was in charge of the palace, and Shebna the secretary, and Joah son of Asaph, the recorder, came to Hezekiah with their clothes torn and told him the words of the Rabshakeh.

A Reading (Lesson) from the First Letter of Paul to the Corinthians [9:1–15]

Am I not free? Am I not an apostle? Have I not seen Jesus our Lord? Are you not my work in the Lord? If I am not an apostle to others, at least I am to you; for you are the seal of my apostleship in the Lord. This is my defense to those who would examine me. Do we not have the right to our food and drink? Do we not have the right to be accompanied by a believing wife, as do the other apostles and the brothers of the Lord and Cephas? Or is it only Barnabas and I who have no right to refrain from working for a living? Who at any time pays the expenses for doing military service? Who plants a vineyard and does not eat any of its fruit? Or who tends a flock and does not get any of its milk? Do I say this on human authority? Does not the law also say the same? For it is written in the law of Moses, "You shall not muzzle an ox while it is treading out the grain." Is it for oxen that God is concerned? Or does he not speak entirely for our sake? It was indeed written for our sake, for whoever plows should plow in hope and whoever threshes should thresh in hope of a share in the crop. If we have sown spiritual good among you, is it too much if we reap your material benefits? If others share this rightful claim on you, do not we still more? Nevertheless, we have not made use of this right, but we endure anything rather than put an obstacle in the way of the gospel of Christ. Do you not know that those who are employed in the temple service get their food from the temple, and those who serve at the altar share in what is sacrificed on the altar? In the same way, the Lord commanded that those who proclaim the gospel should get their living by the gospel. But I have made no use of any of these rights, nor am I writing this so that they may be applied in my case. Indeed, I would rather die than that— no one will deprive me of my ground for boasting!

A Reading (Lesson) from the Gospel according to Matthew [7:22–29]

Jesus opened his mouth and taught his disciples, saying: "On that day many will say to me, 'Lord, Lord, did we not prophesy in your name, and cast out demons in your name, and do many deeds of power in your name?' Then I will declare to them, 'I never knew you; go away from me, you evildoers.' Everyone then who hears these words of mine and acts on them will be like a wise man who built his house on rock. The rain fell, the floods came, and the winds blew and beat on that house, but it did not fall, because it had been founded on rock. And everyone who hears these words of mine and does not act on them will be like a foolish man who built his house on sand. The rain fell, and the floods came, and the winds blew and beat against that house, and it fell—and great was its fall!" Now when Jesus had finished saying these things, the crowds were astounded at his teaching, for he taught them as one having authority, and not as their scribes.

Friday

Psalm 102 [page 731] ❖ *Psalm 107:1–32* [page 746]

A Reading (Lesson) from the Second Book of the Kings [19:1–20]

When King Hezekiah heard the words of the Rabshakeh, he tore his clothes, covered himself with sackcloth, and went into the house of the LORD. And he sent Eliakim, who was in charge of the palace, and Shebna the secretary, and the senior priests, covered with sackcloth, to the prophet Isaiah son of Amoz. They said to him, "Thus says Hezekiah, This day is a day of distress, of rebuke, and of disgrace; children have come to the birth, and there is no strength to bring them forth. It may be that the LORD your God heard all the words of the Rabshakeh, whom his master the king of Assyria has sent to mock the living God, and will rebuke the words that the LORD your God has heard; therefore lift up your prayer for the remnant that is left." When the servants of King Hezekiah came to Isaiah, Isaiah said to them, "Say to your master, 'Thus says the LORD: Do not be afraid because of the words that you have heard, with which the servants of the king of Assyria have reviled me. I myself will put a spirit in him, so that he shall hear a rumor and return to his own land; I will cause him to fall by the sword in his own land.' " The Rabshakeh returned, and found the king of Assyria fighting against Libnah; for he had heard that the king had left Lachish. When the king heard concerning King Tirhakah of Ethiopia, "See, he has set out to fight against you," he sent messengers again to Hezekiah, saying, "Thus shall you speak to King Hezekiah of Judah: Do not let your God on whom you rely deceive you by promising that Jerusalem will not be given into the hand of the king of Assyria. See, you have heard what the kings of Assyria have done to all lands, destroying them utterly. Shall you be delivered? Have the gods of the nations delivered them, the nations that my predecessors destroyed, Gozan, Haran, Rezeph, and the people of Eden who were in Telassar? Where is the king of Hamath, the king of Arpad, the king of the city of Sepharvaim, the king of Hena, or the king of Ivvah?" Hezekiah received the letter from the hand of the messengers and read it; then Hezekiah went up to the house of the LORD and spread it before the LORD. And Hezekiah prayed before the LORD, and said: "O LORD the God of Israel, who are enthroned above the cherubim, you are God, you alone, of all the kingdoms of the earth; you have made heaven and earth. Incline your ear, O LORD, and hear; open your eyes, O LORD, and see; hear the words of Sennacherib, which he has sent to mock the living God. Truly, O LORD, the kings of Assyria have laid waste the nations and their lands, and have hurled their gods into the fire, though they were no gods but the work of human hands—wood and stone—and so they were destroyed. So now, O LORD our God, save us, I pray you, from his hand, so that all the kingdoms of the earth may know that you, O LORD, are God alone." Then Isaiah son of Amoz sent to Hezekiah, saying, "Thus says the LORD, the God of Israel: I have heard your prayer to me about King Sennacherib of Assyria."

A Reading (Lesson) from the First Letter of Paul to the Corinthians [9:16–27]

If I proclaim the gospel, this gives me no ground for boasting, for an obligation is laid on me, and woe to me if I do not proclaim the gospel! For if I do this of my own will, I have a reward; but if not of my own will, I am entrusted with a commission. What then is my reward? Just this: that in my proclamation I may make the gospel free of charge, so as not to make full use of my rights in the gospel. For though I am free with respect to all, I have made myself a slave to all, so that I might win more of them. To the Jews I became as a Jew, in order to win Jews. To those under the law I became as one under the law (though I myself am not under the law) so that I might win those under the law. To those outside the law I became as one outside the law (though I am not free from God's law but am under Christ's law) so that I might win those outside the law. To the weak I became weak, so that I might win the weak. I have become all things to all people, that I might by all means save some. I do it all for the sake of the gospel, so that I may share in its blessings. Do you not know that in a race the runners all compete, but only one receives the prize? Run in such a way that you may win it. Athletes exercise self-control in all things; they do it to receive a perishable wreath, but we an imperishable one. So I do not run aimlessly, nor do I box as though beating the air; but I punish my body and enslave it, so that after proclaiming to others I myself should not be disqualified.

A Reading (Lesson) from the Gospel according to Matthew [8:1–17]

When Jesus had come down from the mountain, great crowds followed him; and there was a leper who came to him and knelt before him, saying, "Lord, if you choose, you can make me clean." He stretched out his hand and touched him, saying, "I do choose. Be made clean!" Immediately his leprosy was cleansed. Then Jesus said to him, "See that you say nothing to anyone; but go, show yourself to the priest, and offer the gift that Moses commanded, as a testimony to them." When he entered Capernaum, a centurion came to him, appealing to him and saying, "Lord, my servant is lying at home paralyzed, in terrible distress." And he said to him, "I will come and cure him." The centurion answered, "Lord, I am not worthy to have you come under my roof; but only speak the word, and my servant will be healed. For I also am a man under authority, with soldiers under me; and I say to one, 'Go,' and he goes, and to another, 'Come,' and he comes, and to my slave, 'Do this,' and the slave does it." When Jesus heard him, he was amazed and said to those who followed him, "Truly I tell you, in no one in Israel have I found such faith. I tell you, many will come from east and west and will eat with Abraham and Isaac and Jacob in the kingdom of heaven, while the heirs of the kingdom will be thrown into the outer darkness, where there will be weeping and gnashing of teeth." And to the centurion Jesus said, "Go; let it be done for you according to your faith." And the servant was healed in that hour. When Jesus entered Peter's house, he saw his mother-in-law lying in bed with a fever; he touched her hand, and the fever left her, and she got up and began to serve him. That evening they brought to him many who were possessed with demons; and he cast out the spirits with a word, and cured all who were sick. This was to fulfill what had been spoken through the prophet Isaiah, "He took our infirmities and bore our diseases."

Saturday

Psalm 107:33–43 [page 748],
Psalm 108:1–6(7–13) [page 749] ❖ *Psalm 33* [page 626]

A Reading (Lesson) from the Second Book of the Kings [19:21–36]

Isaiah the son of Amoz sent to Hezekiah, saying, "This is the word that the LORD has spoken concerning him: She despises you, she scorns you—virgin daughter Zion; she tosses her head—behind your back, daughter Jerusalem. Whom have you mocked and reviled? Against whom have you raised your voice and haughtily lifted your eyes? Against the Holy One of Israel! By your messengers you have mocked the Lord, and you have said, 'With my many chariots I have gone up the heights of the mountains, to the far recesses of Lebanon; I felled its tallest cedars, its choicest cypresses; I entered its farthest retreat, its densest forest. I dug wells and drank foreign waters, I dried up with the sole of my foot all the streams of Egypt.' Have you not heard that I determined it long ago? I planned from days of old what now I bring to pass, that you should make fortified cities crash into heaps of ruins, while their inhabitants, shorn of strength, are dismayed and confounded; they have become like plants of the field and like tender grass, like grass on the housetops, blighted before it is grown. But I know your rising and your sitting, your going out and coming in, and your raging against me. Because you have raged against me and your arrogance has come to my ears, I will put my hook in your nose and my bit in your mouth; I will turn you back on the way by which you came. And this shall be the sign for you: This year you shall eat what grows of itself, and in the second year what springs from that; then in the third year sow, reap, plant vineyards, and eat their fruit. The surviving remnant of the house of Judah shall again take root downward, and bear fruit upward; for from Jerusalem a remnant shall go out, and from Mount Zion a band of survivors. The zeal of the LORD of hosts will do this. Therefore thus says the LORD concerning the king of Assyria: He shall not come into this city, shoot an arrow there, come before it with a shield, or cast up a siege-ramp against it. By the way that he came, by the same he shall return; he shall not come into this city, says the LORD. For I will defend this city to save it, for my own sake and for the sake of my servant David." That very night the angel of the LORD set out and struck down one hundred eighty-five thousand in the camp of the Assyrians; when morning dawned, they were all dead bodies. Then King Sennacherib of Assyria left, went home, and lived at Nineveh.

A Reading (Lesson) from the First Letter of Paul to the Corinthians [10:1–13]

I do not want you to be unaware, brothers and sisters, that our ancestors were all under the cloud, and all passed through the sea, and all were baptized into Moses in the cloud and in the sea, and all ate the same spiritual food, and all drank the same spiritual drink. For they drank from the spiritual rock that followed them, and the rock was Christ. Nevertheless, God was not pleased with most of them, and they were struck down in the wilderness. Now these things occurred as examples for us, so that we might not desire evil as they did. Do not become idolaters as some of them did; as it is written, "The people sat down to eat and drink, and they rose up to play." We must not indulge in sexual immorality as some of them did, and twenty-three thousand fell in a single day. We must not put Christ to the test, as some of them did, and were destroyed by serpents. And do not complain as some of them did, and were destroyed by the destroyer. These things happened to them to serve as an example, and they were written down to instruct us, on whom the ends of the ages have come. So if you think you are standing, watch out that you do not fall. No testing has overtaken you that is not common to everyone. God is faithful, and he will not let you be tested beyond your strength, but with the testing he will also provide the way out so that you may be able to endure it.

A Reading (Lesson) from the Gospel according to Matthew [8:18–27]

Now when Jesus saw great crowds around him, he gave orders to go over to the other side. A scribe then approached and said, "Teacher, I will follow you wherever you go." And Jesus said to him, "Foxes have holes, and birds of the air have nests; but the Son of Man has nowhere to lay his head." Another of his disciples said to him, "Lord, first let me go and bury my father." But Jesus said to him, "Follow me, and let the dead bury their own dead." And when he got into the boat, his disciples followed him. A windstorm arose on the sea, so great that the boat was being swamped by the waves; but he was asleep. And they went and woke him up, saying, "Lord, save us! We are perishing!" And he said to them, "Why are you afraid, you of little faith?" Then he got up and rebuked the winds and the sea; and there was a dead calm. They were amazed, saying, "What sort of man is this, that even the winds and the sea obey him?"

Proper 22   *Week of the Sunday closest to October 5*

Sunday

Psalm 118 [page 760]   ❖   *Psalm 145* [page 801]

A Reading (Lesson) from the Second Book of the Kings [20:1–21]

In those days Hezekiah became sick and was at the point of death. The prophet Isaiah son of Amoz came to him, and said to him, "Thus says the LORD: Set your house in order, for you shall die; you shall not recover." Then Hezekiah turned his face to the wall and prayed to the LORD: "Remember now, O LORD, I implore you, how I have walked before you in faithfulness with a whole heart, and have done what is good in your sight." Hezekiah wept bitterly. Before Isaiah had gone out of the middle court, the word of the LORD came to him: "Turn back, and say to Hezekiah prince of my people, Thus says the LORD, the God of your ancestor David: I have heard your prayer, I have seen your tears; indeed, I will heal you; on the third day you shall go up to the house of the LORD. I will add fifteen years to your life. I will deliver you and this city out of the hand

of the king of Assyria; I will defend this city for my own
sake and for my servant David's sake." Then Isaiah said,
"Bring a lump of figs. Let them take it and apply it to the
boil, so that he may recover." Hezekiah said to Isaiah,
"What shall be the sign that the LORD will heal me, and that I
shall go up to the house of the LORD on the third day?"
Isaiah said, "This is the sign to you from the LORD, that the
LORD will do the thing that he has promised: the shadow
has now advanced ten intervals; shall it retreat ten
intervals?" Hezekiah answered, "It is normal for the
shadow to lengthen ten intervals; rather let the shadow
retreat ten intervals." The prophet Isaiah cried to the LORD;
and he brought the shadow back the ten intervals, by which
the sun had declined on the dial of Ahaz. At that time King
Merodach-baladan son of Baladan of Babylon sent envoys
with letters and a present to Hezekiah, for he had heard that
Hezekiah had been sick. Hezekiah welcomed them; he
showed them all his treasure house, the silver, the gold, the
spices, the precious oil, his armory, all that was found in his
storehouses; there was nothing in his house or in all his
realm that Hezekiah did not show them. Then the prophet
Isaiah came to King Hezekiah, and said to him, "What did
these men say? From where did they come to you?"
Hezekiah answered, "They have come from a far country,
from Babylon." He said, "What have they seen in your
house?" Hezekiah answered, "They have seen all that is in
my house; there is nothing in my storehouses that I did not
show them." Then Isaiah said to Hezekiah, "Hear the word
of the LORD: Days are coming when all that is in your
house, and that which your ancestors have stored up until
this day, shall be carried to Babylon; nothing shall be left,
says the LORD. Some of your own sons who are born to you
shall be taken away; they shall be eunuchs in the palace of
the king of Babylon." Then Hezekiah said to Isaiah, "The

word of the LORD that you have spoken is good." For he thought, "Why not, if there will be peace and security in my days?" The rest of the deeds of Hezekiah, all his power, how he made the pool and the conduit and brought water into the city, are they not written in the Book of the Annals of the Kings of Judah? Hezekiah slept with his ancestors; and his son Manasseh succeeded him.

Acts 12:1–17 [page 767 above]

A Reading (Lesson) from the Gospel according to Luke [7:11–17]

Jesus went to a town called Nain, and his disciples and a large crowd went with him. As he approached the gate of the town, a man who had died was being carried out. He was his mother's only son, and she was a widow; and with her was a large crowd from the town. When the Lord saw her, he had compassion for her and said to her, "Do not weep." Then he came forward and touched the bier, and the bearers stood still. And he said, "Young man, I say to you, rise!" The dead man sat up and began to speak, and Jesus gave him to his mother. Fear seized all of them; and they glorified God, saying, "A great prophet has risen among us!" and "God has looked favorably on his people!" This word about him spread throughout Judea and all the surrounding country.

Monday

Psalm 106:1–18 [page 741] ❖ *Psalm 106:19–48* [page 743]

A Reading (Lesson) from the Second Book of the Kings [21:1–18]

Manasseh was twelve years old when he began to reign; he reigned fifty-five years in Jerusalem. His mother's name was Hephzibah. He did what was evil in the sight of the LORD, following the abominable practices of the nations that the LORD drove out before the people of Israel. For he rebuilt the high places that his father Hezekiah had destroyed; he erected altars for Baal, made a sacred pole, as King Ahab of Israel had done, worshiped all the host of heaven, and served them. He built altars in the house of the LORD, of which the LORD had said, "In Jerusalem I will put my name." He built altars for all the host of heaven in the two courts of the house of the LORD. He made his son pass through fire; he practiced soothsaying and augury, and dealt with mediums and with wizards. He did much evil in the sight of the LORD, provoking him to anger. The carved image of Asherah that he had made he set in the house of which the LORD said to David and to his son Solomon, "In this house, and in Jerusalem, which I have chosen out of all the tribes of Israel, I will put my name forever; I will not cause the feet of Israel to wander any more out of the land that I gave to their ancestors, if only they will be careful to do according to all that I have commanded them, and according to all the law that my servant Moses commanded them." But they did not listen; Manasseh misled them to do more evil than the nations had done that the LORD destroyed before the people of Israel. The LORD said by his servants the prophets, "Because King Manasseh of Judah has committed these abominations, has done things more wicked than all that the Amorites did, who were before him, and has caused Judah also to sin with his idols; therefore thus says the Lord, the God of Israel, I am bringing upon Jerusalem and Judah such evil that the ears of everyone who hears of it will tingle. I will stretch over Jerusalem the measuring line for Samaria, and the plummet for the house of Ahab; I will wipe Jerusalem as one wipes a dish, wiping it and turning it upside down. I will cast off the remnant of my heritage, and give them into the hand of their enemies; they shall become a prey and a spoil to all their enemies, because they have done what is evil in my sight and have provoked me to anger, since the day their ancestors came out of Egypt, even to this day." Moreover Manasseh shed very much innocent blood, until he had filled Jerusalem from one end to another, besides the sin that he caused Judah to sin so that they did what was evil in the sight of the Lord. Now the rest of the acts of Manasseh, all that he did, and the sin that he committed, are they not written in the Book of the Annals of the Kings of Judah? Manasseh slept with his ancestors, and was buried in the garden of his house, in the garden of Uzza. His son Amon succeeded him.

A Reading (Lesson) from the First Letter of Paul to the Corinthians [10:14—11:1]

My dear friends, flee from the worship of idols. I speak as to sensible people; judge for yourselves what I say. The cup of blessing that we bless, is it not a sharing in the blood of Christ? The bread that we break, is it not a sharing in the body of Christ? Because there is one bread, we who are many are one body, for we all partake of the one bread. Consider the people of Israel; are not those who eat the sacrifices partners in the altar? What do I imply then? That food sacrificed to idols is anything, or that an idol is anything? No, I imply that what pagans sacrifice, they sacrifice to demons and not to God. I do not want you to be partners with demons. You cannot drink the cup of the Lord and the cup of demons. You cannot partake of the table of the Lord and the table of demons. Or are we provoking the Lord to jealousy? Are we stronger than he? "All things are lawful," but not all things are beneficial. "All things are lawful," but not all things build up. Do not seek your own advantage, but that of the other. Eat whatever is sold in the meat market without raising any question on the ground of conscience, for "the earth and its fullness are the Lord's." If an unbeliever invites you to a meal and you are disposed to go, eat whatever is set before you without raising any question on the ground of conscience. But if someone says to you, "This has been offered in sacrifice," then do not eat it, out of consideration for the one who informed you, and for the sake of conscience—I mean the other's conscience, not your own. For why should my liberty be subject to the judgment of someone else's conscience? If I partake with thankfulness, why should I be denounced because of that for which I give thanks? So, whether you eat or drink, or whatever you do, do everything for the glory of God. Give no offense to Jews or to Greeks or to the church of God, just as I try to please everyone in everything I do, not seeking my own advantage, but that of many, so that they may be saved. Be imitators of me, as I am of Christ.

A Reading (Lesson) from the Gospel according to Matthew [8:28–34]

When Jesus came to the other side, to the country of the Gadarenes, two demoniacs coming out of the tombs met him. They were so fierce that no one could pass that way. Suddenly they shouted, "What have you to do with us, Son of God? Have you come here to torment us before the time?" Now a large herd of swine was feeding at some distance from them. The demons begged him, "If you cast us out, send us into the herd of swine." And he said to them, "Go!" So they came out and entered the swine; and suddenly, the whole herd rushed down the steep bank into the sea and perished in the water. The swineherds ran off, and on going into the town, they told the whole story about what had happened to the demoniacs. Then the whole town came out to meet Jesus; and when they saw him, they begged him to leave their neighborhood.

Tuesday

(Psalm 120 [page 778]),   *Psalm 121* [page 779],
Psalm 122 [page 779],   *Psalm 123* [page 780]   ❖
Psalm 124 [page 781],   *Psalm 125* [page 781],
Psalm 126 [page 782],   *(Psalm 127* [page 782])

A Reading (Lesson) from the Second Book of the Kings [22:1–13]

Josiah was eight years old when he began to reign; he reigned thirty-one years in Jerusalem. His mother's name was Jedidah daughter of Adaiah of Bozkath. He did what was right in the sight of the LORD, and walked in all the way of his father David; he did not turn aside to the right or to the left. In the eighteenth year of King Josiah, the king sent Shaphan son of Azaliah, son of Meshullam, the secretary, to the house of the LORD, saying, "Go up to the high priest Hilkiah, and have him count the entire sum of the money that has been brought into the house of the LORD, which the keepers of the threshold have collected from the people; let it be given into the hand of the workers who have the oversight of the house of the LORD; let them give it to the workers who are at the house of the LORD, repairing the house, that is, to the carpenters, to the builders, to the masons; and let them use it to buy timber and quarried stone to repair the house. But no accounting shall be asked from them for the money that is delivered into their hand, for they deal honestly." The high priest Hilkiah said to Shaphan the secretary, "I have found the book of the law in the house of the LORD." When Hilkiah gave the book to Shaphan, he read it. Then Shaphan the secretary came to the king, and reported to the king, "Your servants have emptied out the money that was found in the house, and have delivered it into the hand of the workers who have oversight of the house of the LORD." Shaphan the secretary informed the king, "The priest Hilkiah has given me a book." Shaphan then read it aloud to the king. When the king heard the words of the book of the law, he tore his clothes. Then the king commanded the priest Hilkiah, Ahikam son of Shaphan, Achbor son of Micaiah, Shaphan the secretary, and the king's servant Asaiah, saying, "Go, inquire of the LORD for me, for the people, and for all Judah concerning the words of this book that has been found; for great is the wrath of the LORD that is kindled against us, because our ancestors did not obey the words of this book, to do according to all that is written concerning us."

A Reading (Lesson) from the First Letter of Paul to the Corinthians [11:2,17–22]

I commend you because you remember me in everything and maintain the traditions just as I handed them on to you. Now in the following instructions I do not commend you, because when you come together it is not for the better but for the worse. For, to begin with, when you come together as a church, I hear that there are divisions among you; and to some extent I believe it. Indeed, there have to be factions among you, for only so will it become clear who among you are genuine. When you come together, it is not really to eat the Lord's supper. For when the time comes to eat, each of you goes ahead with your own supper, and one goes hungry and another becomes drunk. What! Do you not have homes to eat and drink in? Or do you show contempt for the church of God and humiliate those who have nothing? What should I say to you? Should I commend you? In this matter I do not commend you!

A Reading (Lesson) from the Gospel according to Matthew [9:1–8]

After getting into a boat Jesus crossed the sea and came to his own town. And just then some people were carrying a paralyzed man lying on a bed. When Jesus saw their faith, he said to the paralytic, "Take heart, son; your sins are forgiven." Then some of the scribes said to themselves, "This man is blaspheming." But Jesus, perceiving their thoughts, said, "Why do you think evil in your hearts? For which is easier, to say, 'Your sins are forgiven,' or to say, 'Stand up and walk'? But so that you may know that the Son of Man has authority on earth to forgive sins"—he then said to the paralytic—"Stand up, take your bed and go to your home." And he stood up and went to his home. When the crowds saw it, they were filled with awe, and they glorified God, who had given such authority to human beings.

Wednesday

Psalm 119:145–176 [page 775] ❖ *Psalm 128* [page 783], *Psalm 129* [page 784], *Psalm 130* [page 784]

A Reading (Lesson) from the Second Book of the Kings [22:14—23:3]

The priest Hilkiah, Ahikam, Achbor, Shaphan, and Asaiah went to the prophetess Huldah the wife of Shallum son of Tikvah, son of Harhas, keeper of the wardrobe; she resided in Jerusalem in the Second Quarter, where they consulted her. She declared to them, "Thus says the LORD, the God of Israel: Tell the man who sent you to me, Thus says the LORD, I will indeed bring disaster on this place and on its inhabitants—all the words of the book that the king of Judah has read. Because they have abandoned me and have made offerings to other gods, so that they have provoked me to anger with all the work of their hands, therefore my wrath will be kindled against this place, and it will not be quenched. But as to the king of Judah, who sent you to inquire of the LORD, thus shall you say to him, Thus says the LORD, the God of Israel: Regarding the words that you have heard, because your heart was penitent, and you humbled yourself before the LORD, when you heard how I spoke against this place, and against its inhabitants, that they should become a desolation and a curse, and because you have torn your clothes and wept before me, I also have heard you, says the LORD. Therefore, I will gather you to your ancestors, and you shall be gathered to your grave in peace; your eyes shall not see all the disaster that I will bring on this place." They took the message back to the king. Then the king directed that all the elders of Judah and Jerusalem should be gathered to him. The king went up to the house of the LORD, and with him went all the people of

Judah, all the inhabitants of Jerusalem, the priests, the prophets, and all the people, both small and great; he read in their hearing all the words of the book of the covenant that had been found in the house of the LORD. The king stood by the pillar and made a covenant before the LORD, to follow the LORD, keeping his commandments, his decrees, and his statutes, with all his heart and all his soul, to perform the words of this covenant that were written in this book. All the people joined in the covenant.

A Reading (Lesson) from the First Letter of Paul to the Corinthians [11:23–34]

I received from the Lord what I also handed on to you, that the Lord Jesus on the night when he was betrayed took a loaf of bread, and when he had given thanks, he broke it and said, "This is my body that is for you. Do this in remembrance of me." In the same way he took the cup also, after supper, saying, "This cup is the new covenant in my blood. Do this, as often as you drink it, in remembrance of me." For as often as you eat this bread and drink the cup, you proclaim the Lord's death until he comes. Whoever, therefore, eats the bread or drinks the cup of the Lord in an unworthy manner will be answerable for the body and blood of the Lord. Examine yourselves, and only then eat of the bread and drink of the cup. For all who eat and drink without discerning the body, eat and drink judgment against themselves. For this reason many of you are weak and ill, and some have died. But if we judged ourselves, we would not be judged. But when we are judged by the Lord, we are disciplined so that we may not be condemned along with the world. So then, my brothers and sisters, when you come together to eat, wait for one another. If you are hungry, eat at home, so that when you come together, it will not be for your condemnation. About the other things I will give instructions when I come.

A Reading (Lesson) from the Gospel according to Matthew [9:9–17]

As Jesus was walking along, he saw a man called Matthew sitting at the tax booth; and he said to him, "Follow me." And he got up and followed him. And as he sat at dinner in the house, many tax collectors and sinners came and were sitting with him and his disciples. When the Pharisees saw this, they said to his disciples, "Why does your teacher eat with tax collectors and sinners?" But when he heard this, he said, "Those who are well have no need of a physician, but those who are sick. Go and learn what this means, 'I desire mercy, not sacrifice.' For I have come to call not the righteous but sinners." Then the disciples of John came to him, saying, "Why do we and the Pharisees fast often, but your disciples do not fast?" And Jesus said to them, "The wedding guests cannot mourn as long as the bridegroom is with them, can they? The days will come when the bridegroom is taken away from them, and then they will fast. No one sews a piece of unshrunk cloth on an old cloak, for the patch pulls away from the cloak, and a worse tear is made. Neither is new wine put into old wineskins; otherwise, the skins burst, and the wine is spilled, and the skins are destroyed; but new wine is put into fresh wineskins, and so both are preserved."

Thursday

Psalm 131 [page 785], *Psalm 132* [page 785],
(Psalm 133 [page 787]) ❖ *Psalm 134* [page 787],
Psalm 135 [page 788]

*A Reading (Lesson) from the Second Book of the
Kings* [23:4–25]

The king commanded the high priest Hilkiah, the priests of
the second order, and the guardians of the threshold, to
bring out of the temple of the LORD all the vessels made for
Baal, for Asherah, and for all the host of heaven; he burned
them outside Jerusalem in the fields of the Kidron, and
carried their ashes to Bethel. He deposed the idolatrous
priests whom the kings of Judah had ordained to make
offerings in the high places at the cities of Judah and around
Jerusalem; those also who made offerings to Baal, to the
sun, the moon, the constellations, and all the host of the
heavens. He brought out the image of Asherah from the
house of the LORD, outside Jerusalem, to the Wadi Kidron,
burned it at the Wadi Kidron, beat it to dust and threw the
dust of it upon the graves of the common people. He broke
down the houses of the male temple prostitutes that were in
the house of the LORD, where the women did weaving for
Asherah. He brought all the priests out of the towns of
Judah, and defiled the high places where the priests had
made offerings, from Geba to Beer-sheba; he broke down
the high places of the gates that were at the entrance of the
gate of Joshua the governor of the city, which were on the
left at the gate of the city. The priests of the high places,
however, did not come up to the altar of the LORD in
Jerusalem, but ate unleavened bread among their kindred.
He defiled Topheth, which is in the valley of Benhinnom, so
that no one would make a son or a daughter pass through

fire as an offering to Molech. He removed the horses that the kings of Judah had dedicated to the sun, at the entrance to the house of the LORD, by the chamber of the eunuch Nathan-melech, which was in the precincts; then he burned the chariots of the sun with fire. The altars on the roof of the upper chamber of Ahaz, which the kings of Judah had made, and the altars that Manasseh had made in the two courts of the house of the LORD, he pulled down from there and broke in pieces, and threw the rubble into the Wadi Kidron. The king defiled the high places that were east of Jerusalem, to the south of the Mount of Destruction, which King Solomon of Israel had built for Astarte the abomination of the Sidonians, for Chemosh the abomination of Moab, and for Milcom the abomination of the Ammonites. He broke the pillars in pieces, cut down the sacred poles, and covered the sites with human bones. Moreover, the altar at Bethel, the high place erected by Jeroboam son of Nebat, who caused Israel to sin—he pulled down that altar along with the high place. He burned the high place, crushing it to dust; he also burned the sacred pole. As Josiah turned, he saw the tombs there on the mount; and he sent and took the bones out of the tombs, and burned them on the altar, and defiled it, according to the word of the LORD that the man of God proclaimed, when Jeroboam stood by the altar at the festival; he turned and looked up at the tomb of the man of God who had predicted these things. Then he said, "What is that monument that I see?" The people of the city told him, "It is the tomb of the man of God who came from Judah and predicted these things that you have done against the altar at Bethel." He said, "Let him rest; let no one move his bones." So they let his bones alone, with the bones of the prophet who came out of Samaria. Moreover, Josiah removed all the shrines of the high places that were in the towns of Samaria, which kings of Israel had made, provoking the LORD to anger; he did to them just as he had done at Bethel. He slaughtered on the altars all the priests of the high places who were there, and burned human bones on them. Then he returned to Jerusalem. The king commanded all the people, "Keep the passover to the LORD your God as prescribed in this book of the covenant." No such passover had been kept since the days of the judges who judged Israel, or during all the days of the kings of Israel or of the kings of Judah; but in the eighteenth year of King Josiah this passover was kept to the LORD in Jerusalem. Moreover Josiah put away the mediums, wizards, teraphim, idols, and all the abominations that were seen in the land of Judah and in Jerusalem, so that he established the words of the law that were written in the book that the priest Hilkiah had found in the house of the LORD. Before him there was no king like him, who turned to the LORD with all his heart, with all his soul, and with all his might, according to all the law of Moses; nor did any like him arise after him.

A Reading (Lesson) from the First Letter of Paul to the Corinthians [12:1–11]

Concerning spiritual gifts, brothers and sisters, I do not want you to be uninformed. You know that when you were pagans, you were enticed and led astray to idols that could not speak. Therefore I want you to understand that no one speaking by the Spirit of God ever says "Let Jesus be cursed!" and no one can say "Jesus is Lord" except by the Holy Spirit. Now there are varieties of gifts, but the same Spirit; and there are varieties of services, but the same Lord; and there are varieties of activities, but it is the same God who activates all of them in everyone. To each is given the manifestation of the Spirit for the common good. To one is given through the Spirit the utterance of wisdom, and to another the utterance of knowledge according to the same Spirit, to another faith by the same Spirit, to another gifts of healing by the one Spirit, to another the working of miracles, to another prophecy, to another the discernment of spirits, to another various kinds of tongues, to another the interpretation of tongues. All these are activated by one and the same Spirit, who allots to each one individually just as the Spirit chooses.

A Reading (Lesson) from the Gospel according to Matthew [9:18–26]

While Jesus was saying these things to them, suddenly a leader of the synagogue came in and knelt before him, saying, "My daughter has just died; but come and lay your hand on her, and she will live." And Jesus got up and followed him, with his disciples. Then suddenly a woman who had been suffering from hemorrhages for twelve years came up behind him and touched the fringe of his cloak, for she said to herself, "If I only touch his cloak, I will be made well." Jesus turned, and seeing her he said, "Take heart, daughter; your faith has made you well." And instantly the woman was made well. When Jesus came to the leader's house and saw the flute players and the crowd making a commotion, he said, "Go away; for the girl is not dead but sleeping." And they laughed at him. But when the crowd had been put outside, he went in and took her by the hand, and the girl got up. And the report of this spread throughout that district.

Friday

Psalm 140 [page 796],   *Psalm 142* [page 798]   ❖
Psalm 141 [page 797],   *Psalm 143:1–11(12)* [page 798]

A Reading (Lesson) from the Second Book of the Kings [23:36—24:17]

Jehoiakim was twenty-five years old when he began to reign; he reigned eleven years in Jerusalem. His mother's name was Zebidah daughter of Pedaiah of Rumah. He did what was evil in the sight of the LORD, just as all his ancestors had done. In his days King Nebuchadnezzar of Babylon came up; Jehoiakim became his servant for three years; then he turned and rebelled against him. The LORD sent against him bands of the Chaldeans, bands of the Arameans, bands of the Moabites, and bands of the Ammonites; he sent them against Judah to destroy it, according to the word of the LORD that he spoke by his servants the prophets. Surely this came upon Judah at the command of the LORD, to remove them out of his sight, for the sins of Manasseh, for all that he had committed, and also for the innocent blood that he had shed; for he filled Jerusalem with innocent blood, and the LORD was not willing to pardon. Now the rest of the deeds of Jehoiakim, and all that he did, are they not written in the Book of the Annals of the Kings of Judah? So Jehoiakim slept with his ancestors; then his son Jehoiachin succeeded him. The king of Egypt did not come again out of his land, for the king of Babylon had taken over all that belonged to the king of Egypt from the Wadi of Egypt to the River Euphrates. Jehoiachin was eighteen years old when he began to reign; he reigned three months in Jerusalem. His mother's name was Nehushta daughter of Elnathan of Jerusalem. He did what was evil in the sight of the LORD, just as his father had done. At that time the servants of King Nebuchadnezzar of Babylon came up to Jerusalem, and the city was besieged. King Nebuchadnezzar of Babylon came to the city, while his servants were besieging it; King Jehoiachin of Judah gave himself up to the king of Babylon, himself, his mother, his servants, his officers, and his palace officials. The king of Babylon took him prisoner in the eighth year of his reign. He carried off all the treasures of the house of the LORD, and the treasures of the king's house; he cut in pieces all the vessels of gold in the temple of the LORD, which King Solomon of Israel had made, all this as the LORD had foretold. He carried away all Jerusalem, all the officials, all the warriors, ten thousand captives, all the artisans and the smiths; no one remained, except the poorest people of the land. He carried away Jehoiachin to Babylon; the king's mother, the king's wives, his officials, and the elite of the land, he took into captivity from Jerusalem to Babylon. The king of Babylon brought captive to Babylon all the men of valor, seven thousand, the artisans and the smiths, one thousand, all of them strong and fit for war. The king of Babylon made Mattaniah, Jehoiachin's uncle, king in his place, and changed his name to Zedekiah.

A Reading (Lesson) from the First Letter of Paul to the Corinthians [12:12–26]

Just as the body is one and has many members, and all the members of the body, though many, are one body, so it is with Christ. For in the one Spirit we were all baptized into one body—Jews or Greeks, slaves or free—and we were all made to drink of one Spirit. Indeed, the body does not consist of one member but of many. If the foot would say, "Because I am not a hand, I do not belong to the body," that would not make it any less a part of the body. And if the ear would say, "Because I am not an eye, I do not belong to the body," that would not make it any less a part of the body. If the whole body were an eye, where would the hearing be? If the whole body were hearing, where would the sense of smell be? But as it is, God arranged the members of the body, each one of them, as he chose. If all were a single member, where would the body be? As it is, there are many members, yet one body. The eye cannot say to the hand, "I have no need of you," nor again the head to the feet, "I have no need of you." On the contrary, the members of the body that seem to be weaker are indispensable, and those members of the body that we think less honorable we clothe with greater honor, and our less respectable members are treated with greater respect; whereas our more respectable members do not need this. But God has so arranged the body, giving the greater honor to the inferior member, that there may be no dissension within the body, but the members may have the same care for one another. If one member suffers, all suffer together with it; if one member is honored, all rejoice together with it.

A Reading (Lesson) from the Gospel according to Matthew [9:27–34]

As Jesus went on from there, two blind men followed him, crying loudly, "Have mercy on us, Son of David!" When he entered the house, the blind men came to him; and Jesus said to them, "Do you believe that I am able to do this?" They said to him, "Yes, Lord." Then he touched their eyes and said, "According to your faith let it be done to you." And their eyes were opened. Then Jesus sternly ordered them, "See that no one knows of this." But they went away and spread the news about him throughout that district. After they had gone away, a demoniac who was mute was brought to him. And when the demon had been cast out, the one who had been mute spoke; and the crowds were amazed and said, "Never has anything like this been seen in Israel." But the Pharisees said, "By the ruler of the demons he casts out the demons."

Saturday

Psalm 137:1–6(7–9) [page 792],
Psalm 144 [page 800] ❖ *Psalm 104* [page 735]

A Reading (Lesson) from the Book of Jeremiah [35:1–19]

The word that came to Jeremiah from the LORD in the days of King Jehoiakim son of Josiah of Judah: Go to the house of the Rechabites, and speak with them, and bring them to the house of the LORD, into one of the chambers; then offer them wine to drink. So I took Jaazaniah son of Jeremiah son of Habazziniah, and his brothers, and all his sons, and the whole house of the Rechabites. I brought them to the house of the LORD into the chamber of the sons of Hanan son of Igdaliah, the man of God, which was near the chamber of the officials, above the chamber of Maaseiah son of Shallum, keeper of the threshold. Then I set before the Rechabites pitchers full of wine, and cups; and I said to them, "Have some wine." But they answered, "We will drink no wine, for our ancestor Jonadab son of Rechab commanded us, 'You shall never drink wine, neither you nor your children; nor shall you ever build a house, or sow seed; nor shall you plant a vineyard, or even own one; but you shall live in tents all your days, that you may live many days in the land where you reside.' We have obeyed the charge of our ancestor Jonadab son of Rechab in all that he commanded us, to drink no wine all our days, ourselves, our wives, our sons, or our daughters, and not to build houses to live in. We have no vineyard or field or seed; but we have lived in tents, and have obeyed and done all that our ancestor Jonadab commanded us. But when King Nebuchadrezzar of Babylon came up against the land, we said, 'Come, and let us go to Jerusalem for fear of the army of the Chaldeans and the army of the Arameans.' That is why we are living in Jerusalem." Then the word of the LORD came to Jeremiah: Thus says the LORD of hosts, the God of Israel: Go and say to the people of Judah and the inhabitants of Jerusalem, Can you not learn a lesson and obey my words? says the LORD. The command has been carried out that Jonadab son of Rechab gave to his descendants to drink no wine; and they drink none to this day, for they have obeyed their ancestor's command. But I myself have spoken to you persistently, and you have not obeyed me. I have sent to you all my servants the prophets, sending them persistently, saying, 'Turn now everyone of you from your evil way, and amend your doings, and do not go after other gods to serve them, and then you shall live in the land that I gave to you and your ancestors.' But you did not incline your ear or obey me. The descendants of Jonadab son of Rechab have carried out the command that their ancestor gave them, but this people has not obeyed me. Therefore, thus says the LORD, the God of hosts, the God of Israel: I am going to bring on Judah and on all the inhabitants of Jerusalem every disaster that I have pronounced against them; because I have spoken to them and they have not listened, I have called to them and they have not answered. But to the house of the Rechabites Jeremiah said: Thus says the LORD of hosts, the God of Israel: Because you have obeyed the command of your ancestor Jonadab, and kept all his precepts, and done all that he commanded you, therefore thus says the LORD of hosts, the God of Israel: Jonadab son of Rechab shall not lack a descendant to stand before me for all time.

A Reading (Lesson) from the First Letter of Paul to the Corinthians [12:27—13:3]

You are the body of Christ and individually members of it. And God has appointed in the church first apostles, second prophets, third teachers; then deeds of power, then gifts of healing, forms of assistance, forms of leadership, various kinds of tongues. Are all apostles? Are all prophets? Are all teachers? Do all work miracles? Do all possess gifts of healing? Do all speak in tongues? Do all interpret? But strive for the greater gifts. And I will show you a still more excellent way. If I speak in the tongues of mortals and of angels, but do not have love, I am a noisy gong or a clanging cymbal. And if I have prophetic powers, and understand all mysteries and all knowledge, and if I have all faith, so as to remove mountains, but do not have love, I am nothing. If I give away all my possessions, and if I hand over my body so that I may boast, but do not have love, I gain nothing.

A Reading (Lesson) from the Gospel according to Matthew [9:35—10:4]

Jesus went about all the cities and villages, teaching in their synagogues, and proclaiming the good news of the kingdom, and curing every disease and every sickness. When he saw the crowds, he had compassion for them, because they were harassed and helpless, like sheep without a shepherd. Then he said to his disciples, "The harvest is plentiful, but the laborers are few; therefore ask the Lord of the harvest to send out laborers into his harvest." Then Jesus summoned his twelve disciples and gave them authority over unclean spirits, to cast them out, and to cure every disease and every sickness. These are the names of the twelve apostles: first, Simon, also known as Peter, and his brother Andrew; James son of Zebedee, and his brother John; Philip and Bartholomew; Thomas and Matthew the tax collector; James son of Alphaeus, and Thaddaeus; Simon the Cananaean, and Judas Iscariot, the one who betrayed him.

Proper 23   *Week of Sunday closest to October 12*

Sunday

Psalm 146 [page 803],   *Psalm 147* [page 804] ❖
Psalm 111 [page 754],   *Psalm 112* [page 755],
Psalm 113 [page 756]

A Reading (Lesson) from the Book of Jeremiah [36:1–10]

In the fourth year of King Jehoiakim son of Josiah of Judah, this word came to Jeremiah from the LORD: Take a scroll and write on it all the words that I have spoken to you against Israel and Judah and all the nations, from the day I spoke to you, from the days of Josiah until today. It may be that when the house of Judah hears of all the disasters that I intend to do to them, all of them may turn from their evil ways, so that I may forgive their iniquity and their sin. Then Jeremiah called Baruch son of Neriah, and Baruch wrote on a scroll at Jeremiah's dictation all the words of the LORD that he had spoken to him. And Jeremiah ordered Baruch, saying, "I am prevented from entering the house of the LORD; so you go yourself, and on a fast day in the hearing of the people in the LORD's house you shall read the words of the LORD from the scroll that you have written at my dictation. You shall read them also in the hearing of all the people of Judah who come up from their towns. It may be that their plea will come before the LORD, and that all of them will turn from their evil ways, for great is the anger and wrath that the LORD has pronounced against this people." And Baruch son of Neriah did all that the prophet Jeremiah ordered him about reading from the scroll the words of the LORD in the LORD's house. In the fifth year of King Jehoiakim son of Josiah of Judah, in the ninth month, all the people in Jerusalem and all the people who came from the towns of Judah to Jerusalem proclaimed a fast before the LORD. Then, in the hearing of all the people, Baruch read the words of Jeremiah from the scroll, in the house of the LORD, in the chamber of Gemariah son of Shaphan the secretary, which was in the upper court, at the entry of the New Gate of the LORD's house.

A Reading (Lesson) from the Acts of the Apostles [14:8–18]

In Lystra there was a man sitting who could not use his feet and had never walked, for he had been crippled from birth. He listened to Paul as he was speaking. And Paul, looking at him intently and seeing that he had faith to be healed, said in a loud voice, "Stand upright on your feet." And the man sprang up and began to walk. When the crowds saw what Paul had done, they shouted in the Lycaonian language, "The gods have come down to us in human form!" Barnabas they called Zeus, and Paul they called Hermes, because he was the chief speaker. The priest of Zeus, whose temple was just outside the city, brought oxen and garlands to the gates; he and the crowds wanted to offer sacrifice. When the apostles Barnabas and

Paul heard of it, they tore their clothes and rushed out into the crowd, shouting, "Friends, why are you doing this? We are mortals just like you, and we bring you good news, that you should turn from these worthless things to the living God, who made the heaven and the earth and the sea and all that is in them. In past generations he allowed all the nations to follow their own ways; yet he has not left himself without a witness in doing good—giving you rains from heaven and fruitful seasons, and filling you with food and your hearts with joy." Even with these words, they scarcely restrained the crowds from offering sacrifice to them.

A Reading (Lesson) from the Gospel according to Luke [7:36–50]

One of the Pharisees asked Jesus to eat with him, and he went into the Pharisee's house and took his place at the table. And a woman in the city, who was a sinner, having learned that he was eating in the Pharisee's house, brought an alabaster jar of ointment. She stood behind him at his feet, weeping, and began to bathe his feet with her tears and to dry them with her hair. Then she continued kissing his feet and anointing them with the ointment. Now when the Pharisee who had invited him saw it, he said to himself, "If this man were a prophet, he would have known who and what kind of woman this is who is touching him—that she is a sinner." Jesus spoke up and said to him, "Simon, I have something to say to you." "Teacher," he replied, "speak." "A certain creditor had two debtors; one owed five hundred denarii, and the other fifty. When they could not pay, he canceled the debts for both of them. Now which of them will love him more?" Simon answered, "I suppose the one for whom he canceled the greater debt." And Jesus said to him, "You have judged rightly." Then turning toward the woman, he said to Simon, "Do you see this woman? I entered your house; you gave me no water for my feet, but she has bathed my feet with her tears and dried them with her hair. You gave me no kiss, but from the time I came in she has not stopped kissing my feet. You did not anoint my head with oil, but she has anointed my feet with ointment. Therefore, I tell you, her sins, which were many, have been forgiven; hence she has shown great love. But the one to whom little is forgiven, loves little." Then he said to her, "Your sins are forgiven." But those who were at the table with him began to say among themselves, "Who is this who even forgives sins?" And he said to the woman, "Your faith has saved you; go in peace."

Monday

Psalm 1 [page 585],   *Psalm 2* [page 586],
Psalm 3 [page 587] ❖ *Psalm 4* [page 587],
Psalm 7 [page 590]

A Reading (Lesson) from the Book of Jeremiah [36:11–26]

When Micaiah son of Gemariah son of Shaphan heard all the words of the LORD from the scroll, he went down to the king's house, into the secretary's chamber; and all the officials were sitting there: Elishama the secretary, Delaiah son of Shemaiah, Elnathan son of Achbor, Gemariah son of Shaphan, Zedekiah son of Hananiah, and all the officials. And Micaiah told them all the words that he had heard, when Baruch read the scroll in the hearing of the people. Then all the officials sent Jehudi son of Nethaniah son of Shelemiah son of Cushi to say to Baruch, "Bring the scroll that you read in the hearing of the people, and come." So Baruch son of Neriah took the scroll in his hand and came to them. And they said to him, "Sit down and read it to us." So Baruch read it to them. When they heard all the words, they turned to one another in alarm, and said to Baruch, "We certainly must report all these words to the king." Then they questioned Baruch, "Tell us now, how did you write all these words? Was it at his dictation?" Baruch answered them, "He dictated all these words to me, and I wrote them with ink on the scroll." Then the officials said to Baruch, "Go and hide, you and Jeremiah, and let no one know where you are." Leaving the scroll in the chamber of Elishama the secretary, they went to the court of the king; and they reported all the words to the king. Then the king sent Jehudi to get the scroll, and he took it from the chamber of Elishama the secretary; and Jehudi read it to the king and all the officials who stood beside the king. Now the king was sitting in his winter apartment (it was the ninth month), and there was a fire burning in the brazier before him. As Jehudi read three or four columns, the king would cut them off with a penknife and throw them into the fire in the brazier, until the entire scroll was consumed in the fire that was in the brazier. Yet neither the king, nor any of his servants who heard all these words, was alarmed, nor did they tear their garments. Even when Elnathan and Delaiah and Gemariah urged the king not to burn the scroll, he would not listen to them. And the king commanded Jerahmeel the king's son and Seraiah son of Azriel and Shelemiah son of Abdeel to arrest the secretary Baruch and the prophet Jeremiah. But the LORD hid them.

A Reading (Lesson) from the First Letter of Paul to the Corinthians [13:(1–3)4–13]

> If I speak in the tongues of mortals and of angels, but do not have love, I am a noisy gong or a clanging cymbal. And if I have prophetic powers, and understand all mysteries, and all knowledge, and if I have all faith, so as to remove mountains, but do not have love, I am nothing. If I give away all my possessions, and if I hand over my body so that I may boast, but do not have love, I gain nothing.

Love is patient; love is kind; love is not envious or boastful or arrogant or rude. It does not insist on its own way; it is not irritable or resentful; it does not rejoice in wrongdoing, but rejoices in the truth. It bears all things, believes all things, hopes all things, endures all things. Love never ends. But as for prophecies, they will come to an end; as for tongues, they will cease; as for knowledge, it will come to an end. For we know only in part, and we prophesy only in part; but when the complete comes, the partial will come to an end. When I was a child, I spoke like a child, I thought like a child, I reasoned like a child; when I became an adult, I put an end to childish ways. For now we see in a mirror, dimly, but then we will see face to face. Now I know only in part; then I will know fully, even as I have been fully known. And now faith, hope, and love abide, these three; and the greatest of these is love.

A Reading (Lesson) from the Gospel according to Matthew [10:5–15]

Jesus sent out the twelve with the following instructions: "Go nowhere among the Gentiles, and enter no town of the

Samaritans, but go rather to the lost sheep of the house of Israel. As you go, proclaim the good news, 'The kingdom of heaven has come near.' Cure the sick, raise the dead, cleanse the lepers, cast out demons. You received without payment; give without payment. Take no gold, or silver, or copper in your belts, no bag for your journey, or two tunics, or sandals, or a staff; for laborers deserve their food. Whatever town or village you enter, find out who in it is worthy, and stay there until you leave. As you enter the house, greet it. If the house is worthy, let your peace come upon it; but if it is not worthy, let your peace return to you. If anyone will not welcome you or listen to your words, shake off the dust from your feet as you leave that house or town. Truly I tell you, it will be more tolerable for the land of Sodom and Gomorrah on the day of judgment than for that town."

Tuesday

Psalm 5 [page 588], *Psalm 6* [page 589] ❖
Psalm 10 [page 594], *Psalm 11* [page 596]

A Reading (Lesson) from the Book of
Jeremiah [36:27—37:2]

After the king had burned the scroll with the words that Baruch wrote at Jeremiah's dictation, the word of the LORD came to Jeremiah: Take another scroll and write on it all the former words that were in the first scroll, which King Jehoiakim of Judah has burned. And concerning King Jehoiakim of Judah you shall say: Thus says the LORD, You have dared to burn this scroll, saying, Why have you written in it that the king of Babylon will certainly come and destroy this land, and will cut off from it human beings and animals? Therefore thus says the LORD concerning King Jehoiakim of Judah: He shall have no one to sit upon the throne of David, and his dead body shall be cast out to the heat by day and the frost by night. And I will punish him and his offspring and his servants for their iniquity; I will bring on them, and on the inhabitants of Jerusalem, and on the people of Judah, all the disasters with which I have threatened them—but they would not listen. Then Jeremiah took another scroll and gave it to the secretary Baruch son of Neriah, who wrote on it at Jeremiah's dictation all the words of the scroll that King Jehoiakim of Judah had burned in the fire; and many similar words were added to them. Zedekiah son of Josiah, whom King Nebuchadrezzar of Babylon made king in the land of Judah, succeeded Coniah son of Jehoiakim. But neither he nor his servants nor the people of the land listened to the words of the LORD that he spoke through the prophet Jeremiah.

A Reading (Lesson) from the First Letter of Paul to the Corinthians [14:1-12]

Pursue love and strive for the spiritual gifts, and especially that you may prophesy. For those who speak in a tongue do not speak to other people but to God; for nobody understands them, since they are speaking mysteries in the Spirit. On the other hand, those who prophesy speak to other people for their upbuilding and encouragement and consolation. Those who speak in a tongue build up themselves, but those who prophesy build up the church. Now I would like all of you to speak in tongues, but even more to prophesy. One who prophesies is greater than one who speaks in tongues, unless someone interprets, so that the church may be built up. Now, brothers and sisters, if I come to you speaking in tongues, how will I benefit you unless I speak to you in some revelation or knowledge or prophecy or teaching? It is the same way with lifeless instruments that produce sound, such as the flute or the harp. If they do not give distinct notes, how will anyone know what is being played? And if the bugle gives an indistinct sound, who will get ready for battle? So with yourselves; if in a tongue you utter speech that is not intelligible, how will anyone know what is being said? For you will be speaking into the air. There are doubtless many different kinds of sounds in the world, and nothing is without sound. If then I do not know the meaning of a sound, I will be a foreigner to the speaker and the speaker a foreigner to me. So with yourselves; since you are eager for spiritual gifts, strive to excel in them for building up the church.

A Reading (Lesson) from the Gospel according to Matthew [10:16-23]

These twelve Jesus sent out, charging them, "See, I am sending you out like sheep into the midst of wolves; so be wise as serpents and innocent as doves. Beware of them, for they will hand you over to councils and flog you in their synagogues; and you will be dragged before governors and kings because of me, as a testimony to them and the Gentiles. When they hand you over, do not worry about how you are to speak or what you are to say; for what you are to say will be given to you at that time; for it is not you who speak, but the Spirit of your Father speaking through you. Brother will betray brother to death, and a father his child, and children will rise against parents and have them put to death; and you will be hated by all because of my name. But the one who endures to the end will be saved. When they persecute you in one town, flee to the next; for truly I tell you, you will not have gone through all the towns of Israel before the Son of Man comes."

Wednesday

Psalm 119:1–24 [page 763] ❖ *Psalm 12* [page 597], *Psalm 13* [page 597], *Psalm 14* [page 598]

A Reading (Lesson) from the Book of Jeremiah [37:3–21]

King Zedekiah sent Jehucal son of Shelemiah and the priest Zephaniah son of Maaseiah to the prophet Jeremiah saying, "Please pray for us to the LORD our God." Now Jeremiah was still going in and out among the people, for he had not yet been put in prison. Meanwhile, the army of Pharaoh had come out of Egypt; and when the Chaldeans who were besieging Jerusalem heard news of them, they withdrew from Jerusalem. Then the word of the LORD came to the prophet Jeremiah: Thus says the LORD, God of Israel: This is what the two of you shall say to the king of Judah, who sent you to me to inquire of me: Pharaoh's army, which set out to help you, is going to return to its own land, to Egypt. And the Chaldeans shall return and fight against this city; they shall take it and burn it with fire. Thus says the LORD: Do not deceive yourselves, saying, "The Chaldeans will surely go away from us," for they will not go away. Even if you defeated the whole army of Chaldeans who are fighting against you, and there remained of them only wounded men in their tents, they would rise up and burn this city with fire. Now when the Chaldean army had withdrawn from Jerusalem at the approach of Pharaoh's army, Jeremiah set out from Jerusalem to go to the land of Benjamin to receive his share of property among the people there. When he

reached the Benjamin Gate, a sentinel there named Irijah
son of Shelemiah son of Hananiah arrested the prophet
Jeremiah saying, "You are deserting to the Chaldeans." And
Jeremiah said, "That is a lie; I am not deserting to the
Chaldeans." But Irijah would not listen to him, and arrested
Jeremiah and brought him to the officials. The officials were
enraged at Jeremiah, and they beat him and imprisoned him
in the house of the secretary Jonathan, for it had been made
a prison. Thus Jeremiah was put in the cistern house, in the
cells, and remained there many days. Then King Zedekiah
sent for him, and received him. The king questioned him
secretly in his house, and said, "Is there any word from the
LORD?" Jeremiah said, "There is!" Then he said, "You shall
be handed over to the king of Babylon." Jeremiah also said
to King Zedekiah, "What wrong have I done to you or your
servants or this people, that you have put me in prison?
Where are your prophets who prophesied to you, saying,
'The king of Babylon will not come against you and against
this land'? Now please hear me, my lord king: be good
enough to listen to my plea, and do not send me back to the
house of the secretary Jonathan to die there." So King
Zedekiah gave orders, and they committed Jeremiah to the
court of the guard; and a loaf of bread was given him daily
from the bakers' street, until all the bread in the city was
gone. So Jeremiah remained in the court of the guard.

*A Reading (Lesson) from the First Letter of Paul to the
Corinthians* [14:13–25]

One who speaks in a tongue should pray for the power to
interpret. For if I pray in a tongue, my spirit prays but my
mind is unproductive. What should I do then? I will pray
with the spirit, but I will pray with the mind also; I will
sing praise with the spirit, but I will sing praise with the

mind also. Otherwise, if you say a blessing with the spirit, how can anyone in the position of an outsider say the "Amen" to your thanksgiving, since the outsider does not know what you are saying? For you may give thanks well enough, but the other person is not built up. I thank God that I speak in tongues more than all of you; nevertheless, in church I would rather speak five words with my mind, in order to instruct others also, than ten thousand words in a tongue. Brothers and sisters, do not be children in your thinking; rather, be infants in evil, but in thinking be adults. In the law it is written, "By people of strange tongues and by the lips of foreigners I will speak to this people; yet even then they will not listen to me," says the Lord. Tongues, then, are a sign not for believers but for unbelievers, while prophecy is not for unbelievers but for believers. If, therefore, the whole church comes together and all speak in tongues, and outsiders or unbelievers enter, will they not say that you are out of your mind? But if all prophesy, an unbeliever or outsider who enters is reproved by all and called to account by all. After the secrets of the unbeliever's heart are disclosed, that person will bow down before God and worship him, declaring, "God is really among you."

A Reading (Lesson) from the Gospel according to Matthew [10:24–33]

These twelve Jesus sent out, charging them, "A disciple is not above the teacher, nor a slave above the master; it is enough for the disciple to be like the teacher, and the slave like the master. If they have called the master of the house Beelzebul, how much more will they malign those of his household! So have no fear of them; for nothing is covered up that will not be uncovered, and nothing secret that will not become known. What I say to you in the dark, tell in the light; and what you hear whispered, proclaim from the housetops. Do not fear those who kill the body but cannot kill the soul; rather fear him who can destroy both soul and body in hell. Are not two sparrows sold for a penny? Yet not one of them will fall to the ground apart from your Father. And even the hairs of your head are all counted. So do not be afraid; you are of more value than many sparrows. Everyone therefore who acknowledges me before others, I also will acknowledge before my Father in heaven; but whoever denies me before others, I also will deny before my Father in heaven."

Thursday

Psalm 18:1–20 [page 602]   ❖   *Psalm 18:21–50* [page 604]

A Reading (Lesson) from the Book of Jeremiah [38:1–13]

Shephatiah son of Mattan, Gedaliah son of Pashhur, Jucal son of Shelemiah, and Pashhur son of Malchiah heard the words that Jeremiah was saying to all the people, Thus says the LORD, Those who stay in this city shall die by the sword, by famine, and by pestilence; but those who go out to the Chaldeans shall live; they shall have their lives as a prize of war, and live. Thus says the LORD, This city shall surely be handed over to the army of the king of Babylon and be taken. Then the officials said to the king, "This man ought to be put to death, because he is discouraging the soldiers who are left in this city, and all the people, by speaking such words to them. For this man is not seeking the welfare of this people, but their harm." King Zedekiah said, "Here he is; he is in your hands; for the king is powerless against you." So they took Jeremiah and threw him into the cistern of Malchiah, the king's son, which was in the court of the guard, letting Jeremiah down by ropes. Now there was no water in the cistern, but only mud, and Jeremiah sank in the mud. Ebed-melech the Ethiopian, a eunuch in the king's house, heard that they had put Jeremiah into the cistern. The king happened to be sitting at the Benjamin Gate, so Ebed-melech left the king's house and spoke to the king, "My lord king, these men have acted wickedly in all they did to the prophet Jeremiah by throwing him into the cistern to die there of hunger, for there is no bread left in the city." Then the king commanded Ebed-melech the Ethiopian, "Take three men with you from here, and pull the prophet Jeremiah up from the cistern before he dies." So Ebed-melech took the men with him and went to the house of the king, to a wardrobe of the storehouse, and took from there old rags and worn-out clothes, which he let down to Jeremiah in the cistern by ropes. Then Ebed-melech the Ethiopian said to Jeremiah, "Just put the rags and clothes between your armpits and the ropes." Jeremiah did so. Then they drew Jeremiah up by the ropes and pulled him out of the cistern. And Jeremiah remained in the court of the guard.

A Reading (Lesson) from the First Letter of Paul to the Corinthians [14:26–33a, 37–40]

What should be done then, my friends? When you come together, each one has a hymn, a lesson, a revelation, a tongue, or an interpretation. Let all things be done for building up. If anyone speaks in a tongue, let there be only two or at most three, and each in turn; and let one interpret. But if there is no one to interpret, let them be silent in church and speak to themselves and to God. Let two or three prophets speak, and let the others weigh what is said. If a revelation is made to someone else sitting nearby, let the first person be silent. For you can all prophesy one by one, so that all may learn and all be encouraged. And the spirits of prophets are subject to the prophets, for God is a God not of disorder but of peace. Anyone who claims to be a prophet, or to have spiritual powers, must acknowledge that what I am writing to you is a command of the Lord. Anyone who does not recognize this is not to be recognized. So, my friends, be eager to prophesy, and do not forbid speaking in tongues; but all things should be done decently and in order.

A Reading (Lesson) from the Gospel according to Matthew [10:34–42]

These twelve Jesus sent out, saying, "Do not think that I have come to bring peace to the earth; I have not come to bring peace, but a sword. For I have come to set a man against his father, and a daughter against her mother, and a daughter-in-law against her mother-in-law; and one's foes will be members of one's own household. Whoever loves father or mother more than me is not worthy of me; and whoever loves son or daughter more than me is not worthy of me; and whoever does not take up the cross and follow me is not worthy of me. Those who find their life will lose it, and those who lose their life for my sake will find it. Whoever welcomes you welcomes me, and whoever welcomes me welcomes the one who sent me. Whoever welcomes a prophet in the name of a prophet will receive a prophet's reward; and whoever welcomes a righteous person in the name of a righteous person will receive the reward of the righteous; and whoever gives even a cup of cold water to one of these little ones in the name of a disciple—truly I tell you, none of these will lose their reward."

Friday

Psalm 16 [page 599],   *Psalm 17* [page 600]   ❖
Psalm 22 [page 610]

A Reading (Lesson) from the Book of Jeremiah [38:14–28]

King Zedekiah sent for the prophet Jeremiah and received
him at the third entrance of the temple of the LORD. The
king said to Jeremiah, "I have something to ask you; do not
hide anything from me." Jeremiah said to Zedekiah, "If I
tell you, you will put me to death, will you not? And if I give
you advice, you will not listen to me." So King Zedekiah
swore an oath in secret to Jeremiah, "As the LORD lives,
who gave us our lives, I will not put you to death or hand
you over to these men who seek your life." Then Jeremiah
said to Zedekiah, "Thus says the LORD, the God of hosts,
the God of Israel, If you will only surrender to the officials
of the king of Babylon, then your life shall be spared, and
this city shall not be burned with fire, and you and your
house shall live. But if you do not surrender to the officials
of the king of Babylon, then this city shall be handed over to
the Chaldeans, and they shall burn it with fire, and you
yourself shall not escape from their hand." King Zedekiah
said to Jeremiah, "I am afraid of the Judeans who have
deserted to the Chaldeans, for I might be handed over to
them and they would abuse me." Jeremiah said, "That will
not happen. Just obey the voice of the LORD in what I say to
you, and it shall go well with you, and your life shall be
spared. But if you are determined not to surrender, this is
what the LORD has shown me—a vision of all the women
remaining in the house of the king of Judah being led out to
the officials of the king of Babylon and saying, 'Your trusted
friends have seduced you and have overcome you; now that
your feet are stuck in the mud, they desert you.' All your

wives and your children shall be led out to the Chaldeans, and you yourself shall not escape from their hand, but shall be seized by the king of Babylon; and this city shall be burned with fire." Then Zedekiah said to Jeremiah, "Do not let anyone else know of this conversation, or you will die. If the officials should hear that I have spoken with you, and they should come and say to you, 'Just tell us what you said to the king; do not conceal it from us, or we will put you to death. What did the king say to you?' then you shall say to them, 'I was presenting my plea to the king not to send me back to the house of Jonathan to die there.' " All the officials did come to Jeremiah and questioned him; and he answered them in the very words the king had commanded. So they stopped questioning him, for the conversation had not been overheard. And Jeremiah remained in the court of the guard until the day that Jerusalem was taken.

A Reading (Lesson) from the First Letter of Paul to the Corinthians [15:1–11]

I would remind you, brothers and sisters, of the good news that I proclaimed to you, which you in turn received, in which also you stand, through which also you are being saved, if you hold firmly to the message that I proclaimed to you—unless you have come to believe in vain. For I handed on to you as of first importance what I in turn had received: that Christ died for our sins in accordance with the scriptures, and that he was buried, and that he was raised on the third day in accordance with the scriptures, and that he appeared to Cephas, then to the twelve. Then he appeared to more than five hundred brothers and sisters at one time, most of whom are still alive, though some have died. Then he appeared to James, then to all the apostles. Last of all, as to one untimely born, he appeared also to me. For I am the least of the apostles, unfit to be called an apostle, because I persecuted the church of God. But by the grace of God I am what I am, and his grace toward me has not been in vain. On the contrary, I worked harder than any of them—though it was not I, but the grace of God that is with me. Whether then it was I or they, so we proclaim and so you have come to believe.

A Reading (Lesson) from the Gospel according to Matthew [11:1–6]

When Jesus had finished instructing his twelve disciples, he went on from there to teach and proclaim his message in their cities. When John heard in prison what the Messiah was doing, he sent word by his disciples and said to him, "Are you the one who is to come, or are we to wait for another?" Jesus answered them, "Go and tell John what you hear and see: the blind receive their sight, the lame walk, the lepers are cleansed, the deaf hear, the dead are raised, and the poor have good news brought to them. And blessed is anyone who takes no offense at me."

Saturday

Psalm 20 [page 608],   *Psalm 21:1–7(8–14)* [page 608]   ❖
Psalm 110:1–5(6–7) [page 753],
Psalm 116 [page 759],   *Psalm 117* [page 760]

A Reading (Lesson) from the Second Book of Kings [25:8–12,22–26]

In the fifth month, on the seventh day of the month—which was the nineteenth year of King Nebuchadnezzar, king of Babylon—Nebuzaradan, the captain of the bodyguard, a servant of the king of Babylon, came to Jerusalem. He burned the house of the LORD, the king's house, and all the houses of Jerusalem; every great house he burned down. All the army of the Chaldeans who were with the captain of the guard broke down the walls around Jerusalem. Nebuzaradan the captain of the guard carried into exile the rest of the people who were left in the city and the deserters who had defected to the king of Babylon—all the rest of the population. But the captain of the guard left some of the poorest people of the land to be vinedressers and tillers of the soil. He appointed Gedaliah son of Ahikam son of Shaphan as governor over the people who remained in the land of Judah, whom King Nebuchadnezzar of Babylon had left. Now when all the captains of the forces and their men heard that the king of Babylon had appointed Gedaliah as governor, they came with their men to Gedaliah at Mizpah, namely, Ishmael son of Nethaniah, Johanan son of Kareah, Seraiah son of Tanhumeth the Netophathite, and Jaazaniah son of the Maacathite. Gedaliah swore to them and their men, saying, "Do not be afraid because of the Chaldean officials; live in the land, serve the king of Babylon, and it shall be well with you." But in the seventh month, Ishmael son of Nethaniah son of Elishama, of the royal family, came with ten men; they struck down Gedaliah so that he died, along with the Judeans and Chaldeans who were with him at Mizpah. Then all the people, high and low, and the captains of the forces set out and went to Egypt; for they were afraid of the Chaldeans.

A Reading (Lesson) from the First Letter of Paul to the Corinthians [15:12–29]

If Christ is proclaimed as raised from the dead, how can some of you say there is no resurrection of the dead? If there is no resurrection of the dead, then Christ has not been raised; and if Christ has not been raised, then our proclamation has been in vain and your faith has been in vain. We are even found to be misrepresenting God, because we testified of God that he raised Christ—whom he did not raise if it is true that the dead are not raised. For if the dead are not raised, then Christ has not been raised. If Christ has not been raised, your faith is futile and you are still in your sins. Then those also who have died in Christ have perished. If for this life only we have hoped in Christ, we are of all people most to be pitied. But in fact Christ has been raised from the dead, the first fruits of those who have died. For since death came through a human being, the resurrection of the dead has also come through a human being; for as all die in Adam, so all will be made alive in Christ. But each in his own order: Christ the first fruits, then at his coming those who belong to Christ. Then comes the end, when he hands over the kingdom to God the Father, after he has destroyed every ruler and every authority and power. For he must reign until he has put all his enemies under his feet. The last enemy to be destroyed is death. For "God has put all things in subjection under his feet." But when it says, "All things are put in subjection," it is plain that this does not include the one who put all things in subjection under him. When all things are subjected to him, then the Son himself will also be subjected to the one who put all things in subjection under him, so that God may be all in all. Otherwise, what will those people do who receive baptism on behalf of the dead? If the dead are not raised at all, why are people baptized on their behalf?

A Reading (Lesson) from the Gospel according to Matthew [11:7–15]

As John's disciples went away, Jesus began to speak to the crowds about John: "What did you go out into the wilderness to look at? A reed shaken by the wind? What then did you go out to see? Someone dressed in soft robes? Look, those who wear soft robes are in royal palaces. What then did you go out to see? A prophet? Yes, I tell you, and more than a prophet. This is the one about whom it is written, 'See, I am sending my messenger ahead of you, who will prepare your way before you.' Truly I tell you, among those born of women no one has arisen greater than John the Baptist; yet the least in the kingdom of heaven is greater than he. From the days of John the Baptist until now the kingdom of heaven has suffered violence, and the violent take it by force. For all the prophets and the law prophesied until John came; and if you are willing to accept it, he is Elijah who is to come. Let anyone with ears listen!"

Proper 24   *Week of Sunday closest to October 19*

Sunday

Psalm 148 [page 805],   *Psalm 149* [page 807],
Psalm 150 [page 807]   ∴   *Psalm 114* [page 756],
Psalm 115 [page 757]

A Reading (Lesson) from the Book of Jeremiah [29:1,4–14]

These are the words of the letter that the prophet Jeremiah sent from Jerusalem to the remaining elders among the exiles, and to the priests, the prophets, and all the people, whom Nebuchadnezzar had taken into exile from Jerusalem to Babylon. Thus says the LORD of hosts, the God of Israel, to all the exiles whom I have sent into exile from Jerusalem to Babylon: Build houses and live in them; plant gardens and eat what they produce. Take wives and have sons and daughters; take wives for your sons, and give your daughters in marriage, that they may bear sons and daughters; multiply there, and do not decrease. But seek the welfare of the city where I have sent you into exile, and pray to the LORD on its behalf, for in its welfare you will find your welfare. For thus says the LORD of hosts, the God of Israel: Do not let the prophets and the diviners who are among you deceive you, and do not listen to the dreams that they dream, for it is a lie that they are prophesying to you in my name; I did not send them, says the LORD. For thus says the LORD: Only when Babylon's seventy years are completed will I visit you, and I will fulfill to you my promise and bring you back to this place. For surely I know the plans I have for you, says the LORD, plans for your welfare and not for harm, to give you a future with hope. Then when you call upon me and come and pray to me, I will hear you. When you search for me, you will find me; if you seek me with all your heart, I will let you find me, says the LORD, and I will restore your fortunes and gather you from all the nations and all the places where I have driven you, says the LORD, and I will bring you back to the place from which I sent you into exile."

Acts 16:6–15 [page 815 above]

A Reading (Lesson) from the Gospel according to Luke [10:1–12,17–20]

After this the Lord appointed seventy others and sent them on ahead of him in pairs to every town and place where he himself intended to go. He said to them, "The harvest is plentiful, but the laborers are few; therefore ask the Lord of the harvest to send out laborers into his harvest. Go on your way. See, I am sending you out like lambs into the midst of wolves. Carry no purse, no bag, no sandals; and greet no one on the road. Whatever house you enter, first say, 'Peace to this house!' And if anyone is there who shares in peace, your peace will rest on that person; but if not, it will return to you. Remain in the same house, eating and drinking whatever they provide, for the laborer deserves to be paid. Do not move about from house to house. Whenever you enter a town and its people welcome you, eat what is set before you; cure the sick who are there, and say to them, 'The kingdom of God has come near to you.' But whenever you enter a town and they do not welcome you, go out into its streets and say, 'Even the dust of your town that clings to our feet, we wipe off in protest against you. Yet know this: the kingdom of God has come near.' I tell you, on that day it will be more tolerable for Sodom than for that town." The seventy returned with joy, saying, "Lord, in your name even the demons submit to us!" He said to them, "I watched Satan fall from heaven like a flash of lightning. See, I have given you authority to tread on snakes and scorpions, and over all the power of the enemy; and nothing will hurt you. Nevertheless, do not rejoice at this, that the spirits submit to you, but rejoice that your names are written in heaven."

Monday

Psalm 25 [page 614] ❖ *Psalm 9* [page 593],
Psalm 15 [page 599]

A Reading (Lesson) from the Book of Jeremiah [44:1–14]

The word that came to Jeremiah for all the Judeans living in the land of Egypt, at Migdol, at Tahpanhes, at Memphis, and in the land of Pathros. Thus says the LORD of hosts, the God of Israel: You yourselves have seen all the disaster that I have brought on Jerusalem and on all the towns of Judah. Look at them; today they are a desolation, without an inhabitant in them, because of the wickedness that they committed, provoking me to anger, in that they went to make offerings and serve other gods that they had not known, neither they, nor you, nor your ancestors. Yet I persistently sent to you all my servants the prophets, saying, "I beg you not to do this abominable thing that I hate!" But they did not listen or incline their ear, to turn from their wickedness and make no offerings to other gods. So my wrath and my anger were poured out and kindled in the towns of Judah and in the streets of Jerusalem; and they became a waste and a desolation, as they still are today. And now thus says the LORD God of hosts, the God of Israel: Why are you doing such great harm to yourselves, to cut off man and woman, child and infant, from the midst of Judah, leaving yourselves without a remnant? Why do you provoke me to anger with the works of your hands, making offerings to other gods in the land of Egypt where you have come to settle? Will you be cut off and become an object of cursing and ridicule among all the nations of the earth? Have you forgotten the crimes of your ancestors, of the kings of Judah, of their wives, your own crimes and those of your wives, which they committed in the land of Judah and in the streets of Jerusalem? They have shown no contrition or fear to this day, nor have they walked in my law and my statutes that I set before you and before your ancestors. Therefore thus says the LORD of hosts, the God of Israel: I am determined to bring disaster on you, to bring all Judah to an end. I will take the remnant of Judah who are determined to come to the land of Egypt to settle, and they shall perish, everyone; in the land of Egypt they shall fall; by the sword and by famine they shall perish; from the least to the greatest, they shall die by the sword and by famine; and they shall become an object of execration and horror, of cursing and ridicule. I will punish those who live in the land of Egypt, as I have punished Jerusalem, with the sword, with famine, and with pestilence, so that none of the remnant of Judah who have come to settle in the land of Egypt shall escape or survive or return to the land of Judah. Although they long to go back to live there, they shall not go back, except some fugitives.

A Reading (Lesson) from the First Letter of Paul to the Corinthians [15:30–41]

Why are we putting ourselves in danger every hour? I die every day! That is as certain, brothers and sisters, as my boasting of you—a boast that I make in Christ Jesus our Lord. If with merely human hopes I fought with wild animals at Ephesus, what would I have gained by it? If the dead are not raised, "Let us eat and drink, for tomorrow we die." Do not be deceived: "Bad company ruins good morals." Come to a sober and right mind, and sin no more; for some people have no knowledge of God. I say this to your shame. But someone will ask, "How are the dead raised? With what kind of body do they come?' Fool! What you sow does not come to life unless it dies. And as for what you sow, you do not sow the body that is to be, but a bare seed, perhaps of wheat or of some other grain. But God gives it a body as he has chosen, and to each kind of seed its own body. Not all flesh is alike, but there is one flesh for human beings, another for animals, another for birds, and another for fish. There are both heavenly bodies and earthly bodies, but the glory of the heavenly is one thing, and that of the earthly is another. There is one glory of the sun, and another glory of the moon, and another glory of the stars; indeed, star differs from star in glory.

A Reading (Lesson) from the Gospel according to Matthew [11:16–24]

Jesus began to speak to the crowds concerning John: "To what will I compare this generation? It is like children sitting in the marketplaces and calling to one another, 'We played the flute for you, and you did not dance; we wailed, and you did not mourn.' For John came neither eating nor drinking, and they say, 'He has a demon'; the Son of Man came eating and drinking, and they say, 'Look, a glutton and a drunkard, a friend of tax collectors and sinners!' Yet wisdom is vindicated by her deeds." Then he began to reproach the cities in which most of his deeds of power had been done, because they did not repent. Woe to you, Chorazin! Woe to you, Bethsaida! For if the deeds of power done in you had been done in Tyre and Sidon, they would have repented long ago in sackcloth and ashes. But I tell you, on the day of judgment it will be more tolerable for Tyre and Sidon than for you. And you, Capernaum, will you be exalted to heaven? No, you will be brought down to Hades. For if the deeds of power done in you had been done in Sodom, it would have remained until this day. But I tell you that on the day of judgment it will be more tolerable for the land of Sodom than for you."

Tuesday

Psalm 26 [page 616], *Psalm 28* [page 619] ❖
Psalm 36 [page 632], *Psalm 39* [page 638]

A Reading (Lesson) from the Book of
Lamentations [1:1–5(6–9)10–12]

How lonely sits the city that once was full of people! How like a widow she has become, she that was great among the nations! She that was a princess among the provinces has become a vassal. She weeps bitterly in the night, with tears on her cheeks; among all her lovers she has no one to comfort her; all her friends have dealt treacherously with her, they have become her enemies. Judah has gone into exile with suffering and hard servitude; she lives now among the nations, and finds no resting place; her pursuers have all overtaken her in the midst of her distress. The roads to Zion mourn, for no one comes to the festivals; all her gates are desolate, her priests groan; her young girls grieve, and her lot is bitter. Her foes have become the masters, her enemies prosper, because the LORD has made her suffer for the multitude of her transgressions; her children have gone away, captives before the foe.

From daughter Zion has departed all her majesty. Her princes have become like stags that find no pasture; they fled without strength before the pursuer. Jerusalem remembers, in the days of her affliction and wandering, all the precious things that were hers in days of old. When her people fell into the hand of the foe, and there was no one to help her, the foe looked on mocking over her downfall. Jerusalem sinned grievously, so she has become a mockery; all who honored her despise her, for they have seen her nakedness; she herself groans, and turns her face away. Her uncleanness was in her skirts; she took no thought of her future; her downfall was appalling, with none to comfort her. "O Lord, look at my affliction, for the enemy has triumphed!"

Enemies have stretched out their hands over all her precious things; she has even seen the nations invade her sanctuary, those whom you forbade to enter your congregation. All her people groan as they search for bread; they trade their treasures for food to revive their strength. Look, O Lord, and see how worthless I have become. Is it nothing to you, all you who pass by? Look and see if there is any sorrow like my sorrow, which was brought upon me, which the Lord inflicted on the day of his fierce anger.

A Reading (Lesson) from the First Letter of Paul to the Corinthians [15:41–50]

There is one glory of the sun, and another glory of the moon, and another glory of the stars; indeed, star differs from star in glory. So it is with the resurrection of the dead. What is sown is perishable, what is raised is imperishable. It is sown in dishonor, it is raised in glory. It is sown in weakness, it is raised in power. It is sown a physical body, it is raised a spiritual body. If there is a physical body, there is also a spiritual body. Thus it is written, "The first man, Adam, became a living being"; the last Adam became a life-giving spirit. But it is not the spiritual that is first, but the physical, and then the spiritual. The first man was from the earth, a man of dust; the second man is from heaven. As was the man of dust, so are those who are of the dust; and as is the man of heaven, so are those who are of heaven. Just as we have borne the image of the man of dust, we will also bear the image of the man of heaven. What I am saying, brothers and sisters, is this: flesh and blood cannot inherit the kingdom of God, nor does the perishable inherit the imperishable.

A Reading (Lesson) from the Gospel according to Matthew [11:25–30]

At that time Jesus said, "I thank you, Father, Lord of heaven and earth, because you have hidden these things from the wise and the intelligent and have revealed them to infants; yes, Father, for such was your gracious will. All things have been handed over to me by my Father; and no one knows the Son except the Father, and no one knows the Father except the Son and anyone to whom the Son chooses to reveal him. Come to me, all you that are weary and are carrying heavy burdens, and I will give you rest. Take my yoke upon you, and learn from me; for I am gentle and humble in heart, and you will find rest for your souls. For my yoke is easy, and my burden is light."

Wednesday

Psalm 38 [page 636]   ❖   *Psalm 119:25–48* [page 765]

A Reading (Lesson) from the Book of Lamentations [2:8–15]

The LORD determined to lay in ruins the wall of daughter Zion; he stretched the line; he did not withhold his hand from destroying; he caused rampart and wall to lament; they languish together. Her gates have sunk into the ground; he has ruined and broken her bars; her king and princes are among the nations; guidance is no more, and her prophets obtain no vision from the LORD. The elders of daughter Zion sit on the ground in silence; they have thrown dust on their heads and put on sackcloth; the young girls of Jerusalem have bowed their heads to the ground. My eyes are spent with weeping; my stomach churns; my bile is poured out on the ground because of the destruction of my people, because infants and babes faint in the streets of the city. They cry to their mothers, "Where is bread and wine?" as they faint like the wounded in the streets of the city, as their life is poured out on their mothers' bosom. What can I say for you, to what compare you, O daughter Jerusalem? To what can I liken you, that I may comfort you, O virgin daughter Zion? For vast as the sea is your ruin; who can heal you? Your prophets have seen for you false and deceptive visions; they have not exposed your iniquity to restore your fortunes, but have seen oracles for you that are false and misleading. All who pass along the way clap their hands at you; they hiss and wag their heads at daughter Jerusalem; "Is this the city that was called the perfection of beauty, the joy of all the earth?"

A Reading (Lesson) from the First Letter of Paul to the Corinthians [15:51–58]

Listen, I will tell you a mystery! We will not all die, but we will all be changed, in a moment, in the twinkling of an eye, at the last trumpet. For the trumpet will sound, and the dead will be raised imperishable, and we will be changed. For this perishable body must put on imperishability, and this mortal body must put on immortality. When this perishable body puts on imperishability, and this mortal body puts on immortality, then the saying that is written will be fulfilled: "Death has been swallowed up in victory." "Where, O death, is your victory? Where, O death, is your sting?" The sting of death is sin, and the power of sin is the law. But thanks be to God, who gives us the victory through our Lord Jesus Christ. Therefore, my beloved, be steadfast, immovable, always excelling in the work of the Lord, because you know that in the Lord your labor is not in vain.

A Reading (Lesson) from the Gospel according to Matthew [12:1-14]

Jesus went through the grainfields on the sabbath; his disciples were hungry, and they began to pluck heads of grain and to eat. When the Pharisees saw it, they said to him, "Look, your disciples are doing what is not lawful to do on the sabbath." He said to them, "Have you not read what David did when he and his companions were hungry? He entered the house of God and ate the bread of the Presence, which it was not lawful for him or his companions to eat, but only for the priests. Or have you not read in the law that on the sabbath the priests in the temple break the sabbath and yet are guiltless? I tell you, something greater than the temple is here. But if you had known what this means, 'I desire mercy and not sacrifice,' you would not have condemned the guiltless. For the Son of Man is lord of the sabbath." He left that place and entered their synagogue; a man was there with a withered hand, and they asked him, "Is it lawful to cure on the sabbath?" so that they might accuse him. He said to them, "Suppose one of you has only one sheep and it falls into a pit on the sabbath; will you not lay hold of it and lift it out? How much more valuable is a human being than a sheep! So it is lawful to do good on the sabbath." Then he said to the man, "Stretch out your hand." He stretched it out, and it was restored, as sound as the other. But the Pharisees went out and conspired against him, how to destroy him.

Thursday

Psalm 37:1–18 [page 633] ❖ *Psalm 37:19–42* [page 634]

A Reading (Lesson) from the Book of Ezra [1:1–11]

In the first year of King Cyrus of Persia, in order that the word of the LORD by the mouth of Jeremiah might be accomplished, the LORD stirred up the spirit of King Cyrus of Persia so that he sent a herald throughout all his kingdom, and also in a written edict declared: "Thus says King Cyrus of Persia: The LORD, the God of heaven, has given me all the kingdoms of the earth, and he has charged me to build him a house at Jerusalem in Judah. Any of those among you who are of his people—may their God be with them!—are now permitted to go up to Jerusalem in Judah, and rebuild the house of the LORD, the God of Israel—he is the God who is in Jerusalem; and let all survivors, in whatever place they reside, be assisted by the people of their place with silver and gold, with goods and with animals, besides freewill offerings for the house of God in Jerusalem." The heads of the families of Judah and Benjamin, and the priests and the Levites—everyone whose spirit God had stirred—got ready to go up and rebuild the house of the LORD in Jerusalem. All their neighbors aided them with silver vessels, with gold, with goods, with animals, and with valuable gifts, besides all that was freely offered. King Cyrus himself brought out the vessels of the house of the LORD that Nebuchadnezzar had carried away from Jerusalem and placed in the house of his gods. King

Cyrus of Persia had them released into the charge of Mithredath the treasurer, who counted them out to Sheshbazzar the prince of Judah. And this was the inventory: gold basins, thirty; silver basins, one thousand; knives, twenty-nine; gold bowls, thirty; other silver bowls, four hundred ten; other vessels, one thousand; the total of the gold and silver vessels was five thousand four hundred. All these Sheshbazzar brought up, when the exiles were brought up from Babylonia to Jerusalem.

A Reading (Lesson) from the First Letter of Paul to the Corinthians [16:1–9]

Concerning the collection for the saints: you should follow the directions I gave to the churches of Galatia. On the first day of every week, each of you is to put aside and save whatever extra you earn, so that collections need not be taken when I come. And when I arrive, I will send any whom you approve with letters to take your gift to Jerusalem. If it seems advisable that I should go also, they will accompany me. I will visit you after passing through Macedonia—for I intend to pass through Macedonia—and perhaps I will stay with you or even spend the winter, so that you may send me on my way, wherever I go. I do not want to see you now just in passing, for I hope to spend some time with you, if the Lord permits. But I will stay in Ephesus until Pentecost, for a wide door for effective work has opened to me, and there are many adversaries.

A Reading (Lesson) from the Gospel according to Matthew [12:15–21]

Jesus, aware that the Pharisees took counsel against him, how to destroy him, departed. Many crowds followed him, and he cured all of them, and he ordered them not to make him known. This was to fulfill what had been spoken through the prophet Isaiah: "Here is my servant, whom I have chosen, my beloved, with whom my soul is well pleased. I will put my Spirit upon him, and he will proclaim justice to the Gentiles. He will not wrangle or cry aloud, nor will anyone hear his voice in the streets. He will not break a bruised reed or quench a smoldering wick until he brings justice to victory. And in his name the Gentiles will hope."

Friday

Psalm 31 [page 622]   ❖   *Psalm 35* [page 629]

A Reading (Lesson) from the Book of Ezra [3:1–13]

When the seventh month came, and the Israelites were in the towns, the people gathered together in Jerusalem. Then Jeshua son of Jozadak, with his fellow priests, and Zerubbabel son of Shealtiel with his kin set out to build the altar of the God of Israel, to offer burnt offerings on it, as prescribed in the law of Moses the man of God. They set up the altar on its foundation, because they were in dread of the neighboring peoples, and they offered burnt offerings upon it to the LORD, morning and evening. And they kept the festival of booths, as prescribed, and offered the daily burnt offerings by number according to the ordinance, as required for each day, and after that the regular burnt offerings, the offerings at the new moon and at all the sacred festivals of the LORD, and the offerings of everyone who made a freewill offering to the LORD. From the first day of the seventh month they began to offer burnt offerings to the LORD. But the foundation of the temple of the LORD was not yet laid. So they gave money to the masons and the carpenters, and food, drink, and oil to the Sidonians and the Tyrians to bring cedar trees from Lebanon to the sea, to Joppa, according to the grant that they had from King Cyrus of Persia. In the second year after their arrival at the house of God at Jerusalem, in the second month, Zerubbabel son of Shealtiel and Jeshua son of Jozadak made a beginning, together with the rest of their people, the priests and the Levites and all who had come to Jerusalem from the captivity. They appointed the Levites, from twenty years old and upward, to have the oversight of the work on the house of the LORD. And Jeshua with his sons and his kin, and Kadmiel and his sons, Binnui and Hodaviah along with the sons of Henadad, the Levites, their sons and kin, together took charge of the workers in the house of God. When the builders laid the foundation of the temple of the LORD, the priests in their vestments were stationed to praise the LORD with trumpets, and the Levites, the sons of Asaph, with cymbals, according to the directions of King David of Israel; and they sang responsively, praising and giving thanks to the LORD, "For he is good, for his steadfast love endures forever toward Israel." And all the people responded with a great shout when they praised the LORD, because the foundation of the house of the LORD was laid. But many of the priests and Levites and heads of families, old people who had seen the first house on its foundations, wept with a loud voice when they saw this house, though many shouted aloud for joy, so that the people could not distinguish the sound of the joyful shout from the sound of the people's weeping, for the people shouted so loudly that the sound was heard far away.

A Reading (Lesson) from the First Letter of Paul to the Corinthians [16:10–24]

If Timothy comes, see that he has nothing to fear among you, for he is doing the work of the Lord just as I am; therefore let no one despise him. Send him on his way in peace, so that he may come to me; for I am expecting him with the brothers. Now concerning our brother Apollos, I strongly urged him to visit you with the other brothers, but he was not at all willing to come now. He will come when he has the opportunity. Keep alert, stand firm in your faith, be courageous, be strong. Let all that you do be done in love. Now, brothers and sisters, you know that members of the household of Stephanas were the first converts in Achaia, and they have devoted themselves to the service of the saints; I urge you to put yourselves at the service of such people, and of everyone who works and toils with them. I rejoice at the coming of Stephanas and Fortunatus and Achaicus, because they have made up for your absence; for they refreshed my spirit as well as yours. So give recognition to such persons. The churches of Asia send greetings. Aquila and Prisca, together with the church in their house, greet you warmly in the Lord. All the brothers and sisters send greetings. Greet one another with a holy kiss. I, Paul, write this greeting with my own hand. Let anyone be accursed who has no love for the Lord. Our Lord, come! The grace of the Lord Jesus be with you. My love be with all of you in Christ Jesus.

A Reading (Lesson) from the Gospel according to Matthew [12:22–32]

There was brought to Jesus a demoniac who was blind and mute; and he cured him, so that the one who had been mute could speak and see. All the crowds were amazed and said, "Can this be the Son of David?" But when the Pharisees heard it, they said, "It is only by Beelzebul, the ruler of the demons, that this fellow casts out the demons." He knew what they were thinking and said to them, "Every kingdom divided against itself is laid waste, and no city or house divided against itself will stand. If Satan casts out Satan, he is divided against himself; how then will his kingdom stand? If I cast out demons by Beelzebul, by whom do your own exorcists cast them out? Therefore they will be your judges. But if it is by the Spirit of God that I cast out demons, then the kingdom of God has come to you. Or how can one enter a strong man's house and plunder his property, without first tying up the strong man? Then indeed the house can be plundered. Whoever is not with me is against me, and whoever does not gather with me scatters. Therefore I tell you, people will be forgiven for every sin and blasphemy, but blasphemy against the Spirit will not be forgiven. Whoever speaks a word against the Son of Man will be forgiven, but whoever speaks against the Holy Spirit will not be forgiven, either in this age or in the age to come."

Saturday

Psalm 30 [page 621], *Psalm 32* [page 624] ❖
Psalm 42 [page 643], *Psalm 43* [page 644]

A Reading (Lesson) from the Book of Ezra [4:7,11–24]

And in the days of Artaxerxes, Bishlam and Mithredath and Tabeel and the rest of their associates wrote to King Artaxerxes of Persia; the letter was written in Aramaic and translated. This is a copy of the letter that they sent: "To

King Artaxerxes: Your servants, the people of the province Beyond the River, send greeting. And now may it be known to the king that the Jews who came up from you to us have gone to Jerusalem. They are rebuilding that rebellious and wicked city; they are finishing the walls and repairing the foundations. Now may it be known to the king that, if this city is rebuilt and the walls finished, they will not pay tribute, custom, or toll, and the royal revenue will be reduced. Now because we share the salt of the palace and it is not fitting for us to witness the king's dishonor, therefore we send and inform the king, so that a search may be made in the annals of your ancestors. You will discover in the annals that this is a rebellious city, hurtful to kings and provinces, and that sedition was stirred up in it from long ago. On that account this city was laid waste. We make known to the king that, if this city is rebuilt and its walls finished, you will then have no possession in the province Beyond the River." The king sent an answer: "To Rehum the royal deputy and Shimshai the scribe and the rest of their associates who live in Samaria and in the rest of the province Beyond the River, greeting. And now the letter that you sent to us has been read in translation before me. So I made a decree, and someone searched and discovered that this city has risen against kings from long ago, and that rebellion and sedition have been made in it. Jerusalem has had mighty kings who ruled over the whole province Beyond the River, to whom tribute, custom, and toll were paid. Therefore issue an order that these people be made to cease, and that this city not be rebuilt, until I make a decree. Moreover, take care not to be slack in this matter; why should damage grow to the hurt of the king?" Then when the copy of King Artaxerxes' letter was read before Rehum and the scribe Shimshai and their associates, they hurried to the Jews in Jerusalem and by force and power made them cease. At that time the work on the house of God in Jerusalem stopped and was discontinued until the second year of the reign of King Darius of Persia.

A Reading (Lesson) from the Letter of Paul to Philemon [1–25]

Paul, a prisoner of Christ Jesus, and Timothy our brother, to Philemon our dear friend and co-worker, to Apphia our sister, to Archippus our fellow soldier, and to the church in your house: Grace to you and peace from God our Father and the Lord Jesus Christ. When I remember you in my prayers, I always thank my God because I hear of your love for all the saints and your faith toward the Lord Jesus. I pray that the sharing of your faith may become effective when you perceive all the good that we may do for Christ. I have indeed received much joy and encouragement from your love, because the hearts of the saints have been refreshed through you, my brother. For this reason, though I am bold enough in Christ to command you to do your duty, yet I would rather appeal to you on the basis of love—and I, Paul, do this as an old man, and now also as a prisoner of Christ Jesus. I am appealing to you for my child, Onesimus, whose father I have become during my imprisonment. Formerly he was useless to you, but now he is indeed useful both to you and to me. I am sending him, that is, my own heart, back to you. I wanted to keep him with me, so that he might be of service to me in your place during my imprisonment for the gospel; but I preferred to do nothing without your consent, in order that your good deed might be voluntary and not something forced. Perhaps this is the reason he was separated from you for a while, so that you might have him back forever, no longer as a slave but more than a slave, a beloved brother—especially to me but how much more to you, both in the flesh and in the Lord. So if you consider me your partner, welcome him as you would welcome me. If he has wronged you in any way, or owes you anything, charge that to my account. I, Paul, am writing this with my own hand: I will repay it. I say nothing about your owing me even your own self. Yes, brother, let me have this benefit from you in the Lord! Refresh my heart in Christ. Confident of your obedience, I am writing to you, knowing that you will do even more than I say. One thing more—prepare a guest room for me, for I am hoping through your prayers to be restored to you. Epaphras, my fellow prisoner in Christ Jesus, sends greetings to you, and so do Mark, Aristarchus, Demas, and Luke, my fellow workers. The grace of the Lord Jesus Christ be with your spirit.

A Reading (Lesson) from the Gospel according to Matthew [12:33–42]

Jesus said to the Pharisees, "Either make the tree good, and its fruit good; or make the tree bad, and its fruit bad; for the tree is known by its fruit. You brood of vipers! How can you speak good things, when you are evil? For out of the abundance of the heart the mouth speaks. The good person brings good things out of a good treasure, and the evil person brings evil things out of an evil treasure. I tell you, on the day of judgment you will have to give an account for every careless word you utter; for by your words you will be justified, and by your words you will be condemned." Then some of the scribes and Pharisees said to him, "Teacher, we wish to see a sign from you." But he answered them, "An evil and adulterous generation asks for a sign, but no sign will be given to it except the sign of the prophet Jonah. For just as Jonah was three days and three nights in the belly of the sea monster, so for three days and three nights the Son of Man will be in the heart of the earth. The people of Nineveh will rise up at the judgment with this generation and condemn it, because they repented at the proclamation of Jonah, and see, something greater than Jonah is here! The queen of the South will rise up at the judgment with this generation and condemn it, because she came from the ends of the earth to listen to the wisdom of Solomon, and see, something greater than Solomon is here!"

Proper 25   *Week of the Sunday closest to October 26*

Sunday

Psalm 63:1–8(9–11) [page 670],
Psalm 98 [page 727]   ❖   *Psalm 103* [page 733]

A Reading (Lesson) from the Book of Haggai [1:1—2:9]

In the second year of King Darius, in the sixth month, on the first day of the month, the word of the LORD came by the prophet Haggai to Zerubbabel son of Shealtiel, governor of Judah, and to Joshua son of Jehozadak, the high priest: Thus says the LORD of hosts: These people say the time has not yet come to rebuild the LORD's house. Then the word of the LORD came by the prophet Haggai, saying: Is it a time for you yourselves to live in your paneled houses, while this house lies in ruins? Now therefore thus says the LORD of hosts: Consider how you have fared. You have sown much, and harvested little; you eat, but you never have enough; you drink, but you never have your fill; you clothe yourselves, but no one is warm; and you that earn wages earn wages to put them into a bag with holes. Thus says the LORD of hosts: Consider how you have fared. Go up to the hills and bring wood and build the house, so that I may take pleasure in it and be honored, says the LORD. You have looked for much, and, lo, it came to little; and when you brought it home, I blew it away. Why? says the LORD of hosts. Because my house lies in ruins, while all of you hurry off to your own houses. Therefore the heavens above you have withheld the dew, and the earth has withheld its produce. And I have called for a drought on the land and the hills, on the grain, the new wine, the oil, on what the soil produces, on human beings and animals, and on all their labors. Then Zerubbabel son of Shealtiel, and Joshua son of Jehozadak, the high priest, with all the remnant of the people, obeyed the voice of the LORD their God, and the words of the prophet Haggai, as the LORD their God had sent him; and the people feared the LORD. Then Haggai, the messenger of the LORD, spoke to the people with the LORD's message, saying, I am with you, says the LORD. And the LORD stirred up the spirit of Zerubbabel son of Shealtiel, governor of Judah, and the spirit of Joshua son of Jehozadak, the high priest, and the spirit of all the remnant of the people; and they came and worked on the house of the LORD of hosts, their God, on the twenty-fourth day of the month, in the sixth month. In the second year of King Darius, in the seventh month, on the twenty-first day of the month, the word of the LORD came by the prophet Haggai, saying: Speak now to Zerubbabel son of Shealtiel, governor of Judah, and to Joshua son of Jehozadak, the high priest, and to the remnant of the people, and say, Who is left among you that saw this house in its former glory? How does it look to you now? Is it not in your sight as nothing? Yet now take courage, O Zerubbabel, says the LORD; take courage, O Joshua, son of Jehozadak, the high priest; take courage, all you people of the land, says the LORD; work, for I am with you, says the LORD of hosts, according to the promise that I made you when you came out of Egypt. My spirit abides among you; do not fear. For thus says the LORD of hosts: Once again, in a little while, I will shake the heavens and the earth and the sea and the dry land; and I will shake all the nations, so that the treasure of all nations shall come, and I will fill this house with splendor, says the LORD of hosts. The silver is mine, and the gold is mine, says the LORD of hosts. The latter splendor of this house shall be greater than the former, says the LORD of hosts; and in this place I will give prosperity, says the LORD of hosts.

A Reading (Lesson) from the Acts of the Apostles [18:24—19:7]

There came to Ephesus a Jew named Apollos, a native of Alexandria. He was an eloquent man, well-versed in the scriptures. He had been instructed in the Way of the Lord; and he spoke with burning enthusiasm and taught accurately the things concerning Jesus, though he knew only the baptism of John. He began to speak boldly in the synagogue; but when Priscilla and Aquila heard him, they took him aside and explained the Way of God to him more accurately. And when he wished to cross over to Achaia, the believers encouraged him and wrote to the disciples to welcome him. On his arrival he greatly helped those who through grace had become believers, for he powerfully refuted the Jews in public, showing by the scriptures that the Messiah is Jesus. While Apollos was in Corinth, Paul passed through the interior regions and came to Ephesus, where he found some disciples. He said to them, "Did you receive the Holy Spirit when you became believers?" They replied, "No, we have not even heard that there is a Holy Spirit." Then he said, "Into what then were you baptized?" They answered, "Into John's baptism." Paul said, "John baptized with the baptism of repentance, telling the people to believe in the one who was to come after him, that is, in Jesus." On hearing this, they were baptized in the name of the Lord Jesus. When Paul had laid his hands on them, the Holy Spirit came upon them, and they spoke in tongues and prophesied—altogether there were about twelve of them.

A Reading (Lesson) from the Gospel according to Luke [10:25–37]

A lawyer stood up to test Jesus. "Teacher," he said, "what must I do to inherit eternal life?" He said to him, "What is written in the law? What do you read there?" He answered, "You shall love the Lord your God with all your heart, and with all your soul, and with all your strength, and with all your mind; and your neighbor as yourself." And he said to him, "You have given the right answer; do this, and you will live." But wanting to justify himself, he asked Jesus, "And who is my neighbor?" Jesus replied, "A man was going down from Jerusalem to Jericho, and fell into the hands of robbers, who stripped him, beat him, and went away, leaving him half dead. Now by chance a priest was going down that road; and when he saw him, he passed by on the other side. So likewise a Levite, when he came to the place and saw him, passed by on the other side. But a Samaritan while traveling came near him; and when he saw him, he was moved with pity. He went to him and bandaged his wounds, having poured oil and wine on them. Then he put him on his own animal, brought him to an inn, and took care of him. The next day he took out two denarii, gave them to the innkeeper, and said, 'Take care of him; and when I come back, I will repay you whatever more you spend.' Which of these three, do you think, was a neighbor to the man who fell into the hands of the robbers?" He said, "The one who showed him mercy." Jesus said to him, "Go and do likewise."

Monday

Psalm 41 [page 641],   *Psalm 52* [page 657] ❖
Psalm 44 [page 645]

A Reading (Lesson) from the Book of Zechariah [1:7–17]

On the twenty-fourth day of the eleventh month, the month of Shebat, in the second year of Darius, the word of the LORD came to the prophet Zechariah son of Berechiah son of Iddo; and Zechariah said, In the night I saw a man riding on a red horse! He was standing among the myrtle trees in the glen; and behind him were red, sorrel, and white horses. Then I said, "What are these, my lord?" The angel who talked with me said to me, "I will show you what they are." So the man who was standing among the myrtle trees answered, "They are those whom the LORD has sent to patrol the earth." Then they spoke to the angel of the LORD who was standing among the myrtle trees, "We have patrolled the earth, and lo, the whole earth remains at peace." Then the angel of the LORD said, "O LORD of hosts, how long will you withhold mercy from Jerusalem and the cities of Judah, with which you have been angry these seventy years?" Then the LORD replied with gracious and comforting words to the angel who talked with me. So the angel who talked with me said to me, Proclaim this message:

Thus says the LORD of hosts; I am very jealous for Jerusalem and for Zion. And I am extremely angry with the nations that are at ease; for while I was only a little angry, they made the disaster worse. Therefore, thus says the LORD, I have returned to Jerusalem with compassion; my house shall be built in it, says the LORD of hosts, and the measuring line shall be stretched out over Jerusalem. Proclaim further: Thus says the LORD of hosts: My cities shall again overflow with prosperity; the LORD will again comfort Zion and again choose Jerusalem.

A Reading (Lesson) from the Revelation to John [1:4–20]

John to the seven churches that are in Asia: Grace to you and peace from him who is and who was and who is to come, and from the seven spirits who are before his throne, and from Jesus Christ, the faithful witness, the firstborn of the dead, and the ruler of the kings of the earth. To him who loves us and freed us from our sins by his blood, and made us to be a kingdom, priests serving his God and Father, to him be glory and dominion forever and ever. Amen. Look! He is coming with the clouds; every eye will see him, even those who pierced him; and on his account all the tribes of the earth will wail. So it is to be. Amen. "I am the Alpha and the Omega," says the Lord God, who is and who was and who is to come, the Almighty. I, John, your brother who share with you in Jesus the persecution and the kingdom and the patient endurance, was on the island called Patmos because of the word of God and the testimony of Jesus. I was in the spirit on the Lord's day, and I heard behind me a loud voice like a trumpet saying, "Write in a book what you see and send it to the seven churches, to Ephesus, to Smyrna, to Pergamum, to Thyatira, to Sardis, to

Philadelphia, and to Laodicea." Then I turned to see whose voice it was that spoke to me, and on turning I saw seven golden lampstands, and in the midst of the lampstands I saw one like the Son of Man, clothed with a long robe and with a golden sash across his chest. His head and his hair were white as white wool, white as snow; his eyes were like a flame of fire, his feet were like burnished bronze, refined as in a furnace, and his voice was like the sound of many waters. In his right hand he held seven stars, and from his mouth came a sharp, two-edged sword, and his face was like the sun shining with full force. When I saw him, I fell at his feet as though dead. But he placed his right hand on me, saying, "Do not be afraid; I am the first and the last, and the living one. I was dead, and see, I am alive forever and ever; and I have the keys of Death and of Hades. Now write what you have seen, what is, and what is to take place after this. As for the mystery of the seven stars that you saw in my right hand, and the seven golden lampstands: the seven stars are the angels of the seven churches, and the seven lampstands are the seven churches."

A Reading (Lesson) from the Gospel according to Matthew [12:43–50]

Jesus answered the scribes and the Pharisees, "When the unclean spirit has gone out of a person, it wanders through waterless regions looking for a resting place, but it finds none. Then it says, 'I will return to my house from which I came.' When it comes, it finds it empty, swept, and put in order. Then it goes and brings along seven other spirits more evil than itself, and they enter and live there; and the last state of that person is worse than the first. So will it be also with this evil generation." While he was still speaking to the crowds, his mother and his brothers were standing outside, wanting to speak to him. Someone told him, "Look, your mother and your brothers are standing outside, wanting to speak to you." But to the one who had told him this, Jesus replied, "Who is my mother, and who are my brothers?" And pointing to his disciples, he said, "Here are my mother and my brothers! For whoever does the will of my Father in heaven is my brother and sister and mother."

Tuesday

Psalm 45 [page 647] ❖ *Psalm 47* [page 650], *Psalm 48* [page 651]

A Reading (Lesson) from the Book of Ezra [5:1–17]

Now the prophets, Haggai and Zechariah son of Iddo, prophesied to the Jews who were in Judah and Jerusalem, in the name of the God of Israel who was over them. Then Zerubbabel son of Shealtiel and Jeshua son of Jozadak set out to rebuild the house of God in Jerusalem; and with them were the prophets of God, helping them. At the same time Tattenai the governor of the province Beyond the River and Shethar-bozenai and their associates came to them and spoke to them thus, "Who gave you a decree to build this house and to finish this structure?" They also asked them this, "What are the names of the men who are building this building?" But the eye of their God was upon the elders of the Jews, and they did not stop them until a report reached Darius and then answer was returned by letter in reply to it. The copy of the letter that Tattenai the governor of the province Beyond the River and Shethar-bozenai and his associates the envoys who were in the province Beyond the

River sent to King Darius; they sent him a report, in which was written as follows: "To Darius the king, all peace! May it be known to the king that we went to the province of Judah, to the house of the great God. It is being built of hewn stone, and timber is laid in the walls; this work is being done diligently and prospers in their hands. Then we spoke to those elders and asked them, 'Who gave you a decree to build this house and to finish this structure?' We also asked them their names, for your information, so that we might write down the names of the men at their head. This was their reply to us: 'We are the servants of the God of heaven and earth, and we are rebuilding the house that was built many years ago, which a great king of Israel built and finished. But because our ancestors had angered the God of heaven, he gave them into the hand of King Nebuchadnezzar of Babylon, the Chaldean, who destroyed this house and carried away the people to Babylonia. However, King Cyrus of Babylon, in the first year of his reign, made a decree that this house of God should be rebuilt. Moreover, the gold and silver vessels of the house of God, which Nebuchadnezzar had taken out of the temple in Jerusalem and had brought into the temple of Babylon, these King Cyrus took out of the temple of Babylon, and they were delivered to a man named Sheshbazzar, whom he had made governor. He said to him, "Take these vessels; go and put them in the temple in Jerusalem, and let the house of God be rebuilt on its site." Then this Sheshbazzar came and laid the foundations of the house of God in Jerusalem; and from that time until now it has been under construction, and it is not yet finished.' And now, if it seems good to the king, have a search made in the royal archives there in Babylon, to see whether a decree was issued by King Cyrus for the rebuilding of this house of God in Jerusalem. Let the king send us his pleasure in this matter."

A Reading (Lesson) from the Revelation to John [4:1–11]

After this I looked, and there in heaven a door stood
open! And the first voice, which I had heard speaking to
me like a trumpet, said, "Come up here, and I will show
you what must take place after this." At once I was in the
spirit, and there in heaven stood a throne, with one seated
on the throne! And the one seated there looks like jasper
and carnelian, and around the throne is a rainbow that
looks like an emerald. Around the throne are twenty-four
thrones, and seated on the thrones are twenty-four elders,
dressed in white robes, with golden crowns on their heads.
Coming from the throne are flashes of lightning, and
rumblings and peals of thunder, and in front of the throne
burn seven flaming torches, which are the seven spirits of
God; and in front of the throne there is something like a
sea of glass, like crystal. Around the throne, and on each
side of the throne, are four living creatures, full of eyes in
front and behind: the first living creature like a lion, the
second living creature like an ox, the third living creature
with a face like a human face, and the fourth living
creature like a flying eagle. And the four living creatures,
each of them with six wings, are full of eyes all around
and inside. Day and night without ceasing they sing,
"Holy, holy, holy, the Lord God the Almighty, who was
and is and is to come." And whenever the living creatures
give glory and honor and thanks to the one who is seated
on the throne, who lives forever and ever, the twenty-four
elders fall before the one who is seated on the throne and
worship the one who lives forever and ever; they cast their
crowns before the throne, singing, "You are worthy, our
Lord and God, to receive glory and honor and power, for
you created all things, and by your will they existed and
were created."

A Reading (Lesson) from the Gospel according to Matthew [13:1–9]

That same day Jesus went out of the house and sat beside the sea. Such great crowds gathered around him that he got into a boat and sat there, while the whole crowd stood on the beach. And he told them many things in parables, saying: "Listen! A sower went out to sow. And as he sowed, some seeds fell on the path, and the birds came and ate them up. Other seeds fell on rocky ground, where they did not have much soil, and they sprang up quickly, since they had no depth of soil. But when the sun rose, they were scorched; and since they had no root, they withered away. Other seeds fell among thorns, and the thorns grew up and choked them. Other seeds fell on good soil and brought forth grain, some a hundredfold, some sixty, some thirty. Let anyone with ears listen!"

Wednesday

Psalm 119:49–72 [page 767] ❖ *Psalm 49* [page 652], *(Psalm 53* [page 658])

A Reading (Lesson) from the Book of Ezra [6:1–22]

King Darius made a decree, and they searched the archives where the documents were stored in Babylon. But it was in Ecbatana, the capital in the province of Media, that a scroll was found on which this was written: "A record. In the first year of his reign, King Cyrus issued a decree: Concerning the house of God at Jerusalem, let the house be rebuilt, the place where sacrifices are offered and burnt offerings are brought; its height shall be sixty cubits and its width sixty cubits, with three courses of hewn stones and one course of timber; let the cost be paid from the royal treasury.

Moreover, let the gold and silver vessels of the house of God, which Nebuchadnezzar took out of the temple in Jerusalem and brought to Babylon, be restored and brought back to the temple in Jerusalem, each to its place; you shall put them in the house of God." "Now you, Tattenai, governor of the province Beyond the River, Shethar-bozenai, and you, their associates, the envoys in the province Beyond the River, keep away; let the work on this house of God alone; let the governor of the Jews and the elders of the Jews rebuild this house of God on its site. Moreover I make a decree regarding what you shall do for these elders of the Jews for the rebuilding of this house of God: the cost is to be paid to these people, in full and without delay, from the royal revenue, the tributes of the province Beyond the River. Whatever is needed—young bulls, rams, or sheep for burnt offerings to the God of heaven, wheat, salt, wine, or oil, as the priests in Jerusalem require—let that be given to them day by day without fail, so that they may offer pleasing sacrifices to the God of heaven, and pray for the life of the king and his children. Furthermore I decree that if anyone alters this edict, a beam shall be pulled out of the house of the perpetrator, who then shall be impaled on it. The house shall be made a dunghill. May the God who has established his name there overthrow any king or people that shall put forth a hand to alter this, or to destroy this house of God in Jerusalem. I, Darius, make a decree; let it be done with all diligence." Then, according to the word sent by King Darius, Tattenai, the governor of the province Beyond the River, Shethar-bozenai, and their associates did with all diligence what King Darius had ordered. So the elders of the Jews built and prospered, through the prophesying of the prophet Haggai and Zechariah son of Iddo. They finished their building by command of the God of Israel and by decree of Cyrus, Darius, and King Artaxerxes of Persia; and this house was finished on the third day of the month of Adar, in the sixth year of the reign of King Darius. The people of Israel, the priests and the Levites, and the rest of the returned exiles, celebrated the dedication of this house of God with joy. They offered at the dedication of this house of God one hundred bulls, two hundred rams, four hundred lambs, and as a sin offering for all Israel, twelve male goats, according to the number of the tribes of Israel. Then they set the priests in their divisions and the Levites in their courses for the service of God at Jerusalem, as it is written in the book of Moses. On the fourteenth day of the first month the returned exiles kept the passover. For both the priests and the Levites had purified themselves; all of them were clean. So they killed the passover lamb for all the returned exiles, for their fellow priests, and for themselves. It was eaten by the people of Israel who had returned from exile, and also by all who had joined them and separated themselves from the pollutions of the nations of the land to worship the LORD, the God of Israel. With joy they celebrated the festival of unleavened bread seven days; for the LORD had made them joyful, and had turned the heart of the king of Assyria to them, so that he aided them in the work on the house of God, the God of Israel.

A Reading (Lesson) from the Revelation to John [5:1–10]

I saw in the right hand of the one seated on the throne a scroll written on the inside and on the back, sealed with seven seals; and I saw a mighty angel proclaiming with a loud voice, "Who is worthy to open the scroll and break its seals?" And no one in heaven or on earth or under the earth was able to open the scroll or to look into it. And I began to weep bitterly because no one was found worthy to open the scroll or to look into it. Then one of the elders said to me, "Do not weep. See, the Lion of the tribe of Judah, the Root of David, has conquered, so that he can open the scroll and its seven seals." Then I saw between the throne and the four living creatures and among the elders a Lamb standing as if it had been slaughtered, having seven horns and seven eyes, which are the seven spirits of God sent out into all the earth. He went and took the scroll from the right hand of the one who was seated on the throne. When he had taken the scroll, the four living creatures and the twenty-four elders fell before the Lamb, each holding a harp and golden bowls full of incense, which are the prayers of the saints. They sing a new song: "You are worthy to take the scroll and to open its seals, for you were slaughtered and by your blood you ransomed for God saints from every tribe and language and people and nation; you have made them to be a kingdom and priests serving our God, and they will reign on earth."

A Reading (Lesson) from the Gospel according to Matthew [13:10–17]

The disciples came and said to Jesus, "Why do you speak to them in parables?" He answered, "To you it has been given to know the secrets of the kingdom of heaven, but to them it has not been given. For to those who have, more will be given, and they will have an abundance; but from those who have nothing, even what they have will be taken away. The reason I speak to them in parables is that 'seeing they do not perceive, and hearing they do not listen, nor do they understand.' With them indeed is fulfilled the prophecy of Isaiah that says: 'You will indeed listen, but never understand, and you will indeed look, but never perceive. For this people's heart has grown dull, and their ears are hard of hearing, and they have shut their eyes; so that they might not look with their eyes, and listen with their ears, and understand with their heart and turn—and I would heal them.' But blessed are your eyes, for they see, and your ears, for they hear. Truly I tell you, many prophets and righteous people longed to see what you see, but did not see it, and to hear what you hear, but did not hear it."

Thursday

Psalm 50 [page 654] ❖ *(Psalm 59* [page 665],
Psalm 60 [page 667]) or *Psalm 103* [page 733]

A Reading (Lesson) from the Book of Nehemiah [1:1–11]

The words of Nehemiah son of Hacaliah. In the month of Chislev, in the twentieth year, while I was in Susa the capital, one of my brothers, Hanani, came with certain men from Judah; and I asked them about the Jews that survived, those who had escaped the captivity, and about Jerusalem. They replied, "The survivors there in the province who escaped captivity are in great trouble and shame; the wall of Jerusalem is broken down, and its gates have been destroyed by fire." When I heard these words I sat down and wept, and mourned for days, fasting and praying before the God of heaven. I said, "O Lord God of heaven, the great and awesome God who keeps covenant and steadfast love with those who love him and keep his commandments; let your ear be attentive and your eyes open to hear the prayer of your servant that I now pray before you day and night for your servants, the people of Israel, confessing the sins of the people of Israel, which we have sinned against you. Both I and my family have sinned. We have offended you deeply, failing to keep the commandments, the statutes, and the ordinances that you commanded your servant Moses. Remember the word that you commanded your servant Moses, 'If you are unfaithful, I will scatter you among the peoples; but if you return to me and keep my commandments and do them, though your outcasts are under the farthest skies, I will gather them from there and bring them to the place at which I have chosen to establish my name.' They are your servants and your people, whom you redeemed by your great power and your strong hand. O Lord, let your ear be attentive to the prayer of your servant, and to the prayer of your servants who delight in revering your name. Give success to your servant today, and grant him mercy in the sight of this man!" At the time, I was cupbearer to the king.

A Reading (Lesson) from the Revelation to John [5:11—6:11]

I looked, and I heard the voice of many angels surrounding the throne and the living creatures and the elders; they numbered myriads of myriads and thousands of thousands, singing with full voice, "Worthy is the Lamb that was slaughtered to receive power and wealth and wisdom and might and honor and glory and blessing!" Then I heard every creature in heaven and on earth and under the earth and in the sea, and all that is in them, singing, "To the one seated on the throne and to the Lamb be blessing and honor and glory and might forever and ever!" And the four living creatures said, "Amen!" And the elders fell down and worshiped. Then I saw the Lamb open one of the seven seals, and I heard one of the four living creatures call out, as with a voice of thunder, "Come!" I looked, and there was a white horse! Its rider had a bow; a crown was given to him, and he came out conquering and to conquer. When he opened the second seal, I heard the second living creature call out, "Come!" And out came another horse, bright red; its rider was permitted to take peace from the earth, so that people would slaughter one another; and he was given a great sword. When he opened the third seal, I heard the third living creature call out, "Come!" I looked, and there was a black horse! Its rider held a pair of scales in his hand, and I heard what seemed to be a voice in the midst of the four living creatures saying, "A quart of wheat for a day's pay, and three quarts of barley for a day's pay, but do not damage the olive oil and the wine!" When he opened the fourth seal, I heard the voice of the fourth living creature call out, "Come!" I looked and there was a pale green horse! Its rider's name was Death, and Hades followed with him; they were given authority over a fourth of the earth, to kill with sword, famine, and pestilence, and by the wild animals of the earth. When he opened the fifth seal, I saw under the altar the souls of those who had been slaughtered for the word of God and for the testimony they had given; they cried out with a loud voice, "Sovereign Lord, holy and true, how long will it be before you judge and avenge our blood on the inhabitants of the earth?" They were each given a white robe and told to rest a little longer, until the number would be complete both of their fellow servants and of their brothers and sisters, who were soon to be killed as they themselves had been killed.

A Reading (Lesson) from the Gospel according to Matthew [13:18–23]

Jesus answered the disciples, "Hear then the parable of the sower. When anyone hears the word of the kingdom and does not understand it, the evil one comes and snatches away what is sown in the heart; this is what was sown on the path. As for what was sown on rocky ground, this is the one who hears the word and immediately receives it with joy; yet such a person has no root, but endures only for a while, and when trouble or persecution arises on account of the word, that person immediately falls away. As for what was sown among thorns, this is the one who hears the word, but the cares of the world and the lure of wealth choke the word, and it yields nothing. But as for what was sown on good soil, this is the one who hears the word and understands it, who indeed bears fruit and yields, in one case a hundredfold, in another sixty, and in another thirty."

Friday

Psalm 40 [page 640],   *Psalm 54* [page 659] ❖
Psalm 51 [page 656]

A Reading (Lesson) from the Book of Nehemiah [2:1–20]

In the month of Nisan, in the twentieth year of King Artaxerxes, when wine was served him, I carried the wine and gave it to the king. Now, I had never been sad in his presence before. So the king said to me, "Why is your face sad, since you are not sick? This can only be sadness of the heart." Then I was very much afraid. I said to the king, "May the king live forever! Why should my face not be sad, when the city, the place of my ancestors' graves, lies waste, and its gates have been destroyed by fire?" Then the king said to me, "What do you request?" So I prayed to the God of heaven. Then I said to the king, "If it pleases the king, and if your servant has found favor with you, I ask that you send me to Judah, to the city of my ancestors' graves, so that I may rebuild it." The king said to me (the queen also was sitting beside him), "How long will you be gone, and when will you return?" So it pleased the king to send me, and I set him a date. Then I said to the king, "If it pleases the king, let letters be given me to the governors of the province Beyond the River, that they may grant me passage until I arrive in Judah; and a letter to Asaph, the keeper of the king's forest, directing him to give me timber to make beams for the gates of the temple fortress, and for the wall of the city, and for the house that I shall occupy." And the king granted me what I asked, for the gracious hand of my God was upon me. Then I came to the governors of the province Beyond the River, and gave them the king's letters. Now the king had sent officers of the army and cavalry with me. When Sanballat the Horonite and Tobiah the Ammonite official heard this, it displeased them greatly that someone had come to seek the welfare of the people of Israel. So I came to Jerusalem and was there for three days. Then I got up during the night, I and a few men with me; I told no one what my God had put into my heart to do for Jerusalem. The only animal I took was the animal I rode. I went out by night by the Valley Gate past the Dragon's Spring and to the Dung Gate, and I inspected the walls of Jerusalem that had been broken down and its gates that had been destroyed by fire. Then I went on to the Fountain Gate and to the King's Pool; but there was no place for the animal I was riding to continue. So I went up by way of the valley by night and inspected the wall. Then I turned back and entered by the Valley Gate, and so returned. The officials did not know where I had gone or what I was doing; I had not yet told the Jews, the priests, the nobles, the officials, and the rest that were to do the work. Then I said to them, "You see the trouble we are in, how Jerusalem lies in ruins with its gates burned. Come, let us rebuild the wall of Jerusalem, so that we may no longer suffer disgrace." I told them that the hand of my God had been gracious upon me, and also the words that the king had spoken to me. Then they said, "Let us start building!" So they committed themselves to the common good. But when Sanballat the Horonite and Tobiah the Ammonite official, and Geshem the Arab heard of it, they mocked and ridiculed us, saying, "What is this that you are doing? Are you rebelling against the king?" Then I replied to them, "The God of heaven is the one who will give us success, and we his servants are going to start building; but you have no share or claim or historic right in Jerusalem."

A Reading (Lesson) from the Revelation to John [6:12—7:4]

When the Lamb opened the sixth seal, I looked, and there came a great earthquake; the sun became black as sackcloth, the full moon became like blood, and the stars of the sky fell to the earth as the fig tree drops its winter fruit when shaken by a gale. The sky vanished like a scroll rolling itself up, and every mountain and island was removed from its place. Then the kings of the earth and the magnates and the generals and the rich and the powerful, and everyone, slave and free, hid in the caves and among the rocks of the mountains, calling to the mountains and rocks, "Fall on us and hide us from the face of the one seated on the throne and from the wrath of the Lamb; for the great day of their wrath has come, and who is able to stand?" After this I saw four angels standing at the four corners of the earth, holding back the four winds of the earth so that no wind could blow on earth or sea or against any tree. I saw another angel ascending from the rising of the sun, having the seal of the living God, and he called with a loud voice to the four angels who had been given power to damage earth and sea, saying, "Do not damage the earth or the sea or the trees, until we have marked the servants of our God with a seal on their foreheads." And I heard the number of those who were sealed, one hundred forty-four thousand, sealed out of every tribe of the people of Israel.

A Reading (Lesson) from the Gospel according to Matthew [13:24–30]

Another parable Jesus put before the disciples, saying, "The kingdom of heaven may be compared to someone who sowed good seed in his field; but while everybody was asleep, an enemy came and sowed weeds among the wheat, and then went away. So when the plants came up and bore grain, then the weeds appeared as well. And the slaves of the householder came and said to him, 'Master, did you not sow good seed in your field? Where, then, did these weeds come from?' He answered, 'An enemy has done this.' The slaves said to him, 'Then do you want us to go and gather them?' But he replied, 'No; for in gathering the weeds you would uproot the wheat along with them. Let both of them grow together until the harvest; and at harvest time I will tell the reapers, Collect the weeds first and bind them in bundles to be burned, but gather the wheat into my barn.' "

Saturday

Psalm 55 [page 660]   ❖   *Psalm 138* [page 793],
Psalm 139:1–17(18–23) [page 794]

A Reading (Lesson) from the Book of Nehemiah [4:1–23]

When Sanballat heard that we were building the wall, he was angry and greatly enraged, and he mocked the Jews. He said in the presence of his associates and of the army of Samaria, "What are these feeble Jews doing? Will they restore things? Will they sacrifice? Will they finish it in a day? Will they revive the stones out of the heaps of rubbish—and burned ones at that?" Tobiah the Ammonite was beside him, and he said, "That stone wall they are building—any fox going up on it would break it down!" Hear, O our God, for we are despised; turn their taunt back on their own heads, and give them over as plunder in a land of captivity. Do not cover their guilt, and do not let their sin be blotted out from your sight; for they have hurled insults in the face of the builders. So we rebuilt the wall, and all the wall was joined together to half its height; for the people had a mind to work. But when Sanballat and Tobiah and the Arabs and the Ammonites and the Ashdodites heard that the repairing of the walls of Jerusalem was going forward and the gaps were beginning to be closed, they were very angry, and all plotted together to come and fight against Jerusalem and to cause confusion in it. So we prayed to our God, and set a guard as a protection against them day and night. But Judah said, "The strength of the burden bearers is failing, and there is too much rubbish so that we are unable to work on the wall." And our enemies said, "They will not know or see anything before we come upon them and kill them and stop the work." When the Jews who lived near them came, they said to us ten times, "From all the places where they live they will come up against us." So in the lowest parts of the space behind the wall, in open places, I stationed the people according to their families, with their swords, their spears, and their bows. After I looked these things over, I stood up and said to the nobles and the officials and the rest of the people, "Do not be afraid of them. Remember the LORD, who is great and awesome, and fight for your kin, your sons, your daughters, your wives, and your homes." When our enemies heard that their plot was known to us, and that God had frustrated it, we all returned to the wall, each to his work. From that day on, half of my servants worked on construction, and half held the spears, shields, bows, and body-armor; and the leaders posted themselves behind the whole house of Judah, who were building the wall. The burden bearers carried their loads in such a way that each labored on the work with one hand and with the other held a weapon. And each of the builders had his sword strapped at his side while he built. The man who sounded the trumpet was beside me. And I said to the nobles, the officials, and the rest of the people, "The work is great and widely spread out, and we are separated far from one another on the wall. Rally to us wherever you hear the sound of the trumpet. Our God will fight for us." So we labored at the work, and half of them held the spears from break of dawn until the stars came out. I also said to the people at that time, "Let every man and his servant pass the night inside Jerusalem, so that they may be a guard for us by night and may labor by day." So neither I nor my brothers nor my servants nor the men of the guard who followed me ever took off our clothes; each kept his weapon in his right hand.

A Reading (Lesson) from the Revelation to John [7:(4–8)9–17]

I heard the number of those who were sealed, one hundred forty-four thousand, sealed out of every tribe of the people of Israel: From the tribe of Judah twelve thousand sealed, from the tribe of Reuben twelve thousand, from the tribe of Gad twelve thousand, from the tribe of Asher twelve thousand, from the tribe of Naphtali twelve thousand, from the tribe of Manasseh twelve thousand, from the tribe of Simeon twelve thousand, from the tribe of Levi twelve thousand, from the tribe of Issachar twelve thousand, from the tribe of Zebulun twelve thousand, from the tribe of Joseph twelve thousand, from the tribe of Benjamin twelve thousand sealed.

After this I looked, and there was a great multitude that no one could count, from every nation, from all tribes and peoples and languages, standing before the throne and before the Lamb, robed in white, with palm branches in their hands. They cried out in a loud voice, saying, "Salvation belongs to our God who is seated on the throne, and to the Lamb!" And all the angels stood around the throne and around the elders and the four living creatures, and they fell on their faces before the throne and worshiped God, singing, "Amen! Blessing and glory and wisdom and thanksgiving and honor and power and might be to our God forever and ever! Amen." Then one of the elders addressed me, saying, "Who are these, robed in white, and where have they come from?" I said to him, "Sir, you are the one that knows." Then he said to me, "These are they who have come out of the great ordeal; they have washed their robes and made them white in the blood of the Lamb. For this reason they are before the throne of God, and worship him day and night within his temple, and the one who is seated on the throne will shelter them. They will hunger no more, and thirst no more; the sun will not strike them, nor any scorching heat; for the Lamb at the center of the throne will be their shepherd, and he will guide them to springs of the water of life, and God will wipe away every tear from their eyes."

A Reading (Lesson) from the Gospel according to Matthew [13:31-35]

He put before the disciples another parable: "The kingdom of heaven is like a mustard seed that someone took and sowed in his field; it is the smallest of all the seeds, but when it has grown it is the greatest of shrubs and becomes a tree, so that the birds of the air come and make nests in its branches." He told them another parable: "The kingdom of heaven is like yeast that a woman took and mixed in with three measures of flour until all of it was leavened." Jesus told the crowds all these things in parables; without a parable he told them nothing. This was to fulfill what had been spoken through the prophet: "I will open my mouth to speak in parables; I will proclaim what has been hidden from the foundation of the world."

Proper 26 *Week of the Sunday closest to November 2*

Sunday

Psalm 24 [page 613], *Psalm 29* [page 620] ❖
Psalm 8 [page 592], *Psalm 84* [page 707]

A Reading (Lesson) from the Book of Nehemiah [5:1-19]

There was a great outcry of the people and of their wives against their Jewish kin. For there were those who said, "With our sons and our daughters, we are many; we must get grain, so that we may eat and stay alive." There were also those who said, "We are having to pledge our fields, our vineyards, and our houses in order to get grain during the famine." And there were those who said, "We are having to borrow money on our fields and vineyards to pay the king's tax. Now our flesh is the same as that of our kindred; our children are the same as their children; and yet we are forcing our sons and daughters to be slaves, and some of our daughters have been ravished; we are powerless, and our fields and vineyards now belong to others." I was very angry when I heard their outcry and these complaints. After thinking it over, I brought charges against the nobles and the officials; I said to them, "You are all taking interest from your own people." And I called a great assembly to deal with them, and said to them, "As far as we were able, we have bought back our Jewish kindred who had been sold to other nations; but now you are selling your own kin, who must then be bought back by us!" They were silent, and could not find a word to say. So I said, "The thing that you are doing is not good. Should you not walk in the fear of our God, to prevent the taunts of the nations our enemies? Moreover I and my brothers and my servants are lending them money and grain. Let us stop this taking of interest. Restore to them, this very day, their fields, their vineyards, their olive orchards, and their houses, and the interest on money, grain, wine, and oil that you have been exacting from them." Then they said, "We will restore everything and demand nothing more from them. We will do as you say." And I called the priests, and made them take an oath to do as they had promised. I also shook out the fold of my garment and said, "So may God shake out everyone from house and from property who does not perform this promise. Thus may they be shaken out and emptied." And all the assembly said, "Amen," and praised the LORD. And the people did as they had promised. Moreover from the time that I was appointed to be their governor in the land of Judah, from the twentieth year to the thirty-second year of King Artaxerxes, twelve years, neither I nor my brothers ate the food allowance of the governor. The former governors who were before me laid heavy burdens on the people, and took food and wine from them, besides forty shekels of silver. Even their servants lorded it over the people. But I did not do so, because of the fear of God. Indeed, I devoted myself to the work on this wall, and acquired no land; and all my servants were gathered there for the work. Moreover there were at my table one hundred fifty people, Jews and officials, beside those who came to us from the nations around us. Now that which was prepared for one day was one ox and six choice sheep; also fowls were prepared for me, and every ten days skins of wine in abundance; yet with all this I did not demand the food allowance of the governor, because of the heavy burden of labor on the people. Remember for my good, O my God, all that I have done for this people.

A Reading (Lesson) from the Acts of the Apostles [20:7–12]

On the first day of the week, when we met to break bread, Paul was holding a discussion with them; since he intended to leave the next day, he continued speaking until midnight. There were many lamps in the room upstairs where we were meeting. A young man named Eutychus, who was sitting in the window, began to sink off into a deep sleep while Paul talked still longer. Overcome by sleep, he fell to the ground three floors below and was picked up dead. But Paul went down, and bending over him took him in his arms, and said, "Do not be alarmed, for his life is in him." Then Paul went upstairs, and after he had broken bread and eaten, he continued to converse with them until dawn; then he left. Meanwhile they had taken the boy away alive and were not a little comforted.

A Reading (Lesson) from the Gospel according to Luke [12:22–31]

Jesus said to his disciples, "I tell you, do not worry about your life, what you will eat, or about your body, what you will wear. For life is more than food, and the body more than clothing. Consider the ravens: they neither sow nor reap, they have neither storehouse nor barn, and yet God feeds them. Of how much more value are you than the birds! And can any of you by worrying add a single hour to your span of life? If then you are not able to do so small a thing as that, why do you worry about the rest? Consider the lilies, how they grow: they neither toil nor spin; yet I tell you, even Solomon in all his glory was not clothed like one of these. But if God so clothes the grass of the field, which is alive today and tomorrow is thrown into the oven, how much more will he clothe you—you of little faith! And do not keep striving for what you are to eat and what you are to drink, and do not keep worrying. For it is the nations of the world that strive after all these things, and your Father knows that you need them. Instead, strive for his kingdom, and these things will be given to you as well."

Monday

Psalm 56 [page 662],   *Psalm* 57 [page 663],
(Psalm 58 [page 664])   ❖   *Psalm* 64 [page 671],
Psalm 65 [page 672]

A Reading (Lesson) from the Book of Nehemiah [6:1–19]

When it was reported to Sanballat and Tobiah and to Geshem the Arab and to the rest of our enemies that I had built the wall and that there was no gap left in it (though up to that time I had not set up the doors in the gates), Sanballat and Geshem sent to me, saying, "Come and let us meet together in one of the villages in the plain of Ono." But they intended to do me harm. So I sent messengers to them, saying, "I am doing a great work and I cannot come down. Why should the work stop while I leave it to come down to you?" They sent to me four times in this way, and I answered them in the same manner. In the same way Sanballat for the fifth time sent his servant to me with an open letter in his hand. In it was written, "It is reported among the nations—and Geshem also says it—that you and the Jews intend to rebel; that is why you are building the wall; and according to this report you wish to become their king. You have also set up prophets to proclaim in Jerusalem concerning you, 'There is a king in Judah!' And now it will be reported to the king according to these words. So come, therefore, and let us confer together." Then I sent to him, saying, "No such things as you say have been done; you are inventing them out of your own mind"—for they all wanted to frighten us, thinking, "Their hands will drop from the work, and it will not be done." But now, O God, strengthen my hands. One day when I went into the house of Shemaiah son of Delaiah son of Mehetabel, who was confined to his house, he said, "Let us meet together in the house of God, within the temple, and let us close the doors of the temple, for they are coming to kill you; indeed, tonight they are coming to kill you." But I said, "Should a man like me run away? Would a man like me go into the temple to save his life? I will not go in!" Then I perceived

and saw that God had not sent him at all, but he had
pronounced the prophecy against me because Tobiah and
Sanballat had hired him. He was hired for this purpose, to
intimidate me and make me sin by acting in this way, and so
they could give me a bad name, in order to taunt me.
Remember Tobiah and Sanballat, O my God, according to
these things that they did, and also the prophetess Noadiah
and the rest of the prophets who wanted to make me afraid.
So the wall was finished on the twenty-fifth day of the
month Elul, in fifty-two days. And when all our enemies
heard of it, all the nations around us were afraid and fell
greatly in their own esteem; for they perceived that this
work had been accomplished with the help of our God.
Moreover in those days the nobles of Judah sent many
letters to Tobiah, and Tobiah's letters came to them. For
many in Judah were bound by oath to him, because he was
the son-in-law of Shecaniah son of Arah: and his son
Jehohanan had married the daughter of Meshullam son of
Berechiah. Also they spoke of his good deeds in my
presence, and reported my words to him. And Tobiah sent
letters to intimidate me.

Revelation 10:1–11 [page 629 above]

*A Reading (Lesson) from the Gospel according to
Matthew* [13:36–43]

Jesus left the crowds and went into the house. And his
disciples approached him, saying, "Explain to us the
parable of the weeds of the field." He answered, "The one
who sows the good seed is the Son of Man; the field is the
world, and the good seed are the children of the kingdom;
the weeds are the children of the evil one, and the enemy
who sowed them is the devil; the harvest is the end of the

age, and the reapers are angels. Just as the weeds are collected and burned up with fire, so will it be at the end of the age. The Son of Man will send his angels, and they will collect out of his kingdom all causes of sin and all evildoers, and they will throw them into the furnace of fire, where there will be weeping and gnashing of teeth. Then the righteous will shine like the sun in the kingdom of their Father. Let anyone with ears listen!"

Tuesday

Psalm 61 [page 668], *Psalm 62* [page 669] ❖
Psalm 68:1–20(21–23)24–36 [page 676]

A Reading (Lesson) from the Book of Nehemiah [12:27–31a,42b–47]

Now at the dedication of the wall of Jerusalem they sought out the Levites in all their places, to bring them to Jerusalem to celebrate the dedication with rejoicing, with thanksgivings and with singing, with cymbals, harps, and lyres. The companies of the singers gathered together from the circuit around Jerusalem and from the villages of the Netophathites; also from Beth-gilgal and from the region of Geba and Azmaveth; for the singers had built for themselves villages around Jerusalem. And the priests and the Levites purified themselves; and they purified the people and the gates and the wall. Then I brought the leaders of Judah up onto the wall, and appointed two great companies that gave thanks and went in procession. And the singers sang with Jezrahiah as their leader. They offered great sacrifices that day and rejoiced, for God had made them rejoice with great joy; the women and children also rejoiced. The joy of Jerusalem was heard far away. On that day men were

appointed over the chambers for the stores, the
contributions, the first fruits, and the tithes, to gather into
them the portions required by the law for the priests and for
the Levites from the fields belonging to the towns; for Judah
rejoiced over the priests and the Levites who ministered.
They performed the service of their God and the service of
purification, as did the singers and the gatekeepers,
according to the command of David and his son Solomon.
For in the days of David and Asaph long ago there was a
leader of the singers, and there were songs of praise and
thanksgiving to God. In the days of Zerubbabel and in the
days of Nehemiah all Israel gave the daily portions for the
singers and the gatekeepers. They set apart that which was
for the Levites; and the Levites set apart that which was for
the descendants of Aaron.

A Reading (Lesson) from the Revelation to John [11:1–19]

I was given a measuring rod like a staff, and I was told,
"Come and measure the temple of God and the altar and
those who worship there, but do not measure the court
outside the temple; leave that out, for it is given over to
the nations, and they will trample over the holy city for
forty-two months. And I will grant my two witnesses
authority to prophesy for one thousand two hundred sixty
days, wearing sackcloth." These are the two olive trees
and the two lampstands that stand before the Lord of the
earth. And if anyone wants to harm them, fire pours from
their mouth and consumes their foes; anyone who wants
to harm them must be killed in this manner. They have
authority to shut the sky, so that no rain may fall during
the days of their prophesying, and they have authority
over the waters to turn them into blood, and to strike the
earth with every kind of plague, as often as they desire.

When they have finished their testimony, the beast that comes up from the bottomless pit will make war on them and conquer them and kill them, and their dead bodies will lie in the street of the great city that is prophetically called Sodom and Egypt, where also their Lord was crucified. For three and a half days members of the peoples and tribes and languages and nations will gaze at their dead bodies and refuse to let them be placed in a tomb; and the inhabitants of the earth will gloat over them and celebrate and exchange presents, because these two prophets had been a torment to the inhabitants of the earth. But after the three and a half days, the breath of life from God entered them, and they stood on their feet, and those who saw them were terrified. Then they heard a loud voice from heaven saying to them, "Come up here!" And they went up to heaven in a cloud while their enemies watched them. At that moment there was a great earthquake, and a tenth of the city fell; seven thousand people were killed in the earthquake, and the rest were terrified and gave glory to the God of heaven. The second woe has passed. The third woe is coming very soon. Then the seventh angel blew his trumpet, and there were loud voices in heaven, saying, "The kingdom of the world has become the kingdom of our Lord and of his Messiah, and he will reign forever and ever." Then the twenty-four elders who sit on their thrones before God fell on their faces and worshiped God, singing, "We give you thanks, Lord God Almighty, who are and who were, for you have taken your great power and begun to reign. The nations raged, but your wrath has come, and the time for judging the dead, for rewarding your servants, the prophets and saints and all who fear your name, both small and great, and for destroying those who destroy the earth." Then God's temple in heaven was opened, and the ark of his covenant was seen within his temple; and there were flashes of lightning, rumblings, peals of thunder, an earthquake, and heavy hail.

A Reading (Lesson) from the Gospel according to Matthew [13:44–52]

Jesus answered his disciples, "The kingdom of heaven is like treasure hidden in a field, which someone found and hid; then in his joy he goes and sells all that he has and buys that field. Again, the kingdom of heaven is like a merchant in search of fine pearls; on finding one pearl of great value, he went and sold all that he had and bought it. Again, the kingdom of heaven is like a net that was thrown into the sea and caught fish of every kind; when it was full, they drew it ashore, sat down, and put the good into baskets but threw out the bad. So it will be at the end of the age. The angels will come out and separate the evil from the righteous and throw them into the furnace of fire, where there will be weeping and gnashing of teeth. Have you understood all this?" They answered, "Yes." And he said to them, "Therefore every scribe who has been trained for the kingdom of heaven is like the master of a household who brings out of his treasure what is new and what is old."

Wednesday

Psalm 72 [page 685]   ❖   *Psalm 119:73–96* [page 769]

A Reading (Lesson) from the Book of Nehemiah [13:4–22]

Before this, the priest Eliashib, who was appointed over the chambers of the house of our God, and who was related to Tobiah, prepared for Tobiah a large room where they had previously put the grain offering, the frankincense, the vessels, and the tithes of grain, wine, and oil, which were given by commandment to the Levites, singers, and gatekeepers, and the contributions for the priests. While this was taking place I was not in Jerusalem, for in the thirty-second year of King Artaxerxes of Babylon I went to the king. After some time I asked leave of the king and returned to Jerusalem. I then discovered the wrong that Eliashib had done on behalf of Tobiah, preparing a room for him in the courts of the house of God. And I was very angry, and I threw all the household furniture of Tobiah out of the room. Then I gave orders and they cleansed the chambers, and I brought back the vessels of the house of God, with the grain offering and the frankincense. I also found out that the portions of the Levites had not been given to them; so that the Levites and the singers, who had conducted the service, had gone back to their fields. So I remonstrated with the officials and said, "Why is the house of God forsaken?" And I gathered them together and set them in their stations. Then all Judah brought the tithe of the grain, wine, and oil into the storehouses. And I appointed as treasurers over the storehouses the priest Shelemiah, the scribe Zadok, and Pedaiah of the Levites, and as their assistant Hanan son of Zaccur son of Mattaniah, for they were considered faithful; and their duty was to distribute to their associates. Remember me, O my God, concerning this, and do not wipe out my good deeds that I have done for the house of my God and for his service. In those days I saw in Judah people treading wine presses on the sabbath, and bringing in heaps of grain and loading them on donkeys; and also wine, grapes, figs, and all kinds of burdens, which they brought into Jerusalem on the sabbath day; and I warned them at that time against selling food. Tyrians also, who lived in the city, brought in fish and all kinds of merchandise and sold them on the sabbath to the people of Judah, and in Jerusalem. Then I remonstrated with the nobles of Judah and said to them, "What is this evil thing that you are doing, profaning the sabbath day? Did not your ancestors act in this way, and did not our God bring all this disaster on us and on this city? Yet you bring more wrath on Israel by profaning the sabbath." When it began to be dark at the gates of Jerusalem before the sabbath, I commanded that the doors should be shut and gave orders that they should not be opened until after the sabbath. And I set some of my servants over the gates, to prevent any burden from being brought in on the sabbath day. Then the merchants and sellers of all kinds of merchandise spent the night outside Jerusalem once or twice. But I warned them and said to them, "Why do you spend the night in front of the wall? If you do so again, I will lay hands on you." From that time on they did not come on the sabbath. And I commanded the Levites that they should purify themselves and come and guard the gates, to keep the sabbath day holy. Remember this also in my favor, O my God, and spare me according to the greatness of your steadfast love.

Revelation 12:1–12 [page 650 above]

A Reading (Lesson) from the Gospel according to Matthew [13:53–58]

When Jesus had finished these parables, he left that place. He came to his hometown and began to teach the people in their synagogue, so that they were astounded and said, "Where did this man get this wisdom and these deeds of power? Is not this the carpenter's son? Is not his mother called Mary? And are not his brothers James and Joseph and Simon and Judas? And are not all his sisters with us? Where then did this man get all this?" And they took offense at him. But Jesus said to them, "Prophets are not without honor except in their own country and in their own house." And he did not do many deeds of power there, because of their unbelief.

Thursday

(Psalm 70 [page 682]), *Psalm 71* [page 683] ❖
Psalm 74 [page 689]

A Reading (Lesson) from the Book of Ezra [7:(1–10)11–26]

In the reign of King Artaxerxes of Persia, Ezra son of Seraiah, son of Azariah, son of Hilkiah, son of Shallum, son of Zadok, son of Ahitub, son of Amariah, son of Azariah, son of Meraioth, son of Zerahiah, son of Uzzi, son of Bukki, son of Abishua, son of Phinehas, son of Eleazar, son of the chief priest Aaron—this Ezra went up from Babylonia. He was a scribe skilled in the law of Moses that the LORD the God of Israel had given; and the king granted him all that he asked, for the hand of the LORD his God was upon him. Some of the people of Israel, and some of the priests and Levites, the singers and gatekeepers, and the temple servants also went up to Jerusalem, in the seventh year of King Artaxerxes. They came to Jerusalem in the fifth month, which was in the seventh year of the king. On the first day of the first month the journey up from Babylon was begun, and on the first day of the fifth month he came to Jerusalem, for the gracious hand of his God was upon him. For Ezra had set his heart to study the law of the LORD, and to do it, and to teach the statutes and ordinances in Israel.

This is a copy of the letter that King Artaxerxes gave to the priest Ezra, the scribe, a scholar of the text of the commandments of the LORD and his statutes for Israel: "Artaxerxes, king of kings, to the priest Ezra, the scribe of the law of the God of heaven: Peace. And now I decree that any of the people of Israel or their priests or Levites in my kingdom who freely offers to go to Jerusalem may go with you. For you are sent by the king and his seven counselors to make inquiries about Judah and Jerusalem according to the law of your God, which is in your hand, and also to convey the silver and gold that the king and his counselors have freely offered to the God of Israel, whose dwelling is in Jerusalem, with all the silver and gold that you shall find in the whole province of Babylonia, and with the freewill offerings of the people and the priests, given willingly for the house of their God in Jerusalem. With this money then, you shall with all diligence buy bulls, rams, and lambs, and their grain offerings and their drink offerings, and you shall offer them on the altar of the house of your God in Jerusalem. Whatever seems good to you and your colleagues to do with the rest of the silver and gold, you may do, according to the will of your God. The vessels that have been given you for the service of the house of your God, you shall deliver before the God of Jerusalem. And whatever else is required for the house of your God, which you are responsible for providing, you may provide out of the king's treasury. I, King Artaxerxes, decree to all the treasurers in the province Beyond the River: Whatever the priest Ezra, the scribe of the law of the God of heaven, requires of you, let it be done with all diligence, up to one hundred talents of silver, one hundred cors of wheat, one hundred baths of wine, one hundred baths of oil, and unlimited salt. Whatever is commanded by the God of heaven, let it be done with zeal for the house of the God of heaven, or wrath will come upon the realm of the king and his heirs. We also notify you that it shall not be lawful to impose tribute, custom, or toll on any of the priests, the Levites, the singers, the doorkeepers, the temple servants, or other servants of this house of God. And you, Ezra, according to the God-given wisdom you possess, appoint magistrates and judges who may judge all the people in the province Beyond the River who know the laws of your God; and you shall teach those who do not know them. All who will not obey the law of your God and the law of the king, let judgment be strictly executed on them, whether for death or for banishment or for confiscation of their goods or for imprisonment."

A Reading (Lesson) from the Revelation to John [14:1–13]

I looked, and there was the Lamb, standing on Mount Zion! And with him were one hundred forty-four thousand who had his name and his Father's name written on their foreheads. And I heard a voice from heaven like the sound of many waters and like the sound of loud thunder; the voice I heard was like the sound of harpists playing on their harps, and they sing a new song before the throne and before the four living creatures and before the elders. No one could learn that song except the one hundred forty-four thousand who have been redeemed from the earth. It is these who have not defiled themselves with women, for they are virgins; these follow the Lamb wherever he goes. They have been redeemed from humankind as first fruits for God and the Lamb, and in their mouth no lie was found; they are blameless. Then I saw another angel flying in midheaven, with an eternal gospel to proclaim to those who live on the earth—to every nation and tribe and language and people. He said in a loud voice, "Fear God and give him glory, for the hour of his judgment has come; and worship him who made heaven and earth, the sea and the springs of water." Then another angel, a second, followed, saying, "Fallen, fallen is Babylon the great! She has made all nations drink of the wine of the wrath of her fornication." Then another angel, a third, followed them, crying with a loud voice, "Those who worship the beast and its image, and receive a mark on their foreheads or on their hands, they will also drink the wine of God's wrath, poured unmixed into the cup of his anger, and they will be tormented with fire and sulfur in the presence of the holy angels and in the presence of the Lamb. And the smoke of their torment goes up forever and ever. There is no rest day or night for those who worship the beast and its image and for anyone who receives the mark of its name." Here is a call for the endurance of the saints, those who keep the commandments of God and hold fast to the faith of Jesus. And I heard a voice from heaven saying, "Write this: Blessed are the dead who from now on die in the Lord." "Yes," says the Spirit, "they will rest from their labors, for their deeds follow them."

A Reading (Lesson) from the Gospel according to Matthew [14:1-12]

Herod the ruler heard reports about Jesus; and he said to his servants, "This is John the Baptist; he has been raised from the dead, and for this reason these powers are at work in him." For Herod had arrested John, bound him, and put him in prison on account of Herodias, his brother Philip's wife, because John had been telling him, "It is not lawful for you to have her." Though Herod wanted to put him to death, he feared the crowd, because they regarded him as a prophet. But when Herod's birthday came, the daughter of Herodias danced before the company, and she pleased Herod so much that he promised an oath to grant her whatever she might ask. Prompted by her mother, she said, "Give me the head of John the Baptist here on a platter." The king was grieved, yet out of regard for his oaths and for the guests, he commanded it to be given; he sent and had John beheaded in the prison. The head was brought on a platter and given to the girl, who brought it to her mother. His disciples came and took the body and buried it; then they went and told Jesus.

Friday

Psalm 69:1–23(24–30)31–38 [page 679] ❖
Psalm 73 [page 687]

A Reading (Lesson) from the Book of Ezra [7:27–28;8:21–36]

Blessed be the LORD, the God of our ancestors, who put such a thing as this into the heart of the king to glorify the house of the LORD in Jerusalem, and who extended to me steadfast love before the king and his counselors, and before all the king's mighty officers. I took courage, for the hand of the LORD my God was upon me, and I gathered leaders from Israel to go up with me. Then I proclaimed a fast there, at the river Ahava, that we might deny ourselves before our God, to seek from him a safe journey for ourselves, our children, and all our possessions. For I was ashamed to ask the king for a band of soldiers and cavalry to protect us against the enemy on our way, since we had told the king that the hand of our God is gracious to all who seek him, but his power and his wrath are against all who forsake him. So we fasted and petitioned our God for this, and he listened to our entreaty. Then I set apart twelve of the leading priests: Sherebiah, Hashabiah, and ten of their kin with them. And I weighed out to them the silver and the gold and the vessels, the offering for the house of our God that the king, his counselors, his lords, and all Israel there present had offered; I weighed out into their hand six hundred fifty talents of silver, and one hundred silver vessels, and one hundred talents of gold, twenty gold bowls worth a thousand darics, and two vessels of fine polished bronze as precious as gold. And I said to them, "You are holy to the LORD, and the vessels are holy; and the silver and the gold are a freewill offering to the LORD, the God of your ancestors. Guard them and keep them until you weigh them before the chief priests and the Levites and the heads of families in Israel at Jerusalem, within the chambers of the house of the LORD." So the priests and the Levites took over the silver, the gold, and the vessels as they were weighed out, to bring them to Jerusalem, to the house of our God. Then we left the river Ahava on the twelfth day of the first month, to go to Jerusalem; the hand of our God was upon us, and he delivered us from the hand of the enemy and from ambushes along the way. We came to Jerusalem and remained there three days. On the fourth day, within the house of our God, the silver, the gold, and the vessels were weighed into the hands of the priest Meremoth son of Uriah, and with him was Eleazar son of Phinehas, and with them were the Levites, Jozabad son of Jeshua and Noadiah son of Binnui. The total was counted and weighed, and the weight of everything was recorded. At that time those who had come from captivity, the returned exiles, offered burnt offerings to the God of Israel, twelve bulls for all Israel, ninety-six rams, seventy-seven lambs, and as a sin offering twelve male goats; all this was a burnt offering to the LORD. They also delivered the king's commissions to the king's satraps and to the governors of the province Beyond the River; and they supported the people and the house of God.

Revelation 15:1–8 [page 670 above]

A Reading (Lesson) from the Gospel according to Matthew [14:13–21]

When Jesus heard of John's death, he withdrew from there in a boat to a deserted place by himself. But when the crowds heard it, they followed him on foot from the towns. When he went ashore, he saw a great crowd; and he had compassion for them and cured their sick. When it was evening, the disciples came to him and said, "This is a deserted place, and the hour is now late; send the crowds away so that they may go into the villages and buy food for themselves." Jesus said to them, "They need not go away; you give them something to eat." They replied, "We have nothing here but five loaves and two fish." And he said, "Bring them here to me." Then he ordered the crowds to sit down on the grass. Taking the five loaves and the two fish, he looked up to heaven, and blessed and broke the loaves, and gave them to the disciples, and the disciples gave them to the crowds. And all ate and were filled; and they took up what was left over of the broken pieces, twelve baskets full. And those who ate were about five thousand men, besides women and children.

Saturday

Psalm 75 [page 691], *Psalm* 76 [page 692] ❖
Psalm 23 [page 612], *Psalm* 27 [page 617]

A Reading (Lesson) from the Book of Ezra [9:1–15]

After these things had been done, the officials approached me and said, "The people of Israel, the priests, and the Levites have not separated themselves from the peoples of the lands with their abominations, from the Canaanites, the Hittites, the Perizzites, the Jebusites, the Ammonites, the Moabites, the Egyptians, and the Amorites. For they have taken some of their daughters as wives for themselves and for their sons. Thus the holy seed has mixed itself with the peoples of the lands, and in this faithlessness the officials and leaders have led the way." When I heard this, I tore my garment and my mantle, and pulled hair from my head and beard, and sat appalled. Then all who trembled at the words of the God of Israel, because of the faithlessness of the returned exiles, gathered around me while I sat appalled until the evening sacrifice. At the evening sacrifice I got up from my fasting, with my garments and my mantle torn, and fell on my knees, spread out my hands to the LORD my God, and said, "O my God, I am too ashamed and embarrassed to lift my face to you, my God, for our iniquities have risen higher than our heads, and our guilt has mounted up to the heavens. From the days of our ancestors to this day we have been deep in guilt, and for our iniquities we, our kings, and our priests have been handed over to the kings of the lands, to the sword, to captivity, to plundering, and to utter shame, as is now the case. But now for a brief moment favor has been shown by the LORD our God, who has left us a remnant, and given us a stake in his holy place, in order that he may brighten our eyes and grant us a little sustenance in our slavery. For we are slaves; yet our God has not forsaken us in our slavery, but has extended to us his steadfast love before the kings of Persia, to give us new life to set up the house of our God, to repair its ruins, and to give us a wall in Judea and Jerusalem. And now, our God, what shall we say after this? For we have forsaken your commandments, which you commanded by your servants the prophets, saying, 'The land that you are entering to possess is a land unclean with the pollutions of the peoples of the lands, with their abominations. They have filled it from end to end with their uncleanness. Therefore do not give your daughters to their sons, neither take their daughters for your sons, and never seek their peace or prosperity, so that you may be strong and eat the good of the land and leave it for an inheritance to your children forever.' After all that has come upon us for our evil deeds and for our great guilt, seeing that you, our God, have punished us less than our iniquities deserved, and have given us such a remnant as this, shall we break your commandments again and intermarry with the peoples who practice these abominations? Would you not be angry with us until you destroy us without remnant or survivor? O LORD, God of Israel, you are just, but we have escaped as a remnant, as is now the case. Here we are before you in our guilt, though no one can face you because of this."

A Reading (Lesson) from the Revelation to John [17:1–14]

One of the seven angels who had the seven bowls came and said to me, "Come, I will show you the judgment of the great whore who is seated on many waters, with whom the kings of the earth have committed fornication, and with the wine of whose fornication the inhabitants of the earth have become drunk." So he carried me away in the spirit into a wilderness, and I saw a woman sitting on a scarlet beast that was full of blasphemous names, and it had seven heads and ten horns. The woman was clothed in purple and scarlet, and adorned with gold and jewels and pearls, holding in her hand a golden cup full of abominations and the impurities of her fornication; and on her forehead was written a name, a mystery: "Babylon the great, mother of whores and of earth's abominations." And I saw that the woman was drunk with the blood of the saints and the blood of the witnesses to Jesus. When I saw her, I was greatly amazed. But the angel said to me, "Why are you so amazed? I will tell you the mystery of the woman, and of the beast with seven heads and ten horns that carries her. The beast that you saw was, and is not, and is about to ascend from the bottomless pit and go to destruction. And the inhabitants of the earth, whose names have not been written in the book of life from the foundation of the world, will be amazed when they see the beast, because it was and is not and is to come. "This calls for a mind that has wisdom: the seven heads are seven mountains on which the woman is seated; also, they are seven kings, of whom five have fallen, one is living, and the other has not yet come; and when he comes, he must remain only a little while. As for the beast that was and is not, it is an eighth but it belongs to the seven, and it goes to destruction. And the ten horns that you saw are ten kings who have not yet received a kingdom, but they are to receive authority as kings for one hour, together with the beast. These are united in yielding their power and authority to the beast; they will make war on the Lamb, and the Lamb will conquer them, for he is Lord of lords and King of kings, and those with him are called and chosen and faithful."

A Reading (Lesson) from the Gospel according to Matthew [14:22–36]

Jesus made the disciples get into the boat and go on ahead to the other side, while he dismissed the crowds. And after he had dismissed the crowds, he went up the mountain by himself to pray. When evening came, he was there alone, but by this time the boat, battered by the waves, was far from the land, for the wind was against them. And early in the morning he came walking toward them on the sea. But when the disciples saw him walking on the sea, they were terrified, saying, "It is a ghost!" And they cried out in fear. But immediately Jesus spoke to them and said, "Take heart, it is I; do not be afraid." Peter answered him, "Lord, if it is you, command me to come to you on the water." He said, "Come." So Peter got out of the boat, started walking on the water, and came toward Jesus. But when he noticed the strong wind, he became frightened, and beginning to sink, he cried out, "Lord, save me!" Jesus immediately reached out his hand and caught him, saying to him, "You of little faith, why did you doubt?" When they got into the boat, the wind ceased. And those in the boat worshiped him, saying, "Truly you are the Son of God." When they had crossed over, they came to land at Gennesaret. After the people of that place recognized him, they sent word throughout the region and brought all who were sick to him, and begged him that they might touch even the fringe of his cloak; and all who touched it were healed.

Proper 27   *Week of the Sunday closest to November 9*

Sunday

Psalm 93 [page 722],   *Psalm 96* [page 725]   ❖
Psalm 34 [page 627]

A Reading (Lesson) from the Book of Ezra [10:1-17]

While Ezra prayed and made confession, weeping and throwing himself down before the house of God, a very great assembly of men, women, and children gathered to him out of Israel; the people also wept bitterly. Shecaniah son of Jehiel, of the descendants of Elam, addressed Ezra, saying, "We have broken faith with our God and have married foreign women from the peoples of the land, but even now there is hope for Israel in spite of this. So now let us make a covenant with our God to send away all these wives and their children, according to the counsel of my lord and of those who tremble at the commandment of our God; and let it be done according to the law. Take action, for it is your duty, and we are with you; be strong, and do it." Then Ezra stood up and made the leading priests, the Levites, and all Israel swear that they would do as had been said. So they swore. Then Ezra withdrew from before the house of God, and went to the chamber of Jehohanan son of Eliashib, where he spent the night. He did not eat bread or drink water, for he was mourning over the faithlessness of the exiles. They made a proclamation throughout Judah and Jerusalem to all the returned exiles that they should assemble at Jerusalem, and that if any did not come within three days, by order of the officials and the elders all their property should be forfeited, and they themselves banned from the congregation of the exiles. Then all the people of Judah and Benjamin assembled at Jerusalem within the three days; it was the ninth month, on the twentieth day of the month. All the people sat in the open square before the house of God, trembling because of this matter and because of the heavy rain. Then Ezra the priest stood up and said to them, "You have trespassed and married foreign women, and so increased the guilt of Israel. Now make confession to the LORD the God of your ancestors, and do his will; separate yourselves from the peoples of the land and from the foreign wives." Then all the assembly answered with a loud voice, "It is so; we must do as you have said. But the people are many, and it is a time of heavy rain; we cannot stand in the open. Nor is this a task for one day or for two, for many of us have transgressed in this matter. Let our officials represent the whole assembly, and let all in our towns who have taken foreign wives come at appointed times, and with them the elders and judges of every town, until the fierce wrath of our God on this account is averted from us." Only Jonathan son of Asahel and Jahzeiah son of Tikvah opposed this, and Meshullam and Shabbethai the Levites supported them. Then the returned exiles did so. Ezra the priest selected men, heads of families, according to their families, each of them designated by name. On the first day of the tenth month they sat down to examine the matter. By the first day of the first month they had come to the end of all the men who had married foreign women.

A Reading (Lesson) from the Acts of the Apostles [24:10–21]

When Felix the governor motioned to him to speak, Paul replied: "I cheerfully make my defense, knowing that for many years you have been a judge over this nation. As you can find out, it is not more than twelve days since I went up to worship in Jerusalem. They did not find me disputing with anyone in the temple or stirring up a crowd either in the synagogues or throughout the city. Neither can they prove to you the charge that they now bring against me. But this I admit to you, that according to the Way, which they call a sect, I worship the God of our ancestors, believing everything laid down according to the law or written in the prophets. I have a hope in God—a hope that they themselves also accept—that there will be a resurrection of both the righteous and the unrighteous. Therefore I do my best always to have a clear conscience toward God and all people. Now after some years I came to bring alms to my nation and to offer sacrifices. While I was doing this, they found me in the temple, completing the rite of purification, without any crowd or disturbance. But there were some Jews from Asia—they ought to be here before you to make an accusation, if they have anything against me. Or let these men here tell what crime they had found when I stood before the council, unless it was this one sentence that I called out while standing before them, 'It is about the resurrection of the dead that I am on trial before you today.' "

Luke 14:12–24 [page 605 above]

Monday

Psalm 80 [page 702]   ❖   *Psalm 77* [page 693], *(Psalm 79* [page 701])

A Reading (Lesson) from the Book of Nehemiah [9:1–15(16–25)]

On the twenty-fourth day of this month the people of Israel were assembled with fasting and in sackcloth, and with earth on their heads. Then those of Israelite descent separated themselves from all foreigners, and stood and confessed their sins and the iniquities of their ancestors. They stood up in their place and read from the book of the law of the LORD their God for a fourth part of the day, and for another fourth they made confession and worshiped the

Lord their God. Then Jeshua, Bani, Kadmiel, Shebaniah, Bunni, Sherebiah, Bani, and Chenani stood on the stairs of the Levites and cried out with a loud voice to the Lord their God. Then the Levites, Jeshua, Kadmiel, Bani, Hashabneiah, Sherebiah, Hodiah, Shebaniah, and Pethahiah, said, "Stand up and bless the Lord your God from everlasting to everlasting. Blessed be your glorious name, which is exalted above all blessing and praise." And Ezra said: "You are the Lord, you alone; you have made heaven, the heaven of heavens, with all their host, the earth and all that is on it, the seas and all that is in them. To all of them you give life, and the host of heaven worships you. You are the Lord, the God who chose Abram and brought him out of Ur of the Chaldeans and gave him the name Abraham; and you found his heart faithful before you, and made with him a covenant to give to his descendants the land of the Canaanite, the Hittite, the Amorite, the Perizzite, the Jebusite, and the Girgashite; and you have fulfilled your promise, for you are righteous. And you saw the distress of our ancestors in Egypt and heard their cry at the Red Sea. You performed signs and wonders against Pharaoh and all his servants and all the people of his land, for you knew that they acted insolently against our ancestors. You made a name for yourself, which remains to this day. And you divided the sea before them, so that they passed through the sea on dry land, but you threw their pursuers into the depths, like a stone into mighty waters. Moreover, you led them by day with a pillar of cloud, and by night with a pillar of fire, to give them light on the way in which they should go. You came down also upon Mount Sinai, and spoke with them from heaven, and gave them right ordinances and true laws, good statutes and commandments, and you made known your holy sabbath to them and gave them commandments and statutes and a law through your servant Moses. For their hunger you gave them bread from heaven, and for their thirst you brought water for them out of the rock, and you told them to go in to possess the land that you swore to give them."

"But they and our ancestors acted presumptuously and stiffened their necks and did not obey your commandments; they refused to obey, and were not mindful of the wonders that you performed among them; but they stiffened their necks and determined to return to their slavery in Egypt. But you are a God ready to forgive, gracious and merciful, slow to anger and abounding in steadfast love, and you did not forsake them. Even when they had cast an image of a calf for themselves and said, 'This is your God who brought you up out of Egypt,' and had committed great blasphemies, you in your great mercies did not forsake them in the wilderness; the pillar of cloud that led them in the way did not leave them by day, nor the pillar of fire by night that gave them light on the way by which they should go. You gave your good spirit to instruct them, and did not withhold your manna from their mouths, and gave them water for their thirst. Forty years you sustained them in the wilderness so that they lacked nothing; their clothes did not wear out and their feet did not swell. And you gave them kingdoms and peoples, and allotted to them every corner, so they took possession of the land of King Sihon of Heshbon and the land of King Og of Bashan. You multiplied their descendants like the stars of heaven, and brought them into the land that you had told their ancestors to enter and possess. So the descendants went in and possessed the land, and you subdued before them the inhabitants of the land, the Canaanites, and gave them into their hands, with their kings and the peoples of the land, to do with them as they pleased. And they captured fortress cities and a rich land, and took possession of houses filled with all sorts of goods, hewn cisterns, vineyards, olive orchards, and fruit trees in abundance; so they ate, and were filled and became fat, and delighted themselves in your great goodness."

A Reading (Lesson) from the Revelation to John [18:1–8]

After this I saw another angel coming down from heaven, having great authority; and the earth was made bright with his splendor. He called out with a mighty voice, "Fallen, fallen is Babylon the great! It has become a dwelling place of demons, a haunt of every foul and hateful bird, a haunt of every foul and hateful beast. For all the nations have drunk of the wine of the wrath of her fornication, and the kings of the earth have committed fornication with her, and the merchants of the earth have grown rich from the power of her luxury." Then I heard another voice from heaven saying, "Come out of her, my people, so that you do not take part in her sins, and so that you do not share in her plagues; for her sins are heaped high as heaven, and God has remembered her iniquities. Render to her as she herself has rendered, and repay her double for her deeds; mix a double draught for her in the cup she mixed. As she glorified herself and lived luxuriously, so give her a like measure of torment and grief. Since in her heart she says, 'I rule as a queen; I am no widow, and I will never see grief,' therefore her plagues will come in a single day—pestilence and mourning and famine—and she will be burned with fire; for mighty is the Lord God who judges her."

A Reading (Lesson) from the Gospel according to
Matthew [15:1–20]

Pharisees and scribes came to Jesus from Jerusalem and
said, "Why do your disciples break the tradition of the
elders? For they do not wash their hands before they eat."
He answered them, "And why do you break the
commandment of God for the sake of your tradition? For
God said, 'Honor your father and your mother,' and,
'Whoever speaks evil of father or mother must surely die.'
But you say that whoever tells father or mother,
'Whatever support you might have had from me is given to
God,' then that person need not honor the father. So, for
the sake of your tradition, you make void the word of
God. You hypocrites! Isaiah prophesied rightly about you
when he said: 'This people honors me with their lips, but
their hearts are far from me; in vain do they worship me,
teaching human precepts as doctrines.'" Then he called
the crowd to him and said to them, "Listen and
understand: it is not what goes into the mouth that defiles
a person, but it is what comes out of the mouth that
defiles." Then the disciples approached and said to him,
"Do you know that the Pharisees took offense when they
heard what you said?" He answered, "Every plant that my
heavenly Father has not planted will be uprooted. Let
them alone; they are blind guides of the blind. And if one
blind person guides another, both will fall into a pit." But
Peter said to him, "Explain this parable to us." Then he
said, "Are you also still without understanding? Do you
not see that whatever goes into the mouth enters the
stomach, and goes out into the sewer? But what comes out
of the mouth proceeds from the heart, and this is what
defiles. For out of the heart come evil intentions, murder,

adultery, fornication, theft, false witness, slander. These are what defile a person, but to eat with unwashed hands does not defile."

Tuesday

Psalm 78:1–39 [page 694] ❖ *Psalm 78:40–72* [page 698]

A Reading (Lesson) from the Book of Nehemiah [9:26–38]

Ezra said to the LORD, "Nevertheless they were disobedient and rebelled against you and cast your law behind their backs and killed your prophets, who had warned them in order to turn them back to you, and they committed great blasphemies. Therefore you gave them into the hands of their enemies, who made them suffer. Then in the time of their suffering they cried out to you and you heard them from heaven, and according to your great mercies you gave them saviors who saved them from the hands of their enemies. But after they had rest, they again did evil before you, and you abandoned them to the hands of their enemies, so that they had dominion over them; yet when they turned and cried to you, you heard from heaven, and many times you rescued them according to your mercies. And you warned them in order to turn them back to your law. Yet they acted presumptuously and did not obey your commandments, but sinned against your ordinances, by the observance of which a person shall live. They turned a stubborn shoulder and stiffened their neck and would not obey. Many years you were patient with them, and warned them by your spirit through your prophets; yet they would not listen. Therefore you handed them over to the peoples of the lands. Nevertheless, in your great mercies you did not make an end of them or forsake them, for you are a gracious and merciful God. Now therefore, our God—the great and mighty and awesome God, keeping covenant and steadfast love—do not treat lightly all the hardship that has come upon us, upon our kings, our officials, our priests, our prophets, and our ancestors, and all your people, since the time of the kings of Assyria until today. You have been just in all that has come upon us, for you have dealt faithfully and we have acted wickedly; our kings, our officials, our priests, and our ancestors have not kept your law or heeded the commandments and the warnings that you gave them. Even in their own kingdom, and in the great goodness you bestowed on them, and in the large and rich land that you set before them, they did not serve you and did not turn from their wicked works. Here we are, slaves to this day—slaves in the land that you gave to our ancestors to enjoy its fruit and its good gifts. Its rich yield goes to the kings whom you have set over us because of our sins; they have power also over our bodies and over our livestock at their pleasure, and we are in great distress." Because of all this we make a firm agreement in writing, and on that sealed document are inscribed the names of our officials, our Levites, and our priests.

A Reading (Lesson) from the Revelation to John [18:9-20]

The kings of the earth, who committed fornication and lived in luxury with her, will weep and wail over her when they see the smoke of her burning; they will stand far off, in fear of her torment, and say, "Alas, alas, the great city, Babylon, the mighty city! For in one hour your judgment has come." And the merchants of the earth weep and mourn for her, since no one buys their cargo anymore, cargo of gold, silver, jewels and pearls, fine linen, purple, silk and scarlet, all kinds of scented wood, all articles of ivory, all articles of costly wood, bronze, iron, and marble, cinnamon, spice, incense, myrrh, frankincense, wine, olive oil, choice flour and wheat, cattle and sheep, horses and chariots, slaves—and human lives. "The fruit for which your soul longed has gone from you, and all your dainties and your splendor are lost to you, never to be found again!" The merchants of these wares, who gained wealth from her, will stand far off, in fear of her torment, weeping and mourning aloud, "Alas, alas, the great city, clothed in fine linen, in purple and scarlet, adorned with gold, with jewels, and with pearls! For in one hour all this wealth has been laid waste!" And all shipmasters and seafarers, sailors and all whose trade is on the sea, stood far off and cried out as they saw the smoke of her burning, "What city was like the great city?" And they threw dust on their heads, as they wept and mourned, crying out, "Alas, alas, the great city, where all who had ships at sea grew rich by her wealth! For in one hour she has been laid waste. Rejoice over her, O heaven, you saints and apostles and prophets! For God has given judgment for you against her."

A Reading (Lesson) from the Gospel according to Matthew [15:21–28]

Jesus left that place and went away to the district of Tyre and Sidon. Just then a Canaanite woman from that region came out and started shouting, "Have mercy on me, Lord, Son of David; my daughter is tormented by a demon." But he did not answer her at all. And his disciples came and urged him, saying, "Send her away, for she keeps shouting after us." He answered, "I was sent only to the lost sheep of the house of Israel." But she came and knelt before him, saying, "Lord, help me." He answered, "It is not fair to take the children's food and throw it to the dogs." She said, "Yes, Lord, yet even the dogs eat the crumbs that fall from their masters' table." Then Jesus answered her, "Woman, great is your faith! Let it be done for you as you wish." And her daughter was healed instantly.

Wednesday

Psalm 119:97–120 [page 771]   ❖   *Psalm 81* [page 704],
Psalm 82 [page 705]

A Reading (Lesson) from the Book of
Nehemiah [7:73b—8:3,5–18]

When the seventh month came—the people of Israel being settled in their towns—all the people gathered together into the square before the Water Gate. They told the scribe Ezra to bring the book of the law of Moses, which the LORD had given to Israel. Accordingly, the priest Ezra brought the law before the assembly, both men and women and all who could hear with understanding. This was on the first day of the seventh month. He read from it facing the square before the Water Gate from early morning until midday, in the presence of the men and the women and those who could understand; and the ears of all the people were attentive to the book of the law. And Ezra opened the book in the sight of all the people, for he was standing above all the people; and when he opened it, all the people stood up. Then Ezra blessed the LORD, the great God, and all the people answered, "Amen, Amen," lifting up their hands. Then they bowed their heads and worshiped the LORD with their faces to the ground. Also Jeshua, Bani, Sherebiah, Jamin, Akkub, Shabbethai, Hodiah, Maaseiah, Kelita, Azariah, Jozabad,

Hanan, Pelaiah, the Levites, helped the people to understand the law, while the people remained in their places. So they read from the book, from the law of God, with interpretation. They gave the sense, so that the people understood the reading. And Nehemiah, who was the governor, and Ezra the priest and scribe, and the Levites who taught the people said to all the people, "This day is holy to the LORD your God; do not mourn or weep." For all the people wept when they heard the words of the law. Then he said to them, "Go your way, eat the fat and drink sweet wine and send portions of them to those for whom nothing is prepared, for this day is holy to our LORD; and do not be grieved, for the joy of the LORD is your strength." So the Levites stilled all the people, saying, "Be quiet, for this day is holy; do not be grieved." And all the people went their way to eat and drink and to send portions and to make great rejoicing, because they had understood the words that were declared to them. On the second day the heads of ancestral houses of all the people, with the priests and the Levites, came together to the scribe Ezra in order to study the words of the law. And they found it written in the law, which the LORD had commanded by Moses, that the people of Israel should live in booths during the festival of the seventh month, and that they should publish and proclaim in all their towns and in Jerusalem as follows, "Go out to the hills and bring branches of olive, wild olive, myrtle, palm, and other leafy trees to make booths, as it is written." So the people went out and brought them, and made booths for themselves, each on the roofs of their houses, and in their courts and in the courts of the house of God, and in the square at the Water Gate, and in the square at the Gate of Ephraim. And all the assembly of those who had returned from the captivity made booths and lived in them; for from the days of Jeshua son of Nun to that day the people of

Israel had not done so. And there was very great rejoicing. And day by day, from the first day to the last day, he read from the book of the law of God. They kept the festival seven days; and on the eighth day there was a solemn assembly, according to the ordinance.

A Reading (Lesson) from the Revelation to John [18:21–24]

A mighty angel took up a stone like a great millstone and threw it into the sea, saying, "With such violence Babylon the great city will be thrown down, and will be found no more; and the sound of harpists and minstrels and of flutists and trumpeters will be heard in you no more; and an artisan of any trade will be found in you no more; and the sound of the millstone will be heard in you no more; and the light of a lamp will shine in you no more; and the voice of bridegroom and bride will be heard in you no more; for your merchants were the magnates of the earth, and all nations were deceived by your sorcery. And in you was found the blood of prophets and of saints, and of all who have been slaughtered on earth."

A Reading (Lesson) from the Gospel according to Matthew [15:29–39]

After Jesus had left that place, he passed along the Sea of Galilee, and he went up the mountain, where he sat down. Great crowds came to him, bringing with them the lame, the maimed, the blind, the mute, and many others. They put them at his feet, and he cured them, so that the crowd was amazed when they saw the mute speaking, the maimed whole, the lame walking, and the blind seeing. And they praised the God of Israel. Then Jesus called his disciples to him and said, "I have compassion for the crowd, because they have been with me now for three days and have nothing to eat; and I do not want to send them away hungry, for they might faint on the way." The disciples said to him, "Where are we to get enough bread in the desert to feed so great a crowd?" Jesus asked them, "How many loaves have you?" They said, "Seven, and a few small fish." Then ordering the crowd to sit down on the ground, he took the seven loaves and the fish; and after giving thanks he broke them and gave them to the disciples, and the disciples gave them to the crowds. And all of them ate and were filled; and they took up the broken pieces left over, seven baskets full. Those who had eaten were four thousand men, besides women and children. After sending away the crowds, he got into the boat and went to the region of Magadan.

Thursday

(Psalm 83 [page 706]) or *Psalm 23* [page 612], *Psalm 27* [page 617] ❖ *Psalm 85* [page 708], *Psalm 86* [page 709]

A Reading (Lesson) from the First Book of the Maccabees [1:1–28]

After Alexander son of Philip, the Macedonian, who came from the land of Kittim, had defeated King Darius of the Persians and the Medes, he succeeded him as king. (He had previously become king of Greece.) He fought many battles, conquered strongholds, and put to death the kings of the earth. He advanced to the ends of the earth, and plundered many nations. When the earth became quiet before him, he was exalted, and his heart was lifted up. He gathered a very strong army and ruled over countries, nations, and princes, and they became tributary to him. After this he fell sick and perceived that he was dying. So he summoned his most honored officers, who had been brought up with him from youth, and divided his kingdom among them while he was still alive. And after Alexander had reigned twelve years, he died. Then his officers began to rule, each in his own place. They all put on crowns after his death, and so did their descendants after them for many years; and they caused many evils on the earth. From them came forth a sinful root, Antiochus Epiphanes, son of King Antiochus; he had been a hostage in Rome. He began to reign in the one hundred thirty-seventh year of the kingdom of the Greeks. In those days certain renegades came out from Israel and misled many, saying, "Let us go and make a covenant with the Gentiles around us, for since we separated from them many disasters have come upon us." This proposal pleased them, and some of the people eagerly went to the king, who authorized them to observe the ordinances of the Gentiles. So they built a gymnasium in Jerusalem, according to Gentile custom, and removed the marks of circumcision, and abandoned the holy covenant. They joined with the Gentiles and sold themselves to do evil. When Antiochus saw that his kingdom was established, he determined to become king of the land of Egypt, in order that he might reign over both kingdoms. So he invaded Egypt with a strong force, with chariots and elephants and cavalry and with a large fleet. He engaged King Ptolemy of Egypt in battle, and Ptolemy turned and fled before him, and many were wounded and fell. They captured the fortified cities in the land of Egypt, and he plundered the land of Egypt. After subduing Egypt, Antiochus returned in the one hundred forty-third year. He went up against Israel and came to Jerusalem with a strong force. He arrogantly entered the sanctuary and took the golden altar, the lampstand for the light, and all its utensils. He took also the table for the bread of the Presence, the cups for drink offerings, the bowls, the golden censers, the curtain, the crowns, and the gold decoration on the front of the temple; he stripped it all off. He took the silver and the gold, and the costly vessels; he took also the hidden treasures that he found. Taking them all, he went into his own land. He shed much blood, and spoke with great arrogance. Israel mourned deeply in every community, rulers and elders groaned, young women and young men became faint, the beauty of the women faded. Every bridegroom took up the lament; she who sat in the bridal chamber was mourning. Even the land trembled for its inhabitants, and all the house of Jacob was clothed with shame.

A Reading (Lesson) from the Revelation to John [19:1–10]

After this I heard what seemed to be the loud voice of a great multitude in heaven, saying, "Hallelujah! Salvation and glory and power to our God, for his judgments are true and just; he has judged the great whore who corrupted the earth with her fornication, and he has avenged on her the blood of his servants." Once more they said, "Hallelujah! The smoke goes up from her forever and ever." And the twenty-four elders and the four living creatures fell down and worshiped God who is seated on the throne, saying, "Amen. Hallelujah!" And from the throne came a voice saying, "Praise our God, all you his servants, and all who fear him, small and great." Then I heard what seemed to be the voice of a great multitude, like the sound of many waters and like the sound of mighty thunderpeals, crying out, "Hallelujah! For the Lord our God the Almighty reigns. Let us rejoice and exult and give him the glory, for the marriage of the Lamb has come, and his bride has made herself ready; to her it has been granted to be clothed with fine linen, bright and pure"—for the fine linen is the righteous deeds of the saints. And the angel said to me, "Write this: Blessed are those who are invited to the marriage supper of the Lamb." And he said to me, "These are true words of God." Then I fell down at his feet to worship him, but he said to me, "You must not do that! I am a fellow servant with you and your comrades who hold the testimony of Jesus. Worship God! For the testimony of Jesus is the spirit of prophecy."

A Reading (Lesson) from the Gospel according to Matthew [16:1–12]

The Pharisees and Sadducees came, and to test Jesus they asked him to show them a sign from heaven. He answered them, "When it is evening, you say, 'It will be fair weather, for the sky is red.' And in the morning, 'It will be stormy today, for the sky is red and threatening.' You know how to interpret the appearance of the sky, but you cannot interpret the signs of the times. An evil and adulterous generation asks for a sign, but no sign will be given to it except the sign of Jonah." Then he left them and went away. When the disciples reached the other side, they had forgotten to bring any bread. Jesus said to them, "Watch out, and beware of the yeast of the Pharisees and Sadducees." They said to one another, "It is because we have brought no bread." And becoming aware of it, Jesus said, "You of little faith, why are you talking about having no bread? Do you still not perceive? Do you not remember the five loaves for the five thousand, and how many baskets you gathered? Or the seven loaves for the four thousand, and how many baskets you gathered? How could you fail to perceive that I was not speaking about bread? Beware of the yeast of the Pharisees and Sadducees!" Then they understood that he had not told them to beware of the yeast of bread, but of the teaching of the Pharisees and Sadducees.

Friday

Psalm 88 [page 712]   ❖   *Psalm 91* [page 719],
Psalm 92 [page 720]

A Reading (Lesson) from the First Book of the Maccabees [1:41–63]

The king wrote to his whole kingdom that all should be one people, and that all should give up their particular customs. All the Gentiles accepted the command of the king. Many even from Israel gladly adopted his religion; they sacrificed to idols and profaned the sabbath. And the king sent letters by messengers to Jerusalem and the towns of Judah; he directed them to follow customs strange to the land, to forbid burnt offerings and sacrifices and drink offerings in the sanctuary, to profane sabbaths and festivals, to defile the sanctuary and the priests, to build altars and sacred precincts and shrines for idols, to sacrifice swine and other unclean animals, and to leave their sons uncircumcised. They were to make themselves abominable by everything unclean and profane, so that they would forget the law and change all the ordinances. He added, "And whoever does not obey the command of the king shall die." In such words he wrote to his whole kingdom. He appointed inspectors over all the people and commanded the towns of Judah to offer sacrifice, town by town. Many of the people, everyone who forsook the law, joined them, and they did evil in the land; they drove Israel into hiding in every place of refuge they had. Now on the fifteenth day of Chislev, in the one hundred forty-fifth year, they erected a desolating sacrilege on the altar of burnt offering. They also built altars in the surrounding towns of Judah, and offered incense at the doors of the houses and in the streets. The books of the law that they found they tore to pieces and burned with fire. Anyone found possessing the book of the covenant, or anyone who adhered to the law, was condemned to death by decree of the king. They kept using violence against Israel, against those who were found month after month in the towns. On the twenty-fifth day of the month they offered sacrifice on the altar that was on top of the altar of burnt offering. According to the decree, they put to death the women who had their children circumcised, and their families and those who circumcised them; and they hung the infants from their mothers' necks. But many in Israel stood firm and were resolved in their hearts not to eat unclean food. They chose to die rather than to be defiled by food or to profane the holy covenant; and they did die.

A Reading (Lesson) from the Revelation to John [19:11–16]

I saw heaven opened, and there was a white horse! Its rider is called Faithful and True, and in righteousness he judges and makes war. His eyes are like a flame of fire, and on his head are many diadems; and he has a name inscribed that no one knows but himself. He is clothed in a robe dipped in blood, and his name is called The Word of God. And the armies of heaven, wearing fine linen, white and pure, were following him on white horses. From his mouth comes a sharp sword with which to strike down the nations, and he will rule them with a rod of iron; he will tread the wine press of the fury of the wrath of God the Almighty. On his robe and on his thigh he has a name inscribed, "King of kings and Lord of lords."

*A Reading (Lesson) from the Gospel according to
Matthew* [16:13–20]

When Jesus came into the district of Caesarea Philippi, he
asked his disciples, "Who do people say that the Son of
Man is?" And they said, "Some say John the Baptist, but
others Elijah, and still others Jeremiah or one of the
prophets." He said to them, "But who do you say that I
am?" Simon Peter answered, "You are the Messiah, the
Son of the living God." And Jesus answered him, "Blessed
are you, Simon son of Jonah! For flesh and blood has not
revealed this to you, but my Father in heaven. And I tell
you, you are Peter, and on this rock I will build my
church, and the gates of Hades will not prevail against it. I
will give you the keys of the kingdom of heaven, and
whatever you bind on earth will be bound in heaven, and
whatever you loose on earth will be loosed in heaven."
Then he sternly ordered the disciples not to tell anyone
that he was the Messiah.

Saturday

Psalm 87 [page 711],   *Psalm 90* [page 717]   ❖
Psalm 136 [page 789]

*A Reading (Lesson) from the First Book of the
Maccabees* [2:1–28]

Mattathias son of John son of Simeon, a priest of the family
of Joarib, moved from Jerusalem and settled in Modein. He
had five sons, John surnamed Gaddi, Simon called Thassi,
Judas called Maccabeus, Eleazar called Avaran, and
Jonathan called Apphus. He saw the blasphemies being
committed in Judah and Jerusalem, and said, "Alas! Why
was I born to see this, the ruin of my people, the ruin of the
holy city, and to live there when it was given over to the

enemy, the sanctuary given over to aliens? Her temple has become like a person without honor; her glorious vessels have been carried into exile. Her infants have been killed in her streets, her youths by the sword of the foe. What nation has not inherited her palaces and has not seized her spoils? All her adornment has been taken away; no longer free, she has become a slave. And see, our holy place, our beauty, and our glory have been laid waste; the Gentiles have profaned them. Why should we live any longer?" Then Mattathias and his sons tore their clothes, put on sackcloth, and mourned greatly. The king's officers who were enforcing the apostasy came to the town of Modein to make them offer sacrifice. Many from Israel came to them; and Mattathias and his sons were assembled. Then the king's officers spoke to Mattathias as follows: "You are a leader, honored and great in this town, and supported by sons and brothers. Now be the first to come and do what the king commands, as all the Gentiles and the people of Judah and those that are left in Jerusalem have done. Then you and your sons will be numbered among the Friends of the king, and you and your sons will be honored with silver and gold and many gifts." But Mattathias answered and said in a loud voice: "Even if all the nations that live under the rule of the king obey him, and have chosen to obey his commandments, everyone of them abandoning the religion of their ancestors, I and my sons and my brothers will continue to live by the covenant of our ancestors. Far be it from us to desert the law and the ordinances. We will not obey the king's words by turning aside from our religion to the right hand or to the left." When he had finished speaking these words, a Jew came forward in the sight of all to offer sacrifice on the altar in Modein, according to the king's command. When Mattathias saw it, he burned with zeal and his heart was stirred. He gave vent to righteous anger; he ran and killed him on the altar. At the same time he killed the king's officer who was forcing them to sacrifice, and he tore down the altar. Thus he burned with zeal for the law, just as Phinehas did against Zimri son of Salu. Then Mattathias cried out in the town with a loud voice, saying: "Let every one who is zealous for the law and supports the covenant come out with me!" Then he and his sons fled to the hills and left all that they had in the town.

A Reading (Lesson) from the Revelation to John [20:1–6]

Then I saw an angel coming down from heaven, holding in his hand the key to the bottomless pit and a great chain. He seized the dragon, that ancient serpent, who is the Devil and Satan, and bound him for a thousand years, and threw him into the pit, and locked and sealed it over him, so that he would deceive the nations no more, until the thousand years were ended. After that he must be let out for a little while. Then I saw thrones, and those seated on them were given authority to judge. I also saw the souls of those who had been beheaded for their testimony to Jesus and for the word of God. They had not worshiped the beast or its image and had not received its mark on their foreheads or their hands. They came to life and reigned with Christ a thousand years. (The rest of the dead did not come to life until the thousand years were ended.) This is the first resurrection. Blessed and holy are those who share in the first resurrection. Over these the second death has no power, but they will be priests of God and of Christ, and they will reign with him a thousand years.

A Reading (Lesson) from the Gospel according to Matthew [16:21-28]

From that time on, Jesus began to show his disciples that he must go to Jerusalem and undergo great suffering at the hands of the elders and chief priests and scribes, and be killed, and on the third day be raised. And Peter took him aside and began to rebuke him, saying, "God forbid it, Lord! This must never happen to you." But he turned and said to Peter, "Get behind me, Satan! You are a stumbling block to me; for you are setting your mind not on divine things but on human things." Then Jesus told his disciples, "If any want to become my followers, let them deny themselves and take up their cross and follow me. For those who want to save their life will lose it, and those who lose their life for my sake will find it. For what will it profit them if they gain the whole world but forfeit their life? Or what will they give in return for their life? For the Son of Man is to come with his angels in the glory of his Father, and then he will repay everyone for what has been done. Truly I tell you, there are some standing here who will not taste death before they see the Son of Man coming in his kingdom."

Proper 28 *Week of the Sunday closest to November 16*

Sunday

Psalm 66 [page 673], *Psalm 67* [page 675] ❖
Psalm 19 [page 606], *Psalm 46* [page 649]

A Reading (Lesson) from the First Book of the Maccabees [2:29–43,49–50]

At that time many who were seeking righteousness and justice went down to the wilderness to live there, they, their sons, their wives, and their livestock, because troubles pressed heavily upon them. And it was reported to the king's officers, and to the troops in Jerusalem the city of David, that those who had rejected the king's command had gone down to the hiding places in the wilderness. Many pursued them, and overtook them; they encamped opposite them and prepared for battle against them on the sabbath day. They said to them, "Enough of this! Come out and do what the king commands, and you will live." But they said, "We will not come out, nor will we do what the king commands and so profane the sabbath day." Then the enemy quickly attacked them. But they did not answer them or hurl a stone at them or block up their hiding places, for they said, "Let us all die in our innocence; heaven and earth testify for us that you are killing us unjustly." So they attacked them on the sabbath, and they died, with their wives and children and livestock, to the number of a thousand persons. When Mattathias and his friends learned of it, they mourned for them deeply. And all said to their neighbors: "If we all do as our kindred have done and refuse to fight with the Gentiles for our lives and for our ordinances, they will quickly destroy us from the earth." So they made this decision that day: "Let us fight against anyone who comes to attack us on the sabbath day; let us not all die as our kindred died in their hiding places." Then there united with them a company of Hasideans, mighty warriors of Israel, all who offered themselves willingly for the law. And all who became fugitives to escape their troubles joined them and reinforced them. Now the days drew near for Mattathias to die, and he said to his sons: "Arrogance and scorn have now become strong; it is a time of ruin and furious anger. Now, my children, show zeal for the law, and give your lives for the covenant of our ancestors."

A Reading (Lesson) from the Acts of the Apostles [28:14b–23]

We came to Rome. The believers from there, when they heard of us, came as far as the Forum of Appius and Three Taverns to meet us. On seeing them, Paul thanked God and took courage. When we came into Rome, Paul was allowed to live by himself, with the soldier who was guarding him. Three days later he called together the local leaders of the Jews. When they had assembled, he said to them, "Brothers, though I had done nothing against our people or the customs of our ancestors, yet I was arrested in Jerusalem and handed over to the Romans. When they had examined me, the Romans wanted to release me, because there was no reason for the death penalty in my case. But when the Jews objected, I was compelled to appeal to the emperor—even though I had no charge to bring against my nation. For this reason therefore I have asked to see you and speak with you, since it is for the sake of the hope of Israel that I am bound with this chain." They replied, "We have received no letters from Judea about you, and none of the brothers coming here has reported or spoken anything evil about you. But we would like to hear from you what you think, for with regard to this sect we know that everywhere it is spoken against." After they had set a day to meet with him, they came to him at his lodgings in great numbers. From morning until evening he explained the matter to them, testifying to the kingdom of God and trying to convince them about Jesus both from the law of Moses and from the prophets.

A Reading (Lesson) from the Gospel according to Luke [16:1–13]

Jesus said to the disciples, "There was a rich man who had a manager, and charges were brought to him that this man was squandering his property. So he summoned him and said to him, 'What is this that I hear about you? Give me an accounting of your management, because you cannot be my manager any longer.' Then the manager said to himself, 'What will I do, now that my master is taking the position away from me? I am not strong enough to dig, and I am ashamed to beg. I have decided what to do so that, when I am dismissed as manager, people may welcome me into their homes.' So, summoning his master's debtors one by one, he asked the first, 'How much do you owe my master?' He answered, 'A hundred jugs of olive oil.' He said to him, 'Take your bill, sit down quickly, and make it fifty.' Then he asked another, 'And how much do you owe?' He replied, 'A hundred containers of wheat.' He said to him, 'Take your bill and make it eighty.' And his master commended the dishonest manager because he had acted shrewdly; for the children of this age are more shrewd in dealing with their own generation than are the children of light. And I tell you, make friends for yourselves by means of dishonest wealth so that when it is gone, they may welcome you into the eternal homes. Whoever is faithful in a very little is faithful also in much; and whoever is dishonest in a very little is dishonest also in much. If then you have not been faithful with the dishonest wealth, who will entrust to you the true riches? And if you have not been faithful with what belongs to another, who will give you what is your own? No slave can serve two masters; for a slave will either hate the one and love the other, or be devoted to the one and despise the other. You cannot serve God and wealth."

Monday

Psalm 89:1–18 [page 713] ❖ *Psalm 89:19–52* [page 715]

A Reading (Lesson) from the First Book of Maccabees [3:1–24]

Then Mattathias' son Judas, who was called Maccabeus, took command in his place. All his brothers and all who had joined his father helped him; they gladly fought for Israel. He extended the glory of his people. Like a giant he put on his breastplate; he bound on his armor of war and waged battles, protecting the camp by his sword. He was like a lion in his deeds, like a lion's cub roaring for prey. He searched out and pursued those who broke the law; he burned those who troubled his people. Lawbreakers shrank back for fear of him; all the evildoers were confounded; and deliverance prospered by his hand. He embittered many kings, but he made Jacob glad by his deeds, and his memory is blessed forever. He went through the cities of Judah; he destroyed the ungodly out of the land; thus he turned away wrath from Israel. He was renowned to the ends of the earth; he gathered in those who were perishing. Apollonius now gathered together Gentiles and a large force from Samaria to fight against Israel. When Judas learned of it, he went out to meet him, and he defeated and killed him. Many were wounded and fell, and the rest fled. Then they seized their spoils; and Judas took the sword of Apollonius, and used it in battle the rest of his life. When Seron, the commander of the Syrian army, heard that Judas had gathered a large company, including a body of faithful soldiers who stayed with him and went out to battle, he said, "I will make a name for myself and win honor in the kingdom. I will make war on Judas and his companions, who scorn the king's command." Once again a strong army of godless men went up with him to help him, to take vengeance on the Israelites. When he approached the ascent of Beth-horon, Judas went out to meet him with a small company. But when they saw the army coming to meet them, they said to Judas, "How can we, few as we are, fight against so great and so strong a multitude? And we are faint, for we have eaten nothing today." Judas replied, "It is easy for many to be hemmed in by few, for in the sight of Heaven there is no difference between saving by many or by few. It is not on the size of the army that victory in battle depends, but strength comes from Heaven. They come against us in great insolence and lawlessness to destroy us and our wives and our children, and to despoil us; but we fight for our lives and our laws. He himself will crush them before us; as for you, do not be afraid of them." When he finished speaking, he rushed suddenly against Seron and his army, and they were crushed before him. They pursued them down the descent of Beth-horon to the plain; eight hundred of them fell, and the rest fled into the land of the Philistines.

A Reading (Lesson) from the Revelation to John [20:7–15]

When the thousand years are ended, Satan will be released from his prison and will come out to deceive the nations at the four corners of the earth, Gog and Magog, in order to gather them for battle; they are as numerous as the sands of the sea. They marched up over the breadth of the earth and surrounded the camp of the saints and the beloved city. And fire came down from heaven and consumed them. And the devil who had deceived them was thrown into the lake of fire and sulfur, where the beast and the false prophet were, and they will be tormented day and night forever and ever. Then I saw a great white throne and the one who sat on it; the earth and the heaven fled from his presence, and no place was found for them. And I saw the dead, great and small, standing before the throne, and books were opened. Also another book was opened, the book of life. And the dead were judged according to their works, as recorded in the books. And the sea gave up the dead that were in it, Death and Hades gave up the dead that were in them, and all were judged according to what they had done. Then Death and Hades were thrown into the lake of fire. This is the second death, the lake of fire; and anyone whose name was not found written in the book of life was thrown into the lake of fire.

A Reading (Lesson) from the Gospel according to Matthew [17:1–13]

Six days later, Jesus took with him Peter and James and his brother John and led them up a high mountain, by themselves. And he was transfigured before them, and his face shone like the sun, and his clothes became dazzling white. Suddenly there appeared to them Moses and Elijah, talking with him. Then Peter said to Jesus, "Lord, it is good for us to be here; if you wish. I will make three dwellings here, one for you, one for Moses, and one for Elijah." While he was still speaking, suddenly a bright cloud overshadowed them, and from the cloud a voice said, "This is my Son, the Beloved; with him I am well pleased; listen to him!" When the disciples heard this, they fell to the ground and were overcome by fear. But Jesus came and touched them, saying, "Get up and do not be afraid." And when they looked up, they saw no one except Jesus himself alone. As they were coming down the mountain, Jesus ordered them, "Tell no one about the vision until after the Son of Man has been raised from the dead." And the disciples asked him, "Why, then, do the scribes say that Elijah must come first?" He replied, "Elijah is indeed coming and will restore all things; but I tell you that Elijah has already come, and they did not recognize him, but they did to him whatever they pleased. So also the Son of Man is about to suffer at their hands." Then the disciples understood that he was speaking to them about John the Baptist.

Tuesday

Psalm 97 [page 726], *Psalm 99* [page 728],
(Psalm 100 [page 729]) ❖ *Psalm 94* [page 722],
(Psalm 95 [page 724])

A Reading (Lesson) from the First Book of the Maccabees [3:25–41]

Judas and his brothers began to be feared, and terror fell on the Gentiles all around them. His fame reached the king, and the Gentiles talked of the battles of Judas. When King Antiochus heard these reports, he was greatly angered; and he sent and gathered all the forces of his kingdom, a very strong army. He opened his coffers and gave a year's pay to his forces, and ordered them to be ready for any need. Then he saw that the money in the treasury was exhausted, and that the revenues from the country were small because of the dissension and disaster that he had caused in the land by abolishing the laws that had existed from the earliest days. He feared that he might not have such funds as he had before for his expenses and for the gifts that he used to give more lavishly than preceding kings. He was greatly perplexed in mind; then he determined to go to Persia and collect the revenues from those regions and raise a large fund. He left Lysias, a distinguished man of royal lineage, in charge of the king's affairs from the river Euphrates to the borders of Egypt. Lysias was also to take care of his son Antiochus until he returned. And he turned over to Lysias half of his forces and the elephants, and gave him orders about all that he wanted done. As for the residents of Judea and Jerusalem, Lysias was to send a force against them to wipe out and destroy the strength of Israel and the remnant of Jerusalem; he was to banish the memory of them from the place, settle aliens in all their territory, and distribute their land by lot. Then the king took the remaining half of his forces and left Antioch his capital in the one hundred and forty-seventh year. He crossed the Euphrates river and went through the upper provinces. Lysias chose Ptolemy son of Dorymenes, and Nicanor and Gorgias, able men among the Friends of the king, and sent with them forty thousand infantry and seven thousand cavalry to go into the land of Judah and destroy it, as the king had commanded. So they set out with their entire force, and when they arrived they encamped near Emmaus in the plain. When the traders of the region heard what was said to them, they took silver and gold in immense amounts, and fetters, and went to the camp to get the Israelites for slaves. And forces from Syria and the land of the Philistines joined with them.

A Reading (Lesson) from the Revelation to John [21:1–8]

Then I saw a new heaven and a new earth; for the first
heaven and the first earth had passed away, and the sea
was no more. And I saw the holy city, the new Jerusalem,
coming down out of heaven from God, prepared as a
bride adorned for her husband. And I heard a loud voice
from the throne saying, "See, the home of God is among
mortals. He will dwell with them as their God; they will
be his peoples, and God himself will be with them; he will
wipe every tear from their eyes. Death will be no more;
mourning and crying and pain will be no more, for the
first things have passed away." And the one who was
seated on the throne said, "See, I am making all things
new." Also he said, "Write this, for these words are
trustworthy and true." Then he said to me, "It is done! I
am the Alpha and the Omega, the beginning and the end.
To the thirsty I will give water as a gift from the spring of
the water of life. Those who conquer will inherit these
things, and I will be their God and they will be my
children. But as for the cowardly, the faithless, the
polluted, the murderers, the fornicators, the sorcerers, the
idolaters, and all liars, their place will be in the lake that
burns with fire and sulfur, which is the second death."

*A Reading (Lesson) from the Gospel according to
Matthew* [17:14–21]

When Jesus, with Peter and James and John his brother,
came to the crowd, a man came to him, knelt before him,
and said, "Lord, have mercy on my son, for he is an
epileptic and he suffers terribly; he often falls into the fire
and often into the water. And I brought him to your
disciples, but they could not cure him." Jesus answered,
"You faithless and perverse generation, how much longer

must I be with you? How much longer must I put up with you? Bring him here to me." And Jesus rebuked the demon, and it came out of him, and the boy was cured instantly. Then the disciples came to Jesus privately and said, "Why could we not cast it out?" He said to them, "Because of your little faith. For truly I tell you, if you have faith, the size of a mustard seed, you will say to this mountain, 'Move from here to there,' and it will move; and nothing will be impossible for you."

Wednesday

Psalm 101 [page 730],
Psalm 109:1–4(5–19)20–30 [page 750] ❖
Psalm 119:121–144 [page 773]

A Reading (Lesson) from the First Book of the Maccabees [3:42–60]

Judas and his brothers saw that misfortunes had increased and that the forces were encamped in their territory. They also learned what the king had commanded to do to the people to cause their final destruction. But they said to one another, "Let us restore the ruins of our people, and fight for our people and the sanctuary." So the congregation assembled to be ready for battle, and to pray and ask for mercy and compassion. Jerusalem was uninhabited like a wilderness; not one of her children went in or out. The sanctuary was trampled down, and aliens held the citadel; it was a lodging place for the Gentiles. Joy was taken from Jacob; the flute and the harp ceased to play. Then they gathered together and went to Mizpah, opposite Jerusalem, because Israel formerly had a place of prayer in Mizpah. They fasted that day, put on sackcloth and sprinkled ashes on their heads, and tore their clothes. And they opened the book of the law to inquire into those matters about which the Gentiles consulted the likenesses of their gods. They also brought the vestments of the priesthood and the first fruits and the tithes, and they stirred up the nazirites who had completed their days; and they cried aloud to Heaven, saying, "What shall we do with these? Where shall we take them? Your sanctuary is trampled down and profaned, and your priests mourn in humiliation. Here the Gentiles are assembled against us to destroy us; you know what they plot against us. How will we be able to withstand them, if you do not help us?" Then they sounded the trumpets and gave a loud shout. After this Judas appointed leaders of the people, in charge of thousands and hundreds and fifties and tens. Those who were building houses, or were about to be married, or were planting a vineyard, or were fainthearted, he told to go home again, according to the law. Then the army marched out and encamped to the south of Emmaus. And Judas said, "Arm yourselves and be courageous. Be ready early in the morning to fight with these Gentiles who have assembled against us to destroy us and our sanctuary. It is better for us to die in battle than to see the misfortunes of our nation and of the sanctuary. But as his will in heaven may be, so shall he do."

A Reading (Lesson) from the Revelation to John [21:9–21]

Then one of the seven angels who had the seven bowls full of the seven last plagues came and said to me, "Come, I will show you the bride, the wife of the Lamb." And in the spirit he carried me away to a great, high mountain and showed me the holy city Jerusalem coming down out of heaven from God. It has the glory of God and a radiance like a very rare jewel, like jasper, clear as crystal.

It has a great, high wall with twelve gates, and at the gates twelve angels, and on the gates are inscribed the names of the twelve tribes of the Israelites; on the east three gates, on the north three gates, on the south three gates, and on the west three gates. And the wall of the city has twelve foundations, and on them are the twelve names of the twelve apostles of the Lamb. The angel who talked to me had a measuring rod of gold to measure the city and its gates and walls. The city lies foursquare, its length the same as its width; and he measured the city with his rod, fifteen hundred miles; its length and width and height are equal. He also measured its wall, one hundred forty-four cubits by human measurement, which the angel was using. The wall is built of jasper, while the city is pure gold, clear as glass. The foundations of the wall of the city are adorned with every jewel; the first was jasper, the second sapphire, the third agate, the fourth emerald, the fifth onyx, the sixth carnelian, the seventh chrysolite, the eighth beryl, the ninth topaz, the tenth chrysoprase, the eleventh jacinth, the twelfth amethyst. And the twelve gates are twelve pearls, each of the gates is a single pearl, and the street of the city is pure gold, transparent as glass.

A Reading (Lesson) from the Gospel according to Matthew [17:22–27]

As they were gathering in Galilee, Jesus said to the disciples, "The Son of Man is going to be betrayed into human hands, and they will kill him, and on the third day he will be raised." And they were greatly distressed. When they reached Capernaum, the collectors of the temple tax came to Peter and said, "Does your teacher not pay the temple tax?" He said, "Yes, he does." And when he came home, Jesus spoke of it first, asking, "What do you think,

Simon? From whom do kings of the earth take toll or tribute? From their children or from others?" When Peter said, "From others," Jesus said to him, "Then the children are free. However, so that we do not give offense to them, go to the sea and cast a hook; take the first fish that comes up; and when you open its mouth, you will find a coin; take that and give it to them for you and me."

Thursday

Psalm 105:1–22 [page 738]   ❖   *Psalm 105:23–45* [page 739]

A Reading (Lesson) from the First Book of the Maccabees [4:1–25]

Gorgias took five thousand infantry and one thousand picked cavalry, and this division moved out by night to fall upon the camp of the Jews and attack them suddenly. Men from the citadel were his guides. But Judas heard of it, and he and his warriors moved out to attack the king's force in Emmaus while the division was still absent from the camp. When Gorgias entered the camp of Judas by night, he found no one there, so he looked for them in the hills, because he said, "These men are running away from us." At daybreak Judas appeared in the plain with three thousand men, but they did not have armor and swords such as they desired. And they saw the camp of the Gentiles, strong and fortified, with cavalry all around it; and these men were trained in war. But Judas said to those who were with him, "Do not fear their numbers or be afraid when they charge. Remember how our ancestors were saved at the Red Sea, when Pharaoh with his forces pursued them. And now, let us cry to Heaven, to see whether he will favor us and remember his covenant with our ancestors and crush this army before us today. Then all the Gentiles will know that there is one who redeems and saves Israel." When the foreigners looked up and saw them coming against them, they went out from their camp to battle. Then the men with Judas blew their trumpets and engaged in battle. The Gentiles were crushed, and fled into the plain, and all those in the rear fell by the sword. They pursued them to Gazara, and to the plains of Idumea, and to Azotus and Jamnia; and three thousand of them fell. Then Judas and his force turned back from pursuing them, and he said to the people, "Do not be greedy for plunder, for there is a battle before us; Gorgias and his force are near us in the hills. But stand now against our enemies and fight them, and afterward seize the plunder boldly." Just as Judas was finishing this speech, a detachment appeared, coming out of the hills. They saw that their army had been put to flight, and that the Jews were burning the camp, for the smoke that was seen showed what had happened. When they perceived this, they were greatly frightened, and when they also saw the army of Judas drawn up in the plain for battle, they all fled into the land of the Philistines. Then Judas returned to plunder the camp, and they seized a great amount of gold and silver, and cloth dyed blue and sea purple, and great riches. On their return they sang hymns and praises to Heaven—"For he is good, for his mercy endures forever." Thus Israel had a great deliverance that day.

A Reading (Lesson) from the Revelation to John [21:22—22:5]

I saw no temple in the city, for its temple is the Lord God the Almighty and the Lamb. And the city has no need of sun or moon to shine on it, for the glory of God is its light, and its lamp is the Lamb. The nations will walk by its light, and the kings of the earth will bring their glory into it. Its gates will never be shut by day—and there will be no night there. People will bring into it the glory and the honor of the nations. But nothing unclean will enter it, nor anyone who practices abomination or falsehood, but only those who are written in the Lamb's book of life. Then the angel showed me the river of the water of life, bright as crystal, flowing from the throne of God and of the Lamb through the middle of the street of the city. On either side of the river, is the tree of life with its twelve kinds of fruit, producing its fruit each month; and the leaves of the trees are for the healing of the nations. Nothing accursed will be found there any more. But the throne of God and of the Lamb will be in it, and his servants will worship him; they will see his face, and his name will be on their foreheads. And there will be no more night; they need no light of lamp or sun, for the Lord God will be their light, and they will reign forever and ever.

A Reading (Lesson) from the Gospel according to Matthew [18:1–9]

At that time the disciples came to Jesus and asked, "Who is the greatest in the kingdom of heaven?" He called a child, whom he put among them, and said, "Truly I tell you, unless you change and become like children, you will never enter the kingdom of heaven. Whoever becomes humble like this child is the greatest in the kingdom of heaven. Whoever welcomes one such child in my name welcomes me. If any of you put a stumbling block before one of these little ones who believe in me, it would be better for you if a great millstone were fastened around your neck and you were drowned in the depth of the sea.

Woe to the world because of stumbling blocks! Occasions for stumbling are bound to come, but woe to the one by whom the stumbling block comes! If your hand or your foot causes you to stumble, cut it off and throw it away; it is better for you to enter life maimed or lame than to have two hands or two feet and to be thrown into the eternal fire. And if your eye causes you to stumble, tear it out and throw it away; it is better for you to enter life with one eye than to have two eyes and to be thrown into the hell of fire."

Friday

Psalm 102 [page 731] ❖ *Psalm 107:1–32* [page 746]

A Reading (Lesson) from the First Book of the Maccabees [4:36–59]

Judas and his brothers said, "See, our enemies are crushed; let us go up to cleanse the sanctuary and dedicate it." So all the army assembled and went up to Mount Zion. There they saw the sanctuary desolate, the altar profaned, and the gates burned. In the courts they saw bushes sprung up as in a thicket, or as on one of the mountains. They saw also the chambers of the priests in ruins. Then they tore their clothes and mourned with great lamentation; they sprinkled themselves with ashes and fell face down on the ground. And when the signal was given with the trumpets, they cried out to Heaven. Then Judas detailed men to fight against those in the citadel until he had cleansed the sanctuary. He chose blameless priests devoted to the law, and they cleansed the sanctuary and removed the defiled stones to an unclean place. They deliberated what to do about the altar of burnt offering, which had been profaned. And they thought it best to tear it down, so that it would not be a lasting shame to them that the Gentiles had defiled it. So they tore down the altar, and stored the stones in a convenient place on the temple hill until a prophet should come to tell what to do with them. Then they took unhewn stones, as the law directs, and built a new altar like the former one. They also rebuilt the sanctuary and the interior of the temple, and consecrated the courts. They made new holy vessels, and brought the lampstand, the altar of incense, and the table into the temple. Then they offered incense on the altar and lit the lamps on the lampstand, and these gave light in the temple. They placed the bread on the table and hung up the curtains. Thus they finished all the work they had undertaken. Early in the morning on the twenty-fifth day of the ninth month, which is the month of Chislev, in the one hundred forty-eighth year, they rose and offered sacrifice, as the law directs, on the new altar of burnt offering that they had built. At the very season and on the very day that the Gentiles had profaned it, it was dedicated with songs and harps and lutes and cymbals. All the people fell on their faces and worshiped and blessed Heaven, who had prospered them. So they celebrated the dedication of the altar for eight days, and joyfully offered burnt offerings; they offered a sacrifice of well-being and a thanksgiving offering. They decorated the front of the temple with golden crowns and small shields; they restored the gates and the chambers for the priests, and fitted them with doors. There was very great joy among the people, and the disgrace brought by the Gentiles was removed. Then Judas and his brothers and all the assembly of Israel determined that every year at that season the days of dedication of the altar should be observed with joy and gladness for eight days, beginning with the twenty-fifth day of the month of Chislev.

A Reading (Lesson) from the Revelation to John [22:6–13]

The angel said to me, "These words are trustworthy and true, for the Lord, the God of the spirits of the prophets, has sent his angel to show his servants what must soon take place." "See, I am coming soon! Blessed is the one who keeps the words of the prophecy of this book." I, John, am the one who heard and saw these things. And when I heard and saw them, I fell down to worship at the feet of the angel who showed them to me; but he said to me, "You must not do that! I am a fellow servant with you and your comrades the prophets, and with those who keep the words of this book. Worship God!" And he said to me, "Do not seal up the words of the prophecy of this book, for the time is near. Let the evildoer still do evil, and the filthy still be filthy, and the righteous still do right, and the holy still be holy." "See, I am coming soon; my reward is with me, to repay according to everyone's work. I am the Alpha and the Omega, the first and the last, the beginning and the end."

A Reading (Lesson) from the Gospel according to Matthew [18:10–20]

Calling to him a child, Jesus put him in the midst of the disciples, and said, "Take care that you do not despise one of these little ones; for, I tell you, in heaven their angels continually see the face of my Father in heaven. What do you think? If a shepherd has a hundred sheep, and one of them has gone astray, does he not leave the ninety-nine on the mountains and go in search of the one that went astray? And if he finds it, truly I tell you, he rejoices over it more than over the ninety-nine that never went astray. So it is not the will of your Father in heaven that one of these little ones should be lost. If another member of the church sins against you, go and point out the fault when the two of you are alone. If the member listens to you, you have regained that one. But if you are not listened to, take one or two others along with you, so that every word may be confirmed by the evidence of two or three witnesses. If the member refuses to listen to them, tell it to the church; and if the offender refuses to listen even to the church, let such a one be to you as a Gentile and a tax collector. Truly I tell you, whatever you bind on earth will be bound in heaven, and whatever you loose on earth will be loosed in heaven. Again, truly I tell you, if two of you agree on earth about anything you ask, it will be done for you by my Father in heaven. For where two or three are gathered in my name, I am there among them."

Saturday

Psalm 107:33–43 [page 748],
Psalm 108:1–6(7–13) [page 749] ❖ *Psalm 33* [page 626]

Isaiah 65:17–25 [page 578 above]

A Reading (Lesson) from the Revelation to John [22:14–21]

Blessed are those who wash their robes, so that they will have the right to the tree of life and may enter the city by the gates. Outside are the dogs and sorcerers and fornicators and murderers and idolaters, and everyone who loves and practices falsehood. "It is I, Jesus, who sent my angel to you with this testimony for the churches. I am the root and the descendant of David, the bright morning star." The Spirit and the bride say, "Come." And let everyone who hears say, "Come." And let everyone who is thirsty come. Let anyone who wishes take the water of life as a gift. I warn everyone who hears the words of the prophecy of this book: if anyone adds to them, God will add to that person the plagues described in this book; if anyone takes away from the words of the book of this prophecy, God will take away that person's share in the tree of life and in the holy city, which are described in this book. The one who testifies to these things says, "Surely I am coming soon." Amen. Come, Lord Jesus! The grace of the Lord Jesus be with all the saints. Amen.

A Reading (Lesson) from the Gospel according to Matthew [18:21–35]

Peter came and said to Jesus, "Lord, if another member of the church sins against me, how often should I forgive? As many as seven times?" Jesus said to him, "Not seven times, but, I tell you, seventy-seven times. For this reason the kingdom of heaven may be compared to a king who wished to settle accounts with his slaves. When he began the reckoning, one who owed him ten thousand talents was brought to him; and, as he could not pay, his lord ordered him to be sold, together with his wife and children and all his possessions, and payment to be made. So the slave fell on his knees before him, saying, 'Have patience with me, and I will pay you everything.' And out of pity for him, the lord of that slave released him and forgave him the debt. But that same slave, as he went out, came upon one of his fellow slaves who owed him a hundred denarii; and seizing him by the throat, he said, 'Pay what you owe.' Then his fellow slave fell down and pleaded with him, 'Have patience with me, and I will pay you.' But he refused; then he went and threw him into prison until he would pay the debt. When his fellow slaves saw what had happened, they were greatly distressed, and they went and reported to their lord all that had taken place. Then his lord summoned him and said to him, 'You wicked slave! I forgave you all that debt because you pleaded with me. Should you not have had mercy on your fellow slave, as I had mercy on you?' And in anger his lord handed him over to be tortured until he would pay his entire debt. So my heavenly Father will also do to every one of you, if you do not forgive your brother or sister from your heart."

Proper 29 *Week of the Sunday closest to November 23*

Sunday

Psalm 118 [page 760] ❖ *Psalm 145* [page 801]

A Reading (Lesson) from the Book of Isaiah [19:19–25]

On that day there will be an altar to the LORD in the center of the land of Egypt, and a pillar to the LORD at its border. It will be a sign and a witness to the LORD of hosts in the land of Egypt; when they cry to the LORD because of oppressors, he will send them a savior, and will defend and deliver them. The LORD will make himself known to the Egyptians; and the Egyptians will know the LORD on that day, and will worship with sacrifice and burnt offering, and they will make vows to the LORD and perform them. The LORD will strike Egypt, striking and healing; they will return to the LORD, and he will listen to their supplications and heal them. On that day there will be a highway from Egypt to Assyria, and the Assyrian will come into Egypt, and the Egyptian into Assyria, and the Egyptians will worship with the Assyrians. On that day Israel will be the third with

Egypt and Assyria, a blessing in the midst of the earth, whom the LORD of hosts has blessed, saying, "Blessed be Egypt my people, and Assyria the work of my hands, and Israel my heritage."

A Reading (Lesson) from the Letter of Paul to the Romans [15:5–13]

May the God of steadfastness and encouragement grant you to live in harmony with one another, in accordance with Christ Jesus, so that together you may with one voice glorify the God and Father of our Lord Jesus Christ. Welcome one another, therefore, just as Christ has welcomed you, for the glory of God. For I tell you that Christ has become a servant of the circumcised on behalf of the truth of God in order that he might confirm the promises given to the patriarchs, and in order that the Gentiles might glorify God for his mercy. As it is written, "Therefore I will confess you among the Gentiles, and sing praises to your name"; and again he says, "Rejoice, O Gentiles, with his people"; and again, "Praise the Lord, all you Gentiles, and let all the peoples praise him"; and again Isaiah says, "The root of Jesse shall come, the one who rises to rule the Gentiles; in him the Gentiles shall hope." May the God of hope fill you with all joy and peace in believing, so that you may abound in hope by the power of the Holy Spirit.

Luke 19:11–27 [page 660 above]

Monday

Psalm 106:1–18 [page 741] ❖ *Psalm 106:19–48* [page 743]

A Reading (Lesson) from the Book of Joel [3:1-2,9-17]

The Lord answered and said to his people, "Then, in those days and at that time, when I restore the fortunes of Judah and Jerusalem, I will gather all the nations and bring them down to the valley of Jehoshaphat, and I will enter into judgment with them there, on account of my people and my heritage Israel, because they have scattered them among the nations. They have divided my land. Proclaim this among the nations: Prepare war, stir up the warriors. Let all the soldiers draw near, let them come up. Beat your plowshares into swords, and your pruning hooks into spears; let the weakling say, "I am a warrior." Come quickly, all you nations all around, gather yourselves there. Bring down your warriors, O LORD. Let the nations rouse themselves, and come up to the valley of Jehoshaphat; for there I will sit to judge all the neighboring nations. Put in the sickle, for the harvest is ripe. Go in, tread, for the wine press is full. The vats overflow, for their wickedness is great. Multitudes, multitudes, in the valley of decision! For the day of the LORD is near in the valley of decision. The sun and the moon are darkened, and the stars withdraw their shining. The LORD roars from Zion, and utters his voice from Jerusalem, and the heavens and the earth shake. But the LORD is a refuge for his people, a stronghold for the people of Israel. So you shall know that I, the LORD your God, dwell in Zion, my holy mountain. And Jerusalem shall be holy, and strangers shall never again pass through it.

A Reading (Lesson) from the First Letter of Peter [1:1-12]

Peter, an apostle of Jesus Christ, to the exiles of the Dispersion in Pontus, Galatia, Cappadocia, Asia, and Bithynia, who have been chosen and destined by God the Father and sanctified by the Spirit to be obedient to Jesus

Christ and to be sprinkled with his blood: May grace and peace be yours in abundance. Blessed be the God and Father of our Lord Jesus Christ! By his great mercy he has given us a new birth into a living hope through the resurrection of Jesus Christ from the dead, and into an inheritance that is imperishable, undefiled, and unfading, kept in heaven for you, who are being protected by the power of God through faith for a salvation ready to be revealed in the last time. In this you rejoice, even if now for a little while you have had to suffer various trials, so that the genuineness of your faith—being more precious than gold that, though perishable, is tested by fire—may be found to result in praise and glory and honor when Jesus Christ is revealed. Although you have not seen him, you love him; and even though you do not see him now, you believe in him and rejoice with an indescribable and glorious joy, for you are receiving the outcome of your faith, the salvation of your souls. Concerning this salvation, the prophets who prophesied of the grace that was to be yours made careful search and inquiry, inquiring about the person or time that the Spirit of Christ within them indicated when it testified in advance to the sufferings destined for Christ and the subsequent glory. It was revealed to them that they were serving not themselves but you, in regard to the things that have now been announced to you through those who brought you good news by the Holy Spirit sent from heaven—things into which angels long to look!

A Reading (Lesson) from the Gospel according to Matthew [19:1–12]

When Jesus had finished saying these things, he left Galilee and went to the region of Judea beyond the Jordan. Large crowds followed him, and he cured them there. Some Pharisees came to him, and to test him they asked, "Is it lawful for a man to divorce his wife for any cause?" He answered, "Have you not read that the one who made them at the beginning 'made them male and female,' and said, 'For this reason a man shall leave his father and mother and be joined to his wife, and the two shall become one flesh'? So they are no longer two, but one flesh. Therefore what God has joined together, let no one separate." They said to him, "Why then did Moses command us to give a certificate of dismissal and to divorce her?" He said to them, "It was because you were so hard-hearted that Moses allowed you to divorce your wives, but from the beginning it was not so. And I say to you, whoever divorces his wife, except for unchastity, and marries another commits adultery." His disciples said to him, "If such is the case of a man with his wife, it is better not to marry." But he said to them, "Not everyone can accept this teaching, but only those to whom it is given. For there are eunuchs who have been so from birth, and there are eunuchs who have been made eunuchs by others, and there are eunuchs who have made themselves eunuchs for the sake of the kingdom of heaven. Let anyone accept this who can."

Tuesday

(Psalm 120 [page 778]),   Psalm 121 [page 779],
Psalm 122 [page 779],   Psalm 123 [page 780]   ❖
Psalm 124 [page 781],   Psalm 125 [page 781],
Psalm 126 [page 782],   (Psalm 127 [page 782])

A Reading (Lesson) from the Book of Nahum [1:1–13]

An oracle concerning Nineveh. The book of the vision of
Nahum of Elkosh. A jealous and avenging God is the LORD,
the LORD is avenging and wrathful; the LORD takes
vengeance on his adversaries and rages against his enemies.
The LORD is slow to anger but great in power, and the
LORD will by no means clear the guilty. His way is in
whirlwind and storm, and the clouds are the dust of his feet.
He rebukes the sea and makes it dry, and he dries up all the
rivers; Bashan and Carmel wither, and the bloom of
Lebanon fades. The mountains quake before him, and the
hills melt; the earth heaves before him, the world and all
who live in it. Who can stand before his indignation? Who
can endure the heat of his anger? His wrath is poured out
like fire, and by him the rocks are broken in pieces. The
LORD is good, a stronghold in a day of trouble; he protects
those who take refuge in him, even in a rushing flood. He
will make a full end of his adversaries, and will pursue his
enemies into darkness. Why do you plot against the LORD?
He will make an end; no adversary will rise up twice. Like
thorns they are entangled, like drunkards they are drunk;
they are consumed like dry straw. From you one has gone
out who plots evil against the LORD, who counsels
wickedness. Thus says the LORD, "Though they are at full
strength and many, they will be cut off and pass away.
Though I have afflicted you, I will afflict you no more. And
now I will break off his yoke from you and snap the bonds
that bind you."

A Reading (Lesson) from the First Letter of Peter [1:13–25]

Therefore prepare your minds for action; discipline
yourselves; set all your hope on the grace that Jesus Christ
will bring you when he is revealed. Like obedient children,

do not be conformed to the desires that you formerly had in ignorance. Instead, as he who called you is holy, be holy yourselves in all your conduct; for it is written, "You shall be holy, for I am holy." If you invoke as Father the one who judges all people impartially according to their deeds, live in reverent fear during the time of your exile. You know that you were ransomed from the futile ways inherited from your ancestors, not with perishable things like silver or gold, but with the precious blood of Christ, like that of a lamb without defect or blemish. He was destined before the foundation of the world, but was revealed at the end of the ages for your sake. Through him you have come to trust in God, who raised him from the dead and gave him glory, so that your faith and hope are set on God. Now that you have purified your souls by your obedience to the truth so that you have genuine mutual love, love one another deeply from the heart. You have been born anew, not of perishable but of imperishable seed, through the living and enduring word of God. For "All flesh is like grass and all its glory like the flower of grass. The grass withers, and the flower falls, but the word of the Lord endures forever." That word is the good news that was announced to you.

A Reading (Lesson) from the Gospel according to Matthew [19:13–22]

Then little children were being brought to Jesus in order that he might lay his hands on them and pray. The disciples spoke sternly to those who brought them; but Jesus said, "Let the little children come to me, and do not stop them; for it is to such as these that the kingdom of heaven belongs." And he laid his hands on them and went on his way. Then someone came to him and said,

"Teacher, what good deed must I do to have eternal life?" And he said to him, "Why do you ask me about what is good? There is only one who is good. If you wish to enter into life, keep the commandments." He said to him, "Which ones?" And Jesus said, "You shall not murder; You shall not commit adultery; You shall not steal; You shall not bear false witness; Honor your father and mother; also, You shall love your neighbor as yourself." The young man said to him, "I have kept all these; what do I still lack?" Jesus said to him, "If you wish to be perfect, go, sell your possessions, and give the money to the poor, and you will have treasure in heaven; then come, follow me." When the young man heard this word, he went away grieving, for he had many possessions.

Wednesday

Psalm 119:145–176 [page 775]   ❖   *Psalm 128* [page 783], *Psalm 129* [page 784],   *Psalm 130* [page 784]

A Reading (Lesson) from the Book of Obadiah [15–21]

The day of the LORD is near against all the nations. As you have done, it shall be done to you; your deeds shall return on your own head. For as you have drunk on my holy mountain, all the nations around you shall drink; they shall drink and gulp down, and shall be as though they had never been. But on Mount Zion there shall be those that escape, and it shall be holy; and the house of Jacob shall take possession of those who dispossessed them. The house of Jacob shall be a fire, the house of Joseph a flame, and the house of Esau stubble; they shall burn them and consume them, and there shall be no survivor of the house of Esau; for the LORD has spoken. Those of the Negeb shall possess

Mount Esau, and those of the Shephelah the land of the Philistines; they shall possess the land of Ephraim and the land of Samaria, and Benjamin shall possess Gilead. The exiles of the Israelites who are in Halah shall possess Phoenicia as far as Zarephath; and the exiles of Jerusalem who are in Sepharad shall possess the towns of the Negeb. Those who have been saved shall go up to Mount Zion to rule Mount Esau; and the kingdom shall be the LORD's.

A Reading (Lesson) from the First Letter of Peter [2:1–10]

Rid yourselves of all malice, and all guile, insincerity, envy, and all slander. Like newborn infants, long for the pure, spiritual milk, so that by it you may grow into salvation—if indeed you have tasted that the Lord is good. Come to him, a living stone, though rejected by mortals yet chosen and precious in God's sight, and like living stones, let yourselves be built into a spiritual house, to be a holy priesthood, to offer spiritual sacrifices acceptable to God through Jesus Christ. For it stands in scripture: "See, I am laying in Zion a stone, a cornerstone chosen and precious; and whoever believes in him will not be put to shame." To you then who believe, he is precious; but for those who do not believe, "The stone that the builders rejected has become the very head of the corner," and "A stone that makes them stumble and a rock that makes them fall." They stumble because they disobey the word, as they were destined to do. But you are a chosen race; a royal priesthood, a holy nation, God's own people, in order that you may proclaim the mighty acts of him who called you out of darkness into his marvelous light. Once you were not a people, but now you are God's people; once you had not received mercy, but now you have received mercy.

Mathhew 19:23–30 [page 693 above]

Thursday

Psalm 131 [page 785],   *Psalm 132* [page 785],
(Psalm 133 [page 787])   ❖   *Psalm 134* [page 787],
Psalm 135 [page 788]

A Reading (Lesson) from the Book of Zephaniah [3:1–13]

Ah, soiled, defiled, oppressing city! It has listened to no
voice; it has accepted no correction. It has not trusted in the
Lord; it has not drawn near to its God. The officials within
it are roaring lions; its judges are evening wolves that leave
nothing until the morning. Its prophets are reckless, faithless
persons; its priests have profaned what is sacred, they have
done violence to the law. The Lord within it is righteous; he
does no wrong. Every morning he renders his judgment,
each dawn without fail; but the unjust knows no shame. I
have cut off nations; their battlements are in ruins; I have
laid waste their streets so that no one walks in them; their
cities have been made desolate, without people, without
inhabitants. I said, "Surely the city will fear me, it will
accept correction; it will not lose sight of all that I have
brought upon it." But they were the more eager to make all
their deeds corrupt. Therefore wait for me, says the Lord,
for the day when I arise as a witness. For my decision is to
gather nations, to assemble kingdoms, to pour out upon
them my indignation, all the heat of my anger; for in the fire
of my passion all the earth shall be consumed. At that time I
will change the speech of the peoples to a pure speech, that
all of them may call on the name of the Lord and serve him
with one accord. From beyond the rivers of Ethiopia my
suppliants, my scattered ones, shall bring my offering. On

that day you shall not be put to shame because of all the deeds by which you have rebelled against me; for then I will remove from your midst your proudly exultant ones, and you shall no longer be haughty in my holy mountain. For I will leave in the midst of you a people humble and lowly. They shall seek refuge in the name of the LORD—the remnant of Israel; they shall do no wrong and utter no lies, nor shall a deceitful tongue be found in their mouths. Then they will pasture and lie down, and no one shall make them afraid.

A Reading (Lesson) from the First Letter of Peter [2:11–25]

Beloved, I urge you as aliens and exiles to abstain from the desires of the flesh that wage war against the soul. Conduct yourselves honorably among the Gentiles, so that, though they malign you as evildoers, they may see your honorable deeds and glorify God when he comes to judge. For the Lord's sake accept the authority of every human institution, whether of the emperor as supreme, or of governors, as sent by him to punish those who do wrong and to praise those who do right. For it is God's will that by doing right you should silence the ignorance of the foolish. As servants of God, live as free people, yet do not use your freedom as a pretext for evil. Honor everyone. Love the family of believers. Fear God. Honor the emperor. Slaves, accept the authority of your masters with all deference, not only those who are kind and gentle but also those who are harsh. For it is a credit to you if, being aware of God, you endure pain while suffering unjustly. If you endure when you are beaten for doing wrong, what credit is that? But if you endure when you do right and suffer for it, you have God's approval. For to this you have been called, because Christ also suffered for you, leaving you an example, so that you should follow in his steps. "He committed no sin, and no deceit was found in his mouth." When he was abused, he did not return abuse; when he suffered, he did not threaten; but he entrusted himself to the one who judges justly. He himself bore our sins in his body on the cross, so that, free from sins, we might live for righteousness; by his wounds you have been healed. For you were going astray like sheep, but now you have returned to the shepherd and guardian of your souls.

A Reading (Lesson) from the Gospel according to Matthew [20:1–16]

Jesus said to his disciples, "The kingdom of heaven is like a landowner who went out early in the morning to hire laborers for his vineyard. After agreeing with the laborers for the usual daily wage, he sent them into his vineyard. When he went out about nine o'clock, he saw others standing idle in the marketplace; and he said to them, 'You also go into the vineyard, and I will pay you whatever is right.' So they went. When he went out again about noon and about three o'clock, he did the same. And about five o'clock he went out and found others standing around; and he said to them, 'Why are you standing here idle all day?' They said to him, 'Because no one has hired us.' He said to them, 'You also go into the vineyard.' When evening came, the owner of the vineyard said to his manager, 'Call the laborers and give them their pay, beginning with the last and then going to the first.' When those hired about five o'clock came, each of them received the usual daily wage. Now when the first came, they thought they would receive more; but each of them also received the usual daily wage. And when they received it, they grumbled against the landowner, saying, 'These last worked only one hour, and you have made them equal to us who have borne the burden of the day and the scorching heat.' But he replied to one of them, 'Friend, I am doing you no wrong; did you not agree with me for the usual daily wage? Take what belongs to you and go; I choose to give to this last the same as I give to you. Am I not allowed to do what I choose with what belongs to me? Or are you envious because I am generous?' So the last will be first, and the first will be last."

Friday

Psalm 140 [page 796], *Psalm 142* [page 798] ❖
Psalm 141 [page 797], *Psalm 143:1–11(12)* [page 798]

A Reading (Lesson) from the Book of Isaiah [24:14–23]

They lift up their voices, they sing for joy; they shout from the west over the majesty of the LORD. Therefore in the east give glory to the LORD; in the coastlands of the sea glorify the name of the LORD, the God of Israel. From the ends of the earth we hear songs of praise, of glory to the Righteous One. But I say, I pine away, I pine away. Woe is me! For the treacherous deal treacherously, the treacherous deal very treacherously. Terror, and the pit, and the snare are upon you, O inhabitant of the earth! Whoever flees at the sound of the terror shall fall into the pit; and whoever climbs out of the pit shall be caught in the snare. For the windows of heaven are opened, and the foundations of the earth tremble. The earth is utterly broken, the earth is torn asunder, the earth is violently shaken. The earth staggers like a drunkard, it sways like a hut; its transgression lies heavy upon it, and it falls, and will not rise again. On that day the LORD will punish the host of heaven in heaven, and on earth the kings of the earth. They will be gathered together like prisoners in a pit; they will be shut up in a prison, and after many days they will be punished. Then the moon will be abashed, and the sun ashamed; for the LORD of hosts will reign on Mount Zion and in Jerusalem, and before his elders he will manifest his glory.

A Reading (Lesson) from the First Letter of Peter [3:13—4:6]

Who will harm you if you are eager to do what is good? But even if you do suffer for doing what is right, you are blessed. Do not fear what they fear, and do not be intimidated, but in your hearts sanctify Christ as Lord. Always be ready to make your defense to anyone who demands from you an accounting for the hope that is in you; yet do it with gentleness and reverence. Keep your conscience clear, so that, when you are maligned, those who abuse you for your good conduct in Christ may be put to shame. For it is better to suffer for doing good, if suffering should be God's will, than to suffer for doing evil. For Christ also suffered for sins once for all, the righteous for the unrighteous, in order to bring you to God. He was put to death in the flesh, but made alive in the spirit, in which also he went and made a proclamation to the spirits in prison, who in former times did not obey, when God waited patiently in the days of Noah, during the building of the ark, in which a few, that is, eight persons, were saved through water. And baptism, which this prefigured, now saves you—not as a removal of dirt from the body, but as an appeal to God for a good conscience, through the resurrection of Jesus Christ, who has gone into heaven and is at the right hand of God, with angels, authorities, and powers made subject to him. Since therefore Christ suffered in the flesh, arm yourselves also with the same intention (for whoever has suffered in the flesh has finished with sin), so as to live for the rest of your earthly life no longer by human desires but by the will of God. You have already spent enough time in doing what the Gentiles like to do, living in licentiousness, passions, drunkenness, revels, carousing, and lawless idolatry. They are surprised that you no longer join them in the same excesses of dissipation, and so they blaspheme. But they will have to give an accounting to him who stands ready to judge the living and the dead. For this is the reason the gospel was proclaimed even to the dead, so that, though they had been judged in the flesh as everyone is judged, they might live in the spirit as God does.

A Reading (Lesson) from the Gospel according to Matthew [20:17–28]

While Jesus was going up to Jerusalem, he took the twelve disciples aside by themselves, and said to them on the way, "See, we are going up to Jerusalem, and the Son of Man will be handed over to the chief priests and scribes, and they will condemn him to death; then they will hand him over to the Gentiles to be mocked and flogged and crucified; and on the third day he will be raised." Then the mother of the sons of Zebedee came to him with her sons, and kneeling before him, she asked a favor of him. And he said to her, "What do you want?" She said to him, "Declare that these two sons of mine will sit, one at your right hand and one at your left, in your kingdom." But Jesus answered, "You do not know what you are asking. Are you able to drink the cup that I am about to drink?" They said to him, "We are able." He said to them, "You will indeed drink my cup, but to sit at my right hand and at my left, this is not mine to grant, but it is for those for whom it has been prepared by my Father." When the ten heard it, they were angry with the two brothers. But Jesus called them to him and said, "You know that the rulers of the Gentiles lord it over them, and their great ones are tyrants over them. It will not be so among you; but whoever wishes to be great among you must be your servant, and whoever wishes to be first among you must be your slave; just as the Son of Man came not to be served but to serve, and to give his life a ransom for many."

Saturday

Psalm 137:1–6(7–9) [page 792], *Psalm 144* [page 800] ❖
Psalm 104 [page 735]

A Reading (Lesson) from the Book of Micah [7:11–20]

A day for the building of your walls! In that day the boundary shall be far extended. In that day they will come to you from Assyria to Egypt, and from Egypt to the River, from sea to sea and from mountain to mountain. But the earth will be desolate because of its inhabitants, for the fruit of their doings. Shepherd your people with your staff, the flock that belongs to you, which lives alone in a forest in the midst of a garden land; let them feed in Bashan and Gilead as in the days of old. As in the days when you came out of the land of Egypt, show us marvelous things. The nations shall see and be ashamed of all their might; they shall lay their hands on their mouths; their ears shall be deaf; they shall lick dust like a snake, like the crawling things of the earth; they shall come trembling out of their fortresses; they shall turn in dread to the LORD our God, and they shall stand in fear of you. Who is a God like you, pardoning iniquity and passing over the transgression of the remnant of your possession? He does not retain his anger forever, because he delights in showing clemency. He will again have compassion upon us; he will tread our iniquities under foot. You will cast all our sins into the depths of the sea. You will show faithfulness to Jacob and unswerving loyalty to Abraham, as you have sworn to our ancestors from the days of old.

A Reading (Lesson) from the First Letter of Peter [4:7–19]

The end of all things is near; therefore be serious and discipline yourselves for the sake of your prayers. Above all, maintain constant love for one another, for love covers a multitude of sins. Be hospitable to one another without complaining. Like good stewards of the manifold grace of God, serve one another with whatever gift each of you has received. Whoever speaks must do so as one speaking the very words of God; whoever serves must do so with the strength that God supplies, so that God may be glorified in all things through Jesus Christ. To him belong the glory and the power forever and ever. Amen. Beloved, do not be surprised at the fiery ordeal that is taking place among you to test you, as though something strange were happening to you. But rejoice insofar as you are sharing Christ's sufferings, so that you may also be glad and shout for joy when his glory is revealed. If you are reviled for the name of Christ, you are blessed, because the spirit of glory, which is the Spirit of God, is resting on you. But let none of you suffer as a murderer, a thief, a criminal, or even as a mischief maker. Yet if any of you suffers as a Christian, do not consider it a disgrace, but glorify God because you bear this name. For the time has come for judgment to begin with the household of God; if it begins with us, what will be the end for those who do not obey the gospel of God? And "If it is hard for the righteous to be saved, what will become of the ungodly and the sinners?" Therefore, let those suffering in accordance with God's will entrust themselves to a faithful Creator, while continuing to do good.

A Reading (Lesson) from the Gospel according to Matthew [20:29–34]

As Jesus and his disciples were leaving Jericho, a large crowd followed him. There were two blind men sitting by the roadside. When they heard that Jesus was passing by, they shouted, "Lord, have mercy on us, Son of David!" The crowd sternly ordered them to be quiet; but they shouted even more loudly, "Have mercy on us, Lord, Son of David!" Jesus stood still and called them, saying, "What do you want me to do for you?" They said to him, "Lord, let our eyes be opened." Moved with compassion, Jesus touched their eyes. Immediately they regained their sight and followed him.

Holy Days

St. Andrew *November 30*

<u>MORNING PRAYER</u>

Psalm 34 [page 627]

A Reading (Lesson) from the Book of Isaiah [49:1–6]

Listen to me, O coastlands, pay attention, you peoples from far away! The LORD called me before I was born, while I was in my mother's womb he named me. He made my mouth like a sharp sword, in the shadow of his hand he hid me; he made me a polished arrow, in his quiver he hid me away. And he said to me, "You are my servant, Israel, in whom I will be glorified." But I said, "I have labored in vain, I have spent my strength for nothing and vanity; yet surely my cause is with the LORD, and my reward with my God." And now the LORD says, who formed me in the womb to be his servant, to bring Jacob back to him, and that Israel might be gathered to him, for I am honored in the sight of the LORD, and my God has become my strength—he says, "It is too light a thing that you should be my servant to raise up the tribes of Jacob and to restore the survivors of Israel; I will give you as a light to the nations, that my salvation may reach to the end of the earth."

A Reading (Lesson) from the First Letter of Paul to the Corinthians [4:1–16]

Think of us in this way, as servants of Christ and stewards of God's mysteries. Moreover, it is required of stewards that they be found trustworthy. But with me it is a very small thing that I should be judged by you or by any human court. I do not even judge myself. I am not aware of anything against myself, but I am not thereby acquitted. It is the Lord who judges me. Therefore do not pronounce judgment before the time, before the Lord comes, who will bring to light the things now hidden in darkness and will disclose the purposes of the heart. Then each one will receive commendation from God. I have applied all this to Apollos and myself for your benefit, brothers and sisters, so that you may learn through us the meaning of the saying, "Nothing beyond what is written," so that none of you will be puffed up in favor of one against another. For who sees anything different in you? What do you have that you did not receive? And if you received it, why do you boast as if it were not a gift? Already you have all you want! Already you have become rich! Quite apart from us you have become kings! Indeed, I wish that you had become kings, so that we might be kings with you! For I think that God has exhibited us apostles as last of all, as though sentenced to death, because we have become a spectacle to the world, to angels and to mortals. We are fools for the sake of Christ, but you are wise in Christ. We are weak, but you are strong. You are held in honor, but we in disrepute. To the present hour we are hungry and thirsty, we are poorly clothed and beaten and homeless, and we grow weary from the work of our own hands. When reviled, we bless; when persecuted, we endure; when slandered, we speak kindly. We have become like the rubbish of the world, the dregs of all things, to this very day. I am not writing this to make you ashamed, but to admonish you as my beloved children. For though you might have ten thousand guardians in Christ, you do not have many fathers. Indeed, in Christ Jesus I became your father through the gospel. I appeal to you, then, be imitators of me.

Psalm 96 [page 725],   *Psalm 100* [page 729]

A Reading (Lesson) from the Book of Isaiah [55:1–5]

Ho, everyone who thirsts, come to the waters; and you that
have no money, come, buy and eat! Come, buy wine and
milk without money and without price. Why do you spend
your money for that which is not bread, and your labor for
that which does not satisfy? Listen carefully to me, and eat
what is good, and delight yourselves in rich food. Incline
your ear, and come to me; listen, so that you may live. I will
make with you an everlasting covenant, my steadfast, sure
love for David. See, I made him a witness to the peoples, a
leader and commander for the peoples. See, you shall call
nations that you do not know, and nations that do not
know you shall run to you, because of the LORD your God,
the Holy One of Israel, for he has glorified you.

John 1:35–42 [page 293 above]

St. Thomas *December 21*

MORNING PRAYER

Psalm 23 [page 612],   *Psalm 121* [page 779]

A Reading (Lesson) from the Book of Job [42:1–6]

Job answered the LORD: "I know that you can do all things,
and that no purpose of yours can be thwarted. 'Who is this
that hides counsel without knowledge?' Therefore I have
uttered what I did not understand, things too wonderful for
me, which I did not know. 'Hear, and I will speak; I will

question you, and you declare to me.' I had heard of you by the hearing of the ear, but now my eye sees you; therefore I despise myself, and repent in dust and ashes."

A Reading (Lesson) from the First Letter of Peter [1:3–9]

Blessed be the God and Father of our Lord Jesus Christ! By his great mercy he has given us a new birth into a living hope through the resurrection of Jesus Christ from the dead, and into an inheritance that is imperishable, undefiled, and unfading, kept in heaven for you, who are being protected by the power of God through faith for a salvation ready to be revealed in the last time. In this you rejoice, even if now for a little while you have had to suffer various trials, so that the genuineness of your faith— being more precious than gold that, though perishable, is tested by fire—may be found to result in praise and glory and honor when Jesus Christ is revealed. Although you have not seen him, you love him; and even though you do not see him now, you believe in him and rejoice with an indescribable and glorious joy, for you are receiving the outcome of your faith, the salvation of your souls.

EVENING PRAYER

Psalm 27 [page 617]

Isaiah 43:8–13 [page 437 above]

John 14:1–7 [page 438 above]

St. Stephen   *December 26*

MORNING PRAYER

Psalm 28 [page 619],   *Psalm 30* [page 621]

A Reading (Lesson) from the Second Book of Chronicles [24:17–22]

After the death of Jehoiada the officials of Judah came and did obeisance to the king; then the king listened to them. They abandoned the house of the Lord, the God of their ancestors, and served the sacred poles and the idols. And wrath came upon Judah and Jerusalem for this guilt of theirs. Yet he sent prophets among them to bring them back to the Lord; they testified against them, but they would not listen. Then the spirit of God took possession of Zechariah son of the priest Jehoiada; he stood above the people and said to them, "Thus says God: Why do you transgress the commandments of the Lord, so that you cannot prosper? Because you have forsaken the Lord, he has also forsaken you." But they conspired against him, and by command of the king they stoned him to death in the court of the house of the Lord. King Joash did not remember the kindness that Jehoiada, Zechariah's father, had shown him, but killed his son. As he was dying, he said, "May the Lord see and avenge!"

A Reading (Lesson) from the Acts of the Apostles [6:1–7]

During those days, when the disciples were increasing in number, the Hellenists complained against the Hebrews because their widows were being neglected in the daily distribution of food. And the twelve called together the whole community of the disciples and said, "It is not right that we should neglect the word of God in order to wait on tables. Therefore, friends, select from among yourselves seven men of good standing, full of the Spirit and of wisdom, whom we may appoint to this task, while we, for our part, will devote ourselves to prayer and to serving the word." What they said pleased the whole community, and they chose Stephen, a man full of faith and the Holy

Spirit, together with Philip, Prochorus, Nicanor, Timon, Parmenas, and Nicolaus, a proselyte of Antioch. They had these men stand before the apostles, who prayed and laid their hands on them. The word of God continued to spread; the number of the disciples increased greatly in Jerusalem, and a great many of the priests became obedient to the faith.

EVENING PRAYER

Psalm 118 [page 760]

A Reading (Lesson) from the Book of Wisdom [4:7–15]

The righteous, though they die early, will be at rest. For old age is not honored for length of time, or measured by number of years; but understanding is gray hair for anyone, and a blameless life is ripe old age. There were some who pleased God and were loved by him, and while living among sinners were taken up. They were caught up so that evil might not change their understanding or guile deceive their souls. For the fascination of wickedness obscures what is good, and roving desire perverts the innocent mind. Being perfected in a short time, they fulfilled long years; for their souls were pleasing to the Lord, therefore he took them quickly from the midst of wickedness. Yet the peoples saw and did not understand, or take such a thing to heart, that God's grace and mercy are with his elect, and that he watches over his holy ones.

A Reading (Lesson) from the Acts of the Apostles [7:59—8:8]

While they were stoning Stephen, he prayed, "Lord Jesus, receive my spirit." Then he knelt down and cried out in a loud voice, "Lord, do not hold this sin against them." When he had said this, he died. And Saul approved of their killing him. That day a severe persecution began against the church in Jerusalem, and all except the apostles were scattered throughout the countryside of Judea and Samaria. Devout men buried Stephen and made loud lamentation over him. But Saul was ravaging the church by entering house after house; dragging off both men and women, he committed them to prison. Now those who were scattered went from place to place, proclaiming the word. Philip went down to the city of Samaria and proclaimed the Messiah to them. The crowds with one accord listened eagerly to what was said by Philip, hearing and seeing the signs that he did, for unclean spirits, crying with loud shrieks, came out of many who were possessed; and many others who were paralyzed or lame were cured. So there was great joy in that city.

St. John *December 27*

MORNING PRAYER

Psalm 97 [page 726], *Psalm 98* [page 727]

A Reading (Lesson) from the Book of Proverbs [8:22–30]

The LORD created me at the beginning of his work, the first of his acts of long ago. Ages ago I was set up, at the first, before the beginning of the earth. When there were no depths I was brought forth, when there were no springs abounding with water. Before the mountains had been shaped, before the hills, I was brought forth—when he had not yet made earth and fields, or the world's first bits of soil.

When he established the heavens, I was there, when he drew a circle on the face of the deep, when he made firm the skies above, when he established the fountains of the deep, when he assigned to the sea its limit, so that the waters might not transgress his command, when he marked out the foundations of the earth, then I was beside him, like a master worker; and I was daily his delight, rejoicing before him always.

A Reading (Lesson) from the Gospel according to John [13:20–35]

Jesus said to the disciples, "Very truly, I tell you, whoever receives one whom I send receives me; and whoever receives me receives him who sent me." After saying this Jesus was troubled in spirit, and declared, "Very truly, I tell you, one of you will betray me." The disciples looked at one another, uncertain of whom he was speaking. One of his disciples—the one whom Jesus loved—was reclining next to him; Simon Peter therefore motioned to him to ask Jesus of whom he was speaking. So while reclining next to Jesus, he asked him, "Lord, who is it?" Jesus answered, "It is the one to whom I give this piece of bread when I have dipped it in the dish." So when he had dipped the piece of bread, he gave it to Judas son of Simon Iscariot. After he received the piece of bread, Satan entered into him. Jesus said to him, "Do quickly what you are going to do." Now no one at the table knew why he said this to him. Some thought that, because Judas had the common purse, Jesus was telling him, "Buy what we need for the festival"; or, that he should give something to the poor. So, after receiving the piece of bread, he immediately went out. And it was night. When he had gone out, Jesus said, "Now the Son of Man has been glorified, and God has been glorified in him. If God has been glorified in him, God will also glorify him in himself and will glorify him at once. Little children, I am with you only a little longer. You will look for me; and as I said to the Jews so now I say to you, 'Where I am going, you cannot come.' I give you a new commandment, that you love one another. Just as I have loved you, you also should love one another. By this everyone will know that you are my disciples, if you have love for one another."

EVENING PRAYER

Psalm 145 [page 801]

A Reading (Lesson) from the Book of Isaiah [44:1–8]

Thus says the LORD, your Redeemer, the Holy One of Israel: "Now hear, O Jacob my servant, Israel whom I have chosen! Thus says the LORD who made you, who formed you in the womb and will help you: Do not fear, O Jacob my servant, Jeshurun whom I have chosen. For I will pour water on the thirsty land, and streams on the dry ground; I will pour my spirit upon your descendants, and my blessing on your offspring. They shall spring up like a green tamarisk, like willows by flowing streams. This one will say, "I am the LORD's," another will be called by the name of Jacob, yet another will write on the hand, "The LORD's," and adopt the name of Israel. Thus says the LORD, the King of Israel, and his Redeemer, the LORD of hosts: I am the first and I am the last; besides me there is no god. Who is like me? Let them proclaim it, let them declare and set it forth before me. Who has announced from of old the things to come? Let them tell us what is yet to be. Do not fear, or be afraid; have I not told you from of old and declared it? You are my witnesses! Is there any god besides me? There is no other rock; I know not one.

1 John 5:1–12 [page 468 above]

Holy Innocents *December 28*

<u>MORNING PRAYER</u>

Psalm 2 [page 586], *Psalm 26* [page 616]

Isaiah 49:13–23 [page 174 above]

A Reading (Lesson) from the Gospel according to Matthew [18:1–14]

At that time the disciples came to Jesus, saying, "Who is the greatest in the kingdom of heaven?" He called a child, whom he put among them, and said, "Truly I tell you, unless you change and become like children, you will never enter the kingdom of heaven. Whoever becomes humble like this child is the greatest in the kingdom of heaven. Whoever welcomes one such child in my name welcomes me. If any of you put a stumbling block before one of these little ones who believe in me, it would be better for you if a great millstone were fastened around your neck and you were drowned in the depth of the sea. Woe to the world because of stumbling blocks! Occasions for stumbling are bound to come, but woe to the one by whom the stumbling block comes! If your hand or your foot causes you to stumble, cut it off and throw it away; it is better for you to enter life maimed or lame than to have two hands or two feet and to be thrown into the eternal fire. And if your eye causes you to stumble, tear it out and throw it away; it is better for you to enter life with one eye than to have two eyes and to be thrown into the hell of fire. Take care that you do not despise one of these little ones; for, I tell you, in heaven their angels continually see the face of my Father in heaven. What do you think? If a shepherd has a hundred sheep, and one of them has gone astray, does he not leave the ninety-nine on the mountains and go in search of the one that went astray? And if he finds it, truly I tell you, he rejoices over it more than over the ninety-nine that never went astray. So it is not the will of your Father in heaven that one of these little ones should be lost."

EVENING PRAYER

Psalm 19 [page 606], *Psalm 126* [page 782]

A Reading (Lesson) from the Book of Isaiah [54:1–13]

Sing, O barren one who did not bear; burst into song and shout, you who have not been in labor! For the children of the desolate woman will be more than the children of her that is married, says the LORD. Enlarge the site of your tent, and let the curtains of your habitations be stretched out; do not hold back; lengthen your cords and strengthen your stakes. For you will spread out to the right and to the left, and your descendants will possess the nations and will settle the desolate towns. Do not fear, for you will not be ashamed; do not be discouraged, for you will not suffer disgrace; for you will forget the shame of your youth, and the disgrace of your widowhood you will remember no more. For your Maker is your husband, the LORD of hosts is his name; the Holy One of Israel is your Redeemer, the God of the whole earth he is called. For the LORD has called you like a wife forsaken and grieved in spirit, like the wife of a man's youth when she is cast off, says your God. For a brief moment I abandoned you, but with great compassion I will gather you. In overflowing wrath for a moment I hid my face from you, but with everlasting love I will have compassion on you, says the LORD, your Redeemer. This is like the days of Noah to me: Just as I swore that the waters of Noah would never again go over the earth, so I have sworn that I will not be angry with you and will not rebuke you. For the mountains may depart and the hills be removed, but my steadfast love shall not depart from you, and my covenant of peace shall not be removed, says the LORD, who has compassion on you. O afflicted one, storm-tossed, and not comforted, I am about to set your stones in antimony, and lay your foundations with sapphires. I will make your pinnacles of rubies, your gates of jewels, and all your wall of precious stones. All your children shall be taught by the LORD, and great shall be the prosperity of your children.

A Reading (Lesson) from the Gospel according to Mark [10:13–16]

People were bringing little children to Jesus in order that he might touch them; and the disciples spoke sternly to them. But when Jesus saw this, he was indignant and said to them, "Let the little children come to me; do not stop them; for it is to such as these that the kingdom of God belongs. Truly I tell you, whoever does not receive the kingdom of God as a little child will never enter it." And he took them up in his arms, laid his hands on them, and blessed them.

MORNING PRAYER

Psalm 66 [page 673], *Psalm 67* [page 675]

A Reading (Lesson) from the Book of Ezekiel [3:4–11]

He said to me: Mortal, go to the house of Israel and speak my very words to them. For you are not sent to a people of obscure speech and difficult language, but to the house of Israel—not to many peoples of obscure speech and difficult language, whose words you cannot understand. Surely, if I sent you to them, they would listen to you. But the house of Israel will not listen to you, for they are not willing to listen to me; because all the house of Israel have a hard forehead and a stubborn heart. See, I have made your face hard against their faces, and your forehead hard against their foreheads. Like the hardest stone, harder than flint, I have made your forehead; do not fear them or be dismayed at their looks, for they are a rebellious house. He said to me: Mortal, all my words that I shall speak to you receive in your heart and hear with your ears; then go to the exiles, to your people, and speak to them. Say to them, "Thus says the Lord GOD"; whether they hear or refuse to hear.

A Reading (Lesson) from the Acts of the Apostles [10:34–44]

Peter began to speak to them: "I truly understand that God shows no partiality, but in every nation anyone who fears him and does what is right is acceptable to him. You know the message he sent to the people of Israel, preaching peace by Jesus Christ—he is Lord of all. That message spread throughout Judea, beginning in Galilee after the baptism that John announced: how God anointed Jesus of Nazareth with the Holy Spirit and with power; how he went about doing good and healing all who were oppressed by the devil, for God was with him. We are witnesses to all that he did both in Judea and in Jerusalem. They put him to death by hanging him on a tree; but God raised him on the third day and allowed him to appear, not to all the people but to us who were chosen by God as witnesses, and who ate and drank with him after he rose from the dead. He commanded us to preach to the people and to testify that he is the one ordained by God as judge of the living and the dead. All the prophets testify about him that everyone who believes in him receives forgiveness of sins through his name." While Peter was still speaking, the Holy Spirit fell upon all who heard the word.

EVENING PRAYER

Psalm 118 [page 760]

A Reading (Lesson) from the Book of Ezekiel [34:11–16]

Thus says the Lord GOD: I myself will search for my sheep, and will seek them out. As shepherds seek out their flocks when they are among their scattered sheep, so I will seek out my sheep. I will rescue them from all the places to which they have been scattered on a day of clouds and thick darkness. I will bring them out from the peoples and gather them from the countries, and will bring them into their own land; and I will feed them on the mountains of Israel, by the watercourses, and in all the inhabited parts of the land. I will feed them with good pasture, and the mountain heights of Israel shall be their pasture; there they shall lie down in good grazing land, and they shall feed on rich pasture on the mountains of Israel. I myself will be the shepherd of my sheep, and I will make them lie down, says the Lord GOD. I will seek the lost, and I will bring back the strayed, and I will bind up the injured, and I will strengthen the weak, but the fat and the strong I will destroy. I will feed them with justice.

A Reading (Lesson) from the Gospel according to John [21:15–22]

When they had finished breakfast, Jesus said to Simon Peter, "Simon son of John, do you love me more than these?" He said to him, "Yes, Lord; you know that I love you." Jesus said to him, "Feed my lambs." A second time he said to him, "Simon son of John, do you love me?" He said to him, "Yes, Lord; you know that I love you." Jesus said to him, "Tend my sheep." He said to him the third time, "Simon son of John, do you love me?" Peter felt hurt because he said to him the third time, "Do you love me?" And he said to him, "Lord, you know everything; you know that I love you." Jesus said to him, "Feed my sheep. Very truly, I tell you, when you were younger, you used to fasten your own belt and to go wherever you wished. But when you grow old, you will stretch out your hands, and someone else will fasten a belt around you and take you where you do not wish to go." (He said this to indicate the kind of death by which he would glorify God.) After this he said to him, "Follow me." Peter turned and saw the disciple whom Jesus loved following them; he was the one who had reclined next to Jesus at the supper and had said, "Lord, who is it that is going to betray you?" When Peter saw him, he said to Jesus, "Lord, what about him?" Jesus said to him, "If it is my will that he remain until I come, what is that to you? Follow me!"

Conversion of St. Paul *January 25*

Psalm 19 [page 606]

Isaiah 45:18–25 [page 155 above]

A Reading (Lesson) from the Letter of Paul to the Philippians [3:4b–11]

If anyone else has reason to be confident in the flesh, I have more: circumcised on the eighth day, a member of the people of Israel, of the tribe of Benjamin, a Hebrew born of Hebrews; as to the law, a Pharisee; as to zeal, a persecutor of the church; as to righteousness under the law, blameless. Yet whatever gains I had, these I have come to regard as loss because of Christ. More than that, I regard everything as loss because of the surpassing value of knowing Christ Jesus my Lord. For his sake I have suffered the loss of all things, and I regard them as rubbish, in order that I may gain Christ and be found in him, not having a righteousness of my own that comes from the law, but one that comes through faith in Christ, the righteousness from God based on faith. I want to know Christ and the power of his resurrection and the sharing of his sufferings by becoming like him in his death, if somehow I may attain the resurrection from the dead.

Psalm 119:89–112 [page 770]

A Reading (Lesson) from the Book of
Ecclesiasticus [39:1–10]

How different the one who devotes himself to the study of
the law of the Most High! He seeks out the wisdom of all
the ancients, and is concerned with prophecies; he preserves
the sayings of the famous and penetrates the subtleties of
parables; he seeks out the hidden meanings of proverbs and
is at home with the obscurities of parables. He serves among
the great and appears before rulers; he travels in foreign
lands and learns what is good and evil in the human lot. He
sets his heart to rise early to seek the Lord who made him,
and to petition the Most High: he opens his mouth in prayer
and asks pardon for his sins. If the great Lord is willing, he
will be filled with the spirit of understanding; he will pour
forth words of wisdom of his own and give thanks to the
Lord in prayer. The Lord will direct his counsel and
knowledge, as he meditates on his mysteries. He will show
the wisdom of what he has learned, and will glory in the law
of the Lord's covenant. Many will praise his understanding;
it will never be blotted out. His memory will not disappear,
and his name will live through all generations. Nations will
speak of his wisdom, and the congregation will proclaim his
praise.

A Reading (Lesson) from the Acts of the Apostles [9:1–22]

Saul, still breathing threats and murder against the
disciples of the Lord, went to the high priest and asked
him for letters to the synagogues at Damascus, so that if
he found any who belonged to the Way, men or women,
he might bring them bound to Jerusalem. Now as he was
going along and approaching Damascus, suddenly a light
from heaven flashed around him. He fell to the ground
and heard a voice saying to him, "Saul, Saul, why do you

persecute me?" He asked, "Who are you, Lord?" The reply came, "I am Jesus, whom you are persecuting. But get up and enter the city, and you will be told what you are to do." The men who were traveling with him stood speechless because they heard the voice but saw no one. Saul got up from the ground, and though his eyes were open, he could see nothing; so they led him by the hand and brought him into Damascus. For three days he was without sight, and neither ate nor drank. Now there was a disciple in Damascus named Ananias. The Lord said to him in a vision, "Ananias." He answered, "Here I am, Lord." The Lord said to him, "Get up and go to the street called Straight, and at the house of Judas look for a man of Tarsus named Saul. At this moment he is praying, and he has seen in a vision a man named Ananias come in and lay his hands on him so that he might regain his sight." But Ananias answered, "Lord, I have heard from many about this man, how much evil he has done to your saints in Jerusalem; and here he has authority from the chief priests to bind all who invoke your name." But the Lord said to him, "Go, for he is an instrument whom I have chosen to bring my name before Gentiles and kings and before the people of Israel; I myself will show him how much he must suffer for the sake of my name." So Ananias went and entered the house. He laid his hands on Saul and said, "Brother Saul, the Lord Jesus, who appeared to you on your way here, has sent me so that you may regain your sight and be filled with the Holy Spirit." And immediately something like scales fell from his eyes, and his sight was restored. Then he got up and was baptized, and after taking some food, he regained his strength. For several days he was with the disciples in Damascus, and immediately he began to proclaim Jesus in the synagogues, saying, "He is the Son of God." All who heard him were amazed and said, "Is not this the man who made havoc in Jerusalem among those who invoked this name? And has he not come here for the purpose of bringing them bound before the chief priests?" Saul became increasingly more powerful and confounded the Jews who lived in Damascus by proving that Jesus was the Messiah.

Eve of the Presentation   *February 1*

EVENING PRAYER

Psalm 113 [page 756],   *Psalm 122* [page 779]

A Reading (Lesson) from the First Book of Samuel [1:20–28a]

In due time Hannah conceived and bore a son. She named him Samuel, for she said, "I have asked him of the LORD." The man Elkanah and all his household went up to offer to the LORD the yearly sacrifice, and to pay his vow. But Hannah did not go up, for she said to her husband, "As soon as the child is weaned, I will bring him, that he may appear in the presence of the LORD, and remain there forever; I will offer him as a nazirite for all time." Her husband Elkanah said to her, "Do what seems best to you, wait until you have weaned him; only—may the LORD establish his word." So the woman remained and nursed her son, until she weaned him. When she had weaned him, she took him up with her, along with a three-year-old bull, an ephah of flour, and a skin of wine. She brought him to the house of the LORD at Shiloh; and the child was young. Then they slaughtered the bull, and they brought the child to Eli. And she said, "Oh, my lord! As you live, my lord, I am the woman who was standing here in your presence, praying to the LORD. For this child I prayed; and the LORD has granted me the petition that I made to him. Therefore I have lent him to the LORD; as long as he lives, he is given to the LORD."

A Reading (Lesson) from the Letter of Paul to the Romans [8:14–21]

For all who are led by the Spirit of God are children of God. For you did not receive a spirit of slavery to fall back into fear, but you have received a spirit of adoption. When we cry, "Abba! Father!" it is that very Spirit bearing witness with our spirit that we are children of God, and if children, then heirs, heirs of God and joint heirs with Christ—if, in fact, we suffer with him so that we may also be glorified with him. I consider that the sufferings of this present time are not worth comparing with the glory about to be revealed to us. For the creation waits with eager longing for the revealing of the children of God; for the creation was subjected to futility, not of its own will but by the will of the one who subjected it, in hope that the creation itself will be set free from its bondage to decay and will obtain the freedom of the glory of the children of God.

The Presentation *February 2*

MORNING PRAYER

Psalm 42 [page 643],   *Psalm 43* [page 644]

A Reading (Lesson) from the First Book of Samuel [2:1–10]

Elkanah and Hannah worshiped at Shiloh. Hannah also prayed and said, "My heart exults in the LORD; my strength is exalted in my God. My mouth derides my enemies, because I rejoice in my victory. There is no Holy One like the LORD, no one besides you; there is no Rock like our God. Talk no more so very proudly, let not arrogance come from your mouth; for the LORD is a God of knowledge, and by him actions are weighed. The bows of the mighty are broken, but the feeble gird on strength. Those who were full have hired themselves out for bread, but those who were hungry are fat with spoil. The barren has borne seven, but she who has many children is forlorn. The LORD kills and brings to life; he brings down to Sheol and raises up. The LORD makes poor and makes rich; he brings low, he also exalts. He raises up the poor from the dust; he lifts the needy from the ash heap, to make them sit with princes and inherit a seat of honor. For the pillars of the earth are the LORD's, and on them he has set the world. He will guard the feet of his faithful ones, but the wicked shall be cut off in darkness; for not by might does one prevail. The LORD! His adversaries shall be shattered; the Most High will thunder in heaven. The LORD will judge the ends of the earth; he will give strength to his king, and exalt the power of his anointed."

A Reading (Lesson) from the Gospel according to John [8:31–36]

Jesus said to the Jews who had believed in him, "If you continue in my word, you are truly my disciples; and you will know the truth, and the truth will make you free." They answered him, "We are descendants of Abraham and have never been slaves to anyone. What do you mean by

saying, 'You will be made free'?" Jesus answered them,
"Very truly, I tell you, everyone who commits sin is a slave
to sin. The slave does not have a permanent place in the
household; the son has a place there forever. So if the Son
makes you free, you will be free indeed."

EVENING PRAYER

Psalm 48 [page 651], *Psalm 87* [page 711]

A Reading (Lesson) from the Book of Haggai [2:1–9]

In the second year of King Darius, in the seventh month, on
the twenty-first day of the month, the word of the Lord
came by the prophet Haggai, saying: Speak now to
Zerubbabel son of Shealtiel, governor of Judah, and to
Joshua son of Jehozadak, the high priest, and to the
remnant of the people, and say, Who is left among you that
saw this house in its former glory? How does it look to you
now? Is it not in your sight as nothing? Yet now take
courage, O Zerubbabel, says the Lord; take courage, O
Joshua, son of Jehozadak, the high priest; take courage, all
you people of the land, says the Lord; work, for I am with
you, says the Lord of hosts, according to the promise that I
made you when you came out of Egypt. My spirit abides
among you; do not fear. For thus says the Lord of hosts:
Once again, in a little while, I will shake the heavens and the
earth and the sea and the dry land; and I will shake all the
nations, so that the treasure of all nations shall come, and I
will fill this house with splendor, says the Lord of hosts.
The silver is mine, and the gold is mine, says the Lord of
hosts. The latter splendor of this house shall be greater than
the former, says the Lord of hosts; and in this place I will
give prosperity, says the Lord of hosts.

A Reading (Lesson) from the First Letter of John [3:1–8]

See what love the Father has given us, that we should be
called children of God; and that is what we are. The
reason the world does not know us is that it did not know
him. Beloved, we are God's children now; what we will be
has not yet been revealed. What we do know is this: when
he is revealed, we will be like him, for we will see him as
he is. And all who have this hope in him purify
themselves, just as he is pure. Everyone who commits sin
is guilty of lawlessness; sin is lawlessness. You know that
he was revealed to take away sins, and in him there is no
sin. No one who abides in him sins; no one who sins has
either seen him or known him. Little children, let no one
deceive you. Everyone who does what is right is righteous,
just as he is righteous. Everyone who commits sin is a
child of the devil; for the devil has been sinning from the
beginning. The Son of God was revealed for this purpose,
to destroy the works of the devil.

St. Matthias *February 24*

MORNING PRAYER

Psalm 80 [page 702]

A Reading (Lesson) from the First Book of Samuel [16:1–13]

The LORD said to Samuel, "How long will you grieve over
Saul? I have rejected him from being king over Israel. Fill
your horn with oil and set out; I will send you to Jesse the
Bethlehemite, for I have provided for myself a king among
his sons." Samuel said, "How can I go? If Saul hears of it, he
will kill me." And the LORD said, "Take a heifer with you,
and say, 'I have come to sacrifice to the LORD.' Invite Jesse

to the sacrifice, and I will show you what you shall do; and you shall anoint for me the one whom I name to you." Samuel did what the LORD commanded, and came to Bethlehem. The elders of the city came to meet him trembling, and said, "Do you come peaceably?" He said, "Peaceably; I have come to sacrifice to the LORD; sanctify yourselves and come with me to the sacrifice." And he sanctified Jesse and his sons and invited them to the sacrifice. When they came, he looked on Eliab and thought, "Surely the LORD's anointed is now before the LORD." But the LORD said to Samuel, "Do not look on his appearance or on the height of his stature, because I have rejected him; for the LORD does not see as mortals see; they look on the outward appearance, but the LORD looks on the heart." Then Jesse called Abinadab, and made him pass before Samuel. He said, Neither has the LORD chosen this one." Then Jesse made Shammah pass by. And he said, "Neither has the LORD chosen this one." Jesse made seven of his sons pass before Samuel, and Samuel said to Jesse, "The LORD has not chosen any of these." Samuel said to Jesse, "Are all your sons here?" And he said, "There remains yet the youngest, but he is keeping the sheep." And Samuel said to Jesse, "Send and bring him; for we will not sit down until he comes here." He sent and brought him in. Now he was ruddy, and had beautiful eyes, and was handsome. The LORD said, "Rise and anoint him; for this is the one." Then Samuel took the horn of oil, and anointed him in the presence of his brothers; and the spirit of the LORD came mightily upon David from that day forward. Samuel then set out and went to Ramah.

A Reading (Lesson) from the First Letter of John [2:18–25]

Children, it is the last hour! As you have heard that antichrist is coming, so now many antichrists have come. From this we know that it is the last hour. They went out from us, but they did not belong to us; for if they had belonged to us, they would have remained with us. But by going out they made it plain that none of them belongs to us. But you have been anointed by the Holy One, and all of you have knowledge. I write to you, not because you do not know the truth, but because you know it, and you know that no lie comes from the truth. Who is the liar but the one who denies that Jesus is the Christ? This is the antichrist, the one who denies the Father and the Son. No one who denies the Son has the Father; everyone who confesses the Son has the Father also. Let what you heard from the beginning abide in you. If what you heard from the beginning abides in you, then you will abide in the Son and in the Father. And this is what he has promised us, eternal life.

EVENING PRAYER

Psalm 33 [page 626]

A Reading (Lesson) from the First Book of Samuel [12:1–5]

Samuel said to all Israel, "I have listened to you in all that you have said to me, and have set a king over you. See, it is the king who leads you now; I am old and gray, but my sons are with you. I have led you from my youth until this day. Here I am; testify against me before the LORD and before his anointed. Whose ox have I taken? Or whose donkey have I taken? Or whom have I defrauded? Whom have I oppressed? Or from whose hand have I taken a bribe to blind my eyes

with it? Testify against me and I will restore it to you."
They said, "You have not defrauded us or oppressed us or
taken anything from the hand of anyone." He said to them,
"The LORD is witness against you, and his anointed is witness
this day, that you have not found anything in my hand."
And they said, "He is witness."

*A Reading (Lesson) from the Acts of the
Apostles* [20:17–35]

From Miletus Paul sent a message to Ephesus, asking the
elders of the church to meet him. When they came to him,
he said to them: "You yourselves know how I lived among
you the entire time from the first day that I set foot in
Asia, serving the Lord with all humility and with tears,
enduring the trials that came to me through the plots of
the Jews. I did not shrink from doing anything helpful,
proclaiming the message to you and teaching you publicly
and from house to house, as I testified to both Jews and
Greeks about repentance toward God and faith toward
our Lord Jesus. And now, as a captive to the Spirit, I am
on my way to Jerusalem, not knowing what will happen
to me there, except that the Holy Spirit testifies to me in
every city that imprisonment and persecutions are waiting
for me. But I do not count my life of any value to myself,
if only I may finish my course and the ministry that I
received from the Lord Jesus, to testify to the good news
of God's grace. And now I know that none of you, among
whom I have gone about proclaiming the kingdom, will
ever see my face again. Therefore I declare to you this day
that I am not responsible for the blood of any of you, for
I did not shrink from declaring to you the whole purpose
of God. Keep watch over yourselves and over all the flock,
of which the Holy Spirit has made you overseers, to

shepherd the church of God that he obtained with the blood of his own Son. I know that after I have gone, savage wolves will come in among you, not sparing the flock. Some even from your own group will come distorting the truth in order to entice the disciples to follow them. Therefore be alert, remembering that for three years I did not cease night or day to warn everyone with tears. And now I commend you to God and to the message of his grace, a message that is able to build you up and to give you the inheritance among all who are sanctified. I coveted no one's silver or gold or clothing. You know for yourselves that I worked with my own hands to support myself and my companions. In all this I have given you an example that by such work we must support the weak, remembering the words of the Lord Jesus, for he himself said, 'It is more blessed to give than to receive.' "

St. Joseph *March 19*

MORNING PRAYER

Psalm 132 [page 785]

A Reading (Lesson) from the Book of Isaiah [63:7–16]

I will recount the gracious deeds of the LORD, the praiseworthy acts of the LORD, because of all that the LORD has done for us, and the great favor to the house of Israel that he has shown them according to his mercy, according to the abundance of his steadfast love. For he said, "Surely they are my people, children who will not deal falsely"; and he became their savior in all their distress. It was no messenger or angel but his presence that saved them; in his love and in his pity he redeemed them; he lifted them up and carried them all the days of old. But they rebelled and grieved his holy spirit; therefore he became their enemy; he himself fought against them. Then they remembered the days of old, of Moses his servant. Where is the one who brought them up out of the sea with the shepherds of his flock? Where is the one who put within them his holy spirit, who caused his glorious arm to march at the right hand of Moses, who divided the waters before them to make for himself an everlasting name, who led them through the depths? Like a horse in the desert, they did not stumble. Like cattle that go down into the valley, the spirit of the LORD gave them rest. Thus you led your people, to make for yourself a glorious name. Look down from heaven and see, from your holy and glorious habitation. Where are your zeal and your might? The yearning of your heart and your compassion? They are withheld from me. For you are our father, though Abraham does not know us and Israel does not acknowledge us; you, O LORD, are our father; our Redeemer from of old is your name.

Matthew 1:18–25 [page 78 above]

<u>EVENING PRAYER</u>

Psalm 34 [page 627]

A Reading (Lesson) from the Second Book of Chronicles [6:12–17]

Solomon stood before the altar of the LORD in the presence of the whole assembly of Israel, and spread out his hands. Solomon had made a bronze platform five cubits long, five cubits wide, and three cubits high, and had set it in the court; and he stood on it. Then he knelt on his knees in the presence of the whole assembly of Israel, and spread out his hands toward heaven. He said, "O LORD, God of Israel, there is no God like you, in heaven or on earth, keeping covenant in steadfast love with your servants who walk before you with all their heart—you who have kept for your servant, my father David, what you promised to him. Indeed, you promised with your mouth and this day have fulfilled with your hand. Therefore, O LORD, God of Israel, keep for your servant, my father David, that which you promised him, saying, 'There shall never fail you a successor before me to sit on the throne of Israel, if only your children keep to their way, to walk in my law as you have walked before me.' Therefore, O LORD, God of Israel, let your word be confirmed, which you promised to your servant David."

Ephesians 3:14–21 [page 138 above]

Eve of the Annunciation   *March 24*

EVENING PRAYER

Psalm 8 [page 592],   *Psalm 138* [page 793]

A Reading (Lesson) from the Book of Genesis [3:1–15]

The serpent was more crafty than any other wild animal that the LORD God had made. He said to the woman, "Did God say, 'You shall not eat from any tree in the garden'?" The woman said to the serpent, "We may eat of the fruit of the trees in the garden; but God said, 'You shall not eat of the fruit of the tree that is in the middle of the garden, nor shall you touch it, or you shall die.' " But the serpent said to the woman, "You will not die; for God knows that when you eat of it your eyes will be opened, and you will be like

God, knowing good and evil." So when the woman saw that the tree was good for food, and that it was a delight to the eyes, and that the tree was to be desired to make one wise, she took of its fruit and ate; and she also gave some to her husband, who was with her, and he ate. Then the eyes of both were opened, and they knew that they were naked; and they sewed fig leaves together and made loincloths for themselves. They heard the sound of the Lord God walking in the garden at the time of the evening breeze, and the man and his wife hid themselves from the presence of the Lord God among the trees of the garden. But the Lord God called to the man, and said to him, "Where are you?" He said, "I heard the sound of you in the garden, and I was afraid, because I was naked; and I hid myself." He said, "Who told you that you were naked? Have you eaten from the tree of which I commanded you not to eat?" The man said, "The woman whom you gave to be with me, she gave me fruit from the tree, and I ate." Then the Lord God said to the woman, "What is this that you have done?" The woman said, "The serpent tricked me, and I ate." The Lord God said to the serpent, "Because you have done this, cursed are you among all animals and among all wild creatures; upon your belly you shall go, and dust you shall eat all the days of your life. I will put enmity between you and the woman, and between your offspring and hers; he will strike your head, and you will strike his heel."

Romans 5:12–21 [page 345 above]

or this

A Reading (Lesson) from the Letter of Paul to the Galatians [4:1–7]

My point is this: heirs, as long as they are minors, are no better than slaves, though they are the owners of all the property; but they remain under guardians and trustees until the date set by the father. So with us; while we were minors, we were enslaved to the elemental spirits of the world. But when the fullness of time had come, God sent his Son, born of a woman, born under the law, in order to redeem those who were under the law, so that we might receive adoption as children. And because you are children, God has sent the Spirit of his Son into our hearts, crying, "Abba! Father!" So you are no longer a slave but a child, and if a child then also an heir, through God.

The Annunciation   *March 25*

MORNING PRAYER

Psalm 85 [page 708],   *Psalm 87* [page 711]

A Reading (Lesson) from the Book of Isaiah [52:7–12]

How beautiful upon the mountains are the feet of the messenger who announces peace, who brings good news, who announces salvation, who says to Zion, "Your God reigns." Listen! Your sentinels lift up their voices, together they sing for joy; for in plain sight they see the return of the LORD to Zion. Break forth together into singing, you ruins of Jerusalem; for the LORD has comforted his people, he has redeemed Jerusalem. The LORD has bared his holy arm before the eyes of all the nations; and all the ends of the earth shall see the salvation of our God. Depart, depart, go out from there! Touch no unclean thing; go out from the midst of it, purify yourselves, you who carry the vessels of the LORD. For you shall not go out in haste, and you shall not go in flight; for the LORD will go before you, and the God of Israel will be your rear guard.

A Reading (Lesson) from the Letter to the Hebrews [2:5–10]

God did not subject the coming world, about which we are speaking, to angels. But someone has testified somewhere, "What are human beings that you are mindful of them, or mortals, that you care for them? You have made them for a little while lower than the angels; you have crowned them with glory and honor, subjecting all things under their feet." Now in subjecting all things to them, God left nothing outside their control. As it is, we do not yet see everything in subjection to them, but we do see Jesus, who for a little while was made lower than the angels, now crowned with glory and honor because of the suffering of death, so that by the grace of God he might taste death for everyone. It was fitting that God, for whom and through whom all things exist, in bringing many children to glory, should make the pioneer of their salvation perfect through sufferings.

EVENING PRAYER

Psalm 110:1–5(6–7) [page 753], *Psalm 132* [page 785]

A Reading (Lesson) from the Book of Wisdom [9:1–12]

With my whole heart I said: "O God of my ancestors and Lord of mercy, who have made all things by your word, and by your wisdom have formed humankind to have dominion over the creatures you have made, and rule the world in holiness and righteousness, and pronounce judgment in uprightness of soul, give me the wisdom that sits by your throne, and do not reject me from among your servants. For I am your servant the son of your serving girl, a man who is weak and short-lived, with little understanding of judgment and laws, for even one who is perfect among human beings will be regarded as nothing without the wisdom that comes from you. You have chosen me to be king of your people and to be judge over your sons and daughters. You have given command to build a temple on your holy mountain, and an altar in the city of your habitation, a copy of the holy tent that you prepared from the beginning. With you is wisdom, she who knows your works and was present when you made the world; she understands what is pleasing in your sight and what is right according to your commandments. Send her forth from the holy heavens, and from the throne of your glory send her, that she may labor at my side, and that I may learn what is pleasing to you. For she knows and understands all things, and she will guide me wisely in my actions and guard me with her glory. Then my works will be acceptable, and I shall judge your people justly, and shall be worthy of the throne of my father."

A Reading (Lesson) from the Gospel According to John [1:9–14]

The true light, which enlightens everyone, was coming into the world. He was in the world, and the world came into being through him; yet the world did not know him. He came to what was his own, and his own people did not accept him. But to all who received him, who believed in his name, he gave power to become children of God, who were born, not of blood or of the will of the flesh or of the will of man, but of God. And the Word became flesh and lived among us, and we have seen his glory, the glory as of a father's only son, full of grace and truth.

St. Mark *April 25*

MORNING PRAYER

Psalm 145 [page 801]

A Reading (Lesson) from the Book of Ecclesiasticus [2:1–11]

My child, when you come to serve the Lord, prepare yourself for testing. Set your heart right and be steadfast, and do not be impetuous in time of calamity. Cling to him and do not depart, so that your last days may be prosperous. Accept whatever befalls you, and in times of humiliation be patient. For gold is tested in the fire, and those found acceptable, in the furnace of humiliation. Trust in him, and he will help you; make your ways straight, and hope in him. You who fear the Lord, wait for his mercy; do not stray, or else you may fall. You who fear the Lord, trust in him, and your reward will not be lost. You who fear the Lord, hope for good things, for lasting joy and mercy. Consider the generations of old and see: has anyone trusted in the Lord and been disappointed? Or has anyone persevered in the fear of the Lord and been forsaken? Or has anyone called upon him and been neglected? For the Lord is compassionate and merciful; he forgives sins and saves in time of distress.

A Reading (Lesson) from the Acts of the Apostles [12:25—13:3]

After completing their mission Barnabas and Saul returned to Jerusalem and brought with them John, whose other name was Mark. Now in the church at Antioch there were prophets and teachers: Barnabas, Simon who was called Niger, Lucius of Cyrene, Manaen a member of the court of Herod the ruler, and Saul. While they were worshiping the Lord and fasting, the Holy Spirit said, "Set apart for me Barnabas and Saul for the work to which I have called them." Then after fasting and praying they laid their hands on them and sent them off.

EVENING PRAYER

Psalm 67 [page 675],   *Psalm 96* [page 725]

Isaiah 62:6–12 [page 220 above]

A Reading (Lesson) from the Second Letter of Paul to Timothy [4:1–11]

In the presence of God and of Christ Jesus, who is to judge the living and the dead, and in view of his appearing and his kingdom, I solemnly urge you: proclaim the message; be persistent whether the time is favorable or unfavorable; convince, rebuke, and encourage, with the utmost patience in teaching. For the time is coming when people will not put up with sound doctrine, but having itching ears, they will accumulate for themselves teachers to suit their own desires, and will turn away from listening to the truth and wander away to myths. As for you, always be sober, endure suffering, do the work of an evangelist, carry out your ministry fully. As for me, I am already being poured out as a libation, and the time of my departure has come. I have fought the good fight, I have finished the race, I have kept the faith. From now on there is reserved for me the crown of righteousness, which the Lord, the righteous judge, will give me on that day, and not only to me but also to all who have longed for his appearing. Do your best to come to me soon, for Demas, in love with this present world, has deserted me and gone to Thessalonica; Crescens has gone to Galatia, Titus to Dalmatia. Only Luke is with me. Get Mark and bring him with you, for he is useful in my ministry.

St. Philip and St. James   *May 1*

MORNING PRAYER

Psalm 119:137–160 [page 774]

A Reading (Lesson) from the Book of Job [23:1–12]

Job answered Eliphaz the Temanite: "Today also my complaint is bitter; his hand is heavy despite my groaning. Oh, that I knew where I might find him, that I might come even to his dwelling! I would lay my case before him, and fill my mouth with arguments. I would learn what he would answer me, and understand what he would say to me. Would he contend with me in the greatness of his power? No; but he would give heed to me. There an upright person could reason with him, and I should be acquitted forever by my judge. If I go forward, he is not there; or backward, I cannot perceive him; on the left he hides, and I cannot behold him; I turn to the right, but I cannot see him. But he knows the way that I take; when he has tested me, I shall come out like gold. My foot has held fast to his steps; I have kept his way and have not turned aside. I have not departed from the commandment of his lips; I have treasured in my bosom the words of his mouth."

John 1:43–51 [page 295 above]

EVENING PRAYER

Psalm 139 [page 794]

A Reading (Lesson) from the Book of Proverbs [4:7–18]

The beginning of wisdom is this: Get wisdom, and whatever else you get, get insight. Prize her highly, and she will exalt you; she will honor you if you embrace her. She will place on your head a fair garland; she will bestow on you a beautiful crown." Hear, my child, and accept my words, that the years of your life may be many. I have taught you the way of wisdom; I have led you in the paths of uprightness. When you walk, your step will not be hampered; and if you run, you will not stumble. Keep hold of instruction; do not let go; guard her, for she is your life. Do not enter the path of the wicked, and do not walk in the way of evildoers. Avoid it; do not go on it; turn away from it and pass on. For they cannot sleep unless they have done wrong; they are robbed of sleep unless they have made someone stumble. For they eat the bread of wickedness and drink the wine of violence. But the path of the righteous is like the light of dawn, which shines brighter and brighter until full day.

John 12:20–26 [page 404 above]

EVENING PRAYER

Psalm 132 [page 785]

A Reading (Lesson) from the Book of Isaiah [11:1–10]

A shoot shall come out from the stump of Jesse, and a branch shall grow out of his roots. The spirit of the LORD shall rest on him, the spirit of wisdom and understanding, the spirit of counsel and might, the spirit of knowledge and the fear of the LORD. His delight shall be in the fear of the LORD. He shall not judge by what his eyes see, or decide by what his ears hear; but with righteousness he shall judge the poor, and decide with equity for the meek of the earth; he shall strike the earth with the rod of his mouth, and with the breath of his lips he shall kill the wicked. Righteousness shall be the belt around his waist, and faithfulness the belt around his loins. The wolf shall live with the lamb, the leopard shall lie down with the kid, the calf and the lion and the fatling together, and a little child shall lead them. The cow and the bear shall graze, their young shall lie down together; and the lion shall eat straw like the ox. The nursing child shall play over the hole of the asp, and the weaned child shall put its hand on the adder's den. They will not hurt or destroy on all my holy mountain; for the earth will be full of the knowledge of the LORD as the waters cover the sea. On that day the root of Jesse shall stand as a signal to the peoples; the nations shall inquire of him, and his dwelling shall be glorious.

Hebrews 2:11–18 [page 300 above]

MORNING PRAYER

Psalm 72 [page 685]

1 Samuel 1:1–20 [page 672 above]

A Reading (Lesson) from the Letter to the Hebrews [3:1–6]

Therefore, brothers and sisters, holy partners in a heavenly calling, consider that Jesus, the apostle and high priest of our confession, was faithful to the one who appointed him, just as Moses also "was faithful in all God's house." Yet Jesus is worthy of more glory than Moses, just as the builder of a house has more honor than the house itself. (For every house is built by someone, but the builder of all things is God.) Now Moses was faithful in all God's house as a servant, to testify to the things that would be spoken later. Christ, however, was faithful over God's house as a son, and we are his house if we hold firm the confidence and the pride that belong to hope.

EVENING PRAYER

Psalm 146 [page 803],   *Psalm 147* [page 804]

Zechariah 2:10–13 [page 75 above]

A Reading (Lesson) from the Gospel According to John [3:25–30]

A discussion about purification arose between John's disciples and a Jew. They came to John and said to him, "Rabbi, the one who was with you across the Jordan, to whom you testified, here he is baptizing, and all are going to him." John answered, "No one can receive anything except what has been given from heaven. You yourselves are my witnesses that I said, 'I am not the Messiah, but I have been sent ahead of him.' He who has the bride is the bridegroom. The friend of the bridegroom, who stands and hears him, rejoices greatly at the bridegroom's voice. For this reason my joy has been fulfilled. He must increase, but I must decrease."

St. Barnabas *June 11*

MORNING PRAYER

Psalm 15 [page 599], *Psalm 67* [page 675]

A Reading (Lesson) from the Book of Ecclesiasticus [31:3–11]

The rich person toils to amass a fortune, and when he rests he fills himself with his dainties. The poor person toils to make a meager living, and if ever he rests he becomes needy. One who loves gold will not be justified; one who pursues money will be led astray by it. Many have come to ruin because of gold, and their destruction has met them face to face. It is a stumbling block to those who are avid for it, and every fool will be taken captive by it. Blessed is the rich person who is found blameless, and who does not go after gold. Who is he, that we may praise him? For he has done wonders among his people. Who has been tested by it and been found perfect? Let it be for him a ground for boasting. Who has had the power to transgress and did not transgress, and to do evil and did not do it? His prosperity will be established, and the assembly will proclaim his acts of charity.

A Reading (Lesson) from the Acts of the Apostles [4:32–37]

The whole group of those who believed were of one heart and soul, and no one claimed private ownership of any possessions, but everything they owned was held in common. With great power the apostles gave their testimony to the resurrection of the Lord Jesus, and great grace was upon them all. There was not a needy person among them, for as many as owned lands or houses sold them and brought the proceeds of what was sold. They laid it at the apostles' feet, and it was distributed to each as any had need. There was a Levite, a native of Cyprus, Joseph, to whom the apostles gave the name Barnabas (which means "son of encouragement"). He sold a field that belonged to him, then brought the money, and laid it at the apostles' feet.

EVENING PRAYER

Psalm 19 [page 606], *Psalm 146* [page 803]

A Reading (Lesson) from the Book of Job [29:1–16]

Job again took up his discourse, and said: "Oh, that I were as in the months of old, as in the days when God watched over me; when his lamp shone over my head, and by his light I walked through darkness; when I was in my prime, when the friendship of God was upon my tent; when the Almighty was still with me, when my children were around me; when my steps were washed with milk, and the rock poured out for me streams of oil! When I went out to the gate of the city, when I took my seat in the square, the young men saw me and withdrew, and the aged rose up and stood; the nobles refrained from talking, and laid their hands on their mouths; the voices of princes were hushed, and their tongues stuck to the roof of their mouths. When the ear heard, it commended me, and when the eye saw, it approved; because I delivered the poor who cried, and the orphan who had no helper. The blessing of the wretched came upon me, and I caused the widow's heart to sing for joy. I put on righteousness, and it clothed me: my justice was like a robe and a turban. I was eyes to the blind, and feet to the lame. I was a father to the needy, and I championed the cause of the stranger."

A Reading (Lesson) from the Acts of the Apostles [9:26–31]

When Paul had come to Jerusalem he attempted to join the disciples; and they were all afraid of him, for they did not believe that he was a disciple. But Barnabas took him, brought him to the apostles, and described for them how on the road he had seen the Lord, who had spoken to him, and how in Damascus he had spoken boldly in the name of Jesus. So he went in and out among them in Jerusalem, speaking boldly in the name of the Lord. He spoke and argued with the Hellenists; but they were attempting to kill him. When the believers learned of it, they brought him down to Caesarea and sent him off to Tarsus. Meanwhile the church throughout Judea, Galilee, and Samaria had peace and was built up. Living in the fear of the Lord and in the comfort of the Holy Spirit, it increased in numbers.

Eve of St. John the Baptist   *June 23*

EVENING PRAYER

Psalm 103 [page 733]

A Reading (Lesson) from the Book of
Ecclesiasticus [48:1-11]

Then Elijah arose, a prophet like fire, and his word burned like a torch. He brought a famine upon them, and by his zeal he made them few in number. By the word of the Lord he shut up the heavens, and also three times brought down fire. How glorious you were, Elijah, in your wondrous deeds! Whose glory is equal to yours? You raised a corpse from death and from Hades, by the word of the Most High. You sent kings down to destruction, and famous men, from their sickbeds. You heard rebuke at Sinai and judgments of vengeance at Horeb. You anointed kings to inflict retribution, and prophets to succeed you. You were taken up by a whirlwind of fire, in a chariot with horses of fire. At the appointed time, it is written, you are destined to calm the wrath of God before it breaks out in fury, to turn the hearts of parents to their children, and to restore the tribes of Jacob. Happy are those who saw you and were adorned with your love! For we also shall surely live.

A Reading (Lesson) from the Gospel According to
Luke [1:5-23]

In the days of King Herod of Judea, there was a priest named Zechariah, who belonged to the priestly order of Abijah. His wife was a descendant of Aaron, and her name was Elizabeth. Both of them were righteous before God, living blamelessly according to all the commandments and regulations of the Lord. But they had no children, because Elizabeth was barren, and both were getting on in years. Once when he was serving as priest before God and his section was on duty, he was chosen by lot, according to the custom of the priesthood, to enter the sanctuary of the Lord and offer incense. Now at the time of the incense offering, the whole assembly of the people was praying outside. Then there appeared to him an angel of the Lord, standing at the right side of the altar of incense. When Zechariah saw him, he was terrified; and fear overwhelmed him. But the angel said to him, "Do not be afraid, Zechariah, for your prayer has been heard. Your wife Elizabeth will bear you a son, and you will name him John. You will have joy and gladness, and many will rejoice at his birth, for he will be great in the sight of the Lord. He must never drink wine or strong drink; even before his birth he will be filled with the Holy Spirit. He will turn many of the people of Israel to the Lord their God. With the spirit and power of Elijah he will go before him, to turn the hearts of parents to their children, and the disobedient to the wisdom of the righteous, to make ready a people prepared for the Lord." Zechariah said to the angel, "How will I know that this is so? For I am an old man, and my wife is getting on in years." The angel replied, "I am Gabriel. I stand in the presence of God, and I have been sent to speak to you and to bring you this good news. But now, because you did not believe my words, which will be fulfilled in their time, you will become mute, unable to speak, until the day these things occur." Meanwhile the people were waiting for Zechariah, and wondered at his delay in the sanctuary. When he did come out, he could not speak to them, and they realized that he had seen a vision in the sanctuary. He kept motioning to them and remained unable to speak. When his time of service was ended, he went to his home.

Nativity of St. John the Baptist   *June 24*

Psalm 82 [page 705],   *Psalm 98* [page 727]

A Reading (Lesson) from the Book of Malachi [3:1–5]

See, I am sending my messenger to prepare the way before me, and the Lord whom you seek will suddenly come to his temple. The messenger of the covenant in whom you delight—indeed, he is coming, says the LORD of hosts. But who can endure the day of his coming, and who can stand when he appears? For he is like a refiner's fire and like fullers' soap; he will sit as a refiner and purifier of silver, and he will purify the descendants of Levi and refine them like gold and silver, until they present offerings to the LORD in righteousness. Then the offering of Judah and Jerusalem will be pleasing to the LORD as in the days of old and as in former years. Then I will draw near to you for judgment; I will be swift to bear witness against the sorcerers, against the adulterers, against those who swear falsely, against those who oppress the hired workers in their wages, the widow and the orphan, against those who thrust aside the alien, and do not fear me, says the LORD of hosts.

A Reading (Lesson) from the Gospel According to John [3:22–30]

Jesus and his disciples went into the Judean countryside, and he spent some time there with them and baptized. John also was baptizing at Aenon near Salim because water was abundant there; and people kept coming and were being baptized—John, of course, had not yet been thrown into prison. Now a discussion about purification arose between John's disciples and a Jew. They came to John and said to him, "Rabbi, the one who was with you across the Jordan, to whom you testified, here he is baptizing, and all are going to him." John answered, "No one can receive anything except what has been given from heaven. You yourselves are my witnesses that I said, 'I am not the Messiah, but I have been sent ahead of him.' He who has the bride is the bridegroom. The friend of the bridegroom, who stands and hears him, rejoices greatly at the bridegroom's voice. For this reason my joy has been fulfilled. He must increase, but I must decrease."

EVENING PRAYER

Psalm 80 [page 702]

A Reading (Lesson) from the Book of Malachi [4:1–6]

See, the day is coming, burning like an oven, when all the arrogant and all evildoers will be stubble; the day that comes shall burn them up, says the LORD of hosts, so that it will leave them neither root nor branch. But for you who revere my name the sun of righteousness shall rise, with healing in its wings. You shall go out leaping like calves from the stall. And you shall tread down the wicked, for they will be ashes under the soles of your feet, on the day when I act, says the LORD of hosts. Remember the teaching of my servant Moses, the statutes and ordinances that I commanded him at Horeb for all Israel. Lo, I will send you the prophet Elijah before the great and terrible day of the LORD comes. He will turn the hearts of parents to their children and the hearts of children to their parents, so that I will not come and strike the land with a curse.

A Reading (Lesson) from the Gospel According to Matthew [11:2–19]

When John heard in prison what the Messiah was doing, he sent word by his disciples and said to him, "Are you the one who is to come, or are we to wait for another?" Jesus answered them, "Go and tell John what you hear and see: the blind receive their sight, the lame walk, the lepers are cleansed, the deaf hear, the dead are raised, and the poor have good news brought to them. And blessed is anyone who takes no offense at me." As they went away, Jesus began to speak to the crowds about John: "What did you go out into the wilderness to look at? A reed shaken by the wind? What then did you go out to see? Someone dressed in soft robes? Look, those who wear soft robes are in royal palaces. What then did you go out to see? A prophet? Yes, I tell you, and more than a prophet. This is the one about whom it is written, 'See, I am sending my messenger ahead of you, who will prepare your way before you.' Truly I tell you, among those born of women no one has arisen greater than John the Baptist; yet the least in the kingdom of heaven is greater than he. From the days of John the Baptist until now the kingdom of heaven has suffered violence, and the violent take it by force. For all the prophets and the law prophesied until John came; and if you are willing to accept it, he is Elijah who is to come. Let anyone with ears listen! But to what will I compare this generation? It is like children sitting in the marketplaces and calling to one another, 'We played the flute for you, and you did not dance; we wailed, and you did not mourn.' For John came neither eating nor drinking, and they say, 'He has a demon'; the Son of Man came eating and drinking, and they say, 'Look, a glutton and a drunkard, a friend of tax collectors and sinners!' Yet wisdom is vindicated by her deeds."

St. Peter and St. Paul *June 29*

Psalm 66 [page 673]

A Reading (Lesson) from the Book of Ezekiel [2:1–7]

And the Lord said to me, O mortal, stand up on your feet, and I will speak with you. And when he spoke to me, a spirit entered into me and set me on my feet; and I heard him speaking to me. He said to me, Mortal, I am sending you to the people of Israel, to a nation of rebels who have rebelled against me; they and their ancestors have transgressed against me to this very day. The descendants are impudent and stubborn. I am sending you to them, and you shall say to them, "Thus says the Lord God." Whether they hear or refuse to hear (for they are a rebellious house), they shall know that there has been a prophet among them. And you, O mortal, do not be afraid of them, and do not be afraid of their words, though briers and thorns surround you and you live among scorpions; do not be afraid of their words, and do not be dismayed at their looks, for they are a rebellious house. You shall speak my words to them, whether they hear or refuse to hear; for they are a rebellious house.

Acts 11:1–18 [page 757 above]

Psalm 97 [page 726], *Psalm 138* [page 793]

A Reading (Lesson) from the Book of Isaiah [49:1–6]

Listen to me, O coastlands, pay attention, you peoples from far away! The LORD called me before I was born, while I was in my mother's womb he named me. He made my mouth like a sharp sword, in the shadow of his hand he hid me; he made me a polished arrow, in his quiver he hid me away. And he said to me, "You are my servant, Israel, in whom I will be glorified." But I said, "I have labored in vain, I have spent my strength for nothing and vanity; yet surely my cause is with the LORD, and my reward with my God." And now the LORD says, who formed me in the womb to be his servant, to bring Jacob back to him, and that Israel might be gathered to him, for I am honored in the sight of the LORD, and my God has become my strength—he says, "It is too light a thing that you should be my servant to raise up the tribes of Jacob and to restore the survivors of Israel; I will give you as a light to the nations, that my salvation may reach to the end of the earth."

A Reading (Lesson) from the Letter of Paul to the Galatians [2:1–9]

After fourteen years I went up again to Jerusalem with Barnabas, taking Titus along with me. I went up in response to a revelation. Then I laid before them (though only in a private meeting with the acknowledged leaders) the gospel that I proclaim among the Gentiles, in order to make sure that I was not running, or had not run, in vain. But even Titus, who was with me, was not compelled to be circumcised, though he was a Greek. But because of false believers secretly brought in, who slipped in to spy on the freedom we have in Christ Jesus, so that they might enslave us—we did not submit to them even for a moment, so that the truth of the gospel might always remain with you. And from those who were supposed to be acknowledged leaders (what they actually were makes no difference to me; God shows no partiality)—those leaders contributed nothing to me. On the contrary, when they saw that I had been entrusted with the gospel for the uncircumcised, just as Peter had been entrusted with the gospel for the circumcised (for he who worked through Peter making him an apostle to the circumcised also worked through me in sending me to the Gentiles), and when James and Cephas and John, who were acknowledged pillars, recognized the grace that had been given to me, they gave to Barnabas and me the right hand of fellowship, agreeing that we should go to the Gentiles and they to the circumcised.

Independence Day *July 4*

<u>MORNING PRAYER</u>

Psalm 33 [page 626]

A Reading (Lesson) from the Book of Ecclesiasticus [10:1–8,12–18]

A wise magistrate educates his people, and the rule of an intelligent person is well ordered. As the people's judge is, so are his officials; as the ruler of the city is, so are all its inhabitants. An undisciplined king ruins his people, but a city becomes fit to live in through the understanding of its rulers. The government of the earth is in the hand of the Lord, and over it he will raise up the right leader for the time. Human success is in the hand of the Lord, and it is he who confers honor upon the lawgiver. Do not get angry with your neighbor for every injury, and do not resort to acts of insolence. Arrogance is hateful to the Lord and to mortals, and injustice is outrageous to both. Sovereignty passes from nation to nation on account of injustice and insolence and wealth.

A Reading (Lesson) from the Letter of James [5:7–10]

Be patient, therefore, beloved, until the coming of the Lord. The farmer waits for the precious crop from the earth, being patient with it until it receives the early and the late rains. You also must be patient. Strengthen your hearts, for the coming of the Lord is near. Beloved, do not grumble against one another, so that you may not be judged. See, the Judge is standing at the doors! As an example of suffering and patience, beloved, take the prophets who spoke in the name of the Lord.

EVENING PRAYER

Psalm 107:1–32 [page 746]

A Reading (Lesson) from the Book of Micah [4:1–5]

In days to come the mountain of the LORD's house shall be established as the highest of the mountains, and shall be raised up above the hills. Peoples shall stream to it, and many nations shall come and say: "Come, let us go up to the mountain of the LORD, to the house of the God of Jacob; that he may teach us his ways and that we may walk in his paths." For out of Zion shall go forth instruction, and the word of the LORD from Jerusalem. He shall judge between many peoples, and shall arbitrate between strong nations far away; they shall beat their swords into plowshares, and their spears into pruning hooks; nation shall not lift up sword against nation, neither shall they learn war any more;

but they shall all sit under their own vines and under their own fig trees, and no one shall make them afraid; for the mouth of the LORD of hosts has spoken. For all the peoples walk, each in the name of its god, but we will walk in the name of the LORD our God forever and ever.

A Reading (Lesson) from the Revelation to John [21:1–7]

I saw a new heaven and a new earth; for the first heaven and the first earth had passed away, and the sea was no more. And I saw the holy city, the new Jerusalem, coming down out of heaven from God, prepared as a bride adorned for her husband. And I heard a loud voice from the throne saying, "See, the home of God is among mortals. He will dwell with them as their God; they will be his peoples, and God himself will be with them; he will wipe every tear from their eyes. Death will be no more; mourning and crying and pain will be no more, for the first things have passed away." And the one who was seated on the throne said, "See, I am making all things new." Also he said, "Write this, for these words are trustworthy and true." Then he said to me, "It is done! I am the Alpha and the Omega, the beginning and the end. To the thirsty I will give water as a gift from the spring of the water of life. Those who conquer will inherit these things, and I will be their God and they will be my children."

St. Mary Magdalene *July 22*

MORNING PRAYER

Psalm 116 [page 759]

A Reading (Lesson) from the Book of Zephaniah [3:14–20]

Sing aloud, O daughter Zion; shout, O Israel! Rejoice and
exult with all your heart, O daughter Jerusalem! The LORD
has taken away the judgments against you, he has turned
away your enemies. The king of Israel, the LORD, is in your
midst; you shall fear disaster no more. On that day it shall
be said to Jerusalem: Do not fear, O Zion; do not let your
hands grow weak. The LORD, your God, is in your midst, a
warrior who gives victory; he will rejoice over you with
gladness, he will renew you in his love; he will exult over
you with loud singing as on a day of festival. I will remove
disaster from you, so that you will not bear reproach for it. I
will deal with all your oppressors at that time. And I will
save the lame and gather the outcast, and I will change their
shame into praise and renown in all the earth. At that time I
will bring you home, at the time when I gather you; for I
will make you renowned and praised among all the peoples
of the earth, when I restore your fortunes before your eyes,
says the LORD.

*A Reading (Lesson) from the Gospel According to
Mark* [15:47—16:7]

Mary Magdalene and Mary the mother of Joses saw
where the body was laid. When the sabbath was over,
Mary Magdalene, and Mary the mother of James, and
Salome bought spices, so that they might go and anoint
him. And very early on the first day of the week, when the
sun had risen, they went to the tomb. They had been
saying to one another, "Who will roll away the stone for
us from the entrance to the tomb?" When they looked up,
they saw that the stone, which was very large, had already
been rolled back. As they entered the tomb, they saw a
young man, dressed in a white robe, sitting on the right

side; and they were alarmed. But he said to them, "Do not be alarmed; you are looking for Jesus of Nazareth, who was crucified. He has been raised; he is not here. Look, there is the place they laid him. But go, tell his disciples and Peter that he is going ahead of you to Galilee; there you will see him, just as he told you."

EVENING PRAYER

Psalm 30 [page 621], *Psalm 149* [page 807]

A Reading (Lesson) from the Book of Exodus [15:19–21]

When the horses of Pharaoh with his chariots and his chariot drivers went into the sea, the LORD brought back the waters of the sea upon them; but the Israelites walked through the sea on dry ground. Then the prophet Miriam, Aaron's sister, took a tambourine in her hand; and all the women went out after her with tambourines and with dancing. And Miriam sang to them: "Sing to the LORD, for he has triumphed gloriously; horse and rider he has thrown into the sea."

A Reading (Lesson) from the Second Letter of Paul to the Corinthians [1:3–7]

Blessed be the God and Father of our Lord Jesus Christ, the Father of mercies and the God of all consolation, who consoles us in all our affliction, so that we may be able to console those who are in any affliction with the consolation with which we ourselves are consoled by God. For just as the sufferings of Christ are abundant for us, so also our consolation is abundant through Christ. If we are being afflicted, it is for your consolation and salvation; if we are being consoled, it is for your consolation, which you experience when you patiently endure the same sufferings that we are also suffering. Our hope for you is unshaken; for we know that as you share in our sufferings, so also you share in our consolation.

St. James *July 25*

MORNING PRAYER

Psalm 34 [page 627]

A Reading (Lesson) from the Book of Jeremiah [16:14–21]

The days are surely coming, says the Lord, when it shall no longer be said, "As the Lord lives who brought the people of Israel up out of the land of Egypt," but "As the Lord lives who brought the people of Israel up out of the land of the north and out of all the lands where he had driven them." For I will bring them back to their own land that I gave to their ancestors. I am now sending for many fishermen, says the Lord, and they shall catch them; and afterward I will send for many hunters, and they shall hunt them from every mountain and every hill, and out of the clefts of the rocks. For my eyes are on all their ways; they are not hidden from my presence, nor is their iniquity concealed from my sight. And I will doubly repay their iniquity and their sin, because they have polluted my land with the carcasses of their detestable idols, and have filled my inheritance with their abominations. O Lord, my strength and my stronghold, my refuge in the day of trouble, to you shall the nations come from the ends of the earth and say: Our ancestors have inherited nothing but lies, worthless things in which there is no profit. Can mortals make for themselves gods? Such are no gods! "Therefore I am surely going to teach them, this time I am going to teach them my power and my might, and they shall know that my name is the LORD."

A Reading (Lesson) from the Gospel According to Mark [1:14–20]

After John was arrested, Jesus came to Galilee, proclaiming the good news of God, and saying, "The time is fulfilled, and the kingdom of God has come near; repent, and believe in the good news." As Jesus passed along the Sea of Galilee, he saw Simon and his brother Andrew casting a net into the sea—for they were fishermen. And Jesus said to them, "Follow me and I will make you fish for people." And immediately they left their nets and followed him. As he went a little farther, he saw James son of Zebedee and his brother John, who were in their boat mending the nets. Immediately he called them; and they left their father Zebedee in the boat with the hired men, and followed him.

EVENING PRAYER

Psalm 33 [page 626]

A Reading (Lesson) from the Book of Jeremiah [26:1–15]

At the beginning of the reign of King Jehoiakim son of Josiah of Judah, this word came from the LORD: Thus says the LORD: Stand in the court of the LORD's house, and speak to them all the cities of Judah that come to worship in the house of the LORD; speak to them all the words that I command you; do not hold back a word. It may be that they will listen, all of them, and will turn from their evil way, that I may change my mind about the disaster that I intend to bring on them because of their evil doings. You shall say to them: Thus says the LORD: If you will not listen to me, to walk in my law that I have set before you, and to heed the words of my servants the prophets whom I send to you urgently—though you have not heeded—then I will make this house like Shiloh, and I will make this city a curse for all the nations of the earth. The priests and the prophets and all the people heard Jeremiah speaking these words in the house of the LORD. And when Jeremiah had finished speaking all that the LORD had commanded him to speak to all the people, then the priests and the prophets and all the people laid hold of him, saying, "You shall die! Why have you prophesied in the name of the LORD, saying, 'This house shall be like Shiloh, and this city shall be desolate, without inhabitant'?" And all the people gathered around Jeremiah in the house of the LORD. When the officials of Judah heard these things, they came up from the king's house to the house of the LORD and took their seat in the entry of the New Gate of the house of the LORD. Then the priests and the prophets said to the officials and to all the people, "This man deserves the sentence of death because he has prophesied against this city, as you have heard with your own ears." Then Jeremiah spoke to all the officials and all the people, saying, "It is the LORD who sent me to prophesy against this house and this city all the words you have heard. Now therefore amend your ways and your doings, and obey the voice of the LORD your God, and the LORD will change his mind about the disaster that he has pronounced against you. But as for me, here I am in your hands. Do with me as seems good and right to you. Only know for certain that if you put me to death, you will be bringing innocent blood upon yourselves and upon this city and its inhabitants, for in truth the LORD sent me to you to speak all these words in your ears."

A Reading (Lesson) from the Gospel According to Matthew [10:16–32]

Jesus sent out the twelve, charging them, "See, I am sending you out like sheep into the midst of wolves; so be wise as serpents and innocent as doves. Beware of them, for they will hand you over to councils and flog you in their synagogues; and you will be dragged before governors and kings because of me, as a testimony to them and the Gentiles. When they hand you over, do not worry about how you are to speak or what you are to say; for what you are to say will be given to you at that time; for it is not you who speak, but the Spirit of your Father speaking through you. Brother will betray brother to death, and a father his child, and children will rise against parents and have them put to death; and you will be hated by all because of my name. But the one who endures to the end will be saved. When they persecute you in one town, flee to the next; for truly I tell you, you will not have gone through all the towns of Israel before the Son of Man comes. A disciple is not above the teacher, nor a slave above the master; it is enough for the disciple to be like the teacher, and the slave like the master. If they have called the master of the house Beelzebul, how much more will they malign those of his household? So have no fear of them; for nothing is covered up that will not be uncovered, and nothing secret that will not become known. What I say to you in the dark, tell in the light; and what you hear whispered, proclaim from the housetops. Do not fear those who kill the body but cannot kill the soul; rather fear him who can destroy both soul and body in hell. Are not two sparrows sold for a penny? Yet not one of them will fall to the ground apart from your Father. And even the hairs of your head are all counted. So do not be afraid; you are of more value than many sparrows. Everyone therefore who acknowledges me before others, I also will acknowledge before my Father in heaven."

Eve of the Transfiguration *August 5*

EVENING PRAYER

Psalm 84 [page 707]

A Reading (Lesson) from the First Book of the Kings [19:1–12]

Ahab told Jezebel all that Elijah had done, and how he had killed all the prophets with the sword. Then Jezebel sent a messenger to Elijah, saying, "So may the gods do to me, and more also, if I do not make your life like the life of one of them by this time tomorrow." Then he was afraid; he got up and fled for his life, and came to Beersheba, which belongs to Judah; he left his servant there. But he himself went a day's journey into the wilderness, and came and sat down under a solitary broom tree. He asked that he might die: "It is enough; now, O LORD, take away my life, for I am no better than my ancestors." Then he lay down under the broom tree and fell asleep. Suddenly an angel touched him and said to him, "Get up and eat." He looked, and there at his head was a cake baked on hot stones, and a jar of water. He ate and drank, and lay down again. The angel of the LORD came a second time, touched him, and said, "Get up and eat, otherwise the journey will be too much for you." He got up, and ate and drank; then he went in the strength of that food forty days and forty nights to Horeb the mount of God. At that place he came to a cave, and spent the night there. Then the word of the LORD came to him, saying, "What are you doing here, Elijah?" He answered, "I have been very zealous for the LORD, the God of hosts; for the Israelites have forsaken your covenant, thrown down your altars, and killed your prophets with the sword. I alone am left, and they are seeking my life, to take it away." He said, "Go out and stand on the mountain before the LORD, for the LORD is about to pass by." Now there was a great wind, so strong that it was splitting mountains and breaking rocks in pieces before the LORD, but the LORD was not in the wind; and after the wind an earthquake, but the LORD was not in the earthquake; and after the earthquake a fire, but the LORD was not in the fire; and after the fire a sound of sheer silence.

A Reading (Lesson) from the Second Letter of Paul to the Corinthians [3:1–9,18]

Are we beginning to commend ourselves again? Surely we do not need, as some do, letters of recommendation to you or from you, do we? You yourselves are our letter, written on our hearts, to be known and read by all; and you show that you are a letter of Christ, prepared by us, written not with ink but with the Spirit of the living God, not on tablets of stone but on tablets of human hearts. Such is the confidence that we have through Christ toward God. Not that we are competent of ourselves to claim anything as coming from us; our competence is from God, who has made us competent to be ministers of a new covenant, not of letter but of spirit; for the letter kills, but the Spirit gives life. Now if the ministry of death, chiseled in letters on stone tablets, came in glory so that the people of Israel could not gaze at Moses' face because of the glory of his face, a glory now set aside, how much more will the ministry of the Spirit come in glory? For if there was glory in the ministry of condemnation, much more does the ministry of justification abound in glory! And all of us, with unveiled faces, seeing the glory of the Lord as though reflected in a mirror, are being transformed into the same image from one degree of glory to another; for this comes from the Lord, the Spirit.

The Transfiguration *August 6*

MORNING PRAYER

Psalm 2 [page 586], *Psalm 24* [page 613]

A Reading (Lesson) from the Book of Exodus [24:12–18]

The LORD said to Moses, "Come up to me on the mountain, and wait there; and I will give you the tablets of stone, with the law and the commandment, which I have written for their instruction." So Moses set out with his assistant Joshua, and Moses went up into the mountain of God. To the elders he had said, "Wait here for us, until we come to you again; for Aaron and Hur are with you; whoever has a dispute may go to them." Then Moses went up on the mountain, and the cloud covered the mountain. The glory of the LORD settled on Mount Sinai, and the cloud covered it for six days; on the seventh day he called to Moses out of the cloud. Now the appearance of the glory of the LORD was like a devouring fire on the top of the mountain in the sight of the people of Israel. Moses entered the cloud, and went up on the mountain. Moses was on the mountain for forty days and forty nights.

A Reading (Lesson) from the Second Letter of Paul to the Corinthians [4:1–6]

Since it is by God's mercy that we are engaged in this ministry, we do not lose heart. We have renounced the shameful things that one hides; we refuse to practice cunning or to falsify God's word; but by the open statement of the truth we commend ourselves to the conscience of everyone in the sight of God. And even if our gospel is veiled, it is veiled to those who are perishing. In their case the god of this world has blinded the minds of the unbelievers, to keep them from seeing the light of the gospel of the glory of Christ, who is the image of God. For we do not proclaim ourselves; we proclaim Jesus Christ as Lord and ourselves as your slaves for Jesus' sake. For it is the God who said, "Let light shine out of darkness," who has shone in our hearts to give the light of the knowledge of the glory of God in the face of Jesus Christ.

EVENING PRAYER

Psalm 72 [page 685]

A Reading (Lesson) from the Book of Daniel [7:9–10,13–14]

As I watched, thrones were set in place, and an Ancient One took his throne, his clothing was white as snow, and the hair of his head like pure wool; his throne was fiery flames, and its wheels were burning fire. A stream of fire issued and flowed out from his presence. A thousand thousands served him, and ten thousand times ten thousand stood attending him. The court sat in judgment, and the books were opened. As I watched in the night visions, I saw one like a human being coming with the clouds of heaven. And he came to the

Ancient One and was presented before him. To him was given dominion and glory and kingship, that all peoples, nations, and languages should serve him. His dominion is an everlasting dominion that shall not pass away, and his kingship is one that shall never be destroyed.

A Reading (Lesson) from the Gospel According to John [12:27–36a]

Jesus said to Philip and Andrew, "Now my soul is troubled. And what should I say—'Father, save me from this hour'? No, it is for this reason that I have come to this hour. Father, glorify your name." Then a voice came from heaven, "I have glorified it, and I will glorify it again." The crowd standing there heard it and said that it was thunder. Others said, "An angel has spoken to him." Jesus answered, "This voice has come for your sake, not for mine. Now is the judgment of this world; now the ruler of this world will be driven out. And I, when I am lifted up from the earth, will draw all people to myself." He said this to indicate the kind of death he was to die. The crowd answered him, "We have heard from the law that the Messiah remains forever. How can you say that the Son of Man must be lifted up? Who is this Son of Man?" Jesus said to them, "The light is with you for a little longer. Walk while you have the light, so that the darkness may not overtake you. If you walk in the darkness, you do not know where you are going. While you have the light, believe in the light, so that you may become children of light."

St. Mary the Virgin *August 15*

Psalm 113 [page 756], *Psalm 115* [page 757]

A Reading (Lesson) from the First Book of Samuel [2:1–10]

Hannah prayed and said, "My heart exults in the LORD; my strength is exalted in my God. My mouth derides my enemies, because I rejoice in my victory. There is no Holy One like the LORD, no one besides you; there is no Rock like our God. Talk no more so very proudly, let not arrogance come from your mouth; for the LORD is a God of knowledge, and by him actions are weighed. The bows of the mighty are broken, but the feeble gird on strength. Those who were full have hired themselves out for bread, but those who were hungry are fat with spoil. The barren has borne seven, but she who has many children is forlorn. The LORD kills and brings to life; he brings down to Sheol and raises up. The LORD makes poor and makes rich; he brings low, he also exalts. He raises up the poor from the dust; he lifts the needy from the ash heap, to make them sit with princes and inherit a seat of honor. For the pillars of the earth are the LORD's, and on them he has set the world. He will guard the feet of his faithful ones, but the wicked shall be cut off in darkness; for not by might does one prevail. The LORD! His adversaries shall be shattered; the Most High will thunder in heaven. The LORD will judge the ends of the earth; he will give strength to his king, and exalt the power of his anointed."

A Reading (Lesson) from the Gospel According to John [2:1–12]

On the third day there was a wedding in Cana of Galilee, and the mother of Jesus was there. Jesus and his disciples had also been invited to the wedding. When the wine gave out, the mother of Jesus said to him, "They have no wine." And Jesus said to her, "Woman, what concern is that to you and to me? My hour has not yet come." His mother said to the servants, "Do whatever he tells you." Now standing there were six stone water jars for the Jewish rites of purification, each holding twenty or thirty gallons. Jesus said to them, "Fill the jars with water." And they filled them up to the brim. He said to them, "Now draw some out, and take it to the chief steward." So they took it. When the steward tasted the water that had become wine, and did not know where it came from (though the servants who had drawn the water knew), the steward called the bridegroom and said to him, "Everyone serves the good wine first, and then the inferior wine after the guests have become drunk. But you have kept the good wine until now." Jesus did this, the first of his signs, in Cana of Galilee, and revealed his glory; and his disciples believed in him. After this he went down to Capernaum with his mother, his brothers, and his disciples; and they remained there a few days.

EVENING PRAYER

Psalm 45 [page 647] or *Psalm 138* [page 793], *Psalm 149* [page 807]

A Reading (Lesson) from the Book of Jeremiah [31:1–14]

These are the words which the LORD spoke concerning
Israel and Judah: At that time, says the LORD, I will be the
God of all the families of Israel, and they shall be my
people. Thus says the LORD: The people who survived the
sword found grace in the wilderness; when Israel sought for
rest, the LORD appeared to him from far away. I have loved
you with an everlasting love; therefore I have continued my
faithfulness to you. Again I will build you, and you shall be
built, O virgin Israel! Again you shall take your
tambourines, and go forth in the dance of the merrymakers.
Again you shall plant vineyards on the mountains of
Samaria; the planters shall plant, and shall enjoy the fruit.
For there shall be a day when sentinels will call in the hill
country of Ephraim: "Come, let us go up to Zion, to the
LORD our God." For thus says the LORD: Sing aloud with
gladness for Jacob, and raise shouts for the chief of the
nations; proclaim, give praise, and say, "Save, O LORD,
your people, the remnant of Israel." See, I am going to bring
them from the land of the north, and gather them from the
farthest parts of the earth, among them the blind and the
lame, those with child and those in labor, together; a great
company, they shall return here. With weeping they shall
come, and with consolations I will lead them back, I will let
them walk by brooks of water, in a straight path in which
they shall not stumble; for I have become a father to Israel,
and Ephraim is my firstborn. Hear the word of the LORD, O
nations, and declare it in the coastlands far away; say, "He
who scattered Israel will gather him, and will keep him as a
shepherd a flock." For the LORD has ransomed Jacob, and
has redeemed him from hands too strong for him. They
shall come and sing aloud on the height of Zion, and they
shall be radiant over the goodness of the LORD, over the

grain, the wine, and the oil, and over the young of the flock and the herd; their life shall become like a watered garden, and they shall never languish again. Then shall the young women rejoice in the dance, and the young men and the old shall be merry. I will turn their mourning into joy, I will comfort them, and give them gladness for sorrow. I will give the priests their fill of fatness, and my people shall be satisfied with my bounty, says the LORD.

or this

A Reading (Lesson) from the Book of Zechariah [2:10–13]

Sing and rejoice, O daughter Zion! For lo, I will come and dwell in your midst, says the LORD. Many nations shall join themselves to the LORD on that day, and shall be my people; and I will dwell in your midst. And you shall know that the LORD of hosts has sent me to you. The LORD will inherit Judah as his portion in the holy land, and will again choose Jerusalem. Be silent, all people, before the LORD; for he has roused himself from his holy dwelling.

A Reading (Lesson) from the Gospel According to John [19:23–27]

When the soldiers had crucified Jesus, they took his clothes and divided them into four parts, one for each soldier. They also took his tunic; now the tunic was seamless, woven in one piece from the top. So they said to one another, "Let us not tear it, but cast lots for it to see who will get it." This was to fulfill what the scripture says, "They divided my clothes among themselves, and for my clothing they cast lots." And that is what the soldiers did. Meanwhile, standing near the cross of Jesus were his mother, and his mother's sister, Mary the wife of Clopas, and Mary Magdalene. When Jesus saw his mother and the disciple whom he loved standing beside her, he said to his mother, "Woman, here is your son." Then he said to the disciple, "Here is your mother." And from that hour the disciple took her into his own home.

or this

A Reading (Lesson) from the Acts of the Apostles [1:6–14]

When the disciples had come together, they asked Jesus, "Lord, is this the time when you will restore the kingdom to Israel?" He replied, "It is not for you to know the times or periods that the Father has set by his own authority. But you will receive power when the Holy Spirit has come upon you; and you will be my witnesses in Jerusalem, in all Judea and Samaria, and to the ends of the earth." When he had said this, as they were watching, he was lifted up, and a cloud took him out of their sight. While he was going and they were gazing up toward heaven, suddenly two men in white robes stood by them. They said, "Men of Galilee, why do you stand looking up toward heaven? This Jesus, who has been taken up from you into heaven, will come in the same way as you saw him go into heaven." Then they returned to Jerusalem from the mount called Olivet, which is near Jerusalem, a sabbath day's journey away. When they had entered the city, they went to the room upstairs where they were staying, Peter, and John, and James, and Andrew, Philip and Thomas, Bartholomew and Matthew, James son of Alphaeus, and Simon the Zealot, and Judas son of James. All these were constantly devoting themselves to prayer, together with certain women, including Mary the mother of Jesus, as well as his brothers.

St. Bartholomew   *August 24*

MORNING PRAYER

Psalm 86 [page 709]

A Reading (Lesson) from the Book of Genesis [28:10–17]

Jacob left Beer-sheba and went toward Haran. He came to a certain place and stayed there for the night, because the sun had set. Taking one of the stones of the place, he put it under his head and lay down in that place. And he dreamed that there was a ladder set up on the earth, the top of it reaching to heaven; and the angels of God were ascending and descending on it. And the LORD stood beside him and said, "I am the LORD, the God of Abraham your father and the God of Isaac; the land on which you lie I will give to you and to your offspring; and your offspring shall be like the dust of the earth, and you shall spread abroad to the west and to the east and to the north and to the south; and all the families of the earth shall be blessed in you and in your offspring. Know that I am with you and will keep you wherever you go, and will bring you back to this land; for I will not leave you until I have done what I have promised you." Then Jacob woke from his sleep and said, "Surely the LORD is in this place—and I did not know it!" And he was afraid, and said, "How awesome is this place! This is none other than the house of God, and this is the gate of heaven."

John 1:43–51 [page 833 above]

EVENING PRAYER

Psalm 15 [page 599],   *Psalm 67* [page 675]

A Reading (Lesson) from the Book of Isaiah [66:1–2,18–23]

Thus says the Lord: Heaven is my throne and the earth is
my footstool; what is the house that you would build for
me, and what is my resting place? All these things my hand
has made, and so all these things are mine, says the LORD.
But this is the one to whom I will look, to the humble and
contrite in spirit, who trembles at my word. For I know
their works and their thoughts, and I am coming to gather
all nations and tongues; and they shall come and shall see
my glory, and I will set a sign among them. From them I will
send survivors to the nations, to Tarshish, Put, and
Lud—which draw the bow—to Tubal and Javan, to the
coastlands far away that have not heard of my fame or seen
my glory; and they shall declare my glory among the
nations. They shall bring all your kindred from all the
nations as an offering to the LORD, on horses, and in
chariots, and in litters, and on mules, and on dromedaries,
to my holy mountain Jerusalem, says the LORD, just as the
Israelites bring a grain offering in a clean vessel to the house
of the LORD. And I will also take some of them as priests
and as Levites, says the LORD. For as the new heavens and
the new earth, which I will make, shall remain before me,
says the LORD; so shall your descendants and your name
remain. From new moon to new moon, and from sabbath to
sabbath, all flesh shall come to worship before me, says the
LORD.

A Reading (Lesson) from the First Letter of Peter [5:1–11]

As an elder myself and a witness of the sufferings of
Christ, as well as one who shares in the glory to be
revealed, I exhort the elders among you to tend the flock
of God that is in your charge, exercising the oversight, not
under compulsion but willingly, as God would have you

do it—not for sordid gain but eagerly. Do not lord it over those in your charge, but be examples to the flock. And when the chief shepherd appears, you will win the crown of glory that never fades away. In the same way, you who are younger must accept the authority of the elders. And all of you must clothe yourselves with humility in your dealings with one another, for "God opposes the proud, but gives grace to the humble." Humble yourselves therefore under the mighty hand of God, so that he may exalt you in due time. Cast all your anxiety on him, because he cares for you. Discipline yourselves, keep alert. Like a roaring lion your adversary the devil prowls around, looking for someone to devour. Resist him, steadfast in your faith, for you know that your brothers and sisters in all the world are undergoing the same kinds of suffering. And after you have suffered for a little while, the God of all grace, who has called you to his eternal glory in Christ, will himself restore, support, strengthen, and establish you. To him be the power forever and ever. Amen.

Eve of Holy Cross   *September 13*

EVENING PRAYER

Psalm 46 [page 649],   *Psalm 87* [page 711]

A Reading (Lesson) from the First Book of the Kings [8:22–30]

Solomon stood before the altar of the LORD in the presence of all the assembly of Israel, and spread out his hands to heaven. He said, "O LORD, God of Israel, there is no God like you in heaven above or on earth beneath, keeping

covenant and steadfast love for your servants who walk
before you with all their heart, the covenant that you kept
for your servant my father David as you declared to him;
you promised with your mouth and have this day fulfilled
with your hand. Therefore, O LORD, God of Israel, keep for
your servant my father David that which you promised him,
saying, 'There shall never fail you a successor before me to
sit on the throne of Israel, if only your children look to their
way, to walk before me as you have walked before me.'
Therefore, O God of Israel, let your word be confirmed,
which you promised to your servant my father David. But
will God indeed dwell on the earth? Even heaven and the
highest heaven cannot contain you, much less this house
that I have built! Regard your servant's prayer and his plea,
O LORD my God, heeding the cry and the prayer that your
servant prays to you today; that your eyes may be open
night and day toward this house, the place of which you
said, 'My name shall be there,' that you may heed the prayer
that your servant prays toward this place. Hear the plea of
your servant and of your people Israel when they pray
toward this place; O hear in heaven your dwelling place;
heed and forgive."

*A Reading (Lesson) from the Letter of Paul to the
Ephesians* [2:11–22]

Remember that at one time you Gentiles by birth, called
"the uncircumcision" by those who are called "the
circumcision"—a physical circumcision made in the flesh
by human hands—remember that you were at that time
without Christ, being aliens from the commonwealth of
Israel, and strangers to the covenants of promise, having
no hope and without God in the world. But now in Christ
Jesus you who once were far off have been brought near

by the blood of Christ. For he is our peace; in his flesh he has made both groups into one and has broken down the dividing wall, that is, the hostility between us. He has abolished the law with its commandments and ordinances, that he might create in himself one new humanity in place of the two, thus making peace, and might reconcile both groups to God in one body through the cross, thus putting to death that hostility through it. So he came and proclaimed peace to you who were far off and peace to those who were near; for through him both of us have access in one Spirit to the Father. So then you are no longer strangers and aliens, but you are citizens with the saints and also members of the household of God, built upon the foundation of the apostles and prophets, with Christ Jesus himself as the cornerstone. In him the whole structure is joined together and grows into a holy temple in the Lord; in whom you also are built together spiritually into a dwelling place for God.

Holy Cross Day   *September 14*

MORNING PRAYER

Psalm 66 [page 673]

A Reading (Lesson) from the Book of Numbers [21:4–9]

From Mount Hor they set out by the way to the Red Sea, to go around the land of Edom; but the people became impatient on the way. The people spoke against God and against Moses, "Why have you brought us up out of Egypt to die in the wilderness? For there is no food and no water, and we detest this miserable food." Then the LORD sent poisonous serpents among the people, and they bit the people, so that many Israelites died. The people came to Moses and said, "We have sinned by speaking against the LORD and against you; pray to the LORD to take away the serpents from us." So Moses prayed for the people. And the LORD said to Moses, "Make a poisonous serpent, and set it on a pole; and everyone who is bitten shall look at it and live." So Moses made a serpent of bronze, and put it upon a pole; and whenever a serpent bit someone, that person would look at the serpent of bronze and live.

A Reading (Lesson) from the Gospel According to John [3:11–17]

Jesus answered Nicodemus, "Very truly, I tell you, we speak of what we know and testify to what we have seen; yet you do not receive our testimony. If I have told you about earthly things and you do not believe, how can you believe if I tell you about heavenly things? No one has ascended into heaven except the one who descended from heaven, the Son of Man. And just as Moses lifted up the serpent in the wilderness, so must the Son of Man be lifted up, that whoever believes in him may have eternal life. For God so loved the world that he gave his only Son, so that everyone who believes in him may not perish but may have eternal life. Indeed, God did not send the Son into the world to condemn the world, but in order that the world might be saved through him."

EVENING PRAYER
_____

Psalm 118 [page 760]

A Reading (Lesson) from the Book of Genesis [3:1–15]

Now the serpent was more crafty than any other wild animal that the LORD God had made. He said to the woman, "Did God say, 'You shall not eat from any tree in the garden'?" The woman said to the serpent, "We may eat of the fruit of the trees in the garden; but God said, 'You shall not eat of the fruit of the tree that is in the middle of the garden, nor shall you touch it, or you shall die.' " But the serpent said to the woman, "You will not die; for God knows that when you eat of it your eyes will be opened, and you will be like God, knowing good and evil." So when the woman saw that the tree was good for food, and that it was a delight to the eyes, and that the tree was to be desired to make one wise, she took of its fruit and ate; and she also gave some to her husband, who was with her, and he ate. Then the eyes of both were opened, and they knew that they were naked; and they sewed fig leaves together and made loincloths for themselves. They heard the sound of the LORD God walking in the garden at the time of the evening breeze, and the man and his wife hid themselves from the presence of the LORD God among the trees of the garden. But the LORD God called to the man, and said to him, "Where are you?" He said, "I heard the sound of you in the garden, and I was afraid, because I was naked; and I hid myself." He said, "Who told you that you were naked? Have you eaten from the tree of which I commanded you not to eat?" The man said, "The woman whom you gave to be with me, she gave me fruit from the tree, and I ate." Then the LORD God said to the woman, "What is this that you have done?" The woman said, "The serpent tricked me, and I ate." The LORD God said to the serpent, "Because you have done this, cursed are you among all animals and among all wild creatures; upon your belly you shall go, and dust you shall eat all the days of your life. I will put enmity between you and the woman, and between your offspring and hers; he will strike your head, and you will strike his heel."

A Reading (Lesson) from the First Letter of Peter [3:17–22]

It is better to suffer for doing good, if suffering should be God's will, than to suffer for doing evil. For Christ also suffered for sins once for all, the righteous for the unrighteous, in order to bring you to God. He was put to death in the flesh, but made alive in the spirit, in which also he went and made a proclamation to the spirits in prison, who in former times did not obey, when God waited patiently in the days of Noah, during the building of the ark, in which a few, that is, eight persons, were saved through water. And baptism, which was prefigured, now saves you—not as a removal of dirt from the body, but as an appeal to God for a good conscience, through the resurrection of Jesus Christ, who has gone into heaven and is at the right hand of God, with angels, authorities, and powers made subject to him.

St. Matthew *September 21*

MORNING PRAYER

Psalm 119:41–64 [page 766]

A Reading (Lesson) from the Book of Isaiah [8:11–20]

The LORD spoke thus to me while his hand was strong upon me, and warned me not to walk in the way of this people, saying: Do not call conspiracy all that this people calls conspiracy, and do not fear what it fears, or be in dread. But the LORD of hosts, him you shall regard as holy; let him be your fear, and let him be your dread. He will become a sanctuary, a stone one strikes against; for both houses of Israel he will become a rock one stumbles over—a trap and a snare for the inhabitants of Jerusalem. And many among them shall stumble; they shall fall and be broken; they shall be snared and taken. Bind up the testimony, seal the teaching among my disciples. I will wait for the LORD, who is hiding his face from the house of Jacob, and I will hope in him. See, I and the children whom the LORD has given me are signs and portents in Israel from the LORD of hosts, who dwells on Mount Zion. Now if people say to you, "Consult the ghosts and the familiar spirits that chirp and mutter; should not a people consult their gods, the dead on behalf of the living, for teaching and for instruction?" Surely, those who speak like this will have no dawn!

A Reading (Lesson) from the Letter of Paul to the Romans [10:1–15]

Brothers and sisters, my heart's desire and prayer to God for them is that they may be saved. I can testify that they have a zeal for God, but it is not enlightened. For, being ignorant of the righteousness that comes from God, and seeking to establish their own, they have not submitted to God's righteousness. For Christ is the end of the law so that there may be righteousness for everyone who believes. Moses writes concerning the righteousness that comes from the law, that "the person who does these things will live by them." But the righteousness that comes from faith says, "Do not say in your heart, 'Who will ascend into heaven?'" (that is, to bring Christ down) "or 'Who will descend into the abyss?'" (that is, to bring Christ up from the dead). But what does it say? "The word is near you, on your lips and in your heart" (that is, the word of faith that we proclaim); because if you confess with your lips that Jesus is Lord and believe in your heart that God raised him from the dead, you will be saved. For one believes with the heart and so is justified, and one confesses with the mouth and so is saved. The scripture says, "No one who believes in him will be put to shame." For there is no distinction between Jew and Greek; the same Lord is Lord of all and is generous to all who call on him. For, "Everyone who calls on the name of the Lord shall be saved." But how are they to call on one in whom they have not believed? And how are they to believe in one of whom they have never heard? And how are they to hear without someone to proclaim him? And how are they to proclaim him unless they are sent? As it is written, "How beautiful are the feet of those who bring good news!"

EVENING PRAYER

Psalm 19 [page 606], *Psalm 112* [page 755]

A Reading (Lesson) from the Book of Job [28:12–28]

Job took up his discourse, and said: "But where shall wisdom be found? And where is the place of understanding? Mortals do not know the way to it, and it is not found in the land of the living. The deep says, 'It is not in me,' and the sea says, 'It is not with me.' It cannot be gotten for gold, and silver cannot be weighed out as its price. It cannot be valued in the gold of Ophir, in precious onyx or sapphire. Gold and glass cannot equal it, nor can it be exchanged for jewels of fine gold. No mention shall be made of coral or of crystal; the price of wisdom is above pearls. The chrysolite of Ethiopia cannot compare with it, nor can it be valued in pure gold. Where then does wisdom come from? And where is the place of understanding? It is hidden from the eyes of all living, and concealed from the birds of the air. Abaddon and Death say, 'We have heard a rumor of it with our ears.' God understands the way to it, and he knows its place. For he looks to the ends of the earth, and sees everything under the heavens. When he gave to the wind its weight, and apportioned out the waters by measure; when he made a decree for the rain, and a way for the thunderbolt; then he saw it and declared it; he established it, and searched it out. And he said to humankind, 'Truly, the fear of the Lord, that is wisdom; and to depart from evil is understanding.' "

Matthew 13:44–52 [page 1142 above]

St. Michael & All Angels   *September 29*

MORNING PRAYER

Psalm 8 [page 592],   *Psalm 148* [page 805]

A Reading (Lesson) from the Book of Job [38:1–7]

The LORD answered Job out of the whirlwind: "Who is this that darkens counsel by words without knowledge? Gird up your loins like a man, I will question you, and you shall declare to me. Where were you when I laid the foundation of the earth? Tell me, if you have understanding. Who determined its measurements—surely you know! Or who stretched the line upon it? On what were its bases sunk, or who laid its cornerstone when the morning stars sang together and all the heavenly beings shouted for joy?"

A Reading (Lesson) from the Letter to the Hebrews [1:1–14]

Long ago God spoke to our ancestors in many and various ways by the prophets, but in these last days he has spoken to us by a Son, whom he appointed heir of all things, through whom he also created the worlds. He is the reflection of God's glory and the exact imprint of God's very being, and he sustains all things by his powerful word. When he had made purification for sins, he sat down at the right hand of the Majesty on high, having become as much superior to angels as the name he has inherited is more excellent than theirs. For to which of the angels did God ever say, "You are my Son; today I have begotten you"? Or again, "I will be his Father, and he will be my Son"? And again, when he brings the firstborn into the world, he says, "Let all God's angels worship him." Of the angels he says, "He makes his angels winds, and his servants flames of fire." But of the Son he says, "Your throne, O God, is forever and ever, and the righteous scepter is the scepter of your kingdom. You have loved righteousness and hated wickedness; therefore God, your God, has anointed you with the oil of gladness beyond your companions." And, "In the beginning, Lord, you founded the earth, and the heavens are the work of your hands; they will perish, but you remain; they will all wear out like clothing; like a cloak you will roll them up, and like clothing they will be changed. But you are the same, and your years will never end." But to which of the angels has he ever said, "Sit at my right hand until I make your enemies a footstool for your feet"? Are not all angels spirits in the divine service, sent to serve for the sake of those who are to inherit salvation?

EVENING PRAYER

Psalm 34 [page 627],   *Psalm 150* [page 807]   or
Psalm 104 [page 735]

A Reading (Lesson) from the Book of Daniel [12:1–3]

One having the appearance of a man said to me, "At that time Michael, the great prince, the protector of your people, shall arise. There shall be a time of anguish, such as has never occurred since nations first came into existence. But at that time your people shall be delivered, everyone who is found written in the book. Many of those who sleep in the dust of the earth shall awake, some to everlasting life, and some to shame and everlasting contempt. Those who are wise shall shine like the brightness of the sky, and those who lead many to righteousness, like the stars forever and ever."

or this

A Reading (Lesson) from the Second Book of the Kings [6:8–17]

Once when the king of Aram was at war with Israel, he took counsel with his officers. He said, "At such and such a place shall be my camp." But the man of God sent word to the king of Israel, "Take care not to pass this place, because the Arameans are going down there." The king of Israel sent word to the place of which the man of God spoke. More than once or twice he warned such a place so that it was on the alert. The mind of the king of Aralam was greatly perturbed because of this; he called his officers and said to them, "Now tell me who among us sides with the king of Israel?" Then one of his officers said, "No one, my lord king. It is Elisha, the prophet in Israel, who tells the king of Israel the words that you speak in your bedchamber." He said, "Go and find where he is; I will send and seize him." He was told, "He is in Dothan." So he sent horses and chariots there and a great army; they came by night, and surrounded the city. When an attendant of the man of God rose early in the morning and went out, an army with horses and chariots was all around the city. His servant said, "Alas, master! What shall we do?" He replied, "Do not be afraid, for there are more with us than there are with them." Then Elisha prayed: "O Lord, please open his eyes that he may see." So the Lord opened the eyes of the servant, and he saw; the mountain was full of horses and chariots of fire all around Elisha.

A Reading (Lesson) from the Gospel According to Mark [13:21–27]

Jesus said to the disciples, "If anyone says to you at that time, 'Look! Here is the Messiah!' or 'Look! There he is!'—do not believe it. False messiahs and false prophets will appear and produce signs and omens, to lead astray, if possible, the elect. But be alert; I have already told you everything. But in those days, after that suffering, the sun will be darkened, and the moon will not give its light, and the stars will be falling from heaven, and the powers in the heavens will be shaken. Then they will see 'the Son of Man coming in clouds' with great power and glory. Then he will send out the angels, and gather his elect from the four winds, from the ends of the earth to the ends of heaven."

or this

A Reading (Lesson) from the Revelation to John [5:1–14]

Then I saw in the right hand of the one seated on the throne a scroll written on the inside and on the back, sealed with seven seals; and I saw a mighty angel proclaiming with a loud voice, "Who is worthy to open the scroll and break its seals?" And no one in heaven or on earth or under the earth was able to open the scroll or to look into it. And I began to weep bitterly because no one was found worthy to open the scroll or to look into it. Then one of the elders said to me, "Do not weep. See, the Lion of the tribe of Judah, the Root of David, has conquered, so that he can open the scroll and its seven seals." Then I saw between the throne and the four living creatures and among the elders a Lamb standing as if it had been slaughtered, having seven horns and seven eyes, which are the seven spirits of God sent out into all the earth. He went and took the scroll from the right hand of the one who was seated on the throne. When he had taken the scroll, the four living creatures and the twenty-four elders fell before the Lamb, each holding a harp and golden bowls full of incense, which are the prayers of the saints. They sing a new song: "You are worthy to take the scroll and to open its seals, for you were slaughtered and by your blood you ransomed for God saints from every tribe and language and people and nation; you have made them to be a kingdom and priests serving our God, and they will reign on earth." Then I looked, and I heard the voice of many angels surrounding the throne and the living creatures and the elders; they numbered myriads of myriads and thousands of thousands, singing with full voice, "Worthy is the Lamb that was slaughtered to receive power and wealth and wisdom and might and honor and glory and blessing!" Then I heard every creature in heaven and on earth and under the earth and in the sea, and all that is in them, singing, "To the one seated on the throne and to the Lamb be blessing and honor and glory and might forever and ever!" And the four living creatures said, "Amen!" And the elders fell down and worshiped.

MORNING PRAYER

Psalm 103 [page 733]

A Reading (Lesson) from the Book of Ezekiel [47:1–12]

A man, whose appearance was like bronze, brought me back to the entrance of the temple; there, water was flowing from below the threshold of the temple toward the east (for the temple faced east); and the water was flowing down from below the south end of the threshold of the temple, south of the altar. Then he brought me out by way of the north gate, and led me around on the outside to the outer gate that faces toward the east; and the water was coming out on the south side. Going on eastward with a cord in his hand, the man measured one thousand cubits, and then led me through the water; and it was ankle-deep. Again he measured one thousand, and led me through the water; and it was knee-deep. Again he measured one thousand, and led me through the water; and it was up to the waist. Again he measured one thousand, and it was a river that I could not cross, for the water had risen; it was deep enough to swim in, a river that could not be crossed. He said to me, "Mortal, have you seen this?" Then he led me back along the bank of the river. As I came back, I saw on the bank of the river a great many trees on the one side and on the other. He said to me, "This water flows toward the eastern region and goes down into the Arabah; and when it enters the sea, the sea of stagnant waters, the water will become fresh. Wherever the river goes, every living creature that swarms will live, and there will be very many fish, once these waters reach there. It will become fresh; and everything will live where the river goes. People will stand fishing beside the sea from En-gedi to En-eglaim; it will be a place for the spreading of nets; its fish will be of a great many kinds, like the fish of the Great Sea. But its swamps and marshes will not become fresh; they are to be left for sale. On the banks, on both sides of the river, there will grow all kinds of trees for food. Their leaves will not wither nor their fruit fail, but they will bear fresh fruit every month, because the water for them flows from the sanctuary. Their fruit will be for food, and their leaves for healing."

A Reading (Lesson) from the Gospel according to Luke [1:1–4]

Since many have undertaken to set down an orderly account of the events that have been fulfilled among us, just as they were handed on to us by those who from the beginning were eyewitnesses and servants of the word, I too decided, after investigating everything carefully from the very first, to write an orderly account for you, most excellent Theophilus, so that you may know the truth concerning the things about which you have been instructed.

EVENING PRAYER

Psalm 67 [page 675],   *Psalm 96* [page 725]

A Reading (Lesson) from the Book of Isaiah [52:7–10]

How beautiful upon the mountains are the feet of the messenger who announces peace, who brings good news, who announces salvation, who says to Zion, "Your God reigns." Listen! Your sentinels lift up their voices, together they sing for joy; for in plain sight they see the return of the LORD to Zion. Break forth together into singing, you ruins of Jerusalem; for the LORD has comforted his people, he has redeemed Jerusalem. The LORD has bared his holy arm before the eyes of all the nations; and all the ends of the earth shall see the salvation of our God.

A Reading (Lesson) from the Acts of the Apostles [1:1–8]

In the first book, Theophilus, I wrote about all that Jesus did and taught from the beginning until the day when he was taken up to heaven, after giving instructions through the Holy Spirit to the apostles whom he had chosen. After his suffering he presented himself alive to them by many convincing proofs, appearing to them during forty days and speaking about the kingdom of God. While staying with them, he ordered them not to leave Jerusalem, but to wait there for the promise of the Father. "This," he said, "is what you have heard from me; for John baptized with water, but you will be baptized with the Holy Spirit not many days from now." So when they had come together, they asked him, "Lord, is this the time when you will restore the kingdom to Israel?" He replied, "It is not for you to know the times or periods that the Father has set by his own authority. But you will receive power when the Holy Spirit has come upon you; and you will be my witnesses in Jerusalem, in all Judea and Samaria, and to the ends of the earth."

St. James of Jerusalem   *October 23*

MORNING PRAYER

Psalm 119:145–168 [page 775]

A Reading (Lesson) from the Book of Jeremiah [11:18–23]

It was the LORD who made it known to me, and I knew; then you showed me their evil deeds. But I was like a gentle lamb led to the slaughter. And I did not know it was against me that they devised schemes, saying, "Let us destroy the tree with its fruit, let us cut him off from the land of the living, so that his name will no longer be remembered!" But you, O LORD of hosts, who judge righteously, who try the heart and the mind, let me see your retribution upon them, for to you I have committed my cause. Therefore thus says the LORD concerning the people of Anathoth, who seek your life, and say, "You shall not prophesy in the name of the LORD, or you will die by our hand"—therefore thus says the LORD of hosts: I am going to punish them; the young men shall die by the sword; their sons and their daughters shall die by famine; and not even a remnant shall be left of them. For I will bring disaster upon the people of Anathoth, the year of their punishment.

A Reading (Lesson) from the Gospel according to Matthew [10:16–22]

Jesus sent out the twelve, charging them, "See, I am sending you out like sheep into the midst of wolves; so be wise as serpents and innocent as doves. Beware of them, for they will hand you over to councils and flog you in their synagogues; and you will be dragged before governors and kings because of me, as a testimony to them and the Gentiles. When they hand you over, do not worry about how you are to speak or what you are to say; for what you are to say will be given to you at that time; for it is not you who speak, but the Spirit of your Father speaking through you. Brother will betray brother to death, and a father his child, and children will rise against parents and have them put to death; and you will be hated by all because of my name. But the one who endures to the end will be saved."

EVENING PRAYER

Psalm 122 [page 779], *Psalm 125* [page 781]

Isaiah 65:17–25 [page 578 above]

A Reading (Lesson) from the Letter to the Hebrews [12:12–24]

Lift your drooping hands and strengthen your weak knees, and make straight paths for your feet, so that what is lame may not be put out of joint, but rather be healed. Pursue peace with everyone, and the holiness without which no one will see the Lord. See to it that no one fails to obtain the grace of God; that no root of bitterness springs up and causes trouble, and through it many become defiled. See to it that no one becomes like Esau, an immoral and godless person, who sold his birthright for a single meal. You know that later, when he wanted to inherit the blessing, he was rejected, for he found no chance to repent, even though he sought the blessing with tears. You have not come to something that can be touched, a blazing fire, and darkness, and gloom, and a tempest, and the sound of a trumpet, and a voice whose words made the hearers beg that not another word be spoken to them. (For they could not endure the order that was given, "If even an animal touches the mountain, it shall be stoned to death." Indeed, so terrifying was the sight that Moses said, "I tremble with fear.") But you have come to Mount Zion and to the city of the living God, the heavenly Jerusalem, and to innumerable angels in festal gathering, and to the assembly of the firstborn who are enrolled in heaven, and to God the judge of all, and to the spirits of the righteous made perfect, and to Jesus, the mediator of a new covenant, and to the sprinkled blood that speaks a better word than the blood of Abel.

St. Simon and St. Jude   *October 28*

MORNING PRAYER

Psalm 66 [page 673]

A Reading (Lesson) from the Book of Isaiah [28:9–16]

"Whom will he teach knowledge, and to whom will he explain the message? Those who are weaned from milk, those taken from the breast? For it is precept upon precept, precept upon precept, line upon line, line upon line, here a little, there a little." Truly, with stammering lip and with alien tongue he will speak to this people, to whom he has said, "This is rest; give rest to the weary; and this is repose"; yet they would not hear. Therefore the word of the LORD will be to them, "Precept upon precept, precept upon precept, line upon line, line upon line, here a little, there a little"; in order that they may go, and fall backward, and be broken, and snared, and taken. Therefore hear the word of the LORD, you scoffers who rule this people in Jerusalem. Because you have said, "We have made a covenant with death, and with Sheol we have an agreement; when the overwhelming scourge passes through it will not come to us; for we have made lies our refuge, and in falsehood we have taken shelter"; therefore thus says the Lord GOD, See, I am laying in Zion a foundation stone, a tested stone, a precious cornerstone, a sure foundation: "One who trusts will not panic."

Ephesians 4:1–16 [page 144 above]

EVENING PRAYER

Psalm 116 [page 759],   *Psalm 117* [page 760]

A Reading (Lesson) from the Book of Isaiah [4:2–6]

On that day the branch of the LORD shall be beautiful and glorious, and the fruit of the land shall be the pride and glory of the survivors of Israel. Whoever is left in Zion and remains in Jerusalem will be called holy, everyone who has been recorded for life in Jerusalem, once the Lord has washed away the filth of the daughters of Zion and cleansed the bloodstains of Jerusalem from its midst by a spirit of judgment and by a spirit of burning. Then the LORD will create over the whole site of Mount Zion and over its places of assembly a cloud by day and smoke and the shining of a flaming fire by night. Indeed over all the glory there will be a canopy. It will serve as a pavilion, a shade by day from the heat, and a refuge and a shelter from the storm and rain.

A Reading (Lesson) from the Gospel according to John [14:15–31]

Jesus said to the disciples, "If you love me, you will keep my commandments. And I will ask the Father, and he will give you another Advocate, to be with you forever. This is the Spirit of truth, whom the world cannot receive, because it neither sees him nor knows him. You know him, because he abides with you, and he will be in you. I will not leave you orphaned; I am coming to you. In a little while the world will no longer see me, but you will see me; because I live, you also will live. On that day you will know that I am in my Father, and you in me, and I in you. They who have my commandments and keep them are those who love me; and those who love me will be loved by my Father, and I will love them and reveal myself to them." Judas (not Iscariot) said to him, "Lord, how is it that you will reveal yourself to us, and not to the world?" Jesus answered him, "Those who love me will keep my word, and my Father will love them, and we will come to them and make our home with them. Whoever does not love me does not keep my words; and the word that you hear is not mine, but is from the Father who sent me. I have said these things to you while I am still with you. But the Advocate, the Holy Spirit, whom the Father will send in my name, will teach you everything, and remind you of all that I have said to you. Peace I leave with you; my peace I give to you. I do not give to you as the world gives. Do not let your hearts be troubled, and do not let them be afraid. You heard me say to you, 'I am going away, and I am coming to you.' If you loved me, you would rejoice that I am going to the Father, because the Father is greater than I. And now I have told you this before it occurs, so that when it does occur, you may believe. I will no longer talk much with you, for the ruler of this world is coming. He has no power over me; but I do as the Father has commanded me, so that the world may know that I love the Father. Rise, let us be on our way."

Eve of All Saints *October 31*

EVENING PRAYER
—————————

Psalm 34 [page 627]

A Reading (Lesson) from the Book of Wisdom [3:1–9]

The souls of the righteous are in the hand of God, and no
torment will ever touch them. In the eyes of the foolish they
seemed to have died, and their departure was thought to be
a disaster, and their going from us to be their destruction;
but they are at peace. For though in the sight of others they
were punished, their hope is full of immortality. Having
been disciplined a little, they will receive great good, because
God tested them and found them worthy of himself; like
gold in the furnace he tried them, and like a sacrificial burnt
offering he accepted them. In the time of their visitation they
will shine forth, and will run like sparks through the
stubble. They will govern nations and rule over peoples, and
the Lord will reign over them forever. Those who trust in
him will understand truth, and the faithful will abide with
him in love, because grace and mercy are upon his holy
ones, and he watches over his elect.

A Reading (Lesson) from the Revelation to John [19:1,4–10]

I heard what seemed to be the loud voice of a great
multitude in heaven, saying, "Hallelujah! Salvation and
glory and power to our God." And the twenty-four elders
and the four living creatures fell down and worshiped God
who is seated on the throne, saying, "Amen. Hallelujah!"
And from the throne came a voice saying, "Praise our
God, all you his servants, and all who fear him, small and
great." Then I heard what seemed to be the voice of a
great multitude, like the sound of many waters and like
the sound of mighty thunderpeals, crying out, "Hallelujah!
For the Lord our God the Almighty reigns. Let us rejoice
and exult and give him the glory, for the marriage of the
Lamb has come, and his bride has made herself ready; to
her it has been granted to be clothed with fine linen,

bright and pure"—for the fine linen is the righteous deeds of the saints. And the angel said to me, "Write this: Blessed are those who are invited to the marriage supper of the Lamb." And he said to me, "These are true words of God." Then I fell down at his feet to worship him, but he said to me, "You must not do that! I am a fellow servant with you and your comrades who hold the testimony of Jesus. Worship God! For the testimony of Jesus is the spirit of prophecy."

All Saints' Day *November 1*

MORNING PRAYER

Psalm 111 [page 754], *Psalm 112* [page 755]

A Reading (Lesson) from the Second Book of Esdras [2:42–47]

I, Ezra, saw on Mount Zion a great multitude that I could not number, and they all were praising the Lord with songs. In their midst was a young man of great stature, taller than any of the others, and on the head of each of them he placed a crown, but he was more exalted than they. And I was held spellbound. Then I asked an angel, "Who are these, my lord?" He answered and said to me, "These are they who have put off mortal clothing and have put on the immortal, and have confessed the name of God. Now they are being crowned, and receive palms." Then I said to the angel, "Who is that young man who is placing crowns on them and putting palms in their hands?" He answered and said to me, "He is the Son of God, whom they confessed in the world." So I began to praise those who had stood valiantly for the name of the Lord.

A Reading (Lesson) from the Letter to the Hebrews [11:32—12:2]

What more should I say? For time would fail me to tell of Gideon, Barak, Samson, Jephthah, of David and Samuel and the prophets—who through faith conquered kingdoms, administered justice, obtained promises, shut the mouths of lions, quenched raging fire, escaped the edge of the sword, won strength out of weakness, became mighty in war, put foreign armies to flight. Women received their dead by resurrection. Others were tortured, refusing to accept release, in order to obtain a better resurrection. Others suffered mocking and flogging, and even chains and imprisonment. They were stoned to death, they were sawn in two, they were killed by the sword; they went about in skins of sheep and goats, destitute, persecuted, tormented—of whom the world was not worthy. They wandered in deserts and mountains, and in caves and holes in the ground. Yet all these, though they were commended for their faith, did not receive what was promised, since God had provided something better so that they would not, apart from us, be made perfect. Therefore, since we are surrounded by so great a cloud of witnesses, let us also lay aside every weight and the sin that clings so closely, and let us run with perseverance the race that is set before us, looking to Jesus the pioneer and perfecter of our faith, who for the sake of the joy that was set before him endured the cross, disregarding its shame, and has taken his seat at the right hand of the throne of God.

EVENING PRAYER

Psalm 148 [page 805],   *Psalm 150* [page 807]

A Reading (Lesson) from the Book of
Wisdom [5:1–5,14–16]

The righteous will stand with great confidence in the
presence of those who have oppressed them and those who
make light of their labors. When the unrighteous see them,
they will be shaken with dreadful fear, and they will be
amazed at the unexpected salvation of the righteous. They
will speak to one another in repentance, and in anguish of
spirit they will groan, and say, "These are persons whom we
once held in derision and made a byword of reproach—
fools that we were! We thought that their lives were
madness and that their end was without honor. Why have
they been numbered among the children of God? And why
is their lot among the saints?" Because the hope of the
ungodly is like thistledown carried by the wind, and like a
light frost driven away by a storm; it is dispersed like
smoke before the wind, and it passes like the remembrance
of a guest who stays but a day. But the righteous live
forever, and their reward is with the Lord; the Most High
takes care of them. Therefore they will receive a glorious
crown and a beautiful diadem from the hand of the Lord,
because with his right hand he will cover them, and with
his arm he will shield them.

A Reading (Lesson) from the Revelation to
John [21:1–4,22—22:5]

Then I saw a new heaven and a new earth; for the first
heaven and the first earth had passed away, and the sea
was no more. And I saw the holy city, the new Jerusalem,
coming down out of heaven from God, prepared as a
bride adorned for her husband. And I heard a loud voice
from the throne saying, "See, the home of God is among
mortals. He will dwell with them as their God; they will

be his peoples, and God himself will be with them; he will wipe every tear from their eyes. Death will be no more; mourning and crying and pain will be no more, for the first things have passed away." I saw no temple in the city, for its temple is the Lord God the Almighty and the Lamb. And the city has no need of sun or moon to shine on it, for the glory of God is its light, and its lamp is the Lamb. The nations will walk by its light, and the kings of the earth will bring their glory into it. Its gates will never be shut by day—and there will be no night there. People will bring into it the glory and the honor of the nations. But nothing unclean will enter it, nor anyone who practices abomination or falsehood, but only those who are written in the Lamb's book of life. Then the angel showed me the river of the water of life, bright as crystal, flowing from the throne of God and of the Lamb through the middle of the street of the city. On either side of the river is the tree of life with its twelve kinds of fruit, producing its fruit each month; and the leaves of the tree are for the healing of the nations. Nothing accursed will be found there any more. But the throne of God and of the Lamb will be in it, and his servants will worship him; they will see his face, and his name will be on their foreheads. And there will be no more night; they need no light of lamp or sun, for the Lord God will be their light, and they will reign forever and ever.

Thanksgiving Day

MORNING PRAYER

Psalm 147 [page 804]

Deuteronomy 26:1–11 [page 643 above]

A Reading (Lesson) from the Gospel according to John [6:26–35]

Jesus said to the people, "Very truly, I tell you, you are looking for me, not because you saw signs, but because you ate your fill of the loaves. Do not work for the food that perishes, but for the food that endures for eternal life, which the Son of Man will give you. For it is on him that God the Father has set his seal." Then they said to him, "What must we do to perform the works of God?" Jesus answered them, "This is the work of God, that you believe in him whom he has sent." So they said to him, "What sign are you going to give us then, so that we may see it and believe you? What work are you performing? Our ancestors ate the manna in the wilderness; as it is written, 'He gave them bread from heaven to eat.' " Then Jesus said to them, "Very truly, I tell you, it was not Moses who gave you the bread from heaven, but it is my Father who gives you the true bread from heaven. For the bread of God is that which comes down from heaven and gives life to the world." They said to him, "Sir, give us this bread always." Jesus said to them, "I am the bread of life. Whoever comes to me will never be hungry, and whoever believes in me will never be thirsty."

EVENING PRAYER

Psalm 145 [page 801]

A Reading (Lesson) from the Book of Joel [2:21–27]

Do not fear, O soil; be glad and rejoice, for the LORD has done great things! Do not fear, you animals of the field, for the pastures of the wilderness are green; the tree bears its fruit, the fig tree and vine give their full yield. O children of Zion, be glad and rejoice in the LORD your God; for he has given the early rain for your vindication, he has poured down for you abundant rain, the early and the later rain, as before. The threshing floors shall be full of grain, the vats shall overflow with wine and oil. I will repay you for the years that the swarming locust has eaten, the hopper, the destroyer, and the cutter, my great army, which I sent against you. You shall eat in plenty and be satisfied, and praise the name of the LORD your God, who has dealt wondrously with you. And my people shall never again be put to shame. You shall know that I am in the midst of Israel, and that I, the LORD, am your God and there is no other. And my people shall never again be put to shame.

A Reading (Lesson) from the First Letter of Paul to the Thessalonians [5:12–24]

We appeal to you, brothers and sisters, to respect those who labor among you, and have charge of you in the Lord and admonish you; esteem them very highly in love because of their work. Be at peace among yourselves. And we urge you, beloved to admonish the idlers, encourage the faint hearted, help the weak, be patient with all of them. See that none of you repays evil for evil, but always seek to do good to one another and to all. Rejoice always, pray without ceasing, give thanks in all circumstances; for this is the will of God in Christ Jesus for you. Do not quench the Spirit. Do not despise the words of prophets, but test everything; hold fast to what is good; abstain from every form of evil. May the God of peace himself sanctify you entirely; and may your spirit and soul and body be kept sound and blameless at the coming of our Lord Jesus Christ. The one who calls you is faithful, and he will do this.